MARKETING MANAGEMENT
A STRATEGIC PLANNING APPROACH

McGRAW-HILL SERIES IN MARKETING
CONSULTING EDITOR

Charles D. Schewe, *University of Massachusetts*

Allen, Spohn, and Wilson: Selling Dynamics
Bowersox, Cooper, Lambert, and Taylor: Management in Marketing Channels
Britt, Boyd, Davis, and Larréché: Marketing Management and Administrative Action
Buell: Marketing Management: A Strategic Planning Approach
Buskirk and Buskirk: Retailing
Corey, Lovelock, and Ward: Problems in Marketing
DeLozier: The Marketing Communications Process
Dobler, Lee, and Burt: Purchasing and Materials Management: Text and Cases
Engel: Advertising: The Process and Practice
Guiltinan and Paul: Marketing Management: Strategies and Programs
Guiltinan and Paul: Readings in Marketing Strategies and Programs
Kinnear and Taylor: Marketing Research: An Applied Approach
Loudon and Della Bitta: Consumer Behavior: Concepts and Applications
Monroe: Pricing: Making Profitable Decisions
Redinbaugh: Retailing Management: A Planning Approach
Reynolds and Wells: Consumer Behavior
Russell, Beach, and Buskirk: Selling: Principles and Practices
Schewe and Smith: Marketing: Concepts and Applications
Shapiro: Sales Program Management: Formulation and Implementation
Stanton: Fundamentals of Marketing
Stroh: Managing the Sales Function
Wright, Winter, and Zeigler: Advertising

MARKETING MANAGEMENT
A STRATEGIC PLANNING APPROACH

VICTOR P. BUELL
University of Massachusetts, Amherst

McGraw-Hill Book Company

New York   St. Louis   San Francisco   Auckland   Bogotá   Hamburg
Johannesburg   London   Madrid   Mexico   Montreal   New Delhi
Panama   Paris   São Paulo   Singapore   Sydney   Tokyo   Toronto

MARKETING MANAGEMENT: A Strategic Planning Approach

Copyright © 1984 by McGraw-Hill, Inc. All rights reserved. Printed in the United States of America. Except as permitted under the United States Copyright Act of 1976, no part of this publication may be reproduced or distributed in any form or by any means, or stored in a data base or retrieval system, without the prior written permission of the publisher.

234567890 DOCDOC 8987654

ISBN 0-07-008865-9

This book was set in Cheltenham Light by Black Dot, Inc. The editors were Cheryl L. Mehalik and Gail Gavert; the designer was Charles A. Carson; the production supervisor was Charles Hess. The drawings were done by Fine Line Illustrations, Inc.
R. R. Donnelley & Sons Company was printer and binder.

Library of Congress Cataloging in Publication Data

Buell, Victor P.
    Marketing management.

    (McGraw-Hill series in marketing)
    Includes bibliographical references and index.
    1. Marketing—Management. I. Title. II. Series.
HF5415.13.B775   1984   658.8'02   83-19970
ISBN 0-07-008865-9

ABOUT THE AUTHOR

Victor P. Buell is Professor of Marketing Emeritus, School of Management, University of Massachusetts, Amherst, where he continues with his research, writing, teaching, and consulting.

Before turning to a career in education, Professor Buell was an executive of several international companies. He was corporate vice president, marketing, American Standard, Inc.; vice president, marketing, Archer Daniels Midland Company; manager, marketing division, The Hoover Company; and marketing consultant, McKinsey & Co. He began his marketing career as a college student door-to-door hosiery salesman and crew supervisor.

Professor Buell is the author of *Marketing Management in Action*, *Changing Practices in Advertising Decision-Making and Control*, *Organizing for Marketing/Advertising Success*, and editor in chief of the *Handbook of Modern Marketing*. His books have been published in foreign language editions and distributed worldwide. Other writings have included articles, monographs, and contributed chapters to management handbooks. His article, "The Changing Role of the Product Manager," received the Alpha Kappa Psi award for the best article in the *Journal of Marketing* for 1975.

Professor Buell has served as president of the American Marketing Association; director and executive committee member, Association of National Advertisers; executive committee member, the Department of Commerce national marketing advisory committee; planning council member, American Management Association;

trustee, SME Graduate School of Sales Management and Marketing; member of the board of governors, Parlin Foundation; director, Home Manufacturers Association; chapter officer, Sales and Marketing Executives, International; editorial adviser, *Industrial Marketing*; and member of the editorial review board, *Journal of Marketing*. His professional activities have also included executive training programs, corporate directorships, and consultancies to companies, associations, and government agencies.

A native of Oklahoma, Professor Buell was graduated from the Pennsylvania State University and served with the rank of major in the Quartermaster Corps during World War II.

CONTENTS

Preface   xvii

PART ONE   INTRODUCTION

Chapter 1   The Role of Marketing Management   3

     Why Study Marketing Management?   3
     The Needs for Managers.   The Need for Managers Who Understand Marketing.
     Evolution of Marketing   5
     Production Orientation.   Sales Orientation.   Market Orientation.   Societal Orientation.
     Company Resources and Business Purpose   8
     Purpose Based on Technology.   Purpose Based on Market Strength.   Determining Business Purpose.
     Defining Marketing Management   11
     Further Background Considerations   11
     Company Organization.   Types of Decisions.   Types of Planning.   Consumer and Industrial Marketing.   Marketing of Services.   Dichotomy of the Marketing Management Job.
     Summary   16
     Questions   17
     References   17

Chapter 2   Marketing Definitions and Concepts   18

     What Is a Market?   18
     Market Segments.   Target Market.
     Definition of Marketing   19
     Economic Definitions.   Legal Definition.   Managerial Definitions.
     The Marketing Mix   21
     Product, Price, Distribution   23
     Product.   Price.   Distribution.
     The Promotional Mix   24
     Varying the Promotional Mix.   Push-Pull Strategies.   Sales Promotion.   Publicity.
     Types of Goods   26
     Consumer and Industrial Goods.   Convenience, Shopping, and Specialty Goods.   Classes of Industrial Goods.   Other Goods Classifications.
     Marketing as a System   28
     Nonbusiness Marketing   28
     Acceptance of Marketing Concept.   Nonbusiness Marketing Jobs.

		International Marketing	33

Job Opportunities. Foreign versus Domestic Marketing. Approaches to International Marketing. Key to International Marketing Success.

		A Look at the Future	36
		Questions	37
		References	37

PART TWO UNDERSTANDING THE MARKET AND FORECASTING SALES

Chapter	3	Market Indicators and Market Trends	41

Broad Market Characteristics. Market Indicators and Data Sources.

		Consumer Markets	43

Demographic Data. Significance of Demographic Change. Geographic Population Breakdown. Economic Data. Survey of Buying Power. Need for Discrete Analysis.

		Industrial Markets	57

Identifying Industrial Buyers. Primary Market Research. Relative Industrial Market Potential by Geographic Location. Standard Industrial Classification System.

		Markets for Services	62

Selected Services by Number, Size, and Growth Patterns. Geographic Patterns.

		Summary	63
		Questions	64
		References	64

Chapter	4	Market Segmentation and Market Structure	66
		Market Segmentation	66

Evolution of the Market Segmentation Concept. Strategic Implications. Alternative Segmentation Approaches. Segmentation Criteria. Types of Consumer Market Segments. Reverse Segmentation. Types of Industrial Market Segments. Common Sense Approaches to Segmentation.

		Structural Market Change	75

Cultural Change. Legal and Governmental Controls. Technology.

		Industry Structure	79

Industry Size and Trends. Company Market Share. Industry Product Life Cycle.

		Competitive Structure	82

Quantitative and Qualitative Evaluation. Direct versus Indirect Competition. Oligopolistic and Monopolistic Competition.

		Distribution Structure	85

Available Alternatives. Number, Size, and Location of Intermediaries. Quality of Intermediaries.

		Price Structure	86

Required Market Price Data. Collecting Price Data.

		Company Position in the Market	90
		Summary	90
		Questions	91
		References	91

| Chapter 5 | Buyer Behavior | 92 |

The Role of Buyer Behavior in Marketing ... 92
Types of Buyers.
The Consumer Decision-Making Process ... 93
Low-Involvement Purchases. High-Involvement Purchases. Steps in the Decision-Making Process.
Factors Influencing Consumer Purchase Behavior ... 95
Internal Influences. Measurable Environmental Influences. Random Environmental Factors. Market-Initiated Influences.
Organizational Buying Behavior ... 113
The Organizational Purchase Decision Process. Factors Influencing the Organizational Buying Decision. Models of Organizational Buying Behavior.
Summary ... 117
Questions ... 118
References ... 119

| Chapter 6 | Marketing Research and Marketing Information Systems | 121 |

The Need for Information ... 121
Risk and Uncertainty. The Role of Information in Marketing Planning.
Scope of Marketing Research ... 123
Types of Marketing Research Applications.
Designing the Marketing Research Project ... 127
Defining the Problem. Project Strategy. Project Tactics. Using the Information. Organizing the Marketing Research Function.
The Marketing Information System ... 137
Types of Marketing Information Systems. Design of a Marketing Information System. Operating the Marketing Information System. Building the Marketing Information System.
Summary ... 142
Questions ... 142
References ... 143

| Chapter 7 | Sales Forecasting | 144 |

Sales Forecasting Defined. Uses of Sales Forecasting.
Dimensions of Forecasting ... 145
Time Period. Scope of the Forecast. Assumptions of Forecasting. Costs and Benefits of Forecasting.
Types of Forecasts ... 150
Macro Forecasts. Micro Forecasts.
Forecasting Techniques ... 153
Judgmental Techniques. Survey Techniques. Statistical Techniques. Composite Techniques.
Tracking Performance and Making Revisions ... 157
Summary ... 157
Addendum: Description of Statistical Methods ... 158
Trend Extrapolation. Correlation Techniques. Regression Analysis. Computer Simulation Models.
Questions ... 167
References ... 167

CASES FOR PART TWO

1	Tennis Racket Market Segmentation	169
2	Heublein, Inc.: Environmental Scanning for Strategic Planning	171
3	Heublein, Inc.: Using Environmental Data at Kentucky Fried Chicken	180

PART THREE THE STRATEGIC MARKETING PLANNING PROCESS

Chapter 8 Approach to Strategic Marketing Planning — 187

The Role of Strategic Marketing Planning — 188
Distinction between Strategy and Tactics. Criteria for Identifying Strategies. Short- and Long-Range Planning. Reasons for Adoption of Strategic Planning.
The Planning Environments — 194
Roles of Purpose, Objectives, Strategies, Policies. The Strategic Environments. The Internal Environment. Strategy Formulation.
Strategic Growth Options — 201
Option 1: Present Products, Present Markets. Option 2: New Products, Present Markets. Option 3: Present Products, New Markets. Option 4: New Products, New Markets. Analysis Needed to Select the Best Option.
Other Planning Considerations — 206
Organization. Line and Staff Responsibilities. Planning Guides and Formats.
Summary — 207
Questions — 207
References — 209

Chapter 9 The Situation Analysis — 210

Importance of the Situation Analysis. Scope of the Analysis. Time Period Covered. Topical Outline for Situation Analysis.
Comments on Situation Analysis Outline — 213
A. Economic and Industry Forecasts. B. Business Unit Forecasts. C. The Planning Gap. D. Markets Served and Not Served. E. Buyer Behavior Characteristics. F. Competitive Situation. G. The Marketing Mix. H. Changes in Market Structure. I. Constraints. J. Strengths and Weaknesses. K. Opportunities. L. Summary of Key Problems and Opportunities.
The Hanes' Corporation Case — 222
Situation Analysis—Hanes Corporation — 227
A. Economic and Industry Forecasts. B. Company Forecasts. C. The Planning Gap. D. Markets Served and Not Served. E. Buyer Behavior Characteristics. F. Competitive Situation. G. The Marketing Mix. H. Changes in Market Structure. I. Constraints. J. Strengths and Weaknesses. K. Opportunities. L. Summary of Key Problems and Opportunities.
Summary — 237
Questions — 237

Chapter 10	Selecting Objectives and Strategies	238
	Determining Objectives	239
	Nature of Marketing Objectives. Types of Marketing Objectives. Getting Management Concurrence with Objectives.	
	Developing Alternative Strategies	241
	Getting from One Point to Another. Choosing the Best Alternative. Strategic Approach Difficult for Some. Strategic Alternatives Checklist. Generating and Evaluating Strategic Alternatives.	
	Selecting the Best Strategies	244
	Obtaining Management Approval of Strategies	244
	Selecting Objectives and Strategies at Hanes	245
	Objectives. Alternative Strategies. Recommended Strategies. Rejected Strategies. The Recommended Secondary Strategy. Primary Strategy. Revised Objectives.	
	Summary	253
	Questions	254
	References	254
Chapter 11	Preparing Tactical Plans	255
	The Tactical Marketing Plan	256
	Situation Analysis. Objectives. Strategy. Marketing Programs. Budget Impact. Scheduling and Assignments.	
	Programming by Marketing Functions	259
	Preparing the Tactical Marketing Plan Worksheet	259
	Situation, Objectives, and Strategy. The Tactical Program. Company Price Policy. Profit Impact. Weakness of Promotional Strategies. Meshing Tactical and Strategic Plans.	
	Developing Tactical Programs at Hanes	267
	Summary of Situation, Objectives, and Strategies. Program for 1970. Product. Packaging and Display. Pricing. Distribution. Sales. Advertising. Sales Promotion. Publicity. Service.	
	Summary	273
	Questions	277
	References	277
Chapter 12	Integrating Marketing and Business Plans: Financial Aspects of Marketing	278
	The Annual Marketing Department Plan	279
	Prescribed Planning Format. Constructing the Marketing Plan. Applying the Planning Format. Consolidating Marketing Plans.	
	The Effects of Marketing Plans on Financial Statements	284
	Effect on Financial Statements of Flavor, Inc. Longer-Range Financial Forecasts.	
	Estimating the Financial Impact of Marketing Plans	289
	Essential Financial Data. Computing Net Profit and ROS. Capital Needs and ROI. Understanding Finance.	
	Summary	296
	Questions	296
	References	297

Chapter 13	Strategic Marketing Case Summary	298
	Industry Conditions. Company Performance. Tactical Programs Adopted. Competitive Reactions.	
	Observations on Hanes' Strategies and Tactics	307
	High-Risk Strategy. High-Risk Tactics. Balancing Off the Risks. Summary.	
	Addendum: The Hosiery Industry and Hanes' Position in 1977	309
	Hosiery Industry Situation. Hanes' Situation. Hanes Management Philosophy.	
	Questions	313

CASES FOR PART THREE

4	Spalding Tennis Rackets	314
5	National Relocation, Inc.	321
6	American-Standard: Changing Corporate Strategy	327
7	American-Standard: The Stainless Steel Sink Problem	333

PART FOUR ORGANIZING, DIRECTING, AND CONTROLLING MARKETING OPERATIONS

Chapter 14	Structuring the Marketing Organization	343
	The Classic Organization Model. Importance of Understanding Organization. Definition of Organization. Reasons for Organizational Change.	
	Fundamentals of Organizational Design	345
	Types of Authority. Guidelines to Organization Design. Organizational Charting Guidelines. Developing the Position Description.	
	Alternative Forms of Marketing Organization	354
	The Functional Organization. Organizational Responses to Growth and Diversification. Other Forms of Organization.	
	Summary	365
	Questions	366
	References	366
Chapter 15	Direction, Organizational Behavior, and Managerial Control	368
	Direction	368
	Coordination. Communications. Personnel Administration. Decision Making.	
	Organizational Behavior	371
	Introduction. Group Behavior. Leadership. Motivation.	
	Managerial Control	381
	Types of Control Reports. Types of Control Information. The Corporate Control System. Characteristics of a Good Marketing Control System. Developing the Marketing Control System.	
	Summary	386
	Questions	386
	References	387

READINGS FOR PART FOUR

8	Organizing for Effective Advertising Results—Campbell Soup Company	389
9	New Patterns in Sales Management	392
10	A Sales Manager in Action	403

PART FIVE MANAGING THE MARKETING FUNCTIONS

Chapter 16 Managing the Product Line — 411

Definitions and Descriptions — 411
Product. Product Differentiation. Product Line. Product Mix. Product Attributes. Brand Names, Trademarks, Trade Names. Brands and Nonbrands.

Product Concepts with Strategy Implications — 420
Product Life Cycle. Portfolio Concepts.

Product Strategies — 430
Product Situation Analysis. Product Mix Strategies.

Brand Strategies — 436
Individual Brand Strategy. Family Brand Strategies. Combination Brand Strategies. Brand Extension Strategies. Positioning Strategies. Repositioning Strategies.

Summary — 440
Questions — 441
References — 442

Chapter 17 New Product Planning and Development — 444

The New Product — 444
New Product Failures — 445
Reasons for Failures. Reducing Failure Rates.

New Product Strategies — 446
External Development Strategies. Internal Development Strategies.

Organization for Internal Product Development — 454
The Organizational Problem. Organizational and Procedural Guidelines. Types of Organization.

Internal Development Procedures — 459
New Product Strategy Stage. Idea/Concept Generation Stage. Screening and Evaluation. Business Analysis. Development. Testing. Commercialization. Market Sales Test. Testing and the New Product Process.

Summary — 471
Questions — 472
References — 473

Chapter 18 Pricing Management — 475

What Is Price? — 475
Price and the Marketing Mix.

Key Factors in Setting Price — 476
Demand Factors. Competitive Factors. Cost Factors.

Channel Price Structure — 492

Markup Pricing. Trade Discounts. Quantity Discounts. Payment Terms. Promotional Discounts.
Legal Aspects of Pricing — 496
The Principal Federal Acts. State Laws Affecting Pricing. Pricing Don'ts for Sellers. A Don't for the Buyer. FTC Guidelines for Retail Pricing.
Pricing Strategies — 500
Marketing Positioning Strategies. Cost-Based Strategies. Trade Positioning Strategies. Price Administration Strategies. New Product Strategies.
Summary — 513
Questions — 514
References — 514

Chapter 19 Distribution Management — 516

Changing Channels.
Channel Intermediaries — 518
Wholesale Intermediaries. Retail Intermediaries. Dealer. Service Intermediaries.
Channels of Distribution — 524
Consumer Goods Channels. Industrial Goods Channels. Channels for Services. Multiple Suppliers in Channels. Multiple Channels. Length of Channels. Relative Costs by Channel Length. Channel Conflict. Vertical Channels.
Legal Issues in Distribution — 533
Exclusive Dealing. Exclusive Territories. Tying Sales. Reciprocity. Refusal to Deal.
Distribution Strategies — 534
Distribution Objectives. Market Coverage Strategies. Channel Strategies. Strategies for Cost/Performance Optimization.
Summary — 545
Questions — 546
References — 546

Chapter 20 Sales Management — 548

The Sales Manager's Job — 548
Planning the Sales Functions — 550
Defining the Sales Job.
Organizing the Sales Force — 554
Company Examples.
Directing the Sales Force — 558
Recruiting and Selection. Sales Training. Motivation and Compensation. Designing Sales Territories.
Controlling the Sales Force — 569
Sales Goals. Establishing Quotas. Control Methods. Expense Budgets and Controls.
Sales Strategies — 572
Market Coverage Strategies. Organizational Strategies. Strategies for Targeting Sales Efforts.
Summary — 580

	Questions	581
	References	582
Chapter 21	Managing Advertising, Sales Promotion, and Publicity	583

    Market Communications   583
    The Nature of Advertising   585
    Purposes of Advertising. Classifications of Advertising.
    Classification of Media. Spending by Types of Products.
    Advertiser-Agency Functions and Relationships   589
    Division of Work. Client-Agency Problems.
    Organization and Decision Making by Industry Type   592
    Consumer Packaged Goods Advertising. Consumer Hard Goods and
    Industrial Goods Advertising. Corporate Advertising.
    Strategic Advertising Planning   598
    Advertising Goals. Advertising Strategies. Budgeting.
    Research and Measurement.
    Sales Promotion   607
    Types of Sales Promotion. Problems in Managing Promotion.
    Strategic Sales Promotion Planning   609
    Sales Promotion Goals. Sales Promotion Strategies. Sales
    Promotion Budgets. Research and Measurement.
    Product Publicity   613
    Advantages and Disadvantages. Types of Product Publicity.
    Tactical Planning for Product Publicity.
    Summary   615
    Marketing and Marketing Management.
    Questions   616
    References   616

CASES FOR PART FIVE

11	Paper Mate	619
12	The Gril-Kleen Corporation	626
13	Black & Decker Manufacturing Co., Consumer Power Tool Division	633
14	Eraser Mate	640
15	National High Blood Pressure Education Program	647
16	The Quit-Smoke Company	661
17	The Boston Bolts	663

Appendix: Sources of Business and Marketing Information   666

Indexes   673
    Name and Organization Index
    Cases and Readings Index
    Subject Index

PREFACE

Only a few years ago the U.S. auto industry was the marvel of the world. Textbooks cited it for its examples of good management practice. The Edsel failure was notable because it was the exception.

But what has happened to the auto industry? Blinded by its success, it made the biggest marketing mistake of all—it failed to adapt to the changing needs and wants of the marketplace. Japanese and other foreign auto companies moved in to fill the market void. By the early 1980s General Motors and Ford were losing hundreds of millions of dollars and Chrysler was fighting off bankruptcy.

The auto industry is merely the most visible example. Other industries, individual companies, and institutions (e.g., colleges and hospitals) have gotten into similar trouble. Although there can be contributing factors (such as high labor costs), failure to recognize and adapt to market change has been the most common reason for the decline (and even demise) of once successful companies.

What does this have to do with the study of marketing management? A great deal! To recapture America's industrial leadership, future managers must understand the necessity for market-based decisions. The people attending our schools of management and business administration today will be the future managers of finance, accounting, computer science, engineering, and human resources as well as marketing. The marketing management course is the ideal place for marketing and non-marketing majors alike to learn why and how coordinated management effort is needed to ensure marketing success, and hence, business success.

Text Objectives

This book is the outcome of 13 years of experimenting with ways to help bridge the gap between what students know and what employers expect them to know about management and marketing. Specifically, it is designed to help students:

a. Develop further their understanding of the tools of marketing.
b. Learn where to find and how to use market information for forecasting near-term market potential and longer-term structural market change.
c. Learn how to apply the principles of management—planning (and especially strategic planning), organization, direction, and control—to marketing operations.
d. Understand the interrelationships of marketing with other business functions and how marketing decisions affect profits or other measures of organizational success.
e. Using the above information, practice solving problems faced by real organizations.

Intended Audiences

The text has been designed to serve the needs of both undergraduate students with previous marketing courses and MBA students taking their first course in marketing. The material is well suited for an advanced or capstone course for undergraduate marketing majors. It can also be adapted to marketing strategy and policy courses.

This book is particularly applicable for the first or core graduate marketing course. Both full- and part-time MBA programs are enrolling increasing numbers of students who have had no previous marketing (or other business) courses. The book is designed so those students can learn the basics of marketing and then advance to managerial concepts and applications in the same course.

Chapters and cases have been class tested with several sections of graduate and undergraduate students, and many of their suggestions have been incorporated into the text.

Organization of the Text

Part One: Introduction. Marketing management is introduced in Chapter 1 and the basic terms and concepts of marketing are capsuled in Chapter 2.

Part Two: Understanding the Market and Forecasting Sales. Chapters 3–7 describe the marketing information needed for marketing planning; how it is collected, stored, and retrieved; and how it is used to forecast sales and market change. Three cases illustrate market segmentation and environmental scanning.

Part Three: The Strategic Marketing Planning Process. Students are taken, in Chapters 8–13, step-by-step through a strategic and tactical planning process, illustrated by the Hanes Company. Four cases provide students with practice in applying this planning approach.

Part Four: Organizing, Directing, and Controlling Marketing Operations. Chapters 14–15 show how organization and management direction are used to implement the plans, and how control methods measure progress towards goals. The three readings illustrate how organization structure facilitates decision-making and how leadership styles can affect sales performance.

Part Five: Managing the Marketing Functions. Chapters 16–21 describe the elements of the marketing and promotional mixes and various functional strategies and tactics. Seven more cases highlight individual functions and also show how each is dependent on the marketing mix.

Appendix. This is a practical guide to the principal sources of business and marketing information.

Parts May Be Rearranged. Because parts were designed to stand alone, they can be rearranged to meet the needs of different courses or the preferences of instructors. The planning chapters (Part Three), for example, can be introduced earlier for a marketing capstone or strategy course so that more time can be devoted to cases or term projects. The functional chapters (Part Five) can be moved closer to the beginning for graduate courses enrolling students with no previous marketing training. Or some instructors may prefer to assign the organization, direction, and control chapters (Part Four) last.

Comparison with Other Marketing Management Texts

Principal Similarities

Classic coverage. Like most other texts this one covers the classic subjects of marketing from a managerial point of view. Hence, instructors should feel comfortable with the format.

Specialized subjects. Special subject areas, such as legal aspects of marketing, marketing to government agencies, international marketing, and marketing for nonprofit institutions, have been integrated at appropriate points throughout the text. Both the pricing and distribution chapters, for example, contain sections on legal aspects.

Types of marketing. A consistent effort has been made throughout to deal with industrial as well as consumer marketing, services as well as goods, and with nonprofit organizations. There are more examples from for-profit businesses because this is where marketing has been practiced the longest.

Mathematics and statistics. While this text is not heavily oriented towards mathematical and statistical techniques and models, they are included where needed for completeness of coverage. For example, the addendum to Chapter 7, Sales Forecasting, contains descriptions of relevant statistical methods and computer simulation models.

Theories, concepts, and models. While the more prominent ones have been included, formulas with standardized answers are avoided. Even similar marketing problems usually require different solutions by different companies. While return on investment, for example, may correlate with market share, this fact is meaningful only to the few market leaders in each industry. For the vast majority of companies, the issue is how to improve ROI despite low market share.

Principal Differences

Emphasis on strategic marketing planning. This text differs in several ways from other texts in its treatment of strategic planning:

More discussion than is usual is devoted to strategic and tactical planning. The six chapters and four cases of Part Three, as well as sections of other chapters, deal with the subject thoroughly. The step-by-step approach presented in Part Three teaches students how to plan while the specially designed cases permit them to apply this knowledge. The planning approach (which emphasizes the matching of business strengths and market opportunities) is typical of that used by the business units of many leading companies. The business unit, of course, is where product and market plans are made and where students are most likely to encounter planning in their future jobs. Because the approach is research oriented, fact-based, and analytical, instructors will find it ties in closely with their own training and experiences.

A unique feature of Part Three is the use of a single case through the planning chapters to illustrate how each planning step is applied to a real company.

Although conceptual, matrix, planning models (e.g., portfolio models) are explained thoroughly in Chapter 16, they are not used in this book as the principal approach to strategic planning. These models have declined in popularity since the 1970s because those employing them have found they do not necessarily lead to profitable growth. Their prime contribution has been to help corporate management allocate resources among businesses and products; this book explains how they are used for this important function.

Another unique feature of the planning coverage (found in Chapter 12) shows how strategic and tactical plans are integrated into the annual marketing department plan and how the marketing plan is integrated into the business unit plan. Thus, the planning process moves from strategic thinking to the tactical programs, budgets, staffing, and work assignments that are needed to make a business go.

How marketing decisions impact financial results. While the relationships between finance and accounting and marketing are emphasized throughout, Chapter 12 contains a special section which illustrates how marketing decisions affect profits. A unique feature demonstrates the before-and-after effects of a proposed new strategy on a company's income, balance sheet, and cash-flow statements.

Cases written for this text. Most of the cases for Parts Two, Three, and Five were written especially to tie in with these chapters. They describe real situations and afford students the opportunity to solve problems using knowledge gained from the chapters. The cases for Part Three are particularly appropriate for applying the planning approaches because some real-life companies agreed to permit publication of relevant facts about significant problems requiring new strategies. Hence, students have the same information that management had as a basis for their strategic planning.

For the most part, cases have been written as briefly as possible without sacrificing key information. They are difficult enough to be challenging, yet most students can solve them. None has been published previously except for parts of the Hanes case. Company solutions and results will be supplied separately.

How to spot changes in market structure. Chapters 3 and 4 show how to conduct market analyses that can help to identify likely changes in market structure. The reason for this emphasis is apparent when we consider that failure to anticipate change can mean problems and lost opportunities similar to those experienced by the U.S. auto industry.

How organization affects marketing results. More attention has been given to organization (both from the structural and behavioral standpoints) than in most marketing texts. The reason for this emphasis is that, as important as planning is to successful marketing, the best-laid plans are of little value unless backed up by proper organization and motivated employees. Students may or may not have studied organization in other courses. If they have, they will now be able to see how the principles apply to marketing.

Tying in the 4-Ps with strategies. Marketing functions are described in the six chapters of Part Five. As noted, these can be assigned earlier if desired. Description has been limited to that which seems essential for students new to marketing, even though this has meant omitting a few topics found in principles books. To increase student interest, practical illustrations and applications are cited liberally.

Unique to this book, however, is that substantial portions of these chapters explain product, pricing, distribution, and promotional strategies and show how these tie in with marketing mix strategies. These sections make the study of the basic marketing functions even more interesting and relevant, irrespective of whether students have had previous marketing courses.

Acknowledgments

I wish to thank the many people who helped to make this book what it is. The principal contributor was Professor Peter LaPlaca who prepared Chapters 5, 6, 7, and 18, and who collaborated with me on the Heublein cases. Other key contributors were Professor Hugh O'Neill, who wrote the organizational behavior section of Chapter 15; Professor Chris Allen, who was a skilled advisor on buyer behavior; and Professor Charles Schewe, who provided excellent suggestions and encouragement throughout.

Valuable assistance was provided by a number of other people. Graduate students Philip Lieberman and Debra Lennon assisted with data collection; David O'Leary developed the end-of-chapter questions; and Kris Busche prepared the appendix with the counsel of business librarian Salvatore Meringolo. Professor Ben Branch critiqued the financial section of Chapter 12; Professor Anthony Butterfield, the organization portions of Chapters 14 and 15; and Professor Larry Rosenberg, the channels portion of Chapter 19. Professors Michael Peters and Robert Hisrich prepared the Gril-Kleen and Boston Bolts cases. William Novelli and Pamela Gelfand prepared the National High Blood Pressure Education Program case.

I am indebted to the managements of the following organizations for their cooperation and assistance in providing information for cases: Heublein, Inc.; the Paper Mate Division of the Gillette Company; the Spalding Division of Questor Corporation; the Black & Decker Manufacturing Co.; American Standard, Inc.; the Campbell Soup Co.; and the company represented by the fictitious name, National Relocation, Inc. My thanks go also to the officials of the National Heart, Lung, and Blood Institute, the Gril-Kleen Co., and the Boston Bolts sports organization for their assistance to the contributing case writers. While many people at the McGraw-Hill Book Co. have been very helpful, I have worked most closely with editors Beth Lewis, William Kane, and John Carleo, and with editing supervisor Gail Gavert. My dear wife, Virginia, typed the manuscript drafts and gave help and support in many other ways. Bonnie Webster typed the final manuscript accurately and with good humor.

I wish to thank the reviewers whose criticisms and suggestions have greatly improved this book: Chris T. Allen, University of Massachusetts; Boris W. Becker, Oregon State University; William A. Cohen, California State University; Michael d' Amico, University of Akron; Donald Granbois, Indiana University; Joseph L. Hair, Louisiana State University; Richard Hill, University of Illinois at Urbana-Champaign; A. H. Kizilbash, Northern Illinois University; E. W. Leonard, Emory University; Lynn J. Loudenback, Iowa State University; Robert R. Rothberg, Rutgers University; Charles Schewe, University of Massachusetts; Samuel V. Smith, University of Houston; and Steven D. Thrasher, Pacific Lutheran University.

Finally, this book might never have been completed without the support of my colleagues at the School of Management, University of Massachusetts, Amherst, and particularly Professor Parker Worthing, head of the marketing department, and Dean Harry Allan.

Victor P. Buell

PART ONE

Introduction

CHAPTER 1

The Role of Marketing Management

WHY STUDY MARKETING MANAGEMENT?

In informal discussions with students one of the questions frequently asked is, "Why should I study marketing management?" The student then points out that either (1) he or she does not intend to work in marketing or (2) if the student is a marketing major, his or her first job is unlikely to be at the management level. In the second situation the implied—and sometimes explicit—question is, "Shouldn't I be learning things that are going to help me get and hold that first job?"

These are good questions that deserve answers. A subject is more interesting when students understand how it can be of value to them. Two reasons why you should study marketing management are (1) the need for managers and (2) the need for managers who understand marketing.

The Needs for Managers

Both graduate and undergraduate schools of business emphasize broad training in business functions and managerial decision-making processes. Most companies that recruit business school graduates are looking for people with managerial potential. Successful companies need people whose personal qualities and training will enable them to handle increasing responsibility over time.

For the most part business schools don't attempt to provide training for entry level jobs. In the first place there is no way for the student or the school to know what entry level job the student may obtain. In the second place companies generally are well equipped to provide training for their own entry level jobs. On the other hand, few of even the larger, more sophisticated companies maintain in-house management training programs. Therefore, the college graduate with management training is usually better prepared for advancement.

While new bachelor degree holders probably won't start in managerial jobs, graduates with MBA degrees tend to find themselves in a different situation. Some companies place new MBAs—particularly those with previous work experience—in decision-making positions or in staff-assistant positions working with decision-making executives. A *Business Week* survey found that "many companies are looking for MBAs to whom they can give a lot of responsibility and who will produce immediately."[1]

Appreciation of management training is not limited to business organizations.

Increasingly, government and other nonprofit organizations are recognizing the need to attract people with such training. Not all advancement in profit or nonprofit organizations, of course, is limited to managerial positions. Organizations need functional and staff specialists as well. Specialists, however, usually work in large, complex organizations or for service firms serving such organizations. Those with managerial training should be better equipped to understand the environment in which they operate.

The Need For Managers Who Understand Marketing

If knowledge of management can help your career advancement, why then should one study marketing management in particular? The answer has to do with the role of marketing in a business organization. Management authorities generally agree that business organizations (and most nonbusiness organizations as well) exist to serve markets. One of the best known, Peter Drucker, has said: "The purpose of business is to create a customer. The purpose is to provide something for which an independent outsider, who can choose not to buy, is willing to exchange his purchasing power."[2] Marvin Bower, former managing director of the management consulting firm of McKinsey & Company, often stated that "marketing is the competitive cutting edge of the business."

Marketing: The Focal Point. From the thinking and writing of management authorities has emerged the concept that a business exists to create and serve customers. The marketing function is the focal point for achieving this business purpose. As we shall see, not all marketing functions are performed by the marketing department. In the final analysis, however, almost every business function exists to assist the marketing department in creating and serving customers.

One can conclude, therefore, that understanding the management of marketing is basic to understanding the management of a business as a whole. We're not suggesting that marketing is the most important function of a business or that marketing executives should not understand other business functions. But we want to emphasize that modern companies organize their resources to concentrate on achieving success in the marketplace.

The company organization chart presented in Figure 1-1 shows not only the marketing activities commonly assigned to the marketing department but also those marketing and marketing-related activities commonly assigned to nonmarketing departments. Figure 1-1 presents a typical picture, although the assignment of activities will vary from company to company.

The Coordinating Function of Marketing Management. It would be impossible for the manager of marketing to control all of the firm's marketing activities since all functional areas of the business contribute to the marketing process. The only executive with sufficient authority to exercise such control is the chief executive. This has led some observers to conclude that *the real marketing manager is the chief executive*. Since the chief executive can't do everything, authority and responsibility can be delegated to several functional managers. The marketing manager usually reports to the chief executive, who assigns to the marketing manager direct responsibility for the management of designated marketing activities. The chief executive, furthermore, usually looks to the marketing manager to coordinate marketing activities with other functional departments. The chief execu-

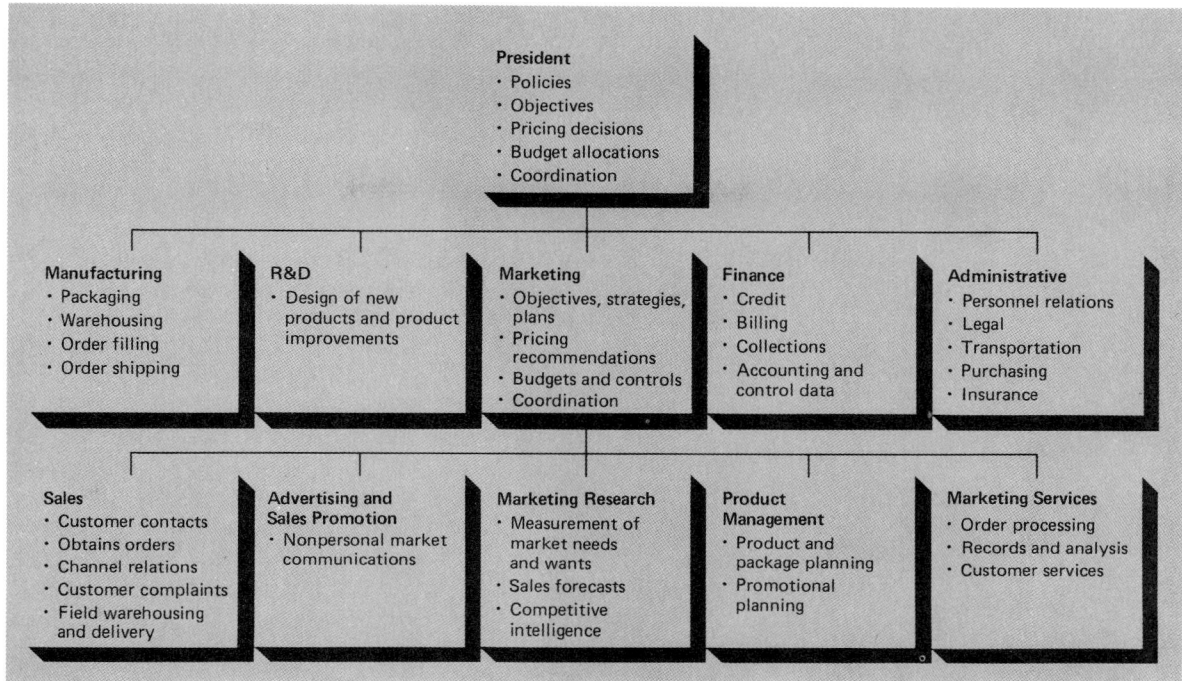

FIGURE 1-1. Company organization chart, showing where marketing and marketing support activities are commonly assigned.

tive steps in personally only when needed to resolve conflict. We will see in Chapter 14 some of the different ways in which companies organize and coordinate their marketing activities.

EVOLUTION OF MARKETING

Marketing has not always held a central role in business organizations. During the developing phases of an industrialized society, the forces of production concentrate on supplying the basic and relatively homogenous needs of a population having limited discretionary income. As the techniques of mass production bring down product costs and workers' incomes go up, demand increases for both quantity and variety of goods. Competition for markets grows as capital availability encourages the establishment of new companies. As consumer discretionary income grows, markets begin to segment. New markets appear, and consumers begin to demand services, education, travel, and other manifestations of more affluent societies.

It is in the latter stages of these developments that marketing assumes the form in which we know it today. If we look at roughly the last century of United States history, we can see three periods of business orientation, each adapted to a stage of economic and social development. These periods can be described as production orientation, sales orientation, and market orientation. Currently, we are in a fourth period—market combined with societal orientation.

Figure 1-2 suggests the approximate time spans these periods covered. Other developed countries have gone through similar periods, usually lagging behind the

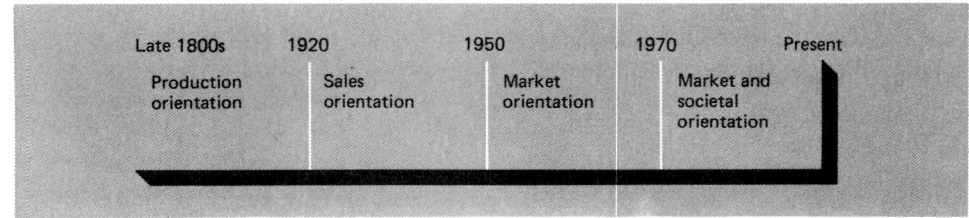

FIGURE 1-2. Changes in business orientation—Approximate time periods.

United States by a few years. Since change occurs gradually over a continuum, the periods actually overlap one another; the brackets, therefore, indicate only the times during which a particular phase of business orientation has been prevalent. A brief description of each period follows.

Production Orientation

Companies were essentially production-oriented from the latter part of the nineteenth century to about 1920. Emphasis was placed on filling the demand for basic commodities. The typical family had little discretionary income and there was little demand for products not associated with filling those basic family requirements. Demand was usually supplied by the producer's perception of what consumers needed. Product design and product line decisions were heavily influenced by manufacturing considerations. Management attention was directed primarily to improving production methods, increasing output, and lowering costs.

Sales Orientation

The period of sales orientation covered roughly the years from 1920 to 1950. With the exception of the years of the Great Depression, this period was characterized by gradually rising discretionary income, emerging demand for differentiated products, increasing competition, and the expansion of distribution channels.

Although product decisions continued to be dominated by what the manufacturing department wanted to make, the role of sales became increasingly important. With the production department capable of turning out increasing quantities of goods through mass production techniques, company success began to turn on the ability of the sales force to move inventories.

Market Orientation

Covering the years from about 1950 to 1970, this period was characterized by a continuing shift in business emphasis to understanding and reacting to changing markets. The dramatic rise in consumer discretionary income following World War II created demand for new products and services. The mobility provided by mass ownership of automobiles encouraged the development of suburbs, new shopping patterns, and changes in distribution methods. Markets became more segmented and more complex. Product life cycles shortened.

With these conditions, production people no longer were in a position to determine accurately what would sell. Selling skills were no longer sufficient to overcome the problems created when products were not attuned to a more discriminant market demand. In order to provide a better fit between market demand

and company offerings—and in order to provide for better coordination of marketing activities—companies reorganized and assigned increased responsibilities to the marketing department.

Marketing took on the role of analyzing markets and interpreting the needs, wants, and preferences of these markets to the engineering, research and development, and manufacturing departments. More sophisticated approaches were developed to fulfill the traditional marketing roles of product promotion and the management of distribution channels. The role of marketing in pricing increased. And finally, the marketing department became the focal point for the development of corporate strategies needed to adjust to market change.

The management of one of the world's largest banks, Citicorp, had this to say about its corporate reorganization designed to serve customers better:[3]

> Our revised operating structure is not a procrustean bed on which customers are cut or stretched to fit our requirements. For the forseeable future we expect to face vigorous competitors—many offering highly specialized financial services with fewer constraints and wider powers than we enjoy. To attract and hold our share of customers in such a market environment, we will have to adjust to their changing needs, not expect them to adapt to ours.

The Marketing Concept. The market-oriented concept for some years has been referred to as the *marketing concept*. General Electric gave impetus to the marketing concept when in the early 1950s its chairman announced publicly that, henceforth, GE would be organized around the customer. Since that time the marketing concept has come not only to mean (1) market, i.e., customer, orientation, but also (2) organization of various marketing functions under a marketing executive.

The marketing concept was not just an altruistic philosophy designed for favorable publicity. It was developed as a business philosophy which assumed that serving the customer better is the best way to earn profit. Carried to the extreme, of course, giving the customer anything desired—prices below cost, for example—could lead to bankruptcy. One of the changes that has occurred in the marketing manger's role under the marketing concept has been a shift from emphasis on sales volume to an emphasis on profitable sales. Without satisfactory profits no company can serve customers over the long run.

Societal Orientation

When managements adopted the marketing concept, they could not foresee the environmental problems or the changes in society's values that would raise questions about the market orientation philosophy. In terms of what we now know about pollution, the finiteness of raw materials, and the apparent inability of our economic system to eliminate poverty, some people question whether what is good for the individual consumer is always good for society. Increasingly, national policy—and, in turn, business policy—is tempering concern for the consumer with concern for society as a whole. Thomas A. Murphy, chairman of General Motors, addressed this dilemma when he said, "We may have let ourselves grow out of touch with the customer's need for continued satisfaction in a time of heightened expectations and the society's concern for environmental improvement and energy conservation."[4]

Marketing policies attuned to serving the market as the market wants to be served continue to represent modern company policy. But we are also seeing market-oriented decisions modified by societal concerns, as a result both of law and of responsible management policies.

COMPANY RESOURCES AND BUSINESS PURPOSE

You might have the impression that all a company needs to do to be profitable is to be market-oriented and give the market whatever it wants as long as this does not conflict with the interests of society. Nothing would be more likely to ensure business failure.

This leads us to the consideration of business purpose. Drucker's definition—the purpose of a business is to create a customer—may now be refined. It would be more accurate to say that *the purpose of a specific business (company) is to create customers for the kinds of products or services that the company is peculiarly well qualified to provide.* These company qualifications are referred to as *company resources*.

Every business venture from its inception has a particular combination of financial, technical, marketing, and human skills and capabilites that circumscribe the markets the company can serve. While these capabilities (resources) may expand and diversify as the company succeeds and grows, there are always limits to the types of markets it can serve.[5]

In the case of Pillsbury, for example, the company's resources have been closely associated with the milling of flour since its inception, over a century ago. With its growing resources in marketing, technology, finance, and people, Pillsbury has expanded its product line to a wide range of convenience foods, although much of its business is still tied to its basic technical resource, the milling of flour. Pillsbury's other business ventures, in the main, have been associated with food for humans and animals. In contrast, a major milling competitor—General Mills—has utilitzed its financial resources and skills at consumer marketing to venture into different fields, such as children's toys.

Purpose Based on Technology

For many businesses, technical capabilities in research, engineering, materials, production, and/or science are critical. This is true of most companies serving industrial markets as well as of some companies serving consumer markets. Many of our best-known corporations concentrate their production on products which utilize their primary technologies. Some examples are:

Company	Major Products
Monsanto	Chemicals
Texaco	Petroleum and other energy sources
General Motors	Transportation
General Electric	Energy creation and energy applications
IBM	Computerized data processing
Kodak	Photographic reproduction
General Foods	Processed packaged foods

Each of these companies has utilitzed or expanded its technology to move into new products and/or new markets. And some have acquired other types of businesses. But one rarely sees these kinds of companies move very far away from their basic technological strengths unless forced to do so by new competing technologies.

Purpose Based on Market Strength

Other companies capitalize on their marketing and distribution strengths and, in order to do so, develop or acquire new technology. Procter & Gamble, for example, built a successful business in soaps and foods based on its fats and oils technology. Subsequently, P&G developed and acquired new technical capabilities to produce products such as dentifrices, household paper products, and coffee. These were products which could be sold through the same distribution channels the company was already using and which could be marketed by the same promotional methods at which the company had become highly skilled.

Gillette, in similar fashion, expanded beyond razor blade technology to move into additional personal grooming products, such as shaving soaps and deodorants, and into less related products, such as writing pens and cigarette lighters. All of these lines utilized the company's strong distribution and marketing resources. The Mosler Safe Company, now a division of American Standard Inc., used its strong relationship with customer banks to market product lines as technologically diverse as security cameras and bank checks.

Holiday Inns, Inc. has come full circle. From a successful hotel chain Holiday diversified into 30 different businesses ranging from furniture manufacturing to the operation of buses. Poor experiences with these diversifications have brought Holiday Inns, back to concentrating on its real capabilities. As chief executive Roy E. Winegardner now says, "Holiday is actually a *hospitality* company—a concept that will limit its scope to food, lodging, and entertainment." Entertainment now includes gambling casino hotels. Mr. Winegardner added that the company in the future will "get into as few businesses as possible, and only those that have good growth, high returns, and are synergistic with our main business—hotels".[6]

Determining Business Purpose

Company capabilites (resources) determine the types of products or services a company is qualified to offer. The second factor in the equation is market opportunity. Matching technical and marketing capabilities with the opportunity to serve specific market needs and wants determines the *business purpose* (or *business charter*, as it is sometimes called). Financial and management capabilities affect how quickly the market opportunity can be developed. See Figure 1-3.

FIGURE 1-3. Determining business purpose.

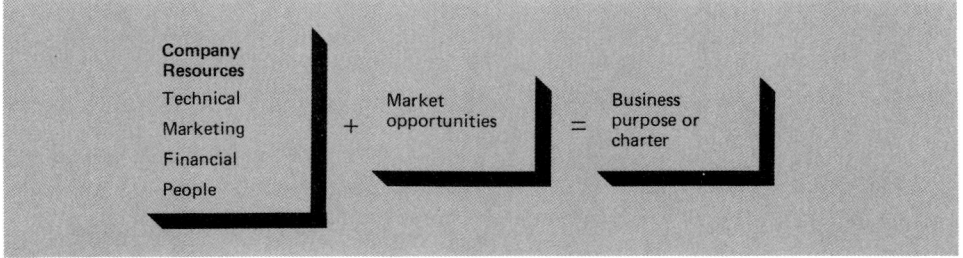

Like many other management tasks, developing the business purpose or charter isn't always simple. You must think broadly enough to recognize potential opportunities for market expansion, and, at the same time, plan realistically within the limits of the firm's current resources.

In his classic article, "Marketing Myopia," Theodore Levitt warned of the dangers of thinking too narrowly of one's business purpose.[7] He thought, for example, that the railroads should have considered themselves as being in the transportation business and the Hollywood movie industry as being in the entertainment business.

Levitt and others have noted how frequently industries have faced obsolescence because new technology was applied by competitors from outside the traditional industry. Classic examples are trucks and airlines in the case of railroads, and television in the case of Hollywood. Combination fiberglass and plastic bathtubs, in another instance, were introduced by companies from outside the plumbing industry. Traditional plumbing equipment manufacturers faced the problem of getting their research and development and their production people, whose whole careers were based on enameled cast iron technology, to think in terms of plastics. The change-over proved to be a slow and painful process.

The fortunes of many firms declined because they were too caught up in their own technology to recognize changing market demand. One of the important roles of marketing management is to sense when new technology needs to be brought in. A firm also can define its purpose too broadly and spread its resources so thin that it excels at nothing. The managers of a gas and oil furnace manufacturing company may be thinking too narrowly when they state that their company's business purpose is to supply home furnaces. They may be going too far afield, however, in defining its purpose as energy generation. A less sweeping definition of the business—home heating and cooling, for example—might help them consider applications of alternative sources of energy, such as solar, before new technologies cause the furnace market to erode.

Adjusting to new or different technology is rarely simple. Not only do furnace and solar heating manufacturing technologies differ, but so do the skills required of dealer-installers. Furnace installers employ sheet metal workers, whereas water-based systems employ plumbers. Thus a company with two different types of heating

FIGURE 1-4. Marketing management model.

Marketing management
Decision making

Planning	Organizing	Directing	Controlling
Policies Goal setting Plans and budgets for attaining goals Changing plans if necessary.	Building the structure for organizing people to carry out plans	Staffing, training, assigning, compensating, coordinating, leading, and motivating people to achieve goals	Measuring progress towards goals

products may find itself with its dealers competing at the customer level. Nevertheless, it is usually better to face such issues early rather than late.

The idea that a company should concentrate on its strengths has been confirmed by McKinsey & Company, a leading management consulting firm. McKinsey listed "emphasis on doing what they know best" as one of the common attributes of ten well-managed companies they studied in depth. McKinsey noted:

> Robert W. Johnson, the former chairman of J&J, put it this way: "Never acquire any business you don't know how to run." Edward G. Harness, CEO at P&G, says, "This company has never left its base." All of the successful companies have been able to define their strengths—marketing, customer contact, new product innovation, low-cost manufacturing—and then build on them. They have resisted the temptation to move into new businesses that look attractive but require corporate skills they do not have.[8]

DEFINING MARKETING MANAGEMENT

The management of any activity involves two broad functions: (1) planning and (2) the execution of plans.

Planning involves setting goals or objectives to be achieved by some future point (or points) in time and determining how these goals are to be reached. *Execution* of plans involves the functions of organizing, directing (and coordinating), and controlling. *Organizing* involves determining activities to be performed, grouping activities into positions, assigning responsibilities and authorities to positions, and staffing the positions with people. *Direction* involves the supervision of people and coordination of their activities; additionally, in the case of marketing management, it includes coordination with those marketing activities assigned to nonmarketing departments. *Control* measures progress toward goals and identifies problem areas when performance en route to the goals is below standard. Part Three of the text expands on the planning function, and Part Four describes the functions of execution. A marketing management model is shown in Figure 1-4.

We now are far enough along to define marketing management in a meaningful way. The first sentence of the definition below is the descriptive statement. The second sentence is the qualifier needed to make marketing management socially justifiable and economically viable. Like any other human endeavor, marketing mangement can be performed poorly or well, nobly or ignobly, with entirely different results.

> Marketing management is the setting of marketing goals—considering company resources and market opportunities—and the planning and execution of activities required to meet the goals. When carried out effectively and honorably, marketing management results in creating and satisfying customers in a manner acceptable to society and leads to profitable growth for the firm.

FURTHER BACKGROUND CONSIDERATIONS

As we get into our study of marketing management, there are several issues which will help you understand the chapters that follow. These have to do with company organization, types of decisions, types of planning, classes of marketing, and the dichotomy of the marketing management job.

Company Organization

Differing organizational forms will be discussed in more detail in Chapter 14. You should be familiar, however, with a few terms that will be used before we get to these chapters. Company organization, when viewed in managerial terms, in contrast to legal terms, is usually of two basic types—functional or divisional.

Functional Organization. In a functional organization the heads of the various functional departments, such as manufacturing, marketing, and finance, report directly to the chief executive. The chief executive performs the coordinating function. In larger companies staff specialists (such as personnel and legal experts), who provide support services to the other functional departments, also report to the chief executive.

Divisional Organization. Companies usually begin with a functional organization which is used until they become too large or too diversified for their chief executives to coordinate effectively. When a company reaches this point, it is divided into two or more divisions, each with its own manufacturing, marketing, and accounting functions. Each division becomes responsible for managing its resources to provide budgeted profits. Staff functions usually continue to report to the company chief executive.

Companies divided in this way are referred to as divisionalized companies. The divisions, in turn, are organized along functional lines. Most large American corporations are divisionalized. Figure 1-5 compares functional and divisionalized organization plans.

Operations. In either type of organization there are *operating functions*, which are directly concerned with production, distribution, and sales, namely, manufacturing and marketing. They contrast with *support functions*—e.g., finance, accounting, control, personnel, legal—which are grouped under the general heading of *staff functions*.

Divisions which perform manufacturing and marketing functions are often referred to as *operating divisions* in order to distinguish them from headquarters staff units, which in some companies may also be called divisions, e.g., the finance division. The term "line" is sometimes used as a synonym for "operating," e.g., line division or line function.

Types of Decisions

Good planning is characterized by deliberate decision making based on careful analyses of internal and external data and assumptions about the future. If planning is to be something more than guesswork, it requires information, analysis, and consideration of alternative methods of reaching goals. Planning decisions must be made with respect to the information to be collected, goals to be sought, and strategies and tactics to be followed in achieving goals.

Implementing Operating Decisions. Despite the importance of planning, most of the marketing manager's time is spent on operational concerns, such as staffing, training, supervising, coordinating, and solving a variety of everyday problems. Many operating decisions must be made ad hoc because there is not enough time

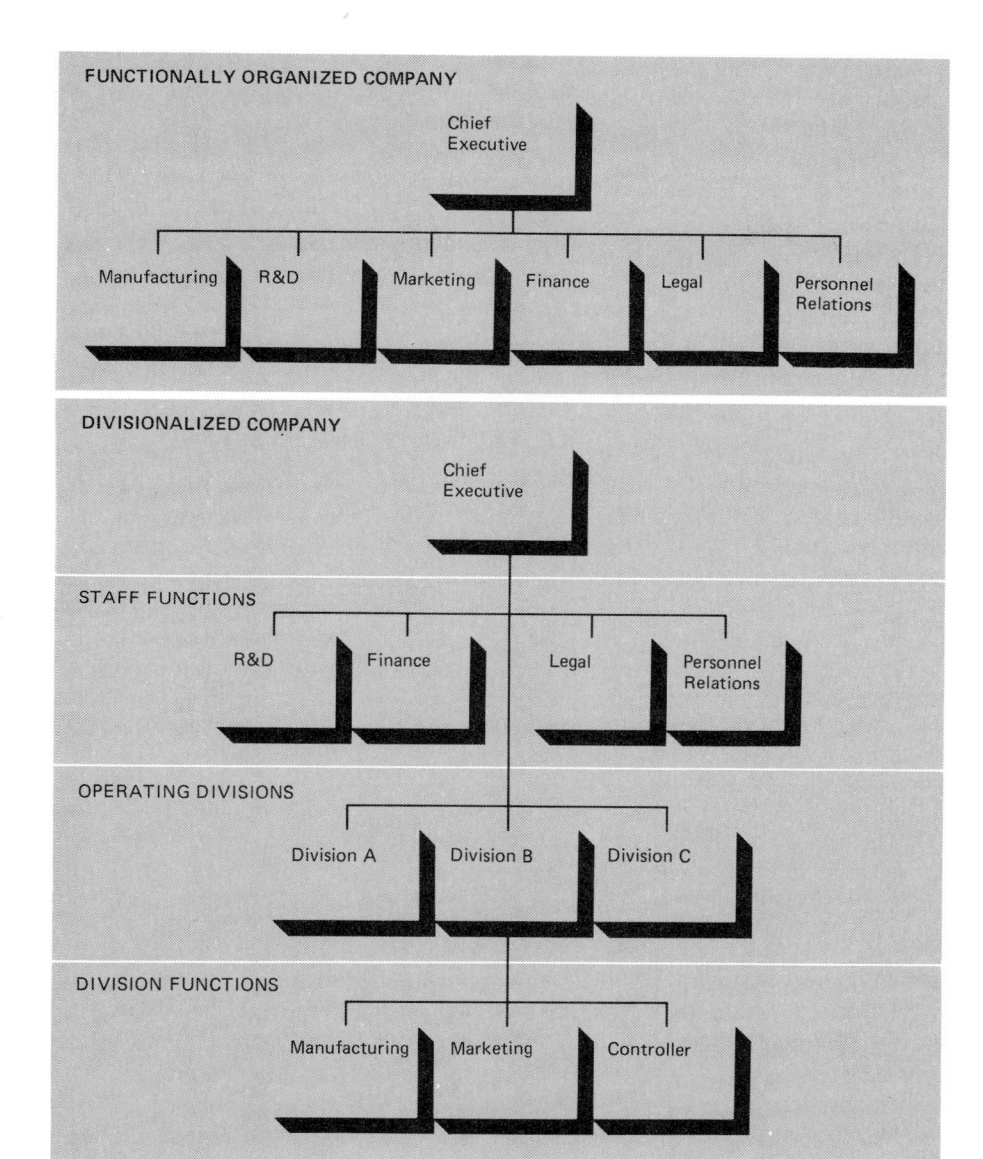

FIGURE 1-5. A functionally organized company and a divisionalized company.

available for collecting desired information, analyzing it carefully, or deliberating over alternative solutions. Experience, judgment, and a willingness to risk making decisions promptly under conditions of uncertainty are important qualities for operating managers to have.

Computerized information systems and mathematical modeling techniques are being used by some companies to attempt to bring more order to the process of decision making. Because of their cost, however, these sophisticated techniques have been used sparingly in marketing management. Their use undoubtedly will increase, however, and students of management would do well to study management science. No matter how sophisticated the managerial tools, however, you should bear in mind that planning and operating management functions—though interrelated—are very different in nature and call for different personal qualities.

Types of Planning

Four types of planning are carried on within modern companies—strategic, tactical, individual, and special project planning.

Strategic Planning. Strategic planning involves development of major, longer-term goals, developing alternative strategies, and selecting the most appropriate strategies. Strategic planning inherently requires top management involvement and, particularly, leadership from the chief marketing executive. Because of its importance, strategic planning is covered in depth in Part Three.

Tactical Planning. Tactical plans are more detailed plans required to implement the broader strategic plans. They are shorter range in nature, usually covering periods of 1 year or less. Whereas strategies may deal with a total business unit, separate tactical plans are prepared for each functional unit, such as sales, advertising, and product development. Also, the plans of each lower unit in the organization supplement the plans of the larger units of which they are a part. For example, the sales department plans supplement the marketing department plans, the sales district plans supplement the sales department plans, and so on. Tactical planning is covered in Chapter 11.

Individual Planning. Personal activities should be planned so that individual responsibilities are carried out. For example, a salesperson plans to cover the assigned territory on a monthly, weekly, and daily basis and also plans individual sales calls. Although a sales position isn't strictly a managerial position, many sales managers stress the importance of the salesperson managing the individual territory to achieve agreed-upon goals. Individual planning will not be covered formally in the text, but it is recognized as a desirable activity in a well-managed company.

Special Project Planning. Strategic and tactical planning are generally done on a regular basis. It is usual for companies to develop formal plans annually prior to the start of the company's fiscal year. The period during which plans are developed may cover only a few weeks. This relatively short period wouldn't be the proper place to study and plan major projects.

New product and product improvement planning, for example, normally are continuing processes requiring organized efforts outside the framework of the annual marketing planning program. The expected results of the product development process, of course, are factored into the annual marketing plan. Other planning projects are needed only occasionally, such as a distribution channel improvement study or a branch office operations study.

Planning Emphasis. We will be emphasizing strategic and tactical marketing planning because of the importance well-managed companies attach to these activities, and because study of this type of planning leads to understanding the interrelationships that are so important to marketing management. Although *annual* strategic and tactical planning are stressed, you should realize that planning permeates the current business organization and is carried out at all levels, both on a regular timetable basis and when needed to deal with special developments.

Consumer and Industrial Marketing

Many companies are engaged only in the marketing of consumer goods, others market only industrial goods, and still others market both types. The planning approaches advocated here are equally appropriate for consumer and industrial marketing. Specific application and points of emphasis, however, are often quite different.

Consumer marketing is concerned with providing products and services for individual consumers. Individual consumers are normally reached through intermediate channels such as wholesalers and retailers, although they may be reached also through other distribution methods, such as direct-to-consumer selling (door-to-door), direct mail, catalog sales, and vending machines.

Industrial marketing is concerned with providing products and services to nonindividual consumers—namely, industrial and commercial businesses, and private and government institutions. Even though government purchasing practices are often different from those of private businesses, for convenience we include government within the industrial marketing classification.

Determining whether marketing is consumer or industrial is based on the buyer or user, and not the product. In practice we speak of consumer products and industrial products, and some are clearly one or the other. Heavy production equipment, for example, would not be bought by individual consumers. Yet many so-called consumer products are properly classified as industrial products when they are sold for use by companies or institutions such as schools and hospitals. Examples are food, clothing, bedsheets, office supplies, petroleum, and automobiles. Computers, which used to be thought of purely as industrial products, now are bought by consumers for use at home. While the products may be the same or similar, consumer and industrial purchasing methods are quite different and the channels used to reach each type of market usually differ. Consequently, while the same planning approaches may be used for both, the marketing methods will differ.

Marketing of Services

Sevices may also be classified as consumer or industrial, depending upon the buyer or user. A market research agency would be unlikely to serve the individual consumer and so would be classified as an industrial service. Other service businesses, such as airlines, banks, and insurance companies, provide similar services to both consumer and industrial markets. These companies are engaged in consumer marketing when serving individual consumers and industrial marketing when serving industrial buyers and users.

For all practical purposes the words *product* and *service* can be used interchangeably when speaking about what a company offers. Companies producing services have their counterparts to the manufacturing department of a product company. In the case of an airline the service is produced by the Operations Department—the department that is responsible for maintaining, scheduling, and flying the airplanes. The service (product) marketed by the airline is a ticket for a seat on a scheduled flight. The marketing planning approaches presented here work equally well for service or product companies, even though channels used and the marketing methods followed may differ.

Dichotomy of the Marketing Management Job

While the two major functions of marketing mangement are planning and execution, there are two other distinguishing characteristics of the marketing management job. One has to do with the sales of established products, and the other is concerned with developing new products and new markets. Both are important and both must go on simultaneously if the company is to grow profitably.

Marketing Established Product Lines. Unless a company is brand-new, the firm will have an established line of products and a certain market position in these products. The products provide the cash flow for company expansion, and their positions in the marketplace must be maintained or improved. The opportunity for sales and profit improvement within the established product line depends to a large extent on (1) where each product is in its life cycle and (2) the intensity of its competition. Maximizing sales and profits from established products demands much of marketing management's attention.

Developing New Products and Markets. Eventually every product reaches the mature and declining periods of its life cycle, when profit margins fall or disappear. Only by finding new products, new markets, or new businesses can a company offset the effects of aging. Companies that have remained profitable and that have grown over a long period of time have mastered the art of using the present to prepare for the future.

Managing Both Established and New Businesses. Few marketing managers are equipped through training, experience, or aptitude to excel in both of these aspects of the marketing management job, though usually they excel in one. But successful marketing managers recognize the dual nature of their responsibilities and organize and staff their organizations to provide the talents needed to accomplish both jobs.

SUMMARY

Since the 1950s American business has been characterized by market orientation. During this period companies have organized with the market as their central focus and have directed their efforts toward creating products and services to meet specific market needs and wants. In the 1970s societal orientation was superimposed on market orientation. Management increasingly must deal with questions of what is right for society, as well as what is right for the consumer. At times these overlap and appear to be in conflict, thus creating new and challenging problems for business management.

Business purpose has been defined as the creation of customers by matching company resources with market opportunities. We have stressed the point that the kinds of markets that can be served effectively by any one company are determined by that company's own mix of technical, marketing, financial, and people resources. The marketing function serves as a two-way communication link between the market and the company. The more effective the communication, the greater the degree of customer satisfaction and the greater the chance of success.

The company operates within constantly changing market and competitive environments. It is through skillful adaptation to change that companies grow and prosper over the long term. Since marketing management is in the best position to observe market and competitive change, it should take the lead in proposing strategies to deal with change.

We have defined the marketing management function as the process of setting marketing goals, after considering company resources and market opportunities, and the planning and execution of activities required to meet the goals. We have suggested that this process should be carried out in a manner acceptable to both customers and to society.

Finally, we have suggested that nonmarketing majors should study marketing and marketing management since every functional area of a business, either directly or indirectly, is involved with the company's goal of creating and maintaining satisfied customers. Marketing majors also should study other business functions, for, in the future, they will need to coordinate their activities with other functional managers. These interrelationships will become more apparent later as we deal with marketing planning and administration.

QUESTIONS

1. Explain the idea that the real marketing manager is the chief executive and describe this person's relationship to the functional marketing manager.
2. Trace the evolution of marketing through the four periods of business orientation during the last century of United States history.
3. What is the basic philosphy behind the marketing concept?
4. Define business purpose and explain how it is determined.
5. Briefly explain the elements of management.
6. Specifically, what is marketing management?
7. Explain the difference between strategic planning and tactical planning.
8. Differentiate between consumer marketing and industrial marketing.
9. In what sense can it be said that the marketing manager's job represents a dichotomy? How does the marketing manager deal with this dual role?

REFERENCES

1. *Business Week*, Feb. 7, 1977, p. 98.
2. Peter F. Drucker, *Managing For Results*, Harper & Row, New York, 1964, p. 91.
3. Citicorp, *Annual Report 1979*, p. 13.
4. From a speech to the National Association of Automobile Dealers, reported by *The New York Times*, Jan. 31, 1977, p. 35.
5. For a discussion of matching a company's unique strengths with the needs of particular markets, see Andrew G. Kaldor, "Imbricative Marketing," *Journal of Marketing*, April 1971, pp. 19–25.
6. *Business Week*, July 21, 1980, p. 104. By special permission, © 1980 by McGraw-Hill, Inc., New York, N.Y., 10020. All rights reserved.
7. Theodore Levitt, "Marketing Myopia," *Harvard Business Review*, vol. 38, July–August 1961, pp. 24–47.
8. *Business Week*, July 21, 1980, p. 205. By special permission, © 1980 by McGraw-Hill, Inc., New York, N.Y., 10020. All rights reserved.

CHAPTER 2

Marketing Definitions and Concepts

This chapter is included for those who have not had a basic marketing course or who need a review of those introductory marketing subjects not covered in Chapter 1. Much of the chapter deals with explanations of terms such as market, marketing, marketing mix, promotional mix, classes of goods, and the marketing system. The latter part of the chapter discusses nonbusiness marketing and international marketing—subjects you may not have had previously. The chapter closes with comments on the challenging role for marketing executives during the balance of the twentieth century.

Most of you have some idea of what marketing is, although perhaps not its scope. On the first day of an introductory course I ask my students to write their definitions of *marketing*. Most of them equate it with advertising and selling. This is natural since we've all experienced advertising and have dealt with salespeople in stores and elsewhere. While advertising and selling are parts of the promotional function of marketing, they by no means represent the whole.

WHAT IS A MARKET?

Before defining marketing we should be sure that we know what a market is. *Market* can be a verb, adjective, or noun. When used as a verb it implies everything that results in a sale. For example, we may say that Goodyear *markets* (sells) its tires to automobile manufacturers as original equipment and to consumers as replacements. Market is an adjective when used as a modifier, for example, market price, market demand, market order.

When used as a noun, market has two meanings. One refers to the market (or marketplace) where exchange occurs, such as the stock market, a farmers' market, or the European Common Market. The second use as a noun is in describing a group of buyers and potential buyers for a specific product or service. This is the way in which market is most frequently used by marketing professionals. We can define this use of market as follows:

> A market represents the aggregate demand of the buyers and potential buyers for a product or service over a specific period of time.

The automotive market, for example, represents all of the people and organizations willing and able to buy an automobile this year.

Market Segments

Market segments (or niches) and the concept of market segmentation will be discussed in Chapter 4. For now we can say that *market segments are those subgroups of a broader market that have different needs, preferences, or buying patterns*. Segments of the car market, for example, would be the:

Economy car market

Chicago car market

Car leasing market

Foreign import car market

Commercial fleet market

Target Market

This term is applied to *the market segment or segments designated by a firm to receive its principal marketing efforts*. Generally a firm will concentrate on segments that represent the largest potential or that otherwise provide the best opportunity. Coca-Cola, for example, may target its advertising primarily to the heaviest consumers of soft drinks—the 13 to 24 age group. Procter & Gamble may target its marketing efforts for Crest toothpaste to the more health-conscious families. American Can may target its efforts toward the beer and soft drink industry—the largest users of cans. While those companies also offer their products to broader segments, they concentrate their marketing efforts where they believe the payoff to be greatest.

DEFINITION OF MARKETING

There seem to be as many definitions of marketing as there are books on the subject. Different perspectives result in different definitions of marketing; it is an evolving, changing discipline, and it is a complex subject not easily captured in a few words. Marketing commonly is defined in economic, legal, or managerial terms.

Economic Definitions

Two classic economic definitions describe marketing (1) as an exchange process and (2) as a creator of utilities.

> **Exchange.** The simplest and most encompassing definition is:

Marketing is an exchange process.

It is the process by which sellers are brought together with buyers to exchange their goods or services for something of value. The virtue of this definition is that it is applicable to every type of society, country, and economy, ranging from simple barter in an agrarian society to the complicated marketing systems of the highly developed societies where few people produce any of the things they consume. It applies to socialist economies, where production and distribution facilities are state-owned, as well as to capitalist, free market economies. It applies to services as well as to products. And it applies to government and institutional services as well as to services provided by business. The concept is portrayed in Figure 2-1.

Utilities. The whole process of producing and distributing products to provide consumer satisfaction can be viewed as the creation of utilities, namely, form, time, place, and possession. Each of these utilities adds value for the buyer or user of the product.

Manufacturing creates *form* utility as raw materials are converted into a finished product. In the case of a soft drink, for example, sweeteners, flavors, and charged water are mixed and packaged to create (i.e., give *form* to) a bottle of soda. But, on a hot day, a can of soda is of no value to you or me if it is sitting in a bottler's plant. To have value it must be at some convenient retail location—such as a vending machine in a school building or service station—at the time we are thirsty and want a soda. Furthermore, to give us the satisfaction we seek, the soda must be refreshingly cold and available at a reasonable price.

It is marketing that adds the utilities of time, place, and possession. To continue with our soda example, *time* and *place* utilities are provided by transportation to retail outlets and inventories of various flavors, so that the soda we want is conveniently available when we are hot and thirsty. *Possession* utility is created when we possess the product and, in this case, when our desire for a cold soda is satisfied at a price that is acceptable.

An easy-to-remember definition which encompasses the utility concept is:

> Marketing is having the right product at the right place at the right time at the right price.

Legal Definition

From the legal standpoint marketing can be viewed as *the process of transferring ownership from the producer to the ultimate consumer or buyer*. In the case of a typical consumer good, for example, legal title is transferred (1) from the producer to the wholesaler, (2) from the wholesaler to the retailer, and (3) from the retailer to the consumer buyer. This process also encompasses the legal right to use a product rather than outright ownership. For example, when one rents or leases a car, one has a legal right to use it.

Managerial Definitions

Rather than give an economic or legal definition, a marketing manager more likely would define marketing as follows:

> Marketing is providing—on a timely basis—products (or services) designed to meet the

FIGURE 2-1. Marketing as an exchange process.

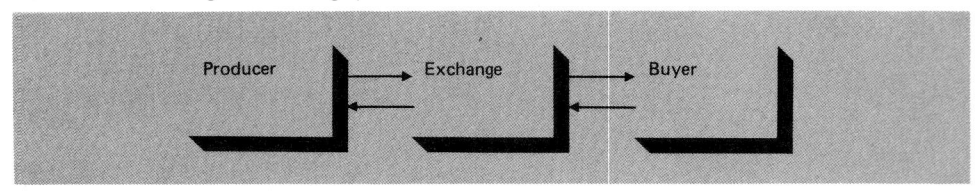

Producer → Exchange → Buyer

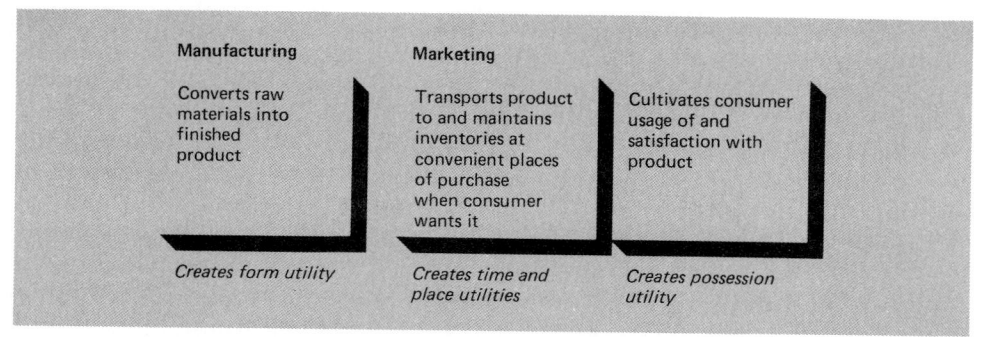

Manufacturing	Marketing	
Converts raw materials into finished product	Transports product to and maintains inventories at convenient places of purchase when consumer wants it	Cultivates consumer usage of and satisfaction with product
Creates form utility	*Creates time and place utilities*	*Creates possession utility*

FIGURE 2-2. Manufacturing and marketing add value to product through creation of utilities.

needs and wants of target markets, and arranging for pricing, distribution, promotion, and postsale service.

This definition represents the way we will look at marketing. It covers the six basic steps experienced marketers follow to develop a satisfied clientele:

1. Determine the target markets to be served.
2. Plan the products or services to be offered, based on knowledge of the markets' wants and needs.
3. Set prices.
4. Select channels of distribution to reach the target markets and persuade channel members to distribute the products or services.
5. Inform potential customers of the firm's offerings and persuade them to buy.
6. Provide needed services after the sale, such as installation, maintenance, repair, and warranty fulfillment.

Much of this text deals with the many functions required to carry out the above six steps in a way that is satisfactory to the customer, acceptable to society, and profitable to the company.*

THE MARKETING MIX

Neil H. Borden, formerly of the Harvard Business School, popularized the idea of the *marketing mix*. According to him and his colleague, Martin Marshall:

> The concept of the Marketing Mix essentially premises that the decision-making executive must analyze certain market forces and certain elements of marketing if the executive is ultimately to determine a sound "mix" of marketing elements—which promises to be effective and profitable.[1]

The market forces were the behavior of consumers, the trade (wholesalers and retailers), competition, and government. The marketing elements Borden and Marshall referred to have been gathered under the following six headings:

*Instead of "profit" one may substitute "within budget" when speaking of non-profit organizations.

Product planning, including branding and packaging

Pricing

Distribution, including channels and physical handling

Promotion, including personal selling, advertising, publicity, and sales promotion

Servicing

Marketing research

The definition has changed in the intervening years, and the scope of the marketing mix now includes only the four marketing elements of product, price, distribution,* and promotion. Service has been subsumed under product, while marketing research has become part of the marketing information system which underlies the marketing planning process. And Borden's market forces are now considered when developing marketing strategies.

Since we'll use the term *marketing mix* to refer to product, price, distribution (or place) and promotion, we define the concept as follows:

> The concept of the marketing mix suggests that the company resources devoted to product, price, distribution, and promotion (and the subsections thereof) should be mixed in varying proportions depending upon the industry category of the firm, its position in the market, and the competitive situation.

For example, the marketing mix of a consumer packaged goods firm such as Gillette will be weighted toward promotion, with particular emphasis on consumer advertising. In contrast, the marketing mix of a primarily industrial goods firm such as Du Pont will be weighted toward product design, technical service, and personal selling.

A company with low market share usually will have to spend a greater share of its income on promotion than will the market leader. Or it may vary its mix by pricing lower than the leader. This means that the company in the weak market position will have a lower profit margin as a result of spending relatively more for promotion and/or receiving lower prices. As shown in Table 2-1, General Motors is the market leader in the automotive industry. GM also outspends its competitors for advertising, although this represents a smaller share of its income than is the case for the smaller

---

*Professor Jerome McCarthy changes "distribution" to "place" and refers to the elements as the "4Ps," which makes them easy to remember—product, price, place, and promotion.

TABLE 2-1

Advertising as a Percent of Sales, Automotive Industry—1980

Market Position	Sales, $ billions	Ad Expenditures, $ millions	% Advertising to Sales
1. General Motors	57.7	316	0.5
2. Ford	37.0	280	0.8
3. Chrysler	9.3	150	1.6
4. American Motors	2.5	46	1.8

Source: *Advertising Age*, Sept. 10, 1981, p. 8.

competitors. If all other things are equal, including price, Chrysler's profit margin will be 1.1 percent lower than General Motors' and American Motors' profit margin will be 1.3 percent lower than GM's.

PRODUCT, PRICE, DISTRIBUTION

In this section we briefly describe the product, price, and distribution elements of the marketing mix. Promotion is described in the following section. The chapters in Part Five are devoted to these subjects.

Product

The *product* offered by an organization is what the business (or nonbusiness) entity is all about. While we tend to think of products as objects we can see and touch, the term product may be used in referring to intangible services and ideas as well.

Because products often have values for buyers that transcend their intrinsic qualities, we define product as follows:

> Product is a marketer's offering as perceived by the market.

The factors that influence buyers' perceptions are described in Chapter 16. The cases in this book deal with organizations that market services and ideas as well as physical objects; all, however, market "products."

Most organizations market more than one product. A group of related products is called a *product line*. Diversified organizations offer multiple lines of products.

Price

To most of us price is the amount we pay a retailer in exchange for a product. Retailers, of course, may charge what they wish since manufacturers legally cannot dictate the retailer's price.*

There are two common methods by which prices are computed—discount and markup. In the *discount method* the manufacturer sets prices for wholesalers and retailers, which represent percentage discounts from an *assumed* retail price. The *markup* method is just the opposite. Here the manufacturer sets the price to be charged to the wholesaler. The wholesaler marks up this price by a percentage when selling to the retailer; the retailer in turn marks up the wholesaler's price by a percentage when selling to the consumer.

The size of discounts or markups varies by product industry and tends to correlate with distribution costs. Discounts or markups for cigarettes, for example, are relatively small because of rapid inventory turnover and low handling costs. Prescription drugs, on the other hand, require relatively large discounts or markups because of slow inventory turnover and the high costs of dispensing through licensed pharmacists.

As consumers we observe that prices for the same or similar product sometimes differ according to the type of retail outlet selling the product. This is primarily because of differences in the amount and quality of services offered. A self-service

---

*Some states require minimum retail markups for certain classes of products.

clothing store with few customer services, for example, sells for less than a department or specialty store offering pleasant surroundings, trained salesclerks, and free alterations. Differences in prices among stores of the same type can vary for other reasons, such as differences in retailers' costs or their pricing policies.

A difficult but important subject, pricing is more involved than this brief introduction can suggest. Chapter 18 will delve into pricing further.

Distribution

Most of the time our mass distribution system provides us with the products we want at the time and place we want them. To appreciate how well our system works, we have to experience life in less developed countries or encounter a major disruption of supply such as a gasoline shortage.

Channels of distribution are the means by which products move from producers to consumers or to user organizations. Channel *intermediaries* in the form of *wholesalers* and *retailers* provide the distribution channel for most consumer products. Wholesalers specialize by classes of products and carry a wide selection of items to meet the varying needs of their retail customers. Wholesalers purchase goods in bulk quantities from a variety of manufacturers, store the goods in warehouses, and deliver in small quantities to retail stores in the geographic area served. A minor portion of consumer goods are channeled *direct* from manufacturers to consumers through such means as mail order, vending machines, or door-to-door salespeople.

Industrial goods (goods bought by organizations for their own use) are distributed either direct from the supplier to the customer or through industrial wholesalers who specialize by classes of goods. Channels of distribution are discussed in Chapter 19.

THE PROMOTIONAL MIX

Marketing teachers and writers use the term "promotion" as an inclusive term covering all activities involved in market communication and persuasion, namely, advertising, personal selling, sales promotion, and publicity. It should be noted, however, that when practicing marketing executives use the term "promotion," they often mean sales promotion. We'll use the term *promotion* in the all-inclusive sense. The elements of promotion are defined as follows:

Advertising—any paid message presented in media, such as TV, radio, magazines, newspapers, or billboards by an identified source.

Personal selling—sales contacts made with the trade, end users, or influencers (nonbuyers who influence brand or product selection) by company sales persons.

Sales promotion—any other communication or persuasive device; a catch-all term which includes things as diverse as coupons, product samples, cents-off deals, displays, trade show booths, contests, and product brochures.

Publicity—any unpaid-for mention of a company, brand, or product by the media.

Varying the Promotional Mix

The most prevalent promotional mix variables are advertising and personal selling. Relative expenditures for advertising and personal selling vary by type of product as shown in Figure 2-3. The ratio of advertising expense to sales expense may run as high as 10 to 1 for some consumer packaged goods and as low as 1 to 10 for some industrial goods.[2]

The reasons for heavy weighting toward advertising for consumer packaged goods is that these products are sold largely through self-service stores. Advertising is needed by Procter & Gamble, for example, to build consumer brand awareness and interest so that the consumer will pick the P&G brand off the shelf. Personal selling by P&G ensures that company brands are on the retail shelf, properly displayed and priced, but this selling expense is less than the national advertising expense.

The ratio of advertising to personal selling approaches equilibrium in the case of consumer hard goods. General Electric, for example, uses national advertising to keep its brand name "in the consumer's mind" so that the consumer will be receptive to the GE brand when the time comes to buy an appliance. But General Electric also must have a sizable sales force to maintain retail distribution for its products and to train retail salesclerks who influence the brand of appliance purchased by the consumer.

In the case of industrial goods sold by one company for use by another, primary emphasis is placed on personal selling. The marketing of many industrial goods, such as the products of U.S. Steel, requires considerable face-to-face discussion between seller and buyer. Advertising helps to maintain a favorable company image, but industrial customers are made and retained by personal contact.

Push-Pull Strategies

Two terms used to indicate the relative importance of advertising and personal selling in consumer goods marketing are pull strategy and push strategy. The *pull strategy* applies to consumer packaged goods sold through self-service stores. Advertising causes consumers to pull the product off the retail store shelf. This triggers replacement orders to be pulled from the manufacturer through the wholesaler to replace the retailer's stock.

The *push strategy* is used for consumer shopping goods (such as appliances, women's coats, and men's suits) sold in situations where the retail salesclerk

FIGURE 2-3. Continuum showing how the ratio of advertising expense to personal selling expense changes as goods go from consumer packaged toward industrial.

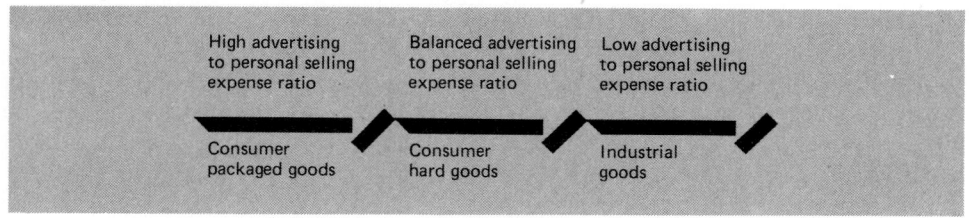

High advertising to personal selling expense ratio	Balanced advertising to personal selling expense ratio	Low advertising to personal selling expense ratio
Consumer packaged goods	Consumer hard goods	Industrial goods

influences product and brand selection. The manufacturer uses personal selling to push the product to the retailer and to encourage the retail salesclerk to push the product to the consumer.

Sales Promotion

Sales promotion is used by most companies, and particularly by those selling consumer packaged goods. Historically, it was considered a supplement to consumer advertising. Recently, however, sales promotion expenditures have risen faster than expenditures for advertising and now total over $50 billion annually. Much of the increase was due to the relative flatness of the U.S. economy, beginning in the mid-seventies, which caused convenience goods companies to offer larger incentives to retailers (for stocking, display, and local advertising) and to promote more deals to consumers (e.g., premiums and discounts). These incentives are a form of temporary price discounting. They allow the manufacturer to maintain list price while modifying the size of the incentives as the market situation warrants.

Publicity

Publicity is a relatively minor form of promotion because the manufacturer has no control over what the media will use. On the other hand, a favorable report by the news media on a company product often will carry more weight than a paid advertising message. Consequently, companies regularly issue press releases on subjects they hope are newsworthy, such as new product introductions. To gain the attention of editors, the Milton Bradley Co. introduced its new Super Simon®* electronic game at Carol Channing's Manhattan town house. Papers across the country printed pictures of the Broadway star playing with the game. The elements of the promotional mix are covered more thoroughly in Chapters 20 and 21.

TYPES OF GOODS

Goods can be classified in several ways. We have already used some of these classifications without explaining them in detail. Here we will describe some of the more commonly used classifications.

Consumer and Industrial Goods

The most basic classification separates goods into consumer and industrial. As you saw in Chapter 1, the basis for the classification is who buys the goods and who uses them. Consumer goods are those bought by individuals for personal or family use. Industrial goods are those bought and used by organizations such as companies, institutions, and government.

The same product may be either consumer or industrial. A typewriter bought by a student for personal use is a consumer good. A typewriter purchased by a university department for typing student records is an industrial good. It is important

---

*Super Simon® is a registered trademark of the Milton Bradley Co.

to understand the basis for classification since consumer and industrial goods usually require different marketing strategies.

Convenience, Shopping, and Specialty Goods

Consumer goods are commonly classified by the way they are distributed and purchased.

Convenience Good. A convenience good is purchased frequently, is relatively low in price, and is available in a wide choice of retail outlets—i.e., is conveniently located. Convenience goods are consumed quickly and bought frequently, and consumers usually will accept a substitute brand rather than search past the first store visited if their regular brand is not in stock.

Many of the products found in self-service stores are convenience goods such as tobacco, packaged foods, nonprescription drugs, and personal toilet articles. In the Hanes case in Part Three we will see how women's hosiery moved into self-service stores when it was recognized that hosiery was a convenience good.

Shopping Good. A shopping good is purchased infrequently, is relatively expensive, and is a sufficiently important purchase that consumers will search for information and the best buy. Cars, major applicances, coats, and suits are examples.

Specialty Good. A specialty good is a unique product or brand for which the consumer will not readily accept a substitute. The consumer, therefore, will search for and even go some distance to obtain the item. Specialty goods are distributed *exclusively* or *selectively* (i.e., they will be stocked in only one or a limited number of stores in a geographic area). They are usually priced higher than more widely distributed brands. Designer clothes, arch-support shoes, medical appliances, and some brands of sports and hobby equipment fall into this category.

Classes of Industrial Goods

Industrial goods can be classified as follows:

1. Raw materials such as fibers and semifinished goods such as unbleached textiles
2. Equipment such as machinery, trucks, and computers
   a. *engineered* equipment (designed to the specifications of an individual buyer or class of buyers—usually made to order)
   b. *multipurpose* equipment (designed for different buyers with common needs—usually inventoried for prompt delivery)
3. Components of finished goods such as motors and hoses
   a. engineered components (see above)
   b. multipurpose components (see above)
4. Supplies such as lubricants, fuel, janitorial needs, and office supplies

Other Goods Classifications

Other commonly used goods classifications include durable, nondurable, packaged, and capital.

Durable Goods. These are goods that are not readily consumed; they last from a few to many years in normal use. They can be primarily consumer (e.g., cars, furniture, appliances) or primarily industrial (e.g., trucks or plant machinery). Consumer durables may be referred to as consumer "hard goods."

Nondurable Goods. These are goods that are consumed relatively quickly by people (e.g., food, tobacco) or by production processes (e.g., fuels, lubricants), or that have limited life in use (e.g., textiles, apparel, paper). The U.S. Census of Manufacturers lists several types of manufactured goods by durable and nondurable classifications. Consumer nondurables, such as textiles and clothing, are sometimes referred to as "soft" goods.

Consumer Packaged Goods. These are prepackaged products, such as food, drugs, and tobacco, sold mainly in self-service stores. Most often they are nondurable goods, though not exclusively so; for example, small durable goods found in hardware stores are prepackaged for self-service.

Capital Goods. These are machinery and tools used in the production of other goods.

MARKETING AS A SYSTEM

Going beyond the definitions of marketing given earlier in the chapter, we can now consider marketing as a *system*. Marketing in a developed country can be viewed as a system because of the interactions that occur within and between the external and internal market environments. An action at any one point in the system causes reactions elsewhere. When information feedback is added to the system, the company can react to changes occurring in the external environment.

The elements of the internal environment—such as production, finance, and the marketing mix—are considered variables that are *controllable* by the company. Elements of the external environment—such as the market, the economy, and competition—are *not controllable* by the company. But knowledge of changes in these uncontrollable variables enables the company to alter its marketing mix to maintain or improve its market position.

Figure 2-4 depicts the marketing system. Side brackets indicate the internal and external variables as well as the distribution channels through which company products meet the market. Distribution channels may or may not be controllable by the company as will be explained in Chapter 8.

NONBUSINESS MARKETING

Many of the marketing principles and concepts developed by business organizations are being adopted by growing numbers of nonbusiness organizations, including governmental, educational, social, cultural, and political agencies. Nonbusiness marketing often is called *social marketing*, although when Kotler and Zaltman introduced the term, they limited its meaning to the marketing of social causes.[3]

The first and most obvious application of marketing by nonbusiness organizations is promotion—primarily advertising. The federal government, for example, is

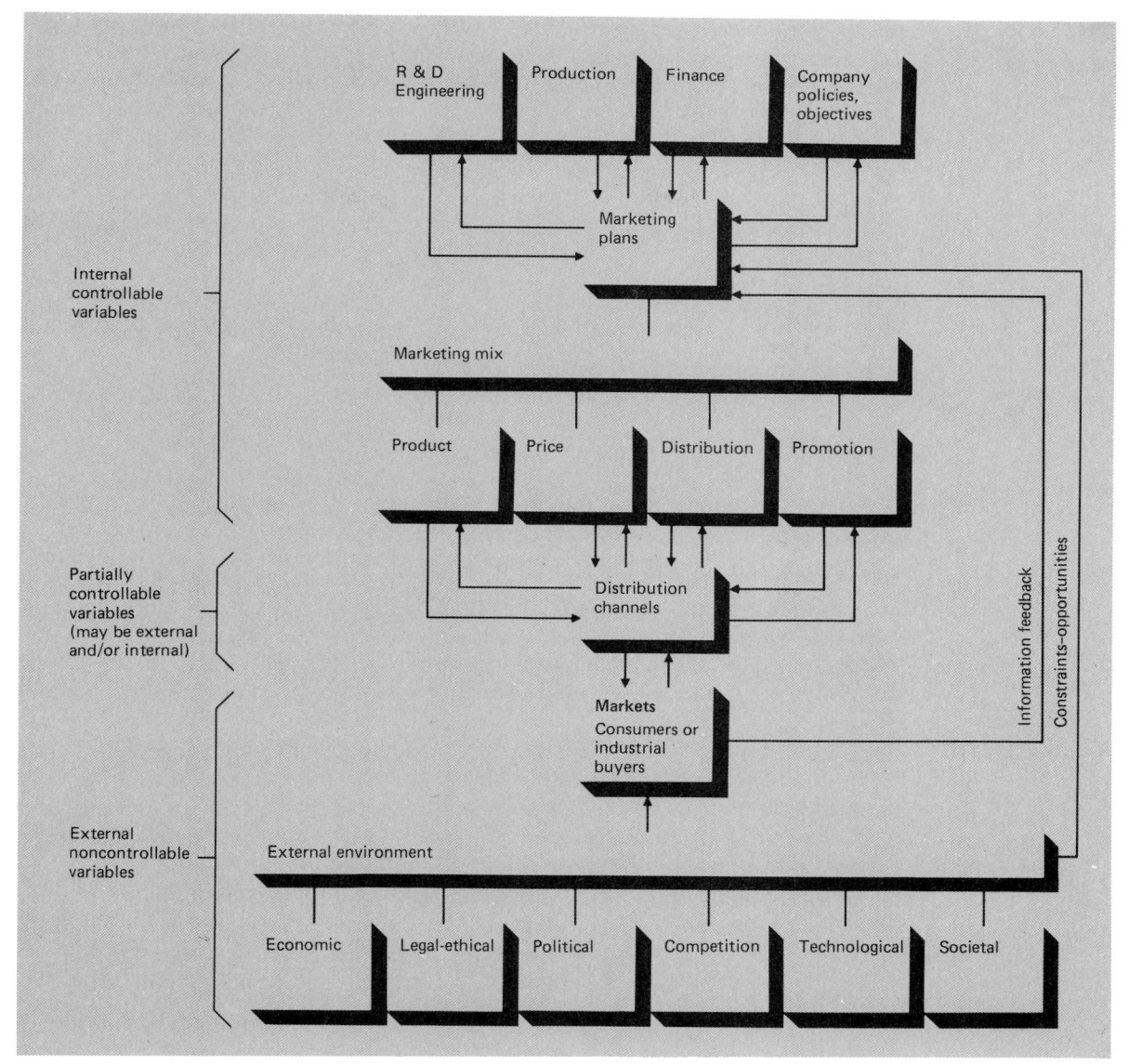

FIGURE 2-4. Diagram of a total marketing system. *Source:* Victor P. Buell, "Marketing Concepts and Systems," in Lester R. Bittel, ed., *Encyclopedia of Professional Management*, McGraw-Hill, New York, 1979, p. 694.

among the top thirty largest U.S. advertisers, with expenditures totalling nearly $200 annually.[4] Rapid acceptance of the use of advertising techniques by the government led William Novelli, head of a Washington based advertising agency, to predict that advertising in the public sector will be the major development in the field of advertising during the 1980s.[5]

Examples of government agencies using advertising and some of the subjects are given in the table on the next page.

EXAMPLES OF GOVERNMENT ADVERTISING

	Subject
Federal agency:	
Department of Defense	Armed services recruiting
U.S. Postal Service	Express mail service
Department of Agriculture	Better eating habits for children
Amtrack	Rail passenger services
Public Service Campaigns*:	
Social Security	Benefits for elderly
Transportation	Seat belt use
Women's credit	How to protect rights
National Heart and Lung Institute	Prevention of high blood pressure
Consumer Product Safety Commission	Safety messages

*Many public service campaigns are arranged by the Advertising Council, a nonprofit industry group whose members furnish creative services and campaign coordination free to selected nonprofit agencies.

Source: Advertising Age, Sept. 6, 1979, pp. 156–157, and Sept. 9, 1982, pp. 176–177.

Acceptance of Marketing Concept

Despite their use of advertising and other promotional techniques, many nonbusiness organizations have not thought of themselves as "marketers." Increasingly, however, these organizations are accepting the idea that organizing to serve the needs and wants of their markets (clients, publics, customers, etc.) is the best way to ensure their success. In essence they are adopting the marketing concept described in Chapter 1.

As this concept is accepted, they begin to adopt other business marketing terms such as target markets, market objectives, and the marketing mix. And they use marketing research to identify, measure, and segment markets, to determine market wants and needs, and to measure the market's satisfaction with the organization's services.

Responding to an article in *Business Week*, headed "Ads Start to Take Hold in the Professions," Dr. Daniel J. Fink of the University of Pennsylvania School of Medicine took issue with advertising by professionals. In so doing, however, he made a forceful statement in support of professionals using marketing in its broader sense. Dr. Fink's letter to the editor read in part:

> If professionals concentrate only on advertising, they are missing the major benefits of the broader aspects of marketing—finding out what the client wants, designing services to meet these wants, and delivering these services.
>
> The successful professional, in an age of increasing competition, will not be the one who advertises well but rather the one who does a solid job of marketing. And, if by marketing, the quality of service and level of satisfaction can be increased, the professional will be acting in a most professional manner.[6]

Table 2-2 shows how marketing can be applied to three nonbusiness institutions —a college, a political candidate, and a government agency. The similarities between business and nonbusiness marketing are greater than the differences. Differences are most pronounced in the areas of *price* and *distribution*. The price of

TABLE 2-2
Examples of Marketing Approaches by Nonbusiness Organizations

Target Markets	Marketing Objectives	Marketing Mix			
		Product (Service)	Price	Distribution	Promotion
EDUCATIONAL: College					
High school seniors the college is best suited to serve	Meet enrollment quotas	Courses, degrees, social and athletic development	Tuition, fees, personal expenses	Faculty; administration; organizations; facilities—living, dining, social, athletic	*External*: bulletins, brochures, letters, advertising, recruiting visits, campus open houses *Internal*: bulletin boards, campus paper
POLITICAL: Political candidate					
Segments are party members, labor, ethnic, minorities, new voters	Winning election	Party candidate	Voters' time in learning of candidate; voter contributions—money, work	Candidate's exposure to voters	Advertising, speeches, handshaking, telephone, direct mail, new releases
GOVERNMENTAL: Office of Cancer Communications, National Cancer Institute					
Women not having regular breast examinations	Increased rate of early detection and treatment of breast cancer	Facts about breast cancer	Cost of visit to doctor; fear associated with possible discovery	Through "intermediaries": American Cancer Society (ACS), unions, churches, health care institutions, mass media	Through "intermediaries": advertising by ACS, articles, brochures, letters, free clinics by others.

some nonbusiness services may be expressed in terms of social costs (time, effort, forgoing pleasure) rather than an outlay of money. Distribution—the means of bringing the service to the customer—usually is through facilities other than retail stores.

The value of applying modern marketing approaches to any organization is the advantage gained from thinking through answers to marketing oriented questions such as:

What is our product (service)?

Who are we trying to serve (target markets)?

What are we trying to accomplish with our clients (our marketing objectives)?

How should our service be priced, distributed, and promoted to effectively achieve our objectives?

Although the conclusions of a nonbusiness organization may be different from the answers a business organization may reach, it is the thought process that is important.

Nonbusiness Marketing Jobs

As nonbusiness marketing grows, the jobs requiring a marketing orientation increase, although they are not as easily spotted as marketing jobs in business. Government and social agencies seem reluctant to use marketing position titles for fear of appearing too commercial. Even so, the use of marketing and marketing related titles continues to grow as the following list shows:

U.S. Postal Service

    Assistant Post Master General/Customer Service

    Director of Commercial Marketing

    Manager, Advertising Branch

Amtrack

    Director of Marketing Services

U.S. Travel Service

    Director, Advertising and Media Services Division

Public Broadcasting Service

    Senior Vice President, Development and Public Information

Community Health Plan, Inc. (Rhode Island)

    Director of Marketing

WGBY-TV, Public Service Channel 57, Springfield, MA.

    Marketing Manager

As people move from business to government and other nonprofit agency marketing jobs, they prove that business concepts can be transferred successfully from the private to the public sector.

INTERNATIONAL MARKETING

We will be concentrating on mastering the basic principles of marketing management. Once gained these can be applied anywhere. Yet, since most of the examples used in the text are from the United States, a brief overview of international marketing may be useful.

Job Opportunities

There are fewer jobs in foreign marketing with American companies than in domestic marketing. With a few exceptions, American companies obtain most of their sales in the United States, or at least on the North American continent. Several reasons can be offered.

Traditional Attitudes. Traditionally Americans have shown less interest in foreign trade than other developed countries. First of all, the vast size of the U.S. market provides sufficient opportunity at home to satisfy most companies. Secondly, U.S. self-sufficiency in raw materials made it unnecessary to sell abroad to obtain foreign exchange to pay for importing raw materials. The second situation has been changing, particularly with respect to oil. The United States has run sizable foreign exchange deficits in recent years, partly because of its long term neglect of exports.

Historically, by contrast, countries short of raw materials—such as the United Kingdom, Japan, and Germany—had to export in order to pay for the imports necessary for their survival. Because foreign trade is in the national interest of such countries, government policies are supportive of private business engaged in foreign marketing. U.S. policies have been much less supportive with the result that U.S. businesses often must compete on unequal terms.

With annual exports of about $200 billion the United States ships more goods abroad than any other country, yet these goods represent a small proportion of gross national product compared with other major exporting nations. The following list illustrates this by comparing exports as percentages of the gross national product of major industrial nations.

EXPORTS AS APPROXIMATE PERCENT OF GNP

Country	%
United States	6
Japan	13
France	17
Germany	24
United Kingdom	25

Source: *Statistical Abstract of the United States*, 1981, pp. 878, 890.

Politics and Trade. The United States sometimes uses its exports as a device for rewarding friends and punishing enemies. This policy is regularly applied to grains and other edible products, but it also affects specialized machinery and manufactured goods. Such policies create uncertainties that discourage private businesses from pushing their foreign marketing efforts. Some U.S.-based multinational* companies also have been criticized for alleged interference in foreign governments.

---

*Multinationals are companies with investments in manufacturing and marketing facilities in other than their home countries. Such companies tend to take a global rather than a domestic view of their opportunities.

This has not helped to improve the climate for the many American companies that do business abroad and avoid involvement in foreign politics. American ideals of fair play at times have created handicaps for American firms dealing in countries with different standards. United States laws against kickbacks to foreign nationals reputedly cause American companies to lose business to those foreign competitors who operate without such restrictions.

Staffing With Nationals. An important reason for the scarcity of foreign marketing jobs in U.S. companies is the prevailing practice of staffing foreign operations with nationals of the countries in which these companies operate. Consequently, marketing people in international departments may spend little time abroad. During a 20-year international career I observed far more U.S. engineers and production people on temporary assignments abroad than I did U.S. marketing people.

Companies staff with foreign nationals for two principal reasons. First, they want to have people in charge who understand the area. Second, it is less costly as a rule to have local managers than to maintain U.S. citizens abroad. Of 100,000 Xerox employees abroad, for example, less than one half of one percent are U.S. citizens.[7] Because of such extras as housing, private school tuition, home leaves, and higher pay to cover higher taxes, it can cost three times as much to keep an American abroad as it does at home.

Language Barriers. English is the international language of business. Consequently, Americans without foreign language skills are not necessarily barred from foreign marketing assignments. On the other hand, communication is far more effective if you speak the language of the area in which your company is marketing.

One finds in foreign economic centers communities of "ex-patriots"—citizens of various countries who work somewhat permanently abroad. These people are usually multilingual. They are less likely to be Americans because less emphasis is placed on foreign language training in the United States than in other countries. Ex-patriots are in demand by international companies because of their understanding of foreign cultures and their willingness to live abroad permanently and move from country to country.

Changing Times. While the above comments may seem pessimistic with respect to jobs in international marketing, you should not be discouraged from trying to work abroad if you are interested. There is little question that U.S. foreign trade will expand. As raw material shortages grow, they will force changes in public and government attitudes. The United States will have to export more in order to survive.

Furthermore, international marketing has become more sophisticated; consequently, better educated people will be needed to manage the international functions of U.S. corporations. The international departments will compete with the domestic departments for good marketing employees. Also, many international companies prefer that their top executives have international experience. We are beginning to see non-Americans move into top management positions in American based multinational companies.

Foreign versus Domestic Marketing

Basic U.S. approaches to marketing apply to any developed country with a market-based economy. The marketing planning approach outlined in Chapter 9, for example, is as applicable in France, Mexico, or Japan as it is in the United States.

Problems in marketing in foreign lands usually are less foreseeable than in your own country and can be disastrous for the unwary. Differences tend to show up in national laws, cultural customs and attitudes, and sometimes in distribution methods. Many American companies in the past have stumbled over such problems, nearly always as the result of ignorance. Information is the key to avoiding mistakes and it can be gathered abroad as it can in the United States. Experienced nationals can be hired to conduct market research, and marketing consultants usually are available.

Some products can be sold throughout the world with little or no change. IBM, for example, designs its computers so that the machinery and parts are interchangeable everywhere. American-Standard, on the other hand, found that with few exceptions it was unable to sell a bathroom product designed for one country in another country. The reasons were differences in building codes and consumers' perceptions of what a fixture should look like. Consequently, American-Standard (known as Ideal-Standard abroad) was denied the advantages of standardized design and centralized mass production (e.g., for the European Common Market) available to a company like IBM.

Approaches to International Marketing

American manufacturing companies have three primary options when doing business abroad: (1) exporting, (2) joint-venture, or (3) local production. A company usually goes through this sequence in the process of becoming multinational, although it may continue to use all three since some are more appropriate for some countries than for others.

Exporting. This involves selling products abroad that are produced in the United States. Sales usually are made through independent export agents.

Joint-Venture. This is an arrangement whereby a U.S. company sets up a jointly owned business with a foreign national company. Each party brings something to the venture. The U.S. company may provide patents, technical know-how, and capital while the indigenous company may provide production and marketing facilities, and local market knowledge.

The Scott Paper Company refers to its foreign joint ventures as "partnerships" or "manufacturing affiliates." Scott's approach to overseas markets is described in Marketing Note 2-1.

Company-Owned Production. In this arrangement the U.S. company owns a controlling interest in local production and marketing facilities. The key is *control* of the business since the laws of countries vary as to the degree and kind of ownership permitted to foreigners. Many companies view local control of production as the best option, but they usually do not go this route until they become experienced in foreign operations.

Franchising. Some American fast-food companies, such as Burger King, market abroad through company-owned outlets and also by franchising others to operate restaurants under the fast-food company's brand.

MARKETING NOTE 2-1	**Scott Paper's Approach to Foreign Operations**

From its earliest days, Scott has sought to serve customers beyond its U.S. borders. In the decades before World War II a substantial export business was carried on through a network of sales agents abroad with whom the Company developed relationships of mutual respect and loyalty.

The knowledge of international markets gained through our dealings with these export agents was a major asset when Scott set out in the 1950s to establish manufacturing affiliates overseas. Our approach was unusual: we sought out highly reputable local partners to share equally with us in affiliate ownership. This partnership concept has speeded our entry into foreign markets, and has assured a thorough understanding of local conditions in affiliate management. Tested now over more than two decades, it is still our preferred approach as we enter into new international ventures.

Executive leadership for our affiliates has been provided in most cases by local nationals selected in concert with our partners, while from its U.S. operations Scott has provided traveling cadres of experienced managers to work with affiliate executives and to help accomplish the transfer of technology and marketing expertise.

The size and growing importance of the international affiliates are evidenced by the fact that their combined sales equal almost one-half the sales of the domestic Company. In most affiliate countries, the markets for sanitary paper products are growing much more rapidly than ours here at home. A number of affiliates are in areas where per capita consumption of sanitary paper is still less than one-fourth that of the United States. The potential is there. And so is Scott.

Source: Excerpted from *The Centennial Edition, Scott Paper Company 1978 Annual Report*. Reproduced with the permission of Scott Paper Company.

Key to International Marketing Success

A basic key to marketing success anywhere is having the information to make good decisions. As in domestic situations, matching market opportunities with internal company resources is crucial. There is rarely any real barrier to gaining needed foreign market information, so long as mangagement is willing to spend the time and money to get it.

A LOOK AT THE FUTURE

Unlike the third quarter of the current century—a period of unparalleled growth—many analysts believe the balance of this century will see relatively slow economic growth. Among the reasons are the leveling off of population, unpredictable energy supplies, and high energy prices.

If this outlook is correct, companies will likely be run by conservative managements, less inclined to take risks than those who were in charge during the years 1950 to 1975. Emphasis will be on greater productivity (more sales at lower relative costs); there will be less tolerance for mistakes; marketing plans will receive closer scrutiny; and new product and other ventures requiring investment capital will have to meet strict financial tests.

This period will create opportunities for marketing executives with general business training and marketing managerial knowledge. Marketing management's role in the strategic direction of the firm will be greater than in the past because the market environment will be the key determinant in corporate strategy. Along with marketing knowledge other managerial requirements will be the ability to lead, to communicate clearly and creatively, and to plan effectively.

Part Two which follows begins our study of marketing management with an approach to understanding the market and forecasting sales. This knowledge will form the foundation for our next experience—learning how to develop strategic marketing plans, which will be taken up in Part Three.

QUESTIONS

1. What is the most common use of the term "market"?
2. Provide two economic definitions of marketing.
3. How is the concept of marketing viewed from a legal standpoint?
4. From the managerial viewpoint, how is marketing defined? What implication does this definition have for the marketing manager?
5. To what does the term "marketing mix" refer and how can it be defined?
6. What are the subsections of promotion? Describe them.
7. The most prevalent promotional mix variables are advertising and personal selling. Describe how these elements can be varied depending on the type of good. Indicate which of these variations is a pull strategy and which is a push strategy.
8. Briefly define the following types of goods:
    (a) consumer
    (b) industrial
    (c) convenience
    (d) shopping
    (e) specialty
    (f) durable
    (g) nondurable
    (h) consumer packaged
    (i) capital

REFERENCES

1. Neil H. Borden and Martin V. Marshall, *Advertising Management*, Irwin, Homewood, Ill., 1959, p. 23.
2. Advertising expenditures for companies can be obtained by reasearch of public documents, whereas personal selling expenditures are rarely reported separately in public reports. Occasional private studies verify the continuum shown in Figure 2-3. For example, see Edwin H. Lewis, "Sales Promotion Decisions," *Business News Notes*, University of Minnesota, Minneapolis, November 1954, p. 2.
3. Philip Kotler and Gerald Zaltman, "Social Marketing: An Approach to Planned Social Change," *Journal of Marketing*, July 1971, pp. 3–12.
4. *Advertising Age*, Sept. 9, 1982, p. 1.
5. Comments made at a conference on "Advertising in the 1980s" sponsored by the American Enterprise Institute for Public Policy Research and *Advertising Age*, Washington, D.C., June 27, 1980.
6. "Reader's Report," *Business Week*, Aug. 14, 1978, p. 4.
7. *The Wall Street Journal*, July 21, 1980, p. 12.

PART TWO

Understanding the Market and Forecasting Sales

Market knowledge is the foundation on which modern marketing is built. It is the basis on which a company plans its line of products or services, pricing, distribution, and promotional programs.

No well-managed company would attempt to develop strategies and the plans for their implementation without first having thoroughly analyzed its markets. All professionals, whether they are surgeons, lawyers, or airline pilots, collect and analyze information prior to applying their technical skills. A surgeon would not operate without first studying a patient's medical history, X rays, and diagnostic test results. Similarly, analysis of the market is the prerequisite for the professional marketing manager.

Developing market information is the process of asking and answering appropriate questions. Paraphrasing the six questions asked by journalists, we would want to know:

1. Who are the buyers and prospective buyers?
2. Where are they located and where do they buy?
3. How many are there and how can they be reached?
4. What is their buying potential?
5. Why do they buy the way they do?
6. When do they buy?

In Chapters 3 and 4 we'll learn about market analyses designed to answer the first four questions above. Chapter 5—Buyer Behavior—will answer the question why. In Chapter 6—Marketing Research and Information Systems—we'll discuss sources and methods for finding and processing the market information covered in Chapters 3, 4, and 5. And in Chapter 7—Sales Forecasting—we'll discuss how market information and company information are used to develop sales forecasts—an essential ingredient of business planning. Chapter 7 will show how seasonal and cyclical buying factors reflect on question

6—when do people buy? In Part Three—*The Strategic Marketing Planning Process*—we will see how these data are used in the development of company marketing plans.

Dealing With Numbers

In the chapters that follow you will see tables and graphs containing numbers and occasional equations. Most of these do not utilize advanced math or statistics. In fact, knowledge of basic arithmetic, common sense, and a little time are all that are needed to understand the data and to draw conclusions from them. While advanced math and statistics have their place, many business decisions do not require them.

Graduate as well as undergraduate students often become tense when faced with numbers. There is really no need for concern here. What most of us need is practice in studying tables of numbers, looking for relationships and signs of change, then practice in developing our own tables during case analyses. A simple table of numbers, arranged to show relationships, often reveals more about a problem or opportunity than do paragraphs of descriptive prose.

The practice of marketing, like management in any type of organization, deals with (1) numbers and (2) people. Success comes with developing skills at handling both. The text provides the opportunity for you to develop your skills in analyzing prearranged tables of numbers, while the cases give you the chance to arrange numbers on your own.

CHAPTER 3

Market Indicators and Market Trends

Effective market analysis begins with an understanding of the broad market indicators that influence the opportunities for all businesses, whether those businesses are serving consumer or industrial markets and whether they are providing goods or services.

Markets for consumer goods and services are affected by trends in the size, makeup, and location of population and by shifts in consumer purchasing power. Industrial goods and services markets are affected by these same trends, since most industrial demand is derived from consumer demand. Markets for industrial goods and services are also influenced by shifts in the industrial side of the economy, specifically by changes in the numbers and location of manufacturing plants and changes in their buying potential.

The market analyst begins by studying these broad market indicators, then moves to more specific analyses of the markets served by the company and the market environment. Finally, the analyst determines the company's position in the market or markets it serves. We will follow this same approach here and in the next chapter. The subjects we will discuss, and their analytic purposes, are listed in the accompanying table.

Subject	Analytic Purposes
1. Broad market characteristics	Measurement of general market size and trends by demographic, geographic, and economic indicators
2. Market segments	Classification of markets for products and services by segments with differing needs and preferences
3. Structural market change	Identification of significant change in the company's markets caused by external, uncontrollable factors
4. Industry structure	Measurement of the industry of which the company is a part—in terms of size, characteristics, and trends
5. Competitive structure	Description of competitive climate and numbers and rankings of competitors
6. Distribution structure	Determination of alternative channels and numbers and quality of intermediaries by location
7. Price structure	Tracking of industry trends in prices, margins, and allowances as well as prices of substitute products and services
8. Company position in the market	Company market share and trends as well as the market's perception of the company and its brands

Broad Market Characteristics

The amount of market data available from public sources, or by purchase from private sources, is so vast that only a fraction can be covered in one chapter. The sampling we offer here is organized by *consumer* markets, *industrial* markets, and markets for *services*. While many texts emphasize consumer marketing, we attempt to give balanced treatment to all three types. The importance of going beyond consumer marketing is apparent when one considers that in the U.S. economy, the value of industrial goods exceeds the value of consumer goods, and the value of services exceeds the value of all goods—both consumer and industrial.

Market Indicators and Data Sources

We will be looking at each market category in terms of its *demographic* (population characteristics), *geographic* (location), and *economic* (buying potential) indicators. Considered together these indicators are useful in estimating market potential, forecasting sales, laying out sales territories, and targeting advertising and sales promotional efforts. Figure 3-1 summarizes the types of information sought for each market category. The chapter follows the pattern revealed in this figure. First we examine trends in consumer markets in terms of demographic, geographic, and economic indicators. Next we examine the same indicators for industrial markets and for service markets. The tables are arranged to reveal the demographic and economic shifts occurring between the northern states (often referred to as the snow belt) and the southern and western states (called the sun belt).

The several federal censuses and government department surveys serve as the

FIGURE 3-1. Broad market characteristics.

Market indicators \ Markets	Consumer goods	Industrial goods	Services
Demographic	Size and makeup of population	Types and numbers of buying units	Same as for consumer or industrial goods according to which market services are sold
Geographic	Where people live	Locations of buying and using units	
Economic	Individual and family purchasing power	Sales potential by classes of buyers or by buying units	

Rates of change

lead to

Understanding some of the underlying factors affecting the specific markets for the company's product or service offerings sources of most of our broad market data. In addition to these public sources, many private organizations sell summaries and analyses of data, which may be of interest to particular companies. These organizations include reference book publishers, trade magazines, trade associations, and market research firms. Both the public sources, and many of the privately published materials, are available in major university and city libraries. When seeking data, experienced market analysts look first among public sources before deciding whether to turn to costlier primary market research studies.

One of the most valuable guides to available public data is the *Statistical Abstract of the United States*, published annually by the U.S. Department of Commerce, Bureau of the Census. The *Statistical Abstract* lists in summary form virtually every type of data developed by the several U.S. censuses and various government agencies. It includes information from many other private and public sources as well. Nearly 1600 tables refer to the original data sources if you need more detailed information. While there are other good reference works, the *Statistical Abstract* provides a convenient, effective, and inexpensive guide to most publicly available data. A guide to other commonly used data sources is provided in the appendix.

CONSUMER MARKETS

Demographic Data

Through the exhaustive decennial *Census of Population*, and its frequent periodic updates based on sampling, the Bureau of the Census provides population data broken into a wide variety of categories. There are breakdowns by age, sex, race, ethnic origin, family, and religion, for example. Vital statistics (such as births, deaths, marriages, divorces, and life expectancy) are also provided.

Figure 3-2, reproduced from the "Recent Trends" section of the *Statistical Abstract*, illustrates some of the trends in population. The decline of the under-18 age segment, for instance, is illustrated by one of the bar charts. The decline in the number of persons per household is shown in another. The lower portion of the figure reveals that the rate of population growth declined in the 1970 to 1980 period. Elsewhere in the *Abstract*, however, you would find that this picture is likely to change during the 1980 to 1990 period because of rising birth and immigration rates and a leveling of the death rate.

Actually the rate of population growth had been trending downward between the years 1960 and 1977. Nevertheless total population grew in absolute numbers during these years. This was because the decline in the rates of infant deaths and deaths from accidents and disease resulted in increased life expectancy. Average life expectancy is now about 74 years, and the median age is projected to increase from 30 in 1980 to 35.5 by the end of the century.

Significance of Demographic Change

Since people represent the base for consumer markets, marketers of consumer goods need to be aware not only of changing rates of population growth but also of the way the declines in birth and death rates affect the size of various age categories

Population

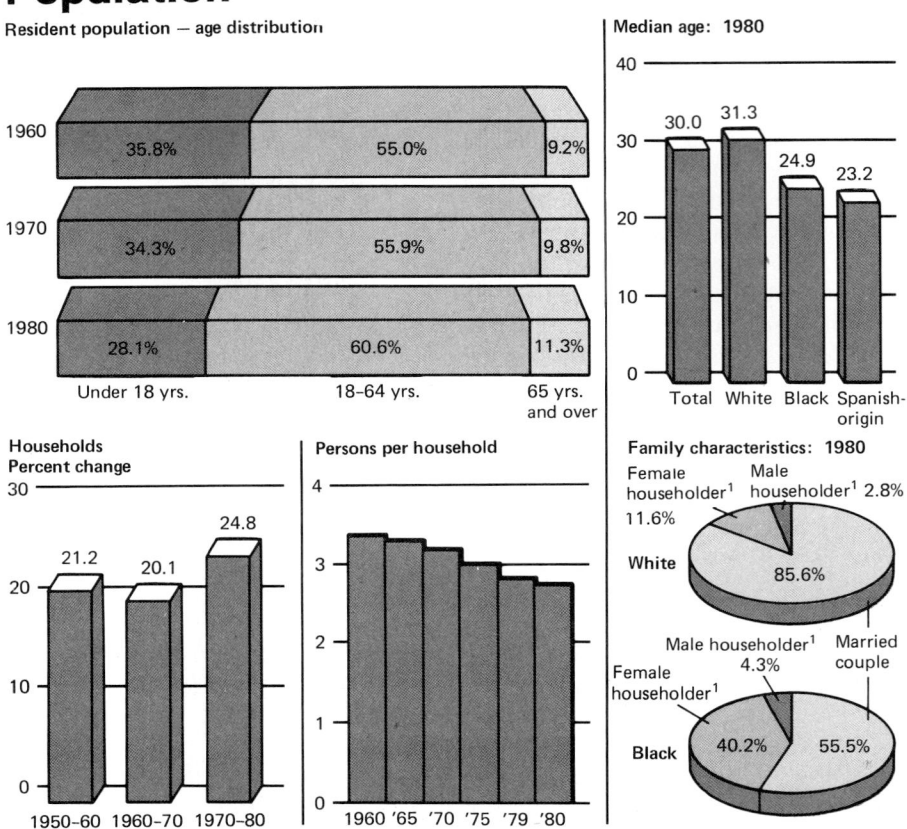

Resident population — age distribution

Year	Under 18 yrs.	18–64 yrs.	65 yrs. and over
1960	35.8%	55.0%	9.2%
1970	34.3%	55.9%	9.8%
1980	28.1%	60.6%	11.3%

Median age: 1980

- Total: 30.0
- White: 31.3
- Black: 24.9
- Spanish-origin: 23.2

Households — Percent change

- 1950–60: 21.2
- 1960–70: 20.1
- 1970–80: 24.8

Persons per household: 1960, '65, '70, '75, '79, '80

Family characteristics: 1980

White:
- Female householder[1]: 11.6%
- Male householder[1]: 2.8%
- Married couple: 85.6%

Black:
- Female householder[1]: 40.2%
- Male householder[1]: 4.3%
- Married couple: 55.5%

Subject	Unit of measure	1960	1970	1980	Percent change 1960–70	Percent change 1970–80
Resident population, total	Millions	179.3	203.3	226.5	13.4	11.4
Under 18 years	Millions	64.2	69.7	63.7	8.5	−8.5
18–64 years	Millions	98.6	113.6	137.2	15.2	20.8
65 years and over	Millions	16.6	20.0	25.5	20.6	27.9
White	Millions	158.8	178.1	188.3	12.1	5.8
Black	Millions	18.9	22.6	26.5	19.7	17.3
Persons of Spanish origin	Millions	(NA)	9.1	14.6	(NA)	61.0
Households	Millions	52.8	63.4	79.1	20.1	24.8
Persons per household	Number	3.33	3.14	2.75	(NS)	(NS)
One person households	Millions	6.9	10.7	17.8	55.1	66.4
Families, total	Millions	45.1	51.6	58.4	14.4	13.3
Married-couple	Millions	39.3	44.8	48.2	13.8	7.7
Female householder[1]	Millions	4.5	5.6	8.5	24.1	52.7

NA — Not available   NS — Not significant   [1] No spouse present

FIGURE 3-2. Examples of population trends. *Source:* U.S. Bureau of the Census, *Statistical Abstract of the United States, 1981*, Washington, D.C., p. 902.

at different times. (See Figure 3-3). Such developments affect companies differently, depending upon where their products fit with respect to age categories. Producers of infant foods such as Gerber and Beechnut were hurt by the decline in the birthrate, and producers of jeans, such as Levi Strauss & Co., benefited as the youth segment expanded in the 1960s and 1970s. Operators of nursing homes and producers of drugs for older people have experienced increased demand as life expectancy continues to increase.

The number and average size of households and families may be more significant than population numbers for goods associated with household operations such as appliances, home furnishings, and hardware. The number of ice cream cones sold is related more to numbers of people; the number of refrigerators sold is related more to the number of households.

For marketing planning purposes, future projections of demographic data are most important. The Bureau of the Census offers projections of populations and other demographic factors, using varying assumptions. The bureau, for example, expects the number of births to increase during the period from the late 1970s to the year 2000, even if the birthrate remains stable. This is because the number of women in the childbearing ages between 15 and 44 will be larger during this period. If the birthrate increases, we could have another baby boom in the U.S. during the last part of this century—which has positive implications for market planners.[1]

Age Change and Beverage Sales. The sales of soft drinks and coffee illustrate how the changing size of age groups affects product markets. Soft drinks have their

FIGURE 3-3. Birth and death rates, 1960 to 1980. *Source:* U.S. Bureau of the Census, *Statistical Abstract of the United States, 1981*, Washington, D.C., p. 57.

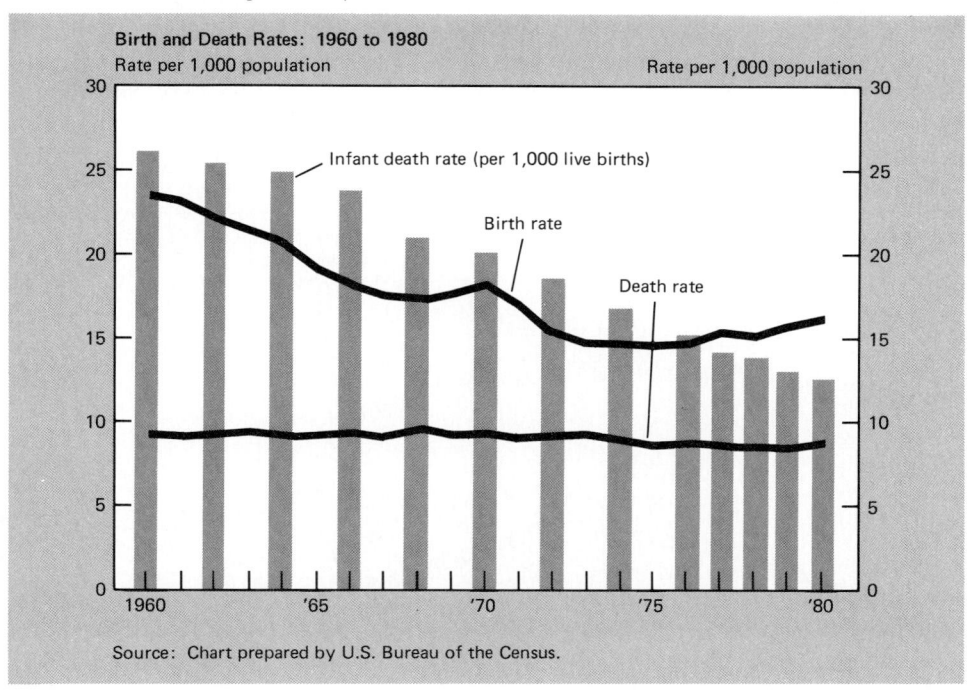

heaviest usage in the teenage to mid-20s age group, whereas coffee has its heaviest usage in the 25-and-over age group. Annual per capita consumption of soft drinks by 13- to 24-year-olds is 823 cans compared to 547 cans for all age groups and 243 cans for persons over 45.[2]

Between 1960 and 1980 the 14 to 24 age group rose from 15 percent to 20.5 percent of total population, an absolute gain of 19.2 million persons. The pattern has changed, however. This age group increased only slightly between 1970 and 1980, and it is projected to drop by 11.7 million between 1980 and 1990, when it will account for only 14.3 percent of total population. (See Figure 3-4.) As the 15 to 24 age group declines in importance, the implications for soft drink companies are obvious. Soft drinks are expected to grow at only 3.5 percent yearly in the 1980s, compared with gains of 8 to 13 percent during the 1960s and 1970s.[3] Such changing age patterns caused the stock market to discount soft drink company stocks; as a consequence, companies such as Coca-Cola and Pepsi-Co revised their strategies by expanding their sales efforts directed to older people and to overseas markets, and by diversifying into new businesses via acquisition.

Coffee processors may see the opposite effect on their sales potential. Per capita coffee consumption has been declining since 1965. Other things being equal, however, as the over-25 age segment begins to grow again, coffee producers could see their sales charts turn up once more.

Marriage and Divorce. Changing attitudes toward marriage and divorce have been altering household and family living arrangements, as you can see in Table 3-1. The number of unmarried couples living together, for example, increased by 545 percent between 1960 and 1980 compared with an increase in all households of only 50 percent. While that dramatic increase received much publicity, the unmarrieds represented less than 2 percent of all households in 1980.

Families headed by a female increased by 90 percent between 1960 and 1980, while total families rose by only 30 percent. Families headed by divorced women, however, rose even faster during the same period—327 percent. There are negative economic implications in these increases when one considers that such families

FIGURE 3-4. Changes in 14 to 24 age group showing 1960–1970 actual and 1980–1990 Census Projection. *Source:* U.S. Bureau of the Census, "Illustrative Projections of State Populations by Age, Race, and Sex: 1975 to 2000," *Current Population Reports,* ser. P-25, no. 796, U.S. Government Printing Office, Washington, D.C., 1979, p. 8; and U.S. Bureau of the Census, *Statistical Abstract of the United States, 1981,* Washington, D.C., table 30.

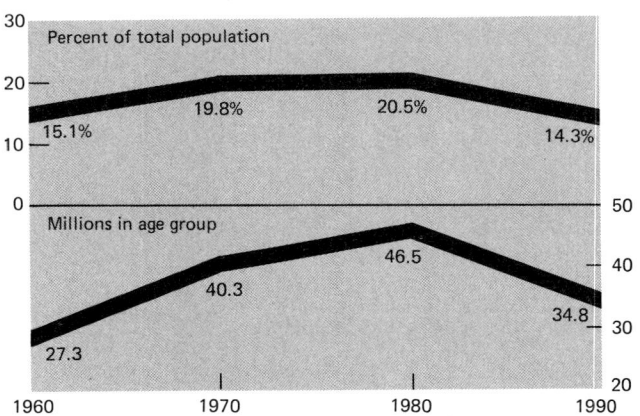

TABLE 3-1
Changes in Households and Families* (1960 and 1980 figures in thousands)

	1960	1980	% Change
Households:			
All households	52,799	79,108	50
Unmarried couples living together	242	1,560	545
Families:			
All families	45,111	58,426	30
With female head	4,507	8,540	90
Headed by divorced women	694	2,960	327

*According to the Census Bureau, a *household* comprises all persons who occupy a housing unit. A *family* refers to a group of two or more persons related by blood, marriage, or adoption and residing together in a household.

Source: U.S. Bureau of the Census, *Statistical Abstract of the United States, 1981*, Washington, D.C., extracted from tables 58, 60, and 72.

have median incomes less than half of those headed by a male, i.e., $12,573 compared to $24,172.[4] This suggests that market analysts should consider not only the changes in the number of household and family spending units but also the composition of these units.

Working Wives. Another reflection of demographic change is the number of working wives. By 1979 this had grown to 53 percent of the 48 million husband-wife families. And husband-wife families with working wives had incomes 34 percent higher than those in which only the husband worked. Demographers have observed that when both partners are working, the husband's income is used more for the essentials of living while the wife's income tends to be spent more for discretionary family purchases such as education, travel, and personal services. Furthermore, several studies have shown that the lifestyle of working wives varies from that of housewives in terms of such things as saving, spending, shopping, media exposure, leisure activities, and influence on family purchases.[5]

The Senior Citizen Market. While increasing life span has obvious implications for markets such as retirement housing and medical care, marketers are looking for new ways to appeal to the senior citizen market. Pfizer test-marketed a shampoo called New Season, intended to meet "the special needs of people over 50." Alberto-Culver has registered the brand names Forty-Plus, Best Years, and My Age for hair-care products. Manufacturers of jeans have introduced fuller-cut lines so that older men, already psychologically comfortable with a more casual style of dress, can be physically comfortable as well.[6]

Decline in Birthrate. Reacting to the declining birthrate, producers of baby foods deemphasized their baby food products or, as in the case of Gerber, have diversified their product lines. Baby foods now represent only 65 percent of Gerber's sales, as a result of the company's diversification into toys, baby clothes, life insurance, and can making.[7] Gerber also made an interesting, but reportedly unsuccessful, attempt to tap the geriatric market with single servings of foods designed for the solitary survivor. Hasbro Industries, a toy concern, has spread its marketing into family games and arts and crafts, which can be enjoyed by a wider age range. Hasbro also diversified into gourmet cooking items.[8]

Geographic Population Breakdown

Figure 3-5 shows the geographic lines of the four Census Regions and the nine Census Divisions. Table 3-2 presents the dispersal of population by Census Regions and Divisions and the annual average rate of change since 1960. While the numbers of people in each Census Division have increased since 1960, certain parts of the country have grown more rapidly than others. The Northeast and North Central Regions (the snow belt) are growing at a slower rate than the country as a whole, while the South and West Regions (which include the sun belt states) are growing at a faster rate.

Despite the fact that the combined population of the two northern regions declined from 54 percent of the total in 1960 to 48 percent in 1980, they remain important markets for consumer products. Analysts also need to look at what is happening within divisions since some states are going against area trends. New Hampshire in the Northeast Region, for example, is growing faster than the country as a whole, whereas West Virginia in the South Region is growing more slowly.

FIGURE 3-5. Census regions and geographic divisions of the United States. *Source:* U.S. Department of Commerce, Bureau of the Census.

TABLE 3-2
Rate of Population Change

Area	Population, millions			Annual Average % Change	
	1960	1970	1980	1960–1970	1970–1980
United States	180.0	203.8	226.5	1.3	1.1
Northeast:	44.8	49.2	49.0	1.0	−.04
New England	10.5	11.9	12.0	1.2	.08
Mid-Atlantic	34.3	37.3	37.0	0.8	−.08
North Central:	51.7	56.7	59.0	1.0	0.4
East north central	36.3	40.3	42.0	1.1	0.4
West north central	15.4	16.4	17.0	0.6	0.4
South:	55.1	63.1	75.0	1.5	1.9
South Atlantic	26.0	30.8	37.0	1.7	2.0
East south central	12.1	12.9	15.0	0.6	1.6
West south central	17.0	19.4	24.0	1.3	2.4
West:	28.3	34.9	43.0	2.1	2.3
Mountain	6.9	8.3	11.0	1.9	3.3
Pacific	21.4	26.6	32.0	2.2	2.0

Source: U.S. Bureau of the Census, *Statistical Abstract of the United States, 1981*, Washington, D.C. Data extracted from table 9, p.10.

Figure 3-6 shows the percentage change in population by state expected between 1980 and 1990. **Marketing Note** 3-1 describes how and why some of these shifts in population are occurring.

Demographic data are also reported by the Census Bureau for counties, cities, towns, and Standard Metropolitan Statistical Areas (SMSAs).* Figure 3-7 shows the geographic location of the SMSAs. Effective market analysis for most consumer goods requires consideration of these smaller geographic market segments. This is because urbanization has resulted in major concentrations of population and buying power within a relatively small proportion of U.S. land area. The 318 SMSAs, for example, comprised only 16 percent of total land area, yet contain about 75 percent of the total population. Although large consumer goods companies normally distribute to all geographic areas, most concentrate their marketing efforts in the major geographic submarkets where the bulk of the population is found.

General Mills, for example, concentrates its marketing efforts in 75 area markets. Also, because of demographic differences and preferences, General Mills and other food companies tailor special marketing programs for each market area. A West Coast food processor has said, "We used to look at one big national market. Now we find we've got 50 markets, with each one now getting different TV ads."[9]

---

*The SMSA has proved to be a useful geographic breakdown for marketing planning purposes. It represents an integrated economic and social unit with a large population nucleus. As defined by the Office of Management and Budget (OMB) in 1980, an SMSA must contain either (1) one city of 50,000 or more inhabitants or (2) an urbanized area of at least 50,000 inhabitants and a total SMSA population of at least 100,000 (75,000 in New England). In 1982 the OMB announced that it was planning to reclassify SMSAs into three categories according to size. Details were not available at the time of printing.

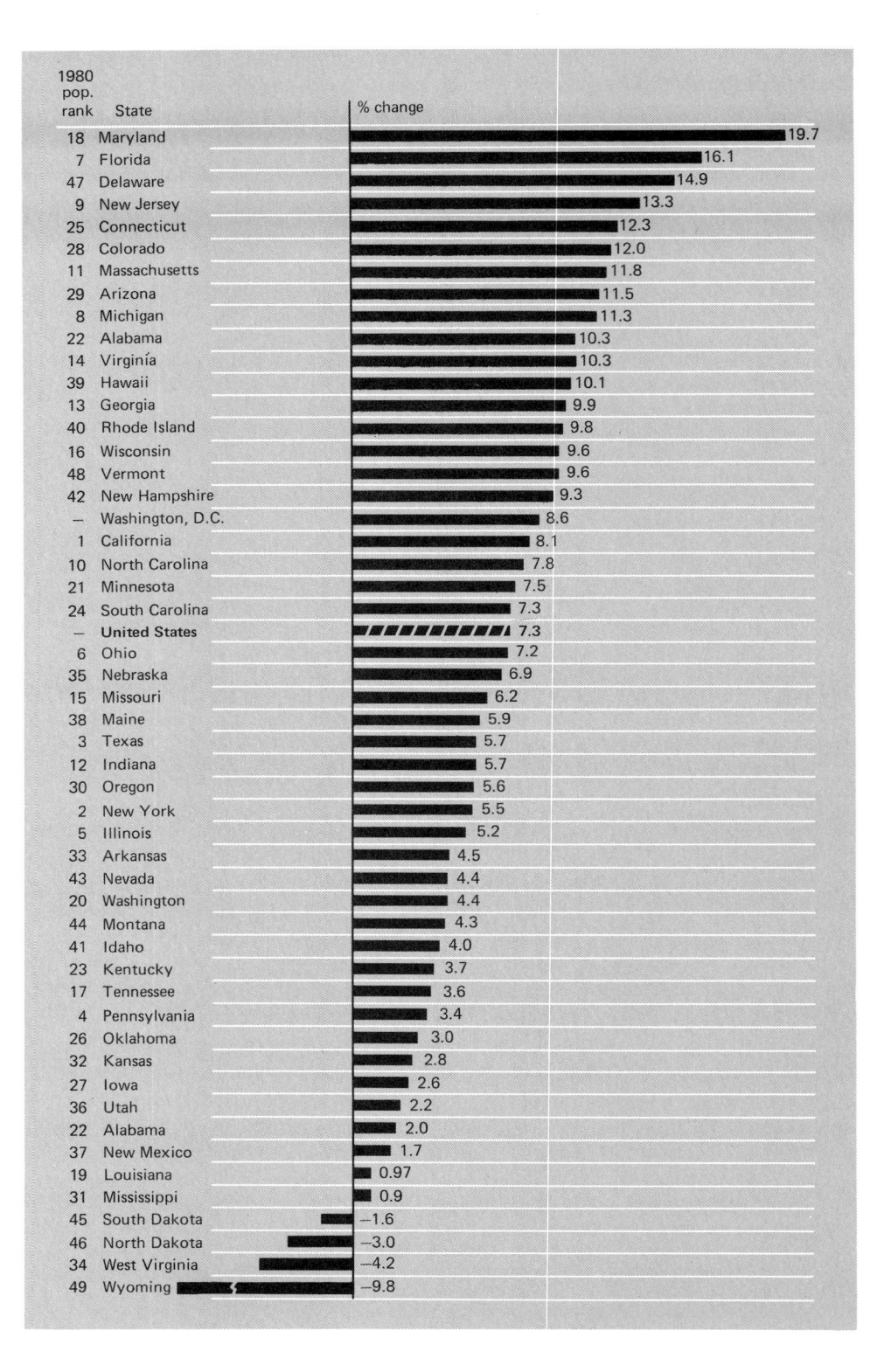

PART TWO
UNDERSTANDING
THE MARKET AND
FORECASTING
SALES

1980 pop. rank	State	% change
18	Maryland	19.7
7	Florida	16.1
47	Delaware	14.9
9	New Jersey	13.3
25	Connecticut	12.3
28	Colorado	12.0
11	Massachusetts	11.8
29	Arizona	11.5
8	Michigan	11.3
22	Alabama	10.3
14	Virginia	10.3
39	Hawaii	10.1
13	Georgia	9.9
40	Rhode Island	9.8
16	Wisconsin	9.6
48	Vermont	9.6
42	New Hampshire	9.3
—	Washington, D.C.	8.6
1	California	8.1
10	North Carolina	7.8
21	Minnesota	7.5
24	South Carolina	7.3
—	**United States**	**7.3**
6	Ohio	7.2
35	Nebraska	6.9
15	Missouri	6.2
38	Maine	5.9
3	Texas	5.7
12	Indiana	5.7
30	Oregon	5.6
2	New York	5.5
5	Illinois	5.2
33	Arkansas	4.5
43	Nevada	4.4
20	Washington	4.4
44	Montana	4.3
41	Idaho	4.0
23	Kentucky	3.7
17	Tennessee	3.6
4	Pennsylvania	3.4
26	Oklahoma	3.0
32	Kansas	2.8
27	Iowa	2.6
36	Utah	2.2
22	Alabama	2.0
37	New Mexico	1.7
19	Louisiana	0.97
31	Mississippi	0.9
45	South Dakota	−1.6
46	North Dakota	−3.0
34	West Virginia	−4.2
49	Wyoming	−9.8

Mobility: Restless America

MARKETING NOTE 3-1

Vance Packard, one of America's most versatile social commentators, reflects on some of the emerging patterns of people on the move. He is author of **A Nation of Strangers, The Status Seekers, The Hidden Persuaders,** *and other books.*

Americans move far more often than the people of any other advanced society, and the rate has been accelerating. More than thirty-six million Americans—nearly a fifth of all U.S. families—now change their residences every year. The most restless people seem to be in the West and Southwest. They tend to move twice as often as people in the Northeast. Americans have traditionally been restless. Today that restlessness is heightened by the propulsive forces of expanding technology. It is heightened also by a new national mood. Recently some striking new patterns have emerged in our moving habits. Here are some of them.

The Shift of Population to the South, Southwest, and West. In the past five years 85 percent of the nation's population growth has been in these states. Arizona grew by one-fourth in a mere half-decade, while New York State actually lost population. More people moved out of North Eastern and North Central States than moved in. The attractions of the South and Southwest include warm weather, generally flat terrain, which reduces building costs, wide open spaces, and generally lower labor and living costs . . . [and] water.

I suspect that the outlook for the Sun-belt is not limitlessly rosy. In my view we are headed for a crunch in energy that will last through most of the 1980's. It will undoubtedly be decided that people living in cold areas need heat for warmth more than people living in hot areas need mechanically-cooled air. Americans will look with new interest to the belt of states running from the Carolinas, through Tennessee and Kentucky to Missouri and Arkansas, and then to the southern highlands of the Rockies. In these areas people can live comfortably year-round with a minimum of energy-treated air.

The Shift of Population Away from Metropolitan Areas. For more than a century progress to young rural Americans meant moving to the big city. In just two decades the farm population was cut in half. Then, in the 1960's, progress came to mean moving to the suburbs of the big cities. It was felt that the suburbs offered the best of both worlds.

By the mid-1970's, a new mood swept America. It began with the young rebels of the counterculture, but spread to all ages. Nature and naturalism became major values of the new life-style. The big city took on a new (unpleasant) image for many; and, many major cities stopped growing or lost population. The new big-city image rubbed off on the suburbs.

A search began for places offering more natural life-styles, places where community was still important, such as Upper Michigan, the Blue Ridge Mountains, Montana, New Mexico, the High Sierra, and British Columbia. Small towns, but not farm areas, are growing briskly.

Moving to rural areas became economically feasible because, as the nation's economy moved increasingly to "service" and "light" industries, it became feasible for companies to settle away from cities. Also, commuter airlines were reaching about every U.S. town of at least 15,000 people.

People Now Move Greater Distances. Moving van officials report that on the average, customers using their services move about one-hundred miles farther each decade. One study shows that major business executives, when they move, now average about 800 miles per move. Moves abroad are also on the upswing. The spectacular growth of multinational corporations has induced hundreds of thousands of Americans to take job assignments overseas. Then there are military families. The United States has about two thousand bases in thirty different countries. The military has sent not only its personnel overseas, but their families as well.

◀ FIGURE 3-6. Expected percentage change in state population, 1980–1990. *Source:* U.S. Bureau of the Census, "Illustrative Projections of State Population by Age, Race, and Sex, 1975 to 2000," *Current Population Reports,* ser. P-25, no. 796, U.S. Government Printing Office, Washington D.C., 1979, table I, p. 25. The percentage change was calculated from state populations for 1980 and forecasts for 1990. The population rank for 1980 is from U.S. Bureau of the Census, *Statistical Abstract of the United States, 1981,* Washington, D.C., table 9, p. 11.

The Shift of Population and Business toward the Great Regional Jet Centers. These centers are the hubs where transfers are made to other airlines, including small feeder lines. The growth of these hubs has had a sizable influence on where people are moving. In the U.S. interior, Atlanta, Minneapolis, Chicago, Memphis, Denver, Kansas City, and Dallas–Fort Worth have emerged as the great regional jet transfer points. There are also major airport centers on the coasts for transfers and for overseas takeoff: New York, Washington, Miami, New Orleans, Houston, Los Angeles, and San Francisco.

The Rise of the Corporate Nomad. Virtually every major city has at least one bedroom town largely populated by corporate nomads. Managers and professionals who move every two or three years tend to end up in such suburban towns. The nation-hopping travels of today's business managers and professionals has developed because big corporations have a far-flung network of plants, offices, and distribution centers.

. . .

These patterns suggest that we will continue to be a nation on the move for years to come. Both individual and collective planning need to take this prospect into account. With nearly a quarter of our population moving every year, we are in danger of becoming a rootless nomadic people. But at the same time, mobility can allow us to share the experiences of our different regions. If we can strike the proper balance between tradition and change, between familiarity and discovery, we can keep moving into the twenty-first century with a firm sense of who and where we are.

Source: Vance Packard, "Mobility: Restless America," *Mainliner*, May 1977. Reprinted by permission of Vance Packard.

Prior to World War II mass merchandising chains such as Sears, Montgomery Ward, and Penney's had their store locations in smaller communities, where they served primarily rural markets. With the postwar shift of population from farms to the cities, these chains now concentrate their stores in metropolitan areas. The more

FIGURE 3-7. Standard metropolitan statistical areas. *Source:* U.S. Department of Commerce, Bureau of the Census.

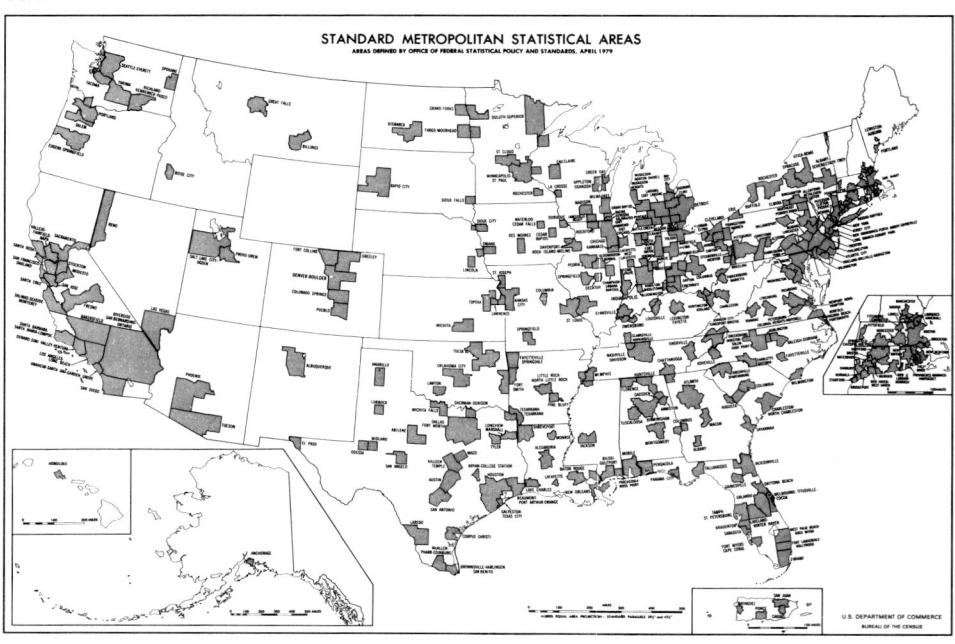

recently created K mart chain located its stores near population centers from the start. Shifts in population patterns influence all chains in deciding where to locate their new stores.

Economic Data

Knowing where the population is concentrated and in what quantities is only part of what needs to be known in order to evaluate market potential. Equally important is where the buying power is concentrated. The Bureau of the Census provides us with a variety of economic measures broken down by the same geographic locations as the demographic data. A few of these are personal income, income per capita; disposable personal income (i.e., income after deducting personal tax and nontax payments to government), savings, and employment. For the nation as a whole, the gross national product (GNP) measures the value of all goods and services *at market prices*.

Table 3-3 shows the changes in some key economic indicators. The continuing rise in the rates of increase for GNP and income are shown in the three right-hand columns, as is the precipitous drop in the rate of personal saving during the 1975 to

TABLE 3-3
Trends in Some Key Economic Indicators

Subject	1960	1970	1975	1979	1980	Average annual % change		
						1960–70	1970–75	1975–80
Gross national product (GNP), $billions	507	993	1,549	2,414	2,626	7.0	9.3	11.1
National income, $billions	416	811	1,239	1,963	2,120	6.9	8.9	11.3
Personal income, $billions	402	811	1,265	1,944	2,160	7.3	9.3	11.3
Disposable personal income, $billions	352	695	1,096	1,642	1,822	7.0	9.5	10.7
Personal saving, $billions	20	56	94	86	101	10.8	10.9	1.5
GNP constant (1972) dollars, $billions	737	1,086	1,234	1,483	1,481	4.0	2.6	3.7
Per capita, $1000	4.1	5.3	5.7	6.6	6.5	2.6	1.5	2.6
GNP implicit price deflator index*	68.7	91.5	125.6	162.8	177.4	2.9	6.5	7.2
Producer price index (PPI)†	94.9	110.4	174.9	235.6	268.8	1.5	9.6	9.0
Consumer price index (CPI)†	88.7	116.3	161.2	217.4	246.8	2.8	6.8	8.9
Food	88.0	114.9	175.4	234.5	254.6	2.7	8.8	7.7
Fuel oil, coal, and bottled gas	89.2	110.1	235.3	403.1	556.0	2.1	16.4	18.8

*1972 = 100. †1967 = 100.
Source: U.S. Bureau of the Census, *Statistical Abstract of the United States, 1981*, Washington, D.C., p. 908.

1980 period. The savings rate dropped, despite the increase in personal income, because of rising inflation [reflected in the table by the change in the consumer price index (CPI)].

When analyzing data that can be affected by inflation (e.g., GNP, personal income, and company sales income), you should consider whether figures are in *current* dollars, which reflect the effects of inflation or deflation, or whether they are in *constant* dollars, which have been adjusted for inflation or deflation. This point is illustrated in Figure 3-8, which compares the GNP in both current and constant dollars.

Geographic Income Data. Table 3-4 shows personal income data by Census Region and Division in constant 1972 dollars. For the total United States, on an average annual basis, we see that the rate of increase in constant dollars has dropped from 5.8 percent in the 1960 to 1970 period to 3.9 percent in the 1970 to 1980 period. When you consider the slowing rate of growth for both population and personal income—measured in constant dollars—it is apparent why the growth rates of many consumer goods companies were slowing. To help overcome these conditions, company managements turned to marketing and strategic planning.

When comparing the rate of growth in personal income by Census Region, the same pattern appears that we saw for population. The Northeast and North Central Regions are growing at a slower rate than the national average, while the South and West Regions are growing at a faster rate. And, as in the case of population, some

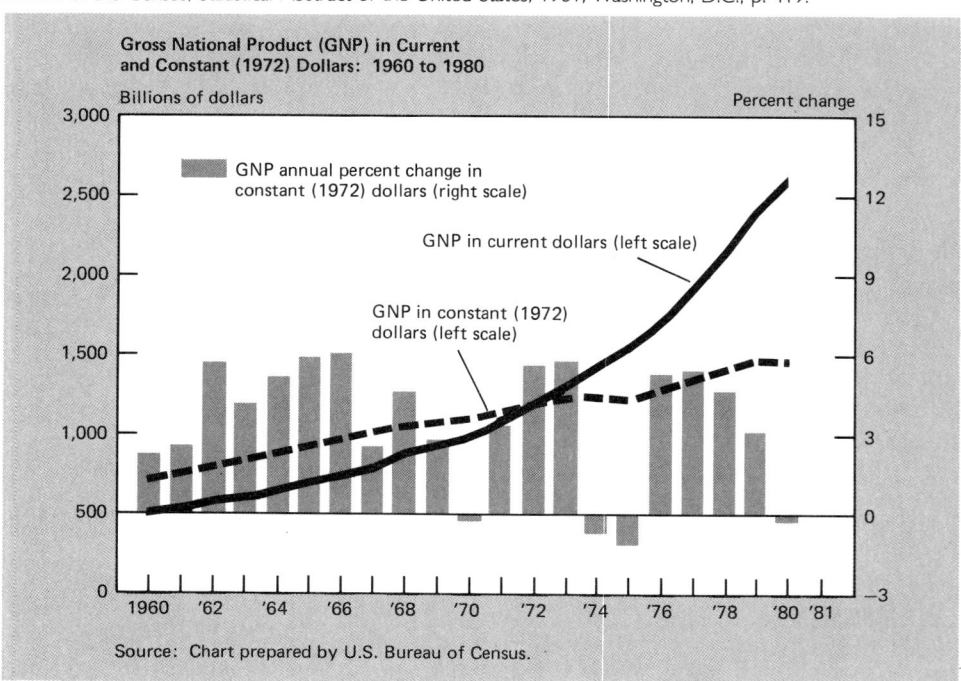

FIGURE 3-8. Gross national product (GNP) in current and constant (1972) dollars, 1960–1980. *Source:* U.S. Bureau of the Census, *Statistical Abstract of the United States, 1981*, Washington, D.C., p. 419.

TABLE 3-4
Changes in Personal Income

Area	Constant 1972 dollars, billions			Annual average % change	
	1960	1970	1980	1960–1970	1970–1980
United States	550.9	869.1	1,209.0	5.8	3.9
Northeast:	157.1	234.9	277.1	5.0	1.8
New England	35.5	55.2	68.3	5.5	2.7
Mid-Atlantic	121.6	179.9	208.8	4.8	1.6
Central:	162.9	244.2	318.2	5.0	3.0
East north central	119.5	178.1	228.3	4.9	2.8
West north central	43.4	66.1	89.9	5.2	3.6
South:	133.9	231.1	363.7	7.3	5.7
South Atlantic	66.6	120.1	181.8	8.0	5.2
East south central	25.0	41.0	61.1	6.4	4.9
West south central	42.3	70.1	120.8	6.6	7.2
West	97.2	159.0	248.3	6.4	5.6
Mountain	19.7	32.6	57.3	6.6	7.6
Pacific	77.5	124.4	191.0	6.3	5.1

Source: U.S. Bureau of the Census, *Statistical Abstract of the United States, 1981*, Washington, D.C. Data extracted from table 10, p. 12.

states are at variance with their regional trends. In 1980 the two northern regions combined accounted for only 49 percent of national personal income, having dropped from 58 percent in 1960.

Just as sophisticated consumer goods companies and major retail chains concentrate their efforts on highly populated regions, so too they concentrate on those places which represent pockets of major income. The 318 SMSAs, for example, account for nearly four-fifths of total disposable personal income.

Family Buying Power. Certain types of companies also pay attention to the buying power of families and households. The highest two-fifths of the families in 1979, for example, received 67 percent of all income; the highest one-fifth received 42 percent while the highest one-twentieth received 16 percent. Some products, such as cigarettes, show little sensitivity to family income; other products, such as automobiles and other consumer durables, are responsive to family and household income levels. In 1980, 58 percent of households with incomes of $25,000 and over owned two or more cars compared to 26 percent in the $10,000 to $14,999 income bracket. Similarly, 30 percent of the $25,000 and over households had air conditioning compared to 23 percent of the $10,000 to $14,999 households. In fact, with the exception of tobacco, family spending for most major categories of household spending (e.g., food, housing, clothing, education, and health care) increase with family income.

Rising Income of Black Families. Buying power increased dramatically between 1960 and 1979 for all families. Although blacks continue to have lower median family income than whites, the incomes of blacks have been rising at a faster rate than whites. See Table 3-5. The significance of the growing purchasing power of blacks (who represent nearly 12 percent of the U.S. population) has not been lost on marketers who now design promotional programs specifically for black consumers.

Survey of Buying Power

The Annual Survey of Buying Power, published by *Sales and Marketing Management* magazine, is a widely used source of consumer market data. The survey selectively presents in convenient form the more pertinent consumer market data gleaned from the censuses, broken out by the 305 largest Metro Areas.*

For each Metro Area (and the counties and principal city within the Area), the survey provides population, population by age group, households, total retail sales broken into six major retail categories, effective buying income, and a buying power index.† The survey's "buying power index" is a widely used single measure of relative market potential for mass consumer products by geographic area. As the survey points out, however, the further a product is removed from the mass market, the greater the need for modification by more discriminating factors such as income, class, age, or sex.

---

*The survey defines a Metro Area as having a city or group of contiguous places with a combined population of at least 44,000, slightly different than the SMSA. The 305 Metro Areas account for about 15 percent of U.S. land area, yet represent approximately 75 percent of population and households and 80 percent of effective buying income and retail sales (about the same as for the 318 SMSAs).

†*Effective buying income* is defined as personal income less personal tax and nontax payments to government and less income paid to personnel on the government payroll while stationed overseas. The *buying power index* is computed by giving weights of 5 to effective buying income, 3 to retail sales, and 2 to population.

TABLE 3-5
White and Black Family Incomes
(Measured in current dollars)

	1960	1979	% Change
MEDIAN FAMILY INCOME			
White	$5,835	$20,502	251
Black and other races	3,230	12,380	283
PERCENT WITH INCOMES OF $25,000 OR MORE			
White	1.0	36.7	
Black and other races	0.1	19.7	
PERCENT BELOW POVERTY LEVEL*			
White	16.5	7.4	
Black and other races	56.0	29.9	

*Annual adjustments are made to the poverty level based on changes in the consumer price index.

Source: U.S. Bureau of the Census, *Statistical Abstract of the United States, 1981*, Washington, D.C. Data extracted from tables 725, 726, and 748.

Need for Discrete Analysis

The analyses we have made merely indicate some of the many types of information that can be gleaned from published data. Some data hold more significance for one company than another. Each company, therefore, needs to search for and analyze what is important and relevant for its situation.

A lawn sprinkler manufacturer, in estimating market potential, will want to know not only the number of households by geographic area, but also the number with lawns. This may be determined approximately from census reports of single family homes on the assumption that single-family homes normally have lawns. And further adjustments can be made for factors such as income (or buying power) and urban or suburban location.

For some products no measures of potential by geographic area can be computed from public data. In such cases primary market research is the only answer. Before going to the expense of private surveys, however, you should determine whether your product can be correlated with some available market measure. The market for hearing aids, for example, may correlate roughly with age. The accuracy of this assumption might be determined by experience with your customers or from available medical studies. With knowledge of the incidence of deafness by age, the company could estimate the total market potential for hearing aids as well as the relative potential by geographic area.

Measures of relative potential sales for specific products rarely are precise in the best of circumstances; nevertheless, reasonable approximations are usually sufficient for planning purposes. The number of variables in any marketing situation is sufficiently large to make it impractical (i.e., too costly) to attempt to obtain exact information for every variable.

INDUSTRIAL MARKETS

As in the case of consumer goods producers, the industrial goods supplier needs to know the types, numbers, and locations of buyers and prospective buyers for the company's products or services, their buying power, and the rates of change within these categories.

Industrial market data are provided by several censuses taken at 5–7 year intervals, namely the Manufacturing, Business (covering retail and wholesale trade and selected service industries), Agriculture, Mineral Industries, and Transportation Censuses. The Housing Census is made every 10 years. Most of these censuses are supplemented by periodic interim reports—some as often as weekly and monthly—and by special studies. While the above represent the broad federal censuses, there are hundreds of other statistical sources useful to industrial marketers. An appendix to the *Statistical Abstract* provides an extensive "Guide to Sources of Statistics."

We broadly define industrial marketing as follows:

> The marketing of goods and services to organizations for use within the organization, or for producing or processing other products or services.

Broad industrial market classifications include manufacturers, wholesalers, retailers, service industries, government, agriculture, forestry, fisheries, construction, and mining.

Identifying Industrial Buyers

The first problem in industrial market analysis is to identify actual users and potential users. This can be relatively simple for a product such as cigarette paper produced specifically for cigarette manufacturers. On the other hand, it is more difficult to identify the users of chemical products for which there often are a variety of applications in a variety of industries.

The second problem is to *locate* users and potential users. Whereas commercial firms, such as banks, office supply dealers, and retailers, can be found in or near population centers, other types of industrial customers are not as easily found. Manufacturing plants are located primarily on the basis of proximity to raw materials, water supplies, transportation facilities, and specific labor skills. Extractive industries are located at raw material sites and the locations are different for lumber, oil fields, ores, and minerals. Agriculture is concentrated in a few regions and states; for example, 40 percent of the nation's vegetables and 25 percent of its cotton are grown in California. Government purchasing offices are concentrated in and around Washington, D.C., state capitals, county seats, major cities, and military bases.

A third problem is to measure market potential. Published data are available for many product industries, yet are not broken out for every industry. Furthermore, companies of medium and small size often serve minor segments of major industries for which data may not be broken out in the census reports.

Primary Market Research

While much useful data are available from the industrial censuses, companies—or their trade associations—often develop additional data using primary market research. Industrial market studies usually can be done more quickly and at less cost than consumer studies for two reasons. First, many industries are composed of a relatively small number of companies. Second, a small percentage of companies in most industries account for the major portion of purchases. Consequently, primary market research often means contacting only a small number of companies. To illustrate the point, only one-third of the approximately 360,000 manufacturing establishments* have twenty or more employees.[10] Furthermore, the 100 largest companies account for 25 percent of all value added by manufacture,† while the largest 200 companies account for 34 percent.[11]

Table 3-6 shows the number of companies and the percentage of shipments (by dollar value) for the eight largest, as well as the fifty largest, companies in selected industries. Most major industries in the United States are considered to be *concentrated* or *oligopolistic*—i.e., a few companies account for the major portion of the output of the total industry. This fact has implications for marketing strategies

---

*The Census use of the term *establishment* signifies a single physical plant site or factory. It is not necessarily identical with the business unit or company, which may consist of one or more establishments.

†"Value added by manufacture" is the best measure available for comparing the relative economic importance of manufacturing among industries and geographic areas. Briefly defined, it is the value of shipments less the costs of materials, supplies, containers, fuel, purchased electricity, and contract work, plus net change in finished goods and work-in-process inventory and value added in merchandising activities.

TABLE 3-6
Percent of Shipments Accounted for by Largest Companies in Selected Industries

Industry	Number of Companies	8 Largest, % of Total	50 Largest, % of Total
Motor vehicles and car bodies	254	99	99+
Tires and inner tubes	121	88	99+
Photographic equipment & supplies	702	86	94
Aircraft	151	81	99+
Soap and other detergents	554	71	89
Toilet preparations	644	56	90
Petroleum refining	192	53	94
Saw and planing mills	6,966	23	49
Bottled soft drinks	1,758	22	50
Commercial printing, letterpress	14,375	19	31
Commercial printing, lithographic	10,964	10	26

Source: U.S. Bureau of the Census, *Statistical Abstract of the United States, 1981*, Washington, D.C. Data extracted from table 1427, pp. 793–794.

which we will examine in Part Three. From the standpoint of market analysis, however, it means that the size and trends of many industries can be measured by firsthand surveys of a few companies in each industry.

More extensive contacts, however, are necessary when gathering data on *nonconcentrated* or *monopolistic* industries—those industries composed of many companies, none of which have a dominant industry share. Examples of such industries in Table 3-6 are sawmills, bottlers of soft drinks, and commercial printers.

Relative Industrial Market Potential by Geographic Location

Census data provide geographic breakdowns by numbers of units and several economic measures for major categories of industry. We will illustrate geographic analyses using the *manufacturing* classification.

While the Northeast and North Central Regions account for nearly three-fifths of all manufacturing, the South and West Regions are growing faster. This is illustrated in Table 3-7 and confirms the publicized shift of industry to the sun belt states. A study by the Academy for Contemporary Problems, however, found that the shift of industry from the snow belt to the sun belt states has been caused less by migration than by the fact that more new industries chose to locate in the sun belt.[12]

The industrial market analyst, of course, must look more closely at where industry is concentrated geographically. Table 3-8 shows that seven states—all but two in the snow belt—account for about half of the value added and nearly half of all manufacturing establishments. Concentrations of industry can be narrowed even further by studying the Area Statistics volumes of the Census of Manufacturers. Ohio, for example, has seventeen SMSAs, but two—Cincinnati and Cleveland—account for 32 percent of the value added and 39 percent of the establishments in the state.

By knowing where manufacturing plants are concentrated in terms of location and buying potential—and by monitoring trends—industrial marketers can plan their

TABLE 3-7
Shift in Manufacturing from the North to the South and West

Area	Number of Establishments 1977	Value added, $ millions 1967	Value added, $ millions 1977	Annual Average % Increase 1967 to 1977
United States	359,893	261,984	585,108	12.3
Northeast:	96,746	76,234	138,747	8.2
New England	25,737	18,972	35,587	8.8
Mid-Atlantic	71,009	57,262	103,160	8.0
North Central:	93,558	91,789	200,844	11.8
East north central	69,237	75,016	160,223	11.4
West north central	24,321	16,773	40,621	14.2
South:	96,675	59,648	160,650	16.9
South Atlantic	47,692	29,313	72,304	14.7
East south central	19,187	13,718	36,234	16.4
West south central	29,796	16,617	52,112	21.4
West:	72,914	34,197	84,867	14.8
Mountain	13,808	4,522	13,622	20.1
Pacific	59,106	29,675	71,245	14.0

Source: U.S. Bureau of the Census, *Staticstical Abstract of the United States, 1981*, Washington, D.C. Data extracted from table 1416, pp. 782–3.

sales coverage, promotional efforts, and supply points. For companies which produce goods used by most manufacturers (e.g., office or maintenance equipment and supplies), knowledge of total manufacturing concentrations may be sufficient for planning purposes. Other producers, who supply only certain types of manufacturing establishments, however, need data broken out by industrial classifications.

Standard Industrial Classification System

The Bureau of the Census and other federal agencies that collect industry data follow the Standard Industrial Classification System (SIC) as prescribed by the *Standard*

TABLE 3-8
The Seven Leading Manufacturing States

	Value Added in 1977, $ millions	Percent	Number of Establishments in 1977	Percent
United States	585,108	100.0	359,893	100.0
California	54,862	9.4	45,289	12.6
New York	44,290	7.6	36,578	10.2
Ohio	43,055	7.4	17,354	4.8
Illinois	40,279	6.9	19,517	5.4
Michigan	37,566	6.4	15,627	4.3
Pennsylvania	36,017	6.2	18,735	5.2
Texas	33,150	5.7	18,107	5.0
7-state total	289,219	49.5	171,207	47.6

Source: U.S. Bureau of the Census, *Statistical Abstract of the United States, 1981*, Washington, D.C. Data extracted from table 1416, pp. 783-4.

Industrial Classification System Manual, published by the U.S. Office of Management and Budget. The SIC system provides uniformity and comparability in the collection and reporting of government data. It allows the market analyst to trace industry data from the aggregate to the specific and vice versa.

The SIC manual lists 99 *Major Industry Groups*, each coded by a two-digit number. These major groups are found within the broad categories of agriculture, forestry, fishing, mining, construction, manufacturing, transportation, wholesale trade, retail trade, finance, insurance, real estate, services, public administration, and nonclassifiable. These *Major Industry Groups* are divided into *Industry Product Groups* designated by a three-digit code number. And finally, the *Industry Product Groups* are divided into approximately 5000 product classifications, each designated with a four-digit number. Table 3-9 illustrates the system applied to manufacturing and wholesale and retail trade.

The Census of Manufacturing Area Statistics volumes provide data by SIC code for Census Divisions, states, counties, and SMSAs. For each they show the number of establishments, cost of materials, value of shipments, and new capital expenditures. If we wanted information on fluid milk production in the Cincinnati SMSA, for example, we would look up SIC Code 2026 in the latest census.

TABLE 3-9

Examples of SIC System Applied to Manufacturing and Wholesale and Retail Trade

SIC Code	Major Group	SIC Code	Industry Product Group	SIC Code	Industry
			MANUFACTURING		
20	Food and kindred products	201	Meat		
		202	Dairy	2021	Butter
				2022	Cheese
				2023	Condensed and evaporated milk
				2024	Ice Cream
				2026	Fluid milk
		203	Processed fruits and vegetables		
		204	Grain mill		
		205	Bakery		
			WHOLESALE TRADE		
51	Non-durable goods	514	Groceries	5143	Dairy products
			RETAIL TRADE		
54	Food stores	545	Dairy products	5451	Dairy products stores

Source: Office of Management and Budget, *Standard Industrial Classification Manual,* Washington, D.C., 1972.

MARKETS FOR SERVICES

Services represent the fastest-growing segment of the U.S. economy and *the value of services now exceeds the value of all goods produced*. Services may be sold to consumer markets or to industrial markets. The Committee on Definitions of the American Marketing Association describes services as follows:

> Activities, benefits or satisfactions which are offered for sale, or are provided in connection with the sale of goods.[13]

Examples of services include airlines, banks, insurance, telephone, credit cards, motels, repair, amusements, and personal services (e.g., beauty shops, funeral parlors, advertising agencies, lawyers, and hospitals). This list can be extended greatly and new types of services appear frequently.

Analyzing markets for services is much the same as analyzing markets for other products. Again we need to know the types, numbers, and locations of buyers and prospective buyers for a company's services, their buying power, and the rates of change occurring. Data can be obtained from a number of sources, including several of the federal censuses. The *Statistical Abstract* provides guides to these varied sources. Services are included in the SIC System, but are not always broken down as finely as we might wish.

Selected Services by Number, Size, and Growth Patterns

The Census of Business provides data on over 300 "Selected Service Industries" subsumed under six general categories shown in Table 3-10. Also shown are the number of establishments for each category, their dollar receipts,* and the percentage increase in receipts between 1972 and 1977.

*Dollar receipts for services are the equivalent of *dollar sales* in a product company. Many service organizations—for example, physicians and auto repair—would not refer to their service charges as sales.

TABLE 3-10

Selected Services Industries/ (Establishments with payroll, 1977)

	Number of Establishments, 1000s	Receipts, $ millions	% Increase in Receipts since 1972
United States	725.1	164,219	72
Hotels, motels, etc.	41.6	17,893	76
Personal services	170.2	15,297	31
Miscellaneous business services	154.8	49,999	79
Auto repair, services, garages	106.2	19,659	80
Miscellaneous repair services	55.0	9,558	98
Amusement, recreation services	61.8	19,756	56

Source: U.S. Bureau of the Census, *Census of Service Industries, 1977*, Washington, D.C. Data extracted from table 1, pp. 52–8 to 52–10 and table 2, pp. 52–11 to 52–13.

Geographic Patterns

For the most part the censuses provide service data broken down in the same way as for consumer and industrial. Table 3-11 shows the relative size and growth rate for selected services by Census Region and Division. We see patterns of geographic change similar to those for consumer and industrial markets.

The Northeast and North Central Regions combined represent 48 percent of total U.S. receipts but are growing at slower rates than the South and West. Since services tend to follow population and industry, it is not surprising to see geographic patterns similar to those for consumer and industrial markets. At variance with this pattern, however, is the fact that selected services in New England are growing slightly faster than the national average. A possible explanation for this is that as industrial growth has slowed there, some of the slack has been offset by efforts to develop travel and recreational services as well as business services such as consulting and commercial and technical research.

SUMMARY

In this chapter we have seen how markets for consumer and industrial goods and services can be measured broadly in terms of *numbers of potential buyers*, their *buying potential, geographic location*, and *rates of change*. Study of these types of data is not terribly exciting until the data are used to identify problems and opportunities for actual companies, at which time their significance becomes apparent. Cases presented later will provide you with this kind of experience.

The figures and tables have presented only a small fraction of the kinds of data available from published sources. They contain mainly summaries, detailed break-

TABLE 3-11

Relative Growth of Selected Service Industries from 1967 to 1977 (Establishments with payroll)

	1967 Receipts, $ millions	1977 Receipts, $ millions	% Increase 1967–1977
United States	55,527	164,219	196
Northeast	18,377	41,610	126
New England	2,723	8,348	207
Mid-Atlantic	15,654	33,262	112
North Central	13,244	36,489	176
East north central	10,058	26,727	166
West north central	3,186	9,762	206
South	12,614	45,793	263
South Atlantic	6,840	24,145	253
East south central	2,011	6,211	209
West south central	3,763	15,437	310
West	11,292	40,326	257
Mountain	2,506	9,943	297
Pacific	8,786	30,383	246

Source: From U.S. Bureau of the Census, *Statistical Abstract of the United States, 1979*, Washington, D.C., table 1376, p. 814; *Census of Service Industries, 1977*, table 4, p. 52–17.

downs of which can be found in government and commercial reference publications. The amount of market information compiled by federal, state, and local governments and other public and private organizations is almost overwhelming in volume and scope. Most university and major city libraries contain files of these reference materials as do U.S. Department of Commerce field offices. Additional sources for more detailed information include trade publications, trade and professional associations, company libraries, and private market research organizations which sell data developed from their own continuing surveys. A list of commonly used data sources will be found in the appendix.

The general rule of analysis is to start with the broad data and move toward the specific. Experienced market analysts search first for published data before buying privately developed data or conducting their own primary market research. For many products and services, the published data are sufficient to provide practical measures of general market characteristics. There are other cases, however, where the published data are not collected in sufficient detail and private studies are required.

No company will find all of the market data it needs from published sources and some companies will find only limited amounts that are pertinent to their situations. Yet, none need plan without adequate market information. The adequacy of data collection is determined largely by the effort and ingenuity of the market analyst and the willingness of management to invest in primary market research when necessary. The latter often involves only modest expenditures, particularly for industrial goods companies. Many medium- and smaller-size companies operate with inadequate market data on the assumption that they are not available or are too costly to collect.

QUESTIONS

1. What are the three general types of markets and what are the broad market indicators that influence the opportunities for all businesses?
2. For what reasons does the text suggest the *Statistical Abstract of the United States* as a valuable guide to available public data?
3. What are SMSAs and why are they of importance to consumer market planning?
4. Describe *The Annual Survey of Buying Power* published by *Sales and Marketing Management* and indicate its importance to consumer goods marketers.
5. What are the sources of industrial market data?
6. What is the Standard Industrial Classification System (SIC)?
7. Describe the markets for services.
8. How are markets for services analyzed and what are the data sources used?
9. Assume that you are opening a retail store and can choose where to put it. Considering information of the types in Tables 3-2 and 3-4 and Fig. 3-6, in what area of the United States would you locate your store? Why?

REFERENCES

1. For a discussion of the market implications of the expected increase in births, see William Lazer and John E. Smallwood, "The Changing Demographics of Women," *Journal of Marketing*, July 1977, pp. 14-22.
2. *Business Week*, May 23, 1977, pp. 68 and 71.

3. *Business Week*, Mar. 14, 1977, p. 84.
4. U.S. Bureau of the Census, *Statistical Abstract of the United States, 1981*, Washington, D.C. Data extracted from table 731, p. 439, and table 738, p. 442.
5. See, for example, Rena Bartos, "The Moving Target: The Impact of Women's Employment on Consumer Behavior," *Journal of Marketing*, July 1977, p. 31, and Suzanne H. McCall, "Meet the Workwife," *Journal of Marketing*, July 1977, p. 55.
6. *MBA*, July-August 1977, pp. 42-43.
7. *Business Week*, June 27, 1977, p. 26.
8. *Wall Street Journal*, Jan. 4, 1972, p. 1.
9. *Business Week*, Mar. 8, 1976, p. 53.
10. U.S. Bureau of the Census, *Statistical Abstract of the United States, 1981*, Washington, D.C., table 1423, p. 787.
11. U.S. Bureau of the Census, *Statistical Abstract of the United States, 1981*, table 1426, p. 793.
12. *The Morning Union*, Springfield, Mass., Dec. 12, 1977, p. 14.
13. Ralph S. Alexander, *Marketing Definitions*, American Marketing Association, Chicago, 1960.

CHAPTER 4

Market Segmentation and Market Structure

In the previous chapter we looked at the first subject in Table 4-1: *broad market characteristics*. We considered the types, numbers, and locations of buyers and prospective buyers for a company's products or services, their buying power, and their rates of change. These broad cuts, however, are not always precise enough for planning purposes, and they don't include all of the factors marketing management must consider. Therefore, we turn now to the other key factors which affect marketing planning. The first is *market segmentation*, following which we will examine the other six subjects listed in Table 4-1. With the completion of this chapter, you will be aware of the market information the professional marketing manager seeks as the foundation for marketing planning.

MARKET SEGMENTATION

Market segmentation is the division of a market into those subgroups which have special needs and preferences and which represent sufficient pockets of demand to justify separate marketing strategies.

It is difficult to think of any consumer or industrial product or service with a single, homogeneous market. Knowledge of market segments relevant to the company's offerings is essential to the development of effective marketing strategies. Yet few companies attempt to serve all market segments. Even IBM, the dominant company in the electronic data processing industry, concentrated primarily on the major business and government segments, leaving to others (at least until now) the

TABLE 4-1
Key Subjects for Market Analysis

1. Broad market characteristics	5. Competitive structure
2. Market segments	6. Distribution structure
3. Structural market change	7. Price structure
4. Industry structure	8. Company position in market

market segments for large engineering and scientific applications, small business systems, and consumers uses. Going further, IBM segmented the business market by type of industry such as manufacturers, airlines, banks, and newspaper publishers. While each of these industries has common computer application needs (e.g., for accounting data and payroll preparation), they also have different needs—manufacturers for inventory control, airlines for ticket reservations, banks for account retrieval, and newspapers for typesetting and page makeup.

Evolution of the Market Segmentation Concept

Companies have long recognized and responded to certain types of market segments such as price, quality, age, sex, geography, application, and use. An early example was the organization of General Motors into the Chevrolet, Pontiac, Buick, Oldsmobile, and Cadillac divisions, arranged to cover automobile price and quality segments from economy to luxury. This was in contrast to Henry Ford's approach. Ford had offered one standardized, low-priced model designed for the mass of potential car buyers.

Widespread acceptance of the concept of market segmentation occurred as the result of (1) increasing awareness of the almost infinite number of ways in which markets can be segmented and (2) growing recognition that separate strategies for separate segments offer opportunities for increased sales and profits. The term *market segmentation* has come to encompass not only identification and measurement of segments, but also the development of separate marketing strategies for dealing with those segments.

Consumer market segmentation is a natural response to the growth of discretionary income and population. Discretionary income enables people to indulge their preferences while large populations create groups of buyers with similar preferences of sufficient size to enable companies to serve them at a profit. *Industrial market segmentation* is a natural response to the growth of manufacturing and service industries, and governmental and private institutions required to serve a growing, affluent population.

Supported by growing population and consumer income, the automotive industry now serves market segments other than those originally observed by General Motors. In addition to price, quality, and brand, the market for automobiles has been further segmented into an enormous variety of design, performance, and use segments. These reflect not only the needs of consumers for basic transportation but their psychic needs as well. Consumers may now choose among thousands of combinations of brands, models, colors, and optional equipment to satisfy their individual preferences. It is a far cry from the early Henry Ford credo: *They may have any color they want so long as it is black.*

Strategic Implications

Wendell Smith, in a pioneering article, introduced strategic implications of market segmentation by pointing out that companies have two basic options: (1) to capture as large a share of the heterogeneous market as possible with a single product offering by attempting to differentiate its brand from all others in the market or (2) to serve one or more of the homogeneous segments with product designed to appeal to the preferences of each segment.[1]

Combining Differentiation with Segmentation. While the strategic options pointed out by Smith do exist, most companies today practice market segmentation and, at the same time, attempt to differentiate their brands from those of competitors within the segments served.

The soft drink industry is a case in point. The two leading brands—Coca-Cola and Pepsi-Cola—compete for the same market segments. Both companies have basically the same users (youth), flavor, low-calorie alternatives, packaging (individual and family sizes, cans and bottles), place of purchase (convenience goods outlets, vending machines, and soda fountains), and geographic locations (including foreign countries). Yet both companies also try to differentiate their brands.

Coca-Cola's uniquely shaped bottle provided an effective means of differentiation for its cola drink until cans replaced much of the bottle market. Pepsi-Cola, a later market entrant, originally built its market share by using price and bottle size to differentiate its product. Later, when Pepsi-Cola priced its products at parity with Coca-Cola, the brands became less distinguishable. Both companies used similar advertising themes to appeal to the heavy usage youth segment.* Now, the battleground appears to have shifted to the local market scene, where the competition is in the form of franchising the strongest bottlers, conducting point-of-sale promotions, and expanding distribution.

There is far more to marketing strategy than market segmentation and product and brand differentiation. Yet these are crucial, and should never be overlooked during the strategic planning process.

Alternative Segmentation Approaches

There are three basic approaches a company can take to market segmentation: (1) serving primarily the larger segments, (2) serving primarily the smaller segments, or (3) serving a cross-section of both.

Concentration on a Larger Segment. Most product markets have a primary or "regular" market segment which accounts for a sizable portion of total industry volume. In the analgesics industry, regular-strength pain relievers account for over two-fifths of the market. Bayer aspirin (Sterling Drug) traditionally has concentrated its efforts on this larger segment. Most of the Bayer 1981 ad budget of $22 million was spent on regular aspirin.[2]

The advantage of concentrating on the larger or largest market segment is that it offers the greater sales potential. The disadvantage is that other major brands are also attracted to the larger segment; consequently, competitive activity is intense, making it more difficult for each company to attain or retain market share.

Concentration on Secondary or Smaller Segments. Concentration on a smaller segment offers less potential sales volume, but usually there are fewer competitors fighting for share. Traditionally, Bristol-Myers has concentrated in the roll-on applicator segment of the underarm deodorant market with its Ban brand, even though this was a secondary segment. Although Bristol-Myers also competed in the larger, but more competitive, spray applicator segment, its strong position in roll-on applicators made this segment the more profitable one for the company.

*However, recently both have directed some advertising to the growing older age segments.

In the electronic computer industry few companies have competed successfully with IBM for the general-purpose "mainframe" (central) systems business, which continues to represent the largest dollar market segment. Even such giant firms as RCA and General Electric were unsuccessful in competing for this major market segment and both withdrew from the industry. Most of the companies that succeeded in gaining a foothold in the computer market did so by concentrating on smaller segments. Examples are Control Data (scientific uses), Digital Equipment (minicomputers), Burroughs (banking applications), and, more recently, Apple and Tandy (personal computers).

Serving Multisegments. The prevailing pattern has been for larger firms to concentrate on major market segments and smaller firms to concentrate on lesser ones. Now larger firms are expanding into smaller segments as well. Tylenol moved into the childrens' and sinus medication segments with its acetaminophen product. IBM moved into the small business applications and consumer segments of the computer market. Multisegment strategies are common also in the markets where the same product is sold to all segments—for example, breakfast cereals.

Segmentation Criteria

Because no two buyers have precisely the same preferences, the smallest market segments would be the individual, family, or industrial buyer. From a practical standpoint, therefore, when we speak of market segments we are referring to groups of buyers with similar preferences. While there are exceptions—such as custom-built homes and machinery designed to the industrial buyer's specifications—a viable market segment in most cases must:

1. Be identifiable and describable in terms of the segment's needs and preferences
2. Be measurable, so that the segment's size and demand potential can be determined
3. Be large enough to enable both producers and distribution channel intermediaries to serve it profitably with a separate marketing strategy

Some maintain that a segment should also be "reachable" with a marketing program. While patently true, normally the segment can be reached if the above three criteria are met.

Identifying Segments. Existing market segments can be recognized either by direct observation or by formal market research. They can also be *created* by developing new products that fulfill latent needs.

Most developed industries are already serving clearly identified segments. One option for a company not serving an already established segment is to compete for this segment. A second option is to develop a new product to create demand in a latent, previously unserved segment. There was no consumer demand for a low calorie beer until it was offered to the market. But a brewer recognized that calorie conscious people were concerned about the fattening qualities of beer. There was no consumer demand for a deodorant treated sock until one was introduced. This market segment was created when a hosiery manufacturer realized that foot odor could be alleviated with a deodorant-treated sock. We continue to see new market segments created by managements willing to engage in market research, creative thinking, and experimental product and market development.

Measuring Segments. Measurement of already established segments is relatively simple since it merely involves measuring existing sales patterns. Published industry data may be available or, if not, measurements can be obtained using standard market research survey techniques. Segment data covering some major consumer products can be purchased from private research firms. Measuring the sales potential of previously *unserved* or *unrecognized* segments is quite another matter, and usually requires sophisticated and costly market research. Expensive and time-consuming test marketing also may be needed to verify the research findings. Measuring and developing new market segments is similar to the steps involved in new product development described in Chapter 17.

Segment Size and Profitability. Serving two or more market segments may be more costly for a company than treating the market as a single entity. The latter approach offers the cost efficiencies associated with mass production and the use of a single promotional program. Segmentation, on the other hand, incurs the added costs of multiproduction lines and multipromotional programs. Selling costs also rise when distribution must be forced through wholesalers and retailers who normally resist providing warehouse and shelf space for additional product lines.

Nevertheless, market segmentation *may* be the more profitable approach. Higher costs may be more than offset by higher prices, greater total unit volume, or the effects of incremental volume in absorbing fixed costs. The decision to adopt a market segmentation strategy should be preceded by careful profit analysis. Once a segmentation strategy has been adopted, special care must be exercised in going after additional segments. Markets can be segmented into smaller and smaller units until they reach the point of no profit return.

Types of Consumer Market Segments

A comprehensive list would contain thousands of market segments. The list shown in Table 4-2 contains some common means of categorizing consumer markets, but is suggestive at best. Each product industry offers its own opportunities for market segmentation and the segments for one industry may be quite different from those for another.

Let's look briefly at some of the segments in Table 4-2.

Geographic. Many companies market locally or regionally; hence, unserved geographic segments offer potential opportunities for expansion. National companies also may move into foreign markets. Geographic variations in weather, topography, water, soil, etc., offer segmentation opportunities for many types of consumer goods (e.g., clothing, sports equipment, and tires).

Demographic. Most consumer markets can be segmented by one or more demographic variables. Food and drink consumers can be categorized by age, race, ethnic background, religion, health, and physical characteristics; buyers of housing can be segmented by personal status; and so on, ad infinitum.

Economic. Income is a useful means of segmenting markets for many products and services, particularly higher-priced items like automobiles, housing, and home

TABLE 4-2
Examples of Consumer Market Segments

GEOGRAPHIC

- Location of population (i.e., by country, region, urban, suburban, rural)
- Climate
- Topography
- Water
- Soil characteristics
- Political

DEMOGRAPHIC

- Sex
- Age
- Race
- Ethnic origin
- Religion
- Education
- Personal status (i.e., single, married, unmarried but living together)
- Health
- Physical characteristics (i.e., height, weight, complexion)

ECONOMIC

- Personal income
- Family, household income
- Occupation
- Income source
- Savings
- Assets
- Price

SOCIAL AND PSYCHOLOGICAL

- Social class
- Reference group
- Lifestyle
- Stage of family life cycle
- Personality

PREFERENCE AND USE

- Usage rate (light user, heavy user)
- Use application
- Quality (performance)
- Benefits sought
- Aesthetic
- Brand loyalty

furnishings. Experienced marketers, however, do not consider income as a sole factor when segmenting markets. Rather, they consider it along with social, psychological, and other factors that also influence purchase behavior. *Demand* results from a combination of *ability to buy and willingness to buy*. Consequently, income is only one element of the demand equation. It is usually fruitful to look beyond income (and other contributors to purchasing power, such as savings, assets, and credit availability) for those other demand factors which determine willingness to buy.

Social and Psychological. Martineau found social class to be a better indicator than income for segmenting markets for savings and investment, travel, and home furnishings.[3] It can even be a key factor in consumers' retail store selections. Reference groups also significantly influence segmentation. Each generation of college students, for example, adopts a mode of dress distinctly its own, yet quickly adapts to the mode of dress of the postgraduate work environment. Stages of the life cycle as well as lifestyles influence purchasing patterns—for example, singles versus couples with children. Personality differences account for the great variety in the demand for items reflecting self-expression, such as clothes, jewelry, or art objects.

Social and psychological segments are easier to identify than they are to measure. The measurement challenge has attracted a number of experimental researchers.

Preference and Use. Variations in *usage rates* represent an important means of segmentation. The study depicted in Figure 4-1 is illustrative. Of the eighteen products measured, between 74 and 91 percent of total purchases were accounted for by the one-half of the users classified as *heavy*. For purposes of marketing planning, the problem is to determine the heavy users' characteristics so that marketing strategies can be devised which will reach the heavy users. Soap and detergent usage rates may correlate with family size, but one can wonder about

FIGURE 4-1. Annual Purchase Concentration in eighteen product catagories. *Source: Chicago Tribune* Consumer Panel, special analysis of 1962 data. Reprinted from Dik Warren Twedt, "The Concept of Market Segmentation," in Victor P. Buell, ed., *Handbook of Modern Marketing,* McGraw-Hill, New York, 1970, p. 2-13.

Product	Nonusers (Households)	Light half	Heavy half
	42%	29%	29%
Lemon-lime	0 (Volume)	9%	91%
Colas	0 / 22	10 / 39	90 / 39
Concentrated frozen orange juice	0 / 28	11 / 36	89 / 36
Bourbon	0 / 59	11 / 20	89 / 21
Hair fixatives	0 / 54	12 / 23	88 / 23
Beer	0 / 67	12 / 16	88 / 17
Dog food	0 / 67	13 / 16	87 / 17
Hair tonic	0 / 52	13 / 24	87 / 24
Ready-to-eat cereals	4 / 48	13 / 48	87
Canned hash	0 / 68	14 / 16	86 / 16
Cake mixes	0 / 27	15 / 36	85 / 37
Sausage	3 / 48	16 / 49	84
Margarine	0 / 11	17 / 44	83 / 45
Paper towels	0 / 34	17 / 33	83 / 33
Bacon	0 / 6	18 / 47	82 / 47
Shampoo	0 / 18	19 / 41	81 / 41
Soaps & detergents	0 / 2	19 / 49	81 / 49
Toilet tissue	0 / 2	26 / 49	74 / 49

household cleaning compounds. In a private study we found that the frequency of kitchen floor washing ranged from *daily* for families that considered "cleanliness next to Godliness" to almost *never* by those who felt that "a little dirt never hurt anybody."

Use applications form the basis for market segmentation for a great many products. Almost from the beginning of the vacuum cleaner industry, the market was considered to be segmented between the suction cleaner (exemplified by the Electrolux tank) and the revolving brush with beater bar type (exemplified by the Hoover upright). Later consumer studies revealed that segmentation really was based on the principal use of the cleaner. The Electrolux was bought mainly by households with movable rugs and partially bare floors while the Hoover was bought mainly by households with wall-to-wall carpeting, even though both companies offered (at extra cost) attachments which simulated the features of the other. Hoover added a suction model to compete for both market segments.

Variations in demand for many products is based on variations in *attitudes toward quality and performance*, which are related, at least partly, to price. With hobby equipment like cameras and sports equipment like tennis rackets, the neophyte often begins with lower-priced, lower-quality-performance equipment and moves up the scale as interest and skill increase. Noncorrelation between price and income is frequently seen in such products. The enthusiast often manages to find the money to obtain the finest equipment, irrespective of income level.

One idea of segmentation is based on *benefits sought*. Table 4-3 shows how the toothpaste market was segmented on this basis.

Reverse Segmentation

As noted earlier, it is possible for an industry to become so segmented that profitability is eliminated. If a little segmentation is good, a lot is not necessarily better. Some companies have returned to treating their heterogeneous markets as single entities. "All-purpose" detergents and "all-purpose" waxes are examples.[4] And

TABLE 4-3
Toothpaste Market Segment Description

	Segment Name			
	The Sensory Segment	The Sociables	The Worriers	The Independent Segment
Principal benefit sought	Flavor, product appearance	Brightness of teeth	Decay prevention	Price
Demographic strengths	Children	Teens, young people	Large families	Men
Special behavioral characteristics	Users of spearmint-flavored toothpaste	Smokers	Heavy users	Heavy users
Brands disproportionately favored	Colgate, Stripe	Macleans, Plus White, Ultra Brite	Crest	Brands on sale
Personality characteristics	High self-involvement	High sociability	High hypochondriasis	High autonomy
Lifestyle characteristics	Hedonistic	Active	Conservative	Value-oriented

Source: Russell I. Haley, "Benefit Segmentation: A Decision-Oriented Research Tool," *Journal of Marketing,* July 1968, p. 33.

Johnson & Johnson has promoted its Baby Shampoo and Baby Powder to all age groups in order to counteract the decline in the size of the baby market. These cases only serve to emphasize the point that marketing strategy formulation is not subject to pat formulas. The facts of each situation and the available options should dictate the company strategy.

Types of Industrial Market Segments

Industrial marketers have long been aware of market segmentation because many goods and services are sold to different industries, each with its own product and service needs. There are also relatively homogeneous markets which can be served with single product lines such as typewriters, lubricating oils, and air transportation. Even homogeneous markets, however, can be segmented by volume and profit potential. Conrail advertises that it "has a highly sophisticated market analysis ranking 60 'lines of business' according to their profit potential," helping Conrail "concentrate our marketing efforts and resources on the services that are in greatest demand—and that will earn enough to justify the costs of providing them."[5]

As with consumer product markets, industrial product markets can be segmented in many ways, although each company need only analyze the particular markets it chooses to serve. Table 4-4 illustrates some common means of segmenting industrial markets. You will remember from our discussion in Chapter 3 that the classes of industrial buyers shown may be segmented by SIC numbers into thousands of additional product and service classes.

Common Sense Approaches to Segmentation

Most of the literature dealing with segmentation research applies (1) to consumer markets and (2) to companies serving large mass markets. For a large consumer goods company competing for market share with large competitors, any information which will give it an advantage is worth considerable investment in consumer

TABLE 4-4
Examples of Industrial Market Segments

GEOGRAPHIC		
Location of buyers and users		
CLASS OF BUYER		
Manufacturers	Construction	Banking
Institutions	Mining	Investment
Government	Retailing	Insurance
Agriculture	Wholesaling	Restaurants, hotels, motels
Transportation	Commericial	Entertainment, recreation
Forestry	Communications	Repair, maintenance
Fisheries	Utilities	
ECONOMIC		
Use rate	Quality and performance requirements	
Price	Service requirements	

research. Not all market segmentation decisions must be based on sophisticated and expensive primary market research, however. Many segmentation opportunities can be evaluated with available data. One does not need research to know that a company operating in one geographic segment may consider the question of expansion into other geographic areas.

General Motors needed only observation and available statistics to know that the small car segment had grown to nearly one-fourth of the total car market, and that it was being developed primarily by foreign companies. Hanes did not need sociological research to recognize that low-priced hosiery was beginning to be sold in supermarkets—a segment Hanes did not serve at that time. A manufacturer of polyethylene film, serving the package manufacturing market, learned from its customers that the privately owned segment—where the company's sales were concentrated—was declining and that the large publicly owned segment—to which it did not sell—was growing.

Basically, we should apply whatever methods are required for the particular situation. Sometimes this will mean sophisticated research; at other times, only common sense, analysis of available data, or relatively simple market research is required. And, despite the fact that most literature deals with consumer markets, remember that segmentation applies to industrial markets as well.

STRUCTURAL MARKET CHANGE

The *market structure* for any product group consists of those elements that determine its size and purchase characteristics, including its segments. Knowing the market structure as it presently exists is important for short-term market planning, whereas understanding the factors that *cause* significant change in the structure is important to longer-range planning. This is why strategic planning emphasizes forecasting market change. Those companies that have maintained leadership positions over many years can be characterized by their ability to adapt to market change.

Important elements of market structure include the demographic, geographic, and economic factors discussed in Chapter 3. Excellent census data make it relatively easy to track and forecast them. Three other important elements of market structure are more difficult to track and forecast, however. These are cultural change, as reflected in social values, attitudes, and lifestyles; legal and governmental controls; and technological developments. Please note that *structural market change refers to significant semipermanent or permanent change in contrast to seasonal or cyclical fluctuation or temporary market aberrations.*

Cultural Change

Examples of cultural or subcultural changes occurring in America and many other Western countries are listed in Table 4-5. There is no assurance that all represent permanent change. Some may be cyclical in nature. Furthermore, because of cultural lag, not all people accept changing values at the same time, and some may never accept them. Yet there is little question that the total impact of cultural change has a direct effect on the structure of consumer markets over time and an indirect effect on industrial markets as well.

TABLE 4-5
Examples of Change in Cultural Values, Attitudes, and Lifestyles

Lengthening years of education	Increase in cults and nontraditional religious experiences
Decline of the family	
Increasing divorce rates	Informality in dress, manners, entertaining
Increase in nonmarried households	Heightened interest in personal privacy
Later childbearing	Back-to-nature movement
Increase in percent of women working	Interest in exercise and physical fitness
Decline of materialism	Increase in humanism
Decline of the work ethic	Distrust of bigness, whether government, business, or labor
Increasing hedonism	Lessening confidence in advertising
Increasing travel	Growing support for rights of minorities
Frequent change of home location	Growth of consumerism
More leisure activities	Increasing support of egalitarianism
Increase in use of sensory stimulants	Aversion to taking risks
Increasing sexual freedom	

Just one aspect of the women's liberation movement—the increase of working wives*—has affected many markets, such as food, appliances, restaurants, and education. A company's sales may be affected positively or negatively by such developments. More eating out because both partners work, for example, is a positive factor for the restaurant and take-out food business, but a negative factor for foods sold for home preparation. Several food processing companies, such as General Mills and Pillsbury, recognized the potential consequences and acquired fast food restaurant chains. An interesting aspect of this phenomenon is the large proportion of working wives in higher income families. Figure 4-2 shows that two-thirds are in families with annual incomes over $20,000. This factor influences the markets for those products and services sensitive to rising family income.

Another example of cultural change is the trend to informality which for several years severely damaged the markets for men's and women's hats while stimulating the growth of the market for hair conditioners. Hats have since made some degree of comeback. Whether informality is a new permanent fixture of the culture or will exhibit the cyclical characteristics of fashion remains to be seen. Rising interest in exercise (encouraged by new medical evidence) helped revive a declining bicycle industry.

Legal and Governmental Controls

The increasing complexity of modern life has led to substantial increases in laws and to a rise in the number of enforcement and regulatory agencies and their activities. These changes affect every aspect of society and some affect business and marketing in particular.

*The percentage of married women working rose from 25 percent in 1950 to 51 percent in 1980. *Source*: U.S. Bureau of the Census, *Statistical Abstract of the United States*, 1981, Washington, D.C., table 652, p. 388.

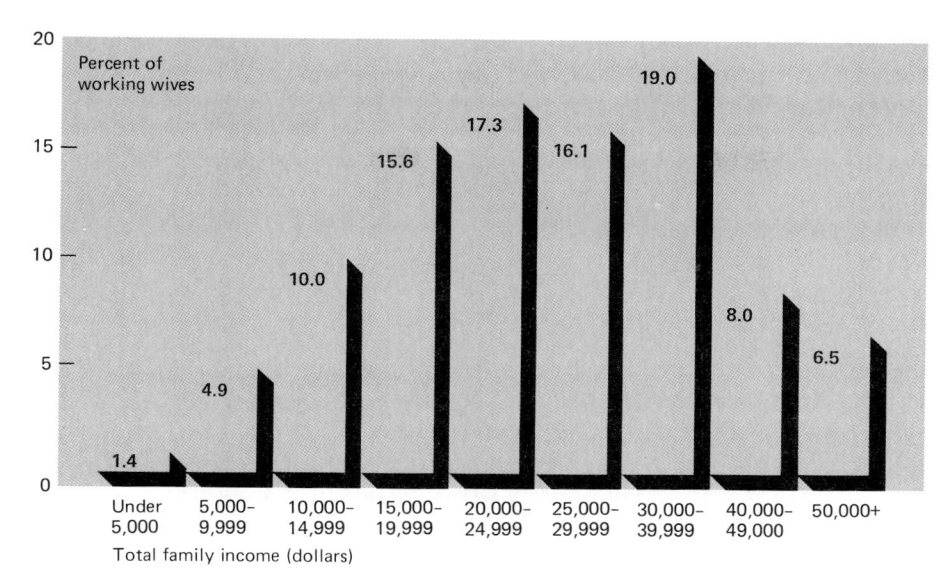

FIGURE 4-2. Percent of working wives by family income. For example, 19 percent of all working wives are in families where the family income is between $30,000 and $39,000. *Source:* U.S. Bureau of the Census, "Money Income of Families and Persons in the United States: 1979," *Current Population Reports,* ser. P-60, no. 129, U.S. Government Printing Office, Washington, D.C., 1981.

Law is a reflection of many aspects of a society. Because fundamental economic, social, and other factors undergo change, it follows that laws and their interpretation by the courts also change. Traditionally, U.S. laws with the greatest impact on marketing have dealt with antitrust, consumer protection, contracts, warranties, and trademarks. We now see an increase in laws designed to protect consumers, workers, and the environment, as well as stepped up involvement in business regulation by the Department of Justice, the Federal Trade Commission (FTC), and the Food and Drug Administration (FDA). American companies involved in international trade also must comply with different laws in each foreign country.

How Laws Affect Markets. Legal and regulatory actions have caused much change. For instance product design, costs, and prices of automobiles have been affected by legislation dealing with safety, pollutant emissions, and minimum miles per gallon of fuel. Pollution control laws have banned certain detergent formulations as well as disposable containers in some states and localities. DDT has been banned and other insecticides strictly limited in their use. Packaging laws have set new standards which have brought about drastic changes in packaging and marketing for many consumer products. Credit policies of merchants, lending agencies, and credit card companies have been changed to correspond with revised credit regulations. Market introductions of new drugs have been delayed or aborted by stricter FDA testing requirements. Energy conservation laws are affecting the design of a host of products, including housing and commercial structures. Standards promulgated by the Consumer Product Safety Commission have caused the redesign of many products, such as safety guards on rotary lawn mowers.

Tighter FTC controls have caused basic changes in advertising policies and practice. The outlawing of cigarette advertising on TV and radio has been cited as a factor in the slower growth rate of cigarette sales. The banning of the sugar substitute cyclamate not only wiped out the cyclamate industry, but also caused a slowdown in the growth of diet foods and drinks.

While marketing executives should understand and keep up to date with the broad aspects and purposes of the laws and regulations affecting marketing, they should also have access to professional legal counsel. Legal counsel is essential because of the growing size and complexity of the legal environment.

Technology

The markets of virtually every industry are subject to periodic technological change. Change can occur slowly or so dramatically that it wipes out an entire industry. Interurban railways, silk hosiery, and vacuum tubes are just a few of the products made virtually extinct by new technologies.

Plastics have invaded the markets of wood, metals, linoleum, paper, and natural textile fibers. Television almost wiped out the movie industry before Hollywood reacted by producing films for that medium. Electronic data processing and transmission have made manual and electrical approaches to data handling increasingly obsolete. Technological developments in agronomy and farm machinery helped to change the United States from an agriculturally based to an industrially based economy within a few decades.

Technological developments from within and without one's industry can have positive or negative results for a company. How they affect the individual company depends, at least in part, on how quickly management recognizes and adapts to the change.

Developments Outside the Industry. Not infrequently, market structure is changed via technological developments imposed by an outside industry that had not previously served the market. Such technology may improve upon, or supplant, the products of the industry that traditionally supplied the market. This kind of market change is among the more difficult for companies to recognize and accept. It has been said that "a visit to a pathology lab of the corporate hospital reveals a common cause of death: killed by a competitor one did not know or did not take seriously."[6]

The electric typewriter was developed by a company from outside the typewriter industry, namely IBM, which succeeded in replacing much of the manual typewriter market with electric models before the former leaders of the typewriter industry developed their own competitive electric models. Fiber glass bathtubs, developed by companies outside the plumbing equipment industry, were viewed by the leading plumbing equipment manufacturers as inferior to the more traditional cast iron and steel tubs until fiber glass had achieved a sizable foothold in the market. Radio and TV stations had invaded the traditional advertising medium held by printed publications before some publishers decided to acquire their own stations to offset the loss of advertising revenues to their publications. The traditional mechanical watch industry was invaded with electronic digital watches produced by manufacturers of transistors who formerly had not manufactured watches.

Technological change from outside one's industry causes a serious type of threat because the traditional companies often do not possess the technology with which to compete. Such situations call for alternative strategies in time to adjust to the outside threats.

INDUSTRY STRUCTURE

We will now consider several market-related subjects which, in combination with the markets themselves, form the environment within which a company operates. The first of these is the industry structure.

An industry is made up of all the companies (or their business units) that produce a similar line of products or services. The terms "industry" and "market" are sometimes used interchangeably, particularly when referring to market share. A product industry and its market, however, while closely related, are not the same. *An industry provides product; the market consumes it.* It is true, however, that industry factory shipments in units (after adjustment for inventories, exports, and imports) equal market purchases in units.

A company producing a single product line will be a part of only one industry. The William Wrigley Jr. Company, for example, is a one-industry company whose products are sold to the various segments of the population that chew gum. General Electric, by contrast, is a multiindustry company. Its products fall into industry categories ranging from home appliances to jet engines. GE products are sold to hundreds of markets and market segments.

Industry structure can be described in terms of (1) the total size and sales trends of the industry, (2) the competing companies within it, (3) the distribution system used to reach its markets, and (4) the industry pricing system. Because competitive, distributive, and price structures have ramifications beyond a single industry, we discuss them separately in the sections that follow.

Industry Size and Trends

It is important that management follow the size and trends of its industry's sales so that it can compare company performance with that of the industry. Except for private market research studies, industry sales recorded as factory shipments are the only available measures of market size and trends. Ideally, product sales should be recorded at the market level, but this is not done for most industries because of the high cost and the problems of data collection. Industry sales data can be obtained from one or more of the following sources:

Census Data. Manufacturers' shipments are recorded by SIC product classifications. All plants are surveyed at the time of the 5-year censuses; monthly projections of factory shipments are made between the general censuses, using sampling methods.

Industry Association Data. Many industry associations collect factory shipment data monthly from their members and report the totals back to their member subscribers. Some also release these totals to the financial and trade press. The advantages of association-collected data, as compared to census data, are that they are reported more quickly, rely less on sampling methods, and often are presented in finer breakdowns.

Private Research Firms. For many years a few private research firms have specialized in collecting sales by product and brand at the wholesale, retail, or consumer level, using sampling methods. This information is sold to subscribers for considerably less than it would cost an individual company to collect the data on its own. Research of this type is carried out principally for high-turnover consumer items such as food, drug, and personal care products.

The advantages of sales data collected in these ways are that they more accurately reflect consumer purchases on a timely basis, and market share is reported for major brands. Furthermore, the data are reported by geographic areas of consumer purchase whereas factory sales are reported by the geographic area in which products are manufactured. And, in the case of data collected by consumer sampling methods, sales also can be broken out by demographic, income, and usage rate segments.

Trade Media. Some trade magazines report product sales information for the industries they serve, using census data and surveys by the magazine and/or private research firms.

In the industrial field, *Sales and Marketing Management* magazine, in its annual "Survey of Industrial Purchasing Power," reports sales at the factory level for all four digit SIC classifications, arranged by county and U.S. total. *Sales and Marketing Management* obtains data from the Census of Manufacturers which in turn are adjusted by supplementary information from a private research firm to overcome the shortcomings of the census data.*

Identification of Industry Data. When using industry sales data, note carefully exactly what is being reported. For example, sales may be reported in dollars (or other national currencies) and also by physical measures (units, pairs, dozens, pounds, tons, etc.). Both of these measures are useful in analyzing industry sales data. Observe also whether sales are reported at manufacturers' prices or at recommended retail selling prices.

To better guage the value of sales going to the domestic market, domestic factory sales must be adjusted for the value of imports and exports. The output of the American shoe industry, for example, is smaller than domestic shoe consumption because shoe imports greatly outnumber shoe exports.

Sales by Industry Segments. It is important for companies to analyze industry sales by product segment as well as by industry total. This is because sales of industry segments may be changing at different rates than the industry average. The writing instrument industry at one point was growing when the fountain pen segment was leveling and then declining because of the popularity of the newer ball point pens. Companies producing fountain pens could have been misled had they looked only at total fountain pen sales and ignored the sales trends of the ball point segment.

Industry segments do not always correspond to market segments since the same product can be sold to multiple segments. In the absence of purchase

---

*For example, census data, in order to avoid identifying an individual establishment, do not include sales of a plant that represents a significant share of county manufacturing activity. Also census data covering plant sales are recorded by the SIC classification of the primary product produced by the plant, which can result in over- or underreporting of an SIC product total.

information by market segment, however, shifts in sales by industry segments often provide clues to what is happening at the market level.

Company Market Share

Perhaps the most valuable use of industry sales data is that it permits a company to compute its approximate market share as frequently as industry data is issued. Tracking one's market share provides a useful means of measuring company performance.

Several conclusions may result from industry sales and market share analyses. If the industry is not growing at a rate consistent with company growth objectives, marketing management either must find ways of increasing market share or consider other alternatives such as diversification. If market share is holding steady, can the company do better? If market share is declining, why is this happening? What corrective measures can the company take? Operating without industry and market share information means that in a growing industry a company may be lulled into thinking it is doing well because its own sales are increasing. Actually, it may be slipping because it is not growing as fast as the industry. Such a situation is illustrated in Figure 4-3.

Industry Product Life Cycle

Plotting annual industry sales on a graph can assist management in determining the current phase of the product life cycle. The *product life cycle concept* is explained in Chapter 16 and so we merely introduce the subject here. (Figure 16-3 illustrates the cycle.)

This concept states that every product industry sales curve goes through a cycle which is divisable into at least four stages: (1) introduction, (2) growth, (3) maturity,

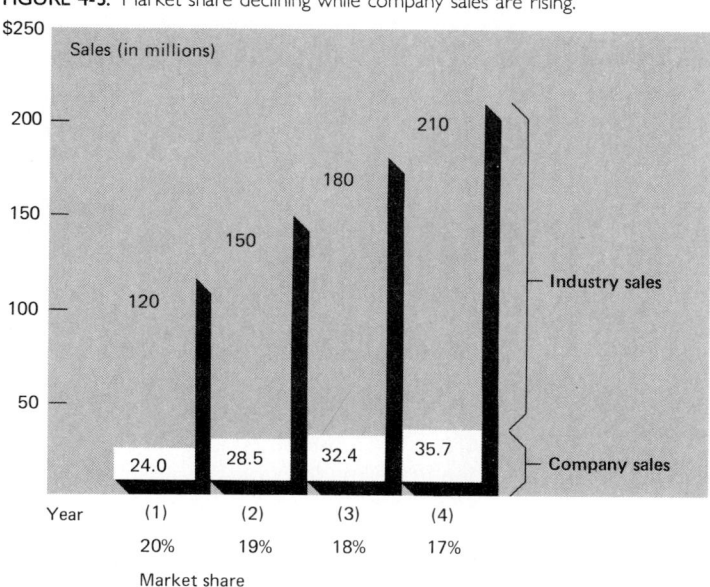

FIGURE 4-3. Market share declining while company sales are rising.

Year	(1)	(2)	(3)	(4)
Industry sales	120	150	180	210
Company sales	24.0	28.5	32.4	35.7
Market share	20%	19%	18%	17%

and (4) decline. The *growth* period usually represents the most profitable portion of the curve, whereas the periods of *maturity* and *decline* usually find profit margins narrowing and weaker companies being squeezed out of the industry.

It is not easy to tell precisely when an industry is moving from one period to another, since cyclical movements or aberrations may temporarily disguise the basic change. For both short- and long-range planning, nevertheless, it is important to estimate which period the industry is in and how much longer it will last. Significantly, at any one time the majority of major industries are in their mature phase.

COMPETITIVE STRUCTURE

Competition inevitably ranks high among executive concerns. Nothing can cause as quick a change of plans as a competitive threat to the company's market position. In analyzing the competitive situation, you should look at competition in both quantitative and qualitative terms, consider indirect as well as direct competition, and be aware of whether your industry is oligopolistic or monopolistic.

Quantitative and Qualitative Evaluation

Information that should be developed about competitors includes:

- Number of competitors.
- Ranking of direct competitors by name in terms of size and market share. Note your company's position.
- Changes in rankings. Are some growing faster than others, and if so, why?
- Strengths and weaknesses of major competitors relative to your company.
- Import competition, if any.
- Names and types of indirect competitors.

If your company is the industry leader, it is important to know whether competitors are gaining and, if so, why. If it is not the leader, compare its strengths and weaknesses with larger competitors to learn what will be needed to overtake them.

If import competition exists, find out what share of industry sales are accounted for by imports, whether the share is growing, who the leading importers are, and what their strengths and weaknesses are. Even giant IBM does not ignore import competition. Frank Cary, IBM board chairman, responding to a shareholder's question, said, "The Japanese firms are very capable. They have good technology and also the support of the Japanese government, which has declared it wants to make data processing an export industry. We are not taking that competition lightly at all."[7] And powerful Xerox announced major price reductions on four of its copiers that faced severe price competition from Japanese made copiers.[8]

Role of Historical Leadership. The leading company or brand in an industry frequently occupies that position because it was one of the pioneers of the industry and has maintained its early advantage. Such companies usually have well-known brand names, substantial market shares, and broad product lines distributed by the leading wholesalers and/or retailers. Examples include RCA, Polaroid, Gillette, American-Standard, Jell-O, Nabisco, Kellogg, Time, and Hertz. Johnson & Johnson's Tylenol, the original brand of acetaminophen pain reliever, maintains a commmanding lead over Bristol-Myers' Datril brand despite lower prices and heavy promotional efforts by Bristol-Myers, itself a highly sophisticated marketer. And Tylenol retained market leadership even after the poisoning scare it suffered in 1982.

Early leadership, of course, provides no assurance of continued success, as witnessed by the demise of the Packard car, *Life* and *Look* magazines, and Lucky Strike cigarettes.* Nor did it prevent the decline in market position of Listerine toothpaste or Camel cigarettes. The would-be challengers should ask how solid is the position of the historical leader and what would be the costs in money, time, and effort (relative to alternative opportunities) to overtake the leader. It may be more sensible to seek second or third place. Avis has made a virtue out of its second place position after Hertz in the car rental industry.

Direct versus Indirect Competition

Normally we think of our competition as other companies selling the same or similar products or services. Such competitors represent *direct* competition from within one's own industry. Of equal importance, however, may be *indirect* competitors—companies in other industries competing with substitute products or representing alternate attractions for consumers' dollars.

U.S. Steel, for example, not only competes directly with other companies in the steel industry, but also with other materials industries such as aluminum, plastics, and wood. Stockbrokers compete directly with other stockbrokers, yet indirectly as well with other industries vying for consumer savings such as banks, corporate bonds, government bonds, and life insurance. American Airlines competes not only with United and TWA for the travel and freight markets, but also with other forms of transportation.

Oligopolistic and Monopolistic Competition

Because neither pure competition nor pure monopoly exists in its classical form in the United States, economists have developed other theories of competition to describe the actual situation. *Oligopoly* and *monopolistic competition* represent two well-known examples, one or the other of which will explain the competitive condition in most U.S. industries.

In Chapter 3 we explained that oligopoly exists in an industry when a few companies have a sizeable combined share of the industry. There are no precise definitions of "a few" or the "size of the combined market share"; rather an industry is considered oligopolistic when it acts like an oligopoly. Monopolistic competition exists where there are a substantial number of companies in an industry but none has a dominant position. The term is used to suggest that each company maintains a "monopoly" on a small geographic or other market segment by virtue of its product

*Both *Life* and *Look* have since been reintroduced.

differentiation, yet has no real monopoly power in the classical sense of that term.* Table 3-6, page 59, contains examples of industries falling into each classification. Figure 4-4 illustrates how monopolistic competition and oligopoly differ from each other and from pure competition and pure monopoly.

A characteristic of an oligopolistic industry is that the leading firms are sufficiently strong to protect their market shares from inroads by competitors. Thus, they normally will meet price cuts or increased promotional effort in kind. Consequently, vigorous price competition usually is not pursued in such industries since company managements know that everyone tends to lose from such actions. The smaller, nonleader firms (of which there may be many) tend to have more freedom of action because changes in their market positions have only minor impacts on the industry leaders. Also the smaller companies in an oligopolistic industry often serve small, specialized market segments for which the industry leaders do not consider it worth their while to compete.

In a *monopolistic, competitive* industry, on the other hand, all companies are relatively free to make competitive moves in terms of product, price, distribution, and promotion. The reason is that one company may achieve a significant increase in its market share (a share, still small, however, in terms of total industry) without

---

*Care should be taken to distinguish between the noun "monopoly" and the adjective "monopolistic." In economic theory, pure monopoly represents the absence of competition since by definition there is only one seller in an industry. Monopolistic competition, by contrast, is present where a number of competing companies each have some degree of monopoly by virtue of their differentiated offerings. Edward Hastings Chamberlin first introduced the theory of monopolistic competition in his doctoral thesis in 1927, and later presented it in his book *The Theory of Monopolistic Competition*, first published by the Harvard University Press in 1933 and followed by numerous subsequent editions. The essence of his theory is that with any degree of product differentiation a seller has an absolute monopoly even though the seller's product is subject to competition from other sellers offering more or less imperfect substitutes. Professor Chamberlin also describes this condition as one of "competing monopolists." Although this is a seeming contradiction in terms, it actually describes a situation common to many industries.

FIGURE 4-4. Market structures and their features. *Source:* Robert J. Holloway and Robert S. Hancock, *Marketing in a Changing Environment*, 2d ed., Wiley, New York, 1973, p.107.

Features	Pure Competition	Monopolistic Competition	Oligopoly	Pure Monopoly
Number of sellers	Very large number	Substantial number	Few	One
Product	Undifferentiated perfect substitutes	Differentiated products with close substitutes*		No close substitute for unique good
Price	No control over price — seller must accept market price	Administered Prices		Much control over price — but can sell only what market will take at his price
		Some price competition can prevail. Price control depends much on degree of differentiation	Pricing in concert is strong tendency. Firms mutually interdependent	
Entry of new firms	Easy	Somewhat easy — but depends on technology and size of firms	Usually difficult because of size of firms and high costs	No entry as resource access is blocked
Marketing effort	None	Very large amount of nonprice competition with heavy emphasis on brands and product differentiation. Wide use of advertising and any marketing activity to build market share		Little, but can enjoy benefits if less product elasticity is created

*Except for undifferentiated oligopoly which is not common in actual market situations.

triggering direct reaction from competitors. The impact of the company's actions is spread over so many competitors that it may not be noticed by any—or if it is, the company may not be readily identified as the one gaining market share.

Industries fall on a continuum running from clearly oligopolistic to clearly monopolistic competition with those toward the center being somewhat difficult to classify. To the extent possible, however, marketing management should determine the competitive classification of its industry. Market strategies should differ depending on the class of industry competition in which one competes, and, in the case of oligopoly, strategies should differ according to whether the firm is one of the leaders or one of the smaller companies.

DISTRIBUTION STRUCTURE

Over the years distribution structure has changed from one in which wholesalers and retailers specialized in distributing the products of a single industry to one in which they distribute the products of several or many industries. While examples of specialization remain, the general switch from monistic to pluralistic distribution has caused the term *distribution structure* to take on wider meaning. Our main discussion of distribution is reserved for Chapter 19. Here we want to point out the key channel factors to be considered during the market analysis.

Principal consumer goods channels are:

1. Manufacturer to consumer
2. Manufacturer to retailer to consumer
3. Manufacturer to wholesaler (or chain warehouse) to retailer to consumer

The most commonly used channel for consumer goods is the last, in which wholesalers and retailers represent the channel intermediaries between manufacturer and consumer. From the viewpoint of the manufacturer, these intermediaries perform two major functions: (1) physical distribution and (2) sales (though the degree of sales effort may vary considerably). Wholesale and retail operations normally are provided by individually owned firms or by chains, although in some cases either or both may be owned by the manufacturer.

The principal industrial goods channels are (1) manufacturer to user and (2) manufacturer to wholesaler to user. Over 60 percent of all industrial goods are distributed direct—i.e., manufacturer to user—in contrast to about 5 percent direct distribution for consumer goods.[9]

For market analysis purposes a company needs to know the alternate channels that are available, and the number, size, location, and quality of channel intermediaries.

Available Alternatives

Channel alternatives can be among those listed above for consumer and industrial goods, or some combination of these. Or there may be other possibilities such as franchised retailers, or company-owned branches in place of independent wholesalers. Few companies use only one channel under all circumstances.

Analysis calls for evaluating the advantages and disadvantages of each alternative and determination of the most appropriate channels for each type of geographic or other market segment served. For example, distribution direct from manufacturer to retailer may be utilized for large city markets, while a wholesaler may be better for less geographically concentrated markets. While companies in most industries tend to follow set distribution patterns, there are enough successful exceptions to suggest that any company may benefit from periodic reexamination of alternate means of reaching the ultimate customer. Hanes found it advisable to add supermarkets and drug stores to its traditional department store and hosiery shop outlets. General Electric had to bypass the electric appliance retailer and sell direct to home builders in order to penetrate the new home, built-in kitchen appliance market.

Number, Size, and Location of Intermediaries

Marketing management needs to know the number and sales volume by market area of the classes of wholesalers and retailers that stock the types of products produced by the company. This information can be found in the Census of Business and the Area Statistics by SIC code. The relative size of individual wholesale and retail establishments, however, will require company or purchased market research.

There are approximately 2 million retail and 300,000 merchant wholesale establishments in the United States.* Their sales by major classes of business are shown in Tables 4-6 and 4-7.

Quality of Intermediaries

Of even more significance is the percentage of available intermediaries carrying the company's product line and the quality of these intermediaries. For companies marketing *convenience goods*, a major distribution objective usually is wide retail coverage, i.e., *intensive* distribution. A sale certainly will be lost whenever a brand is not on the shelf at the time someone wishes to buy that brand. For companies marketing *shopping goods*, distribution through a limited number of specific types of retailers in each local market (called *selective* distribution) is more important than intensity of coverage. This is because the company needs supportive retailers who will give special push to the manufacturer's brand.

Because brands holding leading market shares tend to have the largest and most effective wholesalers and retailers—particularly for selectively distributed products—smaller companies may be locked out of the better intermediaries or their brands may receive less attention when carried. Consequently, distribution strategy becomes a high priority planning item for companies with secondary market positions.

PRICE STRUCTURE

The price setting process brings into focus the risks inherent in marketing strategy selection. Price usually affects volume of sales and volume usually affects cost. The price/volume/cost mix will usually determine the amount of profit to be derived from a strategy.

When General Motors' Chevrolet Division introduced the low-priced Chevette to compete in the foreign dominated U.S. small car market, it not only accepted less

---

*Merchant wholesalers take title to the goods they distribute. They account for about 83 percent of all wholesale establishments.

TABLE 4-6

No. 1466. Retail Trade—Sales, by Kind of Business: 1967 to 1981

[In billions of dollars. Based on 1972 Standard Industrial Classification. Data reflect methodological revision effective Aug. 1977. Based on Current Business Survey, see Appendix III. See also *Historical Statistics, Colonial Times to 1970*, series T 245-271]

KIND OF BUSINESS	1967	1970	1973	1974	1975	1976	1977	1978	1979	1980	1981, Jan.-June [1]
Retail trade, total	293.0	368.4	509.5	541.0	588.1	657.4	725.2	804.7	894.3	956.7	518.6
Durable goods stores, total [2]	88.7	109.2	172.9	169.4	183.0	217.8	248.7	279.8	304.8	297.9	164.3
Automotive dealers	53.8	62.6	103.3	96.5	106.6	129.8	150.0	167.3	177.3	167.0	92.6
Motor veh., misc. automotive dealers	49.7	56.9	94.8	87.5	96.8	118.9	137.1	153.2	161.1	148.8	82.7
Motor vehicle dealers	48.0	55.0	88.6	80.6	89.0	111.3	128.8	144.0	150.8	140.1	(NA)
Motor vehicle dealers, franchised	45.0	51.8	83.5	76.3	84.2	105.2	121.9	135.8	141.4	130.3	(NA)
Auto and home supply stores	4.2	5.6	8.6	9.0	9.9	10.9	12.9	14.0	16.1	18.2	9.8
Building materials, hardware, garden supply, mobile home dealers [2]	13.3	17.6	26.9	27.0	27.0	33.0	38.9	44.8	50.3	48.2	26.9
Building materials, supply stores	9.0	11.2	17.2	17.8	18.0	22.5	27.1	31.5	35.3	33.7	18.9
Hardware stores	2.8	3.2	4.1	4.5	5.1	5.4	6.1	6.9	7.8	7.7	4.4
Furniture, home furnishings, equip.[2]	14.2	17.7	24.3	26.0	26.9	30.0	33.2	36.5	41.9	44.0	23.3
Furniture, home furnishings stores	8.3	10.6	15.2	16.3	16.2	18.0	20.3	22.5	25.7	26.2	14.0
Household appliance, radio, TV	5.0	6.0	7.4	7.6	8.3	9.2	10.0	10.5	12.4	13.2	7.0
Nondurable goods stores, total [2]	204.2	259.2	336.6	371.6	405.2	439.6	476.5	525.0	589.5	658.7	354.4
Apparel and accessory stores [2]	16.3	20.2	27.7	28.9	31.3	33.7	35.6	40.0	42.4	44.5	23.8
Men's, boys' clothing, furnishings	3.4	4.4	5.9	5.9	6.4	6.5	6.9	7.5	7.8	8.0	4.0
Women's clothing, specialty stores, furriers	6.4	7.7	10.6	11.2	12.4	13.4	13.5	15.5	16.2	17.0	9.3
Women's ready-to-wear stores	5.3	6.7	9.5	10.1	11.3	12.3	12.4	14.3	15.0	15.6	(NA)
Family clothing stores	3.1	3.8	5.7	6.2	6.6	7.2	8.1	8.3	8.7	9.1	(NA)
Shoe stores	2.9	3.6	4.5	4.4	4.6	5.0	5.7	6.5	7.4	8.0	4.5
Drug stores and proprietary stores	10.8	13.8	17.0	18.4	19.9	21.6	23.2	25.3	28.1	31.6	16.8
Eating and drinking places	23.5	31.1	40.4	44.7	51.1	57.2	63.3	70.7	79.6	86.6	47.4
Food stores	69.4	88.7	111.4	126.0	138.4	148.0	157.9	174.2	195.8	217.5	116.7
Grocery stores	64.2	81.5	103.5	117.2	129.2	138.2	147.8	162.7	182.4	202.1	108.0
Gasoline service stations	22.6	29.2	37.0	43.0	47.5	52.0	56.5	59.7	73.2	94.5	51.4
General merchandise group stores [2]	41.0	50.3	67.4	71.2	75.7	81.8	90.7	100.8	109.7	116.3	62.2
Department stores	31.1	38.5	52.6	55.4	59.4	65.7	73.6	81.5	88.5	94.2	50.7
Variety stores	5.3	6.6	7.4	7.7	8.0	7.2	7.1	7.5	8.4	8.9	4.6
Liquor stores	6.6	8.3	10.2	11.0	11.8	12.4	13.0	13.6	15.3	16.6	8.3
Mail-order houses (department store merchandise) [3]	2.7	3.5	5.0	5.4	5.6	6.1	6.8	7.1	5.3	(NA)	(NA)

NA Not available. [1] Adjusted for seasonal variation. [2] Includes kinds of business not shown separately. [3] Includes sales made by mail-order catalog desks in department stores or mail-order firms.

Source: U.S. Bureau of the Census, *Current Business Reports*, series BR, *Monthly Retail Trade*.

Reprinted from U. S. Bureau of the Census, *Statistical Abstract of the United States, 1981*, Washington, D. C., p. 812

profit per car but also ran the risk that sales of Chevette would rob sales from other higher-priced and more profitable Chevrolet Division models. J. C. Penney took a calculated gamble with future company profits when it decided to move into higher priced segments, particularly by replacing its basic women's apparel lines with fashion merchandise. Based on analysis of the changing preferences of its women customers, Penney's management made this move despite knowledge that its major competitor, Sears, had decided to pull back from a similar previous move it had made to higher prices.[10]

Pricing strategies are a reflection of a company's overall marketing strategies. Neither strategic nor tactical pricing decisions can be made in a vacuum. Pricing decisions should be made while considering all of the external factors discussed in this and the previous chapter, plus the company's objectives, internal strengths and weaknesses, and position in the marketplace.

Required Market Price Data

Basic information needed on the market pricing structure includes:

1. The prevailing range of prices for products similar to the company's products, and for substitute products

2. Price trends
3. Reasons for price trends such as general economic trends, inflationary costs, changing supply-and-demand relationships, prices of substitutes, entrance or exit of competitors, and change in the product life cycle curve
4. Industry volume shares by price segments such as high, medium, and low (or even finer breakdowns)
5. Industry practice with respect to trade price discounts, promotional discounts, credit terms, and absorption or nonabsorption in the product price of the costs of transportation and services
6. Degree of pricing freedom, depending on whether the industry is oligopolistic or monopolistic
7. Demand elasticity, i.e., the degree to which industry revenue changes in response to changes in price
8. Legal constraints

Factors affecting price are shown in Figure 4-5.

Collecting Price Data

In highly competitive industries company managements deal with pricing issues frequently. Hence, in an established industry management tends to have at hand much of the information listed above.

Companies look to their sales forces to report competitors' price ranges, price changes, and variations in industry pricing practices. Some industry price levels are reported by government agencies, publications, and private research services. Public information contributes to an understanding of the reasons for price changes, and this can be supplemented by company economic and market research.

Whether an industry is oligopolistic or monopolistic can be determined from the published government data for many industries. (See Table 3-6, page 59, for examples.) For industries not included in the government reports, experienced managements usually know whether a large share of industry volume is

TABLE 4-7

No. **1483.** Merchant Wholesalers—Estimated Sales, by Kind of Business: 1967 to 1981

[**In billions of dollars.** Data reflect methodological revision effective August 1977. Based on Current Business Survey, see Appendix III. See *Historical Statistics, Colonial Times to 1970,* series T 280–371, for related data]

KIND OF BUSINESS	1967	1970	1975	1977	1978	1979	1980	1981, Jan.–June [1]
Merchant wholesalers	233.4	287.3	559.5	671.8	776.6	915.2	1,043.9	582.8
Durable goods, total [2]	99.7	127.2	229.5	297.3	354.2	410.0	438.4	243.7
Motor vehicles and automotive equipment	14.1	21.4	39.7	55.1	66.3	75.5	81.6	45.4
Furniture and homefurnishings	4.3	5.5	8.3	11.1	12.6	13.9	15.6	11.8
Lumber and construction materials	9.2	11.6	17.3	27.6	33.7	37.1	33.2	17.4
Electrical goods	12.4	15.0	22.7	30.4	36.2	41.8	46.4	26.4
Hardware, plumbing, and heating equipment	8.7	10.5	15.2	19.9	23.3	26.8	27.6	15.4
Machinery, equipment, and supplies	28.7	33.8	69.2	85.7	99.2	116.0	129.0	71.6
Nondurable goods, total [2]	133.6	160.1	329.9	374.6	422.4	505.1	605.4	339.1
Paper and paper products	6.4	7.4	11.2	15.0	17.0	19.3	21.6	12.2
Drugs, proprietaries, and sundries	4.7	5.6	8.8	10.1	10.7	11.6	13.1	7.5
Apparel, piece goods, and notions	8.9	10.2	14.7	17.9	21.4	23.0	25.8	14.0
Groceries and related products	42.5	54.4	95.8	111.6	125.8	136.5	149.9	81.3
Farm-product raw materials	24.0	24.8	83.3	80.2	92.7	106.4	120.2	64.9
Beer, wine, and distilled beverages	10.4	13.1	19.4	22.4	25.9	29.2	31.7	16.7
Petroleum and petroleum products	(S)	(S)	(S)	59.5	66.9	103.0	158.2	97.7

S Data do not meet publication standards.   [1] Seasonally adjusted.   [2] Includes kinds of business not shown separately.

Reprinted from U. S. Bureau of the Census, *Statistical Abstract of the United States, 1981,* Washington, D. C., p. 822

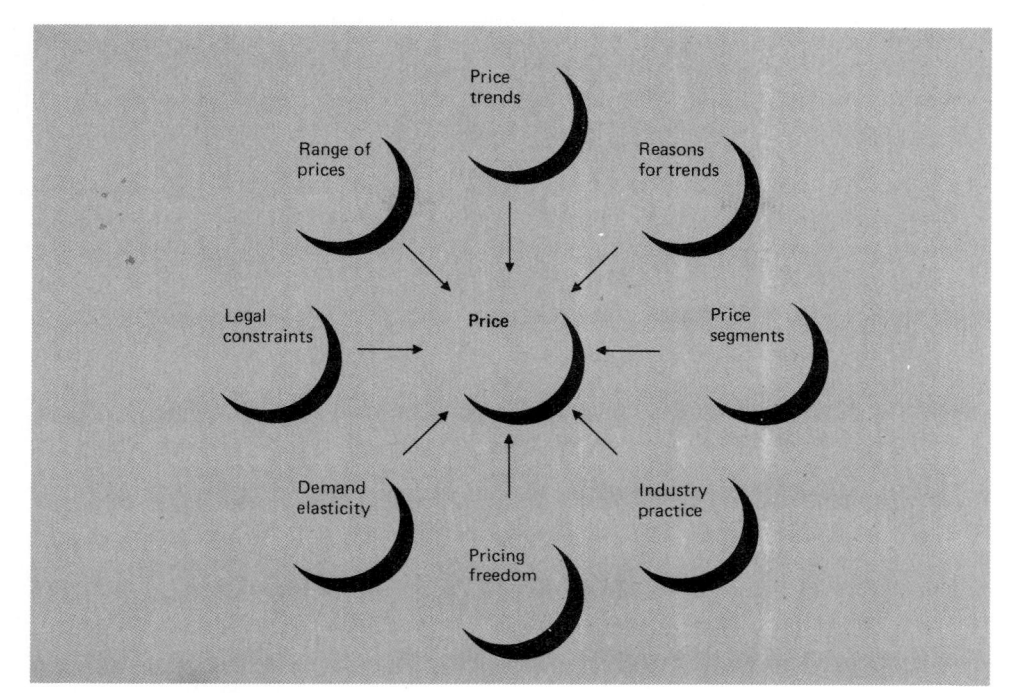

FIGURE 4-5. Information needed to determine product price.

accounted for by a few companies. This information can be developed by market research.

The most difficult pricing information to determine accurately is whether an industry's products are *price elastic* or *inelastic*. Despite the fact that demand sensitivity to price change is accepted economic dogma, it is ironic that few managements are certain about the demand/price relationships of their own industries. Experimentation may have drastic consequences, particularly if a price decrease is not accompanied by an increase in demand. Price elasticity is usually observable in new growth industries as new buyer segments are brought into the market each time industry prices are lowered. However, as an industry approaches saturation of its potential market (i.e., approaches maturity), demand tends to become more inelastic. During periods of inflation, demand tends to be somewhat inelastic for basic (relatively essential) commodities, but more elastic for postponable purchases. Inflationary price rises appear to have little effect on general demand when incomes are rising as fast as prices.

It is important to remember that demand elasticity refers to a total industry and not to the pricing actions of an individual company. Price actions by a single company may result in shifts of market share but are unlikely to affect total industry demand unless the entire industry adjusts to the new price level adopted by the company. A characteristic of oligopoly, of course, is that the industry tends to shift toward the new price levels established by a major company. Pricing actions of leading companies, therefore, are watched closely by all industry members.

Legal constraints on pricing are circumscribed by the antitrust laws. Direct government price controls have been imposed on all industry from time to time, and occasionally on a specific industry. Government imposed requirements for such things as product and industrial safety, pollution abatement, and minimum gasoline mileage for cars, serve to increase production costs and, indirectly, to increase prices.

COMPANY POSITION IN THE MARKET

The last—but by no means the least important—market information needed for planning purposes is an understanding of the company's position in the marketplace. Market position has a significant bearing on the strategies open to a company. It would be unusual to find both strong and weak companies following the same marketing strategies. Principal indicators of a company's position are market share, brand awareness, buyer acceptance, degree of brand loyalty, quality and breadth of distribution, and the attitudes of trade channel members towards the company.

There appears to be an inherent tendency for management to overestimate its company's market strengths and underestimate its market weaknesses. Periodic, objective audits of the company's market position by the company marketing research department or outside consultants in an effective antidote to overconfidence.

Table 4-8 shows a checklist that may be used in auditing a company's market position. Each factor should be looked at in relation to leading competitors since it is relative effectiveness and not perfection that determines position. The company's performance with respect to product, price, distribution, and promotion results in perceptions held by buyers and prospective buyers; perceptions, in turn, affect purchases and company market share. Market share is the single best measure of a company's market position, but it is the result and not the cause of market position.

SUMMARY

We have seen that the study of market segments enables management to decide where it will emphasize its marketing efforts and what marketing mix is appropriate for each market segment served.

TABLE 4-8

Factors Affecting Company Market Position in Relation to Competition

Product	Price	Distribution	Promotion	Market Perceptions
Uniqueness	Segments served (high, medium, low)	Breadth and quality of distribution	Reach and frequency of advertising	Brand awareness
Quality and performance fit with market requirements	Price same, above, or below competition	Product availability at point-of-sale, or when ordered	Effectiveness of advertising	Perceived degree of product differentiation
Breadth of line	Adequacy of trade discounts and allowances	Sales support by channel intermediaries	Effectiveness of sales promotions	Attitudes toward company, brands, products, services
Customer service		Attitudes of channel members towards company	Breadth and depth of sales force coverage	
Effectiveness of packaging				
Market segments served, not served				
Cost efficiency				

Awareness of ever present structural market change ensures that strategic planning considers potential market developments that pose either threats or opportunities over the longer term. Understanding of the industry, competitive, distribution, and price structures are essential to both short- and longer-range planning.

Finally, an objective analysis of the company's position in the market enables marketing management to plan marketing strategies in terms of the company's market strengths and weaknesses in relation to competition.

If a good job has been done of gathering and analyzing this information, management should be aware of market problems to be solved, market constraints to be circumvented, and market opportunities to be exploited. The market environment is by no means the only area to be considered in the development of marketing plans. But it should be apparent by now that it is an essential area and of sufficient depth and scope to require an organized effort to describe and understand it fully.

QUESTIONS

1. Describe market segmentation.
2. What are the tests, or segmentation criteria, that a viable market segment in most cases will meet?
3. What is market structure and what are some of the important elements which determine market structure? How do these elements affect short- and longer range marketing planning?
4. Differentiate between an industry and its market and briefly describe the idea of industry structure.
5. Explain the concept of the industry product life cycle.
6. What are the factors that a marketing manager should consider in analyzing the industry's competitive structure?
7. Describe the channels of distribution for both consumer goods and industrial goods.
8. What are the basic considerations in determining the market pricing structure?
9. Market position has a significant bearing on the strategies open to a company. What are the principal indicators of a company's position?

REFERENCES

1. Wendell R. Smith, "Product Differentiation and Market Segmentation as Alternative Marketing Strategies," *Journal of Marketing*, July 1956, pp. 3-8.
2. *Advertising Age*, Sept. 9, 1982, p. 164.
3. Pierre Martineau, "Social Classes and Spending Behavior," *Journal of Marketing*, vol. 23, no. 2, October 1958, pp. 121-130.
4. Lee Adler, "A New Orientation for Plotting Marketing Strategy," *Business Horizons*, vol. 8, no. 4, Winter 1964.
5. From an advertisement in the Springfield, Mass. *The Morning Union*, Dec. 29, 1977, p. 30.
6. Hugo E. R. Uyterhoeven, Robert W. Ackerman, and John W. Rosenblum, *Strategy and Organization*, Richard D. Irwin, Inc., Homewood, Ill., 1973, p. 31.
7. IBM, *Report to Stockholders*, Annual Meeting, Apr. 25, 1977, p. 13.
8. *Wall Street Journal*, Apr. 5, 1977, p. 6.
9. Kenneth R. Davis, *Marketing Management*, 4th ed., Ronald Press, New York, 1981, p. 408.
10. "J. C. Penney's Fashion Gamble," *Business Week*, Jan. 16, 1978, pp 66-74. By special permission, © 1978 by McGraw-Hill, Inc., New York. All rights reserved.

CHAPTER 5

Buyer Behavior

In the previous two chapters we have learned how to obtain answers to the *where*, *how*, *what*, and *when* questions that should be raised during the marketing planning process. We now turn to buyer behavior to learn *why* people and organizations buy the way they do and *how* they arrive at their purchase decisions. We shift the emphasis from the decision processes of the marketing manager to the decision processes of the buyer. We will discuss the purchase decision-making process and the factors that influence buyer behavior for consumers and for organizations.

THE ROLE OF BUYER BEHAVIOR IN MARKETING

Consumers and organizational buyers are the focal point of companies' marketing efforts. Some critics of marketing complain that marketers attempt to control customers, to make them buy what they really don't need or may not even want. Practicing marketing people, however, do not believe that they could control customers even if they wanted to. They do, nevertheless, follow the efforts of behavioral scientists to *describe*, *understand*, and *predict* buyer behavior. In this way they can better match their activities to meet the wants and needs of their target markets.

Types of Buyers

Buyers can be divided into two broad categories: consumers and organizations. While there are differences between the buying practices of consumers and organizations, these are matters more of degree than of fact. Both types of buyers go through a similar decision process to solve their problems—that is, a process for finding the products or services most appropriate to their needs. Many factors influence the outcome of a specific purchase decision; some are controllable by the marketer and some are not.

Consumers as Buyers. We usually think of the consumer as the buyer of products for personal or family consumption. While the opinions and motivations of the actual buyer may have a significant influence on what is purchased, these factors are tempered by family and other influences. These influences will be discussed later in this chapter.

Whether in organizational or consumer buying situations, people play different roles and participate at different stages in the buying decision process. Some may act as *initiators* or requesters for goods and services. Others may occupy the role of *influencers* and attempt to have the *decider*—the person with the authority and responsibility for making the purchase decision—select the product, brand, or store which they favor. The person who actually makes the purchase is the *buyer*. Those who consume the product are the *users*, and those who judge whether the product's consumption satisfies the needs are the *evaluators*. As a single consumer, you may occupy all of these roles; yet for other purchase situations—such as family, club, or job—you may play only one or some of these roles.

Organizations as Buyers. Organizations represent the other component of buyers and include every type and size or organization, such as factories, schools, government departments, farmers, wholesalers, and retailers. Raw materials, components, supplies, and services are bought by manufacturers. Finished goods are purchased by wholesalers for resale to other organizations and by retailers for resale to consumers. Organizational buying typically is delegated to trained purchasing managers who receive technical support, as needed, from other parts of the organization.

Differences between Consumer and Organizational Buyers. Organizations generally purchase in larger quantities than do consumers; consequently, they exert more influence on vendors. The New York Telephone Company would have greater negotiating strength when buying hundreds of automotive vans, for instance, than would a consumer buying only one. A second difference concerns buying motives. Organizational buying motives tend to be more economic and less emotional than those of consumers. Organizations, therefore, tend to be more objective than consumers in their decisions.

A third difference is that more people usually are involved in the buying decision in an organization. Only a few members would be involved in a family decision, whereas the number of people involved in an organizational purchasing decision will range from one (for a routinely purchased item) to dozens for a major special purchase. Some decisions might involve the using department, research and development, engineering, and the president, in addition to the purchasing department. Because of the need to coordinate the activities of many individuals, a fourth difference is that organizational buying decisions tend to be more structured.

Later we will examine the organizational buying process and buying influences. For now, however, let's look at the consumer buying decision process and the factors that influence consumer behavior.

THE CONSUMER DECISION-MAKING PROCESS

Before discussing a formal model of the consumer buying process we should note that consumer decision patterns vary with the significance of the purchase. This can be illustrated with descriptions of two very different types of purchase decisions—low involvement and high involvement.

Low-Involvement Purchases

Low-involvement purchasing decisions are relatively unimportant to the buyer because they involve (1) low financial risk (paperback book), (2) low social risk (jar of peanuts), (3) low physical risk (going to the movies), or (4) low personal interest (notebook paper). Such purchases tend to be routine and involve little or no formal evaluations of alternatives.

Many of the products or services we buy are habitual purchases. We find an acceptable brand and stick with it. We don't, for example, have to evaluate all restaurants before choosing where to go to lunch; we may just go to McDonald's. Since habitual responses occur as the need to purchase arises, marketers of competitive brands have limited opportunity to influence the outcome. (We do note later, however, the role of repetitive advertising in conditioning consumers to consider advertised brands.)

High-Involvement Purchases

High-involvement purchases are those that are important to the consumer because they entail (1) high financial risk (car or boat), (2) high social risk (home furnishings, wedding dress), (3) high physical risk (mountain climbing equipment), or (4) simply high personal interest (stamp collecting, stereo equipment). Buyers making these types of purchases tend to follow a more structured decision process. This process takes place over time and marketers have more opportunities to influence the outcome. A seemingly impulsive act (the purchase of a new coat or a personal computer for Christmas) may actually be the last act of an extended decision process that began much earlier.

We will now describe the classic steps in the consumer decision-making process, which are more applicable to high- than to low-involvement purchases. Actually purchases fall on a continuum ranging from high to low in importance; the amount of time and thought given to each purchase decision varies accordingly.

Steps in the Decision-Making Process

The consumer decision process can be seen in the five stages portrayed in Figure 5-1.

Problem recognition. This first stage occurs when we realize that we need or want to purchase some product. Any number of things can contribute to an awareness of a problem such as change of income, job, lifestyle, peer pressure, or simply an advertisement.

Information search. There are both internal and external sources of information available to the consumer. The internal source includes memory and previous

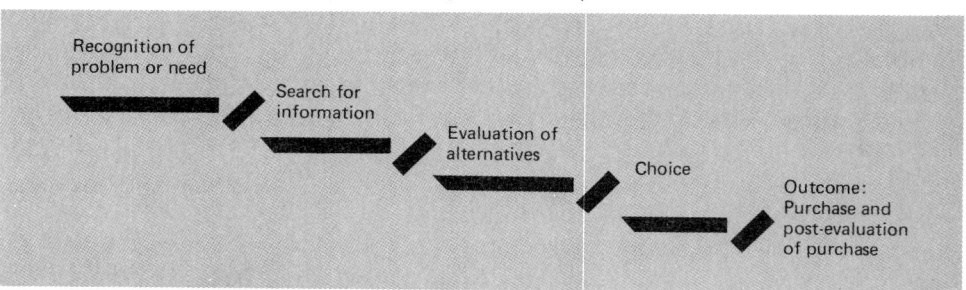

FIGURE 5-1. Basic consumer decision process for high-involvement purchases.

experience. The external source includes environmental influences and marketer initiated influences which we will examine later. The information search may be relatively simple, for example, when buying a new jacket, or complicated, for example, when researching a piece of antique furniture.

Evaluation of alternatives. When evaluating product or brand alternatives, consumers employ criteria such as price, tangible and intangible product attributes and benefits, and place of purchase. Generally, they limit their product evaluations to a narrow subset of brands (the evoked set).

Choice. Choice is made after the alternatives have been evaluated. The product or brand selected may be a clear-cut choice or it may represent a compromise—the one that most nearly meets the consumer's criteria.

Outcome. The outcome includes the decision to purchase, the actual purchase, and postpurchase evaluation. The postpurchase evaluation is stored in the memory to be recalled during the information search stage of a future purchase. The degree of satisfaction or nonsatisfaction will influence whether the same brand is repurchased. Also the buyer's evaluation may be shared with others, thereby influencing the purchase decisions of other consumers.

Consumers do not always go through the above stages in a clearly delineated or sequential manner, nor are they necessarily conscious that they are employing a decision process. And their willingness to search and evaluate will vary with the product. Nevertheless, the decision model helps us understand the typical *hierarchy of effects** leading from problem recognition to the purchase of a high involvement product.

FACTORS INFLUENCING CONSUMER PURCHASE BEHAVIOR

While we can diagram the steps of the buyer decision process with some confidence, we know much less about people's thought processes and why they act as they do. Human beings are complicated organisms influenced by many internal and external stimuli. We have ideas about how these affect people's decisions, but rarely do we have conclusive proof, despite the growing accumulation of research in the behavioral sciences.

In this section we present an overview of the principal factors that are thought to influence purchase behavior. The information is drawn largely from the social sciences. The discussions are necessarily brief and incomplete but should be sufficient to help you understand why marketers need to keep abreast of the findings of behavioral research. We discuss the factors affecting consumer behavior under the headings of internal, environmental, and marketer-initiated influences. The topics and their interrelationships are shown in Figure 5-2.

Internal Influences

As the term implies, *internal influences* are those factors which are internalized to the consumer and, though not directly observable, affect the consumer's selection of products. Since the consumer is an integrated whole entity, these factors must be

---

*"Hierarchy of effects" is a term referring to a model that involves sequential steps leading to a decision. Its forerunner was the Lavidge and Steiner *stair-step* model which described the steps involved in moving a potential buyer from the awareness stage to the purchase stage.[1]

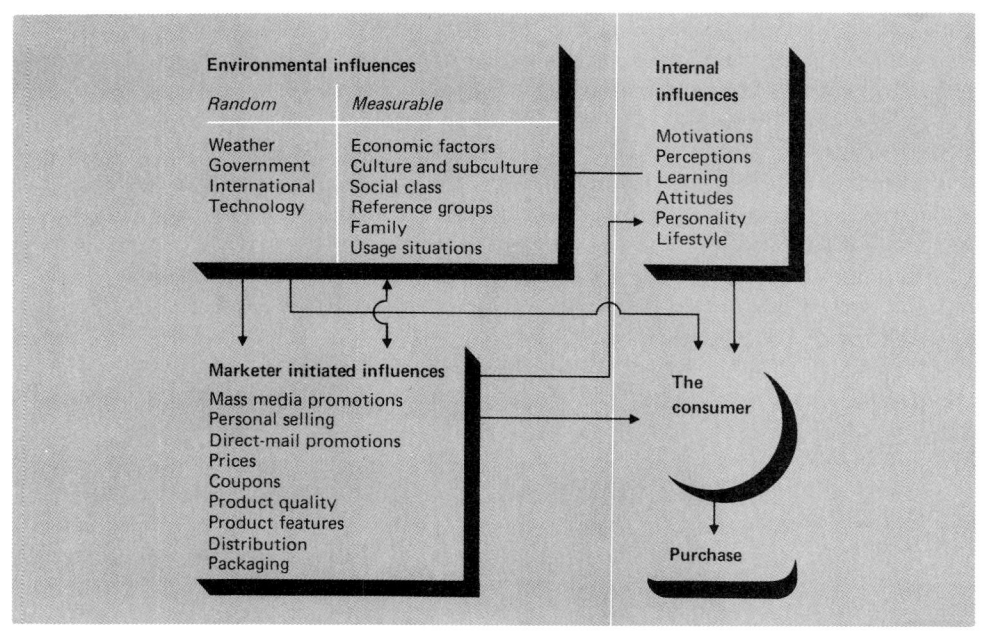

FIGURE 5-2. Influences on consumer purchase behavior.

Environmental influences		Internal influences
Random	*Measurable*	
Weather	Economic factors	Motivations
Government	Culture and subculture	Perceptions
International	Social class	Learning
Technology	Reference groups	Attitudes
	Family	Personality
	Usage situations	Lifestyle

Marketer initiated influences

Mass media promotions
Personal selling
Direct-mail promotions
Prices
Coupons
Product quality
Product features
Distribution
Packaging

The consumer → Purchase

related to one another. For example, if we consider just four of them—motivation, perceptions, learning, and attitudes—we can assume that a general sequence does exist. While none of the four is the only factor influencing any of the others, the following process seems logical. To some extent our level of motivation and our specific motives have an effect on those stimuli we perceive in our environment and on how we perceive them. Information gathered through these perceptions enables us to learn about our environment and the specific products and brands in our environment. Learning in turn is essential for the development of attitudes, which usually precede our behavior and which give it direction. In brief, the sequence is: *motives, perceptions, learning, attitudes, behavior,* although, as we will see later, behavior precedes attitudes in some low-involvement buying situations.

Motives. The intial stage of the consumer decision process is the recognition of a need or problem. Motivation helps us determine our need and involves (1) an energizing force or tension system which gives impetus to behavior and (2) a directional component that gives general direction to a variety of responses serving the same general function for the organism.[2]

A widely held theory of motivation, developed by Abraham Maslow, identifies the five levels of need shown in **Marketing Note 5-1.** According to Maslow, needs are arranged in a hierarchy—from physiological to self-actualization needs. Unless a certain level of need has been satisfied, higher levels of need will not serve to motivate the individual; likewise, once a level of need has been satisfied, it no longer serves as a motivator. The amount of unsatisfied need influences the effort that the individual will expend in seeking need gratification. The object of the individual's behavior is determined also by its ability to satisfy the particular motivating need.

Because many American consumers already have satisfied their *basic* needs, companies often focus their product appeals on *growth* needs. Combination appeals have the potential for satisfying several types of needs. Different consumers may be operating at different need levels; once minimum degrees of need fulfillment have been met, a consumer may pursue parallel need fulfillment. For example, an ad for Betty Crocker cake mix may point out that you could win a prize for the cake (an *esteem* need), that such a cake shows that you care for your family (a *love* need), and that the mix is foolproof (a *safety* need). The actual consumption of the baked cake will provide some caloric intake necessary for *physiological* maintenance.

Perceptions. As consumers we are faced with an increasingly complex environment, which bombards us with thousands of stimuli each day. We cannot possibly cope with all of them. Perception is the process by which these sensory stimuli are selected, organized, and given meaning. Figure 5-3 shows a model of consumer perceptions.

The *psychological set* is made up of the consumer's current levels of needs, information and beliefs about products and brands, likes and dislikes, and intentions. As consumers, we selectively *expose ourselves to media and stimuli* which enhance our ability to get useful information. The *perception* process is comprised of three stages: (1) selective attention, (2) selective comprehension, and (3) selective retention. Selective attention means we tend to favor those stimuli which are consistent with our psychological set and avoid those which are contradictory. Selective comprehension gives meanings to stimuli so that they are consistent with our attitudes and beliefs. Selective retention is remembering those things which are relevant and consistent to our psychological set. However, *new information* may *alter our psychological set* as we experience changes in our beliefs, brand evaluations, and buying behavior.

Maslow's Hierarchy of Needs

The Basic Needs. These are needs necessary to the survival of the organism and the species.

1. Physiological needs: nutritional necessities, sex, sleep, maternal behavior, sensory pleasure, activity and exercise
2. Safety needs: security, stability, dependency, protection, freedom from fear, freedom from anxiety and chaos, need for structure, order, law and limits, strength in the protector

The Growth Needs. These needs are necessary for the advancement of the organism and the species.

3. Belongingness and love needs: to give and receive love and affection, to develop close relationships with others, to experience contact with others, intimacy, to identify with others
4. Esteem needs
    Self-esteem: desire for strength, achievement, adequacy, mastery and competence, confidence, to be useful
    Other-esteem: reputation or prestige, status, fame and glory, dominance, attention, recognition, importance, dignity, appreciation
5. Self-actualization needs: self-fulfillment, to become all one is capable of being, to do what the *individual* is fitted for, to know for the sake of knowing

   Source: Based on Abraham H. Maslow, "A Theory of Human Motivation," *Motivation and Personality,* 2d ed., Harper & Row, New York, 1970. By permission of the publishers.

MARKETING NOTE 5-1

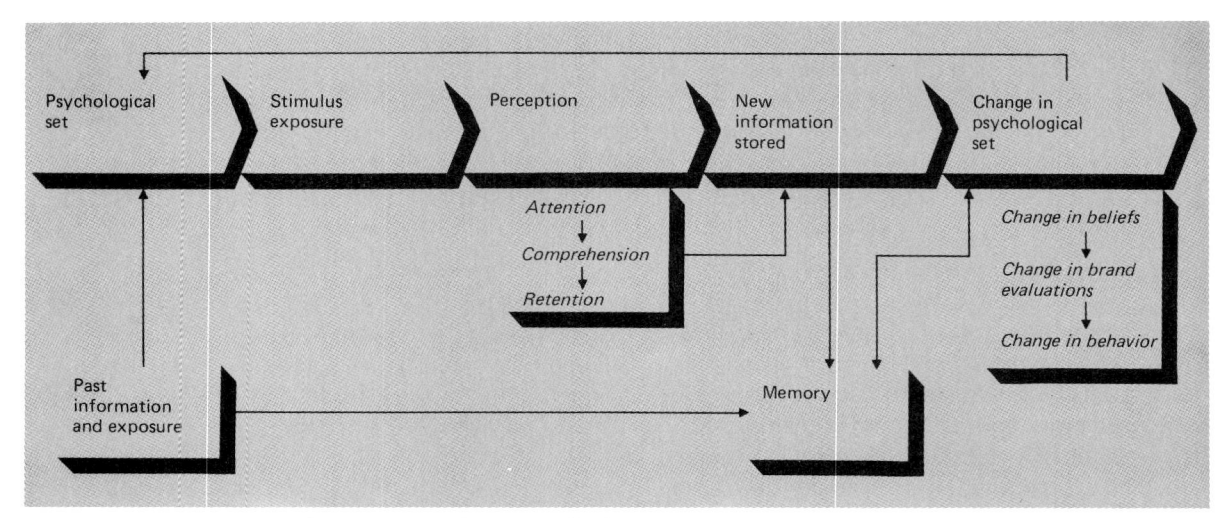

FIGURE 5-3. A high-involvement model of consumer perceptions. *Source:* Henry Assael, *Consumer Behavior and Marketing Action*, Kent Publishing, Boston, 1981, p. 103. Reprinted with permission.

Marketers are concerned with the way we as consumers perceive their product offerings. Our perception of "quality" may be based on known standards of performance (e.g., amount of "distortion" or "flutter" for a stereo set). When there are no objective standards, our perception of quality may be based on subjective factors such as *brand name* (Michelin may suggest to us the best steel-belted radial tires), the *store* in which the product is stocked (Saks Fifth Avenue carries quality merchandise), an *advertising slogan* (quality is suggested by the slogan of Harvey's Bristol Cream Sherry, "when you care enough to serve the very best"), or, for many products, *price* (the $459 stereo *must* be better than one that sells for only $299). As long as purchases based on such surrogate criteria provide satisfaction, consumers will continue to use them in their decision processes.

Learning. Learning may be defined as *a change in the response tendency of an individual because of the effect of experience with the environment*. In other words consumers learn to respond in a particular way (e.g., purchase a particular brand) by studying the consequences of their purchase behavior (e.g., satisfaction with the brand). The more favorable the outcome of the behavior, the more likely the behavior will be repeated. The most significant outcome of a consumer's use of a product is satisfaction with the product. Because of the different ways in which consumers evaluate a product's use, different amounts of satisfaction (called *reinforcement* in learning theory parlance) will be derived. Even a good product may be evaluated poorly if too much was expected of it in the first place.

Three theories derived from psychology help us understand consumer learning. *Classical conditioning* and *instrumental conditioning* represent the behaviorist tradition in psychology, which emphasizes that learning occurs through conditioned responses and rewards. The *cognitive learning* school emphasizes that learning occurs through cognitive or mental processes.

Classical conditioning theory. The principles of classical conditioning hold that learning is a result of an organism learning to associate a conditioned or secondary stimulus with a primary stimulus. In the well-known case of Pavlov's experiments, dogs were taught to associate the sound of a bell (the secondary stimulus) with the presentation of food (the primary stimulus). The dogs had learned to respond to the primary stimulus by salivating—an unconditioned response. Through repeated associations of the bell with the presentation of food, Pavlov was able to condition the dogs to salivate in the presence of the bell only—a conditioned response.

Several studies suggest that classical conditioning may have application to the marketing of low involvement products. In one experiment, for example, it was found that background music (the unconditioned stimulus) can influence the selection of a convenience good (the conditioned stimulus).[3] University students, whose musical likes and dislikes had been predetermined, were broken into two groups. The first group was shown a neutral colored ball point pen while listening to liked music and the same pen of a different neutral color while listening to disliked music. The second group was exposed to similar situations with the pen colors reversed. Later all students were offered a pen and permitted to choose the color they wanted. Seventy-nine percent took the color of pen they had seen when listening to liked music. When questioned later only 3 percent were aware that the music had influenced their choice. These findings suggest that unconditioned stimuli (e.g., music and visuals in advertisements) which generate positive emotions can create positive feelings about a low involvement product and can lead to purchase.

While classical conditioning has less application in high involvement purchases, marketers do view repetitive advertising as an important tool for establishing associations between product symbols (packaging and logos) and brand names, thereby creating familiarity with the product among consumers.[4] These familiar brands are much more likely to be considered by consumers than brands they have not heard of before.

Instrumental conditioning theory. In instrumental conditioning, individuals learn the association between stimulus and response. But unlike classical conditioning, they do not respond to a conditioned stimulus through its linkage to a primary stimulus. Rather, individuals emit behavior for which *they receive rewards or punishments*. If they receive rewards, the probability that they will emit the same behavior again is increased. The probability decreases with punishments. No external agent is presumed to be presenting the stimuli. Rather individuals determine whether their behavior is rewarding or not.

Instrumental conditioning is a better model for explaining some buyer behavior than classical conditioning. It suggests that consumers make decisions on the basis of their positive experiences with products. Satisfaction with a product reinforces the purchase decision and increases the probability that the purchase will be repeated. According to this view, consumer product satisfaction ought to be a major goal of marketing strategy.

Cognitive learning theory. The cognitive learning school differs from the behaviorist tradition in that it assumes that behavior is not the result of a passive response of the individual to stimuli. Rather, cognitive psychologists emphasize the mental or cognitive processes through which individuals solve problems and reach goals. Humans are viewed as active information processors who employ reasoning, form concepts, and acquire knowledge about their environment. Behavior is seen as the outcome of mental processes through which individuals attempt to realize goals.

Marketers should be concerned with how individuals acquire, store, process, and retrieve information about products and brands. Such information may come from the immediate external environment (the price marked on a product), or it may come from memory (a conversation about a particular brand, an advertisement, or a previous product experience).

The behaviorist conditioning theories and cognitive learning theory apply to different types of consumer purchases. The behaviorist tradition with its emphasis on repetition and reinforcement seems to apply more to low-involvement consumer purchases whereas cognitive learning theory applies more to high-involvement purchases in which the consumer undergoes an extensive decision process.

Brand loyalty. Marketers are interested in specific applications of learning theory to questions such as: How does a person learn about a brand? How does brand loyalty develop? What relevant rewards can the marketer employ to enhance learning? What types of learning are susceptible to marketing forces?

Consumers need not know about all brands available before they make a decision. In fact for most consumers the evoked set of brands (the list of brands immediately considered) represents only a few of the brands available, but it is sufficient to offer the buyer a choice and to offer an alternative brand should the first choice be unavailable.

Brand loyalty may be defined as the *greater likelihood that a consumer will purchase a given brand repeatedly*. With brand loyalty the consumer can use the more efficient decision process of automatic response behavior. The consumer even may be aware that other brands might offer greater satisfaction, yet not want—or not be able—to seek out information on those brands. The brand currently being purchased may provide enough satisfaction, and not exploring new brands reduces the consumer's risk of unknown consequences.

Brand loyalty, however, implies more than the repetitive purchasing of a brand over time. Other factors that affect it include psychological commitment, the availability of alternative brands, evaluation of the alternatives, and the purchase decision process. A brand loyal purchase, therefore, can be a high-involvement purchase in contrast to a low-involvement, repetitive purchase based largely on habit, inertia, or lack of alternatives. Although research on brand loyalty is somewhat inconclusive, there are several established propositions:

1. Consumers cannot be characterized wholly as brand loyal or not brand loyal. Rather, a consumer will show brand loyalty in certain product categories but not in others. Products with symbolic social meaning, such as Izod shirts and Harvey's Bristol Cream sherry, are likely to command more brand loyalty than common household products such as paper towels.
2. Consumers who make brand-loyal purchases are more likely to express post-purchase satisfaction.
3. Store-loyal consumers are more likely to make brand-loyal purchases.
4. Certain market structure characteristics influence the degree of brand loyalty. There is less loyalty for brands with many available alternatives, where prices change often, or where the number of purchases and expenditures per buyer are high. There is more loyalty for widely distributed brands and for products where market share is concentrated in the leading brand.

Brand-loyal consumers have been declining. The percentage of adults who agree with the statement "I try to stick to well-known brand names" decreased from 74 percent of women and 80 percent of men in 1975 to 58 percent of women and 65 percent of men in 1981.[5] The erosion of brand loyalty along with the growth of generic (nonbrand) products (estimated at 4 percent of supermarket unit sales)[6] creates challenges for firms that have invested in building brand names.

Attitudes. Attitudes are *learned tendencies to respond consistently toward an object in a positive or negative way*. It is useful for marketers to understand how attitudes toward brands are formed, maintained, and changed since they are important determinants of consumer behavior. Consumers favor products and brands for which they have positive attitudes and avoid those for which they have negative attitudes. The topography of consumer attitudes can be used in developing market segments and in devising and evaluating marketing strategies.

Consumer attitudes toward brands are shaped by a variety of social and personal factors. Attitudes can be learned through instrumental conditioning, for example, when a consumer has a positive or rewarding experience with a particular brand. Attitudes can also be developed through cognitive learning. Consumers who believe that caffeine is harmful may have negative attitudes towards brands of soda which contain it. Attitudes toward products and brands are also shaped by family and peer groups.

As Figure 5-4 shows, there are three components of attitudes—beliefs, evaluations, and a tendency to act. *Beliefs* represent the cognitive components of attitudes. Consumers hold beliefs about the attributes of a particular brand or about the benefits which it provides. For example, a woman believes that Prell shampoo has a pleasant smell, creates lots of lather, rinses out easily (attributes), and makes her hair shiny, aromatic, and attractive (benefits).

Evaluations represent the affective component of attitudes. Consumers make an overall evaluation of a brand on the basis of their beliefs about its attributes or benefits. In the example above the woman would probably have a favorable evaluation of Prell shampoo. Beliefs about brands tend to be multidimensional—that is, the consumer will hold beliefs about a brand along a number of dimensions (attributes and benefits). In contrast, evaluations tend to be unidimensional—that is, the evaluation is along the single dimension of positive to negative, or favorable to unfavorable.

The *tendency to act* is represented by the predisposition to purchase or not purchase. Where consumers have favorable evaluations of brands they tend to

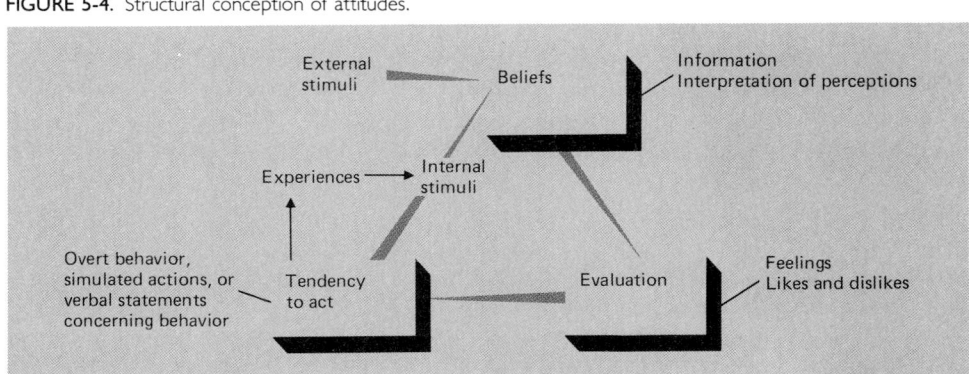

FIGURE 5-4. Structural conception of attitudes.

purchase; where they have unfavorable evaluations they tend not to purchase. Presumably the woman would have a tendency to purchase Prell particularly if her evaluation of the brand is more favorable than for any other.

How does a marketer use attitude theory to better understand the consumer? Again we need to make a distinction between high-involvement and low-involvement purchase decisions.

High-involvement purchases. In high-involvement situations, attitudes are an important determinant of consumer purchase behavior. Buyers tend to seek information which will reduce their risk of making a wrong decision or satisfy their interest in the product. This information is organized and stored in the belief component of the consumer's attitude. Consumers evaluate the product or brand based on these beliefs to form a liking or disliking toward it. And finally they form a tendency to act on the basis of their evaluations. This sequential process is another example of the hierarchy of effects.

The hierarchy of effects suggests that the easiest way to influence attitudes is by influencing the belief component since beliefs are logically prior to the other components. Thus, in introducing a new product, we can attempt to create positive consumer attitudes about it by communicating those product attributes or benefits which are important to consumers in the target market. Topol toothpaste is advertised as the smokers' toothpaste which removes tobacco stains. If smokers value this benefit and believe the claim, they will evaluate the brand favorably and be motivated to try it.

We can also attempt to change beliefs about a product by altering an existing belief. This is often called *repositioning*. Seven-Up's strategy in advertising that its soda contained no caffeine, while pointing out that major competitors Coke and Pepsi did, was an attempt to change beliefs. Though the product itself was not altered, the strategy encouraged consumers to evaluate soft drinks along a new dimension and think more positively of Seven-Up.

We may also attempt to alter attitudes toward a brand's total image rather than towards its specific components. A classic example involved altering the attitudes towards Marlboro cigarettes from a feminine to a masculine image by switching to advertising that associated Marlboro with rugged cowboys.

Low-involvement purchases. The role of attitudes in low-involvement situations is somewhat different. Research indicates that for many low-involvement situations the purchase may not be preceded by a conscious decision process.[7] These situations hold limited opportunity for marketers to influence the decision since they have little personal relevance to the consumer.[8]

Under these conditions the consumer looks at only one or a few product attributes. The marketer's task is to properly identify these relevant product attributes and their benefits (e.g., Charmin toilet paper's emphasis on the softness attribute and Sanka coffee's caffeine-free benefit of less tension), communicate them to the consumer, and provide an opportunity for their easy in-store evaluation. And satisfaction with product use can provide an internal stimulus to help build a positive attitude for subsequent purchases. In these cases attitude development may actually follow rather than precede the purchase.[9]

Personality. Personality is a fundamental aspect of human behavior which probably influences purchase behavior. When we talk about personality, we refer to the way a person acts which makes that person different from others. Some people behave in an aggressive fashion; others are shy. Some are independent; others are dependent. These response tendencies are thought to influence both *what* people buy and *how* they buy it.

In practice, however, marketing researchers have had difficulty in trying to use personality to explain specific consumer purchases. Several studies indicate that marketing strategists may find little benefit in the use of personality traits as predictors of consumer behavior.[10] This is due to the complex nature of personality factors and the discrepancies that occur in trying to measure it. As an alternative, marketers have turned to lifestyle research.

Lifestyles. Rather than being an invisible internal construct guiding behavior, as is the case with personality, *lifestyle* represents a broad composite of what a person does, the way the person lives, what products and services are bought, and how they are used. In short, *lifestyle is what the individual does with available resources (financial, social, and time).* Lifestyle researchers have developed measures of a person's attitudes, interests, and opinions (AIO),[11] called psychographic profiles, which can be used to segment consumers into homogeneous markets based on what they are likely to buy.[12] Perhaps the most significant use of AIO measurements is in the selection of media and promotional strategies.[13] The rapid increase in special interest magazines makes it possible to match lifestyle segments with different advertising mediums.

Psychographic research helps the marketer supplement traditional demographic segmentation with more personalized profiles of product users and nonusers. Table 5-1 provides a demographic breakdown of heavy users of shotgun ammunition, defined as those who spend $11 a year or more. It turns out, for example, that heavy users are younger, lower in income, and more likely to be blue-collar workers and to live in rural areas than nonusers. Such information is useful when estimating the size and composition of the market and when making future market projections.

On the other hand, Table 5-2 provides us with a psychographic profile of heavy users. For example, they love the outdoors, including activities such as hunting, fishing, camping, and outdoor work. They like to eat and play poker. These attitudes and interests, plus indications that users have greater attraction to violence and adventure than nonusers, can help in determining the types of media and programs that heavy users would be most likely to see. Better still, of course, would be to study the media habits of heavy users and nonusers for guidance on advertising strategy.

Measurable Environmental Influences

Many of the internal factors that influence consumers' decision processes are derived from the environment in which they live. Some of these external influences are measurable by objective criteria and some by subjective criteria. Others, which we will discuss later, represent random events which are not always readily measurable or predictable.

Economic Factors. It is quite obvious that consumers cannot spend more money than they have or use more credit than is available to them. Microeconomic theory uses *available income* as the consumer's budget line, subject to which, the consumer attempts to obtain as much satisfaction toward fulfilling needs as possible.[14] The consumer's available income becomes an important influencer of behavior because it can limit total expenditures, eliminate alternatives from the

TABLE 5-1
Demographic Profile of the Heavy User of Shotgun Ammunition

	Heavy Users, %*	Nonusers, %
Age:		
Under 25	9	5
25–34	33	15
35–44	27	22
45–54	18	22
55+	13	36
Occupation:		
Professional	6	15
Managerial	23	23
Clerical-sales	9	17
Craftsman	50	35
Income:		
Under $6,000	26	19
$6,000–$10,000	39	36
$10,000–$15,000	24	27
$15,000+	11	18
Population density:		
Rural	34	12
2,500–50,000	11	11
50,000–500,000	16	15
500,000–2 million	21	27
2 million+	13	19
Geographic division:		
New England–mid-Atlantic	21	33
Central (N, W)	22	30
South Atlantic	23	12
E. south central	10	3
W. south central	10	5
Mountain	6	3
Pacific	9	15

*Persons who spent $11 or more per year on shotgun ammunition; the percentages for the two groups are based on sampling population sizes of 141 for users and 395 for nonusers.

Source: William D. Wells, "Psychographics: A Critical Review," *Journal of Marketing Research*, vol. 12, May 1975, p. 197.

consumer's evoked set, change expectations of product attainments, and even influence the amount of time devoted to gathering information on the alternatives.

Another economic factor influencing consumer behavior is the overall cost of living. If the cost of living (measured by the consumer price index) rises at a rate less than the rate of personal income, consumers either will have a *real* increase in income and will spend their money for more goods and services or will increase their savings. However, if income increases do not keep pace with rises in the cost of living, *real* income declines and consumers find that their paychecks, though larger, do not buy the same amount of goods and services as before. To compensate for this decline in *real* income, they may (among other things) seek less expensive items (e.g., nonbranded, generic products) or retail outlets with fewer services but lower markups.

TABLE 5-2
Psychographic Profile of the Heavy User of Shotgun Ammunition

Base	% Responding Favorably	
	Heavy Users*	Nonusers
I like hunting	88	7
I like fishing	68	26
I like to go camping	57	21
I love the out-of-doors	90	65
A cabin by a quiet lake is a great place to spend the summer	49	34
I like to work outdoors	67	40
I am good at fixing mechanical things	47	27
I often do a lot of repair work on my own car	36	12
I like war stories	50	32
I would do better than average in a fist fight	38	16
I would like to be a professional football player	28	18
I would like to be a policeman	22	8
There is too much violence on television	35	45
There should be a gun in every home	56	10
I like danger	19	8
I would like to own my own airplane	35	13
I like to play poker	50	26
I smoke too much	39	24
I love to eat	49	34
I spend money on myself that I should spend on the family	44	26
If given a chance, most men would cheat on their wives	33	14
I read the newspaper every day	51	72

*Persons who spent $11 or more per year on shotgun ammunition; the percentages for the two groups are based on sampling population sizes of 141 for users and 395 for nonusers.

Source: William D. Wells, "Psychographics: A Critical Review," *Journal of Marketing Research,* vol. 12, May 1975, p. 198.

Cultural Factors. Culture is the broadest of the external social influences on consumer behavior. All other influences—even those internal to the consumer—seldom violate cultural norms. *Culture* is the general pattern of behavior which characterizes a society. This takes place through the widespread acceptance of cultural *values*—beliefs that some general state of existence is personally and socially worth striving for.[15] These values are passed on from generation to generation; that is, values are learned through the process of consumer socialization in which younger members of society, for example, develop attitudes toward products, brands, and the purchasing process. Consumer socialization has both a social and a cognitive component.

Social learning occurs as the result of social influences on consumer behavior. Some learning occurs directly, for example, when a child is taught what to buy or how to shop for bargains. Other social learning results when a child imitates the consumption patterns of family members and peers.

The *cognitive* component of consumer socialization refers to cognitive development, or mental maturation, which occurs in stages. With cognitive development children refine their sensorimotor skills, learn language and conceptual skills, and learn to reason and employ logic around increasingly abstract problems. One outcome of cognitive maturation is that children become increasingly sophisticated about commercial messages and product information.

Cultural values change as society changes. Economic dislocations may alter our attitudes toward savings; technological forces may change our values concerning the work environment; political abuses can affect our attitudes toward authority figures. One observer has noted the following long-term trends in American cultural values.[16]

From	To
Other-centeredness	Self-fulfillment
Postponed gratification	Immediate gratification
Hard work	The easy life
Formal relationships	Informal, open relationships
Religious orientation	Secular orientation

Another notes that Americans place high value on progress, personal achievement, materialism, activity, informality, individualism, and youthfulness.[17] The 1960s saw the rise of a counterculture with a different set of values regarding family patterns, sexual mores, ways and means of earning a livelihood, esthetic forms, and personal identities that were divorced from power policies, the bourgeois home, and the consumer society.[18] By the 1980s some of these countercultural developments had affected the cultural norms.

Foreign cultures. Marketing abroad requires particular attention to cultural variations from country to country. Many companies, when they begin to market abroad, make serious (and sometimes fatal) errors because they are unaware of the often subtle differences in local cultural values. **Marketing Note 5–2** cites examples of the ways in which Brazilians have reacted negatively to products that were successful in the United States.

Skilled international companies usually are able to avoid cultural blunders through cultural research, by using anthropologists as consultants, and/or by employing native managers who are familiar with the mores of their own countries.

Subcultures. Many subcultures exist within the United States. A person raised on San Francisco's Nob Hill can feel out of place in Chinatown. Orthodox Jews, Mormons, and other religion-based subcultures have rules which include what their members can and cannot consume. Enclaves of people of foreign extraction continue to observe native customs for generations after their forebears arrived in the United States. Examples can be seen in the bayous of Louisiana and in the Pennsylvania Dutch section of the country. When subcultures contain enough people, they can be considered as market segments justifying separate marketing strategies.

> **MARKETING NOTE 5-2**
>
> ### What to Look Out for Selling to Brazilians
>
> Rueful advertising and marketing execs in Brazil warn of potential pitfalls in selling to Brazilians. For example:
>
> - Imaginative Brazilians do not always use products in the same way as Americans. "Marketers assume they can segment markets and position products, but Brazilian housewives find multiple uses for things," says Ian Gardner, a former Reckitt & Colman product manager. "If you try to sell a product specifically for cleaning floor surfaces, Brazilians will use it for disinfecting the toilet bowl, cleaning the cat and washing the kids' hair."
>
>   Recently, sales of a certain brand of floor wax dropped mysteriously, says an American adman.
>
>   The perplexed manufacturer soon discovered many Brazilians had been using the floor wax as lighter fluid to ignite their Sunday barbecues.
>
>   When the company added more water to the solvent base, the floor wax became less flammable and Brazilians stopped buying it.
>
> - Products must be tailored to local tastes and customs. In Rio de Janeiro, consumers are used to butter that is usually slightly rancid from the tropical heat.
>
>   Unilever and Anderson-Clayton learned that to sell margarine successfully in Rio, it should taste slightly rancid.
>
>   Advertising as well as the product itself should be directed at the way Brazilians do things. Like washing dishes. Brazilians squirt liquid detergent on a sponge rather than filling the kitchen sink with soapy water and submerging plates and silverware.
>
>   A recent commercial for a successful liquid dishwashing detergent featured a row of nuns, plates in hand, correctly doing the dishes by passing a soapy sponge down the line.
>
> - Why should Portuguese speakers try to pronounce Kentucky Fried Chicken? "Some names are ridiculous, like [Pepsi's] Mountain Dew and [R.J. Reynolds'] Chesterfield," says Mr. Gardner. "Brazilians can't pronounce them."
>
>   Since its introduction in southern Brazil at the end of 1981, Mountain Dew has been working on the pronunciation problem with a pneumonic device. Ads read: *"Peca* [ask for] Mao-Tem-Du," a close approximation of Mountain Dew in a Brazilian accent.
>
>   "If you have to spend lots of money just to teach people to pronounce your product's name, there are much better ways to spend money," Mr. Gardner said.
>
>   Few Brazilians seem to be asking for Mountain Dew. A Pepsi marketing exec said the soft drink started very strong but sales have flattened. "But Brazilians can pronounce the name," he said. "They just need a little help."
>
>   Brazilians may have a similar problem when local beverage manufacturer Antarctica launches the national fruit flavored soft drink—called Guarana and prounounced "Gaw-ra-nuh"—in the U.S. later this year.
>
> *Source*: Laurel Wenz, *Advertising Age*, July 5, 1982, p. m–25. Copyright ©1982 by Crain Communications, Inc. Reprinted with permission.

The black and Hispanic populations are the largest ethnic subcultures in the United States. Not only their size, but also their purchasing patterns can affect marketers' strategies. Studies by Selling Areas-Marketing, Inc. (SAMI), for example, show that blacks (26 million) and Hispanics (15 million) make up about one-fifth of the population. They spend about 25.5 percent of their income on foodstore products—a significantly higher percentage than the rest of the population. The combined spending power of these two groups has grown from $20 billion in 1960 to $145 billion in 1980.[19]

Hispanics represent the fastest growing subculture in the United States. Their attitudes toward brands are often distinct. Marketers such as McDonald's, Procter & Gamble, and Coca-Cola advertise in the Spanish language directly to the Hispanic market via Spanish cable television, radio, magazines, and newspapers with copy specifically prepared to appeal to the target population.

TABLE 5-3
The Influence of Social Class on Buying Behavior

Behavioral characteristics	Purchase behavior	% of U.S. Population
UPPER UPPER CLASS: Socially prominent, with inherited wealth		
Elite club membership Children attend private schools and top colleges Social position in society is secure Can deviate from social norms more than other classes—owing to security of social position	Spend money as if it were unimportant—but not ostentatiously Conservative clothing Elegance in social parties Possessions reflect British aristocracy—English Tudor homes, large lawns, servants	0.5
LOWER UPPER CLASS: People who have "earned" their social position rather than inherited it*		
Socially mobile College educated, but not from top school Active people Highly seeking social esteem and prestigious social interactions Children showered with possessions	"Conspicuous consumption" is the rule Products symbolize their success and wealth: —swimming pools —yachts —furs —large homes —designer-name clothing	2.5
UPPER MIDDLE CLASS		
Motivation centered on career Moderately successful professionals: —owners of medium-sized companies —young junior executives on the rise Highly educated class, but usually from state college as opposed to prestige university "Gracious living" is lifestyle pattern followed Demanding of children Cultivate broad range of interests, from civic to cultural	Purchases reflect quality Want to be seen as fashionable, having a nice home in a nice neighborhood Purchases are conspicuous but not showy Automobile, home, and clothing are symbols of success	12.0
LOWER MIDDLE CLASS: The "typical" American		
Law-abiding Hard-working Church-going Occupations focus on nonmanagerial office workers and blue-collar jobs Continually striving to do a good job Respectability is the key motivation Conformity rather than innovativeness is the rule	Home is central possession —well-painted —respectable area Do-it-yourselfers Buy rather standard home furnishings Rely on magazines and retail literature for home furnishings information Work hard at their shopping; quite price-sensitive	30.0

TABLE 5-3 *(Continued)*

Behavioral characteristics	Purchase behavior	% of U.S. Population
UPPER LOWER CLASS: The "working class"		
Routine day-to-day existence Jobs center on manual skills Reluctant to change Children are highly prized Little social contact outside the home Vacations center on visiting relatives Have little expectations of social movement	Live in declining areas of city, in small houses Purchase behavior is impulsive with new products and brand-loyal with repeat purchases Like national brands	35.0
LOWER LOWER CLASS: Unskilled workers and unemployed		
Characterized as apathetic, fatalistic, and bent on "getting one's kicks" while one can Poorly educated	Impulsive purchasing Often pay too much for products and buy inferior products Do not evaluate quality or search out valuable information	20.0

*Nouveax riches: corporate presidents, successful entrepreneurs, well-to-do lawyers, beginning physicians.

Source: Adapted from Charles D. Schewe and Reuben M. Smith, *Marketing Concepts and Applications,* 2d ed. McGraw-Hill, New York, 1983, fig. 6–3, p. 177 and table 6–2, p. 179.

Social Class. People do not live with uniformly equal status. Every society is stratified into different levels of social status, and it is these different levels, or social classes, which give rise to many of our social motivations. Social classes act as reference groups for our behavior, even to the point of identifying consumptive behavior acceptable to those persons with whom we want to associate. Indeed, one way people attempt to climb the social ladder is by purchasing the "right" products.

Social classes in America are commonly divided into the six classifications described in Table 5-3. These are determined largely on the basis of occupation, education, housing, and source (rather than amount) of income. The lower middle and upper lower classes are the largest groups in America and together represent about two-third of all consumers.

Reference Groups. A *reference group* is any aggregation of people who influence an individual's attitudes or behavior. It may be a group to which one belongs such as family, social club, or school sports team. We may buy Sergio Valenti jeans, for example, because our sorority sisters or fraternity brothers think well of them. Or we may opt for the black leather jackets of our motorcycle club.

A reference group can also be one that we admire or aspire to join such as an honor society or a professional sport. Aspiration is used by sports equipment producers to influence buyer behavior. Some people will buy a Dunlop tennis racket because John McEnroe is seen playing with this brand in televised tournaments; others will buy Converse basketball shoes because Larry Bird wears them.

The family. This reference group is considered to have the greatest influence on purchase behavior. During an individual's formative years, the family has significantly more interaction with the child than any other group. Socialization takes place within the family and social values and cultural norms are transmitted during the formative years. Parents set examples of adult roles and of adult consumers; proper and improper behaviors (and purchases) are rewarded or punished. However, this influence is not a one-way street; parents are often influenced by their children. The child can request a certain brand of cereal or toy seen on television, and parents often seek to please or reward the child by purchasing the item.

Family buying patterns may vary according to the type of products being purchased. One study, for example, found four types of product-specific decision-making arrangements involving husbands and wives:[20]

Type of Decision-Making	Representative Products
1. The husband is the dominant influence.	1. Life and other types of insurance.
2. The wife is the dominant influence.	2. Cleaning products, children's clothing, wife's clothing, and food.
3. Both are equally dominant.	3. Husband's clothing, garden tools, and over-the-counter drugs.
4. Decisions are made jointly.	4. Schooling, vacation, housing, and entertainment.

Changing family patterns, of course, can effect such decision patterns and marketers need to keep abreast of such changes. Working wives, for example, increasingly are making or sharing in decisions once reserved for the husband. A study made in the late 1970s reported that women accounted for 40 percent of automotive purchase decisions. Career-oriented working women, in particular, make an excellent target market for car manufacturers. If the working woman is married, she shares in the car purchase decision; if unmarried, she makes the decision herself. Another reason for her involvement in car buying is that the career-oriented working woman—married or not, with or without children—does the most driving.[21]

Family life cycle. This concept illustrates another influence of the family on purchase decisions. Only brief reflection in needed for you to realize that it is quite normal for the amount and type of products and services purchased to vary by the ages and numbers of family members. Table 5-4 shows a family life cycle with five major stages and several subcategories. This updated version of the *classic* family life cycle takes note of the rising percentages of divorced persons with and without children. Future revisions may incorporate unmarried singles and couples with and without children.

Referring to Table 5-4, it can be seen that the categories "young married with dependent children" and "middle-aged married with dependent children" account for half of the U.S. population.[22] Historically the middle-aged married with dependent

TABLE 5-4

Percent of U.S. Population by Life Cycle Stage

Stage	% Population
Young single	8.2
Young married without children	2.9
Other young:	
Young divorced without children	0.1
Young married with dependent children	17.1
Young divorced with dependent children	1.9
Middle-aged:	
Middle-aged married without children	4.7
Middle-aged divorced without children	0.3
Middle-aged married with dependent children	33.0
Middle-aged divorced with dependent children	1.8
Middle-aged married without dependent children	5.5
Middle-aged divorced without dependent children	0.1
Older:	
Older married	5.2
Older unmarried	2.0
All other*	17.2

*Includes all adults and children not accounted for by the family life cycle stages.

Source: Adapted from Patrick E. Murphy and William A. Staples, "A Modernized Family Life Cycle," Journal of Consumer Research, June 1979, p. 16, table 2.

children category (incorporating one-third of the population) has been a prime target market for many consumer products because of its size, higher income, and increased demands created by the presence of young and adolescent children.*

From changes in family composition such as decreasing family size, increasing divorce rates, increasing life span, and available disposable income, Murphy and Staples have drawn the following implications for marketers:

Declining family size affects marketers who sell products that appeal to large families, i.e., station wagons and large package sizes of groceries.

The young divorced stage may be a good segment for small appliances, life insurance, and personal enhancement services such as health spas and tennis clubs.

Middle-aged childless couples and divorced individuals with no children to support may represent a good market for luxury goods, e.g., expensive restaurants, vacations, and furniture.

Middle-aged divorced parents, with two-household expenses, may seek more low-priced products, e.g., used cars and fast food restaurants.

Increasing longevity means that older people without dependent children (the classic "empty nest" stage), though not necessarily wealthy, will be able to save for vacations, new homes, and home furnishings.[23]

*Husbands and working wives in this age category earn more on average than younger workers.

Usage Situations. In Chapter 4 we discussed how markets for products can be segmented on the basis of consumer usage such as heavy and light users or by special uses (e.g., suction-type vacuum cleaners for bare floor cleaning versus revolving brush sweeper-type vacuum cleaners for carpeted floors).

Henry Assael points out that segmenting a product market on the basis of consumer usage can lead to new and different product positioning and advertising strategies.[24] He notes that it is perfectly reasonable for a consumer to say, "The brand I select depends on how, when, where, and why I'm going to use it." A consumer may prefer one brand of car for family use and another for commuting to work, or one brand of spirits for personal consumption and another when entertaining guests.

The size of each usage segment will determine whether it deserves a separate marketing strategy. A very large usage segment may support a comprehensive strategy including, for example, a product or brand designed specifically to appeal to the segment. Or the segment may not be of sufficient size to justify a major strategy, yet be large enough to justify a separate advertising campaign with copy designed to help position the existing brand for an identified usage situation.

Random Environmental Factors

In addition to the external factors discussed above, random external forces also can shape consumer behavior. *Weather* is one example. Severe blizzards disrupt normal purchase patterns but increase the demand for snow related products (e.g., snow blowers). At the other extreme, spells of hot weather increase the demand for air-conditioners and cooling beverages. Similarly, a disease or sickness can influence our needs for and purchases of medical treatment or medications.

A *government* regulation or announcement also can affect consumer attitudes and purchase behavior. The Food and Drug Administration's announcement of the possible harmful effect of sodium nitrite, a preservative used in bacon and other foods, caused at least a temporary drop in demand for bacon.

International situations can influence consumer behavior. The oil crisis affected the way consumers evaluated automobiles (miles per gallon) and houses (annual energy costs). The energy situation has been a boon to such industries as woodstoves, home insulation, and solar heating.

Changing *technology*, of course, is constantly influencing consumer behavior. Examples include the electronic pocket calculator replacing the slide rule, the plastic eyeglass lens replacing the glass lens, and synthetic fibers replacing natural fibers. Nothing seems more pervasive than technological change which, in turn, causes consumers to reevaluate their purchase patterns.

Marketer-Initiated Influences

Of major interest to marketers are those buyer behavior influences which are controllable by the marketer's own organization—the elements of the marketing program. (The components of the marketing program are covered in Parts Three and Five.) In formulating the firm's marketing program, the marketing decision-maker should view the different components—particularly product, price, distribution, personal selling, and advertising—as an integrated package, which the consumer will perceive as a single offering. Marketing elements are seen by the consumer as only part of the total purchase environment. For example, a price can be high or low relative to the consumer's income, need for quality, and perceived quality of the brand. In the same way perception of a promotional program is conditioned by social and personal factors.

ORGANIZATIONAL BUYING BEHAVIOR

Organizations, like consumers, go through a decision process to select products and services and to select suppliers. The process is followed more formally in those organizations with purchasing departments.

In this section we first examine the organizational purchase decision process and then discuss the internal and external influences on the organizational buyer. We close with a look at some models of organizational buying behavior.

The Organizational Purchase Decision Process

Figure 5-5 depicts the steps in the organizational buying process. The principal difference from the consumer model is the addition of an *internal communications* step needed in larger organizations with numerous departments.

The *recognition of problem or need* occurs in a variety of ways; the most common is when the inventory of an item is running low. In a very small organization, the person concerned will place an order with a vendor. As the size of the organization increases, however, specialization occurs and the task of procurement falls to the purchasing department. The person with the need now must *communicate* with the purchasing department, usually by means of a purchase requisition.

The purchasing manager then identifies suppliers or vendors capable of providing the products or services specified on the purchase requisition (the *search for alternatives*). Where the product requested is a standard or low priced item, the purchasing department usually places the order with the chosen vendor; however, with first-time purchases or large-ticket (high-priced) items, the purchasing department may develop a list of qualified vendors from which the department or individual who made the original request will make the final selection (*evaluation of alternatives* and *choice*). The *purchase* will be made by the purchasing department

FIGURE 5-5. The organizational purchase decision process.

Recognition of problem or need

Establishment and communication of objectives and specifications

Search for alternative means of need satisfaction

Evaluation of alternatives

Choice

Outcome: Purchase and post-evaluation of purchase

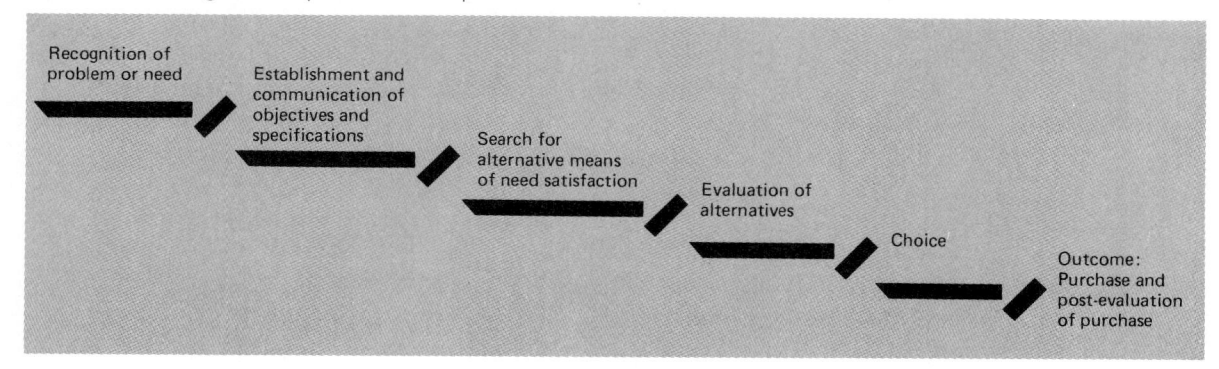

and the *postevaluation of the purchase* will be made by both the purchasing department and by the user department.

Factors Influencing the Organizational Buying Decision

While consumer and organizational decision processes may be similar, the influences are sufficiently different to require separate marketing approaches. Figure 5-6 shows the factors that influence the organizational buyer.

   Personal Influences. Purchasing managers (or buyers) and others involved with the organizational buying decision, being human, are influenced by a host of personal considerations. Their personalities can influence not only the outcome of the purchase decision, but the very nature of the decision process itself. Some may meticulously obtain and process information on purchase alternatives while others may not. Some buyers may have greater vendor loyalty than others, thereby simplifying their buying decisions. Another individual factor is the amount of perceived risk the buyer can tolerate. Those with a low risk tolerance may seek great amounts of information and/or organizational support before selecting a vendor; those with a higher risk tolerance may choose a supplier with only a few facts before them.

   Organizational Influences. The structure of the purchasing function affects the organizational buying process. Some organizations have a *centralized* purchasing function at company headquarters which services the entire organization. All purchase requests are sent to this centralized group. Other organizations *decentralize* their purchasing by placing their buying offices with the operating functions, such as divisions or plants. Some even go so far as to permit individual departments (e.g., engineering or sales) to place orders direct with vendors. In these cases limits usually are placed on the dollar amounts that may be spent without purchasing department approval.

FIGURE 5-6. Factors influencing the organizational buyer's purchase decision.

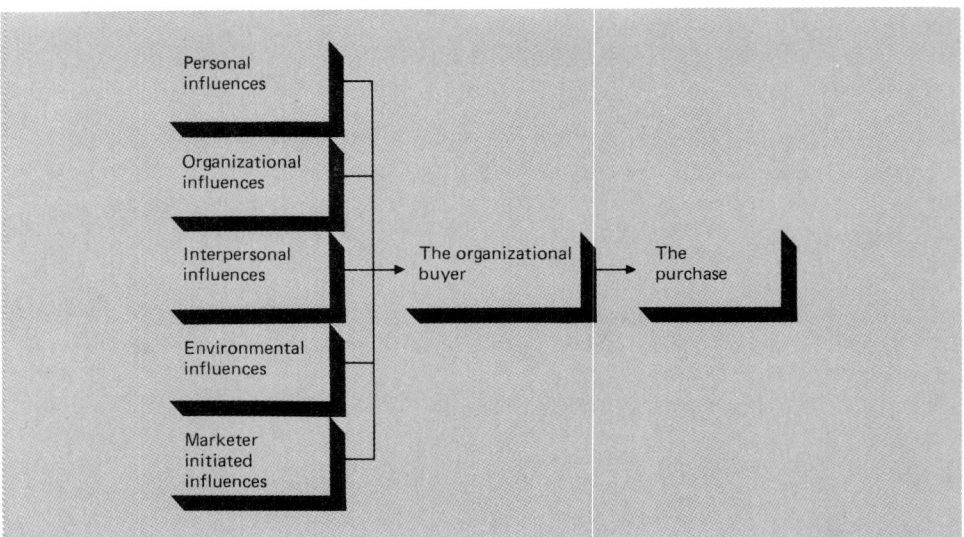

Not all organizations assign the same tasks to their purchasing departments, irrespective of whether they are centralized or decentralized. In some organizations, the purchasing department merely processes orders to vendors who have been chosen by other departments. In other companies, considerable authority is given to the purchasing department. Still others use a combination of the above: the purchasing department may have the authority to decide certain purchases, such as for nontechnical or routine supplies, but have little authority with respect to technical products, such as machinery or computers. Each of these arrangements involves different procedures and attracts employees with significantly different qualifications.

Interpersonal Influences. Purchasing people interact and communicate with each other and with those in the departments where the goods and services are actually used. Each person attempts to influence others to obtain the most favorable outcome from the purchase decision process. In those situations where common goals (outcomes) are sought, this influence is in the form of cooperation and enhances the efficiency of the overall process. However, the opposite can occur when those involved in the purchasing decision do not share a consistent frame of evaluative criteria by which the alternative purchase options are evaluated.

Several distinct roles have been noted for persons involved in the purchase decision process.[25] The first is the *user*. The user initiates the process and may exert a significant influence on product specifications and vendor selection. A second type of role is that of the general *influencers*, who exert a direct or indirect influence on the purchase selection. Research and development people, for example, may influence the purchase of components and raw materials for new products as well as the selection of suppliers.

The actual *buyers*, those who formally deal with vendors, represent a third role in the purchasing process. While the buyers' roles may vary, as a minimum they would place orders and follow up on vendor delivery. When an engineer specifies what is to be ordered, the engineer rather than the buyer has assumed the role of *decider*. A final role is that of the *gatekeeper*. Vendor sales representatives will try to call on anyone in the organization that they think can influence the vendor selection. As gatekeeper the purchasing manager controls who the salesperson may and may not see.

Environmental Influences. Like individual consumers, organizations exist within many overlapping environments, such as physical, governmental, and technological. Concern for the physical environment, for example, may cause one supplier's equipment to be favored for making kraft paper because it is less polluting. Government regulations, such as import quotas or duties, can restrict available supplies or increase their costs. The National Bureau of Standards and the Occupational Safety and Health Administration (OSHA) promulgate product standards which must be considered when selecting some materials.

Changing technology means that many industries have such rapid rates of technological development and innovation that forecasting needed supplies is difficult. Pocket calculator technology advanced so rapidly that new models became obsolete almost immediately. The economic environment also has an impact on organizational buying. Credit terms, inflation, and economic booms and recessions all affect purchasing decisions. And, finally, the cultural environment affects the purchasing process. The values of an American businessperson vary from those of an Arab or Japanese businessperson. Understanding cultural differences can facilitate purchasing supplies from abroad.

Marketer-Initiated Influences. Organizational buyers, like their consumer counterparts, are the targets of marketing efforts. They read advertising and promotional literature and are called upon by sales representatives. They evaluate product quality and vendor service and consider these factors along with price.

As with consumer products, the most important reinforcement for organizational purchases is a satisfactory product experience. However, organizations also give much weight to economic factors, such as productivity, cost and value, or production output.

Organizations frequently have step-by-step procedures for analyzing vendors and their products.[26] These procedures incorporate such considerations as product variables (quality, performance), packaging (ease of handling, product protection), price (including credit terms and discounts), delivery (on-time delivery, acceptance of emergency orders), and vendor capabilities (reputation, past performance). Consequently, sellers' promotional efforts with organizational buyers stress factual information, although emotional appeals may also be used.

Models of Organizational Buying Behavior

Several attempts have been made to develop models of the organizational buying process. We will briefly describe four of these.

The Price Minimizer Model. The simplest model portrays the buyer as the pure price minimizer. It depicts the firm in a competitive environment in which prices are determined by market forces. Since the buying firm has little influence over the prices it receives for its goods, it attempts to maximize profit by minimizing its costs for purchased materials and supplies. However, except for situations where the firm is purchasing undifferentiated commodities (e.g., grains, copper, wood), the price minimization model has limited application.

Vendor-Oriented Models. Other models of organizational buying focus on the vendor. In many large organizations purchasing managers select from a set of "approved" vendors. Government agencies follow this approach and sellers go to great lengths to be placed on their approved vendor lists. Approved vendors, in some cases, may negotiate a master contract with the government and sell their products to all agencies at the negotiated price. This model assumes that the products being offered are essentially equivalent; consequently, price and service become highly significant.

Yoram Wind has studied these factors.[27] Price is an objective criteria which can easily be compared among alternative vendors. Service, on the other hand, can be expressed in several ways: on-time delivery, fast service to minimize downtimes, automatic reordering, frequent and complete training for proper product use, or the ability to adapt the product (or the payment schedule) to the buyer's needs. Since service, unlike price, can be evaluated only after experience with a vendor over a period of time, purchasing managers tend to remain loyal to their proven vendors.

Trial of a new vendor tends to occur only when a current vendor's service deteriorates or when the vendor's prices get out of line.

Buyer-Oriented Models. The price minimizer and vendor models are based on economic criteria. People involved in organizational buying, however, often have motives similar to those of individual consumers. Other things being equal, therefore, salespersons who can enhance the ego and self-esteem of the potential buyer have a competitive advantage.

Theodore Levitt conducted an extensive investigation of the organizational buying process in which he applied the *perceived risk model* of buyer behavior—originally developed for consumers—to organizational buyers. This model assumes that all purchase situations have some degree of risk associated with them. Buyers may seek to minimize this risk by having others in the organization make the decision, staying with the same vendor, or buying from the vendor with the largest market share. Levitt's study was concerned particularly with the influence of "corporate" advertising (advertising designed to build the company reputation rather than sell specific products) and the sales presentation. Levitt found:

- The better a company's reputation, the better are its chances (1) of getting a favorable first hearing for a new product among customer prospects and (2) of getting early adoption of that product.
- The greater the risk the customer is asked to take (product adoption versus merely agreeing to give it a further and closer look), the less important seems to be the vendor's reputation in influencing the customer's decision.
- In the case of complex industrial materials, purchasing agents, who are usually highly competent as professional buyers, may be less influenced by a company's generalized reputation than technical personnel, who are presumably less competent as buyers but more competent as judges of a complex product's merits.
- The quality of a salesman's presentation in support of a product was found to be an important variable in obtaining favorable buyer reactions.[28]

The study was concerned with the initial purchase of a product by a customer. Repeat purchases are largely a function of satisfaction with prior vendor experiences.

The BUYGRID Model. A Marketing Science Institute report concluded that purchase tasks can be classified by degrees of difficulty. As purchasing moves from first time purchases (new tasks) to repeat purchases (straight rebuys), the decision process becomes less complex, fewer persons are involved, and new vendors find it harder to obtain orders.[29]

SUMMARY

Because the buyer is the central focus of the marketing effort, understanding how the buyer makes a purchase decision can be useful to marketing management. Viewing marketing from the buyer's side involves looking at the internal and external factors that influence purchase behavior.

Internal influences on consumer buyer behavior include motives, perceptions, learning, attitudes, personality, and lifestyle. External influences include measurable environmental influences such as economic factors, culture, social class, reference groups (including family), and usage situations. They also include random environmental influences such as weather, government, international conditions, and technology.

Internal influences on organizational buyer behavior include personal, organizational, and interpersonal factors. External influences on the organizational buyer include the physical, governmental, technological, economic, and cultural environments. And finally, both consumer and organizational buyers are influenced by sellers. Each selling company uses its own mix of product, price, distribution, and promotion to attempt to get buyers to purchase its brand.

Both consumer and organizational buyers undergo similar processes when making a decisions leading to a purchase. First there is a recognition of a problem or need on the part of the potential buyer, followed by search and evaluation of alternative means of satisfying the need. Eventually a choice is made and the product is purchased; then the product is used or consumed, followed by an evaluation of the purchase. A favorable evaluation usually means repeat purchases (the marketer's goal); an unfavorable evaluation means a renewed search for a better solution to the buyer's problem or need.

The extent to which the complete process is followed by the buyer is determined by the type of purchase. In the case of high involvement purchases, consumers likely will go through all of the formal decision steps. In the case of low involvement purchases, on the other hand, buying tends to become more routine and it is less likely that consumers will engage in search and evaluation of alternatives. Similarly, when organizations are making first-time purchases, they are likely to engage in search, evaluation of alternatives, and postpurchase evaluation. Buying becomes more routine, however, in the case of repeat purchases when suppliers have performed satisfactorily in the past.

The more we learn about how and why people and organizations buy as they do, the more this knowledge can be used in the development of marketing strategies.

QUESTIONS

1. Name the different roles that consumers may play in the purchase decision process.
2. What are the principal differences in organizational buying compared to consumer buying?
3. Describe the differences between low-involvement and high-involvement purchase situations.
4. Describe the five steps of the consumer decision process for high involvement purchases.
5. Name the internal, external, and marketer-initiated influences on consumer purchase behavior, and explain in general how they are thought to influence buyers' decisions.
6. Describe the hierarchy of effects with respect to attitudes as it leads to purchase. Begin with beliefs.
7. Which reference group has the greatest influence on purchase behavior? Why?
8. Which two stages of the family life cycle combined contain about two-thirds of the U.S. population?
9. What step in the organizational model of the purchase decision process is not found in the consumer model?
10. Name the three internal and two external factors that influence the organizational buyer's purchase decisions.

REFERENCES

1. Robert J. Lavidge and Gary A. Steiner, "A Model for Predictive Measurements of Advertising Effectiveness," *Journal of Marketing*, October 1961, pp. 59–62.
2. Kenneth E. Runyon, *Consumer Behavior and the Practice of Marketing*, Charles E. Merrill, Columbus, Ohio, 1977, p. 177.
3. Gerald T. Gorn, "The Effects of Music in Advertising on Choice Behavior: A Classical Conditioning Approach," *Journal of Marketing*, Winter 1982, pp. 94–101.
4. Michael Ray and Alan Sawyer, "Repetition in Media Models: A Laboratory Technique," *Journal of Marketing Research*, February 1971, pp. 11–14.
5. *Wall Street Journal*, June 7, 1982, p. 23.
6. *Wall Street Journal*, Nov. 12, 1981, p. 31.
7. Richard Olshausky and Donald Granbois, "Consumer Decision Making—Fact or Fiction?" *Journal of Consumer Research*, September 1979, pp. 93–100.
8. Richard Petty and John Cacioppo, "Issue Involvement as a Moderator of the Effects of Attitude of Advertising Content and Context," in Kent B. Monroe (ed.), *Advances in Consumer Research*, vol. 8, Association for Consumer Research, Ann Arbor, 1981, pp. 20–24.
9. Henry Assael, *Consumer Behavior and Marketing Action*, Kent Publishing, Boston, 1981. See chapter 4 for a discussion of conditions under which purchase may precede attitude formulation.
10. See, for example, W. T. Tucker and John J. Painter, "Personality and Product Use," *Journal of Applied Psychology*, October 1961, pp. 325–329; Joel B. Cohen, "The Role of Personality in Consumer Behavior," *California Management Review*, Spring 1968, pp. 67–70; David Sparks and W. T. Tucker, "A Multivariate Analysis of Personality and Product Use," *Journal of Marketing Research*, February 1971, pp. 67–70; Harold H. Kassarjian, "Personality and Consumer Behavior," *Journal of Marketing Research*, November 1971, pp. 409–419.
11. William D. Wells and Douglas J. Tigert, "Activities, Interests, and Opinions," *Journal of Advertising Research*, August 1971, pp. 27–35.
12. R. Ziff, "Psychographics for Market Segmentation," *Journal of Advertising Research*, April 1971, pp. 3–8.
13. Elayn K. Bernay, "Life Style Analysis as a Basis for Media Selection," in Charles King and Douglas Tigert, *Attitude Research Reaches New Heights*, American Marketing Association, Chicago, 1971, pp. 189–195.
14. Edwin Mansfield, *Microeconomics: Theory and Application*, Norton, New York, 1970. See chapters 2 and 3 for an excellent explanation of this mechanism.
15. Milton J. Rokeach, "The Role of Values in Public Opinion Research," *Public Opinion Quarterly*, Winter 1968, pp. 547–549.
16. Philip Kotler, *Marketing Management: Analysis, Planning, and Control*, 4th ed., Prentice-Hall, Englewood Cliffs, N.J., 1980, p. 127.
17. Henry Assael, op. cit., pp. 267–268.
18. Theodore Roszak, *The Making of a Counter Culture: Reflections on the Technocratic Society and Its Youthful Opposition*, Doubleday, Garden City, N.Y., 1969, p. 66.
19. Polly Summar, "Service Scans the Market," *Advertising Age*, April 27, 1981, p. S-49.
20. H. L. Davis and Benny P. Rigaux, "Perception of Marital Roles in Decision Processes," *Journal of Consumer Research*, June 1974, pp. 51–62.
21. Rena Bartos, "What Every Marketer Should Know about Women," *Harvard Business Review*, May–June, 1978, p. 83.
22. Based on the 1970 *Census of Population*.
23. Abstracted from Patrick E. Murphy and William E. Staples, "A Modernized Family Life Cycle," *Journal of Consumer Research*, vol. 6, June 1979, pp. 19–20.
24. Henry Assael, op. cit., chapter 17.

25. Frederick E. Webster, Jr., and Yoram Wind, *Organizational Buying Behavior,* Prentice-Hall, Inc., Englewood Cliffs, N.J., 1972, chapter 6. Copyright © 1972, Reprinted by permission.
26. Richard Hill, Ralph Alexander, and James Cross, *Industrial Marketing,* 4th ed, Richard D. Irwin, Homewood, Ill., 1975. See chapter 6 for a description of vendor analysis.
27. Yoram Wind, "Industrial Source Loyalty," *Journal of Marketing Research*, November 1970, pp. 450–457.
28. Theodore Levitt, *Industrial Purchasing Behavior: A Study of Communication Effects*, Division of Research, Graduate School of Business Administration, Harvard University, Boston, 1965.
29. For a description of the "Buygrid" model, see Patrick Robinson, Charles Faris, and Yoram Wind, *Industrial Buying and Creative Marketing*, Allyn and Bacon, Inc., Boston, 1967.

CHAPTER 6

Marketing Research and Marketing Information Systems

Decision making is a pervasive element of the marketing manager's job. Whether dealing with products, pricing, advertising, personal selling, or distribution, problems arise which require decisions. And these must be made in an environment which places an ever increasing cost on wrong decisions.

We will explore some of the principal means by which marketing management obtains needed information. As we saw in Chapters 3 and 4, information is the key to accurately assessing marketing problems and opportunities. The bulk of the chapter is devoted to marketing research—the traditional approach to market data gathering and analysis. The last section describes the developing field of marketing information systems—a more comprehensive, largely computerized, approach which leads ultimately to alternate solutions to questions of marketing strategy and tactics.

THE NEED FOR INFORMATION

Risk and Uncertainty

Neither marketing research nor marketing information systems can eliminate all uncertainty and risk. Despite the use of marketing research in new product planning, for example, the failure rate of new products remains high. Examples of new product failure include the Lone Star Brewery's Lime Lager beer, Procter & Gamble's Teel Liquid Toothpaste, and General Foods' Gourmet Foods. These errors, and others like them, might not have happened had some manager not decided to take a chance in the face of uncertainty or risk.

A manager can foresee several possible consequences (such as competitive reaction or involvement of a government regulatory agency) which could affect the outcome of a decision. This is known as making a *decision under risk*. Probability theory and decision analysis can be used to suggest the decision which will minimize the risk or maximize the gain. These are illustrated by an example in **Marketing Note 6-1**.

For many decisions the marketing manager can neither assign a probability of occurrence for outcomes nor know all the consequences prior to the decision. Under these conditions the manager is said to be making a *decision under uncertainty*. Advertising campaigns are launched without knowing their exact effects

> **MARKETING NOTE 6-1**
>
> **Decision Making under Risk**
>
> The Jet Power Products Company produces a line of automotive additives that clean the car's carburetor and yield increased gasoline mileage. However, due to the many products offered with similar claims—but which do not perform as promised—many states have halted the marketing of such products. Jet Power must decide whether to try selling its line and risk legal action.
>
> Jerry Pitkin, the regional sales manager, must decide whether to recommend that Jet Power begin marketing in Kansas. If the company begins marketing and then is stopped by the state's consumer protection agency, the resultant negative publicity and dealer reaction would preclude future distribution of the product. Jerry has determined that the following possibilities exist and, for each, has stated the probability of occurrence:
>
> | | State Intervention | | No State Action | |
> |---|---|---|---|---|
> | Alternative | Probability | Consequence | Probability | Consequence |
> | Begin marketing in Kansas | .30% | −$38,000 | .70% | $150,000 |
> | Do not market in Kansas | 0 | 0 | 1.00 | 0 |
>
> On the basis of these assumptions, Jerry has decided to enter the market. He has calculated that if Jet Power begins marketing in Kansas, there is an *expectation* of a profit of $93,600 as follows:
>
> $$(.30)(-\$38,000) + (.70)(\$150,000) = \$93,600$$
>
> This is certainly larger than the expected profit of zero if the company does not enter the state. Note that there is still a 30 percent chance that the state will issue an injunction to stop the product's distribution; however, the expectation is that this will not happen. The risk has been quantified, not eliminated.

on the marketplace. The local bakery must guess the number of loaves and types of bread to bake each day. Such uncertainty cannot be ignored, yet decisions must be made if the firm is to continue to exist. One such decision that paid off was the acquisition and development of Chester Carlson's patents covering the xerographic process by the Haloid Corporation (now Xerox), after IBM and Kodak had turned them down.

The Role of Information in Marketing Planning

When asked to respond to the question: "From the perspective of the Chief Executive Officer, what is the task of the marketing professional?" Stuart D. Watson, Chairman of Heublein, stated:

> In my judgment, the fundamental responsibility is to bring the customer or consumer into the decision structure of the firm—that is, to insure the availability of timely and accurate information about consumers and their environment. A second essential responsibility, of course, is the formulation and effective implementation of marketing strategies and tactics. This total task has remained essentially unchanged during my business career. However, effective implementation is becoming infinitely more difficult.[1]

The development of an effective marketing plan cannot take place without adequate information concerning the needs and desires of the firm's customers. Mr. Watson properly places this information gathering function as the priority task of the marketer. Information is the foundation for planning from which successful marketing programs are launched.

The following example will show some of the different types of information needed at the various stages of the management decision process.

> The Clark Paint Company is a small manufacturer of high quality paints and paint products which are sold exclusively through its five retail outlets, all within 20 miles of the production facility. The sales of paints and other products (wall and floor coverings, brushes, rollers, etc.) at the outlets resulted in 1981 sales of about $4 million. Nathan Clark is concerned about future expansion of the company's operations. In particular, he realizes that (1) only 60 percent of the firm's production capacity is being utilitized, (2) the market for house paint is much larger geographically than a circle of 20 miles radius, (3) paint can be sold in outlets other than Clark Paint Company stores, (4) the name Clark Paint may not be the best name for a paint, and (5) the current policy of pricing below the average of major brands may not be optimal.
>
> Mr. Clark has reached the following tentative conclusions:
>
> - Bulk paint sales to home builders and rental property owners will help utilitze excess plant capacity.
> - Selected paint dealers within a 50-mile radius should be contacted to act as authorized dealers for the company's products.
> - The company name should be changed to the New England Paint Company.
> - The current pricing policy should be continued.
>
> A list of the specific information needed to evaluate these conclusions can be prepared so that each can be researched and tested.

The Clark Paint Company example points out the fundamental purpose of information and of marketing research: (1) *information is that data which are useful to the manager's decision-making process* and (2) *marketing research is not merely the gathering of information but also includes the generation and testing of ideas.*

Each of Mr. Clark's conclusions can be tested or evaluated based on information obtained from dealers, builders, and customers.

SCOPE OF MARKETING RESEARCH

Marketing research is defined as follows:

> The systematic gathering, recording, and analyzing of data about problems relating to the marketing of goods and services.[2]

Table 6-1 shows the types and frequency of use of marketing research activities based on a national sample of 798 companies. This survey found that 73 percent of the firms had a formal marketing research department and that the mean expenditure for marketing research per firm was $473,000. The incidence of marketing

TABLE 6-1
Research Activities of 798 Respondent Companies

	Source of Research			
	Market Research Department, %	Another Department, %	Outside Firm, %	Total, %
Advertising research				
Motivation research	28	3	17	48
Copy research	22	6	21	49
Media research	24	11	26	61
Studies of ad effectiveness	38	5	24	67
Business economics and corporate research				
Short-range forecasting (Up to 1 year)	52	31	2	85
Long-range forecasting (Over 1 year)	50	30	2	82
Studies of business trends	61	21	4	86
Pricing studies	36	44	1	81
Plant and warehouse location studies	30	38	3	71
Acquisition studies	29	38	2	69
Export and international studies	24	25	2	51
MIS (management information system)	26	44	2	72
Operations research	17	42	1	60
Internal company employees	18	41	6	65
Corporate responsibility research				
Consumers "right to know" studies	11	12	3	26
Ecological impact studies	5	25	3	33
Studies of legal constraints on advertising and promotion	12	34	5	51
Social values and policies studies	18	17	5	40
Product research				
New product acceptance and potential	71	7	6	84
Competitive product studies	71	9	5	85
Testing of existing products	49	20	6	75
Packaging research: design or physical characteristics	36	16	8	60
Sales and market research				
Measurement of market potentials	82	7	4	93
Market share analysis	80	9	3	92
Determination of market characteristics	83	6	4	93
Sales analysis	64	24	1	89

TABLE 6-1 *(Continued)*

	Source of Research			
	Market Research Department, %	Another Department, %	Outside Firm, %	Total, %
Establishment of sales quotas, territories	27	48	—	75
Distribution channel studies	31	37	1	69
Test markets, store audits	38	9	7	54
Consumer panel operations	32	5	13	50
Sales compensation studies	14	43	3	60
Promotional studies of premiums, coupons sampling, deals, etc.	34	15	3	52

Source: Dik Warren Twedt, *1978 Survey of Marketing Research,* American Marketing Association, Chicago, 1978.

research departments and the amount spent by company are higher for advertising agencies and consumer products companies than for all companies.

Types of Marketing Research Applications

Market and Economic Analysis. Market analysis includes the analysis of potential for existing market segments. The marketing researcher estimates the market potential for the firm's products within specific segments and assesses the factors which may impinge upon the firm's ability to capture potential sales from those segments. Economic analysis, including economic forecasting, is another activity of the marketing research department. It provides information useful in decisions regarding levels of marketing activity, production, and capital investment.

Product Research. Product research is conducted for new products, improvements of existing products, and product packaging, and for comparisons with competitors' product lines. *Product concept testing* usually begins early in the new product development process to investigate consumer reactions to proposed products or product modifications. Even before a sample is available, potential customers are exposed to verbal or pictorial representations of the proposed product to try to determine whether the concept is worthy of proceeding to laboratory research and development.

As the product development process advances from concept to reality, additional information and customer reaction is needed to refine many aspects of the product's design. *Customer use tests* can be employed to determine reactions to product prototypes. Use tests are applicable to proposed new consumer products and to industrial products as well. A new cake mix may be placed in homes for family testing. A manufacturer of a new machine tool may conduct a field test by installing a prototype in a customer's factory for operator and management evaluation.

As a final precaution, some firms conduct *market tests* in selected areas before deciding to launch a full market introduction. Test marketing is extremely useful for evaluating new products, since the product is exposed to real world competition and offered for sale in a scaled down version of a total marketing program. General Foods test marketed its Maxim freeze-dried coffee for several years before full national marketing was begun.

Market tests are feasible only for products that can be made in test quantities without major investments in plant or equipment. Test quantities of toothpaste can be mixed relatively cheaply in tubs in the laboratory or pilot plant. On the other hand, it would cost several millions of dollars to produce just *one* automobile.

Pricing Research. Systematic pricing research can help to determine the optimal price structure and avoid the problems resulting from incorrect or frequent pricing modifications. The margins between selling prices and the costs of production must be enough to cover operating expenses and profit. Many companies, however, use a standard margin which creates the risk of underpricing or overpricing relative to competition. Marketing research through price/quality and other types of studies can help set prices that achieve company profit goals. It should be noted, however, that pricing decisions often must be made quickly without the benefit of in-depth market research.

Advertising Research. Because advertising is relatively expensive, the funds allocated should be planned and evaluated carefully. Advertising research can be grouped into three segments: content, media, and effectiveness research. *Content research* is concerned with how well an advertisement conveys the intended message. It may be carried out before or after the ad appears in the media. In pretesting TV commercials, samples of potential viewers are questioned after seeing finished or rough versions of the proposed ads. In pretesting print ads, potential readers are shown layouts of proposed ads and then questioned. In posttesting, people who saw the ads are asked to recall specific aspects of the ads as well as give their reactions to the message.

Media research attempts to maximize the efficiency of advertising messages by identifying and evaluating the various media that will reach the intended audiences. One of the most widely used measures of print media is the annual study of the reading habits of the American people conducted by the W. R. Simmons Company. Advertisers use it to select the best mix of magazines for reaching their target markets. The A. C. Nielsen Company provides frequent measurements of TV show audiences.

Advertising effectiveness research attempts to analyze the total impact of the advertising campaign. Of prime concern is the degree to which the ad program helps achieve overall marketing objectives. Unless advertising goals are stated prior to the advertising campaign, research cannot measure the campaign's effectiveness. And studies must be made prior to the start of the ad campaign to learn the benchmark points from which progress will be measured—for example, the percent of viewers who are aware of the brand name.

Sales Research. There are many types of sales research. One is *sales analysis*, which utilizes customer records and outside data sources—such as census reports—to find opportunities for better targeting sales and marketing efforts. Another is *selling research*, which analyzes personal selling tasks. Does the sales presentation create or intensify buyer interest? Are sales brochures and other sales tools as helpful as they might be? How can salespeople close a greater percentage of their sales calls? These and many other questions are studied through selling research.

DESIGNING THE MARKETING RESEARCH PROJECT

The marketing research process is a systematic procedure linking together the marketing researcher, the marketing decision maker, and the sources of relevant information concerning a problem. The key to the process is planning. The marketing research process has its roots in scientific research and the scientific method. In practice, however, marketing research studies range from the "quick and dirty" to carefully planned, systematic empirical investigations of hypotheses.

Figure 6-1 shows the relationships among the components of the scientific marketing research process. The four major components—problem definition, project strategy, project tactics, and use of information—are each comprised of several stages. Each stage may or may not apply to every marketing research problem; however, the researcher should evaluate the appropriateness of each stage for every proposed marketing research project before deciding to eliminate one or more stages.

FIGURE 6-1. The marketing research process.

Problem definition
- What is the overall problem for which the marketing manager needs information?
- What specific decisions will be made on the basis of the information obtained?
- Can the problem be broken down into smaller yet meaningful subproblems which may be easier to analyze?

Project strategy
- Develop possible solutions or hypotheses which may solve the problem.
- Identify the specific information which is needed to solve the problem or to test the solution.
- Determine the method of research to be used.
- Identify and evaluate potential sources of information.

Project tactics
- Collect pertinent data from published or other secondary sources.
- Design a sample for primary data collection.
- Prepare a data collection form.
- Collect the data.
- Analyze the data.

Using the information
- Interpret the findings.
- Report the results.
- Use the results to make a decision.

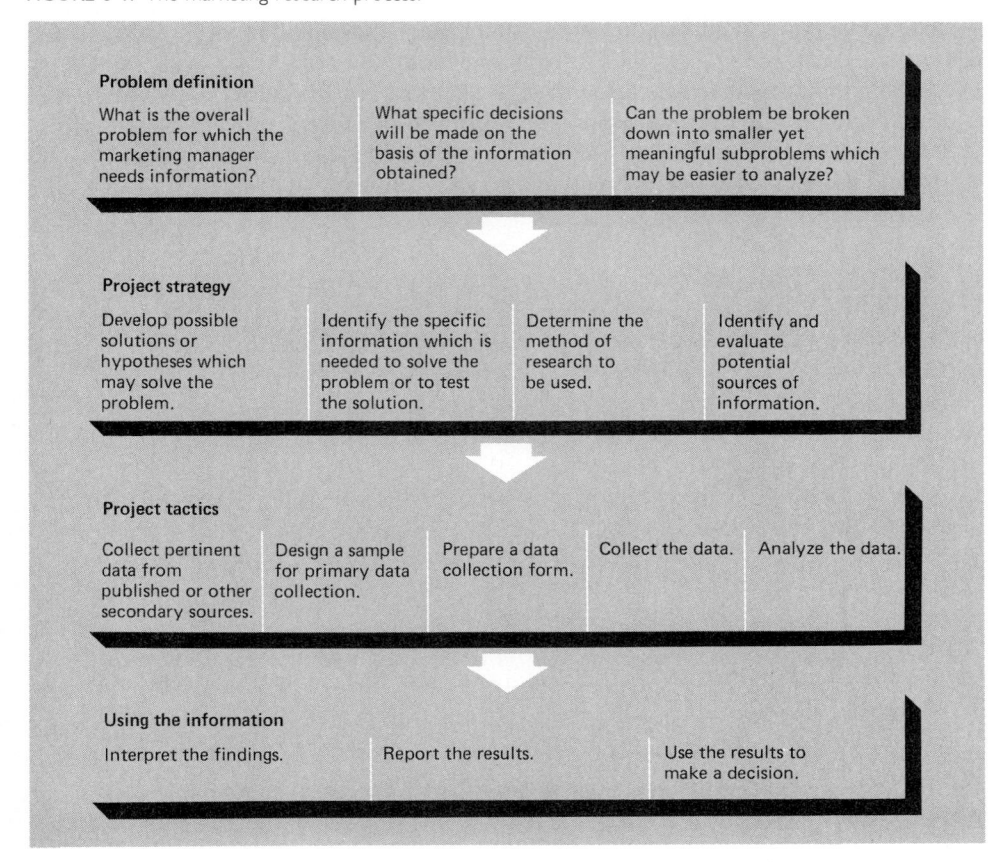

Defining the Problem

Problem definition for marketing research may appear easy. All you have to do is answer the question, "What went wrong?" and then find out why. In practice, however, this approach often proves frustrating and inadequate. Marketing executives are concerned with results, the ability to reach objectives. When the results are less than anticipated, the executive starts waving the red flag. But the problem may not be adequately identified with simple statements like "Sales are down" or "We lost two points in market share." These are *symptoms*, not the real problem. When we have a fever, we take aspirin; however, the fever may have been caused by our body's reaction to an infection. To treat the symptom—the fever—without treating the cause—the infection—can lead to an actual increase in our health problem.

Similarly, a decline in sales results from more basic factors. Separating the symptom from the problem is complicated by the fact that the decision-making executive thinks and speaks in terms of results and performances—areas of symptoms. A useful approach is to divide the factors influencing the problem into those which are environmental and those which are actionable.[3] The first category includes factors in the marketplace which cannot be changed by the marketer—sales that have already occurred, for example. Actionable factors involve those areas where the marketer can make specific decisions, "What would be the effect on sales and profits of a ten percent price cut?" Answering this is much more useful than descriptions of environmental factors, although the latter may help to answer the action question.

When defining the marketing problem, the researcher initially should state it as broadly as necessary. The scope can be narrowed during the preliminary phases of the research, reducing the possibility of investigating too narrow a topic.

Project Strategy

Marketing research should be undertaken with a predetermined strategy in mind. Before developing the strategy, the following questions should be answered:

- What is the information to be generated by this project intended to prove or disprove?
- What specific information is needed?
- By what means will the information be obtained?
- From which sources will the information be sought?

Developing Hypotheses. After defining the problem it also is useful to develop tentative conclusions or hypotheses. Hypotheses provide the researcher with expectations of the outcome of the research, thereby avoiding any surprise results. They also provide a basis for the statistical analysis and testing of possible solutions.

Information Needed. Once the marketing researcher has determined what the research is intended to accomplish, the next step is to specify the exact information needed to test the hypotheses. The tentative answers to the questions under investigation are a starting point. For example, in a research study to ascertain those factors which influence the sales of health and beauty aids (H&BA) in supermarkets, we may have the following hypotheses: (1) The relative location of H&BA in the store influences their sales; or (2) the number of *shelf facings* (retail shelf space allocated to an item) devoted to H&BA influences their sales; or (3) the number of *stockouts* (when the retailer runs out of a regularly stocked item) influences the sales of H&BA.

For each of these alternative hypotheses, we need information on the sales of health and beauty aids in several stores. This may be expressed in a number of ways: total sales, sales per square foot, sales as a percentage of total store sales, and the change in any of these from a similar period a year earlier. Additionally, each hypothesis will require: (1) knowledge of the relative location of H&BA in several stores, (2) knowledge of the number of shelf facings, and (3) information regarding inventory and stock conditions. Analysis of these data will indicate whether the hypotheses were correct. It may be that *none* of the three original hypotheses actually influenced H&BA sales. In this case, new hypotheses must be generated and new data collected and analyzed. The more plausible the hypotheses the better the chance that the right information will be collected.

Means of Collection and Sources. The above example required the collection of facts. Facts are objective. They can be measured directly, and in many instances, are available from secondary sources, such as the census or trade associations. But facts are only one kind of information of value to the marketing manager. Another category of information is *opinion*, or *belief*. Opinions represent a person's attitudes. They may be obtained from pollsters such as Gallup or Louis Harris, or the company may contract for a specific study by a market research firm. Figure 6-2 shows some results of a national survey of public opinion concerning attitudes toward labor, retirement, and discrimination.

FIGURE 6-2. Findings from an opinion survey of a cross section of U.S. heads of households. *Source:* "Study of American Opinion", 1978 summary report, *U.S. News and World Report,* 1978 p. 5.

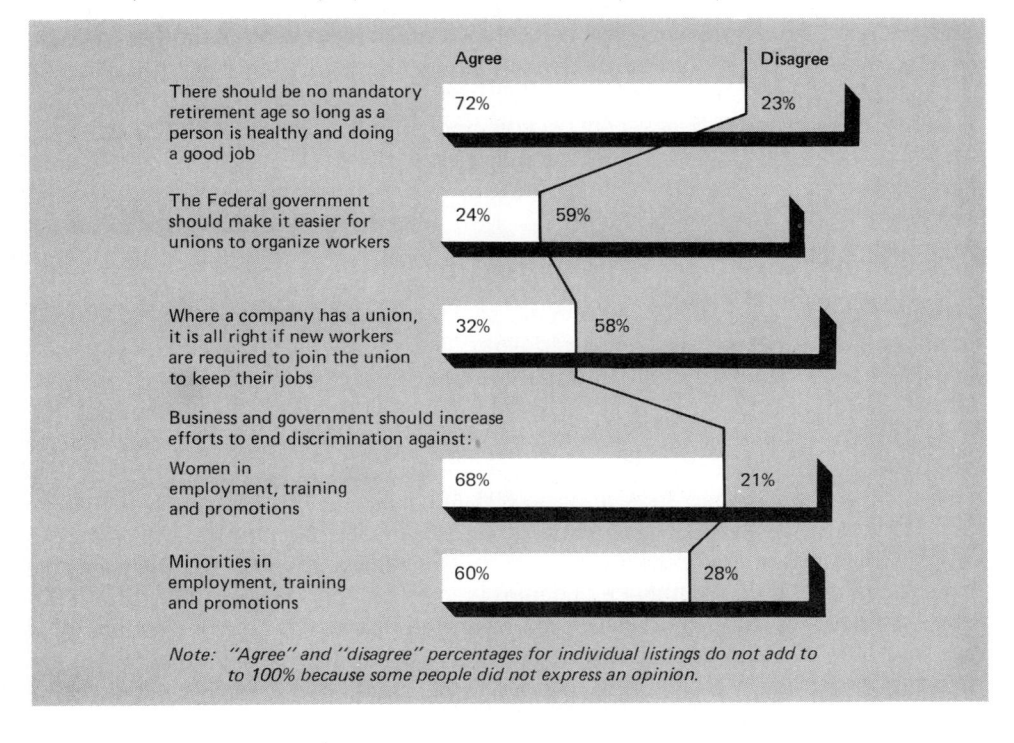

	Agree	Disagree
There should be no mandatory retirement age so long as a person is healthy and doing a good job	72%	23%
The Federal government should make it easier for unions to organize workers	24%	59%
Where a company has a union, it is all right if new workers are required to join the union to keep their jobs	32%	58%
Business and government should increase efforts to end discrimination against:		
Women in employment, training and promotions	68%	21%
Minorities in employment, training and promotions	60%	28%

Note: "Agree" and "disagree" percentages for individual listings do not add to to 100% because some people did not express an opinion.

A third type of information involves *motive*. Motives are reasons why somebody does something. We buy a product without stopping to rationalize it or determine why. Sometimes we do not want to tell why we did it. For example, we may tell someone we bought a small car because it gets good gas mileage or is easy to park. The real reason may be because we simply couldn't afford a larger one. The marketing researcher, therefore, may have to resort to indirect questioning to ascertain real motives. A manufacturer of backyard swimming pools commissioned a study to find out why more families did not buy them. Management was perplexed because it had reasoned that the energy crisis and the high cost of gasoline would force more families to stay at home. *Direct* questioning had indicated that people didn't purchase pools because they were difficult to clean and used costly chemicals. On the basis of this information, the company developed a more efficient, nonchemical filtering system. Sales still did not pick up. *Indirect* questioning showed that people did not want their neighbors to keep bothering them for use of the pool. The pool would rob them of their privacy. A new marketing approach was developed to try to convince people that this was not a real likelihood.

Project Tactics

Following the determination of the project strategy, we move to the tactical portion of the study—the collection and analysis of the data.

Sources of Information. The many places in which a researcher may look for useful information can be grouped into two categories—primary data sources and secondary data sources. *Primary sources* are used to obtain data, specific to your problem, which have not already been collected by others (or, if collected, are not readily available or accessible to you). Common sources are consumers and buying organizations. Primary data are expensive and time-consuming to obtain and should only be used if all other means of solving the problem prove futile.

Secondary sources contain data that were collected originally for other purposes (e.g., industry statistics, census data, and company sales reports). Because of their low cost, the availability of secondary data should be fully explored before committing funds to primary data collection.

Designing the Sample. Assuming primary data are needed, the first task is to pick the sample to be interviewed. Marketers rarely can afford the time or costs to interview everyone. Instead, researchers select samples of the *universe* (the total population or other entities being studied). The samples are then contacted and questioned, and the resulting information is analyzed at costs affordable to the marketer. An extensive science of sampling statistics exists, which enables the researcher to estimate total population information from surveys of much smaller samples. Thus a political pollster can estimate the results of a national election to within ±3 percent from a sample of only 1500 voters.

However, this type of projection is only possible if the sample selected is representative of the population to which the results are to be projected. For consumer surveys this assurance is determined by comparing characteristics of the selected sample to known statistics about the population (e.g., type and brand of car, age of household head, income, or level of education). For industrial surveys typical comparisons may be made for the size of the company, classification of goods produced, or geographic locations of plants.

An initial step in designing the sample is to define the parameters of the sample by:

Sample size—the number of respondents to be included in the final sample.

Sampling unit—the individual elements of the population to be sampled (e.g., head of household, type of retail store, purchasing agent, etc.).

Sampling frame—the lists, indices, maps, or other sources from which the sample will be selected (e.g., telephone book, street directory, census map, or association membership roster).

Sampling method—the specific means by which the sampling units will be selected from the sampling frame. These may be random (probability) or judgmental (nonprobability) methods.

The data collection method to be used can have a significant effect on the type of sampling used. Two very important constraints when doing marketing research are time and money. Since sampling and data collection approaches have different costs, it is important to compare their costs and time requirements with their advantages and disadvantages. Personal, in-depth interviewing, for example, may be necessary to discover motives, but the technique is costly and time-consuming. Sample sizes, therefore, would have to be reduced to make the research project affordable. Mail samples are less expensive to select and contact, but take more time and have lower response rates than telephone samples.

The high costs of conducting marketing research surveys has promoted a search for more efficient sampling procedures. To meet the demands for better information from samples, marketing researchers have attempted to reduce total survey error and response bias and to estimate more accurately any error that remains.[4]

Designing the Data Collection Form. Information rarely exists in a form readily usable by the researcher. This is true for both secondary data sources as well as primary data collected by survey techniques. We need, therefore, to prepare a data collection form which will maximize the usefulness of the information collected. An example of a secondary data collection form is shown in Figure 6-3. In this case the marketing researcher is attempting to estimate the market potential for a product which is a component of several manufactured products. Because differences may exist in projections made by different forecasters, data has been collected from five sources. The researcher can then prepare a composite forecast.

The development of a good questionnaire requires care in planning and testing. The form should be as simple and concise as possible and yet be complete enough to provide the necessary data. Unnecessary questions should be avoided unless they help to increase recall or response rates. The specific question topics, question wording, placement, and means of answering the questions, all have an effect on the response rate and response error of the survey. Figure 6-4 shows a questionnaire for determining the corporate images and brand awareness of oil field supply companies. The respondents were oil field supply purchasing managers and engineers.

Product description:	
Type of component use:	
SIC code:	

Year	Total U.S. shipments from				
	Predicasts	Census of Business	Survey of Business	U.S. Industrial Outlook	Frost & Sullivan
1970					
1975					
1976					
1977					
1978					
1979					
1980					
1981					
1982					
1983					
1984					
1985					
1990					
1995					
Annual growth					

(Years 1970–1983 labeled "Actual"; 1984–1995 labeled "Forecasted")

FIGURE 6-3. Form for collecting secondary data.

The Data Collection Process. Once the sources of information have been identified and the questionnaire designed, the next step is to collect the data. There are three basic methods of obtaining information from respondents. *Personal interviewing* involves direct, face-to-face exchange between the interviewer and the respondent. Although it is the most costly type of interviewing, it may be necessary if complex questions are being asked, if objects or pictures are being shown, or if extensive probing is required. When using personal interviews (or when purchasing the services of an outside marketing research firm), precautions should be taken to minimize interviewer bias and to provide for field interviewing controls (such as following up to ensure that interviews were actually made).[5]

The *focus group* interview (a form of personal interviewing) is a popular and inexpensive method for obtaining ideas about a subject which can be used in planning further research. A trained researcher acts as moderator for a group of from eight to twelve respondents gathered together to discuss a particular topic, such as a new product. Based on this discussion, which may last for two hours or

SURVEY OF OIL FIELD CHEMICAL SUPPLIERS

1. How well do you know each of the following suppliers of oil field chemicals? (Please check one box for each company.)

	Well	Moderately well	I know this company: Somewhat	Hardly at all	Never heard of it
Aquaness	☐	☐	☐	☐	☐
Enjay Chemical	☐	☐	☐	☐	☐
Sinclair	☐	☐	☐	☐	☐
Tretolite	☐	☐	☐	☐	☐
Visco	☐	☐	☐	☐	☐

(Please answer questions 2 through 6 only for those companies you've heard of. If you haven't heard of any, please skip to question 7.)

2. Have you seen or heard any advertising on oil field chemicals recently by any of these companies?

	Aquaness	Enjay Chemical	Sinclair	Tretolite	Visco
Yes	☐	☐	☐	☐	☐
No	☐	☐	☐	☐	☐

3. Please check which of these companies you believe are mainly captive suppliers selling principally to parent crude oil companies, and those which sell to the entire crude oil producing industry. (Please check one box for each company you've heard of.)

	Captive supplier selling mainly to parent company	Sells to entire crude oil producing industry	Don't know
Aquaness	☐	☐	☐
Enjay	☐	☐	☐
Sinclair	☐	☐	☐
Tretolite	☐	☐	☐
Visco	☐	☐	☐

4. Check which of the companies listed to the left uses these brand names. (Only one check mark in each column.)

	Breaxit	Coat	Corexit	Cronox	Drop	Kontol	Surflo
Aquaness	☐	☐	☐	☐	☐	☐	☐
Enjay	☐	☐	☐	☐	☐	☐	☐
Sinclair	☐	☐	☐	☐	☐	☐	☐
Tretolite	☐	☐	☐	☐	☐	☐	☐
Visco	☐	☐	☐	☐	☐	☐	☐
Don't know	☐	☐	☐	☐	☐	☐	☐

(Please turn)

Page 2

5. Please rate each of the following companies using the scale at the left. Take Aquaness, for example. If you think they rate "very good" on product performance, mark the company 5; if you think they're "very poor" mark them 0. Of course you may want to rate them any number in between. Please rate each of the other companies the same way on product performance.

Very good
5
4
3
2
1
0
Very poor

	Aquaness	Enjay	Sinclair	Tretolite	Visco
a) Product performance	___	___	___	___	___

Using the same rating scale above, please rate each of these companies with a number on each of the following factors:

	Aquaness	Enjay	Sinclair	Tretolite	Visco
b) Technical service	___	___	___	___	___
c) Lowest possible cost to do the job	___	___	___	___	___
d) Sales service	___	___	___	___	___
e) Completeness of product line	___	___	___	___	___
f) Reputation as a supplier	___	___	___	___	___

6. For each company, please check the products listed which you believe it offers. Check as many products as apply for each company:

	Aquaness	Enjay	Sinclair	Tretolite	Visco
Bactericides	☐	☐	☐	☐	☐
Demulsifiers	☐	☐	☐	☐	☐
Scale chemicals	☐	☐	☐	☐	☐
Anti-foulants	☐	☐	☐	☐	☐
Paraffin chemicals	☐	☐	☐	☐	☐
Corrosion inhibitors	☐	☐	☐	☐	☐
Surfactants	☐	☐	☐	☐	☐

And now, for tabulating purposes only,

7. What is your job function? (Please be specific, e.g., purchasing department manager, district engineer, etc.)

_____

8. Please check the statement below which most closely defines the degree of your involvement in the selection of individual oil field chemical suppliers. (Please check one.)

Have final say ☐
Make decisions subject to approval ☐
Approve products from a technical point of view only ☐
Place order, but not otherwise involved ☐
Not involved ☐

Thank you for your help.

FIGURE 6-4. Corporate image questionnaire with brand question. *Source:* Paul L. Erdos, *Professional Mail Surveys*, McGraw-Hill, New York, 1970, pp. 531–532.

more, the researcher may discern deep seated attitudes about the subject which may not be brought out in a one-on-one interview.[6] Because the small group is not a representative sample of the universe, it should not be used for predictive purposes.

The second basic method, *telephone interviewing*, is used widely. It offers the advantages of speed, lower cost, and excellent control. Its disadvantages are the limited types of questions which may be asked (no pictures, for instance) and the possibility of the wrong household member being interviewed.

The third basic method of data collection is by *mailed questionnaires*. Lengthy questionnaires can be used, although shorter ones tend to have a higher response rate. Interest in the subject increases response rates. Hence, specific targets (e.g., engineers, accountants, or college professors) may respond to subjects of interest to them at rates of 60 percent or more, whereas rates of 20 percent are considered good for general audiences. The principal advantage of mail questionnaires is lower cost per response. The principal disadvantage is uncertainty over how representative is the sample of those who responded. You always wonder how the 40 to 80 percent who didn't answer would have affected the results. Procedures for reducing this uncertainty raise the cost and lengthen the time frame of the study.[7]

Data Analysis. Once the information has been gathered, it must be analyzed. But first the data are prepared for computer tabulation; they are edited, coded, prepared for computer entry, and validated. Editing clarifies statements, marks, or other uncertainties on the questionnaire form made by either the respondent or the interviewer. Coding classifies respondent information to make it usable by a computer. Codes are then transferred to data processing cards or tapes, or typed directly into a terminal. Data are checked for accuracy before the information is processed by the computer.

The data are now ready for initial analysis. A *frequency distribution** is usually prepared for each question for comparison with anticipated findings. Also, cross tabulations of sets of two or three of the variables may be run to spot possible relationships, which may warrant further analysis or research. Figure 6-5 illustrates this kind of analysis. Collected from a national sample of 1500 licensed sportsmen, this table represents the cross tabulation of product ownership with respondents' occupations. The marketing manager of the sporting goods company which sponsored the study used this information to select specific target markets for a variety of products the company produced.

There are other and more sophisticated statistical means of data analysis which may be appropriate for certain situations. However, relatively simple frequency distributions and cross tabulations suffice for most market research data analyses.

Using the Information

Interpretation of Findings. A marketing research project does not end with analysis of the data. The findings should be interpreted in a way that is most useful to the decision maker. Too often, a voluminous report is submitted with many pages of data but with little about the managerial implications. The key to interpretation is

---

* A "frequency distribution" classifies data by some specific, perceptible characteristics, usually in table or graph form.

Products \ Occupation	Professional or technical	Craftspeople	Manager or proprietor	Laborer	Service worker	Sales or clerical	Business executive	Percentage of total sample owning each product
Backpack	38	14	26	19	19	13	37	25
Boat	1	4	2	0	0	1	8	2
Bow	8	3	4	1	1	2	5	4
Camp axe	15	8	9	5	10	12	24	12
Camp stove	10	3	3	1	4	5	10	6
Canoe	4	3	1	1	0	0	4	2
Compass	16	10	4	2	2	3	12	8
Fishing reel	59	42	30	35	20	18	51	37
Fishing rod	61	42	30	34	22	21	50	38
Handgun	26	5	36	27	10	6	23	20
Hunting knife	22	12	11	11	9	12	24	15
Hunting vest	13	4	4	2	0	1	20	7
Ice skates	17	3	13	2	3	7	18	10
Pellet gun	31	12	24	16	16	10	31	21
Pocket knife	89	93	69	78	51	42	56	68
Rifle	31	20	34	14	8	13	41	24
Shotgun	37	21	31	16	12	18	43	26
Skis	24	10	21	7	8	13	32	17
Tennis racket	51	21	42	18	18	28	51	34
Tent	26	13	21	5	3	10	17	14
Toboggan	8	2	7	2	4	5	9	6

Numbers represent the percentage of respondents in each occupation who own the specific product. For example, 38% of the respondents in a professional or technical occupation own a backpack.

FIGURE 6-5. Crosstabulation of ownership of recreational products with occupation.

relating the findings to the original hypotheses and to the purpose of the research project.

Preparing the Research Report. Results of the research project may be reported orally, in writing, or both. Oral reports are usually made in brief form to a management meeting where questions can be asked and discussion occurs. Written reports are more formal and comprehensive, but should contain summaries for the busy executive not interested in detail. While practices vary, the following is representative of the organization of a report.

Executive Summary

Purpose of the Project

Brief Statement of Methods Used

Findings

Interpretations

Conclusions

Limitations of the Project

Appendices

Details of Methodology

Types of Analyses

Data Tables

Using the Findings to Make a Decision. Marketing research which does not meet the test of applicability does not represent a good use of money. A well planned and well executed study should help with marketing decision making. Yet we need to bear in mind that many factors besides marketing research projects have an impact upon decisions. Marketing research is a tool, not a crutch, for decision making.

Organizing the Marketing Research Function

There is a direct correlation between size of a company and the size of its marketing research department, as shown in Figure 6-6. Size of the company, however, is not the only determinant. The overriding factor is the anticipated benefit associated with the cost of the department; the more extensive and frequent the marketing research analyses required, the larger the personnel and operating budgets. The size of the department also increases as its tasks become more complex. Figure 6-7 shows how this evolution occurs.

FIGURE 6-6. Median number of full-time employees—by company type and size. *Source:* Dik Warren Twedt, *1978 Survey of Marketing Research,* American Marketing Association, Chicago, 1978.

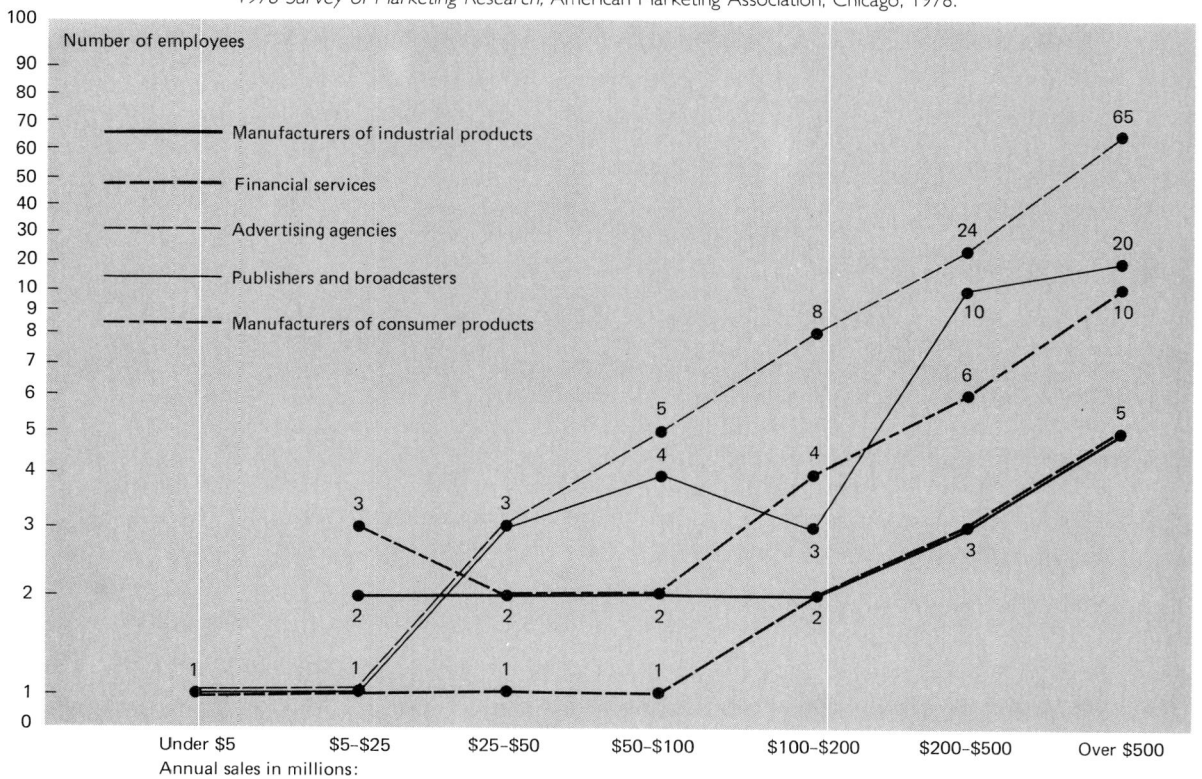

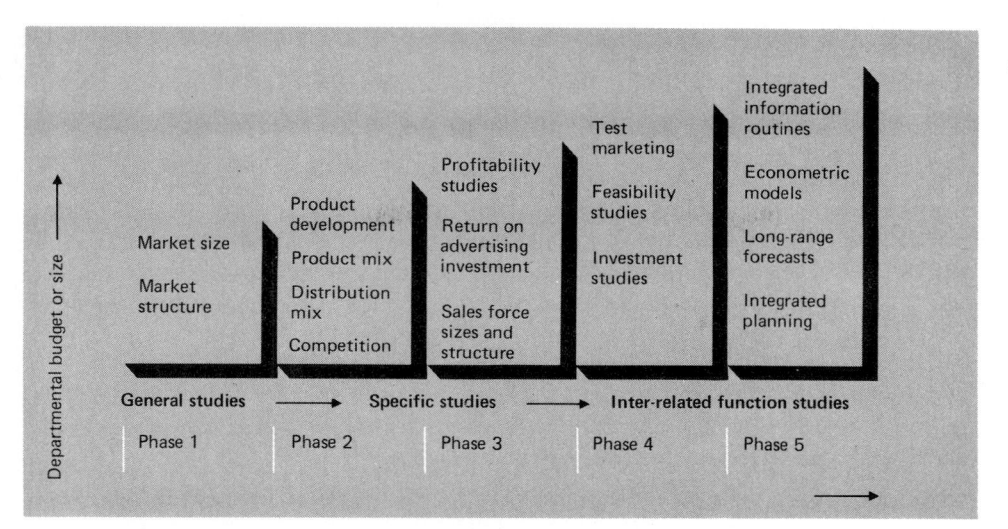

FIGURE 6-7. Evolution of corporate marketing research. *Source:* Lee Adler and Charles Mayer, *Managing the Marketing Research Function,* American Marketing Association, Chicago, 1977, p. 85, as adapted from Aubrey Wilson, Industrial Research Seminar, Toronto, May 18, 1976.

The marketing research manager usually reports to the marketing manager. Marketing research departments normally are located at headquarters in functionally organized companies and at the division level in divisionalized companies. In some divisionalized companies, however, the marketing research function is centralized at corporate headquarters from whence it supplies research services to the divisions.

Wherever it is located in the organization, it is important that the marketing research function complement the marketing information system (if the company has one). Whereas marketing research is an accepted function in most companies, marketing information systems are only in their developmental phase.

THE MARKETING INFORMATION SYSTEM

Marketing research usually is conducted on request to provide information relevant to the solution of specific problems as they occur. The marketing information system (MIS) is designed to provide a continuously updated information base that is readily available as problems occur or when plans need to be made or changed. As marketing becomes more complex, the marketing manager needs more information faster than the traditional marketing research function can offer. The marketing information system attempts to fulfill this need. MIS can be defined as:

> A system which provides a continuous flow of marketing information useful for management decisons.

The MIS gathers data from such sources as the marketing research department, the sales force, customers' orders, shipments, competitors, trade associations, and the government. In a company employing MIS, marketing research is an important source of input to the system but is not limited to this role.

Types of Marketing Information Systems

Marketing information systems generally fall into three categories. The first is simply a massive *data bank*, usually computerized, from which marketing management may request specific pieces of information. It provides procedures for collecting, storing, and retrieving information.

A second type of marketing information system is a *statistical bank* which enables the marketing manager to investigate consequences of a variety of situations. It can respond to "what if" types of questions. For example, a manager may ask, "What would happen if I allowed the sales force to deviate from published prices by more than ten percent?" This type of system utilizes the statistical bank to develop mathematical relationships between variables as an aid in predicting outcomes. Predictions may be *deterministic* (based on specific functional relationships), *stochastic* (based on probabilistic relationships), or *behavioral* (based on relationships of a variety of marketing variables).

A third type of MIS includes a *model bank* and is designed to help marketing management identify optimal solutions to marketing problems. For example, when planning media programs, the advertising manager with a predetermined advertising budget may wish to know what mix of periodicals would maximize the exposure of advertisements to a target market.

Regardless of the type of marketing information system, its function is to support the marketing decision process. The more advanced the system the more it should add to the efficiency with which decisions are made. A key determinant of the system's contribution to the decision process is the way the system is structured.

Design of a Marketing Information System

Components of the MIS. There are five principal components to the MIS: hardware, software, information, procedures, and personnel.[8] The *hardware* component is the physical apparatus used to store the information. While common usage implies the presence of electronic computer facilities, hardware can be anything which has the capacity for containing information. A simple filing system or a library can provide adequate hardware facilities for many marketing applications. However, for efficiency and speed, many marketing information systems utilize computers. In addition to the computer itself, hardware also includes input devices, which feed information to the computer, output devices, which record or display the results, and peripheral storage equipment (e.g., magnetic tapes or disks), which holds information until it is called for by the computer program.

Operating programs, called *software*, instruct the computer to isolate specific sets of data and perform calculations and analyses with them. Regression or correlation analyses and sorting routines are examples of commonly used software programs. The information base consists of the specific bits of data which have been collected for use within the system. Procedure manuals are needed to provide instructions to people who will use the system.

The final component of a marketing information system is the people who make it work. The MIS roll call includes people with titles such as systems analyst, programmer, computer operator, operation researcher, statistician, model builder, and marketing researcher—and their managers.

Structure of the MIS. The schematic representation of a marketing information system, shown in Figure 6-8, places into a consistent framework the five components of the MIS and the three types of systems we have discussed. The users of the system—marketing managers and researchers—interact with it through the input-output unit. Information is stored in the data bank and can be retrieved as it is entered into the system or can be further analyzed. The statistical bank contains computer programs (software) which permit analyses of the data by means of various statistical techniques.

The model bank does not contain an overall model of the firm's interaction with its environment, but rather a variety of specialized models dealing with specific marketing functions or phenomena. Examples of models that might be included in the model bank are distribution locations, sales force allocation, media mix, advertising effectiveness, brand loyalty, attitude change, and product evaluation.[9]

Operating the Marketing Information System

The Inputs. Despite advances in computer hardware and software, statistical analysis, and modeling techniques, the basic determinant of the usefulness of the MIS remains the quality of the data placed in the data bank. These data may be in the form of the results of a special research project, purchased consumer panel or retail

FIGURE 6-8. Structure of a marketing information system. *Source:* Adapted from David Montgomery and Glen Urban, "Marketing Decision-Information Systems: An Emerging View," *Journal of Marketing Research,* May 1970, p. 227.

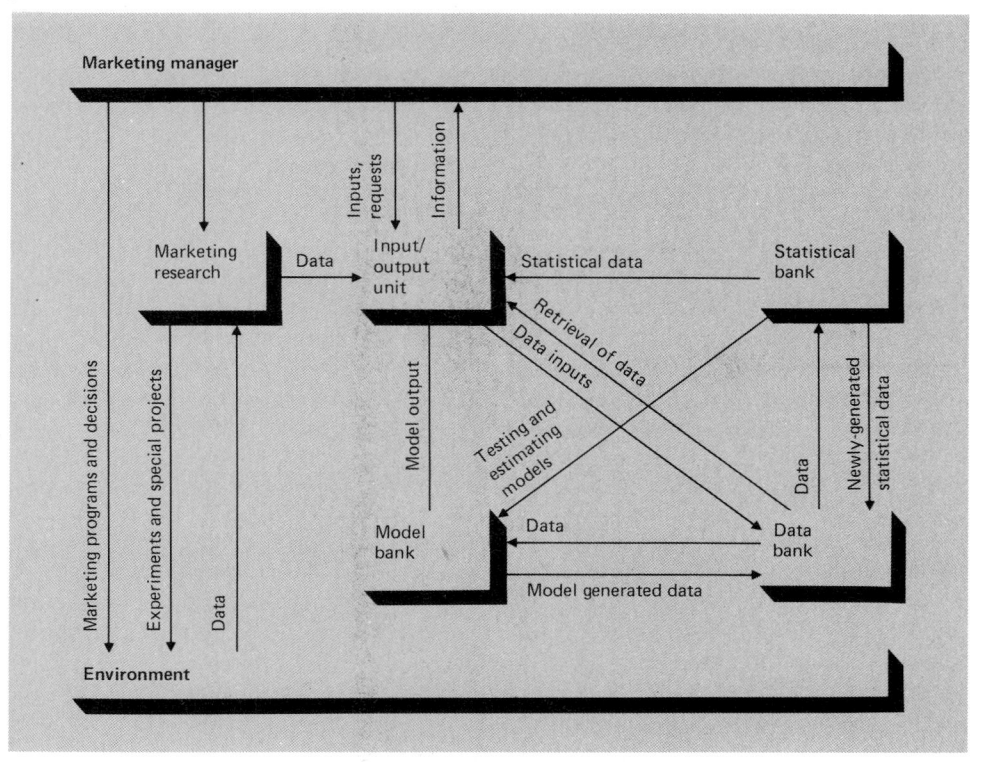

audit data, or periodic reports of orders and deliveries. Details of the firm's marketing programs and their results (prices, margins, promotions, distribution, sales, and market share) should be included as well as similar data on competitors. Increased attention also is being given to scanning uncontrollable environmental factors for additional information inputs. At the end of Part Two, you will see in the Heublein, Inc., cases how environmental scanning is used for strategic planning purposes.

All marketing data may not be of value for decision making; therefore, data should be screened for relevance before being entered in the data bank. Similarly, caution should be exercised before discarding data from the bank, since many models require histories of data.

Retained data should be abstracted to enable system users to determine whether data is relevant to a specific decision without having to read large volumes of data. The abstracts contain brief descriptions of the data, the source, the population from which it was collected, the dates during which it was collected, and procedures to gain access to it. While abstracting reduces the time required for the user to obtain information, it does not provide a quick access mechanism to all relevant data in the system. This is the function of indexing. Indexing is a process in which all data in the MIS are identified by key words or topics. The decision maker can use these key words (or code numbers associated with them) to call out information from the system.

Using the Data. Data contained in the MIS can be recalled by the marketing manager as needed, usually in a summary format such as a frequency distribution (in either tabular or graphical form). All of the original data should be retained, however, to permit further analysis and model development. Storage of only the summary data would greatly reduce the value of the entire MIS.

Developing Models. Frequently the results of basic or even advanced statistical analysis do not provide a meaningful basis for marketing decision-making. Under these conditions the marketing manager can use one or more of the models in the model bank most appropriate for the specific problem. For unique situations the user may be able to combine several different models or develop new ones to obtain the most useful result. In fact, the user can step beyond the capabilities of the firm's MIS by gaining access to a commercial time-sharing computer system containing different models. Several companies provide such services including General Electric's Information Services Business Division which offers access to models through its MARK III time-sharing service.

Building the Marketing Information System

While the persons tending the model bank must have extensive training and experience, the complexity of the models used will depend on the marketing manager's ability and willingness to use them. Model banks normally develop parallel with management interest. **Marketing Note 6-2** shows an evolutionary approach to developing an MIS.

The Preliminary Stage. For a marketing information system to function properly, it needs the support of top management, potential users of the system, and those

Steps to Building a Marketing Information System

MARKETING NOTE 6-2

Preliminary stage:

Communicate intentions to build an MIS

Obtain cooperation from potential users

Obtain top management approval

Prepare an inventory of decisions currently being made, decisions which marketing managers would like to make, and decisions which they are likely to be making in the future

Data bank stage:

Determine information needed to make the decisions inventoried above

Determine current and potential sources of the necessary information

Determine the forms in which the information will be made available

Obtain hardware, software, and personnel needed for the data bank

Train marketing managers in the use and misuse of the MIS

Statistical bank stage:

Determine shortcomings of simple data bank

Select the appropriate statistical techniques and make them compatible with the data bank

Recruit and/or train personnel

Model bank stage:

Determine shortcomings of improved MIS

Determine the subjective models used by marketing management

Obtain commercially available models which will be useful for marketing decision making

Recruit and/or train personnel

Develop specialized marketing models

---

who must help with its development (e.g. operations research and computer specialists). Such backing helps to eliminate false starts, minimize bureaucratic obstacles, and even uncover rudimentary information systems which already exist. In this stage, the decisions that managers are making currently should be classified and recorded along with those they would like to make with the aid of additional and more timely information.

Data Bank. To create the *data bank* the needed information must be identified, gathered, evaluated, abstracted, indexed, and stored. Computer hardware, software, and the people to operate them must be obtained. Marketing managers and other users of the data bank must be trained in its proper use and later in the use of statistical and model banks. Benefits as well as limitations should be made clear. A frequent reason for low usage of an MIS is lack of understanding of what it can and cannot accomplish.[10]

Statistical Bank. As managers become more familiar with the MIS, they will begin asking for more than basic analyses of data. They may ask for mathematical relationships among marketing and buyer variables or for the examination of differences among buyers. These and other similar extensions of the system will necessitate the use of more advanced analytical techniques which must then be collected and integrated within the existing MIS.

Model Bank. As users become even more accustomed to the potential of the MIS, they will look to the system for more help with decision making. Models will be needed, first to assist with routine decisions (e.g., inventory control and media purchases), then to help in the explanation of market phenomena (e.g., brand switching or attitude change models). Managers' own subjective models can become the first components of the model bank. Commercially available models may also be included. And operations researchers can be used for preparing models internally.

SUMMARY

Marketing research provides a link between the marketing decision maker and the firm's marketing environment. Its two basic functions are to gather information and test hypotheses which are useful for marketing decision making. The marketing research process begins with a definition of the purpose of the research. It is followed by developing a study plan, conducting the research, analyzing and interpreting the findings, and it ends when the decision is made. Some examples of marketing research are found in product research, economic and market analysis, advertising research, and pricing and sales research.

Marketing information systems extend marketing research from a project-to-project basis to a continuous management information function. Marketing information systems have evolved from mere data bases, to statistical banks, to model banks, thereby greatly increasing management's ability to utilize vast amounts of information. Models can also be used to test ideas and strategies prior to actual implementation.

Chapters 3 and 4 presented a variety of types of information which the marketing manager should consider when making decisions. Chapter 5 described the ways in which consumers and organizational buyers react to marketing programs. These types of information are gathered through marketing research, environmental scanning, and other means of obtaining market intelligence. They are then stored and analyzed in the MIS, and finally used by marketing management in its decision making. Marketing research processes and marketing information systems are concerned with what *did happen* and what *is happening* in the interactions between the firm and the market environment. Chapter 7 will extend this process to the future—forecasting what *is likely to happen* tomorrow.

QUESTIONS

1. Distinguish between making a decision under risk and making a decision under uncertainty.
2. What is the relationship between information and marketing planning?
3. What is marketing research and what are its principal applications?
4. Describe primary and secondary data sources.

5. What is a marketing information system (MIS)? What are its data sources? What is its purpose?
6. What are the five principal components of the marketing information system?

REFERENCES

1. Stuart D. Watson, "What the Chief Executive Will Require of His Marketing Professionals," in Peter LaPlaca (ed.), *The New Role of the Marketing Professional*, American Marketing Association, Chicago, 1977, p. 19.
2. Ralph S. Alexander, *Marketing Definitions*, American Marketing Association, Chicago, 1963, p. 16.
3. William F. O'Dell, "Problem Delineation," in Robert Ferber (ed.), *Handbook of Marketing Research*, McGraw–Hill, New York, 1974, pp. 2.3–2.10.
4. See for example: Martin L. Frankel and Lester R. Frankel, "Some Recent Developments in Sample Survey Design," *Journal of Marketing Research*, August 1977, pp. 280–293; Clyde L. Rich, "Is Random Digit Dialing Really Necessary?" *Journal of Marketing Research*, August 1977, pp. 300–305; and E. Laird Landon and Sharon K. Banks, "Relative Efficiency and Bias of Plus–One Telephone Sampling," *Journal of Marketing Research*, August 1977, pp. 294–299.
5. For more on data collection and interview forms, see Ed Blair, Seymour Sudman, Norman Bradburn, and Carol Stocking, "How to Ask Questions about Drinking and Sex: Response Effects in Measuring Consumer Behavior," *Journal of Marketing Research*, August 1977, pp. 316–321; Paul L. Erdos, *Professional Mail Surveys*, McGraw–Hill, New York, 1970, p. 123; and J. R. McKinzie, "An Investigation into Interviewer Effects in Market Research," *Journal of Marketing Research*, August 1977, pp. 330–336.
6. Danny Bellenger, Kenneth Bernhardt, and Jac Goldstucker, *Qualitative Research in Marketing*, American Marketing Association, Chicago, 1976; and Bobby Calder, "Focus Groups and the Nature of Qualitative Marketing Research," *Journal of Marketing Research*, August 1977, pp. 353–364.
7. For more on mail questionnaires, see Paul L. Erdos, "Data Collection Methods: Mail Surveys," in Robert Ferber, *Handbook of Marketing Research*, McGraw–Hill, New York, 1974, pp. 2.90–2.104; A. B. Blankenship, *Professional Telephone Surveys*, McGraw–Hill, New York, 1977; Allan Rawnsley, *Manual of Industrial Marketing Research*, Wiley, New York, 1978, p. 36.
8. William King, *Marketing Management Information Systems*, Petrocelli Charter, New York, 1977, pp. 19–24.
9. For discussions of marketing models, see Ralph Day and Thomas Ness, *Marketing Models: Behavioral Science Applications*, Intext Educational Publishers, Scranton, Pa., 1971; Ralph Day and Leonard Parsons, *Marketing Models: Quantitative Applications*, Intext Educational Publishers, Scranton, Pa., 1971; Arnold Amstutz, *Computer Simulation of Competitive Market Response*, MIT Press, Cambridge, Mass., 1967; and Philip Kotler, *Marketing Decision Making: A Model Building Approach*, Holt, Rinehart and Winston, New York, 1971.
10. Charles D. Schewe, "Marketing Information Systems—The Problem of System Usage," *Journal of the Academy of Marketing Science*, Winter 1975, pp. 290–298.

CHAPTER 7

Sales Forecasting

Managers must try to predict future conditions so that their goals and plans are realistic. While no one can predict precisely what lies ahead, management should not reject the notion of forecasting; to assume the continuation of the status quo —given the dynamic and varied conditions of the business and market climate—is both myopic and unreasonable.

Of particular importance is the development of reasonably accurate sales forecasts for each product marketed by the firm. A sales forecast is not a number provided by some soothsayer after gazing into a crystal ball; rather, it is a *reasonable estimate* of the sales likely to occur under anticipated environmental circumstances.

Sales Forecasting Defined

A sales forecast can be expressed in terms of estimated unit sales or dollar revenues, or both. It may be long- or short-term. It may be for each market or for the composite of all markets served by the firm. A sales forecast may be defined as:

> A quantitative estimate—expressed in units and/or dollars—of future sales for a specific time period, under assumed marketing programs and environmental conditions.

The responsibility for the preparation of the sales forecast rests with the chief marketing executive for each division of the company, although the ultimate decision is made by the division manager. The actual work of forecasting will likely be delegated to others: the head of forecasting, chief economist, sales manager, or director of marketing research. Often the task is shared by several people.

Uses of Sales Forecasting

Sales forecasting is the starting point for business planning. It influences the marketing effort required to obtain the forecasted sales; the amounts of raw materials, production, and inventories needed to fill customers' orders; and the amounts of cash needed to finance these operations. Forecasting sales is more than a statistical exercise because the marketing, production, and finance plans themselves influence the sales that will be obtained. Sales forecasting, therefore, begins with assumptions about the market and the business plans of the company. The final forecast may have been modified more than once during the process of crystalizing the business plans. Once the forecast is approved by management, it becomes a key marketing and business objective. In Part Three we will see how sales forecasting is interwoven with the fabric of business and marketing planning. You should bear in mind that although preparing sales forecasts is a responsibility of marketing management, more than marketing considerations are involved in the forecast.

DIMENSIONS OF FORECASTING

Several factors need to be considered before starting the sales forecast. These are the time period to be covered, the scope of the forecast, the assumptions to be used, and the degree of effort and expense to be devoted to the forecast.

Time Period

The period covered by the sales forecast will depend on the purpose of the forecast. Table 7-1 gives examples of uses for five different time periods.

Short-range forecasts are less subject to environmental effects than longer ones and the uses of these shorter forecasts require greater accuracy. Since the firm at any point may be engaged in several types of decision making, it is quite common to find forecasts covering several time periods, such as by month, year, and multiyear. The overlap in these forecasts helps to promote a degree of continuity. Not all firms need to deal with such a multiplicity of time horizons; rather forecasts are developed to meet the informational needs of the particular company. Novelty toys or campaign buttons, for example, require only short-term forecasts, whereas the forest products industry must think about how long it takes a tree to grow.

Scope of the Forecast

In summary form the forecast will list the expected sales for the company by time periods, broken down by divisions or other business units. Depending on how the company is organized and the ways it views its target markets, forecasts may be broken down *geographically* (e.g., by sales region and salesperson's territory), *by type of market* (e.g., consumer, institutional, or industrial), or *by channel of distribution* (e.g., wholesaler, chain, or direct). Forecasts will also be broken out *by individual product* for marketing and production planning purposes.

Another measure of the scope of the sales forecasting effort is the number of forecasts to be prepared. Because it is impossible to foresee all conditions that will affect actual sales, many companies prepare more than one forecast: for example, high, medium, and low forecasts. The high forecast is the estimate of possible sales if all goes right; the medium forecast represents the most likely—or expected—estimate of sales; and the low forecast is the level of sales which can be made in all but the most negative circumstances. In companies using this multiple-range approach, expense budgets are initially developed for the middle, or expected forecast. As the period covered by the forecast moves forward, expenses may be adjusted upward or downward depending upon actual levels of sales, thereby avoiding the embarrassment of missing profit objectives.

TABLE 7-1
Time Periods of Forecasts, Factors Determining Time Periods, and Major Uses

	Time Periods	Factors Determining Time Periods	Major Uses
Very short-range forecast	1–6 months, but sometimes longer	Manufacturing and marketing cycle from ordering materials to shipping finished products to customers and collecting accounts receivable	Planning purchases, inventories, employees' work schedules, production schedules, transportation, and working capital
Short-range forecast	1 or 2 years, often detailed by quarters or months	Company's fiscal year, seasonal fluctuations in business	Budgeting receipts and expenditures and planning employment, working capital, tax actions, and marketing programs
Medium-range forecast	3–5 years (from end of short-range forecast to period covered by long-range forecast)	Length of business cycle, time required to bring new facilities into production, to hire and train workers, to bring new products to a commercial stage	Timing of capital expenditures and planning marketing strategy, personnel development, product and market development, research programs, and acquisitions
Long-range forecast	5–15 years	Economic life of major plants and equipment, product life cycles (from new product stage to mature product stage), remaining life of major patents	Development of company objectives and planning major capital expenditures and specific acquisitions
Very long-range forecast	15–30 years	Life of mineral deposits, oil and gas reserves, and woodlands owned by the company and its suppliers, and time required for revolutionary technological, economic, and social changes	Establishing overall company objectives, planning major raw material sources, planning basic technological development work, and developing acquisition policies

Source: Bay E. Estes, Jr. "Sales Forecasting," in Victor P. Buell (ed.), *The Handbook of Modern Marketing,* McGraw-Hill, New York, 1970, pp. 6–98.

Assumptions of Forecasting

Since a sales forecast is an estimate of some future sales activity, the forecaster bases this estimate on certain assumptions. These should always be stated in the introduction to the forecast. Assumptions can be categorized as economic, demographic and social, political, technological, and competitive.

Economic Assumption. Companies marketing in the entire United States will need to make assumptions about the future of the entire U.S. economy: What will be the gross national product? Will the current rate of growth be sustained or will it decrease? Will family disposable income rise or fall—and by how much? What is the expected rate of unemployment? Experience will indicate to which of these factors the sales forecast is most sensitive and how much deviation from an assumed level can be tolerated before the sales forecast must be modified. Correlation analysis—discussed later in the chapter—can be useful in determining relationships between economic factors and industry sales.

Table 7-2 shows a method of estimating the impacts that possible economic and other events will have on the demand for hospital sales of a variety of medical solutions sold in containers larger than 50 cubic centimeters (cc). The column headed "event number" contains the computer code for the specific event. A brief description of the event is given in the "forecast." The next two columns show the probability that the forecasted event will occur by 1980 or 1990. "Years to first

TABLE 7-2
Events Used in Impact Analysis

Event Number	Forecast	Probability 1980	Probability 1990	Years to First Impact	Years to Maximum Impact	Maximum Impact, %
4162	Recession: GNP does not exceed annual growth rate of 2.5% for at least 2 consecutive years.	.10	.75	0	1	−10
4161	Number of persons age 65 or over increases 29.6% over a 15-year period (1960–1974 increase was 30.8%).	.01	.90	0	1	−1
4119	The federal government institutes control of prices of medical supplies comparable to the maximum allowable costs (MAC) set for reimbursement of patient expenditures for drugs.	.10	.20	0	1	−1
4073	Group buying accounts for 25% of all hospital purchases (1976 = 15%).	.30	.75	1	2	+1
4024	Chemotherapy supplants surgery and/or radiation as treatment of choice for colon, breast, and prostate cancer.	.10	40	1	5	+1
4129	Availability of a scanner which provides more accurate information about mineral and other deficiencies and diseases in bone than is available in 1977.	.10	.30	5	10	+3
4163	National health insurance plan enacted to provide comprehensive coverage for all groups. Poor and aged are covered by government; workers through private insurance.	.30	.75	1	2	+3
4160	Number of persons age 25 to 64 increases 27% over a 15-year period (1960–1974 increase was 3%).	.01	.80	0	1	+4

Source: HS.1 Hospital Sales: Solutions over 50cc, The Futures Group and IMS America Ltd., Glastonbury, Conn., August 1977.

impact" and "years to maximum impact" indicate the time in years before the event will affect the demand for the medical solution sales, if it does in fact occur. Finally, the last column represents the amount of that impact expressed as a percent of forecasted sales.

Demographic and Social Assumptions. Consumer goods firms are most directly affected by the demographics of the marketplace. The sales forecast—particularly the longer-term ones—should make specific assumptions about trends in population and income when developing future sales scenarios. Certainly Gerber must consider anticipated births in developing its forecast of baby food sales. Other demographic factors which may affect sales forecasts are family size, occupation, racial and ethnic background, working spouses, and ownership of major items (such as automobiles and appliances).

Other influencing factors are social trends, which reflect society's changing attitudes toward the world about us. Some current examples are a greater percentage of women in the work force, smaller families, and attitudes toward religious institutions.

A number of far-reaching studies have been made to probe these and other types of trends. **Marketing Note 7-1** is from one such report. Since the impact of a changing trend on a sales forecast may be unknown, it is important for the forecaster to be explicit in stating the assumptions used. With benefit of hindsight you can check the accuracy of some of the projections for the 1980 to 1990 period in Marketing Note 7-1.

Political and Technological Assumptions. Future legal and political actions often are difficult to predict. The halting of further development of B-1 bombers caused great joy at Boeing (builders of the B-52) and an equal amount of agony at Rockwell International (prime contractor on the B-1).[1] Certainly those persons responsible for predicting sales had to make explicit assumptions about the "politics" of the decision. The Michigan Chemical Company, the manufacturer of the product Tris, used in flameproofing children's pajamas, had a serious problem when its product was banned by the Consumer Product Safety Commission.[2] Not only did the company lose future revenues, but it also had to recall all Tris-impregnated garments and reimburse consumers, retailers, and clothing manufacturers.

The United States Federal Aviation Administration developed a series of forecasts of needs for new airports and new types of airplanes, each based on a set of specific assumptions, or scenarios, encompassing population growth, economic growth, and governmental intervention. Figure 7-1 shows the different forecasts of revenue passenger miles for the year 2000 based on each assumption.

The United States for many years led the world in technological innovations. Despite an apparent slowing down of this process, we continue to see a constant stream of new product introductions.[3] The sales forecaster must monitor such changes and realize that a new innovation may render the company's product sales forecast obsolete. Disregard for such influences has caused many forecasters to prepare résumés rather than forecasts.

Competitive Assumptions. A final but highly important external influence about which assumptions must be made is competition. In hotly competitive industries, forecasters often develop multiple forecasts, each based on a different

The Future of Transit in The United States: Some Projections

MARKETING NOTE 7-1

Intermediate Future (1980–1990)

- In 1985, 10 percent of the activities that now require travel will be done through electronic communication.
- There will be a growing trend toward labor strikes that tie up mass transit systems. By 1985, bus riders will experience a 10 percent increase in strike disruptions of services.
- There will be permanent rationing of gas, fuel oil, and gasoline.
- There will be negative incentives for large energy users, the opposite of the present pricing system.
- Driving automobiles will be discouraged and tolls for entering downtown areas will be imposed. In some cities, cars will be banned from downtown areas altogether.
- Lack of adequate highway maintenance will raise insurance rates and cause more accidents.
- Free transit rides will be commonplace by the late 1980s.
- A practical high-density battery or fuel cell will be developed, making electric cars competitive for city use in the early 1980s.
- Small electric vehicles will be mass produced.
- By 1985, 20 percent of personal vehicles will be largely pollution free.
- All eight-cylinder cars will be phased out.

Long-Term Future (1990 on)

- The distances people travel to work on buses or rapid transit will nearly double in the next 30 years.
- Per-capita car ownership will be reduced slightly during the next 30 years, but there will be increased use of rental and leased cars.
- Demand for rapid transit will nearly double by 2005.
- Freeways and expressways are losing their popularity and with more people turning to public transportation, opposition to building new freeways will increase three-fold within the next 30 years.
- One out of four trips that people now make will be handled by electronic devices such as home-to-store communications.
- By the mid-1990s, half of all personal vehicles will be pollution-free. Ninety percent will be by 2005.
- Six-cylinder cars will be phased out.
- There will be widespread use of electric cars for intra-city travel.
- There will be widespread use of electric trains for inter-city travel.
- Moving sidewalks will be used widely by the late 1990s.
- After prolonged experimentation, automated highways will be built for regular usage during 1996–2010.

Source: The Futurist, June 1978, p. 171, published by the World Future Society, 4916 St. Elmo Avenue, Washington, D.C. 20014.

---

likely strategy of the company's major competitors. Price wars, advertising battles, and sales force skirmishes all affect company sales and need to be incorporated into the forecast assumptions.

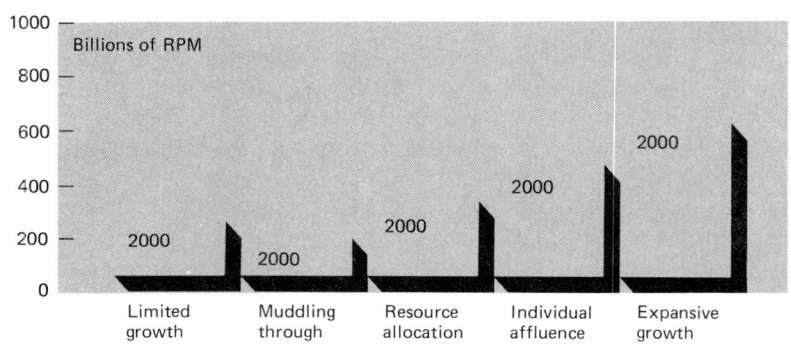

FIGURE 7-1. Alternate FAA forecasts of total domestic U.S. revenue passenger miles by the year 2000 using different assumptions. *Source:* Jerry Richardson, "Tomorrow's Aviation: The Sky Won't Be the Only Limit," *The Futurist,* June 1977, p. 170. Published by the World Future Society, 4916 St. Elmo Avenue, Washington, D.C. 20014.

Costs and Benefits of Forecasting[4]

Sales forecasting, like any business activity, costs money. A simple judgmental forecast may cost little and if there is not much need for high levels of accuracy it may be adequate. However, the cost of inaccuracy may far exceed the cost of even the most sophisticated forecasting techniques. The decision to introduce a new product or expand production capacity may involve millions of dollars of investment. (The ill-fated Edsel car required a commitment of over $100 million by the Ford Motor Company.) On the other hand, a production scheduling decision has a much smaller impact on profits. The new product decision may justify relatively large expenditures for forecasting activities while the scheduling decision would justify a much lower amount.

Determining forecasting budgets and expenses involves several considerations. In addition to the cost of inaccuracy, they include timing, available data, effect of delays, and decision flexibility. A short deadline will preclude the use of sophisticated data collection and analysis. Given greater time, costlier and more accurate techniques can be employed. Forecasting error represents the allowable difference between forecasted and actual sales. The forecaster should know how accurate the forecast is required to be in order to determine how much should be spent and what techniques should be used.

TYPES OF FORECASTS

There are several types of sales forecasts. These can be grouped into macro and micro categories which represent only two labels on a continuum. There is much overlap in both scope and purpose as we move across the continuum from the broad environmental (macro) type of forecast to the specific company (micro) forecast.

Macro Forecasts

Macro forecasts are very broad in scope, encompassing more than the firm's direct environment. Yet a macro forecast can help identify new opportunities for growth which may be overlooked if a narrower perspective is placed on the forecast. We examine four examples of macro forecasts, moving from the very broad to the more specific, namely, world, regional, national economic, and industry.

World Forecast. The broadest scope of forecasting (at least until space travel becomes commonplace) is the planet earth, recognizing as we do the increasing interrelationships of all peoples of the world. World forecasts provide a valuable tool for long-range strategic planning by identifying long-term growth situations. A major shipbuilding facility, for example, may cost hundreds of millions of dollars and would be considered only if a long period of growth in world demand exceeded the projected capacity to meet that demand.[5] World forecasts are prepared by the United Nations, by countries and trade groups, and by multinational corporations. The items most frequently forecasted are those with international consequences, such as population, energy, and food production.

Regional Forecasts. Regional forecasts encompass a narrower geographic spectrum. Regional forecasts are prepared for trade areas (Europe, North Africa, South America, etc.). They provide information about regional trends which would be lost in world statistics.

Like world forecasts, regional projections are prepared by the United Nations and other multinational groups and by corporations. Preparation of both regional and world forecasts is handicapped by the paucity of reliable data for the less developed areas. There was the case, for example, of two population estimates of one Latin American country which were prepared by different agencies and which differed by more than 100 percent.

National Economic Forecasts. For the great majority of U.S. firms, the initial forecast deals with the U.S. economy. The most common types of economic forecasts consist of indicators of future business activity such as gross national product and national income. These forecasts (usually covering periods of from 3 to 18 months) are prepared by the U.S. Department of Commerce, the President's Council of Economic Advisors, large banks, major business periodicals, industry groups, private consultants, and some universities.

All companies are affected by the national economy. A brief look at the concept of the "business cycle" will emphasize this point. Figure 7-2 presents a history of U.S. business conditions spanning a period of 57 years. The business cycle represents the expansion and contraction of business activity. Although different industries and geographic areas are affected to differing degrees, almost all suffer if the contraction is severe or prolonged. Knowledge of anticipated economic conditions can be an important input to managerial planning.

Industry Forecast. The economy is but one of the environments within which the firm operates. It is the condition of the firm's industry that has the greatest influence on company operations. Firms in the same industry share similar environments and can use the same industry forecasts in preparing their own product forecasts. Forecasts are prepared for many (but not all) industries by the Department of Commerce, trade associations, and trade publications. When reliable industry forecasts are available, a common method of forecasting company sales is to multiply the industry forecast by the percent share of industry estimated for the firm.

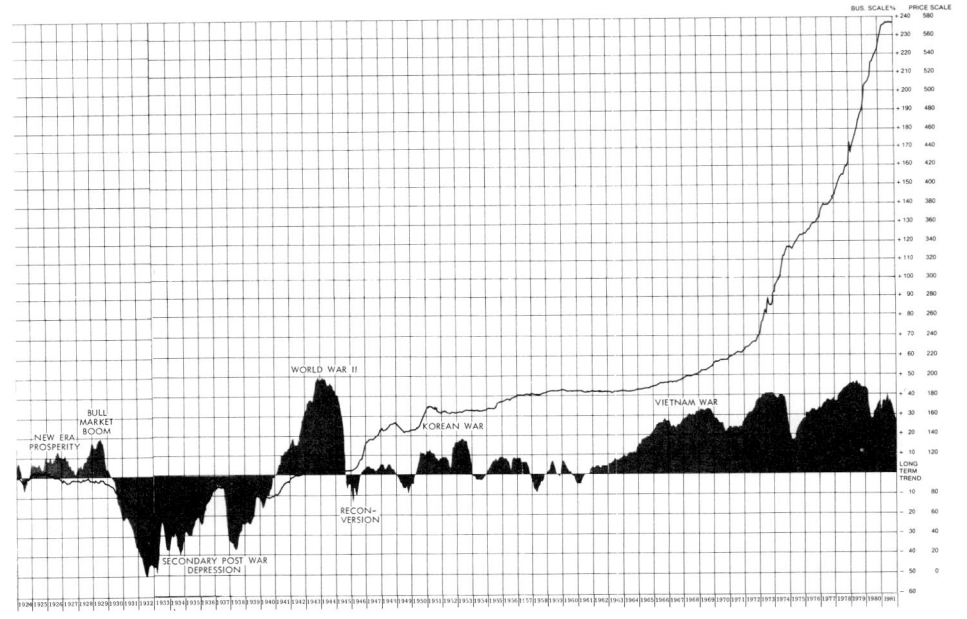

FIGURE 7-2. Index of business activity, 1924–1981. *Source: American Business Activity from 1790 to Today*, 53d ed., July 1982. Reproduced with the permission of the Ameritrust Company, Cleveland, Ohio.

Micro Forecasts

Whereas macro forecasts assess the firm's future operating environment, micro forecasts deal directly with the firm's own sales outlook. Four levels of micro forecasts are presented: company, product, market, and sales territory.

Company Sales Forecasts. The company forecast is the composite of all of the firm's product sales forecasts. In the large multiproduct, multidivisional corporation this total company forecast will be the total of all product sales forecast by each division.

Product Sales Forecast. Usually of short-term duration, the product sales forecast represents the level of planned sales activity for a particular product during the planning horizon. The annual product forecast, for example, may be broken down into quarterly, monthly, or even weekly periods as needed to schedule purchasing and manufacturing activities. Each product forecast is based on marketing strategies and planned tactical programs. Marketing management, of course, would consider the macro forecasts (such as the outlook for the industry and the national economy) when developing the product marketing plans.

Market Sales Forecasts. These are used where the same product is marketed to different types of users or industries, a situation commonly faced by industrial marketers. By identifying different growth rates for sales to these separate industries (markets), marketing efforts can be directed to those with the greatest potential for increased growth and market penetration.

Territorial Sales Forecasts. This is the most disaggregate of the forecasting levels described here. Territorial sales forecasts are used in the setting of territory sales quotas. Quotas are the levels of *expected* sales peformance in a given sales person's territory. They serve as the basis for the evaluation of sales performance and provide criteria for compensation, bonuses, and awards. Individual salesperson's quotas can be combined into larger sales districts and regions for broader levels of management evaluation and control.

FORECASTING TECHNIQUES

The business and sales forecaster has a wide variety of techniques to call upon. Data availability, time available prior to decision, forecasting skills, and the types of decisions to be made will determine the particular forecasting techniques to be used. We will focus on four common forecasting techniques: judgmental, survey, statistical, and composite.

Judgmental Techniques

Despite a virtual explosion of sophisticated forecasting techniques and computer models, the most commonly used sales forecast is derived from executive judgment.[6] Whether the result of the judgment of a single executive in a small firm or a consensus formed by several executives in a large corporation, this type of forecast is a subjective evaluation of future sales performance. The consensus technique is called the "jury of executive opinion" and consists of combining the views of executives from several functional areas (such as sales, production, finance, purchasing and staff operations). These executives may be provided with preliminary forecasts, derived from surveys or statistical methods, which they modify based on their subjective judgments of the effects that the economy, the company's marketing programs, and anticipated competitive actions will have on future sales. The forecast reached in this way is a broad one, usually expressed in dollar sales for a division or for the entire company. This *top-down* forecast is then translated into sales forecasts for specific product lines by personnel at operating levels who themselves will apply their judgments.

Forecasting the company's share of industry sales, discussed previously under the heading "Industry Forecast," is another example of the judgmental technique. Executive judgment is expressed with respect to both the reliability of the industry forecast and the percent share of industry sales the company can expect to obtain. The share of industry approach is more appropriate for mature industries where change is slow than it is for growth industries where change is more rapid. In growth situations the company has more opportunity to influence its market share than it does in industries that are relatively static.

Survey Techniques

Survey techniques involve the collection of opinions about future sales from numerous persons both inside and outside the firm. Surveys of the sales force will involve a series of product-specific sales estimates; surveys of consumer expectations may reflect total sales estimates for the entire economy.

Composite Surveys. This technique requires the collection of estimates of future sales of individual products from the sales force and sales managers. Since not every salesperson deals with all products or all sales territories, this technique requires consolidation and adjustments of the various sales forecasts at higher levels of management.

Salespeople are given standardized forecasting forms to complete. These completed forms are then discussed with the regional sales managers who make appropriate modifications and send the regional forecasts to the next level of management. The headquarters marketing department combines the regional forecasts and compares the result with the sales forecasts made using other forecasting techniques. The sales force forecast may be modified on the basis of planned marketing programs unknown to the sales organization when their forecasts were made. This *bottom-up* forecasting method is a valuable communications device for keeping marketing management in touch with those closest to customers and the trade.

Surveys of Industrial User Expectations. In situations where the major portion of a firm's sales are made to relatively few customers—a situation common to industrial marketing—customers may be asked about their expected purchases. For example, a firm supplying the automobile industry may request purchase estimates from the major automobile manufacturers. Even firms which have large numbers of customers can utilize this technique. Each year the National Lead Company interviews 100 companies by personal visits and another 500 by mail questionnaire to produce an industry forecast from which its own sales forecast is derived.[7]

Surveys of Consumer Expectations. For those firms producing consumer products, surveys of users are neither as readily available nor as reliable as user surveys for industrial producers. General surveys of consumer expectations can be useful, however. One well-known survey is conducted quarterly by the Survey Research Center of the University of Michigan. In it, a national sample of over 1500 households is asked about expectations of personal economic well-being and planned major expenditures (car, major appliances, etc.) over the next twelve months. Since its inception after World War II, the center's Index of Consumer Sentiment has been widely used as a leading indicator of retail sales levels. The center's findings, or those of other surveys of buying intentions, can be used in preparing a firm's annual forecast. Figure 7-3 shows changes in the Index of Consumer Sentiment over a period of years.

Statistical Techniques

Forecasters have available a number of statistical approaches to help with predicting future sales levels. These range from the simple to the complex. Several are described in the addendum to this chapter.

For the most part statistical forecasting techniques are methods of extending sales estimates into the future based on past experience. The strength of these techniques is their ability to extend trend lines accurately after making adjustments for seasonal, cyclical, and other variations in the historical data. Their weakness is that they do not take into account either internal or external changes that can shift future sales above or below the historically based trend line.

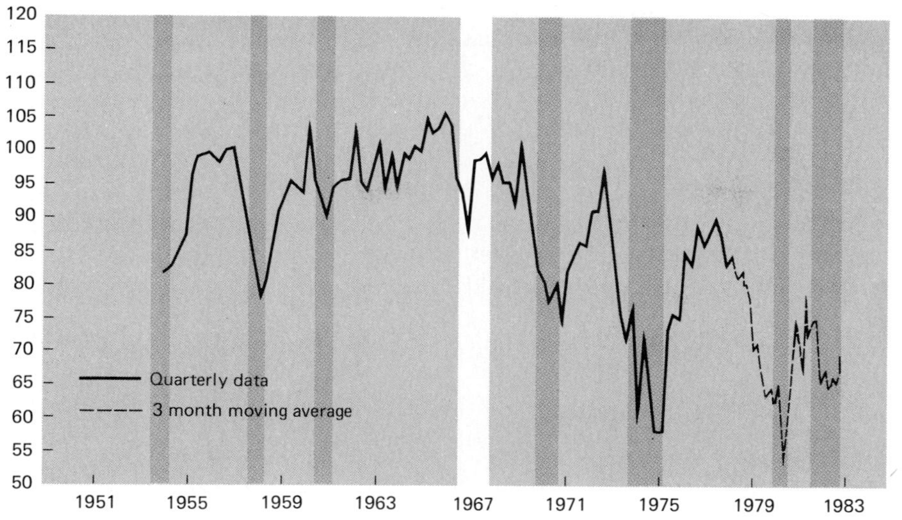

FIGURE 7-3. Index of consumer sentiment, 1954–1982. *Source: Surveys of Consumer Attitudes,* "Tables and Charts, October 1982," Survey Research Center, University of Michigan, Ann Arbor. © 1982 University of Michigan. Reproduced with permission.

The weakness can be an advantage in marketing planning, however. One of the key purposes of strategic marketing planning is to improve sales and profits over what can be expected from extensions of past trends. If trend line forecasting is used as a starting point for planning, it is quite useful. However, it can be misleading if the future external environment or company marketing programs differ from those of the past.

There are newer techniques (e.g., trend impact analysis, cross impact analysis, and the Delphi technique), which are used to modify historically based extrapolations by quantifying the potential impact of expected future events.* Also, forecasting models are providing management with opportunities to consider alternate forecasts, each with a different set of assumptions. From these, management can select what appears to be the most appropriate alternative. These models are also useful for making rapid corrections to the selected forecast when actual future events differ from the assumptions.

Composite Techniques

Most companies do not rely on just one method of developing a sales forecast.[8] Regression techniques (or other methods of extrapolation) may be coupled with trend analyses and then cross-checked with survey or judgmental methods. If there is consistency among the forecasts derived by the various methods, greater confidence can be placed in the recommended forecast. If wide variations exist, the assumptions made in each case must be questioned as well as the data used in each technique.

*These techniques are discussed in Case 2, "Heublein, Inc.: Environmental Scanning for Strategic Planning."

Some techniques can be used only at certain stages in the forecasting process. Each may employ different data and may answer different questions. Different information sources may be employed at each level of forecasting to act as a validity check on the data. Figure 7-4 shows an example of an inverse hierarchy of forecasts used by Combustion Engineering, Inc. to determine sales forecasts for each of 24 major refractory products.

A decision must be made on how to combine the various forecasts developed by different techniques. A simple averaging will weigh all techniques equally and not recognize the particular assumptions inherent in any given method. A better means of combining short-range forecasts would be to assign weights to each forecast

FIGURE 7-4. Flowchart of the Forecasting Problem. *Source:* Elliot D. Ranard, "Use of Input/Output Concepts in Sales Forecasting," *Journal of Marketing Research*, February 1972, p. 54.

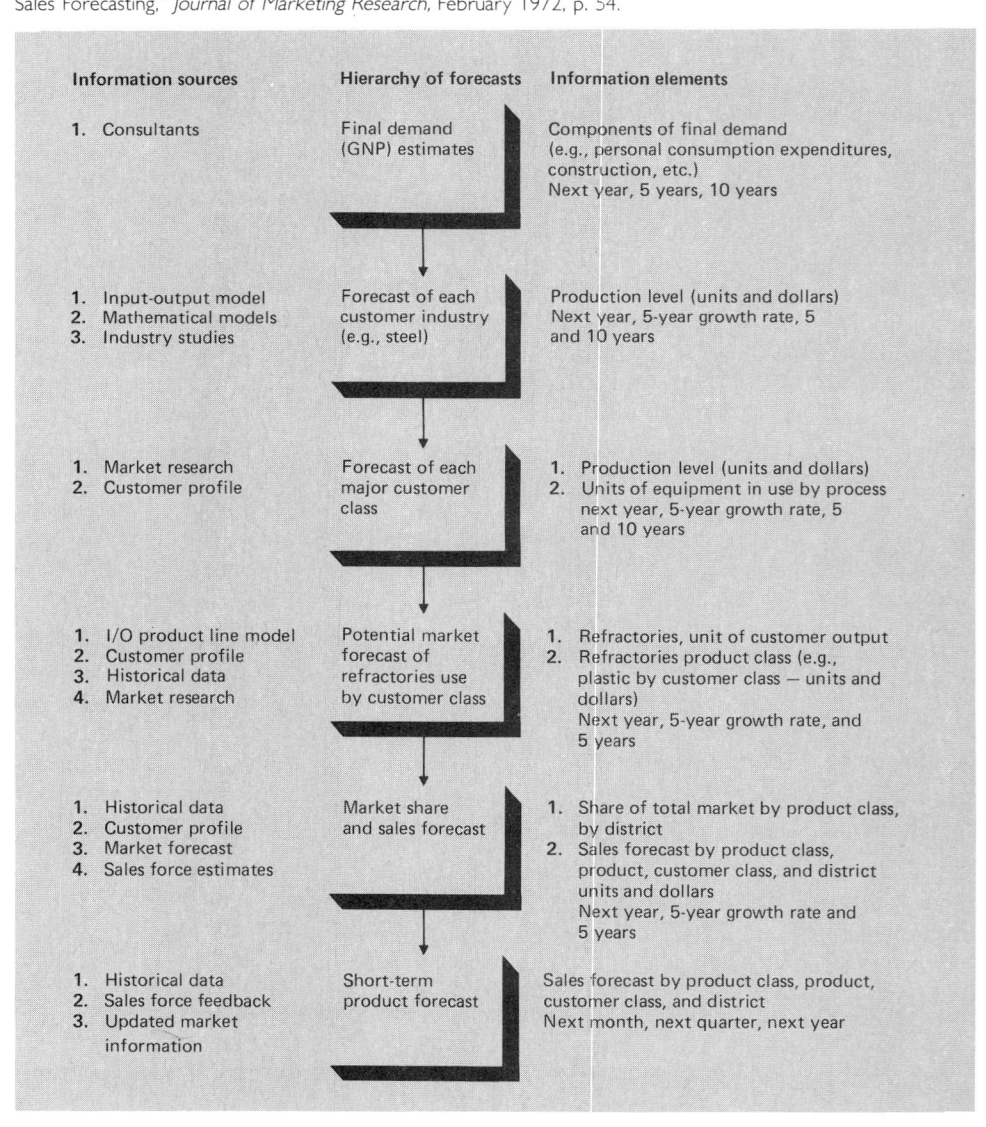

Information sources	Hierarchy of forecasts	Information elements
1. Consultants	Final demand (GNP) estimates	Components of final demand (e.g., personal consumption expenditures, construction, etc.) Next year, 5 years, 10 years
1. Input-output model 2. Mathematical models 3. Industry studies	Forecast of each customer industry (e.g., steel)	Production level (units and dollars) Next year, 5-year growth rate, 5 and 10 years
1. Market research 2. Customer profile	Forecast of each major customer class	1. Production level (units and dollars) 2. Units of equipment in use by process next year, 5-year growth rate, 5 and 10 years
1. I/O product line model 2. Customer profile 3. Historical data 4. Market research	Potential market forecast of refractories use by customer class	1. Refractories, unit of customer output 2. Refractories product class (e.g., plastic by customer class — units and dollars) Next year, 5-year growth rate, and 5 years
1. Historical data 2. Customer profile 3. Market forecast 4. Sales force estimates	Market share and sales forecast	1. Share of total market by product class, by district 2. Sales forecast by product class, product, customer class, and district units and dollars Next year, 5-year growth rate and 5 years
1. Historical data 2. Sales force feedback 3. Updated market information	Short-term product forecast	Sales forecast by product class, product, customer class, and district Next month, next quarter, next year

proportional to the accuracy with which the technique predicted sales for the most recent period. For the longer-range forecast, evaluation of the key assumptions used in the forecast must be made. This is why the responsibility for deciding the sales forecast to be used is usually assigned to a high organizational level.

TRACKING PERFORMANCE AND MAKING REVISIONS

The sales forecast is a very practical tool for business management. For most companies profits are made or lost depending on how closely purchasing and production schedules and finished goods inventory levels correspond to anticipated sales—week by week or month by month.

Sales forecasting is dependent on assumptions based on the external market environment. In a dynamic industry such assumptions are rarely perfect and management expects deviations from the sales forecasts. The final steps in the forecasting process, therefore, are (1) tracking performance and determining reasons for any variance between forecast and actual sales and (2) revising the sales forecast promptly, if necessary.

Thus far we have assumed that the forecast covered some period of time such as the fiscal year. For operating purposes, however, the annual forecast needs to be broken into shorter periods. Sales performance would be measured beginning with the first week or month, as the case may be, of the fiscal year. If performance is over or under plan and marketing management does not expect it to return quickly to the forecast level, a revised forecast should be made so that adjustments can be made in production schedules. And if sales are lagging behind forecast, tactical marketing plans need to be revised to make up for the lag. The sooner the areas of weak sales performance—and their causes—are spotted, the more chance there is to make corrections before profits are seriously affected. The importance of timely information of the right kind cannot be overemphasized.

SUMMARY

Sales forecasting is essential to the development of a marketing plan and is a necessary input for such functions as profit planning, cash flow planning, purchasing, production scheduling, and inventory management. Forecasts can range from the very broad (world demand) to the very narrow (product sales in a sales territory). In general, the forecasting process proceeds from macro to micro forecasts. There are a number of sales forecasting techniques available, ranging from the simple to the complex. These can be categorized as judgmental, survey, statistical, and composite.

Efficient business management is highly dependent on reasonably accurate sales forecasts. In a larger, well-staffed company, sales forecasts usually are developed by functional specialists who obtain help from various sources. Because there is no foolproof method, the wise specialist works into the forecasting model the knowledge and judgments of anyone who can supply useful inputs, whether they be customers, salespeople, or the president. Sales forecasts usually are arrived at with the concurrence of the marketing manager (who is responsible for obtaining the forecasted sales) and the final approval of general management (who are responsible for achieving profit forecasts).

Sales forecasts are based on assumptions about external factors—such as demand and competition—which may prove to be incorrect. It is important, therefore, to provide for close tracking of company sales performance and external conditions as the year progresses so that sales forecasts can be adjusted rapidly if required.

In Part Three, the Strategic Marketing Planning Process, we will see how sales forecasting is used in longer-range strategic planning and annual tactical planning.

ADDENDUM: DESCRIPTION OF STATISTICAL METHODS

Trend Extrapolation

The simplest statistical procedure for forecasting sales is the linear projection of past sales. This assumes that the forces which influenced past sales will continue to operate in the future. While the exact conditions of history are seldom duplicated, the fact that the firm's basic marketing program, capacity, and distribution system normally are not subject to radical change in a single year does give some credence to a simple projection. Where the forecasted item is overall company sales, the simple projection may be quite sufficient, although it may be less reliable when applied to specific products.

The first step in preparing a trend extrapolation is to develop a *scatter diagram*. This is a plot of the actual company sales of the last, say, ten or twelve years. A casual examination of this graph will give the forecaster a feel for future sales expectations. The second step will be to fit a straight line to the points plotted in the scatter diagram. The equation for a straight line is:

$$Y = a + bX$$

where
Y = sales volume
a = point at which line crosses vertical or sales axis
b = slope of line or average rate of change of sales volume over time
X = time variable

By extending the calculated line beyond the time span for which sales volumes have been actually recorded, a projection is obtained. This is shown in Figure 7-5. The *least squares method* (which minimizes the total differences between the line and the scattering of points) for calculating this trend line will give us a confidence interval within which we are 90 or 95 percent sure our forecast will be accurate *in the absence of changes in the firm's environments*.

The disadvantage of this simple linear extrapolation is that all of the data points are weighted equally; sales volume in year (-9) has as much influence in determining a trend line as does the figure for year (-1). Clearly the firm which has strived to build momentum would underestimate next year's sales and, consequently, plan too limited a production, risking stock-outs, and thereby jeopardizing the momentum it had built up. Two ways of correcting for this shortcoming are (1) weighting the data and (2) using a moving average. The former is useful for annual (and longer) forecasts, while the latter is more commonly applied to forecasts of less than a year.

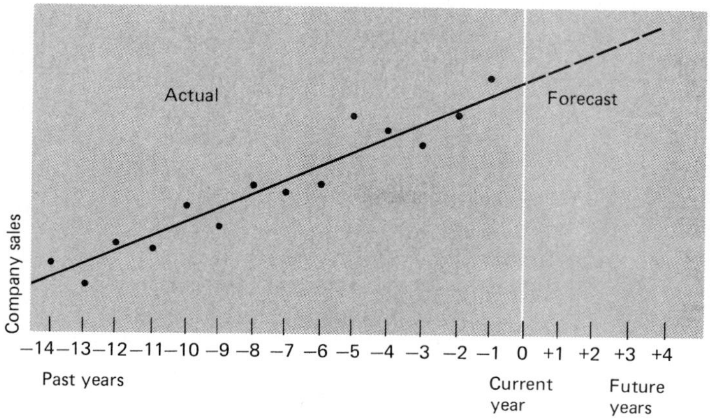

FIGURE 7-5. Scatter diagram of annual sales with fitted trend line.

Using *weighted data* simply recognizes that the more recent sales volume took place in a business environment which is more likely to be similar to next year's than to the previous year's environment. The forecaster assigns weights, or measures of importance, to each year's data and recomputes the trend line. Clearly different forecasts will be derived using different weighted schemes. Table 7-3 shows four different estimates of next year's sales by using different weights for previous annual sales. The forecaster will have to select a weighting carefully to be sure of having a reliable forecast.

The *moving average* technique commonly is used for forecasts of monthly sales. A 3-month moving average, for example, would only use the most recent 3 month's sales in formulating a forecast of the next month's sales.

The data in Table 7-4 represent retail sales for a large department store. The monthly forecast is based on a 3-month moving average of percentage change. For example, the 3-month moving average of 4.0 percent for September's percentage change was calculated by averaging the monthly percentage changes for July,

TABLE 7-3
Linear Extrapolation Using Alternative Weighting Methods

Year	Sales, $1000s	Weight A	Weight B	Weight C	Weight D
−9	1,352	1	1	1	1
−8	1,598	1	2	1	1
−7	1,563	1	3	1	1
−6	1,798	1	4	3	1
−5	1,953	1	5	3	1
−4	2,476	1	6	3	1
−3	3,541	1	7	4	5
−2	3,965	1	8	4	5
−1	4,813	1	9	5	8
Current year	6,138	1	10	10	10
Next year's estimate		7,298	7,451	7,525	7,603

TABLE 7-4
Sales Forecast Using 3-Month Moving Average

Month	Sales ($000)	% Change	3-Month Moving Average	Forecast of the Following Month
Jan.	6,438			
Feb.	5,646	−12.3		
Mar.	6,228	10.3		
Apr.	6,763	8.6	2.20	6,912
May	7,122	5.3	8.07	7,697
June	7,634	7.2	7.03	8,171
July	7,779	1.9	4.80	8,152
Aug.	8,075	3.8	4.30	8,422
Sept.	8,583	6.3	4.00	8,926
Oct.	8,420	−1.9	2.73	8,649
Nov.	9,574	13.7	6.03	10,152
Dec.	11,327	18.3	10.03	12,463
Jan.	10,273	−9.3	7.57	11,050
Feb.	9,363	−6.2	0.93	9,726
Mar.	10,446	8.4	−2.37	10,199

August, and September (1.9 + 3.8 + 6.3)/3. The forecast for October was obtained by multiplying the actual September sales by this 3-month moving average ($8583 × 104% = $8926). Each month's forecast is obtained in the same fashion. The longer the base for which a moving average is calculated, the greater is the importance of earlier time periods and the less is the influence of sporadic sales fluctuations. The use of only a few months will accentuate the effect of recent events.

There are pitfalls in this method. For example, the use of a 3-month moving average of October-November-December to predict January sales may produce an unrealistically high forecast due to the nature of the pre-Christmas selling season. This type of *seasonal* factor is discussed in the section on time series analysis which follows.

Time Series Analysis. Time series analyses are a group of techniques used to analyze chronologically arranged sets of data and to help explain dips and surges from the long-term trend. The data may be in terms of weekly, monthly, quarterly, or annual sales volumes. The time series analysis attempts to determine four separate sets of factors which influence sales: the long-term (growth) trend, cyclical business fluctuations, seasonal variations, and residual changes.

Trend (T)—the long-term movement of the series which can be attributed to such factors as population growth, capital formation, technological development, and sociological evolution. While this long-term trend is fairly stable, it is possible for it to change to produce a "kinked" trend line.

Cycle (C)—a recurrent fluctuation of sales above and below the trend line generally referred to as the business cycle. Cycles do not have a uniform amplitude or frequency and may be different for different industries or sectors of the economy.

Seasonal (S)—a consistent pattern of sales movements within the year. While the most common period used refers to changes induced by the season of the year, seasonal variations can be any *recurrent* and *periodic* hourly, weekly, monthly, or quarterly sales pattern. There are wide differences in the seasonal sales pattern for different products and services.

Residual (R)—any fluctuation in sales not attributable to trend, cycle, or seasonal factors. These fluctuations may or may not be recurrent and are seldom periodic, a combination which makes them highly unpredictable. While of short duration, residual fluctuations can be very severe. They may be caused by strikes, natural disasters, boycotts, unusual weather conditions, war, and other such factors. These factors are sometimes called *irregular* factors.[9]

These four factors are shown in Figure 7-6. Together they combine to produce the current sales levels. They can be combined either additively:

$$\text{Sales} = T + C + S + R$$

or multiplicatively:

$$\text{Sales} = T \times C \times S \times R$$

The multiplicative method assumes that cyclical and seasonal factors are proportional to the trend level: C, S, and R are stated as percentages and trend is in absolute sales. Time series analysis requires many complicated calculations and would be impractical without the use of a computer.

Cycle forecasting. One type of time series forecasting which is not as complex as others is cycle forecasting. Figure 7-7 shows the actual monthly orders for the

FIGURE 7-6. Types of sales fluctuations. *Source:* Robert McLaughlin, *Time Series Forecasting,* American Marketing Association, Chicago, 1962, p. 8.

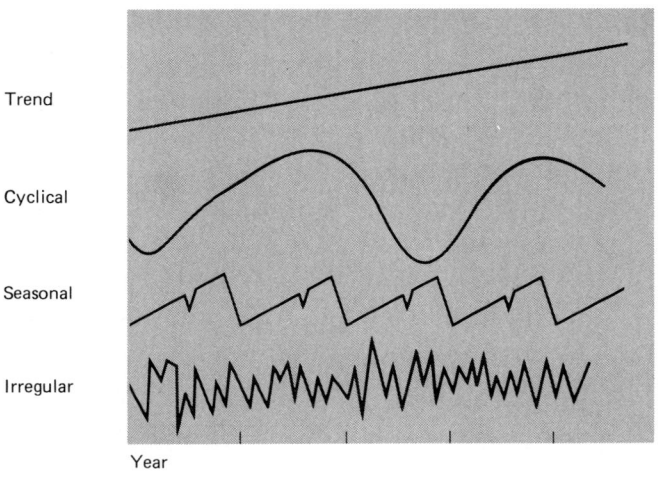

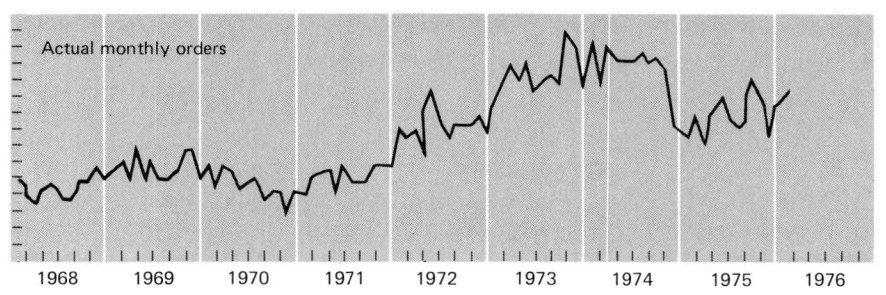

FIGURE 7-7. Monthly orders of metal-working machinery. *Source:* Parker Hannifin Corp. Printed in *Industry Week*, April 25, 1977.

metal working machinery industry as reported by the U.S. Department of Commerce. Any cycle in this figure is hard to discern, making forecasting troublesome. Figure 7-8 shows the same data plotted as the ratio of the most recent 12-month total of orders to the total of orders for the preceding 12-month period. This ratio of orders is called the *12/12 pressure on monthly orders* and represents the momentum (or pressure on the production process) of the industry. Here the cycle is much more pronounced and can be more readily used in forecasting and planning. The Parker Hannifin Corporation has done pioneering work in this area[10] and has developed a series of operating objectives for each state of the business cycle.[11]

Table 7-5 is an example of the computations necessary to determine the 12/12 pressure on monthly orders (although these data are not the same as those used to plot Figures 7-7 and 7-8). The first column shows the actual total of monthly orders placed for one class of machine tools with all companies producing the tools. These orders are then accumulated as successive 12-month totals (called 12-month moving totals) in the second column. The numbers in the third column are derived by dividing the 12-MMT of a month by the 12-MMT of the same month a year earlier. This ratio becomes the index of future industry demand. Note that the 12/12 in April 1974 signaled an upturn in industry demand while actual orders declined from the previous month. The relationship of each of the company's products to the industry cycle is used in determining specific strategies for each product.

Correlation Techniques

Correlation techniques measure the degree of association between two variables whether or not they are linked through causality. They are useful for sales forecasting

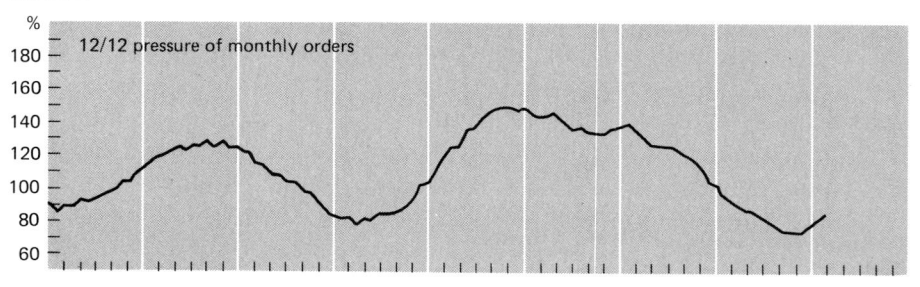

FIGURE 7-8. 12/12 pressure of monthly orders. *Source:* Parker Hannifin Corp. Printed in *Industry Week*, April 25, 1977.

TABLE 7-5
Calculations of 12/12 Pressure from Actual Monthly Orders

	Orders	12-MMT*	12/12
1972			
Jan.	226		
Feb.	284		
Mar.	331		
Apr.	292		
May	301		
June	336		
July	315		
Aug.	277		
Sept.	332		
Oct.	314		
Nov.	335		
Dec.	362	3,705	
1973			
Jan.	370	3,849	
Feb.	407	3,972	
Mar.	498	4,139	
Apr.	411	4,258	
May	406	4,363	
June	421	4,448	
July	387	4,520	
Aug.	382	4,625	
Sept.	393	4,686	
Oct.	487	4,859	
Nov.	423	4,947	
Dec.	500	5,085	137.3
1974			
Jan.	375	5,090	132.2
Feb.	517	5,200	130.9
Mar.	628	5,330	128.8
Apr.	581	5,500	129.2
May	573	5,667	129.9
June	589	5,835	131.2
July	524	5,972	132.1
Aug.	519	6,109	132.1
Sept.	690	6,406	136.7

*12-MMT: 12-month moving totals

Source: Dale W. Sommer, "Cycle Forecasting Spots Trends," Industry Week, April 25, 1977.

when there is a close relationship between sales and other measurable factors in the firm's environment. Correlation is also useful in evaluating the accuracy of forecasts developed through the use of regression analyses discussed in the next section. The higher the correlation between past sales and the factors used in the regression equation, the narrower will be the confidence interval (expected error) in the forecast. The use of environmental factors with high correlations to sales greatly improves the accuracy of sales forecasts.

Table 7-6 shows the sales of central air-conditioning systems and new home

TABLE 7-6
Sales of Residential Air-Conditioning Systems and Building Permits

Quarter	Previous Quarter's Building Permits	Central Air-Conditioning System Units Sold
Winter 1978	1214	48
Spring 1979	2169	117
Summer 1979	2437	123
Fall 1979	1236	55
Winter 1979	937	31
Spring 1980	1222	62
Summer 1980	1938	141
Fall 1980	109	131
Winter 1980	813	43
Spring 1981	1682	139
Summer 1981	2435	186

construction permits in the sales area of a heating and air-conditioning contractor. In order to use these data as an aid to forecasting, the contractor must first calculate the degree of association between the sales of central air-conditioning systems and construction permits. This is accomplished by calculating the *coefficient of correlation r* as follows:

$$r = \left(\frac{n\Sigma xy - \Sigma x \Sigma y}{n\Sigma y^2 - (\Sigma y)^2} \cdot \frac{n\Sigma xy - \Sigma x \Sigma y}{n\Sigma x^2 - (\Sigma x)^2} \right)^{1/2}$$

where

    y = quarterly sales of central air-conditioning systems (in units)
    x = number of building permits for residential construction issued in previous quarter
    n = number of quarters being used in calculations

In our example from Table 7-6, $r = 0.771$. The maximum theoretical value of r is either 1 (a perfect direct relationship) or -1 (a perfect inverse relationship). A value of 0 means there is no relationship at all. In our example r is 0.771, so there is a fairly good relationship between the sales of central air-conditioners and building permits issued the preceding quarter. In fact the contractor can go one step further by squaring r to obtain the *coefficient of determination* which measures the variation in the dependent variable (central air-conditioner sales) which can be explained by changes in the independent variable (building permits). Here r^2 equals $(0.771)^2$ or 0.59, and may be interpreted to mean that 59 percent of the variation in sales is explained by associating sales with building permits.

Regression Analysis

Regression analysis is a statistical technique that determines the relationship between a dependent variable (sales) and one or more independent variables in such a way that the differences between past values of the dependent variable determined by the regression equation and the actual values are minimized. In our earlier discussion of trend extrapolation, we fitted sales (the dependent variable) to time (the independent variable) with the linear relationship $Y = a + bX$. This represents a form of regression equation with one independent variable and is known as a *simple linear regression*. Use of more than one independent variable represents a *multiple regression* technique. Sales, of course, can be regressed with many factors other than time, and the more factors used, usually the less will be the difference between actual sales and predicted sales. Why, then, shouldn't we use as many independent factors as possible to increase the accuracy of the sales forecast?

Normal business events are rarely, if ever, completely explainable and a sales forecaster could search forever without finding all of the reasons why the forecast was is error. Indeed many of the *independent* variables are highly correlated to each other and add little to the sales forecast. Costs are important in determining the number of independent variables to use. One should be careful not to add independent variables to the point where the costs of doing so exceed their benefits.

The exact independent variables selected will depend upon the factors which the forecaster assumes influence sales, availability of data, likelihood of a causal relationship, ability of management to manipulate the factors, and other judgmental criteria. In the following example four factors are used to predict future sales:

$$\text{Sales} = a + b_1X_1 + b_2X_2 + b_3X_3 + b_4X_4$$

where

a = base sales level from which other factors have influence
X_1 = previous year's company sales
X_2 = projected percentage change in GNP from current year
X_3 = planned company advertising as percentage of industry average
X_4 = planned company price as percentage of industry average
and $b_1b_2b_3b_4$ = coefficients of regression. They represent the average change in the dependent variable for a unit change in the appropriate independent variable when other variables are held constant.

To use this type of regression analysis, the sales forecaster will need several years of past data. In general there should be a minimum of four or five data points for each independent factor used. In this example the forecaster will need at least sixteen years of data to obtain a "good" regression equation. The measure of "goodness" used is the *coefficient of determination* r^2, between the series of independent variables and the dependent variable. An r^2 of $\pm.85$ would mean that 85 percent of the sales fluctuations are explained by the combination of variables in the regression. Even an r^2 of 1 does not necessarily imply causation. It has been shown that there is a high correlation between the number of telephones in a town and the number of television sets. However, it would be unwarranted to draw the conclusion that owning a telephone causes one to own a TV; more likely both are caused by the family's disposable income.[12]

Regression analysis is useful for both forecasting and planning. A simple *trend extrapolation* can be used to answer the question, "What will sales be next period assuming present trends continue?" The *four-factor regression method* can be used to answer the question, "What will sales be during the next period if there is a 6 percent decline in GNP, we decrease our price 5 percent, and we raise our advertising by 8 percent?" The four-factor regression method can be used to develop alternatives from which the marketing manager can select the one expected to yield the highest sales.

Shortcomings of Regression Analysis. While regression techniques are quite helpful to the sales forecaster, they do have several shortcomings. First, relevant variables may be overlooked, which could help to improve the accuracy of the forecast. Secondly, values of independent variables which exceed those used to develop the regression coefficients may yield sales forecasts with high degrees of error (e.g., the forecaster could not use an estimate of 150 for company advertising if the highest the number had been in an actual case was only 120). A third shortcoming is caused by the time lag in the reporting of many economic and other statistics, forcing the forecaster to use an *estimate* to calculate an *estimated* sales forecast. This only compounds error. A fourth problem for many firms is *two-way causation*. For example, while advertising may cause sales, the level of advertising expenditures may be set at a predetermined percentage, e.g., 10 percent, of anticipated sales.

Computer Simulation Models

Advances in computer technology have enabled forecasters to develop complex models or mathematical representations for use in forecasting. These range from the very large and very complex models of the entire economy, which are used to forecast growth in GNP and other macro measures of economic growth, to the smaller models used to forecast sales of a single industry. Combustion Engineering, Inc., for example, uses an input/output model to forecast market growth rates for its refractory division.[13] This input-output model, containing ninety sectors of the U.S. economy, determines interrelations among various industries and identifies industry growth rates determined by the technological coefficients used in the model.

Computer models have been developed which incorporate several of the techniques mentioned in this chapter. One such model has been developed by the Pacific Gas and Electric Company to forecast sales of major electrical appliances (refrigerators, dishwashers, electric clothes dryers, electric ranges, and washing machines) in northern California.[14] This model employed the following statistical representation:

$$Q = f(P, P_s, Y, H_s, H_m, T)$$

where

Q = annual retail sales of appliance being considered
P = its average installed price
P_s = average installed price of substitute appliances
Y = California per capita income
H_s = new single–family housing units connected to utilities
H_m = new multifamily housing units connected to utilities
T = trend variable accounting for uniform changes over time

Income and price elasticities were computed for each appliance and short-term sales forecasts were made.

Another model is the Airline System Simulation developed by Lockheed Aircraft Corporation[15] to forecast the market for the supersonic transport. Because of the impossibility of predicting congressional actions, the model has not worked out well for this particular aircraft, but has been used successfully to forecast demand for conventional jet aircraft. Some of the independent variables used in Airline System Simulation are:

- All existing and potential flight routes around the world
- Flight elevations by aircraft types to determine likely aircraft by route, schedule, preference, and airline strategies to optimize revenues
- Flight assignments (which aircraft would be assigned to which flights to optimize earnings)
- Population density at different terminal points

Armour and Company developed a model to forecast the number of cattle it should slaughter to meet market demand.[16] This complex model was based upon independent variables such as past consumption of beef, feed and grazing conditions, steer/corn and hog/corn price ratios, and others. Because of the complexity of the models described and the number of mathematical computations they require, they could not be used without the aid of the computer.

QUESTIONS

1. What is a sales forecast and what are the various uses of a sales forecast within an organization?
2. Name the four factors to be considered before starting the sales forecast.
3. Name the typical categories of assumptions on which a sales forecast is based. Why is it important for the forecaster to be explicit about these assumptions?
4. Briefly differentiate between the two basic types of forecasts, macro and micro.
5. Describe the four basic categories of forecasting techniques.
6. Why is it usually advisable to use more than one technique when developing a sales forecast?
7. What are the final (follow-up) steps in the forecasting process?

REFERENCES

1. "Carter's Decision on Bomber Jars Rockwell and Its Workers," *The New York Times*, July 1, 1977, p. D1.
2. "U.S. Bans a Flame Retardant Used in Children's Sleepware," *The New York Times*, April 8, 1977, p. A14.
3. "The Breakdown of U.S. Innovation," *Business Week*, Feb. 16, 1976, pp. 55–56.
4. See John C. Chambers, Satinder K. Mullick, and Donald D. Smith, *An Executive Guide to Forecasting*, Wiley-Interscience, New York, 1974, chapter 2, for a discussion of the managerial implications of forecasting. This section borrows from that chapter.
5. Peter J. LaPlaca, *Feasibility and Economic Impact Study of the Proposed Shipbuilding Facility in Hanover Parish*, LaPlaca Associates, Vernon, Conn. 1974.

6. Steven Wheelwright and Darral Clarke, "Corporate Forecasting: Promise and Reality," *Harvard Business Review*, November–December 1976, pp. 40–64.
7. George Steiner, *Top Management Planning*, Macmillan, New York, 1969, p. 221.
8. R. A. Lloyd, "Combine Forecasting Methods for Demand Estimates," *Industrial Marketing Management*, 1976, pp. 89–93.
9. Adapted from R. L. McLaughlin, *Time Series Forecasting*, American Marketing Association, Chicago, 1962, pp. 7–9.
10. Dale Sommer, "Cycle Forecasting Spots Trends," *Industry Week*, April 25, 1977.
11. "A Parker Checklist for Cyclical Periods," Parker Hannifin Corp., 1976.
12. William G. Sullivan and W. Wayne Claycombe, *Fundamentals of Forecasting*, Reston, 1977, p. 63.
13. Eliot D. Ranard, "Use of Input/Output Concepts in Sales Forecasting," *Journal of Marketing Research*, February 1972, pp. 53–58.
14. Hoy F. Carman, "Improving Sales Forecasts for Appliances," *Journal of Marketing Research*, May 1972, pp. 214–218.
15. William Gunn, "Airline System Simulation," *Operations Research*, March–April 1964, pp. 206–229.
16. *Forecasting Sales*, National Industrial Conference Board, New York, 1963, pp. 87–90.

Market research is used to identify new market segments.

Case 1

Tennis Racket Market Segmentation

As part of its effort to improve its position in the tennis equipment market, the Spalding Division of the Questor Corporation had authorized a major market research study. Although the study was designed to develop information useful to the overall market planning process, its principal purpose was to identify market segments for tennis rackets.

For years the principal means of segmenting the tennis racket market had been by price or by materials used for the frame (wood, metal, or composite materials). Spalding officials also were aware from market research and observation that different players selected specific brands and types of rackets—according to factors such as their age, sex, income, skill, frequency of play, and peer group influence. But Spalding was unsure as to which combinations of factors constituted a discrete preference group and what the sizes of these groups were.

Background

One of the best known names in sports equipment, the A. G. Spalding Corp.* introduced its first tennis rackets in 1888. Spalding had lost position in the tennis equipment market during the 1950s when management had decided to concentrate on faster-growing sports. By the 1970s, when tennis had become a major growth sport, Spalding ranked a poor third in market share after the Wilson and Head brands. Both Wilson and Head were successful with higher-price rackets sold primarily through tennis pro and specialty shops. Spalding's strength was in lower-priced rackets sold primarily through sporting goods stores and discount department stores. Wilson was a full-line manufacturer selling in all price ranges through all channels. Head concentrated in the higher-price segment.

To build sales volume and raise profit margins, the Tennis Business Unit of Spalding had begun developing higher-quality, higher-price rackets for sale through pro and specialty shops where the more sophisticated tennis players did much of their buying. But Spalding was hampered both by its image as a low-quality manufacturer of tennis rackets and by the aggressive efforts of the market leaders who were determined to hold their positions in the high-price market segment. As a result, Spalding's management found it more difficult than had been anticipated to break into the higher end of the market. It was in this setting that the business unit manager for tennis products, Scott Creelman, authorized a major market research study. Mr. Creelman hoped to identify market opportunities, including market segments, that would lead to more effective tennis racket marketing strategies for Spalding.

The Market Research Study

The study was conducted during 1977 among a national sample of regular tennis players (those who play one or more times a month) by a reputable market research firm. The purposes of the study were to:

1. Identify the various market segments for tennis rackets
2. Identify Spalding's strengths and weaknesses
3. Identify where product improvements were needed
4. Identify new marketing, distribution, and product opportunities.
5. Examine Spalding in relation to its competition and identify competitors' strengths and weaknesses.

Information was collected from each respondent concerning: age; sex; income; geographic area; frequency of purchase; place of purchase; frequency of play; years of play; types of partners; brand owned; future racket purchase intentions by brand, type (such as frame materials), prestrung or unstrung, and price; the player's appraisal of his or her own playing style and degree of skill; and the player's ranking of various racket attributes.

Using statistical techniques designed to correlate and analyze multiple data, the study identified five player segments which in total covered 93 percent of regular tennis players. The player segments were defined essentially on the basis of three factors: (1) degree of playing skill, (2) length of time playing the game, and (3) style of play.

---

*A.G. Spalding Corp. was acquired by Questor Corporation in 1969.

Degree of playing skill and length of playing time were developed from direct questioning. Style of play was determined from respondents' self-appraisals of their games: can hit ball hard, stamina, quick reflexes, aggressiveness, volley, serve, net play, steady coolness, forehand, speed covering court, concentration, confidence, psychology, placement of ball, strategy, consistency, experience, and backhand.

Answers were tabulated by categories of players including male, female, light buyers, heavy buyers, prices paid, price elasticity (degree of willingness to pay more for next racket), and place of purchase.

Once the five segments had been identified on the basis of playing skill, length of time playing the game, and style of play, the segments were analyzed in terms of their relative size, ratio of male to female players, and the price they expected to pay for their next racket. Exhibit 1-1 shows how the segments vary by skill, time, and style. It also shows how the segments break down according to relative size, the male/female ratio, and the percent of players who expect to spend over $40 (a pricing point for more expensive rackets) for their next racket.

Further breakdowns by segments were made for factors which seem to influence selection when buyers purchase new rackets:

1. Preferred racket attributes
2. Preferred frame materials
3. Strung versus unstrung racket
4. Whether racket is used and endorsed by a professional player
5. Professional appearance of the racket
6. Whether racket is recommended by a pro or specialty shop

It was found that the above factors varied for each of the five segments, further reinforcing the idea of segmentation based on skill, time, and style of play.

Uses of Segmentation Findings

Now that the market research findings were available, Mr. Creelman was faced with the question of whether to plan Spalding's tennis racket strategies around the newly defined but unorthodox segments. He and his marketing staff believed that there were essentially two uses of segmentation information:

EXHIBIT 1-1
Characteristics of Tennis Racket Market Segments

Characteristics	Segments				
	A	B	C	D	E
Degree of skill	Highest	Second highest	Average	Second lowest	Least
Time played the game	Longest	Average	Second highest	Second lowest	Shortest
Style of play	Two groups: 1. Play *percentage game:* tactical, methodical. 2. Play *forcing game:* inventive, aggressive.	*Anticipation game:* alert, responsive, anticipates opponent.	*Competitive:* hits the ball hard.	*Careful:* tries to avoid errors.	*Enthusiastic:* tries to overpower and deceive opponents.
Percent of potential	26%	15%	13%	18%	21%
Percent male to female	58/42	50/50	70/30	59/41	53/47
Percent will spend over $40.00 for next racket	50%	64%	62%	27%	40%

1. For product line planning purposes to guide the development of products which would meet the needs and preferences of each segment.
2. For planning promotional programs targeted to appeal to the interests and preferences of each segment

Obviously there would be risk in switching corporate resources from the current marketing strategies, which were tied to the traditional price and type of racket segments. The new segments were intriguing but untested under real market conditions. Yet, if the five segments had been correctly identified, plans could be developed that might clearly differentiate the Spalding brand and give the company a clear-cut marketing advantage. It was believed that Spalding already had rackets well suited for some of the segments, but additional rackets would be needed to satisfy all five segments.

Mr. Creelman and his staff began an intensive review of the pros and cons of the proposed market segmentation.

QUESTIONS

1. Should Spalding use any or all of the five newly defined market segments as a basis for its markeging strategy?
2. How should the rackets be priced by segment?
3. Recommend a name for the racket designed for each segment.
4. Recommend a promotional program targeted to each segment, including ways of reaching the segments.

How Heublein uses forecasts of the external environment in its annual strategic planning process

Case 2

Heublein, Inc.: Environmental Scanning for Strategic Planning

During the winter of 1978-1979, Heublein was engaged in its annual planning process, preparing for the company's 1980 fiscal year which would begin July 1, 1979. Like other large multibusiness companies, Heublein had found it necessary to adopt formal planning programs with increasing emphasis placed on strategic planning.

Management had seen its businesses affected more and more (both positively and negatively) by external environmental developments over which it had little or no control. Attempting to identify and predict environmental change, therefore, was considered one of the keys to the development of effective strategies.

The Company

Heublein, headquartered in Farmington, Conn., was engaged in four major businesses: distilled spirits, wines, specialty grocery products, and fast-food restaurants. The businesses were organized into groups headed by group vice presidents. There was also a vice president for the International Group. Each group had a strategic planning department which maintained a close working relationship with the director of Corporate Planning and Research.

Heublein's brands were among the best known in their respective industries. They included Smirnoff vodka, Inglenook wines, A.1. Steak Sauce, and Kentucky Fried Chicken restaurants. A listing of the company's brands is shown in Exhibit 2-1.

During the 1970s Heublein had enjoyed a good record of growth, until 1977 when the company encountered several problems. Return on equity (ROE) had improved since hitting a low of 12.8 percent in 1977. Further improvement in ROE was one of management's objectives. Financial results in 1970 and 1979 are compared below.

	1979	1970
Sales, $1000s	1,769,074	636,038
Net income, $1000s	68,130	31,925
Earnings per share	$3.19	$1.70
Return on shareholders' equity	15.8%	18.8%

A comparison of sales, operating profits, and assets by the four business segments for the years 1978 and 1979 are shown in Exhibit 2-2. Management was particularly

EXHIBIT 2-1

Heublein Brands of Foods and Beverages. (*Source: Heublein, Inc., Annual Report,* 1979).

Heublein Brands of Foods and Beverages

Listed below are the principal brands of fine foods and beverages marketed by Heublein. When you have occasion to use products of this type, we invite you to order Heublein brands by name — you'll be getting the finest products of their kind.

SPIRITS: Smirnoff Vodkas (80° & 100°) · Smirnoff Silver (90.4°) · Black Velvet Canadian Whisky · Black & White Scotch · Arrow Cordials and Brandies · Bahia Licor de Cafe · Heublein Cocktails · The Club Cocktails · Jose Cuervo Tequila · Cuervo 1800 · Don Q Rum · Irish Mist Liqueur · Milshire Gin · Tullamore Dew Irish Whiskey · Popov Vodka · Relska Vodka · Arrow Ostrova Vodka · McMaster's Scotch and Canadian Whiskies · Matador Tequila · Malcolm Hereford's Cows · Yukon Jack Canadian Liqueur · Boggs Cranberry Liqueur · Vaklova Liqueur

CALIFORNIA WINES: Beaulieu Vineyard Wines · Inglenook Vineyards Wines · Colony Table Wines, Dessert Wines and Aperitifs · Petri Wines · Annie Green Springs Refreshment Wines · T.J. Swann Refreshment Wines · Bali Hai Tropical Flavored Wine · Sangrole · Mission Bell Wines · Santa Fe Dessert Wines · H.M.S. Frost · Esprit · Jacare · G & D Wines and Vermouth · Lejon Champagne and Brandy · Jacques Bonet Champagne and Brandy · Zazie Refreshment Wine

IMPORTED WINES: Lancers Vin Rose, Vinho Branco and Rubeo · Harveys Bristol Cream · Bouchard Pere & Fils Burgundy · Egri Bikaver Hungarian Wine · Tokaji Aszu Hungarian Dessert Wine · Harveys Other Sherries and Ports · Vinya Rose · Kiku Masamune Sake · Taru Sake

CONVENIENCE FOODS: Colonel Sanders' Recipe Kentucky Fried Chicken · Extra Crispy Chicken · Barbecue Style Chicken · H. Salt Seafood · The Colonel's Little Bucket Desserts · Zantigo Mexican-American Foods

SAUCES AND SPECIALTY FOODS: A.1. Steak Sauce · Grey Poupon Mustard · Ortega Tacos, Chiles, Sauces and Mexican-style Foods · Snap-E-Tom Tomato Cocktail · Regina Wine Vinegars and Cooking Wines · Escoffier Sauces · Steak Supreme Sauce · Hart's Dinner Rolls, Muffins and Buttermilk Biscuits

HEUBLEIN INC. FARMINGTON CONNECTICUT 06032

pleased with the improving earnings in the restaurant area, a business which had encountered serious problems in 1977.

Strategic Planning at Heublein

The current planning cycle was the continuation of a corporation-wide planning system which Heublein had begun as a pilot program in 1975. Entering 1978, strategic planning was coordinated by the director of Corporate Planning and Research. The position was filled by Robert W. Pratt, Jr., who had come to Heublein in 1976 from General Electric's strategic planning function to head up Heublein's Economic and Marketing Research.

In this position, Mr. Pratt reported to C. W. Carriuolo, executive vice president. While the development of plans was the responsibility of the business groups, the overall direction, scheduling, and coordination were provided by Mr. Pratt and his staff. The organization of Corporate Planning and Research is shown in Exhibit 2-3.

Environmental Scanning. Mr. Pratt believed that one distinguishing characteristic of strategic planning was its concern with the external environment. Analyzing the environment and forecasting change, therefore, was essential to effective strategy formulation. His views are illustrated by an excerpt from a talk he gave before the Conference Board, a private business research group:

The essential purpose of strategic planning is to make sure that factors that impinge on a particular business are identified and their potential impacts understood, so that the business can be positioned to achieve both its long- and short-term objectives within its environment. The purpose of a strategic planning process is to provide a structured approach that will minimize the probability of making decisions without consideration of factors that could impact the outcome of those decisions.

The initial phase of virtually all strategic planning processes—and this is certainly true for our approach at Heublein—requires some form of environmental

EXHIBIT 2-2
Business Segment Data

	1979, $1000s	1978, $1000s
REVENUES		
Spirits	819,563	742,575
Wines	368,972	324,794
Grocery	114,193	118,160
Restaurants	466,346	434,583
	1,769,074	1,620,112
OPERATING PROFIT		
Spirits	87,599	73,105
Wines	29,422	28,895
Grocery	17,989	17,949
Restaurants	34,966	26,711
	169,976	146,660
IDENTIFIABLE ASSETS		
Spirits	300,605	272,257
Wines	281,969	221,748
Grocery	66,696	61,170
Restaurants	242,266	227,659
Corporate	80,382	100,412
	971,918	883,246

Source: Heublein 1979 *Annual Report.*

EXHIBIT 2-3
Corporate Planning and Research Organization

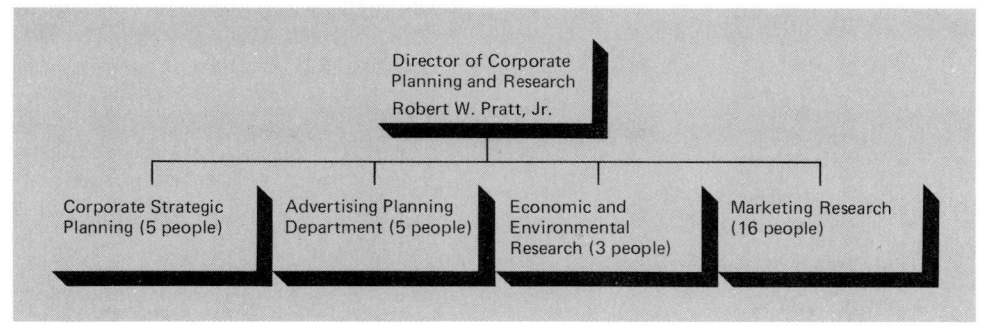

```
                    Director of Corporate
                    Planning and Research
                    Robert W. Pratt, Jr.
        ┌───────────────┬──────────────┬───────────────┐
  Corporate Strategic  Advertising Planning  Economic and         Marketing Research
  Planning (5 people)  Department (5 people) Environmental        (16 people)
                                             Research (3 people)
```

scanning and analysis, with the objective of identifying and understanding external conditions or forces that have the potential for influencing or modifying, either directly or indirectly, the results of specific internal decisions and actions.*

Stuart D. Watson, Heublein's chairman, shared the view that anticipating change in the external environment was important. Mr. Watson had stated on more than one occasion in talks before marketing organizations that what he needed from marketing research was less information about the past and more about the future.

Steps in the Planning Process. Management interest in the future of the external environment had led to environmental scanning and analysis becoming the first step in the year-long planning process. Environmental analysis began at the corporate level with subjects of corporate-wide interest and was followed by environmental analysis at each business group level.

The principal steps in the strategic planning process as they led up to the development and approval of group operating plans and budgets are discussed here and shown in Exhibit 2-4.

1. Corporate Strategic Planning initiates the annual planning process by issuing planning guidelines and preparing an environmental assessment which is reviewed with group planners.
2. Environmental analyses are conducted by each group. These include an analysis of the industry structure, impact of environmental trends and events of group operations and existing strategies, and an analysis of competition.
3a. Corporate management develops overall corporate goals and objectives.
3b. Each group establishes its proposed mission, goals, and objectives, and identifies "critical issues" that represent significant threats or opportunities relative to achieving the goals and objectives.
4. Group goals and objectives are jointly reviewed by group and corporate management as they relate to corporate goals and objectives. This step serves as a required "green light" to continue the strategic planning process.
5. Groups develop strategy alternatives to meet goals and objectives; constraints are identified; areas for direct action and contingencies are identified; and detailed financial implications are developed.
6a. Groups analyze strategies for consistency.
6b. Corporate management reviews and analyzes plans of each group and the business units therein.
7. Group strategies are jointly reviewed by corporate and group managements.
8. Corporate management conducts a strategy analysis based on the entire portfolio of business units. Results are used to establish strategic directions for corporate and group actions (i.e., which businesses to invest in, which to harvest). Results are communicated to each group.
9. As necessary, the Corporate Development Department investigates alternatives for meeting corporate goals and objectives over and above contributions of existing businesses (e.g., acquisitions).
10. Based on strategic directions from corporate management, groups prepare action and contingency plans.
11. Groups prepare operating plans and budgets for the ensuing year.

*"Anticipating the Future: Some Applications of Environmental Research," by Robert W. Pratt, Jr., presented to the 1977 Marketing Conference of the Conference Board, New York, October 27, 1977.

EXHIBIT 2-4
Overview of the 1979 Planning Process

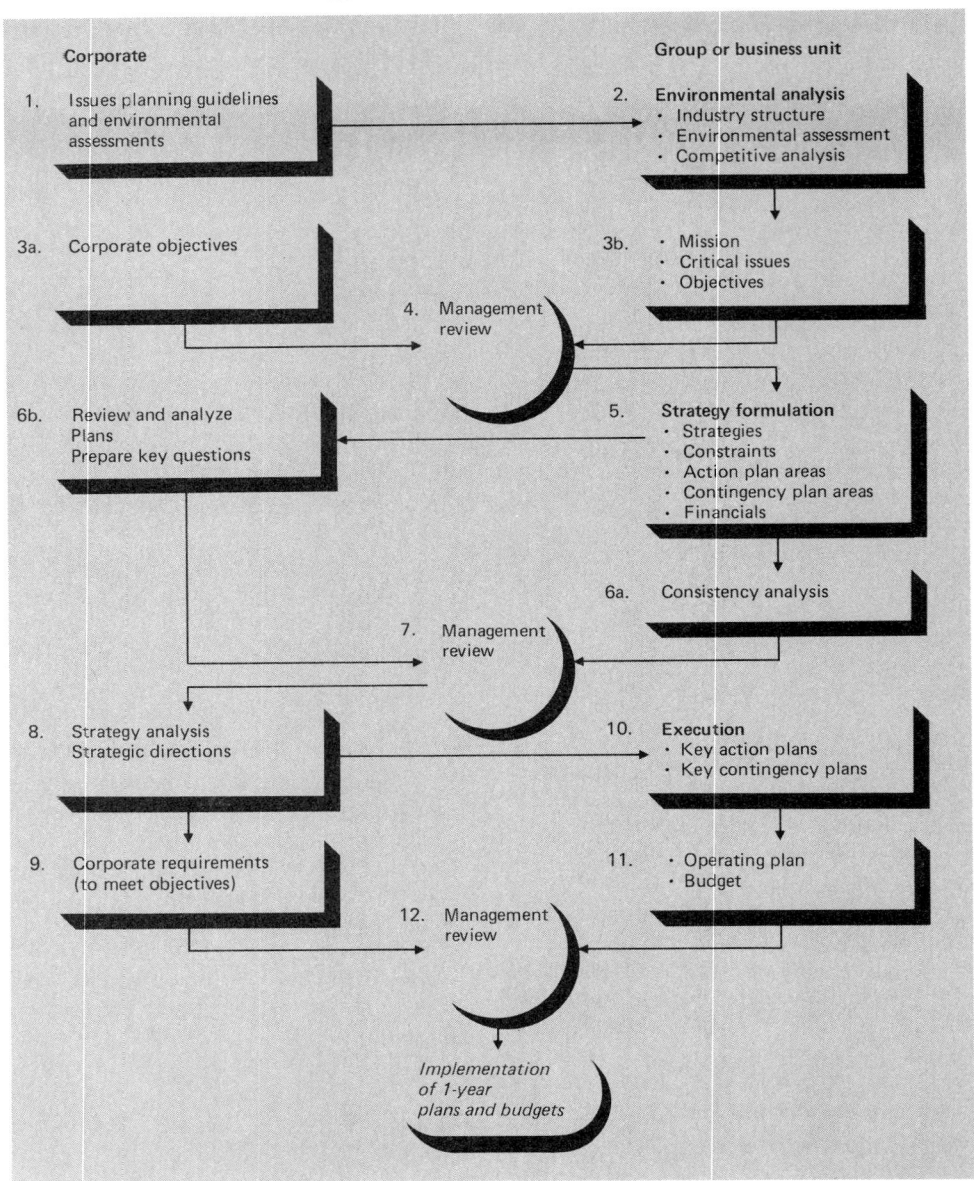

Corporate

1. Issues planning guidelines and environmental assessments

3a. Corporate objectives

6b. Review and analyze Plans
Prepare key questions

8. Strategy analysis
Strategic directions

9. Corporate requirements (to meet objectives)

Group or business unit

2. Environmental analysis
   - Industry structure
   - Environmental assessment
   - Competitive analysis

3b.
   - Mission
   - Critical issues
   - Objectives

4. Management review

5. Strategy formulation
   - Strategies
   - Constraints
   - Action plan areas
   - Contingency plan areas
   - Financials

6a. Consistency analysis

7. Management review

10. Execution
    - Key action plans
    - Key contingency plans

11.
    - Operating plan
    - Budget

12. Management review

Implementation of 1-year plans and budgets

---

12. Corporate and group managements review and adjust, when necessary, operating plans and budgets.

It should be noted that the operating businesses do not prepare their annual operating plans and budgets until their strategies have been approved by corporate management.

The balance of the corporate planning process includes the following: Corporate staff departments prepare their departmental plans and budgets for corporate management review. Corporate development plans are prepared for areas outside the charters of the business groups. Finally, a consolidated corporate budget and summary of strategies and action plans are prepared.

Environmental Analysis at Group Level. The environmental analysis is comprised of three components. The first, industry structure, deals with items such as concentration ratios, barriers to entry, and leverage enjoyed by buyers. The second component of the group's environmental analysis is a complete assessment of the impact of selected environmental factors submitted by Corporate Planning and Research and/or those identified and analyzed by the group (e.g., zoning for fast food, grape supply for wines). Group planners would estimate the impact of energy costs on group sales and operating costs, or they would assess the sales impact of a change in the minimum drinking age in a state.

The third component involves an analysis of competition. What are competitors' programs, strengths, and weaknesses? How prepared are they to meet changes in the environment? Will the anticipated environmental factors have a positive or negative impact on competitors? The analysis also looks at the various types of indirect as well as direct competition. For example, supermarkets compete indirectly with Kentucky Fried Chicken for the consumer's food dollar. Waybest or Purdue brands of chicken sold in stores are less direct. McDonald's and other fast-food outlets compete directly for the fast-food consumer dollar, while chains offering fried chicken, such as Church's, are direct competitors at the brand level.

Environmental Analysis at Corporate Level. In the first year of strategic planning at Heublein, environmental scanning was carried on only by the business groups. Subsequently, scanning of selected environmental areas of interest to two or more groups became the responsibility of corporate planning and research. By 1979 information on over 140 different topics was being provided. Exhibit 2-5 shows a partial listing.

The 1979 Heublein *Environmental Assessment Book* consisted of 300 pages of forecasts and analyses. To assist with the gathering and organizing of this information, Heublein engaged the services of the Futures Group, a consulting firm specializing in environmental analysis. The assessment book analyzed the macroenvironment in which Heublein would operate over the next five years. It was an update of the previous year's environmental assessment and an expansion of critical issues. The assessment book was designed to provide the most relevant set of uncontrollable, macro issues which could offer potentially significant threats or opportunities to Heublein's businesses. Each group was responsible for selection of those events which would have an impact on its businesses, the determination of impacts and financial effects on its businesses, and the determination of events warranting contingency plans. The information contained in the assessment book was intended to complement research done in the groups, thereby allowing more time and effort to be spent on interpreting industry, competitive, and marketing reseach information that relates to strategies and implications for specific businesses.

The initial section of the book was entitled "Scenarios" and provided an overview of the most likely environment for the next five years. Following this were sections dealing with: the economy, raw materials, demography, social change, technology, media trends, and the international environment. Each section contained analyses of numerous factors influencing the particular environment, their probabilities of occurrence, and their potential impacts on Heublein.

Sources of Environmental Information. The Economic and Environmental Research Department uses a wide range of sources to develop its *Environmental Assessment Book*. These can be grouped into five major categories:

1. *Government publications*, from the Environmental Protection Agency; Bureau of Labor Statistics; departments of Energy, Transportation, and Health, Education and Welfare; the Bureau of the Census; Council of Economic Advisors; the Federal Reserve; Bureau of Alcohol, Tobacco, and Firearms; Bureau of Economic Analysis; and others
2. *Industry and trade publications*, such as those of the Conference Board; National Restaurant Association; Consumer Report of Eating Share Trends; National Association of Beverage Importers; and the Distilled Spirits Council of the United States
3. *Periodicals*, including *Futurist*; *Futures*; *Foreign Affairs*; *Business Week*; *Forbes*; *Duns Review*; *Daedalus*; *Social Policy*; *Technology Review*; *Mother Jones*; *MS*; *Business and Society*; *Scientific American*; *U.S. News and World Report*; *American Demographics*; *Commentary*; and *World Business*
4. *Special information sources*, such as the *Yankelovich Monitor*; SRI's *VALS*; University of Michigan's *Monitoring*

EXHIBIT 2-5
Partial List of Environmental Topics Monitored

ECONOMICS	DEMOGRAPHY	MEDIA
Economic highlights	Demographic highlights	Media highlights
Real GNP	Population	Television
Inflation	Births and fertility rates	Radio
Prime interest rate	Population distribution by age	Magazines
Savings rate	Age-income distribution	Newspapers
Unemployment rate	1985 household distribution	Outdoor
Real disposable income	Age-income distribution of	
Real disposable income per household	HH's earning $25+	INTERNATIONAL
Tax and nontax payments as percent of personal income	Age-income distribution of HH's earning $50+	Highlights
		Japan
Heublein annual economic projections	Households	Great Britain
Cyclelong scenario	SOCIAL CHANGE	Canada
Trendlong scenario	Working women	Australia
Pessimistic scenario	Multiearner families	Brazil
RAW MATERIALS	Societal orientation toward conversation	Mexico
Raw material highlights	Generic brands	Exchange rates
Beef	Health and nutrition	U.S. dollar
Broilers	The changing employee	Japanese yen
Corn	Values and lifestyle	French franc
Soybean oil	Legislation and regulation	British pound sterling
Sugar	TECHNOLOGY	Italian lire
High fructose corn syrup	Changing distribution patterns	Canadian dollar
Wheat (KC #1 hard)	New food technologies	Australian dollar
Corrugated fiber boxes	Changes in home technologies	Brazilian cruzeiro
Electricity		Mexican peso
Peroleum		
Natural gas		

Source: Heublein *Environmental Assessment Book,* 1979.

Economic Change Program; *Gallup Economic Service*; Data Resources' *Macroeconomic Service*; Data Resources' *Agricultural Service*; and The Futures Group's *Consumer Prospects*

5. *Miscellaneous publications*, such as from the Brookings Institution; Urban Institute; Congressional Clearing House; brokerage firms; and major banks

Some of the private reporting services to which Heublein subscribed are described below:

The Yankelovich Monitor is a service of Yankelovich, Skelly, and White, Inc. It provides its client companies with an overview of the U.S. social climate and the general implications that specific elements of this social climate may have on market decisions. It is a basic assessment, from survey data, or "what's on the mind of America?" Some of the issues covered by the *Monitor* survey are: attitudes toward the future economic condition of America and of the individual values of the American people; social themes; and attitudes toward social and public institutions. *Monitor* also develops in-depth implications of these elements of the social climate on the specific industries of its client sponsor.

VALS (Values and Lifestyles) is a service of the Stanford Research Institute (SRI). Using a psychological typology based on an elaboration and extension of Maslow's hierarchy of needs, SRI divides the U.S. population into nine segments based on their positions in this hierarchy. For each segment, *VALS* provides demographic characteristics, analysis of values of lifestyles and their changes, and analysis of their impact on buying patterns. Sponsors of the *VALS* service can then use this information to help analyze the impact of changing values on their particular businesses.

The Survey Research Center of the University of Michigan provides monthly measures of consumer sentiment and expectations of future economic conditions. Since what consumers spend their money on now (and how much) is partially a function of what they anticipate their future economic fate will be, measures such as the expectation data are useful in developing estimates of total expenditures and of spending in broad categories such as housing, recreation, and transportation.

Data Resources, Inc. provides macroeconomic data for major segments of the United States economy. These data can be used as input to economic models of those sectors of the economy within which the company operates. DRI provides projections for the near and intermediate planning horizon. Another service of DRI provides information on United States agriculture. This service provides supply and demand projections for agricultural commodities such as wheat, corn, soybeans, hogs, chickens, and beef.

Consumer Prospects, a service of the Futures Group, provides detailed information on consumer demographics. The most recent trends for numerous demographic variables (e.g., age groupings, family size, occupations, marriage and divorce rates) are used to project these variables into the future. Exhibit 2-6 takes examples from the Heublein *Environmental Assessment Book*, June 1979, to show how implications for Heublein's businesses are drawn from demographic projections.

Using Environmental Data in Sales Forecasting

An important part of the strategic planning process is the preparation of demand forecasts for the next fiscal year as well as for the longer term. Robert Pratt believed that environmental influences were an important consideration in sales forecasting. His views were stated in his talk referred to earlier:

Our kit of forecasting techniques has expanded substantially over the last six years. For example, we have witnessed rapid development and expanded application of:

1. Trend impact analysis (TIA), a technique that was developed to modify historically based extrapolations, such as those based on regressions, by quantifying the potential impact of possible unprecedented or unexpected events that may change the historical trend.
2. Cross impact analysis (CIA), a technique that attempts to anticipate the effect that actual occurrence of a specific event could have on the likelihood of occurrence of one or more additional events. The events, of course, may be technological, social, economic, political or any combination of these.
3. The Delphi technique, which offers a systematic approach for gathering and quantifying information, including qualitative judgments, from a group of individuals who are experts in a particular subject area. The technique, or a modified version, is frequently used in completing trend and cross-impact analyses.

These are intended as examples. The use of scenarios and computer simulation models are other techniques that have been gaining wider acceptance during this decade.

The development and expanded application of techniques to quantify judgmental variables, to better understand interactions among variables and to develop and display alternate futures have occurred primarily because conventional forecasting techniques of the 1950s and 1960s are not serving us as well as they once did.

The effectiveness of many of the traditional techniques is premised on the assumption that the future will be like the past. Thus, if we can determine cause and effect using historical data, the same relationships are assumed to be valid looking ahead. This general assumption underlies, for example, most regression forecasts. If there is one lesson we have learned in the 1970s, however, it is that there are trends and events that may not have existed in the recent past, but that are nonetheless likely to have a major impact on future projections. Enter the newer techniques.

I'll close with an observation regarding what I consider to be a logical next step for forecasting. The hypothetical sales forecasts [shown in Exhibit 2-7] include both a standard regression forecast and a band of forecasts generated using trend impact analysis. Note that not one of the TIA forecasts overlaps the traditional regression forecast—not an unusual occurrence.

Also note that there is no most probable projection indicated within the band. Looking ahead, it seems to me that the job of the forecaster may become that of providing management with reasonable bands of uncertainty, but not point estimates. An assessment of the importance of a specific forecast will provide a basis for determining the resources that should be committed to developing the band. A band can be drawn in one minute using a pencil or developed over a period of years using various combinations of the techniques just described.

EXHIBIT 2-6
Examples of Demographic Highlights

	Description 1980–1990	
Trend	Most Likely Direction	Implications
Fertility rate	The rate will probably not show much of an increase above the present lifetime births of 1.8 children per woman. The number of babies born, however, will increase over present levels approximating that of all 1950s in some years (including postponed births, end of marriage squeeze), but will be spread among more families. There is a possibility that the fertility rate may increase toward the end of the decade as a less crowded age cohort reaches the family formation age.	Women will withdraw from the labor force for shorter periods to rear children because of smaller families; higher dual incomes will be maintained for longer periods. The larger number of babies will increase opportunities for child-oriented products and eating facilities; the smaller number per family will enable more to be spent on each child.
Age Groups	The median age of the population will increase as the baby boom moves into the prime age group: 25-44. The 45-55 group, the depression cohort, will decrease and the number of elderly will continue to increase (although) not as a percent of population).	Teenagers will be a declining market (except for blacks). Greatest growth will in 25-44 age segments. This age group eats out more frequently and spends more per meal than other groups; also likely to do more home entertaining. Opportunity exists to appeal to over 55 age group, more affluent and younger acting than previously; also additional market of older people working part-time to replace teenagers, keep up with inflation. "Senior" households spend more annually on food eaten at home than national average. They eat out less often than families headed by younger people, but when they go out, they spend more than the average patron (in both fast service units and atmosphere/specialty restaurants). Market for congregate feeding for elderly, catered food for institutions.
Household formation rate	The household formation rate will decline as the nuber of 18- to 24- year-olds diminishes and as higher housing costs cause more doubling up.	Although rate slowing, opportunity exists to serve large number of dual-income households with members who are well educated and have expensive, gourmet tastes.
Age of household head	Aging of the baby boom population will result in rapid growth of household heads aged 25-45 from 37 percent to 42 percent of all households.	Emphasis on young adult households—more likely to be homeowners and home entertainers.
One- and two-person households	The growth of two-person households is expected to accelerate in the coming decade as the growth of one-person households diminishes.	Single population will not grow as fast, but will still be large.

EXHIBIT 2-6 *(Continued)*
Examples of Demographic Highlights

	Description 1980–1990	
Trend	Most Likely Direction	Implications
Women in the labor force	The participation rate of women in the labor force (now about 50 percent) will continue to increase, but at a slower rate. Driving forces will be economic need, expansion of female-oriented clerical and service jobs, and the fact that highly educated women are more apt to work, regardless of family income. The two-earner household will be the standard.	In fast foods, more working women with higher family income offer tradeup opportunities for menu diversification. Working women exhibit special food shopping, preparation, and eating patterns. They are more likely to eat beef, drink beer and wine with dinner, shop for food less frequently, and spend less time preparing food. They also entertain more often. Although it is always assumed that working women use more convenience foods, a recent survey reports they are more apt to use fresh ingredients. Advertising should increasingly target men and adolescents who are more often doing the family shopping. Advertising funds will likely shift away from daytime TV.

Source: Heublein Environmental Assessment Book, June 1979.

EXHIBIT 2-7

Hypothetical Sales Forecasts. (*Source*: Robert W. Pratt, Jr., "Anticipating the Future: Some Applications of Environmental Research," presented to the 1977 Marketing Conference of the Conference Board, Inc., New York, October 27, 1977).

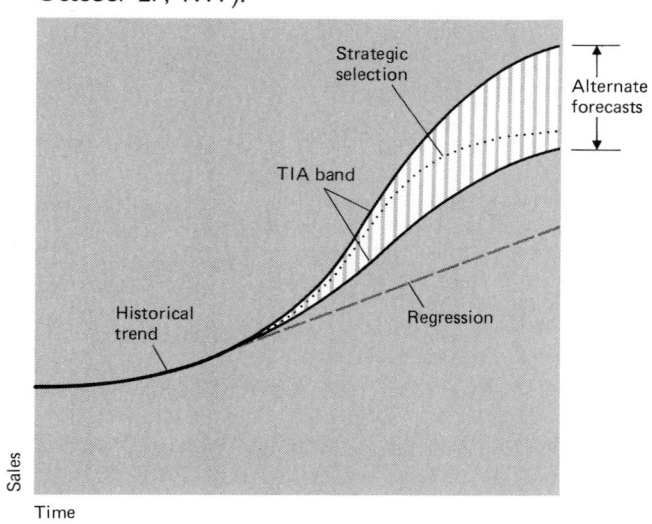

Determining the specific set of points estimates to use within a band should fall to strategic planning. It is strategic planning techniques, not forecasting techniques, that are best able to assess position within a band.*

QUESTIONS

1. Considering separately each of Heublein's four business areas (spirits, wines, specialty grocery products, and fast-food restaurants), which of the environmental topics listed in Exhibit 2-5 is likely to have a significant impact on each of these businesses during the next few years?
2. Pick the three to four most crucial issues for each business and explain what impact they might have, using basic data from census and other library sources in preparing your environmental forecast.

*Op. cit.

Whether the environmental forecast should influence KFC's plans

Case 3

Heublein, Inc.: Using Environmental Data At Kentucky Fried Chicken

In the earlier Heublein, Inc. case, the corporation's planning system and approach to environmental scanning were described. Robert Pratt, Jr., director of Corporate Planning and Research, was reviewing the linkages which division executives had made between environmental factors and actual marketing strategies. He was particularly concerned with the Food Service and Franchising Group. Partly because of several operating problems with Kentucky Fried Chicken, total food operations had a significant reduction in profits in 1977 and 1978 (see Exhibit 3-1). The turn-around which began in the latter half of 1978 continued during 1979. Corporate management wanted to be sure that this trend would continue and that KFC strategies were in tune with environmental changes that could impact KFC operations.

The change in KFC's sales and profits had been due largely to improved operations in the company-owned restaurants. Average annual sales per company-owned outlet were up 14 percent in 1979 to an all-time high.

EXHIBIT 3-1
Domestic Food Operations Revenues and Profits (Millions of dollars)

Revenues	1975	1976	1977	1978	1979
Company-owned KFC	272.4	279.5	245.3	224.8	246.1
Franchise fees and royalties	21.3	25.9	28.0	30.5	33.7
Food service	78.5	96.1	113.9	50.6	20.4
Grocery products	74.6	87.8	100.0	117.8	113.7
Total	446.8	489.3	487.2	423.7	413.9
Operating profit	58.8	57.0	35.8	34.4	38.2

Source: Hueblein 1979 Annual Report.

While improvements from these efforts were expected to continue, there was the question of whether KFC should also open additional outlets to stem its declining share of market.

The Industry

The industry in which KFC operates can be defined along a hierarchy of dimensions: place of service, image, time—convenience/price/menu limitations, on-off premise, food category, and brand. Exhibit 3-2 shows an approach to industry definition used by KFC. As shown in Exhibit 3-3, the rate of growth in consumption of food away from home had slowed markedly. The decline could have been due to several factors including the rising cost of gasoline, rapid increases in menu prices, and declines in real disposable personal income (DPI). In spite of the decline in growth of the food-away-from-home industry, the fast-food sector of the industry had continued to grow at an average rate of 2 percent per

EXHIBIT 3-2
Industry Definition, 1979

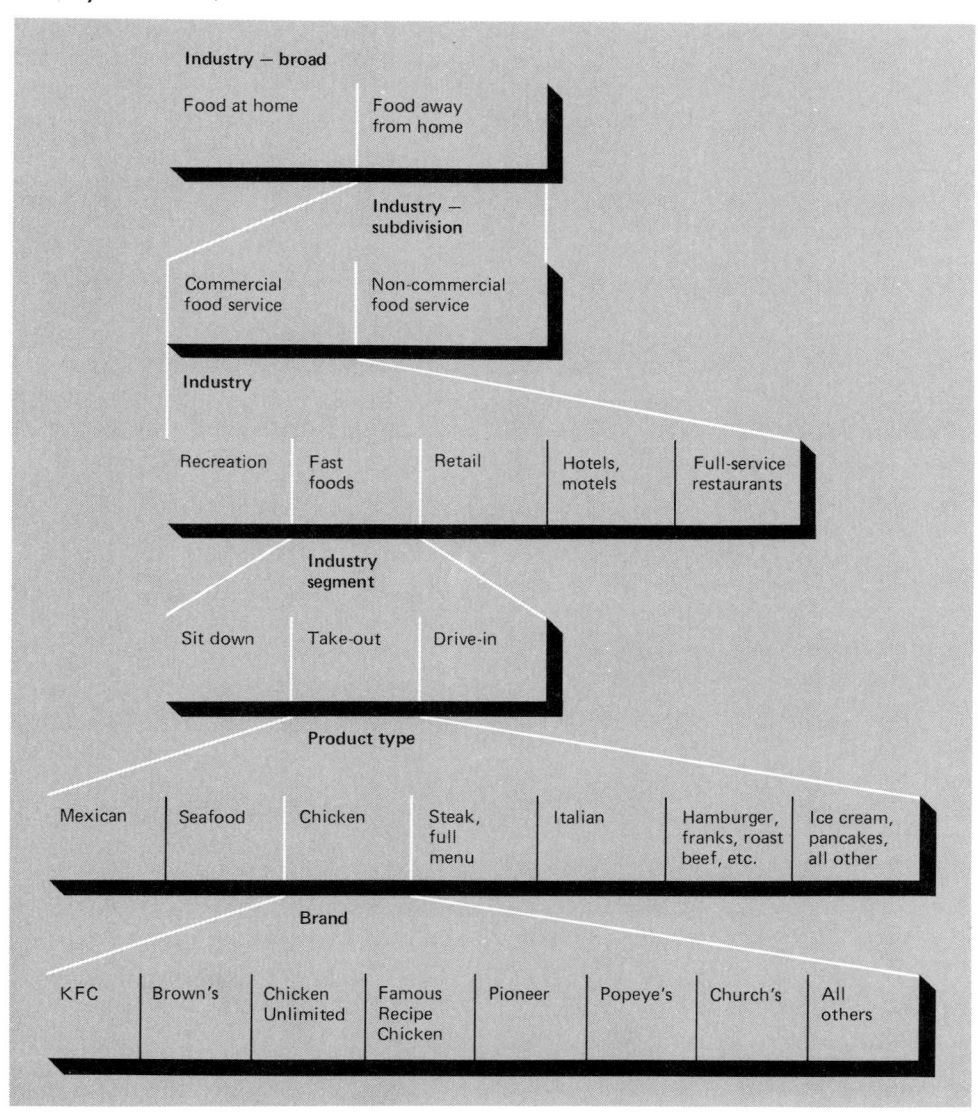

Industry — broad	Food at home; Food away from home
Industry — subdivision	Commercial food service; Non-commercial food service
Industry	Recreation; Fast foods; Retail; Hotels, motels; Full-service restaurants
Industry segment	Sit down; Take-out; Drive-in
Product type	Mexican; Seafood; Chicken; Steak, full menu; Italian; Hamburger, franks, roast beef, etc.; Ice cream, pancakes, all other
Brand	KFC; Brown's; Chicken Unlimited; Famous Recipe Chicken; Pioneer; Popeye's; Church's; All others

EXHIBIT 3-3

Consumption of Food Away from Home (Percentage change from previous fiscal year)

1972	+4.3	1976	+6.6
1973	+5.9	1977	+3.9
1974	+2.1	1978	+2.6
1975	+2.1	1979	+0.7

Source: Foods Group *Environmental Assessment Book.*

year. This was due to unit expansion (more outlets) and new competitors.

The chicken category of fast-food restaurants had a higher percentage of chain-controlled outlets than other categories (Exhibit 3-4). KFC's position as sole member of the industry had declined over the past decade. As shown in Exhibit 3-5, KFC's percentage of all chicken outlets declined from 94 percent in 1967 to 65 percent in 1978. Additionally, more rapid expansion by Church's, Famous Recipe, Pioneer, and others had eaten into KFC's market share of total sales. (Exhibit 3-6.)

The Economic Environment

The general economic picture was not expected to be highly favorable during the 1980s. Overall growth of the economy was expected to be slow, with continued high inflation. Some of the specific assumptions about the economic environment (as of June 1979) were:

Real GNP. At least a mild recession in the next two years, followed by growth averaging 2.7 to 3.0 percent.

Real DPI. A slowdown paralleling that of GNP, followed by growth averaging approximately 3 percent.

EXHIBIT 3-4

Concentration of Chains in Specific Types of Restaurants*

Type	Total Number of Units	Member of Chain-Controlled Units	% of Chain Members
Chicken	10,500	8,400	80
Hamburger	44,000	30,400	69
Ice cream	14,000	9,500	69
Full menu	100,000	13,700	14

*Data adjusted to protect confidentiality.

Source: Foods Group *Environmental Assessment Book.*

EXHIBIT 3-5

Growth of Chicken Restaurants*

	% of Units			
	1967	1972	1977	1978
KFC	94	86	75	65
Church's	2	10	15	21
Famous Recipe	2	2	3	3
Pioneer	—	1	4	4
Total %	98	99	97	93
Total number of industry units	1900	4100	5700	6900

*Data adjusted to protect confidentiality.

Source: Foods Group *Environmental Assessment Book.*

Inflation. Near-term rate at 8.5 percent or higher, with a winding down in the long term to about 7 percent.

Food expenditure. Will continue to grow in real terms while declining as a percent of DPI. Food away from home will grow somewhat more rapidly than food at home.

Prime interest rate. Will peak at 12 percent in FY 1980, but will remain high by historical standards.

Tax and nontax payments to government. Will continue to rise as a percent of personal income.

Demographics

Demographic trends have a significant impact on overall company performance. Fortunately these trends are relatively easy to predict and change only slowly. Some of the demographic trends of concern are:

The median age of the population will rise as the baby-boom group moves into the 25 to 44 age cohort.

The greatest growth will be in the 25 to 44 age segment: this age group eats out more frequently and spends more per meal than do other groups.

The U.S. population will continue to shift to the sunbelt and west.

Family size is decreasing. Smaller families tend to eat out more often. (Persons per household in 1960, 3.33; 1970, 3.14; 1980, 2.75.)

More women will join the work force and will account for 50 percent by 1990. This will result in an increase of dual-income families.

Blacks will increase as a percent of the population because of their higher birthrate. Increases in educa-

EXHIBIT 3-6
Estimated Market Share of Major Competitors*

Brand	Market Share, %	
	1978	1979
KFC	66	58
Church's	15	21
Famous Recipe	3	3
Pioneer	2	3
Popeye	1	2
Chicken Unlimited	1	1
Brown's	1	2
Others	11	10
Total sales, $ millions	1950	2400

*Data adjusted to protect confidentiality.
Source: Foods Group *Environmental Assessment Book.*

tion and training will reduce the gap between earnings of black and whites.

The growth of two-person households is expected to accelerate in the 1980s as the growth of one-person households diminishes.

Social Trends
Social trends reflect the aggregate mood of a culture. They are comprised of many factors including demographics, technology, economics, and lifestyle. Some of the factors which may have an effect on KFC are:

Increasing time pressures will result from continued growth in the number of working wives.

Continued growth in food away from home as eating out is increasingly viewed as a necessity rather than a luxury.

Intensification of consumer interest in nutrition.

Sales of microwave ovens will continue to grow, but at a slower rate.

People are consuming more frozen foods, ethnic foods, vegetables, fish, poultry, and wine.

There has been considerable growth in the following areas: outdoor recreational activities, travel (domestic and foreign), cultural activities (theater, opera, etc.), adult education, and home entertainment.

Interest in gourmet foods and gourmet cooking should continue and possibly grow.

"Senior" households (households headed by retired persons) eat out less often, but spend more when they do (in fast-food outlets as well as in atmosphere/specialty restaurants).

The Legislative and Regulatory Environment
The impact of government regulation seems to increase annually. Some of the new areas in which government will expand its impact are shown below. These are in addition to those areas where government has been involved for many years.

Franchise regulations are likely to become more restrictive for the franchisor.

Due to the energy situation, local, state, and federal regulations may restrict the use of lighted signs, and building temperature may also be controlled by regulation. New building codes will result in more energy-efficient buildings, but at a higher cost per square foot.

The FTC views menus as a form of advertising, and may require nutritional information on even standard menus.

Scheduled increases in the minimum wage may be postponed or canceled as the government attempts to ease unemployment, particularly among young people.

Regulations by the Occupational Safety and Health Administration may require new procedures in food preparation.

Deregulation of the trucking industry could mean lower distribution costs.

The FTC is considering banning "cumulative volume discounts" offered by newspapers and magazines to advertisers. If this happens, advertising costs would increase significantly.

Technology
Several technological trends will affect KFC operations in the next several years. The more significant ones relate to raw materials and store operations.

New breeding techniques continue to reduce the time of maturity for chickens. Chickens can now be harvested in 8 weeks rather than 9 weeks.

New chilling techniques could mean longer shelf life for chickens and other items.

Microwave techniques could provide improved in-store operations. However, changeover would mean large investments in new equipment.

QUESTIONS

1. Should Kentucky Fried Chicken expand its outlets at a rate that would increase—or at least prevent further decline of—its market share? In answering the question, assume that the current rate of profit return is satisfactory to Heublein's management. Explain your answer in terms of the environmental factors provided in the case.
2. If Heublein's long-term objective is to improve profitability, how might your decision be altered?
3. In light of today's environment, how would you update the environmental assessments made in this case? What considerations would you add to the list? Which would you delete?

PART THREE
The Strategic Marketing Planning Process

Any company engaging in marketing planning needs to ask and answer these questions:

1. How have we performed in recent years in terms of sales, profits, and market share?
2. What is our current position? Are we gaining, losing, or holding steady in sales, profits, and share of market?
3. What are our short- and long-range marketing objectives?
4. Will our present strategies enable us to achieve these objectives, or will it be necessary to modify present strategies or adopt new ones?

Planning is an inherent part of the management process in well-managed companies. The annual business plan provides the basis for profit forecasts and for allocating resources and measuring performance of the operating units of the business. For some years formalized marketing planning has been used to improve the management of the marketing function. While it continues to serve this purpose, it also has become the primary foundation upon which all other company planning is based.

The marketing plan culminates in the sales forecast from which production, financing, and profit plans emerge. Companies require outside financing both for current operations and expansion. Lenders decide whether to lend, how much to lend, and what interest rate to charge on the basis of the company's financial position and its profit forecasts. The degree of faith that lenders have in the profit forecasts depends in large measure on the credibility of the marketing plans.

Consequently, skill in planning has become an increasingly important qualification for the marketing manager. For this reason the next six chapters are devoted to this subject. Not only will you learn the marketing planning process, but you also will gain understanding of the interrelationships among the various marketing functions as well as between marketing and other business functions.

Chapter 8 introduces the concept of strategic marketing planning. Chapter 9 covers the situation analysis; it will examine the firm's internal and external situation in order to identify problems and opportunities. In Chapter 10 we will see how strategies designed to fulfill company objectives evolve from the situation analysis. Chapter 11 will explain how tactical plans are developed to implement the strategies. And Chapter 12 will describe how marketing plans are integrated with the annual business plan.

The Hanes case is introduced in Chapter 9 and is used through the balance of Part Three to

PART THREE
THE STRATEGIC MARKETING PLANNING PROCESS

illustrate how the steps of the marketing planning process are applied to a real company. Chapter 13 provides a summary of this case. Additional cases at the end of Part Three have been selected to permit you to apply the planning approach. From your analyses of these cases you will see the practical usefulness of the material presented earlier in Part Two.

CHAPTER 8

Approach to Strategic Marketing Planning

In a report of personal interviews with fifty chief executives, the Conference Board* summarized what planning means to top executives:

Planning is a systematic method for the effective and efficient management of change.

It includes determining where the company is to go as well as how it is to get there, or, more formally, the setting of objectives and goals and the formulation and selection of alternate strategies and courses of action to reach them.

Planning identifies and analyzes opportunities, strengths, weaknesses, problems, and threats, and sets priorities for capitalizing on or overcoming them so that company resources will be put to the best uses.

Planning entails regular measurement of progress toward objectives and goals and the execution of strategies and action programs. Yet it is clearly recognized that plans often have to be altered in the light of new circumstances.

Planning should be a continuing process and not a once-a-year exercise; it should involve all those whose jobs have a significant effect on the fortunes of the company.

It is clearly distinct from forecasting. Forecasting, one of the essential elements of planning, is a prediction of what *will* happen on the basis of certain assumptions; planning is an attempt to determine what *should* happen and then to take steps that will make it likely to happen.[1]

The chief executives were also asked what benefits they received from planning. The most commonly mentioned was, "The company is being run better." More specific benefits were reported as:

Better understanding of the business.

Better discernment and investigation of opportunities and needs.

Better decision making.

---

*The Conference Board, Inc. is an independent, non-profit research organization supported by America's leading companies and other organizations such as governments, unions, and universities.

Improved coordination and integration between operating units and corporate headquarters and among the various operating and staff units of the company.

Guidance for chief executives—a more realistic sense of the future and better control over the company's direction.

Most major companies have adopted strategic planning as a means of dealing with an uncertain external environment. In **Marketing Note 8-1** the chief executive of General Electric explains why the manager of the future will have to be able to plan strategically.

In a subsequent study of marketing planning, involving a sample of 267 companies, the Conference Board found that 261 of these firms do some form of formal marketing planning ranging from plans for individual products to those that are "part of a broader business or strategic plan." In the foreword the president of the Board writes: "The marketing plan embodies, in capsule form, a seller's realistic hopes and intentions for competing successfully in the market place. Such a plan is widely considered to be a necessary and invaluable tool for purposeful marketing."[2]

THE ROLE OF STRATEGIC MARKETING PLANNING

In this chapter emphasis is placed on strategic planning because of its use by companies with good planning practices, and also because it should precede tactical planning, a subject discussed in Chapter 11.

Distinction between Strategy and Tactics

"Strategy," a term borrowed from the military, has crept into common usage almost everywhere, although not everyone using the term understands its meaning. We will use the following definitions of marketing strategy and tactics, which are consistent with the terms as they are used by a number of leading companies.

> *Marketing strategies* are *major* plans (or methods) for achieving *major* objectives or goals.* *Tactics* are the plans or methods devised to implement the strategies.

To illustrate, let's assume that a company's marketing objective is to increase market share by 5 percent over the next 3 years. The marketing strategy for accomplishing this is to broaden the product line to tap additional market price segments. Tactics for implementing the strategy include selecting the specific price points, the specifications for the products to be added, and the promotional and distributional plans for introducing the additional products to the market. Note that there is one broad strategy, but several specific tactics—a normal characteristic of strategic and tactical planning.

Criteria for Identifying Strategies

Anyone engaging in strategic planning for the first time usually experiences some difficulty in distinguishing between strategies and tactics, although this problem

---

*The terms "objectives" and "goals" are used interchangeably in this text.

GE Chief Describes Successful Managers of the Future	MARKETING NOTE 8-1

Certainly the successful managers of the future are going to have technical competence in the basic business functions—marketing, production, finance, employee relations, and so on. They'll understand business planning and organization, and they'll feel at home with the new tools of management—the computer-based information and control systems. These are the traditional areas of management expertise, updated to accommodate modern technology.

But beyond that, there are some new requirements.

The new managers will have a greater intellectual breadth than their predecessors. They will have to feel comfortable in the world of ideas—well read, articulate, and capable of relating their business responsibilites to the larger world around them.

Strategic planning will distinguish the new breed. Seat-of-the-pants management is too risky these days, particularly in businesses that involve large, long-term investments with uncertain payout.

At General Electric we have spent the better part of a decade developing our strategic planning system. At first it was pretty much a paper exercise, and was seen that way by most of our operating management. But over the years, we've eliminated the irrelevant aspects and turned it into an intense, creative experience that involves everybody who can make a contribution. It forces all of us to face up to realities that were hidden behind a smokescreen of wishful thinking and conventional wisdom.

Some feel that such detailed analysis discourages risk-taking, but our experience is otherwise. Because we understand the business better, because we are able to weigh alternatives, our managers seem to be more confident about taking business risks and getting into new areas of opportunity. Without these advantages of strategic planning, the tendency would be to play it safe—selling the same old products from the same old stand. And that won't do in the 1980's.

. . .

The GE chief executive went on to say that the executive of the future also must be sensitive to social responsibilities, politically sophisticated, world-minded, and absolutely scrupulous in matters of law and ethics.

Source: Excerpted from "Managing in the 1980's," speech by Reginald H. Jones, Chairman and Chief Executive Officer, General Electric Company, presented to the student body of The Wharton School of the University of Pennsylvania on Feb. 4, 1980.

tends to disappear with practice. Some guidelines may be helpful in learning to distinguish between the two:

1. *Strategies will be few in number; tactics will be more numerous.* If the plan contains a long list of strategies, the chances are that they are more tactical than strategic. Too many major efforts may result in organizational confusion and dissipation of resources.
2. *Strategies usually affect the functions of two or more departments.* Consequently, strategic plans usually require top management approval and support. Tactics, on the other hand, may be left to the discretion of lower-level managers.
3. *New or revised strategies usually require additional funds or shifts of resources.* These represent additional reasons why strategies call for top management approval.
4. *Strategies tend to be continuing in nature whereas tactics tend to be more short-term.* Strategies, of course, may not be long-lived if they don't work or if upset by unforeseen changes in market conditions.

How broadly one company views its long-term corporate growth strategies is illustrated by a Boise Cascade Corporation advertisement, Figure 8-1.

No businessman likes to talk very specifically in advertising about future plans. Too much of what's to come is beyond his control. And yet we think a company that seeks to convince you of its potential ought to do so. So we've decided to share our long term growth strategies with you.

Strategy Number 1.

We plan to concentrate on our two basic businesses—building materials and paper products.

We plan to invest $1.1 billion in them between 1974 and 1978 while holding to our target debt to equity ratio of 0.6:1.

We plan to generate an average annual return on total investment of <u>at least 12% after taxes</u> on each project within the $850 million we're using to improve and expand our businesses. (The remaining $250 million are being used to keep our facilities well maintained, safe and environmentally sound.)

Rationale.

1. We have a good resource base. Including joint ventures, we own 2 million acres of timberland and have long term harvesting rights on 5 million more.

2. Our resource is renewable. If we manage our forests thoughtfully, they'll supply us eternally.

3. We're able to add to the value of many of our forest products <u>after</u> they leave our paper and wood products mills by converting and distributing them directly to their users.

4. While we're among the leaders in our component businesses, our market shares are small so there's ample room for growth.

Strategy Number 2.

We plan to invest 27% of our capital dollars in our converting and distributing operations in order to maximize the earning power of our forest-originated products.

Rationale.

1. Converting and distributing operations offer very attractive returns on investment. (By converting operations, we mean businesses like manufactured housing and composite cans that <u>convert</u> lumber into single and multi-family homes and paper into packaging.)

2. They also offer excellent opportunities for expansion.

3. Our converting operations have a ready source of supply—our primary manufacturing operations (our paper and wood products mills).

4. Converting and distributing operations are relatively less susceptible to market fluctuations, owing to the range of products and diversity of demand.

Strategy Number 3.

We plan to divide our capital investment about equally between our paper and building materials operations in order to maintain our relatively equal balance between the two.

Rationale.

It's this balance between building materials and paper, together with our balance between manufacturing forest products and converting and distributing them, that enables us to cope with the historical nemesis of forest products companies, cyclicality.

If all this suggests to you that Boise Cascade sees its future in forest-related products, this ad has done its job. We've been manufacturing, converting and distributing them profitably since Boise Cascade was first formed back in 1957. And we intend to continue. We know from experience, money <u>does</u> grow on trees.

For a detailed picture of Boise Cascade, write for our annual report and statistical supplement, c/o Boise Cascade Corporation, Communications Dept., One Jefferson Square, Boise, Idaho 83728. For a more dispassionate view, call your broker.

Boise Cascade Corporation

FIGURE 8-1. Boise Cascade Corporation advertisement. Source: Courtesy of the Boise Cascade Corporation. Reproduced with permission.

Short- and Long-Range Planning

In most cases the short-range plan covers the company's fiscal year. A few years ago a number of leading companies began long-range planning merely by extending the planning period to cover 3 to 5 years, or longer. Usually, the first year plan would be prepared in detail while the plans for succeeding years contained less detail. There was some disenchantment with this process because the longer-range plan essentially turned out to be a projection, made without adequate consideration of possible changes in the external and internal environments.

Dissatisfaction with these long-range planning procedures led to the *strategic planning concept*. Strategic planning comes at the beginning of the annual planning process. The first step is a review of current strategies to see whether they will achieve longer-range goals.

Because strategies are major means of achieving major objectives—and because achievement of major objectives normally requires more than one year—companies using strategic planning have now come full circle. By starting the annual planning process with a strategic review, companies, in effect, begin with long-range planning and follow with the short-range plan. The annual 1-year plan thus has become one of a series of periodic steps in the implementation of the strategic plan.

Reasons for Adoption of Strategic Planning

Corporate planning has evolved over the years. The strategic planning approach is but one step (albeit an important one) in a series of improvements. The adoption of strategic planning was hastened by changes in the market and business environment. During the 1950s and 1960s most well-managed companies enjoyed substantial growth in sales and profits as their markets expanded and as increasingly affluent consumers were willing to try new products and pay more for improved products and services.

Changes in the Business Environment.

Environmental changes that became apparent in the 1970s, however, slowed the growth rates of even the best-managed companies. Slower population and economic growth, changing consumer attitudes towards consumption, rapid inflation (aggravated by enormous increases in the prices of crude oil), and the higher costs for mandated environmental protection measures (costs which companies could not offset with productivity gains) all served to cause business management to reexamine its traditional approaches to growth.

The strategic planning concept has proved useful in meeting these new conditions because it stresses both realistic appraisal of present and probable future conditions and creative thinking about alternate means of attaining corporate objectives. Like any other business concept, it is no better than the quality of the effort put into it. But it appears to offer advantages to the many companies faced with slower growth markets, maturing product life cycles, and customers resistant to higher prices and products without significant differentiation. **Marketing Note 8-2** describes why Citicorp felt it was necessary to reorganize and revise its strategies for the 1980s.

A publishing company's strategic planning model is shown in Figure 8-2. From

MARKETING NOTE 8-2

Citicorp Charts Its Strategies for the Future

In discussing its plans for the 1980s, Citicorp management said:

We recently completed a comprehensive analysis of our corporation and of the changing world in which we will have to operate in the years ahead. Based on this analysis, we have formulated a new strategic plan and reorganized for the future. . . .

The key lesson we learned in our review was that periods of vigorous growth followed each occasion when we correctly defined the developing trends in our marketplace and devised new adaptive strategies. . . .

Our overall strategic plan for the 1980s rests on several working assumptions about Citicorp's function in the world and the kind of world in which we will function. One assumption is that the United States and several other important national markets will continue to evolve through agrarian and industrial economies to postindustrial or service-based economies. . . .

As our present reorganization indicates, preparing for the future has become a serious business throughout the business world. . . . Our own corporate planning function has been enlarged under the reorganization of an Office of Corporate Strategy and Development. The responsibility for implementing Citicorp's overall strategic plan rests with the senior manager of this office, reporting to the chairman. . . .

We have acted *now* because the competitive structure of our industry is changing, the composition of our customer groups is changing, the legal powers of financial institutions are changing, and the societal obligations of a private company of our stature and success are changing. The risk of charting our course now into the uncertain future is only exceeded by the clearer hazard of living in the past.

Source: Excerpted from "Reorganizing for the Future," Citicorp's *Stockholder Report for 1979.*

this model we can see the several steps required in strategic planning and the predominant role played by marketing factors.

Importance of Profit Growth. Failure to improve profits over the longer term leads inevitably to corporate death. The reason is simple. Capital—derived from profit and/or borrowed from outside sources—is essential to the business enterprise. External capital flows to those enterprises with the better prospects for profitable growth and away from those with poor prospects for profits. The corporate graveyard is filled with the corpses of companies that failed to remain profitable and the corporate hospital has patients needing infusions of capital in order to survive.

Profit is not the only goal of responsible corporate management. But it represents a fundamental goal which cannot be ignored. Consequently, we will be concerned in our discussions of planning with the need for longer-term profitable growth. While current profits are important, it is sometimes necessary to forego them in the interest of greater longer-term rewards. Furthermore, significant changes in company growth patterns normally require more than 1 year to achieve.

Continued Need for Short-Term Planning. Strategic marketing planning in no way precludes the need for shorter-range tactical planning. Within established industries, success—by and large—comes to those companies with the best product, pricing, distribution, and promotional plans and to those that are the most skillful in their implementation. Effective penetration of existing markets is normally a marketing strategy with high priority. The point is that with an uncertain business climate both kinds of planning are needed. One study of 99 companies found that marketing strategy was receiving more thoughtful attention than ever before and that a sizable majority of the executives surveyed were working to formalize the linkage between their short-term marketing plans and their future intentions.[3]

193

CHAPTER 8
APPROACH TO
STRATEGIC
MARKETING
PLANNING

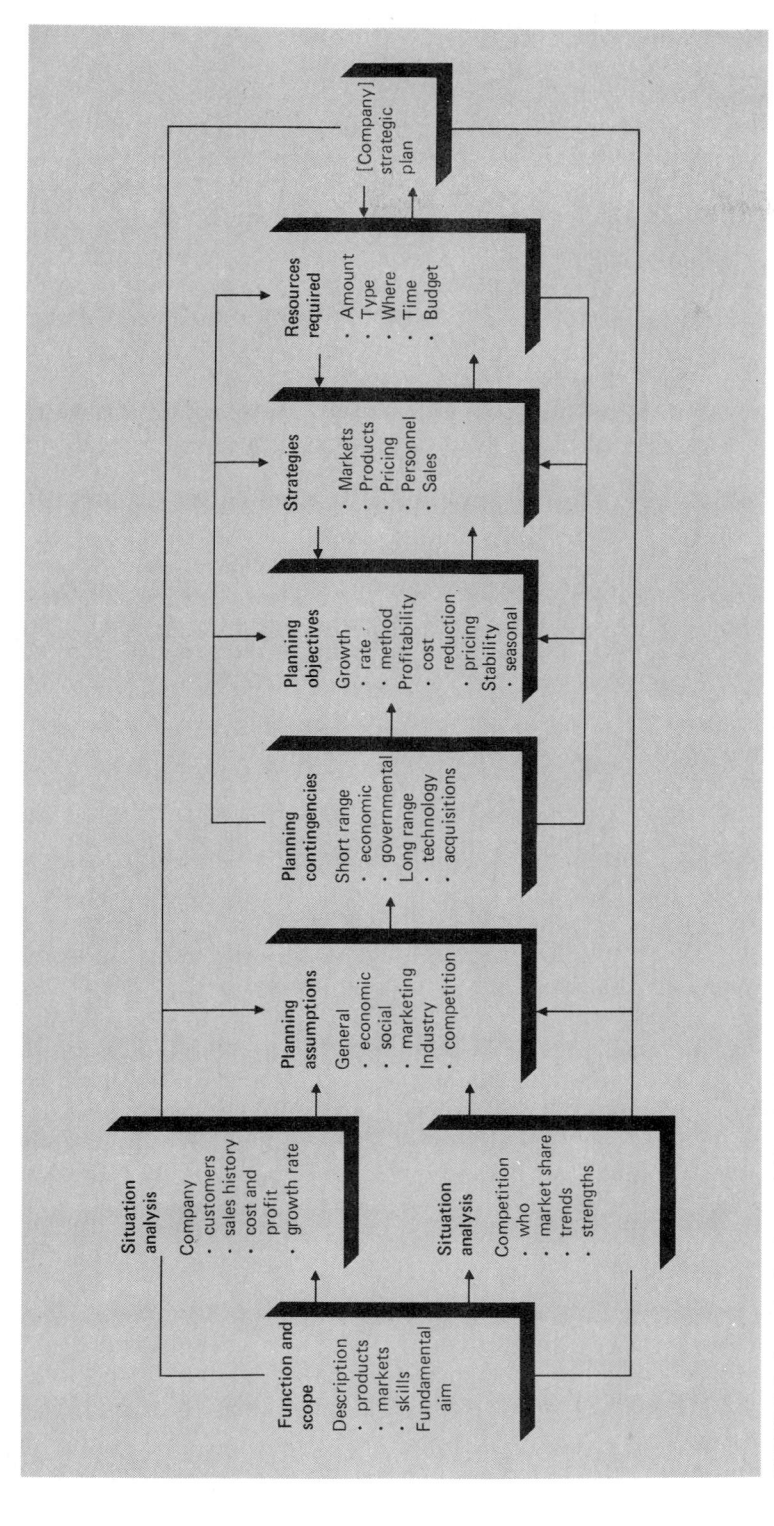

FIGURE 8-2. Strategic planning model for a publishing company. *Source:* Rochelle O'Connor, *Corporate Guides to Long-Range Planning,* report no. 687, The Conference Board, New York, 1976, p. 13.

THE PLANNING ENVIRONMENTS

Chapter 1 introduced the idea that a company's business purpose (or charter or mission) evolves from a matching of company resources with market opportunities. (See Figure 1-3.)

Roles of Purpose, Objectives, Strategies, Policies

An explicit statement of company *purpose* defines the areas of company interest. It does so in broad terms to provide room for expansion; yet a realistic statement of purpose also will circumscribe the areas of interest to prevent diversions that may dilute company resources. Once management has agreed on its business purpose, it needs to determine company objectives, strategies, and policies.

Company *objectives* are precise statements of what the company wishes to attain within specific time periods. *Strategies* are the broad means by which the company expects to reach them. *Policies** provide a framework of principles, rules, and operating guidelines within which management expects the organization to function.

To illustrate, a leading processor of spices has as its business purpose the concentration of its resources in the condiments segment of the food industry, marketing high quality, branded products to consumers and institutions, but not engaging in private branding. One of its marketing objectives is to increase company share of the national condiments market by an average of 1 percent a year over the next 5 years. The principal marketing strategy for accomplishing this objective is to increase promotional efforts to 40 percent of the SMSAs in which the company currently is not the market leader. A company policy states that price cutting is not to be used to "buy" market share. This is to discourage price wars and preclude the use of pricing as a possible strategy for increasing market share.

The Development Process. Company purpose and politics evolve over time, although a new management sometimes brings about abrupt changes in either or both. Purpose and policies may be implicit or explicit, although the larger, professionally managed companies have found that stating them in writing facilitates communication throughout the organization.

Modifications of purpose and policy usually result from changes in resources and market opportunities. The more carefully they are thought through, however, the less frequent is the need for modification. Objectives and strategies, by contrast, are subject to more frequent changes since they must be adapted to the constantly changing external environment. That is why, of course, planning should be a continuous process.

The Strategic Environments

Strategy sometimes is described as the *internal* (company) response to the *external* environment. By examining these two environments and their relationships to one another, we will see how they are used by marketing management in the develop-

---

*Company policy is not to be confused with the term as it is used in business school curricula. *Policy courses* are courses concerned with general management in contrast to functional or methodological courses.

ment of alternate marketing strategies. External environmental variables are generally thought of as uncontrollable, while internal company variables are considered controllable, although this is not entirely so. The economic environment is an external factor over which marketing management has no control, whereas distribution channels represent an external factor over which the marketing manager may exert varying degrees of control.

The External Environment. External variables may be categorized under the following seven headings which we shall examine to see the extent to which each is controllable or uncontrollable by the firm:

- The economy
- Market size and trends
- Competition
- Distribution channels
- Technology
- Legal and government
- Social

The economy. Since marketing management has no control over the economy, it can only try to understand it and anticipate its direction. When analyzing the economy, we look beyond the general economy—as measured by the GNP, for example—to those aspects which have a direct bearing on the sales of the company and its industry.

The demand for new automobile tires, for instance, is derived* from the rate of new car production and the rate of used tire replacements. The replacement tire market is determined by the number of used cars and the average number of miles driven per car. Both new car and replacement tire sales are affected by economic factors such as disposable consumer income, inflation, and gasoline prices. Noneconomic factors, of course, also may affect tire demand. In recent years, for example, technological change (radial tires wear longer than conventional tires), legal change (traffic speed limits reduce tire wear), and social factors (attitudes toward energy conservation affect miles driven) have all affected tire demand.

Market size and trends. The company, of course, has no control over demographic, geographic, or economic variables. Factors such as the number and locations of consumer and industrial buyers, consumer income, or industrial purchasing power represent external variables which the marketer must accept.

When we consider markets in terms of potential buyers for products or services, however, the individual firm and its competitors presumably can influence market size. This particularly is the case during the developing phase of an industry. The market for frozen orange juice, for example, was created largely through the efforts of the then new Birds Eye, Minute Maid, and Snow Crop brands. Their combined marketing efforts not only caused some consumers to switch from freshly squeezed

---

*"Derived demand" is a term usually used in connection with industrial goods. The demand for many industrial products can be traced ultimately to the consumer. The demand for packaging machinery, for instance, is derived from the consumer demand for packaged products.

orange juice to frozen, but, more importantly, they caused many additional consumers to drink orange juice regularly. While these efforts succeeded in increasing market demand for orange juice, the companies' abilities to affect total demand lessened as the industry matured.

Competition. In the United States there are no legal means by which companies can control competition since agreements between competitors violate the antitrust laws. Americans believe that competition represents a desirable means for providing consumers with choice and value. The antitrust laws were designed to encourage vigorous competition by outlawing monopoly and conspiracies to restrain trade.

Distribution channels. The vast majority of consumer goods are distributed through independent channel intermediaries over whom the manufacturer has limited control. Exceptions include firms that sell through company-owned outlets such as Singer (sewing machines) and Thom McAn (shoes), although both sell through independent retailers as well. Other exceptions include catalog, direct mail, and personal selling and delivery direct to the home. Some companies, such as automobile and soft drink manufacturers, distribute through franchised dealers. Although franchised dealerships are independently owned, franchisees operate within specified agreements with the franchisors. The extent of control by the franchisor, however, is limited by law.

Something less than 40 percent of industrial goods is distributed through wholesalers. Most of the balance is distributed direct from manufacturers to their customers, a form of distribution over which the manufacturer has complete control.

The question of how much control manufacturers exert over independent channel intermediaries has been the subject of extensive investigation and reporting. While there is no absolute control over independent wholesalers, the degree of manufacturer influence varies with the importance of the manufacturer's line to the wholesaler's sales and profits. And, in the case of companies following selective or exclusive distribution policies, part of the quid pro quo for being chosen to handle a brand is that the wholesaler and/or retailer agrees to stock, promote, and service in accordance with the policies of the manufacturer. There is a legal question, however, about how far the manufacturer can go in attempting to control independent wholesalers and retailers without running afoul of the antitrust laws.

Where the manufacturer sells to large chains, the shoe often is on the other foot. The buying power of the chain is such that the chain is more likely to influence the manufacturer's policies than the other way around. Here too, however, control by the chain may be considered illegal if it uses its power to obtain deals not available to its smaller retail competitors.

Control of distribution channels by manufacturers can be viewed as a continuum, ranging from negative control over large chains to complete control over company-owned distribution facilities. Figure 8-3 illustrates this continuum. In the final analysis, however, manufacturers and channel members are dependent upon one another for their respective success; consequently, it is to their mutual advantage to develop satisfactory working relationships.

Technology. Companies may exert some control over technology, depending upon how much and how wisely they invest in research and development. Companies such as Polaroid, Du Pont, Western Electric, IBM, and Texas Instruments have brought about internal technological advances. However, most companies—including those named—rely primarily on technology developed on the outside.

Degree of control	Negative (reverse)	Little or no control	Some control	Much control	Complete control
Determined by	Large chains exert control over manufacturer	Manufacturer has weak market position	Manufacturer has strong market position	Manufacturer uses exclusive or selective distribution, or franchises	Manufacturer owns distribution intermediaries or distributes direct to user

FIGURE 8-3. Factors affecting manufacturer degree of control (influence) over distribution channels.

Most company R&D budgets are devoted primarily to development rather than to research.

Of the more than $49 billion spent by industry for R&D, approximately 78 percent goes for development, 19 percent for applied research, and only 3 percent for basic research. Nonindustry sources—namely, colleges and universities, the federal government, and other nonprofit institutions—account for the majority of the funds spent for basic research.[4] General Foods explains its R&D breakdown as follows:

> The $79.1 million General Foods invested in technical research during fiscal 1980 was divided three ways. About half of the funds went toward work on established products—quality improvements, cost reductions, line extensions, as well as safety and compliance work. Another third was invested in new product development projects, with more than a dozen new products technically prepared for market introduction. The remainder was spent on fundamental research—the gaining of basic knowledge and the furthering of emerging technolgoies—and for research support services.[5]

It is apparent that the primary technological role of industry is one of applying scientific discoveries from outside sources to the development of new and improved materials, processes, products, and services. In terms of its size, diversity, and rate of change, technology often appears to be uncontrollable by the individual firm. Nevertheless, it represents an opportunity for the company that makes the first—or best—application of new technology.

The first applications of new technology don't necessarily belong to the companies with the biggest R&D budgets. Larger companies tend to be protective of their investments in current technology, frequently leaving the entrepreneurial breakthroughs to individuals or small companies. A study of sixty important inventions found that more than half came from independent inventors, less than half from corporate research, and even less from large concerns.[6] Small companies discovered and initially produced refrigerators, dryers, dishwashers, the hermetically sealed compressor, vacuum cleaners, deep freezers, steam irons, electric shavers, and hearing aids.[7]

Legal and government. For the most part, laws, court interpretations of laws, and regulation by government agencies are beyond the control of the marketing manager. This is not to suggest that all laws and regulations work to the disadvantage of companies. Many laws are for the protection of business. Furthermore, some laws, such as those concerning pollution control, create new business for those companies—and their suppliers—engaged in producing and installing pollution control equipment. Nevertheless, the enormous growth of new statutes and regulations in recent years appears to have added to the restraints imposed on marketing management's freedom of action.

Social variables. We have already cited numerous examples of change brought about by new social patterns. One aspect we have not discussed is the effect that style and fashion changes have on some industries. Fashion represents a highly uncontrollable external variable. Despite the popular view that fashion changes are caused by designers and producers of fashion goods, the truth is that fashion is cyclical in nature and consumers appear ready to change periodically. Designers attempt to anticipate the timing and direction of impending change by introducing new styles. Consumers may reject a new style completely, accept it enthusiastically as a short-lived fad, or back it with a solid, growing acceptance until it develops into a longer-lived fashion.

Fashions are by no means limited to women's clothing which receives the most fashion publicity. They exist in automobiles, architecture, politics, business decision methods, the stock market, and on the dance floor.[8]

Fashions may have secondary repercussions which are as uncontrollable as the fashions themselves. The fashion in miniskirts, for example, led to the development of pantyhose. While skirts were rising, the women's hosiery industry benefited with increased sales of pantyhose; but when pants became the fashion, replacing the miniskirt, women's hosiery sales suffered uncontrollably. An early marketing authority suggested the uncontrollability of fashion when he said: "Business succeeds when it goes with fashion but fails when it goes against the tide."[9]

The Internal Environment

In theory, at least, the firm has control over its own internal activities, yet there are usually internal constraints which limit actions by marketing management. Organizational rigidities may limit or preclude consideration of certain marketing strategies as may factors such as high production costs, insufficient capital, inadequate plant capacity, or lagging technology. Presumably internal deficiencies can be eliminated or alleviated over time, but at any one period in time, marketing management is usually forced to live with some internal constraints. The key internal factors are company resources, management philosophy, organization, and marketing elements.

Company Resources. No two companies are alike any more than two fingerprints are alike. They vary in terms of their mix of resources, namely, people, finances, and facilities. Many executives believe that a firm's most important asset is its employees and that success is highly influenced by the quality of company management and the skills of its marketing, financial, R&D, and production personnel. Yet the quality of individuals varies between firms and within the same company. A marketing strategy can be no more successful than the competence of the people who carry it out.

For some types of industries, success is heavily dependent on the competence of the people in particular functional areas: *engineering* for capital goods industries such as tooling and production machinery; *finance* for capital intensive industries such as steel and petroleum; and *marketing* for consumer packaged goods companies. A company's financial position, as reflected in its ability to raise short- and long-term capital, is of key importance to strategy formulations. A beautiful marketing strategy that cannot be financed adequately should not be adopted. Physical assets such as plants, warehouses, and laboratories can back up marketing strategies or act as a constraint upon them, depending upon their quality and capacity.

Management Philosophy. Marketing strategies that differ greatly from top management's philosophy have little chance of being approved or of receiving enthusiastic support if they are accepted. In some companies, managements have a growth-oriented philosophy and are willing to use leverage to finance expansion and/or to forego dividends while reinvesting profits in new growth opportunities. Managements with a more conservative philosophy feel more comfortable with steady but unspectacular growth, maximization of cash flow from current businesses, high dividends, and investment in what appear to be sure bets. High-risk strategies stand little chance of approval from this type of management.

Other management philosophies that may affect strategy formulation are attitudes toward recruitment and development of key personnel, R&D investment, innovation, and centralized versus decentralized decision-making authority. The latter is discussed under the next subheading.

Organization. Most large- and many medium-sized companies are divisionalized. Divisions usually are organized as profit centers with division managers held responsible for profits. Companies vary, however, in the degree of decision-making authority delegated by corporate management to the division manager. Furthermore, division managers within the same corporation often vary in the degree to which they delegate authority to their subordinates. To some executives, decentralization means delegation of authority only down to themselves.

The divisions of some companies will be self-sufficient in both production and marketing, while in others, a centrally controlled sales force or production department will serve several or all divisions. The marketing manager in a decentralized, self-sufficient division will likely have more influence on divisional strategic marketing decisions than will the division marketing manager in a more centralized organization.

How decision-making authority can vary by company was reported in a study of twenty of the largest U.S. consumer, industrial, and service companies.[10] Advertising strategies, for example, were approved most frequently at the division manager and marketing manager levels; yet the range of the organizational decision levels for such decisions varied from division middle management to the corporate president or board chairperson. Even in the case of individual advertisements, the approval level ranged from the product manager in one company to the corporate president in another. The key variable in determining where the advertising decision was made was the importance of the product to company sales and profits.

Marketing Elements. Product, pricing, distribution, and promotional decisions are largely controllable internally, although they can be strongly influenced by the external environment. Product decisions and promotional decisions provide more leeway for internal decision making than do pricing and distribution. Even so, product decisions are highly influenced by competitors' offerings. Pricing flexibility

---

MARKETING NOTE 8-3

Strategic Business Planning at the General Electric Company

A GE executive explains that the words "strategic business planning" have been carefully chosen. "To distinguish what was new and different from existing planning activities," he says, "emphasis was placed on the new dimensions of stronger competition and scarce resources. Strategic business planning was designed to add competitive focus, greater alertness to the changing environment, and stronger attention to allocation of scarce resources, thus providing the 'edge' we were looking for."

GE's strategic planning at the corporate level is concerned with, among many other matters, the setting of corporate objectives and goals, and the conducting of "validity reviews" of plans prepared by line managers for each of some 40 strategic business units into which the company's operations have been divided. A strategic business unit (SBU) is defined as "a unit whose manager has complete responsibility for integrating all functions into a strategy against an identifiable external competitor." Thus, the SBU's are of various sizes and fall at various organizational levels.

GE's portfolio strategy is designed to seek to ensure that earnings are sustained in the near term, while investment resources are guided to the better growth opportunities. Rather than merely applying financial measures, such as discounted cash flow/return on investment, management puts emphasis on examining the conditions under which a business can be successful and profitable. An important tool for this purpose is GE's "business screen"—a matrix for which the two dimensions are "business strengths" and "industry attractiveness." Businesses enjoying a medium-to-strong position in an attractive industry fall within the "Invest/Grow" category (dotted area on the accompanying chart). Those engaged in industries that are least attractive, or those whose position in their industry is weak, fall within the "Harvest/Divest" category (the dark area shown in the chart). And businesses on the charted diagonal, ranging from either a weak position in an attractive industry, are in the in-between category dubbed "Selectivity/Earnings."

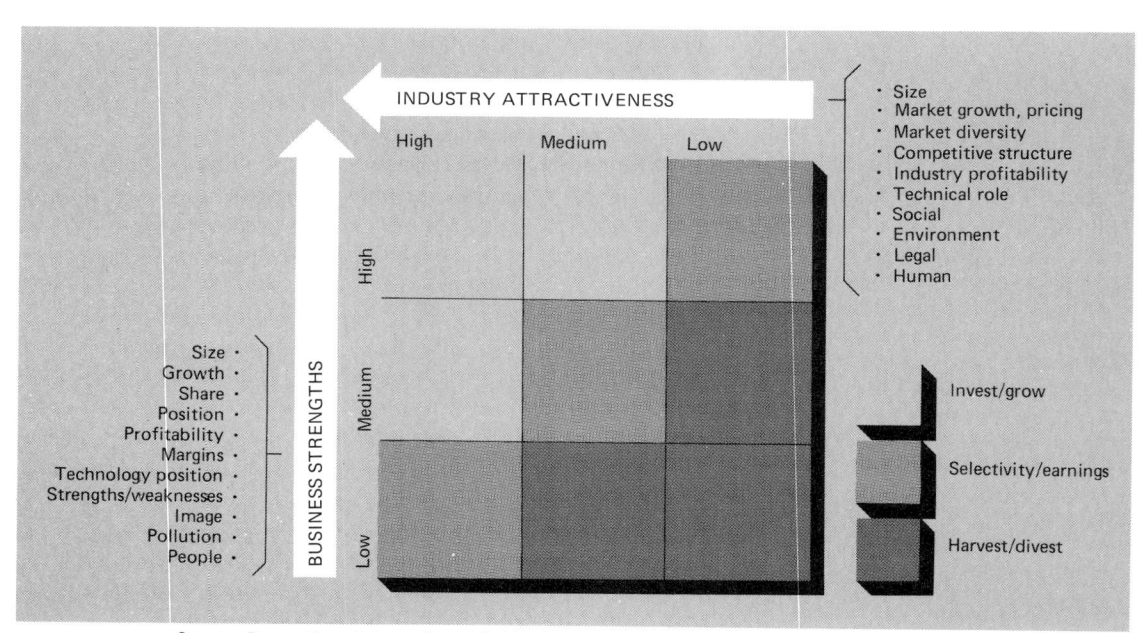

INDUSTRY ATTRACTIVENESS: High, Medium, Low
- Size
- Market growth, pricing
- Market diversity
- Competitive structure
- Industry profitability
- Technical role
- Social
- Environment
- Legal
- Human

BUSINESS STRENGTHS: High, Medium, Low
- Size
- Growth
- Share
- Position
- Profitability
- Margins
- Technology position
- Strengths/weaknesses
- Image
- Pollution
- People

Invest/grow
Selectivity/earnings
Harvest/divest

Source: Reproduced from David S. Hopkins, "Business Strategies for Problem Products," Report No. 714, The Conference Board, New York, 1977, p. 48.

will be constrained by the factors of demand, product cost, and competitors' prices. Management's degree of control over distribution varies from total to none, as we've seen (Figure 8-3). Promotional decisions probably provide the greatest degree of internal flexibility.

Strategy Formulation

When formulating strategies, marketing management considers the strengths and weaknesses of the company's external position in the marketplace—vis-à-vis competition—and the company's internal strengths and weaknesses in marketing, production, finance, R&D, and engineering. An objective evaluation of these factors—along with market opportunity—determines in a large part the range of marketing strategies that should be considered. Options may range from continuing with present strategies to going out of business, although they usually fall somewhere in between.

General Electric calls this process *strategic business planning*. Marketing Note 8-3 explains how GE compares external variables with internal business strengths in order to screen out unattractive investments and focus on the more attractive ones. This is an example of the portfolio approach to corporate strategic planning; it, along with other types of portfolio approaches, is discussed in Chapter 16.

STRATEGIC GROWTH OPTIONS

Setting aside, for the time being, negative options such as dropping products or businesses, or following a defensive, cash-conserving holding pattern, we now look at four strategic growth options shown in the Opportunity Grid, Figure 8-4.

Option 1: Present Products, Present Markets

The first option covers opportunities to improve profits through the increased penetration of present markets using the company's present products. Success depends on such factors as the stage of the product life cycle, the company's position in the market, intensity of competition, and the cost of attaining additional market share.

Most companies devote many of their resources to maintaining and improving their present businesses, since it is these businesses that usually provide the cash flow needed to support optional growth strategies. Option 1 is the least risky option

FIGURE 8-4. The opportunity grid. *Source:* Adapted from the growth vector grid in H. Igor Ansoff, *Corporate Strategy*, McGraw-Hill, New York, 1965, p. 109.

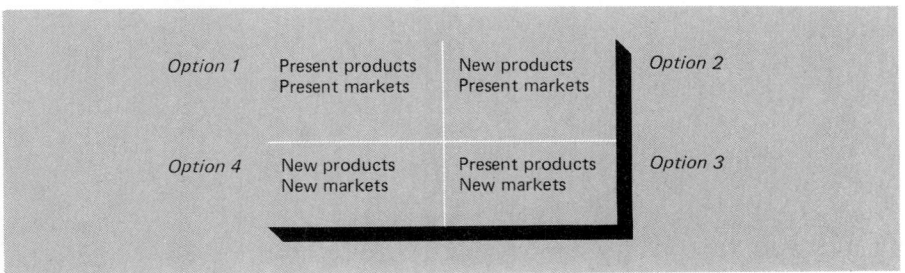

Option 1	Present products Present markets	New products Present markets	Option 2
Option 4	New products New markets	Present products New markets	Option 3

because the company is dealing with known products and with markets in which it has experience.

Examples abound of companies that have improved their position, even in mature industries (usually at the expense of competitors). Figure 8-5 shows several brands that moved ahead of their nearest competitors through the judicious use of advertising and other marketing tools.

Case Example—Option 1

Clarence Eldridge, former vice president, marketing, of General Foods described how some years ago the market position of its product Jell-O was improved dramatically by changes in the quality, price, and promotional mix.[11]

Back in the early thirties, Jell-O, General Foods' brand of gelatin dessert, was encountering very rough going. Not only was Royal cutting heavily into Jell-O's

FIGURE 8-5. Growth and decline of brand usage share within product forms, 1961 and 1973. *Source:* Nariman K. Dhalla and Sonia Yuspeh, "Forget the Product Life Cycle Concept." *Harvard Business Review*, January—February 1976, p. 108.

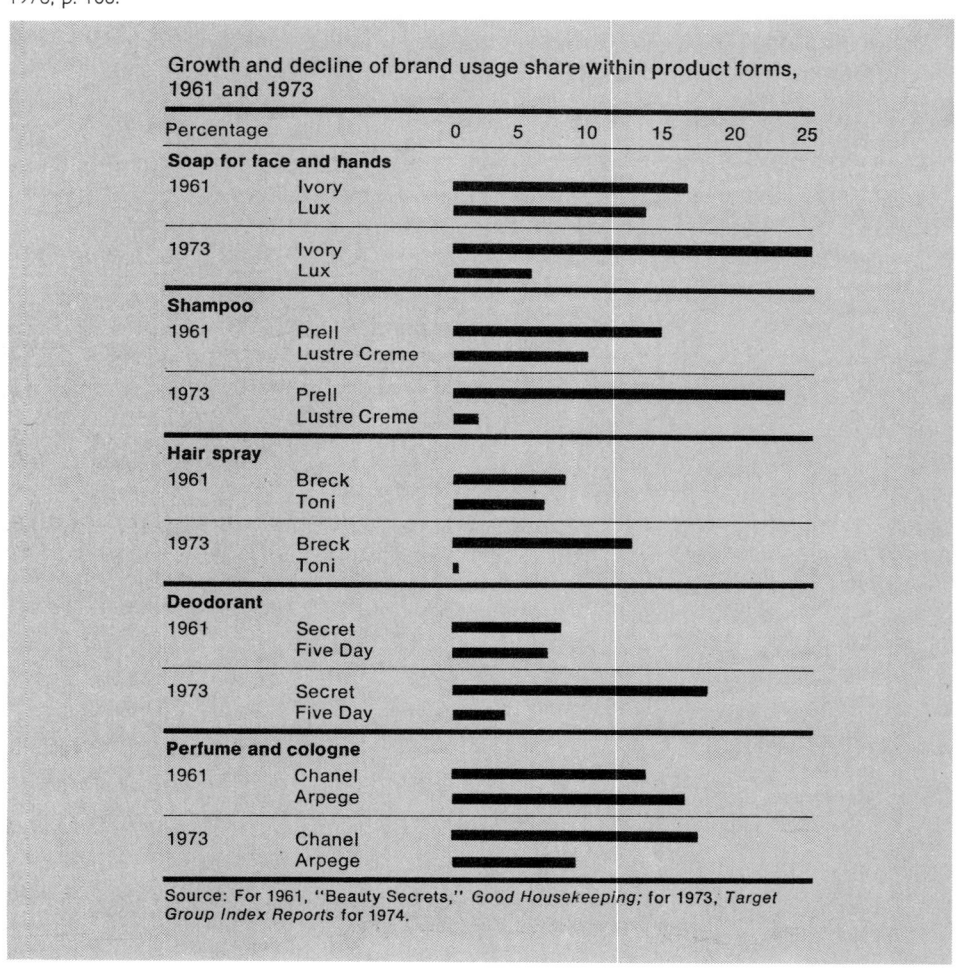

Growth and decline of brand usage share within product forms, 1961 and 1973

Percentage		0	5	10	15	20	25
Soap for face and hands							
1961	Ivory						
	Lux						
1973	Ivory						
	Lux						
Shampoo							
1961	Prell						
	Lustre Creme						
1973	Prell						
	Lustre Creme						
Hair spray							
1961	Breck						
	Toni						
1973	Breck						
	Toni						
Deodorant							
1961	Secret						
	Five Day						
1973	Secret						
	Five Day						
Perfume and cologne							
1961	Chanel						
	Arpege						
1973	Chanel						
	Arpege						

Source: For 1961, "Beauty Secrets," *Good Housekeeping*; for 1973, *Target Group Index Reports* for 1974.

traditional share of the market, but private brands, notably A & P's Sparkle, were making substantial inroads, especially in a broad band of territory in the Middle West. There were a number of possible reasons. One reason for Royal's progress was that Jell-O, when being prepared by the housewife, emitted a rather unpleasant odor; Royal did not. Another was that Jell-O required boiling water; Royal did not.

The reason for the growth of private label competition was not so difficult to detect: the private labels were selling to consumers for 5 cents a package: Jell-O was 6 or even 7 cents. And, finally, no demonstrably effective advertising campaign had been found for Jell-O.

In striving more or less frantically for a solution to the problem, General Foods did three things, virtually simultaneously. It made a drastic improvement in the product, eliminating the offensive odor and making it possible to prepare the product with other than boiling water. It reduced the price so that it could be sold to consumers for 5 cents a package. And it engaged Jack Benny.

The results were nothing less than spectacular. In a matter of weeks the sales curve had turned sharply upward; Jell-O's share of market increased month after month until it completely dominated the market; Royal's share declined proportionately; and the private labels were not only stopped in their tracks but were turned back.

What caused this dramatic turnabout? No one can say for sure; but it is obvious that *in total* "they must have done *some*thing right." I am quite sure that General Foods' Research Department firmly believed that it was the improvement in the product that was primarily, if not exclusively, responsible for the results. Others credited the price reduction, which certainly did help the product vis-à-vis private label competition. And still others have always contended that the credit should go to Jack Benny and his highly popular radio program, and the introductory tune spelling out the letters J-E-L-L-O.

The fact is that General Foods put a three-horse team (if there is such a thing!) to work: an improved and superior product, a competitively attractive price, and a highly popular and effective advertising campaign.

Option 2: New Products, Present Markets

Option 2 provides for new products to be sold to the company's present markets. This is more risky than Option 1 because the company is dealing with a new element (new product) with which it has no experience.

Option 2 is a commonly used approach to growth. Chances for success are good if the company has a strong position in its present markets, can distribute the new product through its present channels, uses its established sales force, if the market is growing, and if the new product can be differentiated from competitors. When companies refer to new products, they usually mean products new to them, not necessarily new to the market. When American auto manufacturers introduced compact cars, for example, they were new cars to the companies but not to the U.S. market which had long been used to foreign compacts. When Procter & Gamble introduced Pampers diapers, it brought to market an improved version of the disposable diaper which had been introduced earlier by others.

Option 3: Present Products, New Markets

Selling present products to new markets is also more risky than Option 1 since the company has no experience with the new markets. While opportunities under this option may not be as obvious as Option 2, the search for new market opportunities can be very rewarding. In essence it is the process of expanding into new market segments.

Dr Pepper grew from a small soft drink syrup and concentrate manufacturer, starting in the southwest in 1923, to a company with $333 million in sales and $27 million in profits in 1980, through the process of steady expansion into new geographic markets. Now that Dr Pepper has become a national brand it is moving into foreign markets. Sunbeam expanded the formerly all-male market for electric shavers by introducing a model designed for women to shave their legs. Applications of nylon, originally developed and promoted by Du Pont, spread from the parachute market to women's hosiery, carpeting, automobile tires, and a number of additional markets.

Expanding into new markets sometimes requires differentiation via modifications in product, packaging, pricing, and/or the use of new distribution channels and market promotions. Consequently, Option 3 should be taken only after careful market study.

Case Example—Options 2 and 3

The Mosler Safe Co. (now a part of American Standard Inc.) is an example of a company that successfully moved out of a slow growth pattern by following Options 2 and 3. Mosler was one of the two leading manufacturers of safes and vault doors whose primary market was the banking industry. A new management redefined Mosler's business purpose as "providing security systems." This broader view of its business led to the addition of new products for its present market—the banks. As the new products succeeded, they became Mosler's present products, which, in turn, were expanded to new markets—namely, any business or institution requiring security systems.

For its traditional bank customers, Mosler first added such new products as electronic surveillance and alarm systems, automatic cameras to record bank holdups, bank furniture, and the printing of personalized checks. Using the know-how gained from these new lines, Mosler's second step was to move beyond the bank market to apply surveillance systems to factories, warehouses, commercial and institutional buildings. Its check-printing operations were expanded into a chain of commercial printers serving broad markets for printing and other graphic arts. Mosler's graphic arts business even included an advertising agency.

Mosler carried out its strategic planning by consciously utilizing the Opportunity Grid. Each step was designed to minimize risk by moving into situations where the company had either product or market expertise. While Mosler continued to serve the bank market with safes and vault doors, its present products and present markets were greatly expanded. Its business purpose continued to broaden as the added products and markets provided new opportunities to diversify even further by again using Options 2 and 3.

Option 4: New Products, New Markets

Entering new products and new markets involves the greatest risk because the company has no experience in either. To reduce the risk the most common approach to Option 4 is via acquisition of existing businesses. Yet even this approach is not without risk as many companies have found to their sorrow. Buying another company is a little like buying a used car; outward appearance often bears little resemblance to what is under the hood.

There are few large companies that have not made acquisitions. Many of our best known corporations are the result of acquisitions and mergers—U.S. Steel, General Motors, General Electric, International Harvester, RCA, General Foods, and General Telephone and Electronics, to name but a few. Most of these grew by acquisitions of, or mergers with, companies in their own industries with which they were familiar. Because of stricter court interpretations of the antitrust laws in recent years, however, most acquiring companies now must seek companies in other industries. Hence, acquisition at the present time usually means following Option 4—new products, new markets. Continental Can Co. (now Continental Group), for example, acquired a life insurance company rather than another can manufacturer.

Case Example—Option 4

Historically, the Raytheon Company was primarily in the defense and space business.[12] More recently it has expanded dramatically through careful, long-range planning and by following a strategy of diversification through acquisition—that is, Option 4.

In the mid-sixties Raytheon management announced 5-year goals for doubling sales to $1 billion and reducing government contract business to 50 percent of its product mix. Both goals were achieved. Later, management set new 5-year goals: $1.8 billion sales, 55 percent commercial volume, and a 50 percent increase in earnings per share—goals which were surpassed within 4 years. While government contract business has continued to grow (Option 1), sales from the new acquisitions (Option 4) have climbed even faster.

Raytheon's top management engaged in 2 years of heated discussions over corporate strategy before adopting its first 5-year plans. Successful acquisitions included two appliance manufacturers, two companies engaged in construction of petrochemical and power plants and services to oil fields, and a road building company. Acquisitions in the educational TV equipment and publishing fields have not been as successful and the former has since been sold. Raytheon also has followed a strategy of applying its defense and space technology to commercial markets (Option 3).

Analysis Needed to Select the Best Option

The above examples were chosen to illustrate applications of the four strategic growth options and are not intended to suggest that one option is superior to another. The options in the Opportunity Grid provide a framework within which to seek out and evaluate opportunities. The fact that risk increases as you move clockwise through the grid should not inhibit consideration of these options. Rather, more information and careful planning are called for as you consider expansion into areas in which the company has no experience.

OTHER PLANNING CONSIDERATIONS

Organization

Corporate plans represent the sum total of approved profit center (division) plans* plus any new ventures the company may be planning exclusive of existing businesses. Divisional plans represent the consolidation of plans for the product lines marketed by the division.

Plans should be developed for separate product lines whenever they require different marketing approaches. Razor blades and personal deodorants, although sold to the same markets by Gillette, require sufficiently different promotional approaches to justify separate marketing plans. Also, it is sometimes best to develop separate plans when the product line is sold to different markets, through different distribution channels, or through separate sales forces. Food companies frequently sell the same product (corn flakes, for example) through retail channels and through institutional channels, using separate sales forces for each channel. How far one should go in developing separate marketing plans is a matter of executive judgment and the internal organizational setup. Product managers may be responsible for developing marketing plans for their assigned product lines, while group product managers will be responsible for consolidating the plans of the product managers reporting to them. At each higher-level management must consider the proportion of available resources to be allocated to each product line.

Planning, when carried out by product managers, flows from the bottom up. Yet planning should flow from the top down as well. Corporate management sets the planning climate and long-range business objectives, establishes companywide policies, and approves the business purpose of each business unit. Some campanies don't take these steps, which results in unnecessary confusion at lower planning levels. Division management should recommend to corporate management the division's business purpose and its short- and long-range objectives. It should assign planning responsibilities within the division. Because the market is of such importance to the planning process, marketing management normally has a key role in the development of the division plan, and, of course, is responsible for the marketing segment of the plan.

Line and Staff Responsibilities

Experience has shown that for planning to be a truly effective management tool, line operating management must be involved in the planning process and participate in the key strategic decisions. The reason is that operating managers usually do not give wholehearted support to plans imposed on them by others—particularly if they have been developed by staff people. Staff personnel can save operating manager's time, however, by preparing for planning discussions, by assembling and analyzing pertinent information, and by preparing written drafts of plans after the key strategic and tactical decisions have been made by operating management. Large companies often have full-time staff planning specialists assigned to assist operating manage-

---

*Another organizational term used to designate planning units is the *strategic business unit* (SBU). While General Electric and others have adopted the term, most major companies refer to their planning units as divisions or profit centers. We will use the term *business unit* to mean any organizational unit operating as a profit center for which separate plans are developed.

Outline for Divisional Marketing Plans—A Large Consumer Products Company

MARKETING NOTE 8-4

I. *Analyze and define the business situation—past, present, and future.* An analysis of where we are, perhaps how we got there. Data and trend lines should reach back three to five years. Suggested items to cover:
   A. The scope of the market (class of trade)
   B. Sales history, by products, by class of trade, regions
   C. Market potential, major trends anticipated
   D. Distribution channels
      1. Identification of principal channels (dealer or class of trade), sales history through each type
      2. Buying habits and attitudes of these channels
      3. Our selling policies and practices
   E. The customer or end user
      1. Identification of customer making the buying decision, classified by age, income level, occupation, geographical location, etc.
      2. Customer attitudes on product or services, quality, price, etc. Purchase or use habits that contribute to attitudes.
      3. Advertising history; expenditures, media and copy strategy, measurements of effectiveness
      4. Publicity and other educational influences
   F. The product or services
      1. Story of the product line, quality development, delivery and service
      2. Comparison with other approaches to serve the customers' needs
      3. Product research; product improvements planned
II. *Identification of problems and opportunities*
   A. In view of the facts cited in (I) above, what are the major problems that are restricting or impeding our growth?
   B. What opportunities do we have for
      — Overcoming the above problems?
      — Modifying or improving the product line, or adding new products?
      — Serving the needs of more customers in our market or developing new markets?
      — Improving the efficiency of our operation?
III. *Define specific and realistic business objectives*
   A. Assumptions re future conditions
      — Level of economic activity
      — Level of industry activity
      — Changes in customer needs
      — Changes in distribution channels
      — Changes beyond our control, increased costs, etc.
   B. Primary marketing objectives (the establishment of aim points and goals). Consider where you are going and how you will get there. Objectives are the necessary base of any plan since a plan must have precise direction.
   C. Over-all strategy for achievement of primary objectives. The division's over-all strategy to accomplish its primary objective—sample: shifting of sales emphasis, products or classes of trade; changes for improvement of sales coverage, etc.
   D. Functional (departmental) objectives. (In this section "explode" your primary objectives into sub-objectives, or goals, for each department. Show the interrelation vertically, by marketing project. Show time schedule on objectives below.)
      1. Advertising and promotion objectives
      2. Customer service objectives
      3. Product modification objectives
      4. New product objectives
      5. Expense control objectives
      6. Manpower objectives
      7. Personnel training objectives
      8. Market research objectives

MARKETING NOTE 8-4 *(Continued)*

IV. *Define marketing strategy and action programs*—to accomplish the objectives.
  A. Here, *detail the action steps,* priorities, and schedules relating to each of the functional objectives above. If, for example, one of your estimates was "an increase in sales of product X from 10,000 to 20,000 units," now is the time to pinpoint specific customers. In order to explain who must do what, and when, you can show the interaction of the departments listed above (III-D) and how their objectives serve to meet this increased demand.
  B. If one of your objectives was to introduce a new product by "x" date, now show the details and deadlines, production schedule, market introduction plans, advertising and merchandising support, sales and service training needed, etc. Define responsibility and dates for each step.
  C. Alternatives—In the event of a delay in a project or program, what alternative plans are available?
V. *Control and review procedures.* How will the execution of the plan be monitored?
  A. What kinds of "feedback" information will be needed?
  B. When and how will reviews be scheduled? (departments, regions, etc.)
  C. Date for full-scale review of progress vs. plan.

Source: David S. Hopkins, *The Marketing Plan,* Report No. 801, The Conference Board, New York, 1981, pp. 50–51.

---

ment. In smaller companies and smaller divisions, however, staff planning may be part-time assignments for persons whose normal duties involve analytical work such as marketing research.

Because planning is a profit-oriented process, functional departments should not conduct their planning in a functional vacuum. During both the developmental and consolidation phases of profit center planning, interchange of information and ideas should be made among the marketing, production, financial, R&D, and engineering departments. Much of this interchange may be handled by staff personnel, but in the final planning stages, division management should bring together the department heads to hammer out final agreements.

Planning Guides and Formats

A study of 83 companies found that corporate planning guides and planning formats varied considerably from company to company according to (1) size and variety of business, (2) style of management, and (3) degree of uniformity desired from organizational units.[13] The study also found that the development of the planning guide is not a one-shot event; rather it takes several planning cycles to arrive at a satisfactory format, and even then, changes may be made from time to time. An example of a marketing plan guide is shown in **Marketing Note 8–4**.

SUMMARY

Marketing planning is closely interrelated with overall business planning both at the divisonal profit center level and at the corporate level. The marketing plan is a key part of the business plan because other functional plans derive largely from the sales forecasts that evolve out of the marketing plan. At the same time, the marketing plan is dependent on manufacturing capacity, product costs, product developments, the ability to finance planned operations, and other factors for which other functional managers have responsibility. Consequently, coordination and cooperation among departments is essential to good planning.

Marketing planning is important also because marketing management must take prime responsibility for interpreting the external market environment. And it must assume a leadership role in (1) determining when new strategies are needed to meet either the threats or opportunities arising out of external change, and (2) analyzing strategic growth options. In a large company, marketing management may receive assistance from staff professionals such as planners and economists. But in the final analysis, the responsibility for recommending marketing strategies rests with the marketing manager.

QUESTIONS

1. Distinguish between marketing strategies and marketing tactics.
2. What is the strategic planning concept?
3. How do company purpose, objective, strategy, and policy relate to one another?
4. Strategy has been described as the internal reponse to the external environment. What are the variables which make up the external and internal environments?
5. Describe the process of strategy formulation.
6. What are the strategic growth options of the Opportunity Grid?
7. Which strategic growth option carries the greatest risk and why?

REFERENCES

1. *Planning and the Chief Executive*, Conference Board Report No. 571, The Conference Board, New York, 1972, pp. 2–3 and 40–41.
2. David S. Hopkins, *The Marketing Plan*, Report No. 801, The Conference Board, New York, 1981, pp. v and 4.
3. Judith Bauer, "Balanced Marketing Planning in a Period of Sudden Change," *The Conference Board Record*, May 1975, pp. 14–17.
4. U.S Bureau of the Census, *Statistical Abstract of the United States, Washington, D.C., 1981*, p. 599.
5. General Foods, *Annual Report*, 1980, p. 13.
6. Dr. Walter Adams (quoting Jawkes, Sawers, and Stillerman, *The Sources of Invention*, chap. IV) in testimony given before the Select Committee on Small Business, U.S. Senate, June 29, 1967; reprinted in Robert J. Holloway and Robert S. Hancock, *The Environment of Marketing Behavior*, 2d ed., Wiley, New York, 1969, p. 154.
7. Ibid., p. 159.
8. Chester R. Wasson, "How Predictable Are Fashion and Other Product Life Cycles?" *Journal of Marketing*, vol. 32, July 1968, pp. 36–43.
9. Paul H. Nystrom, *Fashion Merchandising*, Ronald, New York, 1932, p. 31.
10. Victor P. Buell, *Organizing for Marketing/Advertising Success*, Association of National Advertisers, New York, 1982, chap. 4.
11. Clarence E. Eldridge, "The Marketing Budget and Its Allocation," No. 8 in the series, "The Management of the Marketing Function," Association of National Advertisers, Inc., New York, 1966, pp. 7, 8.
12. "Raytheon's Five Year Plans at Work," *Business Week*, July 14, 1975. By special permission, © 1975 by McGraw-Hill, Inc., New York, 10020. All rights reserved.
13. Rochelle O'Connor, *Corporate Guides to Long-Range Planning*, Report No. 687, The Conference Board, New York, September 1976.

CHAPTER 9

The Situation Analysis

We now begin a step-by-step approach to the marketing planning process. The first step—the *situation analysis*—involves the analysis of all pertinent external and internal information needed to identify short- and long-term marketing problems and opportunities.

Following an explanation of the *situation analysis*, we introduce the *Hanes Corporation* case. Hanes' management faced a set of problems which called for changes in marketing strategies. We will imagine ourselves in the role of Hanes' management to see what conclusions we might have reached had we been in their shoes. By the end of Part Three you should have a good understanding of how to do marketing planning.

Importance of the Situation Analysis

The *situation analysis* is fundamental to the planning process. The more accurate and complete the information gathered for the analysis, the more likely it is that real problems and opportunities will be recognized and that effective strategies will evolve.

FIGURE 9-1. Steps in the marketing planning process.

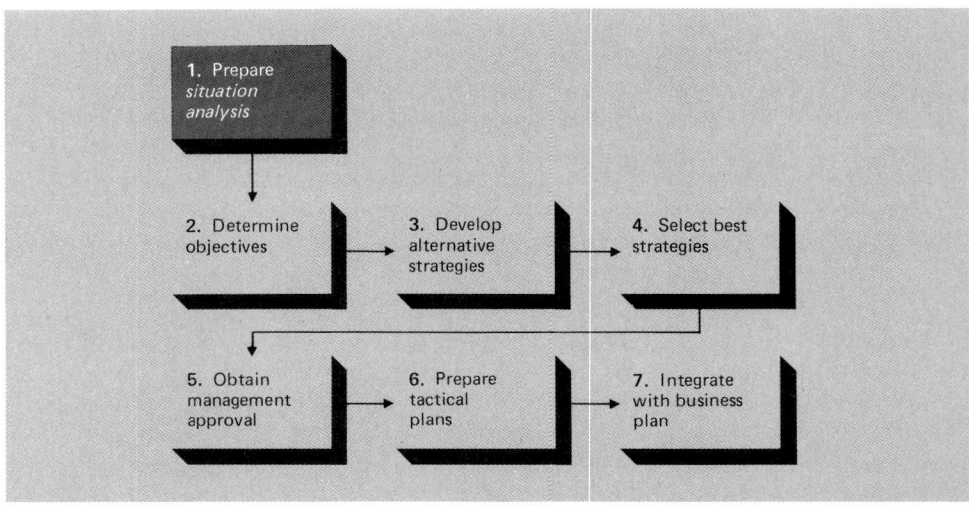

1. Prepare situation analysis
2. Determine objectives
3. Develop alternative strategies
4. Select best strategies
5. Obtain management approval
6. Prepare tactical plans
7. Integrate with business plan

Managements inexperienced in formal planning may skip the *situation analysis* step. Inexperience and lack of accumulated information needed for analysis are two reasons for this oversight. Considerable time and effort is needed, for example, to collect the type of external market data covered in Chapters 3 and 4. If that has not been done beforehand, it is too late to do so when the planning process begins. One of the benefits provided by the marketing information system (MIS) described in Chapter 6 is that it provides much of the information needed for carrying out the *situation analysis*.

In most cases skipping the analysis step leads to ineffective plans, although some managers seem able to identify their problems and opportunities intuitively, utilizing their firsthand observations and experience. By and large, however, professional managements recognize that careful data collection and analysis are needed prior to strategy formulation.

Scope of the Analysis

When writing the *situation analysis* section of an annual marketing plan, there is, inevitably a question about how detailed it should be. The answer is that it should be written in as much detail as is needed to ensure that all persons involved in the development and approval of the marketing plan understand the background facts. Even so, it should be no longer than absolutely necessary. Brevity encourages readership.

Original plans require more detail than updated plans prepared in succeeding years. When updating, emphasis is placed on change from the preceding year. Dynamic organizations have frequent personnel turnover and can't assume that everyone knows all the essential facts. Always consider the needs of your audience.

Time Period Covered

Begin by looking at performance over at least the most recent 5-year period, including the current year, then review a forecast of performance for the next 3 to 5 years. (Of course, some company plans cover a longer span of time.)

Because strategies are major plans for achieving major longer-range objectives, the strategic planning process by its very nature must look several years ahead. In contrast, the shorter-range tactical plan usually covers only the next year and coincides with the corporate budget period—normally the fiscal year.

In a *situation analysis*, the past record of performance and the forecasted future performance should be placed in the same tables or graphs. Forecasting is more meaningful when viewed in relation to the past. Plans which show only the forecasts for future years tend to be unduly optimistic. To encourage realistic forecasting, many corporate planning guidelines require forecasts and past performance to be shown together.

Topical Outline for Situation Analysis

The topical outline in **Marketing Note 9-1** is a guide for preparing *situation analyses* for cases or for actual companies. Some topics may be important to one company but unimportant to another. The outline, however, serves as a checklist to make certain that no topic is overlooked.

Some cases do not contain all of the information needed to answer each topic,

MARKETING NOTE 9-1

Topical Outline for Situation Analysis

A. *Economic and industry forecasts*
   1. Demand factors
   2. Industry sales forecasts
B. *Business unit forecasts*
   1. Sales
   2. Market share
   3. Profits
C. *The planning gap*
D. *Markets served and not served*
E. *Buyer behavior characteristics*
   1. Identify ultimate customers, purchase influencers, and factors influencing purchase
   2. Frequency of purchase
   3. Seasonal and cyclical patterns
F. *Competitive situation*
   1. Rank competitors by market share
   2. Describe competitive environment
   3. Role of imports, if any
   4. Competition from outside the industry
G. *The marketing mix*
   1. Product line
      a. Position with respect to differentiation, quality, breadth, packaging, and customer service
      b. Stage of product life cycle
      c. Private brand offerings, if any
   2. Distribution policies and channels
      a. Channels used and not used
      b. Coverage—quantitative and qualitative
      c. Coverage policy—intensive, selective, exclusive
      d. Sales support for channel members, if any
      e. Trade attitudes towards company
   3. Promotion
      a. Expenditures compared to major competitors
      b. Sales force size, composition, and coverage
      c. Advertising effectiveness
   4. Pricing
      a. Policy and practices with respect to price segments served, and competitiveness of costs, prices, credit policies, trade discounts
      b. Industry situation with respect to pricing leader (if any), demand elasticity, nature of industry (oligopolistic or monopolistic), and price level trends
H. *Changes in market structure*
I. *Constraints*
   1. External
   2. Internal
J. *Strengths and weaknesses*
K. *Opportunities*
   1. Marketing
   2. Cost Efficiency
L. *Summary of key problems and opportunities*

either because the company did not have it or because the case writer could not obtain it. Therefore, assumptions about the missing information may be made and should be noted, unless the information can be obtained from available sources such as libraries or trade associations. Even companies with good marketing information systems rarely have every piece of information needed. Consequently, company plans often contain assumptions which are noted as such.

COMMENTS ON SITUATION ANALYSIS OUTLINE

The comments that follow explain briefly how each topic might affect the company or the business unit's situation. Some subjects may be new to you. If you feel more explanation is needed, refer to the Subject Index for further coverage.

In using the outline for the first time, students occasionally complain of redundancy. A certain amount of duplication and overlap is inevitable when analyzing a market situation. A subject such as cost, for example, may need to be discussed under topic headings such as pricing, competition, constraints, strengths and weaknesses, and possibly others. The planner may need to explain the facts about costs only once, yet note their significance when discussing each topic affected by costs. Experience reveals that redundancy is, in fact, useful as it tends to highlight and reinforce problems and opportunities.

Under the first two outline headings (A and B), we are engaged in forecasting sales and profits for a hypothetical business unit up to five years ahead. We make assumptions about the economic climate and industry sales during that period while assuming no change in the unit's current strategies. The forecasting process covered by A and B leads to heading C where the forecasts are compared with management objectives to see whether there is a difference. If there is, this difference is termed the *planning gap.**

A. Economic and Industry Forecasts

1. Demand Factors. Begin by reviewing the general economic and other related factors believed to influence demand in your industry. The relevant factors will vary by industry. Common examples are: gross national product, inflation rate, production index, population, personal disposable income, retail sales, and segments of the above.

One method of forecasting an industry's sales is to determine whether correlations exist between industry sales and published economic series for which government or private forecasts are issued regularly. Even if a good correlation cannot be found, it still is useful to review the outlook for the next 3 to 5 years, focusing on those economic and demographic factors thought to influence the total market for our products or services.

In the examples that follow, our hypothetical business unit is producing and selling a consumer hard good. Table 9-1 presents the five-year outlook for gross national product (GNP) and durable goods retail sales—a published economic measure with which our product historically has shown a good correlation. Although GNP and durable goods retail sales grow at approximately the same rate over longer periods, they do not grow at the same rate each year. In our example, management—based on government forecasts and its own judgment—assumes that both of these economic series will grow during the next five years at the same average rate as they did for the past five years. After adjusting for the effects of an assumed average inflation rate of 6 percent, the estimated rate of real growth for each is found to be a little over 3 percent per annum.

2. Industry Sales Forecast. Table 9-2 presents industry sales data for the past five years (data collected by the industry trade association). It also contains marketing management's forecast of industry sales for the next five years. Table 9-2

*Some planners refer to this difference as the "strategic gap."

TABLE 9-1

GNP and Durable Goods Retail Sales:
History and 5-Year Forecast

Year	GNP	Durable Goods Retail Sales
HISTORICAL ANNUAL % INCREASE*		
−4	+ 8.2	+ 6.0
−3	+10.2	+ 7.8
−2	+11.6	+11.5
−1	+ 8.1	+11.3
Current	+ 7.3	+ 9.0
Average % increase	+ 9.1	+ 9.2
5-YEAR FORECAST OF ANNUAL AVERAGE % INCREASE		
Actual dollars (before inflation)	+ 9.1%	+ 9.2%
Real annual growth rate (after inflation)†	+ 3.1%	+ 3.2%

*Based on actual dollars not adjusted for inflation.
†Assuming a 6.0% inflation rate.

shows that industry sales are expected to grow at a slower rate than durable goods retail sales, despite the historic correlation between the two series.

The rate of industry sales increases had begun to fall below that of durable

TABLE 9-2

Industry Sales History and 5-Year Projection

Year	Sales, $ millions	% Change from Previous Year
PAST SALES PERFORMANCE		
−4	100.0	+ 6.0
−3	108.0	+ 8.0
−2	119.9	+11.0
−1	132.5	+10.5
Current	143.8	+ 8.5
Average annual % increase		+ 8.8
ESTIMATED SALES PERFORMANCE		
+1	156.0	+ 8.5
+2	168.5	+ 8.0
+3	181.1	+ 7.5
+4	193.7	+ 7.0
+5	206.3	+ 6.5
Average annual % increase		+ 7.5

goods retail sales about three years ago. It is thought that the reason for this variance is that the industry has entered the mature phase of its product life cycle. When adjusted for an assumed rate of 6 percent inflation, real industry growth is expected to approach zero by the fifth year (6.5 percent dollar growth less 6.0 percent inflation equals 0.5 percent real growth). This provides our first indication of a potential problem. Slower industry growth will mean slower growth for the business unit, assuming no change in the unit's strategies.

B. Business Unit Forecasts

Table 9-3 shows the sales and market share history for the business unit and the forecast of sales and market share for the next five years. Estimated sales were arrived at by multiplying estimated industry sales by the business unit's average share of market for the past five years. Because the industry rate of growth is declining, a similar decline should occur for the business unit, assuming no change in strategies. Assuming a 6 percent inflation rate, sales in constant dollars will be virtually flat by the fifth year.

Table 9-4 shows that profit growth also has been slowing. Actual dollar profits are expected to peak in the second year of the planning period and decline thereafter. The unsatisfactory profit outlook is due to:

1. The slowing rate of sales growth.
2. Inflationary cost increases that cannot be offset either by the economies of scale that would flow from real sales growth or price increases. Price increases are prevented by the competitive pressures characteristic of the mature phase of the product life cycle.

TABLE 9-3
Business Unit Sales and Industry Share: History and 5-Year Forecast

Year	Sales, $ millions	% Change in Sales from Previous Year	% Share of Industry
	ACTUAL		
−4	20.0	6.0	20.0
−3	21.1	5.5	19.5
−2	24.0	13.7	20.0
−1	27.2	13.3	20.5
Current	29.4	8.1	20.5
Average annual share			20.0
	ESTIMATED		
+1	31.2	6.1	20.0
+2	33.7	8.0	20.0
+3	36.2	7.4	20.0
+4	38.7	6.9	20.0
+5	41.3	6.7	20.0

TABLE 9-4

Business Unit Net Profit: History and 5-Year Forecast*

Year	Profit, ($ millions)	% Change in Profit from Previous Year	% Return On Sales
	PAST PERFORMANCE		
−4	3.2	7.0	16.0
−3	3.0	(6.2)	14.0
−2	3.6	20.0	15.0
−1	3.9	8.3	14.5
Current	4.1	5.1	14.0
Average ROS			14.7
	ESTIMATED PERFORMANCE		
+1	4.2	2.4	13.5
+2	4.4	4.8	13.0
+3	4.3	(2.3)	12.0
+4	4.3	0	11.0
+5	4.1	(4.7)	10.0
Average ROS			11.9

*Profit before tax but after deducting corporate charges.

Note. Some managements prefer to show profits as a return on some defined measure of investment (ROI) in addition to the return on sales (ROS) as used in this example.

C. The Planning Gap

We are now in a position to compare the forecasted profits over the next five years with what management would like them to be. Their goal is to increase profits at a compound rate of 10 percent annually.

Figure 9-2 plots management's yearly profit goals compared to estimated actual profits (from Table 9-4). It can be seen that the shortfall for the fifth year would be $2.2 million ($6.3 million less $4.1 million). The cumulative shortfall over the 5–year period would be $5.4 million.

The difference between performance goals and estimates of actual performance represents the planning gap. When such a gap occurs, management has two options: (1) lower the goals, or (2) develop new strategies for achieving the goals. Most managements will opt for the new strategies, a decision which adds challenge to the planning process. Occasionally a company's outlook is so favorable there is no planning gap, but such a case is an exception.

D. Markets Served and Not Served

List each known market segment for our product line in order of size. Show dollar value and approximate share of total market if known. Indicate which segments we

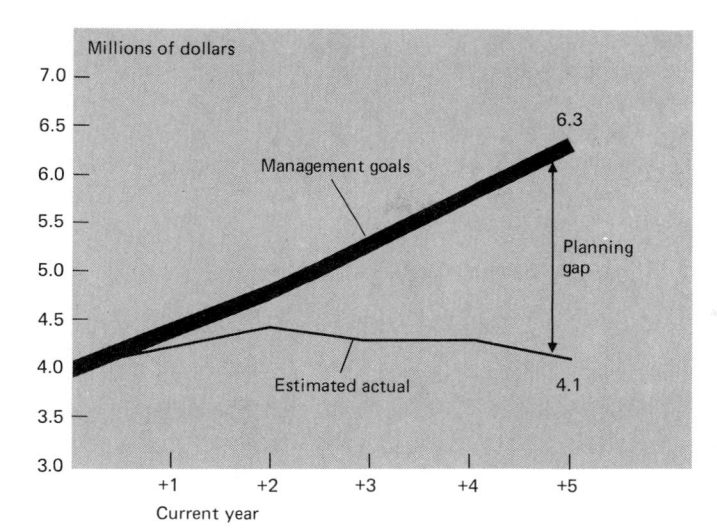

FIGURE 9-2. Gap between profit goals and estimated actual profit.

market to and which we do not. Discuss whether we should enter any segments we don't serve, or get out of any we do serve.

E. Buyer Behavior Characteristics

In this section we identify who the buyers and users of our products are, what factors influence their purchases, and how frequently they purchase. We also note whether seasonal or cyclical purchase patterns exist.

It is important in marketing planning to think of the ultimate buyers and users as our customers rather than the wholesalers or retailers who may actually buy the product from us. Although channel intermediaries are important, market success depends on how well we understand and serve the needs and wants of the ultimate buyers and users. Marketing planning, therefore, really begins with the ultimate buyer and user and builds from that base.

1. **Identify Ultimate Customers.** The buyers and users of consumer goods may or may not be the same person. A parent, for example, may buy food or clothing for use by children or spouse. Or one person may purchase something as a gift for another. In organizational buying the purchasing department places the order but usually at the request of the using department.

2. **Identify Purchase Influencers.** Other members of the family usually influence (or may dictate) what the shopper will buy. This is particularly true for food and clothing, but it also exists in varying degrees for durable goods purchases such as appliances, home furnishings, and cars. Peers, relatives, and pets may also influence family purchases. Medical doctors dictate the purchase of prescription drugs and influence the purchase (or nonpurchase) of nonprescription drugs. Reporters and editors may influence the selection of particular products or brands. In planning our consumer advertising and other promotional programs, therefore, we should consider reaching significant influencers as well as the actual buyers.

Professional buyers for organizations seek the best buy from among acceptable offerings, although supplier selection often is influenced by or dictated by using departments. Purchasing departments have greater authority when buying undifferentiated commodities but less authority when buying products where special performance characteristics are needed. Knowing who really controls the buying decision for our product is essential to planning our personal selling effort and is also useful in targeting our advertising and sales promotion.

3. **Identify Other Factors Influencing Purchase.** Other influencing factors may include demographic, economic, social, psychological, lifestyle, fashion, and brand preference. These, of course, will vary according to the product or service.

4. **Frequency of Purchase.** How often the purchaser buys our type of product is an important determinant of our product category, and, in turn, the marketing mix we choose. In consumer marketing, for example, frequently purchased convenience goods lend themselves to intensive distribution and promotional strategies that help to *pull* the product through the channels of distribution. Infrequently purchased shopping goods, on the other hand, lend themselves to selective or exclusive distribution and promotional strategies that help to *push* the product through the channels.

5. **Seasonal and Cyclical Variations.** Most industries have minor seasonal sales variations which have no significant impact on marketing planning. Other industries, however, such as snow tires or lawn and garden equipment, have significant seasonal sales variations. Companies with seasonal lines have the option of living with the situation or of diversifying into product lines with offsetting seasonal variations. A novel approach to the seasonal problem is taken by the Provincetown–Boston airline with serves the Cape Cod area in the summer but moves its planes south in the winter where its Naples Airlines Division provides connecting flights between cities in Florida.

Whereas seasonal variations occur within the year, cyclical variations occur over periods of several years. Durable goods are more subject to cycles than nondurables. Many industries have cycles that correspond to the ups and downs of the national and world economies, while others—such as home construction—have cycles that run counter to the general economy. One of the strategic alternatives for companies in cyclical businesses is acquiring companies in industries that run counter-cyclical to their own.

F. Competitive Situation

There is probably nothing more important in a *situation analysis* than an objective examination of the competitive situation. We should:

1. Rank principal competitors, including our product or brand, by market share.
2. Note changes in rankings that may be occurring.
3. Discuss strengths and weaknesses of major competitors.
4. Describe the competitive environment. Determine, if possible, the degree to which the industry is oligopolistic or monopolistic and indicate what effect this has on our marketing planning.

5. Check imports. Imports may or may not be significant. If they are, their effect on our marketing planning should be discussed.
6. Analyze competition from outside the industry. It is important to be alert to competitive developments from outside our industry. These are usually technological in nature and are introduced by companies with different technologies. Examples are IBM's invasion of the mechanical typewriter industry with its electric typewriter and Texas Instrument's invasion of the mechanical watch industry with its electronic digital watch. Technological competition from the outside is often more serious than competitive developments within the industry.

G. The Marketing Mix

1. Product Line. Since our line of products or services is what we have to offer in exchange for customer dollars, we need to make an objective appraisal of our product line, particularly in comparison with our major competitors.
   a. *Position.* What is the market's appraisal of our products in relation to competition?
      (1) Are our products differentiated, and if so, how? If not, what might be done to differentiate them?
      (2) How good is our quality and performance for the market segments we are serving?
      (3) How broad is our line? Should it be expanded or pruned?
      (4) How effective is our packaging from the viewpoint of the customer (protection and information) and the trade* (information, handling and shelf stacking).
      (5) What customer services do we provide, and how are they viewed by customers and the trade? Are they adequate? Are they properly priced?
   b. *Stage of product life cycle.* State the estimated present stage of the industry product life cycle and when the industry might enter the next stage. State the implications of the product life cycle for our planning.
   c. *Private brand offerings.* Do we manufacture private brands? If yes, why? If no, why not? Should private branding be considered a potential strategy for us?
2. Distribution Policies and Channels. Consider the effectiveness of our present channels and how effective our policies are in dealing with the trade:

   List *available channels* used and not used by us.

   Evaluate our *coverage* of wholesalers, retailers, or direct customers in terms of number and quality.

   Does our policy embrace the use of intensive, selective, or exclusive *distribution*, and why?

   Do we (or should we) provide *sales support* for channel members (e.g., training of wholesale salespeople or making missionary calls on retailers)?

   How does the *trade view* us as a supplier?

---

*The "trade" is a term often used in industry to denote wholesalers and/or retailers.

3. **Promotion.** Here we evaluate our promotional efforts in terms of expenditures and quality, relative to our major competitors. Should we cut expenditures or should we spend more? Can the productivity of our promotion be improved?
   a. *Expenditures.* Show expenditures for advertising, personal selling, and sales promotion by amount and as a percentage of sales for the past five years. Compare with estimated expenditures of major competitors. Note any change in trends of our own or competitors' expenditures.
   b. *Sales force.* Describe our sales force in terms of size, composition (e.g., company salespeople or manufacturers' representatives), and adequacy of account coverage compared to major competitors.
   c. *Advertising.* Evaluate the effectiveness of our advertising in terms of reach, frequency, and performance compared to objectives.
4. **Pricing.** We should review our pricing policies and practices in relation to the industry pricing situation.
   a. *Pricing policies and practices*
      (1) What price segments do we serve and not serve?
      (2) How competitive are our prices compared to major competitors?
      (3) How competitive are costs relative to major competitors?
      (4) Are our credit policies and trade discounts competitive?
   b. *Industry pricing situation*
      (1) Who is the industry price leader, if any?
      (2) Are industry products demand-elastic?
      (3) Is pricing affected by the oligopolistic or monopolistic nature of the industry?
      (4) What are the trends in price levels?

H. Changes in Market Structure

One of the distinctions between strategic and tactical planning is that strategic marketing planning attempts to look beyond the current environment (which may appear static to the casual observer). The purpose is to spot basic structural changes that may represent potential threats or opportunities for our business. Consider topics such as: (1) *geographic*, (2) *demographic*, (3) *economic*, (4) *cultural*, (5) *legal and governmental*, and (6) *technological* changes.

I. Constraints

Every marketing manager is faced with conditions which limit options. These will be found in both the external market environment and the internal company environment. The purpose of this section is to bring the constraints into the open so that external constraints can be circumvented in the planning process and internal company constraints can be resolved.

No list of potential constraints can be offered which would be representative because they will vary according to each company's situation. External constraints, however, might include government action, pressure groups, environmental conditions, or fashion. Internal constraints might include limited production capacity, high production costs, or inadequate capital. Management policies and attitudes may represent a constraint if a proposed strategy runs counter to past practice. An example of both an internal and external constraint would be the case of a company whose current stock price is relatively low. The company would be constrained from adopting an acquisition strategy which required exchange of stock because it would prove too costly for stockholders.

A constraint may develop when a new strategy is considered. Current production capacity could constrain a proposed strategy that would increase sales substantially. This constraint can be removed, of course, by building more capacity. Nevertheless, the constraint should be noted as soon as it is identified.

J. Strengths and Weaknesses

Here we list as objectively as possible the strengths and weaknesses of the business unit as compared to competition in terms of market position, product line, costs, people, finance, and technology. Good planning calls for emphasizing strengths and minimizing weaknesses, while at the same time working to correct the weakness.

K. Opportunities

1. **Marketing Opportunities.** As a result of the subject matter covered in the analysis to this point, the planner is now in a position to list possible marketing opportunities. Reasonable selectivity should be applied here; that is, one should list only ideas that appear to have merit and feasibility. The purpose at this point is to list possible opportunities that have occurred to the analyst without going into all the pros and cons. Later in the planning process these ideas can be evaluated as possible strategies. Examples (which may or may not apply) include: (a) new products, (b) product improvements, (c) line broadening, (d) entering new (or unserved) market segments, (e) utilizing new (or unused) distribution channels, (f) improvements in customer service, (g) diversification, (h) forward integration into company-owned or franchised distribution, (i) raising performance in below-par geographic segments, (j) improving promotional programs, (k) emphasis on products with higher profit margins.

2. **Cost Efficiency Opportunities.** Ideas for increasing volume are usually more exciting to marketing executives, but opportunities to increase profits by improving efficiency should not be overlooked. Most businesses that have been in operation for a period of time offer good cost-cutting opportunities. Companies find themselves in markets or market segments which offer low profit potential and from which they should withdraw. Most companies benefit from periodic pruning of product lines which have grown too large. And most companies can benefit from coordinated logistical programs which attempt to balance the interrelated—but competitive—needs of production scheduling, inventories, warehousing, transportation, and customer services.

These types of cost reduction opportunities are usually subjects for study by special task forces. They are too involved to attempt solutions during the annual marketing planning process. They are included in the *situation analysis* outline, however, so that they will not be overlooked.

L. Summary of Key Problems and Opportunities

This section is the highlight of the *situation analysis*. Here we draw conclusions about the significant issues revealed by the analysis: What are the major problems? What has caused them? What might be done to solve them?

Avoid making a long list of every apparent problem uncovered in the analysis. Most minor problems can be dealt with in the tactical plans covering the marketing functions. What we are trying to isolate here are the conditions that might prevent the business from reaching its long-range objectives. Usually these are few in number. In the case of our hypothetical company, for instance, we saw that (1) there was a gap between profit objectives and estimated profits, as a result of (2) a decline in the forecast rate of industry and business unit growth, caused by (3) the industry reaching maturity. If this were an actual company, and we had followed through with its *situation analysis*, we might have discovered other problems needing correction. The chances are, however, there would be nothing approaching the scope of the problem created by declining industry demand.

The major opportunities for this company might be: (1) to increase sales by taking market share from other companies, or (2) to utilize the company's technology and market know-how to develop new products for its present markets or new market applications for existing products, or (3) to diversify into new businesses.

THE HANES' CORPORATION CASE

In 1969 the management of the Hanes Corporation of Winston-Salem, North Carolina, a leading manufacturer of women's hosiery and men's and boy's underwear, was reviewing its marketing strategies. The women's hosiery line, which accounted for about two-thirds of company sales, had shared in the growth of the hosiery industry during the last half of the 1960s—a growth which had been tied to the increasing popularity of the miniskirt.

As skirts became shorter, the traditional thigh-length hosiery no longer adequately covered the leg. This led to the introduction of pantyhose, a one-piece stocking which covered the body from toe to waist. Pantyhose sales were rising rapidly, accounting for nearly half of total women's hosiery production, and were expected to exceed 70 percent by 1970.

Despite the recent growth of hosiery sales, Hanes' management was not complacent. Although company sales had increased at an average annual rate of nearly 10 percent since 1965, profit margins had been declining. Industry prices had softened as a result of competition created by low-price private brands. The general competitive situation had required an increasing percentage of income to be allocated to company promotional expenditures.

One concern was that supermarkets had begun to offer hosiery under their own private brand names. Not only were they taking sales from the traditional outlets (department and specialty stores) used by Hanes, but they were also selling hosiery at markedly lower prices: as low as 29 cents a pair compared to $2.50 to $3.00 a pair for branded hose. Food supermarkets accounted for 12 percent of industry sales in 1968 while drug stores accounted for 6 percent.

While Hanes did not market a supermarket brand, it did produce private label

TABLE 9-5
Industry Shipments of Women's Hosiery

Year	Millions of Dozen Pairs	Per Capita Consumption
1966	101.6	16.7
1967	116.4	19.0
1968	123.4	19.9
1969	133.1	21.1

products, some of which were sold to mass merchandisers. Tables 9-5 and 9-6 show industry and company performance data.

Characteristics of the Women's Hosiery Market

Hosiery is worn by women beginning in their teenage years. It is purchased frequently, with per capita consumption ranging from 15 to 21 pairs annually. The heavy usage segments are the 18- to 49-year age group, socially active women, and women in white-collar occupations. The population of women in the 18 to 49 age bracket is expected to increase by 20.7 percent during the next decade—from 42.9 million in 1970 to 51.8 million in 1980—compared to a 9.3 percent increase for the female population as a whole.

Nylon is the preferred yarn because its elasticity and strength allow for sheerness and a smooth fit. At various times hosiery styling has been expressed in terms of color, type of knit (e.g., mesh), sheerness, and toe style. Knee-length hosiery with elastic tops (called knee-highs by the industry) are a minor part of industry sales.

Pantyhose appeal to women of all ages because of their greater protection, warmth, and the fact they do not require garters. They are expected to replace regular length hosiery even after mini miniskirts are out of fashion.

Hosiery market segments can be viewed in several ways. For each category shown in Table 9-7, segments are ranked in order of size.

The slowest purchasing season is during the summer months when many women go without hosiery. Geographic purchases are somewhat lower than average in warmer sections of the country. Hosiery normally is purchased by the wearer except for gift occasions and when mothers purchase for daughters. Factors influencing the type and amount of hosiery purchased are income levels, fashion

TABLE 9-6
Hanes Corporation Performance Data

Year	Sales, $ millions	After-Tax Profit, $ millions	% Profit Return on Sales	Earnings per Share	% Market Share
1965	113	9.0	8.0	2.31	5
1966	121	9.3	7.7	2.40	5
1967	131	7.6	5.8	1.95	5
1968	145	8.1	5.6	2.09	6
1969 (estimate)	155 to 160	4.0 to 5.0	2.5 to 3.2	1.00 to 1.30	6

TABLE 9-7
Hosiery Market Segments

PLACE OF PURCHASE	SHEERNESS	SIZE
*1. *Department and specialty stores*	*1. *Regular*	*1. *Average*
2. Mass merchandising chain stores	*2. *Extra-sheer*	*2. *Outsize*
3. Food and drug chain stores		*3. *Petite*
4. Mail order	STYLE	
5. Vending machines	*1. *Stocking (regular length)*	PRICE RANGE
	*2. *Regular pantyhose*	*1. *Medium*
BRANDED/NONBRANDED	*3. *Knee highs*	2. Low
*1. *Advertised brands*	*4. *Support (elasticized) pantyhose*	*3. *High*
*2. *Private brands*		

*Indicates the market segments in which Hanes competes.

consciousness, working versus nonworking status, and lifestyle (active versus inactive social life, frequency of travel). Socks and peds (foot covering only) are occasionally worn as stocking substitutes. There is also a small core of nonwearers.

Leading hosiery brands are advertised in media directed primarily to women. Brand selection is influenced by quality of the products, pricing, and brand image. Hosiery is normally packaged with one pair contained in a transparent, open-ended, polyethylene envelope which enables the buyer to see the color and examine the stocking. Brand name, features, color and size are printed on an opaque or translucent portion of the envelope.

Competition

The mass merchandising chains—J. C. Penney and Sears—together account for about 16 percent of the market, while the six other leading manufacturers' brands represent about 24 percent. In total the top eight companies have approximately 40 percent of the women's hosiery market. There has been no significant change in market share by any individual company. Ranking by share is shown in Table 9-8.

Major competitive actions by one of the companies manufacturing advertised brands is usually followed by the others. Several smaller competitors have estab-

TABLE 9-8
Shares of Women's Hosiery Market

Rank	Hanes and Competitors	Estimated % Market Share	
1	J. C. Penney	9.0	16
2	Sears-Roebuck	7.0	
3	Hanes	5.5	
4	Kayser-Roth	5.5	
5	Burlington	4.0	24
6	Adams-Millis	3.0	
7	Bear Brand	3.0	
8	J. P. Stevens	3.0	
All others	(Approximately 215 companies)	60	
Total		100	

lished strong positions in specific market segments such as geographic area, low price, and private label. A factor contributing to Hanes' position is that women's hosiery represents its major business. Kayser-Roth Corporation and Burlington Industries are considerably larger companies but more diversified, with women's hosiery representing a smaller segment of their total sales.

Neither imports nor exports are significant because other countries have well-established hosiery companies offering a wide range of products and pricing.

Distribution

Women's hosiery is distributed through a variety of outlets—department stores, specialty stores, mass merchandising chains, food and drug stores, mail order houses and vending machines. Distribution to retail stores is by independent distributors, chain warehouses, and direct from the manufacturer to the retailer.

Hanes distributes its branded lines through independent distributors to the better department and specialty stores in each market. The Hanes brands are well regarded by the trade and carried by most major department and specialty stores. Average discounts are 45 to 47 percent to retailers, and 17 percent to distributors (i.e., 17 percent of distributor selling price to the retailer). Hanes' price to the distributors, therefore, is about 55 percent off list.

Hosiery departments of department and specialty stores are staffed with sales clerks who assist the customer. Some counter display is provided for self-selection purposes, but hosiery—particularly the more expensive brands—is also displayed in glass-enclosed cases with backup stock behind the counter. Mass merchandising chains and supermarkets use self-service racks.

Product Line

As indicated by the market segments served, Hanes carries one of the broadest lines in the industry, including a wide range of sizes and an assortment of colors. Nevertheless, Hanes primarily produces quality hosiery, designed for upscale market appeal, while avoiding the lowest-priced segments. Hanes products are sold under the following brand names: Hanes, Beauty Mist, and Today's Girl. The multiple-brand policy is designed to appeal to different market segments with different features and prices.

Hanes' manufacturing costs are thought to be competitive with other major manufacturers. Because of the high fixed costs invested in knitting machines, dyeing processes, and other equipment, manufacturing costs are sensitive to fluctuations in sales volume. In addition, over 1000 items are carried in the Hanes line, resulting in short runs for many items.

Promotional Program

Hanes' promotional expenditures—measured as a percent of sales—are in line with leading competitors. The company's financial report combines advertising and sales expense with administrative expense into one figure. Promotional and administrative expenses had risen from 9.4 percent of sales in 1965 to 12.3 percent in 1968 and was expected to reach 13.8 percent in 1969.

Hanes' hosiery sales force of approximately fifteen persons calls on both wholesale and major retail accounts. Hosiery advertising is placed primarily in women's magazines catering to medium and upper income groups. Local co-op

TABLE 9-9
Consolidated Balance Sheet as of Dec. 31, 1968 (In thousands of dollars)

Assets		Liabilities	
Cash	4,699	Notes payable	19,875
Net receivables	22,157	Accounts payable	4,540
Inventories	34,790	Income taxes	1,736
Total current assets	61,646	Accruals	5,106
Net property, etc.	50,206	Total current liabilities	31,257
Investments and advances to subsidiaries	582	Notes payable	3,125
Deferred charges, etc.	748	Deferred compensation	1,127
Total assets	113,182	Deferred income tax	5,910
		Common stock ($1.00)	4,510
		Paid-in-surplus	3,842
		Retained earnings	70,862
Net current assets	30,389	Reacquired stock	(7,451)
Net stockholders' equity	71,763	Total liabilities	113,182

advertising is offered to retailers. National advertising features beautification of the leg with Hanes hosiery.

Market Research

Prior to its marketing strategy planning sessions in 1969, Hanes had researched the pros and cons of private brand hosiery sales in supermarkets and drug stores. The research revealed that many women liked the convenience of buying hosiery while doing their weekly shopping but did not trust the unknown labels. They were skeptical of the quality. Stockouts often caused them to return to traditional channels. Research of the food and drug channels showed that there were over 600 brands offered. There was no brand loyalty. Price represented the primary inducement to purchase; stockouts were common, and the rate of turnover did not satisfy chain managements.

Hanes' management was looking for additional ways to increase sales and profits. The question of moving into supermarket channels, however, raised serious

TABLE 9-10
Consolidated Income Account, Year Ended Dec. 31, 1968 (In thousands of dollars)

Net sales	145,356
Cost of sales	109,402
Gross profit	35,954
Selling, etc., expense	17,904
Interest	1,313
Other deductions, net	168
Income before tax	16,569
Income taxes	8,469
Net income	8,100

TABLE 9-11
Recent Hanes Stock Price Range*

Year	High–Low
1969	44 ¼–14 ¼
1968	48 ¾–23 ⅛
1967	28 ¾–19 ½
1966	29 ½–19 ⅜

*Hanes is listed on N.Y. Stock Exchange.

policy issues and appeared fraught with risk. Management decided that an intensive analysis of the total situation was called for, to be followed by an examination of all feasible alternative strategies that might lead to long-term sales and profit improvement.

Tables 9-9 to 9-11 show recent financial data and prices of the company stock.

SITUATION ANALYSIS—HANES CORPORATION*

A. Economic and Industry Forecasts

1. *Demand Factors.* The basic determinants for women's hosiery demand are thought to be (1) female population between the ages of 18 to 49, (2) disposable personal income (DPI), and (3) women's fashions.
    a. *Population.* Between 1970 and 1980 female population in the 18 to 49 age group is projected by the census to grow more than twice as fast as the total female population—20.8 percent versus 9.3 percent—and at an annual rate of 2.1 percent.
    b. *Disposable personal income.* Table 9-12 shows our forecast of the percent increase in DPI for the next 4 years, both in current (inflated) dollars and constant (1958) dollars. The rate of increase in DPI in constant dollars is trending downward steadily as a result of the rising rate of inflation. We expect inflation will continue to have a slowing effect on real DPI; consequently, we forecast DPI in constant dollars to grow at an average annual rate of 3 percent during the next few years compared to a 4.1 percent average during the past four years.
    c. *Fashion.* Women's hosiery sales traditionally have been strongly influenced by the prevailing length of skirts. Shorter skirts cause an increase in hosiery demand while longer skirts have the opposite effect. The current miniskirt fashion has helped women's per capita hosiery consumption rise from 16.7 pairs annually in 1966 to an estimated 21 pairs this year (1969).
    During the next 4-year planning period, a major question is whether and when the popularity of short skirts will end. From past experience we would

*Information for this analysis is from the case itself, from census data available in 1969, and from my assumptions. The *situation analysis* is presented as though it were a part of the Hanes marketing plan. The pronouns "we" and "our" refer to comments that might have been made by Hanes' planners in their writing of the plan.

TABLE 9-12

Disposable Personal Income

Year	% Increase	
	DPI in Current Dollars	DPI in Constant 1958 Dollars
PAST FOUR YEARS		
1966	7.5	4.9
1967	7.4	4.6
1968	8.2	4.5
1969 (estimate)	6.8	2.5
Annual average % growth	7.5	4.1
FORECAST FOR THE PERIOD 1970–1973		
Annual average % growth	8.0	3.0

expect the current trend to reverse itself within the next year or two. We already are seeing attempts by leading fashion designers to introduce mid-calf length skirts, although with little success so far. Some observers believe that pants for women may be the next major fashion which could dampen hosiery demand even more than longer skirts.

2. **Industry Sales Forecast.** In view of the foregoing we expect an 8 percent increase in industry sales for next year (1970), following the strong gain for this current year (1969). We forecast the fashion change to begin during 1971, leading to a decline in industry sales in 1972 and 1973. See Table 9-13.

TABLE 9-13

Industry Shipments of Women's Hosiery

Year	Millions of Dozen Pairs	% Increase	Per Capita Consumption
ACTUAL			
1966	101.6		16.7
1967	116.4	14.5	19.0
1968	123.4	6.0	19.9
1969 (estimated)	133.1	7.9	21.1
FORECAST			
1970	143.7	8.0	22.0
1971	148.0	3.0	21.0
1972	143.5	(3.0)	20.0
1973	139.2	(3.0)	17.5

B. Company Forecasts

Table 9-14 presents our forecasts of sales, profits, and market share. Sales are based on the industry sales forecast and a continuation of our present market share of roughly 6 percent. The constant market share assumes no change in present marketing strategies.

Despite an increase in company sales during the past four years, profits have been declining and are expected to suffer a severe drop this year. The unsatisfactory profit picture results from declining profit margins. We have been unable to raise prices to offset inflationary cost increases because the competition from low-price private brands has had a softening effect on the prices of branded hosiery. Also, we have had to increase marketing expenses in order to maintain our market share in the face of stiffening competition.

We have forecast relatively flat earnings for the next 4 years on the assumption that profit return on sales can be held at the current rate of 2.6 percent. This may be an optimistic assumption in view of the rapidly deteriorating competitive environment.

C. The Planning Gap

In view of the impending downturn in industry sales and the continuing price competition, it is unlikely that profit margins will return to their pre-1969 levels. However, with tighter internal controls, management should be able to raise return on sales (ROS) to 4 percent. If sales could be increased 10 percent a year, a 4 percent ROS would raise profits to $9.1 million by 1973. In fact, management's primary objective is to return annual profits to the 1965–1966 levels of over $9 million.

The planning gaps, in Figure 9-3, show that if there is no change in strategies there will be a shortfall in sales in 1973 of $62 million and a shortfall in after-tax

TABLE 9-14
Company Forecasts

Year	Sales $ millions	% Change in Sales	% Market Share	Profit after Tax, $ millions	% Profit ROS
		ACTUAL			
1965	113		5	9.0	8.0
1966	121	7.1	5	9.3	7.7
1967	131	8.3	5	7.6	5.8
1968	145	10.7	6	8.1	5.6
1969 (estimated)	157	8.3	6	4.1	2.6
		ESTIMATED			
1970	170	8.0	6	4.4	2.6
1971	175	3.0	6	4.5	2.6
1972	170	(2.9)	6	4.4	2.6
1973	165	(3.0)	6	4.3	2.6

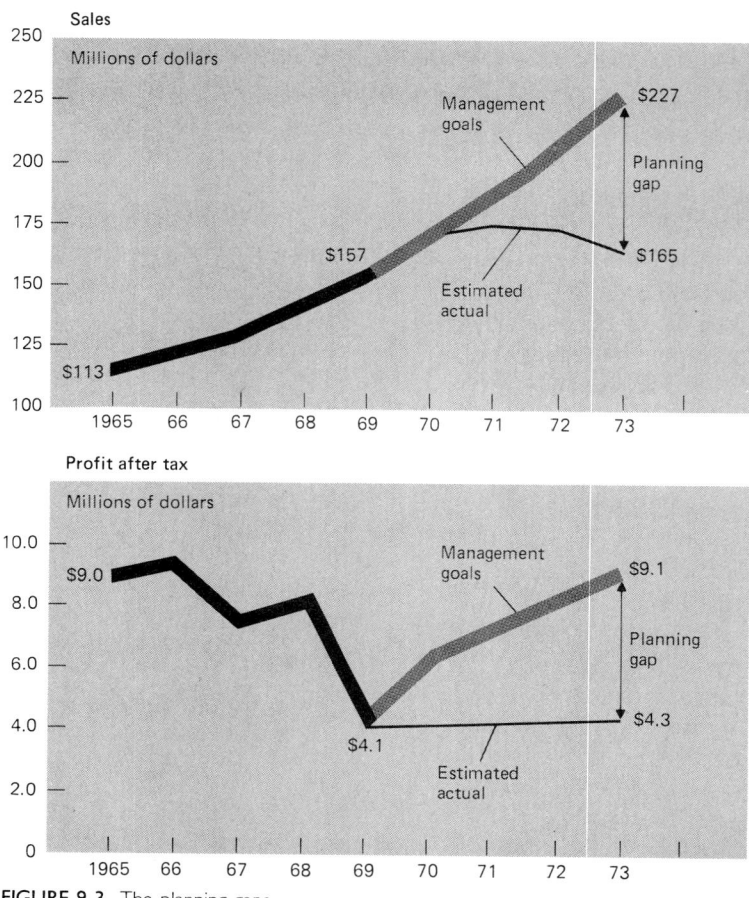

FIGURE 9-3. The planning gaps.

profit of $4.8 million. In the balance of the *situation analysis* we look for market opportunities that could help to overcome our dilemma.

D. Markets Served and Not Served

The hosiery market can be segmented in several ways, as was shown in Table 9-7. Hanes competes quite broadly in the various market segments with the exceptions of (1) the low-price segments and (2) the channel segments other than department and specialty stores. The low-price market offers an opportunity to expand market share, but is not attractive from a profit standpoint. Furthermore, low-price hosiery could harm the Hanes image unless sold under a brand name not identified with Hanes.

Mass merchandisers and food and drug chains sell hosiery packaged under their own private brand names. Hanes can justify producing for private brands only on the basis of incremental pricing (pricing the private brand to cover all variable costs and some portion of fixed costs). While incremental pricing may contribute to company total profit, it obviously is not as desirable as the sale of products that cover total costs plus profit (as in the case of Hanes' branded lines). The mail order and vending machine channels may offer some opportunity for a company brand not identified with Hanes. Some mail order houses sell only their own private brands while others offer advertised brands. However, we would probably have to offer new brand names to these channels to avoid damaging relations with our regular channel accounts.

1. **Private Brand Growth in Chains.** In our planning we must be concerned with the growing importance of private brand hosiery sold through food and drug chains. Sales through these channels accounted for 18 percent of all hosiery sales last year and are expected to continue to increase. Food chains particularly are attracted to hosiery because it carries a higher markup than the average food item. The growth of hosiery business through chains not only takes sales away from department and specialty stores (and hence from us), but the lower prices also make it difficult for us to raise prices on our branded hosiery.

An option we should consider is to go into the food and drug channels with a new brand not identified with Hanes. The problem, of course, is that it would have to be priced much lower than our present brands in order to compete with chain private brands. This raises the question of how profitable it would be.

E. Buyer Behavior Characteristics

1. **Ultimate Customers.** Hosiery is worn by women of all ages beginning with the teenage years. While purchased primarily by users, it is also purchased for gift giving and by mothers for their younger daughters.

2. **Purchase Influencers.** Although hosiery buying is largely a matter of personal choice, peers do exert influence in terms of brand, style, color, and place of purchase.

3. **Other Purchase Influences.** Although hosiery is worn somewhat less in warmer climates, geography is not a highly significant factor. Demographics are significant in that the heaviest users are between the ages of 18 and 49. While income is a factor, it is less important than lifestyle since purchases are highest among socially active women and working women.

As already noted, fashion affects per capita purchasing. It also affects the types of hosiery purchased. The miniskirt fashion created the need for pantyhose. According to the National Association of Hosiery Manufacturers, pantyhose accounted for 14 percent of all women's hosiery production last year (1968) and will rise to about 46 percent this year (1969). Modesty is the basic appeal of pantyhose. However, women also appear to like them for their warmth, and the fact they eliminate the need for garters. Consequently, pantyhose are expected to become the number one style and remain popular even when the miniskirt fashion ends. Women's knee-length hosiery and anklets account for minor sales at present, but could grow if mid-calf skirts or pants become popular.

Preferences for advertised brands exist among well-dressed women who buy medium and higher priced hosiery in department and specialty stores. Hanes' brands—Hanes, Beauty Mist, and Today's Girl—are well known and have a loyal core of customers.

4. **Frequency of Purchase.** Hosiery is purchased frequently in quantities of one or two pairs at a time. Average annual consumption ranges from 15 to 21 pairs. Women's hosiery can be described as a convenience good since it is relatively low in price, is purchased frequently in small quantities, and the consumer usually will

accept a substitute brand if her favorite brand is out of stock. The major manufacturers of advertised brands traditionally have treated hosiery as a specialty good. The food and drug chains are demonstrating that it can be merchandised as a convenience good.

F. Competitive Situation

1. Rankings By Market Share. (See Table 9-8.)

2. Competitive Environment. The industry is not a clear cut example of either oligopolistic or monopolistic competition.* There is no dominant leader and the six largest manufacturers account for only about 24 percent of the market. Nevertheless, the six leading manufacturers produce most of the nationally advertised brands; innovations by one are likely to be followed by the others. A significant phenomenon of this industry is that private brands (mass merchandisers plus the growing brands in food and drug chains) outsell the leading manufacturers' brands in terms of pairs sold.

3. Imports or Other Outside Competition. Neither imports nor exports are significant in the hosiery industry. We are aware of no substitute products that would threaten the hosiery industry.

G. The Marketing Mix

1. Product Line
   a. *Hanes' position.* Our products are well known and well accepted and are differentiated on the basis of brand names, quality, construction, price, packaging, breadth of line, and the quality of retail outlets used. Customer service is good.
   b. *Product life cycle.* Women's hosiery has long been in the mature phase of its product life cycle. The recent strengthening of demand is caused by rising skirt lengths and cannot be expected to last. The lower-priced hosiery sold in supermarkets has not increased demand; rather, women have merely switched their place of purchase from the more traditional outlets. And, the lower supermarket prices have contributed to a lowering of the average industry selling price.
   c. *Private brand offerings.* Our reason for producing private brands is to utilize excess production capacity which helps to absorb fixed overhead. We would prefer to utilize this capacity for higher margin branded products.

2. Distribution Policies and Channels
   a. *Type of distribution.* Hanes' retail distribution is selective in that we sell to the better and larger department and specialty stores in each market.
   b. *Channels used and not used.* Hanes' hosiery is distributed to retailers through independent wholesale distributors. Except for the private brands produced by the company, Hanes products are *not* distributed through mass merchandisers, food or drug outlets, mail order, or vending machines.

---

*This term should not to be confused with pure monopoly. See Chapter 4, pages 83–85, for a discussion of the meaning of monopolistic competition and oligopoly.

c. *Sales support of channel members.* Our national sales force of fifteen can provide only a limited amount of sales support to distributors. However, the sales force does call on direct retail accounts in major cities to encourage orders for distributors and to get retailers to participate in company promotional programs.

d. *Trade attitudes.* Hanes' trade relationships are good as a result of our co-op advertising and merchandising programs, service, margins, and selective distribution policies.

3. **Promotion.** Promotional expenditures for advertising, personal selling, and sales promotion are in line with those of major competitors. In order to maintain market share, however, we have had to steadily increase promotional expenditures. Promotion and administrative expenses combined (as they are reported in the company's Annual Report) have risen from 9.4 percent to 13.8 percent during the past five years.

Promotion and Administrative Expense as a Percentage of Sales

Year	%
1965	9.4
1966	10.3
1967	10.8
1968	12.3
1969 (estimated)	13.8

The sales force of fifteen persons is effective for its size but is only large enough to maintain distributor contacts and calls on major retail accounts. A larger sales force could make wider and more frequent retail calls which should produce increased sales as a result of stimulating retailer promotional activity.

Although advertising reach and frequency are not all that we would wish, the quality and continuity of advertising have made the Hanes name and the company's brands well-known among buyers of quality hosiery.

4. **Pricing.** The pricing situation is highly competitive as is to be expected in a mature industry. Profit margins have declined because we have not been able to recover cost increases with price increases. Our net profit is declining because sales volume has not increased enough to offset the decline in margins. Our dilemma, we believe, is shared by our major competitors whose *costs* are similar to ours.

No significant changes have occurred in our credit arrangements or *margins* offered to the trade. Trade margins are reasonably generous. They average 17 percent for distributors and 45 to 47 percent for retailers and are in line with industry practice for the channels used.

a. *Industry price leader.* There is no industry price leader.

b. *Demand elasticity.* Women's hosiery demand tends to be inelastic. Price reductions have not increased total industry demand and the lower-priced hosiery purchased in supermarkets appears merely to rob sales from other types of retailers.

c. *Price trends.* Prices in department and specialty stores have been showing weakness as a result of rising low-price hosiery sales in food and drug chains. We see little likelihood of prices firming any time soon.

H. Changes in Market Structure

The single significant change in market structure is the growth of hosiery sales through food and drug chains. This development is hurting sales through other channels, including those we use, because of the aforementioned inelastic demand.

The trend appears to be for continued growth of food and drug channel sales to the detriment of department and specialty stores. Our market research confirms this trend and indicates also that women like the convenience of buying hosiery while doing their weekly food shopping (although they are not completely satisfied with the quality of the brands offered or with the stockouts encountered). It is apparent that continued growth of hosiery sales through food and drug retail channels has serious implications for Hanes.

I. Constraints

The hosiery industry is relatively free of external environmental constraints except for fashion. As we have seen, the fashion cycle for women's skirts affects hosiery demand; and fashion is beyond the industry's or Hanes' control. If women's pants become popular for general wear, the effect on hosiery sales will become even more severe.

A change in company strategies, of course, could create new constraints for Hanes. If, for example, we should enter food and drug retail distribution, we would have to lower our prices considerably. Our present costs, therefore, could represent a constraint. A further constraint conceivably could be alienation of our present distribution channels since we would be competing with them through channels which offer lower prices.

J. Strengths and Weaknesses

In terms of our present method of doing business, we have no serious weaknesses. Our position in department and specialty store distribution channels is strong, as is our reputation with consumers. Our costs are competitive with other companies distributing through channels similar to ours, our financial position is sound, and our technical knowledge of hosiery production is extensive.

Our people are knowledgeable and effective with respect to our present business methods. A potential personnel problem might arise, however, if we went into food and drug chain channels since our marketing experience with self-service retail stores is limited.

K. Opportunities.

1. Market Opportunities. We see no substantial opportunities in the areas of our present product line, pricing, promotion, service, or geographic segments. Forward integration into our own hosiery shops does not appear feasible because of high investment requirements, a questionable profit return, and the loss of sales

through our present distribution outlets if we went into direct competition with them.

The market opportunities that stand out from this review of our situation are as follows.

    a. *Diversification.* Diversify into other product areas, preferably textile products, which would utilize our manufacturing know-how and which could be distributed through our present channels, and

    b. *Adding additional channels.* Add additional channels, namely food and drug chain outlets—where hosiery sales are growing fastest.

2. Cost Efficiency Opportunities. We are aware of no significant cost efficiency opportunities with the possible exception of some pruning of the product line. With over 1000 items, it appears that inventory and manufacturing costs could be reduced by dropping nonessential items that show a loss or a low profit return. Consideration, of course, should be given to adverse customer reactions and the contribution that even low profit items make to fixed costs.

L. Summary of Key Problems and Opportunities

1. Key Problems. Our company faces two major and quite serious problems.

The first problem stems from the mature phase of the hosiery industry, which for us means (a) slow growth, (b) rising production costs not offset by either volume efficiencies or higher prices, and (c) higher promotion expense required to maintain market share. The result has been a decline in our net profit. It is distressing to see company profit declining at a time when the industry is enjoying increased demand—albeit temporary. Our profit problems may become more severe in a year or so when the industry will again be caught in the downdraft of the women's skirt fashion cycle.

Our second problem stems from the increasing share of industry sales going through food and drug retail channels. At least part of this increase is at the expense of department and specialty store channels. This will lead to future decline in Hanes' sales.

Unless steps can be taken to offset the effects of industry maturity and hosiery purchases in food and drug channels, we see falling company sales accompanied by a further drop in net profit.

2. Key Opportunities. Based on the *situation analysis* we see two principal opportunities to counteract or offset the problems discussed above. The first is to diversify into other businesses having profitable growth potential.

The second opportunity is to increase our share of the total hosiery market—and our total sales volume—by adding food and drug chains to our existing channels.

Either move would be a major change in company strategy. The opportunities are not necessarily exclusive, but each is sufficiently major to require the concentration of company resources to bring about successful change. Both have pros and cons and would entail significant risk. These alternatives, along with others, will be examined under the Alternative Strategies section of this marketing plan. Table 9-15 provides a summary of findings and conclusions for the twelve major subjects covered in the Hanes *situation analysis.*

TABLE 9-15
Summary of Hanes *Situation Analysis*

A.	Economic and industry forecasts	Industry hosiery sales to decline owing to expected fashion change.
B.	Company forecasts	Sales decline. Market share to hold at 6%. Profit—continues at low level.
C.	Planning gap	Shortfall in fourth year of $62 million sales and $4.8 million profit.
D.	Markets served and not served	Department and specialty stores the only retail segment served. Low-price segment not served.
E.	Buyer behavior characteristics	Purchasers: women; heaviest usage among 18–49 age group, the socially active, and white-collar workers. Purchase influence: fashion—hosiery sales rise and fall with skirt lengths. Place of purchase: shifting towards self-service convenience goods outlets.
F.	Competitive situation	Highly competitive—223 companies. Hanes leading manufacturer with 5–6% share. Many private brands. Penney's and Sears each outsell leading manufacturers.
G.	Marketing mix: Product	Hosiery in mature phase of product life cycle. Hanes brands well known and well accepted. Hanes produces for some private brand chains.
	Distribution	Selective, through wholesalers to better department and specialy stores. Limited missionary sales efforts, but Hanes well regarded by trade.
	Promotion	Expenditures in line with competitors and increasing to maintain market share.
	Pricing	Inelastic demand. Unable to raise prices due to supermarket competition. Margins narrowing as manufacturing and promotional costs rise.
H.	Changes in market structure	Growth of low-price, private brand hosiery sales through food and drug chains is taking market share from other retail segments, including those used by Hanes.
I.	Constraints	Pants and lowering skirt lengths cause decline in hosiery use.
J.	Strengths and weaknesses	No weaknesses for present businesses, but have little experience in distributing through food and drug chains.
K.	Opportunities: Marketing	Diversification. Add other channels, primarily food and drug outlets.
	Cost efficiency	Reduce number of product line items.
L.	Summary: Key problems	Slow long-term industry growth due to maturity; near-term decline due to fashion change. Rising production costs not offset by higher volume or price increases. Rising promotion expense to maintain market share.
	Key opportunities	Diversify into businesses with higher profit growth potential. Increase market share by adding food and drug chain channels.

SUMMARY

The *situation analysis* is the first step in the strategic marketing planning process. The *situation analysis* outline provides for consideration of the several factors—external and internal—that affect the market success of a company or one of its business units. Carefully filling in the outline usually results in:

1. Determining the planning gap between management goals and likely actual performance—if indeed such a gap exists.
2. Identifying the problems that cause the planning gap.
3. Identifying external and internal constraints to goal achievement which must be removed or worked around if they are beyond the control of the company.
4. Identifying opportunities for improving future sales and profits, either by solving the problems and/or by exploring new marketing approaches.

The case of the Hanes Corporation was introduced, a case which we will continue to use to illustrate the application of the various steps of the marketing planning approach. By filling in the *situation analysis* outline for Hanes we were able to identify the planning gap, the serious problems and constraints with which the company was faced, and the possible opportunities for turning in new directions to help management achieve its longer-range goals.

While the *situation analysis* serves to highlight problems and opportunities, it also fulfills another important function. It provides management with background that can be used to think through all aspects of potential marketing strategies. As we shall see, good planning comes from a combination of knowledge and creative thinking. Knowledge provided by the *situation analysis* acts as a stimulant to creative ideas and at the same time acts as a restraining leash so that creativity is kept within the bounds of realism.

We are now ready for Chapter 10 which covers the planning steps of setting objectives, analyzing alternate strategies, and selecting the most appropriate strategies for recommendation to top management.

QUESTIONS

1. What is the purpose of the *situation analysis?*
2. What is a planning gap and what are its implications?
3. What is involved in identifying buyer behavior characteristics?
4. What factors should be looked at when analyzing the competitive situation?
5. What are the basic types of opportunities that a company should evaluate?
6. What were the key problems and opportunities that surfaced from the Hanes *situation analysis?*

CHAPTER 10

Selecting Objectives and Strategies

With the *situation analysis* completed, marketing management can begin strategy development. This involves thinking through alternative strategies, then selecting the best to recommend to top management. Tentative objectives should be established first, however, since objectives are the targets which strategies are designed to reach.

The question of whether objectives or strategies should come first is similar to the chicken or the egg dilemma. Objectives and strategies are very much interrelated. We establish objectives in order to plan how to reach them. But, while developing the plans (strategies), we may find that the objectives are not attainable or that they can be exceeded and will need to be lowered or raised accordingly. Since we must begin somewhere, the commonly accepted place is with objective or goal setting.

The *situation analysis* normally is prepared by staff personnel. Objectives, on the other hand, will be set by marketing management together with (or at least with the concurrence of) business unit management. Developing strategic alternatives also is a job for marketing management, although staff personnel will be called on to assist. The executive responsible for carrying out strategies and achieving the

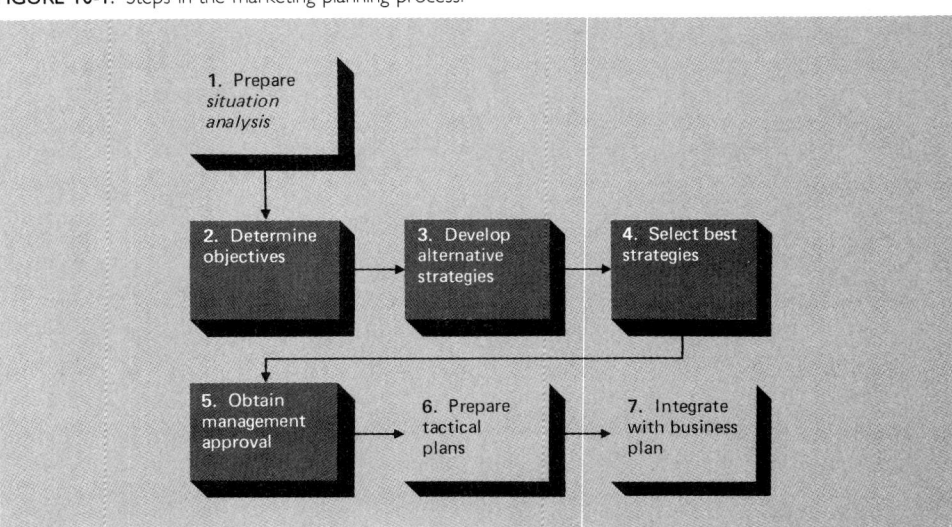

FIGURE 10-1. Steps in the marketing planning process.

objectives will be more supportive of them if that executive has participated in their development and is in agreement with them.

DETERMINING OBJECTIVES

Since objectives were needed earlier for establishing the planning gap, you may wonder why we're dealing with objectives again at this point. This is because the planning process continues to evolve; ideas are refined as more information is made available and thought through. The objectives used in computing the planning gap would have been assumptions of the staff planner or could have been taken from previous statements by top management. Furthermore, approximations of objectives were sufficient for the purpose at that stage of planning.

Management, however, should be prepared to accept or modify the earlier objectives now that it is examining the plan in more depth. Even so, the newer objectives remain tentative until strategies have been formulated and the effects of the strategies calculated.

Nature of Marketing Objectives

Objectives will vary according to the organizational unit proposing them, the time period covered, and whether they are stated in quantitative or qualitative terms.

Organizational Unit. Objectives should be set for every unit of the organization for which performance can be measured, ranging from the total corporation to an individual sales territory. This is called *management by objectives*. But for strategic planning we are talking only about objectives for units covered by marketing plans such as a company (in the case of a nondivisionalized company), a business unit (e.g., a division or profit center of a divisionalized company), or a product line managed by a product manager or group product manager.

Time Period. Objectives may be set for attainment by the end of the current strategic planning period (e.g., 3 to 5 years forward) or in terms of annual progress (e.g., the average percentage change in sales per year). Objectives for a strategic plan normally will cover more than 1 year, whereas objectives for tactical plans normally will be for 1 year or less. Objectives for an annual plan are but one step on the way to the longer-range objectives.

Quantitative versus Qualitative. Wherever possible, objectives should be stated in quantitative rather than qualitative terms. Quantitative objectives are specific; consequently, progress toward their attainment can be measured specifically. A sales objective, for example, should be stated in dollars or units to be sold or shipped by a definite time or expressed as a percent increase in dollars or units over the previous time period. A quantitative market share objective might call for an increase of 5 percent within 4 years, or an average increase of 1.25 percent annually.

Qualitative objectives sometimes are seen in planning documents; for example, "We will increase sales each year." It would be more specific to say, "We will increase sales by 10 percent per year." Certain types of objectives are more difficult to quantify, such as, "We plan to upgrade the quality of our sales force." Even here, however, the upgrading might be put into quantitative criteria such as level of education, years of experience, or number of training courses completed.

Types of Marketing Objectives

Marketing objectives are related to business unit objectives, and business unit objectives are related to corporate objectives. A marketing objective set without regard for what the business unit or corporation is trying to do may run into trouble when the marketing plan comes up for management review. A marketing objective to increase market share (acceptable in many situations) may not be approved if corporate management's objective is to maximize short-term profits or to conserve cash. The reason is that there is usually a time lag between an increase in promotional expense designed to gain market share and the actual change in share.

There are two types of marketing objectives. Primary objectives are essential and are common to most business situations. Secondary objectives supplement primary objectives.

Primary Objectives. Examples are (1) sales, (2) market share, and (3) profit.

Since sales income is the number one responsibility of marketing, sales inevitably will be included with the marketing objectives. Market share is frequently (but not always) found among the marketing objectives. The reason is that market share is a key measure of performance in relation to competition and in relation to market opportunity.

Not every marketing plan lists profit among its objectives since marketing management does not control all of the business functions which affect profit. The growing number of companies that do include profit (or some specific element of profit) among the marketing objectives do so because they want marketing management to consider the effect of its plans on profits. In some companies marketing management is measured by a *merchandising profit*—the difference between sales income and manufacturing cost plus marketing expense. Marketing management can influence the amount of merchandising profit by managing factors under its control such as price, units sold, and marketing expense.

Secondary Objectives. The supplementary objectives we call secondary can vary widely. Examples are (1) sales by market segment or class of trade account, (2) shifts in the product mix toward high profit margin products, (3) pricing to increase profit margins, and (4) raising brand awareness.

Attitudes toward secondary objectives vary among planners. Some would consider the above examples to be strategies rather than objectives; that is, they are really ways to reach primary objectives. Others would class them as subobjectives appropriate for sections of the marketing plan such as personal selling, sales promotion, or advertising. Raising brand awareness, for example, could be an objective for advertising. Keeping the major (or primary) objectives few in number has the advantage of focusing on a few major strategies. What constitutes a major objective or a major strategy, of course, is a matter of individual opinion. There are no hard and fast rules; consequently, there are a variety of interpretations.

Getting Management Concurrence with Objectives

Marketing management and business unit management should work together in setting marketing objectives. This is particularly important when marketing is expected to contribute to profits as well as to produce sales. Sales objectives will be the same for marketing and the business unit. Profit objectives may not be identical.

The business unit will be measured on total profit while marketing may be measured by merchandising profit. Market share is essentially a marketing objective.

One of the key differences between strategic marketing planning and the older forms of marketing planning is that marketing strategies are an inherent part of overall business strategies. Therefore, marketing and general management should have a meeting of the minds about the objectives before going on to the development of strategic alternatives.

DEVELOPING ALTERNATIVE STRATEGIES

Strategic planning and the older planning processes it replaces can be differentiated as follows.

> The *conventional* planning process concentrates on doing things better, whereas *strategic planning* concentrates on the best things to do.

The development of alternative strategies is a creative, freethinking approach based on two assumptions: (1) there is more than one way to get from one point to another and (2) some ways are better than others. A simple example will illustrate.

Getting from One Point to Another

Let's assume you want to go from Hartford to St. Louis. You can go by air, train, bus, auto, motorcycle—you can even hitchhike or walk. There are tradeoffs with the chief one being cost versus time. Your decision may be influenced by such factors as the weather or your traveling companions, and whether you're going for business or pleasure.

After deciding how you will travel, there are other choices to be made. If you're flying, do you want to go first class, coach, or night coach? If you select a nonstop flight, you will have fewer flights to choose from. Flights with intermediate stops leave more frequently but take longer to arrive in St. Louis. Hartford departures that require change of flights en route offer an even larger selection but take still longer to arrive at your destination.

Choosing the Best Alternative

One combination of alternatives for getting from Hartford to St. Louis may be better for one person than for another. And so it is with companies. Different firms will require different combinations of strategies, even to reach similar goals. Furthermore, today's best alternative may not be the best under some future set of circumstances. Hence, careful analysis is required to select the most appropriate strategy for the circumstances.

Strategic Approach Difficult for Some

The formal strategic planning approach forces managers down the line to think in terms of alternatives. This is not easy for those who have always served in operating assignments. Their natural tendency is to try to make the present system work better. They often find it hard to explain their present strategy. They were taught the present method of operating but never encouraged to question why it is the way it is. Present strategies are nearly always identifiable, however.

Strategic Alternatives Checklist

The viable alternatives open to any one business unit at any one time can be quite varied. They may differ considerably even from the alternatives open to another business unit in the same corporation. There are some standard alternatives, however, that planners use as a checklist even though none may apply to a specific situation: (1) no change in present strategy, (2) dispose of business, (3) specialize, (4) diversify, (5) integrate vertically, (6) expand geographically (including to foreign countries), and (7) improve current operations.

No Change. If present strategies are working and there is no planning gap, there is no reason to change. Management hopes this will be the case at the time of the annual planning review where it finds that the strategies adopted earlier are working according to plan.

There are other times when—despite the existence of a planning gap—management decides to stay with its present strategies. It may decide to ride out an economic storm, for instance, by "trimming the sails and battening down the hatches." However, decisions *not* to change strategy are more the exception than the rule. Certainly, the no change alternative should be selected only after failing to find better alternatives.

Dispose of Business. This seemingly negative alternative actually may be a very positive one. There are times when a business is no longer viable and the best thing to do is to close it out and retrieve whatever assets are salvageable. There are other times when a business unit does not fit well with the company's primary business and it is better sold to a more appropriate owner. The positive aspect of disposal is that the assets retrieved (cash in the case of a sale) can be redeployed into more profitable uses. American Standard raised its profits from $3 million to $44 million within 5 years by disposing of several low-potential businesses and reinvesting the assets in its more profitable businesses.

Ego is the principal stumbling block for the disposal alternative. The management of the business unit may be reluctant to admit that it can't run the business successfully and it may be afraid of being fired. Or, if the present corporate management acquired the business in the first place it is often reluctant to admit that it made a mistake. Often a change in top management occurs before the disposal decision is made and implemented.

Specialize. A company may diversify to the point where it becomes "a jack of all trades but master of none." There is much to be said for being very good at something—being the industry leader or the leader of some segment of the company's industry.

When, for example, William R. Hartman became chairman of Interpace Corporation he decided to zero in on just one of the company's several industries—building and construction materials—and to pare back the company's unrelated businesses. Interpace, a leading producer of water and sewer pipe, had diversified into several businesses as unrelated as dinnerware and salt. For the 6 years prior to the decision to specialize, Interpace had shown virtually no earnings growth.

But, within 3 years after the decision, earnings had increased 80 percent and return on equity had grown from 7.4 to 11.2 percent.[1] The PIMS (profit impact of market strategies) studies have shown a strong correlation between high market share and a high rate of profit return on investment, and vice versa.[2] Specialization is one approach to attaining high market share and presumably a high profit rate.

Diversify. The opposite of specialization is diversification. As we saw in the Opportunity Grid, diversification can be by product, by market, or both. Diversification is a commonly used strategy that may be quite appropriate under certain conditions, such as when the company is doing as well as it can in its primary business, when growth is limited because of industry maturity, or when diversification can improve the company's present return on investment.

Mobil's acquisition of Montgomery Ward, Exxon's move into word processing, and Continental Group's (formerly Continental Can Co.) move into insurance are examples of very large companies looking for means to maintain or improve profits because growth of their primary industries is slowing. What companies should avoid is diversifying into low potential businesses or getting into more businesses than can be managed effectively.

Integrate Vertically. A less common strategy is for a company to integrate backward or forward from its place in an industry. A manufacturer, for example, would be integrating backward if it acquired control of raw materials sources or performed processing steps that occur prior to its own manufacturing operations. It would be integrating forward if it acquired control of later processing or assembly operations, or of distribution channel intermediaries. The Champion International Corp., manufacturers of paper and lumber products, is integrated backward through ownership of forests and wood processing facilities and is integrated forward through ownership of paper and lumber distributors. The Singer Co. is integrated forward into company-owned retail stores for its sewing machines and other home appliances.

Questions of forward integration into company-owned or franchised distribution facilities would be considered in the marketing plan. This would be a major decision for most manufacturers because of the large investment required and the likely alienation of the company's present channel intermediaries. For most manufacturers, ownership or franchising of distribution outlets is the exception rather than the rule.

Expand Geographically. It is questionable whether any company ever ran out of geographic opportunities for expansion. Widespread international companies find some countries, like China, closed to them at certain times but open at others. Russia finally agreed to let PepsiCo open bottling plants there if PepsiCo would market Russian vodka in the United States. Many developing nations are expanding to the point where they represent good market potential.

Not all companies distribute in every part of the United States; therefore, domestic expansion opportunities exist for them. And the vast majority of American companies do little or no marketing abroad. Opportunity, of course, does not necessarily equate with desirability. Whether geographic expansion is a good alternative depends on the results of the marketing analysis.

Improve Current Operations. There are few companies whose marketing operations cannot be improved. The *situation analysis* usually spots improvement opportunities within the present business. Consequently, a common strategy is to try to improve in areas such as product, pricing, distribution, and promotion. Companies in highly competitive industries have to improve constantly just to hold their own because competitors are also striving to improve. Therefore, the improvement strategy, while desirable, usually is not sufficient to ensure attainment of high goals.

Generating and Evaluating Strategic Alternatives

Ideas for alternatives come from the *situation analysis* and from suggestions by management and staff personnel. *Brainstorming* sessions are also useful. These are freewheeling sessions in which no idea is rejected outright on the theory that ideas lead to other ideas and that a sound idea may grow out of the thought processes started by an imaginative but impractical idea.

Once all ideas are on the table they are screened. Only ideas which might contribute toward the objectives are included in the written plan. Each is accompanied by a discussion of its pros and cons and conclusions about its relative value. Then the final selection of recommended strategies is made.

SELECTING THE BEST STRATEGIES

Following analysis of the alternatives, marketing management selects the one strategy or the few strategies which appear to have the best chance of attaining the objectives. These preferred strategies are listed again and an explanation given of why they were chosen over the others. Achievement of goals may require only one strategy or it may require a combination of two or three. Recommended strategies should be few in number. If the list contains more than three or four strategies some are likely to be tactics rather than strategies. Even if they are genuine strategies, the list must be narrowed further because no company can afford to dissipate its resources by initiating too many actions simultaneously.

Strategies always carry the risk of failure as well as success. A judicious management will not risk more at one time than it can afford to lose if the strategy fails. One study[3] has emphasized that strategies do not always produce the expected results. It cites as examples General Foods' experience with its acquisition of Burger Chef, Rohr Industries' move into mass transit, Mattel's acquisition of Ringling Bros., Outboard Marine's diversification into snowmobiles, and Singer's development of business machines—all of which resulted in multimillion dollar writeoffs. This list could be expanded.

OBTAINING MANAGEMENT APPROVAL OF STRATEGIES

The sales, profit, and market share forecasts used to set objectives were based on general estimates and reasoning. These forecasts may be revised again when tactical plans have been formulated; hence, the forecasts made up to this point are not yet as refined as they will be later.

Rough estimates, however, normally are sufficient for strategy discussions with corporate management, since it is the broad directions of the business that are of concern to higher management. Prior to meeting with top management, the recommended marketing strategies and forecasts of performance will have been reviewed with other functional managers of the business unit, such as those responsible for manufacturing, accounting, and finance. And, of course, the general manager of the business unit will have participated. Consequently, the sales and profit forecasts are the result of a jury of executive opinion. In older planning procedures the annual profit or business plan was completed before reviewing it with top management. But, with strategic planning there are several benefits to be gained from getting top management's agreement with strategies before proceeding to the development of tactical plans, budgets, and profit forecasts, and the preparation of a detailed business plan. The benefits are:

- It provides top management input to the planning while there is still time to influence the choice of strategies.
- It increases the likelihood that top management will approve the completed business plan since it already has agreed with the strategies in the plan.
- It avoids time lost in preparing a complete business plan that top management disapproves because it does not agree with the strategies.

If top management is to make a contribution to the planning process, it is most likely to be at the strategy level. Corporate management usually is not close enough to each business to contribute to the tactical plan. Competent corporate managements concentrate on policies, goals, and strategies while leaving the details of implementation to managers of the business units.

Strategy discussions with corporate management usually result in agreement with (or modifications of) the proposed strategies. Disapproval is also possible, although agreement to adopt different strategies is more likely than outright rejection. Once strategies have been agreed upon, business unit management can proceed with confidence to develop tactics and the balance of the business plan. However, in the event no strategies are approved, business unit planners must go back to the drawing board.

SELECTING OBJECTIVES AND STRATEGIES AT HANES

We continue with the marketing planning process as it might have occurred at the Hanes Corporation. The objectives and strategies that follow are drawn from the findings in the Hanes' *situation analysis*.

You will recall that Hanes' profits had fallen from $9 million to an estimated $4.3 million during the previous 5 years, and that profits were expected to grow marginally at best during the next 4 years. There is an estimated 1973 planning gap of $62 million in sales and $4.8 million in net profits, assuming no change in company strategy. Hanes' management would not have been satisfied with this outlook and would have been searching for alternative means of wiping out the planning gap. We will look at objectives and strategies that might achieve this.

Remember that although our planning deals only with hosiery, approximately one-third of Hanes' sales came from other products, principally men's and boys' underwear. If the case had provided separate sales and financial data for hosiery, the data related to the alternative strategies would deal with hosiery alone. Since they don't, the assumption is made that all proposed changes in company sales and earnings would be the result of hosiery strategy and that the relative effect of other products would remain constant throughout.

In the sections of the plan that follow, the pronouns "we" and "our" refer to comments as they might have been made by the Hanes' planners.

Objectives

Our principal objective for 1973 is to have earnings at the level of the record year of 1966, or $9.3 million. This assumes sales of $265.7 million and an average ROS (return on sales) of 3.5 percent—slightly more realistic, we believe, than the 4.0 percent ROS used earlier for the planning gap.

SUMMARY OF OBJECTIVES FOR 1973

Sales, $ millions	265.7
Profits after tax, $ millions	9.3
Market share, %	9.7

Our longer-range objective (beyond 1973) is to increase earnings over and above $9.3 million. First, however, we must stop the current deterioration of earnings before we can start upward again. We estimate that it will take about 4 years to make the turnaround and get back to the 1966 level.

Alternative Strategies

We have seriously considered seven strategic alternatives. They are listed below along with the pros and cons of each and our estimate of the probability of success for each.

1. **No Change.** To continue with our present strategies might be the safest course, but it would offer no opportunity to significantly improve profits during the next 4 years. By tightening our company belt, we could reduce expenses, maintain the current profit margin, delay capital investments, and conserve cash. The purpose would be to maintain a strong balance sheet while we ride out the fashion cycle of longer skirts and (possibly) pants, and await the return of short skirts sometime within the next four years. This time, however, we cannot expect as much benefit from the return of short skirts as in the past because an increasing share of industry sales will have shifted to channels we do not sell through. Although industry sales will go up again, our channels will see a smaller share of the increase.

   Advantages
   a. Low risk—good probability that company will survive to benefit from next short skirt cycle.
   b. Would maintain cash reserves to invest in market development when industry sales turn up again.

   Disadvantages
   a. Offers no chance to reach 1973 objectives.
   b. Several years of low profits and low stockholder dividends while awaiting cyclical upturn in sales.

    c. Possibility of financial loss, if:
       (1) Industry sales continue their rapid shift to food and drug channels.
       (2) Prices and margins continue to deteriorate.
       (3) Competitors force us to spend to maintain market share, thereby preventing proposed reduction of marketing expense.

Conclusion
    a. Low probability of either financial losses or company failure.
    b. Zero probability that we would meet 1973 objectives.
    c. This strategy should be considered further only if no positive strategy can be developed.

    2. **Expand into Foreign Markets.** Hanes hosiery is sold in most of Canada, and since 1967 Hanes stockings have been marketed in Europe through a joint venture company—Hanes Hin Int'l—formed with Kousenfabricken of Holland. However, foreign income has not been significant. Hosiery is produced in most developed countries and our landed costs are higher than local manufacturers. Consequently, to compete on even terms, we would have to build or acquire manufacturing facilities abroad.

    Quite frankly, we do not have sufficient information on foreign markets to recommend or not to recommend foreign expansion as a strategy. Our opinion is that expansion of this type would not wipe out our planning gap. Hosiery markets are competitive in western European countries and the industry must cope with fashion cycles similar to ours. Acceptance of the miniskirt in England, for example, predated its acceptance in the United States by several months, and its acceptance in France followed the United States by a few months. Even so, the patterns and timing were similar. Had we been producing in those countries, we would not have benefited from offsetting volume due to different cycles.

    Advantages. None that we see based on present knowledge.

    Disadvantages. Would use our available capital for projects about which we have insufficient knowledge.

    Conclusion. Conduct foreign market studies before considering this strategy further.

    3. **Seek Additional Private Brand Business.** We have no trouble selling private label production as long as we are willing to meet price competition. Buyers will pay little or nothing in the way of premiums for our high quality merchandise, however. Although we do not receive full cost on this business, it does contribute to profit by helping to absorb fixed costs which would have to be charged entirely to our branded hosiery, if it were not for the private brand production.

    It makes sense to use idle capacity for private brand production as long as we have no better use for our manufacturing capacity. However, we will not erase the planning gap in this way. Furthermore, private brand prices can be expected to drop as industry sales level off and decline. Competitors can be expected to lower their prices as they seek to utilize growing idle plant capacity.

    Advantages
    a. Absorbs fixed costs and thereby contributes modestly to profits.
    b. Helps prevent work force layoffs.

    Disadvantages. Does little to erase the planning gap.

Conclusion. Risk is low but payoff is low also. We should produce for private brands as long as there is available production capacity, but we should concentrate on finding a strategy that will make more profitable use of facilities.

4. **Introduce Low-Price Brand to Present Channels.** One of the few market segments in which we do not compete is the low-price segment. The proposed strategy would be to introduce a new low-priced Hanes brand into department and specialty store accounts. While this strategy should increase the number of pairs sold, it also has some negative aspects. Sales of the low-priced brand would cannibalize sales from our high-priced brands, thereby lowering average profit margins. It would invite low-priced competition from other manufacturers. It would also lower the average hosiery profit margin earned by our retail accounts for the same reason our margin would be lowered. We would cause our accounts to accept lower average margins in exchange for a potential (but undetermined) increase in sales volume.

Advantages
  a. Might draw some business away from mass merchandising, food, and drug chains.
  b. Should increase unit sales, thereby substituting some higher contribution production for lower contribution private label production.

Disadvantages
  a. The new lower-price brand would cannibalize sales from our higher price, higher margin brands.
  b. Would have limited effect on profit improvement.
  c. Might damage our reputation with present accounts.

Conclusions. Low probability of profit improvement with some risk of harming Hanes' acceptance with current accounts.

5. **Expand Hanes Brands to Additional Channels.** There may be an opportunity to distribute existing advertised Hanes brands through other channels such as mass merchandising, food and drug retail outlets, and via mail order houses. We would avoid the lowest quality discount operators. We would not expect to convert Penney or Sears from their policies of selling only their own brands. But there are other good quality chains and mail order houses that would welcome the chance to carry Hanes advertised brands.

There are potential problems with this strategy. We could expect discounting from recommended retail prices by the chains and mail order houses. Our current accounts would not be happy with the new competition which could result in the loss of some accounts and less support from others. It is uncertain how much the net gain in sales would be.

Advantages
  a. Would increase sales of our high margin branded lines at least temporarily.
  b. Would increase profits at least temporarily.

Disadvantages
  a. Would lose at least some of our present accounts and the loyalty of others.
  b. Over a longer period of time, losses of sales to present accounts could offset sales to new channel accounts.

Conclusions. A high-risk strategy with a less than 50–50 probability of long term improvement in profits.

6. **Special Brand for Food and Drug Stores.** This strategy calls for developing a new line of hosiery for sale through food and drug retail outlets which would:

- Be an advertised brand but not identified with the Hanes name. (Many packaged goods in other industries are sold by brand and not identified with the company name.)
- Have distinguishing features from other Hanes brands.
- Be priced somewhere between low-priced food chain private brands and medium-priced advertised brands sold in department and specialty stores.

Food and drug chains have clearly demonstrated that hosiery can be sold in self-service outlets just like other packaged convenience goods. It appears that the time is right for these chains to take on a line of quality hosiery offered at reasonable prices, with a brand name supported by advertising, and backed by in-store inventory and merchandising programs designed to increase turnover and store profits. We can be the first hosiery company to seize this opportunity. It will, however, require a change in our historic thinking which has been that hosiery should be treated as a specialty. The key to successful penetration of supermarkets is to merchandise our product like other packaged goods sold through these self-service channels.

We believe this strategy has none of the drawbacks of the previous ones discussed, and that it likely will result in reaching our 1973 objectives. This strategy would:

- Take us into the fastest growing segment of the hosiery industry.
- Replace low profit private brand production with higher margin, advertised brand production.
- Require little or no additional capital investment.
- Minimize antagonism from our current accounts since our new brand would neither compete directly with department and specialty stores nor be identified with Hanes.
- Permit us to follow two strategies simultaneously—(1) our present strategy, which serves those consumers who prefer to shop for prestige brands in department stores and specialty stores, and (2) the new strategy, which would serve those consumers who prefer the convenience and savings of buying in supermarkets.

There are two uncertainties connected with this proposed strategy—profitability and price competition.

We believe that our supermarket brand will have to sell at about half the retail price of our current brands, or between $1.25 and $1.50 per pair. This price range would appear to result in a low profit margin for this line of hosiery as compared to margins for our regular brands. The problem is not necessarily as great as it first appears, however. In the first place supermarkets operate on lower markups than our current channels which means that our discount from recommended retail price will be less for the new brand. Secondly, by selling direct to chains, distributor discounts are eliminated. Thirdly, as already mentioned, the new brand will replace private brand hosiery on our production lines. And, finally, the expected high unit volume multiplied by smaller margins will produce high actual profit dollars. Return on investment should improve also since little or no new investment in production facilities or equipment will be needed.

The second uncertainty has to do with competitive reaction from other manufacturers of advertised brands, particularly with respect to pricing. We assume that major competitors will follow our lead into food and drug channels. The question is, will they choose to compete by lowering price? We do not necessarily believe that they will undersell us but they might think it necessary if we are already well established by the time they enter the market. Low-priced competition from advertised brands would take some of our market share or would force us to lower price. Our best protection, we believe, is to go in with a low penetration price, build brand awareness through a strong consumer advertising program, and pursue an in-store merchandising program that will create retailer preferences for our brand.

Advantages
   a. A major increase in sales volume that may eventually exceed volume going through our current channels.
   b. A major increase in total profit and a higher return on investment, even though average margins will be lower.
   c. An established brand in a large channel segment assures more control over our future than, for example, production of private brands.
   d. Will cause minimal antagonism on the part of current accounts.

Disadvantages
   a. Major financial and organizational commitments must be made without extensive market testing of the strategy because we do not want to provide our competitors with the opportunity to prevent or quickly follow our strategy. If the strategy doesn't work, we will incur a sizable loss. Offsetting this disadvantage to some extent, however, is that we could stop our losses fairly quickly by pulling out of the market.
   b. The possibility that major competitors would compete on a price basis.

Conclusions. We estimate the probability of successful penetration of food and drug channels with this strategy to be between 60 and 70 percent. We estimate the probability of reaching our financial objectives with this strategy at between 50 and 70 percent. We would rate profit attainment at closer to 80 percent except for a 20 percent probability that competitors will engage in price competition.

In summary we see the probability of overall success—both market and financial—as fairly good. And, should the strategy fail the results would not be fatal for the company. No unusual capital investment will be required and expenses can be curtailed rapidly if it becomes necessary to withdraw the program.

7. **Diversification.** A strategy of diversification would reduce Hanes' reliance on the women's hosiery industry. Because the industry is mature and cyclical, company sales increases must come largely from gains in market share. While we believe that entering the food and drug channels will gain market share for us, a complementary strategy of diversification would make for a more balanced and stronger company.

Two diversification options are open to us: (1) new products for our present markets or (2) new products for new markets. The first option could capitalize on Hanes' good relations with distributors and department and specialty store accounts. If the new products were knitwear—such as socks and sportswear—we could also capitalize on our technical and manufacturing knowhow. The problem with other knitwear products, however, is that they too represent mature industries.

The second option—new products in new markets—probably would require acquisition of other businesses. The appeal of this option is that we can search for businesses in the early stages of their industry growth cycles. These are not easily found and will require an organized program of search and analysis.

A possible problem with going the acquisition route at this time is financing. While our balance sheet probably would permit borrowing to purchase a medium sized business for cash, a larger acquisition probably would require an exchange of stock. The depressant effect that lower earnings are having on the price of our stock would not make acquisition for stock a desirable approach at this time. This situation would change, however, if the new hosiery channel is adopted and is successful. Planning for acquisition, therefore, should begin now so as to be ready to act when financial market conditions are right.

Advantages
a. Presents opportunities to enter higher growth markets with good profit growth possibilities.
b. Would reduce dependence on the slow growth, cyclical women's hosiery industry.

Disadvantages
a. It is difficult to find new businesses with high growth prospects, either that can be developed internally or acquired on favorable financial terms.
b. Acquisitions which would take us into new products and new markets carry higher risk because of our inexperience with these businesses.
c. Adding new products to be sold to our present markets carries less risk but also offers less profit potential.

Conclusions. Hanes should find the means for diversifying into new businesses to offset our heavy reliance on women's hosiery. Diversification plans should be made, however, only after careful analysis of alternative approaches and means of financing. A careful approach may postpone the benefits of diversification but will reduce the risks inherent in this strategy.

Recommended Strategies

After reviewing the seven previous alternatives we recommend development of a "Special Brand for Food and Drug Stores" as the *primary* strategy and "Diversification" as the *secondary* strategy. We also recommend continuation of our present strategy of selling branded hosiery through department and specialty stores and development of private brand production to the extent of unused productive capacity. Ideally, the new hosiery brand will succeed in utilizing all of our capacity and allow us to phase out of private label production entirely.

Rejected Strategies

We reject the other alternative strategies for the following reasons:

No change. It is too negative now that we have developed more promising alternatives.

Expand into foreign markets. It does not appear viable at present. We do recommend, however, that a task force be appointed to study foreign market opportunities.

Introduction of low-priced brand to present channels. It might lead to a lowering of average prices and margins. It would provide little profit improvement and could lead to damaging our reputation with current accounts.

Expand Hanes brands to additional channels. Although we believe that other channels would stock our brands, this strategy would antagonize our current accounts. Consequently, any new business gained from new channels might be offset by business lost from our present accounts.

The Recommended Secondary Strategy

"Diversification" is our suggested secondary strategy because of timing and not because it is of secondary importance. Studies by a task force will delay activating this alternative. In the meantime, resources can be marshaled to implement the primary strategy. By the time diversification plans are ready, the profits from the primary strategy should be reflected in an improved stock price which will provide us with the option of acquiring new businesses via exchange of stock.

Along with the diversification strategy, we recommend a new objective: profits in terms of return on investment to be derived—within from 5 to 7 years—50 percent from women's hosiery and 50 percent from other products. The purpose is not to downplay hosiery but to upgrade the role of other products.

Primary Strategy

We believe that moving into food and drug channels while continuing our efforts in the department and specialty store channels can be the means of reaching profit objectives by 1973.

The keys to the success of the new primary strategy are timing, tactics, and resources. We want to have the advantage of being the first advertised brand in supermarkets. Our tactical plans must be such that the food and drug trade will stock our brand, display it effectively, and maintain good inventory backup. Innovative packaging, point-of-sale promotions, and media advertising will be needed to attract consumers to our displays and to get them to try our brand. We will need additional personnel with successful experience in the marketing of packaged goods through food and drug channels.

We estimate that it will take approximately eighteen months to reach breakeven because heavy expenses will be required for product, package, and market development, and for inventory buildup. Later, as sales volume expands and the breakeven point is reached, we foresee a rapid rise in profits; however, top management should be prepared to expect losses during the first year or two.

Revised Objectives

In the process of arriving at the recommended primary and secondary objectives we are making a modest revision in our sales and market share objectives for 1973 as shown below. We have lowered the average profit margin and raised the sales and market share objectives. The profit objective remains unchanged. And we have added a new diversification objective.

	Previous Objectives	Revised Objectives
Sales, $ millions	265.7	286.2
Profit after tax, $ millions	9.3*	9.3†
Market share, %	9.7	10.4
Diversification		A beginning made toward achieving a 50–50 balance in ROI between hosiery and other products by 1974–1976

*Assumes 3.5 percent net profit margin.   †Assumes 3.25 percent net profit margin.

SUMMARY

We have now covered the first five steps of the marketing planning process—preparing the *situation analysis*, determining objectives, developing alternative strategies, selecting the best strategies from among the alternatives, and obtaining management approval of our recommended objectives and strategies.

We have seen that objectives and strategies grow out of the problems and opportunities revealed by the *situation analysis*. We learned that while strategies are means for achieving objectives, strategies may also result in modifications of the objectives. This is but one of the several interfaces characteristic of strategic planning.

Plans are not born fully developed. Effective planning is a creative process which produces a series of ideas that are shaped into tentative strategies, either to be discarded or further refined. The first purpose of alternative strategy development is to make certain that no reasonable means is overlooked for getting the business from where it is now to where management wants it to be. The most junior member of the staff may have as good an idea as the most senior executive. The second purpose is to examine the alternatives, compare them with one another, and zero in on the best ones.

In applying this process to the Hanes case we came up with two major but quite different strategies. The first may achieve company goals by the end of the 4-year planning period, while the second strategy (to be activated later) may take the company to new heights in the years beyond. The primary strategy of entering food and drug channels with a new brand is a bold move that could be foolhardy in an oligopolistic industry. Yet it may work well in an industry as fragmented as the women's hosiery industry in which much of the business is done under private labels. The second strategy—diversification—requires careful study and preparation before activating. These preparations can be made while the company marshals its forces to get the primary strategy under way.

Finally we explained that one of the advantages of strategic planning is that corporate management can be brought into the process when strategies are being finalized. Not only does this afford top management the opportunity to contribute, but also increases the probability that it will approve the final business plan. And, knowing top management's attitude is helpful to marketing management as it proceeds with the planning process.

In the next chapter we will see how tactical plans evolve from the approved strategies.

QUESTIONS

1. Discuss the nature of marketing objectives and why they vary.
2. Marketing objectives are related to what other objectives?
3. Distinguish between primary and secondary marketing objectives.
4. How is strategic planning different from the older forms of planning?
5. The idea that alternate strategies should be developed is based on what assumptions?
6. Give some examples of strategic alternatives.
7. When and why should top management become involved with business unit strategies?

REFERENCES

1. "Interpace: Zeroing in on a Single Product Line to Induce Growth," *Business Week*, July 17, 1978, pp. 88–89. By special permission, © 1978 by McGraw Hill, Inc., New York, N.Y., 10020. All rights reserved.
2. Sidney Schoeffler, Robert D. Buzzell, and Donald F. Heany, "Impact of Strategic Planning on Profit Performance," *Harvard Business Review*, March–April 1974, p. 137.
3. Ronald N. Paul, Neil B. Donovan, and James W. Taylor, "The Reality Gap in Strategic Planning," *Harvard Business Review*, May–June 1978, pp. 124–130.

CHAPTER 11

Preparing Tactical Plans

There is no reason why a company could not develop strategies and tactics at any time during the year and begin to implement them immediately. In practice, however, the planning cycle is such that the plan becomes effective at the start of the fiscal year,* which for the typical company is January 1. The planning period, which precedes the start of the fiscal year, runs from September into December for the majority of companies, although some begin even earlier.[1] In the larger sense, of course, planning is continuous since changes in the external situation can cause changes in the plan as the fiscal year progresses.

The annual marketing plan follows the same cycle as the business unit or company profit plan of which it is an integral part. It is a comprehensive document, containing not only the tactical plans in support of the strategies but also the ongoing activities and budgets of the several departments that report to the marketing manager. We will discuss the departmental plan in the next chapter. Our emphasis here will be on the tactics (or action programs) for carrying out the

*The fiscal year can be any 12-month period established for accounting purposes.

FIGURE 11-1. Steps in the marketing planning process.

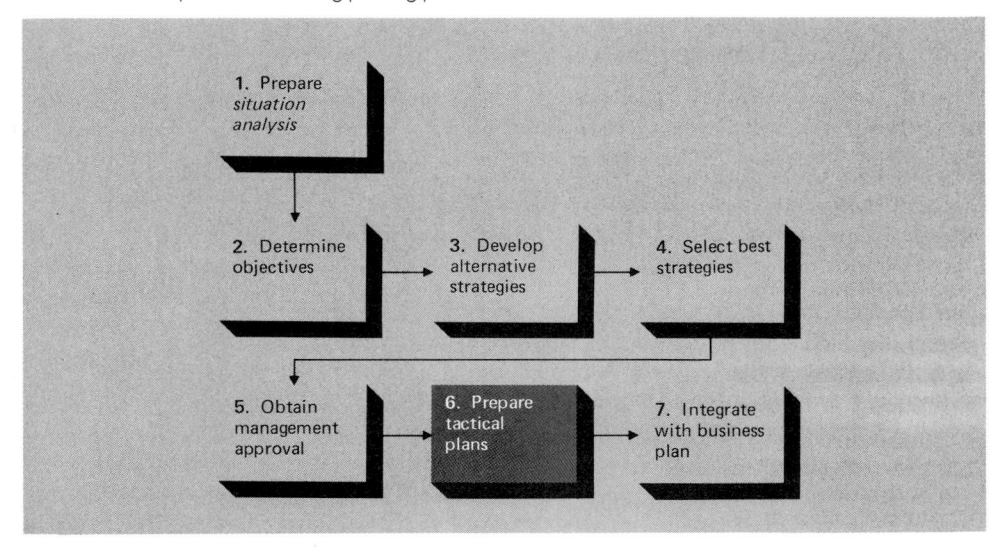

1. Prepare situation analysis
2. Determine objectives
3. Develop alternative strategies
4. Select best strategies
5. Obtain management approval
6. Prepare tactical plans
7. Integrate with business plan

strategies. To assist with this we introduce a planning worksheet and illustrate its use with two company examples.

THE TACTICAL MARKETING PLAN

A Conference Board survey of the annual marketing planning practices of 267 companies reveals a variety of planning formats. According to the board's report, "Marketing plans come in all manner of styles and flavors, so that no ideal 'cookbook'—let alone a single recipe—for preparing marketing plans can cover all individual company circumstances."[2] Despite the differences, however, topics recur with enough frequency to conclude that the marketing planning format in a typical company will include:

- *Situation analysis*
- Objectives
- Strategy
- Programs and their budget impact
- Schedules and assignments

Companies often include a sixth point—"review and revision." Since this comes after the plan is in effect, we treat it as a control rather than a planning function and discuss it later in Chapter 15.

Where strategic planning has preceded the development of the annual tactical plan (as it should), the *situation analysis,* objectives, and strategy can be abstracted from the strategic plan and adapted to the annual plan. These, in turn, lead to the tactical programs for each marketing function, followed by estimates of any extra costs the programs will incur. Time schedules are set, and the responsibility for each program is assigned to individuals or organizational units.

The tactical marketing plan worksheet (Figure 11-2) is a useful device for bringing together plans for the various marketing functions. It begins with summaries of the *situation analysis,* objectives, strategy, and tactical programs, and is followed by plans for each marketing function.

Situation Analysis

The worksheet leads off with a summary of the major problems uncovered by the *situation analysis.* The type of analysis described in Chapter 9 provides the background information for short-term (annual) tactical planning as well as for longer-term strategy development. Much of the more specific information contained in the *situation analysis* is not used in strategy development because the emphasis is on identifying broad problems and opportunities. Annual tactical plans, by way of contrast, contain detailed action programs; consequently, they will utilize the detailed information found in the *situation analysis.*

Objectives

The objectives for the annual tactical marketing plan cover one segment of the longer time period represented by the strategic objectives. This does not necessarily

CHAPTER 11
PREPARING
TACTICAL PLANS

TACTICAL MARKETING PLAN WORKSHEET — 19 __
For: (Product), (Product line), or (Market)

Summary of
Situation Analysis: _____

Objective: _____

Strategy: _____

Marketing Program: _____

Functions	Objectives	Programs	Budget impact	Schedules	Assignment
Product					
Price					
Distribution					
Sales					
Advertising					
Sales promotion					
Publicity					
Service					

FIGURE 11-2. Tactical marketing plan worksheet.

mean that the objectives for 1 year will represent one-fifth of a 5-year objective. An objective of the Hanes Corporation, for example, specified a profit figure to be reached in 4 years, yet the strategic plan pointed out that the new strategy actually would have a negative impact on profits for the first year or two.

The top portion of the worksheet lists the overall objectives for the product or market plan that is the subject of the plan. Specific objectives for the several marketing functions are listed in the lower portion of the form. Each functional objective should be related to, and supportive of, the overall annual objective and strategy.

Just as strategy development is geared to achieve multiyear objectives, tactical program development is geared to achieve the annual objectives. Normally there are alternative ways (programs) by which the annual objectives can be achieved. The annual planning process is concerned with selecting the best, or optimum, programs from among the alternatives.

Strategy

The strategy shown in the upper portion of the worksheet is merely a restatement of the longer-term strategy.

Marketing Programs

The top portion of the worksheet also has a place for a brief statement of the overall marketing program. Programs for each marketing function are listed in the lower portion.

Programs Essential to Strategies. To say that strategies are no better than the tactical programs that support them would be a gross understatement. With the current emphasis on strategic planning some writers tend to obscure, if not ignore, programming for implementation. Marketing management cannot afford to let this happen. While the development of strategies enhances planning effectiveness, strategies cannot take the place of programming.

Organizationally, program development will be carried out by product or market managers and by functional managers such as the heads of sales, advertising, market research, and services. The marketing manager will need to coordinate the several programs into a cohesive whole; yet it is important to delegate program planning to the specialists who know the most about the products, markets, and specialized functions.

Budget Impact

Programs in support of strategies often incur added costs over and above current operating expenses. Many times, however, a program can be implemented by people already carried on the departmental payroll; for example, the company's sales force could implement some of the plans. Realism is added to planning when the planner considers the added costs of each proposed program. This is not to say that the least costly plan is necessarily the best. Program A, for example, may cost more than program B, yet contribute a relatively greater amount of profit. In such a case, and with all other things being equal, program A would be more desirable even though it costs more. Knowing the costs and the potential profit helps in determining whether the program is really essential or whether a lower-cost program should be substituted.

In Figure 11-2 the total of the column headed "budget impact," when compared to expected added sales and profit contribution, will give the marketing manager an approximate idea of the financial effect of the programs. It will be approximate because marketing programs can affect the costs (positively or negatively) of other business functions, such as manufacturing. Financial statements are needed to measure the true impact of the results (such as added sales) and the added costs of marketing programs. More will be said on this in the next chapter. Nevertheless, estimating the budget impact will help the planner to select programs and also will help the accountant or financial analyst to prepare the financial statements.

Scheduling and Assignments

Scheduling of the functional programs is essential if everything is to come together at the point of market impact. For purposes of management control it is important that the responsibility for each step in each program be assigned to someone or some unit. The worksheet provides space for time schedules (such as completion dates) and space for the name of the person or department with responsibility for seeing that the assignment is carried out on schedule.

PROGRAMMING BY MARKETING FUNCTIONS

Marketing strategies will require implementing programs for some or all of the following broad marketing functions: product, pricing, distribution channels, sales (the personal selling function), advertising, sales promotion, publicity, or services.

While not every strategy requires a change in the way the function is currently handled, it is useful to consider each function and decide whether it requires new or changed programs. The strategy might require no change in product, for example, yet require a change in packaging—a subfunction of the product category. The strategy would not be likely to refer to packaging; consequently, the planner would have to determine whether the packaging change was needed to help implement the strategy.

There is, of course, no way to prescribe the appropriate programs in the absence of knowledge of the situation, the objectives, and the strategies. Even so, a checklist can be useful in stimulating ideas for alternative programs. For an example, see **Marketing Note 11-1**.

PREPARING THE TACTICAL MARKETING PLAN WORKSHEET

To illustrate how the tactical marketing plan worksheet is used to develop annual functional programs in support of the longer-range strategy we'll use Flavor, Inc., as an example. This company processes condiments (mustard, spices, and other flavor enhancers of food).*

Situation, Objectives, and Strategy

The situation analysis can be summarized as follows. Flavor is the leading brand of condiments in 60 percent of the 318 Standard Metropolitan Statistical Areas (SMSAs), but holds a second place or lower position in the remaining 40 percent, representing 127 SMSAs. Flavor's average national market share has remained constant in recent years.

Management's objective is to increase the company's national market share by 5 percent over the next 5 years. The strategy for accomplishing this is to maintain share in the markets where Flavor is the leader while increasing promotional efforts in the markets where it is weak. Management is aware that leadership in every

---

*This is a hypothetical company, but the situation is based partly on fact.

MARKETING NOTE 11-1

Checklist of Ideas for Tactical Marketing Programs

The following list of subjects—organized by marketing function—can help to stimulate ideas for tactical programs. While the list is extensive, the number of programs chosen per function should be relatively brief.

Product Programs

1. Product development
   a. New product
   b. Product improvement
   c. Product change
2. Product introduction
3. Package development
4. Package introduction
5. Brand name selection
6. Phasing out products
7. Introduction or deletion of private brands manufacturing
8. Changes in warranty
9. Value analysis (to reduce product cost)
10. Searching out candidates for acquisition or merger

Pricing Programs

1. Change in price
   a. For the end customer
   b. Trade discounts
2. New product price
   a. Market skimming
   b. Market penetration
3. Change in price policy
4. Pricing to include or exclude services
5. Incremental pricing
6. Change in credit policies
   a. Discounts for quantity or prompt payment
   b. Extended terms to encourage early season shipment
7. Annual or longer-term pricing contracts including or excluding escalation clauses
8. Consignment (manufacturer retains title to product while in the channels and until the sale is made to end customer)
9. Rental or leasing

Distribution Programs

1. Change in channels used, for example:
   a. Adding or deleting classes of wholesalers or chains
   b. Adding or deleting classes of retailers
   c. Adding or deleting catalog
   d. Adding or deleting vending machine
   e. Adding or deleting direct-to-consumer (door-to-door)
   f. Adding or deleting direct mail
   g. Change from direct-to-user to going through wholesaler or vice versa
   h. Change from wholesaler to direct-to-retailer or vice versa
2. Change in distribution policies, for example:
   a. Manufacturer sells some end customers or accounts direct, others through wholesalers
   b. Wholesaler takes on some customer service functions
   c. Shift from intensive, selective, or exclusive distribution to one of the others
   d. Shift from independent middlemen to company-owned outlets
   e. Shift from company-owned to franchised outlets
3. Improving quality of wholesale and retail representation
4. Adding company-owned or leased field warehouses to provide better service to trade channels
5. Adding or deleting company branch warehouses for shipping direct to end consumers

MARKETING NOTE 11-1 *(Continued)*

Sales Programs

1. Redefine the sales job
2. Revise plan of sales organization
3. Revise territory layout
4. Revise compensation plan
5. Change number of sales personnel
6. Personnel improvement programs
    a. Qualifications sought
    b. Recruiting
    c. Selection
    d. Training
    e. Promotion
    f. Incentives
7. Training programs for trade channel salespeople
8. Adding new accounts
9. Developing sales potential by market, county, or other control unit
10. Allocating or reallocating sales effort by account potential and location
11. Reporting competitive intelligence
12. Missionary sales effort
    a. With influencers (e.g., architects, doctors)
    b. In-store promotional effort

Advertising Programs

1. Advertising policies
2. Agency selection or change of agency
3. Advertising campaigns
    a. Objectives
    b. Target market
    c. Product positioning
    d. Copy theme
    e. Media
    f. Reach and frequency
    g. Commercials and local co-op ads
    h. Testing commercials
4. Measurement of advertising performance
5. Special events programs (e.g., sponsored sports contests)
6. Coporate image advertising

Sales Promotion Programs

1. Programs for consumers
    a. Coupons
    b. Cents-off offers
    c. Sampling with product
    d. Contests
2. Programs for trade channels
    a. Point-of-sale materials
    b. Store demonstrations
    c. Store displays
    d. Dealer premiums
    e. Dealer mailings
    f. Dealer contests
3. Programs for sales force
    a. Product catalogs
    b. Sales presentation materials
    c. Samples
    d. Arrangements for trade shows
    e. Selling aids
    f. Price lists
    g. Mailings of advertising and promotional materials to buyers and buying influencers
    h. Sales contests

Publicity Programs

1. Announcements to the media
    a. New products
    b. Product improvements
    c. New ways to use product
    d. New business ventures
    e. Research findings
    f. Market expansion
    g. Customer success story
    h. Industry success story
    i. Financial news
    j. Corrective, explanatory stories to offset unfavorable news story

> **MARKETING NOTE 11-1**
> *(Continued)*
>
> 2. Educational background meetings with media
> 3. Sponsoring events of public interest
> 4. Arranging for company products as prizes on TV shows
>
> ### Service Programs
>
> 1. Customer service programs
>   a. Installation
>   b. Start up of new equipment
>   c. Maintenance
>   d. Repair
>   e. Replacement
>   f. Adjustment
>   g. Technical service
>   h. Warranty administration
>   i. Field service stations
>   j. Replacement parts inventories
> 2. Wholesaler and dealer service programs
>   a. Service policies
>   b. Training of trade service people
>   c. Order fulfillment
>   (1) Order acknowledgement
>   (2) On-time deliveries
>   (3) Controlling shipping errors
>   (4) Controlling back orders
>   (5) Providing information on delayed orders
>   (6) Claims and allowances
>   (7) Handling complaints
> 3. Internal services, assisting with production scheduling and inventory control
>   a. Breaking down sales forecast by line item by week or month
>   b. Notifying manufacturing of special sales promotions
>   c. Recommending field inventory levels
>   d. Recommending reorder points
>   e. Coordinating field inventories with factory inventories

market is not always possible and may not even be profitable in some markets where the local competition is very strong. For the time being, therefore, the objective is stated in terms of market share.

First-Year Objective. Management has set the objective for the ensuing year as one-fifth of the 5-year objective—i.e., a 1 percent increase in national market share. Assuming share in the leadership markets remains constant, it is estimated that the average share of the weaker markets will need to be increased by 2.5 percent in order to achieve the national increase of 1 percent.

The Tactical Program

For its overall program (or tactic) marketing management has chosen to run a 5-month "picnic time" promotional blitz in the weaker markets between April 1 and Labor Day, a period which accounts for roughly 70 percent of industry sales of products such as mustard and barbecue sauce.

It is expected that the promotion will increase sales to present customers of Flavor products and that it will attract new purchasers as well. Based on past experience, it is estimated that one-third of the new purchasers will continue using Flavor products. The promotion, therefore, should result in a relatively permanent increase in market share for Flavor, although some of this advantage could be lost as the result of counter-promotions by competitors.

The heart of the blitz will be a cents-off deal on mustard and barbecue sauce—the two largest selling products in the Flavor line. The mustard deal will run from April 1 to June 15. The barbecue sauce deal will run from June 15 to Labor Day. By not running both deals simultaneously, two sales approaches can be made to the trade to argue for the ordering of extra stocks of Flavor products to back up the expected increase in consumer buying. The more the Flavor sales force can get accounts to commit orders to back up Flavor promotions, the less open-to-buy these accounts will have for competitive brands.

Company Price Policy

One of the company's policies is that price cutting is not to be used to "buy" market share—a policy designed to discourage price wars. Although the proposed cents-off deal provides a temporary price reduction to the consumer, it does not involve changing Flavor's price list; therefore, it is not considered a violation of management's pricing policy.

On the company's income statement the costs of the cents-off deal will be included with "Discounts and Allowances" and subtracted from gross sales income in arriving at net sales income. For planning purposes these costs also are shown in the "budget impact" column of Table 11-1 opposite the "sales promotion" function.

Profit Impact

The added costs listed in the "budget impact" column (over and above the discounts) total $584,000. These represent $544,000 in variable marketing expense, plus $40,000 in variable interest expense. Interest expense covers loans to finance additional inventory. Variable manufacturing costs are estimated at $1 million for the added units needed to fill the orders expected from the promotion. Variable marketing expenses added to the variable manufacturing costs total $1,584,000. Subtracting these total variable costs from net sales of $1,700,000 leaves a net profit contribution and net cash flow of $116,000. If a portion of fixed costs are deducted from profit contribution, an *accounting* loss occurs. The calculation is as follows:

Gross sales	$2,000,000
Less: Promotional discounts	(300,000)
Net sales	1,700,000
Less: Variable costs	(1,584,000)
Profit contribution	116,000
Less: Proportionate share of fixed costs	(200,000)
Net loss	$ (84,000)

The accounting loss will be greater than $84,000 if a deduction is made also for some undetermined amount of income lost from sales that would have been made at full price if there were no promotion. The promotion probably can be justified from a financial standpoint, however, in view of the $116,000 contribution to already existing fixed costs. And financial management will be happy with the positive cash flow. Even so, to make a significant contribution to the 5-year strategy the promotion will have to attract permanent new customers to Flavor products. If, in fact, this is the result of the promotion, it will serve to implement the strategy and represent a step toward reaching the long-range objective.

TABLE 11-1
Flavor, Inc., Tactical Marketing Plan Worksheet - 19__ (Condiments product line)

Situation Analysis:	Company has leading market share in 60% of SMSAs; is nonleader in balance. National market share has remained constant for past 5 years.
Objective:	Increase national market share by 5% in 5 years—by 1% next year (or $2 million increase in sales).
Strategy:	Increase promotional effort in 40% of SMSAs where company is not the market leader to obtain average of 2.5% gain in share for these markets.
Marketing Program:	Run a 5-month special "picnic time" blitz in these 127 SMSAs while continuing usual marketing program in balance of country. (Note: 70% of mustard and barbecue sauce purchases are made between April 1 and Labor Day.)

Function	Objective	Program	Budget impact, $	Schedule	Assignment
Product	No change in product line.	No change			
	Packaging—pack mustard and barbecue sauce with removable cents-off label.	Design and order label and issue instructions to manufacturing department.	+5,000	1/15	Sales promotion
Price	Maintain price unless price moves are made by local leaders.	Monitor pricing of competitive leaders.		Continuing	Sales
Distribution	Raise active account level of key chains from 70% to 90%.	Shift 3 national account managers to target markets for 3-month blitz.	+15,000 extra travel	1/1–3/31	Sales
Sales	Sell promotional program to 90% of key chain and distributor headquarters. Obtain retailer agreement to order extra stock and participate in promotions (90% Class A accounts, 75% Class B, 50% Class C).	Make special presentation to all chain and distributor accounts and to all Class A, B, C retailers.		2/1–3/15	Sales
		Hire 25 temporaries to assist sales force with setting up store displays.	+100,000	4/1–7/15	Sales
		Train sales force to sell special promotion.	+1,500	1/15–1/30	Sales
		Sales force to train distributors' salespeople.		2/15–3/15	Sales

Advertising	Attain 66% household awareness of company "picnic time" promotion, including cents-off deal.	+400,000	4/15–Labor Day	Advertising
	Conduct telephone survey in 10 markets to measure awareness.	+5,000	7/5	Market research
	Prepare co-op ad mats.	+2,000		Advertising
Sales Promotion	Arrange for cents-off deals Mustard promotion Barbecue sauce promotion	+150,000 +150,000	1/1–9/6 4/1–6/15 6/15–9/6	Sales promotion Sales promotion Sales promotion
	Assist sales force in selling promotion and utilizing point-of-sale materials to move product off the shelves.	+10,000	1/15–5/1	Sales promotion
Publicity	Stimulate public interest in outdoor cooking (camping, picnics, backyard).	+5,000	2/15 4/15 6/15	Public relations
	Prepare 3 illustrated press releases featuring fun of outdoor cooking and recipes (including mustard, barbecue sauce, and spices).			
Service	Provide accurate and on-time delivery of product to stocking accounts; also, prompt handling of reorders.		1/1	Marketing services
	Provide manufacturing department with weekly product shipments forecast.			
	Increase inventory levels in field warehouses.	+40,000	3/1–8/15	Marketing services
	Stress the importance of adhering to order filling standards; maintain follow-up control.		2/15–8/30	Marketing services

Weakness of Promotional Strategies

Flavor's experience serves to illustrate in financial terms the potential drawback of concentrating solely on a market share objective. It also points up the potential financial disadvantages of a marketing strategy based primarily on increases in promotional expenditures. The classic illustrations of marketing strategy in many marketing textbooks involve increased promotional expenditures (via personal selling, advertising, or sales promotion) to attain market share objectives.

Inexperienced marketing planners usually are drawn first to the use of additional promotion as a strategy, apparently because they perceive marketing as being essentially a promotional function. Financially oriented top managements, however, look skeptically at strategies that do not improve current cash flow—or that cause a drain on it—even though the strategies and programs offer promise of future cash flow benefits. They know that strategies based on promotion alone often invite competitive response in kind and result in no permanent change in market share. This is why the search for alternative strategies has been emphasized in the planning chapters of this text. Frequently one can find more promising strategies than the strategy of increasing promotional effort. It is one of the reasons why the Hanes strategy is so interesting. Despite an expected temporary negative effect on cash flow, the Hanes strategy appears far more promising in the long run than merely slugging it out with competitors on the promotional front.

We are not suggesting that the Flavor strategy is wrong; it may have been the best alternative open for this company. And the idea of singling out the company's weaker markets for improvement appears sound. Nor do we suggest that a strategy of increasing promotion should automatically be rejected. If the company has real advantages to promote, such as a better product, promotion is the logical means of getting new buyers—buyers who will probably remain loyal after they experience the product's advantages over their previous brands.

Meshing Tactical and Strategic Plans

Corporate turnarounds of deteriorating situations, or improvements in traditional patterns of corporate performance, normally are not accomplished quickly. Major business and marketing objectives, therefore, usually extend past 1—or even several—years as do the major strategies for achieving the objectives. Tactical marketing programs, on the other hand, normally cover only the company's fiscal year and tie in with the annual business or profit plan. The annual marketing plan, in effect, becomes one segment of the longer-range strategic plan. And the annual plan may be broken into even shorter segments, such as quarters or months, for purposes of management control.

Planning moves from the broad and longer-range to the specific and shorter-range. The longer-range objectives and strategies provide the framework for the short-range plans. Yet the programs planned for activation in the near future (next month, next quarter, next year) are designed consciously to support the longer-range strategy. These relationships are portrayed in Figure 11-3.

The situation may change during the planning cycle, thereby requiring new or revised strategies and/or annual tactical plans. Well thought out strategies, however, are not likely to require major change since strategies should be designed to respond to long-term trends in the market environment. Tactical plans are more likely to

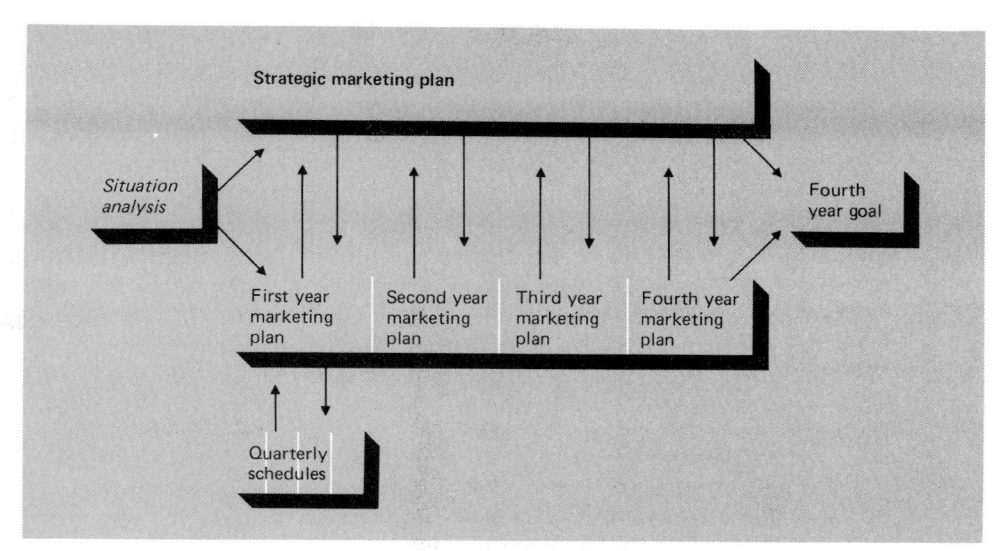

FIGURE 11-3. Relationship of the strategic marketing plan to the annual marketing and tactical plans, and of the annual plan to the quarterly schedules.

require modification in order to respond to short-range competitive actions. Modification of tactical plans can be made during the annual marketing planning process or at any time that market conditions so dictate.

DEVELOPING TACTICAL PROGRAMS AT HANES

As we left the Hanes case in Chapter 10, the marketing plan had recommended the adoption of two strategies. The primary strategy called for entering food and drug channels with a new advertised brand of women's hosiery not identified with Hanes, while at the same time continuing to market the company's other advertised brands through the company's traditional department and specialty store channels. The secondary strategy called for diversification, but recommended that this strategy be postponed until studies of diversification opportunities were completed and until conditions for financing of acquisitions were more favorable.

As we continue with the marketing planning process, we assume that top management has approved the primary strategy and that marketing management is undertaking to develop tactical programs to implement this strategy. The tactical plan presented here represents what marketing management at Hanes might have considered at the time.

Summary of Situation, Objectives, and Strategies

Hanes was confronted with the dual problems of a mature industry and with industry sales shifting to food and drug channels. As a result, Hanes was experiencing a severe decline in profits. The outlook was made no brighter by the realization that industry sales probably would decline in the near future due to the expected cyclical change in women's skirt lengths.

Hanes' primary long-term objective was to return net profits to their previous high level by the year 1973—namely, to $9.3 million after tax. The objective for 1970—the first year of strategy implementation—was to introduce a new brand into the new channels by October 15. It was recognized that development costs would result in a reduction of net income for the year.

The strategy was to broaden consumer exposure to the company's hosiery products at the retail level. Specifically, it was to introduce a new advertised brand into food and drug outlets which currently were selling only low-priced private hosiery brands. The new brand was to be priced higher than the private brands but lower than advertised brands sold through department and specialty stores. To avoid drawing sales from other Hanes brands or damaging relationships with current accounts, the brand was not to be identified with Hanes. The idea was to take share from the private brands sold in supermarkets rather than to cannibalize sales from Hanes brands sold in department and specialty stores.

Program for 1970*

Additional marketing research, planning, decision making, test marketing, and other actions affecting marketing, manufacturing, and other departments of the company are needed promptly if the new strategy is to be operational by October 15.

The strategy involves more than introducing a new brand into new channels. It involves acceptance of the idea that hosiery is a convenience good, subject to the marketing techniques used for other convenience goods sold in self-service stores—goods such as packaged foods, drugs, and personal care products. The approach must take into account the needs of the trade as well as the needs of consumers. Self-service retailers operate on the basis of high volume, high turnover, and low margins. They look at products in terms of profit per square foot of floor space. Consequently, Hanes' tactical programming for the new strategy will have to be viewed from a different perspective than that used in the past.

Product

Basic to the success of the new strategy is the introduction of a product that will be perceived by consumers and trade as different from any other brand. The perception of difference must be enhanced by means of brand name, packaging, advertising, and in-store display.

New Product Available. Fortunately, a new technical development is available —a superstretch pantyhose with superior qualities of fit. One size adapts to different foot lengths and leg shapes and is applicable to about 75 percent of all women. A quick decision will have to be made whether to adopt this product if the manufacturing department is to have inventory ready for an April 1 market test and an October 15 rollout† into selected target markets. Furthermore, all other marketing planning will be affected by the product decision. The pros and cons must be considered.

---

*At this point the Hanes marketing plan continues from where it left off in Chapter 10. It is presented as if it were written by Hanes marketing planners. This portion of the plan covers development of programs and schedules for the first year of strategy implementation (1970).

†In marketing jargon *rollout* means to extend a new product from test market into additional markets. Rollout may be gradual or it may be a full-scale national introduction.

On the positive side, the product is truly differentiated in that it fits better and looks better on the leg than conventional hosiery; it eliminates the need for a range of foot sizes; and it greatly reduces stock keeping units (SKUs) for company and channel members. This last benefit will reduce inventory costs for both company and channel members and require less display area, thereby increasing retailers' turnover and profit per square foot of floor space.

The major negative feature is that the product is unsightly off the leg. Regular hosiery is "boarded" in the final stages of manufacturing—shaped and pressed so that the hosiery which the consumer sees when she opens the package is smooth, flat, and attractive. Because of its elastic characteristics, the new product contracts when not on the leg to a small twisted object unlike anything consumers are used to.

Tentative Conclusion. We should probably choose this product, subject to review of more refined cost estimates. The advantages of better fit seem to outweigh the disadvantages of appearance off the leg. However, a major communications effort may be needed to prepare consumers for the initial exposure to the product when it is removed from the package. We will complete by early January the consumer use tests already begun to make certain that consumers do indeed perceive the product benefits and to learn whether the appearance off the leg affects consumer attitude.

Brand Name Selection. We need a brand name that is distinctive and bears no relationship to present Hanes brands. An important part of our strategy implementation is to differentiate the new brand completely from anything else on the market. Immediately, brainstorming sessions will be conducted with our own employees, and we will solicit ideas as well from our advertising agency and from our design consultant.

As soon as the brand name is selected, we will have patent counsel conduct a search—to make sure there is no infringement of other brand names—and then register the name with the U.S. Patent Office. Prior to that we will ship the product in interstate commerce with the new brand name affixed. This is a precautionary measure to strengthen Hanes' claim on the name by establishing the first date of use in the event someone else at a later date should claim rights to the name.

Packaging and Display

Packaging and display programs will be developed together since they must be compatible in the retail store. The package should help differentiate the product, attract attention, stack easily in the display rack, inform the consumer of its contents, and protect the product from handling prior to purchase. The protection criterion is desirable since self-service stores—unlike department stores and specialty store hosiery departments—do not hire salesclerks to supervise the handling of a fragile product which is subject to snags from rough hands and fingernails.

If we adopt the new superstretch hose, the traditional polyethelene envelope with transparent window is neither necessary nor appropriate since the rather shapeless hose would not show up well in a transparent container. Furthermore, the polyethelene package is not the best method for preventing handling of the product prior to purchase. The situation presents the opportunity to take an entirely different approach to hosiery packaging. In addition to the other features mentioned, it also provides the opportunity to utilize a size and shape that discourages pilferage.

The major design objectives for the display rack are to maximize the amount of inventory displayed while minimizing the floor space used. This means making maximum use of vertical space. The display should enhance product differentiation, attract attention, and provide space for pricing, product features, and sales messages since no salesclerk is present to help the consumer make her selection.

We are engaging a leading creative design consultant experienced in self-service store packaging and display. The product decision should be made prior to the designer beginning work, since the product will influence the design.

Pricing

Finalization of the recommended retail price and trade discount structure must await selection of product and distribution method since both affect costs. We see the need for a retail price ranging between $1.25 and $1.50—a price we believe will be low enough to encourage consumers to trade up beyond the 39 to 89 cents store brand range, yet high enough to provide a profit.

As soon as product and distribution decisions are made and cost estimates refined, we will prepare breakeven charts using various prices and estimated demand curves. Before the final price is chosen we will have some test market experience to help with our decision.

Trade Discounts. The answer to the question of what percentage of trade discounts to offer rests with the method of distribution. Higher margins must be offered if we go through chain warehouse and wholesale channels than if we deliver direct from the retail store and stock the displays ourselves. In either event, however, discounts can be set at lower levels than those used with our present channels. Self-service food/drug chains are accustomed to operating on lower margins than retail outlets, such as department and specialty stores, which incur the added costs of personal sales services.

Retail Price Maintenance. In order to build a quality image it is important that our brand not be discounted by retailers. To discourage discounting we have two options: (1) preprint the retail price on the package and direct our sales force to urge the trade to maintain the price or (2) register our product in each of the 38 states with fair trade laws.*

We plan to follow the fair trade approach even though we know that it is not completely effective and that several states have repealed these laws, and others are considering doing so. However, we believe the psychological effect of our decision to use fair trade pricing will be such that retailers will be impressed with the seriousness of our feelings about retail price maintenance.

---

*Fair trading was abolished in 1976 when Congress repealed the Miller-Tydings Act of 1937 and the McGuire-Keough Act of 1952, acts which had permitted states to enact retail price maintenance laws known as Fair Trade laws. At the time of the Hanes' case fair trade was legal in thirty-eight states. A company could register its retail price under the state law, then require all retailers to sell at that price. However, it was up to the company to enforce retail price maintenance, resorting to the courts if necessary. Because of the difficulty of policing thousands of stores, price maintenance under fair trade usually was not wholly effective.

Distribution

National introduction on October 15 will be nearly impossible, irrespective of the distribution method chosen. It will be more realistic to enter selected markets initially and expand as rapdily thereafter as market reaction and available resources dictate. This approach will also reduce risk. We have purposely limited the period for test marketing to give as little time as possible for competitors to follow our lead. Consequently, a market-by-market rollout beginning October 15 will, in effect, extend our test marketing, provide further opportunity to correct errors, make improvements, or pull back in the unlikely event that our basic strategy proves unsound.

Distribution Objectives. The market research department will recommend forty markets (SMSAs), excluding metropolitan New York. Selection will be based primarily on (1) demographic factors, (2) geographic representation in all Census Divisions, and (3) the availability of good retail chains in the market area. Our objective will be to obtain distribution in 65 percent of the major food and drug outlets in each market within 6 weeks after initial entry. We will not schedule New York until our approach is proven, and we have the people power to do it right. We are selecting markets for early entry in each section of the country to have a series of bases from which to expand rapidly in case a competitor seeks to capture a geographic area ahead of us.

Distribution Options. We have three feasible distribution options: (1) distribution through chain warehouses and independent wholesalers, (2) distribution through rack jobbers, or (3) distribution direct to retail store by our own trucks.

Chain and wholesale distribution. This would be the normal and most obvious method for reaching the tens of thousands of food and drug stores scattered throughout the entire country. It is the lowest-cost method and would be the fastest way to get to national distribution.

The disadvantage of this method is the limited merchandising support our brand would receive from chain headquarters and local stores. Hosiery is not a highly important item to supermarkets and receives minor attention. This is already apparent from the relatively poor job chains do in stocking and merchandising their own private brands. It would be necessary for us to employ brokers or develop a large missionary sales force of our own to make regular retail calls to encourage ordering the product, introduce displays, help to keep displays stocked, and monitor pricing and competitive activity.

Rack jobbers. Rack jobbers may represent a better method than the first option. From their own trucks rack jobbers take over the job of maintaining stocks in supermarket displays of nonfood products such as housewares, hardware, and health and beauty aids. The rack jobber's usual practice is to place inventory on consignment account with payment collected as store inventory is sold.

The disadvantages of using rack jobbers are (1) they are relatively expensive compared to regular wholesale distribution; and (2) because they carry a large number of items, they could not be expected to give our product the attention we would like.

Direct delivery. Similar to the rack jobbers, but providing for more control, would be direct delivery by our own trucks with our drivers trained to sell and service the product as well as deliver. Such a combination would enable us to control every aspect of marketing and distribution including sales effort with retailers, store inventory, pricing, display and in-store promotion, subject, of course, to agreement by chain headquarters.

The major drawback to this method is that it represents the highest cost because of the capital investment required for trucks, field warehousing, and field inventory, as well as the expense of a large driver/sales force. It would also require the longest time to achieve national distribution since we would have to start from scratch. Offsetting the higher costs to some extent would be the lower trade discounts we could offer, since we would eliminate for the chains the costs of ordering, warehousing, and store-delivery. Similarly the retail store would be relieved of the costs of ordering, handling, and stocking. If we were to offer stock on consignment,* it would preclude the need for working capital that trade accounts normally have invested in inventory.

We plan to cost out each alternative distribution method. We also plan to review the experiences of noncompetitive companies—such as Nabisco and Keebler—that use combination driver/sales people for direct store delivery and in-store merchandising.

Sales

Decisions with respect to the sales organization depend upon which distribution method is chosen. The sales job would be different for each of the three distribution alternatives discussed above. The sales manager, therefore, will be closely involved with the distribution decisions. If direct distribution is chosen, using combination driver/sales people, it will require building an entirely new sales organization.

Advertising

Brand Identification System. Since the new brand is not to be identified with Hanes, we need a complete brand identification system including the logotype, (name, symbol, and/or trademark) as it is to be used on packaging, sales promotion materials, displays, signs, letterheads, and advertising. The advertising manager is responsible for development and administration of the system and will look to the advertising agency and/or design consultant for graphic designs. Graphic design necessarily must follow selection of the brand name. Registration of the trademark and its use in interstate commerce will be made as soon as possible.

Advertising Program. The advertising agency will develop an introductory advertising campaign to be run in the test markets via local media. Based on test market experience, the ad program will be finalized to support the market by market rollout beginning October 15. Brand positioning and an effective copy theme are important supports in the product differentiation effort. TV spot commercials and newspapers will be used. The advertising objective will be to obtain 70 percent consumer awareness of the brand with 50 percent recall of the theme within 2 months of introduction. Measurements are to be made by the Marketing Research

---

*Consignment in this context means that Hanes would retain ownership of the stock *consigned* to the store. The store would not be required to pay for the merchandise until purchased by the consumer.

Department via telephone surveys of a sample of consumers in ten markets beginning December 15.

Sales Promotion

The Sales Promotion Department is responsible for having display racks manufactured according to the approved design and shipped to field distribution points. It is also responsible for the design and production of other point-of-sale materials as well as selling aids to assist the sales force in securing orders.

An introductory offer is needed as an incentive to consumers to try the new brand. The Sales Promotion Department is to recommend a plan at a cost not to exceed 35 cents per pair.

Publicity

Introduction of the first advertised hosiery brand into food and drug channels should be newsworthy. The Public Relations Department is responsible for news releases which initially will go only to local media in the target markets; later, as market coverage becomes broader, publicity releases will go to national media.

Service

Marketing services is responsible for coordinating with the appropriate departments to see that a superior inventory control system is ready to go along with the distribution method selected. The objective will be to have sufficient initial and replacement inventories available at each point in the distribution system and to have trade account orders filled accurately and promptly. Once new accounts are being served well, attention will be directed to controlling inventory and distribution costs consistent with continued good service.

If direct distribution is selected, Marketing Services will work with the Credit and Billing Departments to develop new credit, billing, and collection procedures to match the new form of distribution.

Table 11-2 summarizes Hanes' tactical plans and schedules using the tactical marketing plan worksheet.

SUMMARY

In this chapter we have seen how tactical marketing programs make up the short-term plans for supporting the longer-term strategies. Annual tactical plans are needed to help move the major strategic plans toward achievement of their longer-term objectives.

We introduced the tactical marketing plan worksheet to show how the tactical plan is divided into plans for each of eight marketing functions. Spaces are provided to list for each marketing function its objective, programs, budget impact, time schedules, and assignments of responsibility. The overall tactical plan is the sum of the plans for each marketing function. Summarizing the functional plans on one worksheet helps to highlight the interrelationships among functions and foster cooperation among departments and individuals.

TABLE 11-2
Hanes Corporation Tactical Marketing Plan Worksheet, 1970 (Hosiery line for sale through food and drug stores)

Situation Analysis: Slow growth industry; falling company profits. Food and drug chains' private hosiery brands are accounting for increasing share of industry sales. Hanes sells its advertised brands only through department and specialty stores.

Objectives: By 1973: earnings $9.3 million; sales $286.2 million; market share 10.4%. Next year: Maintain status quo in present businesses while implementing new strategy beginning 10/15/70.

Strategy: Introduce a differentiated, advertised hosiery brand (not identified with Hanes) to the food and drug trade, priced between supermarket brands and advertised brands.

Marketing Program: Develop product, packaging, display, pricing, distribution, promotion, and service programs; test market 4/1–9/15; begin rollout to target markets on 10/15/70.

Functions	Objective	Program	Budget Impact, $1000s	Schedule	Assignment
Product	Have a differentiated product with promotable features and benefits.	Determine manufacturing costs of new pantyhose.		1/5	Production manager
		Complete consumer testing.	1–10	1/5	Market research
		Make product decision; provide sales forecasts to manufacturing.		1/15	President and marketing manager
		Order test market quantities.	10–100	2/1	Product manager
	Have a distinctive brand name that suggests no relationship to Hanes.	Brainstorm ideas utilizing advertising agency and designer; select brand name.	1–10	2/1	Product manager
		Ship product with name in interstate commerce.		2/10	Product manager
		Apply for registration at U. S. Patent Office.	1–10	2/15	Legal
Packaging and Display	Develop package to differentiate product and meet other criteria; develop display rack to hold maximum inventory in minimum space.	Engage design consultant experienced in self-service packaging and display.	10–100	1/1	Product manager; marketing manager
		Select package and display rack.		2/15	Product manager; marketing manager
Price	Select retail price that will maximize sales and profit.	Prepare breakeven charts using various price and estimated demand curves.		2/15	Accounting; marketing manager

Category	Task	Details	Range	Date	Responsible
	Select trade discounts that will attract accounts, yet only pay them for actual functions performed.	Research food and drug discount structures; calculate value to trade if we provide delivery, stocking, and consignment.		2/15	Market research; marketing manager
	Discourage price cutting at retail level.	Register retail price in states with fair trade laws.	1–10	6/15	
Distribution	Determine and adopt best method of distribution.	Evaluate pros and cons of (1) chain and wholesale, (2) rack jobbers, (3) direct delivery. Select method.		1/15	Sales manager
				2/1	Sales manager; marketing manager
	Obtain distribution in 65% of major food and drug outlets in initial target markets by 12/31/70.	Test selected method in 4 markets; evaluate.	10–100	4/1–9/15	Sales manager
		Recommend target markets and target accounts.		4/1	Market research
		Develop account coverage plan.		4/15	Sales manager
Sales	Develop a sales organization that will ensure good distribution coverage, retail inventory and in-store display and merchandising.	Organize sales program for four test markets.	10–100	3/15	Sales manager
		Determine type and size of sales organization needed for national program. Implement for initial target markets.	100–1000	5/15–8/15	Sales manager
Advertising	Develop trademark and other graphics for package, advertising, and other forms of communication.	Assign to agency or design consultants. Select from proposed designs.	10–100	2/15	Advertising manager; marketing manager
		Ship in interstate commerce and register with patent office.	1–10	3/1	Legal
	Attain 70% consumer awareness of brand and 50% recall of copy theme by 12/15 in initial target markets.	Have agency develop proposed advertising program and media recommendations for test markets.	10–100	3/1	Advertising manager
		Approve program for initial target markets.	100–1000	8/15	Advertising manager
		Conduct consumer survey in Dec. to measure impact.	10–100	12/15	Market research

275

TABLE 11-2 (continued)

Functions	Objective	Program	Budget Impact, $1000s	Schedule	Assignment
Sales Promotion	Provide effective selling aids and point-of-sale materials.	Design and produce materials:			
		For test markets	1–10	3/15	Sales promotion manager
		For target markets	10–100	8/1	Sales promotion manager
	Have display racks available when and where needed.	Arrange for production shipment:			
		To test markets	1–10	3/15	Sales promotion manager
		To target markets	10–100	9/1	Sales promotion manager
	Arrange for introductory consumer promotion; cost limit 35 cents a pair.	Evaluate deals and develop for test markets.	1–10	3/1	Sales promotion manager
		Finalize deal for target markets.	10–100	8/1	Sales promotion manager
Publicity	Obtain publicity on new brand in target markets.	Prepare and release stories for local media.		9/15	Public relations manager
	Obtain national publicity at 60% national distribution mark.	Plan for announcements to national media to be made in 1971.		12/15	Public relations manager
Service	Provide manufacturing with line item forecasts based on sales forecasts approved by management.	Estimate beginning inventory needs by line item.		2/1	Marketing services manager
	Provide accurate, on-time delivery of product to field warehouse points and prompt servicing of account orders.	Arrange for inventory levels, reorder points, shipping schedules, and troubleshooting:			
		For test markets	10–100	3/1	Marketing services manager
		For target markets	100–1000	8/15	Marketing services manager
		If direct delivery is chosen, develop appropriate credit, billing, and collection procedures.		8/15	Marketing services manager; credit and billing departments

A proposed tactical plan for Flavor, Inc. was used as an example of how to prepare the worksheet. In addition to showing objectives, programs, schedules, and assignments we used the total of the "budget impact" column in a financial analysis of the tactical plan. By comparing the added costs of the programs (the budget impact) with a forecast of added sales volume we discovered that, although there would be a net accounting loss, the plan would make a contribution to fixed costs and produce a favorable cash flow. The financial forecast aids management in deciding whether to approve the tactical plan.

The chapter concluded with a description of how tactical programming might have been carried out for the initial year of the Hanes Corporation's new strategy. A worksheet was used to illustrate recommended programs for each functional marketing area.

In the next chapter we conclude our discussion of the marketing planning process by showing how marketing tactics are incorporated with the annual marketing department plan and how this plan is integrated with the business unit plan.

QUESTIONS

1. What is the usual planning cycle for the annual marketing plan?
2. What are the topics that would be covered by the typical tactical marketing plan?
3. Marketing strategies will require implementing tactical programs for which broad marketing functions?
4. How do the strategic and tactical marketing plans work together?
5. Why are inexperienced marketing planners often drawn to additional promotion as a strategy? What is the potential drawback of this strategy?

REFERENCES

1. *The Short Term Marketing Plan,* The Conference Board, New York, 1972, p. 7.
2. David S. Hopkins, *The Marketing Plan,* The Conference Board, New York, 1981, p. 16.

CHAPTER 12

Integrating Marketing and Business Plans: Financial Aspects of Marketing

Having emphasized how marketing strategies and tactics are developed, what remains is to explain how these plans are incorporated into the annual plans of the marketing department and how, in turn, those plans are integrated into the annual plan of the business unit. The annual marketing plan provides for *all* of the marketing department's activities, some of which may not be directly related to strategies and tactics. In addition to plans for a number of continuing activities, the plan includes the marketing budget as well as organization and staffing plans. Finally, all of this must be placed into a format which can be consolidated with the plans of other departments in the business unit's annual profit plan.*

This chapter will show how the annual marketing plan, incorporating the tactical plans in support of the strategies, is developed in a form that permits

---

*The terms *profit plan* and *business plan* are used interchangeably to mean the annual plan for a company or one of its business units such as a division. This plan includes the financial forecasts along with supporting functional plans.

FIGURE 12-1. Steps in the marketing planning process.

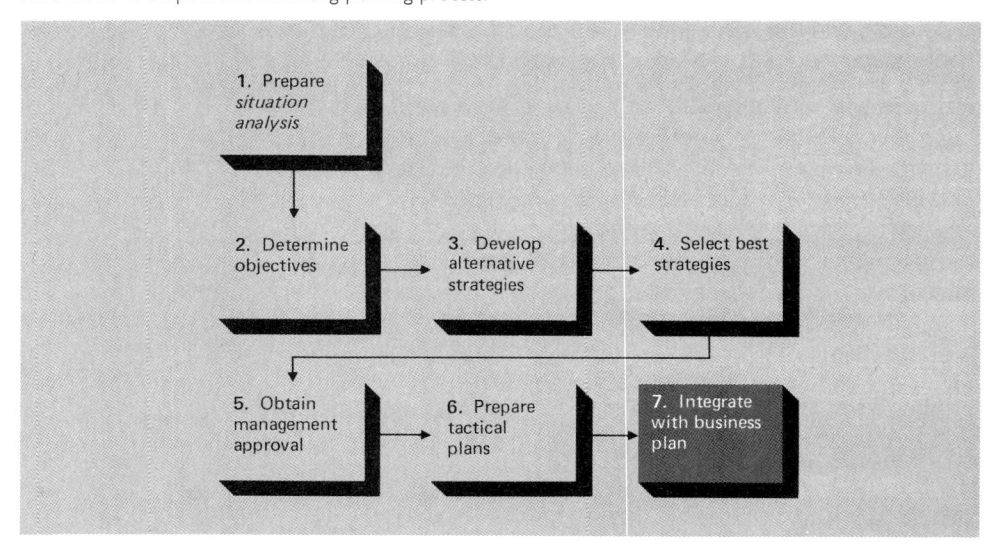

1. Prepare situation analysis
2. Determine objectives
3. Develop alternative strategies
4. Select best strategies
5. Obtain management approval
6. Prepare tactical plans
7. Integrate with business plan

integration with the business unit's profit plan. We will then discuss how and why marketing strategies, tactics, and budgets have important financial impact on the business unit.

THE ANNUAL MARKETING DEPARTMENT PLAN

In a multidivision company each division or business unit usually is made up of several functional departments such as marketing, manufacturing, engineering, and finance.* This functional type of organization provides for specialization as well as a means for business unit management to control the business. The general manager of the business unit (1) exercises control by comparing departmental performance with departmental goals and plans and (2) coordinates the plans of the functional departments to make certain that together they will lead to achievement of the business goals.

Prescribed Planning Format

To achieve the desired coordination, each major functional department normally will be required to submit its annual plan in a prescribed format. A typical format would tie in with the business unit's goals and strategies (see Figure 12-2).

It is only when all of the departmental plans are brought together that business unit management can prepare financial forecasts. The end product of the annual business unit plan is the financial forecast for the coming year expressed in terms of a year end income statement, balance sheet, and cash flow statement. From these

*Finance at the division level may be represented by the division controller or chief accountant.

FIGURE 12-2. Departmental plans format.

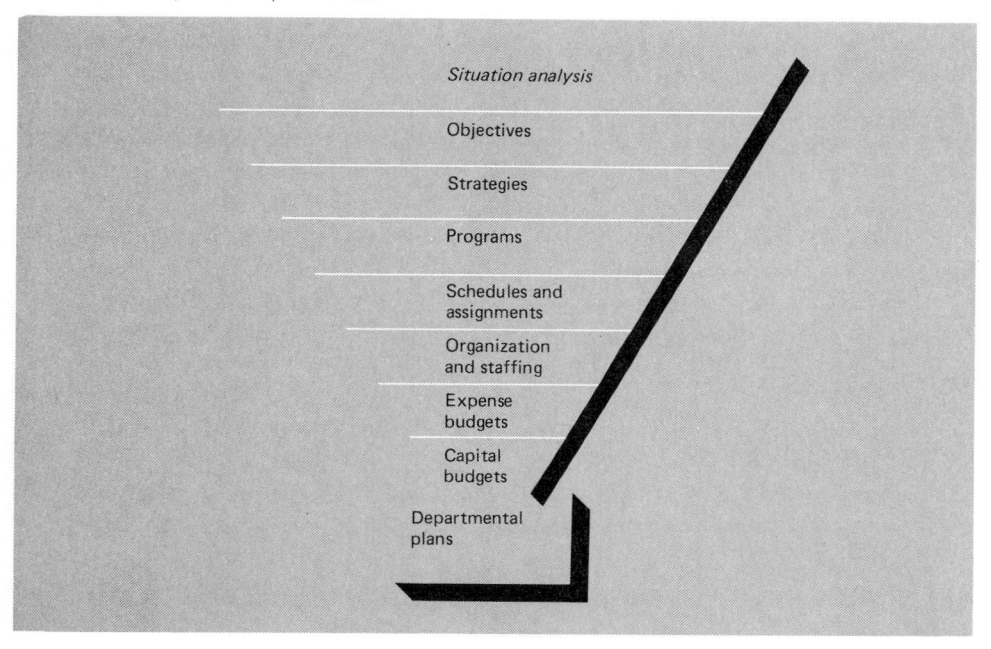

- Situation analysis
- Objectives
- Strategies
- Programs
- Schedules and assignments
- Organization and staffing
- Expense budgets
- Capital budgets
- Departmental plans

documents, expected profit for the year can be computed as a percent of sales (ROS) and as a percent of capital invested (ROI). When the above financial statements are broken down monthly, they provide the basis for forecasting the periods during the year when the business unit will have a positive cash flow and when it will have a negative cash flow. With this information the corporate financial officer can anticipate whether borrowing will be needed to supply cash and make plans accordingly.

The departmental plans provide the inputs for the financial analyses. Sales forecasts are taken from the marketing department plan while expense and capital budgets are obtained from the plans of all departments. Estimates of assets, liabilities, and cash flow are made by the financial executive.

Constructing the Marketing Plan

The marketing department plan normally will be prepared from the plans of the organizational units making up the department, such as sales, advertising, sales promotion, marketing research, and marketing services. If the department contains product or market managers, they also submit plans. Departmental unit plans will follow the same format as the marketing department plan, thereby facilitating consolidation into the department plan. The unit plans, of course, support the objectives and strategies of the marketing department, just as the marketing department's plan supports the objectives and strategies of the division or business unit.

How are the tactical programs in support of marketing strategies incorporated into the marketing plan? If the tactical marketing plan worksheet described in the last chapter is used, tactical plans can be transferred from this worksheet to the plans of each unit of the marketing department. In this way tactical plans are incorporated into the marketing plan along with the continuing programs of the marketing department. Figure 12-3 illustrates how the marketing planning process moves in several steps from objectives to the annual business plan.

Applying the Planning Format

We illustrate how the planning format might be applied to a unit of the marketing department using the Sales Department as an example. In a well-managed marketing planning program the sales manager will be familiar with the marketing *situation*

FIGURE 12-3. The development of marketing plans leading to incorporation into the business plan.

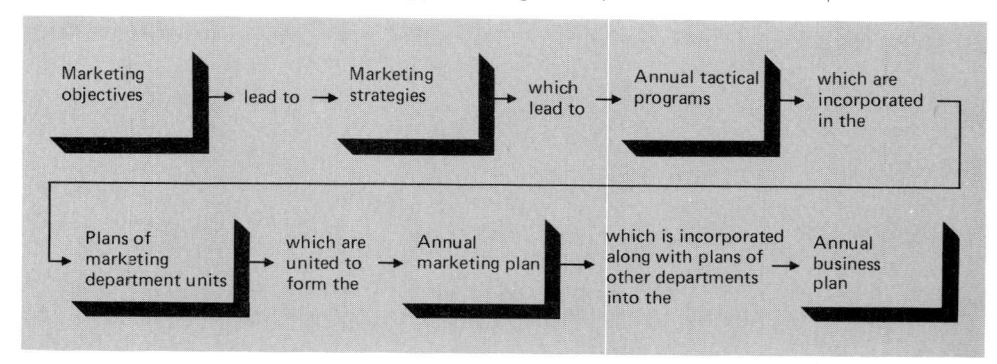

analysis and will have participated in the development of the marketing objectives and the annual tactical programs. The marketing manager will have provided the sales manager with the general, if not the specific, budget limits for the sales department.

Working within this general framework the sales manager's plan is developed first to assist with attainment of the marketing department's goals and second to provide specific sales goals and plans for the guidance of the personnel of the Sales Department. Marketing Note 12-1 shows the kind of information that might be covered in the Sales Department plan. The comments below expand on this subject matter.

Situation Analysis. This summarizes the marketing situation as it relates to the selling situation including the industry outlook, competitive conditions, and special sales problems and opportunities.

Objectives. In terms of sales income, the sales objectives would be identical with those of the marketing department. But there might also be a number of subobjectives such as sales by product and by market, account coverage, new

---

MARKETING NOTE 12-1

Planning Format Summary: Sales Department Example

Situation Analysis
Summarize the marketing situation as it applies to the personal selling function

Objectives
Total sales
Sales by product line and by sales district
Frequency of account calls
New accounts to be added
Increase share of business with specified target accounts
Obtain a specified percent distribution for new product

Strategies
Summary of marketing strategies
Sales strategies needed to support marketing strategies

Programs
To carry out sales strategies
To attain sales objectives
To maintain continuing departmental responsibilities

Schedules and Assignments
Times for starting, attaining intermediate goals, and completing programs
Assignment of program responsibility to individuals

Organization and Staffing
Planned changes in sales organization
Chart of proposed organization
Proposed changes in number of positions with reasons

Expense Budget
Proposed expenses by line items with justification of changes from previous year

Capital Budget
Total proposed capital expenditures by
   Type
   Total dollar amount
   Portion to be spent by month

account development, increased share of the purchases of target accounts, and sales objectives pertaining to new product introductions and product promotions.

Strategies. The Sales Department plan would include a brief restatement of the marketing strategies. There may or may not be a need for sales strategies to back up the marketing strategies. In the Hanes case it appears that there was a need for new sales strategies to help introduce the new brand of hosiery into food and drug channels.

There was a question, for example, whether (1) to make the rollout to one target market in each geographic area of the country with later expansion from these bases or (2) to obtain extensive distribution coverage in one geographic area before moving into a second geographic area, and so on. Alternative (2) would be a more conventional approach and would be simpler to control. Alternative (1), on the other hand, would help to prevent competitors from preempting a geographic area before Hanes got there. Hanes would be able to counter the competitor's move by bringing in a sales task force to expand quickly from its existing base into other markets in that geographic area.

A second question of sales strategy for Hanes would be whether (1) to assign one sales person to develop each designated target market or (2) to use mobile strike forces to move in and develop a target market quickly and then move on to the next one to do the same thing. As soon as the strike force accomplished its initial development objectives, a salesperson would be assigned to the market to maintain it and begin development of nearby markets. Alternative (1) would permit developing a number of markets simultaneously, whereas alternative (2) would provide more thorough and more rapid development of each target market by a team of highly trained salespeople who would become more skilled with each succeeding assignment.

A third question of sales strategy would be whether (1) to expand Hanes' existing sales force to sell both the new brand as well as existing brands or (2) to develop a separate sales force to concentrate only on the new brand. Alternative (2) would appear to be the preferred strategy since the existing sales force could well have difficulty adjusting to selling through the new channels. Furthermore, these salespeople would likely be biased toward the existing channels and not go after the new business with the desired enthusiasm. A disadvantage of alternative (2), however, is that with two sales forces two salespersons would be covering the same geography.

Programs. Programs would include those already developed and assigned to the Sales Department by the tactical marketing planning worksheets. Also included would be programs for products and markets not covered by the strategies. In the Flavor case, for example, programs are needed for maintaining sales in the 60 percent of the SMSAs where Flavor is already the market leader. These markets will not receive the "picnic time" promotional blitz. There might be no need to change the existing sales program in the leadership markets, in which case the sales plan would merely note this fact.

Schedules and Assignments. Schedules and assignments pertaining to sales also will be transferred from the tactical marketing plan worksheet to the Sales Department plan. Additionally, schedules and assignments will be made as needed for other sales programs not included in the worksheet. They will also be made for special programs such as training programs for company sales personnel and channel members. Sales objectives will likely be broken down by organizational unit (region, district, salesperson's territory) with schedules for attainment on a monthly or weekly basis.

Organization and Staffing. The Sales Department organization plan will be shown in chart form, accompanied by explanations of any proposed changes. Names of persons filling the positions may be shown on the organization chart or on a separate listing.

The staffing plan shows the numbers of positions proposed compared to the current and prior year. Explanations are made for any changes in numbers. Problems in filling vacant positions, if any, are described as well as plans for correcting them.

Expense Budget. The proposed Sales Department expense budget would normally be submitted on a company form such as that shown in Figure 12-4. Explanations for significant changes on the proposed budget would be included as would explanations for any unusual change by account number.

Figure 12-4 illustrates a *line item* approach to budgeting. Each line in the "account title" column represents an item in the budget. A different approach used by some companies is the *program budget*. In this form of budgeting a total sum is allocated to the manager of a program, such as the Sales Department program, who uses the budget as needed to achieve the program's objectives.

Capital Budget. If they occur in the marketing budget, capital budget items are most likely to come from the Sales Department. This is because many companies purchase cars for their salespeople. Cars would be considered a capital item to be depreciated over the useful life of the car, rather than as an expense. Furthermore, some companies operate company-owned branch offices and/or branch warehouses for which capital expenditures must be made for land, building, equipment, and major repairs. If the facilities are leased on a long-term basis rather than owned, the leases normally would be capitalized on the balance sheet.

The sales manager would be expected to explain the need for any capital items listed in the budget, although not in detail. Capital budgeting is used for cash flow planning purposes. Company managements normally would not approve or disapprove capital proposals until they are submitted with supporting data during the year. An unessential capital expenditure may be postponed if it appears the business will be short of cash when the expenditure would have to be made. Also, if the proposal is for a major amount of money, management will require extensive justification to accompany the proposal at the time of its submittal.

Consolidating Marketing Plans

After review and any needed adjustments by the marketing manager, the plans of the various units are consolidated into the marketing department plan. The marketing manager may prepare two plans: (1) a consolidated plan containing the detailed plan of each marketing department unit and (2) an abbreviated plan for submission to business unit management. The abbreviated plan would list the marketing department's objectives and strategies; proposed changes in organization, staffing, and budgets; and a summary of major programs.

| | Department _____ | | No. _____ |

Marketing Budget Worksheet

Account Title	Account No.	Next Year's Proposed Budget	This Year's Estimated Actual Expenses	Last Year's Actual Expenses
Payroll	101			
Fringe benefits	102			
Sales force incentives	103			
Direct mail advertising	201			
Magazines and newspapers	202			
Conventions, trade exhibits	203			
Radio and television	204			
Cooperative advertising	205			
Displays and posters	206			
Films	207			
Samples	208			
Selling aids	209			
Publicity	210			
Misc. promotion	211			
Travel and entertainment	301			
Fleet operating costs	302			
Freight	401			
Telephone and telegraph	501			
Supplies	502			
Consultantships	503			
Surveys	504			
Legal services	505			
Other professional services	506			
Outside clerical services	507			
Rentals	508			
Petty cash	509			
Contributions	510			
Dues and subscriptions	511			
Total expenses				
Number of employees				

FIGURE 12-4. Typical budget worksheet. *Source:* Jerome M. Minkin, "Developing the Market Budget," in Victor P. Buell, ed., *Handbook of Modern Marketing,* McGraw-Hill, New York, 1970, p.9-27.

The more detailed consolidated plan would be retained by the marketing manager for purposes of coordinating the various departmental programs and for measuring the progress of each unit against its goals.

THE EFFECTS OF MARKETING PLANS ON FINANCIAL STATEMENTS

Marketing management must understand how marketing strategies and tactics affect the financial statements. Marketing actions influence the financial statements directly in the form of income produced and marketing expenditures. They also influence the financial statements indirectly in terms of their effect on cost of sales (primarily production costs), the business unit's assets and liabilities, the need for borrowing, and—in the final analysis—the net value of the business. In view of the impact marketing actions have on the financial health of the business, it would be foolhardy for marketing management to recommend plans without recognizing their likely effect on the financial statements. The marketing manager cannot know their precise effects until the financial statements are prepared. Yet by being aware of how marketing plans influence financial statements, the marketing manager can make proposals that are most likely to produce favorable financial results.

Effect on Financial Statements of Flavor, Inc.

To illustrate we show the entries on Flavor's income statement, balance sheet, and cash flow statement that would be affected by the first-year program of the proposed marketing strategy.* The program called for a "picnic blitz"—a cents-off promotion on mustard and barbecue sauce during the outdoor picnic season—to be run in the 127 SMSA markets in which Flavor did not hold a leadership position.

Income Statement. Table 12-1 shows the estimated year end income (or profit and loss) statement of Flavor, Inc., before and after considering the effects of the

*Sales and costs used in the financial statements are from Flavor's tactical marketing planning worksheet, Table 11-1, pp. 264 and 265.

TABLE 12-1
Estimated Income Statement, Flavor, Inc. (Showing before and after effects of the proposed promotional program)

Entries	Without Promotion		With Promotion	
	$1000s (1)	% Gross Sales (2)	$1000s (3)	% Gross Sales (4)
1. Gross sales	50,000	100.0	52,000	100.0
2. Less: returns, allowances, discounts	2,000	4.0	2,300	4.4
3. Net sales	48,000	96.0	49,700	95.6
4. Cost of sales	30,000	60.0	30,680	59.0
5. Gross profit (margin)	18,000	36.0	19,020	36.6
6. Operating expenses				
(a) Marketing	8,000	16.0	8,544	16.4
(b) Administration	2,000	4.0	2,000	3.9
(c) R & D	750	1.5	750	1.4
(d) Engineering	750	1.5	750	1.4
7. Total operating expenses	11,500	23.0	12,044	23.1
8. Operating profit (margin)	6,500	13.0	6,976	13.5
9. Interest expense	2,000	4.0	2,040	3.9
10. Net profit before tax	4,500	9.0	4,936	9.6
11. Taxes	2,000	4.0	2,080	4.0
12. Net profit after tax	2,500	5.0	2,856	5.6

recommended marketing program. Columns (1) and (2) show the statement without the promotion; columns (3) and (4) show it after incorporating the promotion. The comments that follow are keyed by number to the numbered entries on the income statement.

Entry 1. Gross sales will increase by the $2 million in extra sales expected from the promotion, i.e., from $50 million to $52 million in annual sales.

Entry 2. Deductions from gross sales will rise by $300,000 which is the estimated cost of the cents-off discount.

Entry 3. Net sales will increase by approximately $1,700,000 ($2 million gross sales less $300,000 discount).

Entry 4. Cost of sales will increase due to the added production needed to supply the added sales. Average unit manufacturing costs should go down, however, because only variable costs will increase; fixed costs will not be affected by the production increase planned for this year. As average manufacturing costs go down, the cost of sales as a percent of gross sales will decline from 60 percent without the promotion to 59 percent with the promotion.

Entry 5. The gross profit margin will increase from the 36 to 36.6 percent because of the reduction in the percent of cost of sales.

Entry 6(a). Marketing expenses associated with the promotion will increase by $544,000, thereby raising total operating expenses (entry 7) from $11,500,000 to $12,044,000.

Entry 8. Operating profit will increase by $476,000 (entry 5 less entry 7).

Entry 9. Interest expense will rise by $40,000 due to the increase in bank loans required to finance the larger inventory and accounts receivable needed to support the additional sales.

Entries 10, 11, and 12. Net profit before tax will increase by $436,000 (entry 8 less entry 9) and net profit after tax will increase by $386,000 (entry 10 less entry 11).

To properly evaluate the profit impact of the promotion, more information is needed than just added sales income and marketing costs. Important additional information is provided by the income statement, namely, the effects of changes in cost of sales and the additional interest costs.

While the Flavor promotion affected only the marketing entry (6a) under operating expense, some types of marketing programs could effect other operating expenses such as administrative, R&D, or engineering.

Balance Sheet. Table 12-2 shows an estimated year end balance sheet for Flavor, Inc. before and after considering the influence of the picnic blitz promotion. Again, the comments that follow are keyed to the numbered entries.

Entry 3. Accounts receivable will rise by an estimated $1 million because higher sales will require that more credit be extended to the trade.

Entry 4. Inventory dollar value will rise by an estimated $800,000 for the added inventory needed to service the higher sales.

TABLE 12-2
Estimated Balance Sheet, Flavor, Inc. (Showing before and after effects of the proposed promotional program)

	Without Promotion, $1000s	With Promotion, $1000s
1. Assets		
2. Cash and marketable securities	765	765
3. Accounts receivable	6,118	7,118
4. Inventory	10,233	11,033
5. Total current assets	17,116	18,916
Fixed assets (land, buildings, machinery)	7,098	7,098
Allowance for depreciation	5,453	5,453
Net fixed assets	1,646	1,646
Other assets	3,675	3,675
6. Total assets	27,889	29,689
7. Liabilities and Capital		
(a) Accounts payable	6,171	6,876
(b) Accrued expenses	344	344
(c) Accrued taxes	939	939
8. Loans payable	2,536	3,275
9. Total current liabilities	9,990	11,434
10. Long-term debt	7,870	7,870
11. Stockholders equity		
(a) Common stock (par value)	2,470	2,470
(b) Retained earnings	7,559	7,915
12. Total stockholders equity	10,029	10,385
13. Total liabilities and capital	27,889	29,689

Entry 5. Total current assets will rise by $1,800,000 as the result of the increases in entries 3 and 4. Total assets will rise by the same amount (entry 6).

Entry 7(a). Accounts payable will rise by an estimated $705,000 because of the added raw materials and supplies needed to produce the additional units.

Entry 8. Loans payable will increase by $739,000 to help finance the larger inventories and accounts receivable.

Entry 9. Total current liabilities will rise by $1,444,000 due to the increases in entries 7(a) and 8.

Entry 11(b). Retained earnings will rise by the estimated increase in after tax net profits of $356,000. (From entry 12 of the Income Statement.) This will cause Stockholders Equity (entry 12) to rise by the same amount.

Although Flavor's current assets and liabilities will rise during the first year of the strategy, it is unlikely that long-term assets or liabilities will be affected immediately. As time goes on, however, and if the 5-year strategy is successful, other changes will occur in the balance sheet: (1) fixed assets will rise in the form of additions to plant and equipment needed to supply the increased order demand; (2) additional working capital will be needed to finance rising inventories and receivables; and, (3) because current earnings probably will not be sufficient to finance items (1) and (2) above, long-term debt in the form of borrowing will have to be raised or additional stock sold, thereby increasing total liabilities.

An increase in production and distribution facilities not only would affect the balance sheet but the income statement as well. The increase in fixed assets would raise unit production costs and thereby increase cost of sales as a percent of total sales.

Source and Application of Funds. Table 12-3 shows an estimated year end statement of cash flow before and after considering the effects of the proposed Flavor promotion.

Entry 2. Cash from net earnings will increase by the $356,000 added profits expected from the promotion (Table 12-1, entry 12).

Entry 4. Cash needed to finance inventory will require increased borrowing of $739,000 (Table 12-2, entry 8).

Entry 5. Total cash available will rise by $1,095,000 as a result of the effects of entries 2 and 4.

Entry 7. Additional cash in the amount of $739,000 will be used for payments on current loans (Table 12-2, entry 8).

Entry 9. Total uses of cash will rise by the $739,000 used for current loan payments.

Entry 10. The promotion would result in a better net cash balance at the end of the year—$270,000 compared to a negative $86,000 if there is no promotion.

TABLE 12-3

Forecast of Cash Flow, Flavor, Inc. (Showing before and after effects of the promotional program)

	Without Promotion, $1000s	With Promotion, $1000s
1. *Cash beginning of year*	700	700
Sources of cash		
2. Net earnings	2,500	2,856
3. Depreciation	1,000	1,000
4. Borrowings	500	1,239
5. Total cash available	4,700	5,795
Uses of cash		
6. Capital expenditures	1,000	1,000
7. Payments on debt	2,536	3,275
8. Dividends	1,250	1,250
9. Total uses of cash	4,786	5,525
10. *Cash at end of year*	(86)	270

Cash, of course, is needed to pay wages, bills, taxes, and interest when due and to maintain the company in a liquid condition. It is possible to have a profitable business on an accrual basis,* yet still not have sufficient cash when payments are due. Consequently, managing cash flow is an extremely important aspect of effective management. Although the year end statement provides an interesting summary, cash flow planning actually must be done as often as needed for a particular business. This may be as often as monthly, weekly, or even daily.

Managing cash flow is a responsiblity of financial management. It is of less immediate concern to the marketing manager than the income statement or balance sheet, unless there is a serious cash problem. If there is a need to conserve cash, for instance, it could place restrictions on marketing strategies or tactics that require expenditures prior to receipt of income—as most marketing expenditures do.

On the basis of the estimated results shown by the Income Statement, Balance Sheet, and Cash Flow Statement, the proposed "picnic blitz" promotion would likely be viewed favorably by management in terms of financial considerations.

Longer-Range Financial Forecasts

Until now we have concentrated on showing how annual marketing plans can be integrated with annual business plans. The annual plans have been used in order to illustrate the process of integration. From a practical standpoint, all functions *must* be integrated in the annual plan if the immediate goals are to be achieved.

We should remember that strategic marketing plans are longer-range in nature and require integration with the business planning over the period covered by the strategic plans. As one means of achieving this integration, companies involved in strategic planning require their business units to prepare proforma (estimated) financial statements covering periods beyond the next year. Some companies require these statements to be prepared for each year of the strategic plan, while others require them only at intervals of 3 or 5 years. The longer-range the plans, the more they must be based on assumptions about the future environment. Because of this uncertainty about future conditions, some managements believe that annual plans and statements beyond a year or two involve unnecessary work. They also feel that detailed annual proforma financial statements suggest a degree of certainty abut the future that is unwarranted. These managements find that periodic looks at the financial impact of strategies at longer intervals, such as every 5 years, are sufficient for longer-range strategic planning.

ESTIMATING THE FINANCIAL IMPACT OF MARKETING PLANS

The preparation of financial statements is a time-consuming function and requires information from all parts of the business unit. It is not practical, therefore, to prepare statements to determine the effects of each marketing strategy under consideration. Consequently, marketing management needs some shortcut methods for evaluating the financial impact of alternative plans.

---

*A standard accounting practice which accrues and allocates income and expenses to the period when they occur rather than when cash is actually received or paid out.

Essential Financial Data

For each proposed marketing strategy top management typically will want to look at the four pieces of financial information shown in Figure 12-5. If the amount of net profit, the return on sales (ROS), the amount of capital required, or the return on capital to be invested (ROI) does not meet management's goals or minimum standards, or sense of rightness, the strategy is likely to be rejected no matter how much it promises in the way of sales, market share, diversification, or other potentially desirable results. These four financial measures, of course, are not the only ones that managements are concerned with, but they do serve as key indicators.

ROI is the preferred means of measuring divisional performance among the majority of large corporations; a substantial minority, however, use ROS as a performance measure, either alone or in combination with ROI.[1] Proposed strategies would probably be evaluated in the same way.

Reasons for Management Interest. Management is interested in the total amount of net profit per year over the expected life of the strategy. The ratio of net profit to sales (ROS) is considered important by many managements although, viewed in isolation, ROS can be a potentially misleading index of performance. Different industries produce varying rates of return on sales in large part because different industries are able to generate different levels of output relative to the resources that they have to work with. What management looks for, therefore, is whether the new strategy promises ROS that ranks favorably with industry performance, and whether it is higher than the business unit's current performance.

Like ROS, the importance of the rate of profit return on capital investment (ROI) alone should not be overemphasized as an indicator of financial performance. Management will be interested in proposals that promise higher ROI than the current average for the business unit and ROI that ranks well above the industry average. Management will be interested also in the amount of capital required. Since no company has unlimited capital resources, it would prefer to apportion capital among alternate proposals on the basis of rate of return and spread of risk.

Evaluating the Key Financial Measures. Assuming that a strategy considers total profit and required capital for the business, management usually will look at both ROS and ROI. Together they indicate the rate that profit will accrue to the business and the productivity of the capital employed. Not all marketing strategies,

FIGURE 12-5. Important financial indicators.

Forecasts of	
Net profit	Net profit as a percentage of sales income (ROS)
Capital to be invested	Return (either net profit or net cash received) as a percentage of capital invested (ROI)

of course, require new capital investment, in which case management will consider primarily total profit and ROS.

Let us now examine briefly how the marketing planning team might develop estimates of net profit, ROS, capital investment requirements, and ROI. These financial forecasts need be prepared only for those strategic alternatives that have not been ruled out for other reasons during the screening process. In Chapter 10, for example, we saw that several of the alternative strategies Hanes was considering were rejected for other than financial reasons. Two were rejected because of their possible adverse effect on the company's standing with wholesalers and retailers; foreign expansion was rejected because of inadequate information and experience.

Computing Net Profit and ROS

The formula for obtaining net profit before income taxes is

$$\text{Sales income less total costs} = \text{net profit before taxes}$$

Estimating sales and costs is relatively uncomplicated when marketing strategies deal with increasing sales and profits from present products sold into present markets (Option 1 of the opportunity grid). But estimates become more complicated when strategies involve the other options: new products in present markets, present products in new markets, or new products in new markets. Estimates for Option 1 can be based on company experience, whereas the other options involve one or more elements with which the company has had no experience.

Even in the areas of limited experience, however, reasonably accurate estimates can be made with the help of marketing research and assistance from production, engineering, and financial personnel. These rough estimates should be accurate enough to rule out financial misfits during the screening process. Before strategies are recommended for final adoption, however, they should be subjected to more sophisticated estimating procedures. Figure 12-6 diagrams the process for narrowing down to the best strategies by means of increasingly rigorous forecasts of sales, costs, investments, and financial performance.

Estimating Costs. Costs fall into three categories: operating expenses, interest expense, and production costs. As shown in Table 12-1, *operating expenses* are incurred by functions such as marketing, administration, R&D, and engineering. Marketing planners can estimate marketing expenses. Other operating expenses can be estimated by the appropriate department.

Interest expense will be primarily for the short-term loans needed to finance accounts receivable and inventory. The amount of borrowed funds needed can be estimated from company experience ratios of (1) accounts receivable to sales and (2) inventories to sales. The finance department will know the current and forecasted interest rates.

Production Costs. Estimating production costs will require input from production and accounting personnel. These estimates are fairly simple to make if the new sales are for current or similar products. Also, if there is unused plant and machinery capacity, production costs will be affected favorably by the added volume. This is because *fixed costs*, such as supervision, heat, light, and depreciation, probably will

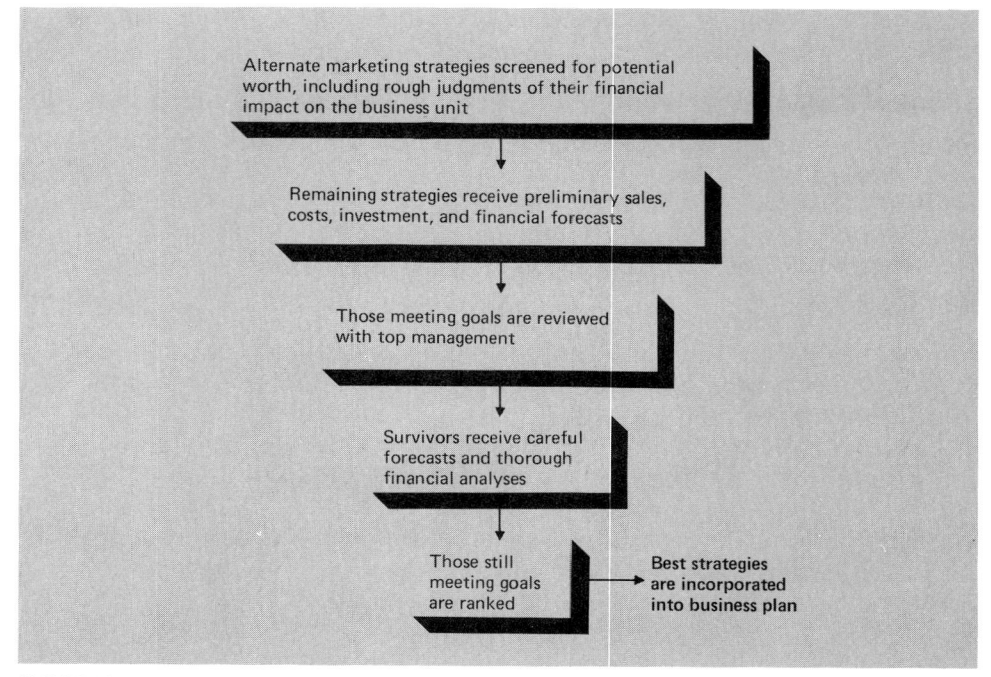

FIGURE 12-6. Screening process for alternate marketing strategies.

not rise; only the variable costs, such as direct labor and materials, will rise in relation to the additional units produced. As volume and capacity utilization rise, therefore, cost per unit generally will go down. This can be illustrated with the data from Figure 12-7 where the fixed cost is $40.00 and the variable cost per unit is 30 cents. As calculated below, the cost of one unit, for example, would be $40.30 while the cost for the 100th unit would be only 70 cents.

Cost for 1 unit:
$40.00 fixed cost + $.30 variable cost ÷ 1 = $40.30

Cost for the 100th unit:
$40.00 fixed costs + $30.00 variable costs ÷ 100 = $.70

Charging Strategy with Total or Variable Costs. When added volume results only in a rise in variable costs, there are two ways to evaluate the profit contribution of the proposed strategy. One is to charge the strategy with the *full production costs* (variable cost plus a share of fixed costs); the other is to charge it with only the *incremental* (i.e., variable) *costs.*

Preferably, a strategy should meet its profit goals after charging it with full production costs. Even if this is not possible, however, the strategy should not be rejected out of hand unless there is a better use for the excess capacity. The income from the added units will increase the gross profit margin for the business unit. And net profit will increase also, as long as the added gross profit exceeds the variable operating and interest costs chargeable to the added units.

This can be seen for the Flavor "picnic blitz" promotion in Table 12-1 which shows the before and after comparative Income Statement. The added gross profit

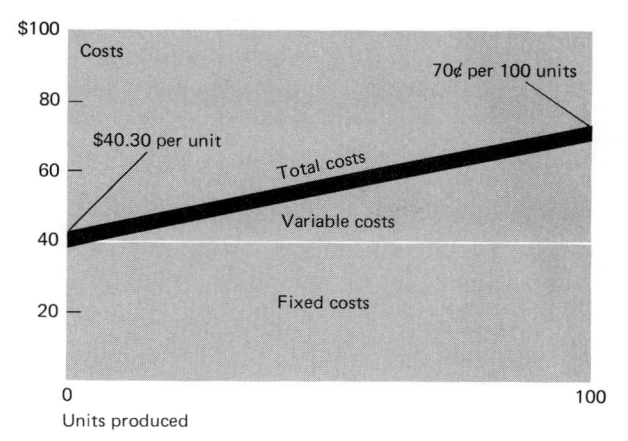

FIGURE 12-7. Fixed costs become a smaller proportion of total costs as units produced increase.

from the promotion is $1,020,000 (entry 5). When the added marketing expense of $544,000 (entry 6a) and the added interest expense of $40,000 (entry 9) are subtracted from the added gross profit, the result is an increase in net profit before taxes of $436,000 (entry 10).

Caution should be exercised, however, in estimating whether and when sales from the new strategy will increase to the point where plant capacity is fully utilized. As plant capacity is approached, manufacturing operations become less efficient and variable unit costs rise. More importantly, when plant capacity is realized, capital will have to be invested in additional fixed assets in the form of new plant and equipment. When this happens, the added sales will be charged with full costs (variable and fixed), thereby lowering the average profit return for the strategy.

Estimating ROS. When the sales forecasts and cost estimates have been made and net profit determined, ROS is computed as follows:

$$\frac{\text{Net profit}}{\text{Sales income}} = \% \text{ ROS}$$

For example, for a net profit of $10,000 and sales income of $100,000:

$$\text{ROS} = \frac{10,000}{100,000} = 10\%$$

ROS should be computed for each year of the strategic planning period and an average taken for the period. It is well to look at the average, since the rate will vary over the years. Typically, ROS will be at a negative or low rate in the early months or years when sales are low and market development costs are high; the rate rises as the strategy succeeds; and sooner or later, it lowers as the market environment becomes less friendly. A typical ROS curve is shown in Figure 12-8. It should be noted, however, that the curve can vary according to the internal and external variables affecting each strategy. Since the curve will hardly ever be flat, it is useful to look at the average expected rate of return when evaluating a proposed strategy.

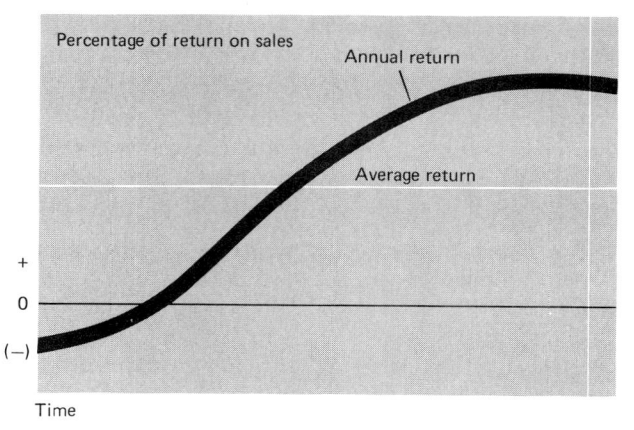

FIGURE 12-8. Profitability curve of a successful strategy measured as rate of return on sales.

Capital Needs and ROI

Capital investment refers to those major projects that require capital for fixed assets (e.g., land, buildings, machinery) plus the operating capital (cash, accounts receivable, inventory) needed to make the fixed assets productive.

Current earnings are rarely sufficient to fund major capital investments. Similarly, the earnings from the capital investments themselves are seldom sufficient since they are not received in time to provide the initial capital needed. Capital is required early to pay for fixed assets, whereas earnings develop later as the assets are used to produce income. Usually, therefore, at least a portion of the needed capital must be obtained from equity issues (such as the sale of additional company stock) or—more commonly from long-term loans.

Strategies requiring capital investment—although essential if a company is to grow—involve the type of risk inherent in any commitment made for the longer-term, uncertain future. Top management, therefore, examines strategies requiring capital investment more closely than those which require only short-term financing.

There are two principal approaches to computing ROI. The traditional method still used by many companies is the average rate of return approach. The newer approach is the discounted cash flow approach. We will examine briefly these two approaches.

Average Rate of Return. In this approach the average annual investment and the average annual net profit are compared over the expected life of the strategy. The formula is

$$\frac{\text{Average annual net profit}}{\text{Average annual investment}} = \% \text{ ROI}$$

For example, for an average annual net profit of $20,000 and an average annual investment of $100,000:

$$\text{ROI} = \frac{20,000}{100,000} = 20\%$$

Management would compare the expected ROI against the business unit's current ROI or the unit's ROI objectives. It would also compare expected return against the cost of capital, particularly in times of high interest rates. For a strategy to be attractive to management it would have to indicate a rate of return in excess of the minimum rate designated by management. Financially speaking, strategies with the highest expected rates of return over the designated minimums would be the most favored strategic alternatives.

Discounted Cash Flow. There are two principal arguments offered by those who favor the discounted cash flow approach over the average rate of return approach. The first argument is that it is more realistic to measure the rate of return on net cash received than on net profit. Real cash can be put to use, whereas net profit is an accounting figure that does not necessarily represent cash in hand.

The second argument has to do with the time value of money. It is argued that a dollar earned in the future is worth less than a dollar earned today. This is due to the *lost opportunity cost* of the earnings that could have been derived from today's dollar (assuming it had been invested in interest-bearing instruments). Since a capital investment requires cash to be invested today, the future cash flow from the investment—so the argument goes—should be discounted by the amount of lost opportunity costs. The net result is that a discount approach will show a lower rate of return than a nondiscount approach such as average rate of return. This, in turn, is thought to encourage a more realistic look at the expected return vis-à-vis the cost of capital and to encourage the search for alternate uses of capital.

The degree of risk represents another consideration of management when ranking strategies requiring capital investment. If higher risk projects are adopted, it is usually because they promise higher payoffs; yet higher risk projects usually entail paying higher rates for the borrowed capital. One way of neutralizing the effect of risk when ranking capital proposals is to discount the expected cash flow of each by a *risk-adjusted rate*, i.e., the expected cash flow of one project versus another, knowing that each has been adjusted for its relative cost of risk capital.

Importance of Forecasts. Irrespective of the approach used to measure ROI, the idea is to select those strategies which will (1) meet or exceed the business unit's goals and (2) improve the unit's rate of return on capital employed after considering the degree of risk acceptable to management. None of the financial analyses, however, is any better than the forecasts cranked into the calculations. Obtaining accurate forecasts of sales, costs, and capital required is considerably more difficult than making ROI calculations.

Of the several forecasts needed none involves more uncertainties than the sales forecasts because of the uncontrollable and often unpredictable variables of the external environment. The study of hundreds of capital investment proposals over the years shows that estimates of fixed assets and operating capital are relatively accurate, even though they often fail to allow enough leeway for inflation and construction delays. In constructing these figures engineers and cost accountants are dealing with what is largely factual data. Actual costs are known or can be obtained for items such as land, buildings, machinery, inventories, and accounts receivable. Clearly many capital projects do not attain their forecast ROIs. Post audits have shown the most common cause of failure to be that sales income did not reach the forecasted level. Responsibility for the financial soundness of marketing strategies involving capital investment, therefore, rests largely with marketing management.

Understanding Finance

There is a need for marketing managers who understand finance and other business functions, and who understand how to develop marketing plans that integrate well with the business plan. This does not mean that the marketing manager must be a skilled financial analyst since financial experts can be hired for the marketing staff or borrowed from the finance department during planning periods. However, the marketing manager who can think in financial as well as marketing terms will produce the more profitable marketing strategies.

SUMMARY

The present chapter has shown how the tactical programs are incorporated into the annual marketing department plan and how the department plan is integrated with the annual business plan. This was followed by two sections on the financial aspects of marketing planning. The first illustrated how strategies affect the key accounting statements of the business unit: income, balance sheet, and cash flow.

Although proforma accounting statements provide estimates of the financial effects of marketing strategies, for time and cost reasons it is not feasible to prepare statements for each marketing strategy considered during the planning process. Therefore, we showed how the marketing planning team can screen alternative strategies using rough estimates of key financial indicators, namely, profit as a return on sales and profit as a return on investment. After the list of strategies is narrowed, more refined financial analyses can be used to evaluate the remaining ones. The best strategies are selected and integrated into the business unit strategy.

Skill in using the planning approach will improve as you acquire marketing knowledge and experience. By following an approach, such as the one presented in Chapters 9 through 12, you are more likely to come up with useful ideas and avoid the superficial solutions that often result from disorganized approaches.

Planning is hard work. People experiencing planning for the first time usually are surprised at the amount of work involved, the amount of information to be gathered, the depth of analysis required, and the give-and-take discussions that are part and parcel of marketing planning. But the rewards can be large for the company and highly satisfying for the people involved.

In Chapter 13 we will review the decisions made in the Hanes planning process and see what effects they had on the company's market and financial positions.

QUESTIONS

1. What makes up the annual marketing plan?
2. Who has the responsibility of bringing together the plans of the functional departments? What happens after the various plans are brought together?
3. What units provide the inputs to the marketing department plan?
4. What are the components of the departmental plans format?

5. How do marketing strategies and tactics affect the business's financial statements?
6. How are the strategic marketing plans integrated with the business planning over the period covered by the strategic plans?
7. What are the four important pieces of financial information for each strategy that top management will typically want to see?

REFERENCES

1. See, for example, a report of a study among the *Fortune* 1000: James S. Reece and William R. Cool, "Measuring Investment Center Performance," *Harvard Business Review*, May–June 1978, particularly exhibits I, p. 29, and XIII, p. 46. This study also discusses other measures of performance being used and the variety of investment bases used by different companies to compute divisional ROI.

CHAPTER 13

Strategic Marketing Case Summary

Beginning in Chapter 9 we described the Hanes situation in 1969, when management was beginning its strategic planning. In Chapters 10 and 11 we told how Hanes went about developing its strategic and tactical plans. We now report what actually happened between 1970 and 1973, the period covered by the plan.

Hanes, in fact, did introduce a new advertised brand into food and drug stores in late 1970. But before describing how this was done, we'll look at how industry conditions changed and how Hanes' sales and financial performance improved.

Industry Conditions

Industry factory shipments of hosiery fell off sooner and more precipitously than had been forecast in the *situation analysis*. This can be seen in Table 13-1 and Figure 13-1. Industry shipments peaked in 1969 as did the miniskirt fashion. The cyclical shift to longer skirt lengths began in 1970, 1 year before the forecast, and long pants for women became popular as well.

Hosiery shipments dropped mainly because of the shift away from short skirts, since other factors affecting hosiery demand remained positive; for example, disposable personal income grew to an average annual rate of 9.3 percent, while growth in GNP remained strong and the numbers of women in the 18 to 49 age bracket increased at the average rate of 1.9 million per year.

Table 13-2 shows how pantyhose continued to grow at the expense of regular

TABLE 13-1
Industry Shipments of Women's Hosiery

Year	Millions of Dozen Pairs	% Change
1966	101.6	
1967	116.4	14.5
1968	123.4	6.0
1969	133.1	7.9
1970	116.6	(12.4)
1971	96.2	(17.5)
1972	104.6	8.7
1973	100.5	(3.9)

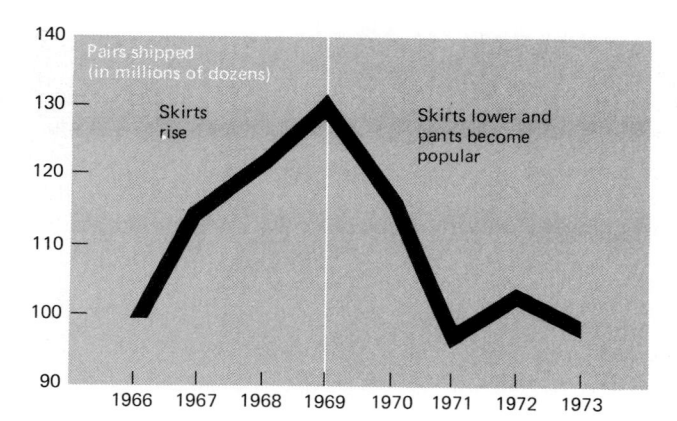

FIGURE 13-1. Industry shipments of women's hosiery, 1966-1973, suggesting relationship with shirt fashion cycle.

hosiery. By 1973, however, sheer knee-high hosiery and anklets, responding to the popularity of pants, were beginning to take share from pantyhose, a trend that continued. By 1973, food and drug stores were accounting for about 26 percent of all industry unit sales, up from 18 percent in 1969.

Company Performance

Sales and Profit Objectives. By 1973 Hanes had attained its profit objective of $9.3 million after taxes. Sales were slightly under objective, but this condition was offset by higher margins than forecast.

The performance record from 1966 through 1973 is shown in Table 13-3. As expected, the costs of implementing the new strategy caused after tax profit to decline in 1971. The positive effects of the new strategy became apparent in 1972 and 1973 when sales and earnings rose dramatically. Gross profit rose from 20.8 percent in 1969 to 38.4 percent in 1973, reflecting a relative drop in manufacturing cost due to higher volume, improved cost control, and replacement of some low margin private brand business with the higher margin newly advertised brand.

Market Share Objective. Hanes' share of the hosiery industry rose to 20 percent in 1973, almost double the objective of 10.4 percent. Hanes' total dollar sales rose by 75 percent between 1969 and 1973, while industry unit shipments were declining by 25 percent.*

*It should be noted that we are not comparing precisely the same things when we compare company dollar sales and industry units. Nevertheless, as Hanes' sales grew and industry sales fell, Hanes' market share improved.

TABLE 13-2
Percent of Hosiery Production by Type

	1967	1968	1969	1970	1971	1972	1973
Stockings (regular length)	100	86.1	54.0	29.1	28.9	16.7	15.6
Pantyhose		13.9	46.0	70.8	68.9	78.8	75.1
Sheer knee-highs and anklets				0.1	2.2	4.5	9.3

TABLE 13-3
Company Performance

Year	Sales, $ millions	% Market Share	% Gross Profit	Profit after Tax, $ millions	% ROS
1966	121	5		9.3	7.7
1967	131	5	22.7	7.6	5.8
1968	145	6	25.0	8.1	5.6
1969	157	6	20.8	4.1	2.6
1970	177	NA	23.1	4.5*	2.5
1971	176	10	26.5	3.5	2.0
1972	245	NA	34.2	8.2	3.4
1973	276	20	38.4	9.4	3.4

*Before extraordinary credit of $1.2 million.

Hanes' new brand alone accounted for 10.5 percent of total industry sales and 30 percent of all hosiery sold through food and drug channels. While the new brand had a major impact on Hanes' total industry share, the company's share of department and specialty store sales also increased. Hanes' regular brands sold in department and specialty stores now accounted for 6.5 percent of industry sales, suggesting that Hanes maintained efforts in the old channels with its regular brands, while pursuing its new strategy in food and drug stores.

Diversification. Hanes had also begun a diversification program in 1969 by acquiring a 42 percent interest in the Bali Company, Inc., makers of swim wear and foundation garments. The remaining 58 percent was acquired on December 31, 1971, through an exchange of stock. The Pine State Knitting Co., makers of men's sweaters, was also acquired in 1969. The proportion of sales by major product lines in 1973 is shown in Table 13-4.

Change in Financial Condition. In addition to substantial improvements in sales and profits following the low period 1969–1971, Hanes also ended 1973 with a strong balance sheet. Table 13-5 presents the balance sheet for the years 1973 and 1968 (the last high profit year before the severe drop in profits in 1969).

Table 13-6 presents several financial comparisons between 1968 and 1973.

TABLE 13-4
Hanes Sales By Product Group—1973

Product Group	Sales, $ millions	% of Total
Women's hosiery	173	63
Knitwear products	70	25
Foundation garments	30	11
Other products	3	1
Total	276	100

TABLE 13-5
Consolidated Balance Sheets as of Dec. 31, 1968, and 1973
(In thousands of dollars)

	1968	1973
Assets		
Cash	4,699	4,043
Receivables, net	22,157	35,314
Inventories	34,790	69,504
Prepayments		419
Total current	61,646	109,280
Net property, etc.	50,206	61,662
Investments and advances to subsidiaries	582	1,047
Deferred charges, etc.	748	
Excess acquisition cost		15,067
Total assets	113,182	187,056
Liabilities		
Notes payable	19,875	86
Accounts payable	4,540	14,225
Income taxes	1,736	2,736
Accruals	5,106	9,948
Total current	31,257	26,995
Long-term debt	3,125	54,959
Deferred compensation	1,127	1,237
Deferred income tax	5,910	5,776
Common stock ($1)	4,510	4,292
Paid-in surplus	3,842	10,768
Retained earnings	70,862	84,062
Reacquired stock	(7,451)	(1,033)
Total liabilities	113,182	187,056

Significant increases had been made in net assets and in stockholders' equity. Improvements had occurred in equity per common share, the current ratio, and in turnover of receivables. Seemingly less favorable comparisons showed up in the form of declines in return on equity, debt to equity ratio, and inventory turnover.

If we compare the 1973 return on equity with 1969 instead of with 1968, however, we see that the percentage was actually improving and that the trend was in the right direction:

Year	% Return on Equity	Year	% Return on Equity
1968	11.3	1971	4.0
1969	5.7	1972	8.9
1970	5.8	1973	9.6

The increase in the debt to equity ratio was due to the increase in long-term debt from $3 million to $55 million (see balance sheets, Table 13-5). Current liabilities actually were lower in 1973 than in 1968 as short-term notes were converted to

TABLE 13-6
Comparisons of Financial Data for 1968 and 1973

Item	1968	1973
Net current assets, $1000s	$30,389	$82,285
Net stockholders equity, $1000s	$71,763	$98,089
% Return on equity	11.3%	9.6%
Equity per common share	$18.91	$23.43
Debt to stockholders equity ratio	0.47:1	0.84:1
Current ratio	2:1	4:1
Receivables turnover (times yearly)	6.6	7.8
Inventory turnover (times yearly)	2.9	2.4

DEFINITIONS

Net current assets (or working capital): Current assets less current liabilities

Net stockholders equity: Common stock + paid-in surplus (capital) + retained earnings (−) reacquired stock

% Return on equity: Net earnings (exclusive of extraordinary items) ÷ stockholders equity

Equity per common share: Net stockholders equity ÷ number of common shares outstanding

Debt to stockholders equity ratio: Current liabilities + long-term debt ÷ stockholders equity

Current ratio: Current assets ÷ current liabilities

Receivables turnover: Annual sales ÷ year-end net trade accounts receivable

Inventory turnover: Cost of goods sold ÷ average inventory

---

long-term debt. The rise in long-term borrowing was necessary, of course, to finance the larger inventories required to support the expanded sales and to provide the capital for manufacturing expansion and the new direct distribution facilities. The 1973 ratio of 0.84:1, shown in Table 13-6, does not appear out of line for a rapidly expanding hosiery manufacturer.

The unfavorable drop in inventory turns from 2.9 to 2.4 times per year appears to have been caused by the expansion of brands and the shift to direct distribution, including store inventories on consignment. With the exception of inventory turnover, Hanes' financial ratios were as good as or better than other women's hosiery manufacturers.

Tactical Programs Adopted

Product. Hanes selected the new superstretch hose as the product with which to enter food and drug distribution.

The brand name selected was L'eggs—a highly creative choice. L'eggs suggests the product (hosiery covers legs) and ties in with the egg-shaped plastic package. The unique name and package combined with the distinctive new superstretch product created immediate product differentiation. Certainly, L'eggs could not be confused with any other brand.

An egg-shaped display was adopted. It combined height with small diameter (2 feet) and held 288 pairs of hosiery. It also showed the hosiery colors which were keyed to color names on the package, because the hosiery could not be seen through the opaque package. The rack, which Hanes called the L'eggs Boutique, featured the brand name and provided space for sales messages. It is shown in Figure 13-2.

Hanes initially introduced L'eggs in the one size which fit 75 percent of all women. The only variations in inventory stocked, therefore, were for purposes of offering various colors. Later L'eggs Queensize was introduced. Note that Hanes did not designate its larger product as "outsize" or "extra-large" as some companies did.

Price. A price of $1.39 was selected after test marketing. Though considerably higher than chain store brands, the $1.39 price proved to be no obstacle to sales when backed up by introductory promotions and heavy advertising featuring the product's benefits. After 6 months L'eggs was the leading brand in each test market where it was the regular brand worn by 25 percent of the women.

The trade discount was set at 35 percent with Hanes providing direct delivery and floor stocking and inventory placed on consignment. The 35 percent discount was attractive to self-service stores accustomed to operating on low margins; furthermore, Hanes assumed all of the delivery, display stocking, and inventory carrying costs, costs which are assumed by the channels in normal wholesale/retail distribution.

Distribution. Deliveries were made in L'eggs vans (also shown in Figure 13-2) by specially trained, attractively dressed women who wore colorful uniforms. Despite the higher costs of this method of distribution, it provided a high degree of company control over sales at the retail trade level, maintenance of retail stocks, positioning of the display rack, price maintenance, and retail promotions. Hanes retained ownership of the display racks. It placed inventory in the store on consignment which meant that the inventory belonged to Hanes until it was sold by the retailer. The retailer was not billed for the product until after it was sold.

FIGURE 13-2. (left) L'eggs store display and (right) a sales representative making a store delivery. Source: Courtesy of Hanes Corporation.

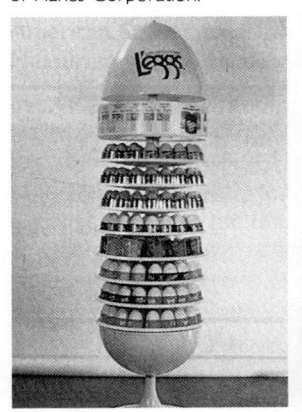

The product was shipped directly from the factory to field warehouse points which supplied the delivery vans. By the end of 1973 Hanes used 41 leased service distribution warehouses at various locations throughout the country. This distribution method offered advantages few retailers could resist. No doubt it contributed to Hanes' success in breaking into food and drug channels where the retailer initially might be reluctant to give space to a product that would compete with the store's own brand.

Sales. By the end of 1973 the L'eggs brand was available in 90 percent of the United States and displayed in some 70,000 stores. Sales of L'eggs products at retail increased from $8.8 million in 1970 to $162 million in 1973.

The sales force consisted of approximately 700 route sales representatives and administrative personnel. Sales to chain buying offices were made by national sales representatives and regional sales managers. Route sales representatives made sales calls on retail stores and delivered the product as well. The L'eggs sales organization chart is shown in Figure 13-3.

While we do not have the selling expense for L'eggs alone, Table 13-7 shows the change in selling and administrative expense for the company between 1969 and 1973, both in total and as a percent of net sales. Sales and administrative expense rose significantly from $14.6 million in 1969 to $45.2 million in 1973. Sales and administrative expense as a percent of net sales rose for the comparable years from 9.3 to 16.3 percent reflecting, no doubt, the increased cost of direct to store delivery and in-store service.

Advertising. As shown in Table 13-8, total company advertising expense rose

FIGURE 13-3. L'eggs sales organization.

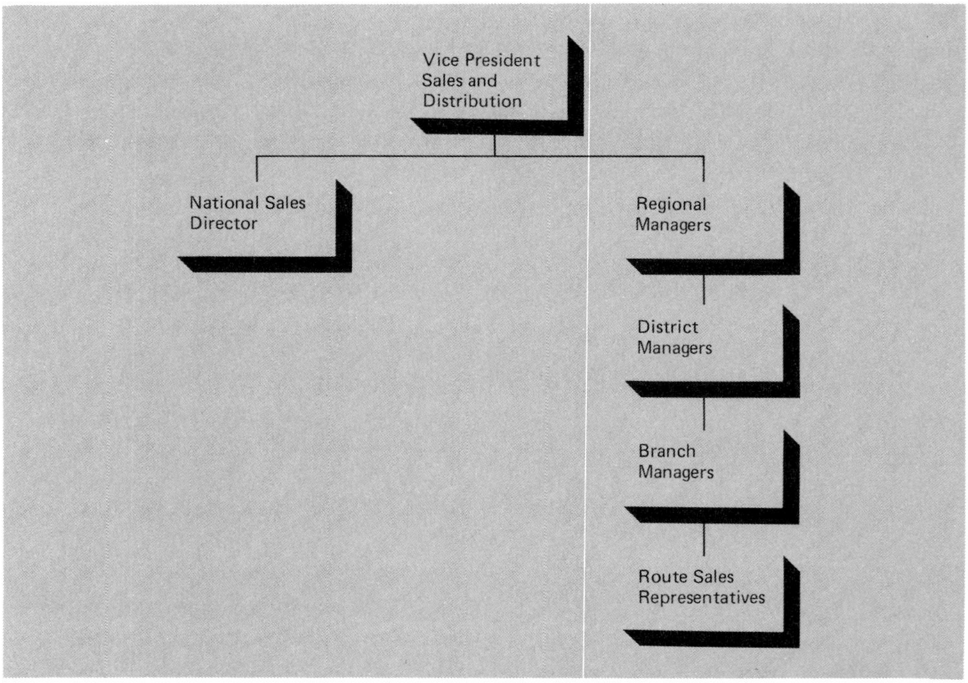

TABLE 13-7
Hanes Sales and Administrative Expense as Percent of Net Sales after Tax

Year	Sales and Administrative Expense, $ millions	As % of Net Sales
1969	14.6	9.3
1970	17.0	9.6
1971	21.1	11.9
1972	37.5	15.3
1973	45.2	16.3

from $7.3 million in 1969 to $40.6 million in 1973. L'eggs accounted for a little over half of this expenditure in 1973. All major media were used, although network and spot TV accounted for about 70 percent of the expenditures in measured media. Not only did total company advertising expense rise, but advertising expense as a percent of net sales also increased from 4.6 percent in 1969 to 14.7 percent in 1973, indicating the importance of advertising in the marketing mix for L'eggs and other Hanes brands.

L'eggs advertising positioned the product as the better fitting hose. "Our L'eggs Fit Your Legs" was the advertising theme with copy stressing the fit and beauty of L'eggs hosiery. The theme was also applied to promotional materials, display boutiques, and delivery van identification.

Market research revealed that brand awareness reached an amazing 80 percent in test markets within 2 months of introduction. The word L'eggs, cast in its distinctive lettering form, was registered as the brand trademark.

Sales Promotion. An introductory deal using direct mail coupons worth 35 cents off the regular $1.39 price was used for the first 13 weeks of the L'eggs introduction into a new market. Other types of promotions were run several times a year.

Publicity. A public relations firm was engaged to generate publicity for the L'eggs program. This activity consisted of placing articles in newspapers and

TABLE 13-8
Hanes Advertising Expense as Percent of Net Sales after Tax

Year	Advertising Expense, $ millions	As % of Net Sales
1969	7.3	4.6
1970	10.6	6.0
1971	15.0	8.5
1972	28.4	11.6
1973	40.6	14.7

magazines about L'eggs pantyhose, the route sales representatives, and how the egg-shaped package could be used in handicraft projects.

Service. A computerized inventory and information system was designed and installed with the aid of a consulting firm. The system was keyed to a very basic information source—the reports of inventory sold from store displays between calls by L'eggs delivery/sales personnel. These reports provided the information needed to plan manufacturing schedules and inventories for the factory, field warehouses, and individual van routes.

From the manufacturer's point of view, direct delivery plus the computerized inventory control system overcame one of the drawbacks of wholesaler/chain warehouse distribution, because it provided store inventory and stock movement rates on a frequent and regular basis. Such information is difficult for a manufacturer to obtain using distribution systems other than company-owned retail outlets. Although market research studies reporting sales and inventory can be purchased for certain types of convenience goods, they are not as precise or as frequently reported as the data provided by the L'eggs system.

Better control of warehouse and inventory costs of the L'eggs system to some extent served to offset the higher costs of direct distribution. Furthermore, well maintained floor inventories with few stockouts at the store level contributed to the increase in sales. The L'eggs computerized system also provided the inputs for billing and accounts receivable purposes and provided additional information for continuous market analyses.

Competitive Reactions

By 1971 Hanes' two major competitors, Kayser-Roth Corporation and Burlington Industries, had entered food and drug store distribution. Each attempted to differentiate its brand from L'eggs.

Kayser-Roth featured quality at a lower price—99 cents compared to L'eggs $1.39. Advertising for its No-Nonsense brand stressed the product's quality features, while emphasizing that its lower price was possible because of its no-nonsense approach to packaging and distribution. No-Nonsense hosiery was packaged in bright orange plastic pouches which were displayed on bright orange racks. It was distributed through chain warehouses and carried a trade discount of 42 percent plus inventory allowances.

Burlington copied the L'eggs pattern by introducing its Activ brand into supermarkets with direct store delivery provided by "Activ Girls" who stocked Activ retail displays. Activ differentiated its brand by using bright red for its packaging, delivery vans, and uniforms, and also by pricing at $1.00. Like Hanes, it offered a 35 percent discount to retailers. Burlington, however, went a step further. Activ distribution was expanded into tobacco channels (such as tobacco stores and magazine stands) by using the distribution facilities of the General Cigar Co.

Hanes' Response. Hanes responded to these competitive moves in three principal ways: (1) it continued strong advertising, promotion, and distribution efforts for L'eggs, (2) it maintained the $1.39 fair trade price, and (3) it market tested a new brand called First to Last for food and drug outlets at a retail price of 99 cents. The new, cheaper brand was market tested in 1971 and introduced into selected markets in 1972.

OBSERVATIONS ON HANES' STRATEGIES AND TACTICS

In view of the outlook for the women's hosiery industry Hanes' management can be credited with having made very bold strategic and tactical decisions in 1969. Yet it also took precautions to reduce the degree of risk and to hedge its bets.

High-Risk Strategy

The decision to try to increase sales and market share in a static industry about to enter the downside of its fashion cycle was highly risky.

Hanes could expect strong competitive reaction, with the possibility of price cutting. The advertised brands segment of the hosiery industry consisted primarily of six companies, several of which were larger and more diversified than Hanes. Hence, one might expect a strong reaction by competitors to prevent declines in their own market shares. And, of course, that is what happened.

Kayser-Roth and Burlington followed Hanes' lead into food and drug channels and did so with lower prices than Hanes. To the credit of Hanes' management it did not immediately follow its competitors' prices; rather, it continued to hold its price while concentrating on a marketing mix composed of product, packaging, advertising, sales promotion, and distribution.

High-Risk Tactics

If Hanes' strategy was risky so were its tactics. In the implementation of its strategy Hanes broke with several industry patterns:

Product: Innovated with a one-size, stretch hose.

Packaging: Used an opaque, sealed, plastic carton which did not show the product, or color, or permit handling of the product.

Display: Developed free-standing aisle display unit designed for the company's product only.

Promotion: Offered cents-off deals.

Advertising: Spent much more heavily than had been the past industry practice.

Distribution: Used direct-to-store delivery, stocked floor displays, and placed inventory on consignment.

Hanes' preresearch of consumers and retailers, plus the fact that the tactics were largely borrowed from successful practices of other convenience goods industries, may have cushioned the risk. But any break with standard patterns means a chance of failure as well as success.

Perhaps the greatest financial risk was taken with the decision to go to direct delivery because of the capital investment and/or capitalized leases required for warehouses, equipment, and delivery vans. Ownership of or leases for facilities and equipment involve long-term commitments that are costly to withdraw from if such action becomes necessary. Wholesale and chain warehouse distribution, by contrast, can be cut back fairly quickly.

Balancing Off the Risks

Although the strategy and tactics involved risks, Hanes' decision could hardly be called foolhardy for several reasons.

Good Informational Base. In the first place the decisions were made using a base of excellent information. Hanes was willing to spend the money necessary for thorough marketing research, ranging from purchase of market reporting services—such as those provided by A. C. Nielson and Market Research Corporation of America—to private market studies. Hanes reportedly spent $400,000 for market studies prior to the L'eggs decision. Consequently, it had detailed knowledge of the industry, the trade, the competition, and the consumer before devising strategies and tactics.

Market Tests. Secondly, Hanes market tested its strategy and tactics before making the decision to roll out. When it did roll, Hanes followed a market-by-market approach. This approach may have been Hanes' only alternative once the decision was made to deliver direct.

The market-by-market approach was slow, but also had advantages. First, improvements could be made for each new market introduction on the basis of previous experience. Second, the progressive approach strung out the investments required for the direct delivery system. Each new increment of investment could be evaluated in terms of the results of the previous investments. Hence, Hanes could speed up, slow down, or cease its new market investments accordingly.

Packaged Goods Experience. As a third means of risk reduction, Hanes brought into the company marketing executives with successful experience in marketing convenience-packaged goods through self-service food and drug channels. They also engaged consultants. While the strategies and tactics were innovations in the apparel industry, they were devised and executed under the direction of people who knew how to use these methods.

It is interesting to note that prior to 1969 Hanes' chairman and board of directors had hired a new president from a packaged food company that sold and distributed direct to retail stores. Apparently, top management had foreseen the need for infusion of experience from outside the apparel industry.

Support of Other Businesses. Finally, Hanes hedged its bets by continuing to work to improve its other businesses while it pursued its new strategy. It actually strengthened its competitive hosiery position in department and specialty stores. It maintained its position in men's and boys' underwear and continued to produce private hosiery brands. And it diversified into the foundation garment business. Had its new strategy failed, Hanes would have been forced to write off losses resulting from disposal of inventory and equipment, yet undoubtedly could have survived with enough financial strength to pursue other strategies.

Summary

The soundness of Hanes' new strategy and tactics is apparent from the market and financial results achieved by 1973. In retrospect the decisions made in 1969 seem quite logical. But these decisions were not easily made at the time, and management must have experienced periods of doubt during the first few months following the basic strategic decision.

There have been several write-ups of the Hanes experience. Most have stressed the highly creative decisions embodied in the L'eggs name, the packaging, the advertising, and the direct distribution to stores by attractive young women. We emphasize, however, that these more obvious aspects of Hanes' actions were *tactical* decisions that would not have been made except for the basic *strategic* decisions which preceded them. If courage was displayed by Hanes' management (as many industry observers think), it was in the decision to choose the higher risk strategy from among the several alternatives available.

ADDENDUM: THE HOSIERY INDUSTRY AND HANES' POSITION IN 1977

We now report on developments during the 4 years following 1973 and ask whether Hanes' business purpose, objectives, and strategies required change as a result of the new conditions existing in 1977.

Hosiery Industry Situation

Industry shipments continued flat with no indication of returning to the level of the peak year of 1969 when 133.1 million dozen pairs were shipped. (See Table 13-9a.)

Food and drug stores together had become the leading outlets for hosiery sales when measured in units, although department and specialty stores combined were still in first place when measured in dollars rather than units. Table 13-9b shows the

TABLE 13-9
Hosiery Industry Situation

(a) Industry Hosiery Shipments		(b) Percent of U.S. Unit Hosiery Sales by Type of Retail Outlet (January 1977)	
Year	Millions of Dozen Pairs	Type of Retail Outlet	% of Unit Sales
1973	100.5	Food and drug	29.4
1974	92.2	Discount*	21.7
1975	99.1	Department and specialty	18.7
1976	106.1	Penney and Sears	11.3
1977	103.4	Variety	7.2
		Mail order/shoe	4.6
		Others	7.2
			100.1

(c) Percent of Hosiery Production by Type

	1969	1973	1976
Stockings (regular length)	54.0	15.6	6.7
Pantyhose	46.0	75.1	61.8
Sheer knee-highs and anklets		9.3	31.5

*Includes mass merchandisers except for Penney and Sears.

share of hosiery sales by types of retail outlets as measured in units for the first half of 1977.

The mix of hosiery continued changing with sheer knee-highs and sheer anklets taking share from both stockings and pantyhose. (See Table 13-9c.) Several new developments in pantyhose had resulted in fragmentation of this category into regular, support (elasticized leg), control top (girdlelike properties), and panty/pantyhose (pantyhose with panty built in).

Before the end of 1974 Burlington had withdrawn the Activ brand from food and drug stores, noting that its attempt to compete in these channels had not proved profitable.

The number of women's hosiery companies in operation had continued to decline—from 301 in 1965 to 121 in 1976.

Hanes' Situation

Financial Position and Market Share. Hanes' performance continued to improve in sales, net profit, return on sales, and share of market as shown in Table 13-10. Gross profit reached a high of 42.0 percent in 1976 and appeared to be leveling.

L'eggs' Continued Success. With a 15.2 percent share of the total hosiery market, L'eggs in 1977 was the largest-selling single hosiery brand in the United States. L'eggs accounted for 38 percent of hosiery sold in food and drug stores.

The L'eggs product line had expanded to meet changing market demand and in 1977 included all the categories into which the market had fragmented.

Despite several years of inflation, the original regular L'eggs continued to sell at $1.39 retail. Prices for other L'eggs models varied; the Sheer Energy support hose brand, for example, sold for $2.99. The larger line and increased volume required larger display racks which retailers accepted because of the already demonstrated profit per square foot produced by L'eggs. Larger delivery vans were also needed.

Hanes' Regular Brands. Hanes was the leader in department and specialty stores with the Hanes brands representing 21 percent of sales through these channels and 7.4 percent of all retail hosiery sales. The Hanes line had also expanded and now included several other brands such as Alive (support pantyhose) and Underalls (panty/pantyhose).

TABLE 13-10
Hanes Performance, 1973–1977

Year	Sales, $ millions	% Market Share	% Gross Profit	Profit after Tax, $ millions	% ROS
1973	275.9	20	38.4	9.4	3.4
1974	288.8	22	39.7	(4.1)*	
1975	314.8	25	39.7	10.6	3.4
1976	372.3	26	42.0	18.4	5.0
1977	414.2	27	41.3	20.8	5.0

*After $14.3 million write-off of goodwill.

Other Hosiery. Today's Girl brand was being sold in mass merchandising, variety, and budget department stores. Private brand sales accounted for 1.6 percent of total company sales.

A mail order business had been developed for products such as L'eggs Nurse White and Better Than Panty Hose which were not offered through normal distribution channels.

With hosiery sold through every distribution channel, Hanes' hosiery was now available virtually wherever consumers purchased hosiery. Hanes was following an *intensive* distribution policy in contrast to the *selective* policy followed prior to 1970.

Other Products. In 1977 Hanes was expanding its line of men's and boys' underwear and had stepped up distribution and sales efforts for these products. The Pine State Knitwear Co. had been acquired and was producing men's sweaters under the Pine State brand and private labels. The wholly owned Bali Company had increased its share of the brassiere market from 8.5 percent in 1973 to 11 percent in 1977. A line of cosmetics sold through food and drug stores was in test market. This was Hanes' first venture outside of the apparel industry. Earlier the company had withdrawn lines of men's underwear and family socks following unsuccessful test marketing in food and drug stores.

Performance by Product Group. Hosiery sales, as a percent of total company sales, were 63 percent in 1977 compared with 66 percent in 1969. Although Hanes had been diversifying and working hard at its other businesses, success of the hosiery lines had been such that hosiery still represented nearly two-thirds of sales and over two-thirds of profits. In Table 13-11 note that hosiery outperformed the other product categories in rates of profit return.

Promotional Expense vis-à-vis Profit. Hanes' management believed in spending promotional funds to make money. This can be seen in Table 13-12. Whereas marketing expense rose from $21.9 million in 1969 to $131.9 million in 1977 (502 percent), net earnings rose from $3.1 million to $20.8 million (570 percent). Marketing expense as a percent of sales had risen from 14.0 percent in 1969 to 31.8 percent in 1973 at which point it began to level off, suggesting that an optimum balance had been struck.

TABLE 13-11
Hanes' Performance by Product Group, 1977

Product Group	Sales, $ millions	% of Total Sales	Earnings after Tax, $ millions	% ROS	% ROI*
Women's hosiery	261	63.0	19.0	7.3	19
Knitwear products	113	27.3	6.6	5.8	13
Foundation garments	37	9.0	2.5	6.8	15
Other products	3	0.7	(1.6)	—	—
Total	414	100.0	20.8†	5.0	15.9

*Percent return on primary investment (receivables, inventories, and fixed assets less current liabilities).

†After deduction of corporate expenses.

TABLE 13-12
Hanes' Marketing Expense Compared with Net Earnings

Year	Marketing Expense,* $ millions	Marketing Expense as % of Net Sales	Net Earnings, $ millions
1969	21.9	14.0	3.1
1971	36.1	20.5	3.5
1973	85.8	31.1	9.4
1975	103.7	32.9	10.6
1977	131.9	31.8	20.8

*Sum of advertising expense plus selling, administrative, and miscellaneous expense from Hanes' *Annual Reports.*

Hanes Management Philosophy

Hanes' performance between 1969 and 1977 demonstrated the soundness of its strategies and tactics and its ability to carry them out effectively. The following excerpts from the Hanes *Annual Report* for 1977 provide insight into management's philosophy:

> Through the disciplined application of proved consumer marketing techniques over the past seven years, Hanes Corporation has the first or second largest brand in three industries—women's hosiery, men's and boys' underwear, and brassieres—each of which represents a billion dollars or more in annual retail sales. Hanes Corporation expects to expand its market share in each of these industries in 1978. It is anticipated that entries will be made into other product areas where the Corporation's consumer marketing and distribution capabilities can be utilized. . . .
>
> No dramatic gains are foreseen for 1978. The continued success of existing brands and further efficiencies in manufacturing should allow Hanes Corporation to achieve a modest rate of growth in sales and earnings in 1978 and meet its goal of earning a 15% return on shareowners' equity. . . .
>
> In 1970 management decided to change its corporate orientation from that of a traditional apparel manufacturer to that of a consumer goods marketing company. With the introduction of L'eggs brand hosiery in 1970, Hanes began to implement this strategy. . . .
>
> The Corporation's marketing strategy is, first, identify consumer needs through extensive research; second, develop products which satisfy those needs; and third, test the viability of the new products in consumer discussion groups and actual trial in the marketplace. The products which indicate they have the potential to meet the Corporation's volume and profit requirements are presented directly to the consumer through extensive media advertising and promotional programs.
>
> The key element in this process is discipline. No product bearing a Hanes Corporation brand is presented to the marketplace before evaluation indicates it is likely to succeed. This process recognizes that not all products developed will survive testing. Even those products which survive testing do not always achieve satisfactory sales levels in the actual marketplace. However, if the pretesting process is followed through with discipline, the probabilities of success are greatly increased. . . .
>
> The hosiery industry continues its recent trend of fragmentation away from nonsupport pantyhose into such categories as support, control-top, combination

panty/pantyhose garments and knee-highs. Rather than attempt to resist this fragmentation, Hanes Corporation utilizes consumer research to anticipate new developments and moves to take advantage of them. This strategy was apparent in all the Corporation's hosiery brands during the year. . . .

The Hanes brand has a 15% unit share of the all-cotton segment of men's and boys' lightweight underwear. The all-cotton segment represents 52% of total industry unit sales. Potential exists for further increases in Hanes brand sales by expanding its present 4% unit share of the blended cotton and polyester segment of the market, which accounts for 37% of total industry unit sales. . . .

Bali has 21% of the underwire segment of the brassiere market which accounts for 12% of total brassiere industry sales. Soft-cup brassieres represent 80% of all sales, but Bali has only a 3% share of this segment. Opportunities for future growth of the Bali brand are in increasing its share of the soft-cup category.

QUESTIONS

The eight years following 1969 saw dramatic success and significant changes come to the Hanes Corporation. It was no longer the company it was when management made its strategic decisions.

1. *Business purpose.* In Chapter 1 we offered the following formula for determining business purpose:

$$\text{Company resources} + \text{market opportunity} = \text{business purpose}$$

   Were Hanes' company resources and market opportunities different in 1977 than in 1969? If so, how would you describe Hanes' apparent business purpose in 1977?
2. *Corporate objectives.* In the company's *Annual Report* the chief executive stated that the 1978 goal was to earn a 15 percent return on corporate equity. In addition to this immediate goal what longer-term objectives might be appropriate in view of your revised estimate of Hanes' business purpose?
3. *Corporate strategies.* Beginning in 1970 the primary strategy was to enter food and drug stores with a new advertised hosiery brand. This was highly successful and appears to have led to a broadening of the company's overall hosiery strategy in succeeding years. The secondary strategy of diversification was implemented through acquisition of Pine State Knitwear and the Bali Company. Efforts to diversify through internal developments were also underway. Hanes' management states that its overall strategy is to be a consumer goods marketing company. Under this umbrellalike strategy what specific strategies do you think Hanes was following in 1977?

Problems in implementing strategies for repositioning Spalding in the tennis racket market.

Case 4

Spalding Tennis Rackets

Scott Creelman, manager of the tennis products business at the Spalding Division of Questor Corporation,* was searching for a plan that would significantly improve Spalding's position in the tennis racket market. The strategy which had been followed since 1975 had not improved Spalding's third-place industry position; in fact, its percentage share had declined. Furthermore, the business was feeling the effects of excess industry production capacity and high inventories at the wholesale and retail levels. These had put pressure on prices and profit margins. If Spalding's tennis racket business was to achieve its objectives in sales, profit, and market share, Mr. Creelman knew that either the present strategy had to be implemented better or a new strategy had to be adopted.

Background

The A. G. Spalding Co. had been formed more than 100 years ago. Spalding was one of the most respected brand names in sports equipment. From the time of its entry into tennis equipment in 1888, Spalding had played a leading role in the tennis industry until about 1950. Tennis equipment, however, was not a major business at Spalding, since tennis had never been a sport for the masses. It had not enjoyed the postwar growth in popularity that was characteristic of golf and a number of team sports. In the early 1950s, for example, there were less than 3 million tennis players in the United States. Consequently, Spalding management had decided to place its major resources behind the faster-growing sports.

The tennis picture had changed by the late 1960s, however, as the game grew in popularity. By 1976, 23.5 million people were playing tennis. Although interest in the sport was still increasing, the rate of growth had begun to slow, as can be seen in Exhibit 4-1.

The increase in tennis players was, of course, reflected in industry sales of rackets. This can be seen in total manufacturers' sales in Exhibit 4-2 and in consumer purchases in Exhibit 4-3. It will be noted that manufacturers' sales were growing at a faster rate than consumer purchases. This resulted in a buildup of inventories at the wholesale and retail level. Dealers' efforts to bring their inventories into line with consumer purchases caused a significant drop in manufacturers' sales in 1975. Consumers continued to buy more rackets each year, although the rate of growth dropped off in 1975.

The problem was that the industry was continuing to produce rackets in excess of consumer demand. Spalding executives, however, believed that the oversupply was primarily in the low-end price segment. There was no serious price cutting in the high-end price segment where product features and brand image were more important than price to the discriminating buyer.

EXHIBIT 4-1
Total U.S. Tennis Players (In millions)

	1972	1973	1974	1975	1976
Players	13.8	15.8	19.4	21.5	23.5
% change		+14	+23	+11	+9

Source: 1976 Business Unit Plan, Tennis Equipment.

EXHIBIT 4-2
Manufacturers' Sales of Tennis Rackets

	1972	1973	1974	1975	1976
Sales at manufacturer's prices, $ millions	50.0	71.5	100.0	85.8	96.6
% change		+43	+40	−14	+13
Units, millions	5.0	6.5	9.0	7.8	9.2
% change		+30	+39	−13	+18

Source: 1976 Business Unit Plan, Tennis Equipment.

*The organization of the Spalding Division (including the organization for tennis products) is shown in Exhibit 4-8 at the end of the case.

EXHIBIT 4-3
Rackets Purchased by Consumers at Retail

	1972	1973	1974	1975
Sales at retail prices, $ millions	79.2	104.1	142.5	191.1
% change		+31	+37	+35
Units, millions	4.0	4.9	6.6	7.9
% change		+23	+35	+20

Source: 1976 Business Unit Plan, Tennis Equipment.

Characteristics of the Tennis Market

Sex and Age. In 1975 the ratio of men to women players was 58/42 and was expected to reach 50/50 by 1980. Historically, per person average equipment purchases had been higher for men than for women.

Nearly four-fifths of all tennis players were between the ages of 15 and 34. Although the 25 to 34 age groups accounted for one-third of all players, it can be seen from Exhibit 4-4 that the 15 to 17 age group had the highest percent of players per age year. The percent of players by age year drops steadily thereafter.

EXHIBIT 4-4
Age Distribution of Tennis Players in 1975

	Men		Women	
Age Group (1)	% in Group (2)	% by Age Yr.* (3)	% in Group (4)	% by Age Yr.* (5)
15-17	17.9	6.0	17.7	5.9
18-24	26.0	3.7	25.2	3.6
25-34	33.4	3.3	34.2	3.4
35-49	17.6	1.2	17.4	1.2
50+	5.1	†	5.5	+
	100.0		100.0	

*Represents % in age group (columns 2 and 4) divided by the number of years in age group (column 1).

†Less than 1%.

Source: 1976 Business Unit Plan, Tennis Equipment.

EXHIBIT 4-5
Metal* versus Wood Racket Purchases at Retail

	1972	1973	1974	1975	% Share in 1975
UNIT SALES (millions)					
Wood	2.6	3.5	4.8	4.9	62
Metal	1.4	1.4	1.8	3.0	38
Total units	4.0	4.9	6.6	7.9	100
SALES ($ millions)					
Wood	39.1	62.7	94.0	98.1	51
Metal	40.1	41.4	48.5	93.0	49
Total sales	79.2	104.1	142.5	191.1	100

*Includes composite materials.

Source: 1976 Business Unit Plan, Tennis Equipment.

Frequency and Place of Play. Frequency of play was once a month or less for 37 percent of players, two to four times a month for 38 percent, and two or more times per week for 25 percent. About four-fifths of participants played on outdoor courts only. Most of the balance played on both outdoor and indoor courts. A small percentage used indoor courts only.

A higher proportion of the population in the south and west played tennis. The highest concentrations were found in Florida and California. Nearly half of all tennis professional and specialty shops were located in Florida and on the west coast.

Racket Type and Price. Although wood rackets outsold metal/composite* rackets, the more expensive metal/composite rackets were growing at a faster rate than wood. (See Exhibit 4-5.) Metal/composite rackets in 1975 accounted for 38 percent of units sold but 49 percent of dollars spent at retail. Players did considerable switching from one racket to another but with the primary switch from wood to metal/composite.

There was a shift in purchase pattern from lower- to higher-price rackets as players upgraded their equipment. (Shown in Exhibit 4-6.) In 1975 55 percent of all wood rackets were sold for below $20 retail, whereas only 24 percent of all metal/composite rackets were sold for under $20.

*A category which includes frames made either of metal or of a composite of materials such as foam, fiberglass, and graphite.

EXHIBIT 4-6

Percent of Racket Sales by Price Group, 1974 and 1975 (In units)

	Under $10	$10–20	$21–30	$31–40	$41+	Don't know	Total
WOOD SALES, %							
1975	16	39	16	7	6	16	100
1974	21	38	14	9	4	14	100
METAL SALES, %							
1975	3	21	21	27	20	8	100
1974	0	25	25	25	16	9	100
TOTAL COMBINED SALES, %							
1975	11	32	18	15	11	13	100
1974	17	34	16	12	7	14	100

Source: 1976 Business Unit Plan, Tennis Equipment.

Place of Purchase. Using consumer responses to questions as to the origins of racket purchases, consumer market researchers had found the following percent of player racket purchases by type of outlet:

Type of Outlet	% Purchasing
Sporting goods stores	32
Department stores	22
Discount stores	16
Pro/specialty shops	9
Other	12
Don't know	9
	100

Approximately 76 percent of rackets were purchased prestrung, with the balance strung by the dealer at time of purchase. The percentage of dealer-strung rackets was much higher for rackets bought in pro shops and somewhat higher for those bought in sporting goods stores. Stringing by the dealer increased the price of the racket, but provided the customer with a racket that met the customer's perceived needs.

Features Sought and Buying Influences. Among the features looked for in rackets, the most important for men was balance; for women it was grip. Players' rankings of the major features were as follows:

Feature	% Ranking the Feature Highest	
	Men	Women
Grip	24	35
Balance	32	26
Control	21	13
Price	10	11
Power	9	7
Appearance	2	3
Don't know	2	5
	100	100

Market research also found the players were influenced in their brand selections by recommendations of friends and family, store clerks, advertising, observation of other players, and pro shop recommendations—in that order.

Competition

Hypothetical* market shares—measured by dollar volume—of rackets by brand for the year 1975 were:

*Hypothetical data used in the case are roughly proportional to the actual.

Brand	Parent Company	% Share
Wilson	Pepsi-Co	33
Head	AMF Corp.	11
Spalding	Questor Corp.	10
Bancroft	Colgate-Palmolive Co.	7
Dunlop		5
Davis		4
All others		30
		100

Brand	Advertising Dollars, 1000s	% of Total
Wilson	1184	32
Bancroft	851	23
Spalding	629	17
Head	370	10
Penn*	370	10
Dunlop	296	8
	3700	100

*Tennis balls only.

Wilson had long dominated the tennis racket market with a complete line of wood and metal rackets sold to all price segments. Wilson made good products, maintained a large sales force, and had advertised and promoted tennis rackets aggressively for years. It had continued to push tennis equipment during the years when Spalding had deemphasized it.

Head featured high-quality metal and the newer composite material frames sold primarily to the higher-price market segments. Spalding historically had sold wood rackets to the lower-price segments. Only recently had it added higher-quality wood and metal frames in order to go after the higher-price segments.

Bancroft, recently acquired by Colgate-Palmolive Company, had begun marketing rackets aggressively, as indicated by its advertising spending which was second only to Wilson in 1975. Dunlop also had begun to advertise more aggressively. Davis was less aggressive and was reputed to be losing market share.

Both Wilson and Spalding had lost market share recently in the low-price market segments due to price cutting by domestic suppliers and an increase in low-priced imports. (Approximately 70 percent of the tennis rackets sold in the United States were made in Pakistan and Taiwan as private brands for U.S. manufacturers, chains, and distributors.)

Technical developments were appearing in frame materials and designs. In addition to wood and metal (steel and aluminum), frames were being offered in fiberglass, graphite, and other materials. Oversize frames had been introduced to provide a larger hitting area. The major manufacturers were moving toward full lines incorporating the various materials and designs.

Competitive Advertising. Six advertisers accounted for most of the advertising dollars spent for both balls and rackets in 1975. Hypothetical expenditures and percent of total were:

Distribution and Sales

Like other major sporting goods manufacturers, Spalding distributed its tennis rackets direct to retail accounts. Some smaller manufacturers distributed through sporting goods wholesalers. Spalding accounts were served by the company's five regional warehouses.

The Spalding sales force, consisting of approximately 100 sales representatives, was organized so as to specialize by the following types of retail accounts: professional golf shops; major dealers (sporting goods and department stores); national accounts (chains such as Sears, Penney, and K mart); and military base outlets.

Spalding's Position

By 1975 Spalding's tennis business was in a period of transition. The tennis business unit had developed a long-term plan, which included marketing strategies and tactics. Prior to recommending the plan, the marketing department had summarized the Spalding market situation as follows:

- A poor image in tennis rackets.
- Poor quality products.
- Emphasis on low-end products. Low-priced rackets had accounted for 86 percent of unit sales in 1974.
- No serious promotional support. Tennis products received only $130,000 in advertising in 1974 compared to an estimated $950,000 for Wilson (a 1:7.3 ratio).
- No active involvement in the sport (such as tournaments) and few player consultants used.

The general objective of the long-term marketing plan adopted in 1975 was to build a highly profitable tennis business based on better-quality products and a solid position of leadership in the sport. The major marketing strategy was:

Shift emphasis to the high end (high-priced segment) of the tennis racket market where brand and product differentiation was important to buyers and where profit margins were highest.

Tactical actions in support of the strategy in 1975 included:

1. Introduction of a new and improved wood product line. These were high-end wood rackets equal to the best of competition.
2. Endorsement by the WCT (World Championship Tennis Tournaments).
3. New consultants (name tennis professionals) were added.
4. Support from the company's sales force had been increased.
5. Advertising expenditures increased to $629,000, compared to $1,184,000 for Wilson (a 1:1.9 ratio).

The 1976 Business Unit Plan (Tennis Rackets)

1976 Business Objectives. The sales objective for 1976 was to increase racket sales by 17 percent. Profit objectives were to increase gross margins by 27 percent and the gross margin to sales ratio by 3.3 points. A comparison of the 1976 objectives with hypothetical performance for the three previous years is shown in Exhibit 4-7.

1976 Marketing Objectives:

1. Convince the trade and the influential core tennis community that Spalding makes top-quality, high-performance tennis products.
2. Achieve 75 percent distribution of premium rackets in tennis pro and specialty high-end dealer accounts.
3. Complete development of and introduce a high-end metal racket bearing the WCT endorsement.

Marketing Strategy. The marketing strategy was to remain the same: to shift emphasis to the high end of the tennis racket market (while continuing to compete, with less emphasis, in the low end of the market).

Tactical Programs:

1. Focus marketing effort on the new (high-end) Gonzales Autograph racket.
2. Keep prices "sharp" on low-end rackets.
3. Concentrate selling effort against pro shops, tennis specialty shops, and other high-end dealer accounts.
4. Facilitate product acceptance by capitalizing on Spalding's association with World Championship Tennis Tournaments and with the tennis professional Pancho Gonzales and other key consultants.
5. Concentrate the limited dollars available for advertising against the core tennis audience and against the highest potential regional areas. (The approved advertising budget was 32 percent lower than budgeted for 1975).

The Situation in 1977

During the latter part of 1977, Scott Creelman was reviewing the results from the racket strategy which had been adopted in 1975. Despite Spalding's best efforts, sales and margins had continued to decline. Hypothetical figures for 1976 and estimates for 1977 were as follows:

EXHIBIT 4-7

Tennis Racket Financial Performance (Hypothetical 1976 objectives and results for 1973–75)

Year	Sales, $ millions	% Change	Gross Margin, $ millions	% Change	% Gross Margin to Sales
1973	$ 7.0		3.08		44.0
1974	9.1	30.0	3.96	28.6	43.5
1975	8.6	(5.5)	3.44	(13.1)	40.0
1976 objective	10.1	17.4	4.37	27.0	43.3

Source: 1976 Business Unit Plan, Tennis Equipment. Data have been disguised to preserve confidentiality but are useful for case analysis.

	1976	Change	1977	Change
Sales	$6.1 mil.	−30.1%	$5.9 mil.	− 3.3%
Gross margin	$2.3 mil.	−33.1%	$1.8 mil.	−21.8%
Gross margin	37.7%	− 3.3 pts	30.5%	− 5.6 pts

Market Share. Spalding's 1977 dollar share of the racket market had fallen since 1975 while Wilson had continued to gain. Hypothetical brand share comparisons for the two years were as follows:

	% of Market	
Brand	1975	1977
Wilson	33	37
Head	11	11
Spalding	10	6
Bancroft	7	6
Dunlop	5	5
All other*	34	35
	100	100

*Davis included in all others.

Player Participation. Although exact figures were not yet available, it was believed that the total number of players had peaked in 1976 and would show a slight decline for 1977.

Preliminary research reports indicated that the falloff in players had been in the 15 to 17 age category. When viewed by income segments, changes in player participation were as follows:

Under $15,000: declining

$15,000 to $25,000: holding steady

Over $25,000: increasing

Industry Sales. Racket sales at retail were reported at $184 million in 1976, a decline of 4 percent from peak sales in 1975. The fast-growth phase of the industry appeared to be ending with maturity setting in. Total unit sales were expected to level off or decline. Modest gains were expected in dollar sales, however, resulting from a continued shift of buyers to higher-priced rackets.

Spalding Product Line. Spalding's line had been broadened with the addition of quality wood rackets and a WCT approved steel racke in the over-$25 category. Additional rackets were under development for the over-$25 segment. These included frames made of wood and a graphite composite; also a large frame wood and composite racket.

Several low-priced rackets had been dropped from the line, although Spalding continued to offer a wide selection of lower-priced rackets. Suggested retail prices for the company's rackets ranged from a low of $12.95 to a high of $79.00.

Strategic Planning for 1978 and Beyond

In preparation for the upcoming business planning period, Scott Creelman reflected on developments since the adoption of the present marketing strategy. The disappointing results in terms of sales, profits, and market share appeared to be due to such factors as:

1. The slowing of market growth.
2. Depressed margins resulting from continued oversupply, particularly in the lower-priced market segment where Spalding's market position was strongest.
3. The difficulties encountered in breaking into the higher-priced market segment. The reasons for these difficulties seemed to be:
    a. The long time needed to develop a complete, high-quality, high-price line equal to or better than competitors'.
    b. Problems in overcoming Spalding's image as a producer of low-end rackets.
    c. Difficulty in convincing pro and specialty shops that Spalding was now a serious contender in the high-end market.
    d. Inadequate sales force efforts among pro and specialty shops.*
    e. Reductions in the national advertising budget that had been made to help offset declining profit margins.
    f. The continued aggressive efforts of the two leading competitors—Wilson and Head—to improve their own positions in the high-end racket market segment.

The original strategy of shifting efforts to the high-end racket segment where profit margins were higher still appeared sound in view of the continued shift of market purchases toward higher-priced rackets. Actually, Spalding had made some good progress in this market,

---

*One sales representative had been assigned to selling tennis pro and specialty shops in 1976, and a second was assigned in 1977. The tennis business unit felt that ten tennis specialists were needed.

although not enough to offset the low-margin portion of its business. All the same, Spalding clearly had underestimated the time and costs involved in converting to the new strategy as well as the extent to which competitors would go to protect their own market shares in the high-end segment.

There was now the question of whether Spalding could afford the time and further financial investment to pursue the strategy to a successful conclusion. Consequently, Mr. Creelman had to decide whether to stick with the current strategy—and find better ways of implementing it—or to find a new strategy.

Alternate Strategy. One new strategy he was thinking about was:

Positioning Spalding to both the trade and consumer as the tennis manufacturer of "Middle America," offering quality at an attractive price, with a broad distribution base.

With such a strategy, Spalding would avoid both extremes of the market—the lowest- and highest-price segments. Except for those segments, it would offer a complete range of rackets sold primarily through sporting goods, discount, and department stores. Efforts would continue to shift sales to the over $25 category, but with less emphasis on the highest-price frames sold through pro and specialty shops. Some of the advantages of such a strategy appeared to be:

1. Capitalizing on the brand name in that segment of the market where Spalding was best known as a quality supplier of sports equipment.
2. Selling through the same retail outlets used by Spalding's other sporting goods products.
3. Using the Spalding sales force more effectively, since it already spent most of its time calling on these same retail outlets.
4. Continuing with the directional shift from lower- to higher-margin products while avoiding the high promotional costs that would be needed to crack successfully the high-end segment sold through pro and specialty shops.

Scott Creelman was reluctant to change strategies unless a new one was clearly superior to the present one. Much of the money and effort that had gone into the present strategy would be wasted if it were dropped. At the same time, he knew that something had to be done to stem the downslide in sales and profits.

In preparing the business plan for 1978 and beyond, Mr. Creelman directed his staff to analyze carefully the present strategy, the alternative strategy described above, and any new strategies that might seem appropriate. He stated that the 1978 objective was to reverse the decline in sales and profit margins. The objective for the second to third year was to return to the sales and gross profit levels of 1974. Longer term, the objective was to

EXHIBIT 4-8

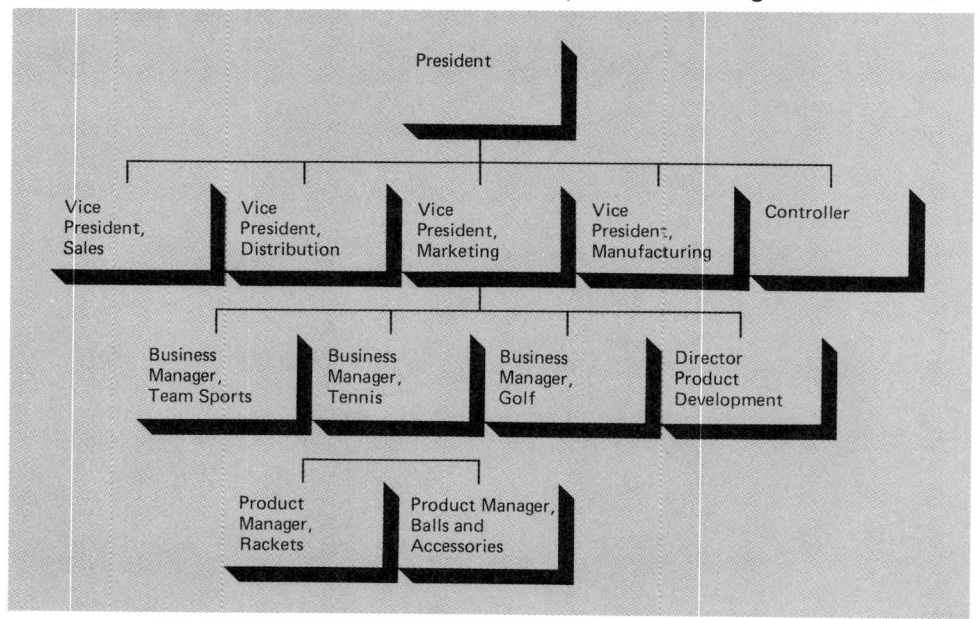

Organization of the Spalding Division, Questor Corporation, Including Tennis Products

become highly profitable and to strengthen position in the tennis racket market.

In approaching the strategy review, Scott Creelman requested his staff to conduct a thorough *situation analysis*, considering all pertinent external and internal data, to make sure that the key problems and opportunities had been identified. The staff also was to list the pros and cons of each strategy under consideration and to recommend to him the most appropriate strategy or strategies.

PROBLEMS

1. Using the outline in Chapter 9, develop a *situation analysis* using information in the case through 1977.
2. Considering results through 1977 and the three-year objectives stated by Scott Creelman for 1978 through 1980, should Spalding continue with the present strategy or change to the proposed new strategy? Or would you recommend a different alternate strategy? Explain your choice.
3. Using the tactical marketing plan worksheet in Chapter 11 as a guide, develop a tactical plan to implement the strategy you chose in 2 above.

Losing its number one position, an employee relocation service firm looks for new strategies to regain industry leadership.

Case 5

National Relocation, Inc.

Robert A. Anderson, senior vice president of Webster Group, Inc., received the report of a task force formed to study National Relocation, Inc., a wholly owned subsidiary of Webster Group. Webster Group, founded in 1951 and now headquartered in Richmond, Va., is a business services management company and the country's leader in special equipment management and leasing. National Relocation is the pioneer in an industry which provides relocation management services to corporations and various real estate and moving services to the employees they transfer.

Although National Relocation had grown rapidly since 1972 when it was acquired by Webster Group, growth in earnings had not kept pace with growth in revenues. (See Exhibit 5-1.) Furthermore, as competitors entered the industry with aggressive pricing strategies, National Relocation's share of the market had been dropping. In fact, by 1977 National Relocation was in danger of losing

*This case is based on real events but names have been disguised.

EXHIBIT 5-1
Financial Results for National Relocation, Inc.

Year	Revenues, $1000s	Operating Profit, $1000s	% ROR*	Assets $1000s	% ROA†
1976	27,100	800	3.0	83,600	0.9
1975	24,400	1,100	4.5	50,100	2.2
1974	23,900	950	4.0	42,000	2.3
1973	22,100	1,000	4.5	37,000	2.7
1972	24,600	1,100	4.5	38,300	2.9

*Return on revenues: operating profit ÷ revenues

†Return on assets; operating profit ÷ assets

its leadership position to a faster-growing competitor. Webster Group had engaged a management consulting firm to work jointly with National Relocation management as a task force to see what could be done to improve market position while maintaining rapid growth in revenues and earnings.

Background

National Relocation was the outgrowth of a firm organized in 1958 by Jonathon O'Day as a result of problems he and his family experienced when transferred by his company to New York City. He began his new firm by organizing a network of reputable realtors in major metropolitan areas to provide "new area counseling and homefinding assistance" to assist people moving to unfamiliar parts of the country. O'Day named his new firm American Transfer Associates. (It is now a wholly owned subsidiary of National Relocation; both are headquartered in Newton, Mass.)

Coordinated by American Transfer Associates, the realtor handling the sale of the family's present home would notify an affiliated realtor at the new location of the family's preferences and financial capabilities. Armed with this information, the destination realtor would show the family only the most suitable areas and homes during the first visit to the new location. O'Day directed his marketing efforts to realtors who specialized in listing and selling corporate transferee housing and to large companies that relocated many employees.

Growing Need to Help Transferees. With postwar corporate expansion and diversification, more and more corporate employees were being transferred from one geographic location to another. To ease relocation-caused financial burdens on their employees and to shorten the family-transfer process, companies began offering to buy the homes of their transferees for appraised market value. Upon acceptance of a corporate home purchase offer, a transferee received the equity* in his or her home and was also freed from the financial and other burdens connected with managing and selling it. A growing number of companies also began to help employees with the movement of household goods and in locating new housing.

Formation of National Relocation, Inc. Aware of these trends O'Day founded a second company named National Relocation, Inc. (NRI). Working on a contract basis with corporations, NRI would relieve them of the many details associated with buying, managing, and selling employees' homes. NRI's services ranged from helping individual families relocate to handling mass company moves, such as when a major oil company transferred 2,400 employees from New York to its new home offices in Houston.

In addition to buying and selling transferees' homes, NRI also manages household goods shipments and—through American Transfer Associates' nationwide network of affiliated realtors—helps families settle into new areas. NRI grew rapidly, finding many companies open to the idea of paying a third party to take over a service which they were often ill equipped to handle efficiently and economically on their own.

National Relocation's Services. When taking over a transferee's home, NRI immediately paid the full equity and assumed the mortgage interest, maintenance, and tax obligations until the property was sold. Appraisals were made by reputable local appraisers, and homes were listed for sale with reputable realtors familiar with local markets.

If employees elected to sell their homes to someone other than NRI, the firm—upon receipt of a valid sales contract—would advance equity, manage the home if vacant, and assume responsibility for closing the employee's sale. Employees were therefore financially and administratively free to move, while their employers were spared from tying up capital in employee housing and from the details of administering the service.

Financing Arrangements. NRI's contracts with corporate clients required that they protect NRI against loss. A corporation agreed to pay for all of the direct costs of buying, carrying, and selling employee homes plus a profit and a prorated portion of NRI's indirect costs (overhead). NRI obtained the capital needed to finance its inventory of homes from banks and insurance companies through an *indenture of trust* set up by a leading New York bank. The trust required that borrowed funds be guaranteed by the corporate clients of NRI and invested only in properties formerly owned by their employees. It also permitted NRI to invest any excess funds in short-term government securities approved by the trustee. The trust was a seemingly excellent arrangement for a new company without sizable capital of its own. As time went by, however, the trust proved restrictive as better-financed competitors offered more flexible, and sometimes cheaper, pricing arrangements—arrangements which called for the relocation firm to share some of the risks with its clients.

---

*The cash difference between the remaining unpaid mortgage balance and the offer price for the property, generally reinvested in housing at the new location.

Situation Analysis

The task force study began with a *situation analysis* to identify NRI's principal problems and opportunities.

Industry Outlook. Nearly 700 companies used relocation management firms services in 1976, compared to 90 in 1971. Over 400 of the firms were on *Fortune's* list of the 1300 largest U.S. companies. The annual number of corporate employee transfers was estimated at 250,000, of which about 65 percent involved homeowners. Prospects for future growth were bright, since only about 16 percent of this potential market (of 163,000 annual transfers by homeowners) was being serviced by relocation management firms.

Home ownership among transferees varied by industry, ranging from a high of nearly 80 percent in petroleum to a low of 50 percent in retailing, with most transfer activity reported by the petroleum, chemical, computer, and auto industries; the least by publishing, mining, and textiles.

Rising Costs of Employee Transfers. Management attention was increasingly being drawn to employee-relocation problems due to rising costs and growing employee resistance to transfer.

The average total cost of relocating a family of four 1000 miles, to and from $50,000 homes, had risen from $6,000 in 1960 to $15,000 in 1977; costs were expected to reach $30,000 by 1980. A cost breakdown is shown in Exhibit 5-2. Costs were largely influenced by inflation, interest rates, and the liberalization of relocation policies designed to reduce employee resistance to moving.

Market Shares. NRI had retained its leadership position in the industry through 1977. However, several smaller relocation firms—some started by former NRI employees—had been purchased by large life insurance, title insurance, and financial services firms (such as Equitable Life and Merrill Lynch*). Backed by their parent company's substantial capital resources and branch office networks, these firms began to compete

*"Job Transfer Blues," *Wall Street Journal*, Jan. 6, 1982, p. 1.

EXHIBIT 5-2
1977 Costs of Relocating an Employee

Following is an itemization of employer/employee activities and expenses typically incurred throughout the relocation process. The figures are averages drawn from numerous corporate policy and relocation expense management studies; they assume the 1,000 mile relocation of a family of four to and from $50,000 housing.

Activity	Cost	Expenses Involved
Initial interview	$ 200	Travel, lodging, meals, etc.
House hunting	770	Travel, lodging, meals, etc.
New home purchase and closing	720	Legal fees and financing charges
Sale of present home	4,925	Broker and legal fees; mortgage prepayment and other charges; inspection requirements; transfer taxes, etc.
Temporary living:		
Employee	1,455	Travel, lodging, meals, etc.
Family	1,275	Travel, lodging, meals, etc.
Moving household goods	2,310	Packing, shipping, temporary storage, delivery
Family travel to new location	260	Travel, lodging, meals, etc.
Miscellaneous expenses	1,250	Vehicle licensing and registration; utility connection costs; decorating, etc.
Old-new mortgage difference	665	Principal and interest
Tax on reimbursements	1,170	
Total relocation cost*	$15,000	

*Varies with the value of housing bought and sold; real estate and financing market conditions at the old and new locations; the distance of the move; and characteristics of possessions shipped.

aggressively, featuring flexible pricing and contract arrangements and their local service delivery capabilities. By 1977 METCO edged past NRI in home inventory units handled, although NRI continued to maintain leadership in profitability. The estimated market share positions of the major firms are shown in Exhibit 5-3.

Business Definition. The task force concluded that for strategic planning purposes, NRI competed in three distinct strategic business units (SBUs):

- Relocation management services
- Destination area counseling and homefinding services —incorporating realtor referrals
- Consultative services

Each SBU had different competitors, different customers, and used different selling channels. Only NRI and METCO competed in all three business areas.

The task force defined NRI's "product" (service) lines as:

- Home purchase, management, and sale
- Rental management (maintaining and renting the home of employees relocated on a short-term basis)
- Property management (appraising, managing, and/or selling corporate-owned employee housing)
- Community and site selection studies for companies planning facility moves
- Household goods shipment management

A client company might contract for any or all of these services. Home purchase, management, and sale were considered NRI's primary "product," however.

NRI's "customers" were, first, corporations and, second, transferees. (It can be argued whether a corporation or the employee it asks to relocate is the *real* customer. Although an employee is not eligible for NRI's services until the employer contracts for them, it is the employee who decides whether or not to use the services offered. Furthermore, the degree of employee satisfaction with services used is a factor in determining whether the company stays with the same relocation firm.)

NRI's "selling channels" were described as:

To corporations. National Relocation had a small sales force headquartered at the home office which solicited new corporate accounts.

To tranferees. The Transferee Services Unit was a group of specialists working out of the home office who contacted transferring employees (mainly by long-distance phone) to acquaint them with the available services and to instruct them as to how to utilize the services.

In 1977, NRI had only one office, the home office in Massachusetts, while the American Transfer Associates subsidiary maintained eight field offices.

Strengths and Weaknesses versus Competitors'. The task force attempted to compare NRI's strengths and weaknesses with those of its major competitors. Based on a client perception analysis, they concluded that corporations evaluated relocation service firms differently depending on the degree of experience they had with them. The task force compared the degree of interest on the part of older, more experienced clients to that of newer, less experienced clients with respect to several criteria. They found that as clients "aged" (became more experienced), their interests shifted from the relocation firm's personal style and reputation to its comparative costs, responsiveness to client needs, and flexibility. NRI's strong and weak points appeared to be as follows:

Strongest

- High level of personal integrity and a strong corporate reputation.
- Acceptable level of financial stability.

Weakest

- High prices. NRI is the "Cadillac" of the industry.
- Inflexibility in pricing and financing.
- Perception of no local service delivery capability outside the Boston area and an inflexible approach to working with clients.

EXHIBIT 5-3
Market Share in Units (Employee moves handled)*

	Units	% Share
METCO	8,500	32.7
National Relocation	8,000	30.8
Global Relocation Service	3,500	13.5
Employee Relocation Company	2,500	9.6
ADS Relocation Services	1,500	5.8
Executive Transfer Company	1,000	3.8
Diversified Relocation Services	1,000	3.8
	26,000	100.0

*Estimated for 1977.

The task force suggested that as the industry matured, more and more clients would choose relocation firms based on criteria where NRI was weakest.

Financial and Pricing Considerations. Large sums of capital are required to sustain a relocation management company. The more successful a relocation firm becomes, the larger its inventory of homes and the more capital it needs. Funds are required to pay transferees the equity in their homes and to cover interest charges on equity payment borrowings. Funds are also needed to make mortgage, property tax, insurance, maintenance, and other typical homeowner payments while homes are in inventory. Finally, funds must be available to pay the various realtor, legal, and mortgage lender fees connected with selling homes, transferring ownership, and processing them out of inventory. All relocation management companies employ their revenues and borrowed capital mainly to cover the *direct costs* associated with buying, managing, and selling corporate transferee housing—and costs can vary significantly in national and local real estate and financing markets.

Relocation management company *indirect costs* are largely governed by the personnel, facilities, and support systems needed to serve clients and to manage direct cost performance. The extent of profits (except under guaranteed-profit pricing arrangements) is determined by the degree to which the relocation firm can keep its total (i.e., direct and indirect) costs below its billings (charges) to its clients.

In 1977 four different pricing structures were being used within the industry. They ranged from conservative cost-plus pricing to high-risk fixed-fee pricing. (See Exhibit 5-4.) The various pricing structures are:

1. Cost-plus pricing. Client guarantees direct costs and indirect costs plus a predetermined profit.

2. Risked-profit pricing. Client guarantees direct and indirect costs, but profit is derived only to the extent that total costs remain lower than billings.

3. Management fee pricing. Client guarantees direct costs only; profits are derived only to the extent that direct costs are kept lower than billings.

4. Fixed-fee pricing. Client pays a predetermined fixed percentage of the value of each inventory unit handled, or of the aggregate value of all units handled during the course of a year. The fee represents maximum cost exposure to the client, and the relocation firm can profit only the the extent that its costs are lower than the fee.

As noted earlier, the indenture of trust prevented NRI from entering any pricing arrangements in which the client company did not guarantee to cover direct and indirect costs. As such, NRI was unable to offer the higher-risk forms of pricing. NRI's more experienced clients and some potential clients were aware that NRI's pricing arrangements could be more costly for them. Competitors, with financing arranged by their parent companies, had more freedom to offer flexible pricing arrangements. METCO, for example, offered to share some unforeseen high costs with the clients, and actively promoted various forms of management fee pricing.

The actual costs of buying, managing, and selling employee housing did not vary significantly between relocation management companies. However, one competitor—in an attempt to increase market share—proposed a fixed fee of 13.5 percent of the appraised value of homes handled. By contrast, NRI's price to clients averaged 14.5 to 15.5 percent of the value of homes handled.

On several occasions, NRI had to forfeit potential clients to competition because the clients' sealed bids specified management fee or fixed-fee pricing arrangements. The task force concluded that strategies must be developed to counter the restrictive covenants of the indenture of trust.

Service Delivery Considerations. The task force spotted two opportunities to improve service to transferees while also increasing NRI's income and reducing costs.

EXHIBIT 5-4

Pricing Structures (The degree of risk and cost-sharing increases for the relocation firm as its pricing structure moves from left to right).

Cost plus	Risked profit	Management fee	Fixed fee
Conservative			High risk
• Most advantageous to relocation firm			• Most advantageous to client
• Greatest risk and cost exposure to client			• Greatest risk and cost exposure to relocation firm

The first opportunity was to increase the *regular acceptance rate* on offers to buy employees' homes.

Transferred employees could use NRI's "regular acceptance" plan, selling their homes to NRI for appraised market value; or they could opt for the "assigned acceptance" plan, selling their homes themselves and assigning to NRI their valid sales contracts and the job of closing these sales. Regular acceptances were preferred, since they required more services and therefore produced more income. Anything to increase the rate of regular acceptances above the normal average of 50 to 55 percent would increase revenues and profits.

The second opportunity involved shortening the *authorization-to-offer* period—the period between the day NRI was notified that an employee was moving until the day NRI offered to buy the employee's home. The average elapsed time of 19 days was thought to be longer than that of some competitors. One competitor used its parent company's field office network to speed up the authorization-to-offer period. Without field offices, it was difficult for NRI to exercise local control over appraisers' scheduling and work. Contributing to the problem was NRI's practice of requiring that appraisals be submitted in writing, which involved time spent on mail preparation and delivery.

Market Share and the Experience Curve.* The consultants believed that leadership in market share allows a company to achieve lower costs than competitors. Superior market share permits the accumulation of more experience and also results in more rapid cost reduction through *experience effects* such as greater economies of scale.

NRI's indirect costs (those overhead costs not directly related to the purchase, management, and sale of homes) had risen steadily and were higher than two of its competitors. Furthermore, it was losing its leadership in market share to METCO. The implication was that to improve its competitive position, NRI needed to be the clear-cut market leader and gain the benefit of lowered costs.

Situation Analysis Summary

After reviewing the *situation analysis*, the task force determined that regaining market leadership would require solution of the following problems:

1. *Cost disadvantage.* Indirect costs were too high and were not benefiting from the experience curve. Also, direct costs were higher than some competitors' due to the lack of local control over home purchase and sale operations.
2. *Lack of pricing flexibility* due to the restrictions of the indenture of trust.
3. *Major external financing needs* were foreseen due to expected growth of the relocation industry.
4. *Need for local service.* Clients perceived that the field offices of title and life insurance companies enabled competitors to provide better service to transferees.
5. *Major potential change in the competitive environment* was foreseen as the result of major companies acquiring relocation service firms.

Strategy Recommendations

The principal problem-solving strategy recommendations were:

1. *Problem:* Price and cost disadvantage.
   Strategies:
   a. Communicate home purchase offers to transferees verbally—rather than in writing—to reduce the "authorization-to-offer" period and increase the rate of "regular" acceptances, thereby increasing profits without increasing prices.
   b. "Manage down the experience curve" by reducing prices to increase volume, thereby reducing the indirect costs per housing unit handled.
   c. Set up a field force to better manage the direct costs of home purchase, management, and sale.
2. *Problem:* Lack of pricing flexibility.
   Strategies:
   a. Offer client companies alternate pricing arrangements by (1) restructuring the indenture of trust to liberalize the restrictions which precluded nonrisk pricing, and/or (2) creating a new subsidiary company capable of borrowing needed capital independently of the trust.
3. *Problem:* Major financing needs.
   Strategies:
   a. Develop new sources of financing.
   b. Reduce dependency on the parent company for financing.

---

*The *experience curve* is similar to the "learning curve" and to "economies of scale"—the idea that costs go down as the number of units produced increases. The principle has long been accepted with respect to manufacturing costs; the company's consultants, however, maintain that the experience curve applies as well to other costs, including overhead, marketing, advertising, and development.

4. *Problem:* Need for localized service delivery and operating controls.
   Strategies:
   a. Set up a field force at strategic locations.
   b. Open a west coast office.

The recommended strategies were accompanied by detailed plans for implementation.

Management Review
In reviewing the recommendations of the task force, Robert Anderson recognized the validity of the problems stated and the need to revise strategies. It seemed that the recommendations could be condensed to one master strategy: Increase volume, market share, and profits through lower—or more flexible—prices and by creating a specialized field force to provide local services and help control costs.

The assumptions behind this strategy were that: (1) costs can be reduced with experience; (2) higher market share helps to create the experience advantage which allows larger cost-reduction efficiencies; (3) these efficiencies will outweigh the costs required to implement the strategy; and (4) the resulting added volume and lower costs will substantially increase profits.

Because of the investment required to implement the strategy, Robert Anderson pondered the risks as he prepared to discuss the report with Webster Group's president and board of directors.

QUESTION
Should Robert Anderson support the recommended strategies? In arriving at your answer:
1. Develop a situation *analysis* following the outline in Chapter 9.
2. Develop your summary of the major problems and opportunities which may or may not be the same as those identified by the task force.
3. Select market share, revenue, and operating profit objectives you think NRI should try to reach within three years.
4. Evaluate the recommended strategies of the task force, including other alternatives if you prefer them to those of the task force.

A multibusiness company finds it must retrench in order to move forward again.

Case 6

American-Standard: Changing Corporate Strategy

In August of 1971 the new president and chief executive of American Standard, Inc., William Marquard, was discussing a change in corporate strategy with Alan Root, vice president for corporate planning. Mr. Marquard had been thrust into the chief executive's role at a critical time in the company's history. American-Standard's financial position was deteriorating rapidly. The board of directors were looking to Mr. Marquard for a new strategy and plan of action for turning the company around.

Company History
The American Radiator and Standard Sanitary Corporation was formed in 1929 as a holding company made up of the American Radiator Company and the Standard Sanitary Manufacturing Co. Both companies had been founded in 1899. American Radiator was the leading domestic manufacturer of boilers and radiators for the heating of single-family homes, apartment houses, and large buildings. It also held a strong competitive position in the European heating market, having begun manufacturing operations in France at the turn of the century. Standard Sanitary was the leading manufacturer of plumbing equipment in the United States and Canada.

In 1939 the two subsidiaries merged into a single operation. The rationale for the merger was the commonality of markets for the products of both companies and the commonality of distribution channels used. The principal distribution system was through plumbing and heating wholesalers and plumbing and heating dealers to residential, commercial, and industrial building contractors.

The plumbing and heating dealers not only performed an intermediary role in the distribution of the products but also contracted to install them as well. American Radiator's position in Europe also provided the opportunity for the production and sale of Standard Sanitary's plumbing equipment. In time the company had heating and plumbing equipment plants in all of the principal European countries and the United Kingdom.

The foreign-based companies operated under the name Ideal-Standard. "Ideal" was the brand name used for heating equipment, and "Standard" the brand name used for plumbing equipment. In 1967 the U.S. parent company name was shortened to American Standard, Inc. The brand name in the U.S. and Canada was American-Standard.

Cast iron (used for boilers, radiators, and bath tubs) and ceramics (used for toilets, urinals, and lavatories) represented the primary technologies and plant investments for both the European and U.S. businesses, although some additional technologies and facilities had been added as a result of diversified acquisitions made in the United States.

Postwar Developments. Since the end of World War II the European companies had provided a disproportionately higher share of corporate earnings relative to sales. They had engaged in massive rebuilding programs for their bombed-out cities, and these were coupled with modernization of existing buildings. Ideal-Standard's sales and profits grew with the demand for their plumbing and heating products, which were designed according to the preferences of each country.

In the postwar United States, the building industry grew in line with the expanding economy, and American-Standard's sales reflected this growth. The company's domestic profit margins, however, were adversely affected by two market developments. The first was that two large segments of the housing market were composed of (1) low-cost housing developments in the suburbs and (2) government-subsidized low-income multifamily dwellings in the cities. Price-conscious builder-developers demanded low-priced, low-margin plumbing and heating products which were difficult for a high-quality producer such as American-Standard to supply at a profit.

The second market development was that the warm air furnace was rapidly replacing hydronic (hot water) methods of heating. To compete with the furnace, more compact boilers had been developed and cast-iron radiators replaced with cheaper (but less profitable) metal baseboard convectors. The forced-air furnace, however, had the added advantage of easy conversion to air cooling so as to provide all-weather air conditioning. Heating and cooling systems in large buildings also were shifting from large central boilers and air-cooling units to a wide variety of packaged units as well as self-contained room units. Although American-Standard had acquired companies making most of the newer heating and cooling products, these proved to be less profitable than cast iron had been when it was in demand. Many of the company's resources remained tied up in cast iron, however.

In an attempt to offset adverse developments in plumbing and heating, the company had diversified to some extent into other businesses. In addition to plumbing, heating, and air conditioning equipment, American-Standard in 1960 listed among its product lines: processing equipment, heat transfer equipment, fluid drives, pressure and temperature controls, valves, switches, aerospace instruments, and molded-plastic and stamped-steel products. Despite management's efforts to modernize and diversify, profits and margins had declined between 1950 and 1960, though they turned up again by 1965 (see Exhibit 6-1).

Situation in the Sixties. In the mid-1960s the company received another jolt. Profit margins from the European companies began to decline. Not only had growth leveled off as the postwar housing deficit was erased, but heating products were changing also. Lower-cost steel radiators had largely replaced cast-iron radiators, a fact that became dramatically evident as the supply of heating equipment caught up with demand. Steel also began to compete with cast iron for bathtubs and plastic bathroom equipment was introduced in England. (Both developments had begun earlier in the United States.) Furthermore, forced-air heating and cooling systems

EXHIBIT 6-1

American Standard, Inc.—Net Sales and Income after Taxes and Percent Return on Sales

Year	Sales, $ millions	Income, $ millions	% ROS
1945	120.0	5.7	4.8
1950	284.8	28.5	10.6
1955	339.6	22.6	6.7
1960	480.2	13.2	2.7
1965	552.6	18.4	3.3

were being introduced into central Europe by Scandinavian companies. The Ideal-Standard companies were left with their assets largely tied up in cast-iron facilities which were rapidly becoming obsolete due to the changing product demand.

Despite these problems, the situation for American-Standard was far from hopeless. The company produced consistent, if not spectacular, profits and paid dividends regularly. It had maintained the U.S. leadership position in plumbing equipment with strong distribution and an excellent product reputation. The balance sheet was sound. Debt and interest costs were low.

The company was in a position to implement a new strategy if one could be found. At least two mergers with large companies had been attempted but rejected. Management was concerned that the company, with its sound balance sheet and depressed stock price, would become a target for a takeover.

The 1960s had seen acquisition and merger become a common avenue to corporate growth. Acquisitions would be financed by stock issues and cash obtained by long-term borrowing. Then the newly acquired assets would provide the leverage for still further borrowing so that additional acquisitions could be made, and so on ad infinitum. The stock market traded up the stock of the acquiring companies, enabling them to make bargain buys by trading their stock for assets. Heavy debt—a condition to be avoided in well-managed companies in the past—became the new trademark of the high-flying managements of the 1960s. Because the antitrust laws precluded companies with strong market positions from acquiring similar businesses, acquisitions were made in a variety of nonrelated businesses. The term "conglomerate" describes such a company.

New Top Management. It was in this economic and business climate that in 1967 the directors of American Standard elected a new president from outside the company to replace the retiring chief executive. The newcomer had considerable experience in acquisition and merger. His new corporate goals called for a more balanced product line, less dependence on construction markets, and a consistent increase in earnings per share. The strategy was to acquire established companies with profitable growth potential. Since the company's depressed common stock prices did not offer a bargaining tool, cash would be raised through long-term borrowing and preference stock would be issued.

Within two years, two major companies and a number of smaller ones had been acquired. The first large company, acquired largely for cash in 1967, was the Mosler Safe Co.—a leading manufacturer of bank vault doors and security systems. Mosler also was a printer of bank checks and business forms. Banks represented its primary market.

The second company was the Westinghouse Airbrake Co. (WABCO), acquired in 1968 primarily through exchange of American-Standard preference stock* for the common stock of WABCO. WABCO sold to the railway transportation, mining, and construction markets with products such as airbrakes, signaling and communications devices, oil-drilling equipment, coal-mining equipment, pneumatic tools, heavy-duty trucks, and earthmoving equipment. In Europe WABCO also produced airbrakes for the heavy-truck industry.

With these acquisitions American-Standard's product lines could be grouped into four major classifications. These are shown in Exhibit 6-2 along with the sales and profit contributions of each for the year 1970. Product lines are shown in Exhibit 6-3; operating groups, divisions, and subsidiaries are listed in Exhibit 6-4.

By 1970 it was clear that the new strategy had resulted in American-Standard's financial position deteriorating further. From Exhibit 6-5 it can be seen that by 1970 net income had fallen to $3.1 million and long-term debt had grown to $352.1 million. Total interest expense of $41.8 million plus the current portion of long-term debt due—$31 million—exceeded the operating profit of $52 million.

Situation in 1971. Essentially this was the situation when William Marquard became the new chief executive in 1971. It provided the backdrop for his discussions on corporate strategy with his vice president for corporate planning, Alan Root.

William Marquard, a graduate of the Wharton School, University of Pennsylvania, had joined the Mosler Safe Co. in 1952 and was its president when Mosler was acquired by American-Standard in 1967. He continued as president of Mosler and was also an executive vice president of American-Standard. Mr. Marquard had long believed in planning. Mr. Root, with a background in marketing, had been Mr. Marquard's principal planning assistant at Mosler. Prior to its acquisition by American-Standard, Mosler's growth in earnings had stemmed from carefully thought out objectives supported by strategic and tactical plans.

During the sixties American-Standard had not been without sophisticated planning procedures. Corporate management required annual profit plans from its divi-

---

*A special fixed-dividend stock issue ranked below the preferred stock.

EXHIBIT 6-2

American Standard, Inc.—Percent of Sales and Income by Major Business Group in 1970 Compared with Total

Business Group	Sales, $millions	% of Total Sales	Income, $millions	% of Total Income
Building products	672.1	47	11.1	16
Transportation systems	238.2	17	23.8	35
Industrial and construction products	250.5	18	15.3	22
Security and graphic arts	190.8	13	26.3	39
Miscellaneous	66.2	5	(8.3)	(12)
Total	1,417.8	100	68.2*	100

*Net income was $3.1 million after adding other income and deducting interest and corporate expenses, taxes, and extraordinary charges.

Source: 1970 Annual Report.

sions and subsidiaries which were subject to in-depth reviews by corporate management. Strategic planning was introduced in 1967.

The Economic Recession. Some analysts believed that the company's financial problems in 1970 had been due more to unfortunate timing than to the absence of good management. Had American-Standard begun the aggressive acquisition program several years earlier, the strategy might have succeeded. As it happened, however, the economic recession of 1970 caught the company with its financial flank exposed. Overextended with debt and with heavy payments of interest and principal, there was inadequate working capital and no investment capital left to support the profitable segments of the business. Many other conglomerates had been caught in similar circumstances.

New Corporate Strategy

Mr. Marquard, after reviewing the available alternatives, set forth a new corporate strategy designed to stem the negative cash flow and get the company back on a growing profitable basis. The strategy had four interrelated parts:

1. Sell off those businesses that fall into specified categories.
2. Use the proceeds to reduce debt, thereby reducing interest payments.
3. Discontinue unprofitable products and shut down marginal facilities.
4. Concentrate resources on those business areas where the company had strong market positions.

The president's letter to shareholders in the 1971 annual report read in part:

Philosophy

A philosophy of consolidation was adopted in 1971, in contrast to the one of rapid expansion that had prevailed in the past several years. It became apparent that economic conditions, both domestic and international, which had supported expansion through acquisition had changed materially. It was also recognized that our

EXHIBIT 6-3
Product Directory

BUILDING PRODUCTS
American-Standard & Ideal-Standard
Hydronic Heating Equipment
Baseboard Panels
Boilers
Convectors
Radiators

Plumbing Products
Bathtubs
Bidets
Drinking Fountains
Faucets
Fittings
Hospital Fixtures
Lavatories
Sinks
Showers
Toilets and Toilet Seats
Urinals

Majestic
Fireplaces
Indoor Barbecue Equipment

Moderncote
Wall Coverings

Modernfold
Folding Doors
Operable Walls
Partitions

Mutschler
Kitchen Cabinets
School Cabinets

Peabody
School Seating
Space Dividers

Steelcraft
Perma-Door Residential Doors
Steel Doors and Frames—Commercial

CONSTRUCTION EQUIPMENT
WABCO
Graders
Heavy-duty Trucks
Scrapers

GRAPHIC ARTS MATERIALS AND SERVICES
Advertising
Audio-visual Services
Business Forms
Cartons
Checkbooks
Checks
Commercial Printing
Computer Print-out Forms
Deposit Tickets
Marketing Communications
Optical Scan Documents
Packaging Materials
Tabulating Cards

INDUSTRIAL PRODUCTS
American-Standard
Electrostatic Precipitators
Dust Collectors
Fans and Blowers
Fluid Drive Power Transmissions
Heavy Duty Heat Transfer Coils
Steam Generators

WABCO & WABCO WESTINGHOUSE
Aero-Space Relays
Fluid Power
 Accessories
 Cylinders
 Filters
 Lubricators
 Regulators
 Valves

American-Standard & WABCO WESTINGHOUSE
Shell and Tube Heat Exchangers

SECURITY SYSTEMS/ BANK PRODUCTS
Mosler
Alarm Systems
Automated Teller Systems
Automatic Conveyor Systems
Camera Surveillance Systems
Depositories
Drive-up Windows
Electronic Security Systems
Government Security Containers
Locks
Pneumatic Tube Systems
Remote Transaction Systems
Safe Deposit Boxes
Safes
Telelift® Materials Handling Systems
Vault Doors
Vaults

TRANSPORTATION SYSTEMS
WABCO & WABCO WESTINGHOUSE
Automotive Braking Systems (Europe)
Mass Transit Braking and Control Systems
Railway Braking Systems
Railway Classification Yard Systems
Railway Draft Gear
Railway Radio Systems
Railway Remote Control Systems
Railway Signaling Systems
Railway Slack Adjusters

EXHIBIT 6-4
Operating Groups

Building Specialties
- Majestic Company, Huntington, Ind.
  - Condon King Division, Lynwood, Wash.
- Modernfold Industries, New Castle, Ind.
  - Moderncote Division, New Castle, Ind.
  - Modernfold Division, New Castle, Ind.
  - Modernfold, Canada
  - Modernfold G.m.b.H., Germany
- Mutschler, Nappanee, Ind.
- Peabody, N. Manchester, Ind.
- Steelcraft Manufacturing Co., Cincinnati, O.
- Bob Lench Company, Santa Ana, Calif.

Construction & Mining
- WABCO Construction and Mining, Peoria, Ill.
  - WABCO Australia Pty. Limited, Australia
  - WABCO Brasil Equipamentos Limitadas, Brazil
  - WABCO Manufacturing, S.A., Belgium
  - WABCO Equipment Division, Canada

European Industrial Products
- Westinghouse Bremsen- und Apparatebau G.m.b.H., Austria
- International Brake and Rectifier, S.A., Belgium
- Compagnie des Freins et Signaux Westinghouse, France
- Westinghouse Bremsen- und Apparatebau G.m.b.H., Germany
- Westinghouse Remmen en Apparatuur B.V. Holland
- Compagnia Italiana Westinghouse Freni e Segnali, Italy
- Dimetal, S.A., Spain
- Westinghouse Broms- och Reglerteknik A.B., Sweden
- S.A. des Freins et Signaux Westinghouse, Switzerland
- Wabco Westinghouse (U.K.) Ltd.

European Plumbing and Heating
- Ideal-Standard G.m.b.H., Austria
- Ideal-Standard, Benelux
- Ideal-Standard Limited, England
- Ideal-Standard, S.A., France
- Ideal-Standard G.m.b.H., Germany
- Ideal-Standard S.A.I., Greece
- Ideal-Standard S.p.A., Italy
- Oertli-Standard A.G., Switzerland
- Affiliate: Compania Roca-Radiadores, S.A., Spain

Western Hemisphere Plumbing and Heating
- American-Standard Plumbing & Heating (U.S.), New Brunswick, N.J.
- Amstan Supply, New Brunswick, N.J.
- American-Standard Export Division, New Brunswick, N.J.
- American-Standard, Canada
- Ideal-Standard S.A.—Industria e Comercio, Brazil
- Ideal-Standard S.A. de C.V., Mexico
- Affiliates:
  - Industria Ceramica Centroamericana, S.A., Nicaragua;
  - Industria Ceramica Costarricense, Ltda., Costa Rica;
  - Sanitary Wares Manufacturing Corp., Philippines;
  - American-Standard Sanitaryware (Thailand) Ltd.

American Standard Credit Inc. / Pittsburgh, Pa.

Graphic Arts
- Bank Check Division, Baltimore, Md.
- American Bank Stationery Co., Baltimore, Md.
- Bankers Lithographing Co., Pittsburgh, Pa.
- Business Forms Division, Hunt Valley, Md.
- Bedinghaus Business Forms Co., Cincinnati, O.
- Forms, Inc., Willow Grove, Pa.
- Litho Formas, S.A., Mexico
- Pioneer Business Forms, Inc., Tacoma, Wash.
- Woehrmyer Printing Co., Denver, Colo.
- Commercial Printing Division, Hunt Valley, Md.
- Adcrafters, Inc., Baltimore, Md.
- Frye & Smith, Ltd., San Diego, Calif.
- Graphic Services, Detroit, Mich.
- Keller-Crescent Co., Evansville, Ind.
- Lebanon Valley Offset Co., Cleona, Pa.
- Stern Majestic Press, Philadelphia, Pa.
- Twin City Press, N. Plainfield, N.J.

Land and Shelter
- A-S Development Inc., Newport Beach, Calif.
- Kendall Development Division, Newport Beach, Cal.
  - Arizona Division
  - California Division
  - New Jersey Division
- Builders Homes, Dothan, Ala.

Power and Controls
- General Industry Products
  - Fluid Power Division, Lexington, Ky.
  - General Sales Division, Dearborn, Mich.
  - Heat Exchanger Division, Buffalo, N.Y.
  - Air Quality Control Division, Dearborn, Mich.
  - Industrial Products Division, Dearborn, Mich.
  - American-Standard Industrial Products, Canada

Security and Business Systems
- The Mosler Safe Company
  - Airmatic Systems Division, Wayne, N.J.
  - Bank & Commercial Division, Hamilton, O.
  - Counter Systems Division, Buffalo, N.Y.
  - Dropository Division, Kansas City, Mo.
  - Hermann Safe Company, San Francisco, Calif.
  - Electronic Systems Div., Danbury, Conn.
  - Sales & Service Division, Hamilton, O.
  - Mosler Internacional S.A., Hamilton, O.
  - Mosler Hidraulica, S.A. de C.V., Mexico
  - Productos Mosler, S.A. de C.V., Mexico
  - Mosler de Puerto Rico
  - Affiliates: Fuji Seiko Co. Ltd., Japan; Chubb-Mosler and Taylor Holdings, Ltd., Canada

Transportation
- Westinghouse Air Brake Company
  - Westinghouse Air Brake Division, Wilmerding, Pa.
  - Union Switch & Signal Division, Swissvale, Pa.
  - WABCO Ltd., Canada
  - Cardwell Westinghouse Co., Chicago, Ill.
  - Canadian Cardwell Division, Canada
  - Freios e Sinais do Brasil, S.A., Brazil

debt level and interest costs were impeding the progress of the company and, therefore, had to be reduced.

Strategy

Our revised strategy calls for us to concentrate on several important business areas in which we have strong market positions and to develop the normal growth of these businesses through reinvestment of earnings after providing reasonable dividends to our stockholders.

Asset Redeployment

We adopted a program of asset redeployment which was described to you . . . [earlier]. One part of this program, related to debt reduction, involves the sale of certain of our businesses that fall into one of three categories: (1) those that are peripheral to our main lines of endeavor; (2) those that require more additional capital than we deem it advisable to invest; or (3) those that do not have the future profit potential to warrant the existing investment. The other part of the program, designed to improve profitability in our basic businesses, will involve a number of facility shutdowns, consolidations, and product eliminations.

Extraordinary Charge

An extraordinary 1971 charge to earning of $97 million, after $25 million of tax benefit, is to provide for estimated expenditures and losses that will be sustained in carrying out the foregoing asset redeployment plan. The implementation of this program is moving forward. In 1971 we adopted an operations plan that purposely restricted sales volume at some sacrifice in profits in favor of an intense emphasis on overhead cost cutting and reduction of funds tied up in working capital. A substantial reduction was made in 1971 operating expenses. Our concentration on cash management resulted in a debt reduction of $56 million.

In the first two months of 1972, arrangements were made for the sale of three operations for approximately

EXHIBIT 6-5
American Standard, Inc.—Comparative Financial Data (In millions of dollars except for earnings per common share)

Year	Net Sales	Net Income after Tax	Earnings per Common Share	Long-Term Debt	Interest Expense
1950	284.8	28.5	$2.80		0.2
1955	339.6	22.6	1.65		
1960	480.2	13.2	1.10	15.4	0.1
1965	552.6	18.4	1.81	21.0	1.0
1970	1,417.8	3.1*	(.53)†	352.1	41.8

*After extraordinary charges of $10 million.

†Indicated as a loss because preferred and preference stock dividend requirements exceeded net income.

Source: Company annual reports.

EXHIBIT 6-6
Abstract of the Annual American-Standard Strategic Planning Guidelines Issued to Operating Units

General Approach and Scheduling

The *Strategic Plan* covers a five-year period and is prepared by each group, division, subsidiary, or other designated profit center. Corporate management reviews the strategic plans during the third calendar quarter of the year preceding the beginning year of the plan.

As the strategic plan of each business unit is approved, it is followed by the preparation of a detailed *Profit Plan* for the first year of the five-year strategy plan. Reviews of profit plans are scheduled by top management for the months of November and December.

Management reviews are held with each business unit the second quarter of the following year to compare first quarter performance against profit plan and the forecast for the balance of the year.

Forecast of Environment
1. Economic Indicators
   a. Assumptions
   b. Quantitative forecasts
2. Markets
   a. Assumptions
   b. Quantitative forecasts by major segments
   c. Segments to be added or abandoned
3. Technological
   a. Anticipated changes
4. Resource Analysis
   a. Strengths and weaknesses of
      (1) Marketing
      (2) Technical capability
      (3) Physical facilities
      (4) Management skills

Objectives
1. Scope/Charter
   a. Define business mission
   b. Rank potential future alternative missions
2. Business Objectives
   a. List top 3 to 5

3. Marketing
   a. For each major market segment, estimate
      (1) Segment sales
      (2) Business unit's share
      (3) Business unit's sales
4. Strategies, Programs, Schedules
   a. In support of each business objective
5. Functional Objectives
   a. List top 3 for
      (1) Engineering/R&D
      (2) Manufacturing
      (3) Employee/Community relations
      (4) Other

Financials
1. By profit centers and summarized by group
   a. Sales and income statement
   b. Capital outlay
      (1) New
      (2) Carry-overs
   c. Balance sheet
   d. Return on assets
   e. Cash flow

Note: The strategic and profit planning instructions issued in 1979 were essentially the same as the above except for these additional analyses:

1. Social and political assumptions
2. Products to be dropped
3. Key competitors
4. Value added objectives
5. Employment cost objectives

Some of the analyses were more sophisticated than those called for in the 1970 plan, and more graphics were to be used in presenting data.

$57 million. These were the Environmental Comfort Systems Group, the Drilling Equipment Division, and the Pneumatic Equipment Division. The proceeds will be used to reduce debt further.

Marquard and Root were familiar with the strengths and weaknesses of the various businesses, having studied the strategies, profit plans, and financial records of the operating units. Operating unit plans—originally designed as road maps for growth—now became valuable tools in planning for contraction and redeployment of assets. An outline of the company's strategic and business plan (shown in Exhibit 6-6) indicates the kinds of information that were available for each unit.

It was apparent that a tourniquet was needed to stop the outflow of cash and that speed was essential. It was agreed that Mr. Root would recommend a set of criteria for determining businesses to be retained or disposed of. The criteria were to incorporate the longer-term as well as the shorter-term aspects of each division. Mr. Marquard would discuss the criteria with the management committee. Once agreed upon, Mr. Root was to recommend that each business and product line be placed in one of three classifications—retain, sell, or discontinue—and then be ranked in order of priority.

Mr. Marquard was to clear the recommendations with the management committee and the board of directors. Specific recommendations would be discussed with affected operating managers and opportunity provided for opposing views to be heard. He knew this process would not be easy. Every business or product scheduled for divestment would have champions at both operating and corporate levels. While every effort would be made to treat people humanely, some would have to be terminated. Morale would suffer until the period of uncertainty was over. Mr. Marquard was certain that the sooner the plan was agreed to, explained to the organization, and actions taken, the better it would be for all concerned.

QUESTIONS

1. What alternate strategies might Mr. Marquard have considered after becoming president?
2. Evaluate the strategy that was adopted.
3. What specific types of data from the strategic plan (Exhibit 6-6) would be most helpful to Mr. Root in classifying the company's products and businesses by (1) retain, (2) sell, or (3) discontinue, and for ranking them in order of priority?

*Management must decide whether to divest a product line
or develop a new strategy for it.*

Case 7

American-Standard: The Stainless Steel Sink Problem

Between 1971 and 1978, American-Standard had followed through with the strategy announced in 1971 by President William Marquard. The results had been nothing less than spectacular.

In essence the strategy, as described in the previous case, involved (1) divestiture of those businesses and products that did not meet—or show promise of meeting—management criteria, and (2) redeployment of the assets, freed up by these moves, into the remaining businesses in which the company had strong market positions.

By 1978 American-Standard had got out of a number of businesses, including heating (one of the company's original main businesses), air conditioning, drilling equipment, pneumatic equipment, control and power equipment, land and shelter development, and sixty-nine company-owned plumbing and heating wholesale outlets. Funds obtained from the disposal of these businesses and the operating capital no longer needed to run them had been used to reduce debt and to improve the company's four main businesses:

EXHIBIT 7-1

Major Product Lines	Major Customers	Plant Locations
TRANSPORTATION PRODUCTS		
WABCO braking systems for heavy trucks	Heavy truck manufacturers, repair and spare parts distributors, and service outlets	Germany, Austria, England, France, Italy, Sweden, and Brazil
Westinghouse air brakes and Cardwell draft gears for freight cars, locomotives, and mass transit cars	Railroad car builders	United States, Canada, Brazil, Italy, France, Belgium, and Germany
Union Switch & Signal systems for train monitoring and control	Railway companies, mass transit systems, and national railways	United States and Italy
Industrial products (e.g., fluid power devices, heat exchangers, industrial fans, and fluid drives)	Utilities, marine manufacturers, and other capital goods industries	United States, Canada, Germany, France, Italy, and England
BUILDING PRODUCTS		
American-Standard and Ideal-Standard plumbing fixtures and fittings	Residential and nonresidential building contractors and owners usually served through wholesale distributors	United States, Canada, Mexico, Brazil, Belgium, England, Germany, Greece, and Italy
Majestic fireplaces, Modernfold movable walls and partitions, and Steelcraft steel doors and frames	Residential and nonresidential building contractors and owners usually served through wholesale distributors	United States
CONSTRUCTION AND MINING EQUIPMENT		
HAULPAK off-highway trucks (35-ton to 250-ton) and WABCO scrapers and graders	Construction, road, and earthmoving contractors generally served through distributors; open-pit mining operators	United States, Canada, Brazil, Australia, and Belgium
SECURITY AND GRAPHIC PRODUCTS		
Mosler safes, vaults, electronic alarms, cameras, and associated security equipment	Financial institutions, primarily banks; commercial organizations; and government agencies	United States and Mexico
Bank checks and stationery (American Bank Stationery)	Financial institutions	United States
Business forms	Industrial and commercial organizations	United States
Commercial printing (e.g., advertising, packaging, annual reports, etc.)	Industrial and commercial organizations	United States

Compare this exhibit with Exhibits 6-3 and 6-4 to see which businesses were divested.

- Transportation products
- Building products
- Construction and mining equipment*
- Security and graphic products

The makeup of these four businesses is shown in Exhibit 7-1. The company's annual report for 1978 characterized the four major businesses:

1. Most have long histories, high reputations, and meet essential needs such as safety and sanitation.
2. They are global in scope.
3. They have positions of market leadership or are among the top three in their industries.
4. They require highly skilled workers, artisans, and significant capital investment.
5. They have growth rates close to the GNPs of the economies in which they operate.
6. They generate more cash than needed for reinvestment in each business.
7. None is losing money (See Exhibit 7-2).

The Divestment Planning Process

American-Standard's management believed that the analysis of marginal businesses for possible pruning should be a continuing aspect of the strategic-planning process. Evolutionary and revolutionary changes in markets and technologies inevitably would affect investment priorities. Furthermore, products would likely continue to surface which could not meet (short of uneconomic infusions of capital) the company's market objective of being among the top industry leaders. Consequently, the annual strategic- and profit-planning process was used to identify products for divestment consideration as well as for opportunities for sales and profit improvement. One such product line that came under scrutiny during the planning period for 1979 was stainless steel sinks, a line that had not been profitable for several years.

The Plumbing Products Situation. Stainless steel sinks represented one of the product lines of the U.S. Plumbing Products Group which in turn was a part of the Building Products Business. This product line had never had an important share of the stainless steel sink market, but had been carried to support a sales policy that called for supplying the company's plumbing distributors with a full American-Standard line.

American-Standard had long been the leading U.S. manufacturer of plumbing products and carried the most complete product line of any manufacturer. The Plumbing Products sales force believed that the completeness of the line was an important reason for the company's strong distribution. Over 1200 independent distributors featured the American-Standard line of high-quality plumbing products. (Distributors normally carried one first-quality brand of a general-line manufacturer and secondary lines of lower-priced brands which specialized in one category of plumbing product.)

Approximate brand market shares for the plumbing products industry are shown in Exhibit 7-3. The "All Others" category is generally made up of brands that specialize by product category, such as Elkay in stainless steel sinks and Moen in single-lever faucets.

Exhibit 7-4 shows estimated industry sales for 1977 by category and by American-Standard's share of each category. Stainless steel sinks with sales of $66.5 million represented the smallest industry category. American-

EXHIBIT 7-2
American Standard, Inc.—Key Performance Measurements

	1971	1975	1978
Sales, $ millions	1,410	1,622	2,111
Net income, $ millions	13.2	44.8	101.0
Return on sales, %	0.9	2.8	4.8
Debt to equity ratio	.99	.46	.43
Return on equity, %	3.8	11.0	23.4

Source: Company annual reports.

EXHIBIT 7-3
Approximate Market Shares in Plumbing Products Industry, 1977

Brand	% Share
American-Standard	20
Kohler	16
Eljer	10
Universal Rundle	5
All others	49
	100

*Replaces the Industrial and Construction Products Classification used in 1971.

EXHIBIT 7-4

Estimated Industry Sales by Product Category and American-Standard Share, 1977

Product Category	Industry Sales, $ millions	American-Standard % Share
Vitreous china	341.4	31
Plumbing fittings	279.4	14
Enameled iron	166.3	29
Plastic	207.7	10
Enameled steel	75.5	14
Stainless steel	66.5	5
	1,136.8	20

EXHIBIT 7-6

Private Housing Starts—Actual and Forecast

Actual		Forecast	
Year	Number, 1000s	Year	Number, 1000s
1972	2,357	1979	1,650
1973	2,045	1980	1,860
1974	1,338	1981	1,970
1975	1,160	1982	1,950
1976	1,538	1983	1,650
1977	1,987		
1978	2,000		

Source: U.S. Plumbing Products Group.

Standard had both its lowest dollar sales and lowest market share in this product category—$3.3 million sales and 5 percent market share.

Stainless Steel Sinks. Demand for stainless steel sinks, like other building products, is tied closely to housing construction, a cyclical industry whose volume of new housing starts is greatly affected by changes in interest rates. (See Exhibit 7-5 for a graph of housing starts from 1965 to 1977.) Exhibit 7-6 shows the Plumbing Products Group's 5-year forecast of housing starts.

Housing represents the largest single industry in the United States. It is a relatively mature industry, however, tied to population growth and family formations. There were 74 million occupied housing units in 1976. The average annual growth rate was 2.6 percent between 1970 and 1976. (Growth is the result of new units minus units removed by fire, demolition, etc.) Plumbing products sales tend to lag housing starts by about three months. Plumbing products sales do not reach the extreme peaks and valleys of new home starts, because in periods of low building activity, some of the slack is taken up by remodeling.

Exhibit 7-7 shows the Plumbing Products Group's forecast of stainless steel sink industry sales in units and dollars. The differences in rate of annual change between units and dollars are unexplained, but may be due to price changes.

Assuming no change in strategy, the Plumbing Products Group's forecast was for rising sales and share of market for its stainless steel sinks until 1983. The share of market had risen in the past three years as a result of special sales efforts, but there was some doubt as to whether this could continue with no change in strategy. Even if the forecast turned out to be correct, there would be a "planning gap" in market share, since American-Standard management considered 10 percent as a minimum acceptable market share. Forecasts in both units and dollars are shown in Exhibit 7-8. Market share in dollars is higher than in units because American-Standard's prices were higher than the industry average.

Reasons for Stainless Steel Sink Problem. The primary reason for the position of this product line was that American-Standard had never made the investments in

EXHIBIT 7-5

New Housing Units Started 1965 to 1977. *Source:* U.S. Bureau of the Census, *Statistical Abstract of the United States,* Washington, D.C., 1978, p. 778.

EXHIBIT 7-7
Stainless Steel Sink Industry Sales—Actual and Forecast

	Actual			Forecast				
	1976	1977	1978	1979	1980	1981	1982	1983
Units, 1000s	2659	3310	3546	3377	3407	3702	3722	3414
% Change		24.5	7.1	(4.8)	0.9	8.7	0.5	(8.3)
Dollars, millions	63.4	68.8	77.5	78.8	85.3	99.9	106.6	104.0
% Change		8.5	12.6	1.7	8.2	17.1	6.7	(2.4)

Source: 1979 Strategic Plan, U.S. Plumbing Products Group.

design, production facilities, and market development necessary to bring sales to a level that would permit an acceptable profit return. Without competitive designs and manufacturing costs it was impossible to attain the lower unit manufacturing costs that would accompany higher production rates.

The historical background of these conditions was that American-Standard's traditional technology and investments, in its plumbing and heating businesses, were associated with vitreous china, cast iron, and enameled iron. The company, for example, had a profitable market position in enameled-iron kitchen sinks. Consequently, it had tried to fight the invasion of stainless steel in kitchen sinks with enameled iron. This turned out to be a losing battle, since stainless steel has lower costs when produced in quantity, yet provides essentially the same sanitary qualities as enamel. Neither was stainless steel as easily damaged in kitchen use as enameled iron. The latter was subject to chipping or cracking when hit by a hard object. The principal disadvantage of stainless steel was that it was more noisy under conditions of kitchen use than was enamelware.

By the time American-Standard decided to "join 'em rather than fight 'em," strong market positions had already been staked out by others. The American-Standard reaction to stainless steel was typical of what has happened in other industries when invaded by technological competition from outside industries. In this case competition came from companies with technology and investment in steel-stamping facilities. The steel-stamping industry was far more able to utilize mass production techniques than was the cast-iron industry. In the final analysis, the American-Standard Plumbing Group's excellent sales force and its good relations with its distributors were no match for the new technology and its economies of scale.

Industry Competition. The principal competitor was Elkay, a company that specialized in stainless steel sinks for home, commercial, and institutional use. Just, Jensen, and others in the business were also specialists. American-Standard was the only general-line plumbing company offering stainless steel sinks. Estimated market shares for 1978 are shown in Exhibit 7-9.

EXHIBIT 7-8
Sales Forecast of American-Standard Stainless Steel Sinks and Share of Market

	Actual			Forecast				
	1976	1977	1978	1979	1980	1981	1982	1983
Units, 1000s	59	114	140	195	204	240	240	175
SOM, %	2.2	3.4	3.9	5.8	6.0	6.5	6.5	5.1
Dollars, millions	1.9	3.2	4.1	6.0	6.5	8.1	9.0	7.2
SOM, %	3.0	4.7	5.3	7.6	7.6	8.1	8.4	6.9

Source: 1979 Strategic Plan, U.S. Plumbing Products Group.

EXHIBIT 7-9
Approximate Brand Shares of Stainless Steel Sink Market, 1978

Brand	% SOM
Elkay	60
Just	8
Jensen	6
American-Standard	4
All others	22
	100

Elkay produced quality products and offered the widest line in the stainless steel sink industry. It had excellent distribution including many distributors who featured American-Standard as their quality full-line plumbing product brand. Some American-Standard distributors did not carry American-Standard stainless steel sinks, but did carry Elkay.

Despite its higher production costs, American-Standard found it necesary to meet Elkay's prices. American-Standard carried two price lines with a total of thirty-one models. The premium line accounted for 25 percent of sales, and the lower price line 75 percent. Elkay offered similar price lines for the home market. Elkay was generally considered to be the industry leader in terms of design and quality.

Strategic Alternatives

During the strategic-planning process for the 1979–1983 plans period, the Plumbing Products Group considered four alternate strategies:

1. Continue as is. While the 5-year forecasts showed increasing sales levels, the financial forecasts showed that losses would continue during the 5 years. (See

EXHIBIT 7-10
Financial Forecasts—Stainless Steel Sinks

	1975	1976	1977	1978	
	HISTORY				
Market, 1000s of units	2313	2659	3310	3546	
A-S sales, 1000s of units	65	59	114	140	
% share of market	2.8	2.2	3.4	3.9	
Net sales, $ millions	2.0	1.9	3.2	4.1	
Operating income, $ millions	(0.2)	(0.6)	(0.6)	(0.2)	
Operating income, %	(10.0)	(31.6)	(20.2)	(3.7)	
Net assets, $ millions	1.1	1.2	1.5	1.4	
RONA	(19.2)	(48.9)	(43.1)	(10.4)	
	1979 Plan	1980	1981	1982	1983
	FORECAST*				
Market, 1000s of units	3377	3407	3702	3722	3414
A-S sales, 1000s of units	195	204	240	240	175
% share of market	5.8	6.0	6.5	6.5	5.1
Net sales, $ millions	6.0	6.5	8.1	9.0	7.2
Operating income, $ millions	(0.2)	(0.3)	(0.2)	(0.3)	(0.3)
Operating income, %	(3.9)	(4.0)	(3.0)	(3.0)	(4.0)
Net assets, $ millions	2.4	2.7	3.3	3.6	3.2
RONA	(9.6)	(9.5)	(7.4)	(7.6)	(9.4)

*Assuming the stainless steel sink business unit continues as per 1978 strategy without major investment for expansion.

Source: Analysis prepared by the U.S. Plumbing Products Group, 1979.

Exhibit 7-10.) There would also be rising needs for manufacturing capital investment and operating capital to support the higher sales. The advantage of the "continue-as-is" strategy would be that a full plumbing products line could continue to be offered to distributors.

2. Attempt to reduce losses, and eventually make at least some profit. Several ideas were considered, although none was thought to be sufficiently productive that it would cause the product line to attain corporate profit standards.

a. Attempt to shift the mix ratio to a higher proportion of the higher-priced, higher-margin line.
b. Raise prices.
c. Cease manufacture, and purchase product from outside sources for resale under American-Standard brand name.
d. Sell to the do-it-yourself market through retail outlets such as hardware and mass merchandising stores. (American-Standard's normal channel was through distributors to plumbing contractors who sell and install for builders and homeowners.) It was thought this might add some 20 to 35 percent more unit sales, but could also antagonize the traditional distributors and contractors. Plumbing products distribution channels are shown in Exhibit 7-11.
e. Drop the low-price line and sell only the high-price line.
f. Reduce the number of models offered.

3. Divest the product line. It was estimated that $1 million in cash could be recovered from liquidated assets and that $900,000 in unrecovered assets could be recorded as a pretax book loss.

The sales department was strongly opposed to this solution. Sales executives argued that when distributors could order a full line from a single source, distributors saved on the combined shipments. It was believed that this helped the sales force sell distributors the full line, including the profitable products. However, as noted previously, this presumed advantage had not kept many distributors from favoring Elkay as their prime supplier of stainless steel sinks.

4. Invest what would be required to bring the line up to company profit standards. This would require infu-

EXHIBIT 7-11
Distribution Channels for Plumbing Products Installed in Housing

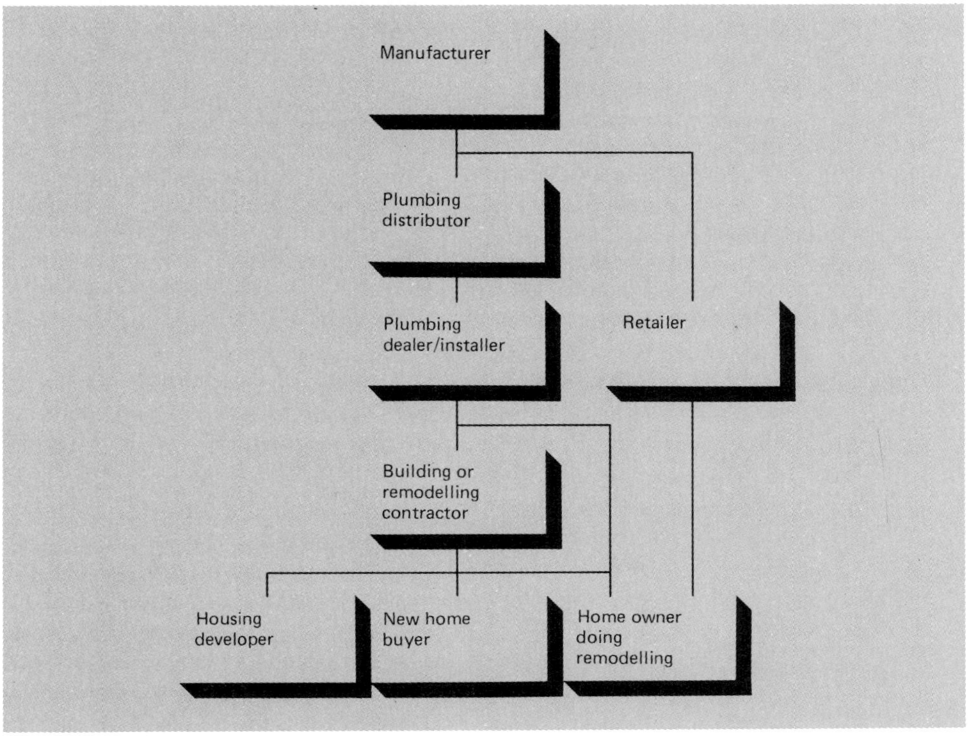

sion of capital for product redesign, line broadening, new tooling, plant modernization, and market development—actions which could require several years to accomplish.

Rough estimates of new capital requirements totaled $2 million. Share of market would have to increase to about 11 percent before units would be sufficient to provide the necessary economies of scale to make product costs competitive.

PROBLEMS

1. Work up a *situation analysis*.
2. Evaluate the strategic alternatives.
3. Recommend one of the alternate strategies, and support your choice with reasons.

PART FOUR
Organizing, Directing, and Controlling Marketing Operations

*T*he classic functions of management include planning—the determination of goals, strategies, and tactical plans and programs; organizing—developing and maintaining structures within which people can work together to carry out the plans and achieve the goals; directing—the activities the manager must take to ensure that people carry out the plans; and controlling—measuring and reporting progress towards goals. The figure shows how the four functions of planning, organizing, directing and controlling form a marketing management model.

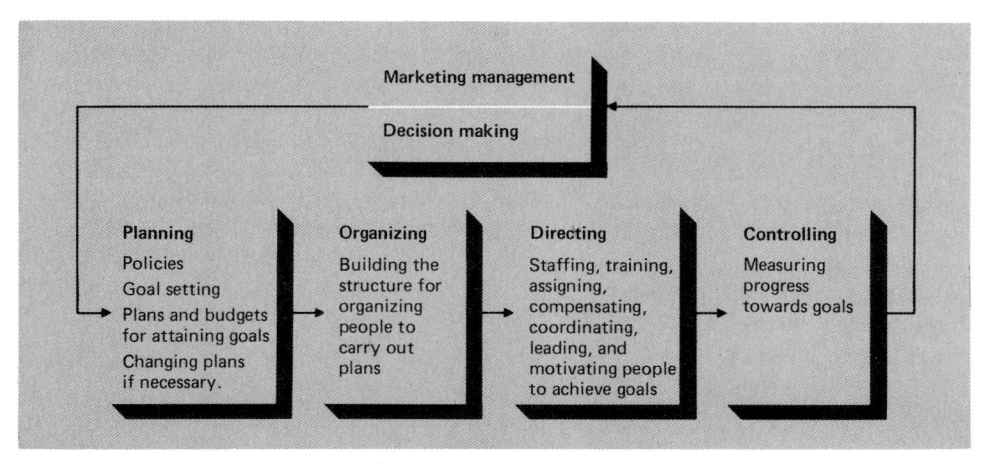

```
                    Marketing management
                    ─────────────────────
                       Decision making

   Planning           Organizing          Directing            Controlling
   Policies           Building the        Staffing, training,  Measuring
   Goal setting       structure for       assigning,           progress
   Plans and budgets  organizing          compensating,        towards goals
   for attaining goals people to          coordinating,
   Changing plans     carry out           leading, and
   if necessary.      plans               motivating people
                                          to achieve goals
```

Marketing management model.

Chapter 14 deals with the structuring of the marketing organization. Modern organization practice is based on some old and classic principles which have been modified to meet the needs of today's large, complex, changing companies. We explain why and how company and marketing organization must be restructured to meet changing situations. This chapter will help you to recognize the type of organization structure used by the company you work for. It will also help you to learn when an organization needs changing.

Chapter 15 covers both direction and control. Direction is discussed in terms of coordination, communication, personnel administration, decisionmaking, and organizational behavior. Organizational behavior is emphasized because it is a subject of increasing importance to marketing managers. Managers must understand how to lead rather than drive

PART FOUR
ORGANIZING, DIRECTING, AND CONTROLLING MARKETING OPERATIONS

people to the achievement of organizational goals. We will discuss the subject in terms of theories dealing with group behavior, leadership, and motivation.

Chapter 15 concludes with a discussion of managerial control. Although control is an essential function of effective management, we will limit our discussion to the purpose and role of control, types of control information, and the characteristics of a good reporting system. Normally, the controller's office provides much of the control information, but marketing management should specify the information it needs.

In Part Four of this text we are trying to make sure that you understand the importance of executing plans effectively and that you are exposed to the principal managerial tools used for this purpose. The best marketing plans are of little value unless the marketing manager is skilled at getting the plans carried out in an effective manner. To do this the manager needs to understand organization, direction, and control.

CHAPTER 14

Structuring the Marketing Organization

In a one-person enterprise no organizational structure exists nor is one needed. The moment a second person is added, however, the need for organization is created. The duties, responsibilities, and authority of each person must be agreed to and working relationships established. The arrangement can be quite informal when there are only a few employees and the boss is present to provide supervision.

The situation changes, however, when the firm grows so large that the boss no longer can supervise everyone personally. At that point a more formal organizational structure becomes essential. People must be grouped according to the particular functions they perform. Supervisors for the groups must be appointed and assigned responsibilities for accomplishing certain goals. Some of the boss' authority must be shared with the supervisors so that they can carry out their responsibilities without constant checking with the boss. Employees need to know their own functions and responsibilities as well as those of others with whom they interact.

The Classic Organization Model

Corporations generally follow a hierarchical form of organization borrowed from the military and the Roman Catholic church. A classic model is shown in Figure 14-1. Lines of authority run from the manager at the top of the pyramid through each managerial level. Orders flow downward through these channels to the workers; communications flow upward through the same channels. This is sometimes called

FIGURE 14-1. Hierarchical form of organization.

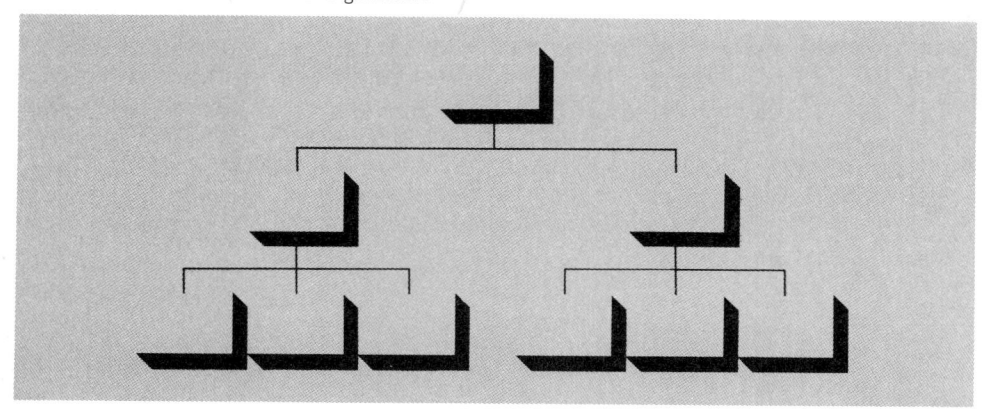

the *chain of command*. In the classic hierarchy one person reports to one boss which is known as *unity of command*.

Companies have made modifications to the model as they have grown in size and diversity. The strict concepts of authority, supervision, and communication attributed to the classic hierarchy provide insufficient flexibility for today's complex business organizations operating in an environment of competition and change. Out of necessity most modern corporations now use a *modified hierarchical* structure in which top management's authority is delegated to lower levels of management and informal communication across organization lines is encouraged. The formal authority structure remains, however, to be used as needed to fulfull top management's fiducial and legal responsibilities.[1]

Importance of Understanding Organization

One cannot understand management without understanding organization. As a minimum you should be familiar with concepts of authority, organizational guidelines, the rules for charting, and common forms of organization, each of which is described in this chapter. Some near term practical benefits for you are:

1. It will help you to understand and solve cases.
2. When job hunting it will help you to understand differences in companies and where a position being applied for fits within the overall organization.
3. On the job it will help you to understand your role and how things get done in the company.
4. It may help you get promoted. As a supervisor or as a staff assistant to an executive, you will likely become involved with planning and charting changes in organization.

Definition of Organization

Working together in an organization, people can accomplish things they could not accomplish working alone. A formal definition of organization is:

> *Organization* is the framework or structure within which people are assigned tasks, responsibilities, and authority, and their work is coordinated to carry out plans and achieve goals.

Two aspects of organization require emphasis. One is *structure*, the organizational framework within which people work; the other is *organizational behavior*, how people act within the structure. The formal structure of organization can be communicated visually by means of charts and position descriptions. Organizational behavior, covered in the next chapter, is less easily portrayed. Structure and behavior are but two sides of the same coin, however, and both should be considered in the study of organization.

Reasons for Organizational Change

Organizational change occurs frequently in any successful, growing company. The basic form of organization may remain the same but changes within the basic model can occur at any time. Annual business and marketing plans, for example, often include proposals for modifying the organization plan. Change can be caused by:

1. Growth in sales which results in more employees, more supervisors, and more levels of supervision
2. Need for specialists brought about by the complexities of size, new technology, new business functions, and new laws and government regulations
3. Addition of new products
4. Entry into new markets
5. Diversification into new businesses
6. Decisions to centralize or decentralize decision-making authority
7. Need to contract the organization as a result of falling sales, deemphasis of some part of the business, or desire to get out of certain businesses altogether

FUNDAMENTALS OF ORGANIZATION DESIGN

Later we will look at various types of organizations. But first we examine fundamentals of organization design which will help you to interpret charts and better understand the reasons why different forms are used in different situations.

Types of Authority

Two basic types of authority commonly are used in business organization—line and functional. A third type is advisory, which has no direct authority over others.

Line Authority. This is the authority managers have over the people assigned to them. Traditionally, line authority includes the authority to hire, assign, direct, make changes in pay, or fire employees. Largely because of laws affecting minorities, women, and union contracts, however, managers at lower levels normally must obtain approval from the personnel department and/or higher levels of management before taking personnel actions involving change of status (hire, fire, pay change, promotion.) The line manager, however, retains considerable influence over personnel actions and, of course, directs people in their work assignments.

The chief executive has line (command) authority over everyone in the organization. In practice, however, chief executives delegate most of this authority to the executives reporting to them, who in turn delegate some of their authority to the next lower level, and so on down the line to the lowest level. Figure 14-2 shows that the chief executive has direct line authority over the seven positions shown in the shaded blocks, as indicated by the solid lines connecting these positions to the chief executive. The shaded block positions in turn have line authority over the positions reporting to them as illustrated by the solid lines connecting the manager of one division (B) with the division managers of manufacturing and marketing and the controller.

Accountability for Results. Although managers delegate responsibility and authority through the chain of command, higher management still holds managers accountable for the actions and performance of their people. Even the chief executive is held accountable by the board of directors for everything that happens in the organization. This is a basic precept of modern business organization. The

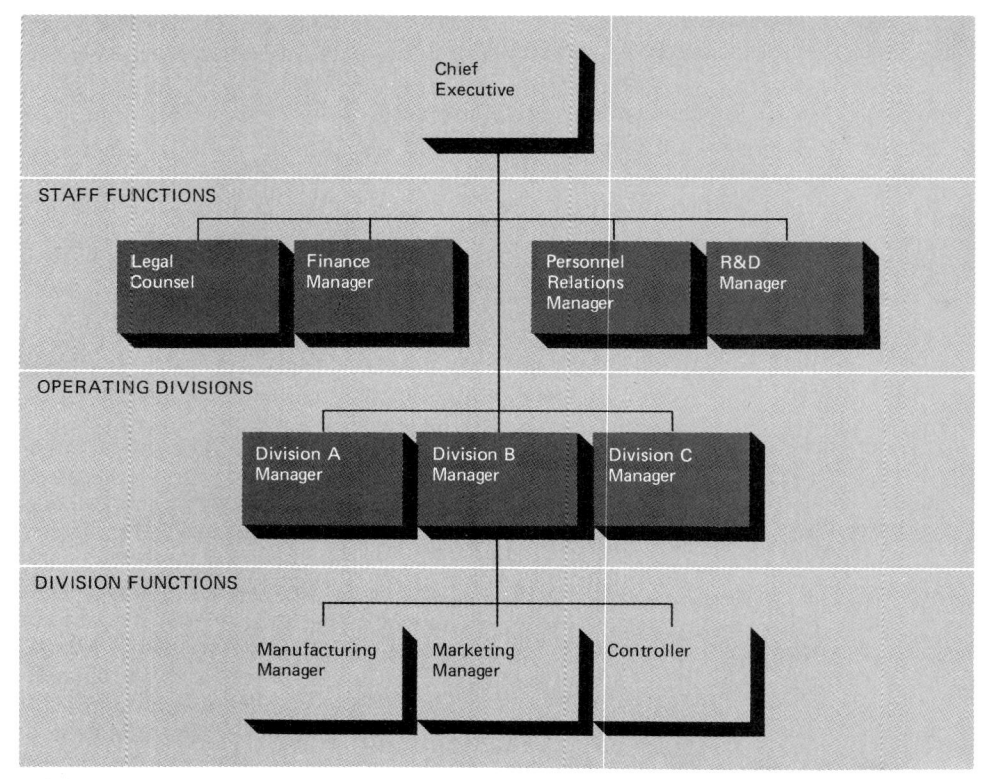

FIGURE 14-2. Line reporting relationships between the chief executive and the staff and operating division manager positions, also between a division manager (B) and managers of the division functional departments.

degree to which managers delegate responsibility and authority varies to some extent with company policy and practice, but primarily with the individual style of the manager. Generally speaking, the manager who can delegate to others successfully is more productive than the manager who insists on making most of the decisions.

Staff Authority. In a business organization there are two types of positions—*operating* and *staff.* Operating* positions are those concerned with production, distribution and sales—namely, manufacturing† and marketing. Those functions that provide support for operations—such as finance, accounting, personnel, and legal—are generally considered staff positions.

Two types of authority are associated with staff positions—*advisory* and *functional.* A staff position may hold only one type of authority or both. There are also staff positions, such as the "assistant to" an executive, which have no authority except the "assistant to" may act as a conduit, transferring directives from the boss.

---

*The term "line" is sometimes used as a synonym for "operating" in referring to positions, functions, or organizational units.

†In a service organization where manufacturing is absent, operating positions would be those involved in providing the service.

Advisory Authority. Staff specialists exist to provide expert advice, such as legal counsel. They may give specialized information, such as the data the marketing research manager provides from market studies. They also may assist others, such as the engineering department helping the production department to solve technical problems.

Staff specialists generally have no direct authority to require others to accept their advice. Their authority is measured by their influence in getting others to accept their recommendations. Staff specialists carry implied authority, however, because of their expertise. Operating managers who ignore the specialist's advice do so at their peril.

Functional Authority. As the management of the modern corporation becomes more complex (including dealing with more and more laws and regulations), it becomes essential that some staff departments be authorized to give directions to others not under their direct control. This authority should be limited to specified functions to be exercised *only* over those parts of the organization named by the chief executive. For example, the finance executive (through such deputies as the treasurer, chief accountant, or controller) commonly is authorized by the chief executive to instruct operating and staff departments how they will handle cash, accounting records, and control reports. The personnel officer may be authorized to specify and enforce the rules covering personnel actions.

In a large company a line manager receives directions from several functional staff departments. A district sales manager, for instance, may be obliged to carry out orders received from such staff departments as accounting, credit, personnel relations, and sales training. Nevertheless, the district sales manager knows that the regional sales manager is the line boss. Furthermore, the regional manager is accountable for the total performance of the district sales manager, including the carrying out of directives from the functional staff departments.

Combinations of Authority. It is not unusual to find staff executives exercising two or more types of authority. This need not create problems as long as the executives and those they deal with know which type of authority is being used in specific situations.

The corporate vice president of marketing for one large, diversified company uses *advisory authority* when he personally or through staff assistants provides specialized advice and assistance to corporate and division executives. *Functional authority* is used by his major accounts manager who coordinates the efforts of multiple divisions selling product systems to a common customer. The vice president exercises *line authority:* (1) over the staff people reporting to him and (2) over new business ventures which are not assigned to divisions.

Guidelines to Organization Design

Organization design guidelines can be observed from the practices of successful corporations. Nonobservance of any of the ten guidelines listed in **Marketing Note 14-1** and explained below does not mean necessarily that the company management is ignorant of the rules or is acting incorrectly. Rather the guidelines represent the norms of organization design. Once you understand the rules for normal situations, you will recognize variations and can examine the reasons for them.

MARKETING NOTE 14-1	***Guidelines of Organization***

1. Each person should report to only one boss.
2. Authority should be commensurate with responsibility. ("Responsibility and authority should go hand-in-hand.")
3. The number of people reporting to one manager should be limited to the number that can be surpervised effectively. This is called *span of control*.
4. Levels of supervision should be as few as possible, consistent with span of control.
5. The organization plan should be developed around functions rather than around people.
6. Communications should cross organizational lines freely and not be limited to the formal chain of command.
7. Decision-making authority should be assigned as close to the scene of action as possible. For marketing this means as close to the market as possible.
8. Line and staff relationships should be made clear.
9. People should know their own duties, responsibilities, authorities, and reporting relationships as well as those of the people with whom they are expected to work.
10. Marketing organization should be developed from the bottom up as well as from the top down.

One Person–One Boss. This guideline assumes that no person can serve two masters equally well, that the employee could become confused and frustrated by conflicting orders from two or more bosses, and that the employee will feel more secure and be more productive when looking to one boss for direction, support, and approval or disapproval of performance.

While observance of this rule creates simple, straightforward relationships, it may lead to organizational rigidity and slow decisionmaking when applied literally. Well-managed companies, therefore, make exceptions when situations call for them. Functional authority also modifies the one-person–one-boss rule to the extent that the employee will receive orders from more than one person, that is, from the employee's line boss and from functional staff personnel.

Whether an employee has one or more bosses is not as important as everyone involved knowing what set of rules is being employed and why.

Responsibility and Authority. When people are asked to achieve certain results, they should also have the authority to make the decisions and give the orders necessary to achieve the results. While this guidelines is obviously sound and reasonable, it too—if followed without exception—can lead to organizational rigidity in complex situations. We will look at some reasons for exceptions later in the chapter.

Span of Control. There is a limit to the number of people a manager can supervise beyond which the manager's effectiveness declines. The limit will vary with the level and complexity of the positions supervised. For most managerial positions, however, it will fall somewhere between three and ten persons.

Levels of Supervision. The more levels of supervision between the worker and the top boss, the greater the problems of communication between the top and bottom, and vice versa. Therefore, the rule is to use as few levels of supervision as possible. It can be seen, however, that this rule conflicts with the previous rule. When a manager's span of control is exceeded, the obvious answer is to create a new level of supervision. To solve one problem, therefore, another is created. Obviously, these two guidelines must be considered together in order to find the compromise arrangement most appropriate for each situation.

Organizing around Functions. Good organization planning calls for establishing positions to perform functions and then filling the positions with people whose talents match the requirements of the positions. The opposite approach—assigning functions to people—generally is not sound.

Efficiency is increased when like functions are grouped into positions and when similar positions are supervised by a common (functional)manager. It is tempting to assign a variety of different functions to a person with a variety of talents. This may work in a small professional organization, such as a consulting or research and development group, but in a large organization it would result in chaos.

Nearly every company, of course, has some talented mavericks who, if forced into the organizational mold, would lose their efficiency or quit in frustration. Creative people, needed in such areas as new product development and promotion, do not function at their best in a hierarchical mold. Successful managers will go to great lengths to find ways to accommodate them without losing complete control over their work assignments.

Open Communications. In the classic hierarchical organization lines of communication follow the chain of command. This, of course, is not the case in modern business organizations. Nothing but bottlenecks would result if people in two different parts of the organization were required to funnel their information through the executive in charge of both parts. In some cases communications would even have to pass through the chief executive's office. Effective managers encourage *direct* communication between people who need to communicate, irrespective of their positions. Such managers only want to be kept informed of pertinent information, including potentially serious problems.

Decentralization of Authority. In small organizations decisions are made by executives who are close to the scene of operations, including the marketplace. In large companies, however, higher executives are insulated by intervening layers of supervision. Decisions made at high levels, therefore, are not based on firsthand knowledge; furthermore, decision-making is delayed while decisions work their way up. Companies solve these problems by delegating decision-making to the lowest point where all pertinent information is available.

Line and Staff Relationship Clarified. People need to know what their relationships will be with one another and what types of authority each position has. Failure to make these things clear can result in bad feelings, wasted time, and a general inability of the organization to perform effectively.

Clarifying the Roles of All Positions. Not only should line and staff relationships be clarified, but all people in the organization should know what is expected of them. They need to know their duties, responsibilities, and authority (if any), and similar information about their supervisors and others with whom they work. People must work in a coordinated and, hopefully, cooperative fashion with others to achieve common organizational goals. This is more likely to happen if people understand the organization structure and their roles in it. Organization charts and position descriptions help to develop this understanding.

Organizing from the Bottom Up. Conventional organization planning often proceeds from the top down, that is, from the chief executive to the lowest level.

Marketing organization, on the other hand, should be guided by what is needed to deal with the market. Hence, the first positions to be determined should be those that perform functions at the first level where contact is made with the market, such as the sales representative. Levels of supervision are then determined as well as supporting staff positions. Practically speaking, the chief marketing executive must also consider the organization from the top down; but the emphasis in marketing organization should always be on how best to organize at the lower levels.

Organizational Charting Guidelines

The following is a list of dos and don'ts of charting as practiced by sophisticated companies. Awareness of good practice will help you to read charts as well as draw acceptable charts yourself.

Rules of Charting

1. A solid line is used to designate a line reporting relationship between the supervisor and the person supervised. Usually the lines flow downwards from the supervisor although occasionally we see a supervised position coming off the supervisor's position in a horizontal line. The position titles also give clues as to who reports to whom. In Figure 14-3 the solid lines tell us that the marketing research, sales, and advertising managers have a line reporting relationship with their boss, the marketing manager. Likewise, the three regional sales managers report on a line basis to the sales manager. There is no significance to lines connecting positions on the same reporting level, such as the marketing research, sales, and advertising managers. They do indicate, or course, that all three have a common boss.

2. Broken lines (dotted or dashed) indicate nonline relationships. In Figure 14-3, for example, the dashed line running between the advertising manager and the advertising agency indicates that the ad manager is responsible for relationships

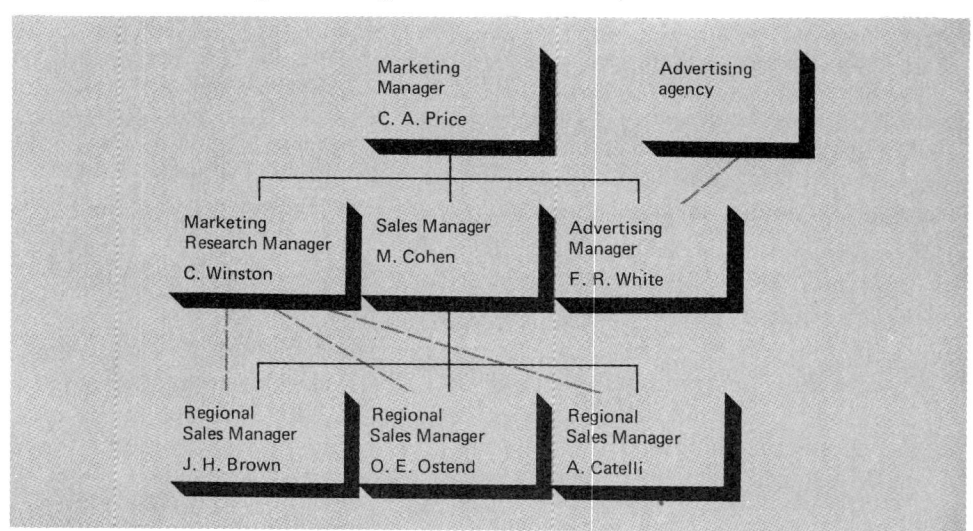

FIGURE 14-3. Classic charting form showing line and nonline relationships.

with the agency and that the ad manager is the agency's point of contact within the company. The dashed lines running between the marketing research manager and the three regional sales managers indicate either a functional or advisory relationship, or both. It could be that regional sales managers report competitive information directly to the marketing research manager while the marketing research manager sends reports on industry and economic trends directly to the regional sales managers. Broken lines should be used sparingly. If used at all, they should be reserved for points of special emphasis. There are so many nonline relationships within the typical organization that any attempt to show them all with broken lines would be more confusing than enlightening.

3. Positions reporting to the same supervisor should not be placed at different levels for the purpose of indicating that one position is more important than another. Because of space limitations, it is not always possible to get all of these positions on the same level. The chart maker should be allowed flexibility in deciding their placement as long as the line reporting relationships are shown correctly. For example, in Figure 14-2, the fact that the staff positions are placed above the operating divisions does not mean that the chief executive considers one more important than the other.

4. In conventional charting, positions are shown by squares or rectangles. Connecting solid lines are drawn vertically and horizontally with right angle turns. Occasionally we see positions portrayed by circles and connected by diagonal lines. These are less practical for extensive charting because circles do not hold as much nonmenclature as squares of rectangles of similar sizes. And diagonal lines are less flexible when it comes to arranging a number of positions on one chart.

5. Position blocks should contain the proper position titles without abbreviation unless space does not allow for spelling out words in full. Many companies also like to include the name of the position incumbent as in Figure 14-3.

6. Avoid trying to put too much on one chart. Use additional charts as needed to show different levels. Company chart books typically contain many charts with each following chart tying in with the preceding one. Several charts, for example, could be made out of Figure 14-3. One chart would show the marketing manager and the positions reporting to this manager. A follow-on chart would show the sales manager and the positions reporting to this executive. Another would show the organization for the marketing research manager's group, and so on.

What Charts Show and Don't Show. Charts don't tell all we would like to know. They can tell us (1) the positions in the organization; (2) the person assigned to each position; (3) the line reporting relationships; and (4) the nonline reporting relationships (functional and advisory), although these should be limited to items of special emphasis.

What an organization chart does not tell us is how the informal organization works. For example, it does not tell us:

1. Who really works with whom to get things done, i.e., beyond the designated line and staff relationships.
2. Who does and does not have the real authority, clout, influence, or leadership ability to make things happen. The capacity of an individual to get or not get

MARKETING NOTE 14-2

Sample Position Description

The Blue Company
Food Products Division
Marketing Manager

Purpose of Position.
To develop marketing strategies and plans for reaching long-range divisional sales and profit objectives; to manage ongoing marketing operations so as to attain current annual division goals.

Reporting Relationships.
Reports to: Division manager
Positions Supervised: Managers of sales, advertising and sales promotion, marketing research, product planning, and marketing services.
Functional Relationships: Internal relationships include working with other divisional functional managers—R&D, manufacturing, controller, and personnel relations—in developing marketing plans and coordinating functions involved in serving customers and maintaining good customer relations. Utilizes the services of the office of the corporate marketing vice president, including the staff economist, public relations, media planning, and corporate planning.

External relationships include major wholesale and chain accounts, institutional customers, industry association leaders, and appropriate contacts with government officials.

Duties and Responsibilities.
Planning
1. Participates with the division manager in the development of division policies, long-range strategies, and the annual business plan.
2. Provides for the continuing study of the external market environment to ensure that product development and marketing strategies and programs are geared to the changing wants and needs of the market.
3. Develops, with the aid of the marketing staff, annual marketing plans that will implement the division's long-range strategy and attain sales and profit goals for the current year.

Organization
4. Develops and implements changes in marketing organization structure needed to carry out marketing plans.
5. Maintains up-to-date organization charts and position descriptions for the Marketing Department.

Direction
6. Participates in weekly meetings of the division Management Committee.
7. Holds weekly meetings with the marketing staff to review programs, communicate internal and external developments, and resolve problems.
8. Delegates to the marketing staff the responsibility and authority for carrying out their respective parts of the annual marketing plan. The marketing manager, however, reserves the authority to approve major decisions relating to new products, pricing, advertising campaigns, and over-budget or nonbudget expenditures.
9. Provides the supervision and coordination needed to ensure that marketing operations are moving toward attainment of annual objectives.
10. Provides for the staffing, training, compensation, and motivation of the people in the marketing department.
11. Provides for open communication channels within the department and between marketing and other departments.
12. Participates as a member of the New Products Planning Committee and works closely with all functional department heads to achieve new product development goals.
13. Plans periodic calls on major customers, or sees them at trade shows and meetings, to demonstrate personal interest in their businesses and to learn about problems and new developments.
14. Participates in industry and trade association and government meetings to promote the welfare of the industry and the company.

> **MARKETING NOTE 14-2** *(continued)*
>
> *Control*
> 15. Works with the controller and members of the marketing staff in developing control reports that provide timely measurement of marketing performance.
> 16. Reviews progress periodically and takes actions to correct performance if needed.
> 17. Provides revised sales forecasts and expense budgets during the year if it appears that sales will exceed or fall below budget.
>
> *Authority.*
> The marketing manager has the authority to carry out approved marketing plans within approved budget limits, subject to corporate and division policies. While this authority is sufficient to cover most day-to-day operating decisions, the marketing manager is expected to check with the division manager before making major changes in such areas as pricing, advertising, new product direction, or customer policies. Personnel decisions made by the marketing manager will normally be honored, but corporate policy requires that they be approved by the personnel relations manager before implementation to ensure that laws, regulations, and union contracts are not violated.

things done may have little relationship to the person's formal position title or job description. Some are reluctant to exercise the authority they do have. Others, by virtue of force of personality, length of service, stock ownership, politics, or nepotism, can have influence far beyond that implied by their position title.

Organization charts, even when supplemented by position descriptions, are not enough to explain how a particular organization works. Training sessions, observation, and guidance from experienced employees are also needed.

Developing the Position Description

Nearly all companies use organization charts, whereas it is mainly the large- and medium-size companies that use position (or job) descriptions. Small companies are less likely to use position descriptions because of the cost of developing and maintaining them.

The purpose of position descriptions is to tell employees what is expected of them, with whom they are expected to have working relationships, and the extent of their authority. When used in conjunction with the organization chart, position descriptions also help employees understand where they fit within the overall organization structure.

There is no standard format for a position description, although most companies include the types of information shown in the following outline. A filled in outline can be seen in **Marketing Note 14-2**.

Company, Division, and Department
Position Title

A. Purpose of Position
B. Reporting Relationships
   1. Reports to:
   2. Positions supervised:
   3. Functional relationships:

C. Duties and Responsibilities
1.
2.
3.
    etc.
D. Authority

ALTERNATIVE FORMS OF MARKETING ORGANIZATION

One is unlikely to find two company organization charts that look exactly alike, because no two companies even in the same industry are identical in terms of their size, policies, objectives, product lines, or market position. Nevertheless, there are only a few *basic* organization models. When you can recognize the basic models and understand the advantages and disadvantages of each, you can work at organizational planning—a necessary task for every marketing executive.

We will begin with a description of the most basic form—the functional organization. Following this we look at mutations that have occurred for dealing with company change in terms of size, diversity, and complexity. These include organizing by product or market, divisionalization, geographic decentralization, and the matrix.

The Functional Organization

In this form of organization the heads of the major functional departments report directly to the chief executive who coordinates the functional activities and makes the overall decisions. An example is seen in Figure 14-4 where the managers of the functions of manufacturing, research and development, marketing, finance, and personnel report to the chief executive as indicated by the connecting solid lines.

The advantage of this form is that it provides for specialization by function and permits the chief executive to be personally involved in the management of the

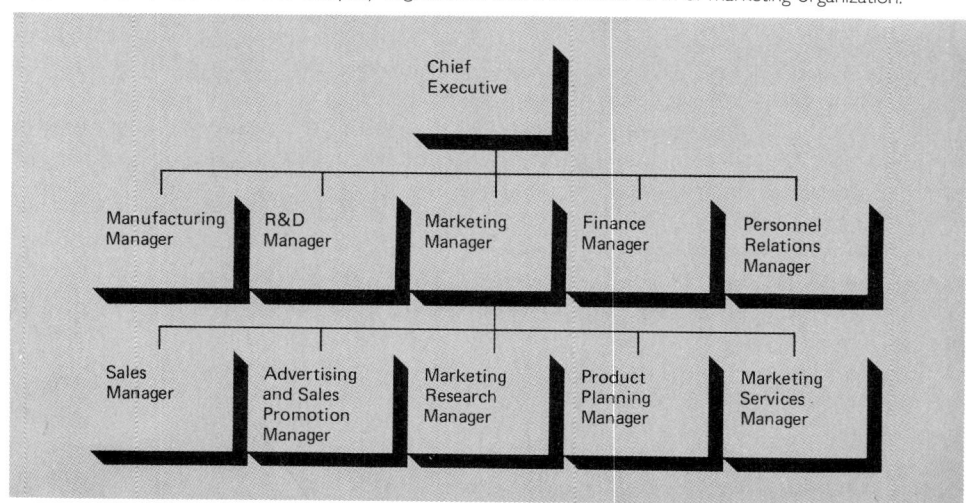

FIGURE 14-4. Functional form of company organization with a functional form of marketing organization.

business. The chief executive can delegate to the department heads the authority they need to carry out their functional responsibilities and at the same time retain overall management control of the business. This is the simplest and most direct form of organization. Even so, it can serve even very large businesses as long as only one or a few product lines, markets, and channels of distribution are involved. Examples are found in large petroleum and soft drink companies. It is when product and/or market proliferation occurs that the functional form begins to lose its effectiveness.

The Functional Marketing Organization. The functional form works equally well for marketing when only a few products, markets, and channels are involved. Figure 14-4 shows the heads of sales, advertising and sales promotion, marketing research, product planning, and marketing services reporting to the marketing manager. The marketing manager delegates authority to these functional specialists while coordinating their activities and maintaining ultimate control over the total marketing operation.

Separating Sales from Other Marketing Functions. Bringing all marketing functions under the marketing manager, as in Figure 14-4, became standard practice for most companies as a result of growing acceptance of the marketing concept. Some companies, however, still consider sales and marketing as separate functions. Figure 14-5 and 14-6 illustrate two of the ways in which sales and marketing are sometimes separated.

Arrangements such as these occur more often in companies where personal selling is the predominant marketing function (e.g., industrial goods) or where it is considered equally as important as advertising and sales promotion (e.g., consumer hard goods). Consumer packaged goods companies, on the other hand, generally place sales under marketing, as shown in Figure 14-4, because they consider personal selling less important than advertising and sales promotion. Many marketing authorities believe that marketing is coordinated more effectively when all marketing functions, including sales, report to the marketing manager, irrespective of the relative importance of personal selling in the marketing mix.

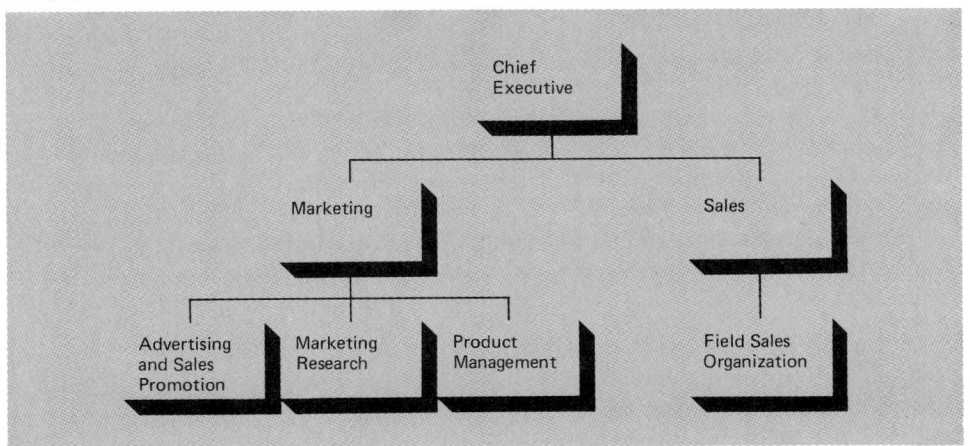

FIGURE 14-5. Organization in which marketing and sales report separately to the chief executive (or to a division manager).

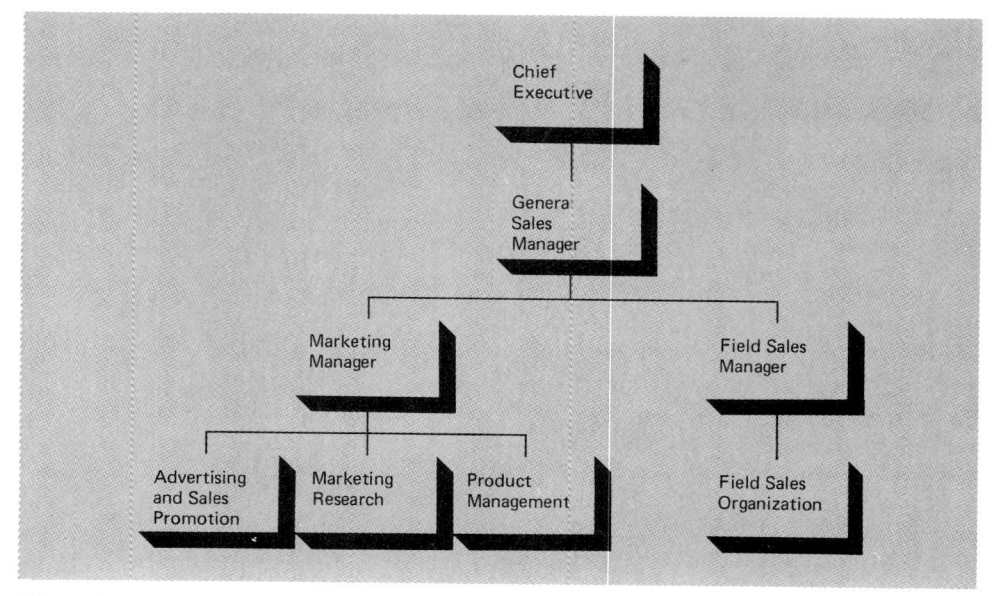

FIGURE 14-6. Organization in which marketing reports to the general sales manager.

A look at the company's organization chart will usually tell you something about how management views marketing and sales. It is well to remember that the term "marketing" does not mean the same thing to everyone.

Organizational Responses to Growth and Diversification

As companies grow, the strain on the functional organization increases. Neither the chief executive nor the marketing manager is able to devote sufficient time to the planning and management of each product, market, or business. The three principal organizational responses to this problem have been product management, market management, or divisionalization.

Product Management. When the organizational strain is caused by too many products, product managers may be introduced to the marketing department to assume part of the workloads of the chief executive and the marketing manager. Each product manager is assigned a product or product line.

> The *product manager** is responsible for developing the product marketing plan, coordinating the implementation of the plan with functional departments, and monitoring performance against the objectives of the plan.

As shown in Figure 14-7 product managers report to the marketing manager. Product managers have multiple relationships as illustrated by the dashed lines. While the dashed lines lead to functional departments, each product manager's

---

*The terms "product manager" and "brand manager" are virtually synonymous. *Brand manager* is likely to be used in consumer packaged goods companies that market multiple brands of their generic products. Procter & Gamble, for example, might have one brand manager for Crest toothpaste and another for Gleem toothpaste.

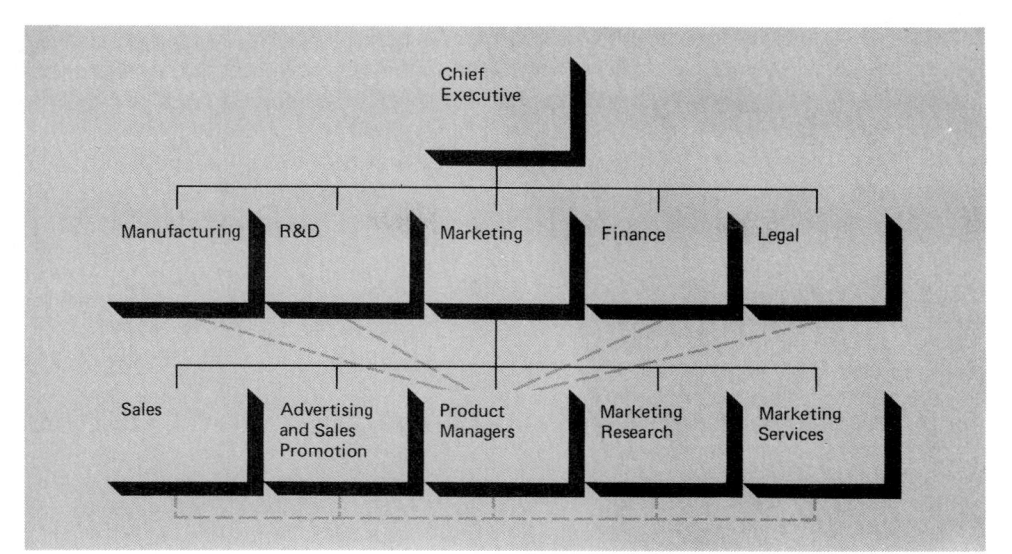

FIGURE 14-7. Product manager form of organization showing nonline relationships (dashed lines) between product managers and other functions.

relationships are more likely to be with those persons directly concerned with the product manager's assigned product. In the case of manufacturing, for example, the major contact likely will be the manager of the plant producing the product manager's assigned product or product line.

As the number of product managers increases an intervening level of *group product managers* is inserted between the product manager and the marketing manager.

Advantage and disadvantage of product management. The big advantage product management brings to multiproduct companies is that each product receives the full attention of one responsible person, much as was the case when the company had only one product. The disadvantage is that the product manager has no line or functional authority over any of the functional departments that design, produce, distribute, finance, or sell the assigned product. There is no practical way to give such authority, since it would result in many product managers giving conflicting orders to each functional department. Each product manager, of course, wants to get the lion's share of attention from each functional department.

Yet the product management form of organization is widely used. A survey of over 400 companies found that product managers are used by nine out of ten consumer packaged goods companies, one-third of other types of consumer goods companies (such as hard goods), and more than half of industrial goods companies.[2] It also found that more companies were moving to product management than were moving away from it.

Why do so many companies use this form of organization? Two studies[3] suggest reasons:

1. As companies gain experience with product management, the functional departments learn that top management expects them to cooperate with product managers in making their products profitable marketing successes.

2. Product managers get to know more about their products and markets than anyone else and have an advantage when dealing with functional managers who have only partial, specialized knowledge. One study found the power of the product manager's expertise to be an important influence in gaining acceptance among functional departments.[4] Furthermore, the more success a product manager has (often moving up to the management of more important products) the more clout the manager has with all types and levels of management.
3. Top managements have become more realistic about what can be expected of product managers. The product manager's roles as the product expert, planner, coordinator, and monitor of results are emphasized but major product and marketing decisions are reserved for higher levels of management.

Differences in consumer and industrial product managers. Whereas the functions of planning, coordinating, and monitoring are common to product managers in all types of companies, there are differences of emphasis to be found between consumer goods and industrial goods companies.

Product managers in consumer packaged goods companies concentrate their efforts on promotional planning, particularly advertising, since promotion is the key to success in the marketing of convenience goods. In fact, a number of large packaged goods companies have eliminated their advertising departments altogether and transferred the contacts with their advertising agencies to their product managers.

By contrast, in industrial goods firms, where personal selling is important but advertising is relatively unimportant, product managers are more concerned with coordinating company efforts in solving customer problems. Their internal contacts primarily are with research and development, manufacturing, sales, and technical services. Their job emphasis is on product, pricing, and customer services.

Jobs in product management. Product manager jobs are of keen interest, particularly to many young people. Product management provides broad experience and is considered a stepping stone to higher management.

Market Management. A second way in which the organizational stress resulting from company growth and diversity can be relieved is by introducing market managers. This model is appropriate when markets are diverse and different channels are used to reach the different markets.

Examples of industries where market management would be applicable include textiles, industrial goods, communications services, and automobile tires, batteries, and accessories (TBA). TBA equipment manufacturers, for example, sell and ship direct to original automotive equipment manufacturers (OEM) and they also sell the same or similar products to the consumer replacement market. The consumer market is reached through multiple channels including tire dealers, service stations, catalogs, and mass merchandising chains. Separate market managers might be assigned to the OEM and consumer replacement markets.

Industrial companies often sell the same or similar products to several classes of companies, each with different application needs. The industrial seller may distribute direct as well as through different classes of wholesalers serving different industry segments. Monsanto, for example, distributes its resin products direct to such manufacturing industries as paper, adhesives, coatings, and safety glass sheeting. The Bell telephone companies have reorganized in order to market their communications services on a market-by-market basis, including consumer, industrial, government, and institutional organizations.[5]

An example of a market manager form of organization is shown in Figure 14-8. This is similar in appearance to the product manager organization plan shown in Figure 14-7 except that the market managers in this model represent consumer markets and industrial markets respectively; also, the sales force is divided into consumer and industrial sales, an arrangement which facilitates the planning, coordination, and monitoring activities of the market managers.

A second example of organizing with market managers is shown in Figure 14-9. Here three market managers report to the marketing manager. Whereas the market managers in Figure 14-8 are staff positions with no line or functional authority, the market managers in Figure 14-9 have line authority over the sales and promotional functions dealing with their respective markets.

In Figure 14-9 the market managers depend on the Marketing Research Department for market information and look to the Product Planning Department for handling product related issues with the corporate functional departments. Where market potential is sufficient to justify separate sales and/or advertising and sales promotion organizations for each market, this arrangement can be very effective. While the product planning manager handles internal product problems, for example, the market manager is able to concentrate on obtaining sales income.

Despite the inherent appeal of organizing around markets, it is a more difficult model to operate successfully than organizing around products. The market manager approach is more effective when the product lines sold to each market are the same or similar, as in the examples of TBA, resins, and telephone services.

FIGURE 14-8. Market manager organization in which market managers act as planners, coordinators, and monitors. Broken lines indicate nonline relationships.

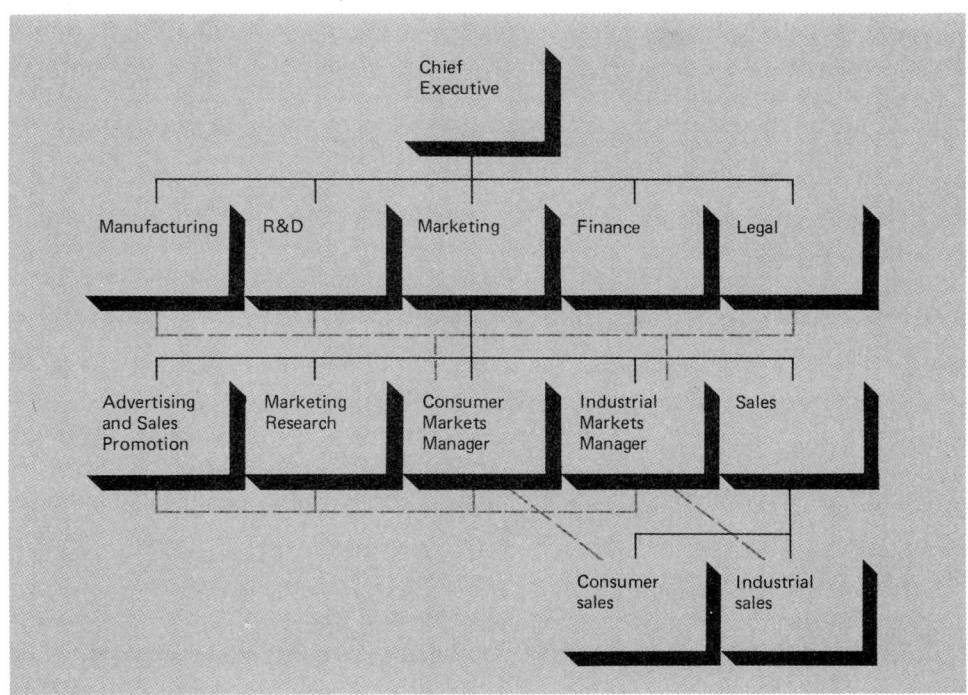

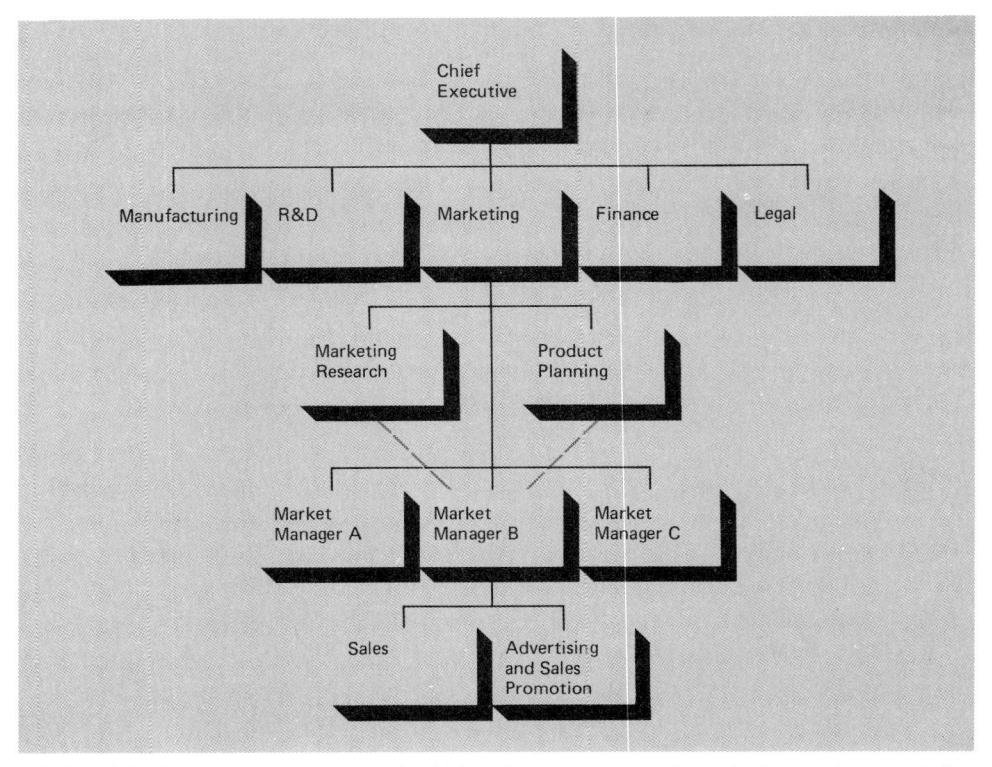

FIGURE 14-9. Market manager organization in which market managers have line authority over functions dealing with selling and promoting products to their assigned markets.

Divisionalization. If a company using product or market management forms of organization continues to grow and diversify, it eventually reaches the point where product or market management solutions are no longer adequate. Companies in this situation usually divide their operations into two or more business units, commonly called divisions. Each division is designated as a profit center, with the divisional managers responsible for meeting profit goals. An example of a divisionalized company is shown in Figure 14-10.

One of the questions arising with divisionalization is: Which functions should the division manager have authority over in order to be held responsible for profits? The more functions assigned to the division, of course, the more control division management has over the factors that determine profits. The two most important functions, however, are marketing and manufacturing (or operations), since these permit the division manager to exercise control over income and operating costs. Divisions normally will have control and accounting functions reporting on a line basis to the division manager and on a functional (broken line) basis to the corporate finance officer. A division containing manufacturing, marketing, and a controller is called an *integrated* division. In the early stages of divisionalization other functions, such as research and development and personnel relations, are provided by the corporate staff. As division sales increase, however, the division acquires more functional staffs of its own.

Decentralized marketing divisions with centralized manufacturing. While the integrated division illustrated in Figure 14-10 shows a common arrangement, some

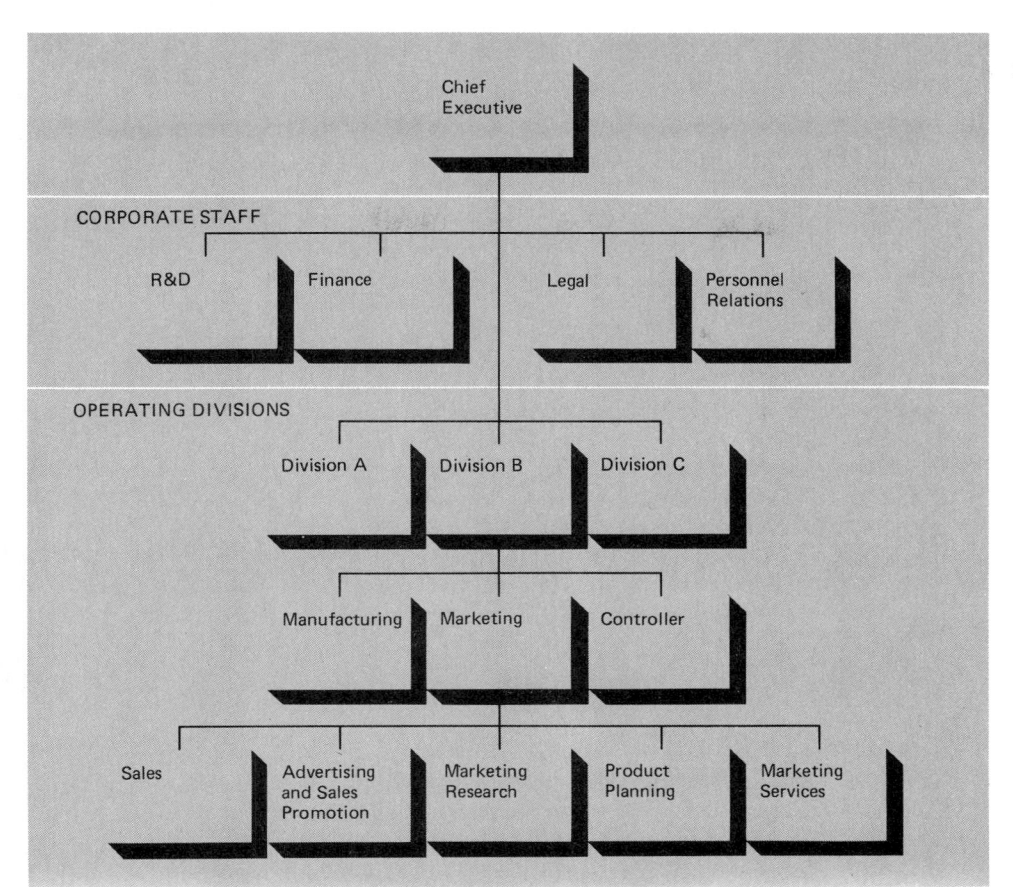

FIGURE 14-10. Company organized by integrated divisions.

companies prefer variations. In Figure 14-11 we see a company in which decentralized divisions are set up primarily for managing marketing operations. Products are supplied to the marketing divisions by a centralized manufacturing division. This arrangement often is found in consumer packaged goods companies (such as General Foods' convenience foods group) where marketing is the principal key to success. In such companies manufacturing may be relatively uncomplicated, but control of manufacturing costs will be highly important. This arrangement occurs less frequently in industrial and consumer hard goods companies where manufacturing is more complicated and where there is greater need for close coordination of manufacturing and marketing.

When marketing and manufacturing divisions are separate, however, some method must be agreed upon for charging product manufacturing costs to the marketing division. This can be on the basis of actual cost, standard cost, or a negotiated price. Charging actual manufacturing costs provides little incentive for the manufacturing division to be cost efficient. Charging at standard cost (an estimated target cost) may cause the manufacturing division to resist marketing suggestions that would raise costs. The negotiated price overcomes some of the disadvantages of the other two methods, but it also poses the sometimes sticky problem of two divisions agreeing on the transfer price. Once the

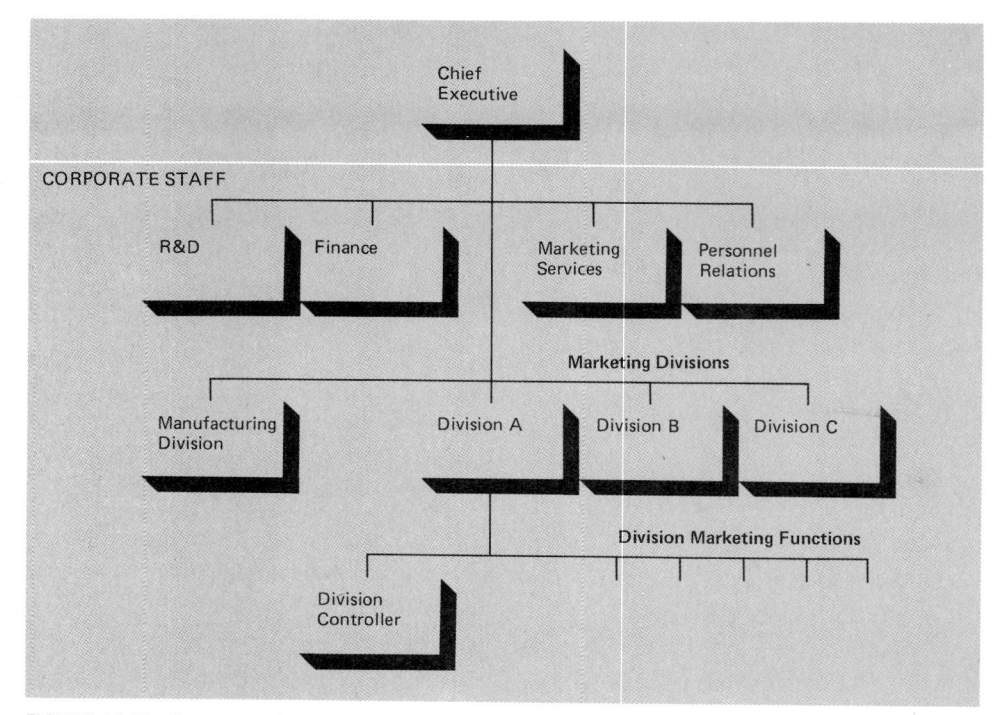

FIGURE 14-11. Company with marketing divisions served by one central manufacturing division.

method of charging for the product is resolved. the profitability of the marketing division can be measured in the normal way, i.e., sales income less all applicable costs.

Integrated divisions with centralized sales. Another arrangement is for the operating division to have control of manufacturing plus all marketing functions except sales. A centralized sales force sells the products of two or more divisions—products which go to similar markets through the same or similar channels. Campbell Soup uses this plan. The advantage of this arrangement is that it lowers average selling costs because duplicate calls on the same accounts are avoided. The disadvantage is that the division has less control over the important function of sales. This arrangement sometimes breaks down when more products are assigned to the sales person than can be handled effectively on each sales call. It was for this reason that General Foods switched from one central sales force to group sales forces which specialize by product categories.

Functional organization at the divisional level. When a company utilizing product or market management goes to divisionalization, the divisions usually organize on a functional basis as can be seen in Figure 14-10. The functional organization is feasible again because the number of products and/or markets is fewer. The division manager, with the help of the marketing manager, now can effectively plan for each product and market and can coordinate all functions. But as divisions grow and diversify, as usually occurs with success, history repeats itself. The divisions reach the point where they must go to a product or market form of organization. Subsequently, some divisions even grow to the point where they must be broken into two or more divisions.

Some observers think that the use of functional and product management forms of organization is declining. But this probably is an incorrect interpretation of what is happening. It is more likely that functional and other forms of organization are appropriate for different periods of corporate life. Models will be adopted, dropped, and readopted ad infinitum according to the company's needs at different times. And it is not unusual for a large company to use several models of organization in different parts of the corporation at the same time.

Marketing functions at division and corporate levels. Some divisionalized companies assign all marketing functions to the divisions. Others have corporate staff marketing services, as shown in Figure 14-11. These marketing services groups provide specialized services such as marketing research and design and production of sales promotion materials. They may also make joint purchases of space in advertising media for several divisions. The functions of central marketing services departments are explained further in Chapter 21.

Other Forms of Organization

We have now completed our discussion of the most common forms of organization and have seen that they are largely determined by marketing factors. The conditions under which each of these models is most appropriate are illustrated in Figure 14-12. We now look briefly at less prevalent models, namely, the geographic and matrix models.

Geographic Organization. When products must be manufactured close to their geographic markets, it often makes sense to decentralize marketing functions as well. Companies tend to locate their manufacturing plants close to regional markets when the finished product is costly to ship because of weight (such as rolls of polyethylene film), bulk (such as cans or cartons), or when the product has a limited life due to spoilage (such as baked goods or fresh milk).

The division manager for a region usually will be responsible for the manufac-

FIGURE 14-12. Typical combination of conditions which suggest choice of organization model. Circled items represent variations from the basic functional model.

Organization model	Number of products	Products: Similar or diverse	Markets: Similar or diverse	Number of channels used
Functional	Few	Similar	Similar	One or very few
Product management	(Many)	Similar	Similar	One or very few
Market management	Any number	Similar or diverse	(Diverse)	(Several)
Divisional	(Many)	(Diverse)	Similar or diverse	(Several)

turing, control, and sales functions. Because each regional plant produces the same product line, there is no need to decentralize marketing functions such as advertising or product planning. These functions can be run more efficiently and at less cost when centralized at company headquarters.

Matrix Organization. A newer development in organizational design is the matrix model. In terms of a corporation, matrix organization can be described as follows:

> The *matrix* is an organizational form in which two or more business managers utilize the company's (or division's) functional departments to produce and market the products or services for which the business managers have profit responsibility.

A distinguishing characteristic of the matrix is that the department managers in charge of subfunctions report to two or more bosses. The functional managers take directions from both their functional bosses and the business managers. The matrix attempts to retain the benefits of the functional organization even while engaging in multiple businesses.

One form of the matrix is illustrated in Figure 14-13. It is intended to show that three business managers, in charge of product lines A, B, and C, respectively, have line authority over subfunction department managers who report to functional

FIGURE 14-13. Matrix organization showing that supervisors of subfunctions (represented by the circles) receive orders from both their functional bosses and their business manager bosses.

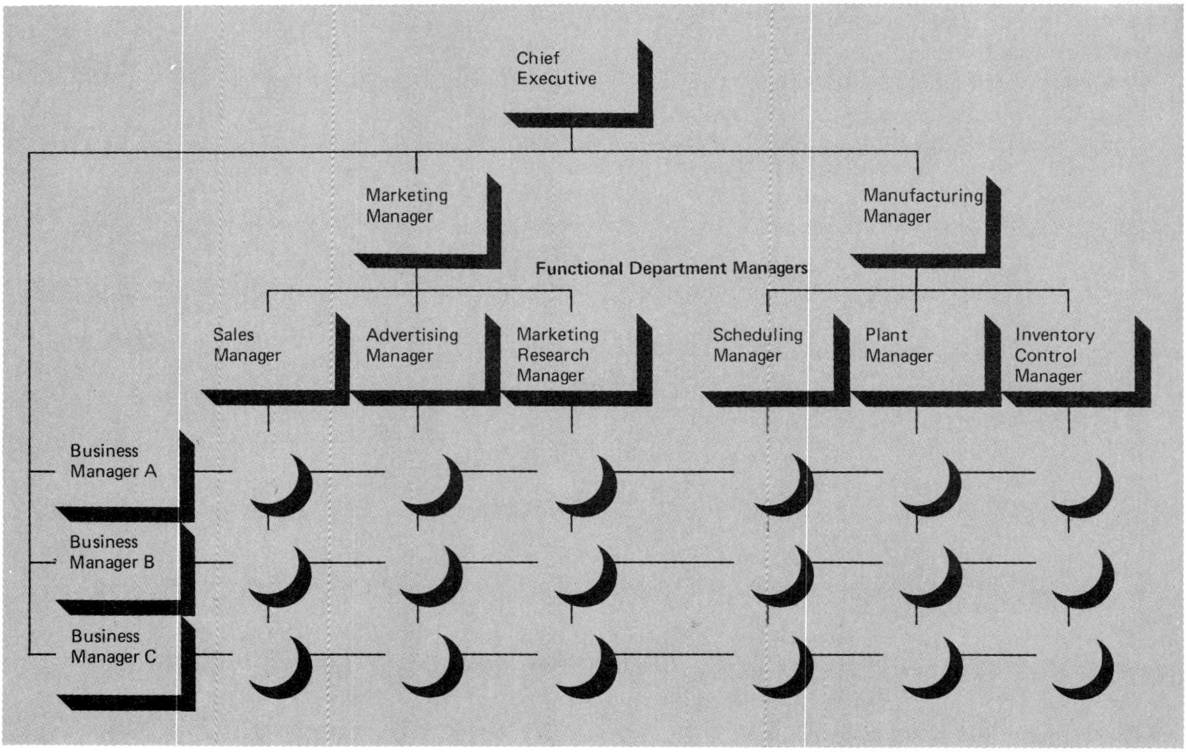

managers in charge of sales, plants, etc. The subfunction department managers are represented by circles.

To illustrate how the matrix works, let's look at the sales area. Assume that each circle represents a product sales supervisor who receives directions from the business manager and the sales manager. When orders from the multiple bosses are not in conflict, all goes well. But when contradictory orders are received, the sales supervisor is expected to work out solutions with each manager. If necessary, the product sales supervisor will bring the multiple bosses together to resolve the problem.

Proponents of the matrix organization believe that the proper place to resolve conflict is at the point where function and business goals overlap. They maintain that this is preferable to letting problems filter to the higher levels of a hierarchical organization. Better and faster decisions are believed to be the result when they are made by the people who will have to carry out the compromise decisions.

The matrix in professional organizations. Matrix works well in professional organizations such as consulting firms where it is unlikely that a project team member will receive contradictory orders from the functional boss and the project team leader. On the other hand, matrix has not worked uniformly well in industrial companies.

The matrix in industrial organizations. Several product and service companies, including General Electric, Equitable Life Insurance, and Shell Oil,[6] have experimented with the matrix in parts of their organizations. Davis and Lawrence find it "an exceedingly complex form of organization that is not for everybody. To put it bluntly," they say, "if you do not really need it, leave it alone."[7] Under the right conditions, however, they believe it can be highly effective.

We don't yet know whether matrix will come into common use. Not all companies that have tried it have stayed with it. In a study of twenty major corporations, however, 40 percent were using matrix in one or more divisions. All planned to keep it as one of their organizational options.[8]

SUMMARY

Organization is one of the most important functions of management. Organization is the structure through which plans are implemented. It is so fundamental to managing that the subject absorbs much of the attention of operating executives, staff executives, and management consultants.

In this chapter we have seen that organizational change is a natural outgrowth of company change, particularly when that change is the result of growth, diversity, and general complexity. We have shown that the most basic form, functional organization, is quite appropriate until growth in products, businesses, and/or markets exceeds the capacity of the chief executive and the marketing manager to coordinate everything effectively. One solution is to redistribute part of the management workload to either product or market managers. A successful organization, however, eventually grows to the point where the only solution is to break the company into smaller pieces, usually called divisions. Divisions are assigned profit responsibility for their assigned product lines, businesses, and/or markets. Divisions often adopt the functional form of organization initially, but as they succeed and grow, they may find it necessary to shift to product or market management models. Eventually large divisions need breaking up and the cycle repeats itself.

Business firms in the main use the classic hierarchical form of organization, although they have modified it to make it more flexible and to allow decision-making to be decentralized to lower levels and closer to the market. The ten organizational guidelines presented in the chapter describe the modified hierarchical organization. These guidelines can be modified further to meet special conditions.

The principal types of authority found in business organizations are line and functional. Line authority is held by managers over their subordinates. Functional authority, assigned to a staff specialist by the chief executive, may be exercised over personnel not reporting on a line basis to the staff specialist. The chapter also provided a list of dos and don'ts of organizational charting and an outline for developing position descriptions.

With the information provided in this chapter you should be able to draw organization charts, write up position descriptions of existing jobs, and—using company organization charts—be able to identify the form or forms of organization the company follows. These skills alone will not qualify you as an expert. Deciding when to switch from one organizational model to another is a complicated management decision and should be made only after careful analysis. Even so, knowing common forms of organization, and when each is most appropriate, as shown in Figure 14-12, provides you with a good background against which to make the analysis.

QUESTIONS

1. What is organization? Name two aspects of organization that require emphasis.
2. What are the basic types of authority commonly used in business organizations?
3. What are the important things that organization charts can and cannot show?
4. What are the purposes of position descriptions?
5. What is the most basic organization form? Describe how it works and its principal advantage.
6. Describe the purpose and functions of the product manager.
7. What are the reasons for divisionalization?

REFERENCES

1. For more in-depth treatments of organization see: Stephen R. Michael, George Odiorne, Fred Luthans, Spencer Hayden, and Warner Burke, *Techniques of Organizational Change*, McGraw-Hill, New York, 1981; Jay R. Galbraith, *Organization Design*, Addison-Wesley, Reading, MA, 1977; J. O'Shaughnessy, *Patterns of Business Organization*, Allen & Unwin, London, 1976; and Derek Newman, *Organization Design*, Edward Arnold, London, 1973.
2. *Current Advertising Practices: Opinions as to Future Trends*, Association of National Advertisers, New York, 1974.
3. See: Victor P. Buell, "The Changing Role of the Product Manager in Consumer Goods Companies," *Journal of Marketing*, July 1975, pp. 3–11; and Victor P. Buell, *Organizing for Marketing/Advertising Success*, Association of National Advertisers, New York, 1982, chap. 5.

4. Gary R. Gemmill and David L. Wileman, "The Product Manager as an Influence Agent," *Journal of Marketing*, January 1972, pp. 26–30.
5. Parts of this section were adapted from Victor P. Buell, "Marketing Organization," *Executive*, vol. 4, no. 3, Cornell University, 1978, p. 32
6. *Business Week*, Jan. 16, 1978, p. 82
7. Stanley M. Davis and Paul R. Lawrence, *Matrix*, Addison-Wesley, Reading, Mass., 1976, pp. 7–8.
8. Buell, *Organizing for Marketing/Advertising Success*, pp. 40–44.

CHAPTER 15

Direction, Organizational Behavior, and Managerial Control

We have now covered two of the four classic functions of management, planning and organization. In this chapter we will discuss the remaining two—direction and control.

Direction is concerned with how management gets things done through the people in the organization, how plans get carried out, and how objectives are achieved. In short, *direction is the management of people to achieve organizational goals.*

Because of fundamental changes in attitudes toward work, the management of people has changed over the years. This has been particularly noticeable in the larger, more complex organizations where "getting a full day's work in return for a full day's pay" has been a major problem. Methods used to get people to perform their jobs effectively now rely less on direct authority and more on such concepts as group behavior, leadership, and motivation. These methods are encompassed in a field of management study known as *organizational behavior.* While covering the management function of direction, we will include some important organizational behavior concepts.

Managerial control is concerned with the measurement of organizational performance. Management not only sets goals and prepares plans for reaching them, it also measures progress toward the goals so that adjustments to plans can be made if necessary.

DIRECTION

There was an office manager who never seemed to have anything to do. Whenever anyone walked into his office, he would be sitting back in his chair behind a clean desk, hands folded, looking out the window. When chided for his inactivity, he would reply that his operations were well organized and staffed with good people, were running well, and that he spent his time thinking up improvements. And, in fact, he was right. He did run a good show.[1]

In theory that's the way management is supposed to work. The manager who plans, organizes, and controls effectively should be able to sit back and think or go play golf. But it's hard to find a marketing manager who can emulate that office manager. The reason is that marketing is a dynamic, fast moving, and constantly changing function. In addition to planning, organizing, and controlling, the marketing manager must provide the spark that makes the organizational engine run. The manager must solve problems, meet emergencies, and perform a variety of activities not covered by the other managerial functions.

Unexpected occurrences not covered in the plans seem to be the normal situation. Another company hires a key member of the marketing staff; a competitor introduces a good, new, lower-priced product; customer deliveries are held up by a plant work stoppage; a defect shows up in the new product that had been counted on for increased volume. These and many other problems must be dealt with promptly. They make the marketing manager's task of directing especially challenging.

Direction includes the activities involved in coordination, communication, personnel administration, and decision-making. These functions are discussed briefly below. Direction also can be considered in terms of group behavior, leadership, and motivation. These aspects will be discussed in a later section on organizational behavior.

Coordination

Teamwork is essential in sports such as football and basketball. It is also essential in a successful marketing department. Unless everyone is pulling together, there will be only mediocre results. Neither athletes nor marketing people coordinate their efforts automatically. With every other element for successful team operation present, a group usually does not work smoothly together without a leader to direct its efforts. One of the reasons for bringing the several marketing functions together under the direction and coordination of the marketing manager is to improve the chances for good teamwork. As we shall see later, some types of organizational groups require more or less direction and coordination than others, but it is questionable whether any can be left completely undirected for very long.

Communications

A good marketing communications system will facilitate the flow of information both upward and downward through the chain of command. It will encourage two-way horizontal flow of information between departments. And it will provide for two-way communication between the company and its channel intermediaries and customers.

A communications challenge occurs whenever one person wants to be understood by another. Speaking, writing, or demonstrating often is not sufficient to bring about understanding. The problem is magnified in marketing because of the large numbers of people involved, their dispersed geographic locations, and the several layers of organization. Common barriers to communication are differences in background, education, and training; the emotional state of the expositor or listener; status differences; and the failure—or absence of the opportunity—to ask questions. **Marketing Note 15-1** offers some suggestions for neutralizing the barriers.

MARKETING NOTE 15-1

Improving Communications

At the risk of oversimplifying a complicated subject here are a few rules followed by successful managers in improving marketing communications.

1. *Be communications-conscious.* Recognize that communications barriers are ever present but that they can be reduced in intensity.
2. *Build a climate for the free exchange for ideas.* Recognize that it is more difficult for information to flow upward than downward. To get ideas and accurate information, negative as well as positive, to flow upward, people must believe that their ideas are wanted and that they will not be penalized for telling the truth. Beware of the NIH (Not Invented Here) reaction—an automatic negative attitude to anything not thought up by the boss.
3. *Establish and promulgate policies.* In a large marketing organization, thousands of daily decisions are made by hundreds of people. The only assurance the marketing manager has that decisions will be made intelligently is when the people making them know and understand the company's policies.
4. *Put yourself in the other person's shoes.* How much background does the other person have for understanding what you are trying to get across? A close associate may understand a grimace. The person at the end of the line may require extensive and patient explanation.
5. *Show and tell.* Don't rely on just one form of communication. Put instructions in writing; supplement them with graphics; explain verbally where possible; test to see if your message is understood.
6. *Be a good listener.* Most everyone knows this, but busy executives under pressure often find the rule difficult to follow. Yet, really effective communication almost always involves two-way communication.

Personnel Administration*

Because the marketing manager's objectives are achieved through people, personnel matters can occupy a lot of time. These matters include turnover, training, and performance reviews.

Turnover. Personnel turnover is normal. People die, retire, become ill, shift to other departments, or move to another company. Filling a vacancy creates a chain reaction as people are promoted up the line. Each vacancy involves selection, compensation, and training decisions, and—at some point—recruiting of a new employee.

Training. Training new people for entry level jobs usually is standard procedure. Training people who are *promoted* to higher-level jobs, however, often is neglected on the mistaken assumption that they already possess the necessary competence and experience. It can be argued that the more important the job, the more important it is that the incumbent receive proper training. While most major companies will underwrite the cost of outside training seminars and part-time college training, only a relative few provide formal in-house management training programs.

Performance Appraisal. Performance reviews of people reporting to the marketing manager represent a part of the personnel administration process. It is important that people know how they are doing. Furthermore, the compensation plan usually is tied to the performance review.

A system that facilitates performance appraisal is known as *management by*

---

*Some companies use the term "human resources administration" in place of "personnel administration."

objectives (MBO). With the MBO system employees set their own objectives with the boss's concurrence. Employees periodically report progress to their supervisors who respond with their opinions of employee performance. They then agree on areas that may need improvement or change.[2]

Decision Making

In earlier chapters we discussed the decisions marketing managers make in connection with planning and organization. Important as these are they represent only a small portion of the total number of decisions made. Decisions are a part of the everyday life of marketing managers. They often report that their days seem to be filled with meetings where they learn about problems and discuss possible solutions. As we noted in Chapter 1, the ability and willingness to make decisions is a characteristic of an effective manager. Timely decisions keep an organization tuned to a fine pitch. Vacillation creates confusion and allows more alert competitors to move ahead.

ORGANIZATIONAL BEHAVIOR

Organizational behavior has received increasing attention in the study of management. Interest in individual and group performance has heightened with advances in behavioral theory and practice and with changes in society itself. Understanding *why* individuals and groups behave as they do, and knowing *how* to use this information, is important to all managers—and especially to the marketing and sales managers who must deal with large numbers of people.

We'll now look at three important aspects of the subject that can be useful to marketing managers—theories of group behavior, leadership, and motivation. For perspective we'll begin with a brief overview. Many of the behavioral experiments we will discuss have been done with production workers. While more research needs to be done with employees in nonproduction departments, many of the findings reported here appear to be applicable to the marketing department.

Introduction

The study of organizations can be traced to the beginnings of the industrial revolution during the middle of the eighteenth century. Adam Smith first publicized the benefits of the division of labor. Max Weber wrote about the protestant ethic and the benefits of bureaucracy in contrast to the feudal methods of economic organization. In the nineteenth century Karl Marx argued against the capitalistic form of organization. The earlier theorists were concerned with the social effects of organizations but had little to say about the skills of management. Before the systematic study of the processes of management began, many suspected that management skill was an accident of birth. Weber wrote of the charismatic leader whose personality influenced others to follow. Unfortunately, few people are born with this magic personality. Organizational behavioralists, however, have attempted to train managers in leadership.

The most successful analyst of behavior in organizations in the early 1900s was Frederick Winslow Taylor. The popular view of Taylor is that he was little more than an efficiency expert. A more balanced view of Taylor is that he introduced the use of the scientific method of research to determine the most efficient forms of working and that he attempted to improve the lot of both the worker and management.[3]

The scientists who followed Taylor provided the foundation for much of the modern theory of organizational behavior. Hugo Munsterberg, the father of industrial psychology, applied the systematic analysis of psychology to such problems as worker selection and training. The Hawthorne studies* (circa 1927–1932) first considered the effects that change in the work environment might have on the production output of individuals in the organization. Kurt Lewin, the father of group dynamics, contributed greatly to the understanding of the behavior of groups.

Human Relations versus Human Resources. The study of behavior is a value-laden process. Most analysts who study behavior hope that their efforts will lead to improvements of the human condition. This admirable philosophy can lead to some difficulties for the practicing manager, however. Improvements in the human condition are important and valuable. But if they come at the cost of decreased productivity, they may lead to unpleasant consequences. We applaud the manager who makes our work more enjoyable; we curse the manager who makes us unemployed. Thus, there is a judgment necessary in the application of the ideas of behavioral theorists. Do the proposed methods lead to productivity? Some theorists believe that unless behavioral skills produce productive results they are of little practical value.

Practicing managers view the findings of behavioral scientists from two different perspectives. On the one hand, managers see themselves as human resources who should have every opportunity for self-direction and self-control. On the other hand they may view their subordinates as incapable of self-direction and self-control. The thesis is that managers use the findings of behavioral scientists to improve their human relations skills with their subordinates while using the same findings to improve their own positions as resources within the firm.

This two-sided view of behavioral science and of human nature serves as an introduction to the findings of behavioral scientists. Our own values and our own perceptions influence what we see and what we think. The professional manager avoids this perceptual trap, substituting for it an objective observation of the situation. Common sense suggests that the chosen approach must produce results. The manager will use human relations skills to satisfy the work group, if such satisfaction will improve performance. Similarly, the manager will use workers as resources if such use will improve the performance of the work group.[4]

Group Behavior

The marketing manager is a member of several groups with the marketing department as the primary group. The manager also meets formally or informally with peers and serves on committees composed of marketing and nonmarketing personnel. Few managers can avoid meetings, since they help to provide the coordination an organization needs to achieve its goals.

In the functional organization, coordination is often achieved through meetings between members of the different functional departments. For example, managers

---

*These studies were named after the Hawthorne, Illinois, plant of the Western Electric Company where they were conducted.

from the production, marketing, and engineering departments might meet to discuss new product development. In a divisionalized company there would be meetings between functional departments within the same division, multidivision meetings, and meetings with corporate headquarters executives. In the matrix organization, teams of functional specialists might meet with business managers to solve problems.

Interdepartmental Conflict. In general, we are loyal to the group with which we spend most of our time. When the group is threatened, we defend it. Now, imagine a meeting of several department heads gathered to discuss a new product. Each department has its own special interest in the new product. For marketing, the product may represent sales opportunities if it can be sold at a low price. For production, the product may help to justify additional manufacturing facilities that the department wants badly, although the higher overhead costs would raise product costs beyond what marketing feels would be competitive. Research and development may want a change in design that would seriously delay the planned introduction date. The departments appear to be competing with one another rather than with the company's competitors. The internal competition, in fact, is real and can even be destructive.

The new product will have little chance of success unless the departments coordinate their efforts. In the classical hierarchical model this coordination should be provided by the nearest common superior. In most practical applications, however, this does not work. The nearest common superior is the president of the company or the division. By the time the conflict has traveled through the chain of command, the problem may have reached crisis proportions. Both theorists and executives have sought ways to overcome departmental barriers to cooperation.

Linking Pin Concept. The *linking pin concept* helps explain the problems of—and possibly means of improving—interdepartmental cooperation and coordination. Rensis Likert recognized that a manager needs communication links to other parts of the organization so that agreements can be reached on joint goals, responsibilities, and shared resources.[5] This interdepartmental linking is a process of group behavior. Since groups usually meet for only short periods of time, it is difficult to build cohesion. Furthermore, group work often is viewed as extra work, and some members may resent the assignment.

Lawrence and Lorsch called this process of linking *integration*.[6] Departments in organizations often operate under different styles. The production department, for example, usually follows a more autocratic style. It applies tight controls, has short-range goals, and gets quick feedback on results. A research department, on the other hand, will often be more democratic. Researchers operate under long-range goals, are not tightly controlled, and management does not get quick feedback on results. Production people see themselves as doers, while researchers see themselves as thinkers. When members of these departments meet, it is difficult for them to adjust to each other's style. Thus, it is difficult to link or integrate. An analogy from marketing would be salespeople, who view themselves as doers, trying to link with market researchers, who consider themselves analyzers and thinkers.

Structural Barriers. Workers and managers who specialize in a particular area, such as production, sales, or research, become identified with the norms and expectations of their departments. While departmental specialization is necessary in any large organization, it does lead to problems in coordination due to the structural barriers between departments.

Many solutions have been proposed to overcome the barriers. They include the use of joint goals, use of people specially trained in the coordination process, professional development of managers, increased skill in merging the styles (meeting half-way), and rotating assignments for managers. It would seem that any lasting solution must include an understanding by management of individual or group behavior. Management needs to recognize that the organization is a system with different requirements for its different parts. Differences in style grow out of the unique needs of each part of the system. Effective management of the system calls for recognition of the differences and for flexibility in dealing with them. Nevertheless, dealing with the complexities of individual and group behavior is not easy, even when the problems are recognized.

The successful manager performs the complex task of designing organizations and directing individuals and groups to goal attainment. Two important tools the manager can use in this process are leadership and motivation.

Leadership

Direction is leadership; all managers must direct; therefore, all managers are leaders. If this were true, few of us would ever have that common experience of finding that our bosses are not leaders. The statement would be more nearly accurate if we said: Direction requires leadership; successful managers can direct; therefore, all successful managers are leaders.

Research in the behavioral sciences has pursued several paths in attempting to explain the phenomenon of leadership. We will look at three of these: (1) studies of *personality traits* to try to find out whether there is some personality trait, or set of traits, which distinguishes leaders from nonleaders; (2) studies of *behavioral style* to learn whether some types of behavior make people more successful leaders; and (3) studies of the *work situation* to see whether there is some relationship between successful leaders, their behavior, and the work situation.[7]

Trait Theory. It is not difficult to identify great leaders. The pages of history books are filled with them. In trying to identify the keys to leadership, trait theorists start with the personal attributes of the leaders themselves.

Any list of great leaders would include such people as Abraham Lincoln, Susan B. Anthony, Franklin Roosevelt, and Adolf Hitler. Yet there are few traits these people had in common other than the fact that they were leaders. Differences are seen in their physical, social, and personality traits. In fact, taken as a whole, leaders do not appear to have many traits in common except that they tend to be a little taller and a little heavier than nonleaders. Also, they tend to score higher on tests of intelligence, extroversion, confidence, and dominance.[8] Even so, quite a bit of variation across these traits is found in different leaders. It cannot be stated that these differences are essential or that they are even causal factors in the success of leaders who possess them. The chance to exercise leadership, for example, may increase confidence or promote extroversion—not vice versa.

The weakness of trait theory is that it ignores two important parts of the leadership situation: first, every leader has followers. Second, every leader works in a specific context. The great leaders of World War II might not have been effective in the Vietnam war. Clearly, leadership is a complex process which requires more than trait theory to explain success. (For additional readings on trait theory, see reference 9 at the end of the chapter.)

Behavioral Style. Other analysts have attempted to identify leadership based on what leaders do, i.e., their specific behavior characteristics. The most distinctive difference between leaders may be in their style. Some leaders are very authoritarian; other leaders tend to be very democratic. In a classic study to determine effective leadership style, schoolchildren were organized into groups and given tasks to perform.[10] In some groups the style of task management was democratic, in others autocratic, and in others laissez faire. Both the autocratic and the democratic groups outperformed the laissez faire groups. The autocratic and democratic groups were about equally productive. However, when the autocratic leader left, this group's productivity declined. The study also reported that the groups with democratic leaders were more satisfied than those with autocratic or laissez faire leaders.

Researchers at Ohio State University isolated two important dimensions of leadership behavior—initiating structure and consideration.[11] *Initiating structure* refers to the behavior of the leader which is task related. The leader, for example, sets guidelines, deadlines, rules, standards of performance, and checks the work of followers for conformance to standards. *Consideration* refers to the behavior of the leader when relating to people. The leader with consideration is friendly, provides support, expresses concern, and builds rapport with the followers.

Blake and Mouton[12] developed the Managerial Grid, shown in Figure 15-1. They labeled one axis of their grid "concern for people" and the other "concern for production." Each of these dimensions can be scored on a scale from 1 to 9. Managers have been found to score in all areas of the grid. Although the "ideal" manager scores 9,9, there are some work situations that do not require the ideal.

A leadership behavior theory which takes explicit account of the work situation is the Life-Cycle Theory[13] depicted in Figure 15-2. A leader might show a high level of both task- and employee-related behavior, a low level of both task- and employee-related behavior, or be high on one dimension and low on the other. This theory suggests that the appropriate style depends upon the group of followers. If the group is immature, a style high in task-oriented behavior and low in relationships (employee consideration) is necessary. If the group is of average maturity, a style high in both task and employee relationships is appropriate. But if the group is highly mature, a style low in both employee relationships and task concern is appropriate, since this group can work well independently of the leader.

As with trait theory, there is no conclusive evidence to support the hypothesis that one dimension of leader behavior is more or less important than another. Leaders can be successful in the absence of consideration, yet consideration does contribute to success. While leaders can be successful without initiating structure, initiating structure also can contribute to success.

In summary the findings seem to tell us that both initiating structure and consideration are important, yet their relative importance depends on the situation, and managers must be flexible in their leadership styles.

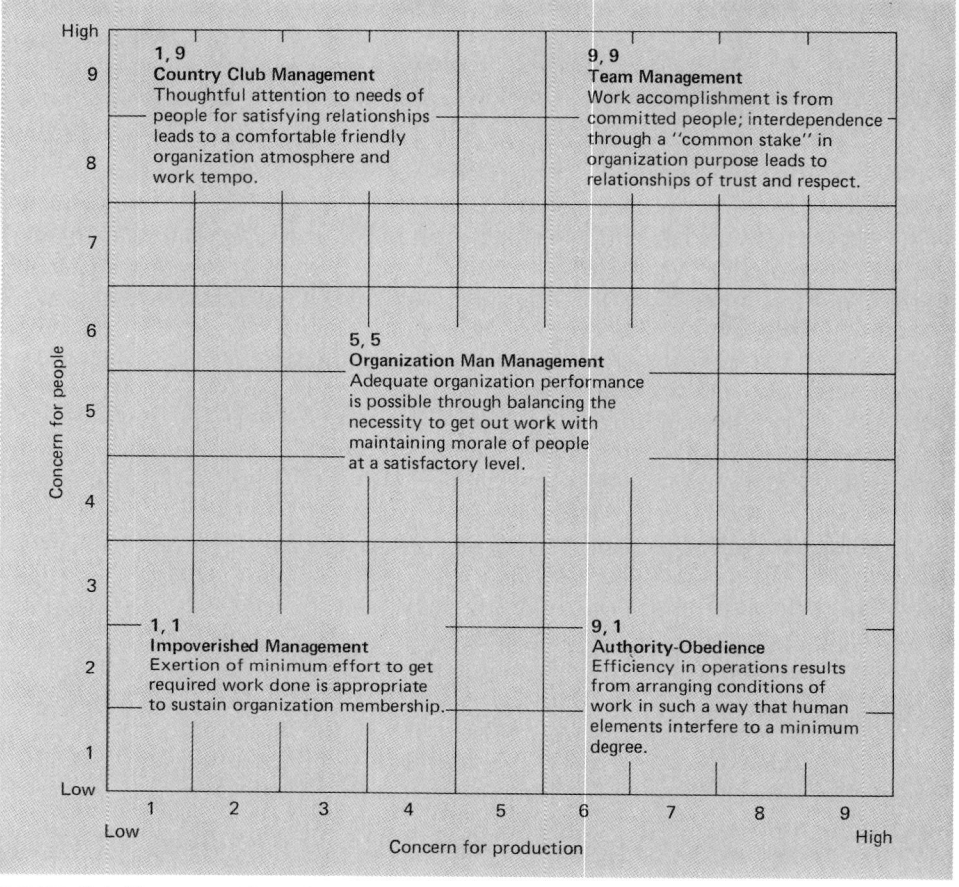

FIGURE 15-1. The managerial grid. *Source:* Robert R. Blake and Jane Srygley Mouton, *The New Managerial Grid,* Gulf Publishing, Houston, 1978, p. 11. Reproduced with permission.

The Work Situation. Others have looked at the relationship between the work situation and leadership style. Consider the successful military leader during wartime. The depth of the crisis and the dangerous nature of the situation dictate that this leader be a stern taskmaster. Few people in war expect their leader to take time to build cohesive feelings in the group. The threat of enemy attack builds all the cohesion necessary. A stern leader, who emphasizes initiating structure over consideration for people, may be very successful. The same leader in different situations may be totally ineffective. General George Patton captured the imagination and support of his troops during World War II. Few, however, would be likely to work for him in a marketing research group. They would resent his firm discipline and pressure tactics.

But let's assume that George Patton *had* become a marketing research manager. How could he have been effective? Obviously he'd have to develop his skills in the area of consideration. It is possible, but not likely, that General Patton could have switched gears. The idea that not everyone—perhaps no one—can change natural leadership styles led Fred Fiedler to develop his contingency model of leadership effectiveness.[14]

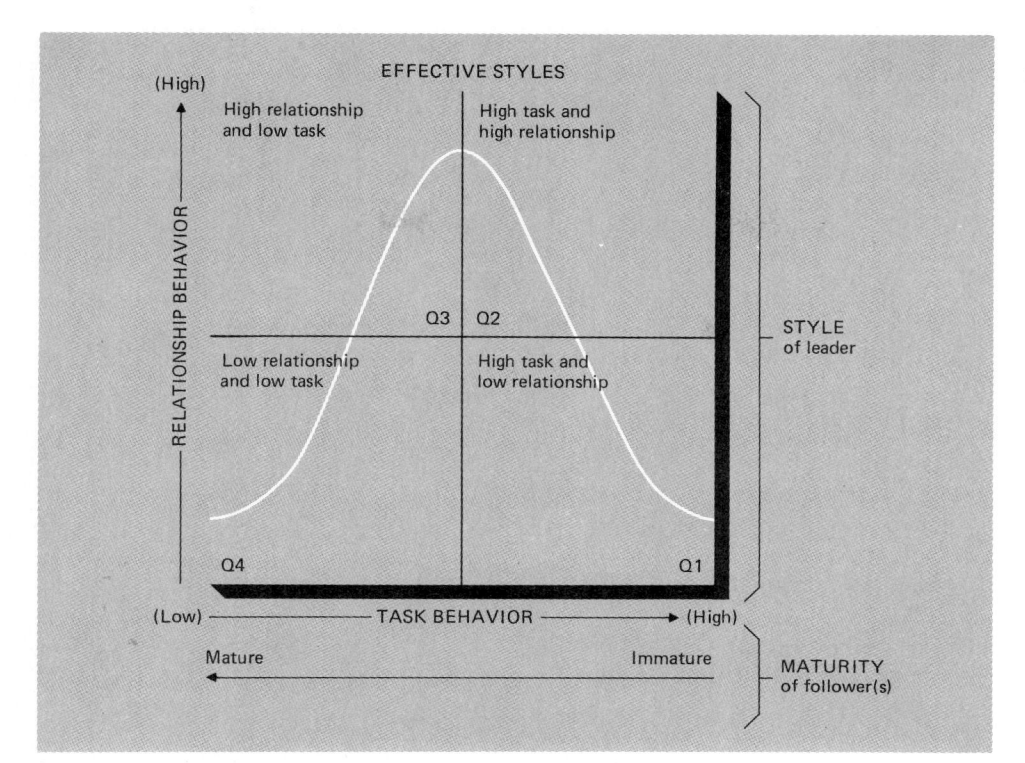

FIGURE 15-2. Situational leadership (or life cycle) theory. *Source:* Paul Hersey and Kenneth H. Blanchard, *Management of Organizational Behavior: Utilizing Human Resources*, 3d ed., Prentice-Hall Englewood Cliffs, 1977, p. 164. Reproduced with permission.

The Fiedler Contingency Model. The Fiedler contingency model stresses that a leader must be matched to the appropriate situation. A leader's style is determined by his or her score on a questionnaire called the LPC (least preferred co-worker). A manager who scores high on this questionnaire is concerned with maintaining good relationships (consideration), while a manager who scores low on this questionnaire is concerned with task success (initiating structure). The theory rates the situation in terms of its favorability for the leader. Favorability is measured by leader-member relations, the structure of the task, and the power of the leader.

The theory holds that the nature of the work situation affects the relationships between leadership style and group effectiveness. In situations of moderate favorability, the high-consideration leader is more effective. In situations of low or high favorability, the task-centered leader is more effective. The performance of this theory in the studies designed to test it has been inconsistent. Some studies find a significant relationship, some do not. Most find some relationship.

Leadership is a complex process which no one has yet explained adequately. We know it when we see it because the successful leader gets results from the group. However, the fact that leaders with different styles can be successful intrigues theorists, and the search for an explanation continues. Present wisdom suggests that leadership is an interactive process between the leader, the followers, and the situation and that the effective leader will consider all three.

Motivation

Motivation is the study of how behavior gets started and how it is stopped.[15]

This definition only hints at the complexity of the process. To date psychologists and management theorists have not reached a clear understanding of the process of motivation, although no one underestimates its importance. We'll limit this brief discussion to motivation as a management function.

Vroom identified four classes of variables which can be used to help explain motivation: (1) outcomes, (2) desire for outcomes, (3) comparison of outcomes with the outcomes of other workers, and (4) amount of outcome expected.[16] These provide a convenient framework for describing motivation as a management task.

Outcomes. Motivation is the task of managing outcomes for workers and has been described as a three-step process of (1) defining goals, (2) clearing obstacles, and (3) providing payoffs. The third step, the payoffs, are the outcomes.[17]

A manager has direct control over the outcomes a worker receives. These include money, status, prestige, personal growth, praise, advancement. There can also be negative outcomes such as fatigue, dismissal, punishment, and admonishment. Several theories have been developed about the nature of the outcome and its effect on motivation.

One study found that certain outcomes lead to motivation. These outcomes include responsibility, achievement, advancement, the work itself, recognition, and the possibility of growth.[18] Unmet needs can also motivate, and these needs can be arranged in a hierarchy. This hierarchy includes physiological, security, social, egoistic, and self-actualization needs.*

Given these outcomes, how does the manager use them? Some outcomes can be more readily adopted than others. Some can be provided by design and some by the manager's behavior after a job is completed.

Job Design. Responsibility, growth, and achievement can be built into a job by careful design. A job that has independence, variety, and identification with the work will increase the amount of job responsibility. Independence can be introduced through the process of mutual goal setting, such as in management by objectives. Variety can be introduced through the process of rotating assignments. Task identity can be built into the job through public recognition of an individual's contribution. Designing motivation into jobs is not easy because it is different for each job. Furthermore, the manager must weigh loss of control of the workforce against the advantages of having an independent workforce.

Recognition. The manager can utilize outcomes such as praise, prestige, and status. Money is one way of providing prestige and status, although some studies show money to be low on the list of motivating factors. Monetary rewards will motivate high performance only when the reward is clearly tied to high performance. Otherwise money has little value as a motivating device. In large institutions and bureaucratic organizations, for example, salaries often are determined by length of service and type of background. Those workers with the same length of service and education may receive the same salary regardless of their level of performance. In

---

*See Marketing Note 5–1 for a description of Maslow's hierarchy of needs.

this case, money will not serve as a motivating factor. But compensation tied to performance can be a strong incentive and explains the common use of incentive compensation plans for salespeople.

Praise for excellent performance is another powerful motivating tool. Successful sales managers make frequent use of this device. But praise doesn't work with everyone. For these people negative outcomes may be better motivators.

The effectiveness of praise as a motivating factor has been demonstrated by behavior modification programs, first proposed by B. F. Skinner. In industrial applications of the method, managers learned to reinforce, i.e., praise, workers for good performance. The effect of the consistent and judicious use of this simple technique led to a dramatic increase in the daily performance level of the workers.[19] Managers who find this technique effective say that if you see a good performance and you want to see it again, give public recognition to it.

Desire for outcomes. An important variable in the process of motivation is the worker. Not all workers want the same thing; when they do they may not have the same level of desire. Any scheme that uses the same outcomes as a motivational device for all workers will have limited success.

There have been several explorations of the relationship between personal characteristics and desired outcomes. One found that rural workers are more concerned about filling needs of higher order on the job than are urban workers.[20] Another identified three categories of workers: The *organizationalist* is highly committed to the organization. The *externalist*, by contrast, is not highly committed to the organization, would rather be elsewhere, and does not see the work environment as a critical part of life. The *professional* is highly committed to work but is not necessarily committed to the organization.[21] People in each of these categories would prefer different outcomes.

The fact that different workers prefer different outcomes introduces a new degree of complexity to the task of motivating employees. The best approach is to hire people who prefer the outcomes that the organization offers. But this is not always possible. Screening devices for differentiating workers according to outcome preference do not yet exist. Even the most successful interviewers are able to screen effectively only part of the time. Thus the manager should attempt to find motivational schemes which will fit different types of outcomes. The problem is commonly encountered by sales managers who find that salespeople do not respond uniformly to the same incentive plans.

While the task is difficult, it is not impossible. The first step is to discover those rewards which motivate the workers being managed. Since workers often don't know or won't say what motivates them, options need to be tested. They might include praise, money, different assignments, opportunity for promotion, office perquisites, competition, and cooperative work efforts. Some people do not respond to any reward schemes. Others have their own built-in motivational systems such as receiving some intrinsic reward from their work. This type of high performer is the *self-actualized person*, or the *professional*. The self-driven high performer, however, is the exception rather than the rule.

Outcomes of other workers. One aspect of the motivation process that the wise manager understands is the outcomes provided by other organizations. Men and women are social animals. We learn, adapt, and build expectations by watching others. Consciously or unconsciously, we build expectations for ourselves and put ourselves into hierarchies. When the outcomes (such as pay) provided by our organization are similar to the outcomes other organizations provide for the same work, we are satisfied. When other organizations provide higher outcomes, we are dissatisfied. Indeed, economic theory teaches that we will be motivated to move to the organization which provides the higher outcome.

Two theories which help explain the importance of the outcomes of other workers are equity theory and expectancy theory. *Equity theory* proposes that workers compare the ratio of their inputs into work with their outcomes from work.[22] Where the ratio is inequitable, the worker strives to balance the inequity. This inequity can occur in either direction; that is, a worker might strive to reduce input to make it equitable with outcome received, or the worker might try to increase outcome.

Expectancy theory proposes that a worker compare the effort required for performance, the probability that a particular performance will lead to a particular outcome, and the value of that outcome.[23] Simply put, the worker estimates the chances of attaining a reward for a particular outcome and compares them with the value of that outcome. This expectancy model is important because it clarifies the influence of other workers in the motivation process. If other workers have not been able to attain the required performance, have not been rewarded for the required performance, or get higher rewards for mediocre performance, the worker will not be motivated.

Level of desired outcome. Frustrated expectations lead to dissatisfaction. Fulfilled expectations lead to satisfaction. The manager may not know what workers expect when they perform at a certain level. This can be corrected through careful attention to the work environment.

The environment includes the physical and social surroundings in the work area. Work provides a multiplicity of outcomes, both good and bad. Motivation can be raised if the bad outcomes in the work environment are changed. In the Hawthorne studies it was learned that workers responded with more productivity each time there was any type of change in the work environment.[24] If the norms of the work group are lower than management desires, there are several methods for changing the norms: (1) break up the group, (2) change the group, (3) use group incentives instead of individual incentives, and (4) hire individualists who are not responsive to group pressures. Many managers choose the group incentive option. The Scanlon and Lincoln pay plans, for example, have been developed to reward group performance. The Scanlon plan offers bonuses for employees if the company performs well during the year.[25] The Lincoln plan offers bonuses based on company performance plus the individual's contribution to that performance.[26] To encourage cooperative efforts Procter & Gamble pays bonuses to its district salespeople based on the performance of the sales district.

Removing obstacles is a direct attempt to decrease the amount of negative outcomes in the performance of work. In many instances, the poor design of work leads to decreased performance. In general, the manager can remove obstacles by supplying proper training which can lead to achievement of higher work expectations and greater work satisfaction.

Managers must see that employees are motivated. Motivation is a difficult subject because it is a dynamic process. A few generations ago the manager could use the *stick* to motivate. Fear of hunger brought people to work, and fear of dismissal kept them there. With changing social and economic environments, fear declined as a motivating process and the *carrot* took over.

Today, however, several factors operate to lessen the effectiveness of the carrot. First, we tire of even the most enjoyable rewards and, as we do, they lose their effectiveness. Secondly, as rewards become more and more expensive they begin to cost more than the increment in performance they encourage. Thirdly, inflation has led to increased expectations and more costly rewards. As a result, the effectiveness of monetary rewards is decreasing.[27]

The answers to motivation of the work force in the future will probably be found through innovation in the work world. In addition to material needs people need to achieve, to feel competent. Many people thoroughly enjoy their work. Even lucrative retirement programs sometimes cannot lure workers into quitting their jobs. Work can provide social interaction, challenge, identity. The challenge to management is to define the desired outcomes and to provide them in the proper manner.

MANAGERIAL CONTROL

The final link in the marketing management process is *control*. Control procedures for measuring progress against goals need to be set up so that corrective actions can be taken if performance is running below goal. Action also needs to be taken if performance is running ahead of plan; for example, new sales forecasts must be made to justify the increase in production needed to supply the increased demand. On the other hand, if sales are below plan, revisions in marketing tactics are needed to improve sales performance; or, if that is not feasible or possible, sales forecasts need to be lowered so that production and inventories can be cut back. Since the more serious problem is below goal performance, our definition of managerial control is as follows:

> *Managerial control* of marketing operations is the means by which marketing management measures progress toward attainment of marketing goals so that timely actions can be taken to improve performance (or modify the goals) if performance is not in accordance with plans.

Types of Control Reports

There are two principal means of managerial control, formal reports and informal communications. Effective marketing managers use both.

Formal Reports. Formal controls take the form of periodic printed reports (usually computer printouts or terminal readouts), plus written reports. *Written reports* contain both quantitative and qualitative information and are prepared by analysts, managers at different levels in the organization, and sales representatives. *Printed reports* of interest to marketing management will show, for the current period and the year to date, the planned goal, the actual performance, and the percent of variance from plan. Figure 15-3 is an example of a control report showing summary, or aggregated, data of interest to the marketing manager. Some managers prefer to see information portrayed graphically as in the sales performance example in Figure 15-4.

Since it is not feasible to obtain all control information through the computer, periodic written reports may be required by different levels of management. The first level sales supervisor, for example, may want daily or weekly reports from sales representatives reporting the results of account calls and including any market

Performance Report for May (month)
(Thousands of dollars)

Item	This Month			Year-to-Date		
	Plan	Actual	% Actual to Plan	Plan	Actual	% Actual to Plan
Sales	$3,500	$4,000	+14.3%	$12,500	$15,000	+20.0%
Profits	245	240	–(2.0)	875	900	+ 2.9
Expenses	280	300	+ 7.1	1,000	1,125	+12.5
Pricing variances	0	–(5)	Negative variance	0	25	Positive variance
Finished inventory	5,000 units	4,500 units	–(10.0)	5,000 units	4,500 units	–(10.0)
Order backlog	4 days	3½ days	Positive* variance	4 days	5 days	Negative variance

*Positive because the service objective of this company is to ship promptly from inventory. For engineered (made-to-order) industrial goods, on the other hand, *higher* than anticipated backlogs would be considered a positive variance.

FIGURE 15-3. Example of a summary control report for the marketing manager.

intelligence learned. The general sales manager may want weekly written reports from regional sales managers citing problems, competitive actions, and developments with major accounts.

Informal Communications. Informal contacts via telephone, face-to-face conversations, and group meetings serve to alert marketing management to market developments before they are reflected in the formal reporting system. A price cut or new promotion by a major competitor foretells a likely drop that will occur in company sales unless something is done quickly to counteract the competitive moves. Customers and wholesale and retail channel executives often know of market competitive and economic developments before they become general knowledge. Or if the falloff in sales is not spotted until it shows up in the formal reporting system, field contacts often can provide clues to the causes.

Consequently, alert marketing managers maintain open communications with the marketplace, and encourage their subordinates (particularly their sales managers) to do likewise. In summary, both the formal reporting system and the informal communications system serve to supplement one another.

Types of Control Information

The type and quantity of information will vary by the company and the individual preferences of marketing managers. Most marketing managers, however, will want to see *aggregated* data covering sales, profits, marketing expenses, pricing variances,

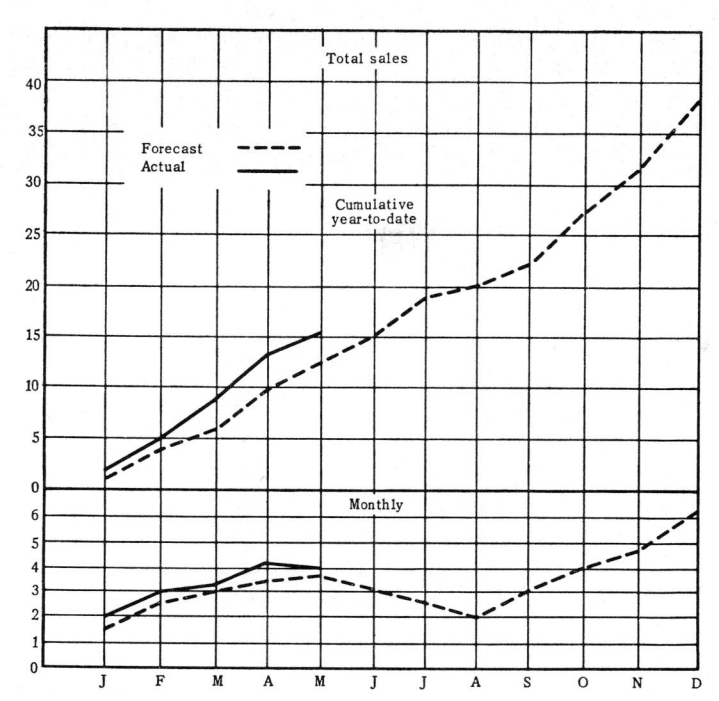

FIGURE 15-4. Actual sales compared to forecast by month and cumulatively. *Source:* Victor P. Buell, *Marketing Management in Action*, McGraw-Hill, New York, 1966, p. 176. Used with permission.

inventories, and order backlogs, as illustrated in Figure 15-3. As a member of the top corporate or division management team the marketing manager also will want to see other information, even though it may report activities outside of the marketing manager's control. Examples would include production costs, delinquent accounts, and warranty costs. These three examples represent control information of direct interest to the managers of manufacturing, credit, and quality control, respectively. Indirectly, of course, they may affect areas for which marketing management is responsible.

Aggregate and Disaggregate Data. An effective control system will provide both aggregate and disaggregate data. The aggregate data tell the marketing manager quickly and simply whether performance in general is running in accordance with the plan. If it is, the marketing manager can work on other things. In Figure 15-3, for example, things seem to be going well except that profits for the most recent month are off by 2 percent. While this is not large it bears watching, since it could signal a softening of prices or a change in the planned product sales mix (as suggested by the negative pricing variance).

If the aggregate data indicate a potential problem, the *disaggregate* information may help pinpoint the specific area where the problem lies. For example, a drop in total sales may be the result of declining sales of one product while sales of the rest of the products are meeting their goals; or sales may be down in one geographic area; or the decline may reflect the loss of one major account. Identifying the problem area, of course, does not correct the situation. Marketing management must still find the underlying causes, correct them if possible, or make adjustments if the causes (such as economic conditions) are beyond the control of marketing management.

This system of locating and dealing with the specific problem area allows the manager to *manage by exception*. The manager, in essence, does not tinker with the engine when it is running well; when it is not, efforts are directed toward finding and solving the specific problems causing the poor performance. This approach avoids upsetting the entire organization when the cause of the problem is in a specific sector and beyond the control of others in the organization to do anything about it. The sales manager, for example, need not exhort the entire sales organization to greater effort because total sales are below goal when the problem is known to be in the eastern region.

Figure 15-5 illustrates the differences between aggregate and disaggregate data for six of the types of information important to the typical marketing manager. Data that are disaggregate for the marketing manager may, of course, be aggregate for someone else. The marketing manager, for example, may not wish to see sales by product as long as overall sales are on target; yet the product manager definitely will want to see sales by product. Similarly, sales performance by district may not be of immediate concern to the marketing manager, yet it would represent essential control information for the general sales manager and the district sales managers.

FIGURE 15-5. Examples of aggregate and disaggregate marketing control data.

Aggregate data	Disaggregate data

1. Sales
   a. Total dollar sales
	1. Sales by
	   a. Product
	   b. Market
	   c. Geographic area (e.g., region, district, territory)
	   d. Major accounts

2. Profit
   a. Net profit
	2. Profit contribution by:
	   a. Product
	   b. Market
	   c. Geographic area
	   d. Major accounts

3. Expenses
   a. Total marketing
	3. Expenses by:
	   a. Subdepartments of marketing
	   b. Sales regions, districts, territories

4. Pricing variances
   a. Total
	4. Pricing variances by
	   a. Product
	   b. Market
	   c. Geographic area

5. Finished inventories	5. Finished inventories in units by:
	   a. Product
	   b. Plant
	   c. Field warehouse

6. Order backlog in excess of standard time to fill by:
   a. Total dollar value
   b. Average number of days over standard
	6. Order backlog in excess of standard time to fill by:
	   a. Product
	   b. Average days over standard by product

In addition to their primary use—measuring performance and identifying problem areas as the year progresses—control reports can also be useful to the marketing planner. Analysis of disaggregate data may reveal opportunities for profit improvement with the next marketing plan. Even though this may be so, control reports should not be designed to serve a dual purpose. Controlling current operations and planning for the future are two different activities. By and large planning and controlling require different types of informational data.

The Corporate Control System

Marketing control should be an integral part of the corporate control report system. Unless there is a planned corporate (or division) system, the reporting situation can become chaotic. Managers at all levels besiege the accounting department, the computing department, and other data sources for the particular reports they want. At a minimum the unfavorable results are duplication of efforts and high costs. Managers often have too much information (information overload), yet still do not have what they really need to exercise effective control.

In companies with good control systems the controller is usually responsible for setting up and supervising the system. The controller determines from managers the information they need and how frequently they need it. A system of reports is then developed from a common data base. In general, data are provided in the most disaggregate form to the lowest levels of management; the data are then increasingly aggregated for each higher level of management. The idea is to give each executive what is needed, yet avoid overloading anyone with unnecessary information.

Characteristics of a Good Marketing Control System

A good marketing control system will provide both formal and informal means of measuring performance and identifying potential and actual problem areas. The *informal* system is largely a system of oral communication between individuals and will vary according to the individual manager's particular style. The effective *formal* report system, on the other hand, will meet certain standard tests. It will:

1. Reveal variations from planned results early enough to allow for taking corrective actions
2. Help identify the specific areas where variations may be occurring that affect the overall performance
3. Permit management by exception
4. Be an integral part of the corporate or division control system
5. Limit information provided each manager to what each manager needs
6. Provide information primarily for control purposes and only incidentally for planning purposes

Developing the Marketing Control System

There are three steps to developing a formal marketing control system: (1) deciding what information is needed, (2) deciding who needs what information, and (3) arranging for the collection and distribution of information.

Step 3 is a job for the corporate or division controller. Step 2 is a decision to be made jointly by marketing managers and their staffs. Step 1 is largely determined when the marketing plan is adopted since the annual marketing plan contains the quantitative goals broken down by time periods. The control information needed, therefore, is that which will measure progress toward the goals set forth in the plan.

These simple steps belie the difficulty companies experience when trying to establish their first integrated reporting system. The process is made much easier, however, when it is preceded by the development of a good planning system with plans that contain quantitatively stated goals.

SUMMARY

The discussions of direction and control in this chapter complete our formal treatment of the classic management functions of planning, organizing, directing, and controlling. Planning has been emphasized in this text because it provides an integrative process for learning how the various aspects of marketing fit together. Furthermore, strategic planning is receiving increasing attention in well-managed companies. At the same time, as we learn about marketing management, it is important that we do not neglect management functions such as direction, which is used to carry out (execute) the plans.

While planning and organizing can be learned in the classroom, direction is not so easy to learn off the job. This is because it is largely involved with getting people, usually groups of people, to perform effectively in carrying out plans and achieving organizational goals. We can teach and learn good administrative practices, but we don't yet know how to teach leadership. Behavioral scientists are unwilling to acknowledge that leadership is a trait that a person is born with; yet they haven't been able to prove that leadership can be learned. Knowledge of group behavior and individual motivation, however, should help the potential manager develop and apply the managerial style appropriate to varying organizational situations. How a manager can or will develop into an outstanding leader remains a mystery.

Control is not the least important management function although it is probably the easiest to learn. Because controllership has become a specialized area in business organizations, marketing managers usually do not need to know the mechanics of developing and operating control systems. Marketing management should understand the use of control reports and how a good control reporting system can help ensure that marketing goals are attained. It should determine the information it needs to measure progress, and identify problem areas, and then make sure that the executive in charge of the control reporting system understands what is wanted. In addition to the formal control system we have pointed out that effective marketing managers also develop their own informal control systems to supplement the formal ones.

QUESTIONS

1. To what does the managerial function of direction refer?
2. With what is managerial control concerned?
3. What is the essence of present wisdom concerning leadership?
4. From the managerial viewpoint, what is motivation?
5. What are the principal means of managerial control?

6. What is the meaning of management by exception?
7. What are the steps in developing a formal marketing control system?

REFERENCES

1. Parts of this section are drawn from Victor P. Buell, *Marketing Management in Action*, McGraw-Hill, New York, 1966, chap. 9.
2. For authoritative information on the subject, see the writings of George S. Odiorne, especially: *MBO II: A System of Managerial Leadership for the 80's*, Fearon Pitman, Belmont, Calif., 1979.
3. Daniel A. Wren, *The Evolution of Management Thought*, Ronald Press, New York, 1972, p. 146.
4. Raymond E. Miles, "Human Relations or Human Resources?", *Harvard Business Review*, July–Aug., 1965. Reprinted by permission. Copyright © 1965 by the President and Fellows of Harvard College; all rights reserved.
5. For further discussion of the linking pin concept, see Rensis Likert, *New Patterns of Management*, McGraw-Hill, New York, 1961; and *The Human Organization: Its Management and Value*, McGraw-Hill, New York, 1967.
6. For more on integration theory see Paul R. Laurence and S. W. Lorsch, *Organization and Environment Managing, Differentiation and Integration*, Irwin, Homewood, Ill., 1969, p. 11.
7. For a complete review of leadership studies, see Ralph M. Stogdill, *Handbook of Leadership: A Survey of Theory and Research*, Free Press, New York, 1974.
8. See Victor H. Vroom, "Leadership," in Marvin D. Dunnette (ed.), *Handbook of Industrial and Organizational Psychology*, Rand McNally, Chicago, 1976, p. 1529.
9. Ghisselli, E. E., *Explorations in Managerial Talent*, Goodyear, Pacific Palisades, CA, 1971; Thomas Carlyle, *Lectures on Heroes, Hero-Worship, and the Hero in History*, P. E. Parr (ed.), Oxford, Clarendon Press, 1910.
10. Kurt Lewin, Ronald Lippitt, and R. K. White, "Patterns of Aggressive Behavior in Experimentally Related Social Climates," *Journal of Social Psychology*, vol. 10, 1939, pp. 271–299.
11. Andrew W. Halpin and B. James Winer, "A Factoral Study of the Leader Behavior Descriptions" in Ralph M. Stogdill and Alvin E. Loons (eds.), *Leader Behavior: Its Description and Measurement*, Bureau of Business Research, College of Commerce and Administration, Ohio State University, Columbus, Ohio, 1957, pp. 41, 42.
12. Robert R. Blake and Jane S. Mouton, *The New Managerial Grid*, Gulf Publishing, Houston, 1978, p. 11.
13. Paul Hersey and Kenneth H. Blanchard, *Management of Organizational Behavior: Utilizing Human Resources*, 3d ed., Prentice-Hall, Englewood Cliffs, NJ, 1977, p. 164. Reprinted by permission.
14. For a more complete description, see F. E. Fiedler and M. M. Chemers, *Leadership and Effective Management*, Scott, Foresman, Glenview, Ill., 1974.
15. For a broader definition and discussion of motivation, see Edward E. Lawler, *Motivation in Work Organizations*, Brooks/Cole, Monterey, Calif., 1973, p. 10.
16. Victor Vroom, "Industrial Social Psychology," in G. Lindsen and E. Aronson (eds.), *The Handbook of Social Psychology*, 2d ed., Addison-Wesley, Reading, Mass., 1969, pp. 200–208.
17. George S. Odiorne, *Executive Skills*, MBO Inc., Westfield, Mass., 1974, pp. 126–127.
18. Frederick Herzberg, Bernard Mausner, and Barbara Brock Snydermann, *The Motivation To Work*, 2d ed., Wiley, New York, 1959.
19. "Productivity Gains From a Pat on the Back," *Business Week*, Jan. 23, 1978, pp. 56–62.
20. C. R. Hulin and M. R. Blood, "Job Enlargement, Individual Differences, and Worker Responses," *Psychological Bulletin*, vol. 69, 1968, pp. 41–45.

21. H. L. Tosi and S. J. Carroll, *Management: Contingencies, Structure, and Process*, St. Clair Press, Chicago, 1976, pp. 82–91.
22. J. S. Adams, "Toward an Understanding of Inequity," *Journal of Abnormal Psychology*, vol. 67, 1963, pp. 422–436.
23. Edward E. Lawler, op. cit., p. 49.
24. Daniel A. Wren, op. cit., pp. 276–277.
25. F. G. Lesieur (ed.), *The Scanlon Plan*, MIT Press, Cambridge, Mass., 1958.
26. J. F. Lincoln, *Incentive Management*, Lincoln Electric Co., 1951.
27. For a discussion of these issues, see Peter Drucker, *Management: Tasks Practices, Responsibilities,* Harper & Row, New York, 1974, pp. 231–245.

The company's marketing organization plan and the role of product management

Reading 8

Organizing For Effective Advertising Results—Campbell Soup Company

We shall deal with the role of the brand manager or product manager system and its abilities in obtaining effective advertising.

The product or brand manager system has blossomed in recent years as companies have diversified into many product lines. And to a large extent, these systems have made diversification possible.

While a limited line of products can be successfully marketed under the vertical [or functional] sales department–marketing department concept, the complexity of an expanding product line demands a coordinated marketing approach for each product under a unified authority.

Thus managerships have been created for each product or for groups of allied products, with the manager as the focal point for all marketing functions with respect to the product. At this point, I want to explain that I draw no distinction between the title "product (or brand) manager" used by many companies and the "product marketing manager" which is the position title we use. Also, our product marketing managers are supervised by product marketing directors—positions which other companies frequently designate "group product managers."

The product marketing director's influence spreads in many directions:

1. Planning and recommending to management the path the product should follow over the forthcoming year and years
2. Product line extension development and improvement of present products
3. Labeling and packaging
4. Marketing research—in sales, consumer, and advertising research
5. Product promotion
6. All aspects of consumer advertising and publicity
7. Marketing budget management
8. Pricing and profit, although top management retains final profit control in order to be in a position to meet corporate objectives

Organization

With this as background, I will describe our organization plan. Line marketing is divisionalized. Each major division has a vice president, marketing—or an individual with a similar title and the same responsibilities. The division vice president, marketing reports to the division president. Also reporting to the division president is the vice president, operations who manages overall plant operations.

The various marketing support groups are part of the Corporate Marketing Services Department. This includes Advertising Services, Product Promotion, Market Research, Home Economics, Design Center, and New Products. The Marketing Services Department is directed by the corporate vice president, marketing . . . who reports to the president of the company.

The sales function is organized as a separate division—the Campbell Sales Company. The Campbell Sales Company has its own president (reporting to the president of the Campbell Soup Company). Within the Campbell Sales Company, sales managers are assigned to the various divisions. The field sales force is organized separately to handle canned foods, frozen foods, and special products (food brokers).

Line Marketing. The Canned Foods Division marketing is organized into four groups under the division vice president, marketing: (1) Red & White Soup and Soup For One; (2) Chunky Soup; (3) Juices/Beans; and (4) Franco-American. Each group has a product marketing

This reading was presented originally as a talk by Robert L. Kress at an advanced advertising management course sponsored by the Association of National Advertisers. It has been updated for this text by Herbert M. Baum, Campbell's vice president, marketing. It describes the marketing organization at Campbell as of July 1980 and provides insight into the workings of the product management form of organizaion.

director* who supervises product marketing managers† and assistants.

The Swanson Frozen Food Division marketing is divided into two groups under the division vice president, marketing: (1) Established Products and (2) New Products. Each group has a product marketing director who supervises product marketing managers and assistants.

Corporate Marketing. The line marketing groups are serviced by the previously mentioned marketing services departments—each headed by a director—whose functions are to advise, assist, and execute for the division marketing groups.

Advertising Services. This department administrates the company's general advertising policy including contracts with advertising agencies, radio and television networks, print media, etc. The director of Advertising Services, who heads up this department, has a key position in view of the fact that he coordinates the corporate advertising wealth that is generated through each division marketing group and counsels with the intent that this large sum of money will be spent most efficiently in regard to discounts and in line with the overall image the company wishes to maintain. However, decisions with respect to advertising strategy and execution are made by the line divisions.

Home Economics. This department is staffed with home economists, whose function is to advise and interpret from the consumer's point of view regarding existing products, new product ideas, recipes, and preparation directions. This department is also charged with the preparation of publicity material in the interest of promoting the company's products with food editors, dieticians, and teachers.

Marketing Research. This department conducts all phases of research into the acceptance and consumer attitude for the company's products, analyzing and interpreting data received from outside organizations, company records, and independently developed sources. Research also assists in forecasting market potential for new products and sales results for existing products, and helps to evaluate effectiveness of promotion programs, merchandising ideas, and advertising campaigns.

Product Promotion. This department cooperates with the division marketing groups in planning, coordinating, and instituting special consumer and trade promotions. It also coordinates and executes the purchase of printed display and promotional material for use in promotional campaigns.

Design Center. This department develops and executes package design, point-of-sale materials, the company annual report, meeting presentations, collateral materials, package photography, and other design work necessary to service the division marketing groups.

New Products. New products (with the exception of line extensions) are a corporate function as part of the Marketing Services Department. New products are managed by Marketing Services until national introduction when they are assigned to the appropriate division.

Delegation of Authority

Each one of the division product groups is headed by a product marketing director, whose responsibility in all areas of marketing has already been outlined. The product marketing director collaborates with the Sales Company, the advertising agencies, and the service or staff departments just outlined. Each one of the product marketing directors has a product marketing manager and, in some cases, an assistant product marketing manager.

With this or similar product management systems, each product marketing director is set up to pursue the group's marketing activities. One of the most important of these activities is, or course, to obtain meaningful and effective advertising for their products. Now comes a major question: How well does the product management system function in obtaining strong performance from the agency?

The key to this, as it is in the manager's ability to obtain results in every other facet of marketing, is tied to the responsibility and authority that management invests in the marketing groups.

In some companies, the product marketing manager may be little more than an advertising clerk, approving estimates, schedules, and invoices, checking proofs and answer prints, and riding herd on agency promises. This type of manager may have little to do with setting advertising policy and approving basic advertising concepts for advertising strategies. Such a person has little, if any, authority and makes decisions only at the direction of the marketing director, marketing vice president, or a committee of superiors.

This kind of product marketing manager has the title but not the prerogative of the manager, and can do little to help the administration or building of effective advertising campaigns. This person can't tell you where to go,

---

*Called *group product manager* in many companies.

†Called *product* (or *brand*) *manager* in many companies.

only how you can't get there. Without belaboring this point further, this situation is the result of too little delegation of authority by management. It stems from management's lack of confidence in the product manager or, more often, their unwillingness to delegate any real authority. Sometimes, too, it stems from not enough assumption of authority on the part of the product manager.

Now, in relating ability to obtain effective advertising, there is another trap of which even a marketing manager with stature can be a victim. Most top managements reserve for themselves final approval of *major* advertising decisions. Due to the size and importance of the advertising investment, this is perfectly understandable, and the product manager can operate effectively within this framework. The problem I speak of arises when top management people go beyond approval of major decisions and insist on injecting themselves into the day-by-day areas of execution. Then you have a problem.

But let's say that a good product marketing director is in a position to recommend advertising programs to top management for their approval and has gained their confidence so that they have given the director authority for the execution of the approved programs. Hopefully this person not only has such authority, but management has learned to depend on him or her for guidance within all marketing areas for the assigned products.

Collaborating with the Agency

Now, with real responsibility and authority, this product marketing director can be effective in collaboration with the advertising agency.

1. The director should be the most knowledgeable person in the company on all aspects of the assigned products.
2. The director should provide the agency with complete information on all aspects of assigned products and in detail concerning all areas of marketing. It is not wise for the agency to plan with only half the story.
3. The director should find and use as many means as possible to stimulate the agency's creative thinking in both advertising and marketing areas.
4. The director should learn to use a funnel, not a shovel, on the agency. You stand to get more than your share of agency thinking on important problems by making sure they are not constantly cluttered with trivia.
5. The director should be sure that certain client-agency relationships are well in the groove and that the respective parties have constant communication and mutual respect. These are the relationships of the product marketing director and the agency counterpart, the account supervisor, and of the product marketing manager with the agency account executive.

What is the difference in responsibility of these two levels? Simply put, the product marketing director and the account supervisor deal more with planning the campaign, and the product marketing manager and account executive more with the execution.

Incidentally, there is usually one more important agency-client relationship in which a top agency executive is teamed to think along with and advise your management. The product marketing director should never create any block to this relationship, as these meetings between managements serve to keep one another aware of their respective company-wide strategies and goals. Of course, the less seen of this agency executive, usually the better the product marketing director is doing his or her job.

6. The director should, in as many areas as possible, represent to the agency the ultimate decision maker; the more areas, the better. And in those areas where top management retains certain prerogatives, the product marketing director should be a good anticipator and interpreter of what the real decision maker is thinking and be a good, firm salesman of what the product marketing director and the agency believe.
7. The director should have more time to work with the agencies and their ideas by having a marketing department system which does not require the product marketing director to administrate the various service or staff departments. In other words, Promotion or Market Research or Home Economics can have their own departmental heads to administrate the work load, personnel, and everyday routine.
8. To obtain effective advertising, the director should train his or her own staff so that they are not used just as information centers for media, copy, and research. More thought and ingenuity will result if these individuals are given their own areas of responsibility and authority and are encouraged to become decision makers. In this regard, it is a blessing if simplicity of the product marketing director's staff can be maintained. Not only does it save administrative time which can be devoted to the creative effort, but it keeps the clear-cut lines between the product group and the agency intact.

We are sold on the product manager system because we have seen it help us expand our business as well as those of other manufacturers with many products or brands. A major satisfaction has been the system's ability to obtain strong performance from our advertising agencies.

The Future

We all work for companies who have planned their futures for quite a few years ahead. And as the future calls for even more expansion of brands or products, so must the future of the product manager system be considered in its ability to handle this new growth. It is my belief that there is enormous elasticity in this system to handle a company's future growth and that additional brand or product manager divisions can be added as warranted. Of course, it may be necessary to divide the number of product marketing directors into two or more groups and have them report to their own group marketing director rather than directly to a vice president. Perhaps it will be necessary to establish separate service or staff departments for each of these marketing groups. It might even be necessary to employ additional advertising agencies so that all products within a company get a fair share of attention and assistance in the creative sphere.

Regardless of how the system expands, we will have to be extremely careful that the individual product marketing director's level of responsibility and authority is not reduced. I would like to repeat that effectiveness starts when management recognizes that the product marketing director is the focal point for all marketing aspects of the product and when this person is given meaningful responsibility and authority to manage, operate swiftly, and make the product grow.

PROBLEMS

1. Draw an organization chart of the Campbell Soup Company. Show the positions reporting to the president of the Sales Company and the corporate vice president, marketing. Show the marketing organization of the Canned Foods Division.
2. What organizational model (or models) does Campbell use?
3. Develop a position description for the product marketing director.

A noted authority discusses the benefits of a nonhierarchical style of sales management.

Reading 9

New Patterns in Sales Management

Rensis Likert

From our research at the Institute for Social Research, University of Michigan, and from the research going on at other places, there is steadily emerging a clearer pattern of the differences in the management principles and practices used by the high-producing and low-producing managers. The evidence demonstrates that the high-producing managers in American industry are gradually evolving a more effective—and also more complex—system of management. These high-producing managers are deviating in important ways, too, from the underlying assumptions upon which the standard operating procedures of their companies are based.

It is possible to integrate the principles used, on the average, by the highest-producing managers into an overall system of management which I call the *newer theory—or system—of management*. This theory and the research findings upon which it is based are described in *New Patterns of Management*.*

I shall summarize some of the important operating

This is an edited and slightly revised version of an article which appeared in *Changing Perspectives in Marketing Management*, edited by Martin R. Warshaw (Ann Arbor, Mich.: The University of Michigan, Bureau of Business Research, 1962). The substance of the article has not been altered. All exhibits have been adapted from the same source. Reprinted by permission.

*Rensis Likert, *New Patterns of Management*, McGraw-Hill, New York, 1961. (Exhibits are from the same source.)

characteristics of the newer system of management. Then I shall examine some research findings that test the extent to which this newer system appears to be applicable to sales management. After this, I shall discuss briefly some of the principles and practices which the theory calls for when applied to the management of a sales organization.

The general pattern of the high-producing managers differs significantly from that of the low-producing managers. The high producers are achieving higher performance and lower costs with less feeling of hierarchical, or unreasonable, pressure on the part of their subordinates. The subordinates have more freedom to pace themselves in their job. They are more enthusiastic about their work. There is better teamwork among the subordinates, less anxiety, less conflict, and less stress.

That the high-producing managers are creating a more powerful social system can be seen from the data shown in Exhibit 9-1. These data are from a service operation and involve thirty-one different departments located in five major metropolitan areas. The departments vary in size from about twenty to seventy-five employees. The nonsupervisory employees belong to a union.

The data shown in Exhibit 9-1 deal with the employees' perception of how much influence their manager has on what goes on in the department—the capacity of the manager to exercise control or influence. To obtain these data we asked the employees the following questions: "In general, how much say or influence do the employees have as to what goes on in the department? How much does the manager have? The plant management? Higher management?" To each question the employees could answer, "Little or no influence," "Some," "Quite a bit," "Great deal," or "A very great deal." Exhibit 9-1 gives the composite scores for the ten most productive departments and the ten least productive departments of the thirty-one.

The same question was asked of the managers, and their answers yielded the same general pattern and conclusions as the employees'. The only appreciable difference was that the managers saw themselves as having more influence than any other hierarchical level.

The data in Exhibit 9-1 show that the high-producing managers have created a more powerful social system in which they have a greater capacity to exercise influence and coordination than is the case with the low-producing managers. An important characteristic of this social system created by the high-producing managers is that *everyone* can exert more influence than can the people in the less productive social system. The managers have more influence, but so too do the employees; there is greater capacity for upward, as well as downward, influence. In support of this important finding, we have data which show that high-producing managers are far more effective in communicating upward to higher management such information as problems of equipment, material, and scheduling, ideas for improving the operation, complaints, and grievances. These high-producing managers are also more effective in getting constructive action from their superiors on these and similar problems than are the low-producing managers. Both communication and the exercise of influence are performed more effectively.

Let's ask ourselves, then, what kind of organization the high-producing manager is building. What characterizes this more effective system of management with its better communication, better decision making based on more accurate information, more cooperative motivation, and greater coordination?

An essential characteristic of this more effective system of management is that it harnesses human motives so that their forces are mutually reinforcing, rather than being blunted because different motives are calling for conflicting behavior. This newer system taps the noneconomic motives so that they reinforce and increase the motivational forces arising from the economic motives. This is in contrast to the traditional systems of management where the motivational forces from the noneconomic motives are often in opposition to those forces from the economic motives and as a consequence reduce the effectiveness of the motives. This

EXHIBIT 9-1. Relation of department productivity to average amount of influence actually exercised by various hierarchical levels (as seen by nonsupervisory employees).

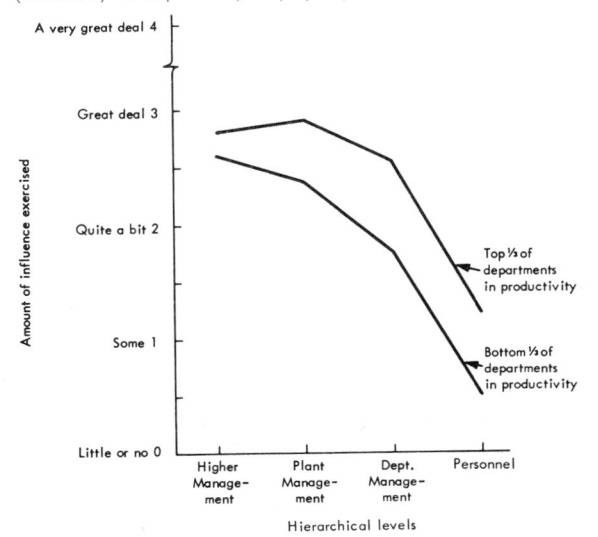

occurs, for example, when direct hierarchical pressure for increased production or cost reduction creates hostile attitudes and resentful behavior which in turn leads to restriction of output, slowdowns, or wildcat strikes.

The high-producing managers realize that merely buying a person's time and issuing instructions does not yield the best results. Similarly, they realize that relying on economic motives alone will not achieve the best performance.

If these same general principles hold in the case of selling, then reliance on economic motives alone should yield less satisfactory results than when the noneconomic motives are used to reinforce the economic. This, as we shall see, is the case. The highest motivation and the best sales performance occur when powerful noneconomic motives reinforce the economic.

It is now possible to assist the top management of any company to build its organization into a newer kind of management system in which the noneconomic motives reinforce the economic. Such a development requires many steps, but one which is fundamental is to apply throughout the organization the *principle of supportive relationships*. This principle should be used to derive appropriate operating procedures and practices and to serve as a general guide to the day-to-day operation of the system. This principle can be stated as follows: *The leadership and other processes of the organization must be such as to ensure a maximum probability that in all interactions and all relationships with the organization each member will, in the light of the person's background, values, and expectations, view the experience as supportive and one which builds and maintains a sense of personal worth and importance.*

In applying this principle to company operations it is well to keep in mind that the relationship between the superior and subordinate is crucial. This relationship should, as the principle specifies, be one which is supportive and ego-building. At times circumstances may prevent a superior from behaving in a supportive manner but such behavior should be held to the absolute minimum; the more often the behavior is ego-building rather than ego-deflating, the better will be its effect on organization performance. It is essential also in applying this principle to keep in mind that the interactions between the leader and the subordinates must be viewed in the light of the subordinate's background, values, and expectations. The subordinates' perception of the situation, rather than the supervisor's perception, determines whether or not the experience is supportive. The superior's behavior and the situation must be such that the subordinate, in the light of the subordinate's background and expectations, sees the experience as one which contributes to a sense of personal worth and importance, one which increases and maintains a sense of significance and human dignity.

You can test whether the superior's behavior is seen as supportive by asking such questions as the following. If the principle of supportive relationships is being applied well, a subordinate will answer each question with a reaction favorable to the superior:

1. To what extent does your superior try to understand your problems and do something about them?
2. How much is your superior really interested in helping you with your personal and family problems?
3. How much help do you get from your superior in doing your work?
    a. How much is your superior interested in training you and helping you learn better ways of doing your work?
    b. How much does your superior help you solve your problems constructively—not tell you the answers but help you think through your problems?
4. To what extent is your superior interested in helping you get the training which will assist you in being promoted?
5. To what extent does your superior try to keep you informed about matters related to your job?
6. How fully does your superior share information with you about the company, its financial condition, earnings, etc.?
7. How much confidence and trust do you have in your superior? How much do you feel your superior has in you?
8. Does your superior ask your opinion when a problem comes up which involves your work?
    a. Does your superior value your ideas and seek them and endeavor to use them?
    b. How well does your superior listen to you?
9. Are group meetings held with subordinates and are such meetings worthwhile?
    a. Does your superior help the group develop its skill in reaching sound solutions?
    b. Does your superior help the group develop its skills in effective interaction, in becoming a well-knit team rather than hostile sub-factions?
    c. Does your superior use the ideas and solutions which emerge and help the group apply its solutions?
10. To what extent does your boss convey to you a feeling of confidence that you can do your job successfully? Does your boss expect the "impossible" and fully believe you can and will do it?

11. To what extent is your boss interested in helping you to achieve and maintain a good income?
12. Is your boss friendly and easily approached?

It is a sobering experience to ask a subordinate these questions and independently to ask his superior to estimate the subordinate's answers and then to compare the two sets of answers. The discrepancies between the two sets of answers all too often are so great as to make one think that the superior and the subordinate cannot be reacting to the same situation. There are important forces causing the subordinate not to reveal to the superior many of his or her reactions. Nevertheless, to apply effectively the principle of supportive relationships, the superior must be able to estimate with reasonable accuracy the subordinate's reactions and perceptions.

From the principle of supportive relationships an important derivation can be made having direct applicability to building a management system in which the noneconomic motives reinforce the economic motives. This derivation states that full use of the potential present in the manpower resources of an organization will occur only when the organization consists of overlapping, highly effective work groups, with each group having high group loyalty and high performance goals.

The traditional organizational structure does not use this group form of organization, but consists of a person-to-person model—superior to individual subordinate (Exhibit 9-2a). In this model the president has full authority and responsibility and delegates to each vice-president specific authority and responsibility and holds each accountable. Vice-presidents in turn do the same with their subordinates. The entire process—stating policy, issuing orders, following up, checking, etc.—involves person-to-person interaction.

The newer system of management in applying the derivation from the principle of supportive relationships calls for an overlapping group form of structure (Exhibit 9-2b). When the group process of supervision is used properly, clear-cut responsibilities are established, decisions are arrived at, and functions performed rapidly and productively. Problems are solved in an efficient fashion, with focused discussion and a minimum of idle talk. There is confidence and trust, full but succinct communication adequately understood. Important issues are recognized and dealt with.

I want to emphasize that when I talk about the group method of supervision I am not talking about the "wishy-washy," "common denominator" sort of committee, about which the superior can say, "Well, the group made this decision and I couldn't do a thing about it."

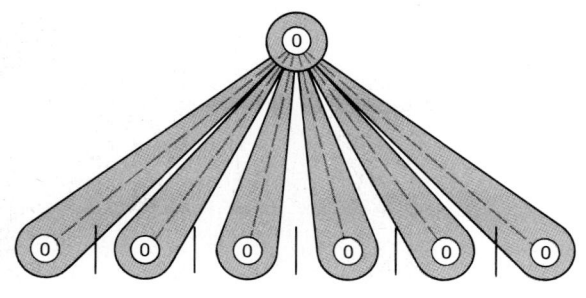

(a) Person-to-person pattern of organization

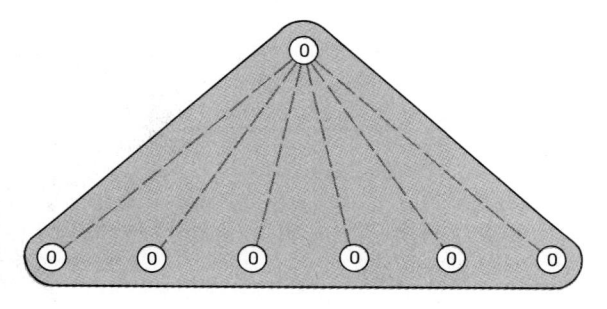

(b) Group pattern of organization

EXHIBIT 9-2. Person-to-person and group patterns of organization.

Quite the contrary! The group method of supervision requires the superior to be fully responsible for decisions and for building subordinates into a group which makes the best decisions. *The superior is fully responsible for the decisions that emerge and for the results accomplished.*

The overlapping group form of organization is structured so that the superior of one group is a subordinate in the next higher group, thus forming a "linking pin" between hierarchical levels, as shown in Exhibit 9-3. We have clear-cut evidence that if a manager is going to do a competent job of leadership, he or she must be able to influence the decisions of his or her peers and his or her superior. Without sideward and upward influence, downward effectiveness is seriously handicapped.

The application of the principle of supportive relationships and the multiple overlapping group form of organization are two essential characteristics of the newer system of management in which the noneconomic motives are mobilized so as to reinforce the economic. Another important characteristic is that managers and supervisors have high performance goals and feel a reciprocal responsibility to the total organization as well as to their own employees.

Let us turn now to the questions: Is this newer system applicable to sales management? Can it be used to help

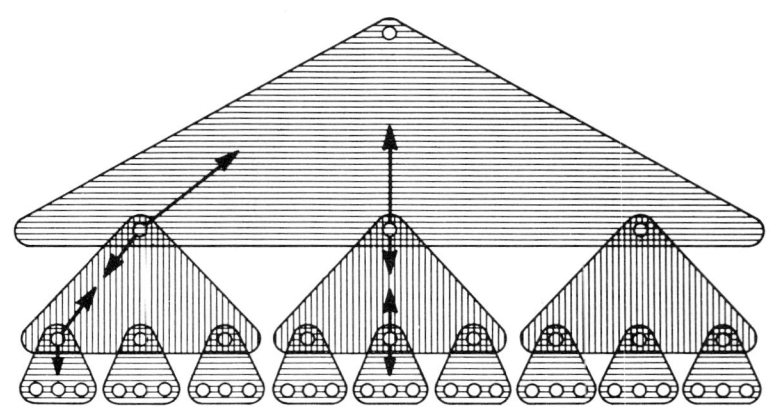

EXHIBIT 9-3. The linking pin (arrows indicate linking pin function).

sales managers improve sales performance significantly?

Sales managers quite generally are saying to us in our interviews with them that the most important problem they face is how to motivate sales representatives. When we ask managers to compare their best salesperson with their poorest, time and again they say that the poorest one knows just as much about the technical aspects of the job (e.g., markets, products, etc.) as does the best one, but the poorer one just does not get out and call on prospects and does not make sales presentations. And calls that are made are often on poorer prospects. This salesperson makes fewer closings on poorer prospects and so gets appreciably less business.

What sales managers are saying, in essence, is that if they had some way of spurring their salespeople on, of tapping the noneconomic motives so that these motives reinforced the economic, they would get significantly better results. This, of course, is precisely what the newer theory of organization makes possible.

Let us look at the motivational consequences and the results achieved when different systems of management are used. What happens when a sales manager uses the traditional system of management and relies on direct hierarchical pressure, or only upon economic motives in the form, for example, of commissions? What happens when the manager uses the newer system and applies the principle of supportive relationships and the overlapping group form of organization?

Presented in Exhibit 9-4 are data from an operation involving forty different independent sales units under relatively independent management but all part of a large company which operates nationally. Geographically these units are widely scattered throughout the nation. They vary in size from eight to fifty salespeople, with a supporting staff of clerical and supervisory personnel.

These forty units consist of twenty pairs of units picked from a total of approximately one hundred such units in the company. One unit of each pair comes from the best units in the company. The top sales management of the

EXHIBIT 9-4. Salespersons' performance goals versus sales managers' performance goals.

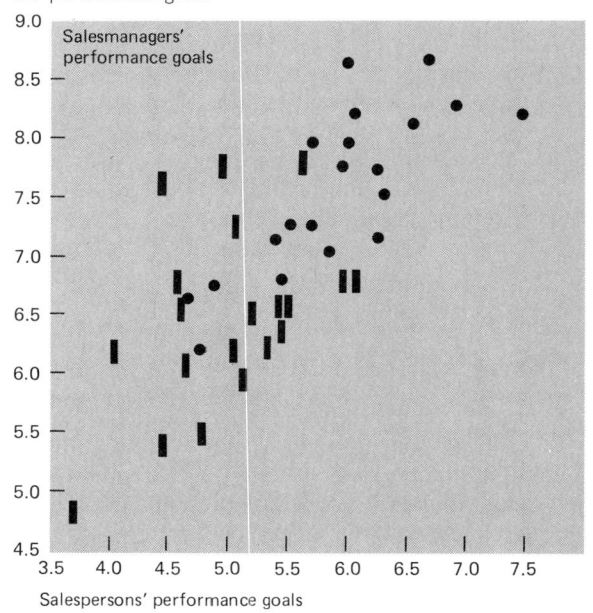

company selected these units on the basis of such criteria as sales volume, costs, quality of business sold, and development of manpower. Each of these units was matched by size and type of market with another unit which was not among the top twenty. Some of these other matching units were about average; some were below average. In Exhibit 9-4 the twenty superior units, which we shall refer to as "better units," are indicated by a large black dot, and the "poorer units" are shown by a vertical bar.

The two axes in Exhibit 9-4 deal with measurements based on information obtained from the salesperson. The vertical axis reflects the extent to which they feel their sales manager has a well-organized sales plan and sales goals for the unit. I have combined a well-organized sales plan and level of sales goals into a single index called *Sales Managers' Performance Goals*. This will simplify our presentation and save time.

The horizontal axis shows comparable measurements as to the extent the people feel the unit has a well-organized plan of work and has high sales goals. As with the managers, these two variables are highly correlated for the employees. The mean (average) score for all of the people in a sales unit is shown in Exhibit 9-4 and is called the *Sales Representatives' Performance Goals*.

The numbers assigned to the two axes shown in Exhibit 9-4 are comparable, since identical questions were used to obtain employees' reactions to the job organization and sales goals of their manager on the one hand and to the job organization and sales goals of their colleagues on the other.

An examination of Exhibit 9-4 reveals many important facts. There is a marked relationship between the performance goal scores of the managers and those of the salespeople in their units. The higher the performance goals of the manager, the higher in general are the performance goals of the people in the sales unit. There is not a single unit in which the manager has low performance goals and the people have high performance goals.

On the average, the performance goals of the people in a unit are appreciably lower than those of their manager. As Exhibit 9-4 shows, the mean performance goals score of the salespeople in a sales unit is about one to one and one-half points lower than the performance goal score of the manager of that unit.

These results demonstrate that it is necessary for a sales manager to have high performance goals if the people in the sales unit are to have high goals. The manager's goals and job organization are very important in determining people's goals and job organization. Moreover, it is necessary for the manager to have higher goals on this combined dimension than those sought for the sales representatives. This is shown by the fact that although the salespeople's scores tend to be high if the manager's is high, and low if the manager's is low, the average score for the salespeople is *lower in every sales unit* than that of the manager of the unit.

A fundamental finding revealed by Exhibit 9-4 is that the better units (black dots) are overwhelmingly in the upper right-hand part of the figure and the poorer units (vertical bars) are in the lower left-hand portion. If a sales unit is to achieve outstanding performance, it is necessary for *both* its manager and its employees to have high performance goals. Both manager and employees need to have a well-organized plan of operation and high sales goals. As Exhibit 9-4 shows, it is *not* sufficient for the manager alone to score high on job organization and performance goals.

There are three sales units in Exhibit 9-4 where the managers have high performance scores but the people have below average scores, and all three are poorer units. These results raise the questions: What must a manager do, in addition to having high performance goals, to create high performance goals on the part of the organization? How does a manager assist people to develop well-organized plans of work and to establish high sales goals for themselves while also having high goals as the manager?

The results in Exhibit 9-5 help to answer the questions.

EXHIBIT 9-5. Salespersons' versus sales managers' performance goals with reference to specific units.

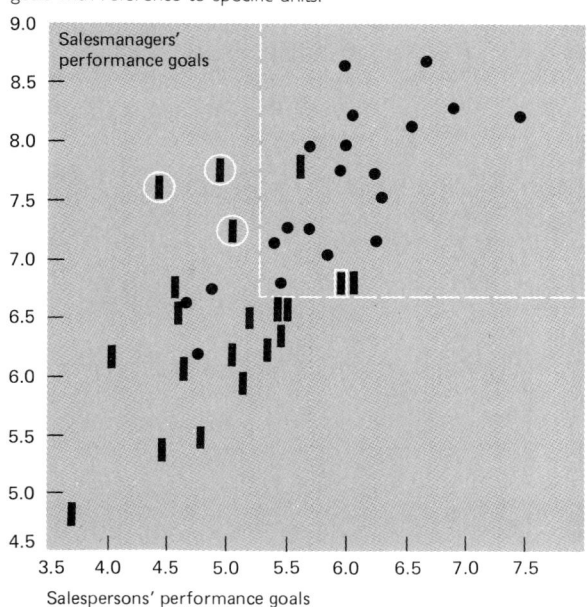

Exhibit 9-5 is exactly the same as Exhibit 9-4 except for the added dotted lines, rectangle, and circles. The dotted lines in Exhibit 9-5 mark off the upper-right quadrant of the figure. The managers in the sales units marked off in this manner are behaving differently from the rest of the sales managers. Every one of the sales managers in the units in this upper-right quadrant, except one, are using group methods of supervision in managing their sales organization. The one exception is the poorer unit enclosed in the rectangle. Of the nineteen units in which the manager uses group methods of supervision, seventeen are better units; only two are poorer.

The management practices of the other twenty units contrast sharply with the practices used by the managers of the twenty units which we have just examined. None of the managers of these other units, namely, those not in the upper-right quadrant, uses group methods of supervision. It is significant that these other units are characterized by having lower employee performance goals and by being predominantly poorer sales units. Seventeen of these twenty units are poorer units.

It may be well to describe briefly what is meant by "group methods of supervision." The exact process varies appreciably from unit to unit but typically is likely to be about as follows. The salespeople meet regularly in group meetings. The number varies but usually does not exceed twelve or fifteen. They are likely to meet at regular intervals every two weeks or every month. As a rule, the sales manager or a sales supervisor presides. Each salesperson, in turn, presents to the group an activity report for the period since the last meeting. It describes such things as the number and kinds of prospects obtained, calls made, the nature of the sales presentations used, the closings attempted, the number of sales achieved, and the volume and quantity of total sales. The others in the group analyze the salesperson's efforts, methods, and results. Suggestions from their experience and know-how are offered. The outcome is a valuable coaching session. For example, if sales results can be improved through better prospecting, this is made clear, and the steps and methods to achieve this improvement are spelled out.

After this analysis by the group, each person with the advice and assistance of the group sets goals concerning the work and the results to be achieved before the next meeting of the group.

The manager or supervisor acts as chairperson of the group, but the analyses and interactions are among the salespeople. The chairperson keeps the orientation of the group on a helpful, constructive, problem-solving basis, seeing that the tone is helpful and supportive and not ego-deflating as a result of negative criticisms and comments.

Each salesperson, as a consequence of the group meeting, feels a commitment to the group to do the work and achieve the desired results. Motivation is often stimulated by having members of the group remind the salesperson in a friendly and even forceful way of goals and commitments if they see the person lagging. Moreover, because of the group loyalty created by the meetings, a salesperson can, if needed, obtain coaching on some problem or assistance on a case not only from the supervisor but also from the other people who had discussed the problem or offered a relevant suggestion in the previous meeting. Each salesperson has available the technical know-how of the supervisor or manager and also that of colleagues. Salespeople derive two important benefits from effective group meetings: they set and strive to achieve higher sales goals—goals which more nearly reflect their own potentiality—and they receive more technical assistance in selling, obtaining help from both their superior and their peers.

These group meetings are effective when the manager (or supervisor) does a competent job of presiding over the interactions among the people. The results are generally disappointing and are largely a waste of time whenever the manager uses the meeting only for personal interaction between himself or herself and each person individually. This occurs when the manager analyzes each person's performance and results and sets goals for each. Such meetings, dominated by the manager, do not create group loyalty and are likely to have an adverse rather than a favorable impact upon the employee's motivation. Moreover, the sales know-how among the group is not used.

The group method of supervision was used initially in this company only for the new people, i.e., those with less than three years with the company. In many sales units, however, the advantages of the group process were recognized by the established salespeople and at their request it was extended to include them. The most successful sales units, i.e., those with largest volume and lowest costs, are now using group processes of supervision for both new and established salespeople. As a rule, each of the different groups within a sales unit consists only of new salespeople or established salespeople. This has proved desirable since many of the problems of new people are different from the problems of established people.

The salespeople in the forty units represented in Exhibit 9-5 are paid on a commission basis. The plan of compensation seeks to use the economic motive in the most effective way possible. But as the results demonstrate, adding the power of the noneconomic motives significantly improves performance over that achieved when economic motives alone are tapped.

Among the most powerful of the noneconomic motives is the desire to achieve and maintain a sense of personal worth and importance. It can be used in many different ways as a source of motivational forces. Some ways are appreciably better than others in using more of the total potential motivational forces available and using these forces more constructively. Procedures such as contests or the manager's giving recognition for outstanding sales performance, appear to harness less of the available motivational forces and of the know-how possessed by the sales organization than when group forces are mobilized through the use of group methods of supervision. Competitive procedures, such as contests, pit people against people and reward keeping know-how to oneself. This stimulates each salesperson to keep confidential all that has been learned about how better to promote the product, to sell successfully against competing products, and to achieve high levels of sales volume. This sharing of know-how, which the group supervision method encourages, can be an important factor in enabling an entire sales organization to attain outstanding performance, rather than having a limited number of people do so.

Managers of the sales units in the upper-right quadrant of Exhibit 9-5 are behaving consistently in their efforts to harness the full power of noneconomic motives. They use group methods of supervision and they apply well the principle of supportive relationships. Both of these general principles and their related procedures appear important in the success of the managers. These two general principles both derive their fundamental motivational force from the desire to achieve and maintain a sense of personal worth and importance.

As seen by their people, the managers who use group methods of supervision are doing a significantly better job of applying the principle of supportive relationships and score appreciably higher in supportive behavior than do the managers who are not using group methods of supervision.

In contrast to the sales units in the upper-right quadrant, the people in the three sales units in Exhibit 9-5 which are circled have relatively low performance goals. The managers of these three units are similar to the managers of units in the upper-right quadrant in having high performance goals, but unlike the latter, these three managers have not been successful in encouraging their people to set high performance goals for themselves. The people in these three units are rejecting the high performance goals of their managers. As might be expected, there are substantial differences in the management principles employed by these three managers in comparison with the managers of the units in the upper-right quadrant.

The managers of the three circled sales units are not employing group methods of supervision. Their methods of management involve person-to-person interaction and dominance. Moreover, these three managers are not applying the principle of supportive relationships. Much of the behavior of these managers violates this principle. This is shown by the poor score of the three units with regard to the managers' application of this principle; they rank thirty-three, thirty-seven, and thirty-eight, out of forty.

In these three circled units the employees not only reject high performance goals for themselves but they also feel to a greater extent than those in the other units that their sales managers are putting unreasonable pressure on them to produce. Direct managerial pressure for high performance and high performance goals quite consistently evokes this feeling on the part of the employees.

In the light of all these facts, it is not surprising that these three circled units are, as Exhibit 9-5 shows, among the poorer sales units.

In contrast to these three circled sales units is the one at the extreme right of Exhibit 9-5. This is the unit in which the salespeople have the highest performance goals of any unit. As might be expected from the preceding discussion, the manager of this unit applies the principle of supportive relationships well and, in comparison with the other managers, places the greatest emphasis on teamwork and group methods of supervision. This manager strives hard to build a sales unit whose members pull together toward commonly accepted goals. The employees respond by setting and achieving high goals for themselves. This is one of the better units.

There is a substantial body of research findings which demonstrates that the greater the loyalty of the members of a group toward the group, the greater is the motivation among the members to achieve the goals of the group and the greater is the probability that the group will achieve its goals. If the goals of such groups are low, they will restrict production; if the goals are high, they will achieve outstanding performance.

These findings suggest that it is important for a sales manager to know how to develop high group loyalty and assist employees to establish performance goals commensurate with their potentiality. How, then, can a manager proceed so as to develop high group loyalty in the organization?

The results shown in Exhibit 9-6 shed important light on this problem. The loyalty of the salespeople in a unit toward each other was measured and is called *peer group loyalty score*. This score is plotted along the vertical axis of Exhibit 9-6. The forty sales units were divided into four groups of ten each on the basis of the extent to which the sales manager is applying the principle of supportive relationships *(Sales Managers' Supportive Behavior Score)*. The four bars in Exhibit 9-6 present data for these four groups of ten sales units each.

The bar on the right in Exhibit 9-6 shows the mean (average) peer group loyalty score for the ten sales units whose sales managers are doing the best job of applying the principle of supportive relationships. The left-hand bar in Exhibit 9-6 shows the results for the ten units whose managers score lowest on applying the principle of supportive relationships. The intermediate bars show average peer group loyalty scores for the two intermediate groups of ten sales units.

Exhibit 9-6 shows the marked differences in peer group loyalty scores in relationship to the managers' supportive behavior. In units whose managers are applying the principle of supportive relationships most effectively, the peer group loyalty scores are appreciably higher than in the units whose managers achieve a low supportive behavior score.

The number in parentheses above each bar shows the extent to which the managers in each group of ten units are using group methods of supervision. In the right-hand bar, ten of the ten units are using group methods of supervision; in the next group, seven of the ten; in the next, two of the ten; and in the left bar group, none of the ten.

In the bar under the number (7), i.e., next to the bar on the right, there is a large dot opposite a peer group loyalty score of sixty-one. This is the mean (average) peer group loyalty score for the three sales units in that cluster of ten whose managers do *not* use group methods of supervision. Under the number 2 and above the second bar from the left there is another large black dot opposite a peer group loyalty score of seventy-six. This is the mean peer group loyalty score for the two sales units whose managers *do* use group methods of supervision. In both bars in the center of the chart, that is, the one under (7) and the one under (2), the managers who use group methods of supervision achieve higher levels of peer group loyalty than the managers who do not. This is consistent with the data shown by the bars on the right and the left.

As the data in Exhibit 9-6 show, managers who use group methods of supervision and also effectively apply the principle of supportive relationships are much more likely to have high peer group loyalty among the people

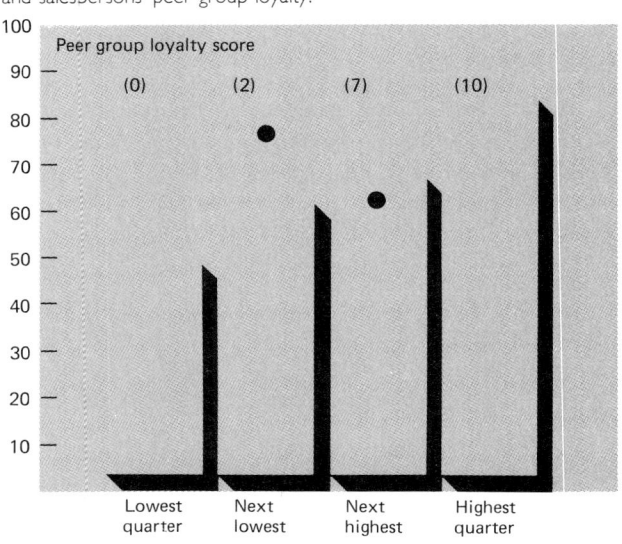

EXHIBIT 9-6. Relationship between sales managers' supportive behavior and salespersons' peer group loyalty.

in their units than are the managers who do not follow these principles and practices of management. Both group methods of supervision and the effective use of the principle of supportive relationships are required since neither one alone produces as good results as the combination.

As might be expected from the preceding discussion, managers who apply well the principle of supportive relationships and also have high performance goal scores are much more likely to have better sales units than are the managers who display the opposite behavior. This is shown in Exhibit 9-7. As will be observed, all of the sales units whose managers' supportive behavior scores are above twenty-five and whose managers' performance goals are above seven are better performing units (shown by black dots). Moreover, every one of the managers of these sales units is using group methods of supervision. All of the units except one, whose manager's supportive behavior score is below twenty-two, are poorer performing units (shown by vertical bars). None of these sales units have managers who are using group methods of supervision. Again, as would be expected, all of the mean (average) peer group loyalty scores of the salespersons in the former group of units (i.e., above 25) are higher than the highest for the ten sales units whose managers' supportive behavior scores are less than twenty-two.

The eight sales units with circles around them in Exhibit 9-7 fall in the top ten of all the units with regard to the extent to which the men feel the manager is putting unreasonable pressure on them to produce. These units tend, in relation to the other units, to be toward the lower-right part of the figure. These are, therefore, units whose managers have relatively high performance goals in comparison with the extent to which they are applying effectively the principle of supportive relationships. These data demonstrate that direct, hierarchical managerial pressure for production produces a feeling of unreasonable pressure in the employees and fails to yield the high levels of sales performance which the managers who apply the pressure desire.

The results presented in Exhibits 9-4, 9-5, 9-6, and 9-7 point to a fundamental conclusion: Sales managers who, as seen by their salespeople, have a well-organized plan of operation, high sales goals, use group methods of supervision, and apply the principle of supportive relationships are appreciably more likely to have better sales units under their direction than are the managers who, as seen by their salespeople, display the opposite pattern of behavior. The latter are much more likely to be in charge of poorer sales units.

I started this presentation by briefly describing a newer system of management based on the principles and practices used by the managers who are achieving the highest productivity and lowest costs in American business. I then mentioned a few of the basic characteristics of this newer system. As we have seen, the results from a major study of sales management show, as do data from other studies of sales management, that the fundamental principles of this newer system are applicable to the management of sales organizations.

Sales managers, consequently, have available to them today two broadly different systems of management. One, of course, is the system in general use today based on traditional theories of management. The other is the newer system of management based on the principles and practices of the highest producing managers. This newer system is available because of the creativity of the higher-producing managers and the contribution of quantitative social science research, which is making clear the nature of the principles used by these high-producing managers.

Exhibit 9-8 schematically presents the two contrasting courses of action open to a sales manager. There are, of course, intermediate courses of action which also are likely to yield intermediate results so far as sales volume, costs, and overall performance are concerned.

This newer system of management has been applied in

EXHIBIT 9-7. Sales managers' performance goals versus sales managers' behavior scores.

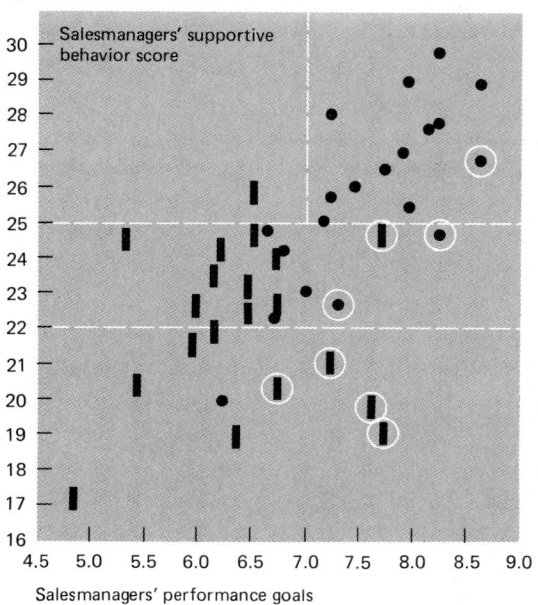

EXHIBIT 9-8
Well-Organized Plan of Operation via Traditional Systems and New Management System

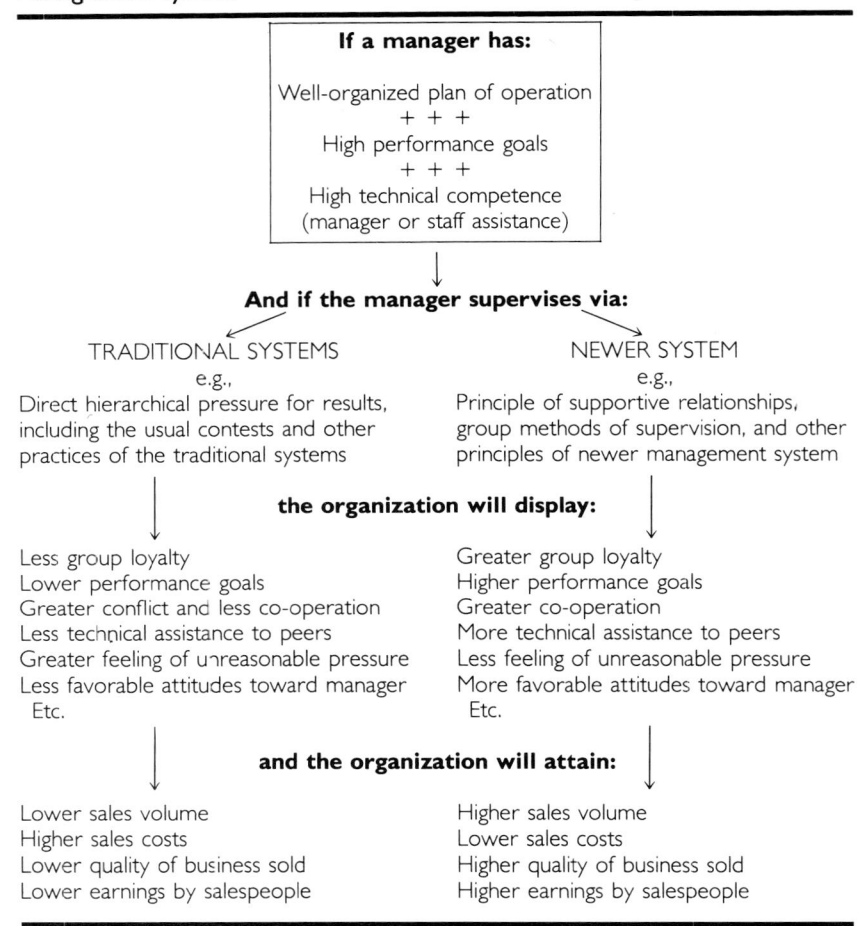

If a manager has:

Well-organized plan of operation
+ + +
High performance goals
+ + +
High technical competence
(manager or staff assistance)

↓

And if the manager supervises via:

TRADITIONAL SYSTEMS	NEWER SYSTEM
e.g.,	e.g.,
Direct hierarchical pressure for results, including the usual contests and other practices of the traditional systems	Principle of supportive relationships, group methods of supervision, and other principles of newer management system

the organization will display:

Less group loyalty	Greater group loyalty
Lower performance goals	Higher performance goals
Greater conflict and less co-operation	Greater co-operation
Less technical assistance to peers	More technical assistance to peers
Greater feeling of unreasonable pressure	Less feeling of unreasonable pressure
Less favorable attitudes toward manager	More favorable attitudes toward manager
Etc.	Etc.

and the organization will attain:

Lower sales volume	Higher sales volume
Higher sales costs	Lower sales costs
Lower quality of business sold	Higher quality of business sold
Lower earnings by salespeople	Higher earnings by salespeople

---

a regional sales organization involving about three hundred people and within two years dramatically demonstrated its superiority over the traditional systems.

QUESTIONS

1. Summarize the key differences in the two management styles which Rensis Likert calls "traditional systems of management" and "newer system of management."
2. According to Likert, what benefits accrued to the company sales units that were managed by sales managers who applied the "newer system of management"?
3. What is your opinion of the "new system of management"? Would you prefer to manage in this way?

The management style of a successful district sales manager

Reading 10

A Sales Manager in Action

Robert T. Davis

This report concerns a field sales manager who "turned" a sick district into a profitable one in 12 months—who converted a group of salesmen with low morale and low performances into a team which exceeded quota in four successive quarters and gained an impressive 20 percent in market share. Our examination of this manager details a number of his behavioral traits—his activities, his attitudes, his interactions with others, and his decisions. Some of his behavior was exemplary, but some was looked upon unfavorably by top management. The sum total, however, was performance well above the ordinary.

No one, of course, can claim that a single case study is more than just that. Indeed, the reader who is experienced in management will recognize that the manager being described exemplifies but one of a number of possible management styles. His behavior, moreover, must be interpreted against a backdrop of a fairly friendly environment. The previous manager was so inadequate that any positive change was bound to bring improvement.

Nonetheless, a single, detailed study can provide understanding and insight into the function of field sales management. Many aspects of this one manager's behavior are relevant to other situations in management. It is the writer's opinion, in fact, that the manager being described possesses most of the characteristics of successful sales managers; the reader, however, is left to draw his own conclusions.

The Setting

The Andrews Food Company manufactured a full line of packaged consumer goods. The annual sales volume of $400 million was distributed directly (40 percent) and through food wholesalers (60 percent) to food stores in the United States. A sales force of 200 operated out of 20 branch offices and was expected: (1) to sell direct to the largest retail outlets; (2) to sell through wholesalers to smaller outlets; (3) to service individual stores, including rotating the stock, building displays, checking prices, revamping shelves, picking up "spoils," and so on.

Ordinarily, selling was based upon the presentation of dealer promotions, usually every six weeks. Although Andrews supported a substantial national advertising program, the critical determinant in getting the order was believed to be the extensive retailer promotion program. Retailer promotions included buying allowances, display allowances, advertising allowances, and label packs. Company expenditures for promotions were approximately the same as for national advertising. Both types of expenditures were controlled by brand managers at the home office. Each of the eight brand managers was accountable for profits in his line. Acceptance of the various promotions by the retailers depended upon several variables including the attractiveness of the offer relevant to competitive offers, past relationships, the retailers' inventory situation, and the selling ability of the field sales force.

The brand managers reported to the marketing vice president through a merchandising manager. The salesmen, on the other hand, reported to the marketing vice president through branch managers, area managers, and a national sales manager. The brand sector was, in effect, the inside "merchandising" group; the sales sector took care of the execution.

This case study centers on an intensive investigation of two managers, one described by senior executives as "our best branch manager," the other as "the worst." The performance records of the two men supported these descriptions:

From Harper W. Boyd and Robert T. Davis, *Readings in Sales Management* (Homewood, Ill.: Richard D. Irwin, 1970), pp. 259–268. Copyright © 1970 by Richard D. Irwin, Inc. Reprinted by permission.

Performance Criteria during past 16 Quarters	Best Manager	Worst Manager
1. Quota attained	15 out of 16 quarters	6 out of 16 quarters
2. Change in market share	Increase from 2% to 11%	Decrease from 12% to 11%
3. Annual rate of salesman turnover	None—except for promotion to better jobs	50%

Top management concurred that the environmental conditions in the two branches were about the same. The difference in results, therefore, was presumably brought about by the local personnel (including the manager).

Because the weaker manager was within two years of retirement, The Andrews Company chose to retire him immediately. The "best" manager was moved into the "worst" manager's branch. During his first 12 months on the new assignment, the strong manager accomplished the following: quota was made in four consecutive quarters (in two of them, the branch was No. 1 in the United States), and market share increased 20 percent. These gains were made, moreover, with a minimum of changes in personnel. One salesman (out of 17) was fired, one key account manager (out of 2) was dismissed, and one supervisor (out of 2) was promoted to branch manager in another part of the country. How did the manager bring about such a remarkable improvement in the branch in such a few months? What was his behavior? Behavior can be categorized into four parts:

1. *Activities.* How does the manager spend his time? What relative importance does he place upon his various tasks?
2. *Sentiments or attitudes.* How does the manager talk about himself and his job? His salesmen? His customers? His competition? Higher management?
3. *Interactions.* With whom does the manager interact, and what role does he play?
4. *Decisions.* What kinds of decisions does the manager make, and on what basis are the decisions made?

The Behavior of the Good Manager

Activities. During the year under study, the branch manager spent 55 percent of his time in the field (where he worked primarily with his account managers in key retail outlets) and 45 percent in the office (dealing with competitive analyses and recommendations to the region for special deals and promotions, planning strategy for major blocs of business, and organizational problems). Specifically, the manager allocated his 250 working days as follows:

71 days (28%) with account managers
60 days (24%) with salesmen
8 days (3%) with sales supervisors
111 days (45%) in the office

It is significant that the manager spent so much less time with his supervisors than with the account managers and salesmen. The manager's logic is evident: he wanted to control key account volume, have firsthand knowledge about developments in the trade, and learn the retailer's reactions to proposed promotions. Obviously, the manager assumed that his supervisors were competent (which confidence, in reality, was justified).

His office time was spread over a number of activities which were hard to separate. He spent many hours in informal discussions with any of the salesmen who "dropped by." These discussions might solicit opinions on future strategy, trade developments, competitive programs, or any other problem currently on the manager's desk. Sometimes, the sessions were for counseling purposes. Whatever their format, the informal meetings were the manager's major technique for communicating and for giving the salesmen a sense of participation in district affairs.

As a supplement to these informal contacts, the manager expected regular telephone calls from his men concerning competitive activities. A complete flow of intelligence was critical to the manager. He used these data for recommending special promotional programs for the district. The cornerstone of his personal policy was to gain more than his share of the company's promotional funds—an objective which required detailed knowledge of competitive action, as well as programs for offsetting the action. It follows that our manager was in touch with his superior (the area manager) 3 or 4 times each week. Most often, these contacts were by phone but sometimes in the form of handwritten notes. The purpose, however, was always the same: to gain support for the branch's programs.

Although the manager relied primarily upon informal channels of communication, he did write a weekly bulletin for the salesmen. Additionally, he held monthly planning sessions with his supervisors and account managers.

The manager spent a significant part of his time on such organizational matters as a review of the branch's territory coverage plan, development programs for individual men, and a continuous evaluation of sales performance. Occasional special reports were prepared for the home office, and much personal interaction took place with the warehouse manager concerning local supply and shipping problems. The manager gave no time to trade association activities, a characteristic not shared by his predecessor.

Sentiments. Much can be learned about the branch manager by considering his attitudes or sentiments. In brief, he defined his mission as building the Andrews franchise through continuous competitive analyses; aggressive, "no-holds-barred" selling; and personal control over key account volume. He stressed the need for team effort and for each salesman to act as if he were "sales manager" for his accounts. In the manager's words: "Selling is easy. The real job is to see that the product moves through the store to the housewife. This requires intensive in-store work, merchandising ideas, and attention to the retailer's problems." The manager, moreover, was steadfast in his conviction that the "name of the game" was to "clobber" competition—that anything he could do to gain the upper hand was desirable. This dedication to victory meant that, in many respects, the manager believed that the end justified the means.

So much for a general summary of the manager's attitudes. Some selected quotations make the specifics clearer.

1. *Attitudes about his job:*
He had a direct-action philosophy:

My job is to produce sales. I don't care how. I'll act today and worry about the problems tomorrow.

He could verbalize a basic selling strategy clearly:

You build a franchise by selling features, which requires a dollar advantage and control of the shelves. You control shelves because competition is lax in this regard, and shelf position enhances features since the housewife typically goes first to the shelf.

He had a clear understanding of the need for open communication:

A two-way flow of information is essential so the salesmen can manage their accounts and so that I can argue for the proper deals and promotions. I always tell the men in advance about pending deals. This means that we can activate any promotion the first day because the salesmen have known how to treat their accounts during the previous two weeks.

He was self-sufficient. He argued, for example, that the branch manager should make his own decisions, that local problems should be solved on the spot.

Don't ask for help unless you also have a solution.

He was flexible and ingenious. In these respects, he rarely tackled an argument head-on if he could "get around" the resistance by some alternative course.

He was "man-oriented." He made himself freely available to the salesmen on the basis that:

Salesmen need confidence. You develop this by demonstrating *how* when a man is finally stuck. I try to inspire my men, to set an example and not push them too directly.

He was ready to go with them personally on any tough call.

He was dedicated to his job. In all conversations, this manager was constantly intrigued with matters of business. He was forever probing for new ideas, inquiring, seeking alternatives, "thinking aloud" about better strategy and how to lick competition.

He believed that a manager must be positive, optimistic, energetic, self-confident, and more competent than the men whom he supervised.

He believed in direct intervention on major accounts. Although the manager never visited a major customer without the accounts manager, he felt that his title and personal skills were legitimate weapons for gaining key customer support.

2. *Attitudes about the salesmen:*

He was convinced that the secret to success was to hire aggressive, intelligent men and force their growth with early responsibility. Each man was treated as an individual and motivated on a personal basis.

Prove to me by your [the noncollege salesman] sales performance that I can recommend you for the special program at Michigan State. Prove to me that I should recommend you [the man who came from an advertising background] for product management.

Each man was respected for his ideas and knowledge. For example, the salesmen were openly invited to suggest strategic moves, to assess branch progress and needs, and to volunteer any other ideas relevant to the operations.

His standards were explicit:

Our job is to sell. Selling is easy. Either you sell or you get out. I'm here to help you sell.

Each salesman, in this respect, was expected to gain a competitive edge in his accounts by aggression, service, imaginative selling, displays, shelf control, and postsale merchandising. He did not tolerate mediocre performance and was quick to put any man "on warning" who was not working up to his abilities.

He relied heavily upon "bonus earnings" as a continuing spur to the salesmen.

I remind them that every sale they lose is bread out of their mouths.

They are all excited about these large bonus checks.

He expected each man to be business-oriented and to manage his accounts without constant supervision.

3. *Attitudes about competition:*

It has already been stated that the branch manager had strong feelings about competition. As he said:

Competition is the enemy. We give no quarter nor expect any. I train my men to demoralize competition, to beat them off the shelf, to spread rumors about them, to keep them off balance and on the run.

The intensity of the manager's feelings was evident in much of his behavior. He warned his salesmen, for example, to avoid personal contacts with competitors. He followed the same rule. He had no patience with arguments that the competitors were better and, in fact, was convinced that Andrews Food would put them all to rout.

One could almost conclude that the branch manager was less concerned with meeting the needs of his customers than he was with beating the competition. The at least partial truth of this statement will be discussed later.

4. *Attitudes about selling:*

We have seen that our manager looked upon increasing sales as his responsibility. Selling, therefore, was the pivot of the manager's world. He had strong feelings about it. To be specific, he believed that selling was easy and fun. It was, moreover, the key ingredient to building a franchise. The manager knew that competitive deals were essential, but their specifics—the way in which they were presented, the competitive edge in the separate stores, the strategies for gaining trade support—were all dependent upon personal effort. Strong selling makes the deals work—that was the branch's chief point of view.

Selling was considered as more than gaining the large orders. The men were reminded often:

You can always make sales if you have a plan to move the merchandise out of the store.

To repeat, the men were expected to move the merchandise *in* and *through* the stores.

The inevitable consequence of this selling orientation was that the manager also assumed sales responsibilities, although on an indirect basis. He kept an eye on the major customers. In fact, when he took over the poor branch, his early emphasis was upon plans and presentations for capturing key volume. This personal control was another important aspect of the strong manager's behavior.

5. *Attitudes about company policy:*

Because the district manager was dedicated to results, fast action, and local autonomy, it is no surprise to learn that he took a liberal view of company policies. By his standards, policy was a *general* guide, not an operational dictum. Policy required local interpretation due to competition and other pressures. "Wheeling and dealing" were justifiable if they increased market share and if "you get your money's worth from the retailer every time you stretch the rules." Moreover, this manager's dedication to his company and product meant that he saw his behavior as "best for the company."

Interrelationships. The third aspect of management behavior has to do with personal interaction and with the role assumed by the manager during these interrelationships. By way of summary, a number of things can be said about our manager. In the first place, he was a man who *listened*, who went out of his way to seek alternatives and new ideas. Secondly, he was an effective communications link between the field salesmen and the home office. He "translated" home office directives into the language of his men and correspondingly translated field requests into home office language. Between himself and his men, he ensured open communications. He was as frank with them as he expected them to be with him. Thirdly, the manager "put himself on the line." He never hesitated to intercede on behalf of his men and considered such intercession a prime responsibility. Let us examine the nature of the manager's interpersonal behavior more specifically:

1. *Relationship with his staff:*

We saw earlier that the manager concentrated his attention upon the accounts managers, and we know why. What was the nature of this relationship?

The branch manager played the role of peer when discussing key account strategy with the others. Thus, the two men would exchange thoughts and information about the characteristics of the account, the idiosyncracies of the buyers, and the details of a proposed strategy.

But the manager became "the expert" when making a joint call upon a key buyer. The two men normally planned the part of the presentation that each would make. The manager's major emphasis was upon the basic message: "We are here to show you how to sell three times as much Andrew," but he carefully left the impression that the salesman was responsible for the account. "I will back 100 percent any commitments the accounts manager makes to you."

Once the account was under control, the branch

manager left most of the selling to the account manager. During this stage, his role was that of advisor.

The staff (account managers and sales supervisors) was the manager's prime agency for recommending strategy, promotions, and customer tactics. He met with the group formally twice each month in so-called "planning" meetings. But he met with the four informally more often. Whenever they passed the office, he would invite their suggestions. His role was again as fellow discussant. But he was all business and rarely allowed the discussions to drift into generalizations or social discourses.

Needless to say, he took the staff fully into his confidence (such as revealing the pending deals) and implicitly assumed that they would treat the knowledge with discretion.

2. *Relationships with the salesmen:*

The intriguing aspect of the manager's relationship with his men was how he could seemingly treat them as peers, maintain an informal relationship with each, and yet protect his position as supervisor. To each of the salesmen, the manager was equally available, and from each, he sought advice and suggestions. He kept them all informed about future deals and correspondingly expected them to keep him informed about competition. The benefits of this open rapport warrant repetition. The manager was assured of the evidence about competition he needed to obtain promotional funds from company headquarters, and the men felt that they were important contributors to branch operations.

Because the salesmen knew that their manager would personally intercede whenever they had trouble, they had little hesitation about "going along" with the manager's plans. As one new man said, "Because of the manager's support, I soon learned that there's no reason to fear retailer reactions. All they can do is yell at you."

Perhaps the best way to sum up this aspect of the manager's behavior is to say that he was a superb supervisor. He was able to lead and inspire his men.

3. *Relations with the home office:*

Just as the manager worked at keeping the channels free between himself and his men, he worked hard at maintaining a two-way flow between himself and the area manager. He most often used the telephone but did not neglect written and personal contacts. Commonly, he initiated the contact. Most of the interchange concerned competition and recommendations for promotional programs. Additionally, the manager kept the home office fully informed about any noteworthy achievements by the salesmen.

The manager, it must be noted, did not pass along all of his problems to higher management. If it could be solved locally, that was always the manager's first choice. For example, there were some differences of opinion between the branch and the warehouse manager. Rather than appeal for top management intervention, the branch manager worked out acceptable compromises with the warehouse manager which were then passed up the line for approval. This was a distinguishing characteristic of the manager. He rarely asked for assistance until he had a solution firmly in mind. In his words: "I try not to ask for action until I've got my ducks lined up."

4. *Relations with key buyers:*

We have already seen that a major aspect of the manager's behavior was personal involvement in key accounts. This was how he attempted to build a franchise and ensure quota attainment. There is no need to repeat the data already presented regarding the manager's role in these relationships. Suffice it to say that his great personal selling skill was used to advantage and his contribution was supplementary to that of the account manager's.

Decisions. Our manager was decisive. He was action-oriented and believed that some activity was better than none. Some of his decisions can be neatly categorized. For example, many were intended to change the status quo whenever the environment operated to the manager's disadvantage. Others were intended to create excitement in the trade and to keep competition off balance. Rarely, we know, did he worry about the precision of company policies. His objective was to get results, and, in this regard, his behavior was single-minded.

The manager would adopt any reasonable action which produced sales or provided a competitive edge. He believed that his abilities could overcome the problems any precipitate action created. When he sold to an anticipated deal, as in one case, and the ensuing terms were less advantageous to the retailer than promised, he and his men managed to calm most of the buyers personally. His later rationalization was that the early promises to the trade resulted in major volume gains which more than offset the resulting customer complaints (which were not, in reality, too numerous).

A vital part of the manager's "deal policy" was the use of display allowances. He used these to ensure in-store movement, to "sweeten the pot," and to give Andrews a public reputation of being "on the move."

Some of his major decisions related to steps for gaining momentum by cracking important accounts. Such early successes were used as testimonials for persuading other reluctant retailers.

The manager made equally important decisions among

the wholesale accounts. He wanted their support in order to counterbalance the direct selling advantages of his competitors. Moreover, by working through wholesalers, he was able to pyramid deals into longer-time periods.

He also tried to do "dramatic" things in order to pull away from his competition. He pushed to be the sponsor of the local professional team, to introduce 5-pound sizes, to execute "Operation Pitchout" (convincing the retailer that he should drop slowly moving competitive lines), and to "blitz" the smaller stores periodically with a task force of salesmen.

This manager was equally decisive about manpower. He would not tolerate below-par performers. He initiated local incentive programs to reward men for obtaining competitive intelligence, and he instituted indirect sales budgets in order to encourage their missionary efforts among wholesalers.

QUESTIONS

1. What management style do you think the field sales manager in this case was using? What were the strong and weak points of his style?
2. If he was not following the "newer system of management" described in the previous case, why was this field sales manager so successful?
3. In this and the previous case you have seen two very different management styles, each apparently applied with successful results. Which would you prefer? Why?

PART FIVE

Managing the Marketing Functions

In the final six chapters we will deal with the management of the principal functions of marketing, namely, product, price, distribution, and promotion. Although we have discussed these subjects earlier, we will now examine them more deeply. Because each chapter will concentrate on a single function, let's run through briefly the concepts of marketing mix and promotional mix, described in Chapter 2.

It should be clear by now that all marketing functions are closely interrelated. We cannot discuss one function for very long before becoming involved with the others. Awareness of these interrelationships led to the concept of marketing mix—the idea that the marketing plans for any business at any particular time period call for a specific mix of products, price, distribution, and promotion. In the same way, a particular mix of the elements of personal selling, advertising, sales promotion, and publicity (the promotional mix) are needed to achieve the goals of the marketing plans. A case history will help illustrate how this happens.

Using the Mix to Improve Market Performance

The market development manager for Keebler, a national bakery products manufacturer, described how his department develops improvement plans for below-par markets. His annual budget includes funds for studies of specified local markets where the company has a weak market share. The first task is to learn why performance is below par. The reasons usually are two or more of the following:

1. The national brand leader and strong regional bakers dominate the local market, leaving Keebler in third or fourth place.
2. There may be local and regional consumer product preferences that are not addressed in the company's national advertising and promotion program.
3. The market did not receive adequate sales and distribution support in the past.
4. The company has problems with the trade (independent retailers and retail chains).
5. Consumer awareness of the company's brand may be low.

To identify the problem, a market development department team analyzes such things as market demographics, growth patterns, sales by store, performance in key accounts, MRCA research data on share of market, and Majers' audits of retail advertising.* They learn the merchandising philosophies of the chains serving the area and look for problems in the

---

*Market Research Corporation of America (MRCA) and Majers Corporation are research firms that specialize in collecting and reporting market information.

company's sales organization or the distribution system (the company delivers its products directly to stores). They authorize a local research study to learn of consumers' awareness of the brand.

After identifying the problems and consulting with corporate sales, distribution, and promotion personnel, the market development team develops a long-term marketing plan designed to increase market share. The plan may include giving higher case allowances (price discounts) to the trade; using consumer promotions to increase consumer trial, such as sampling, direct mail, or couponing; increasing brand advertising using local print and broadcast media; and strengthening the sales and distribution forces. The plan is then submitted to marketing management with budgets and a pay-back forecast.

The approach has been very successful. It recognizes that the national marketing mix is not necessarily right for problem markets. Little can be done about changing the product line if that is part of the local problem. However, emphasis can be placed on promoting those products in the line that are well liked locally. In summary, problems in local markets are cured by finding the reasons for below-par performance, then tailoring marketing and promotional mixes to the needs of each market.*

Several cases at the end of Part Five illustrate the handling of problems in specific functional areas such as new product development or distribution. Here too we will see that identifying and solving problems of one marketing function inevitably involve one or more of the other functions.

In the chapters that follow we discuss the issues that functional managers deal with, including functional strategies. Also included are descriptions of terms and concepts that relate to the functions. We emphasize that functional strategies should be planned within the context of the broader marketing strategy. A personal selling strategy, for example, should support the marketing strategy and be coordinated with other functional strategies such as distribution and advertising. While marketing management has the overall responsibility for coordinating functional plans, the final marketing plans are better when functional managers understand how their strategies fit into the marketing plans.

*Information courtesy of The Keebler Company.

CHAPTER 16

Managing the Product Line

In this text we have emphasized the importance of matching company resources with market opportunities as a major strategy for business success. The principal way in which this is carried out is by offering products that fulfill the needs and wants of selected market segments that the company is best qualified to serve. Consequently, the management of the existing product line, making improvements in existing products, and the development of new products are among the most important responsibilities of marketing and business unit management.

Earlier we noted that the PIMS* studies have shown a high correlation between market share and profit. They also have revealed that the factors most affecting gains in market share (and, therefore, profits) are increases in (1) new product activity, (2) relative product quality, and (3) promotional expenditures, relative to the growth rate of served markets.[1] Note that two of the key factors that affect market share involve product.

Later in this chapter we will present two major concepts that serve as underpinnings for product strategies. Following this we will discuss strategic and tactical product alternatives with emphasis on the existing product line. But first we will define and explain product terms and concepts that provide a foundation for the managerial discussions that follow. New product strategies and development are covered in Chapter 17.

DEFINITIONS AND DESCRIPTIONS

Most of us think of products as physical objects that have been made or modified by humans, such as toothpaste, letter paper, hamburger, or gasoline. But in a generic sense products can be intangible *services* or *ideas* as well as tangible objects. In fact products may be perceived by potential buyers as offerings of a *bundle of benefits*, both tangible and intangible. If these benefits are viewed by buyers as capable of satisfying their needs and wants, the potential for product purchase is created.

Dentifrice buyers may expect tangible benefits such as whiter teeth or fewer cavities. Intangible benefits may be in the form of sensual pleasure or more self-confidence in social situations. The tangible product offered by a college is a

---

*PIMS is an acronym for Profit Impact of Market Strategies, an ongoing program of research and analysis on business strategy conducted by the Strategic Planning Institute using data supplied by over 200 corporations. See page 243 for an earlier reference to the market share/profit relationship and Figure 16-4 of this chapter for a chart showing these relationships.

diploma certifying the earned degree. The degree may lead to an even more tangible benefit such as a job. Intangible benefits may include the satisfaction gained from personal achievement, social experiences, or increased self-confidence. The National Cancer Institute uses fear of breast cancer as the intangible but powerful idea for persuading women to make regular self-examinations and have periodic medical checkups. If the idea is successful, it leads to the examinations—the tangible product.

Product

We can define product broadly as follows:

> A *product* represents a marketer's offering as it is perceived by potential customers. The offering represents a bundle of benefits, both tangible and intangible, designed to satisfy the needs and wants of target markets. A product may be a physical object, a service, an idea, or some combination thereof.

Not all buyers, of course, perceive a product or brand offering in the same way. The fragrance of a perfume may be admired by some and hated by others. An unbranded (generic) product may be perceived as a smart buy by one consumer while another rejects it as inferior to branded merchandise.

Product Differentiation

The above definition of "product" incorporates the concept of product differentiation, defined as follows:

> *Product differentiation* is any perceived difference in a product or brand when compared with others.

People tend to interpret product differentiation literally as meaning some physical difference. In reality it is anything that causes people to see one product or brand as different from another. Smirnoff is a successful brand of vodka. Why? Is it because of the quality of the liquid in the bottle? Is it the brand name which suggests Russia, a country noted for its fine vodka? Is it because of the image portrayed by the packaging, labeling, advertising, and high price? Probably all of these things contribute to the perception that Smirnoff is the brand that particular people choose when they want to please themselves or impress their guests. Jack Daniels is a bourbon whiskey with a distinctive flavor. Although other distillers try to emulate this brand, the Jack Daniels image as a fine, old Tennessee whiskey has kept sales growing—despite its high price—at a time when bourbon and other "nonlight" whiskies are losing market share.

Many other brands and trade names have achieved special status in the minds of consumers for various reasons. Examples include such diverse brands as Hallmark, Harvard University, Morgan Guaranty Bank, American Express, and Campbell Soup. Some of the factors—in addition to the quality of the product itself—that help differentiate products and brands include the types of people who buy; appearance and packaging; endorsements by celebrities; price; reputation; and the attitudes of the buyer's peers. For products sold through retailers we can add the factors of type and quality of retail outlets used.

Favorable product differentiation is one of the best assets a product or brand can possess. Consequently, astute marketers strive to achieve it for their products and brands. Ralston-Purina, a leading producer of pet foods, when criticized by the grocery trade for introducing parity products, announced that henceforth its strategy would be aimed at "strengthening existing brands and introducing new products with *meaningful differences*."[2]

Parity Products. Over time, competing products in a free market tend toward sameness, or *parity*. This is inevitable as competitors adopt one another's product improvements until ideas for improvement are exhausted. (See Figure 16-1.) When parity is reached, differentiation for reasons other than product differences becomes the deciding influence in brand preference. This situation further explains why marketers try for more than one means of product differentiation, particularly during the product's growth period. When a brand achieves a degree of market preference, for whatever combination of reasons, this preference tends to carry on even after product parity is reached.

Augmented Products. Levitt[3] believes that everything can be differentiated. To accomplish this he suggests viewing a product from three perspectives—generic, expected, and augmented.

For example, a basic type of steel (e.g., 72-inch hot-rolled strip) represents a *generic* product. The *expected* product would be the generic product plus minimal customer expectations such as delivery, terms, and support efforts. The *augmented* product would represent the expected product plus what the supplier offers that is more than the buyer expected or may even have considered. Examples of augmentation might be better ways of fabricating and coating the steel strip or reducing thickness to cut its weight. Since the needs of customers change, changes in the seller's augmented offerings are required from time to time.

Augmentation and Convenience Goods. While the augmentation concept appears valid for many types of products, it may be more difficult to apply to convenience goods such as packaged foods and health and beauty aids. Services for most of these products are neither needed nor expected by consumers (although trade channels may value augmented services provided by manufacturers). It is in these categories that we see so many products move toward parity. Significant

FIGURE 16-1. How adoption of competitive improvements leads eventually to product sameness or parity. A typical industry would show numerous companies interacting with one another's improvements.

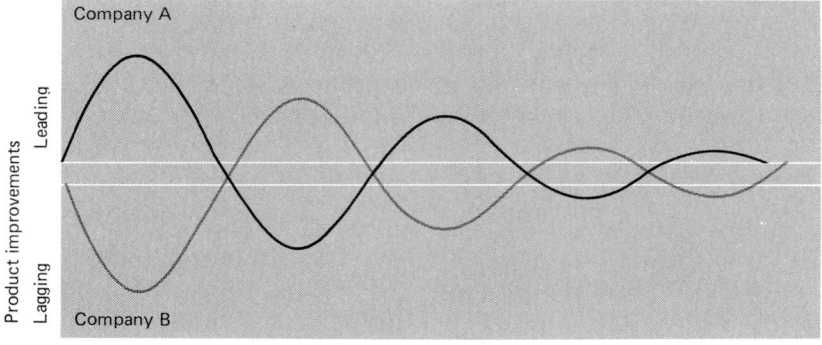

product differences are not easily created for aspirin or coffee, for example, despite intensive research for product improvements.

Product Line

A new company usually begins with one product. If things go well, a product line is created through the additions of models, sizes, colors, flavors, etc.. Additions are made to satisfy current customer segments, attract business from new segments, and counteract actions of competitors. These related products comprise what we commonly think of as the product line. The following definition suggests additional criteria:

> *Product Line*—a group of products that are closely related either because they satisfy a class of need, are used together, are sold to the same customer groups, are marketed through the same type of outlets, or fall within given price ranges. Example, carpenters' tools.[4]

Line Item. An *item* is any single unit in the product line such as a model, color, size, etc.. An item may be referred to as a *line item* or an *SKU* (stock keeping unit). One product line can have from two items to hundreds.

Product Mix

Successful expansion of the product line often is followed by diversification into other product lines. All of the products and product lines offered by a business unit are referred to as its *product mix*.

Product Attributes

That product differentiation is based on something more than the product's distinctive features does not lessen the need to distinguish the product via its tangible attributes. Every advertising copywriter's delight is the product with clearly superior advantages for which substantiated claims can be made.

Attributes, of course, are not limited to tangible features. Anything that buyers perceive as characterizing a product offering would be one of its attributes. Yet there are certain traditional attributes that most manufacturers consider as fundamental: function, quality, price, service, design, and packaging. For some types of products the warranty or guarantee represents an important attribute.

Functions. Competitive versions of established products tend to possess similar basic functions. Consequently, companies strive to create new or improved functions that can be featured in their promotions. Examples abound, including more fuel-efficient motors, speedier office copiers, slow-release medications, and light-sensitive glasses. Unless the functional attribute is patentable, the innovator's advantage may last only until competitors copy it. And as we have noted earlier, it is difficult to come up with new functional improvements for parity products.

Quality. A key measure of quality is how well the product performs for its intended use. A penknife will perform well with a blade made of low-grade steel, whereas a butcher's knife requires a high-carbon-steel blade that can be honed to a sharp edge. A farm tractor requires a higher-horsepower motor than a garden tractor.

But within the area of intended use, differences in quality can make for differences in performance. Improvements in product quality and performance are sought by most manufacturers, since they make for effective promotion. Exceptions to this general rule are found in low-end lines where price is featured rather than quality.

Price and Service. We save discussions of price for Chapter 18. We list it here, however, because in relation to quality, performance, and service, price affects buyers' perceptions of value. We have already discussed service as one means of product differentiation. Service is a more important attribute for some products than for others. It is highly important for mechanical products such as built-in dishwashers or plant machinery where buyers expect services such as installation, maintenance, and repair.

Design. Product design deals with the way a product is styled and the way it is arranged to increase its value to the end user. Styling is concerned with esthetics, including the use of color, materials, texture, and form. Ease of operation and repair as well as economies in production, storage, and transportation are also subjects for design consideration.

Design is also a factor in the presentation of ideas and services. Interior design can enhance the appeal of shops, offices, and airliner interiors and exteriors. Graphic design enhances the effectiveness of trademarks, signs, insurance policies, and awards.[5]

Design, quality, and performance should be decided with consideration given to the health and safety of the buyer, the public, and the natural environment. A continuing challenge to design, engineering, and R&D departments is to develop products that are not harmful to users or to the public at large, but which are not so costly as to price themselves out of the market. The economically viable product nearly always represents a compromise between the ideal and that which customers are willing to pay for.

Packaging. The package serves two primary functions: (1) product protection and (2) information about the product and its use. Superior package design may be enough to attract buyers even when the package contains a parity product.

Packaging should *protect* the product in transit and in the warehouse; on the retail shelf; and in the home or workplace until the contents are consumed. Packaging *information* will include some or all of the following: product and brand identification; price; promotional message; instructions for use; and warranty.

In addition to protection and information, good design calls for packages that stack well in warehouses and on the retail shelf. One also sees creative ideas applied to customer use—opening, closing, and pouring devices and secondary uses of the package after the contents have been consumed. Soft-margarine cartons are examples of the latter. They not only fulfill the basic protection and information requirements, but also have continuing uses such as for storing leftover foods in the refrigerator.

Warranties. Every manufacturer carries the obligation that its goods will perform as promised. For many of the everyday products we buy, performance is promised via an *implied warranty* which assures that the goods are fit for the purpose intended. A pipe tobacco will burn; a garden hose will not leak; a bar of soap will lather. Implied warranties are provided legally by the Uniform Commerical Code and do not need to be stated.

Express warranties, on the other hand, are statements guaranteeing that a product will perform as claimed over a stated period of time. Express warranties are of particular interest to buyers of durable goods. Producers of appliances, cars, and machinery normally state explicitly what is guaranteed and what the remedies for failure will be, such as paying for repair parts and/or labor. Or a warranty may specify a trade-in allowance for products that fail to last a guaranteed length of time (e.g., a battery) or number of miles (e.g., a tire). Express warranties usually serve the manufacturer both as a selling feature and as protection against unreasonable demands from buyers.

Warranty requirements were made more specific with the passage of the Magnuson-Moss Warranty–Federal Trade Commission Improvement Act in 1975. This act gives the FTC the power to make rules for warranted products costing over $5. If warranted products cost over $10, their written (express) warranties must be designated as either *full* or *limited*. A limited warranty must spell out its limitations. A manufacturer is not required to offer an express warranty; but if it does not do so, it forfeits this product attribute.

Increasingly, regulatory agencies, judges, and juries are holding producers more accountable, particularly where safety is concerned. *Caveat emptor* (buyer beware) has been giving way to *caveat venditor* (seller beware).[6]

Brand Names, Trademarks, Trade Names

Nations, families, military units, political parties, and others have long used graphic symbols for quick identification and for portraying images. Business symbols appear in the form of brand names, trademarks, and trade names. Understanding the meanings of these terms will help when we discuss branding strategies later in the chapter.

Brand name. A word or combination of words used to identify a product and differentiate it from other products. All brand names are trademarks, but not all trademarks are brand names.

Trademark. As defined in the United States Trademark Act of 1946, "any word, name, symbol, or device or any combination thereof adopted and used by a manufacturer or merchant to identify his goods and distinguish them from those manufactured or sold by others." Some trademarks are not brand names. For example, Elsie, the cow is a trademark symbol, but the brand name is "Borden's." The slogan "Good to the Last Drop" is a trademark, but the brand name is "Maxwell House."

Trade name. This term is frequently and erroneously used as a synonym for either "brand name" or "trademark." A trade name is the name of a business. A trade name may also be a brand name, but in such a case it serves two separate purposes. "Cluett Peabody & Co., Inc." is solely a trade name for the maker of Arrow shirts; "Gant" is both a trade name for a shirtmaker and the brand name for its shirts.[7]

Selection. The ideal trademark should be short, easily pronounced and understood, and adaptable for display in a wide variety of media. It should be a proper adjective that modifies the product name (example: Head & Shoulders shampoo). The cardinal legal principle in choosing a trademark is to avoid conflict with the existing rights of another company.[8] With thousands of trademarks in use, it is not easy to find good ones that do not somehow infringe on others.

Coming up with ideas for trademarks and brand names is a creative process. Computer programs can be designed to identify many combinations of letters for consideration. ("Exxon" reportedly is the result of a computer search.) But often the "right" name comes from the mind of an employee of the company or its advertising agency. Procter & Gamble's "Ivory Soap" is said to have been the inspiration of a P&G executive while in church during the reading of Psalms 45:8: "All thy garments smell of myrrh, and aloes and cassia, out of the *ivory* palaces whereby they have made thee glad."[9] If inspiration is the source for the idea, the design of the trademark is a job for the industrial designer skilled in graphic representation.

Legal Protection. Trademarks, brand names, and trade names have little value to a company unless they are protected from use by others. Protection involves three key steps:

1. Search of registrations on file at the U.S. Patent Office to make sure the proposed mark is not already registered.
2. Registration with the U.S. Patent Office.
3. Use of the mark in interstate commerce. A trademark is not completely legal until it has been in use for 5 years from the time of registration.

Rights to a trademark can be lost unless it is used constantly in a prescribed manner. One of the biggest dangers for a successful trademark is that it becomes so well known that the public uses it to identify the generic product. "Aspirin," "escalator," and "cornflakes" were trademarks that lost their legal protection because they became generic.

Brands and Nonbrands

There are two principal types of brands competing in the marketplace. The first includes manufacturer-owned and -promoted brands, often referred to as "national," "regional," or "advertised" brands. The second type includes brands owned by others. These commonly are called "private" brands or "private labels." Most often the private brand is owned by a wholesaler or a retail chain. But one manufacturer also may buy products from another manufacturer and sell them under its own "private" brand name. Many of the major oil companies, for example, sell their own brands of tires which are made for them by tire manufacturers.

The fight for shelf space between manufacturers' brands and private chain brands is very intense in some channels (such as grocery) and has been called "the battle of the brands."

Manufacturers' Brands. From the manufacturer's standpoint, brands represent a means of identifying the company's products and of building consumer brand preference. From the consumer's standpoint, manufacturers' brands imply levels of quality and consistency that make shopping easier and reduce uncertainty. From the retailer's standpoint, nationally advertised brands draw customers to the store and help to build store prestige.

The importance of advertised brands to consumers, however, varies by types of products. The J. Walter Thompson advertising agency found that the frequency of shopping by brand name is highest for personal care products and lowest for paper towels. (See **Marketing Note 16-1**.)

Private Brands. Private branders obtain products for sale under their own labels in three principal ways.

From their own production facilities. Some wholesalers and retail chains own production facilities, but usually for only a few of the products they sell. (Wholesalers carry such a wide range of product lines that it would be impossible for them to manufacture everything they sell.) Others have a financial interest in some of their suppliers. Sears' part ownership of Whirlpool Corporation is an example.

Purchased by specification from independent manufacturers. Through contract specifications, the private brander controls the features and quality of products purchased. For goods such as tires, appliances, or building products, the private brander may ensure control over the product through ownership of the tooling or molds.

By shopping for the best buy. Many types of products, however, are bought from different manufacturers at different times. Canned foods represent an example. Manufacturers—depending upon their capacity utilization at a particular time—may or may not want private brand business. Their prices vary accordingly. When a middleman buys from different suppliers without setting specifications, quality can vary and result in lower consumer confidence in the private brand.

As a rule private brands sell for less than nationally advertised brands—about 20 percent less on average in supermarket chains. This price differential attracts some consumers away from higher-priced advertised brands. Middlemen normally obtain a higher profit margin from their private brands. Hence, retail chains usually feature their own brands.

Manufacturers who supply private brands usually do so to fill any production capacity not used for their own advertised brands. The manufacturer is able to sell for less because (1) its manufacturing costs are less (incremental variable costs only), (2) there is little or no advertising cost, and (3) sales costs are minimal. A few manufacturers, however, make *only* private brand merchandise. Design and Manufacturing Corp., for example, makes dishwashers only for others. Its clients include Sears, Western Auto, Gambles, Roper, Magic Chef, Caloric, and Tappan.[10] For many years Yard-Man, Inc. supplied lawnmowers exclusively to Sears, Roebuck and Co., although later it switched to producing its own advertised brand.[11]

An advertisement soliciting private brand business which appeared in a trade magazine is shown in Figure 16-2.

Nonbranded Generic Products. Whereas private brands have been around for many years, *generic* products did not appear in U.S. supermarkets until the late 1970s. Introduced first in Europe, generics are nonbranded consumer goods sold in plain packages containing only the generic name, such as "salad oil." Generics are priced on average about 20 percent below private brands and 40 percent below national brands.[12] By the early 1980s generics were in one-third of U.S. grocery stores and 163 generic products were being offered in total.[13]

In a study of twenty broad categories of generics sold in supermarkets, the A. C. Nielsen Company found their average shares of market to be 13.4 percent. The generics' share had been taken from both national and private brands. Table 16-1

How Important Is a Brand Name?

MARKETING NOTE 16-1

It depends on what you're selling.

Follow a typical consumer through a shopping center, and you'd find some unusual patterns of choice. She (or he) buys a brand name toothpaste instead of the lower-priced stuff, but watches her pennies on paper towels and shoes. To do the wash, she'll buy a well-recognized brand of detergent, but she'll have other considerations—of price and choice, say—when it comes to luggage for a midwinter vacation.

We asked people how they shopped for thirteen different types of products—whether they looked for one, several, or no particular brands. We included items of personal care, household goods, hard goods, food, and apparel, and we tried to gauge the importance of price. As a group, personal care products were most shopped for by brand name: Six out of ten of the people surveyed said they looked for particular brands of such items. Toothpaste had the highest rating among such items, with slightly more than two-thirds of the people saying they looked for just one particular brand. Only one consumer in twenty didn't appear to be attached to any brand of toothpaste, and only one out of ten shopped for bargain-priced dentifrices, apparently making the final choice at the toothpaste display in the store.

The consciousness of brands remained about the same for deodorants, antiperspirants, and mouthwashes. It dropped only slightly for toilet soaps, where about half of he people said they shopped for just one brand.

Apparently consumers associate strong (and positive) characteristics of fulfillment with specific brands of personal care products. Once they find the brand that fills those requirements, they tend to look for that label first rather than for the price tag or the bargain corner.

In household products, it's another ball game altogether. Six out of every ten people we talked to looked for a specific brand of laundry detergent—a consciousness level right up there with toothpaste and mouthwash. But paper towels drew less than half that recognition level—only about a fourth said they shopped for a particular brand of toweling. Instead, the emphasis was on bargains by a very wide margin—four out of every ten saying they shopped price. This may be one reason paper towel makers use such advertising devices as spokespeople with distinctive personalities, dramatic spill tests, and comparative demonstrations—all ways to dramatize brand awareness.

For television sets and cameras, it's clear some manufacturers have established images of high quality and dependability. More than three-fourths of the people surveyed said they shopped for one or, at most, two brands of TV sets. For cameras, the figure is nearly two-thirds. In fact, close to half of all those surveyed claimed they look for only one particular brand of television or camera. Clearly the higher prices of these products do not lead to a penny-pinching mentality.

In the dairy case, the picture isn't clear, and that may have something to do with the fact that many dairy basics, such as milk and eggs, are not national brands. Still, recognition of at least one dairy item ranked up there with the best of personal care. Nearly half the people we surveyed said they looked for one particular kind of butter, for example. More people, in fact, said they looked for a single brand of butter than for a single brand of soft drink—this despite the strong advertising support given to specific soft drink brands. It may well be, however, that consumers look for several soft drink brands when they shop, to accommodate different tastes in the family. At any rate, only about two people of every ten said price was the prime consideration in soft drink purchases—about the same as it is for butter.

Finally, in shoes, brand names rank comparatively low. Only about one person in four said they looked for one brand. Two people out of every ten either look for bargains or shop for a couple of brands. The largest group of shoe buyers by far (about a third) said they look for bargains first. That does not necessarily mean they all aren't brand-conscious, though, because sales of brand-name shoes are a seasonal staple, and many people wait for them like they do for the January white sales.

Source: From "Change in the Marketplace," J. Walter Thompson Co., January 1977. Reprinted by permission.

shows the percent of supermarket sales in four product categories by private brand, generics, and manufacturers' brands. Nielsen found that 44 percent of consumers had tried generics and that 70 percent would buy them again. Contrary to what consumers say, however, Nielsen found from store movement studies that generic

FIGURE 16-2 An advertisement soliciting private brand business.

product shares rise in the early months after introduction and then begin to decline.[14]

The future of generics remains in question. The Nielsen study "has caused some supermarket executives to question whether generic products are really a long-term, viable alternative to private label or national brands."[15] Other observers believe generics will level off at 13 to 15 percent of supermarket sales.[16]

PRODUCT CONCEPTS WITH STRATEGY IMPLICATIONS

Two concepts have proved particularly useful when developing or reevaluating product and marketing strategies: the *product life cycle* and the *product portfolio.* Neither is a strategy per se. Rather, each provides a framework within which alternate strategies can be evaluated.

TABLE 16-1
Market Share of Brands and Generics—Selected Products (Based on supermarkets carrying generic products, February 1979)

Product Group	% of Market Share		
	Private Brand*	Generic	Manufacturers' Brands†
Paper towels	9.5	16.9	73.6
Dishwashing liquids	12.5	13.8	73.7
Salad oil	14.4	13.2	72.3
Mayonnaise	11.0	12.2	76.8

*Nielsen uses the term "controlled brands," defined as "private label as well as wholesale label and franchise brands."
†Nielsen uses the term "remaining brands," presumably manufacturers' brands.
Source: Adapted from The Nielsen Researcher, no. 3, A. C. Nielsen Co., 1979.

Product Life Cycle

The product life cycle (PLC), pictured in Figure 16-3, assumes that a product will go through four stages during its lifetime: (1) introduction, (2) growth, (3) maturity, and (4) decline.

Normally sales are slow during the period of *introduction* when attempts are made to gain a market foothold. If the product is accepted by the market, at some point it takes off into a period of relatively rapid *growth*. This is followed by *maturity*, a period which begins as the rate of sales increase starts to slow. Finally, sales *decline* as product obsolescence sets in.

Profit margins are low during introduction because sales income is low and market development costs are high. The profit margins improve as sales increase during the growth period and as market development costs are shared by a number of competitors. Margins usually peak in the late stages of growth, then level off or fall during maturity as companies compete for shares of a relatively static market. Margins narrow or disappear in the decline phase as the surviving companies vie for a smaller and smaller market.

FIGURE 16-3. The product life cycle.

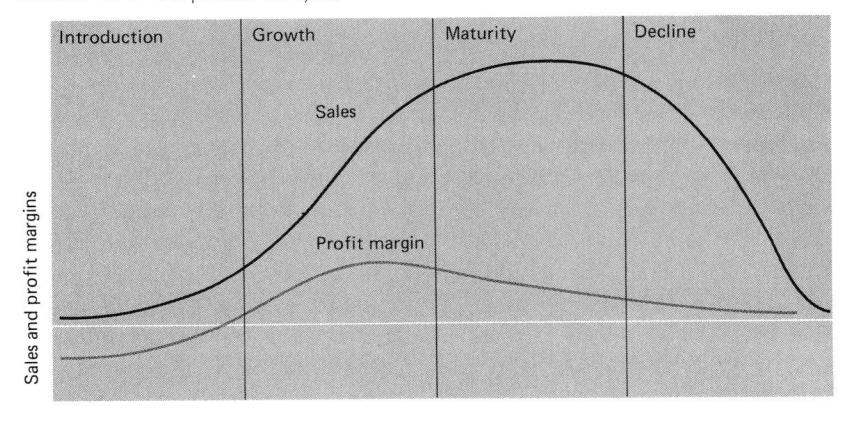

The rate of change and duration of the phases vary by type of product. Novelty toys or faddish clothing may complete their cycles in a matter of months, whereas basic commodities such as bread, beer, and lumber continue in the mature phase indefinitely.

Value for Planning Purposes. The PLC concept is not without controversy. Some enthusiasts have tended to oversell it by suggesting that companies should react to life cycle phases in specific ways. Others feel that while product strategy clearly is influenced by the life cycle, its value in planning should come from understanding how and why competitive conditions change with each phase of the cycle, and understanding the implications these conditions have for the product. Table 16-2 lists conditions typical of life cycle stages. The strategy implications are discussed below. Since conditions will vary by industry, strategic implications will vary by company.

Introduction Period. This is the high-cost and low-profit (or loss) period that the innovator must survive while attempting to gain market acceptance. This period may range from weeks to many years. One theory about why some products take longer than others to reach takeoff is based on the amount of *learning* required before buyers accept a new product.[17] Wasson suggests that learning new habit patterns is a painful process. Thus, we will more readily accept a new version of a familiar product than we will a new product requiring the development of new habit patterns. We might accept a 5-speed bicycle over a one-speed, for example, before we would accept a moped.[18]

Other companies may join the initiating company in the introductory period to gain an early foothold, although many wait to see whether and when the product will take off. The television industry sat back for years while RCA carried the costly burden of introducing color TV.

Examples of products in their introductory stages include those coming from

TABLE 16-2
Typical Conditions by Stage of Product Life Cycle

	Introduction	Growth	Maturity	Decline
Number of companies	One or few	Many entering	Some dropouts	Many dropouts
Sales growth rate	Low	High	Leveling	Declining
Marketing costs as % of sales	High	Lowering	Stabilizing or lowering*	Modest, but depends on number of companies left
Production costs as % of sales	High	Lowering	Stabilizing or lowering†	Modest, but depends on number of companies left
Profit margins	Negative	Rising	Stabilizing or declining‡	Low to negative, but can be high for sole survivor
Company marketing objectives	Obtain market acceptance	Gain market share	Hold market share	Withdraw, or if remain, minimize expense

*Depending on the intensity of competition.

†Depending on whether, and how much, costs are affected by the experience curve or by economies of scale.

‡Depending on competitive price pressures.

the life sciences (genetic engineering), such as plant-growth regulators and defenses against human diseases. Others are products made possible by developments in microelectronics such as telecommunications and office automation systems.

Growth Period. As sales take off, other companies enter the industry, often with improved products coming out of studies of market reactions to the initiator's product. Some companies fight for the market leadership position during this period in the belief that high market shares will ensure good profit margins on into the mature phase. Also, gain in market share can be obtained from increments of market growth rather than by having to take it from competitors.

In theory, average industry margins are highest in the growth phase. Even strong companies, however, do not always find the going profitable in a growth industry; witness the withdrawal of the giant electronic firms, GE and RCA, from the mainframe computer business when they could not take enough share from IBM to make their computer businesses profitable.

Products that appear to be in their growth stages include microwave ovens, personal computers, wines, and plastic bottles. Major product industries in their growth stages include electronic communications equipment, plastics, and cable television.

Maturity Period. Because most industries are in their mature phases, most companies are concerned with strategies for mature products. This period of the product industry is characterized by intensive competition as companies fight to protect market shares already gained and to pick up shares from companies that drop out. Emphasis by company may vary from product improvement to differentiation to cost cutting to innovative promotion. Despite the theory that margins decline during this period, *market leaders* often remain profitable because of lower costs resulting from the experience curve and or economies of scale. Individual company strategies vary from continued aggressive fighting for share to withdrawal from the industry. An in-between strategy is to "milk" or "harvest" the product, investing the excess cash flow from the mature product into better profit opportunities. The Continental Group elected to treat its can business (with sales in excess of $1 billion annually) as a mature product line, using a large proportion of the cash flow from cans to invest in more profitable growth businesses.[19] The B. F. Goodrich Co. "decided five years ago to milk its tire business to finance potentially more profitable ventures into chemicals, plastics, and other products."[20]

Generally it is the older industries that are in the mature stages. Examples include many foods, beer, health aids (analgesics, cold remedies), cosmetics, kitchen appliances, autos, and steel. One can speculate as to whether education, professional sports, fast-food restaurants, or airlines are in or are entering their mature phases.

Reasons for maturity. Market saturation is the most common reason cited for the onset of maturity. This is, however, more the case with certain products than with others. Household durable goods, such as electric appliances, tend to have sustained industry growth until most of the households that will buy have done so. After the practical saturation level is reached, future sales come from new household formations, replacements of worn-out products, and additional appliances per household (e.g., two refrigerators). Although saturation affects all products to some degree, there can be other reasons for the onset of market maturity, as shown below.

For planning purposes, it is important to understand the key reasons for industry maturity, since they can influence strategy formulation.

Type of Product	Contributory Reasons for Industry Maturity
Convenience goods	Slowing population growth
Soft drinks	Decline of the 13 to 24 age group
Cigarettes	Health concerns
Tennis equipment	Decline in number of players
Electric floor polisher	Increase in carpeting and "no-wax" resilient flooring
Candy	Decline in youth population, and health warnings regarding sugar and tooth decay

Decline Period. Decline is characterized by falling sales and profits, which cause most companies to drop out of the product industry. Few industries die, however, at least in the medium term. After the shakeout, the industry often stabilizes, with a few surviving companies making modest profits. The Diamond Tool and Horseshoe Co. of Duluth, Minn., for example, continues to produce horseshoes. It serves the pleasure, racehorse, and residual workhorse population as well as the horseshoe-pitching sport.

Product industries that are either in the decline stage or facing it include cigars, CB radios, railroads, urban newspapers, wood, and rubber-working machinery.

Life Cycle Renewal. Product life cycles sometimes get second lives after maturity (and even decline) have set in. Some examples are listed below. These were the result of new technology or environmental change, except for nylon, which went through a series of renewals as it successfully obtained new market applications.[21]

Products Experiencing Renewed Life Cycles	Reasons for Renewal
Television	Renewed demand for color sets is tied to the growth of telecommunications—home recorders, players, games, computers, etc.
Bicycles	Increased interest in adult exercise
Wood stoves and coal	High costs of oil and gas
Bus travel	Higher costs of driving private car
Life insurance	Increase in women working and heading households
Nylon	Original success was in replacing silk in women's hosiery. As this market matured, new applications were made in tires, textiles, etc.

Use of PLC in Strategy Formulation. The stage of the PLC should always be considered during marketing planning and strategy formulation. To avoid it being overlooked, the PLC was included in the *situation analysis* outline in Chapter 9. While a change in the stage of PLC may call for change in strategy, it should not be to a preordained strategy.

Let's assume, for example, that a product is moving from maturity to the decline stage and that three of the several competing companies are considering changes in their strategies. Each has a different position in the market, rate of profit, and investment opportunity. Depending on these and other conditions affecting each company, it might be good strategy for one to drop out now; for another to milk its product and phase it out later; and for the third to remain and compete intensively for increased market share.

A special issue of the *Journal of Marketing* addressed "the long-standing controversy over the managerial value of the product life cycle concept." In the overview article George Day argues against those who would misuse the PLC in formulating strategy.

> The derivation of generalized strategic prescriptions for each stage of the life cycle has been widely criticized—and for good reason. Such prescriptions are bound to be misleading, for they assume a single role for the life cycle as a determinant of strategy, structure, and performance. Unfortunately this role is implicitly endorsed by a majority of marketing textbooks through an emphasis on strategic guidelines appropriate to the various stages. A more realistic view is that life cycle analysis serves several different roles in the formulation of strategy, such as an enabling condition, a moderating variable, or a consequence of strategic decisions.[22]

In short, we should consider the PLC during strategy formulation, but not look to it for automatic answers.

The Product-Evolution Concept. Tillis and Crawford[23] have proposed an interesting alternative to the PLC which they call the "product-evolution concept" (PEC). Rather than viewing products as passing through life cycles, the PEC assumes that products are in a *state of constant evolution* motivated by market dynamics, managerial creativity, and government intervention. A major premise of the PEC is that product growth is partly the result of the strategy adopted, and not the reverse.

Portfolio Concepts

Product and business portfolios have proven useful for developing strategies in multiproduct companies. In essence the portfolio approach involves classifying the company's products into categories which are subject to different strategies and different resource allocations. Nine different portfolio models have gained acceptance.[24] The best known of these has been closely identified with the Boston Consulting Group (BCG). We will illustrate the portfolio concept with the BCG model.

The BCG Product Portfolio. This portfolio approach makes use of three concepts we have discussed previously: (1) product life cycle, (2) cash flow, and (3) the market share/return on investment correlation. Figure 16-4 shows how return on investment (ROI) changes with market share; the percentages are averages for the businesses participating in the PIMS program.

The BCG model assigns the company's product to four quadrants of a grid according to relative market share (the horizontal scale) and relative growth rate of the market (vertical scale), as shown in Figure 16-5. Products with high market shares in high-growth markets fall into the upper left quadrant of the matrix in Figure 16-5. They are called *stars*. However, they require more cash than they produce because of the high marketing costs needed to obtain high market share.

As market growth rates slow (i.e., as the mature phase of the PLC occurs), stars

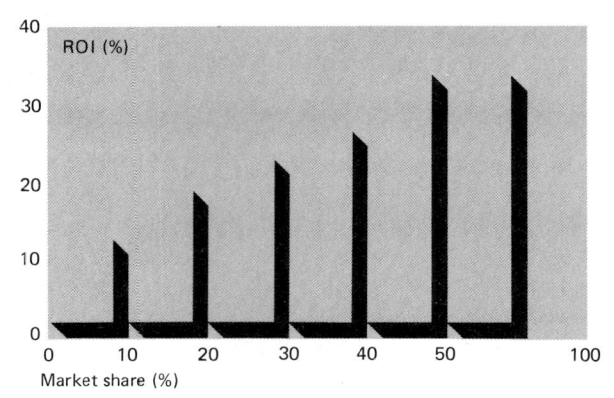

FIGURE 16-4. The relation of ROI to market share. *Source:* Bradley T. Gale and Ben Branch, "The Dispute about High-Share Businesses," *The Pimsletter on Business Strategy,* no. 19, Strategic Planning Institute, 1979.

shift to the lower left quadrant where they are called *cash cows*. The cash cow presumably generates more cash than it needs to maintain its market position in a mature market. The excess cash can be used to finance new stars (new products in growth industries) or to help *problem children* become stars. Problem children, with low market shares in high-growth markets, are placed in the upper right quadrant.

The lower right quadrant in Figure 16-5 is for the *dogs*—products with low market shares in low-growth markets. According to the portfolio concept, these become candidates for milking (harvesting) or divestment. An ideal implementation of the product portfolio concept would be to maintain an inflow of new products in growth markets balanced by a stable of cash cows. As markets for the cash cows move to the decline phase of their product life cycles, they would be divested before they become dogs, and the cash obtained thereby would be reinvested in future stars. The process would be repeated ad infinitum.

Because so many variations of the BCG model have been published by others, we have reprinted the BCG's own version in **Marketing Note 16-2**.

Limitation of the product portfolio. The market share, market growth portfolio has its greatest appeal for large, multiproduct companies that hold market leadership positions or that have the potential for attaining them. Yet even the most

FIGURE 16-5. Product portfolio matrix.

The Product Portfolio

MARKETING NOTE 16-2

To be successful, a company should have a portfolio of products with different growth rates and different market shares. The portfolio composition is a function of the balance between cash flows. High-growth products require cash inputs to grow. Low-growth products should generate excess cash. Both kinds are needed simultaneously.

Four rules determine the cash flow of a product:

- Margins and cash generated are a function of market share. High margins and high market share go together. This is a matter of common observation, explained by the experience curve effect.
- Growth requires cash input to finance added assets. The added cash required to hold share is a function of growth rates.
- High market share must be earned or bought. Buying market share requires an additional increment of investment.
- No product market can grow indefinitely. The payoff from growth must come when the growth slows, or it never will. The payoff is cash that cannot be reinvested in that product.

Products with high market share and slow growth are "cash cows." Characteristically, they generate large amounts of cash, in excess of the reinvestment required to maintain share. This excess need not, and should not, be reinvested in those products. In fact, if the rate of return exceeds the growth rate, the cash *cannot* be reinvested indefinitely, except by depressing returns.

Products with low market share and slow growth are "pets" [or "dogs"]. They may show an accounting profit, but the profit must be reinvested to maintain share, leaving no cash throwoff. The product is essentially worthless, except in liquidation.

All products eventually become either cash cows or pets. The value of a product is completely dependent upon obtaining a leading share of its market before the growth slows.

Low market share, high-growth products are the "question marks" [or "problem children"]. They almost always require far more cash than they can generate. If cash is not supplied, they fall behind and die. Even when the cash is supplied, if they only hold their share, they are still pets when the growth stops. The question marks require large added cash investment for market share to be purchased. The low market share, high-growth product is a liability unless is becomes a leader. It requires very large cash inputs that it cannot generate itself.

The high-share, high-growth product is the "star." It nearly always shows reported profits, but it may or may not generate all of its own cash. If it stays a leader, however, it will become a large cash generator when growth slows and its reinvestment requirements diminish. The star eventually becomes the cash cow, providing high volume, high margin, high stability, security, and cash throwoff for reinvestment elsewhere.

The payoff for leadership is very high indeed, if it is achieved early and maintained until growth slows. Investment in market share during the growth phase can be very attractive, if you have the cash. Growth in market is compounded by growth in share. Increases in share increase the margin. High margin permits higher leverage with equal safety. The resulting profitability permits higher payment of earnings after financing normal growth. The return on investment is enormous.

The need for a portfolio of businesses becomes obvious. Every company needs products in which to invest cash. Every company needs products that generate cash. And every product should eventually be a cash generator; otherwise it is worthless.

Only a diversified company with a balanced portfolio can use its strengths to truly capitalize on its growth opportunities. The balanced portfolio has:

- Stars whose high share and high growth assure the future
- Cash cows that supply funds for that future growth
- Question marks to be converted into stars with the added funds

Pets are not necessary. They are evidence of failure either to obtain a leadership position during the growth phase or to get out and cut the losses.

MARKETING NOTE 16-2 *(Continued)*

The Matrix
Market share

	High	Low
High Growth	★ Star	? Question mark
Low	$ Cash cow	× Pet

Optimum Cash Flow
Market share

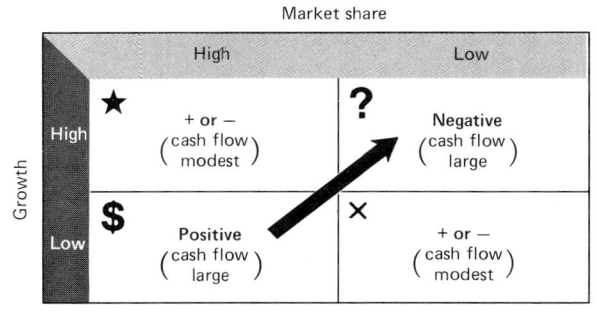

	High	Low
High Growth	★ + or − (cash flow modest)	? Negative (cash flow large)
Low	$ Positive (cash flow large)	× + or − (cash flow modest)

Success Sequence
Market share

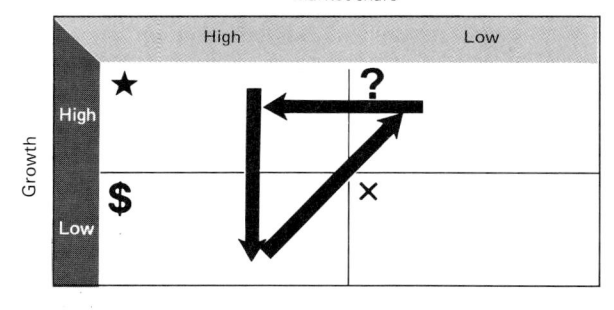

	High	Low
High Growth	★	?
Low	$	×

Disaster Sequence
Market share

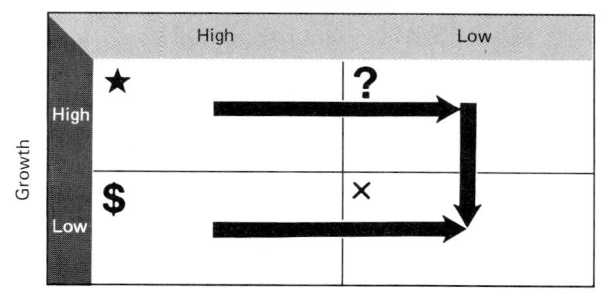

	High	Low
High Growth	★	?
Low	$	×

Source: Perspectives, "The Product Portfolio," The Boston Consulting Group, Inc., Boston, MA, © 1970.

successful have difficulty coming up regularly with new stars, for reasons that will be examined in the next chapter. Consequently many follow a strategy of continuing to invest in building market share for their cash cows. Witness the intensive marketing efforts of successful companies to increase market share for flagship brands which are in mature industries. Examples include Anheuser-Busch (Budweiser, Michelob), Procter & Gamble (Tide, Charmin), and General Foods (Jell-O, Maxwell House). "General Foods still derives 40% of its sales and one-third of its earnings from its coffee business. It has no choice but to compete vigorously and effectively in the coffee industry."[25]

Since only one company or a few can have high market shares of a product industry, the balance must operate with low shares. This does not mean, however, that there is no hope for these companies. One study found that in many industries, companies with low market shares consistently outperformed their larger rivals and showed very little inclination to either expand their share or withdraw from the fight. While acknowledging that high share is better than low share, the authors of this study conclude that not all low-share businesses are dogs. They cite Crown Cork & Seal (metal cans) and Union Camp (forest products) as examples of low-share companies having better than average return on equity as compared to their much larger industry rivals. The authors found that successful small-share companies are content to remain small, emphasize profits rather than sales growth or market share, and specialize by product and market segments rather than diversify.[26]

A small-business expert believes that overemphasis on sales growth is a mistake for small companies as well as for some large companies. He concludes that for many companies emphasis placed on improving return on the capital employed is a better way to profits than is sales growth.[27]

Users of any kind of portfolio approach stress that slotting a product into a matrix is only a start in planning, a *first cut* at strategy that helps to point the planners in the right direction and ensure that a uniform method of product evaluation is followed.[28]

The Multifactor Assessment Portfolio. The General Electric Company uses a portfolio which ranks products and businesses according to industry attractiveness and business strengths. (See Figure 16-6.) Products are then classified into three general strategic categories: invest/grow, selectivity/earnings, or harvest/divest (not unlike BCG's stars, cash cows, and dogs). GE's description of this approach may be seen in **Marketing Note 8-3, page 200**.

The GE approach differs from that of BCG in that it uses several factors in addition to market growth and market share in assessing the relative business strengths and industry attractiveness.

Other companies have developed portfolios using their own list of factors for classifying their products or businesses. Like General Electric, General Foods and H. J. Heinz classify their products into three categories. General Foods aims at balancing its portfolio across categories whose objectives are summed up as maximize growth, maintain franchise, and optimize cash. Heinz divides its product groups into those managed for growth (the so-called market makers), for earnings (maintenance products), and for cash flow (milkers).[29]

Impact of Portfolio Concepts. There is little doubt that product/business portfolio concepts have had an impact on strategic planning. Cash cows and dogs have become a part of business jargon. Companies are trying harder to get into

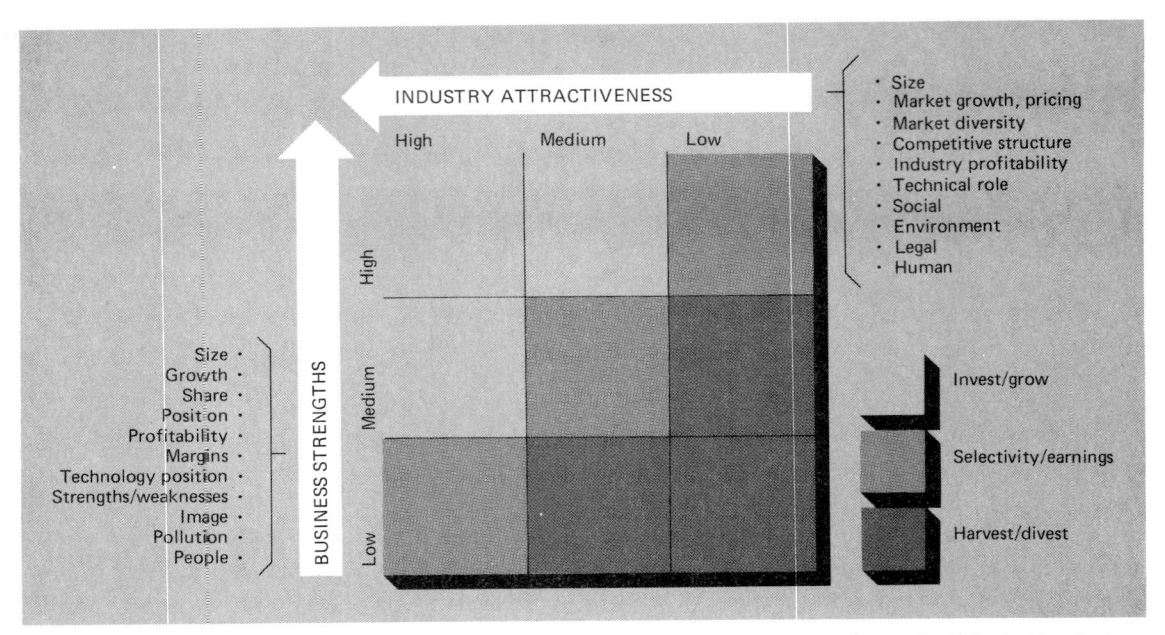

FIGURE 16-6. General Electric's business screen and multifactor assessment. *Source:* David S. Hopkins, *Business Strategies and Problem Products,* The Conference Board, New York, 1977, p.48.

growth businesses. There is more emphasis on market share. And there seems to be more willingness to get rid of dogs. However, not all companies have embraced the idea of spending only enough on cash cows to maintain market share. One reason is the scarcity of new growth businesses in which to build stars. (One study of 345 companies concluded: "Portfolio planning seems unable to successfully address the issue of new business generation."[30]) Another reason is that many mature businesses continue to grow, albeit more slowly. With the market still growing, continued share growth remains feasible; so, in the absence of better opportunities, many large and successful companies continue trying to increase the market shares of their leading brands. In addition to increases in market promotion, they also try for product improvements and brand or line extensions.

The product life cycle is useful in analyzing the individual product situation, and product portfolios are helpful in planning the product mix. The principal value of each, however, is in aiding the thought processes that lead to product and marketing strategies.

PRODUCT STRATEGIES

An ongoing company or business unit usually will have at least one product line (and perhaps several) containing a range of items. Product lines must be managed carefully if the business is to attain anything near its maximum profit potential. Present products must be kept competitive, profit detractors deleted, and new products added.

From the planning chapters in Part Three, we have seen that products are important aspects of the broad marketing strategy. Product planning, however, should not be limited to the annual strategic planning process. Rather, products should be under continuous review by product managers, group product managers, and product planning managers. Several aspects of product management raise strategic and tactical issues. We will discuss these under the headings of "Product Mix" and "Brands." First, however, we emphasize again (as we do for all planning) that the *situation analysis* should precede the development of product strategies and programs.

Product Situation Analysis

Current information similar to that listed in Chapter 9 should be assembled and analyzed for products and product lines: market growth rates; market segments served and not served; market shares; product life cycles; profitability by product; strengths and weaknesses of internal resources; and comparisons of company products with competitors. If the product portfolio concept is used by company management, product planners should know the categories into which products have been placed.

Product Mix Strategies

Managing the product mix involves developing strategies and programs for product lines which will keep them competitive, of optimum size, and pruned of deadwood. And there should be an inflow of new products to offset declining products and provide additional company growth. We will discuss several product strategies: keeping the present line competitive, leaders versus followers, full versus limited lines, line stretching, line pruning, and adding new products.

Maintaining Competitiveness of Present Lines. Product offerings should be equal or superior to those of principal competitors. This requires persistent attention to attributes, particularly quality. Trite though it may be, advertisers know that "new and improved" sells products.

As noted at the beginning of this chapter, the PIMS studies have found that an increase in relative quality is one of the three strategic factors behind market share gains. Observe that the findings refer to *relative* quality. "Quality improvement does not necessarily imply offering deluxe products. . . . Quality, like beauty, is relative; and in most markets, offering better value—especially in the moderate-priced sector where volume is usually concentrated—is most important."[31] Of course, attributes other than quality (e.g., functions, price, services, design, packaging, and warranties) can also influence buyers' perceptions of value.

Organizing for product improvements. An important function of product managers is to evaluate their own and competitors' products. They arrange for marketing research studies to learn of improvements buyers may want, evaluate the market reception given to competitors' improvements, and evaluate improvements that have been developed within the company.

The research and development department is responsible for responding to the marketing department's requests for product upgrading and for ongoing programs of product improvement and cost reduction. Many companies assist R&D by using a team approach to identifying product improvements and cost reductions, called *value analysis*. Teams may be put together for different products, and are composed of people from research and development, engineering, manufacturing, purchasing, and marketing. Suppliers may be encouraged to submit ideas.

Leader versus Follower Strategies. Whether a company is to be a leader or follower should be a strategic decision, because management must decide the amount of resources it will commit to market and technical research and development. *Leaders* must invest heavily in these functions. Generally product leadership implies being first to market with both new *and* improved products often enough to gain recognition as a leader. (No company is likely to always be first to market.)

The *follower* relies on the leader to supply product answers to market needs and wants and to develop the market. The follower may be primarily a *copier* who invests only enough in technical functions to be able to produce "me-too" products. Whereas the leader hopes to profit from higher initial prices and/or from obtaining high market share, the copier hopes to profit from lower costs, even though it sells at lower prices.

Another type of follower is the *hedger* who invests somewhere in between what the leader and the copier do, in hopes of gaining some of the advantages enjoyed by the others, while at the same time lowering its risks. A common version of the hedger strategy is to invest enough in technical research and development to be able to introduce improvements on those innovations by the leader that appear to be meeting with market acceptance. Many well-known companies follow a hedger strategy, although they may not acknowledge it publicly.

Full- versus Limited-Line Strategies. To figure out how broad and how deep a product line should be requires both strategic and tactical decisions. A strategic decision is needed to answer the question of whether to offer a *full line* or a *limited line*. Tactical decisions answer the questions of what items to offer within the full- or limited-line strategy.

Whether a line is full (in breadth and depth of items carried) or limited (only selected items carried) is a matter of degree. Few full-line manufacturers attempt to provide items for every market niche. And few limited-line manufacturers would refuse to add an item if it were demanded by customers. Each strategy has its advantages and disadvantages:

Advantages to the full line. (1) More items provide more sales opportunities. (2) Dealing with one source simplifies buying for channel intermediaries and industrial customers. (3) By combining shipments of many items, the average unit transportation costs are lowered. (4) A full-line offering can enhance the manufacturer's image. (5) For products such as furniture and kitchen appliances, a full line enables the manufacturer to offer coordinated sets of products (a matched set including refrigerator, stove, and dishwasher, for example).

Disadvantages of the full line. (1) Manufacturing costs are higher due to shorter production runs and more frequent machine changeovers caused by the lower volume items. (2) More technology is required to handle a greater variety of products. (3) There are higher inventory costs due to many SKUs. (4) It is difficult to compete costwise with limited-line manufacturers who have the advantages of specialization and economies of scale.

Advantages of the limited line. (1) The manufacturer can choose to offer only high-volume products or those with high profit margins. (2) When high-volume products are selected, it makes for lower costs through economies of scale. (3)

Products can be designed to appeal to a specific market segment or to a specific distribution channel. (4) Limited lines may have greater appeal to chain buyers looking for selected high-volume items at lower prices.

Disadvantages of the limited line. (1) Sales opportunities are lost because of items not offered. (2) It is difficult to sign up the strongest wholesalers or retailers, who often are tied to a full-line manufacturer. (3) Transportation costs are higher because of fewer items per shipment. (4) The manufacturer cannot offer coordinated sets in products such as kitchen appliances. An example of the latter is KitchenAid, a limited-line appliance manufacturer. KitchenAid is at a disadvantage when trying to get its dishwashers into new homes because developers can buy package deals of all kitchen appliances from a full-line appliance manufacturer such as General Electric.

Both full- and limited-line strategies are shown in the lawn and garden sprinkler industry matrix in Figure 16-7. *Breadth of line* (shown on the horizontal scale under the heading "product type") is made up of the types of models of sprinklers offered. *Depth of line* (vertical scale) is indicated by the heading "quality/price levels." Sprinkler quality (performance) is judged by such things as (1) maximum area of water coverage; (2) the extent to which the size and shape of water coverage can be varied; (3) whether water flow is intermittent, a feature which permits better soaking of the soil; and (4) the extent to which materials and workmanship provide trouble-free operation.

Stationary sprinklers generally carry the lowest prices; traveling sprinklers the highest; and the other three types are priced in between. However, the three price/quality levels shown for the vertical scale in Figure 16-7 are relative measures which apply to each product type. A high price for a stationary sprinkler, for example, would be less than a low price for an impact sprinkler.

It can be seen that Company A is a full-line manufacturer offering all types of the product at all price levels.* The other four manufacturers offer limited lines. B offers oscillating sprinklers only. D competes only in the low-price segments, C only in the medium segments, and O only in the high-price segments.

Line-Stretching Strategies. A limited-line business has the options of extending to a full line or something short of a full line. This can be done by *stretching* the line by breadth, by depth, or by both. It is not unusual for limited-line businesses to move toward full line without committing themselves to go all the way. Whether a limited-line business should stretch in either direction should be decided only after a careful situation analysis, a review of long-term goals, and financial analyses of the various options.

Looking again at Figure 16-7, Company B, which makes only oscillating sprinklers, could stretch by breadth into other types of sprinklers. Company C, which offers all types of sprinklers but only in the medium-price range, could stretch downward to the low-price segment, upward to the high-price segment, or both ways. If it stretched only one way, it would still have a limited line, but if it went both ways, it would become a full line. Company D, which makes only low-price sprinklers, could stretch upward to the medium- and high-price segments. Company O is an actual company that decided to stretch by depth.

---

*Except for traveling sprinklers, which generally are not available at the low price/quality level.

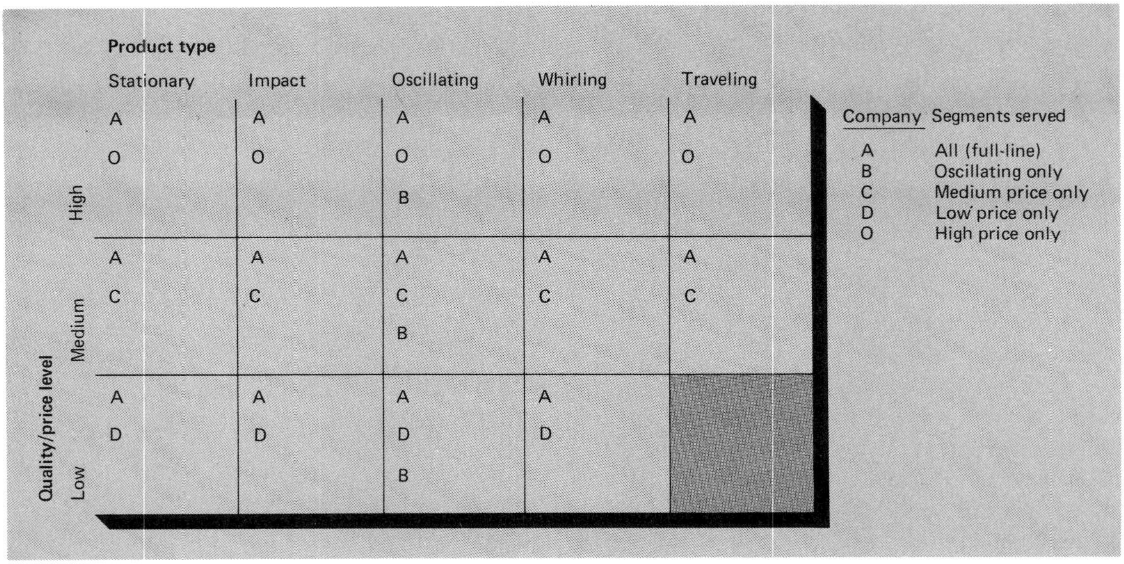

Quality/price level		Product type						Company	Segments served
		Stationary	Impact	Oscillating	Whirling	Traveling		A	All (full-line)
High		A O	A O	A O B	A O	A O		B C D O	Oscillating only Medium price only Low price only High price only
Medium		A C	A C	A C B	A C	A C			
Low		A D	A D	A D B	A D				

FIGURE 16-7. Competitive product line matrix, lawn and garden sprinklers.

Company O, one of the pioneer companies in the lawn and garden sprinkler industry, had always concentrated on the high-price/quality end of the business. Its brand, which enjoyed an excellent reputation, was distributed primarily through hardware and garden equipment channels. Following a change of company ownership, the new management undertook a thorough situation analysis which revealed (among other things): (1) the high end of the market represented the smallest and slowest growth segment; (2) while Company O ranked first in market share in the high end of the market, it was a poor second to Company A in total market share (measured in dollars); (3) for several years consumers place of purchase for sprinklers had been shifting to chains (mass merchandising, variety, food, etc.) from hardware and garden stores; and (4) chain volume sales were largely in the medium- and low-price/quality sprinklers.

Management decided to stretch its line selectively into the middle and the upper end of the low-price segments. The situation analysis had identified the *high-volume price points* for each type of sprinkler. Company O developed products to be priced at these points, avoiding the lowest half of the low-price/quality segment, which offered products below the company's minimum acceptable quality level. About two years were required to implement the line-stretching strategy, which included getting representation in chain outlets. The result? Within three years of the decision, sales had tripled. profits had doubled, and Company O was pushing Company A for market share leadership. Profits had not risen as fast as sales, because margins on the new products were lower than those on O's traditional higher-priced line.

An important reason for the success of Company O's strategy was the decision to use the company's brand name on the new models. Chains liked offering products with the quality image of Company O that could be sold at the price levels featured by the chains.

Company D's low-quality image, by contrast, could hinder this company should it try to stretch upward into the medium- or high-price segments. However, additional brands might be used to overcome this problem. To get a foothold in the high-price watch market, for example, Bulova (at the time a well-known manufacturer of popular-price watches) decided to use a different brand name, Accutron, on its new high-quality watch. Initially Accutron was featured on the face of the watch while the Bulova name was imprinted unobtrusively on the back. As the Accutron watch succeeded, Bulova gradually increased the presence of the Bulova name until finally the watch was called the Bulova Accutron. Later Bulova was able to introduce other high-priced watches, such as the Bulova Quartz watch, with Bulova as a part of the brand name.

Line-Filling Tactics. Gaps occur in a product line either because an existing void has not been filled or because new voids appear due to competitors' introductions or customers' requests for new items. Before filling a gap in the line, certain questions should be asked and answered: (1) Will the new item on its own produce a satisfactory return on investment? (2) Will it cannibalize sales from other items in the line? (3) Will it help to get orders for items presently in the line? (4) Will trade channels be willing to stock it? (5) If the gap is not one that has been created by competition, will competitors be likely to fill it if we don't? (6) How serious will it be if we don't act? The tactical decision should be made only after weighing the relevant factors.

We have described how Company O moved to a full-line status in lawn and garden sprinklers by offering each type of product in all three price/quality levels. Like other industries, the sprinkler industry also offers *assortments* of sizes and shapes in each type of product. Stationary sprinklers, for example, may be made of brass, copper, aluminum, or plastic. Different models provide different water coverage: full circle, half circle, square, or rectangle. Company O did not attempt to offer every type of item in its initial move toward a full line. Gradually, however, it added additional items to fill gaps in its product assortments.

Line-Pruning Strategy. An important aspect of maintaining a healthy product mix is getting rid of products that no longer contribute to profitable growth. It is inevitable over time that some products will turn to deadwood and require pruning. Yet few companies have organized programs or personnel regularly assigned to this unpopular and difficult task. People tend to view it as an undertaker's job—necessary but unpleasant. The American-Standard case (6) in Part Three described how it took a profitability crisis and a change of top management to jolt the company into a product-pruning program.

One of the difficulties with product deletion is that full cost data by individual product are rarely accurate. Generally there is no good way of allocating pooled expenses such as advertising, personal selling, distribution, and overhead.[32] But even after agreement has been reached as to the items not earning their way, getting product deletion decisions is still difficult. There are three common reasons why.

The product defenders. Every product, no matter how low its sales or profits, seems to have one or more defenders vigorously opposed to deletion. It may be a salesperson, wholesaler, dealer, customer, or company executive. Executives of one company had difficulty getting the company chairman to agree to closing the last remaining plant still producing the company's original, but by then unprofitable, product. He had been through the glory years with this product and could not bring himself to accept its inevitable demise.

It helps to sell the profitable products. This argument may be valid, but often turns out to be exaggerated. In the American-Standard case (7) in Part Three, the plumbing sales department argued against dropping the unprofitable stainless steel sink line because it helped to get wholesalers to carry the balance of the product line.

It contributes to overhead. This argument maintains that the product contributes to the profitability of the balance of the line by absorbing overhead that otherwise would be charged to the other products. While this can be a valid argument, it usually is not a justification for retaining dying products. It is better to transfer the resources tied up in these products to present or new products with profitable growth potentials. Ideally, deletion should be made when incremental costs exceed incremental revenues. Unfortunately, this point is often passed before action is taken.[33]

A number of approaches to product pruning have been suggested.[34] Most call for an analysis not unlike the *situation analysis* described in Chapter 9. Once it is suspected that a product needs pruning (usually because of low sales and/or profits), the following steps should be taken: make a forecast of sales and profits for 3 to 5 years; estimate the planning gap between forecast and goals; identify the reasons for unsatisfactory performance; and search for alternate solutions to the problem.

Possible solutions might be to raise the price, improve the product, improve the marketing effort, or milk the product for its cash flow as long as possible. If none of these solutions is feasible, management must make the difficult decision to prune. It is possible, however, that an unprofitable product will be retained because it helps with closing sales on profitable products. Or it may be retained for its contribution to overhead until it can be replaced with profitable products.

New Product Strategies. There can be no doubting the importance of new products. Infusions are needed to offset the profit falloff that occurs when older products enter the mature and decline phases of their life cycles. And they are needed to provide the future stars and cash cows of the product portfolio. Consequently, most companies conduct regular searches for new products from both internal and external sources.

New products can range from unique innovations to minor modifications of existing products. How a company perceives its new product goals and how it goes about reaching them is reflected in its new product policies, strategies, organization, and procedures. The subject is of such importance that we devote the next chapter to new product planning and development.

BRAND STRATEGIES

Major brand strategies include the questions of whether to use individual or family brands, or both; whether to extend existing brands; where to position new brands; and whether to reposition old brands.

Individual Brand Strategy

With this strategy each product has its own brand name. Procter & Gamble, for example, has individual brand names for its laundry cleaning products including Tide, Cheer, Ivory Snow, and Oxydol. The major advantage of this strategy is that a company may increase its overall market share by having its own brands compete for share with one another as well as with competitors' brands. The major disadvantage is that high promotional costs are required to build and maintain separate brands. Many companies feel they cannot afford this strategy. It has proved to be a profitable alternative for P&G, however. Despite large advertising expenses (over $100 million in 1980 for thirteen laundry cleaning brands, over $40 million for four dishwashing products, and $46 million for six bath soaps[35]), P&G continued to increase its net earnings.

Individual brands can also be used to target marketing efforts to different market segments. This is one of the market-share-gaining strategies followed by P&G and others. Anheuser-Busch, for example, competes for the beer market in the price/quality segments with its Michelob and Budweiser brands, in the low-calorie segment with its Bud Light and Michelob Light brands, in the popular-price segment with Busch, and in the import segment with Wurzburger-Hofbrau.

Family Brand Strategies

Family brand strategies may be used to sell all company products under the corporate brand name or to apply different brand names to different categories of products. Examples of the former include Travelers insurance, Campbell soups, and General Electric consumer, industrial, and service products. A company may also use individual product brand names along with the family brand, such as the GE Light & Easy™ Self Clean™ Steam & Dry Iron.

The second type of family brand strategy is illustrated by General Foods, which applies family brands to categories of products such as Post cereals, Jell-O desserts, and Birds Eye frozen fruits and vegetables. Armstrong World Industries uses brand names for product categories, but under the Armstrong family umbrella, for example, Armstrong Solarium no-wax flooring. Companies using family brands for categories may or may not use the corporate name. Armstrong does, while General Foods places the GF trademark in a secondary position to the family brand.

The major advantages of a family brand strategy are that (1) the combined promotion of all products in the family contributes to strengthening the brand name, and (2) the strengthened brand name rubs off on each product in the family. The second advantage is particularly useful when introducing new products. The principal disadvantage of a family brand strategy is that it is more difficult to differentiate individual products of the family than it is to differentiate products sold under individual brand names. It is for this reason that GE uses product brands along with the corporate family brand.

The corporate family brand can be a disadvantage when offering products with different prices and qualities. This drawback can be overcome partially, at least, by using different family brands for different price categories and playing down (or not showing at all) the corporate brand. Automobile companies have long used family brands for different price/quality categories. While the owner knows the identity of the company that made the car, brand identification on the car often does not reveal the corporate or division name.

Combination Brand Strategies

Diversification has forced companies to reexamine their brand strategies. Many companies now use both family brand and individual brand strategies. Gillette, for example, features the corporate brand name on its traditional razors and blades; it applies the Papermate family brand to its writing instruments; and it uses individual brand names on toiletries such as Right Guard deodorant and Toni home permanents. Eastman Kodak applies the Kodak brand to its large family of photographic products, but uses individual or category brands for its industrial products such as Kodel polyesters and Tenox antioxidants.

A brand's image is often the deciding factor as to whether to apply it to other products. "Kodak" would probably be of little help in selling industrial chemicals. And Johnson & Johnson's famous Band-Aid brand is so closely associated with the product that it would be difficult to transfer it to the company's other health care products. On the other hand, the well-known Noxema brand readily transfers to other skin products such as shaving cream and liquid skin cleanser. Yet there are no absolute rules. We even see some companies applying a brand name associated with one product category to entirely different categories. Bic, known for its low-priced, throwaway pens, applied the Bic brand to its new lines of lighters and razors (thereby making "Bic" a corporate family brand name.) Although the Bic product lines are quite different, the common denominators are disposability and low price.

Brand Extension Strategies

Bic also represents an example of brand extension. Brand extensions occur when (1) individual brands are extended to create a family brand, (2) related products are added to an existing family brand, or (3) an individual or family brand is extended to unrelated products. Number 1 is illustrated by the extension of the Jell-O brand from a gelatin dessert to a line of desserts. Number 2 is illustrated by Cheseborough-Pond's extension of its classic Vaseline petroleum jellies into Vaseline hair tonics, baby oils, baby oil wipes, and skin lotion. Number 3 is illustrated by the Bic example and also by Stouffer, which extended from restaurants to frozen foods to hotels.

The flat economy of the early 1980s created new interest in the strategy of brand extensions into related products, by extending an individual brand or a family brand. With corporate emphasis on cost control, the brand extension into related products has two principal advantages: lower product and market development costs; and lower risk, since a brand extension utilizes existing internal and external company know-how. The vice president of a major packaged goods company emphasized lower risk when he stated, "Our philosophy is to stick with what we do best; we have learned to stay away from businesses with which we are unfamiliar."[36] Even P&G, which historically has favored individual brands, extended the Crest brand to include a gel toothpaste.[37]

Positioning Strategies

Brand positioning is a strategic management decision with respect to where a brand (or product) is to compete in the market environment—where it wants to carve out its market niche. The decision utilizes the concepts of market segmentation and product differentiation. Which price, age, or other segment shall the brand compete for? And how shall it be differentiated from competitive brands? Approaches to positioning range from (1) market research of consumers' preferences (for product attributes, for example) and of consumers' perceptions of brands on the market, to (2) the intuition of the creative copywriter (whose ideas may or may not be subjected to advertising copy testing).

Preference and perceptual mapping. This research approach can assist management with its positioning decision. An example of mapping is shown in Figure 16-8. The Chicago beer market was studied for nine brands of beer on each of thirty-five attributes.[38] The researchers found that the two dimensions shown on the matrix (price/quality and relative lightness or mildness*) accounted for approximately 90 percent of the discrimination among images of the nine brands. The circles represent clusters of ideal points of preference by different groups of consumers. Circle size represents the relative size of the clusters. The location of each brand indicates consumers' perceptions of where the brand falls on the two dimensions. Miller, for example, is perceived as a relatively light (i.e., mild) beer and relatively far out on the premium-quality/price scale. Presumably the closer a brand is to a larger circle, the better its market position. The researchers saw an opportunity for a new brand, which would be on the heavy side and approximately neutral in price/quality.

While preference and perceptual mapping provides a basis for brand position-

*Lightness in this study did not refer to low calorie beer.

FIGURE 16-8. Preference/perception mapping—Chicago beer market. *Source:* Richard M. Johnson, "Market Segmentation: A Strategic Management Tool," *Journal of Marketing Research,* February 1971, pp. 13-18.

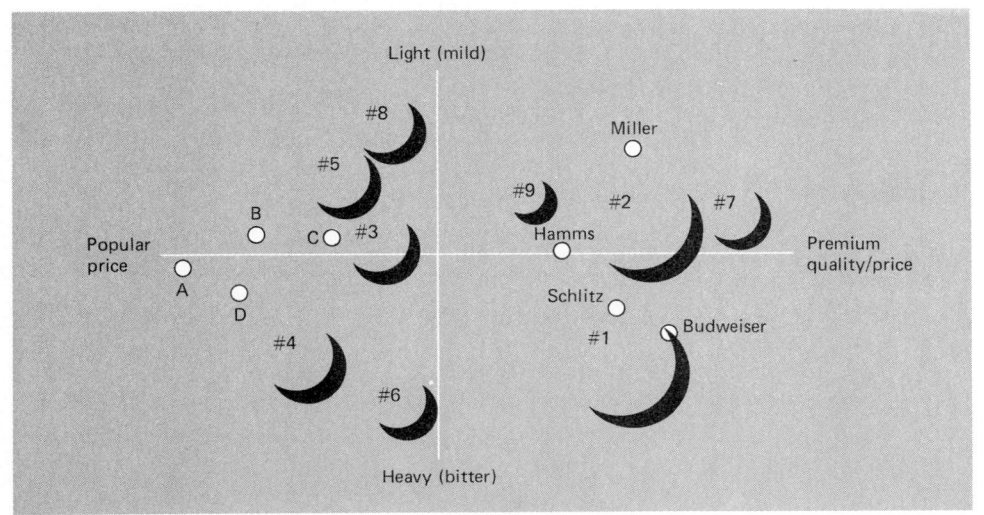

CHAPTER 16
MANAGING THE
PRODUCT LINE

ing, a company should consider all relevant factors before deciding overall brand strategy. A brand may seem to be well-positioned, for example, yet not do well because of competitors' stronger positions in market share, distribution, and expenditures for promotion. Clearly, positioning is only one aspect of marketing strategy.[39]

Repositioning Strategies

It is not unusual for a brand to be repositioned as a result of changes in competitive and market situations that appear in a mapping study. Repositioning involves changing the markets' perceptions of a product or brand so that the product or brand can compete more effectively in its present market or in other market segments. Changing market perception may require changes in the tangible product or in its selling price. Often, however, the new differentiation is accomplished mainly by a change in the promotional message. J&J's Baby Shampoo, Avis rental cars, and Marlboro cigarettes are examples of the latter.

Johnson and Johnson repositioned its Baby Shampoo from a product for the baby to one for the whole family after discovering that adults also liked the fact that it did not irritate the eyes. The gentleness of the product also was found to appeal to those people who washed their hair frequently. Avis decided to make a virtue of its perennial second-place position in rental cars by advertising that it had to "try harder" to please because it was number 2. A famous case of repositioning involved Marlboro cigarettes. Marlboro's image was changed from a lady's to a man's cigarette by consistent advertising showing the brand being smoked by rugged cowboys.

Some grocery product brands have been repositioned from medium price to low price in an effort to limit the inroads of generic products. Ralston-Purina, for example, repositioned Mainstay as a low-price dog food.[40] Beer brand A in Figure 16-8 may be a candidate for repositioning, because its image places it farthest from any cluster of consumer preferences. Repositioning this beer probably would require changes in product quality, price, packaging, and advertising.

A brand should be analyzed for possible repositioning whenever it begins to slip in sales growth because of a maturing market or a decrease in market share. It should be considered even for a healthy brand when it is suspected that buyer habits or preferences are changing.

SUMMARY

A basic company strategy should offer products that fill the needs and wants of selected market segments that the company is qualified to serve. To implement this requires continuous efforts directed to improving the existing product line and developing new products.

A product is more than a physical object. It represents the total offering of benefits and values, both tangible and intangible, as seen by the buyer. If the offering promises to fulfill the buyer's needs and wants, the potential for exchange is created. The product can be a physical object, a service, an idea, or some combination of these.

Product differentiation exists when a product or brand is perceived by buyers as being different from that of competitors. One way of differentiating is to augment the product by offering features or services that are beyond what buyers might normally expect. Traditional attributes that are considered by producers when developing products include functions, quality, price, service, design, packaging, and warranties, although attributes are not limited to these.

Brands can be either manufacturers' brands or private brands. The latter are most commonly products produced by others for sale under the brand names of wholesalers or retail chains. Both manufacturers' and private brands compete for market share against nonbranded, low-price, generic products.

The product life cycle and product portfolios provide conceptual frameworks for developing product/marketing/business strategies. Like living organisms, products are born and they grow, mature, and die. Different product and marketing strategies are required for each phase of the cycle. Product portfolio models assist multiproduct companies in classifying their products into categories which call for different strategies and different levels of resource support. Although portfolio models vary in their numbers of categories and in the factors used for classification, many companies, in the final analysis, assign their products to categories requiring growth, maintenance, or harvest/divest strategies. While the categories' names suggest broad strategies, specific product strategies will vary depending upon the situation of the product and the company.

Product strategies were treated under the headings of "Product Mix" and "Brand" strategies. Product mix strategies in turn were classified by present products and new products. Present product strategies dealt with issues such as maintaining *competitiveness*; whether to be a product leader or follower; whether to offer a full or limited-line; whether to use line stretching; and whether and when to prune. New product strategies are covered in the next chapter. However, present and new product objectives and strategies should be coordinated, since they are part and parcel of the broad strategy of filling the needs and wants of target markets.

Brand strategies raise questions of whether to follow individual, family, or combination brand strategies; whether to emphasize brand extensions; how to position new products and brands; and whether or when to reposition existing brands. Brand strategies should be tied in closely with present and new product objectives and strategies.

QUESTIONS

1. What are the three major product responsibilities of marketing management?
2. Define the following terms: product, product differentiation, parity products, augmented product, product mix.
3. Name the six traditional product attributes that most manufacturers consider fundamental.
4. Name three steps a manufacturer must take to legally protect its trademarks, brand names, and trade names.
5. Name the four stages of the product life cycle. What are the strategic implications of the product life cycle?
6. Name the four quadrants of the BCG product portfolio grid, beginning with stars. Explain how these can be used to form a product strategy.
7. What are the advantages and disadvantages of a full-line versus a limited-line strategy?
8. What are the advantages and disadvantages of an individual versus a family brand strategy?

9. What is meant by brand positioning? How can preference/perceptual mapping be used to help in positioning or repositioning a brand?

REFERENCES

1. Robert D. Buzzell and Frederick D. Wiersema, "Successful Share Building Strategies," *Harvard Business Review*, Jan.–Feb. 1981, pp. 135-144. Copyright © 1981 by the President and Fellows of Harvard College; all rights reserved.
2. *Advertising Age*, Jan. 25, 1982, p. 84.
3. Adapted from Theodore Levitt, "Marketing Success Through Differentiation of Anything," *Harvard Business Review*, Jan.–Feb. 1980, pp. 83-91. Copyright © 1980 by the President and Fellows of Harvard College; all rights reserved.
4. Ralph S. Alexander, *Marketing Definitions*, American Marketing Association, Chicago, 1960, p. 18.
5. For more on product design, see Edgar A. Pessemier, *Product Management Strategy and Organization*, Wiley, New York, 1977, chap. 5; Richard S. Latham, "The Role of the Industrial Designer in Product and Package," in Victor P. Buell (ed.), *Handbook of Modern Marketing*, McGraw-Hill, New York, 1970; Seymour W. Herwald, "Building the Prototype Model," in *Developing a Product Strategy*, AMA Management Report No. 39, American Management Association, 1959; D. A. Saporito, "New Product Success Through Industrial Design," in Brand, Gruber and Co. (eds.), *The Professionals Look at New Products*, Bureau of Business Research, The University of Michigan, 1968.
6. For more on warranties and handling consumer complaints, see C. L. Kendall and Frederick A. Russ, "Warranty and Complaint Policies: An Opportunity for Marketing Management," *Journal of Marketing*, April 1975, pp. 36-43; also Laurence P. Feldman, "New Legislation and the Prospects for Real Warranty Reform," *Journal of Marketing*, July 1976, pp. 41-47.
7. From Thomas C. Collins, "Selecting and Establishing Brand Names," in Victor P. Buell (ed.), *Handbook of Modern Marketing*, McGraw-Hill, New York, 1970, p. 13-70.
8. Abstracted from Sidney A. Diamond, "Establishing and Protecting Trademarks," in ibid., pp. 17-21 and 17-22.
9. Collins, op. cit., p. 13-75.
10. *Business Week*, Oct. 9, 1978, p. 137.
11. Stewart H. Rewoldt, James D. Scott, and Martin W. Warshaw, *Introduction to Marketing Management*, rev. ed., Richard D. Irwin, Homewood, Ill., 1973, p. 446.
12. From studies by Ken Kono and Michael D. Bernacchi, reported in the *Marketing News*, Aug. 22, 1980, pp. 6, 7.
13. *Advertising Age*, Feb. 22, 1980, p. 7.
14. From *The Nielsen Researcher*, no. 3, 1979. Copyright © 1979 by A. C. Nielsen Co. Reproduced by permission.
15. *Advertising Age*, Feb. 22, 1980, p. 7.
16. Ibid.
17. Chester R. Wasson, "How Predictable Are Fashion and Other Product Life Cycles," *Journal of Marketing*, vol. 32, July 1968, pp. 36–43.
18. A two-wheeled vehicle similar to a bicycle except that pedaling is supplemented by a low-powered motor.
19. See the 1973 annual report of The Continental Can Co.; also "How Continental Can is Packaging Growth," *Business Week*, Mar. 3, 1975, pp. 40-41.
20. "Goodrich's Cash Cow Starts to Deliver," *Business Week*, Nov. 14, 1977, p. 77.
21. Theodore Levitt, "Exploit the Product Life Cycle," *Harvard Business Review*, Nov.–Dec. 1965, pp. 81-94. Copyright © 1965 by the President and Fellows of Harvard College; all rights reserved.

22. George S. Day, "The Product Life Cycle: Analysis and Applications Issues," *Journal of Marketing*, fall 1981, p. 65.
23. Gerald J. Tellis and C. Merle Crawford, "An Evolutionary Approach to Product Growth Theory," *Journal of Marketing*, fall 1981, pp. 125-131.
24. Yoram Wind and Vijay Mahajan, "Designing Product and Business Portfolios," *Harvard Business Review*, Jan.–Feb. 1981, p. 155. Copyright © 1981 by the President and Fellows of Harvard College; all rights reserved.
25. Richard G. Hamermesh and Steven B. Silk, "How to Compete in Stagnant Industries," *Harvard Business Review*, Sept.–Oct. 1979, p. 167. Copyright © 1979 by the President and Fellows of Harvard College; all rights reserved.
26. Richard G. Hamermesh, M. J. Anderson, Jr., and J. E. Harris, "Strategies for Low Market Share Businesses," *Harvard Business Review*, May–June 1978, pp. 99-102. Copyright © 1978 by the President and Fellows of Harvard College; all rights reserved.
27. Herbert H. Woodward, "Management Strategies for Small Companies," *Harvard Business Review*, Jan.–Feb. 1976, pp. 113-121. Copyright © 1976 by the President and Fellows of Harvard College; all rights reserved.
28. David S. Hopkins, *Business Strategies for Problem Products*, The Conference Board, New York, 1977, p. 47.
29. Ibid., p. 46.
30. Phillippe Haspeslagh, "Portfolio Planning: Uses and Limits," *Harvard Busines Review*, Jan.–Feb. 1982, p. 60. Copyright © 1982 by the President and Fellows of Harvard College; all rights reserved.
31. Buzzell and Wiersema, op. cit., p. 138.
32. For approaches to dealing with cost allocation, see Martin I. Isenberg, "Dissecting for Profits," *Lybrand Journal*, vol. 49, no. 2, 1968, pp. 2-10; Frank H. Mossman, Paul M. Fischer, and W. J. E. Crissy, "New Approaches to Analyzing Marketing Profitability," *Journal of Marketing*, April 1974, pp. 43-48; and Paul W. Hamelman and Edward M. Mazze, "Improving Product Abandonment Decisions," *Journal of Marketing*, April 1972, pp. 20-26.
33. Walter J. Talley, Jr., "Profiting from the Declining Product," *Business Horizons*, spring 1964, pp. 77-84.
34. For an analysis of six approaches, see Parker M. Worthing, "Improving Product Deletion Decision Making," *MSU Business Topics*, summer 1975, pp. 29-38.
35. *Advertising Age*, Sept. 10, 1981, p. 124.
36. Victor P. Buell, *Organizing for Marketing/Advertising Success*, Association of National Advertisers, New York, 1982, p. 21.
37. *Wall Street Journal*, Jan. 26, 1982, p. 37.
38. Richard M. Johnson, "Market Segmentation: A Strategic Management Tool," *Journal of Marketing Research*, February 1971, pp. 13-18.
39. John P. Maggard, "Positioning Revisited," *Journal of Marketing*, January 1976, pp. 63-66.
40. *Advertising Age*, Jan. 25, 1982, p. 84.

CHAPTER 17

New Product Planning and Development

Marketing management's major product responsibilities are (1) to manage the existing product line to achieve short-range marketing objectives and (2) to add new products to keep the line competitive and the business growing over the longer term. We will discuss the second of these responsibilities in this chapter.

New products are the lifeblood of a business. A study of 148 companies by the Conference Board, Inc.[1] found on the average that 15 percent of their current sales volume came from products introduced during the previous five years; the range was from zero to over 50 percent. Staple, commodity businesses introduced fewer new products than specialty product businesses. The median number of products introduced during the previous five years was eight for industrial goods and six for consumer goods companies. The number per company ranged from one to hundreds. Greater dependence on new products over the next five years was expected by two-thirds of the companies.

Having new products ready for introduction when they are needed to maintain a consistent profitable growth record is not easy. Most large companies have ongoing programs for both internal product development and external acquisition. Yet, even with the best of programs, they worry about having *successful* new products when needed. Luck can play a part as well as skill and effort.

THE NEW PRODUCT

There is no universally accepted definition of "new product." One market-oriented view is that a new product is any product that does not duplicate an existing market offering.[2] Companies, on the other hand, see new products more from an internal orientation. Many consider a new product as anything new to the company, including revisions of existing products. This has been confirmed in a study of 700 companies by the management consulting firm of Booz-Allen & Hamilton (BA&H).[3] The total product introductions of all 700 companies during the previous five years were classified as follows:

10 percent—New to the world

19 percent—New product lines (i.e., new to the companies)

26 percent—Additions to existing product lines

26 percent—Revisions/improvements to existing products

11 percent—Cost reductions

7 percent—Repositioning

For our purposes we will consider a new product as follows:

> A *new product* is any product or brand that is new to the company, irrespective of its degree of newness to the market.

This definition encompasses the first three categories above (totaling 55 percent of the introductions), but excludes the last three categories (44 percent). We should remember that the term "new product" has different meanings for different people.

NEW PRODUCT FAILURES

Studies have shown wide differences in new product failure rates, with some running as high as 80 percent. The differences appear to be due to the way "new product" is defined and what is considered success or failure.

Defining a successful new product as one that "met management's original expectations for it in all important respects," the Conference Board study found that 37 percent of the companies consider their results "highly acceptable" and 52 percent consider them "disappointing but still acceptable."[4] (See Table 17-1.) Defining success as having "met or exceeded objectives outlined prior to its introduction," the BA&H study found that companies classified 65 percent of their new product introductions as successful.[5] Both studies, however, suggest that new product development remains a problem for the majority of companies.

Reasons for Failures

Companies report that the most common causes of new product failure are: *poor market research* (the misreading of customers' needs, too little field testing, and overly optimistic forecasts of market needs and acceptance); *technical problems* (problems growing out of design and production); and *poor timing* (such as because the market changes before the new product can be introduced or the company enters the market too early or too late in the product life cycle). Other reasons cited were inadequate top management involvement; assigning inadequate resources to market development; getting too far away from the company's technical or marketing expertise; underestimating competitive reaction; underestimating the diffusion rate (the time it takes for a new product idea to be communicated and accepted); and inadequate knowledge of costs.[6]

Marketing Note 17-1 describes how Procter & Gamble nearly failed with its entry into the disposable-diaper market. This account illustrates the importance not only of having the right product, but also of having good marketing plans that include all elements of the marketing mix.

Reducing Failure Rates

The new product process is costly. It requires substantial investments in finding and screening ideas, market research and business analysis, technical research and

TABLE 17-1
Acceptability of New-Product Success Rate (Figures are percents)

Management Feeling Regarding Company's Relative Rate of Success	Total, All Reporting Companies	Companies Selling Primarily to		Companies Whose Past Success Rate Was*			
		Industrial Markets	Consumer Markets	Much Above Average	Somewhat Above Average	Somewhat Below Average	Much Below Average
Highly acceptable	37	33	44	79	42	15	5
Disappointing, but still acceptable	52	57	44	21	53	73	67
Unacceptably low	11	10	12	—	5	12	28
	100	100	100	100	100	100	100

*The three quartile values, which divide the distribution into four equal parts, were used to categorize companies' success rates during the past five years. "Much above average" thus means higher than the third quartile value; and "average" refers, of course, to the median.

Source: David S. Hopkins, *New Products Winners and Losers*, The Conference Board, New York, 1980, p. 7.

development, testing, market introduction, market development, and management time in planning, coordination, and control. Since many new products fail, there is obvious risk in introducing a new product. But, of course, there is the greater risk of declining company profits if successful new products are not found.

Because some companies have better records than others, there are things we can learn from the more successful ones. No company turns out only winners. The objective is to reduce the failures and increase the percentage of winners. Let's now look at how successful companies utilize strategies, organization, and procedures to improve their new product performance.

NEW PRODUCT STRATEGIES

A company can obtain new products from its own *internal* research and development or from *external* sources such as acquisitions. A basic strategic question is whether to use one source or the other, or both. The 3-M Company has obtained most of its long-term, steady growth via a strategy of internal new product development. ITT, on the other hand, became one of the world's largest companies (with over 200 businesses) primarily through acquisition of other companies. No one can depend entirely on acquisitions for growth, however, since the acquired businesses will need internal R&D support if they are to remain healthy. Many large firms follow internal and external development strategies simultaneously.

Figure 17-1 shows several types of new product strategies under the broad headings of internal and external development strategies. Since the major emphasis of this chapter is on internal development, we will not dwell on the external approaches. We will, however, describe briefly the three external strategies listed in Figure 17-1 and note their advantages and disadvantages as substitutes for, or supplements to, internal development.

MARKETING NOTE 17-1

Developing the Pampers Disposable Diaper:
How a Skillful Marketer Nearly Failed with a New Product

Although Pampers is one of Procter & Gamble's most talked about successes, it was a failure originally. The idea was generated in the Advertising Department after observing the way disposable tissues had largely replaced handkerchiefs. The challenge of P&G was whether it could develop a disposable diaper that was better than cloth diapers and, if it could, whether parents' diapering habits could be changed. Disposable diapers up to that time had not sold well; they were not absorbent enough, tore easily, chafed the baby's skin, and were used mainly when traveling.

A Brand Group in the Advertising Department, working on new products, was assigned the job of coordinating the development process. The job of creating a workable product was assigned to the Product Research and Development Department. The Market Research Department carried out studies to learn the average baby's size; the average daily diaperings; and whether the diaper should be perfumed and, if so, with what scent. Manufacturing and Sales were consulted at different times.

The product developed by R&D had these advantages over cloth diapers: for the mother it was disposable (even flushable) and eliminated daily washing; for the baby it meant dry skin because of a top sheet which allowed moisture to pass to the absorbent material underneath; it minimized leakage, and it contained a plastic back sheet which eliminated the need for plastic pants.

The challenge to the Brand Group was to get the new product accepted by mothers. With the help of the advertising agency, the brand name, package, price, advertising, media plan, and the sales promotion plan were developed. However, after nine months in test market the product was considered a failure. Analysis revealed these reasons:

- It was *overpriced* in relation to cloth diapers.
- The *package* did not hold a large enough supply of diapers.
- *Sales promotion* was inadequate to reach the continual stream of new parents using diapers for the first time.
- The *advertising* did not generate parent involvement.
- There was an unsolved retail problem of getting the right *location* within the store and adequate *shelf space* for a bulky product.

Corrective actions taken were: (1) reducing the price by narrowing margins, which, it was hoped, would be offset by high volume; (2) increasing the contents of the package from a 1-day to a 4½-day supply; (3) achieving a high rate of trial by supplying new mothers with samples as they left the hospital; (4) changing to "slice-of-life" commercials (after testing twelve advertising strategies and executions), which out-scored the original advertising by 50 percent; and (5) convincing food chain managements to rebuild the baby food section to provide space for stacking and display of Pampers.

With these modifications Pampers was placed in new test markets where it captured 10 percent of all diaper changes, which amounted in retail dollars to more than half of all baby food sales. Later when national distribution was completed, and after the entry of competitors, disposable diapers accounted for about half of all diaper changes. Leading in market share, P&G continued to make improvements in fit, containment, absorbency, and fastening (using tape instead of safety pins). The company had created a successful new business by offering parents a better solution to an old problem.

Source: Abstracted from a brand management recruiting presentation by the Procter & Gamble Company.

External Development Strategies

Part of the appeal of acquisition of other companies is that it is a quick way to add product lines. Other external sources—patents, licenses, and new product

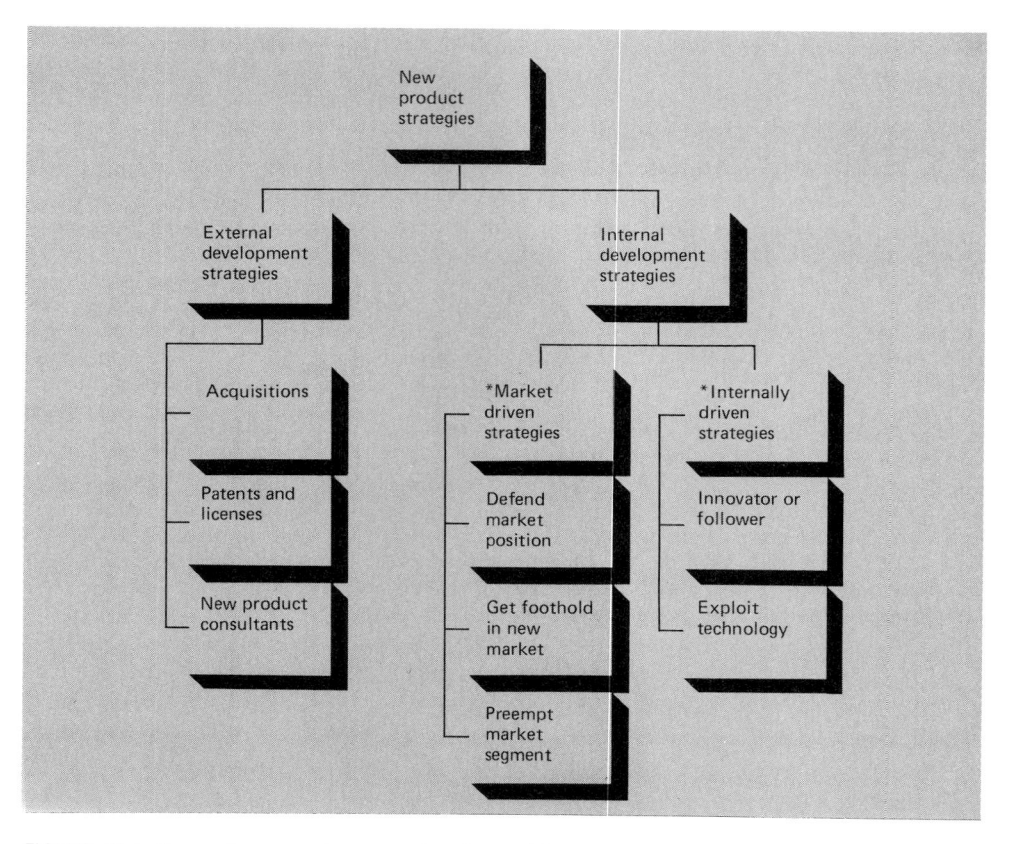

FIGURE 17-1. Types of new product strategies. *Source:* Market-driven and internally driven strategies* are adapted from *New Products, Best Practices—Today and Tomorrow,* Booz-Allen & Hamilton, Inc. New York, 1982, p.8.

consultants—generally take longer and yield new products one at a time. Although these sources are external to the company, they usually are considered as supplements to the internal development process.

Acquisition. Acquisition strategies range from the broadening of a company's regular product line to complete product diversification. Acquisition of an established business usually is a less risky way of acquiring new products than through internal development. The financial records and market position of the company under consideration for acquisition can be verified beforehand, whereas one can never be sure how the internally developed product will turn out. Though a premium based on estimated future earnings will have to be paid for the new company, it will contribute earnings to its new parent almost immediately. By contrast, profits from acquired patents or patent rights may be delayed while technical development is undertaken to bring the patented product to market-ready condition.

There are some disadvantages to acquisitions. One is the aforementioned high purchase price. In the competitive bidding that goes on for companies, sometimes too high a price is paid. More serious, however, is the long period usually needed for the acquired company to adapt to the parent company's management philosophies and systems. The worst problem occurs when acquisitions turn out to be mistakes. Eventually, mistakes have to be sold at a loss or liquidated. The American-Standard case (6) in Part Three revealed how corporate indigestion resulted from too many problem acquisitions. There is also the possibility of government antitrust action. The antitrust laws discourage acquisitions that lead toward monopolization in an industry. While the legal issues in each case can be complex, the general rule is that an already dominant company in an industry should not be allowed to acquire another business if the result would be to give it more market share and thereby lessen competition.

Whereas internal product development involves many people and functions, acquisitions may be handled by one person or by a small department reporting to a high-level executive. Acquisitions may not be the result of planning or of an organized search. Often they appear suddenly in the form of opportunities to be seized or rejected quickly before competing acquirers have acted. Acquisition goals and predetermined criteria can help in evaluating acquisition opportunities when they occur, however. Careful acquisition searches may also be made for businesses that will help fulfill preplanned diversification goals. Yet the handling of acquisitions does not require the same across-the-board organizational and procedural planning and coordination that are essential for internal new product development success.

Patents and Licenses. Patents may be bought from inventors who do not have the resources to develop and market their inventions or who prefer to concentrate on inventing. Or patents may be purchased from companies with patented discoveries which lie outside of their own business interests. While looking for a better water valve, American-Standard's research laboratory discovered an improved gas valve. Since it was not in the gas-control business, American-Standard sold the patent to a company which produced valves for gas pipeline transmissions. This valve became a new product for the gas valve company.

Licenses are the rights to the use of the patent of others through payment of royalty fees to the owners.[7] These usually are voluntary arrangements, but they also can result from court action—as was the case when Du Pont was ordered to share its nylon patents with others. Licenses often are available to companies that manufacture and sell similar products in countries where the patent holder does not operate. Glasrock, a producer of porous pen nibs (points), sold to Bic the patent rights to manufacture the nibs in Bic's U.S. plants. Bic used the nibs in a pen named the Bic Banana.

Because attractive patent and licensing opportunities appear somewhat erratically, a company cannot rely on them to supply all of its new product needs. Nevertheless, a strategy of consistently seeking new inventions and the rights to the use of new developments usually will produce opportunities that the company might not otherwise have had. Richardson-Vicks' highly successful skin emollient Oil of Olay came from acquiring the rights to the product. Xerox's success in copiers was due to its acquisition of the rights to the xerographic process. Hoover's original entry into vacuum cleaners in the United States and into washing machines abroad came via patents purchased from inventors.

New Product Consultants. Outside consultants serve as sources for creative new product ideas and for products developed in their own laboratories. Companies may contract with them to perform different tasks such as idea generation, taking a product from the idea stage through the development stage, advising on the application of new techniques, or operating on a regular basis as an extension of the company's own internal research and development department. Booz-Allen & Hamilton, Arthur D. Little, and Battelle Memorial Institute provide a full range of services. Other firms such as Kahn/Larsen/Walsh, Inc. do not provide technical development; rather they turn over new product profiles to the client's R&D department. This firm was responsible for products such as Swift's Soup Starter, Kimberly-Clark's Lightdays feminine pads, and Mobil's Hefty trash bag. **Marketing Note 17-2** presents a case history on how Soup Starter was developed.

The advantage of external consultants is that they supplement the company's creative and technical resources without adding to fixed costs. The disadvantage is the high fees they charge; the fees, however, can become unimportant when a new product developed by the consultant has a high payoff for the client.

Internal Development Strategies

Figure 17-1 shows internal development broken down into market-driven strategies and internally driven strategies. The BA&H study reported these as the most frequent strategic roles filled by the successful new products of the companies surveyed.[8]

MARKETING NOTE 17-2

New-Product Development: Homemade Soup Starter

The success of Hamburger Helper prompted Swift to examine the potential for new packaged dinner mixes. Kahn felt that while the category was already oversaturated with Hamburger Helper imitations, the consumers' continuing shift away from planned meals to quick, informal one-dish meals indicated a real need for a new generation of packaged dinner products. The specs we developed for a hypothetical new packaged dinner product were:

1. To deliver "real meal" satisfaction rather than make a lesser version of a familiar well-liked dish; i.e., Hamburger Helper makes a skillet version of lasagna that is much inferior to real.
2. To use meats other than hamburger. (Most frequent complaint about hamburger dinner mixes is that "there is nothing to sink your teeth into.")
3. To avoid "boxed dinner" form and imagery. Boxed dinners generically are considered highly artificial, poor-tasting, nonnutritious.

Kahn felt that hearty meat and chicken soups were among the types of end dishes that would meet all of the consumer specs. And the consumer was serving 8 billion portions per year of homemade meat soup as a dinner main course.

Homemade Soup Starter allows the housewife to add her own beef or chicken to make two quarts of hearty homemade-type soup. It's called a "starter" rather than a mix to avoid boxed dinner imagery. It's as the ad says: "everything you need for homemade soup 'cept the meat!"

Soup Starter is a $35mm brand.

Source: Courtesy of Kahn/Larsen/Walsh, Inc.

Market-Driven Strategies. These are new product strategies that grow out of market- and product-planning processes: the annual marketing plan *situation analysis* or product portfolio, line stretching, and brand-extension analyses. Three strategies are discussed in order of their reported frequency of use.

Defend a market position. A strong market share position is a business asset that must be defended against competitive onslaughts. Strong market position usually is the outcome of a company having followed good product and marketing strategies over the years. Yet aggressive actions by competitors or structural market change may force the leader to reevaluate its strategies. New products often are chosen as a part of the defensive strategy.

Witness the response of the big three auto makers (GM, Ford, and Chrysler) to the inroads of foreign cars into the U.S. market. Imports had risen from 6 percent of U.S. car sales in 1965 to over 21 percent by 1973, largely due to growing demand for smaller, more fuel-efficient cars. Yet it was not until after the oil crisis of 1974 that the big three seriously began to defend their eroding market positions by designing lighter, more fuel-efficient cars of their own (a decision reinforced by a federal law requiring the companies to attain higher average fuel efficiencies by specified dates). By the time the U.S. auto companies had their new cars available for sale, imports were approaching a 30 percent market share. This experience shows that even large, powerful companies can lose market positions to competitors who offer products that better correspond to changing market preferences.

The National Broadcasting Company held the leading share of network television viewers during the 1960s and much of the 1970s, followed closely by the Columbia Broadcasting System. Third place American Broadcasting Company took over the network leadership position in the late 1970s by offering new programming (*products*) with greater appeal for viewers. Both NBC and CBS fought back vigorously with new programs of their own, and the leadership positions changed from quarter to quarter. During the 1980s all three of the major networks will be defending their positions against the new competition from cable networks which are winning market share by offering specialized programming.

IBM, for much of its history, held the dominant position in electric and electronic computers by virtue of its leadership in large (mainframe) computers. However, the mainframe share of the computer market has been dropping from 83 percent in 1975 to an expected 36 percent in 1985.[9] The drop in mainframe share was caused by the growth of minicomputers developed by newer companies such as Digital Equipment and Data General. This structural change in the computer market forced IBM into a defensive position. Unlike the auto companies, however, IBM responded relatively quickly to the new competition by offering its own line of minicomputers. It also introduced microcomputers for small business and personal home use. Even though IBM's overall share of the computer market was declining, its aggressive defense against increased competition maintained its position as the clear-cut market leader.

Gain foothold in new market. This is an obvious strategy for the innovator company, assuming that it has the resources and marketing skills to develop the market for its new product. And it is a potential strategy for would-be followers. Strategic decisions for a follower include the question of when, as well as whether, to enter the new market. Shall it rush in for an early foothold, or shall it wait to see how the market develops before making its move?

An interesting example is offered by the emerging market for applications of the new gene-splicing technology (variously called genetic engineering, bioengineering, and biotech.)[10] Several new venture companies (including Genentech, Inc.) were formed in the early 1980s to try for footholds in this unproven but potentially large new industry. (Early applications were seen in regulating plant growth and in fighting disease.) The risks of early entry were high because of the uncertainty over how long it would take for the market to develop to a profitable size. In contrast to the new venture firms, established companies (such as Monsanto and Shell) followed more conservative approaches. They took equity positions in some of the venture companies so they could monitor industry developments. And they built up their own biotech research capabilities. They were positioning themselves so they could move into the embryonic market at the most propitious time.

Other examples are seen in the burgeoning energy conservation market which was expected to reach $30 billion by 1985.[11]

The market for building management systems is expected to grow from $300 million annually today to $1.8 billion by 1990. Honeywell Inc., the largest supplier, has sold more than 7,000 systems since the 1973 oil embargo. A Cambridge (Mass.) company, Count Digital Inc., recently began marketing a similar system for the home that can be used with home steam or hot water heating systems. It uses a tiny computer to turn each room's radiator enclosure into an individual "furnace." The system costs $2,000 and is said to be capable of reducing home heating bills in the northeast as much as 40 percent.[12]

Preempt a market segment. Seizing a market segment ahead of others in order to dominate it is not easily done except when the preemptor is the patent holder for a new-to-the-world product (as was the case with Du Pont nylon and Polaroid instant film). The potential advantage to the preemptor is the reward (usually high ROI) that goes with high market share. The disadvantage is that the cost of developing the market falls entirely on the preemptor.

Even a patent holder may have a limited time advantage because competitors often can work their way around the patent. Xerox successfully preempted the market for plain paper copiers as a result of the patents it acquired for the xerographic process, yet found itself a market defender even before its patents expired. Du Pont became a defender of its market position after being forced by the government to license other companies to produce nylon.

Preemption becomes more difficult in the absence of patent protection. Apple Computer and Tandy (owner of the Radio Shack chain of stores) attempted to preempt the personal computer market by moving early and aggressively, but they were soon faced with competition from large computer companies such as IBM.

Procter & Gamble preempted the disposable diaper market but succeeded in defending it against strong competitors such as Kimberly Clark, Scott Paper, and Johnson & Johnson. Scott and J&J dropped out of the fray, leaving P&G with over 70 percent of the market.[13] [Review Marketing Note 17-1 for how P&G did it.]

Although market preemption appears on the surface to be a desirable strategy, its success (in the absence of good patent protection) depends on the willingness and ability of the preempting company first to establish and then to defend its position against potential strong competitors.

Internally Driven Strategies. In contrast to market-driven new product strategies, *internally driven* strategies grow out of management policy decisions and from research and development.

Maintain position as product innovator. This is another expression of the product leader strategy discussed in the last chapter. As noted there, innovative improvements of existing products and innovative new products are both required to obtain and maintain positions of market leadership. The *product innovator* strategy is closely related to the market-driven strategy "defend a market position," since innovative new products can be very helpful in combating competitive attacks. Adoption of the product innovator strategy requires a management commitment to heavy, continuous technical research and development with more emphasis placed on laboratory research than is the case with most companies. It also means a willingness to finance marketing efforts in the sometimes long, unprofitable introductory phase of the new product's life cycle. The payoff for innovative products should be a high market share position and the higher profit return that usually goes with it.

Commitment to innovation and product leadership can be seen in IBM's product policies: (1) lead in new developments; (2) be aware of advances made by others and better them when IBM can, or be willing to adopt them whenever they fit IBM's needs; and (3) produce quality products of the most advanced design and at the lowest possible cost.[14] In number 2, however, we can see that even the computer industry's leader does not expect to create *all* of the innovations.

The follower alternative. As noted in the previous chapter, many profitable companies are not positioned as product leaders or innovators. And many companies that lead in one product area are not the leaders in others: Kodak is the leader in commercially developed film, but ranks a poor second behind Polaroid in instant film; RCA leads in color television but not in video discs; IBM leads in computers but not in office copiers.

Only one or a few companies in an industry can be the industry leaders by virtue of the innovator strategy. Although this was one of the favored strategies named in the BA&H study, we must point out that many profitable companies do not use it. The follower strategy (followers may be either copiers or hedgers), described in Chapter 16, is more common. There are even industry leaders who do not attempt to be the product innovators. A case in point is the Caterpillar Tractor Company, the clear-cut market share leader in earth-moving equipment.

> With research geared almost exclusively to existing products, Caterpillar is rarely the first to come up with a new offering in its markets. But being on the leading edge has never been one of the company's goals. It has built its reputation by letting other companies go through the trial-and-error process of introducing new products. Caterpillar later jumps in with the most trouble-free product on the market.[15]

Exploit technology in new way. Many companies use their basic technological know-how to lead them into new products. The research and development department has the primary job of implementing this strategy. Even so, new products based on technology transfers must be matched up with market opportunities if they are to succeed.

CPC International, a *Fortune* 100 company, built its business as a wet corn miller. CPC has used its wet corn milling technology to expand into consumer products such as Mazola corn oil and Niagara starch. It has also transferred this technology to industrial products such as a fructose corn sweetener (used in the manufacture of soft drinks) and ethanol, an ingredient in gasohol.

Motorola expanded its technology (used in consumer radios and television sets) to space-age electronics. Eighty percent of its business is now in communications (such as land-based mobile radios) and semiconductors.[16]

Walt Disney created a successful movie business using animated characters—a combination of art and technology that was developed to a high form of imagery. Capitalizing on the public's love affair with Mickey Mouse and his animated friends, Walt Disney Productions combined their technology of imagery with their knowledge of entertainment to create the highly successful Disneyland and Disney World amusement parks.

ORGANIZATION FOR INTERNAL PRODUCT DEVELOPMENT

There may be no greater management challenge than finding the right organization for new product development and then managing it so that it turns out the new products needed to successfully implement the company's new product strategies.

The Organizational Problem

The functional organization used by companies at the operating level was developed to perform the day-to-day functions needed to bring in cash this week, this month, and this year. The marketing department is striving to reach current sales goals; manufacturing is producing to meet current shipping schedules; and finance is managing the cash flow to support the on-going operations of marketing and manufacturing. The overall division and company goal is to attain this year's profit objective. Everyone knows that preparing for the future is important; yet without earnings now, the company might not be around to enjoy the future.

In contrast to current operations, new product development is concerned with providing future profits. It is not necessarily popular with operating people. It spends money now, but doesn't create income now. It competes for company resources as well as for the time and attention of those whose principal interests are with current operations. In essence, the new product organization is superimposed on the regular organization. And therein lies the inherent problem faced by every management. How does it "rationalize"* competing demands on the organization so that both short- and long-range goals are achieved?

The organizational issue is suggested by the matrix shown in Figure 17-2. Here each person or group in charge of a new product is calling for the support of people in research and development, marketing, production, and finance—people who

---

*A useful British management term for describing the process of resolving or harmonizing conflicting issues.

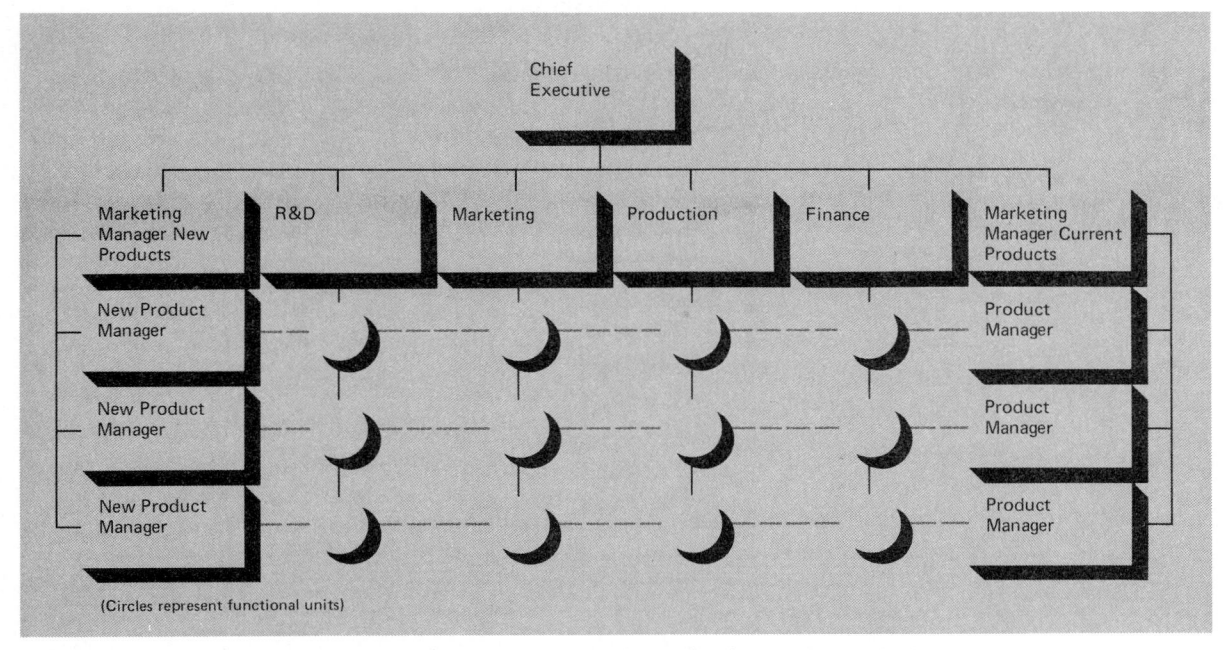

FIGURE 17-2. Matrix showing how managers of new and current products utilize the same functional units.

spend much of their time in support of current operations. The extent of the problem is illustrated by a survey of companies that have been relatively successful with new products. More than four out of five of these companies listed "organization" as their most significant problem area in developing new products.[17]

Organizational and Procedural Guidelines

There are four things that new product organization and procedures should provide to the new product process:

- Assignment of responsibility for scheduling each project from initial screening to the decision whether to commercialize
- Coordination of the tasks performed by each functional department so that critical schedules are met
- Control and follow-up to see that go/no-go decisions are made at each stage of the process
- Involvement of top management in resolving conflicts and making the decision as to whether to commercialize

Later we will look at the procedures for processing a new product project through a series of stages from the initial idea to commercialization. This process involves continuous evaluation that will drop out a product at any stage where it is judged to be not commercially viable. First, however, we will examine several alternate means of organizing for new product planning and development.

Types of Organization

New product organization is usually built around one or more of the following: (1) product managers; (2) new product managers; (3) a new product department (headed by a director of new products); (4) a new products committee; (5) task forces; or (6) new venture teams. Two or more of these forms may be used by the same company. For example, a company might have new product managers along with a new product department and a new product committee.

Product Managers. The role of the product/brand manager position, as we described it in Chapter 14, is to plan, coordinate, and monitor the marketing of an existing product. Few companies today place the added responsibility of new product development on their product managers. Those which do, argue that (1) the product manager is in the best position to see ways in which the current product line can be supplemented, and (2) the product manager's knowledge of the market is more likely to produce ideas that are viable. Ralston-Purina uses regular product managers for new product planning for reasons such as these. The drawback to placing new product responsibility with the current manager is that it is not likely to spawn ideas outside of the current product area managed by the product manager.

Companies that do not use the product manager for new product development believe that (1) the job of managing the regular product demands all of the product manager's time and that (2) new product development is a specialized activity requiring different talents.

New Product Manager. This position most often is found in consumer packaged goods companies where marketing issues are predominant. A typical arrange-

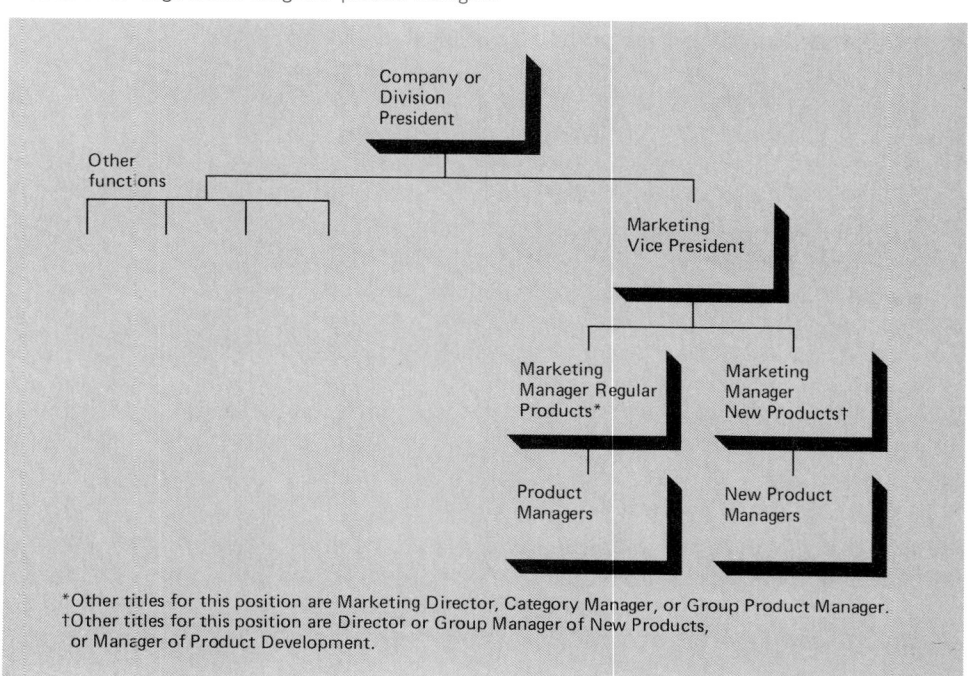

FIGURE 17-3. Organization using new product managers.

*Other titles for this position are Marketing Director, Category Manager, or Group Product Manager.
†Other titles for this position are Director or Group Manager of New Products, or Manager of Product Development.

ment is seen in Figure 17-3 and can be found in companies such as Bristol Myers, Heublein, and Richardson-Vicks.

These managers are chosen partly for their creativeness, since they are expected to create new product ideas. Their jobs can be illustrated by a new product manager at Bristol-Myers who had the idea that a larger head for the Ban roll-on deodorant would be more efficient in applying the deodorant. Rather than disturb the existing market for Ban, a new brand, Tickle, was introduced with the larger head. The new product manager was involved with the testing of the concept, the development and testing of the product and package design, the product ingredient formula, the number of scents, and the market positioning (young in spirit, different, pleasant). While Tickle cannibalized some of Ban's market, the two brands together increased Bristol-Myers share of the roll-on deodorant market.

New Products Department. This arrangement also may be called new product development department. The department is headed by a director, who may be a vice president. Usually the director will report to the company or division chief executive (as shown in Figure 17-4), although we occasionally see this position reporting to the marketing manager.

The principal advantage of this organizational arrangement is that the responsibility for new products is placed at a senior level where (1) the director of new products can work with the other functional heads as an equal and (2) where direct access to the chief executive means that the clout of that position can be called on as needed to break logjams. The director may work alone or with a small staff in coordinating the new product efforts of the functional departments. Or the new products director may have an organization of market research and/or technical people who supplement the work of the regular functional departments. With this

FIGURE 17-4. Organization showing a new products director (department) and a new products committee.

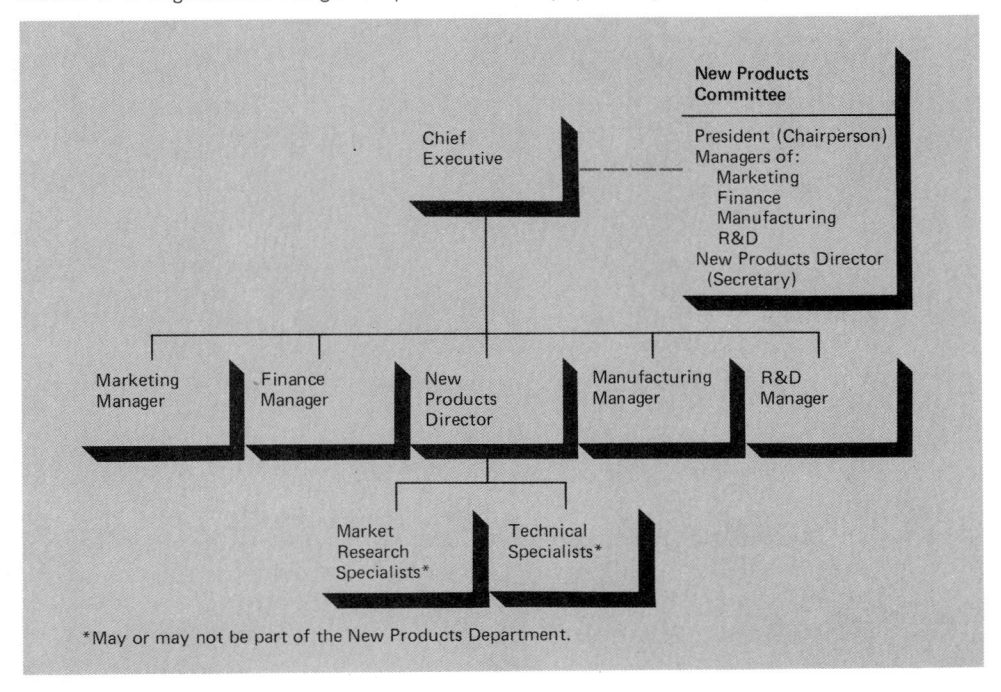

New Products Committee
President (Chairperson)
Managers of:
 Marketing
 Finance
 Manufacturing
 R&D
New Products Director (Secretary)

Chief Executive

Marketing Manager | Finance Manager | New Products Director | Manufacturing Manager | R&D Manager

Market Research Specialists*
Technical Specialists*

*May or may not be part of the New Products Department.

type of arrangement the new products department may perform the market and technical research and evaluation up to the point where a decision is made whether to proceed with full-scale development. Assuming the decision is to go ahead, the regular functional departments become involved and the new product department's role changes to one of scheduling and coordinating their efforts.

S. C. Johnson & Son, Inc., known for its line of floor and furniture waxes, organized a new products department with its own staff of specialists. It also used task forces to lead the new product through the various stages of development.[18] The company was able to expand successfully into insecticides, automotive care products, air fresheners, laundry products, and other household cleaners.

New Products Committee. Normally this committee operates under the aegis of the company or division chief executive, who also is its chairperson. Committee membership is composed of the functional department heads, with the new product director serving as the secretary who schedules the meetings and arranges the agenda. (See Figure 17-4.) Essentially this was the arrangement at the Hoover Company when it was trying to diversify beyond vacuum cleaners.

The new products committee provides the vehicle for setting and reviewing new product policy, establishing the priorities for projects, reviewing progress, dealing with logjams, and deciding whether to commercialize. When the CEO, or other high-level officer with decision-making power, chairs the committee, momentum to the program is provided and the key go/no-go decisions are made as needed.

Committees have been criticized by some as invitations to inaction. There is no question that they are ineffective as substitutes for product departments or new product managers, who should have the responsibility for carrying out day-to-day scheduling and coordination. New product committees can be quite effective, however, when made up of high-level executives who set policies and priorities and who make the major go/no-go decisions. A Booz-Allen & Hamilton study found no incompatibility between properly structured committees and new product departments.[19]

Task Forces. This is an organizational device used by some companies to overcome the problem of getting support from functional departments. A task force is set up for each new product to shepherd it through the various stages to the point of commercialization, at which time it is turned over to the marketing department. The task force usually is composed of representatives from marketing, research and development, and finance, and may be supplemented with others as it moves closer to commercialization. Members may handle their task force assignment on a part-time basis or they may be placed on temporary leave from their regular departments so as to give full time to the project until completed. The task force may report to the new products director, a marketing executive, or (occasionally) to a research and development executive.

The task force (which may be called by other names such as sponsor group, new product team, or marketing action team) has two principal advantages: (1) it provides continuous attention to a new product until it is either abandoned or approved for commercialization; and (2) by bringing functional specialists together to work as a team, it forces them to resolve differences which are not as readily resolved when the same people are working within their respective departments.

The major problem with the task force approach is that there are never enough competent, experienced people available to staff all of the new product projects. And the junior people who often are assigned may not have sufficient clout to get needed tasks carried out within their own departments.

New Venture Teams. This team is similar to the task force, but with an important difference; the functional specialists assigned to the venture team are independent of any functional department. This independent role is crucial because the concept of the venture team is to provide an entrepreneurial environment unencumbered by the bureaucracy of the regular organization. The basic idea is to develop a *new business* which may or may not be similar to the existing corporate businesses. New venture teams characteristically take their product all the way through test marketing and commercialization. In fact, the team members may be assigned to manage the new business. To encourage the entrepreneurial spirit, team members may be paid incentives tied to the success of the new business.

In a study of over 100 venture teams, this organizational concept was found to be uniquely suited to the task of product innovation because of its simple mission, unstructured relationships, insulation from the daily routines, and its entrepreneurial thrust.[20] And venture teams were found more appropriate for totally new products than for me-too products. They are not for the typical "new product" situations. Payoff, if any, is long term; so the project is of little interest to regular functional managers. Consequently, venture teams usually are funded by top management and report to a nonoperating executive at the corporate level. Monsanto's Astro-Turf was assigned to a new venture team. The new enterprise group of which it was a part reported to the president.[21]

It is difficult to say whether one organizational arrangement is superior. Each has its value in certain situations. New product managers seem to work well in consumer packaged goods companies where new product concepts can be thought up and market researched prior to technical development. A combination of new product department and task forces appears more appropriate for durable goods, where coordination of technical and marketing functions is required over long periods. New venture teams are useful when a totally new product needs to be nurtured into a new growth business.

One study reports that new products departments are found in 86 percent of the companies with new product programs, often supplemented by new product teams (task forces) and new product committees.[22]

INTERNAL DEVELOPMENT PROCEDURES

Development of a new product inside the company starts with a new product strategy, is followed by a search for product ideas, and proceeds through several stages to commercialization (unless the idea is screened out along the way). Figure 17-5 shows seven stages that make up the process. If the idea survives the initial screening and evaluation stage, it becomes a candidate for business analysis. At each succeeding step, management decides whether it will go on to the next. Market research, performance testing, and market testing are done along the way to help with decision making.

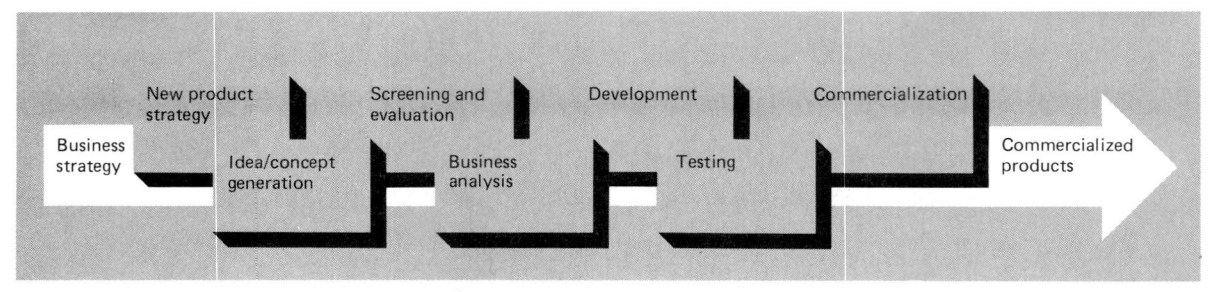

FIGURE 17-5. Seven stages of product evolution. *Source: New Products, Best Practices—Today and Tomorrow,* Booz-Allen & Hamilton, Inc., New York, 1982, p. 8.

Booz-Allen & Hamilton found that on the average it takes seven ideas to yield one successful new product, ranging from sixteen for consumer packaged goods to five for consumer durable goods companies.[23] Most ideas are dropped out at the initial screening and evaluation stage. New product development can be viewed as a continuing screening process, as portrayed by the inverted pyramid in Figure 17-6.

Initially ideas are screened using judgment. From there on, decisions are aided by new increments of knowledge supplied from technical and market research, financial analyses, and customer use tests. The process has been compared to a poker game where you ante small amounts at first, then more as you learn more about your hand from successive deals of the cards. At some point you decide to stay in or drop out.

The importance of information and good judgment is evident when we consider the disappointing results of many new product programs and the high costs of the development, testing, and commercialization stages. These stages account for 80 percent of new product spending. (See Figure 17-7.) Experienced managements, consequently, emphasize screening out the weak products as early as possible, even at the risk of missing an occasional winner. We now examine the principal activities of each of the procedural stages shown in Figure 17-5.

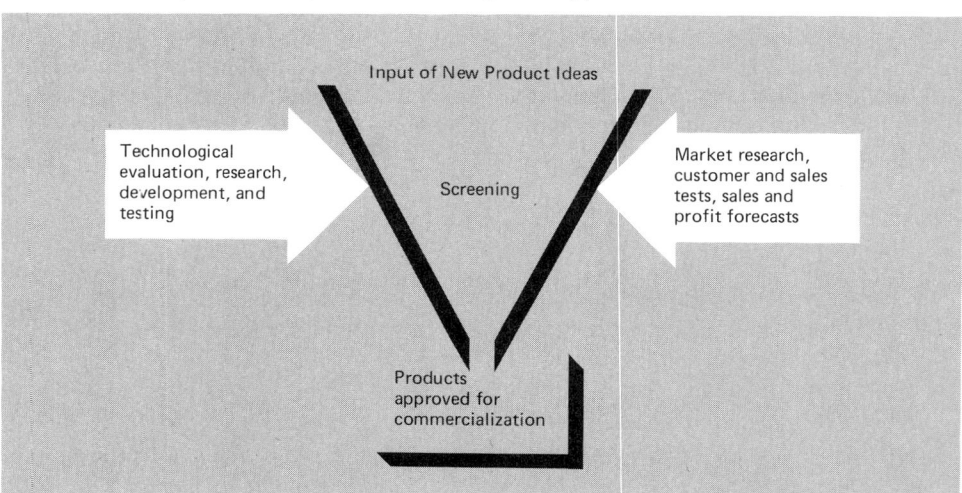

FIGURE 17-6. New product development as a continuing screening process.

```
Strategy,
idea generation,    20%
business analysis

Development         35%

Testing,            45%
commercialization
```

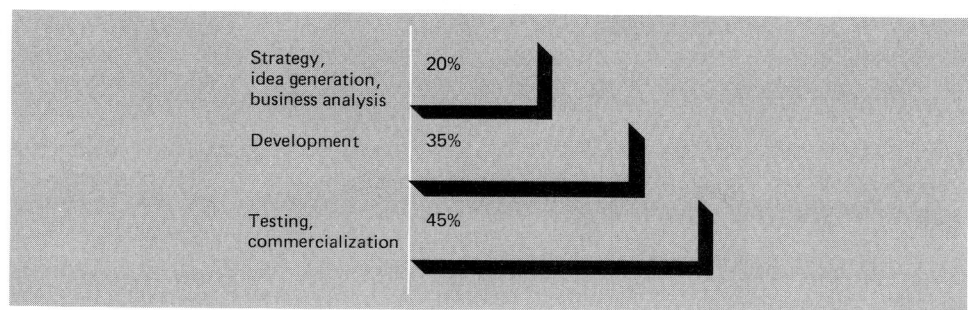

FIGURE 17-7. Percent of new product spending. *Source: New Products, Best Practices—Today and Tomorrow,* Booz-Allen & Hamilton, Inc., New York, 1982, p. 8.

New Product Strategy Stage

Strategic business planning has had an impact on new product development. Companies appear to be placing more emphasis on the earlier stages of the new product planning process—strategy, idea generation, and screening. The result is that fewer but better ideas move to the expensive development stage.

Despite the obvious advantages of tying new product search to specific product strategies, this approach should not be followed slavishly to the exclusion of open-ended approaches. Employees should not be discouraged from considering creative ideas and technological discoveries just because they do not fit a specific new product strategy. So as not to overlook breakthroughs that could open potential new business opportunities, it is not uncommon for new product directors and research directors to permit their people to spend a portion of their time pursuing ideas and technologies not directly related to their new product assignments.

Idea/Concept Generation Stage

Ideas for new products come from both unsolicited and solicited sources. Table 17-2 shows some common sources of each type.

Unsolicited Ideas. Most companies receive gratuitous new product suggestions from many sources. Most are inappropriate for the company's product

TABLE 17-2
Sources of New Product Ideas

Unsolicited Ideas	Solicited Ideas
Employees	Technical and research departments
Customers	Customer service departments
Advertising agency	Technical service departments
Wholesalers and retailers	Published reports
Stockholders	Competitive intelligence
The public	Technology reviews
Inventors	Marketing research
Brokers and agents for	Creative thought
inventors and licensers	Focus groups

objectives, but are examined so that the occasional gem is not discarded inadvertently. Caution must be exercised in the handling of nonpatented ideas received gratuitously.[24] Many times these ideas are already under consideration by the company. If the idea is commercialized, the company may be sued by the submitter who assumes the idea was plagiarized. Company lawyers prescribe procedures for handling submissions, even going so far as to recommend return of all nonpatented submissions without examination.

Solicited Ideas. In order to get a steady input of potentially good ideas, growth-minded companies supplement their idea pools through sources such as those described below.

Technical research departments. These can include R&D, engineering, medical (in the case of drug companies), and home economics departments. Research personnel are encouraged to develop ideas in product areas that support the strategic marketing plans. At Gillette (which produces Paper Mate pens) a company researcher got the idea of trying rubber cement as the vehicle for ink when he was erasing rubber cement from a piece of paper and noted that the cement had not been absorbed by the paper. Although the idea was not the result of direct research, the researcher was aware that Paper Mate wanted to market a pen with erasable ink.

Customer service department. Complaints received by this department are recorded, analyzed, and reported by frequency of occurrence. These serve as ideas for product improvements which sometimes lead to entirely new products.

Technical service department. Technical service people in industrial goods companies assist customers with their complaints and problems. With their technical training and firsthand customer experiences, technical service representatives often come up with ideas for improvements and new products that will better serve their customers.

Published reports. Government reports, such as those describing newly registered patents, are sources of ideas, as are reports of new products printed in trade magazines and the offerings of private reporting services.

Competitive intelligence. The published reports referred to above represent only a small part of the information available on competitors' new product developments, much of it readily accessible through legitimate search. Some companies (Scott Paper, for example) name a person or department to collect this information on a continuing basis and to prepare forecasts of competitive activity.[25]

Technology reviews. Much in the way of technological developments is reported in major newspapers and scientific journals, at scientific meetings, and by scientific abstracting services. Companies assign the responsibility of tracking technology to a technology department or to the research and development department. Developments in microelectronic technology led Texas Instruments into mass-produced wrist watches and hand-held electronic calculators. Pro Brush (owned by Rexall) turned its plastic technology, developed to produce toothbrush handles, into the successful production and sale of computer cabinets.

Marketing research. Through competitive analyses, forecasts of product growth patterns, and segmentation studies, the marketing research department is in a position to identify areas offering new product opportunities.

Creative thought. Companies with effective new product programs are always looking for creative people for their new product positions. This is particularly the case in consumer packaged goods companies, where concepts are conceived and then subjected to quick and inexpensive focus group tests to see whether they are worth further consideration.

A new products organizational unit would likely check on a regular basis with all of the above idea sources plus others (e.g., studies of consumers' perceptions of the attributes of the best-selling brand; possible line or brand extensions; and augmenting the value of present products by adding services or providing combinations of functions, such as an all-purpose kitchen appliance). Although it seems prudent to check all sources for ideas, the group new product manager of a health and beauty aids company told me, "There is no substitute for creative thought, whether it is done alone, in groups, or in brainstorming sessions" (free-wheeling group discussions where notes or tapes are scanned later for feasible ideas).

Some companies mix outside experts with internal people in their brainstorming sessions. In attempting to come up with ideas for new packaging products for the fast-food restaurant market, one company brought in the following outsiders to participate in what it called an "innovative session": a Ph.D. physicist; the director of market research for a large packaging materials/components firm; a Ph.D. food scientist; an industrial designer; a publisher of dining-out magazines; and the president of an advertising agency.[26] Guidelines for an innovative (brainstorming) session are given in **Marketing Note 17-3**.

Businesses begin and prosper by offering creative answers to old and new market wants and needs. The Wright Line Company offers creatively designed

---

MARKETING NOTE 17-3

Guidelines for a Productive Innovation Session

Rule	Caveat
1. There are a number of "right" answers.	1. Don't seek "the" answer.
2. You have a piece of a lot of "right" answers. Say your piece.	2. Don't be shy.
3. Others have other pieces. Listen, and let them have their say. "Build on." Respond.	3. Don't dismiss or ignore others' contributions.
4. Stay positive! Support, modify, improve.	4. Don't criticize or shoot down.
5. Keep moving! Seek quantity, variety!	5. Don't dwell. Don't be boring!
6. Take a lead off base. Try way out!	6. Don't be constrained by convention.
7. Talk to the subject, not to a person.	7. Don't subgroup—don't whisper to your neighbor.
8. One at a time.	8. Don't interrupt.
9. Stay loose. Relax. Enjoy.	9. Don't be "careful" or cover your flank.
10. Keep punching! Hang in!	10. Don't shoot all your bullets and give up.

Source: Frederick D. Buggie, *New Product Development Strategies*, AMACON, New York, 1981, p. 87.

products to help companies deal with their growing computer operations. This successful firm combines in-house customer studies with creative thinking to design furniture and devices for supporting, storing, protecting, and transporting computer tapes, disks, cards, and accessories.

The profitable Treasure Masters Corporation was formed by a husband-and-wife team who had been working for greeting card companies. They develop unique ideas for bridal accessories, baby gifts and accessories, fashion jewelry, and fragrances. New items are introduced every year, such as for the bridal custom of wearing something old, something new, something borrowed, something blue.

Focus groups. As consumers we are not productive sources of new product ideas. When asked, most of us can't think of new products we would like to see. But we can react to ideas presented to us. Discussions in focus groups* sometimes lead to better ideas. The Hoover Company did time studies of common household tasks such as floor washing, rug shampooing, and window washing. Focus group discussions were then held to learn peoples' attitudes toward these tasks and to get their reactions to concepts of products that could help to ease or speed the completion of these distasteful jobs. During these discussions participants came up with ideas for other needs, such as better ways of removing leaves from gutters.

Screening and Evaluation

The first screening of new product ideas is based on the judgments of new product managers, new product departments, or screening committees composed of marketing and technical people and (sometimes) patent attorneys. Ideas outside the competence of these people may be referred to marketing and technical research departments for brief investigations.

New Product Criteria. Screening is greatly facilitated if management establishes criteria on which to evaluate the appropriateness of new ideas and concepts. Many companies believe that to ensure success a new product should have one or more advantages over competition, such as:

- Better quality, performance, or other attributes
- Lower cost (for survival in a price war or for investing the higher margin in market development)
- A stronger company market position in terms of such things as brand name, broad representation, or strength of distribution

Criteria can be adopted that discourage introduction of me-too products (unless there is a special reason for doing so, such as filling out a line). Even strong and skillful marketers have not done well with parity products. Bristol-Myers' Datril was unable to take much share from McNeil Laboratories' Tylenol, even with lower prices and heavy promotion. And neither giant IBM nor Kodak gained substantial shares of the copier market from Xerox despite their strong distribution systems and heavy promotional efforts.

Company examples. Criteria should relate to a company's strategies and

---

*This research method is described on page 132.

strengths. Consequently, criteria will be different for different businesses and may change from time to time even for the same business.

A Caterpillar Tractor Company executive says that new product ideas must meet three tests before they are even considered for discussion: "Unless a product is highly capital-intensive, will benefit from high-level technology, and is marketable through our current distribution system, it won't fit our product-development strategy."[27]

The Hoover Company decided to mount a new product effort to help offset the company's heavy reliance on its principal product, the vacuum cleaner. After months of studying and evaluating markets, competition, and product alternatives, a study team recommended the following criteria for selecting ideas to be developed:

The product must be in the company's present or related field of endeavor (such as electric home appliances).

It must utilize two or more of the company's strengths, which were considered to be electrical and cleaning technology, broad retail distribution, selling skills, and a brand name widely known for quality.

The selling price was to fall within a specified range. (This was to discourage expansion in the high-priced major or low-priced (kitchen-type) appliances, since markets for these products were already dominated by strong brands.)

The product should be able to reach breakeven and a minimum ROI within specified time periods.

The product must be new to the market or, if not, be in the early growth stage of the product life cycle.

If the product already is on the market, Hoover's entry must perform better than competitors', have lower costs, be able to capitalize on the Hoover reputation, or be in a position to utilize the company's distribution strengths; preferably all of these.

The proposed product should require substantial capital investment so as to avoid competition from "garage"-type (small, local, low-overhead) operators.

These guidelines led the way to a program of line broadening of vacuum cleaners and new products such as electric floor polishers, rug shampooers, and floor washers. The high-capital-investment criterion was enough to keep Hoover from creating a chain of rug cleaning service operations because it feared low-price competition from local entrepreneurs who could enter this business with little capital.

Business Analysis

Product ideas that survive the initial screening move next to the business analysis stage, where preliminary profit forecasts are made. First, however, product development and manufacturing costs must be estimated, market potential estimated, and sales forecasts made using assumed prices. This process may be simple or complicated depending on the uniqueness of the product and the company's knowledge of the technology involved.

Ranking of Ideas. Companies often have more product ideas that have survived the initial screening than can be developed at the same time. Consequently, projects need to be ranked in order of their potential for success. A scaled checklist can be devised to help with these rankings. An example is shown in Table 17-3.[28] On this rating form each new product criterion is rated on a scale of one to three (the raw score), then multiplied by the weight (i.e., the relative importance given to each criterion) to get the total score for the criterion. The sum of the criteria scores is then compared with a minimum passing score (presumably based on experience with previous products that went to market). A passing score will not ensure automatic advancement into the development stage if there are products with better scores. And even a product with a high score may possess some inherent *knockout factor*. A new dessert with a good rating score, for example, was eliminated when the product was shown to the company's food brokers who were convinced it would not sell well. Without their support the product would have had little chance for success.

Rating scales have appeal because they reduce several variables to a single number. We can readily rank new products by number. But some analysts believe scales are unreliable except for spotting products at the extremes on a successful-unsuccessful continuum.[29] Consequently, they should be used to assist with decision making and not as substitutes for management judgment.

Development

In the initial stage of development, the R&D or engineering department creates working models of the new products. (These also are referred to as *prototypes* and

TABLE 17-3
A Typical Scoring Form For Ranking New Products

Criterion	Raw Score*			Weight	Total Score
Annual market growth	5-9% 1	9-15% ②	15%+ 3	1	2
Potential profitability (ROI)	Below average 1	Average ②	Above average 3	2	4
Likely emergence of competition	Within a year 1	1-2 Years ②	2+ years 3	1	2
Product life cycle	3 years 1	3-6 years 2	6+ years ③	1	3
Susceptibility to influence of recession	Greater than average 1	Average 2	Less than average ③	2	6
					17

Minimum score for advance to next stage = 15   Pass ✓   Reject

*Author's note: Circled items represent the raw scores for the hypothetical product in this example.

Source: H. Ronald Hamilton, "Screening Business Development Opportunities," *Business Horizons*, August 1974, p. 21. Copyright, 1974, by the Foundation for the School of Business at Indiana University. Reprinted by permission.

breadboard or *bench* models.) The product's appearance may be crude, since the purposes at this stage primarily are to find out whether the original concept is workable, how long it will take to develop the product fully, and how much the manufactured cost will be. The manufacturing and accounting departments assist with the cost estimates. The prototype models are laboratory tested under conditions that often are more severe than would be expected in customer use. No matter how careful the lab testing is, however, unanticipated failures may show up when consumers use the products.

Use Tests. If the product tests well in the laboratory and if it is a nondurable class of product, it usually is placed with consumers or industrial customers for trial. Products that can be produced in vats in the laboratory or pilot plant—such as toothpaste, dog food, and industrial chemicals—can be made relatively quickly and cheaply and then packaged for test purposes.

Durable goods such as appliances and cars generally are not use tested because of the great expense. The costs of breadboard models in test quantities are prohibitive. Factory production would require expensive tooling that would become obsolete if the tests proved that the prototype required changes. Notice that new models of cars, planes, and elevators often develop "bugs" which must be corrected by the manufacturer. In durable goods industries, the new product usually gets its first use test under real market conditions *after* the product is introduced.

If the results of initial development and business analysis to this point are positive, the product will be considered for advanced development. The purpose of advanced development is to get a finished model ready for manufacture. Industrial designers give the product attractive and useful form. Packaging is developed. Concurrently, manufacturing starts to prepare production plans and marketing begins the development of market introduction plans.

Testing

Figure 17-5 shows testing as falling between the development and commercialization stages. Actually tests may be employed at any stage to help management decide whether to proceed to the next stage. Concept tests, for example, may be run during the idea-generation stage; laboratory and use tests during development; and market tests prior to commercialization. After our discussion of the commercialization stage, we will explain types of market tests.

Commercialization

The final stage is commercialization, which occurs when management approves the product's introduction to the market. The decision to commercialize sets several tasks in motion: ordering production materials and equipment, production startup, building inventories, shipping product to field distribution points, training the sales force, announcements to the trade, and advertising to potential customers. The period between decision and introduction may run from a few weeks for simple products made on existing equipment to several years for highly technical products such as airplanes or computers.

Six phases of IBM's new product development process, which together take from three to five years, are described in **Marketing Note 17-4**.

MARKETING NOTE 17-4

The Product Development Process at IBM

The planning and development of a significant hardware or software product at IBM is structured so that the process takes place in a series of phases known as the Phase Review Process. It begins with a statement of objectives by the product manager, which includes estimates of price, delivery, time, market demand, specifications, and forecast assumptions. Each phase and its basic purpose is as follows:

Phase I—Study. The objective is to authorize the commitment of funds for the product.

Phase II—Design. The objective is to design the product and to make internal commitments to management and marketing that the product will be announced.

Phase III—Development. The objective is to get approval to release the product for external announcement.

Phase IV—Preproduction. The purpose is to release the product for entry into regular manufacturing.

Phase V—Production. The purpose is to authorize the first shipment to a customer.

Phase VI—Qualification. During this period the product must meet cost, performance, and reliability projections.

During the Phase Review Process some products could be subject to review by as many as 2200 people in ninety-four worldwide locations for their reactions, objections, and suggestions. A formal review is held at the end of each phase. Before the product can proceed to the next phase, the product manager must either resolve all of the outstanding issues or demonstrate that there are plans to resolve them. Nonconcurrences may be escalated to higher management, even to the Corporate Management Committee.

All efforts may be terminated at any point in the Phase Review Process or the product may be returned to an earlier phase. The process for a significant product could last from three to five years. For example, the IBM 3330 disk drive completed its phases as follows:

Phase I—November 1968

Phase II—June 1969

Phase III—April 1970 (announced in June)

Phase IV—February 1971

Phase V—May 1971 (first shipped to a customer in August)

Phase VI—March 1973

Source: Abstracted from a 1978 statement by Thomas M. Liptak, who at that time was president of IBM's General Technology Division.

Market Sales Test

A widely used though controversial practice is to test to learn how the new product will sell under real or simulated market conditions prior to making the commercialization decision. Testing under real market conditions is controversial because of cost, delay in commercializing, exposure to competitors, and the fact it does not always result in accurate sales forecasts. Simulated market tests are controversial because they are not conducted under real market conditions. Nevertheless, many companies use one or both because the alternative of going to market without testing seems worse. For the same reasons given earlier for customer use tests, market sales tests are not practical for durable goods. Most test marketing occurs with consumer packaged goods.

Test Marketing. Market sales tests may range in scope from a single market test with limited objectives to multimarket tests with multiple objectives. In either case, the primary purpose is to learn how the product sells in the competitive marketplace. Other objectives can be to learn the demographic characteristics of buyer segments, purchase rates, and the best mix of price, consumer promotion, and trade promotion. The dilemma of whether or not to test market can be appreciated if we compare the advantages with the disadvantages.

Advantages

1. Sales performance can be measured under real market conditions, including trial, repurchase, and purchase-frequency rates.
2. Weaknesses in product or package not discovered earlier should show up.
3. It provides purchase rates by demographic segments to help determine target markets.
4. It provides the opportunity to test different mixes of price and promotion.
5. Trade reactions will indicate what will be necessary to get trade support if the product is commercialized.

Disadvantages

1. Competition is alerted and may react by:
   a. Quickly copying the new product
   b. Confusing the test market results with special promotions of its own competing products
   c. Being ready to counterattack when the new product is put on general sale. Cheesebrough-Ponds (maker of Vaseline Intensive Care) saw that Procter & Gamble was test marketing a new skin conditioner, Wondra, and was ready with heavy consumer and trade promotions of its own when Wondra was introduced.
2. It is costly in terms of:
   a. Out-of-pocket costs which exceed the income from test market sales. Test marketing costs can run into the hundreds of thousands of dollars and more.
   b. Lost opportunity costs. Profits are lost on the sales that might have occurred during the test period if the product had been on national sale.
3. Misleading results. Good test marketing requires management to commit resources and to have the patience to wait six months or more for meaningful results. It requires skill in planning, execution, control, measurement, and interpretation. And most importantly, it requires a body of experience with previous market tests and commercialization against which to compare the results of the current test. Many companies cannot claim all of these qualifications, and many have had poor results from test marketing. However, research firms sepcializing in market testing are available to act as consultants or to actually run the test market program for your company.

Conditions favoring test marketing. Because the question of whether or not to test market must be answered prior to commercialization, it is useful to review some circumstances which seem to favor test marketing:

- When both the sales potential and risk are high

- When the product is truly new or novel
- When the costs of producing test quantities are not large
- When the cost of market failure would be greater than the costs of test marketing
- When competition is not likely to be able to copy the product quickly
- When all previous testing suggests a successful product in hand.[30]

The characteristics of a good test marketing program are listed in **Marketing Note 17-5**.

Simulated Test Marketing. Controlled laboratory tests may be substituted for real test marketing or they may be used as a pretest to help decide whether to go to test marketing. The cost is low, compared to test marketing, and the product is not exposed to competitors.

A typical approach is to invite consumers to a test laboratory which is equipped with interviewing rooms, a theater, and a facsimile of a self-service store. The process may go like this: groups are (1) invited to the laboratory; (2) interviewed to obtain demographic information; (3) ushered into the theater to see an entertaining film interspersed with commercials, one of which is for the new product; (4) taken to the store and given discount coupons that can be used along with their own cash to purchase any item in the store; and (5) reinterviewed regarding their purchases. Purchasers of the new product may be interviewed by phone later for their evaluations and their intentions to repurchase. Since the sample is not representative of the total population, the data are weighted to help compensate for this deficiency.

MARKETING NOTE 17-5

Characteristics of Good Test Marketing

- Selection of markets that are representative and that have not been overtested
- Measurement of trade outlets to learn the percent of stores stocking the product and the extent of shelf facings, stockouts, in-store promotions, and competitive brand activity
- Avoidance of artificial conditions, by using sales methods and promotions that would be used in a national rollout.
- Use of several markets so that different marketing mixes can be tried
- Testing long enough to learn what the normal level of sales will be after the initial introductory surge is over
- Measurement of sales results
- Using consumer research to learn:
  Percent who try the new product
  Percent who repurchase
  Frequency of repurchase
  Objections of people who don't buy or don't repurchase
  Demographic characteristics of purchasers to find rates of usage by segment
  The effectiveness of advertising, i.e., brand awareness, interest, intent to buy

Well-planned and well-executed test marketing should lead to reliable sales forecasts, efficient production planning, identification of target markets, effective sales plans for getting the product into the trade channels, selection of the optimum marketing mix, and (possibly) clues to likely competitive reactions.

Firms offering this type of service claim that it produces reasonably accurate forecasts of what will happen in a real market situation. They maintain that accuracy increases as experience with tests accumulates. Paper Mate used the Yankelovich Laboratory Test facilities on Long Island, N.Y. to sales test its new erasable pen. Laboratory testing was chosen over market testing to avoid exposing this unique development to competitors.

Another means of simulated market testing is to send a mobile van, equipped like a store and containing the new product, into neighborhoods that have received promotional material about the new product. Consumers are provided with incentives to shop in the van. Their purchases are noted, and interviews are held. Data are weighted and analyzed much as in the controlled laboratory test.

Testing and the New Product Process

We mentioned several types of tests as we described the various stages of the new product evolution process. We'll now recapitulate the types and purposes of these tests, including some not mentioned earlier, in the approximate order of their occurrence:

Concept testing: to test a product idea before investing in product development

Laboratory test: to evaluate competitive products

Laboratory test: to test the performance of the company's new product at preliminary and advanced development stages

Employee use test: conducted with employees for a quick, cheap, confidential test to see whether the product is ready to go out for test with potential customers

Customer use test: conducted with potential customers to obtain their reactions to the product and opportunities for improvement

Simulated market test: conducted before commercialization and (sometimes) before test marketing to help forecast sales and identify market targets

Test market: prior to commercialization, to learn how the product will sell to buyer segments under real market conditions

Tests are an aid to decision making. Rarely are they conclusive in and of themselves. Consequently, the decision to drop the new product, study or test it further, or move to the next stage is a decision for management to make based on judgment and the available evidence.

SUMMARY

New products are essential to the long-term health of a company. They are needed to provide growth and to offset the inevitable leveling or decline of sales from present products. New product development is not easy, and almost all companies have experienced costly failures. While no one expects winners in every case, companies incur more new product failures than they would like to see. They believe the causes are poor market research, technical problems, bad timing of market introductions, and a number of other reasons. Companies that do well at managing new products direct their development activities in support of specific new product strategies. Many also support searches outside of the strategies in hope of finding entirely new products with which to start new businesses.

Companies may obtain new products through external and internal sources. External strategies include acquisition of other companies, acquiring patents and licenses, and using new product consultants. Internally developed products may be in response to market-driven strategies (such as defending a market position, gaining a foothold in a new market, or preempting a market segment) or internally driven strategies (such as taking a position as innovator or follower, or exploiting company technology in a new way).

Four-fifths of all companies report problems with organizing for internal new product development. We discussed six ways to organize the new product effort and listed the pros and cons of each. The categories are: product managers, new product managers, new products departments, new products committees, task forces, and new venture teams. The underlying organizational problem is how to rationalize the competing demands made on the company's functional specialists by managers who manage the current product line for near-term profits and managers who develop new products for future profits.

Products developed internally go through a multistage process as follows: new product strategy, idea/concept generation, screening and evaluation, business analysis, development, testing, and commercialization. Tests occur at appropriate points along the way, and real or simulated test marketing may be conducted prior to commercialization. Management decides at each stage whether to drop the product or continue. Everyone prays that the products surviving the process will prove to be winners.

QUESTIONS

1. Name the most common causes listed by companies for their relatively high rates of new product failure.
2. Name three external development strategies. What are the advantages and disadvantages of adding new products via the acquisition of established businesses?
3. Internal development strategies can be divided into market-driven and internally driven strategies. Name two examples of each.
4. Explain the problem of organizing for new product development. Why is new product development often not popular with operating people?
5. What organizational and procedural guidelines should management follow for effective internal new product development?
6. The new product manager form of organization appears to work well for what class of goods? Why? A combination of new product department and task forces appears more appropriate for what other class of goods? Why?
7. Name the seven stages of the internal new product development process. Which stages are the most costly?
8. One or more of which three new product criteria are needed to increase the chances of success over competition?
9. What are the major advantages and disadvantages of test marketing?
10. Why did P&G's new product, Pampers, fail in its initial market tests?

REFERENCES

1. David S. Hopkins, *New Product Winners and Losers*, research report no. 773, The Conference Board, New York, 1980.
2. Edgar A. Pessemier, *Product Management Strategy and Organization*, Wiley, New York, 1977, p. 11.
3. *New Products, Best Practices—Today and Tomorrow*, Booz-Allen & Hamilton, New York, 1982, p. 5.
4. Hopkins, op. cit., p. 4.
5. *New Products, Best Practices*, p. 4.
6. Hopkins, op. cit., digested from pp. 12-20.
7. For more on licensing, see Enid Baird Lovell, "Licensing: Reasons, Royalties, Dangers," *Domestic Licensing Practices*, The Conference Board, New York, 1968; and Bernard J. McNamee, "A Primer on Patent, Trademark, and Know-How Licensing," *MSU Business Topics*, summer 1970, pp. 11-20.
8. *New Products, Best Practices*, p. 9.
9. *Business Week*, Feb. 15, 1982, p. 78.
10. See "High Technology: Wave of the Future or a Market Flash in the Pan," *Business Week*, Nov. 10, 1980, pp. 85-98.
11. See "Energy Conservation Spawning a Billion-Dollar Business," *Business Week*, Apr. 6, 1981, pp. 58-69.
12. Quoted from *Business Week,* Apr. 6, 1981, pp. 59-60. By special permission, © 1981 by McGraw-Hill, Inc. New York. All rights reserved.
13. *Advertising Age*, Sept. 10, 1981, p. 124.
14. From a 1978 statement by Thomas M. Liptak, who at the time was president of IBM's General Technology Division.
15. Quoted from *Business Week,* May 4, 1981, p. 77. By special permission, © 1981 by McGraw-Hill, Inc. New York. All rights reserved.
16. *Advertising Age*, Aug. 3, 1981, p. 4.
17. *Management of New Products*, Booz-Allen & Hamilton, undated, p. A-17.
18. Samuel Johnson and Conrad Jones, "How to Organize for New Products," *Harvard Business Review*, May-June 1957, pp. 49-62. Copyright © 1957 by the President and Fellows of Harvard College; all rights reserved.
19. *Management of New Products*, p. A-22.
20. Richard M. Hill and James R. Hlavacek, "The Venture Team: A New Concept in Marketing Organization," *Journal of Marketing*, July 1977, pp. 44-50.
21. Pessemier, op. cit., p. 443.
22. *Management of New Products*, pp. A-20–A-21.
23. *New Products, Best Practices*, p. 6.
24. See C. Merle Crawford, "Unsolicited Product Ideas—Handle With Care," *Research Management*, January 1975, pp. 19-24, for business practices in handling ideas received gratuitously.
25. Sources of competitive information are contained in David I. Cleland and William R. King, "Competitive Business Intelligence Systems," *Business Horizons*, December 1975, pp. 19-28; Robert Hershey, "Commercial Intelligence on a Shoestring," *Harvard Business Review*, September-October, 1980, pp. 22-30, and David B. Montgomery and Charles Weinberg, "Toward Strategic Intelligence Systems," *Journal of Marketing, fall 1979, p. 46.*
26. Frederick D. Buggie, *New Product Development Strategies*, AMACOM, New York, 1981, pp. 91-92.
27. "Caterpillar," *Business Week*, May 4, 1981, p. 76.
28. Other examples of rating scales can be seen in Barry M. Richman, "A Rating Scale for

Product Innovation," *Business Horizons*, summer 1962, pp. 37-44; John S. Harris, "New Product Profile Chart," *Chemical & Engineering News*, Apr. 17, 1961, pp. 110-118; and John J. O'Meara, Jr., "Selecting Profitable Products," *Harvard Business Review*, Jan.-Feb. 1961, pp. 83-89.

29. See, for example, Allan D. Shocker, Dennis Gensch, and Leonard S. Simon, "Toward the Improvement of New Product Search and Screening," Conference Proceedings, American Marketing Association, fall 1969, pp. 168-175.

30. Adapted from N. D. Cadbury, "When and Where to Market Test," *Harvard Business Review*, May-June 1976, pp. 96-105. Copyright © 1976 by the President and Fellows of Harvard College; all rights reserved. Mr. Cadbury has written an excellent article on test marketing based on his experiences with Cadbury Schweppes Ltd.

CHAPTER 18

Pricing Management

Price is such a key element of the marketing mix that many top managements reserve for themselves the authority to decide prices. When pricing authority *is* delegated, it usually is limited and subject to review.

While there are many reasons for management's direct involvement, the principal ones have to do with *profit* and the *law*. Price is one-half of the profit margin equation: price − cost = profit margin. It is not that simple, of course, since several factors influence cost, and management considers more than profit margins when setting prices. We will look at several of these influences in this chapter.

Management is concerned with the law because it is not uncommon for legal suits involving pricing to be brought against sellers by the government, competitors, or customers. Losing a case can be very costly, sometimes requiring payment of treble damages and including jail terms for executives. Interpretations of laws affecting pricing are so varied and so complicated that managements trying to do the right thing may find they have broken the law unintentionally. Later we examine some of the legal issues surrounding price.

WHAT IS PRICE?

Price can take many forms, but in the final analysis it is what a buyer pays a seller for a product, service, license, or future obligation. A product price may be termed list, sale, special, or markdown price. A price for services may be referred to as a fee, fare, or tuition.

The price that wholesalers and retailers pay a manufacturer is usually the assumed retail price less a trade discount. Channel members may be eligible for other discounts for such things as delivery charges, taxes, dealer preparation costs, and warranty reserves.

Manufacturers' brands sell for more than nonbrands or private brands. Yet the majority of people pay the higher prices for the manufacturers' brands because of the greater confidence they have in branded merchandise. Even industrial buyers do not necessarily purchase from the lowest-price vendor. Often they will pay more to the vendor who has earned their confidence with consistent quality and on-time deliveries.

Because of the many ways that both the price and the offering can be viewed, we will simply define *price* as follows:

Price is the net payment by the buyer for the seller's offering.

This is similar to the *exchange* definition of marketing that we discussed in Chapter 2. Payment need not be in money, although this is most common; it might take the form of goods, services, or favors.

Price and the Marketing Mix

Classical economic theory assumes the presence of pure competition and undifferentiated products with perfect substitutes. Under these conditions price could be considered as the main determinant of demand. But widespread use of product differentiation has changed that situation, if indeed it ever existed. We now know that many factors enter into our buying decisions in addition to price. Nevertheless, price remains an important element of the marketing mix, and we dare not treat it lightly.

For the consumer, price serves as a quick and simple indicator of differences between the similar offerings of competitors. It also serves to distinguish among the grades of product offered by a single seller (e.g., Sear's good, better, best). It indicates when bargains are available, for example, during store "sales," or when seasonal factors reduce the prices of products such as fresh fruits and vegetables. Although price is not always an accurate reflection of quality or quantity, much of the time it tends to take the place of time-consuming comparison shopping in convenience goods stores. Even for shopping goods, reliable stores follow the practice of *price lining* to indicate different quality levels (such as lines of suits priced $149, $179, and $199).

The large purchases made by organizations make it worth their while to analyze and test competing vendors' products for quality and performance. All other things being equal, the professional buyer normally will select the lowest-price vendor. But all things rarely are equal. Industrial as well as consumer goods producers practice product differentiation. Consequently, price usually is not the sole determinant in organizational buying.

Price differs from the other elements of the marketing mix in that it can be changed more quickly. Decisions to change product, distribution, or promotion will take from weeks to years to implement and for the results to become apparent. When fast actions are needed to counteract competitive moves or shifts in demand, price has the advantage that changes can be implemented in a matter of hours or days.

In this chapter we look first at the three key factors that should always be considered when setting price—demand, competition, and cost. Following this we examine a fourth factor, channel price structure, that is always present when channel intermediaries are used. After gaining an understanding of these factors, we turn to a brief overview of the laws dealing with price and a summary of the things companies cannot do legally. And finally we will examine several pricing strategies.

KEY FACTORS IN SETTING PRICE

We would like to set a price for our product that will maximize profit. To do this we need to know what the demand for our product will be at different price levels, what competitors' prices are, how competitors will react to our price, and what effect different sales volumes will have on our costs. As the demand for our product rises, the lower our unit costs should be. But if competitors' prices are lower than ours, demand for our product will fall and our costs will rise. And unless we price higher than our costs, we eventually will go broke. Thus we can see that setting an optimum price is not really feasible. Because we are dealing with imperfect information, we will have to base our calculations partly on assumptions. If we have past experience with the industry, this will help with our assumptions. But experience won't be available to help us price new products. Despite the difficulties, it's not hopeless. There are theory, practice, and research to help. We will consider these as we discuss the subject.

Demand Factors

Market demand for a product sets the upper limit for the marketer's pricing decisions. Products cannot be priced higher than potential customers are willing to pay.

> Demand is the total quantity of product purchased in dollars or units during a given time period.

The key question for the marketing planner is what demand will be in the future. From our previous discussions we know that future demand for the company's product will be based on market, competitive, and other environmental conditions, plus how the company uses the marketing mix. In this discussion, however, we will concentrate on price as it affects demand, even though we know that in the real world price is only one influence.

Forecasting demand is difficult enough, but forecasting changes in demand based only on changes in price is even more so. Let's review the concept of elasticity of demand, since it can be a key element in price forecasting.

Elasticity of Demand. No aspect of demand arouses more interest than the concept of elasticity. Different products respond differently to changes in price. A slight decrease in the price of one product will increase demand greatly, while the demand for another will vary only slightly with changes in price.

> Elasticity is a measure of the relative change in total revenue (price × quantity purchased) resulting from a change in product price.

Table 18-1 shows how the raising of price can affect total revenue for two products in different ways. For product A total revenue decreases when price is raised. Where price and revenue move in opposite directions, as they do for product A, price is said to be *elastic*. When they move in the same direction, as for product B, demand is said to be *inelastic*. Notice that in both examples the quantity demanded decreased as price increased. The key variable in determining price elasticity, therefore, is total revenue. When *revenue* does not vary with price, a product is said to have *unit elasticity*. When the *quantity* demanded does not change with price, demand is said to be *totally inelastic*. Figure 18-1 presents a graphic representation of these four demand situations. A formula for computing elasticity of demand is

$$\text{Elasticity} = \frac{\%\text{ change in quantity demanded}}{\%\text{ change in price}}$$

TABLE 18-1
Effect of Price on Quantity Sold and Total Revenue

	Product A			Product B	
Price, $	Quantity Sold	Total Revenue, $	Price, $	Quantity Sold	Total Revenue, $
30	15	450	17	300	5100
35	12	420	18	290	5220
40	9	360	19	280	5320
45	7	315	20	270	5400
50	6	300	21	260	5460
55	5	275	22	250	5500
60	4	240	23	240	5520

When the result of the calculation is 1, we have *unit elasticity*. When it is greater than 1, total revenue increases and demand is *elastic*. When it is less than 1, total revenue decreases and demand is *inelastic*.

Sensitivity to price change is not always known for a product industry, but when it is, this knowledge can be very useful. Steak, for example, is considered to be price elastic. Although steak is preferred by many people, there are cheaper substitutes such as hamburger or chicken. Hence a rise in the price of steak is likely to produce a larger percentage drop in quantity demanded. A drop in price, on the other hand, would likely produce a larger percentage increase in quantity demanded.

Table salt is thought to be inelastic because it is a necessity for most people and there is no good substitute. An increase in price is not likely to lower quantity demanded by the same percentage; likewise, a decrease in price is not likely to be accompanied by as large a percentage increase in quantity demanded. If the above assumptions are correct, then it follows that revenue would be increased from raising the price of salt and lowering the price of steak. Obviously, the marketer of salt should consider the effect an increase in price will have on customer goodwill, and the processor of meat will have to consider the cost of the steak when deciding the amount of the price reduction (since revenue − cost = profit).

Forecasting Demand Based on Price. Forecasting product demand at the company level is what we term *sales forecasting*. As we saw in Chapter 7, the sales forecaster considers a number of internal and external factors of which price is only one.

The sales forecast for the annual marketing and business plans will contain assumptions about price. In "normal" times price may be assumed to remain constant. It is more likely, however, that changes in price will have to be assumed because of inflation, economic cycles, or fluctuations in the supply of raw materials (e.g., a shortage of coffee beans due to the freezing weather or an excess of vegetable oil due to farmers shifting their plantings from corn to soybeans).

Price changes resulting from supply/demand and cost factors tend to spread rapidly throughout an industry. While it helps to correctly anticipate industry price changes, failure to do so is not necessarily crucial for the company, since the sales

a. Elastic

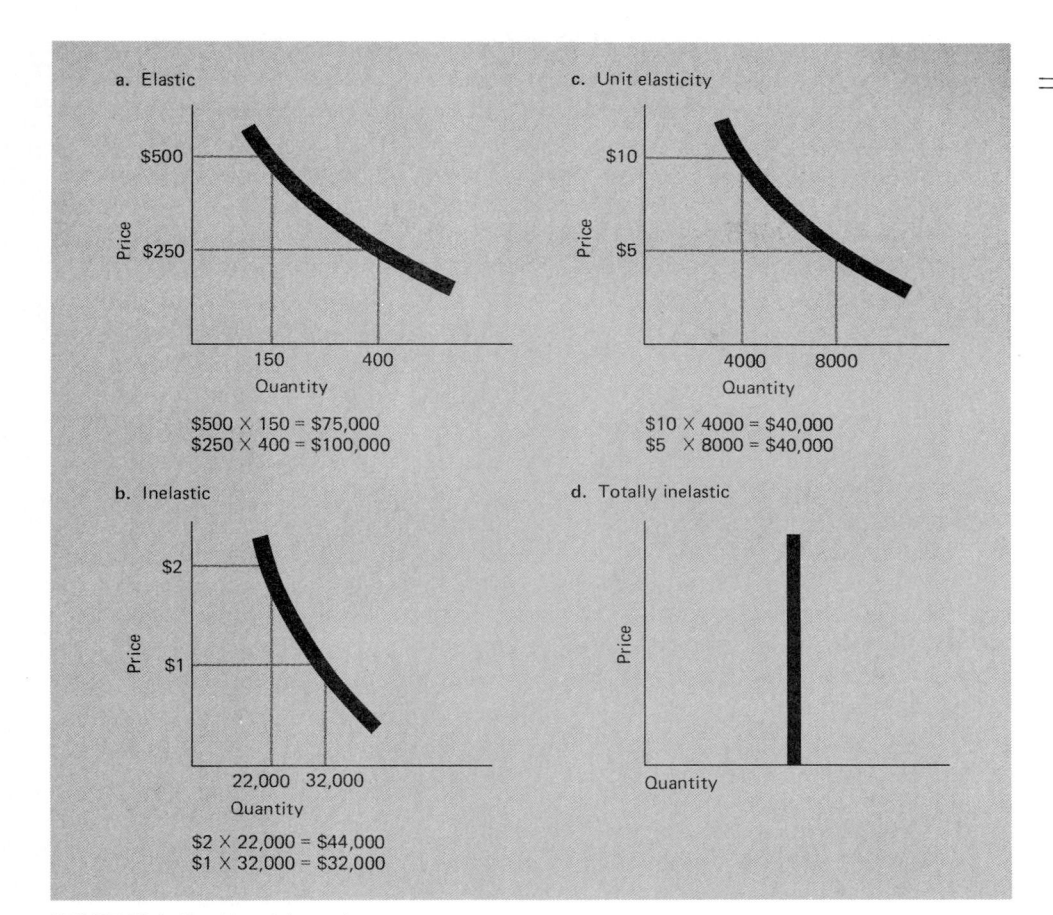

$500 × 150 = $75,000
$250 × 400 = $100,000

b. Inelastic

$2 × 22,000 = $44,000
$1 × 32,000 = $32,000

c. Unit elasticity

$10 × 4000 = $40,000
$5 × 8000 = $40,000

d. Totally inelastic

FIGURE 18-1. Elasticity of demand.

forecast can be updated at the time price changes occur. This is not the case, however, when introducing new products or when attempting to use price as a strategy. In these situations accurate price forecasting can mean profits instead of losses. Although management judgment is always a factor in these decisions, there are aids to judgment such as pricing research, statistical methods, customer surveys, and simulated and real test marketing. Pricing research and statistical methods are the most helpful in setting price strategy for existing products. Surveys and test markets are the most helpful in setting new product prices.

Pricing research. This function is largely one of maintaining records of company, industry, and competitive pricing and sales data over time. This information can be used for statistical methods of forecasting, developing pricing models, and for background information and analysis in assisting management judgment. Responsibility for gathering, storing, and analyzing the information may be assigned to the pricing, market research, or the marketing information systems departments. Examples of the kind of information that should be collected by product on a regular and continuing basis are:

1. Company prices along with price changes by dates
2. Competitors' prices along with price changes by dates

3. Company and competitors' shares of market measured periodically (to see whether price affected market share)
4. Company sales records; also competitors' sales records, such as from annual stockholders' reports
5. Monthly (or more frequent) records of industry sales
6. Records of general and industry price levels
7. Trends of raw materials and labor costs
8. Indexes of economic factors that affect customers' ability to buy the company's product
9. Past records of competitive reactions to price changes initiated by others
10. Periodic interviews with end customers, the trade, and the product sales force for attitudes which could affect buying response to price changes

Analysis of these types of information can indicate the degree of demand elasticity, show whether an industry pricing pattern exists, and provide information for statistical price forecasting and pricing models.

Statistical methods. The addendum to Chapter 7 explains statistical techniques for sales forecasting such as trend extrapolation, time series analysis, and regression analysis. The pros and cons that were listed for these techniques also apply to price forecasting. Generally speaking, statistical approaches to price forecasting are useful means of forecasting the future based on the past, but are unreliable if future conditions turn out to be very different from the past.

Forecasting models which permit price to be used as a variable are difficult to construct, but can be useful as decision tools. The value of a pricing model improves over time with experience. Forecasts of the effects of price changes can be compared with actual results, and the model adjusted accordingly.

Customer surveys. Surveys of customers are of limited value in predicting the effects of price changes for established products because of the likelihood of biased answers, that is, the tendency of customers to favor lower prices and dislike higher prices. Also, consumers often can't remember what they normally pay for products. When S.C. Johnson & Son, Inc., asked consumers what they paid for air fresheners, only 28 percent were within 15 percent of actual prices, 39 percent were off by more than that, and 33 percent had no idea what they paid.[1]

On the other hand, consumer surveys may provide advance warning by uncovering recent market developments not yet reflected in sales statistics. They are useful also in gauging customer attitudes and sensitivity to price. Regular studies by organizations such as the University of Michigan Survey Research Center help companies gauge consumer sentiment toward spending as it may be affected by price.

Customer surveys can provide more help in setting prices for new products. Care must be taken when projecting the findings of these surveys, however, since opinions are obtained in an artificial, nonmarket situation. Before questioning about price, it is essential to decide first whether the interviewee would be likely to buy the product if offered. Once a potential prospect is identified, the interview is continued to learn at what price level the prospect would be most likely to buy.

In a market survey designed to gauge the sales potential of its proposed electric floorwasher, the Hoover Company exposed prospects identified as likely buyers to different prices—$49.95, $59.95, $69.95, and $79.95. To avoid the bias in favor of low price that would occur if prospects were asked what they would be willing to pay, only one price was mentioned when the prospect was asked about the likelihood of buying. The results indicated that the $69.95 price would produce the highest revenue (quantity × price), even though the greatest quantity would be bought at $49.95.

Simulated market tests. These tests were described in the previous chapter. They provide a more reliable means of finding the optimum price for a new product than do customer surveys. In a test using a simulated store, for example, the product price can be changed for each consumer group taken through the store, and the rates of purchase compared for each price. Paper Mate found this method useful in pricing its new erasable ink pen. Even though demand was inelastic up to a price of $1.95, product management recommended a price of $1.69. This is an example of management judgment being added to research findings.

Test markets. Real market tests are better for testing price for new products than are either simulated market tests or customer surveys, since they test consumer reaction under real market conditions. The new product is tested in more than one market simultaneously, using a different price in each. For these tests to be reliable, the test markets must be similar, price must be the only variable, and adjustments are required for any differences in competitive activity by market during the test period. Additional information can be learned by interviewing nonpurchasers to find out whether price was a factor in their failure to purchase.

Management judgment. Pricing decisions normally are made at higher management levels. Management judgment is always an important input, irrespective of whether the previously described tools have been used. Management normally would not rely completely on a pricing model even if the model represented the most sophisticated pricing decision tool available. The more experience management has had with its own industry, the more confident it is when making pricing decisions for existing products. The less experience it has had, such as with new products, the more it tends to rely on research and market tests.

Competitive Factors

Competitive prices often are the overriding consideration in setting and maintaining price. Other things being equal, you will have difficulty attracting customers if your price is much higher than competitors'; if your price is much lower, you may start a price war in which both you and your competitors end up with reduced profit margins and possibly losses.

Companies usually offer products to compete in one or more of three price segments: high, medium, or low. Price competition occurs even more within segments than between segments. Prices tend to fall within a relatively narrow range around the midpoint or average (the *market price*) for each price segment. Patterns develop in which the strongest companies usually (but not always) price at the higher end of the range and weaker companies price at the lower end. In a well-established market these relationships tend to hold even as industry price levels change in response to changes in demand or costs. The Church brand, for example, has long been the market leader in toilet seats. (Its slogan is "The Best Seat in the House.") Historically, Church obtained about a 10 percent price premium over its principal competitors. Whether price changes (up or down) were initiated by Church or others, the 10 percent differential tended to hold.

The pattern may be upset, however, by a current competitor (or a new entrant in the industry) who prices aggressively to gain market share. This may be done by cutting price below what appears justified by changes in demand or materials costs; or it can be caused by a company not following an industrywide price increase. Other companies must then decide whether they will meet the competitor's price cut. Several external and internal factors can affect the decisions. Let's assume that one or more of your competitors (not the market leader) suddenly reduce price by 10 percent with no apparent reason other than to gain market share. Should you also cut price, take no action, or try to offset the aggressor's moves with nonprice actions? Your answer can be influenced by a number of factors, examples of which are listed in Table 18-2. We will discuss each of these briefly.

Price Sensitivity. Some product categories are more price sensitive than others. A category is *price sensitive* when brand preferences are not strong enough to prevent customers from switching to a brand that drops its price below the market. Such products are perceived as homogenous or only slightly differentiated. Examples include gasoline, cigarettes, paper towels, and automobile tires. Many people, for instance, will switch gasoline brands for a difference of as little as 2 cents per gallon.

Product categories with *low price sensitivity* are those in which people will not readily switch from their favorite brands when there is a price cut by another brand. Such brands tend to be highly differentiated; or buyers tend to have high personal involvement in the product purchase. Examples include wines, cigars, home furnishings, clothes, and professional services. Many people will not switch from a designer sport shirt even when a nearly identical chain store brand sells for several dollars less.

There can be other reasons that distinguish a product category by its degree of market price sensitivity. Most companies know from experience and observation pretty much where their industry is positioned. In fact, we should use caution in categorizing an industry on the basis of anything other than the way it acts. We might

TABLE 18-2
Conditions Influencing Pressure to Respond to Competitors' Price Cuts

Conditions of High Pressure	Conditions of Low Pressure
Product market is highly price-sensitive	Product market is not highly price-sensitive
Your market position is weak	Your market position is strong
You serve low- or medium-price segments	You serve the high-price segment
You offer a "me-too" or parity product	Your product is differentiated
Industry is oligopolistic	Industry is monopolistic
Nonprice options are few	There are good nonprice options
Quality and/or service are of low importance	Quality and/or service are of high importance

reason, for instance, that a generic product category such as aspirin would be highly price sensitive, since all aspirin is the same. Yet Bayer, the highest-price brand, continues to have the largest market share (although it has lost some share over time to lower-price brands). A similar situation exists with acetaminophen pain relievers, where Tylenol, the market leader and the highest-priced brand, has lost little of its commanding market share* to lower-priced Datril (although Tylenol did reduce price somewhat). Observation of the pain-reliever market suggests that price differentials have little to do with brand market shares.

Market Position. The stronger your position in terms of market share, the less pressure there is for you to respond in kind to price cuts, particularly if they are made by a weaker competitor. Usually you have time to assess your situation, since many customers will remain loyal to your brand, at least in the short run. If you think that the competitor's price cut is likely to be temporary, you may decide to wait it out or try to offset the competitor's price advantage with nonprice strategies such as more advertising or promotional deals. On the other side of the coin, if your market position is weak, you may have no choice but to respond to another's price cut, particularly if it has been initiated by a stronger competitor.

Sometimes even the market leader may not be able to withstand aggressive price competition. Initially Xerox held its price when its dominant position in the office copier market was challenged by much lower priced Japanese brands. Eventually Xerox slashed its own prices as it became apparent that the Japanese were making serious inroads into its share of the small-copier market. According to Dataquest, Inc., Xerox's share of the U.S. market for plain copiers fell from 75 percent in 1975 to 42 percent in 1981.[2]

Price Segments Served. There is more pressure to respond to competitors' price cuts in the medium- and low-price segments than in the high-price segment. The low-price segment in particular attracts buyers who are sensitive, whereas the high-price segment attracts buyers who are more interested in nonprice factors such as style, performance, and prestige. If Toyota lowers price, it puts pressure on other manufacturers of compact cars to respond. But a price cut by Cadillac may cause no immediate reaction from Mercedes Benz or Rolls Royce.

Product Differentiation. The closer a product is to commodity status, the more pressure there is to respond to price cuts. The prices of undifferentiated products sold on commodity market exchanges, such as grains, hogs, sugar, and metals, reflect traders' expectations of future supply and demand. Producers of these commodities cannot influence price. Their only choice is to withhold the product from the market or accept the market price. Vendors of component materials (sheet steel, newsprint, cement) have somewhat more opportunity to influence price (by differentiating with augmented services), even though their industry prices are also tied closely to supply and demand.

Manufactured products offer the greatest opportunity to vary price (or resist price competition) because they can be differentiated through design, services, and advertising. Highly differentiated brands such as Jack Daniels whiskey, Crest

---

*Except temporarily after poison was found in some Tylenol packages in drug stores. Tylenol returned to its leadership position after being reintroduced in tamper-proof packages.

toothpaste, and the *New Yorker* magazine seem to be little affected by competitors' price cuts.

Type of Competition. A characteristic of *oligopoly* is that the dominant companies in the industry will protect their market shares by meeting price cuts made by any of the other large companies. (They may not respond to cuts by small companies, which don't have much impact on the shares of the larger companies.) Hence we can conclude that the pressure to respond to price cuts in an oligopolistic industry is great. As a practical matter, however, price cuts to gain market share usually do not occur in this type of industry. Everyone knows that others will respond in kind and that the initiator will end up with no gain in market share.

While oligopoly effectively precludes price as a competitive weapon, it does provide a vehicle for making needed changes in industry price levels in response to cost changes or seasonal and cyclical fluctuations in demand. Often (though not always) the *price leader* is the largest company in the industry (e.g., U.S. Steel) or the strongest regional competitor (e.g., Standard Oil of Indiana in the midwest). If the leader guesses right on the size and timing of the price change, other companies follow. If, however, a large competitor does not agree with the price change and does not follow, the leader is forced to back down. To illustrate, U.S. Steel may raise the price of cold-rolled steel by $5 a ton, but Bethlehem Steel follows with an increase of only $3. To prevent Bethlehem from taking market share, U.S. Steel backs down to $3. We see a similar pattern in the auto industry when new annual models are introduced or when rising costs force price changes during the model year. General Motors or Ford usually set the new price for a new model. Competitors will price the same, higher, or lower. The leader then resets its price as necessary to be at a competitive market level.

Monopolistic competition is quite another matter. Here there is less pressure to respond to price cuts, since most of these smaller companies do not compete directly with one another because of geographic separation or product differentiation. Also, any gain in market share by one is not large enough to have a significant effect on the many others in the industry.

Nonprice Options. Unless forced to by a significant change in economic conditions, many companies prefer not to reduce their list prices, not only because these actions reduce their profit margins, but also because it is difficult to raise prices later when market conditions improve. A stronger company may try to avoid meeting a competitive price cut by using nonprice actions such as more advertising, sales promotion, or augmented services.

After responding to the price cuts of Japanese competitors, Xerox avoided further cuts (at least for a time) by using its strong financial position to lend money at bargain rates to customers for purchasing Xerox's equipment. This was a particularly effective nonprice option during a period when high interest rates were hurting industry sales.[3]

Nonprice options can also be used as substitutes for price increases. For many years candy companies lowered the size of their candy bars to offset rising costs rather than depend entirely on price increases. When bars got so small that it became impractical to reduce them further, Mars took the opposite tack by increasing the size of its bar while holding price steady. Hershey, however, responded with an increase in the size of its bars, and a "size" war broke out.[4]

When no effective nonprice options are left to be tried, a company may have to reduce its price to meet competitors' cuts. This happened in the latter stages of the deep economic recession of 1981-1982 when many strong companies could no longer avoid making price cuts.

Quality/Service. When quality and/or service is of lesser importance, there is more pressure to respond to competitors' price cuts. This is the case for industrial materials and supplies purchased according to specifications (set by government, industry, or the buyer). Examples are lubricating oils, industrial alcohol, plain boxboard cartons, and typewriter paper. Not only is product quality the same, but these products often require no special services. As long as the product meets the *specs* (and on-time delivery is assured), organizational buyers tend to accept the lowest price offer. In such circumstances sellers find it difficult not to respond quickly to competitors' price cuts.

Yet there are many situations in which quality or service far outweigh a bargain price. These occur for both consumer and industrial goods. As buyers we tend not to deal with price cutters where safety and health are involved, such as when buying a parachute or leasing a blood dialysis machine. Neither are we attracted much to discounted merchandise when buying clothing for important events such as a wedding or a job interview. And manufacturers place more emphasis on product performance and vendor services than on price when buying plant machinery where the cost of production line breakdowns can outweigh machine price differentials.

Although quality and service are means of differentiating products, there can be other factors in the selection of the supplier. Let's assume that the buyer opts for quality/service rather than price savings. Once that decision has been made, selection then rests on other perceived differences among those sellers who meet the basic tests of quality and service (such as personal friendships built up over a long period with a particular supplier).

We offer no absolute rules for responding to price changes in the several situations that have been discussed under the heading "Competitive Factors." Nevertheless, knowledge that some conditions create more pressure to respond than others can be helpful in planning alternative pricing strategies.

Cost Factors

If demand and competition set the upper limits for our prices, costs set the floor under which we cannot price without losing money. However, we should remember that costs will vary depending on such things as units produced, experience, and the efficiency of plant and equipment. The discussions of break-even analysis will show how differences in the quantity of units produced can affect cost.

Several kinds of costs can be seen in most business organizations. These can be classified in terms of their relationship to a unit of output (direct or indirect) as well as their relationship to the total volume of this output (fixed or variable).

Examples of *direct costs* (directly traceable to a unit of output) are costs such as labor, raw materials, components, and sales commissions. Examples of *indirect costs* (those not traceable to a unit of output) are maintenance of production machines, building rent (or depreciation if the building is company owned), research and development, and sales offices costs. Both direct and indirect costs may have components that vary with the production process. Thus *variable costs* are those costs which vary with the number of units produced and sold. *Fixed costs* exist even when no production or sales occur. While there are exceptions, most direct costs are viewed as variable and most indirect costs are viewed as fixed.

These general statements about costs are sufficient background for discussing break-even analysis. It should be noted, however, that classification of costs are accounting decisions based on the facts of each situation. Cost information for break-even and other price-related analyses are provided by the cost accounting system.

Break-even Analysis. Break-even analysis uses fixed and variable costs, units produced, and estimated sales revenue to determine the break-even point—the point at which revenue equals total costs. It also shows the profit to be gained as revenues rise above total costs. These relationships can be seen in the break-even chart, Figure 18-2. A break-even chart is a practical tool used to compare the potential profitability of various estimated demand curves, each assuming a different unit sales price. It does not ease the task of estimating demand at different prices, but does tell us which demand curve would be the most profitable.

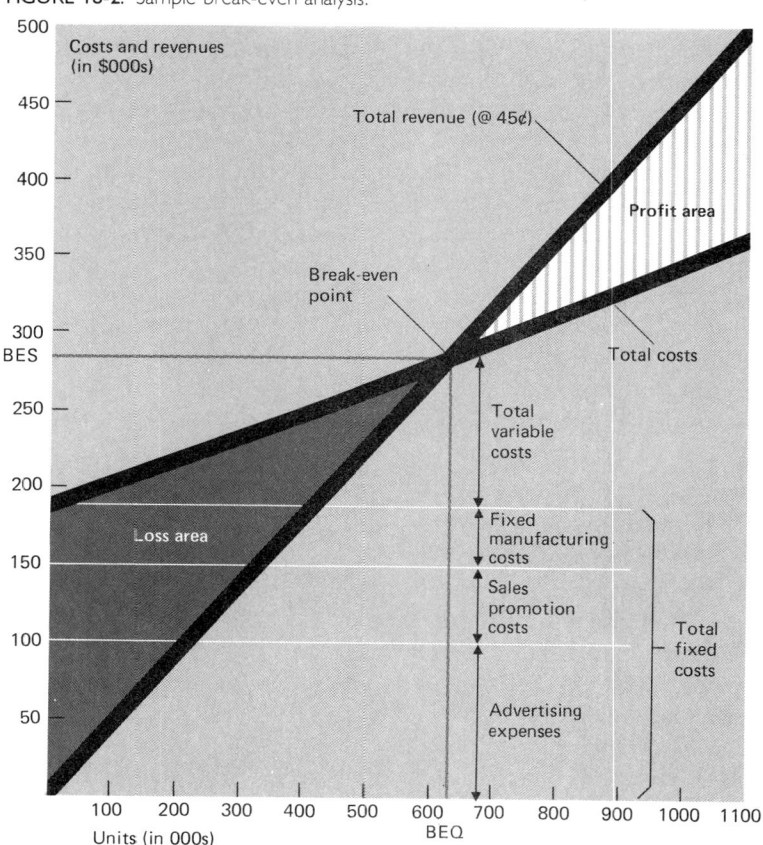

FIGURE 18-2. Sample break-even analysis.

BES = Break-even sales
BEQ = Break-even quantity

Let's look at a manufacturer of a frozen yogurt dessert stick to illustrate how break-even points are computed, charted, and analyzed. This company spends $100,000 for advertising and $50,000 for sales promotion per year. Its fixed manufacturing costs are $40,000 and the variable cost per unit is 15 cents. The price per unit is 45 cents. Assuming that the advertising and sales promotion expenditures are held fixed during the year, the break-even quantity can be calculated as follows:

$$BEQ = \frac{FC}{P - VC}$$

where
BEQ = break-even quantity
FC = total fixed costs
VC = variable cost per unit
P = price per unit

In this example break-even quantity is

$$BEQ = \frac{\$100{,}000 + \$50{,}000 + \$40{,}000}{\$.45 - \$.15}$$

$$= \frac{\$190{,}000}{\$.30}$$

$$= 633{,}333 \text{ units}$$

This means that the manufacturer must produce and sell 633,333 units to cover all costs. At the sales price of 45 cents, this represents total sales of $285,000.

An alternative method of determining the break-even point is to use dollar sales volume rather than quantity of unit sales:

$$BES = \frac{FC}{PM}$$

where
BES = break-even sales
FC = total fixed costs
PM = profit margin (as percent of selling price)

and

$$PM = \frac{P - VC}{P}$$

In the current example

$$PM = \frac{.45 - .15}{.45} = .6667\%$$

and

$$BES = \frac{\$100{,}000 + \$50{,}000 + \$40{,}000}{.6667}$$

$$= \$285{,}000$$

Dividing the break-even sales by the selling price will give the break-even quantity

$$BEQ = \frac{BES}{P}$$
$$= \frac{\$285,000}{.45}$$
$$= 633,333 \text{ units}$$

The profit margin ratio is used to examine the impact of a change in price on the break-even point. For example, a price reduction to 35¢ will result in a lower profit margin:

$$PM = \frac{.35 - .15}{.35} = .5714\%$$
$$BES = \frac{\$190,000}{.5714} = \$332,500$$
$$BEQ = \frac{\$332,500}{.35} = 950,000 \text{ units}$$

At a 35¢ price the company will have to sell 316,667 more units in order to break-even than it would at 45¢ (950,000 less 633,333). Figure 18-3 shows the impact of various price changes (60 cents, 50 cents, 45 cents, 40 cents, 35 cents) on the break-even point.

Break-even analysis is also useful for showing the impact of different decisions about costs. If the $50,000 in sales promotion were changed from a fixed amount to a variable one (say 10¢ per unit), it would affect the break-even point as follows:

$$FC = \$140,000$$
$$VC = .25$$
$$P = .45$$
$$BEQ = \frac{\$140,000}{.45 - .25} = \$700,000 \text{ units}$$
$$\text{and } PM = \frac{.45 - .25}{.45} = .4444\%$$
$$BES = \frac{\$140,000}{.4444} = \$315,000$$

Another decision may be to increase the automation of production by buying a $60,000 piece of machinery. This would have the effect of increasing fixed costs to $250,000, while reducing costs from 15 cents to 11½ cents. The new break-even point with this equipment installed would be

$$BEQ = \frac{250,000}{.45 - .115} = 746,269 \text{ units}$$
$$BES = \frac{\$250,000}{.7444} = \$335,841$$

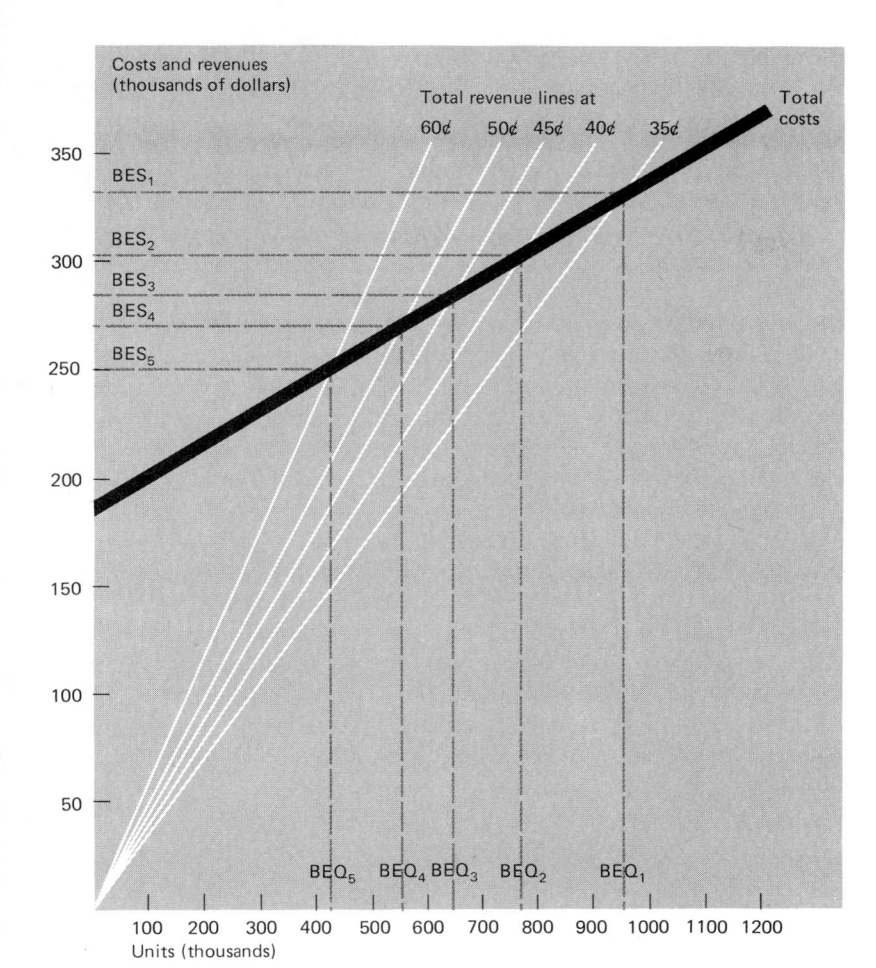

FIGURE 18-3. Impact of different prices on break-even points.

BES = Break-even sales
BEQ = Break-even quantity

Deciding to purchase the equipment or change price cannot be made using break-even analysis alone; it must be combined with demand to develop estimates of profitability. The total revenue line of the break-even chart is simply an assumed price multiplied by the estimated quantity to be sold at that price. In our example, the marketing research department made estimates of demand at different prices:

Price, ¢	Estimated Unit Demand
25	2,200,000
30	1,800,000
35	1,450,000
40	1,100,000
45	800,000
50	600,000
55	450,000
60	350,000

With this information we can now compute profitability at each price. As can be seen in Table 18-3, the maximum profit is $100,000, obtained by selling 1,450,000 frozen dessert sticks at a price of 35 cents.

Profit Analysis. The above analysis is most relevant to the analysis of different decisions and their impact on costs, prices, volume, and profits. Thus, for example, the profit contribution of a $1000 increase in volume on the frozen yogurt dessert manufacturer would be $1000 × PM. In the first instance (a price of 45¢ and VC of 15¢) the PM was .666 and the profits, generated from the new $1000 volume, are $666. This addition to profits results from the fact that the fixed costs have already been paid for by the BEQ and BES levels and every additional increase in sales must only cover variable costs. The remainder is profit.

This logic is particularly useful when evaluating price changes in a multiproduct company. Rather than maximize sales revenues, the company should examine the PM of each product and then assess changes in price and volume based on the resulting change in PM. Obviously any change resulting in a higher PM ratio would contribute more to profits once the BES have been achieved. A change in fixed costs will not affect PM, but rather increase the BES and BEQ. An increase in price (or a reduction in VC) can offset a change in fixed costs. Thus a company which evaluates the usefulness of switching from direct labor (VC) to labor-saving devices (partly FC and partly VC) can achieve a higher PM ratio and the same amount of profits if volume remains the same. A useful implication of the above is the potential for evaluating price increases and their impact on profits. To maintain profits at current levels, the sales change must not exceed

$$\Delta TR = \frac{\Delta P}{PM + \Delta P}$$

where
- ΔTR = percentage change in total revenue
- ΔP = percentage change in price
- PM = profit margin

Using our example, an increase of 10 percent in price (from 45¢ to 50¢) will not affect profits so long as sales do not decline by more than 13 percent:

$$\frac{.10}{.6667 + .10} = \frac{.10}{.7667} = .13$$

An important advantage of profit analysis is the opportunity it provides to calculate the impact of various pricing decisions. On the other hand, profit analysis is no better than the cost data and the sales forecasts that go into it. Consequently, profit-oriented marketing management is highly dependent on good accountants, good sales forecasters, and good internal report systems.

Environmental Effects on Costs. Costs change almost constantly due to a variety of factors: inflation, labor contracts, government regulations, interest rates,

TABLE 18-3
Finding the Price That Maximizes Profit

Price, $	BEQ	BES	Estimated Unit Demand	Total Revenue, $	Total Costs, $	Profit, $
.25	1,900,000	475,000	2,200,000	550,000	520,000	30,000
.30	1,266,666	380,000	1,800,000	540,000	460,000	80,000
.35*	950,000	332,500	1,450,000	507,500	407,500	**100,000**
.40	760,000	304,000	1,100,000	440,000	355,000	85,000
.45	633,333	285,000	800,000	360,000	310,000	50,000
.50	542,857	271,429	600,000	300,000	280,000	20,000
.55	475,000	261,250	450,000	247,500	257,500	(10,000)
.60	422,222	253,333	350,000	210,000	242,500	(32,500)

*Price that maximizes profit.

and the effects of economic cycles and seasonal fluctuations on supply and demand. Consequently, organizations review their product costs periodically and consider whether price changes are needed.

Some factors such as economic cycles, seasonal fluctuations, and interest rates affect costs both upward and downward. Others, however, tend to provide steady upward pressures on costs, such as inflation and government regulations. Inflationary cost increases represent a long-term trend, but it is when these costs exceed productivity gains that economic hardship results. Modest cost increases during the 1950s and 1960s were offset by increases in productivity; consequently, prices rose slowly, actually dropping in some years. However, the sharp rise in oil prices beginning in 1974 substantially exceeded the growth in productivity and led to high rates of inflation.

Consumer pressures, accompanied by rising public concern for the natural environment and public health and safety, resulted in a marked increase in government regulations during the 1960s and 1970s. Most resulted in increasing the costs of operating all types of institutions, including businesses, schools, hospitals, and all levels of government. Billions of dollars have been spent for things such as pollution-control equipment, safety devices, noise abatement, and access ways for the disabled. As socially desirable as these regulations are, they represent additions to cost unaccompanied by productivity improvements. The result is higher prices and higher taxes.

Just as inflation is not as serious for some families as for others, neither does it impact all organizations equally. Organizations selling petroleum, medical services, and computers, for example, usually are able to pass along inflationary cost increases in the form of higher prices. Marketers of nonnecessities (entertainment and luxury items), on the other hand, may have to absorb some or all inflationary cost increases. Producers of durable goods (autos and appliances) representing postponable purchases also have difficulty passing along inflationary costs, and their profit margins suffer accordingly.

It is a rare situation where a business can pass along *all* cost increases with impunity. An apparent exception was a highly profitable manufacturer of tools used in the construction industry. This firm's products were so good and its distribution so strong that it held a commanding share of its market. And it raised its prices fairly regularly. When the executive vice president was asked how price decisions were made, he explained that the income statement was reviewed at the end of each quarter; if margins appeared to be narrowing, prices were raised to bring margins into line. At that time building contractors did not resist the higher prices, since they were passed along to the real estate developers who had no problems selling their houses and buildings. The tool company management's casual approach to pricing was possible because of the inelasticity of demand for its products and the absence of strong competition. This company's pricing decisions became more difficult when construction activity turned down later.

Many companies do not *automatically* pass along cost increases in the form of higher prices. They give serious consideration to the effects the increases would have on demand and what the pricing reactions of their competitors might be.

CHANNEL PRICE STRUCTURE

A manufacturer that distributes through wholesalers and/or retailers has two basic prices to establish: (1) the *list price* (the recommended price to the end customer, or retail price), and (2) the manufacturer's price to the wholesaler (or retailer if distribution is direct to the retailer).

The list price is determined first, since it should represent what the manufacturer thinks is the proper price to the final buyer after considering demand and competition. In most situations the manufacturer cannot legally dictate the retailer's selling price; therefore, the manufacturer's list is a suggested price only. Full-service retailers may sell at the suggested list, whereas others will systematically discount the manufacturer's list price.

The difference between the retail price to the consumer and the manufacturer's price to the wholesaler is what channel intermediaries receive for their services. These are called *trade discounts*. How they are structured represents an important decision for the manufacturer. Before getting into the widely used trade discount approach and other types of manufacturer discounts, we'll first discuss the *markup pricing* process used by retailers and some manufacturers.

Markup Pricing

While the markup method of pricing is more commonly associated with retail trade, it is used by some manufacturers as well. It begins with a percentage markup (for profit) being added to the manufacturer's costs. This becomes the *manufacturer's selling price* to the wholesaler. The wholesaler adds a percent markup to the manufacturer's price, which becomes the *wholesale price* to the retailer. The retailer then adds a percent markup to the wholesale price, which becomes the *retail price* to the consumer. A common variation of this method is to compute markup on selling price rather than on cost.* This is normal in the retail trade.

---

*Tables are available which convert markup on cost to markup on selling price and vice versa. Table 18-4 includes an example in which markups on selling price are used. Their equivalents in markup on cost are shown on the next page:

The advantage to the manufacturer of using markups on cost is its simplicity. To determine price the manufacturer has only to add the desired rate of profit to the estimated product cost. The disadvantage is that this can lead to unrealistic pricing in terms of demand and competition. If a manufacturer's costs are high and if wholesalers and retailers take their standard markups, the manufacturer's products will be offered to the final buyer at prices higher than competitors. If the manufacturer's price is too far out of line, it will be reflected in low demand from wholesalers. To remain in business the manufacturer will have to sell at break-even or a loss until costs can be reduced.

The trade discount form of pricing is more externally oriented to the realities of the market.

Trade Discounts

These are also called *functional discounts* because they represent payments by the manufacturer for distribution functions performed by wholesalers and retailers. These functions include warehousing, inventory financing, customer credit, delivery (by wholesalers primarily), display and promotion. These are functions that the manufacturer would have to perform and pay for if channel intermediaries were not used. Companies that distribute direct to the end buyer must, in fact, add the costs of their own distribution to their other costs before determining price.

Trade discounts normally are expressed as retailer discounts and wholesaler discounts. Table 18-4 illustrates how discounts are applied to arrive at the manufacturer's selling price. This table also shows the markup approach using similar data. In both examples the manufacturer has assumed discounts or markups that are standard for the product industry. In reality wholesalers and/or retailers may for competitive reasons not follow the standard.

Series of Discounts. The manufacturer will quote a discount to the wholesaler that will include both the retailer's discount (if there is a retailer in the distribution channel) and the wholesaler's discount. Thus, in the example in Table 18-4, the manufacturer's total discount to the wholesaler would be 48 percent (.48 × 500 = $240). Instead of the single discount of 48 percent, the manufacturer may quote a series of percentage discounts, expressed as 40-15-6 and computed as follows: $500 less 40 percent = $300; less 15 percent = $255; less 6 percent = $240.

Wholesaler discounts expressed as a series are common in industrial distribution where no retailer is involved. There are two principal reasons for using the series of discounts. The first is that discounts may be added or subtracted depending

% markup on selling price	% markup on cost
10	11
20	25
40	66⅔

The formulas for conversion are

$$\% \text{ markup on cost} = \frac{\% \text{ markup on selling price}}{100\% - \% \text{ markup on selling price}}$$

$$\% \text{ markup on selling price} = \frac{\% \text{ markup on cost}}{100\% + \% \text{ markup on cost}}$$

TABLE 18-4

Trade Discount Compared with Markup Approach to Channel Pricing

DISCOUNT APPROACH	
Estimated list price to final buyer	$500.00
Less: retail discount (40%)	200.00
Price to retailer	300.00
Less: wholesale discount (20%)	60.00
Manufacturer's price to wholesaler	$240.00
MARKUP APPROACH*	
Manufacturer's cost	$216.00
Add: markup (10%)	24.00
Price to wholesaler	240.00
Add: wholesaler's markup (20%)	60.00
Price to retailer	300.00
Add: retailer markup (40%)	200.00
List price to final buyer	$500.00

*Markup computed on selling price.

on the number of functions performed by different classes of wholesalers.[5] Some wholesalers, for example, provide customer repair services or supplement the manufacturer's promotional efforts, for which they might receive an extra 5 or 10 percent discount. The second reason is that, in a market where prices fluctuate, it is quicker and simpler to change price by adding or dropping the last 5 percent discount, for example, than it is to print and distribute new price lists.

Discounts by Trade and Product Classes. Discounts vary by type of retail distribution and by product class. Retailers' costs vary according to the services performed and the rate of inventory turnover. A self-service food store has lower costs per sales dollar and operates on smaller discounts than an apothecary shop. The food store's self-service feature reduces the need for, and costs of, store sales clerks. The inventory turnover is rapid because merchandise is delivered to the store frequently and most items move off the shelf quickly. Thus average inventory investment costs are low.

The apothecary shop, on the other hand, bears the cost of having a pharmacist on duty at all times. Average prescription drug turnover is slow—and inventory costs high—because the shop must be able to fill all doctors' prescriptions immediately, even if a drug is prescribed infrequently. Drug manufacturers' trade discounts, therefore, must be considerably larger than those of manufacturers of groceries.

The rate of product movement also influences the size of the trade discount, as does the floor space required per dollar of sale. Ladies' hosiery will carry a much higher trade discount than cigarettes, for example, even though both are sold in a supermarket. Total discounts (for the wholesaler and retailer combined) commonly range between 20 and 55 percent from the list price. And exceptions occur on either side of the range.

Discount patterns differ by industry as a result of variations in distribution costs and tradition. These discount structures tend to become the norms which most companies observe.

Quantity Discounts

Manufacturers usually give discounts for larger purchases, since per unit selling, handling, and shipping costs are less. A sample discount schedule might be:

Units Ordered	% Discount
1 - 9	0
10 - 49	3
50 or more	5

Discounts may also be offered on cumulative purchases over a period such as a quarter or a year. Another form of quantity discount is to ship freight prepaid for any order over a certain size. Quantity discounts may also be used as a means of classifying customers into large-quantity buyers whom the seller is willing to serve direct and small-quantity buyers to be served through wholesalers.[6]

Payment Terms

Discounts are offered by most sellers to encourage prompt payment by the buyer. Discount terms are expressed as (for example) 2/10, net 30, meaning the purchaser may deduct 2 percent from the amount of the invoice if payment is made within 10 days. If the discount is not taken, the net (full amount of the invoice) is due within 30 days.

Discounts for prompt payment are sometimes referred to as *cash discounts,* a term going back to the days when purchasers were encouraged to pay cash on delivery. Virtually all business transactions today are based on credit. Both the seller and the buyer consider the cost of money; the seller when setting terms, and the buyer when deciding whether to accept the terms. As interest rates rise, the seller may liberalize the discount as an incentive for accounts to pay promptly and reduce the seller's need to borrow. The buyer will try to use the seller's money as long as possible by such means as waiting until the last day to take the discount (or wait even longer in hopes the seller will not object overtly). The buyer may forego the discount entirely if the discount is less favorable than bank rates.

Payment terms are used as incentives in various ways. In the Black & Decker case we will see that B&D considered raising its discount and lengthening the period for net payment as an incentive for larger orders.* Companies producing seasonal products offer extended terms (called *dating*) to encourage wholesalers to accept merchandise ahead of the season. If the wholesaler accepts garden hose in February, for example, it may not have to pay until June. The hose manufacturer saves the costs of warehousing and gets the cost advantage of maintaining normal manufacturing schedules during the off-season.

---

*The Black & Decker Manufacturing Co. case (13) at the end of Part Five also provides examples of the use of trade discounts, quantity discounts, dating terms, and promotional discounts.

Promotional Discounts

A promotional discount, or *allowance*, may be offered to wholesalers and/or retailers in exchange for such things as local advertising, special displays, or guaranteed shelf space. These may take the form of a percentage reduction in price or as an outright cash payment either to the channel member or to the promotional vehicle, e.g., a local newspaper.[7] From an accounting standpoint, discounts may be treated as allowances which are deducted from gross sales to arrive at net sales. Or they may be treated as promotional expenses, in which case they become part of the total marketing expense.

LEGAL ASPECTS OF PRICING

No area of marketing is more involved with the law than pricing. Understanding the law is not easy since the statutes are not always clear. Furthermore, the laws have been subject to many court interpretations over the years, and new applications of existing statutes are tested from time to time by the Department of Justice, the Federal Trade Commission, and other federal and state departments and agencies. Marketers can no longer rely on their personal interpretations of these laws, but need the advice of specialized legal counsel. Nevertheless, it is essential that marketers understand the broad intent and main provisions of the laws that affect pricing.

No legislative acts that we will discuss deal with price alone. They were designed to promote competition, protect buyers and sellers, and regulate certain business practices. We'll describe briefly those portions of the principal acts that deal with or affect pricing, out of which we will draw some general pricing guidelines for marketers.[8]

The Principal Federal Acts

The principal federal acts are the Sherman Antitrust Act, the Federal Trade Commission Act, the Wheeler-Lea Act, the Clayton Act, and the Robinson-Patman Act. Additionally there are many state laws and some city laws directed at pricing. Marketers are subject as well to administrative actions with respect to pricing by the Federal Trade Commission (FTC) and state and city regulatory agencies.

Sherman Antitrust Act (1890). The Sherman Act outlaws contracts, combinations, or conspiracies in restraint of trade and prohibits monopoly or attempts to monopolize in interstate commerce. One of the outcomes of this law has been to ban price fixing. Conspiracies by companies to restrain trade through price fixing are automatic violations. Common pricing actions having the effect of fixing prices also may be ruled violations, even when no overt conspiracy is proven to exist. Careful managements, therefore, not only abstain from collusion, but also avoid actions that might appear to be attempts to fix prices. The law applies to manufacturers, wholesalers, and retailers when they are involved in interstate commerce.

Federal Trade Commission Act (1914). This act established the Federal Trade Commission (FTC), giving it broad powers to deal with unfair methods of competition in interstate commerce. The Wheeler-Lea Act (1938) increased the scope of the FTC Act by outlawing "unfair or deceptive acts or practices." Also the new restrictions applied to sellers' actions as they affected consumers; formerly, they applied only to sellers' actions as they affected competing companies.

Clayton Act (1914). This supplemented the Sherman Antitrust Act by making it unlawful to discriminate in price between different purchasers of commodities when the effect was to lessen competition or tended to create a monopoly. Price discrimination between different purchasers of *commodities* was declared illegal per se. (Services were not mentioned.) The act authorized three legal defenses, with the burden of proof to be on the seller: (1) when there were differences in the grade, quality, or quantity of the commodity sold; (2) when there were differences in the costs of selling or transportation; and (3) when offers were made in good faith to meet competition.

Robinson-Patman Act (1936). This act amended the Clayton Act and extended the injury-to-competition clause to include buyers as well as sellers. It was passed largely to protect the independent merchant from the rising power of chain stores. The law, however, has been broadly applied to all types of transactions, including those between industrial goods sellers and buyers.

Taken together the Robinson-Patman and Clayton Acts explicitly declare several discriminatory pricing practices to be illegal. But they also include certain ways in which price discrimination can be legally justified.

Fictitious brokerage payments. The brokerage section does not prohibit payments to legitimate brokers. Rather, it forbids payment of fees, discounts, or allowances which might be made to chains or other large buyers as disguised price concessions.

Disporportional promotional offers. Sellers are not permitted to offer allowances for promotional services or facilities to customers (e.g., wholesalers or retailers) unless they are offered to all competing customers on "proportionately equal terms." This provision has not been easy to apply, although it seems intended to ensure that smaller wholesalers and retailers have the same access as large ones to manufacturers' promotional offers.

Price Discrimination Defenses. The defenses against price discrimination are (1) cost justification and (2) good faith. *Cost justification* requires proof that the sale was based on differentials in the costs of manufacture, sale, or delivery. Total costs—not marginal costs—must be used. With good cost accounting records, manufacturers usually can justify quantity discount schedules based on the differences in selling, handling, and delivery costs by size of order.[9] It is difficult, however, to prove manufacturing savings on individual orders unless production is for a specific order, such as in the case of engineered products built to a customer's requirements. Consequently, there have been few court cases where the manufacturing cost defense has been used successfully. But Kent Monroe argues that more companies could make successful cost defenses if they maintained cost accounting records that identify indirect marketing expenditures instead of lumping them into a general overhead category.[10]

The Robinson-Patman Act attempts to clarify the conditions under which the *good faith* offer can be used as a defense. These are as follows: (1) the competitor's price offering must be lawful; (2) the seller's price must be a temporary one to meet the competitor's offer and not part of a continuing price plan; (3) the seller's price must be for a specific quantity; and (4) the seller's price cannot be lower than the competitor's offer. Hard evidence often is difficult to obtain, however, as buyers have been known to exaggerate the competitor's offer in order to get an even lower price from the seller. Also, the competitor's offer may have been orally given. Without written evidence of a competitor's offer, the seller runs the risk of not being able to prove its defense. Marketing Note 18-1 suggests steps that management can take to ensure having valid defenses against price discrimination in case they are needed.

Buyer Inducement. It is not lawful for any person to induce or knowingly receive a discriminatory price. Presumably buyers violate the law when they pressure the manufacturer for prices they have reason to believe cannot be granted legally. This was an important amendment restricting the freedom buyers had enjoyed heretofore to pressure sellers for discriminatory prices where the only legal risk was carried by the sellers.

State Laws Affecting Pricing

In 1976 the federal fair trade laws authorizing resale price maintenance were repealed by Congress. Some states still have laws permitting the manufacturer to specify the retail price under certain conditions, although their number is declining as a result of court and legislative actions. Generally, manufacturers feel it is no longer practical to try to enforce price maintenance at the retail level even in states where it is legal.

More than half the states have laws requiring minimum markups by retailers, which are designed to help protect the small retailer. Also many states have specific laws setting minimum liquor prices and some states permit liquor sales only through state-operated stores.

Because federal laws apply only to interstate commerce, many states have their own versions of the federal antitrust laws which prohibit price fixing and price discrimination intrastate. State law is enforced by the state attorney general and the state courts, and largely affects local businesses that do not come under the

---

MARKETING NOTE 18-1

Guidelines for Justifying Price Differentials

How to Avoid Leaving Compliance with the Robinson-Patman Act to Chance

1. Provide a published price list that includes the price breaks and discount eligibility criteria.
2. Establish all discount schedules on a cost-justified basis.
3. Communicate to all sales personnel the policy of adhering to the established price lists and discount schedules.
4. Provide for specific procedures when departing from the established prices and discount schedules.
5. Develop a program for cost-justifying discount schedules and other sources of price differentials.
6. Instruct sales personnel to obtain, whenever possible:
   a. Copies of competitor's offers, price lists, discount schedules, invoices from customers
   b. Signed statements from customers about claimed price concessions provided by competitors
   c. Memoranda of conversations with customers who report competitive offers
   d. A list of customers lost because of lower competitive offers
7. Provide for periodic review of all price concessions granted to meet competition.

Source: Kent B. Monroe, *Pricing: Making Profitable Decisions,* McGraw-Hill, New York, 1979, p. 265. Monroe says the guidelines are adapted from: Ronald M. Copeland, "The Art of Self-Defense in Price Discrimination," *Business Horizons,* vol. 9, winter, 1966, pp. 71-76; Paul H. LaRue, "Meeting Competition and Other Defenses under the Robinson-Patman Act," *The Business Lawyer,* vol. 25, April 1970, pp. 1037-1051; John E. Martin, "Justifying Price Differentials," *Management Accounting,* vol. 47, November 1965, pp. 56-62.

interstate commerce provisions of the federal laws. Generally, marketers need to be aware of state as well as federal laws that affect pricing.

Pricing Don'ts for Sellers

A layperson's list of what sellers cannot do about pricing legally is bound to be oversimplified because of the many ramifications of the laws, exceptions, and acceptable defenses. Nevertheless, the following guide should help you to understand generally what should be avoided and why practicing marketers should check with their legal counsel. Penalties for violation of the laws can be serious, ranging from fines for corporations to fines and imprisonment for executives, and to payment by corporations of treble damages to injured parties.

Legally a seller cannot:

1. Agree to, or go along with, any scheme that results in fixing prices with competitors.
2. Refuse to sell to a retailer who will not agree to maintain the manufacturer's list price (with possible exceptions in some states).
3. Discriminate by charging different prices when the effect would be to injure, destroy, or prevent competition in either the buyers' or sellers' markets. The law allows three defenses, with the burden or proof being on the seller:
   a. Where there are differences in grade and quality of products offered to different customers
   b. Where discounts for quantity purchases can be justified by differences in costs
   c. Where (under specified conditions) offers are made in good faith to meet (but not go lower than) competition
4. Pay brokerage fees to large buyers as a means of making price concessions. Such fees may only be paid to legitimate brokers for services performed.
5. Discriminate with promotional offers; these must be made to competing buyers in proportionately equal terms.
6. Take, or encourage others to take, pricing actions that are deceptive or unfair to companies or consumers.

A Don't for the Buyer

The buyer may not induce the seller to give a discriminatory price when the buyer has reason to believe that this would be an indefensible act on the part of the seller.

FTC Guidelines for Retail Pricing

The FTC from time to time has issued guides for retailers as to what are considered deceptive pricing practices. Local better business bureaus also offer guides (since new deceptive practices spring up periodically), as do some state and local regulatory agencies. Guides do not have the effect of law, but are designed to encourage good business practice. The following examples are extracts from the FTC guidelines.[11]

> Guide I—*Former Price Comparisons.* A reduction ("sale" price) must be made from a bona fide prior price used by the retailer. Fictitious former prices are not allowed.

Guide II—*Former Retail Comparisons.* When a retailer announces a price which is lower than the "usual" price, local competitive stores should be checked to make sure that they actually charge the "usual" price.

Guide III—*Advertising Referring to Manufacturer's List Prices.* When a retailer does not normally sell at the manufacturer's suggested list price, products should not be advertised as reductions from list.

Guide IV—*Bargains Offered with Tie-in Sales.* Any bargain where an item is offered "free" with the purchase of another item must be explicitly stated in the advertisement. Examples of these sales are "2 for 1" or "second item only 1¢."

Guide V—*Miscellaneous Price Comparisons.* Retailers should not:

- Advertise a retail price as a "wholesale" price
- Represent as "factory" prices when not selling at prices paid by those who purchase directly from the manufacturer
- Offer seconds or irregulars at reduced price without disclosing that the higher comparative price refers to perfect merchandise
- Offer an advance sale when the retailer does not in good faith expect to increase the price at a later date, or make a "limited" offer which, in fact, is not limited

PRICING STRATEGIES

As noted earlier, the PIMS studies of approximately 2000 businesses found a close correlation between market share and profit as measured by return on investment (see Figure 16-4). Yet they find no statistical relationship between price and market share.[12] This is a surprising finding when we consider the high degree of attention that pricing receives from marketing and corporate managers. PIMS reported that fewer than 10 percent of the businesses in its data base raised or lowered prices by as much as 3 percent per year.[13]

Buzzell and Wiersema have offered a possible explanation for this seeming anomaly. They note that most of the businesses studied by PIMS operate in relatively mature competitive environments rather than in embryonic industries and that the opportunities to gain volume through aggressive price reduction are rare where technology and marketing practices are well established.[14]

Yet we know of the tremendous impact that lower-priced Japanese products have had on U.S. industries such as automobiles and office copiers. And we have noted earlier how companies such as Texas Instruments dominated the hand calculator market, and Black & Decker the consumer power tool market, with low penetration prices based on the experience curve concept.

It appears that the importance of price in marketing strategy varies according to a number of factors: the stage of the product life cycle, intensity of industry competition, the company's market position, company resources, type of competition (oligopolistic or monopolistic), stage of the economic cycle (boom or bust), degree of price elasticity, whether a new product is innovative or of the me-too variety, and whether sales promotion is a practical alternative to reducing list price. Any business should evaluate its pricing options when planning its marketing strategy. The alternative would seem to be a succession of unplanned responses to competitors' price moves. Since pricing strategies will vary by product, industry conditions, and the company's market position, multibusiness companies may have several different pricing strategies at any one time.

Let's now look at six categories of pricing strategies that can be considered by marketing planners. As in all other types of planning, the alternatives selected in each case will depend on the *situation analysis*. Table 18-5 lists the six categories and typical options for each.

Marketing Positioning Strategies

A key marketing strategy is to decide where the business should be positioned in its product markets. Pricing and product line offerings are important factors in this decision. We need to answer these questions: What price segments do we want to compete in? What image do we want to portray within the chosen segments? What should be the role of trade pricing in gaining the support of our channel intermediaries?

Positioning by Price Segment. Price is one of the more commonly used means of segmenting a market. The broad segments are high, medium, and low. The medium segment is usually the largest and the one where most well known companies concentrate their efforts.

The principal advantages of the *high-price segment* are that it contains the fewest competitors and has the widest profit margins. Buyers seeking top quality or prestige products are less price sensitive. Rolls Royce and Pepperidge Farm produce excellent products and charge accordingly. The disadvantage is that the high-price segment is relatively small and offers limited opportunity for sales expansion.

The principal advantage of the *medium-price sector* is its relatively large size, which offers the potential of high sales volume and production economies of scale. Although margins are narrower than in the high-price segment, profits come from

TABLE 18-5
Pricing Strategies with Options

Strategy	Typical Options
1. Positioning by price segment	High-, medium-, low-, or multiple-price segments
2. Positioning within price segments	At, above, or below market price
3. Cost-based	Cost-plus, target-return, or marginal cost
4. Trade positioning	a. Discount or markup pricing (normal or variations therefrom)
	b. Variations in price discounts for quantity purchases
	c. Variations in payment terms
5. Price administration	Maintenance, flexible, or negotiated pricing
6. New product	Skimming or penetration

selling more units. Campbell Soup, Johnson & Johnson, and Dow concentrate their efforts in the medium-price sector, although each markets some higher-price specialties. The main drawbacks to the medium-price segment are that it is where competition is the most intensive and where the barriers to entry are highest.

The attraction of the *low-price segment* is the opportunity it offers for low-cost producers and companies with weak brand names. The disadvantages are the intensive price competition and low margins. Many well-known brands avoid this sector because the lower margins make it difficult to support the higher promotional costs of maintaining brand image. Successful exceptions, however, include Bic, McDonald's, Toyota, and Timex.

Multiple price segments. Most companies begin by marketing to one price segment. And if they succeed, they move into one or two additional price segments as part of their growth strategy. The pros and cons of these extensions were discussed under "Product Line and Brand Strategies" in Chapter 16. Briefly, the major benefits are the opportunities to expand sales volume and (possibly) to reduce costs through economies of scale. The problem is that companies may not achieve the same degree of success in the new segments. For example, a company which has succeeded by producing high-quality products, supported with heavy promotion, may find that its personnel do not adjust well to serving a low-cost segment where the emphasis is on cost cutting and price deals.

Nevertheless, many companies have succeeded in all three price segments, including Kodak (in cameras), General Motors, Anheuser-Busch, and Revlon. Deere & Company successfully markets a broad line of tractors ranging from garden tractors selling for a few hundred dollars to computerized and environmentally controlled farm tractors selling for over $75,000 each.

Companies that have done well in two segments (medium and high) include General Foods (regular and gourmet foods), Hallmark cards (Hallmark and Ambassador labels), and American Airlines with its first class and tourist class fares. (If we count special fares such as late night and promotional offers, it might be said that American also competes in the low-price segment. Strictly speaking, however, these are not the equivalent of the low, *one-fare,* no-frills airlines operating regular schedules.)

Many companies marketing in the medium- and high-price segments have avoided the low-price segment for fear of harming their brand image. A few have attempted to avoid the stigma, yet still get the added volume, by using separate brands for their low-price lines (i.e., Kimberly Clark's Hi-Dri and Summit paper towels). Others tap into some of the low-price volume by producing private brands or generic products for chains.

Positioning Within Price Segments. Once price segment decisions have been made, the next strategic decision is where to price within each segment. Should we price at market, above, or below market? The answer depends largely on the *strength of our market position.* Generally the market share leader can command a higher price (one of the reasons why companies with high market shares enjoy a higher ROI), whereas companies with low shares must price below market. Yet this generalization can be modified under certain conditions.

The situation, for example, is somewhat different under *oligopoly,* since the few larger companies that dominate the market tend to price at about the same level.

However, the smaller companies in an oligopolistic industry usually must price at levels below the industry leaders. The exception is the small company that obtains a higher price by offering a differentiated product to an industry subsegment too small to interest the larger companies.

Positioning may also be different in the *growth stage* of the product life cycle when companies are competing for market share positions. With sufficient financial strength, any company can compete for share using price as one of its share-building strategies.

As the product enters the *mature phase* of the life cycle, however, market shares begin to stabilize, with price levels tending to correlate with market strength, as described earlier. Gains in market share are more difficult to achieve in mature markets whether price or other marketing strategies are used. A typical example is the rental car industry where National and Budget have difficulty taking share from the market leaders (Hertz and Avis) even when offering equivalent cars at lower prices.

It is the exceptions that draw the attention of the marketing world. Using low price as a competitive weapon, Fuji was able to capture a significant portion of the U.S. film market before Kodak fought back with lowered prices and more aggressive promotion of its own. Seiko used a unique pricing approach to gain entry into the U.S. watch market. Initially it offered a high-quality product at high prices. Once it had established a quality brand image, however, Seiko went after market share by lowering price. When market leaders in mature industries become complacent, they open the door for more aggressive competitors to move in. Even so, it is not easy to displace those with stronger positions, and efforts to do so frequently fail.

Cost-Based Strategies

While positioning is useful for choosing the *price levels* at which to compete, management needs a method for setting a specific price for each product. Or at least it needs a means of finding a base point from which the final price decision can be made.

Prices must be set for new products. They must also be reset (possibly many times) for existing products for reasons such as design changes (product improvements, materials changes), cost changes, shifts in the stage of the product life cycle, restructuring of the product line, and others (both internal and external) that may arise over the product's lifetime. We will discuss three well-known approaches to price setting: cost-plus, target-return, and marginal cost.

Cost-Plus Pricing. This approach involves determining the product's full cost (based on estimated or standard volume assumptions) and then adding a percentage for the profit margin. Full costs include variable production and marketing costs plus the product's fair share of fixed costs. Since it is difficult to allocate fixed costs accurately to a single product, a predetermined percentage of total variable costs may be added to cover fixed costs and profit. Cost-plus is thought to be the most commonly used method for setting price.

The advantages of this approach are that it is simple, easily understood, and *seems* to assure profitability. (If you cover your total costs and add something more, you should end up with a profit.) The weakness of cost-plus pricing is that it does not consider the effects of demand and competition. Therefore, you may price a product to produce a nice profit margin, but if it doesn't sell, it won't produce the revenues needed to pay the bills. Price alone cannot assure profit, since it is only part of the profit equation:

$$\text{Profit} = \text{revenue (price} \times \text{units sold)} - \text{cost}$$

The cost-plus approach worked well for Xerox during the years when it was the unchallenged leader of the office copier market. (Xerox priced so as to achieve a certain percentage return on sales.) But this strategy lost its usefulness when low-price foreign competition forced the company to drop its prices to try to prevent further losses in market share.

The cost-plus approach can also result in too low a price. Consumers' *perceived value* of a product may have little to do with what it actually costs. The prices of designer clothes, prestige brands of perfumes and cosmetics, and seats behind home plate at the ballpark are not based on product cost. To the contrary, higher prices often contribute to the perceived value of such products and serve to increase rather than decrease the demand for them. **Marketing Note 18-2** describes cases where there is little relationship between costs and price.

Despite its weaknesses, cost-plus can be a useful device if it serves as a base point. If the formula comes up with a price that is competitive and that is expected to produce satisfactory demand, well and good. If not, it should be seen as a signal that something else needs to be done, such as improve the product and/or reduce its costs. It may even mean that a new product should be withheld from the market or an existing product phased out of the line. Following the cost-plus formula slavishly is likely to result in something less than optimum profit.

Target-Return Pricing. This strategy is designed to set prices that will provide a predetermined profit return on the capital employed to produce and market each product. It is based on the belief that the single best measure of business performance is the profit earned on (or cash flow received from) the capital invested. Presumably if all products are priced to equal the company's ROI objective, then the company will achieve its total profit objective. This pricing strategy suffers from the same flaws as the cost-plus strategy. But before discussing these, let's see how target-return prices are formulated.

We will have to know the full costs, standard volume (the expected units to be produced over a period such as a year), and the estimated capital employed during that period for each product being priced. The equation for finding the selling price required to meet a target return is:[15]

$$P_r = \text{DVC} + \frac{F}{X} + \frac{rK}{X}$$

where
P_r = selling price determined when the target-return formula is used
DVC = direct unit variable costs
F = fixed costs
X = standard unit volume

r = profit rate desired
K = capital (total operating assets) employed

For an application of the equation, let's assume the following data:

    Direct unit variable cost, $8.00
    Total fixed cost, $400,000
    Standard unit volume, 200,000 units
    Desired rate of return, 15%
    Capital employed, $1,000,000

$$P_r = \$8.00 + \frac{\$400{,}000}{200{,}000} + \frac{.015(\$1{,}000{,}000)}{200{,}000} = \$10.75$$

To summarize, the product would have to be priced at $10.75 to obtain a target return of 15 percent.

The advantage of the target-return strategy is that it encourages thinking about price (as well as other marketing decisions) in terms of maximizing return-on-invested capital. But as with cost-plus pricing, its weakness is that the resulting price may be unrealistic when competition and demand are taken into consideration. On the other hand, if the formula is used as a starting point for the pricing exercise, it can lead to realistic actions like those described for cost-plus pricing. One of the potential dangers of using a formula, however, is that the people who prepare the estimates of costs, capital requirements, and sales may "force" (e.g., underestimate costs, overestimate sales) the figures to conform with top management's expectations for ROI.

In economic theory, target-return pricing is based on the assumption that companies in concentrated (oligopolistic) industries have so much market power that they can *administer* prices; that is, set prices without regard to demand. A role model has been the U.S. automotive industry where for years the major auto companies set prices to meet their profit objectives, yet demand kept on growing. More recently, however, doubt has been cast on the validity of this economic theory as the result of several studies which found that large companies, in fact, do not base their prices on target-return objectives.[16] It was apparent by 1980 that falling demand and strong foreign competition had forced U.S. auto companies to abandon target-return pricing.

The rate-of-return principle can play a reverse role when setting price for capital equipment. The seller's price is set so as to create an attractive rate of return on the *purchaser's investment*. The resulting selling price will not necessarily meet the seller's target-return rate.

Marginal Cost Pricing. Sometimes called *contribution pricing,* a marginal cost strategy is one in which orders are taken at prices which cover all variable costs and some portion of fixed costs. With excess production capacity, for example, a company may be better off taking orders at prices that make some contribution to

MARKETING NOTE 18-2

Pricing of Products is Still an Art, Often Having Little Link with Costs

At $4.50 a 750-milliliter bottle (about a fifth), Fleischmann's gin was losing ground. More gin drinkers were drinking at home. Fewer were patronizing the bars and cocktail lounges where much of Fleischmann's gin flowed. So Fleischmann's over a period of two years raised its price by $1 a bottle to $5.50.

"The strategy helped incredibly," Ferdie Falk gloats. He's the executive in charge of Nabisco Brands Inc.'s beverage group, which markets Fleischmann's. "Sales were deteriorating; now they're coming up. Sales are considerably above last year." Fleischmann's bottle sales and revenue from gin increased although the gin itself remained the same. Only the price—and the bottle, belatedly—was changed to attract liquor-store patrons. The bottle has a new and apparently more salable oblong shape.

Although merchants of just about everything devote a great deal of time and study to determine what prices to put on their products, pricing often remains an art. In some cases, it does involve a straightforward equation: Material and labor costs plus overhead and other expenses, plus profit, equals price. But in many other cases the equation includes psychological and other factors so subtle that pricing consultants, themselves high-priced, are retained to help assay what the market will bear.

$9.86 versus $9.99. One such firm is Management Decision Systems Inc., Waltham, Mass., which uses consumer surveys and computer models to help manufacturers determine the most marketable price on products. The firm usually measures consumer reaction to two different prices on the same product. It usually discovers that the lower price is preferred, but, as in the case of Fleischmann's gin, not always. "The higher you price certain products, like a Mercedes-Benz, the more desirable they become," says Gerald Katz, an MDS vice president.

To decide prices, manufacturers usually weigh costs, and prices, on similar products, and then, as an apparel maker puts it, "take a good guess." Herbert Denenberg, a promoter of consumer causes in Philadelphia and former Pennsylvania state insurance commissioner, says that "everybody thinks people go about pricing scientifically. But very often, the process is incredibly arbitrary."

At its twenty factory outlet stores, Cowden Manufacturing, a subsidiary of Interco Inc., St. Louis, prices jeans at just $9.86. Why the 86 cents? "When people see $9.99 they say, 'That's $10.'" says James McAskill, Cowden's general sales manager. "But $9.86 isn't $10. It's just psychological."

Higher prices seem to suggest higher quality. The relation is dubious. The price on a higher quality product may be considerably higher than the product's extra quality. In 1979, University of Iowa professor Peter C. Reisz tried to relate the prices of 679 brands of packaged foods with their quality ratings as determined over 15 years by Consumers Union. His conclusion: "The correlation between quality and price for packaged food products is near zero."

Marketing men, however, sense that consumers are buying more than a mere commodity when they buy some goods. A $100 bottle of perfume may contain $4 to $16 worth of scent. The rest of the price goes for advertising, packaging and profit. Such perfume sells. "Women are buying atmosphere and hope and the feeling they are something special," says Henry Walter Jr., chairman of International Flavors & Fragrances, Inc., a major scents manufacturer. "There are very few people who are willing to settle for what will satisfy pure needs."

Low prices also sell. Or so J. C. Penney Co., the big retailer, hopes in the case of its bargain $13.50 "plain pockets" jeans and its $18 leisure shirts with fox emblems. Penney does more than concede that the clothes are knockoffs of Levi Strauss & Co.'s $17 jeans and Lacoste's $23 alligator shirts. It *insists* that they are practically identical. Levi Strauss asserts that the Penney jeans are inferior. Lacoste executives decline to dignify the question by discussing it.

Premium Profit. If different companies sell substantially the same product at different prices, they may also sell their own substantially identical products at different prices. Heublein Inc., for example, believes that consumers want a variety of prices on vodka. Last year, it "repositioned" its Popov brand by raising its price by 8 percent to an average $4.10 a fifth at retail without changing what went into the fifth. Popov lost 1 percent of its market share. Heublein moans all the way to the bank; its Popov profits increased by 30 percent because of the higher price. "We are not going to leave money on the table," says John Powers, a Heublein senior vice president.

Popov remains less expensive than Heublein's premium Smirnoff vodka. Securities analysts and other scoff at Heublein's claim that there is a difference between the vodkas. "U.S.-made vodkas are colorless, odorless and tasteless," says Marvin Shanker, publisher of Impact, a wine and spirits newsletter. "The cost of producing vodka is pretty consistent irrespective of brand name."

Marketers say that consumer preference for higher prices extends especially to "ego-sensitive" merchandise such as perfume and other personal care products and goods that one way or another are kept on display. That suits the marketing men fine. "Almost invariably, there's more profit in premium products," says John Keon, a New York University marketing professor. "That's why so many companies want to go to the premium end."

MARKETING NOTE 18-2 (Continued)

Price on Labels. SCM Corp.'s Proctor-Silex appliance subsidiary makes, among other things, fabric irons. Its most expensive model retails for $54.95, or $5 above the next most expensive. The wholesale price is $26.98 against $24.20, a difference of only $2.78. And the extra cost of producing the top model is "less than a dollar," says Ronald Glatz, a Proctor-Silex marketing manager. The top model has a light that signals when the iron is "ready." "There is a segment of the market," Mr. Glatz says, "that wants to buy the best despite the cost."

On some items the label alone fetches a higher price. Various labels with the name "Rogers" have so come to mean quality in silver plate that "you can take any silver item, put 'Rogers' on it, and get $2 more for it," says Irwin Shavel, vice president of sales for the F. B. Rogers division of National Silver Industries Inc. Besides, he says, "Some things like silver sell as well or better at a higher price."

A few years ago, to build volume in its lagging silver department, a New York department store offered a five-piece silver coffee set for only $60, just above the store's cost. Thousands of sets sold at that price, but no more sold than also sold after the store raised the price to $70 a set.

The store might have got in trouble had it advertised the higher $70 price as a "sale" price, however. R. H. Macy & Co.'s New York division recently was accused by the New York City consumer affairs department of doing just that kind of thing. According to the city, Macy's advertised a type of carpeting for $15 a square yard in March 1980 and the next month put it on "sale" for $17 a square yard. Macy's couldn't persuade the city that the "regular" price had been higher than that for any reasonable length of time. Macy's New York denied it had done anything wrong, promised to refrain from doing it in the future and paid $1,500 in partial settlement of the city's complaint.

On many goods, retailers first set prices merely by more or less doubling the price they pay wholesale. If the goods don't sell at that price, the retailers mark them down.

Proctor-Silex and other manufacturers are legally prohibited from fixing retail prices, but they do set their wholesale prices with an eye toward their retail customers' pricing policies. A distributor buying directly from the King of Prussia, Pa., manufacturer usually tacks on 12 percent when he resells the product to a retail merchant. The merchant typically adds another 30 percent although most stores eventually discount all appliances that remain on hand. Otherwise an iron that Proctor-Silex sold at wholesale for $24 will cost about $35 at retail.

Proctor-Silex knows that, and it also knows that a customer who will pay $40 for an iron is a different customer from the one who will pay only $30. The same retail store might not wish to attract both customers for fear of losing its quality reputation with one and its price reputation with the other. That's why Proctor-Silex and its competitors in industry make so many variants of the same product. "Our products are designed and priced with different types of consumers in mind," says a spokesman for General Electric Co.'s major appliance group.

On the other hand, many shoppers appear to pay little attention to price. Last spring, S.C. Johnson & Son Inc., Racine, Wis., maker of Johnson wax products, asked 800 shopping-mall customers what they pay for air fresheners. Only 28 percent quoted figures within 15 percent of actual prices, 39 percent quoted figures that were off by more than that, and 33 percent had no idea at all what they paid.

"We conclude that when you ask consumers if they are interested in buying a new product at a particular price," says Johnson marketing research director Richard F. Chay, "there's going to be a lot of error."

Source: Jeffrey H. Birnbaum, "Pricing of Products is Still an Art, Often Having Little Link with Costs," *Wall Street Journal,* Nov. 25, 1981, sec. 2, first page. Reprinted by permission. Copyright © Dow Jones & Company, Inc., 1981. All rights reserved.

fixed costs rather than lose orders at prices that cover full costs. If all products are sold at less than full costs, however, the company will go broke eventually. A marginal costing strategy, therefore, would likely be appropriate only in a multiple product business where most products are sold at full cost or higher.

Situations where marginal costing strategies might be applied include: (1) producing private brands; (2) pricing low initially to gain acceptance for a new product (or to build market share in a growth market) with the assumption that prices will be raised later to cover full costs; (3) using a low penetration price for introducing a new product on the assumption that high volume and the experience curve will cause costs to fall below the selling price later; and (4) for offering *loss leaders* designed to help sell other more profitable products in the company's line. One of the most common uses of marginal costing as a continuing strategy, however, is to attract added volume to utilize idle capacity. This can be idle plant capacity or underutilized equipment, such as long-distance telephone lines during nights and weekends or empty seats on late night airline flights. You should remember that full and not marginal costs are required under the Robinson-Patman Act to defend a discriminatory price used to meet a competitor's price.

The principle of marginal cost pricing can be used in a variety of situations. The Southern New England Telephone Company, for example, used it to lower the costs of operating its audiovisual center where it makes sales presentations to prospects for commercial telephone systems. Because the facility was underutilized, the excess space was leased to other firms. Charges for leased space were set to cover the additional variable costs that would be incurred (insurance, utilities, and equipment) plus a contribution to overhead (depreciation, building and grounds maintenance, and administration). The result was an attractive price for the lessees and lower costs for the telephone company.

The principal strategy aspects of marginal cost are (1) whether to use it at all (some managements believe that nothing should be sold at less than full cost) and (2) if so, under what conditions. When judiciously applied, marginal costing can improve overall profits by helping absorb fixed costs that would otherwise be charged to products carrying full costs. The disadvantage lies in its potential for overuse. It can become a crutch for inadequate product design and for ineffective selling. And there is the danger that an ambitious manager may allow it to be used to meet a competitor's price illegally.

Trade Positioning Strategies

In our earlier discussion of trade discounts we noted that discounts as a percentage of list price will vary by product class and distribution channel. The first step in setting trade discounts, therefore, is to identify the normal discount pattern for our industry. The next step is to decide whether we should vary our discounts from the normal. The following list suggests the conditions which might favor a higher than normal discount strategy and a lower than normal strategy.

Higher Trade Discounts

To help the company with a weak market position sign up wholesalers and retailers to represent the product line

To encourage wholesalers to provide extra push when the company has no sales force for missionary (promotional) work at the retail level

To get extra wholesaler sales push with industrial prospects when the company has inadequate sales-force coverage at the user level

To help convince channel intermediaries to stock and promote a new product whose sales potential is unknown or where there are already several similar competing brands

Lower Trade Discounts

When a company's position is so strong that wholesalers and retailers want to carry the product. Examples are when:

Brand advertising *pulls* the brand through the channels

The manufacturer's missionary sales force and promotional programs stimulate store traffic and sales for the retailer

The company's industrial sales force stimulates demand at the user level and turns orders over to wholesalers

Once the relative level of discount is established, a further step is to decide whether to use *quantity discounts.* Quantity discounts are usually needed to attract larger intermediaries (such as major wholesalers and chains). We should remember, however, that to be legally defensible, discount schedules must be based on differences in costs.

Another means of attracting good intermediaries is to offer *payment terms* that are more generous than the average. Whether we can do this will depend on our own financial resources. Whether it is necessary to do so will depend on our own market strength. The greater our product demand, the stricter our payment terms can be; the less our product demand, the more generous our terms may have to be.

Price Administration Strategies

Once we know the price we want to get, how do we go about getting it? Shall we hold firmly to list price? Or shall we price as flexibly as necessary to meet competition and customers' demands? Or if we are negotiating contracts to build complicated products, what pricing options should we consider?

Price Maintenance. Although any company would prefer to hold to its established price, there are times when even the stronger ones may have to retreat. One of the reasons for positioning at the appropriate price level in the first place is to minimize pressure from customers and the sales force to discount from the list price. But even an appropriate list price does not provide immunity from such pressures. Buying organizations vary in how aggressively they go after price discounts. Often the largest and most desirable accounts are the most demanding. Strategies of different sellers, therefore, vary between strict adherence to list price, on the one hand, to highly flexible pricing on the other.

There are several advantages to the strict price maintenance strategy: it (1) preserves profit margins, (2) reduces the pressure from customers and the sales force to cut price, (3) encourages company efforts to maintain good product value,

(4) encourages the sales force to sell on the basis of features and benefits rather than price, and (5) reduces the danger of violating the antitrust laws. The principal disadvantage is that we will have to forego some business that we might have got using a more flexible strategy.

Flexible Pricing. Flexible (or variable) pricing implies a willingness to adjust price to the ups and downs of market demand and to vary price when needed to obtain orders from individual customers. The advantages of this strategy are that it (1) permits a more competitive stance so that desirable business is not lost and (2) it helps to balance order input with plant capacity and thereby keep production costs down. The disadvantages are (1) lower margins, (2) much management time spent in making individual price decisions, and (3) the difficulty of avoiding legally indefensible, discriminatory pricing.

Conditions Affecting Maintenance and Flexibility. Periods of high demand and short supply make it easier to practice price maintenance. Even companies with flexible strategies firm up their prices during such periods. Low demand, of course, creates the opposite situation, although companies with high market shares are better able to resist price cutting than those with lower shares.

The larger the company's sales force and the more customers it has, the more difficult it is to practice a flexible pricing strategy. This is because of the large numbers of individual pricing decisions required. Some companies try to solve the problem by delegating pricing decisions to the field sales organization. However, it is difficult to provide decentralized locations with all of the facts needed to make profitable decisions, or to maintain controls that will prevent discriminatory pricing. Decentralized pricing seems to work best when a regional sales force sells the output of a regional plant and when production and pricing are coordinated by the local manager who is responsible for profits.

Consumer goods marketing. Price maintenance strategies are more effective when marketing consumer goods, largely because advertising, sales promotion, and product differentiation can be used to offset price competition. Furthermore, pressures by large distributive organizations for price discounts from the manufacturer are illegal under the Robinson-Patman Act. Large intermediaries, nevertheless, benefit from quantity discounts, company contributions to co-op advertising, and sales promotional deals. Even though the latter two must be offered proportionately to all buyers under the Robinson-Patman Act, as a practical matter, it is the large organizations (primarily the chains) that make the most use of them. The net result is that suppliers can adapt to competitive situations by offering promotional incentives to intermediaries while maintaining their list prices.

Industrial goods marketing. Flexible pricing is more feasible in industrial goods marketing because (1) there are fewer buyers and fewer transactions which make for fewer management decisions; and (2) professional buyers are less influenced by advertising, are more likely to buy on price after ascertaining that quality and service are satisfactory, and are skilled at playing off one supplier against another. Avoiding discriminatory pricing is difficult under these conditions, even by the most reputable sellers. For the most part the huge number of daily transactions by many buyers and sellers make for ineffective law enforcement. Many price deals are made that probably would be difficult to defend in court.

Flexible pricing is by no means the universal strategy of industrial goods companies. Many large and successful industrial companies follow a price maintenance strategy. IBM, for example, historically has held strictly to its list prices for office equipment products, and its salespeople have been trained to emphasize value (quality and service at a fair price). Large computer systems, on the other hand, are more likely to be priced by negotiation or competitive bidding.

Negotiated Pricing. The buying and selling of complicated products and systems involve negotiation well beyond dickering over price. Long and intensive negotiation may be carried on before price can even be estimated for such projects as bridges, special machinery, military hardware, or weapons systems.

Buyers may negotiate with more than one vendor before awarding the contract. But where negotiation will be long and complicated, steps are taken to narrow selection to a single contractor before starting the negotiating process. Narrowing may be accomplished through preliminary bids, quotations, or discussions with potential vendors. Or the vendor may be selected on the basis of reputation and previous experience. Price may be less important to the buyer in these circumstances than the assurance that the contract will be fulfilled.

Contracts may be awarded on a cost-plus arrangement (cost plus a percentage of cost, or cost plus a fixed fee) or at a fixed price. Cost-plus contracts are appropriate when neither the buyer nor the seller can predict cost accurately and when design changes are likely to be made as the project moves along. Incentives for the vendor to keep costs down may be a part of the agreement.

Contracts may be awarded at fixed prices when reliable cost estimates are possible. The seller takes more risk under a fixed price contract, but also has the opportunity to make more profit if costs are well controlled. The Bath Iron Works has built a reputation for quality shipbuilding at fixed prices. This company has been so successful at managing costs that it is not unusual for it to rebate part of its savings to the buyer (usually the government) after the contract is completed.

Strategies for negotiating fixed price contracts will vary according to how badly the vendor needs the business or how dependent the buyer is on obtaining a contractor with special skills. In the first instance the vendor will have to price as low as it deems necessary to be assured of getting the contract, whereas in the second instance the vendor can hold out for a high price.[17]

New Product Strategies

Pricing your new entry into an existing product industry is relatively simple, since the existing price pattern can be observed. The principal question is whether to price above, below, or at market. The answer will depend on the effectiveness of your new product's differentiation, its costs relative to competitors', and the marketing resources to be put behind the market introduction. Test marketing at different prices can be helpful in spotting the optimum price.

Pricing the *unique* new product is more difficult, however, because there is no experience to go on. Nevertheless, we must try to estimate demand, cost, and potential competition as accurately as possible under the circumstances.[18]

Estimating *demand* involves two steps: (1) finding the price range that will make the product economically attractive to buyers (i.e., identifying the price segment), and (2) estimating sales volume at various price points in this range (or segment).

The price range will be determined by the competition of substitutes, since the novel new product merely plugs a gap in the chain of substitutes. The best way to predict sales volume at the various price points is by market testing them in different but similar markets. Though less precise than test marketing, quicker and cheaper methods include surveys of potential buyers, and simulated market tests. Ideally the new product "should be seen through the eyes of the customer and priced just low enough to make it an irresistable investment in view of [the customer's] alternatives."[19]

The role of *cost* is to set a reference base from which to seek the most profitable price. The only pertinent costs are incremental ones (the added costs of going ahead at different plant scales), since the costs of R&D and market testing are *sunk costs* and hence irrelevant.

Competition should be evaluated in terms of (1) possible price retaliation from companies whose products the new entry is intended to displace and (2) the possibility that competitors will enter the market with products similar to yours. You should consider: the strength of your patents and/or know-how, and how long these might protect you; the size of the potential market; the likely impact of your product on competitors' profits; and how competitors have responded in the past to the new products of others. Potential reactions should be evaluated from the viewpoint of competitors, just as demand should be viewed through the eyes of potential buyers.

Your conclusions regarding demand, costs, and competition will then be used to determine the best pricing point. The options run from the high to the low end of the acceptable range. We will use two well-known pricing strategies—skimming and penetration—to examine the pros and cons of pricing high or low.

Skimming Pricing. Under this strategy the new product is introduced at a *high price,* with market promotion aimed at early adopters and those with low sensitivity to price. The idea is to "skim the cream" before lowering the price at later intervals to capture the increasingly price-sensitive segments. Air travel, television, and personal computers were new industries where price skimming was utilized by the innovator companies.

Skimming is an appropriate strategy when (1) there is an *elite* market segment not highly sensitive to price, (2) there are other market segments with different price elasticities, (3) there is uncertainty over how much costs can be reduced through increased volume, or (4) competitors aren't likely to be able to copy your product quickly. When there is uncertainty about price elasticity, a high initial price may serve as a *refusal* price (from which downward adjustments can be made).

The principal *advantages* of the skimming strategy are that it (1) provides high unit margins initially, (2) speeds the payback of funds invested in the new product's development, (3) provides cash for further production and market development, and (4) may help to protect a quality image. Restraining demand in the early stages of introduction also allows for time to *debug* production and promotional programs and to correct any product deficiencies not discovered earlier. It also means that we can hold back on further plant, equipment, and inventory investments until it is evident that the product will succeed in the market.

The major *disadvantage* of the strategy is that it encourages competitors to come in under the skimmer's *price umbrella.*

Protected by its patents, Polaroid followed a successful skimming strategy, bringing prices down over a period of years from several hundred dollars to under $40.00. In the chemical market Du Pont tends to focus on high-margin specialty products. At first it prices high, then gradually lowers the price as the market builds and competition grows.[20] Du Pont's Dacron took twenty years to drop from $2.25 a pound to the 40-cent range. And Qiana, its synthetic silk, floated down by 35 percent in the first five years.[21]

Penetration Pricing. This strategy calls for introducing the new product at a *low price* to develop the market quickly. While unit margins will be narrow and the break-even point delayed, under certain conditions penetration can be more profitable than the skimming strategy in the long run. It is a more appropriate strategy than skimming when (1) the product is price sensitive in the early stages; (2) there are opportunities to reduce costs through economies of scale; (3) there is likely to be early strong competition (because of the absence of patent protection, for example, or because the market is potentially large); or (4) there is no *elite* segment willing to pay a higher price to obtain the newest and best.

The major advantages of the penetration strategy are (1) that slim unit profit margins may discourage competition from entering the market, and (2) if competition does enter, you have the opportunity to preempt the dominant market share position.

The major disadvantages are that (1) the low unit margins and heavy expenses for market development will delay the pay-back of invested capital and (2) an all-out commitment to invest in production facilities must be made before you are certain that the product will have mass appeal.

Black & Decker followed a penetration strategy when introducing the first power tools to the do-it-yourself consumer market. Low prices helped to create sales volume early, which enabled B&D to lower its costs through economies of scale. The low-cost status enabled it to compete with the chain private labels and the Japanese brands that followed B&D into consumer power tools. Dow Chemical practices penetration pricing in contrast to Du Pont's skimming approach. Dow prices low, builds a dominant market share, and holds on for the long pull.[22]

The penetration strategy is not limited to new product introductions, but may be adopted at any time. When Bic entered the already established disposable pen market, it took market share leadership away from Write Brothers and Lindy, using a low penetration price of 19 cents.[23] Bic obtained the lowest costs in the industry through investing in highly efficient production facilities.

SUMMARY

Under normal market conditions, price is determined primarily on the basis of three factors: competition, costs, and demand. Of the three, competition is usually the most powerful, since it pretty much sets the upper limits of a seller's price. Furthermore, competition has a powerful—though indirect—effect on sellers' costs. The simple fact is that, in time, a company that cannot get its costs in line with competition will be forced out of business; it will not be able to price competitively so as to create demand for its products.

We can see that competition, costs, demand, and price are interdependent. Because no one knows where the ideal balance is at any one time for a particular company, setting price is a difficult management decision. It is apparent why pricing decisions are not as a rule delegated very far down the management ladder. Because of competitive actions, demand, and other market variables, management is rarely in complete control of its own pricing. Even so, opportunities usually exist to use price in marketing strategy. It can be used to help build market position. And once a strong market position is attained, price (along with good products) can be used to improve profit margins.

The law imposes restrictions on management's pricing freedom. Beginning with the Sherman Act in 1890, the thrust has been to promote competition and discourage monopoly by outlawing conspiracies such as price fixing. As law has developed further, it has become more specific with respect to price discrimination, protection of small businesses, and the prevention of unfairness and deception. Unfortunately, the law has become so complicated that honest intentions are no longer good enough to keep managers out of trouble. Skilled legal help is now essential.

Despite the many variables and restrictions, strategies can help to reduce some of the uncertainties surrounding pricing. Strategies, for example, can be chosen from among options such as those in the following areas: (1) market positioning by high-, medium-, or low-price segments; (2) positioning within price segments; (3) cost approaches to price setting, including cost-plus, target-return, and marginal costing; (4) positioning by levels of trade discounts and payment terms; (5) administration according to strict price maintenance, flexible prices, or negotiation; and (6) pricing new products by using skimming, penetration, or some in-between approach.

As in other areas of marketing planning, facts are needed for the development and administration of effective price strategies. At a minimum it is essential to know the competitive market situation, to know yours and your competitors' costs, and to have good estimates of market demand at different prices.

QUESTIONS

1. What are the three key factors that should always be considered when making pricing decisions? What other factor is present when using channel intermediaries?
2. What is elasticity of demand, and how can it affect pricing decisions?
3. Why may competitors' prices be of overriding importance when setting and maintaining your price?
4. What factors will influence your decision whether to respond to a competitor's price cut?
5. How does a break-even chart help us find the most profitable demand curve?
6. What are the differences between the trade discount and markup approaches to channel pricing?
7. Name the three allowable defenses to discriminatory pricing allowable under antitrust law.
8. Name six categories of pricing strategies and the typical options under each.
9. Describe marginal costing and situations where it might be used for price setting.

REFERENCES

1. "Pricing of Product is Still an Art, Often Having Little Link to Costs," *Wall Street Journal,* Nov. 25, 1981, sec. 2, p. 1.
2. "Casting Executives as Consultants," *Business Week,* Aug. 30, 1982, p. 51

3. "To Prop Sales, Xerox Gives Bargain Loans," *Wall Street Journal,* Jan. 8, 1981. p. 21.
4. "Mars Replaying the 'Bigger-Is-Better' Ad Pitch," *Advertising Age,* Aug. 9, 1982, p. 24.
5. Kent B. Monroe, *Pricing: Making Profitable Decisions,* McGraw-Hill, New York, 1979, p. 169.
6. Richard M. Hill, Ralph S. Alexander, and James S. Cross, *Industrial Marketing,* 4th ed., Richard D. Irwin, Homewood, Ill., 1975, p. 332.
7. Monroe, op. cit., p. 169.
8. Some of the information in this section has been abstracted from ibid., chap. 16; Ray Werner, "The Laws Affecting Marketing," in Victor P. Buell (ed.), *Handbook of Modern Marketing,* McGraw-Hill, New York, 1970, pp. 17-3 to 17-17; Robert N. Corley, Robert L. Black, and O. Lee Reed, *The Legal Environment of Business Law,* 5th ed., McGraw-Hill, New York, 1981; and Kenneth R. Davis, *Marketing Management,* 4th ed., Wiley, New York, 1981, chap. 13.
9. Monroe, op. cit., chap. 16.
10. Ibid.
11. Bureau of Industry Guidance, *FTC Guidelines Against Deceptive Pricing,* Federal Trade Commission, Washington, D.C., 1964.
12. Robert D. Buzzell and Frederick D. Wiersema, "Successful Share-Building Strategies," *Harvard Business Review,* Jan.-Feb. 1981, p. 142; (c) 1981 by the President and Fellows of Harvard College; all rights reserved.
13. Ibid.
14. Ibid.
15. The equation and example are from Monroe, op. cit., p. 214.
16. For a summary of some of these studies and more discussion of target-return pricing, see Gilbert Burck, "The Myths and Realities of Corporate Pricing," *Fortune,* April 1972. For more on auto pricing see "Auto Makers Rethink Pricing Policies to Woo Still-Reluctant Buyers," *Wall Street Journal,* Oct. 23, 1981, p. 1.
17. Hill et al., op. cit., p. 84
18. The balance of this section is based in part on Joel Dean, "Techniques on Pricing New Products and Services," in Buell, op. cit., pp. 5-51 to 5-61.
19. Ibid., p. 5-61.
20. David J. Luck and O. C. Ferrell, *Marketing Strategy and Plans,* Prentice-Hall, Englewood Cliffs, N.J., 1979, p. 207.
21. "Pricing Strategy in an Inflation Economy," *Business Week,* Apr. 6, 1974, pp. 43-49.
22. Luck and Ferrell, op. cit.
23. C. Schewe and R. Smith, *Marketing Concepts and Applications,* 2nd ed., McGraw-Hill, New York, 1983, p. 373.

CHAPTER 19

Distribution Management

Distribution is the process of getting products and services from producers to consumers and users when and where they are needed. It provides time, place, and possession utilities and the transfer of legal ownership.

Distribution occurs through a variety of *channels* which fall into one of two classifications: (1) *direct*—from the producer to the consumer or industrial user, and (2) *indirect*—through intermediaries, the most common of which are wholesalers and retailers. Industrial goods manufacturers most frequently use the direct channel because usually there are relatively few customers to serve. Consumer goods manufacturers, on the other hand, commonly use indirect channels because there are large numbers of geographically dispersed consumers to be reached. Services mostly are distributed direct, although more and more service organizations are adding indirect channels. Often these must be created, since existing wholesalers and retailers are not always appropriate intermediaries for distributing many types of services. Chains such as Sears, Roebuck & Co., on the other hand, increasingly are offering their own services through their branch stores; these include insurance, optical exams, dental treatment, and income tax preparation.

Changing Channels

Distribution channels sometimes seem not to interest management as much as marketing elements like product, pricing, and advertising—at least not until trouble occurs. This is explained in part by the relatively slow rates of change that channels undergo. More to the point, however, once a company has chosen its channels and developed relationships with its intermediaries, there is a reluctance to do anything that might upset the arrangement. Indeed, there *is* risk in channel change. Concern over the effect of channel change on present intermediaries was seen in the cases in Part Three dealing with American Standard stainless steel sinks and Hanes hosiery.

Though they may occur slowly, distribution patterns do change in response to environmental change and changes in buyers' needs. There has been the shift from downtown city shopping to suburban shopping and from service to self-service stores, the growth of retail chains and franchise operations, and the growth of shopping malls attracting customers from wide geographic areas. Higher transportation costs and other changes, however, may lead to counterdevelopments. Some experts believe that electronic marketing enabling consumers to shop without leaving home will be the next major retail development.

The distribution of bank services has undergone several changes, from central walk-in banks to the addition of branch banks, drive-up windows, and self-service electronic banking. Refrigerated trucks and railroad cars have revolutionized the distribution of perishable foods and changed our eating patterns. It is now commonplace to have fresh lettuce from California in our salad anywhere in the United States during the winter. Industrial goods distribution also has been affected by transportation developments. Super-highways and truck depots have made possible truck deliveries to widely separated points, ranging in time from overnight to one or two days. This has increased the proportion of distribution going direct from producer to user. Air freight, tied in with local truck delivery, has made overnight cross-country shipments feasible for high-value products.

Because buying patterns and channels change somewhat slowly, and because there is the risk of antagonizing present intermediaries if the company makes changes, it is not uncommon for managements to react too slowly in adjusting to the needs of end customers. Problems and lost opportunities can be the result. This is why the *situation analysis* outline in Chapter 9 includes a review of the distribution system.

Examples of Company Distribution Changes. Firms will shift their channels, however, when necessary to meet changed conditions. To illustrate let's look at three major companies whose actions made headlines in the business press.

> IBM traditionally had sold and distributed its products direct to the customer. With the introduction of personal computers, however, it was not feasible for this company to deal directly with its expanding new markets composed of thousands of small businesses and (potentially) millions of consumers. Consequently, IBM opened its own retail stores which offered office machines and small computers. It also distributed the IBM Personal Computer through Sears, Roebuck business systems stores and the Computerland retail chain.[1] Whether these initial channel moves will prove to be temporary or permanent, it is apparent that some form of indirect distribution is needed to serve IBM's new and broader markets.
>
> To increase sales of its jeans, Levi Strauss added the J. C. Penney and Sears, Roebuck chains to its traditional channels (department stores and boutiques). Adverse reactions from some traditional retail outlets caused market analysts to question whether the company would gain or lose market share as a result of this action. The answer was thought to depend on whether the Levi brand was popular enough with consumers to prevent store defections.[2]
>
> For years American Express card holders could charge for travelers checks and obtain cash at American Express offices in larger cities around the world. At best, however, this was inconvenient for the customer. Now American Express gold card holders can obtain checks and cash from automatic tellers at selected banks,[3] a potentially large new distribution channel for credit card services.

Marketing Note 19-1 reports how a major bank views the changes in distribution of financial services.

In this chapter we will describe the functions of the principal types of intermediaries; the principal channels for consumer goods, industrial goods, and services; and the legal issues affecting distribution. We will then examine several distribution strategies.

> **MARKETING NOTE 19-1**
>
> **CITICORP Describes Evolving Distribution System for Financial Services**
>
> One distinctive characteristic of service businesses is that the customers participate in the production of the services they use. A patron in a McDonald's restaurant, for example, produces a good share of his own service by acting as his own waiter and busboy. This reduces McDonald's cost of doing business, shortens transaction time, and gives the consumer more convenience and some control over how the service is delivered.
>
> Translated into banking, this means that historical intermediation—namely, waiting in large granite buildings for customers to bring in deposits, then lending it out to other customers—is becoming less important. Evolving a distribution system that will provide individuals and companies with financial services at time and places where they are of maximum usefulness and convenience for the user is becoming more important.
>
> This could mean placing a bank debit card in the wallet of an individual customer or a cash-management terminal on the desk of a corporate treasurer. In either case, it is the user of the service who determines the time, place, and type of financial transaction. Then it occurs within the customer's operational environment, not the intermediary's.
>
> In service-based economies, more and more, the customer is going to participate in and control the intermediation process at his own convenience and discretion. Through the resulting patterns of usage, customers will effectively redesign financial services themselves. In the intensely competitive financial services industry, business will flow to the intermediaries who are the quickest to recognize and utilize such user input.
>
> *Source*: Citicorp Annual Report 1979, pp. 9 and 12.

CHANNEL INTERMEDIARIES

Channel intermediaries, or middlemen, for goods (in contrast to services) fall into the two broad categories of wholesale and retail trade. *Wholesale intermediaries* are the links between producers on the supply side and retailers and industrial users on the buying side. *Retail intermediaries* are the links between the wholesale intermediaries and consumers.

Wholesale Intermediaries

Wholesale intermediaries are of three principal types: wholesalers, manufacturers' sales branches, and agents.

Wholesalers. In the business world wholesalers may be referred to as *wholesalers*, *distributors*, *jobbers*, or *supply houses*, according to the practice of the industry they serve.* They take title to the merchandise they sell. Normally this merchandise is carried in stock, although the wholesaler may also arrange for *drop-shipments* to be made directly from the manufacturer to the wholesaler's customers.

Several types of wholesalers have developed to serve different customer needs. Some offer full services, while others offer only limited services. The *full service* wholesaler provides its customers with such services as delivery, credit, personal sales calls, advice, and (where the nature of the product requires) assembly or repair. *Limited service* wholesalers offer fewer services, take a lower margin, and sell at lower prices. A *cash-and-carry* wholesaler, for example, sells for cash at its warehouse dock. *Feeder* wholesalers specialize in providing chain stores with products the chains do not order in bulk quantities direct from the manufacturer. The feeder wholesaler works on a high-volume, "no-frills," low-margin basis.

*We will use the term "wholesaler" to mean any of these unless otherwise noted.

The *rack jobber* is a mobile wholesaler that has emerged to relieve the supermarket manager of running such nonfood departments as housewares, health and beauty aids, magazines, and toys. The rack jobber calls frequently at the store location with a truck of merchandise, replenishes the department racks and shelves, and prices the merchandise. The merchandise is placed on *consignment* (ownership retained by the jobber), and the jobber is paid by the store only for merchandise sold.

The *wholesaler voluntary chain* occurs when an independent wholesaler enlists independent retailers to join in a voluntary arrangement. In return for regular purchases by the stores, the wholesaler operates on low markups and provides (for a fee) services such as store identification, store layout plans, advertising mats, and business management counsel. Some of these "voluntaries"—like Super Value and IGA in groceries, Cotter (True Value) in hardware, and Ben Franklin in variety stores—are larger than many corporate chains.

The *retailer cooperative* occurs when a group of independent retailers form a *jointly owned wholesale operation* and share in any profits from this operation. The co-op headquarters staff may provide management and other services similar to those described for the wholesaler voluntary chain. Associated Grocers in foods and Rexall in drugs are examples.[4]

Manufacturers' Sales Branches/Offices. This classification covers manufacturers who sell through their own sales forces direct to retailers or to industrial users, bypassing wholesalers. This approach may be used where (1) wholesalers are not needed (e.g., in the case of special machinery, or where large users order in truckload quantities), (2) where the manufacturer's specially trained salespeople are needed (e.g., for chemicals), or (3) where local sales and distribution are required but good wholesalers are not available to the manufacturer. When local inventories are needed to service customers, companies that distribute directly set up their own field warehouses or distribute through public warehouses.*

Agents. Agents negotiate sales for others for a fee or commission. Unlike wholesalers, agents do not take title to the goods and usually do not carry inventories. They may be called manufacturers' agents, manufacturers' representatives, brokers, selling agents, or sales agents. They substitute for, or supplement, company sales forces when it is uneconomic for the company to maintain its own sales people in some or all markets.

Manufacturers' agents or *representatives* specialize by products and/or markets. Some supply national coverage, but most operate on a limited geographic basis. They sell noncompeting products for two or more manufacturers in specified areas and are paid a commission on orders obtained. By carrying several product lines they are able to operate more efficiently than the small (or even the large) company with a limited line. Because manufacturers' agents are paid only for what is sold, the client's selling expense is variable. This avoids the relatively fixed costs that are incurred when a sales force is composed of employees paid base salaries.

In the grocery industry manufacturers' agents are called *brokers*. In addition to obtaining orders from chains and wholesalers, they may also do merchandising

---

*Public warehouses (or public distribution centers) do not take title to the merchandise, but for a fee will provide inventory, delivery, and billing services for manufacturers.

work in grocery stores, such as building displays, placing point-of-sale materials, and getting the retailer to use the client's co-op advertising program.

Selling or *sales agents* take the responsibility for selling (for a fee or commission) the entire output of one or more producers who may or may not be competitors. Unlike manufacturers' agents who sell under terms set by their clients, selling agents operate without restriction of territory and have more control over the marketing process, including the determination of prices, advertising, and sales promotion. They may even provide financial assistance to small clients who operate seasonal businesses such as the canning of fruits and vegetables.

Chain Buying Offices and Warehouses. When we speak of *chain stores* we are referring to a corporate form of ownership of a group of stores (such as A&P, Sears, or K mart)* in contrast to voluntary chains (wholesaler voluntaries and retail cooperatives). Though classified with *retail trade*, chain store organizations (at least the larger ones) perform wholesale as well as retail functions. They buy from suppliers, maintain inventories at field warehouses, fill orders, and deliver to company store locations. Many chain headquarters give considerable latitude to their store managers to select the items and brands to be carried and the promotions they will use. Consequently, chain headquarters merchandise managers may have to persuade ("sell") store managers to accept their recommended programs. One of the things that manufacturers' missionary sales forces do is try to convince managers of individual stores to implement brand promotions previously approved by their chain headquarters.

Some chain headquarters do not purchase; rather they approve the suppliers from whom their branches or local stores may buy and the terms of sale. Getting on the approved list provides the supplier with a "hunting license" for soliciting orders at the chain's decentralized store locations. Generally, however, manufacturers in their marketing approaches must treat chains much the way they do wholesalers with respect to personal selling, quantity shipments, pricing, and sales promotions. Chains account for approximately one-third of all retail sales. In some categories, they are so important that no manufacturer can be among its industry's leaders without strong representation in them. Note, for example, the percentages of total retail sales accounted for by chains in selected retail classifications:[5]

Retail Classification	% of Sales Accounted for by Chain Stores
Department	94
Variety	80
Grocery	57
Drug and Proprietary	50
Shoe	48

Retail Intermediaries

A retail intermediary is a business unit that sells to consumers. Retail stores account for about 97 percent of all retail sales. The balance is made up of mail order, vending machines, and direct-to-home sales. Operators of retail stores are called retailers.

*The Bureau of the Census classifies a chain as an organization operating eleven or more stores.

A *retailer* is a merchant who buys from producers or wholesalers, takes title to the merchandise, and resells to consumers.

Retail Stores. Total retail store sales break down as follows: franchised stores, 35 percent; chain stores, 33 percent; and nonfranchised independent stores, 32 percent. The long-term trend has been toward growth in franchised and chain stores at the expense of the nonfranchised independent store.[6] The nonfranchised independent retailer may operate completely independently or may affiliate with a retailer cooperative or a wholesaler voluntary chain.

We have already described chain stores. The Bureau of the Census defines *franchising* as: "A form of marketing or distribution in which a parent company [the franchisor] customarily grants an individual or a company [the franchisee] the right, or privilege, to do business in a prescribed manner over a certain period of time in a specified place."

Franchising in 1980 accounted for sales of $338 billion of which 84 percent were from franchisee-owned establishments. (The balance of sales were from stores owned by the franchisors.)

Eighty-five percent of all franchise sales are accounted for by auto dealers (49 percent), gasoline stations (23 percent), fast-food restaurants (9 percent), and food and convenience stores (4 percent). The balance are from soft drink bottlers (4 percent) and services (11 percent).[7]

Franchising has expanded rapidly because it offers advantages to both franchisors and franchisees. It provides the franchising company with the opportunity to expand its business rapidly, using investment capital provided by franchisees.* Franchisor earnings, which come from the fees and royalties paid by the franchisees, can increase just as rapidly as the franchisor can manage its expansion.

The franchisee benefits from entering a business that has already been proven successful, that is already known to consumers, and that provides management training and assistance by the franchisor. Although not all franchisor/franchisee transactions have turned out well, the success of franchising has been such as to support a healthy growth rate for this type of retail operation.

Despite franchising's rapid growth, it has not been a common channel for manufacturers' brands (with the major exceptions of auto and gasoline producers who together account for 72 percent of all franchise sales). Franchisors and their franchisees, of course, may be major customers for producers' products (such as foods for restaurants and office equipment for tax preparation services). As a rule, however, the typical manufacturer of branded merchandise will get more consumer exposure by using established retail channels than it will by limiting its distribution to its own franchised outlets. Also, a store stocked only with one manufacturer's products often will not produce enough volume to make the retail operation profitable for the franchisee.

Mail Order, Direct to Consumer, and Vending. Together these forms of retailing account for only about 3 percent of total retail sales. They fill special needs for some

---

*Capital can be sizable. *Business Week* (June 7, 1982, p. 120) reports that land and building costs for a new Burger King fast-food restaurant run to $350,000 while the franchise fee and working capital require another $300,000.

consumers and continue to grow at about the same rate as store retailing, so that their percentage of sales has not changed significantly over time.*

Mail order performs a service for shut-ins (invalids and others unable to shop in stores) and people in rural areas and small towns who do not have access to large selections of merchandise in nearby stores. It also is used to promote specialty goods, which even retailers in cities are not always willing to stock.

Direct-to-consumer ("door-to-door") sales fill a similar role. It has also been a useful means of introducing new products and selling higher-priced, infrequently purchased products (encyclopedias, for example) which require trained salespeople. **Marketing Note 19-2** gives some little-known information about this form of sales and distribution.

Vending machines (also called "automatic merchandising") render a service by broadening the availability of convenience goods such as cigarettes, candy, soft drinks, and toilet articles beyond what would be available if limited to retail store distribution. They also provide food service in remote factories and offices where it is not practical to have an in-house restaurant.

Electronic Retailing. Some authorities believe that ordering from the home via two-way electronic transmission will be the next major development in retailing.[8] Referred to as "telecommunication shopping" or "teleshopping," one version of how the process will work goes like this:

> Consumers with accounts at the telecommunication merchandiser will shop at home for a variety of products and services. Using an in-home video display catalog, they will order products from a participating retailer. When the order is received on its computer, this retailer will assemble the goods from a fully automated warehouse. Simultaneously, funds will be transferred from the customer's to the retailer's bank account. Customers will choose between picking up the order at a nearby distribution point or having it delivered to their door. There will be no fee for picking up the order. However, there may be a delivery charge. The charge will depend on the amount of the order and delivery time requirements (whether the next day at the company's convenience or at a confirmed time when the customer is at home).[9]

Ordering by telephone or mail in response to retail store or direct-shipment merchandiser television ads is not new. Teleshopping, however, would utilize a two-way TV computer setup in the home. By selecting a specific cable TV station and pressing the proper button, the category of merchandise selected would be displayed on the home screen. The technology is available and has been market tested. The question is whether enough consumers will be willing to invest in the home equipment required and order sufficient amounts of merchandise to support this new form of retailing. The advantages to the consumer of this method of shopping would be convenience as well as savings in time and transportation costs.

This type of retailing is seen as more appropriate for the "non-ego-intensive" types of goods now purchased routinely in food, drug, and variety stores. It appears less appropriate for "ego-intensive" purchases (e.g., dresses, gifts, wines) now made in department and specialty stores where there are knowledgeable salespeople and personal relationships between sales clerks and buyers.[10]

---

*There appears to be increased mail order activity, but so far census information shows it to have made only a slight gain as a percent of total retail sales.

> **Little Known Facts About Direct-to-Consumer Marketing**
>
> **MARKETING NOTE 19-2**
>
> - Over two million people sell direct. Most are independent contractors (agents or dealers) rather than employees of the companies they sell for.
> - Most work part time. Median hours per week: 9.
> - Median earnings per week: $27 (in 1976 dollars).
> - While 8900 companies engage in direct selling, only 800 are "primary marketing units" (firms owning or controlling trade names and trade styles).
> - Estimated value of direct sales in 1975 was $5.8 billion, representing 1 percent of all retail sales and 2 percent of the product categories in which direct selling competes with retail stores.
> - About half of all households purchase from a direct salesperson through these sales approaches:
>   Door-to-door (60 percent)
>   Home party where salesperson demonstrates to guests and takes orders (15 percent)
>   At workplace (8 percent)
>   By telephone (6 percent)
>   Other (11 percent)
> - About one-fourth of adults like shopping via the direct selling method.
> - Consumers consider convenience as the prime benefit; concern over dealing with strangers as the major drawback.
> - Legally consumers may cancel within three business days any order of $25 or more purchased from a direct seller (the FTC's so-called cooling off regulation).
> - While total direct-to-consumer sales amount to only about 1 percent of all retail sales, they are relatively more important in certain categories of products, such as the following:
>
> | Industry | Estimated Direct Selling Share of Industry, % |
> |---|---|
> | Security systems | 75.0 |
> | Encyclopedias, reference books, Bibles | 57.0 |
> | Costume jewelry | 39.0 |
> | Cosmetics, personal care items | 17.0 |
> | Magazine subscriptions | 10.0 |
> | Hearing aids | 5.0 |
> | Toys, crafts, hobby items | 2.0 |
>
> *Sources*: Studies by Louis Harris and Associates, and Tyson, Belzer and Associates for the Direct Selling Association and the Direct Selling Education Foundation (DSEF), Washington, D.C., 1977; and U.S. Bureau of the Census, *Statistical Abstract of the United States*, 1981, p. 818.

Dealer

"Dealer" is an ambiguous term. It is defined as "a firm that buys and resells merchandise at either retail or wholesale."[11] There seems to be no reason other than historical practice that some retailers are normally referred to as, for example, automobile dealers or news dealers. Some dealers, such as building supply dealers, sell both to consumers at retail prices and tradespeople—such as carpenters, plumbers, or electricians—at wholesale price (or at least at a discount from the retail price). In such cases "dealer" is a useful all-purpose term.

Service Intermediaries

Services have no clear-cut intermediaries such as wholesalers and retailers that distribute goods. Until recently little attention was paid to channel intermediaries for services. The reasons are that services are intangible, cannot be stored, transported, or inventoried, and often are inseparable from the person or seller.[12]

Many services are created and distributed simultaneously as in the case of haircuts, shoe shines, or medical treatment. The channels for these services can be described as direct. Nevertheless a growing number of service industries are turning to *indirect* channels, as we will see later (in Table 19-1). In the absence of standardized channels, service marketers must turn to creative solutions for broadening their exposure to potential customers.

CHANNELS OF DISTRIBUTION

Channels of distribution are the means by which products get from the producer to the consumer or industrial user.

Consumer Goods Channels

Figure 19-1 illustrates the principal channels for consumer goods. Channel 1, "direct from the manufacturer to the consumer," is used by mail order and direct-to-home sellers. Many firms using these methods do not, strictly speaking, distribute directly. Catalog and other types of mail order houses, for example, normally buy merchandise from manufacturers and resell it to consumers, thereby acting as retail intermediaries. Most direct-to-home sellers (such as Avon, Amway, and Stanley Home Products) operate through independent contractors. These are either *agents*

FIGURE 19-1. Principal channels of distribution for consumer goods.

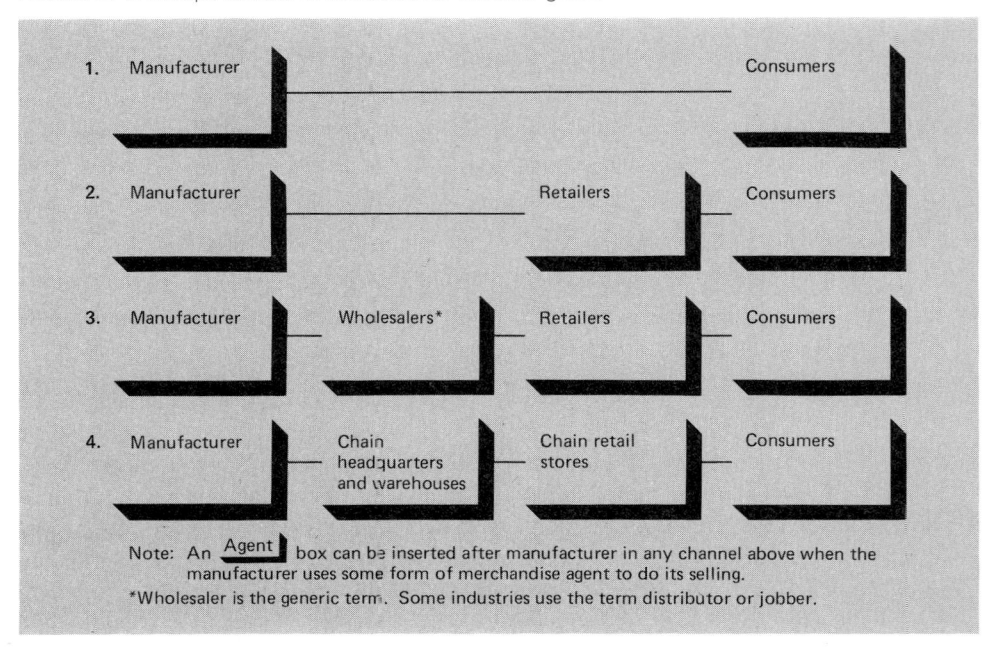

1. Manufacturer → Consumers
2. Manufacturer → Retailers → Consumers
3. Manufacturer → Wholesalers* → Retailers → Consumers
4. Manufacturer → Chain headquarters and warehouses → Chain retail stores → Consumers

Note: An **Agent** box can be inserted after manufacturer in any channel above when the manufacturer uses some form of merchandise agent to do its selling.
*Wholesaler is the generic term. Some industries use the term distributor or jobber.

who sell for the manufacturer on a commission basis or *dealers* who buy from the manufacturer and resell to consumers (although the companies may call them something else). Years ago manufacturers who sold direct to the consumer did so through their own company sales forces. However, with the advent of minimum wage laws, pension plans, and social security taxes, these companies switched to independent sales contractors (nonemployees) to avoid the rising costs of these fringe benefits. Direct-to-consumer selling is characterized by high turnover among very large numbers of salespeople (Avon is reputed to have over 1,000,000 representatives[13] and Amway reports 750,000[14]), most of whom work only part time. The costs of having salespeople classified as *employees* under these conditions became prohibitive for the direct selling companies. Although mail order and direct-to-consumer sellers continue to be classified as using the direct channel, the truth is that some should not.

Channel 2, "direct from the manufacturer to retailers," is used primarily in three special types of situations. The first is when a manufacturer seeks to *control its retail distribution* by owning its own stores (i.e., through forward vertical integration). Examples are Singer sewing machines and Thom McAn shoes. The second situation applies to *fashion merchandise*, such as women's clothing. Manufacturers of fashion merchandise need direct contact with retailers so they can determine which newly introduced items consumers are buying. They then quickly increase production of the "hot" items and rush the goods direct to retailers. A wholesaler would only get in the way of this process. The third situation applies to *perishable goods*, such as milk, bread, and potato chips, where freshness is important. Companies in these businesses normally distribute from regional plants direct to retailers via their own trucks. It is questionable whether direct delivery is still needed, since preservatives and airtight packaging now extend the shelf life of perishables. Despite its higher cost, however, companies like Nabisco and Keebler continue to distribute direct because of the greater control they get over retail shelf space by having their own sales and delivery people in the stores regularly.

The longer channels, 3 and 4, are the most important ones for goods that are widely distributed through such retail outlets as food, drug, liquor, hardware, stationery, and gasoline. Channel 3 uses independent wholesalers (including wholesale voluntaries) and retailers, while channel 4 includes corporate chains and retailer cooperative chains. Because of the large numbers of retail outlets needed to supply consumers with convenience goods, wholesalers and chain warehouses are essential to their efficient and economical distribution.

Industrial Goods Channels

Figure 19-2 shows the principal channels for industrial goods.

Channel 1, "direct from the manufacturer to industrial users," is the most commonly used channel for industrial goods. It may be used when (1) the manufacturer's customers are large enough to take shipments direct from the manufacturer in carload, truckload, or tankload quantities; (2) orders are made to customer specifications and shipped direct to the customer when ready; (3) the manufacturer's plant is located near a concentration of industrial customers from whence regular truck deliveries can be made direct from the plant; or (4) the manufacturer distributes through its own branch warehouses. In these situations the

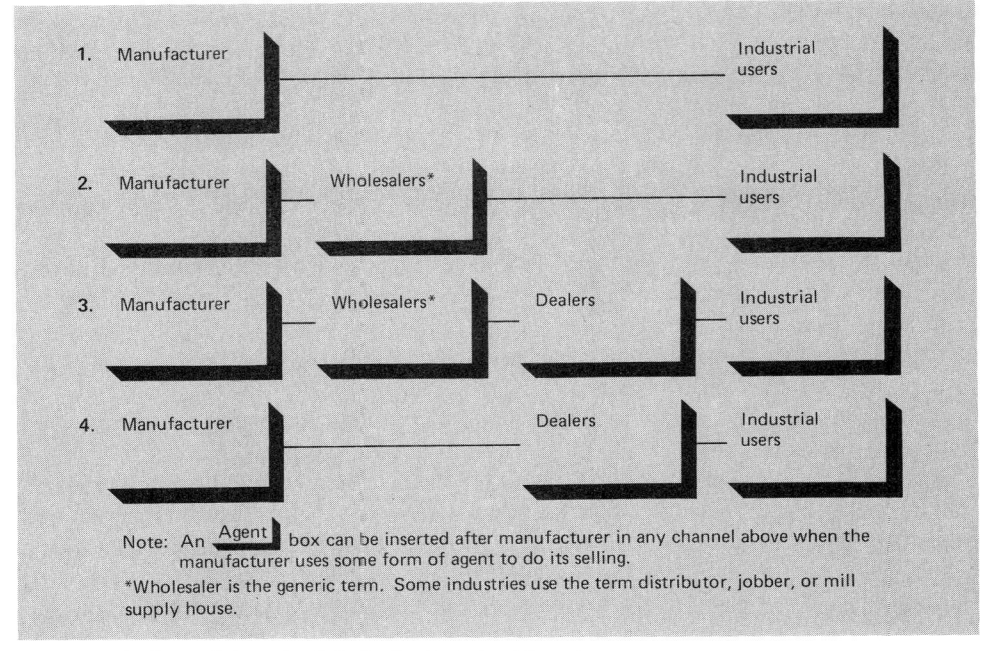

FIGURE 19-2. Principal channels of distribution for industrial goods.

Channel 1 shows: Manufacturer → Industrial users.
Channel 2 shows: Manufacturer → Wholesalers* → Industrial users.
Channel 3 shows: Manufacturer → Wholesalers* → Dealers → Industrial users.
Channel 4 shows: Manufacturer → Dealers → Industrial users.

Note: An Agent box can be inserted after manufacturer in any channel above when the manufacturer uses some form of agent to do its selling.
*Wholesaler is the generic term. Some industries use the term distributor, jobber, or mill supply house.

manufacturer normally will use its own sales force or will contract with agents (usually manufacturer's representatives) to sell its products. Consequently, there is no function for the wholesaler to perform, neither selling *nor* physical distribution.

Channel 2, "manufacturer to wholesalers to users," is the second most common industrial channel. Wholesalers are used where (1) there are many users (such as for office and maintenance equipment or supplies); (2) users are geographically widespread; (3) spare parts must be readily available near users' plants or offices; or (4) sales calls on users are of minor importance, such as for unbranded commodities.

Channel 3, "manufacturer to wholesalers to dealers to users," is used for distributing certain types of industrial goods. Agricultural chemicals, for instance, are distributed from the manufacturer to agricultural chemicals distributors, to farm supply dealers, to industrial users (farmers). Hardware and electrical fixtures are sold through wholesalers to dealers who sell to tradespeople as well as to consumers. And office supplies and equipment may go through wholesalers to dealers who sell to commercial businesses, professional offices, and consumers.

Channel 4, "manufacturer to dealers to users," has developed more recently as manufacturers of computers, copiers, and word processors began to design equipment for small businesses, professional offices, and consumers. Some foreign (and smaller domestic) producers who did not have large sales forces initiated the distribution of their products in the United States using office supply dealers. Now major companies like Xerox and IBM (who formerly had only distributed direct to users) are selling and distributing through their own company stores and through specialized chain stores.

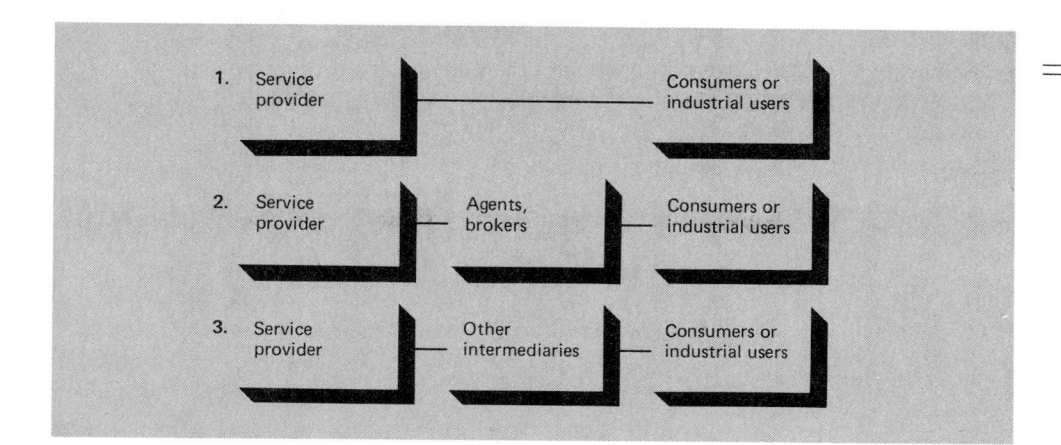

FIGURE 19-3. Channels of distribution for services.

Channels for Services

Figure 19-3 shows the principal channels for services. Many common types of services (e.g., hospital and legal) are created and distributed simultaneously—that is, *directly*, as in Channel 1. Channel 2, "service provider to agent or broker to consumer or industrial users," is illustrated by the use of travel agents for airline tickets and stock brokers for corporate securities. Channel 3, "service producer to other intermediaries to consumer or industrial users," is illustrated by the American Express Company using banks to distribute its travelers checks.

It is becoming clear that services are not necessarily limited to one channel of distribution. Additional examples of direct and indirect channels used to distribute services are shown in Table 19-1.

Multiple Suppliers in Channels

Textbook diagrams of consumer and industrial channels (including those in Figures 19-1 and 19-2) are simplistic representations. They do not portray the fact that a wholesaler buys from many manufacturers and sells to many retailers, or that a retailer buys from several wholesale supply sources and sells to a variety of customers. We suggest the magnitude of the process with hardware industry examples in Figures 19-4 and 19-5.

There is intense competition among manufacturers for the wholesaler's business and among wholesalers for the retailer's business. A hardware industry survey shows us that, out of twenty product lines studied, the median numbers of brands carried by hardware *wholesalers* are as follows: locks—3; carpentry tools—2; shears and scissors—2; and seventeen other products—1. The median number of brands carried by hardware *retail dealers* in each of the twenty product categories is 2.[15]

There are many competing manufacturers producing each product line. Imagine the competition among them to be the sole supplier to those wholesalers typically carrying one brand. And imagine the competition among wholesalers to supply at least one of the two brands carried by the typical retailer. The fact that competing manufacturers and wholesalers continue to exist, of course, is because not all retailers carry the same two brands in each product category.

TABLE 19-1

Examples of Direct and Indirect Distribution Channels for Selected Services

Service	Direct Distribution Channel	Indirect Distribution Channel through Intermediaries
Airline tickets	Airport, ticket counters, 800 telephone numbers	Travel agents, corporate travel departments
Banks	Central bank, U.S. mail, telephone	Branch banks, remote-location electronic tellers
Bank credit cards	Bank locations, mail order	Retail stores
Travel checks	Branch offices	Banks, corporations (for issuance to own employees), airport vending machines
Life insurance	Mail order	Agents, banks, vending machines in airports and hotels
Corporate stock		Brokers, banks, stock exchanges, transfer agents
Laundries, dry cleaners	Plant site service counter	Shops for receiving and delivery
Libraries	Central library	Branches, traveling bookmobiles
Telephone service	Home and commercial installations	Coin-operated booths, hotel switchboards, government installations, etc.

Multiple Channels

Few companies use only one channel, for the simple reason that one channel usually will not reach all of a brand's target markets. Furthermore, even the stronger companies cannot always obtain the quality of intermediaries desired in every market and, therefore, have to consider alternate channels. This may mean having to set up a company-owned wholesale branch. The use of two channels by a company is called *dual distribution* and the use of three or more is called *multiple distribution*.

Length of Channels

Channel length is a means of indicating the number of intermediaries between the manufacturer and its end customers. The fewer the intermediaries, the shorter the channel. The greater the number of intermediaries, the longer the channel. For example:

Short channel—manufacturer to consumer

Medium channel—manufacturer to retailer to consumer

Long channel—manufacturer to wholesaler to retailer to consumer

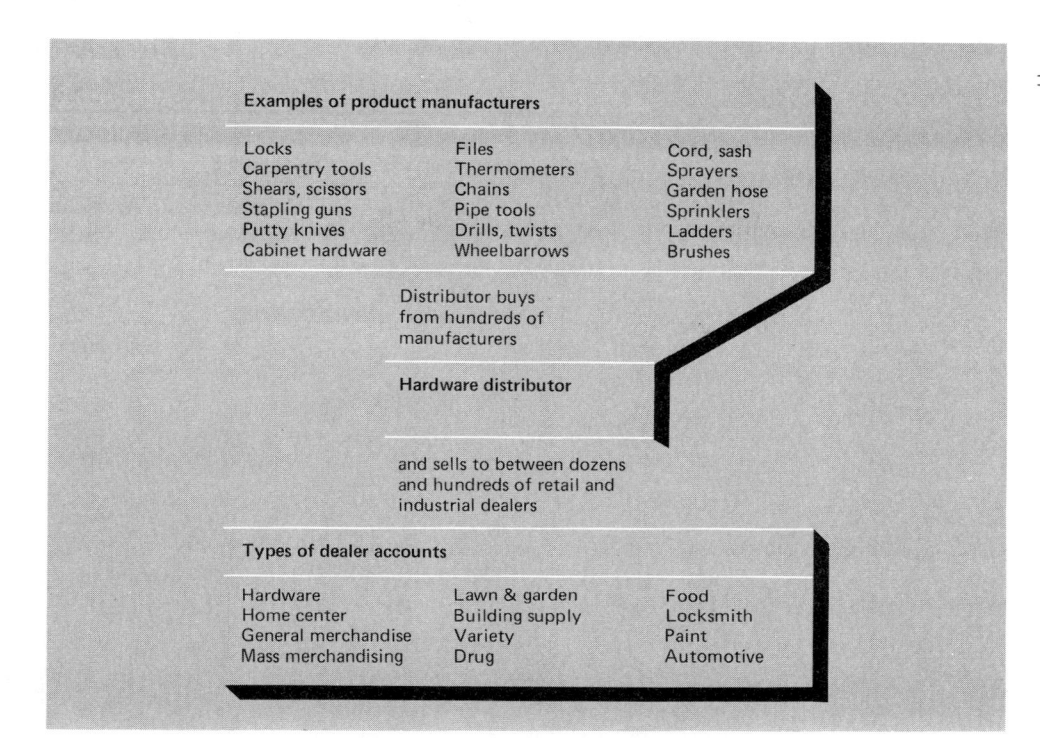

CHAPTER 19
DISTRIBUTION
MANAGEMENT

Examples of product manufacturers

Locks	Files	Cord, sash
Carpentry tools	Thermometers	Sprayers
Shears, scissors	Chains	Garden hose
Stapling guns	Pipe tools	Sprinklers
Putty knives	Drills, twists	Ladders
Cabinet hardware	Wheelbarrows	Brushes

Distributor buys from hundreds of manufacturers

Hardware distributor

and sells to between dozens and hundreds of retail and industrial dealers

Types of dealer accounts

Hardware	Lawn & garden	Food
Home center	Building supply	Locksmith
General merchandise	Variety	Paint
Mass merchandising	Drug	Automotive

FIGURE 19-4. Supply sources and customers of the hardware wholesale distributor.

Relative Costs by Channel Length

Generally speaking, the shorter the channel, the higher the manufacturers' distribution costs, particularly for those consumer products which are distributed to large numbers of people. This is surprising news to most people, who have often seen or

FIGURE 19-5. Supply sources and customers of the hardware dealer.

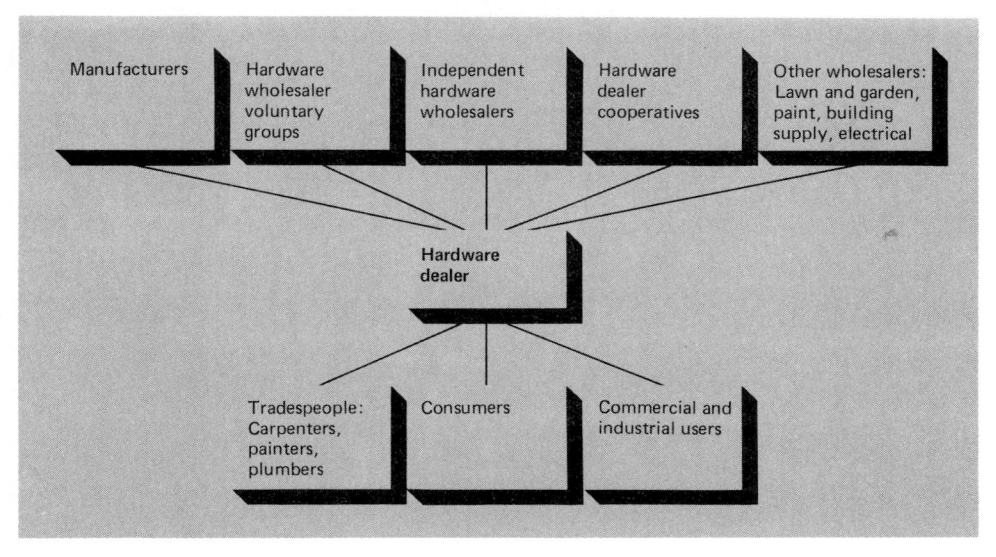

Manufacturers → Hardware wholesaler voluntary groups / Independent hardware wholesalers / Hardware dealer cooperatives / Other wholesalers: Lawn and garden, paint, building supply, electrical

→ **Hardware dealer** →

Tradespeople: Carpenters, painters, plumbers / Consumers / Commercial and industrial users heard ads which say "we can sell it to you cheaper because we cut out the middleman." To realize the fallacy of this argument, all we need to remember is that all distribution functions have to be performed by someone, irrespective of whether a short, medium, or long distribution channel is used. Eliminating intermediaries merely shifts the functions to someone else, usually the manufacturer. There are at least three reasons why it costs less to use intermediaries when distributing to large numbers of end customers: (1) there are fewer transactions, (2) transportation costs are lower, and (3) efficiency is increased through specialization.

Fewer Transactions. There are costs associated with each exchange transaction which are roughly the same whether the transaction is for one or a thousand items. Functions common to each exchange transaction are selling; transmitting the order; checking customer credit status; processing the order; preparing the invoice; and collecting payment. The fewer the transactions, the fewer the functions performed and the lower the costs. How the number of transactions is lowered by the use of an intermediary is illustrated by Figure 19-6.

Lower Transportation Costs. The larger the shipment, the lower the transportation cost per item. Manufacturers ship to the wholesaler or chain warehouse in

FIGURE 19-6. How transactions are reduced by use of an intermediary.

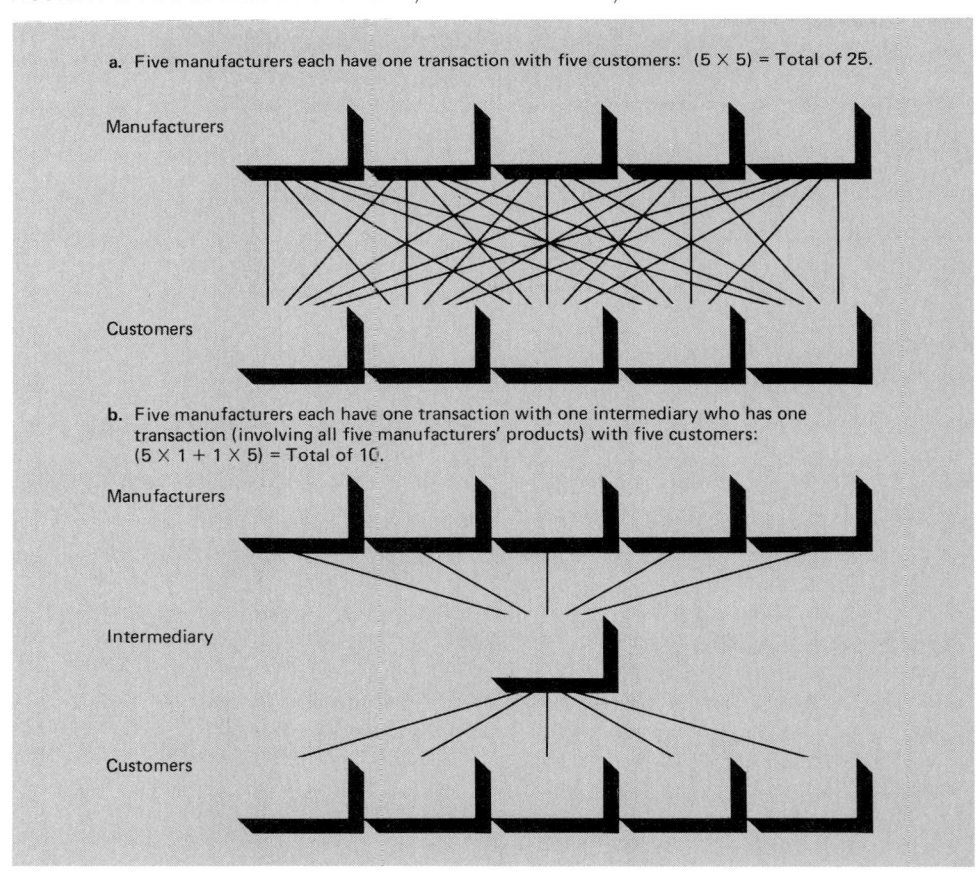

a. Five manufacturers each have one transaction with five customers: (5 × 5) = Total of 25.

b. Five manufacturers each have one transaction with one intermediary who has one transaction (involving all five manufacturers' products) with five customers: (5 × 1 + 1 × 5) = Total of 10.

truckload or less than truckload quantities. Less than truckload shipments are combined at truck terminals with other manufacturers' shipments destined for the same area or customer. Wholesalers in turn combine their customers' order for several items and deliver to customers by truck at regular intervals. The cost of transportation from manufacturer to market average 4.3 percent of the selling price.[16] This percentage would be much higher if all manufacturers' shipments were made direct to individual customers via parcel post or parcel delivery service, for example.

Efficiency through Specialization. Intermediaries generally are more efficient than manufacturers in performing their particular specialties—wholesalers in distributing to retailers, and retailers in distributing to consumers. One of the reasons is that a manufacturer is distributing only a relatively few items of its own manufacture and does not benefit from the economies of scale enjoyed by wholesalers and retailers who handle large numbers of items.

The greater efficiency of intermediaries relative to manufacturers lessens as the number of end customers lessens. In fact, it turns in favor of the manufacturer when it comes to shipping truckload quantities or high-value products (such as machinery) directly to customers.

Cost Is Not the Only Factor. If the long channel is the least costly method of reaching large numbers of end customers, why then do some companies choose the more expensive shorter channels? The answer is that the manufacturer may be willing to accept higher distribution costs in exchange for greater control over its distribution channels. The closer the manufacturer comes to direct contact with its end customers, the more control it can exercise over the implementation of its marketing plans. By distributing L'eggs to stores via company driver-salespeople, Hanes was able to get good floor location and avoid out-of-stock items in its displays. By selling cosmetics, jewelry, and other products direct to the consumer, Avon has more freedom in deciding which products to offer and feature than if it were to sell through retail stores.

Channel Conflict

Wholesalers and retailers would not exist without manufacturers to supply them with products to distribute. Nevertheless, the objectives of manufacturers are often different from those of wholesalers and retailers. The manufacturer wants the intermediary to promote as well as stock and distribute its products. The intermediary is interested in promoting those products that seem to be most preferred by its customers. The intermediary's role has been seen primarily as that of purchasing agent for its customers and only secondarily as selling agent for suppliers.[17] These differences in viewpoint lead to controversy between manufacturers and intermediaries, one of the elements in *channel conflict*. The closer the manufacturer's products meet the intermediary's objectives, the more harmonious the relationship. The further apart they are, the more likely it is that conflict will occur. Also, it has been noted that conflict often occurs because the manufacturer's national or regional point of view is in conflict with the retailer's local view.[18] Channel conflict also occurs when intermediaries resent manufacturers' policies with respect to multiple distribution, selective distribution, trade discounts, or services. Conflict can also exist among wholesalers or retailers competing in the same market.[19]

Vertical Channels

The classical vertical channel is one in which the manufacturer integrates forward through ownership of its wholesaling and/or retailing outlets. Examples of manufacturer-owned retail outlets are Sohio gas stations, Goodyear tire, Sherwin-Williams paint, and Thom McAn shoe stores. Examples of company-owned branch wholesale operations that deliver directly to chain and independent retailers include Nabisco, Keebler, and the L'eggs Division of Hanes.

The principal reason companies go to vertical channel integration is to gain more control over their channels. Another reason sometimes offered is to be able to add the wholesaler or retailer profit to the manufacturer's profit. In practice, however, the secondary reason rarely works out. Many manufacturers have found that the return on capital invested in company-owned wholesale and/or retail operations has been below that obtained from manufacturing. This fact, and the difficulty of instilling an entrepreneurial spirit in nonowner store managers are factors that have led to the decreasing popularity of manufacturer-owned stores.

Vertical Marketing Systems. In recent years the idea of the classic vertical channel has been broadened to include three categories of what are now called *vertical marketing systems*.[20] Together they supply an estimated two-thirds of the market for consumer goods.

The *corporate system* includes the types of manufacturer-owned wholesalers and retailers discussed above and it also includes corporate retail chains. The *controlled system* includes wholesaler-sponsored chains, retailer cooperative chains, and franchised operations.

The *administered system* includes arrangements wherein independent wholesalers and retailers agree to cooperate with a manufacturer's marketing program. The stronger the brand, of course, the more willing independent intermediaries are to participate in the manufacturer's programs, since effective promotions increase the intermediary's sales and profits along with those of the manufacturer. Hallmark cards, for example, are distributed through 6000 *independent* Hallmark dealers who agree to follow Hallmark's inventory, pricing, promotion, and store layout programs in exchange for the privilege of selectively representing a brand that commands nearly half of the greeting card market.[21]

Impact on producers. The growth of vertical marketing systems has brought changes in the way producers deal with their intermediaries. Many of these distributive networks are larger and more powerful than the manufacturers whose products they distribute. They include corporate chains such as A&P and K mart; voluntary chains like IGA and Cotter; and large, multibranch wholesalers such as Foremost-McKesson which distributes drugs, foods, wines, spirits, and industrial chemicals nationally through more than fifty drug distribution centers and over seventy chemical warehouses.

Often these distributive organizations are the *channel captains*,* who may greatly influence producers' distribution policies. To get their products and promotional programs accepted by these networks, suppliers must tailor their marketing plans to meet the requirements of the networks. And they must organize their sales

---

*A term sometimes used to denote the entity in a channel system that controls the others. The captain may be a manufacturer, a retail chain, or a wholesaler, and it may be different in different markets.

forces to work cooperatively with buyers and merchandise managers who may be located at decentralized geographic locations as well as at the network's central headquarters.

Most of the remaining one-third of consumer goods continue to be distributed through nonvertical systems, namely, regional and local wholesalers who sell to independent local retailers. They represent the more traditional channel composed of the smaller, independent middlemen. The producer's sales representatives or agents must call on these entities and negotiate transactions individually. The producer is more likely to be the channel captain in this relationship, yet must be sufficiently flexible to adjust to the needs of merchants servicing the differing demands of local markets. Even though individual orders are small (compared with those of the vertical networks), the combined volume of this distribution segment is too large for most manufacturers to ignore.

LEGAL ISSUES IN DISTRIBUTION

The Sherman and Clayton Acts, described in Chapter 18, are the principal laws affecting distribution. These laws do not make any distribution practices illegal per se. Rather, a company's distribution practices may be declared illegal when shown to be restraining trade or tending to create a monopoly in interstate commerce. As is the case with pricing, marketing management is dependent on competent legal counsel when setting distribution policies. We'll discuss briefly five types of practices that have been ruled illegal in some, but not all, court cases.[22]

Exclusive Dealing

Exclusive distribution is an arrangement whereby the dealer agrees not to carry a competing brand. Section 3 of the Clayton Act prohibits exclusive dealing contracts *only* where the effect "may be to substantially lessen competition or tend to create a monopoly in any line of commerce." Court cases have been won and lost depending on the facts of each situation.

Exclusive Territories

Exclusive dealing arrangements often provide for protected territories whereby none of the company's dealers is allowed to sell in the designated geographic territory of another. Such arrangements permit dealers to concentrate on competing against other manufacturers' brands. As in the case of exclusive dealing, exclusive territory agreements are not illegal per se. Court cases have been decided for and against such arrangements depending on whether competition was thought to be unduly lessened.

Tying Sales

Tie-in arrangements occur when the seller makes the purchase of an item conditional on the purchase of other items (usually less-desirable ones). It violates the tying provision of the Clayton Act, however, only if it contributes to monopolistic behavior. A variation of tying is "full-line forcing" in which the seller of a desirable brand will sell only to the dealer who agrees to carry the seller's whole line.

Tying arrangements were common during World War II when there were shortages of many products, including grain whiskeys. Dealers were forced to buy a certain amount of rum, for example, in order to get a case of bourbon. The dealer in turn would not sell a bottle of bourbon unless the customer purchased one or two bottles of rum as well.

Reciprocity

This is an arrangement, explicit or implicit, whereby two companies buy one another's products—a case of "you scratch my back and I'll scratch yours." This was a common practice described as a strategy in most marketing texts until the late 1960s when the FTC began charging some companies with using reciprocity as an anticompetitive practice. These companies signed consent decrees with the FTC agreeing not to engage in the practice in the future. While no law forbids reciprocity per se, many companies now publish policies prohibiting the practice and have set up internal controls to enforce the policy. Irrespective of the legal issues, some marketing managers have avoided the practice in the belief that it is an unsound method of securing business.

Refusal to Deal

One of the stickier problems for marketing management is knowing under what conditions it can refuse to deal with or cut off sales to a retailer. The law presumably gives sellers the right to select customers on the basis of reasonable criteria they choose to establish and announce. Yet a manufacturer cannot *threaten* to cut off a product from a dealer for reasons of noncompliance with the manufacturer's policies, nor can refusal to deal result from collusive action on the part of the seller or group of resellers.

A manufacturer may refuse to deal *only* on the basis of its unilateral decisions. Presumably a dealer can be dropped for nonperformance. But it might be difficult to drop a dealer for price cutting in states where there is no price maintenance law. Refusal to deal is a subject about which marketing management needs good legal counsel when establishing policies and practices for its sales force.

DISTRIBUTION STRATEGIES

As noted earlier, producers are hesitant to risk changing or adding channels for fear of alienating their intermediaries whose cooperation and support they have worked hard to get. Yet change often is forced on companies by buyers changing their place of purchase. Examples include (1) consumers shifting many hardware purchases from hardware stores to mass merchandising outlets and (2) consumers shifting their place of magazine purchase from newsstands to supermarkets. Additions of new products also may require producers to add new channels, as when Kodak introduced industrial chemicals and office copiers in addition to its photographic lines. Citicorp had to find new channels when it added credit cards and travel checks to its traditional line of banking services.

Ideally a company should anticipate the need for change in its distribution methods. One way is to evaluate distribution during the annual marketing planning process by answering the questions raised in the *situation analysis* outline, Chapter

9. While problems may be uncovered during this analysis, finding solutions often requires more time than can be given during the annual planning period. Consequently, it is not unusual for changes in distribution strategies to be preceded by a special study.

Distribution Objectives

No two companies are likely to have identical distribution objectives; furthermore, distribution objectives often will vary for different products and different markets served by the same company. However, there are three objectives which seem to apply to most any situation. By measuring performance against these, the company is alerted to the need for changes in distribution strategies or for better implementation of current strategies. They are:

1. To maintain the desired coverage of target markets, both quantitatively and qualitatively
2. To ensure that channels provide good customer delivery, services as needed, and adequate product promotional support
3. To optimize the distribution cost/performance ratio

Market Coverage Strategies

The first distribution objective is to maintain the desired coverage of target markets. Market coverage for consumer goods can be classified as intensive, selective, or exclusive, according to the relative numbers of retail outlets used for each geographic market. (See Figure 19-7.) *Intensive* coverage calls for distribution through many retail outlets; *selective* coverage, through a few retail outlets; and *exclusive* coverage, through only one retail outlet per geographic area.

To a large extent, the type of consumer good being marketed suggests the type of market coverage and length of channel that will be needed. Figure 19-8 shows that as we move from *convenience* to *shopping* to *specialty* goods (horizontal scale), market coverage moves from intensive toward exclusive (right-hand vertical scale) and length of channel moves from long toward medium (left-hand vertical scale).

FIGURE 19-7. Intensity of distribution: Market coverage classified according to the number of retail outlets used in each geographic area.

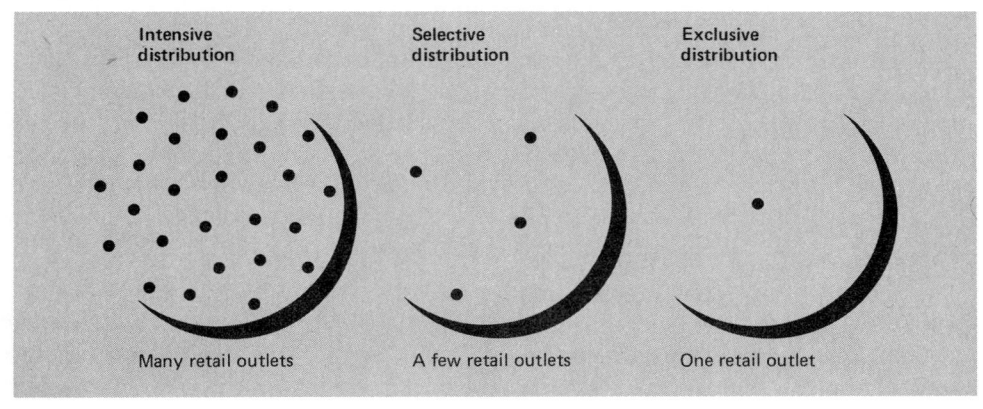

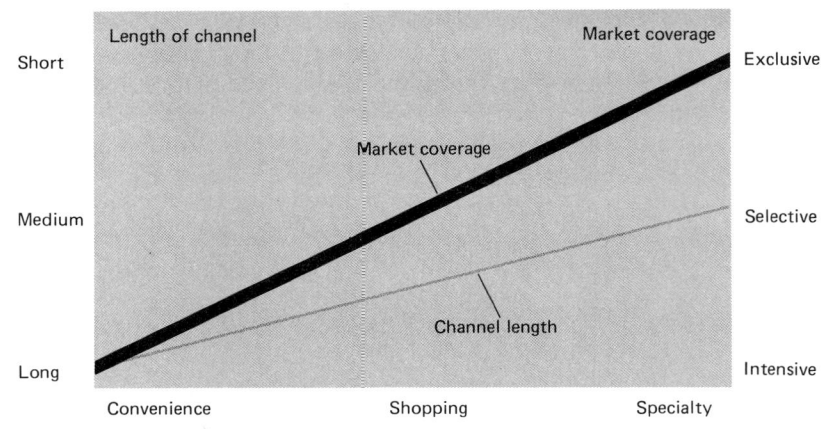

FIGURE 19-8. Relationships between type of consumer good, market coverage, and channel length.

Similar patterns apply for industrial goods. As we move from *multiple-purpose* (made for inventory) goods toward *high-value* and *engineered* (made-to-order) goods, coverage shifts from intensive toward selective or exclusive coverage; and channel length shifts from medium (manufacturer to wholesaler to user) to short (manufacturer to user).

Intensive Coverage. The use of many retail outlets is appropriate for convenience goods because these goods should be widely available to meet the regular, frequent shopping needs of consumers. Wide availability suggests the need for long channels, including retail chains, wholesalers, and independent retailers.

Crest toothpaste, for example, can be bought just about anywhere. It is sold in grocery, drug, department, and mass-merchandising stores; in news and tobacco shops, including those in airports, hotels, and motels; and in vending machines. The advantage of the intensive coverage strategy is that the more available the brand at places where consumers buy, the more likely it is to be purchased. The disadvantage is that the quality of distribution lowers as distribution intensifies—quality in the sense that retailers feel little loyalty toward a product that is stocked by multiple competitors. Unless the manufacturer goes to the expense of employing a missionary sales force, it has little control over retail stockouts or the ways in which the brand is displayed and promoted.

The industrial counterparts of consumer convenience goods are standardized, multipurpose products such as screws, nuts, and bolts; janitorial supplies; and office supplies. Medium-length (wholesalers) or long (wholesalers and dealers) channels, as well as intensive or selective coverage, are needed to reach the large numbers of potential industrial customers in each geographic area. Armstrong World Industries uses wholesalers and dealers to get its ceiling and floor covering products distributed to contractor/installers. The advantages and disadvantages of intensive coverage are much the same as for consumer goods.

Selective Coverage. The use of a few selected retail outlets is appropriate for shopping goods, since by definition consumers are willing to search for shopping goods. And because the number of outlets is limited, it is feasible to use the medium-length channel (manufacturer to retailer to consumer). Examples of brands that distribute selectively include Zenith television, Maytag appliances, Raleigh bicycles, SCM typewriters, Yamaha stereo, and Glidden paints.

The advantage to the manufacturer of a selective coverage strategy is that it results in higher-quality coverage. The manufacturer, can select the larger, financially stronger retailers who will give support to its brand. Also retailers can be selected who complement the brand image that the manufacturer seeks to project. And since retailers benefit from being among the few outlets carrying the brand, they will cooperate by helping the manufacturer achieve its brand sales objectives. The disadvantage is that the selective strategy provides less consumer exposure than the intensive strategy.

The counterpart of selective coverage for industrial goods is found in companies selling to the construction industry. Examples are producers of plumbing equipment, electrical equipment, and lumber. Usually such companies distribute through a limited number of wholesalers and/or dealers in each geographic market. (Weyerhaeuser, for example, distributes its lumber products selectively.) The construction industry has many small contractors in almost every geographic market, which would seem to suggest the need for an intensive coverage strategy. However, larger contractors, though fewer in number, account for a large share of total construction. The stronger wholesalers and dealers are better able to compete for the business of these large contractors. The advantages of selling through a few large intermediaries, therefore, seem to outweigh the disadvantages of selling through many smaller ones.

Exclusive Coverage. The appointment of one retailer in each market is an appropriate strategy for some specialty goods and some high-value shopping goods. Producers of such specialty goods as designer clothes and premier brands of cameras and stereos may seek exclusive retailers. But since a specialty good can be considered as any brand for which there is a loyal following of buyers who will not accept a substitute, selective (or even intensive) distribution may be a better strategy for certain specialty products. Examples might be special drugs or remedies, rare Scotch whiskey, or meershaum pipes. The point to remember is that exclusive coverage is desirable for some specialties but not necessarily all.

High-value shopping goods frequently sold through exclusive retailers include pianos, high-quality men's suits, china, and jewelry. When specialty and shopping goods are sold exclusively, a medium-length channel is generally used so as to facilitate close relationships between manufacturer and retailer. Exclusive distribution is also seen in the form of franchised dealers for such high-value services as U-Haul truck rentals.

Exclusivity is a matter of degree. It might mean one outlet in a small city or one outlet in different sections of a metropolitan area. If the sections of the metropolitan area represent separate trading areas, de facto exclusivity is achieved.

A manufacturer following an exclusive distribution strategy has the advantage of being able to attract the strongest retailer available in a market area, and can expect the retailer's full cooperation in exchange for protecting it from competition from other retailers carrying the same brand. The disadvantage is that exposure to potential buyers is more limited than when selective distribution is used.

Industrial goods exclusive dealers. Exclusive industrial goods dealerships are found in heavy equipment industries such as farm, road, and drilling equipment.

Dealers must make substantial capital investments in order to maintain essential facilities and inventories and sizable sales, repair, and administrative payrolls. The quid pro quo for the dealer is a protected territory. A description of Caterpillar Tractor Company's dealers illustrates why exclusive dealership arrangements are almost essential for attracting and holding good dealers.

> Caterpillar's distribution organization of 93 domestic and 137 overseas dealerships is considered one of the company's greatest strengths. Independently owned, the average dealer has sales of $100 million and a net worth of $4 million. An archetypal dealer has represented Caterpillar for fifty years, operates three branches, has over 400 employees, rebuilds engines, refurbishes tractors, and sells rebuilt parts as well as new ones.
>
> Linked by computer to Caterpillar's distribution center, dealers get overnight delivery of spare parts. A dealer owns a fleet of specially equipped trucks which provide 24-hour service to customers in the field, and some own airplanes for even speedier parts delivery. Service is the key to the dealer's business, since downtime is very costly for a contractor. Competitors believe that the service network provided by Caterpillar dealers is responsible for the company's commanding share of market.[23]

Geographic Coverage Strategies. Manufacturers of consumers goods have three options with respect to geographic coverage strategies: regional, national, or selected metropolitan markets. The smaller producer will have little choice but to limit distribution, at least initially, and may never go national. There are many sound, profitable companies that have remained regional. Examples are found in beer, soft drinks, coffee, and foods. A second alternative is to seek national distribution, a strategy followed by many of the large, well-known brand name companies.

A third alternative is to distribute only in selected markets, usually the larger metropolitan markets which account for much of the nation's population and buying power, and to forego lesser markets which often are unprofitable to serve. Oil companies, for example, have pretty much abandoned the strategy of national distribution. They have learned that it is not profitable to distribute in markets where they do not have strong market positions. Texaco, a long-time national marketer of petroleum, is withdrawing from several states; also Gulf, a former national petroleum marketer, is withdrawing from the entire west coast and Rocky Mountain areas.[24]

Many companies with national distribution of their present lines choose to introduce new products or line extensions on a regional or market-by-market basis. This approach has the advantage of market testing the product and promotional approaches during the rollout; but the disadvantage is that it permits competitors to prepare countermeasures for those markets not yet entered. After buying Folgers, a regional coffee brand, Procter & Gamble moved slowly in expanding to other geographic areas because of the regional strengths of other coffee brands. General Foods' Maxwell House brand was prepared with a strong promotional campaign to greet Folgers when it moved into eastern markets. Increasingly, manufacturers appear to be placing less importance on the questionable prestige of a national distribution position and placing more emphasis on distributing in those areas which are the most profitable for them.

Channel Strategies

There are two basic strategic decisions that manufacturers must make concerning channels: (1) whether to use direct or indirect channels; and (2) if the decision is to go indirect, whether to use single or multiple product channels. Conditions may dictate the answer in some situations, whereas careful research and thought will be needed in others. Decisions usually hang on the three issues discussed earlier under distribution objectives: (1) the type of coverage needed to reach target markets, (2) the type of promotion and customer service needed, and (3) the cost/performance tradeoffs.

Direct Channel for Consumer Goods. Whether to distribute direct-to-consumer is a question rarely faced by established companies.* Most direct-to-consumer businesses were begun by individual entrepreneurs. The founder of Mary Kay Cosmetics, with current sales of over $200 million, began with a sales force of nine people. Tupperware, with sales of nearly $1 billion, was started by the owner of a small plastics container factory. Amway, with sales of over $1 billion, was created by two partners working out of their homes. Stanley Home Products (Stanhome) began in the home of its founder, a former Fuller Brush representative. Despite the success of these and other direct selling companies, this form of distribution continues to represent less than 1 percent of all retail sales. Its success rests on a rare talent: the ability to build and maintain very large sales forces made up of many thousands of part-time representatives.

Indirect Channels for Consumer Goods. Data from the Bureau of the Census show that sales through retail stores account for over 97 percent of all retail sales. The balance is accounted for by mail order, vending machines, and direct-to-consumer sales.[25] Therefore, barring the exceptions discussed above, a consumer goods manufacturer will choose indirect channels. The next important question, whether to use single or multiple product channels, will be discussed later.

Direct Channels for Industrial Goods. Whether to distribute through direct or indirect channels is a question that is more likely to be faced by industrial goods producers. Direct distribution accounts for about three-fifths of industrial sales, a figure swelled by big-dollar car and truckload shipments of raw materials made direct to customers and by direct shipments of such high-value goods as machinery, large trucks, and engineered products.

In general the direct channel is appropriate for industrial goods (1) when there are relatively few customers, (2) when products are of high value, (3) when transportation costs are low relative to product value, or (4) when orders are infrequent. Plant machinery, large computers, and engineered products fit some or all of these criteria. Other factors that may favor the direct channel are proximity to customer locations of the producer's plants or warehouses, and situations where sales and customer services require more technically trained field representatives than those usually provided by wholesalers or dealers.

---

*There was a spate of attempts in the 1950s by well-known cosmetics firms to try to emulate Avon's success by adding new brands to be sold by newly created direct-to-consumer sales forces. Most of these attempts failed, although these firms continued to market their established brands through traditional retail channels.

An alternative distribution strategy is to ship original orders directly, but distribute spare parts indirectly—i.e., though wholesalers or dealers who are able to give faster service because of their proximity to customers.

Indirect Channels for Industrial Goods. In general indirect distribution through wholesaler and/or dealer intermediaries is appropriate (1) when customers are many, geographically dispersed, and not in proximity to the producer's plants; (2) when the products are of relatively low value; (3) when transportation cost is high relative to product value; and (4) when orders are frequent. Products which meet some or all of these criteria include semifinished goods, component parts, multipurpose products, and supplies such as lubricants and cleaning and office supplies. In general such products can be made for inventory and sold to a variety of customers. It is practical to use wholesalers or dealers in these circumstances, since they can provide better customer service at lower cost; also their sales people can answer the usual range of customer inquiries (although highly technical questions may have to be answered by company technicians).

If large customers insist on buying direct from the manufacturer (which is not unusual), a dual distribution strategy may be necessary: (1) direct distribution for the larger customer and (2) indirect through wholesalers for all others. Large customers who can order in truckload quantities want the savings from quantity discounts and lower transportation costs. Often, however, they will order fill-in quantities and spare parts from wholesalers.

Whether an industrial goods producer should use direct, indirect, or dual distribution strategies comes down to weighing the factors of coverage, service, promotion, distribution costs, and the company's market position and manufacturing costs relative to competitors.

Single versus Multiple Product Channels. If the indirect channel has been chosen, the next question is, "Should the manufacturer use one product channel or multiple product channels?" An over-the-counter drug, for example, might be sold through a single product channel such as drug wholesalers and drug retailers, or it might go through multiple product channels made up of drug, food, and variety wholesalers and retailers.

The growth of "scrambled merchandising" (stores of a primary product class, such as food, selling other product classes, such as health and beauty aids and magazines) has led to multiple channels becoming the norm for many products. However, there can be situations where limiting a product to a primary product channel has advantages.

Product channel strategy should not be confused with *market coverage strategy*. Let's assume that the single product channel strategy (drug channel) has been chosen for an over-the-counter drug. The manufacturer now must choose a coverage strategy. It could opt for intensive coverage (all drug stores) or selective coverage (a few drug stores) in each geographic area. Similar options would be available if the decision had been to use multiple product channels. In this product example, exclusive coverage (one drug store per geographic area) would not appear to be a practical alternative.

Single product channel. Sometimes only one product channel is available. In those states where packaged liquor may be sold only through state-owned stores, for example, a distiller has no choice but to use this channel. Oil companies have little choice but to distribute gasoline to consumers through service stations, although they may choose between company-owned or franchised outlets. Auto manufacturers appear to have little choice but to distribute through franchised auto dealers. The reasons are (1) the need to provide warranty service throughout the country, since new car owners may live or drive in areas not close to the place of purchase; and (2) the felt need of the manufacturer to exercise close control of the sales and service performance of its dealers.

Some manufacturers choose to distribute only through a predominant channel. Forest products companies, for example, often sell only through building supply dealers because this channel represents the primary place of lumber purchase for most consumers and contractors. For similar reasons, a mobile home manufacturer may sell only through mobile home dealers.

The desire for dealer loyalty may be the reason for choosing a single product channel. This was the argument used by Bulova for staying with jewelry stores at a time when Timex was expanding rapidly into multiple channels. Bulova was willing to forego the wider consumer exposure of multiple channels in order to strengthen its positions with the professional jewelers. Jewelers were biased against those brands sold at discount in channels such as drug and mass merchandising. American Standard has remained with the traditional plumbing equipment channel (plumbing wholesalers and dealers who sell to contractors and builders) while eschewing the do-it-yourself market which buys from retail hardware and home center channels. This was decided not only because of the factor of dealer loyalty, but also because the traditional channel is the predominant channel.

Multiple product channels. The trend appears to be away from the single product channel to multiple channels. Most consumer products are carried by a variety of wholesale and retail outlets. Many of the industrial products distributed through indirect channels are carried by different categories of wholesalers who specialize by market segments rather than by product class. And many service firms are searching for additional channels for reaching their customers.

Whether to use multiple channels is less the question than is which channels to use. The answer depends largely on (1) where our target markets buy and in what proportions and (2) which outlets we want to be in. From Figure 19-9, for example, we can see that consumers may purchase paint brushes in a variety of retail outlets—independent stores, chain stores, and manufacturer-owned paint stores. Brushes are usually bought at the time and place of paint purchase. Some consumers are loyal to one paint dealer, while others buy at the most convenient location or where they feel they can get the best bargain. Many paint brush manufacturers offer a range of quality and price and seek distribution wherever paint is sold. Others, however, sell only high-quality brushes through better paint and hardware stores. And still others sell only low-price brushes, primarily through discount chains.

Traditional channels are not always the best way to reach target markets. Both Procter & Gamble and Kimberly-Clark turned to direct mail to distribute their disposable briefs for incontinent people after test marketing showed that prospects were too embarrassed to buy the product in retail stores.[26]

In order to get a foothold in the U.S. Market, Lego, the Danish producer of plastic bricks for toy construction kits, licensed Samsonite Corp. (the luggage company) as its distributor. The need for wider distribution in toy channels, however, led Lego

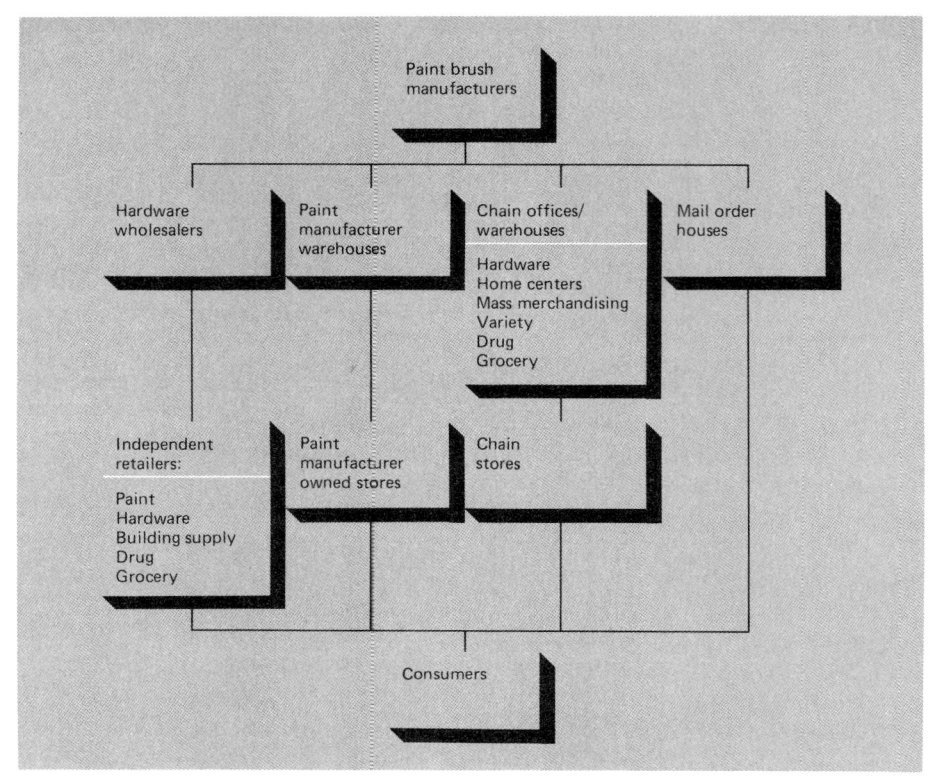

FIGURE 19-9. Multiple channels for paint brushes.

later on to replace Samsonite. It formed a U.S.-based subsidiary with a sales force that would concentrate on toy channels. Using multiple distribution, including toy, department, mass merchandising, and variety stores, Lego has captured over half of the U.S. market for construction toys.[27]

When producers of high quality products seek to reach additional market segments by adding lower-price lines, they risk alienating their present channels. One strategy for moderating this problem is to create a new brand to be sold through other channels which cater to lower-price buyers. Hallmark Cards, Inc., for example, uses the Hallmark brand on its "carriage trade" cards sold through 6,000 independent dealers. But to reach the lower-price market it uses the Ambassador label on cards distributed through 13,000 supermarkets and discount houses.[28]

Strategies for Cost/Performance Optimization

Earlier we said that a common distribution objective is to try to optimize cost/performance ratios. Ideally a manufacturer would like to achieve the desired coverage of its target markets and control of its intermediaries at low cost. But since coverage and control are achieved partly as a result of the manufacturer's expenditures, a practical strategy is one which arrives at the best tradeoff between costs on the one hand and peformance on the other. We will illustrate with three strategies: the first two deal with promotional approaches to the trade, and the third describes a coordinated physical distribution strategy.

Trade Incentives. To get the trade to stock and promote its brand, a manufacturer may offer one or more of the following incentives: (1) higher than average price discounts; (2) stocking discounts (paying the trade to carry the brand as in the case of magazine publishers paying supermarkets for floor space near the checkout counter); (3) promotional discounts to obtain desirable shelf space, floor displays, and cooperative participation in local store advertisements; or (4) extra services as envisioned by the *augmented product* concept described in Chapter 16.

In convenience goods channels, such as packaged foods and health and beauty aids, one or more trade incentives amount to almost a mandatory entry fee. Stronger brands may not have to offer as generous concessions as lesser brands, but all must offer something. Even powerful Procter & Gamble responded to trade pressures to liberalize its trade allowances.[29]

Yet for some product categories, manufacturers may have the options of offering or not offering special trade incentives. The need for incentives is less pronounced in such categories as electric appliances, hardware, stationery and office supplies, and even in the case of highly differentiated drugs or remedies which have achieved specialty status because of their loyal consumer followings. The manufacturer who spends more than the average for trade incentives in categories such as these expects more trade support and higher sales as a consequence. The manufacturer who uses no trade incentives, or spends less than the average, is willing to trade lower sales for higher profit margins.

Supplemental Missionary Efforts. Personal selling and distribution strategies are closely interrelated.[30] One sales/distribution strategy is to supplement the uncertain (and often minimal) sales efforts of the retailer with in-store merchandising efforts by the manufacturer's missionary sales force (or by commissioned agents such as food brokers).

The supermarket manager is concerned with thousands of items, and has little reason to feature a brand unless given some reason to do so. The missionary salesperson often is able to enlist the store manager's cooperation by showing the advantages of tying in with trade and consumer promotions. The salesperson will suggest co-op ads and other forms of retail promotion. If a chain store's rules do not prohibit it, the missionary representative will stock shelves and build displays. Retail promotions, when coordinated with brand advertising and consumer incentives, usually result in more products moving through the channels than when manufacturers rely only on advertising or consumer deals.

But missionary sales forces are costly. Optional strategies to missionary selling include spending more for consumer advertising, offering higher trade and consumer incentives, or minimizing expenditures and settling for lower sales at higher margins. The optimum strategy cannot be determined precisely. Judgment, observation, and experimentation, however, can help a firm get close to the optimum balance between costs and performance.

Physical Distribution Strategy. In addition to trade incentives and missionary selling strategies, a systems approach to physical distribution offers a different but important strategy for optimizing cost/benefit tradeoffs.

Because the decisions that affect distribution cost and performance are made in several departments of a manufacturing firm, a systems approach can be used to coordinate these decisions. Usually it is administered by a centralized distribution department reporting to a top-level executive. Spalding, for example, has a vice president for distribution who reports to the president. The divisional vice president of distribution for Kodak reports directly to the general manager of the U.S. and Canadian Photographic Division.

Figure 19-10 shows a typical distribution diagram tracing the flow of materials, beginning with raw materials and ending with the delivery of finished products to end customers. Departments concerned with this process include purchasing, transportation, manufacturing, finance, and marketing.

The *purchasing department* is responsible for the procurement of materials used in the production process. The *transportation department* arranges for the shipping of inbound materials and outbound products. The *manufacturing department* warehouses incoming materials and finished products. The *finance department* is concerned with having capital available to finance inventories. The *marketing department* forcasts sales by time periods, works with intermediaries in establishing inventory levels, and—in some companies—is in charge of field inventories and shipments to customers. Often intermediaries or industrial customers try to push inventory carrying backward to the manufacturer and demand more frequent deliveries in order to lessen their own inventory costs. Marketing must find solutions to these demands.

Potential for interdepartmental conflict. The objective of a physical distribution system is to provide acceptable customer service (the definition of "acceptable" will vary by different classes of goods and by competitive conditions) at lowest cost. But attaining this objective requires coordination, because each functional department has its own priorities which often are in conflict with those of other departments.

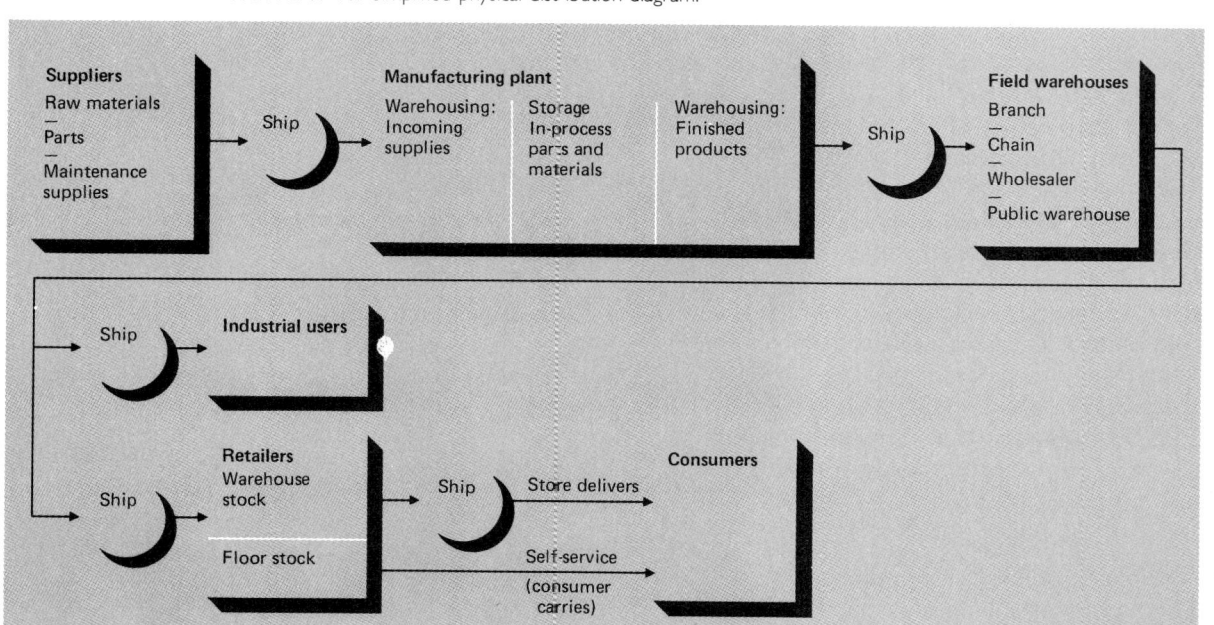

FIGURE 19-10. Simplified physical distribution diagram.

Supplies purchased in quantity are cheaper, but must be stored for longer periods until used; saving from purchasing in large quantities, therefore, may be offset by higher raw material inventory and warehousing costs. Long manufacturing runs reduce production costs, but may result in large inventories of finished product and thereby increase finished inventory and warehousing costs. Raw materials and finished products shipped by the cheapest means (whch usually are the slowest ones) may result in higher inventory costs or unsatisfactory customer service. Efforts by the finance department to reduce capital needs and interest costs by insisting on lower inventories may result in poor customer service and lost sales. The desire of zealous salespersons to give high levels of customer service may result in shorter but higher-cost production runs or the need for higher inventory levels of finished products.

Systems and organization approaches. Many companies now use systems approaches to find the best tradeoffs among the conflicting functional interests. Operations research teams study the problems and devise mathematical models for optimizing the customer service/distribution cost tradeoff. Once objectives are agreed upon, much of the process can be routinized through computer programs. But some organizational arrangement is needed to deal with exceptions which can be expected to occur with regularity.

A distribution department is usually established to oversee the physical distribution system. This may be a staff department responsible for monitoring the system and keeping it up to date. Or it may have the functional authority to issue directives to the several functional departments involved. In some cases it is given line responsibility for the management and distribution of finished inventories. An effective physical distribution system directed by a central department can be of great assistance to the marketing manager. Although the marketing department should make important inputs to the system, such as sales forecasts and recommending customer service levels, a well-managed physical distribution department can free the marketing department to concentrate on business getting activities.

SUMMARY

Companies often seem reluctant to challenge their distribution methods for fear of disturbing relationships with their customers or current channel members. While concern is warranted, delaying too long in adapting to changes in buying patterns can have a negative impact on company sales and market share.

Manufacturers have a choice of direct or indirect distribution channels (e.g., wholesalers and retailers). Indirect channels are used for the vast majority of consumer goods while the direct channel is used for about 60 percent of industrial goods. The direct is the primary channel for services, although there is increasing use of indirect channels.

The concept of vertical marketing systems recognizes the shift from independent wholesalers and retailers to large distribution networks composed of corporate chains, cooperative chains, franchised chains, and large wholesalers who operate regionally or nationally with multiple branches. These large networks move such large quantities of merchandise that it is essential for successful manufacturers to use them.

Channel length designates the approximate number of intermediaries between the manufacturer and end customer. Medium and shorter channels provide for better manufacturer control and closer relationships with end customers, but tend to be more costly than the long channel.

The principal legal issues in distribution involve exclusive dealing, exclusive territories, tying sales, reciprocity, and refusal to deal. Though not automatically illegal, they may be so ruled if they result in restraint of trade or in monopolization.

Distribution strategies are concerned with achieving specific objectives in terms of market coverage, services to customers, product promotional support, and optimization of cost/performance ratios. Channels strategies are concerned with whether to distribute direct or indirect, and if the latter, whether to use single or multiple channels. Cost/performance optimization strategies recognize that effective distribution, as measured by volume of sales to end customers, is achieved at a cost. The objective is to get the best balance between cost and performance.

Planning and implementing distribution strategies are never easy, since distribution tends to be far more complicated than our simplified textbook diagrams indicate. While distribution may not seem as exciting as new product development and product promotion, a strong distribution system is one of the most important assets a company can have.

QUESTIONS

1. Distinguish between direct and indirect distribution.
2. Define wholesale intermediaries and retail intermediaries.
3. Chain store organizations perform some of the same functions as wholesalers. What are they?
4. List the four principal channels of distribution for consumer goods.
5. List the four principal channels for industrial goods.
6. How do channels for services differ from those for goods?
7. Why do some manufacturers prefer the higher-cost shorter channels over the lower-cost longer channels?
8. Name the advantages and disadvantages of intensive, selective, and exclusive market coverage strategies. Which type of good is most likely to use each strategy?
9. Under what conditions is a company most likely to follow a direct or indirect channel strategy?
10. Why is the trend away from the single to the multiple product channel strategy?
11. What has Citicorp learned from McDonald's about the marketing of services?

REFERENCES

1. IBM Annual Report, 1981, p. 4.
2. *Wall Street Journal*, Mar. 1, 1982, p. 43; and *Business Week*, Mar. 8, 1982, pp. 77-78.
3. *Wall Street Journal*, Sept. 1, 1981, p. 21.
4. Donald J. Bowersox, M. Bixby Cooper, Douglas M. Lambert, and Donald A. Taylor, *Management in Marketing Channels*, McGraw-Hill, New York, 1980, p. 276.
5. U.S. Bureau of the Census, *Statistical Abstract of the United States*, Washington, D.C., 1980, pp. 840, 841.
6. Derived from tables 1493, 1495, and 1505 in ibid.
7. Ibid., p. 847.
8. See Larry J. Rosenberg and Elizabeth C. Hirschman, "Retailing Without Stores," *Harvard Business Review*, July-August 1980, pp. 103-112; and Malcolm P. McNair and Eleanor G.

May, "The Next Revolution of the Retailing Wheel," *Harvard Business Review*, Sept.-Oct. 1978, pp. 81-91.
9. Rosenberg and Hirschman, op. cit., p. 105. Copyright © 1980 by the President and Fellows of Harvard College; all rights reserved.
10. McNair and May, op. cit., pp. 81-91. Copyright © 1978 by the President and Fellows of Harvard College; all rights reserved.
11. *Marketing Definitions*, American Marketing Association, Chicago, 1960, p. 11.
12. James H. Donnelly, Jr., "Marketing Intermediaries in Channels of Distribution for Services," *Journal of Marketing*, January 1976, pp. 55-57.
13. *Wall Street Journal*, Apr. 21, 1980, p. 20.
14. 1980 Amway Annual Report, p. 7.
15. Victor P. Buell, *Marketing Characteristics of the Hardware Industry*, Department of Marketing, University of Massachusetts, Amherst, June 1976.
16. Wendell M. Stewart, "Physical Distribution," in Victor P. Buell (ed.), *Handbook of Modern Marketing*, McGraw-Hill, New York, 1970, p. 4-55.
17. Phillip McVey, "Are Channels of Distribution What the Textbooks Say?" *Journal of Marketing*, January 1960, p. 64.
18. Bert C. McCammon, Jr., and Robert W. Little, "Marketing Channels: Analytical Systems and Approaches," in George Schwartz (ed.), *Science in Marketing*, Wiley, New York, 1965, pp. 345, 346.
19. For more on channel conflict see Bruce Mallen, "Conflict and Cooperation in Marketing Channels," in George L. Smith (ed.), *Reflections on Progress in Marketing*, American Marketing Association, 1964; and Bert Rosenbloom, "Conflict and Channel Efficiency: Some Conceptual Models for the Decision Maker," *Journal of Marketing*, July 1973, pp. 26-30.
20. See, for example, William R. Davidson, "Post-1970 Developments" (in vertical marketing systems), *Marketing News*, Mar. 7, 1980, p. 12, and "Changes in Distributive Institutions," *Journal of Marketing*, January 1970, pp. 7-10; also Bert C. McCammon, Jr., "Perspectives for Distribution Programming," in Louis P. Bucklin (ed.), *Vertical Marketing Systems*, Scott, Foresman, 1970, pp. 32-51.
21. *Wall Street Journal*, Mar. 17, 1982, p. 1; and *Business Week*, May 29, 1978, p. 57.
22. Some of the information for this section has been abstracted from Robert N. Corley, Robert L. Black, and O. Lee Reed, *The Legal Environment of Business*, McGraw-Hill, New York, 1981, chaps. 7 and 8; Ray O. Werner, "Marketing and the United States Supreme Court," *Journal of Marketing*, spring 1982, pp. 73-81; Donald J. Bowersox, M. Bixby Cooper, Douglas M. Lambert, and Donald A. Taylor, *Management in Marketing Channels*, McGraw-Hill, New York, 1980, chap. 5; Stewart H. Rewoldt, James D. Scott, and Martin R. Warshaw, *Introduction to Marketing Management*, 3d ed., Irwin, Homewood Ill., 1977, pp. 382-391; and Ray Werner, "The Laws Affecting Marketing," in Buell, *Handbook of Modern Marketing*, pp. 17-3 to 17-17.
23. *Business Week*, May 4, 1981, p. 77; and *Wall Street Journal*, Apr. 17, 1976, p. 1.
24. *Wall Street Journal*, Mar. 5, 1981, p. 52.
25. Calculated from U.S. Bureau of the Census, *Statistical Abstract of the United States*, Washington, D.C., 1981, table 1746, p. 818.
26. *Advertising Age*, Nov. 30, 1981, p. 1.
27. *Los Angeles Times News Service, The Morning Union*, Springfield, Mass., Mar. 27, 1982, p. 20; and *Business Week*, Sep. 6, 1976, p. 80.
28. *Business Week*, May 29, 1978, p. 8.
29. *Business Week*, June 7, 1982, pp. 60, 61.
30. For a coordinated treatment of sales and distribution, see Joseph P. Guiltinan and Gordon W. Paul, *Marketing Management Strategies and Programs*, McGraw-Hill, New York, 1982, chaps. 11 and 12.

CHAPTER 20

Sales Management

In this chapter, we will deal with the management of the personal selling function, one of the four important promotional mix activities we described in Chapter 2. While a few companies rely entirely on personal selling to get their products sold, most use advertising, sales promotion, and publicity as well (we'll cover those subjects in the next chapter). As we discuss sales force management, do bear in mind that its activities are normally coordinated with the other promotional functions.

With the exception of direct mail firms, nearly every company uses salespeople. Sales accounts for six million workers, or 7 percent of the total U.S. work force. About one quarter work part-time, primarily in retailing, which employs about half of all sales workers. When compared with an estimated 180,000 people in advertising and 24,000 in marketing research, we see that sales represent by far the largest proportion of all marketing jobs.[1] The numbers of salespeople by major categories are shown in Table 20-1.

Categories most likely to hire college graduates are manufacturers, securities firms, and a variety of service firms, including those shown as a footnote to Table 20-1. Though not classified as managers, outside salespeople carry greater responsibilities than some managerial personnel in other parts of the business. The sales representative is the company's direct link to its customers and often is the only company person who customers know personally. The salesperson creates customers, maintains relationships with them, and sees that any problems with the company are resolved.

We will discuss sales management principally from the viewpoint of the manufacturer. Although manufacturers employ only 7 percent of all salespeople, they account for a much greater percentage of total sales. Also, they normally use all elements of the marketing mix, which makes them a good springboard for discussing sales management in a promotional context. We treat sales management in terms of the management functions of planning, organization, direction, and control. First, however, let's find out what a sales manager does.

THE SALES MANAGER'S JOB

The job of the sales manager calls for special talents in managing large numbers of people spread over a wide geographic area and working with little or no day-to-day

TABLE 20-1
Estimated U.S. Sales Workers by Principal Categories*

Categories	Number of Workers
Retail trade	2,800,000
Wholesale trade	840,000
Real estate agents and brokers	550,000
Manufacturers' sales	400,000
Gas station attendants	340,000
Route drivers	200,000
Auto sales	158,000
Securities (stocks, bonds, etc.)	110,000
Models (photographic)	60,000
Travel agents	19,000

*Does not include people selling services such as advertising space, commercial bank services, hotel and motel accommodations, transportation, and consulting.

Source: U.S. Department of Labor, Bureau of Labor Statistics, *Occupational Outlook Handbook*, 1980–1981 edition, March 1980.

supervision. More than in most managerial jobs, the sales manager must be a leader, motivator, and expert communicator. Managers of inside functions, such as production, accounting, and advertising, can supervise their people directly on a person-to-person basis. Sales managers, on the other hand, must communicate by phone and in writing, with only occasional face-to-face contact.

Salespeople work alone and often must be away from home during the week. They can become discouraged from the inevitable rejection they receive from some customers and prospects. Successful sales managers have to find the right people, train them properly, and build and maintain their enthusiasm for carrying out plans and achieving objectives week after week. They use more incentives and morale-building devices than other managers.

The personal qualifications and skills needed for sales management are not the same as those needed for selling. While a sales manager should have had sales experience, the star salesperson is no more the ideal candidate for manager than is the star athlete for coach. This is why many major companies look for managerial potential in their college recruiting programs. College graduates are hired for selling jobs with the expectation that many will demonstrate the qualities needed for sales management.

Sales is a common starting point for those who make it to the top marketing executive job and often to top corporate management. Present and former chief executives who began their careers in sales include John Opel of IBM, James McFarland of General Mills, Lee Bickmore of Nabisco, Francis Lucier of Black & Decker, and John Fox of United Brands.

Responsibilities of Procter & Gamble's field sales managers (in charge of districts and units) are reproduced in **Marketing Note 20-1**.

PLANNING THE SALES FUNCTIONS

The general sales manager assists the marketing manager to develop marketing strategies and has the key role in developing tactical sales plans to help implement those strategies. A key planning function is defining the sales job. This is not always done regularly or thoughtfully, yet it is the foundation on which most other sales management decisions are (or should be) based, such as types of sales people needed, sources for recruits, selection procedures, training, sales territory layout, compensation, and organization.

Defining the Sales Job

Defining the sales job is the process of deciding what personal selling functions are to be performed within the context of the overall promotional mix. Selling functions will vary because of the types of products sold, distribution channels used, the company's position in the market, and the role that advertising plays in the sale. Once the required selling functions have been determined, the decision is made where to assign them. All may be performed by each sales representative; or they may be divided among two or more sales representatives; or they may be split between sales representatives and sales supervisors. Position descriptions are then written to describe each salesperson's and each sales supervisor's functions, responsibilities, and places in the organization.

The sales job should be reviewed each time there is a significant change in marketing strategy or changes in the product line, markets, competition, or

---

MARKETING NOTE 20-1

Responsibilities of Field Sales Managers

The general responsibility of a field sales manager (district or unit manager) is to develop and increase the business on his or her products within the marketing area. This can be subdivided into five areas of *basic* responsibility:

1. To ship an annual sales quota
2. To provide leadership and motivation
3. To accept personal sales responsibility
4. To create and test new methods and techniques
5. To provide the company with facts, forecasts, and recommendations

Specifically, the major activities involved in meeting these responsibilities are:

1. To develop sales strategy, execute programs, and evaluate results. This may involve the introduction of new products, new merchandising methods, sales techniques, etc.
2. To analyze all aspects of the business, such as sales results, market trends, promotion and advertising programs, competitive activity, trade coverage, population trends, sales expenses, and training programs.
3. To provide the company with recommendations, estimates of future sales, and vital data about the marketing area.
4. To manage a recruiting program that utilizes newspaper ads, employment agencies, and visits to college campuses.
5. To implement a program for the training of both new and experienced sales representatives, including the development of people to positions of greater responsibility.

MARKETING
NOTE
20-1
(Continued)

6. To provide leadership by setting high standards in the handling of personal sales responsibility.
7. To motivate his or her organization through personal contact, to establish challenging but realistic objectives, to recognize success, to encourage subordinates after failure, and to maintain discipline.
8. To administer effectively the funds available for the District's merchandising program.
9. To maintain records that provide quick analysis of brands, customers, and the organization.
10. To investigate the causes of lack of progress, and to take or recommend corrective action.
11. To keep the organization informed of all matters affecting work.
12. To plan and conduct sales meetings.
13. To make revisions in the geographical organization of territories in the marketing area, and to establish a plan for the proper coverage of the trade.
14. To assume a responsibility to the trade by providing information and recommendations which will help these customers run their businesses more profitably. This might include suggestions for more economical warehouse handling or the development of a program for better training of store personnel.

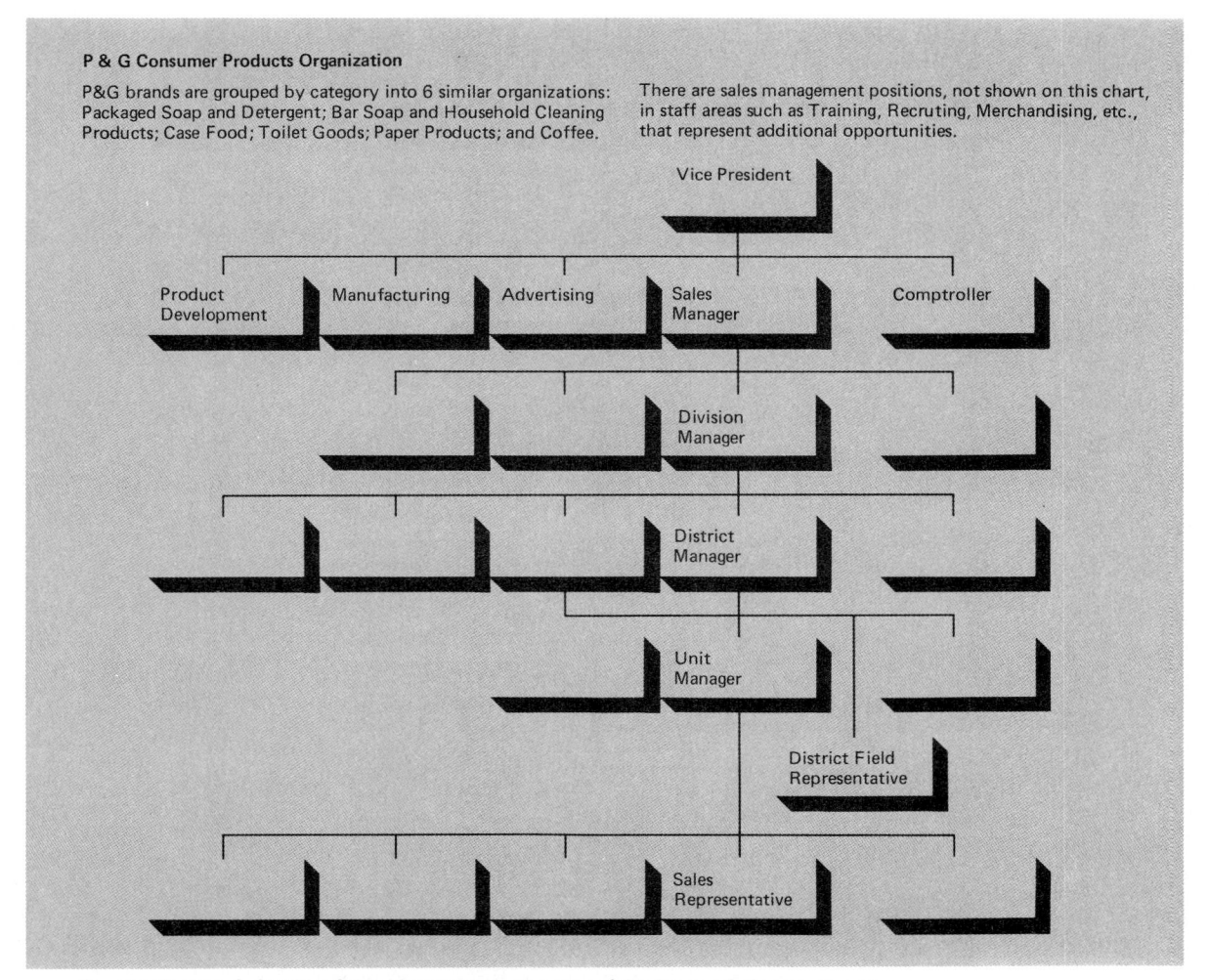

P & G Consumer Products Organization

P&G brands are grouped by category into 6 similar organizations: Packaged Soap and Detergent; Bar Soap and Household Cleaning Products; Case Food; Toilet Goods; Paper Products; and Coffee.

There are sales management positions, not shown on this chart, in staff areas such as Training, Recruiting, Merchandising, etc., that represent additional opportunities.

```
                              Vice President
                                    |
    ┌───────────┬───────────┬───────┼───────┬───────────┐
 Product    Manufacturing Advertising  Sales      Comptroller
Development                         Manager
                                    |
                              Division
                              Manager
                                    |
                              District
                              Manager
                                    |
                              Unit
                              Manager
                                    |
                              District Field
                              Representative
                                    |
                              Sales
                              Representative
```

Source: "Procter & Gamble: Sales Management, courtesy of the Procter & Gamble Company.

economic conditions. If sales management does not redefine the sales job when changed conditions require it, salespeople will do it for themselves. In consulting assignments, it is not unusual to find a marked difference between what sales managers think their salespeople do and what they actually do. The result is that organization, recruiting, and training practices get out of line with the realities of the marketplace and the needs of the sales force.

Selling Functions. The following activities are common to many selling jobs:

1. Locating customers, potential customers, and buying influences and determining their needs and preferences
2. Classifying accounts by potential volume
3. Planning frequency of call by class of account
4. Determining routing of calls on accounts
5. Obtaining interviews with buyers and buying influences
6. Presenting the sales proposition
7. Writing orders or contracts, or making arrangements for orders to be submitted to company
8. Arranging for credit and payment terms (may include collections)
9. Arranging for delivery and service
10. Handling complaints
11. Reporting activities, performance, and market conditions to higher levels of supervision
12. Receiving and digesting information from supervisors and home office
13. Participating in other activities such as trade shows, conventions, meetings, and training courses[2]

"Accounts" in the above list refers to wholesalers and retailers where intermediaries are used, or to end users if sales are direct. Activities will vary according to the products sold and markets served, and some sales jobs will call for specialized activities not shown in the list. Different applications can be seen in several types of selling.[3]

Direct Selling. When industrial products are sold direct to other companies and shipment is made direct from the supplier's factory or warehouse to the customer's plant, the salesperson must perform all key selling functions.

Customers and potential customers must be located, classified, and called on with the necessary frequency. Buyers and buying influences in each account must be identified, their needs and interests determined, and selling propositions made to them. The first sales step in an industrial sale frequently is to get the prospect to test the product and to approve the salesperson's company as a source of supply. Orders may be placed by the purchasing department, but the actual decision to buy may be made by the research, engineering, or manufacturing departments or by higher management levels.

The selling proposition includes not only the quality, performance, utility, and price of the product, but also credit, delivery, and service. These latter considerations may be of greater importance to the customer than the product itself when competitive products are similar in design, quality, and price. Orders may be written by the salesperson or placed directly with the factory by the customer. This sales job may include handling complaints, following up on delayed shipments, and arranging for changes in specifications to meet customers' needs.

Selling Through Intermediate Channels. Whereas selling direct to the using customer requires the salesperson to perform nearly all sales functions personally, selling through intermediate channels of distribution, such as wholesalers and retailers, transfers some of the selling functions to the intermediaries.

Selling through wholesalers or retailers involves two main tasks. The first is to secure market coverage by obtaining the desired quality and quantity of wholesalers and/or retailers. The second is to assist the channel intermediaries in making sales to the ultimate consumers or users. Both tasks may or may not be performed by the same salesperson. In selling packaged foods, for example, sales to chain store headquarters may be made by one salesperson while in-store merchandising is performed by someone else.

Selling to an intermediate channel of distribution is only half the battle. In the final analysis, the size of the company's sales is determined by the amount of product purchased by end users. The sales manager should plan the sales job to ensure that the product moves through, as well as to, intermediate channels of distribution.

Missionary Selling. This type of personal selling includes only some tasks from the list above. Its purpose is to influence the ultimate sale rather than to make the sale itself. Prescription drugs, for example, can be sold only on a doctor's orders. Drug companies, therefore, utilize missionary sales representatives to call on doctors to explain the company's products, distribute samples and literature, and encourage them to prescribe their products.

The food sales representative who carries out promotional work in the retail food store is a form of missionary salesperson. Although missionary sales representatives do not as a rule write orders, they exert a definite influence on the placement of orders.

Manufacturers' Agents. Rather than sell through its own sales force, a company may use manufacturers' representatives or agents. The manufacturer's agent usually carries product lines for more than one company. There are arguments pro and con for the use of company people as opposed to agents. As a rule, however, companies will utilize their own people when the potential volume supports the costs and will use agents when it does not. By selling several products to the same customers or channels of distribution, the agent can make a satisfactory income in territories that would not support a company salesperson with only one product line.

A sales management function must be performed whether company sales people or agents are utilized. In either case, salespeople must be recruited, trained, directed, and motivated. In multiagent organizations, these functions may be performed by the agency head, but the company sales manager must be sure that the functions are performed.

Importance of Defining the Sales Job. The first requirement of successful sales job definition is to determine who the end customers are, how they can be influenced to buy, and how the product can be made available to them most efficiently and conveniently. The second requirement is to determine what selling tasks must be performed to achieve these objectives.

A third requirement is to establish the salesperson's work load. Work load is determined by estimating the time required to handle each class of account; the frequency of call, travel, and waiting time; and the time for ancillary tasks such as reports and service.

ORGANIZING THE SALES FORCE

Once the sales job has been defined, management can proceed to the organization plan. Organization will be influenced by whether the salesperson is to sell the full product line to all accounts in a geographic territory or specialize by products, markets, or types of accounts. If specialization is chosen, a decision must be made whether to specialize only at the sales representative level or at sales supervisory levels as well.

Company Examples

Later in the chapter we will look at the pros and cons of alternate sales organization strategies that affect sales organization. For now we will examine sales organization plans from three major companies which illustrate several forms of organization.

Gillette Safety Razor Division. Each major division of The Gillette Company (e.g., Safety Razor, Personal Care, Paper Mate) has its own sales force. Figure 20-1 shows the field sales organization plan of the Safety Razor Division. This is an example of a business unit that follows a geographic sales plan with no specialization. Each management level and each sales representative is responsible for selling the full line of division products.

The national sales manager reports to the division vice president of sales. Five regional field sales managers report to the national sales manager, and each regional manager supervises four district sales managers whose headquarters are in the cities indicated on the chart. District managers supervise the field sales representatives assigned to their respective districts.

The national accounts manager is responsible for contacts with the headquarters of those retail chains whose operations transcend regional boundaries. Regional and district managers are responsible for contacts with the field office of such national accounts.

Figure 20-2 shows the sales headquarters organization under the direction of the Gillete Safety Razor Division's vice president for sales. In addition to the *line* national sales manager—whose organization is shown in Figure 20-1—there are four *staff* managers reporting to the vice president. This chart illustrates the scope of functions needed to back up the sales force of a large national business. (This division's annual sales exceed $800 million.)

Marketing Note 20-2 is a statement of responsibilities for the key managers in the division. Comparing these statements of responsibilities with the positions shown in Figures 20-1 and 20-2 will help one to understand how this successful sales organization operates.

Richardson-Vicks Toiletry Products Division. Like the Gillette Company, the major divisions of Richardson-Vicks, Inc. have their own sales forces. The Toiletry Products

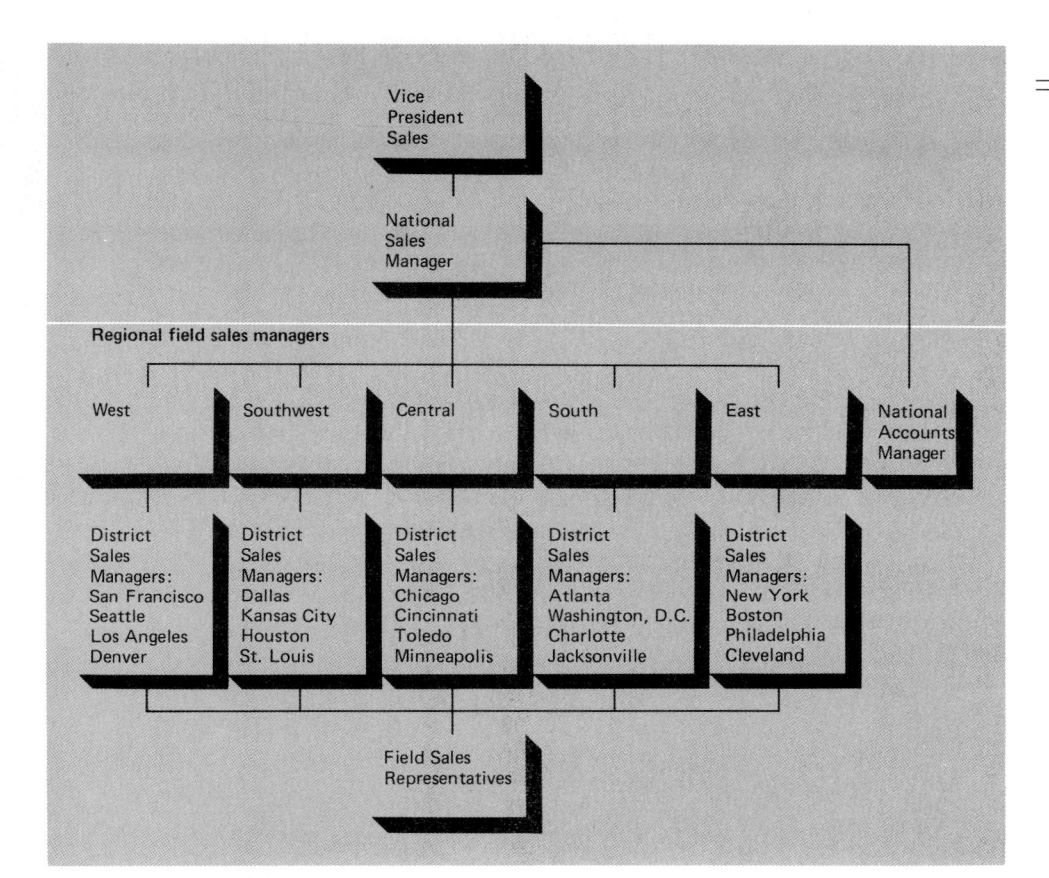

FIGURE 20-1. Safety Razor Division field sales organization.

Division sales organization plan (Figure 20-3) illustrates market specialization based on types of accounts. There are two sales forces. The national field sales manager, shown in the left-hand block, is responsible for sales of all division products to wholesale and chain store accounts. This manager's organization is divided geographically into regions and divisions. The full-line sales representatives report to division managers. The national accounts manager performs a similar function to that described for the Gillette Safety Razor Division's national accounts manager.

The national retail manager, shown in the right-hand block, is responsible for missionary sales activities in retail stores. Like the national field sales manager's organization, the retail organization is divided geographically by regions and divisions, with representatives reporting to division managers.

The activities of the two line sales managers are coordinated by the division vice president of sales. Supporting staff functions are provided by the director of business development and trade relations (center block).

A Steel Company. Figure 20-4 shows a steel company that uses all three types of sales forces—full line as well as specialized by product and market. The sales force (under the sales managers for the western and eastern regions) sells the full line of basic steel products to a variety of steel-using industries such as auto, appliance, can, and pipe.

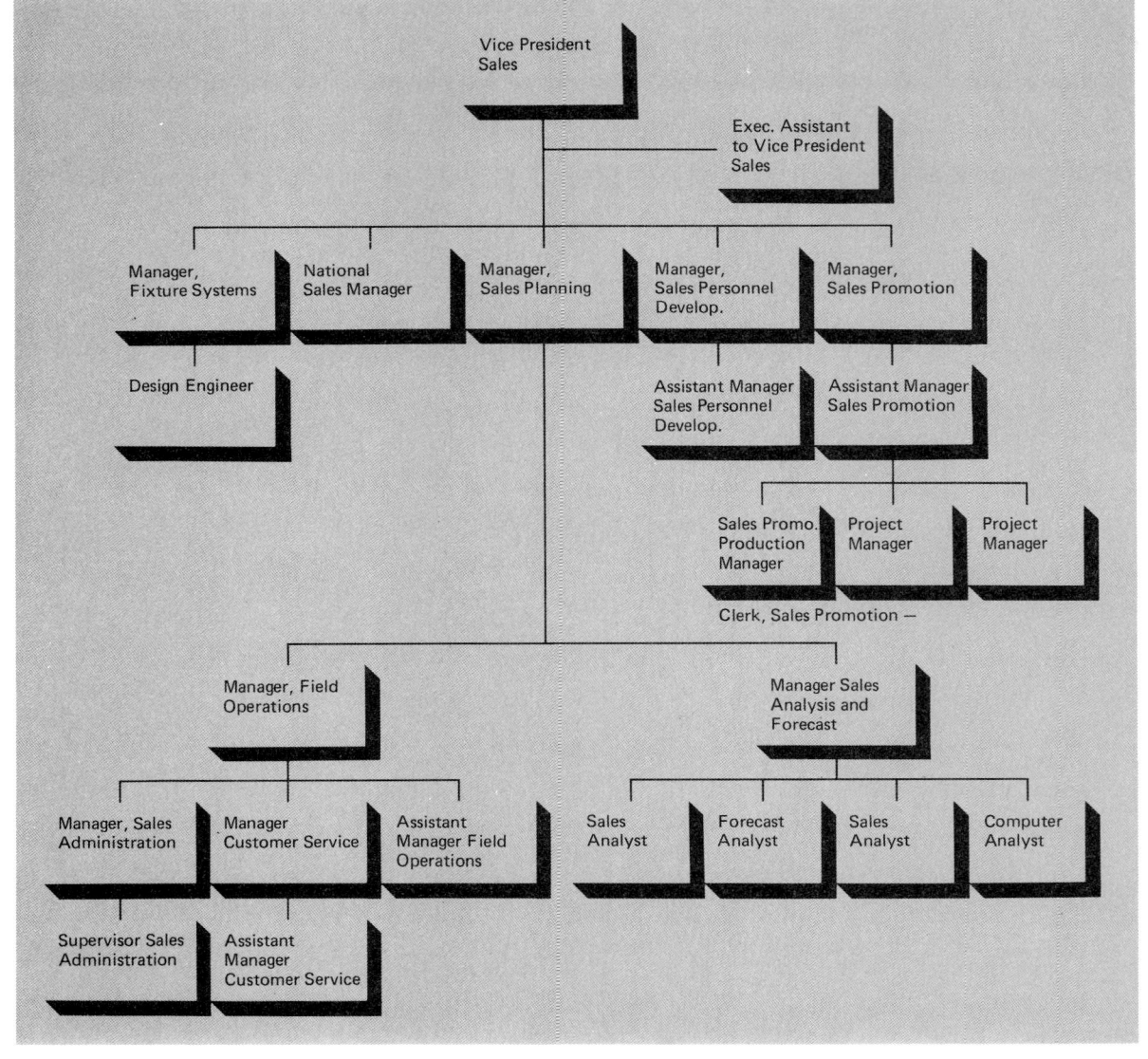

FIGURE 20-2. The Gillette Company Safety Razor Division sales headquarters.

Product specialization is provided by the product managers responsible for rolled, coated, tin plate, and tubular steel, who report to the manager of product sales.

Another sales force, with six regional managers reporting to the manager of sales and marketing, sells prefabricated products designed for the construction industry. Market specialization is provided by the three managers (reporting to the marketing manager) who are responsible for the building, construction, and highway market segments. Sales representatives reporting to the regional managers also specialize by these market segments.

Sales Department Outline of Position Responsibilities: Safety Razor Division, The Gillette Company

MARKETING NOTE 20-2

Vice President, Sales. Responsible for

1. Developing and implementing plans for the distribution, display, and promotion of Safety Razor Division products as approved by the president
2. Recruiting, training, and developing sales personnel
3. The coordination of sales programs with Marketing Research, Product Management, and Fixture Systems via joint planning and communication

National Sales Manager. Responsible for developing and implementing the sales policies and programs necessary to achieve optimum effective distribution and sales of the division's product line. Has the responsibility for all field selling and training activities including the National Accounts' group.

Executive Assistant to the Vice President, Sales. Responsible for assisting the vice president, sales, in the administration and operation of the Sales Department. This includes the preparation of the budgets, monitoring the policies, procedures, sales activities, and the analysis with recommendations that are required to meet established objectives.

Regional Field Sales Manager. Responsible for the overall operation of the Safety Razor Division field sales force in accordance with the policies, plans, and procedures established by headquarters. Primary responsibility is to meet and exceed the regional sales and personnel goals within the regional expense budget.

District Sales Manager. Responsible for training, developing, and motivating field sales representatives; maximizing distribution and display of Gillette products; implementing marketing and sales programs in order to attain sales volumes at levels consistent with assigned goals.

National Accounts Manager. Responsible for maximum development and maintenance of the distribution and display of Gillette products in headquarters' accounts which transcend regional boundaries.

Sales Personnel Development Manager. Responsible for establishing and implementing training programs for field and headquarters' sales personnel; procedures and hiring practices for district managers, assistant district managers, assistant to the regional field sales managers, and territory sales representatives.

Manager, Sales Planning. Under the direction of the vice president, sales, responsible for providing guidance and direction in the development of sales planning activities and creation of sale promotion concepts and ideas. Further assists in directing the activities of field sales personnel.

Manager, Field Operations. Direct, plan, organize, coordinate, and schedule the operation of the field sales administration, service and order processing activities necessary to provide effective and efficient field sales support.

Manager, Sales Promotion. Responsible for the creation, execution, and production of all sales promotional materials. Supervision of all charges and payments of promotional monies and the implementation of the division's sales promotion strategy and goals. Directs and supervises the activities of the sales promotion personnel.

Manager, Fixture Systems. Responsible for the development and review of the division's fixture/display production including the design and production of standard and custom blade, razor, lighter, and new product fixtures.

MARKETING NOTE 20-2 (Continued)

Manager, Sales Analysis and Forecast. Responsible for
1. Developing merchandising programs to be implemented by field sales based on sales objectives, promotional plans, and new product introductions
2. Developing the short-term sales forecast by product following interpretation of available historical data and field projections of promotional and nonpromotional sales

Source: Courtesy of the Sales Department, Safety Razor Division, The Gillette Company.

DIRECTING THE SALES FORCE

In Chapter 15 we explained how management *direction* encompasses coordination, communication, personnel administration, and decision making. All apply to the job of directing the sales force, but none more so than personnel administration.

In this section we describe four major activities: recruiting and selecting new sales personnel; training; motivation and compensation; and designing sales territories. While they may be performed by different levels of sales management—from the general sales manager to the first line of supervision—ordinarily they are shared.

Recruiting and Selection

Recruiting of salespeople occurs fairly regularly due to company growth and the need to fill vacancies. Growth may come from industry expansion, increasing market share, or adding new products. A decision to divide the sales force by specialization

FIGURE 20-3. Sales organization, Toiletry Products Division, Richardson-Vicks, Inc..

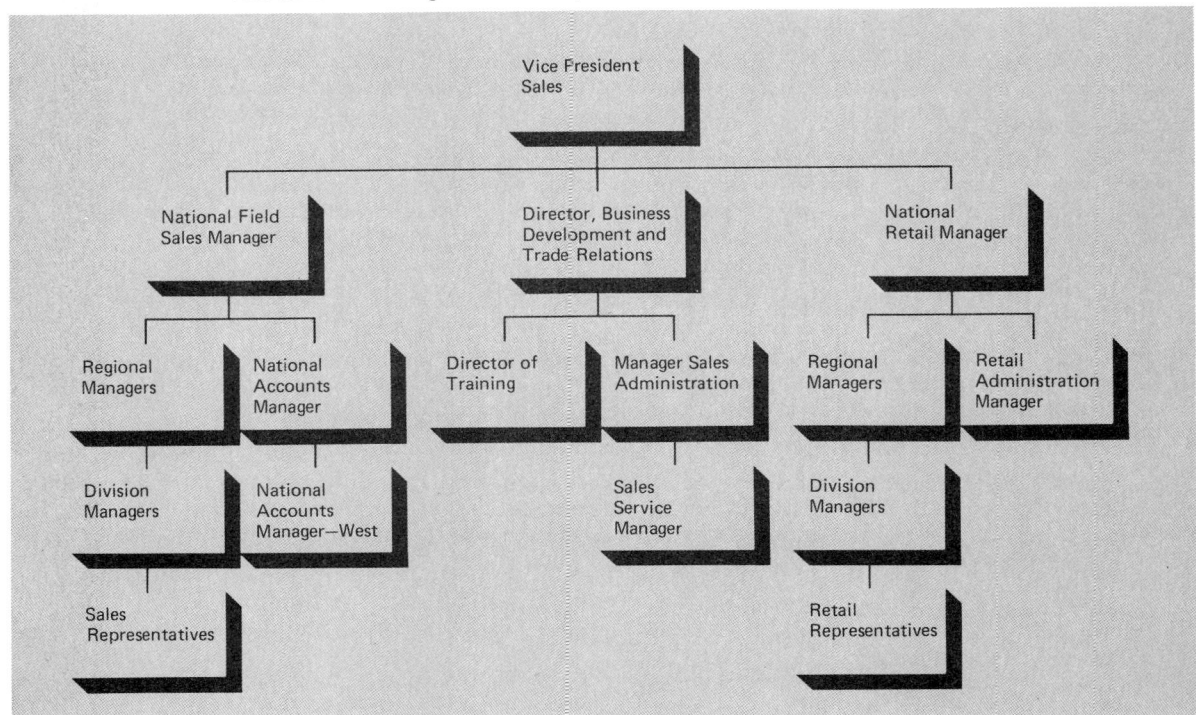

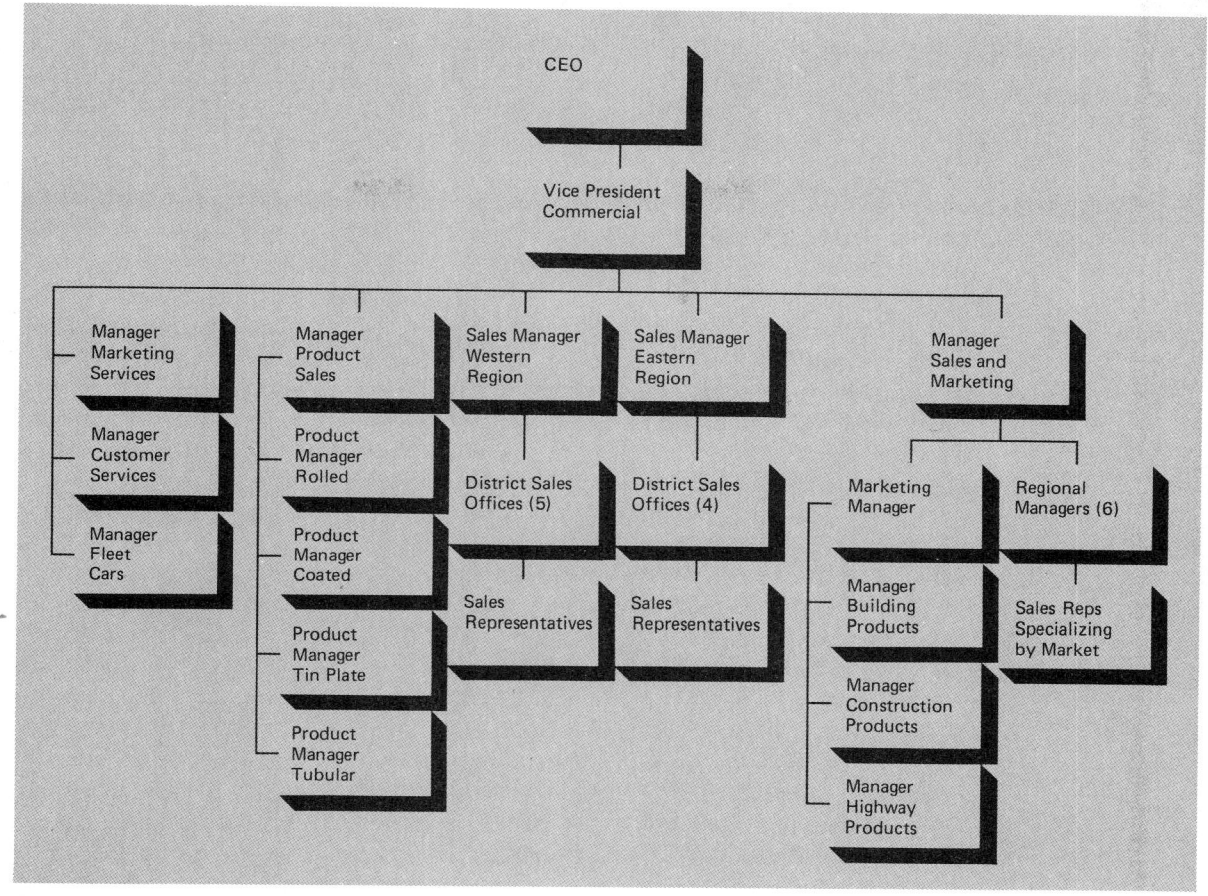

FIGURE 20-4. A steel company sales organization.

will also increase the need for salespeople. Vacancies occur because of retirement, illness, resignation, dismissal, and promotion.

Recruiting is the active search for the best available candidates for a sales position. Recruiting is usually necessary because fewer people voluntarily apply for sales than for other jobs with similar pay. Also, good salespeople seem to have qualities not found in everyone. And since not all qualified people want to sell, recruiting often requires convincing those people to apply.

Once the sales job has been defined, the organization planned, and job descriptions prepared, three basic steps remain to be taken in order to find and hire the best person for the position; (1) determine the desired personal qualifications for the position; (2) identify the likely sources for locating recruits; and (3) establish selection methods.

Determining Qualifications. Basic personal attributes expected of all candidates for outside selling jobs include good health and physical stamina, initiative, industriousness, dependability, integrity, and a degree of ambition appropriate to the particular job. Employers must not discriminate on the basis of race, religion, color, nationality, age, or sex. People with physical handicaps should not be rejected automatically. There can be bona fide reasons for discrimination, but if so, employers must be prepared to substantiate them.

Education. Educational requirements may vary from an ability to read and write for some route sales jobs to an engineering or chemistry degree for some industrial sales jobs. Employers often are flexible with respect to the level of education depending upon an applicant's experience and other qualifications. Even so, a college degree has taken on increased importance for salespeople calling on buyers who are college graduates. As purchasing people have become better educated, so too have sales people.[4]

Experience. Some companies require sales experience while others don't. Large companies with many sales people usually don't require it; their annual rates of turnover create enough openings to justify the expense of training departments and regular recruiting programs. These companies have the financial strength to maintain reserves of newly trained people ready to fill openings as they occur. They are the companies often seen recruiting on college campuses.

Most medium- and small-size companies, on the other hand, prefer sales experience. These companies hire individual salespersons as openings occur. They cannot justify the expense of training departments or keeping people on the payroll until needed. Industrial companies in particular look for mature, experienced salespeople, since sales calls are made on mature, experienced buyers and buying influences. Some managers insist on specific industry sales experience. Others merely want evidence of proven sales performance, on the assumption that the successful salesperson will be able to adapt to their industry.

Other qualifications. Many sales jobs require special qualities in addition to education, experience, and the other basic attributes. Selling in ethnic neighborhoods may require the ability to speak a foreign language. Geographic familiarity may be important, as may adaptability to regional cultures. Someone raised in Brooklyn may not do well in Baton Rouge, or vice versa. Jobs that pay straight commission require entrepreneurs willing to risk the investment of time and money in the hopes of high financial reward.

Knockout factors. There are also attributes that employers try to avoid. Because salespeople work alone, must deal with discouragement, and often are away from home, a stable personality is desirable, as is the relative absence of distracting personal pressures. Consequently, alcoholics, drug addicts, and people with high debts, poor credit records, and marital problems are commonly avoided. Unwillingness to accept geographic transfer may be considered a reason not to hire.

Since no one is likely to possess all desired qualifications, the ideal merely serves as a benchmark against which to evaluate candidates. Table 20-2 suggests how different sales jobs require different qualifications.

Validity of qualifications. A study of 18,000 salespeople in fourteen industries compared relative sales performance with several criteria.[5] No statistically significant differences were found among those ranked in the upper quartile of their sales forces on the basis of whether they were under or over 40; male or female; black or white; whether they had high school diplomas or less versus one or more college degrees (except in certain industries); or whether they had no sales experience (assuming they received training and supervision) versus two or more years of experience.

The one criterion that showed a statistical relationship was whether the

TABLE 20-2
Qualifications by Type of Sales Job

	Education	Sales Experience	Physical Condition	Initiative	Earnings Needs	Willingness to Travel	Knockout Factors
Route sales	Ability to read and write	None	Strong back	Low	Low	Low	Hernia; suspended driver's license
Life insurance	Some college	Desirable	Moderately healthy	High	Moderate to high	Low	Introversion
Ethical drugs (calling on doctors, hospitals)	Chemistry or pharmacology major	Not necessary	Good health	Moderate	Moderate	High	Persistent cough; chain smoking*

*The drug salesperson spends much time in doctors' waiting rooms among patients.

candidate was matched with the particular position; for example, if the job required a large amount of detail or involved teamwork (e.g., with technicians), was the candidate suited to these requirements?

While this and other studies raise questions about the qualifications sales managers often seek, many managers remain convinced that certain levels of education or experience are needed for their sales jobs. This study points out that more attention should be paid to ascertaining the requirements of each sales job (part of the job definition) and searching for people whose personalities, aptitudes, and abilities harmonize with them.

Recruiting Sources. Once the desired qualifications are established, management needs to identify the most likely sources for people with these qualifications.

Schools are appropriate where certain education is desired but sales experience is not essential. Classified advertising widens job exposure, but may attract unqualified people. Prescreening is aided, however, if the ad lists key qualifications. Employment agencies may know of candidates not generally available through other sources. The agency also screens out unqualified people, thus saving the sales executive's time.

In-house transfers can be good sources since current employees know the company and something is known of their attributes. It is not unusual for sales forces to contain accountants, engineers, or chemists who preferred to exchange their inside jobs for the greater freedom and challenges of outside sales work. Wholesalers and retailers sometimes can suggest good prospects. Some companies pay bonuses to employees who recommend people that are hired.

As we have noted, some companies prefer to hire inexperienced people and develop them on their own. Others hire experienced people, which means that they are hiring them away from other companies. Students often sense something unethical about this. Yet it is common practice among business, government, and institutional employers to hire people already employed by others. If this were not the case, our rights to better ourselves by changing jobs would be greatly impaired.

Selection Procedures. If recruiting has gone well, there should be several prospective candidates to select from. There are three principal steps to selection: prescreening, interviewing by executives, and post-interview verification.

Prescreening. The obviously unqualified candidates can be screened out by reviews of resumes and application forms or by telephone questioning. Prescreening may be done in the field by personnel department recruiters or by field sales supervisors. Standard tests, questionnaires, and essays are sometimes used as aids to this process. Prescreening saves executive time and avoids the expense of bringing nonqualified applicants to the home or regional office for further evaluation.

Executive interviews. Applicants surviving prescreening are brought to district, regional, and/or home offices for interviews with sales executives (and perhaps with personnel executives). These are of two principal types: (1) *nondirected* interviews, which are unstructured, free-flowing discussions, and (2) *directed* interviews, which provide a standardized approach for evaluating candidates where multiple interviewers are used. Interview forms list the subjects to be covered and provide space for the interviewer's notes. Interviewers then fill in rating sheets for each candidate, from which average scores can be developed. Candidates are then ranked, their strong and weak points are reviewed, and a tentative hiring decision is made. An example of an applicant rating sheet is shown in Figure 20-5.

Postinterview verification. Most experienced sales executives have been fooled more than once by clever applicants. Consequently, a formal offer to a candidate that survives the executive interviews may be withheld pending verification checks. These may include checks with personal references and former employers, a physical exam, and an investigation by an independent agency. Psychological testing may be introduced at this point, although some companies prefer to see such test results earlier.

Psychological testing has long been a controversial subject in personnel selection, but continues to be used by many companies. Sales executives and consulting psychologists alike maintain that tests should never be used as the sole determinant for selection; rather, they should be used as aids to the overall selection process. Some court cases have arisen over the possible discriminating aspects of testing. Personnel tests are not illegal, however, if they have been professionally developed and validated as measuring the relevant qualifications required for the job. They should not screen out a disproportionately large number of women or minorities.[6]

Sales Training

Sales training should fill the gap between what the salesperson knows and what he or she needs to know. Consequently, training will differ for the neophyte and the experienced salesperson as well as by type of sales job. The average total cost to train a manufacturer's salesperson is $12,633.[7]

Initial training may range from a few hours to several months depending on management philosophy and the degree of technical product knowledge required. In the case of technical products, in particular, some companies require sales trainees to spend time in such departments as production, research and development, purchasing, order processing, and customer service.

SALES APPLICANT EVALUATION SUMMARY

Name: Ronald Jones   Date: 1/22

Refer to the guidelines in the Sales Manpower Development Manual for evaluating each characteristic. As you interpret the records, indicate your findings by marking (X) in the appropriate column below.

GENERAL:	Above Requirements	Meets Requirements	Marginal	Unacceptable
Appearance		X		
Manner		X		
Mentally alert, free of Strain		X		
Health		X		
Vitality		X		
Experience	X			
Education		X		

CHARACTER TRAITS:	Very High	High	Low	Very Low
Stability		X		
Industry		X		
Perseverance		X		
Ability to get along with others		X		
Loyalty		X		
Self-reliance	X			
Emotional maturity		X		

JOB MOTIVATIONS:	Very High	High	Low	Very Low
Money		X		
Security			X	
Competition		X		
Intellectual Curiosity			X	
Perfection			X	
Service		X		
Status			X	
Power			X	

Other Strengths: Has strong desire to join our company

Other Weaknesses: None that I can see

Matches Profile: ☐ Perfect ☑ Good ☐ Marginal ☐ Poor   Hiring Recommendation ☑ Yes ☐ No

Rated By: O.S.W.

FIGURE 20-5. Sales applicant evaluation summary.

Some companies (particularly where products are nontechnical) feel that training is more effective if trainees "get their feet wet" in actual field selling as soon as possible. After a few hours of basic orientation, the new recruit travels with an experienced representative or supervisor and then goes it alone in a territory. This is followed by periodic inside instruction and on-the-job training.

The Training Program. The basic elements of an initial sales training program should include company orientation, market orientation, and selling techniques. All companies provide orientation covering procedures, policies, and company products. This information is essential for experienced as well as inexperienced salespeople. In some companies this may be the only training offered. Better-managed companies, however, instruct their new salespeople about the markets they serve, placing particular emphasis on the needs of their accounts. They also provide information on the strengths and weaknesses of competitors' products.

Relatively few companies provide training on selling techniques, although some will pay the costs of their salespeople attending selling technique seminars. Larger companies (hiring inexperienced people) usually have professional trainers capable of teaching selling skills. Those companies that hire only experienced people assume (often incorrectly) that the person hired knows proper selling techniques.

The initial training schedule for one company's retail sales force is shown in Table 20-3. New representatives begin selling alone in the third week, but spend part of their time in formal training during the next seventeen weeks.

Training Methods. Inside training covers company and market orientation and (in some companies) selling techniques. It may be done at field sales offices, the home office, or training centers. Tours of offices, plants, and laboratories may be

TABLE 20-3
Steps in the Training Program

The sales training program starts when a salesperson is employed, and it continues indefinitely. The training is divided into amounts that the salesperson can handle and is scheduled in such a way that each step can be assimilated before the next one is tackled. The training steps are shown below. Fix them firmly in your mind, so you will at all times have a clear picture of the overall program. It is understood, of course, that these specific training steps are in addition to personal contacts and close overall supervision of training by the district manager.

Schedule	Training Activity	Duration
When employed	Give salesperson the sales manual, price list, and assignment	
SALES TRAINING		
1st and 2nd Week	Orientation	2 days
	Initial field sales training	5 to 7 days
3rd Week		
4th Week	Initial field sales training follow-up (1 day); Chain supermarket account follow-up (1 day)	2 days
5th Week		
6th Week	Cash merchandising allowances; new promotion training	2 days
7th Week		
8th Week	General follow-up; sales analysis and progress review	2 days
SECTION MANAGEMENT TRAINING		
10th Week	Section management I	2 days
12th Week	Follow-up	1 day
14th Week	Section management II	2 days
16th Week	Follow-up	1 day
18th Week	Section management III	2 days
20th Week	Follow-up	1 day

scheduled as well as meetings with top executives. Inside training can consist of self-study, lectures, films, practice presentations, and role playing. As noted earlier, orientation in various company departments may be required.

Outside field training may include travel with experienced salespeople. It should also include the sales supervisor working with the trainee; the two of them may alternate in making sales presentations followed by critiques. Periodic on-the-job coaching by the supervisor may continue indefinitely. Continuing training for all sales representatives is carried on in sales meetings and training meetings led by sales supervisors, home office executives, or staff specialists.

Motivation and Compensation

Salespeople differ as to what motivates them to meet or beat their assigned quotas. For some it is monetary reward, although repeated studies have shown that money does not top the list of the things salespeople look for in their jobs. More important to many are intangibles such as achievement and self-esteem.

One study of industrial salespeople found that self-esteem is the key determinant of performance and that it is enhanced by recognition and monetary rewards. Little relationship was found between job satisfaction and job performance.[8] Another study suggests that the most important determinants of salesperson motivation are (1) the clarity of the task, (2) the salesperson's need for achievement, and (3) incentive compensation.[9] Points 1 and 2 are closely related. If the job goals are not clear and performance cannot be measured and reported, the need for recognition and sense of achievement cannot be fulfilled.

Most experienced sales managers utilize both monetary and nonmonetary rewards. Some believe that motivation programs are best when tailored for the individual, since all salespeople do not respond alike to the same incentives.

Compensation Plans. Sales compensation is paid in one of three basic methods.[10] The frequency of use is as follows:

Straight commission	19 percent
Straight salary	22 percent
Combination (salary plus incentive)	59 percent

Combination plans can be salary plus commission, salary plus bonus, or salary plus commission and bonus. Over the years, the use of straight commission plans has declined and straight salary plans increased. If we add together the percentage of companies using commission and combination plans, over three quarters of all sales payment plans offer direct performance incentives. Straight commission plans offer the greatest incentive to the salesperson. Straight salary plans are favored where performance cannot be measured directly (such as in group sales or missionary sales) or where sales are consummated after long periods of effort (such as for industrial machinery). Combination plans offer the security of a regular salary plus extra pay for above-average performance.

Earnings and fringe benefits. The average experienced salesperson working for a producer of products or services earned $32,165 in 1981.* Experienced people on

*Based on experience during the preceding 10 years, you can add between 5 and 10 percent a year to this figure to get the approximate average pay level for the current year.

straight salary earned an average of $29,120; those on straight commission, $32,658; and those on combination plans, $33,110. The differences suggest that incentives improve individual performance and/or attract better salespeople.

Most companies reimburse their salespeople for travel expenses—the exceptions are those on straight commission who often pay their own expenses. Nearly all companies pay all or part of group health, accident, and life insurance premiums. Many provide other fringe benefits such as pensions, educational assistance, and personal use of the company car.

Compensation plan objectives. A good sales compensation plan should:

1. Attract and hold salespeople with the desired qualifications
2. Fairly reward salespeople for their performance
3. Permit the company to make a fair profit
4. Influence the salesperson to concentrate on the functions the company wants performed (based on the definition of the sales job)

A combination plan is most likely to achieve these objectives. Developing a combination plan is tricky, however. A poor plan can have devastating effects on sales performance and sales force morale. Consequently, many companies turn for help to compensation consultants, who have experience with what does and does not work.

Other Motivational Devices. Frequently used incentives are contests and honor awards. Contests are used to stimulate general sales performance or to promote special activities and events over short time spans (from one day to three months). The payoff may be for such things as exceeding sales quota, adding new customers, or increasing sales of new or laggard products. Rewards may be in the form of cash, merchandise, or holiday trips for the salesperson and spouse. Contests and rewards are limited only by the sales manager's ingenuity. At a morning sales meeting, for example, the sales manager of a Chrysler dealership offered two tickets to a Laker's playoff game for every car sold that day.[11]

Honor awards are made for sales leadership at local, regional, and national levels. Performance may be measured in terms of total sales or percentage over quota. IBM honors branch office sales leaders by inviting them to attend the national sales convention. Awards can take many forms: framed certificates, plaques, pins, and rings, for example. Winners may be announced at sales meetings, on an honor roll in the sales manager's office, on bulletin boards, and in the company newsletter. The Equitable Life Insurance Company of Iowa annually publishes the pictures of its million dollar roundtable members in a full page ad in the *Wall Street Journal.*

Designing Sales Territories

Like a good compensation plan, well-designed sales territories help in achieving sales goals and maintaining sales force morale. Once they are hired and trained, salespeople are assigned to a designated geographic area—the sales territory.

When companies are new, territories can be laid out roughly, then refined with experience over time. Geographic expansion occurs along with company growth. Once all geographic areas are covered, however, further growth of existing product sales must come from more intensive development of sales territories. As this occurs, more attention must be paid to designing territories based on market and sales potentials.

In established companies the need for territory changes occurs more frequently than you might expect. In addition to more intensive market development, reasons include the addition of new products, the growth or decline of area market potentials, and the shifts from full-line to specialized sales forces.

Objectives of Territory Layout. The ideal sales territory will:

1. Have sufficient *sales potential* (the share of market potential that a company expects to achieve) in order to:
   a. Support satisfactory current income for the sales representative
   b. Make a contribution to profit after deducting all costs of maintaining the sales person (compensation, car, travel expenses, etc.)
   c. Leave sufficient potential for growth so that the territory does not have to be realigned (or the salesperson transferred) too frequently
2. Be laid out geographically to minimize travel time and permit the necessary frequency of calls on key accounts
3. Be relatively equal in potential with other territories. This objective is not fully observed in practice in established organizations, however, since salespeople vary in sales ability. Some can handle territories with more than average potential; some can only handle those with less.

Information Needed. The most precise way of laying out sales territories is to use building blocks which can be arranged in patterns that come the closest to achieving territory objectives.

Building blocks (or control units). There are designated geographic areas for which market data are collected by government agencies, such as states, counties, SMSAs, metro areas, cities, and—within cities—postal zip code areas. Building blocks are called *control units.* Information needed by control units includes market potential, company sales, and the number and location of accounts.

Actual or relative market potential. Since industry sales rarely are reported by control units, companies must resort to *surrogate* measures to provide approximations of the relative market potential by control unit. For example, population is a good surrogate measure for many types of consumer goods sales. If a county contains 1 percent of the population, we would expect it to account for about 1 percent of all table salt sales. Other commonly used surrogates for consumer goods are personal income, retail sales, and retail sales by categories such as food, drug, or automotive. Typical surrogate measures for industrial goods are the number of manufacturing plants, number of production employees, and value of factory shipments (in total or by SIC number).*

Company sales. Often there is a considerable gap between the company's actual sales in a control unit and the potential sales. It is useful, therefore, to consider

---

*Refer to Chaps. 3 and 4 for a description of the *Survey of Buying Power* and the *Survey of Industrial Purchasing Power*, which publish annual updates of useful surrogates for potential by several control units (such as state, county, and metro area).

actual as well as potential sales when designing sales territories. Unfortunately, companies do not always have this information, particularly if their sales go through wholesalers. A wholesaler may be located in one area but deliver to accounts in other areas. With computerization of wholesalers' billing, it is possible to get company shipments by control unit if the wholesaler will cooperate. A consulting firm, Distribution by Design, of Roslyn, New York, helps companies set up computerized data files of their sales by geographic area.

Number and location of accounts classified by size. This information helps in developing the work load—where and how frequently the salesperson must call. If the sales job is to call on retail accounts, the representative will have to travel over most of the territory, since retailers locate close to consumers. But if the sales job requires calling only on wholesalers, there will be less travel. Wholesalers tend to locate near regional transportation hubs from whence their trucks deliver to accounts located within a one-day round-trip distance.

Highway maps. Geographic distances and topography must be considered in determining work load as well as the number, location, and size of accounts. Travel distances between cities and accounts can vary greatly. A large state such as Wyoming, for example, has about one-third the population of Rhode Island. Rivers, lakes, and mountain ranges affect driving time. Even in a heavily populated state like New York, driving times between population centers such as Albany and Buffalo are substantial.

Description of the sales job. The sales job should be defined and the position description prepared before laying out sales territories. Such information as who is to be called on and with what frequency, what is to be done on calls, and the average time needed per call is essential to developing the work load (as is location of accounts and travel time between them).

Most companies find it uneconomic to have their salespeople call on all accounts. The principal ways of adjusting the account work load are: (1) call on accounts located only in major markets (e.g., SMSAs), (2) call only on key accounts, (3) call on accounts of various sizes but with different frequencies, or (4) some combination of these.

Laying Out the Territories. To lay out sales territories, two sets of maps are needed: (1) highway maps and (2) plain maps that contain only outlines of the control units to be used, such as counties and states. Information is entered within the county outlines, such as percent of market potential, company sales (if known), and number of accounts. (A list showing accounts by relative size and city location is also needed.) While referring to the highway map for travel information, contiguous counties are grouped into territories that meet the objectives of potential and work load.

Designing territories is not an easy task, even when you have all of the desired information. It is something like solving a giant puzzle. You experiment with different layouts and inevitably make compromises with the ideal layout. Computerized programs can speed up the process of experimenting with various combinations of control units. But maps must still be consulted and judgments made with respect to travel, the sales job definition, competitive conditions, and the characteristics of the salesperson available to fill each territory.

Other methods. The procedures just described are for the company (usually consumer goods) trying to achieve intensive development in the geographic areas in which it markets. Many companies, however, are not yet in a position to afford a sales force large enough to attempt complete coverage. For them, a less precise approach will suffice.

The geographic area to be covered is divided into the same number of territories as there are sales representatives (or as many as are planned if the sales force is new or presently expanding). If there are to be twenty salespeople, for example, the average territory will contain 5 percent of total potential. Control units are then combined to form territories of approximately 5 percent of total potential. Geography and highways also are considered. Since these territories will exceed an individual's work-load capacity, more attention must be paid as to how the territory should be worked. The usual approach is to "skim the cream" until such time as salespeople can be added and average territory potential reduced.

The above methods are applicable for industrial companies with large numbers of accounts and where geographic territories are appropriate. But where accounts are relatively few in number and in scattered locations, a modified approach is needed. In this case the account becomes the control unit. The sales potential is estimated for each account. Accounts are then combined which add up to the desired potential and make for an efficient work schedule. Territories may consist of lists of accounts with their locations, rather than a geographic area laid out on a map.

CONTROLLING THE SALES FORCE

We learned in Chapter 15 that control is the means by which management measures progress toward goals so that timely actions can be taken if performance is lagging.

Sales Goals

Sales force goals are called *sales quotas*. Quotas may be by total dollar sales, product, profit, activities, or some combination thereof.

Dollar Volume Quotas. This is the most common form of quota. The salesperson is measured by the total dollar volume of sales made, irrespective of the mix of products sold. The simplicity of this approach is its virtue, but it does nothing to encourage selling the more profitable items.

Product Quotas. This approach encourages the sale of a product mix that will maximize profit. Without control over sales by product, salespeople tend to sell the most popular products, which often are the ones with the lowest prices and the lowest profit margins.

Profit Quotas. A quota tied to some measure of profit, such as gross margin, tries to reward salespeople for being profit-oriented rather than volume-oriented. Ideally a profit quota should emphasize selling high-margin products, discourage requests for price cuts, and hold down sales expense. Such plans, however, limit management's freedom to control volume. At times, volume of throughput can be more important to profit than profit margins. Furthermore, the idea of selling what the company wants to sell rather than selling what the market wants is contrary to the marketing concept. Consequently, many managements prefer dollar volume quotas. Some use other means to adjust the product mix if and when required, such as product quotas, instructions to the sales force, and temporary incentives.

Activity Quotas. These are designed to encourage performance of certain functions, such as obtaining new customers, increasing the frequency of demonstrations to prospects, and selling larger orders. And they are used to set goals for missionary salespeople, such as the number of product floor displays to be set up in retail stores each week.

Establishing Quotas

The basis for the sales quota is the sales forecast. As we saw in Chapter 7, the sales forecast is proposed by marketing management and approved by top management. Sales management will also have participated in the development of the sales forecast.

After receiving the national sales forecast, the national sales manager apportions it among the next level of sales managers, such as regional. Regional managers apportion their quotas among district managers who in turn assign quotas to sales representatives. The quotas may add up to more than the sales forecast, since each management level may add something as a safety factor. If they are going to err, sales managers would prefer to err by exceeding their goals.

Quotas are not necessarily apportioned equally. If the national quota is 10 percent higher than the previous year, for example, some regions, districts, and territories may receive quotas that are more or less than 10 percent higher. In setting quotas, factors such as sales potential, sales trends, economic, and competitive conditions are considered for each area. Good management practice calls for the quota being assigned only after discussion between the person receiving the quota and the manager making the assignment. Morale can suffer if a quota is considered unfair, especially if incentive compensation is tied to performance related to quota. A good quota should call for extra effort, but not be beyond reach.

Control Methods

Measurements of results compared to quota is obtained by formal reports and by other, more informal methods of feedback.

Exercising Control with Reports. Most companies have computerized reporting systems that report orders received and orders shipped by territory, district, and region on a daily or weekly basis. These may be broken down further into sales by product and by account. Reports measure performance for the current period and accumulatively for the year. If total sales are running below quota, the problem areas (geographic, product, or account) are revealed by these reports. This permits management to search for the reasons so that corrections can be initiated.

Other Types of Control. Even closer controls may be employed by district managers. They may require territory representatives to submit daily or weekly reports listing calls made and results obtained, noting any problems. One company's call report form is shown in Figure 20-6. Daily telephone reports may be required. Weekly sales meetings may be held if the distances between territories and the

SALES CALL REPORT

Sales Rep ______________________ No. ____________ Week Ending ____________

Date	Customer	City/State	TIME SPENT AT ACCT.	TYPE CALL 1-IN PERSON 2-TELEPHONE	CUSTOMER TYPE 1-COMMERCIAL 2-ESP 3-SCHOOL 4-CONSUMER 5-NEW PROSPECT 6-OTHER	APPROX. VALUE OF ORDER	OFFICE USE ONLY CUSTOMER POTENTIAL

SIGNIFICANT COMMENTS (INCLUDE COMPETITIVE INFORMATION):

DISTRIBUTION: ORIGINAL - MKT. RESEARCH
YELLOW - SALES MANAGER
PINK - SALES REP

FIGURE 20-6. Sales call report.

district office are not too great. The district manager may visit with salespeople in their territories and call on major and problem accounts. These formal and informal methods are for the purpose of identifying problems and potential problems before the symptoms appear on the computer reports in the form of below-quota sales performance. The ideal situation is when the district manager has already solved the problem by the time higher management learns of it.

Expense Budgets and Controls

Expense budgets are apportioned to the several management and territory levels, such as was described for sales quotas. Travel and entertainment expenses are the usual costs incurred by sales representatives.* Expenses are controlled by management approval of weekly expense reports. An example of a company's expense report is shown in Figure 20-7. Expense limits are set by management and are not to be exceeded except by prior permission. Branch office expenses are budgeted by month, by quarter, and for the year. Monthly control reports, developed from payroll and expense vouchers, show period and accumulative expenses compared to budget.

SALES STRATEGIES

We now turn to discussions of sales strategies that deal with market coverage, sales force organization, and targeting of sales efforts.

*Some companies will pay no entertainment expense, however; not even lunch for a buyer.

FIGURE 20-7. Travel expense report.

TRAVEL EXPENSE REPORT

LODGING		MEALS FOR SELF (INCLUDE TIPS)	ENTERTAINMENT		TRANSPORTATION AND AUTO EXPENSE						OTHER REIMBURSABLE EXPENSE		
						AUTO EXPENSE							
DATE	AMOUNT		AMOUNT (INCL. TIPS)	IDENTIFY GUESTS	TRAVEL ROUTE	MILES	GAS/OIL LEASED CARS	CAB PARKING TOLLS	FARES PAID	FARES CHARGED	PHONE	OTHER	IDENTIFY
MON		B			FROM/TO								
/		L											
		D											
TUE		B			FROM/TO								
/		L											
		D											
WED		B			FROM/TO								
/		L											
		D											
THU		B			FROM/TO								
/		L											
		D											
FRI		B			FROM/TO								
/		L											
		D											
SAT		B			FROM/TO								
/		L											
		D											
SUN		B			FROM/TO								
/		L											
		D											

TOTAL													
LODGING 1.	MEALS 2.	ENTERTAIN. 3.	LEASED CAR PERSONAL MILEAGE CREDIT 4. MILES @ =	LEASED CAR WEEKLY CHARGE 5.	TOTAL MILES 6. @ ¢ =	GAS/OIL 7.	C. P. T. 8.	FARES PAID 9.	FARES CHG. 10.	PHONE 11.	OTHER 12.	TOTAL EXPENSES 13.	

FOR ACCOUNTING USE

VOUCHER NO.	DUE DATE	A C
CHECKED BY	**APPROVED**	**TERMS**

ACCOUNT NO.	DISTRIBUTION AMOUNT

NAME	DEPARTMENT	WEEK ENDING	WEEK NO.	LESS: CHARGED EXP. 14.
REASON FOR EXPENSE AND DETAIL OF UNUSAL ITEMS:				TOTAL CASH EXP. 15.
				LESS: ADVANCE (IF APPLICABLE) 16.
ACCOUNTING COPY				DUE EMPLOYEE 17.
SIGNATURE				
APPROVAL				DUE COMPANY 18.

CURRENT WEEK		PERIOD-TO-DATE	
ACTUAL	BUDGET	ACTUAL	BUDGET

AC008

Market Coverage Strategies

Sales force strategies are needed to achieve two of the basic distribution objectives listed in the previous chapter: (1) to maintain the desired coverage of target markets and (2) to see that channels provide adequate product promotional support as well as delivery and other basic customer services. Different sales strategies are needed according to whether the distribution strategy calls for intensive, selective, or exclusive distribution.

Intensive Coverage. It is the sales force that must attain the wide distribution among channel intermediaries that is required by an intensive coverage strategy. It calls for convincing intermediaries to stock the product line and participate in the company's product promotional programs. A look at the grocery products industry will illustrate the scope of the sales job under an intensive distribution strategy.

There are approximately 38,000 grocery wholesalers and 179,000 grocery stores in the United States.[12] If a grocery manufacturer's sales strategy included monthly calls on all of these accounts, it would need 1903 sales people, 333 for wholesale calls and 1570 for retail calls. (This is calculated assuming an average of six account calls per day per salesperson working an average of nineteen days per month.)

Because a sales force of this size would be too costly, alternative strategies must be considered for balancing the work load with the size of sales force the company can afford; for example: (1) limit sales calls to wholesale accounts only,* or (2) call only on selected wholesale and retail accounts.

Nearly all grocery stores order from wholesale accounts. Therefore, if a product is stocked by wholesalers, there is a good chance that retailers will order it, assuming that consumer demand exists for the brand. Hence, reasonably wide retail coverage can be attained with a much smaller sales force than that required when the sales strategy also includes calls on retailers. The disadvantage of selling only to wholesalers is that the product will receive inadequate promotional support. This is because grocery wholesalers stock so many products that they can spend little time promoting manufacturers' special deals to retailers; and, as a rule, they do not provide retailers with in-store merchandising assistance.

Selectively calling on both wholesale and retail accounts is a sales strategy that overcomes the promotional weakness of the first strategy while achieving fairly complete coverage. There are several ways in which this strategy can be implemented: (1) classify both wholesale and retail accounts by size, then call only on certain classes such as large and medium size stores; (2) vary the frequency of calls by classes of account, such as biweekly for large accounts and bimonthly for smaller accounts; (3) limit account calls to major markets, such as all or some SMSAs*†; or (4) a combination of some or all of the above. By including retailers in the sales call

---

*In this discussion the term "wholesale accounts" is used to include chain store buying offices as well as independent wholesalers.

†Most wholesalers and chains locate their buying offices and warehouses in or near the larger cities of the geographic areas they serve. From there they may distribute within a radius of 100 miles or more. Hence a manufacturer may achieve wide distribution even though its sales calls to wholesalers are limited to major cities. The situation is not quite the same if the strategy includes sales calls on retailers, since retailers locate near to where people live. Even so, the vast majority of retail stores are found within the 318 SMSAs which contain 75 percent of the population in only 15 percent of the land area.

coverage plan, salespeople can perform missionary sales activities to help move products through to consumers.

Another advantage of a selective account call strategy is that the call plan can be adapted to the size of sales force that the company can afford at each stage of its development. As the company grows, the sales force can be increased in size to cover more accounts in more geographic markets.

Marketing Note 20-3 describes a change in sales coverage strategy for Hanes underwear products. Hanes, in expanding its account calls to include retailers, took the bold step of tripling the size of its sales force in one year. This brought an almost immediate major increase in sales expense—one that many companies would more likely choose to make gradually over a longer time period.

Selective or Exclusive Distribution Coverage. Sales strategy for selective and exclusive coverage is different than that for intensive coverage. Intensive coverage emphasis is on *quantity* of outlets, whereas the emphasis for the other two is on *quality* of outlets. You will recall that selective and exclusive coverage is appropriate for shopping and specialty goods. The sales job for selective and exclusive strategies is similar.

Let's look at the sales job for the *selective strategy* first. The essential sales tasks are to (1) identify the most appropriate dealers in a market area, (2) sign agreements with a select few, and (3) help the selected dealers promote the product line to consumers. If the plan is to bypass the wholesaler and sell direct to selected dealers, the sales tasks will be carried out by the company territory representative. If products are to be distributed through a selected wholesaler, the tasks of screening and

---

MARKETING NOTE 20-3

Change in Sales Strategy at Hanes Knitwear Division

The Hanes brand's 10.8 percent unit market share of men's and boys' lightweight underwear makes it the second largest selling manufacturer's brand in the nation and the largest selling brand in department stores.

Low gross margins inherent in underwear make the application of consumer marketing techniques more difficult than in other segments of the corporation's business. Because of that difficulty, Hanes Corporation in 1975 began an extensive review of how Hanes brand underwear was being distributed, marketed, and sold at retail. Special attention was devoted to the more than 65 percent of the Hanes brand which was then distributed to retailers through independent distributors.

The structure of that system caused difficulties in compiling accurate market data and in implementing intensive sales and marketing programs to retailers. To overcome these problems, the corporation first initiated a comprehensive market analysis, which showed Hanes brand products were in about 30 percent of all underwear outlets. Of these, 90 percent carried the brand's all-cotton line, but only about 20 percent carried its cotton/polyester blended line which is the industry's growth area.

Once an accurate retail profile was developed, the corporation's knitwear sales force was expanded during 1976 from 30 to some 100 representatives as a "sales overlay" to implement an aggressive merchandising program supporting the efforts of existing distributors. The program opened 6,845 new retail accounts or line extensions, an increase of 84 percent over 1975.

Since this sales overlay was completed in August 1976, the corporation has launched major promotions behind Hanes Blue Label blended underwear and Hanes Black Label colored underwear products. As a result, shipment of these two products in 1976 increased 130 percent over their 1975 levels.

Source: The 1976 Annual Report, Hanes Corporation.

signing up dealers can be done by the representative and the wholesaler together.

A sales force objective is to appoint strong retailers who will maintain good inventories and give enthusiastic promotional support to your brand. The quality of the dealers that can be signed tends to equate with the market position of the brand. Leading brands will attract the leading dealers; secondary brands will have to sign with dealers of secondary quality. Part of the continuing territory sales job is to try to improve the quality of the appointed dealers. With good products, good marketing programs, and effective sales representation, your company's brand position in a market can be developed to the point where stronger dealers will want to carry your line.

The sales force objective under the exclusive distribution strategy is to obtain the single best dealer available in the market area. There is less room for error when area sales depend entirely on the one dealer selected. It is not easy to cancel an exclusive dealer contract, and even if it can be canceled, time is lost in getting out of the contract and changing over to a new dealer. Therefore, it is important to select the right dealer in the first place.

The contract will provide for an exclusive territory which protects the dealer from competition from other company dealers. But the contract will not necessarily preclude the dealer from carrying competitive brands. The company's legal policy may not permit exclusive dealing. And even if it does, the more desirable dealer may be unwilling to limit itself to your product line. In any case, your sales representative should try to sign a strong dealer who will give enthusiastic support to the brand. For mechanical goods this may mean that the dealer is to provide maintenance and repair services as well as sales programs.

Once the dealer is signed, the sales representative's job is to work closely with the dealer on inventory control, display, local advertising, pricing, training of the dealer's salespeople, and implementing company promotional programs. A strong, exclusive dealership backed up by effective promotional programs can be a profitable arrangement for both dealer and manufacturer.

Organizational Strategies

Earlier in this chapter we looked at the sales organization plans of three companies which illustrate specialized and nonspecialized selling. The Gillette Safety Razor Division (Figure 20-1) shows an organization in which sales representatives sell the full product line in geographic territories—an example of a nonspecialized sales strategy. The organization plan of the Toiletry Products Division of Richardson-Vicks (Figure 20-3) is an example of the strategy of specialization by account; one sales force specializes in sales to wholesale and chain buying accounts and the other specializes in missionary selling to retail accounts. The steel company plan (Figure 20-4) illustrates three types of sales strategies within one large company: full-line selling and specialization both by product, and by market. We will now examine the pros and cons of the full-line (nonspecialization) strategy and the strategies of specialization by product, market, and account.

The Full-Line Strategy. In this arrangement sales representatives are assigned to geographic territories and are responsible for selling all products to all accounts. It is an appropriate strategy when the following conditions are present: (1) products are sold to the same customers through the same distribution channels, (2) products and their applications are not highly technical or difficult to explain, and (3) products are not too numerous for one salesperson to handle.

Packaged convenience goods often fit these criteria. Let's use the Gillette Safety Razor Division as an example. Razors and blades are sold to the same customers—male and female shavers—through the same convenience goods channels. The products are few in number and easily understood. The sales job is to maintain wide distribution supported by retail displays and other forms of sales promotion. National advertising performs the job of selling consumers on product benefits.

Full-line selling may also be done by industrial sales forces. Monsanto's Crop Chemicals Division, for example, sells its full product line through agricultural distributors who sell to farm supply dealers who sell to farmers. Farmers and the trade are less interested in technical explanations than they are in proven product benefits. And the division's product line is not too large for one sales representative to handle.

The advantages of the full-line sales strategy are simplicity and lower costs (i.e., lower than the costs of specialized sales forces, which require more salespeople and higher travel expenses because of duplicate territory coverage). Also, management can better hold the sales representative responsible for territory sales results. There are no disadvantages (compared to the alternatives) as long as the criteria are met.

Specialized Selling Strategies. It may be necessary to use some form of sales force specialization when products are complicated, numerous, sold to different types of markets or accounts, or sold through different channels.

Product specialization. Breaking the sales force into groups of product specialists may be appropriate when (1) different products and their applications require different types of technical expertise or (2) the product line becomes too large and varied for one person to sell it effectively. The first reason applies to complicated industrial products that require the salesperson to deal with technical people in customer organizations. Examples of product lines which often require more than one type of product expert include plant machinery, metals, chemicals, construction equipment, and space vehicles, along with their support equipment. The second reason is illustrated by successful convenience goods companies, such as Procter & Gamble and Richardson-Vicks, who have created product divisions with sales forces specializing in the products of the division.

The advantages of product specialization come from having salespeople with different types of technical knowledge when such is required, or from increasing the effectiveness of present salespeople by reducing their work loads. The disadvantage is the higher costs for the additional salespeople that specialization requires and for duplicate travel expenses.

Market and account specialization. Part of a successful growth pattern usually includes selling present and new products to new markets. Since the new markets have different characteristics and often are served by different channels, market-oriented sales forces may be the preferred approach. Another reason for specialization is when companies have both consumer and industrial goods businesses. It would be the exception where the same sales representatives would sell to both.

Many companies use market specialized sales strategies for some if not all of their businesses. The Packaged Products Division of the Scott Paper Company has separate sales forces for its consumer and commercial markets; likewise, Kodak has them for its consumer and professional finishing markets. As AT&T broadened from a telephone company to a data processing and transmission company, it became necessary to switch from a full-line to a specialized sales strategy. Despite the technological character of its products, AT&T management decided that market orientation was the key to its future market success. Consequently, it created specialized sales forces for major markets such as consumer, government, and several industry categories.

Another form of market specialization is by account. Procter & Gamble, for example, specializes by classes of trade accounts. National account specialists call on major chain headquarters, field sales managers call on regional chain and wholesaler buying offices, and field sales representatives call on retail stores. Major food companies normally have separate salespeople calling on consumer and institutional trade accounts. Some industrial accounts purchase in such large quantities that suppliers may assign only one or two accounts to a senior sales representative. Tire companies follow this practice with their automotive customers who buy millions of tires for their new cars and trucks.

Product or market specialization? Whether to specialize by product or market is a question faced by businesses as they outgrow the criteria which apply to full-line selling. The decision, however, does not always come down to selecting one or the other; rather it is a case of where to place the emphasis. If there is a trend, it appears to be in favor of market specialization, except where the need for technical product knowledge is overriding.

Centralized versus decentralized sales forces. As explained in Chapter 14, company growth eventually leads to divisionalization. This raises the question of whether each division should have its own sales force or whether divisional products should be sold by a single sales force reporting to group or corporate management.

Divisional sales forces are appropriate when (1) divisions sell different products to different markets through different channels and (2) when divisions are large enough to afford their own sales organizations. The disadvantage is that multiple sales forces cost more in total than a single sales force. The advantages of the centralized sales force are that it saves money (by eliminating duplicate managers and duplicate calls on accounts) and it attracts the best talent to fill the fewer and better-paid sales management positions. The disadvantage is that the marketing managers of the several divisions must negotiate with sales management over the sales force time to be alloted to each product, a process that is less than satisfactory to each party in the negotiations.

The Campbell Soup Company traditionally has used a central sales force. Because of the large numbers of products to be sold, however, it is now organized to handle separately the products of the major divisions. By way of contrast, most General Electric divisions have their own sales forces. General Foods uses both methods. The huge Maxwell House (coffee) Division has its own sales force. But a central sales force (reporting to a group executive) sells the products of the other six packaged convenience foods divisions. The central sales organization is broken into three sales forces, each of which sells the products of two divisions.

Strategies for Targeting Sales Efforts

When companies compare individual territory sales with market potential (industry sales), they nearly always find uneven results. If a firm's overall market share is 10 percent, for example, it is not unusual to find individual territory market shares ranging between 4 and 30 percent. Sometimes the range is wider. If we consider 10 percent as par, then a territory with less than 10 percent share reflects sub-par performance and one with higher than 10 percent reflects above-par performance.

Any improvement in territory market shares will raise a company's total market share. The alternate strategies for targeting sales efforts to bring about this improvement are (1) overcoming territory weaknesses and (2) building on territory strengths. The first is favored by those who believe that the most substantial improvements can be made by finding and correcting the causes of weak territory performance. The second strategy is favored by those who feel that the best way is to increase efforts in those territories which already enjoy a strong position.

Territory Situation Analysis. Before deciding to carry out either strategy, territories must be analyzed separately, since the reasons for variations from par may be different in each. Generally speaking, an insufficient number of skilled people is available to study more than a few territories per year. In the introduction to Part Five it was noted that Keebler's market development department allocates funds for studying specified local markets each year. Because a number of territories may be candidates for analysis, management judgment can be used to set priorities. This will speed things along because territories with the highest or lowest performance compared to par are not necessarily those with the best near-term opportunities for improvement.

Territory analysis should include a look at the entire marketing mix, particularly promotion and distribution. As a rule, personal selling will not provide the entire explanation for territory variances. While sales may not be the principal cause, the territory representative normally will play a key role in implementing the improvement program. Advertising and sales promotion may represent the main problems and opportunities where convenience goods are concerned. But for shopping goods (with their push strategies) and for industrial goods (in the case of those sold direct to end users), personal selling is likely to be the key factor.

Strengthen Weak Territories. The territory situation analysis should reveal the reasons for weakness and lead to the development of corrective programs. We will discuss five common causes of below-par performance and some potential tactics for combatting the problems. We are assuming that prices and product quality are uniform throughout the company's market area and therefore would not explain territory variations.

Uneven territory potential. This is the most common cause of differences in territory market shares. If territory A produces sales that represent 20 percent of its $1 million market potential, but territory B produces sales that represent only 10 percent of its $2 million market potential, territory A has the best performance even though both territories produce the same amount of sales—$200,000. Let's now assume that instead of 10 percent, territory B produces 12 percent, or sales of $240,000. Based on sales volume, it appears to be doing better than territory A; but when measured against its opportunity, it is not doing as well.

Earlier we listed an objective of sales territory layout as having territories roughly equal in market potential. A firm almost certainly will have territories of unequal potential unless they were designed properly at one time and followed up with periodic revisions that reflected market changes and company growth.

In the example above, territories should be realigned to obtain roughly equal potentials. One solution would be to make two territories out of B, each with market potential of $1 million. In due time, two representatives in place of one should raise market share to 20 percent, thereby doubling sales coming out of the former B territory from $200,000 to $400,000. Before adding a salesperson, however, we should ascertain that the expected added sales volume will contribute to profits. This will happen if the increase in gross profit, or the variable profit contribution, from the extra $200,000 of sales exceeds the fixed costs of the added salesperson.

Quality of sales personnel. Wide variations in market share among territories of equal potential may be caused by differences in the competence of salespeople. These may be due to variations in experience, aptitude, motivation, effort, personal problems, or relationships with buyers. The reasons for relatively poor sales performance are best determined by the immediate sales supervisor by means of discussions with the salesperson, on-the-job observation, and interviews with account personnel. Before releasing an inept sales representative, the supervisor should consider trying additional sales training (including on-the-job demonstrations and coaching) and offering help in resolving personal problems.

Poor account relationships. Poor relationships with accounts (either trade or end user) can be the cause for poor territory performance, although they may not be the fault of the territory representative. A few large accounts may buy little or nothing because of previous unsatisfactory experiences with the company. This can greatly reduce the territory potential actually available. The territory representative acting alone may not be able to overcome this type of problem. What is needed is to verify the facts, followed by sales management working out a special strategy to reactivate the accounts. Most buyers will respond to the sincere efforts of a supplier to resolve past grievances if accompanied by assurances of proper treatment in the future. But if the strategy does not work, account or territory changes should be made so that the representative's sales efforts can be targeted on potentially productive areas.

Inadequate technical backup. In industrial selling situations that require technical product and applications knowledge, sales forces often include salespeople with wide differences in technical training and experience. Some need more backup assistance from company technicians than others. Assuming the salesperson is otherwise qualified, the below-par territory performance may be due to insufficient technical help. The immediate answer is to arrange for additional technical assistance. The longer-range answer may be more training for the incumbent salesperson or better salesperson-selection procedures.

Strong competition. Competition in a below-par territory may be so strong that it is beyond the ability of the territory representative to overcome it. A competitor's commanding market position may be due to one or more of the following conditions: (1) it was the original company to serve the territory, enabling it to take an early leadership position which it never lost; (2) it is able to give superior customer service because it has a plant or distribution center in or near the territory; (3) it has lower landed costs because of a favorable plant location, enabling it to deal from a position of strength with competitors who choose to use price or promotion as competitive weapons; (4) it has had a long succession of strong territory representatives and sales supervisors who have maintained good relations with accounts; or (5) it is willing to spend what is necessary to defeat attempted onslaughts by competitors.

To chip away at the competitor's dominance, management must devise a coordinated strategy which may consist of such things as special prices and other incentives, augmented services, increased local advertising, or assignment of a highly competent salesperson. The sales representative's efforts may be supplemented by executives calling on accounts, inviting key account personnel to visit plants and company headquarters, entertaining account personnel, and enlisting the advice of accounts in developing products and marketing plans.

Building on Territory Strengths. Performance in our own above-par territories will have derived from conditions similar to those just listed for strong competitors. It is important to understand why we are strong, so that we can further capitalize on those strengths. It is also important to identify competitors' territory weaknesses so that we can take advantage of them.

Defensive strategy is important as well, although defense is partly achieved through the offensive strategy. However, being ready with plans for prompt counteractions to potential competitive thrusts should be a part of the defensive strategy. The territory representative should maintain close relationships with account personnel so as to learn quickly of changes in competitors' strategies. With sales managements' attention taken up by many problems, there is always the danger that strong territories will be taken for granted. Complacency opens the door for competitors to make gains before we can react. It is, of course, harder to recover lost ground than to hold it in the first instance. Therefore, the annual sales plan should call for a review of territory defensive strategies so that they are not overlooked.

Following Both Strategies. Among companies using territory improvement strategies, the more common approach is to overcome weaknesses. However, there is no reason why the build-on-strength approach should not be used as well. The annual sales department plan should list the territories for study which offer the best opportunities for improvement. The objective should be to increase company market share using the strategy that is most appropriate for each territory designated for study. The important point is that strategies and programs should be tailored for each selected territory.

This does not mean that sales management should avoid broader strategies for achieving increased market share throughout its total selling area. After all, there should be continuing efforts to raise performance overall, including improvements in the average territories (those which represent par). What we have been discussing are additional strategies for targeting sales efforts to those territories which represent special opportunities.

SUMMARY

People are aware of the role of advertising in marketing because it is so visible. Few, however, realize how extensive the role of personal selling is in getting products into distribution channels and consummating sales to ultimate buyers. The six million U.S. sales workers, representing about nine out of every ten marketing jobs, attest to the size of the personal selling function.

Because companies are dependent on sales income, the job of the general sales manager is one of the most important in the company. The reasons are apparent in industrial goods companies where personal selling is the principal element of the promotional mix. But even in those consumer packaged goods companies where advertising is the principal element, it is personal selling that gets the products sold to channel intermediaries and sees that promotional programs are accepted and implemented. When young people first move into company management circles, they often are surprised to learn of the sales manager's high status. We stress this point because in our efforts to portray the broad role of marketing, we often unintentionally underrate the importance of personal selling.

The management of selling represents one of the most interesting management jobs. Not only does it call for the usual skills in planning, organization, and control, but it calls also for unusual skill in leadership. Keeping large numbers of people motivated to attain ambitious goals is a leadership challenge in itself. But the challenge is even greater because salespeople usually are dispersed geographically and work alone without close supervision. To build and maintain a dependable sales organization results from consistently doing the right things over long periods of time. Executives who can do this are highly regarded by their top managements.

The starting point for a successful sales force is the definition of the sales job—that is, deciding the selling functions required to implement the marketing and promotional strategies. This definition forms the basis for decisions with respect to organization, recruiting, training, compensation, and territory layout. When sales management has the right people in the right places doing the right things, the manager with leadership qualities adds the final ingredients for success—instilling desire to reach high goals. In this and other respects, the analogy drawn between sales management and the coaching of sports teams is not unwarranted.

Although sales strategies are closely interrelated with promotional mix and marketing mix strategies, areas do exist that offer strategic sales options. Three of these were discussed: (1) implementing intensive, selective, or exclusive distribution coverage strategies; (2) organizing the sales force to sell on a nonspecialized (full-line) basis, or specializing sales efforts by product, market, or account; and (3) targeting special sales efforts to selected territories with above- and below-par market share performance.

QUESTIONS

1. How does the sales manager's job differ from most other management positions, and what special talents does it demand?
2. Defining the sales job is the foundation for what other sales management decisions?
3. Why is it necessary to actively recruit new salespeople?
4. Name the three principal steps in new salesperson selection procedures.
5. Name the three types of sales compensation plans. Which is the most popular, and why?
6. Name the three objectives of territory layout and the reasons for them.
7. Sales strategies tie in closely with distribution strategies. What is the role of the sales force, in support of intensive, selective, and exclusive market coverage?
8. What are the reasons for organizing the sales force by full-line, product specialization, or market and account specialization strategies?
9. Targeting sales efforts to specific territories to improve their market shares can utilize one of two strategies. Name them.
10. Name five reasons why a territory may be suffering below-par performance.

REFERENCES

1. Figures are from U.S. Department of Labor, Bureau of Labor Statistics, *Occupational Outlook Handbook*, 1980–81 edition, March 1980, except for figures on people in advertising, which are from the 1977–1978 edition.
2. Victor P. Buell, "Sales Management," in H. B. Maynard (ed.), *Handbook of Business Administration*, McGraw-Hill, New York, 1967, p. 8–114.
3. The balance of this section has been adapted from ibid., pp. 8–115 and 8–116.
4. Hugh D. Menzies, "The New Life of a Salesman," *Fortune*, Aug. 11, 1980, p. 180
5. Herbert M. Greenberg and Jeanne Greenberg, "Job Matching for Better Sales Performance," *Harvard Business Review*, Sept.–Oct. 1980, pp. 128–133. Copyright © 1980 by the President and Fellows of Harvard College; all rights reserved.
6. William J. Stanton and Richard H. Buskirk, *Management of the Sales Force*, 5th ed., Irwin, Homewood, Ill., 1978, p. 160.
7. John P. Steinbrink and William B. Friedman, summary of "Dartnell's 21st Biennial Survey of Sales Force Compensation," Copyright © 1981. Courtesy of the Dartnell Corporation, Chicago.
8. Richard P. Bagozzi, "Performance and Satisfaction in an Industrial Sales Force: An Examination of Their Antecedents and Simultaneity," *Journal of Marketing*, spring 1980, pp. 65–77.
9. Stephen X. Doyle and Benson P. Shapiro, "What Counts Most in Motivating Your Sales Force?" *Harvard Business Review*, May–June 1980, pp. 133–140. Copyright © 1980 by the President and Fellows of Harvard College; all rights reserved.
10. Compensation and fringe benefit data in this section are from Steinbrink and Friedman, op. cit.
11. Stanton and Buskirk, op. cit., p. 395
12. U.S. Bureau of the Census, *Statistical Abstract of the United States*, Washington, D.C., 1981, pp. 820, 818.

CHAPTER 21

Managing Advertising, Sales Promotion, and Publicity

In the previous chapter we discussed the management of personal selling. Now let's turn to the management of the impersonal elements of the promotional mix.

Advertising is any paid message presented in media by an identified sponsor.
Sales Promotion is any communication or persuasive device—other than personal selling, advertising, or publicity—designed to increase the flow of orders.
Publicity is any media mention of a company, brand, or product which is not paid for.

Unfortunately, accounting practices in most companies fail to record expenditures according to those defined areas. Holdover habits from the early days of business accounting mean that some companies charge all marketing costs to sales; others charge everything to advertising except for sales force costs; still others charge some sales promotion functions to advertising and some to sales. In addition, publicity may be charged to advertising or to public relations. The result is that marketing management often does not have accurate cost data for measuring performance by elements of the promotional mix. Nationally collected data have similar problems in that different reporting services use different definitions. Some of these data are included, however, to give you an idea of the approximate size of national expenditures for promotion and year-by-year changes.

For most companies advertising and personal selling represent the more important elements of the promotional mix. Sales promotion and publicity are considered supplements to advertising and selling, even though some companies spend more for sales promotion than for advertising. Before proceeding with our discussions of advertising, sales promotion, and publicity, let's examine a conceptual model of the market communications process which highlights the basic steps involved in message transmission.

MARKET COMMUNICATIONS

Market communication is the process by which messages are developed by the marketer and transmitted to intended receivers (the target market audience). Effectiveness is measured by how well the messages are received, understood, and acted upon. Figure 21-1 shows a classic market communications model and how it

	Source	Encoding	Channel	Receiver	Decoding	Response
Communications model			Feedback ←			
Translation	Sender of message — the marketer	Developing message for target audience	Medium for transmitting message	Target audience	How message is perceived by audience	Audience reaction to message
	Planning	Planning and Implementation		Performance Measurement		
Managing the advertising communications process	Target audience defined; goals set for advertising message	Copy strategy decided; ad created	Media strategy decided; ad placed in selected mediums	What percent of target audience was exposed to message?	How clearly was message understood?	Audience response compared to goals of message

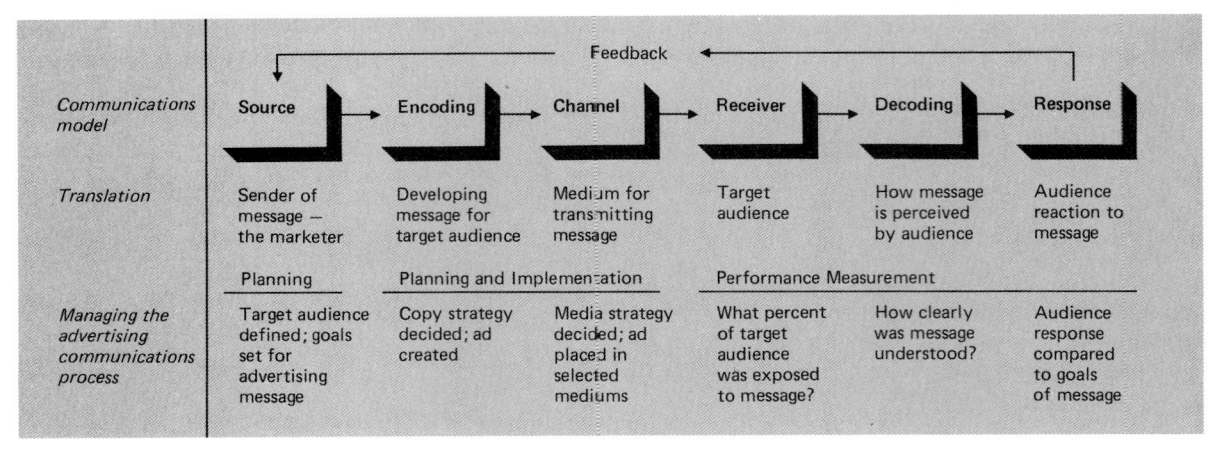

FIGURE 21-1. Application of a market communications model to managing advertising communications.

can be applied to the management of the advertising communications process. The model is relevant to all forms of market communications when they are controlled by the marketer, including personal selling, sales promotion, and package labeling.

The *source* of the message is the sender. Commonly, in the case of advertising, the source is an organization with a product to promote. The organization must decide what it wants to communicate, to whom, and for what purpose. *Encoding* is the use of symbols to communicate the message. Symbols may be words, pictures, sounds, animation, or mood setting. When developing an advertisement, encoding would include the copy strategy and the actual creation of the ad.

The *channel* is the medium used to deliver the message; for example, television, radio, magazine, or newspaper. Media strategy and copy strategy must be coordinated, since an advertisement prepared for one medium may not work well in another. An advertisement developed for printing in a magazine, for example, would be unsuitable for television. The *receiver* represents the target audience with whom the sender seeks to communicate, such as women over 40, medical doctors, or metal-finishing companies.

Decoding is how the receiver perceives the symbols and interprets the message.* Few messages are understood as precisely or as completely as the sender would like. Many are misunderstood, and some are even perceived negatively. This is one of the reasons why alternate advertisements frequently are pretested among samples of target audiences before the final ad is selected. One study found that nearly all viewers (96.5 percent) misunderstand some part of what they see on television, whether it is a program, advertisement, or a public service announcement.[1]

Response is how the receiver reacts to the message. The response can vary from a change in awareness to outright purchase. Company management is concerned with how well the message performs in terms of encoding and response by the receiver. *Feedback* is the transmittal of performance measurement back to the

---

*Unlike some communications models, this one places the *receiver* before *decoding*, on the assumption that the receiver must be exposed to the message before decoding can occur.

source. This information may come from sales records, marketing research, or the sales force.

THE NATURE OF ADVERTISING

Advertising in the aggregate is big business. Total annual expenditures for all types of advertising (including some that we would classify as sales promotion) exceed $55 billion.[2] Expenditures of the five largest advertisers in 1981 (in millions of dollars rounded) were: (1) Procter & Gamble—$672; (2) Sears, Roebuck—$544; (3) General Foods—$457; (4) Philip Morris—$433; and (5) General Motors—$401. Number 100 in advertising expenditures was Canon U.S.A., with $37 million.[3]

Companies would prefer to send a salesperson to deliver every sales message, but it would not be economical to do so. Despite its high total costs, advertising represents the least expensive way to get sales messages to the largest number of prospects. The cost of an advertising message directed toward a mass audience, such as all U.S. households, is a fraction of a cent per exposure, whether the medium is radio, television, magazine, or a city newspaper. Even for more specialized segments the cost is only pennies per exposure. In the case of industrial advertising, where audiences are smaller, the cost per exposure is higher. Even here, however, the average cost per exposure using business publications is 16¢, compared to $137.02 for the average call by an industrial salesperson.[4] The cost per individual advertising exposure is so small that the media quote their prices as cost per thousand (CPM) exposures.

Purposes of Advertising

Advertising is used for many nonbusiness purposes such as disseminating government information or promoting political and social causes. Advertising by business, however, far exceeds other uses. U.S. government advertising expenditures for all purposes in 1981, for example, were exceeded by twenty-five companies.[5]

The end purpose of business product advertising is to create sales. Yet, because advertising is only one of the marketing forces that influence purchase, it often is assigned a more limited role in the sales creation process. This role may be different at different times. The role of advertising at Procter & Gamble, the nation's leading advertiser, is described in **Marketing Note 21-1**.

Three common purposes of product advertising are to create awareness, induce action, and maintain continuing buying interest.

Creating Awareness. Using advertising to create awareness of company trade name, brand, and/or product is referred to as *brand image* or *brand personality advertising*. Its purpose is to make consumers aware of a new product or cognizant of an older product. This is an important early step in paving the way toward eventual purchase.

Inducing Action. Ideally, advertising creates enough interest, conviction, and desire to induce purchase. This is most likely to happen in the case of convenience goods sold in self-service stores. Advertising often can influence the consumer to pick the product off the shelf or display rack for trial. In the case of shopping goods, however, the desired action more likely would be to get the consumer to consider

> **MARKETING NOTE 21-1**
>
> *Marketing at P&G*
>
> While advertising and selling are terribly important, we have never been able to build a successful brand through these skills alone. Advertising and selling skills can get consumers to try the product, but after that the health of the brand depends entirely on satisfaction with its performance. If consumers are happy with the product, then we have the basis of a healthy brand. If they do not perceive any real performance benefits in the brand, then no amount of ingenious advertising and selling can save the brand. This is the way it has been in our business since our company was founded in 1837.
>
> When we introduce a new product, the largest part of our initial marketing investment is usually in the form of introductory sampling. We know that we must get consumers to try the product in their own homes and to determine for themselves whether they prefer its performance characteristics. There is no substitute for consumer experience with the product. Only when satisfied consumers have had firsthand experience with the product will the other elements of the marketing mix, such as advertising and selling, be fully productive. . . .
>
> If you can accept my main premise that product performance is the key to marketing success, then what is the role of advertising? For our kinds of products, advertising performs a number of vital functions. It tells the consumer that the product is available in the first place. It tries to attract those consumers who will be interested in the product and it tries to tell them about the performance characteristics which will interest them.
>
> Advertising gains trial from those consumers who will like the product and will make repeat purchases. Our products live on regular customers, not on trial. To be effective, our advertising must help to win regular customers. For this reason, we want our advertising to be informative. We want to tell consumers what to look for in the product so that they will become regular customers. With our kinds of products . . . the advertising is wasted on those consumers whose experience with the product contradicts what is said in the advertising. This is the principal reason why misleading advertising is so utterly unproductive.
>
> *Source:* "Some Basic Beliefs About Marketing," a talk by the chairman of the board, Procter & Gamble Co.

the company's brand when next shopping for the product. For an industrial product the desired action would be to get the buyer to inquire about the product or grant an interview when the company's salesperson calls.

Maintaining Buyer Interest. For repetitively purchased products, advertising is used to maintain buyer interest in order to offset competitive advertising and the tendency of people to forget. This is called *reminder* advertising. Maintaining that interest over a long period of time is a great challenge to copywriters. It is easier when noteworthy product improvements can be featured periodically. Tide laundry detergent, for example, has had "55 significant modifications during its 30-year lifetime."[6] Ivory Soap, on the other hand, has undergone few changes since its introduction more than a century ago; yet it remains "the volume leader in the toilet soap category,"[7] at least in part as the result of regular use of reminder advertising.

Other Purposes. Some of the many other reasons for the use of advertising are to promote special events, attract new dealers, stimulate dealer interest, build sales force and company employee morale, create store traffic, reach buying influences not accessible to sales persons, obtain sales leads, or offset a seasonal sales slump. A key purpose of much industrial advertising is to prepare the buyer for the salesperson's call. This is illustrated by Figure 21-2. This classic ad has been run for many years; only the model portraying the buyer has been changed.

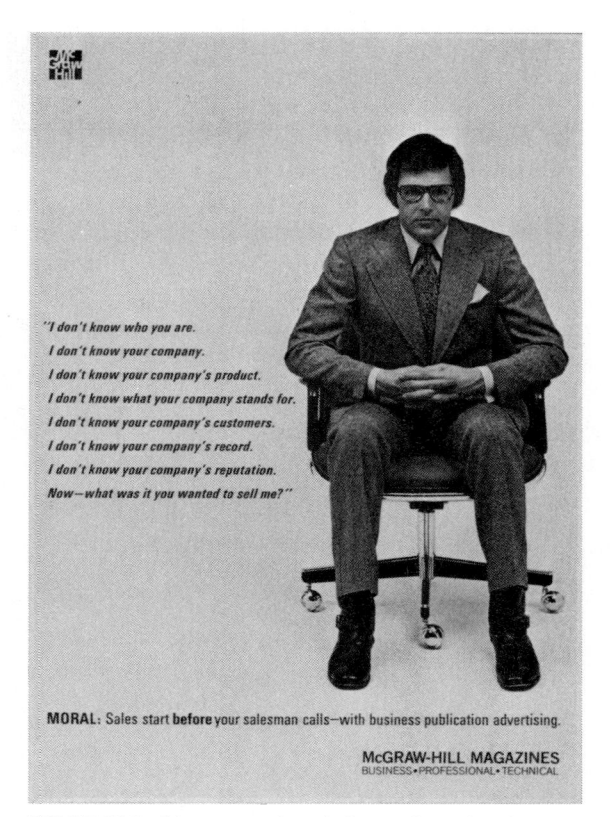

FIGURE 21-2. Sales preparation ad. *Source:* Reproduced by permission of McGraw-Hill, Inc.

Classifications of Advertising

We should be aware of the meaning of terms used to designate different general classes of advertising.

National and Local Advertising. National advertising is sponsored by producers, whereas local advertising is sponsored by retailers. Producers' advertising is classified as "national" even though it may run only regionally or locally. Retail advertising is "local" (even though it may be sponsored by a national retail chain) as long as the advertising is placed in local media and is identified with the local dealer. National advertising accounts for about 55 percent of all advertising, and local accounts for 45 percent.[8]

The basic rationale behind the national and local classifications is for purposes of media billings. National advertising is commissionable to advertising agencies, whereas local advertising is not. Producers' national advertising usually is placed by advertising agencies who receive a commission from the media, whereas retailers usually place their advertising directly with the local media and receive as a discount the commission that otherwise would be given to an agency. In general, national advertising is designed to promote the brand so that a favorable climate for puchase is created. Local retail advertising, in general, is designed to build store traffic by featuring new merchandise and special deals, although prestige retailers may concentrate on maintaining store image.

Cooperative Advertising. "Co-op" advertising is run locally by the dealer but paid for cooperatively with the manufacturer when the ad refers to the manufacturer's product. The proportion paid for by each varies, but commonly is 50-50. The local media charges the manufacturer at the higher national rate and the retailer at the lower local rate. From the manufacturer's standpoint, co-op advertising supplements the national advertising by helping the retailer build store traffic so that more consumers will be exposed to the manufacturer's brand. Or a special deal may help to increase brand purchases. Unless the brand is featured in the ad (usually it is not, except where the dealer is the exclusive local dealer), co-op advertising does little to enhance brand image.

Classification of Media

Table 21-1 shows the percentage of advertising expenditures by the principal types of media. Because television advertising is so ubiquitous, you may be surprised to learn that it accounts for only one-fifth of all media expenditures. Newspaper

TABLE 21-1

Percentage of Advertising Expenditures, by Medium

Advertising Medium		Percentages
Newspapers		28.5
National	4.3	
Local	24.2	
Television		20.7
Network	9.2	
Spot	6.1	
Local	5.4	
Direct mail		13.9
Radio		7.0
Network	0.3	
Spot	1.4	
Local	5.3	
Magazines		5.8
Weeklies	2.6	
Monthlies	1.8	
Women's	1.4	
Business papers		3.1
Outdoor		1.1
Farm Publications		0.2
Miscellaneous		19.7
Total		100.0

Source: U.S. Bureau of the Census, *Statistical Abstract of the United States, 1981,* Washington, D.C., p. 572, compiled by McCann-Erikson, Inc., for Crain Communications, Inc., in *Advertising Age* (copyright).

advertising is the largest medium, as it has been for many years, representing 28.5 percent of all media expenditures. In its early days television took market share from other mediums, particularly radio and magazines, which, taken together, now account for less than television alone.

The proportion accounted for by each medium has leveled off, except that for direct mail. Although the total dollars spent for direct mail have increased, its proportion of all media expenditures dropped from 15.2 percent in 1965 to 13.9 percent in 1980. *Direct mail* advertisements are displays or letters sent directly to individuals in their homes or offices. It should not be confused with *direct response marketing*, which is designed to secure orders directly by return mail or phone. Some compilers list direct mail advertising under sales promotion since it does not meet the strict definition of a *paid* message presented in media.

Spending by Types of Products

The relative importance of advertising to the sale of different types of goods and services is shown in Table 21-2. From the company examples we can see that the percentage of advertising expense to sales income is highest for consumer packaged goods and considerably lower for consumer hard and industrial goods. The services company examples suggest that the importance of advertising can vary widely within this category.

We also see from Table 21-2 that the percentage of sales spent for advertising by these advertisers has declined over the years. Economy of scale is the primary reason for the decline in the ratio and the resulting increase in advertising productivity. After sales reach a certain level, it is not necessary to maintain the same ratio of advertising to sales to earn sales increases. This is illustrated by the company in Table 21-3 whose sales have increased faster than advertising expense.

A different explanation is that some companies have diversified into different businesses that require a lower ratio of advertising to sales. Revlon, a leading cosmetics company, diversified into ethical drugs. The result was a lowering of the overall company ratio of advertising to sales income, because advertising is much less important to the promotion of ethical drugs than it is to the promotion of cosmetics.

ADVERTISER-AGENCY FUNCTIONS AND RELATIONSHIPS

The unique aspect of advertising management is that for most companies it involves working with an independent agency that creates and places the advertising for the company. Only a small minority of advertisers perform one or both of these functions in-house, using their own company agency. Originally the advertising agent was a space broker who brought advertisers and media together. Today's advertising agency is an organization of specialists who work for the advertiser. Most of the agency's compensation, however, still comes from the commission (or discount) that the agency receives from the medium. An agency typically buys space or time from the medium at 85 percent of the list price and bills the client for 100 percent of list. The 15 percent commission long has been a bone of contention between many clients and their agencies; some have now modified this arrangement or use other forms of compensation such as a fixed fee.

TABLE 21-2

Advertising as a Percentage of Sales Income for Selected Companies

	% of Sales Income Spent for Advertising		
Company	1963	1969	1980
PRIMARILY CONSUMER PACKAGED GOODS			
Bristol-Myers	39.9	12.5	6.5
Wm. Wrigley, Jr.	15.2	13.6	9.3
Gillette	12.8	10.3	6.5
Revlon	12.1	7.9	4.8
Coca-Cola	11.1	5.3	3.1
Procter & Gamble	10.4	9.2	5.7
PRIMARILY CONSUMER HARD GOODS			
(Plus Services and Industrial Goods)			
Eastman Kodak	3.6	1.8	0.9
RCA	1.9	2.4	2.1
General Motors	1.0	0.7	0.5
PRIMARILY INDUSTRIAL GOODS			
(Plus Some Consumer Goods)			
Du Pont	2.4	1.4	0.7
Union Carbide	1.1	1.0	0.7
General Electric	1.4	0.9	0.6
PRIMARILY SERVICE			
Loews*	N.A.	8.7	2.9
American Express	N.A.	1.3	1.1
AT&T	0.6	0.6	0.5

*Businesses and products include insurance, hotels, theaters, tobacco, watches.

Source: "100 Leading Advertisers," *Advertising Age*, special issues, 1964, 1970, 1981.

Division of Work

In simplest terms the development of advertising involves deciding (1) what message is to be communicated, (2) to whom it is to be communicated, (3) how it is to be presented, and (4) where the message is to be placed so that it will reach the target audience. These correspond to the source, receiver, encoding, and channel steps in the market communications model (Figure 21-1). From the managerial viewpoint, these and other advertising development functions fall under the broad classifications of planning, creative, media, and coordination. In the typical arrangement, creative and media are the responsibility of the agency while planning and coordination are responsibilities of both the client and the agency.

Client Functions. While the client looks to the agency for communications expertise, the client expects the advertising recommendations to tie in with client product marketing plans.

TABLE 21-3

Drop in Ratio of Advertising Expenditures to Sales Income at Bristol-Myers*

	1972	1974	1976	1978	1980
Sales, $ billions	0.9	1.6	2.0	2.5	3.2
Advertising, $ millions	115	150	189	193	196
Advertising as % of sales	12.0	9.4	9.5	7.8	6.2

*As a result of sales income rising at a faster rate than advertising expenditures.

Source: "100 Leading Advertisers," *Advertising Age*, special issues, 1973, 1975, 1977, 1979, 1981.

Marketing research is a primary responsibility of the advertiser, since market information is essential to the development of marketing strategies and plans. Marketing planning (based on marketing research and the *situation analysis*) results in marketing strategies and advertising budgets which are transmitted to the agency. The agency is also furnished information on the market environment, target markets, the company's position in the market, products to be promoted, and product attributes. (However, smaller companies with inadequate marketing staffs may look to their agencies for help in developing marketing plans.)

Evaluations and approvals of the agency's recommended advertising strategies and advertisements are carried out by the client. Several meetings and discussions normally occur, at which time the agency's proposals are reviewed and changes suggested. Approvals are given when the client is satisfied. Coordination on the part of the client includes providing the agency with needed information, scheduling presentations of agency proposals, and approving and processing agency invoices. Day-to-day coordination typically is assigned to product managers.

Agency Functions. The agency's job is to develop advertising strategies and programs (within budgets established by the client) that contribute to the success of the client's marketing plans. The agency may suggest changes if it feels the client's plans or budgets are inadequate.

Marketing research may be conducted by the agency to supplement the research provided by the client (including purchased research services); for example, it may feel that it needs more information on how consumers view the products of the client and those of its competitors. (The agency may be the principal source of marketing research for smaller clients.) The agency also arranges for pretesting and posttesting of advertisements, unless the client prefers to make these arrangements.

Creative functions involved with the development of advertisements include copywriting, art direction, production, and traffic (scheduling). Media functions include the development of media plans and the buying and scheduling of space in print mediums and time in the broadcast mediums.

Coordination with the agency's clients is the responsibility of account managers who maintain communication with their assigned accounts. Overall coordination of internal agency functions is carried out by top agency management, while the account managers follow up on work in process for their clients. Before a recommendation is made to a client, it is reviewed, critiqued, and finally approved by a board of top agency executives.

Client-Agency Problems

Placing advertising in the hands of an independent agency has its good and bad points. It does permit the advertiser to seek out the best talent available and avoid the need to have creative specialists on its own payroll. On the negative side is the difficulty of achieving effective working relationships. Part of the problem is inherent. An advertisement is a creative form of art that triggers emotional responses. Often client and agency react quite differently, and these differences are not readily resolved. A variety of other problems can arise which have been described in a study by Weilbacher.[9]

Despite their problems, some advertiser and agency executives believe that relationships between agencies and clients are improving as each understands the other's role better. A corporation chairman with long experience on both the agency and client side sees a growing recognition of the special skills of each:

> Company people know a lot about their products, markets, and competition. Agencies can't tell them much about these. But agencies have specialized skills in creative communication and media which make important contributions to the company.[10]

ORGANIZATION AND DECISION MAKING BY INDUSTRY TYPE

The advertising decision-making pattern for the typical consumer packaged goods company is different from that of the typical consumer hard goods or industrial goods company, a factor which may not be apparent from organization charts.[11]

Marketing plans and decisions normally are made by the executives responsible for managing operating units (usually division marketing managers and division general managers). But advertising is a frequent exception. Ad decisions may be made at higher levels for a variety of reasons, including the high costs of advertising, the difficulty of measuring advertising performance, the heavy reliance on judgment in advertising decisions, and high emotional involvement by company executives.

Consumer Packaged Goods Advertising

Many of the largest users of advertising are the marketers of packaged convenience goods. They include products such as foods, detergents, health and beauty aids, soft drinks, beer, liquors, cigarettes, and pet foods. Most of the larger companies are organized into groups and divisions. A typical organization plan is shown in Figure 21-3. Variations from this pattern include manufacturing reporting to the group manager or sales reporting to the division manager.

Product Manager Manages Advertising. Over the years the advertising department has been discarded by most packaged goods companies and the responsibility divided among the product managers. Product managers now are the prime contacts with the advertising agencies, and provide them with marketing objectives, plans, and advertising budgets.

Decision Levels. Product managers in packaged goods companies have been criticized by agencies because they are often relatively inexperienced. Typically the product manager has an MBA degree, little or no advertising training, and about two years' experience as an assistant product manager. Company managements are

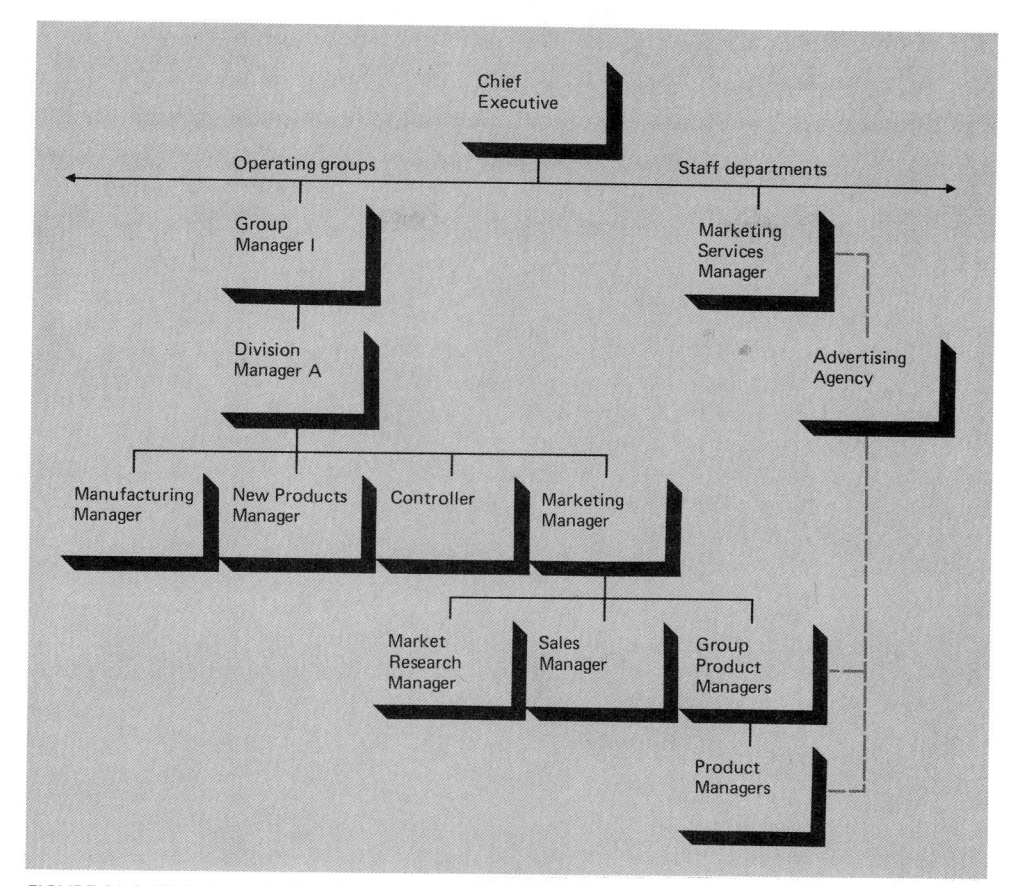

FIGURE 21-3. Typical organization plan, large consumer packaged goods company.

aware of the problem, but continue to use product managers as a practical means of bringing individual management attention to each company product.

Because of the typical product manager's limited experience, however, and because advertising budgets can run into millions of dollars for a single product, the agency's recommendations are approved at higher management levels. While advertising normally is approved by the division marketing manager and the divisional general manager, it is not unusual for ads for important products to be approved by the group executive or the chief executive officer. Although not permitted to approve advertising, as the "gate keeper" the product manager has some control over the ads that higher management sees. Occasionally an agency will go over the product manager's head, but it cannot resort to this tactic too often.

Marketing Services. The organization in Figure 21-3 shows a marketing services department at the corporate staff level. It provides common services to line marketing management in the operating divisions. The most frequent service is media planning and coordination of media buying to ensure that all of the company's advertising is combined to obtain quantity discounts from the media. When a company uses multiple agencies, one agency is designated to place all advertising. The marketing services department coordinates this activity with the agency.

Another commonly offered service is sales promotion planning and development. Specialists assist the product manager with the planning and design of sales promotions. After the promotional plan is approved, the promotional materials are created in-house or the work is contracted to outside design firms and print shops. Marketing services then oversee the distribution of the promotional materials to the field. Other services offered by some but not all marketing services departments include: package design, control of advertising production costs, advertising research, creative services, advertising claims substantiation, and advertising and sales promotion management for small divisions with limited marketing personnel. Figure 21-4 shows the organization of the marketing services department at Richardson-Vicks, Inc. (Vicks Formula 44, Oil of Olay, etc.).

Although the marketing services department typically reported to corporate management in the past, some companies now are assigning it to a group manager or division manager for administrative purposes. No matter where it reports, however, this department provides services to all company divisions.

Consumer Hard Goods and Industrial Goods Advertising

Companies marketing consumer hard goods (e.g., electrical appliances and automobiles) and industrial goods (e.g., chemicals and metals) have organization structures

FIGURE 21-4. Organization of the Marketing Services Department, Richardson-Vicks, Inc..

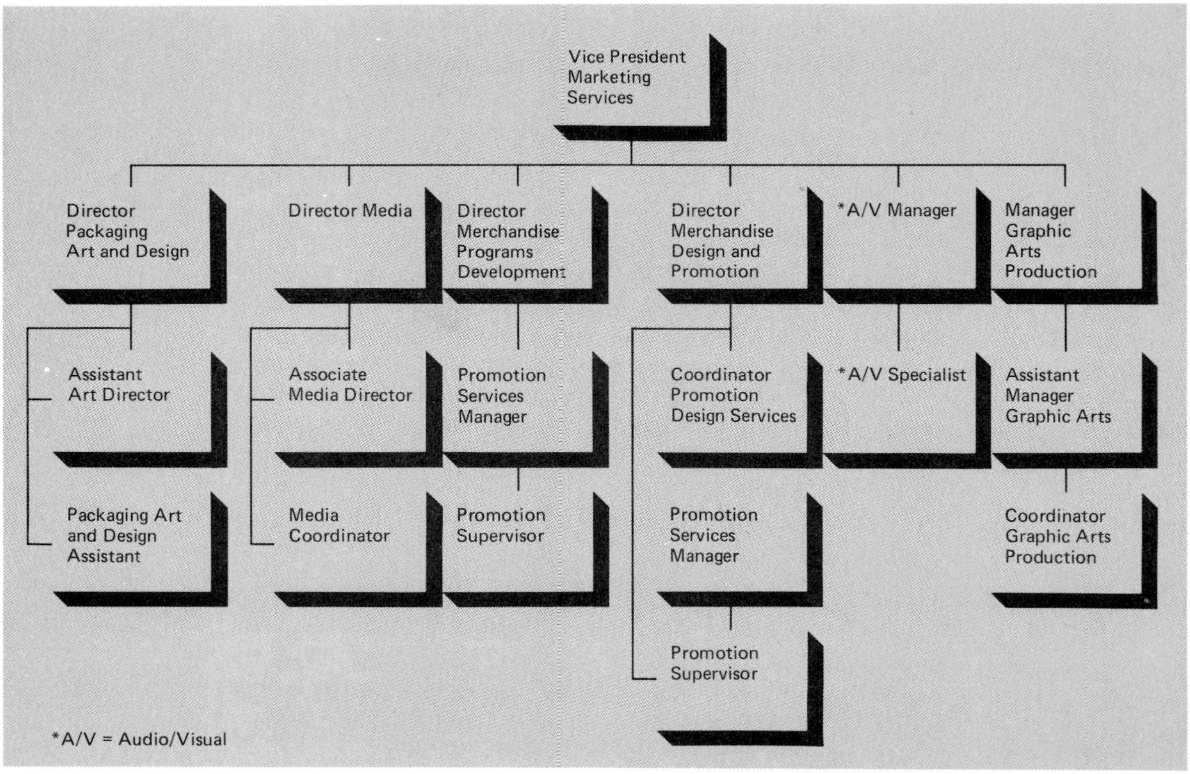

*A/V = Audio/Visual

similar to packaged goods companies, but they manage their advertising differently. Usually they assign it to advertising and sales promotion departments staffed with trained advertising managers who serve as the connecting links between division line marketing management and advertising agencies.

Centralized or Decentralized Advertising. Figures 21-5 and 21-6 show different locations for the advertising and sales promotion department. In Figure 21-5 advertising is centralized in a corporate staff department, whereas in Figure 21-6 it is decentralized to the division marketing department.

In a centralized setup, the central advertising and sales promotion department helps line marketing management in each division develop strategies and programs. In a decentralized setup, these functions are performed by an advertising and sales promotion department located within each division. When advertising management is decentralized, a corporate advertising and sales promotion services department provides divisional services like those described for packaged goods companies.

Decision Making. Advertising plans, budgets, and advertisements are approved by divisional line marketing management irrespective of whether the advertising and sales promotion staff function is centralized or decentralized. A representative of the advertising and sales promotion department participates during the initial stages of the division's annual marketing planning process. Once marketing objectives and tentative promotional budgets have been established, the department representative coordinates with the assigned advertising agency, which develops advertising

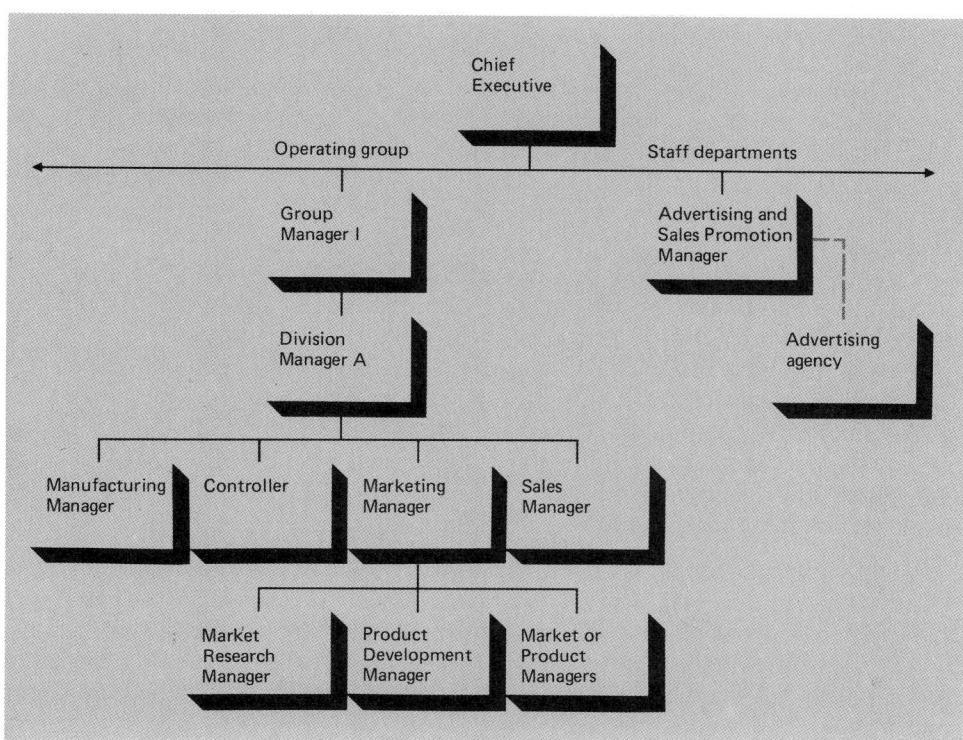

FIGURE 21-5. Typical organization plan, large consumer hard goods or industrial goods company with centralized advertising department.

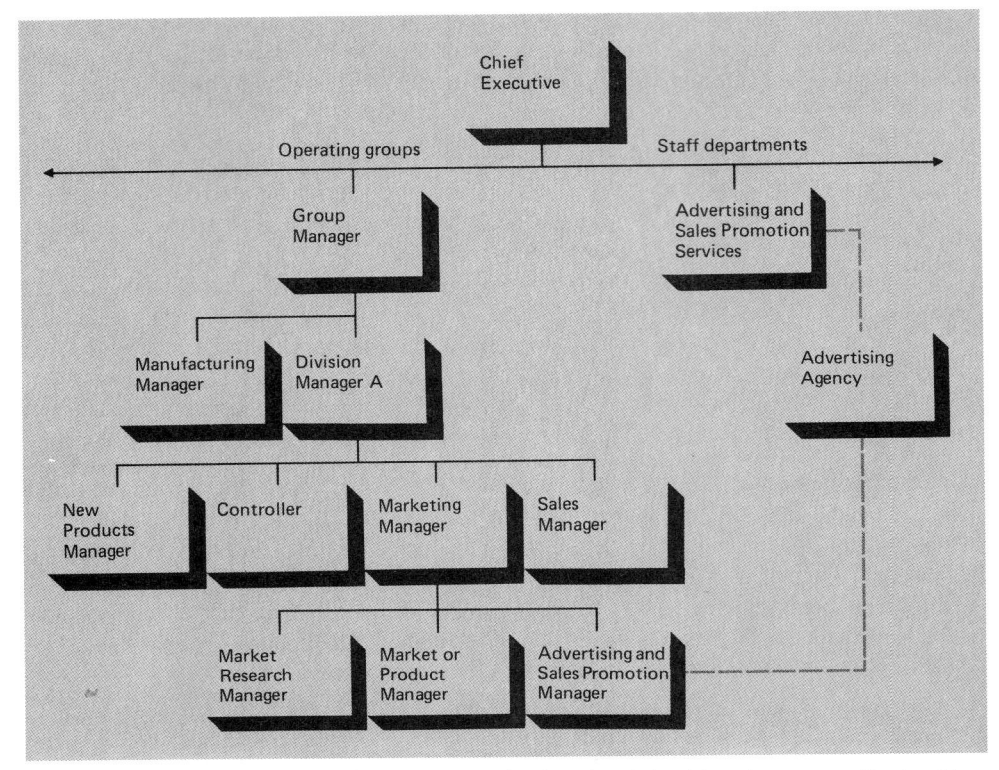

FIGURE 21-6. Typical organization plan, large counsumer hard goods or industrial goods company with advertising decentralized to the divisions.

recommendations. (Sales promotion plans may be developed by the agency or developed internally by the advertising and sales promotion department.) When the advertising and sales promotion department is satisfied with the agency's proposals, it recommends them to division marketing management. Marketing management normally accepts them if they are within budget and support the marketing strategies.

There are fewer hassles over advertising decisions in consumer hard and industrial good companies than in packaged goods companies. This is because advertising plays a lesser role in the promotional mix. Also product, market, and marketing managers usually have sales backgrounds and are inclined to accept the advice of advertising professionals. This does not mean that they are uninterested in advertising; rather, they tend to view it as a supplement to personal selling. As is the case with packaged goods companies, higher-level executives take a personal interest in advertising, and it is not unusual for division, group, and/or corporate management to be included in the review and approval process.

Other Organizational Differences. Figures 21-5 and 21-6 also illustrate differences other than in the placement of advertising. The division manager in Figure 21-5, for example, is responsible for both manufacturing and marketing operations, whereas the division manager in Figure 21-6 essentially is in charge of marketing. In this arrangement manufacturing is located at the group level, where it produces products for all divisions.

Note that in both charts the sales and marketing departments report separately to the division manager. This is a common arrangement in consumer hard and industrial goods companies which consider personal selling as highly important.

Corporate Advertising

Corporate or institutional advertising promotes the company's name and image, while product advertising concentrates on the sale of products and services. Messages may be directed to the general public or to segments such as the financial community (brokers, analysts, business editors, and investors), local communities (where the company has operations), corporate executives (who influence purchases but who may not see product ads in trade magazines), and to influencers in and out of government (who influence the public policies which affect the company's business). Organizationally, corporate advertising usually is managed by the corporate advertising or marketing services department. Objectives, strategies, and advertisements are approved by top corporate management.

Condé Nast Publications, publisher of several women's magazines, ran a corporate campaign in *The New York Times* which was directed at advertisers and stressed the importance of the working women's market. An ad from this series is reproduced in Figure 21-7. While the campaign listed the company's magazines, it was designed to promote and build the Condé Nast image, leaving each magazine to

FIGURE 21-7. Condé Nast ad. *Source:* Reproduced with the permission of Condé Nast Publications.

THE LADY OF THE HOUSE HAS PASSED AWAY.

She's bringing home the bacon. Not just frying it. She's augmenting the family income and spending it. She's selecting the make of car, not just the color. You'll find her packing for her business trips, not his.

She's the 25 million leader-readers of the Condé Nast Package. The 23% the 77% follow. Now she can be reached all in one place, all in one package.

Every month, Vogue, House & Garden, Glamour, Mademoiselle, Bride's and Self provide information and stimulation to those 25 million women readers. What car to drive? A new dressing idea for salad. Where to take those frequent vacations? What bank to bank on?

Whether you're selling an airline reservation, a hotel room, a convenience food, a disposable diaper or a nice bottle of wine, the women of the Condé Nast Package want to know about it.

For more information on the changing women's market, get a copy of the booklet, *The Lady Of The House Has Passed Away*. Call Neil Jacobs at (212) 880-8329.

THE CONDÉ NAST PACKAGE

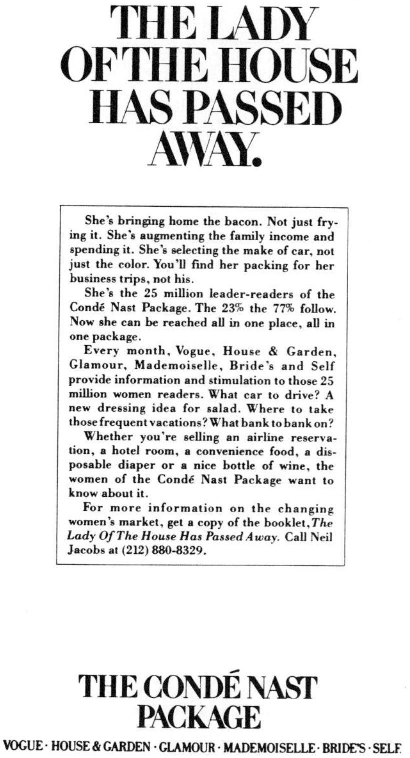

VOGUE · HOUSE & GARDEN · GLAMOUR · MADEMOISELLE · BRIDE'S · SELF

run its own promotion directed to the particular segment of the women's market it serves.

Marketing Note 21-2 describes a corporate advertising program run by ITT, a highly diversified company with most of its businesses in industrial products with which the general public is unfamiliar.

STRATEGIC ADVERTISING PLANNING

The advertising plan is a part of the annual marketing plan, which was described in Chapter 12, and is designed to support the marketing strategy. We discuss it in terms of advertising goals, strategies, budgets, research, and measurement.

Advertising Goals

As noted earlier, the general goal or purpose of product advertising is to produce sales. But we also know that advertising is only one of the elements that influences sales results. Sometimes a change in sales can be attributed directly to a change in the quantity or quality of advertising. More often, however, a direct, immediate cause-and-effect relationship is not evident. Consequently, advertising goals need to be stated in terms that are measurable.

In his definitive work on defining advertising goals and measuring performance, Russell Colley says: "To measure the accomplishments of advertising, a company must first have a clear understanding of the specific results it seeks to accomplish through advertising."[12]

Before setting advertising goals it is essential to know your target market and overall marketing goals. Two case examples show how advertising goals tie in to the marketing goals.[13]

CASE EXAMPLE: BUILDING MATERIALS	
Market	25,000 architects, 125,000 builders, 1 million prospective purchasers of single family dwellings
Marketing goal	Increase share of residential insulation industry from 10% to 14% in three years
Advertising goal	Register message of all-around economy with 40% of architects; register speed of installation message with 30% of builders; attain 50% of brand identity among prospective owners.
CASE EXAMPLE: RAZOR BLADES	
Market	Males 15 and over
Marketing goals	Maintain present share of razor blade market; increase consumption among present users; establish blade shaving habit among youth market
Advertising goals	Area I: Maintain high-level (90%) consumer awareness to hold present share of industry Area II: Convey "buy-a-spare" message to 75% of market Area III: Register "special occasion" blade message among 40% of teenage youths

Source: Russell H. Colley, *Defining Advertising Goods for Measured Advertising Results*, Association of National Advertisers, New York, 1961, pp. 77 and 105.

> **Corporate Advertising at ITT**
>
> MARKETING NOTE 21-2
>
> From extensive research we found that our general high regard for ourselves was not reflected by our various publics. Our past advertising efforts had barely made a ripple in the pond. In fact, if the public knew us at all, we were probably confused with AT&T. Two out of three adults in households with $15,000 annual income or more knew nothing about us. And when people don't know a large company, it's hard to think well of it. In fact, it is very easy to believe any negatives you hear. . . . As *Fortune* magazine pointed out: "*The success of a corporation* nowadays *depends* not only on how it makes and markets its products, but also *on how it is perceived by the public.*"
>
> So we made some decisions. *First*, we had to increase awareness of the corporation among a broad cross section of prosperous Americans who obviously didn't know what ITT stood for. . . . *Second*, we would have to increase substantially our media dollars, not only in print, but in television. . . . *Third*, . . . we had to create better public attitudes by demonstrating that:
>
> 1. ITT makes a large and continuing investment in research and development which produces a wide diversity of products and services, many of them in highly technical fields;
> 2. And that these products and services help improve the quality of our lives.
>
> Initially, we chose a scatter plan of TV spots in evening prime time, news spots, and sports to reach as broad and diverse an audience as possible. In fact, in terms of $15,000-plus households, we reached 28 million adults, with a frequency of 2.8 times in every 4-week period. And we backed that up with a regular schedule in print to reach the infrequent television viewers. . . .
>
> Some of our products shown in commericals included electronic binoculars that see in the dark, circuitry for a heart manikin, a fiber optic communications systems, and a railway control system. Each one was an unusual, demonstrable subject—which is why we chose them, of course—even though 99 percent of the public will never buy or have anything directly to do with most of these products. All of them were supported by print advertisements in a wide range of general and specialized publications. How did we do? Here are some results about a year and a half into this campaign:
>
> - Awareness and familiarity with ITT had increased from 34 to 59 percent.
> - "Develops many new products" went from 46 to 75 percent.
> - "Leader in technology," from 49 to 81 percent.
> - "Leads in R&D to improve products," from 46 to 71 percent.
> - "Makes quality products," from 54 to 82 percent.
> - "Reliable," from 48 to 73 percent.
> - "Cares about general public," from 31 to 50 percent.
> - "Good stock to buy or own," from 52 to 72 percent.
>
> *Source:* From a talk to the Incorporated Society of British Advertisers, November 1980, by J. Paul Jannuzzo, director, Advertising and Sales Promotion, International Telephone and Telegraph Corporation.

Advertising Strategies

Strategies for achieving advertising goals include decisions about product positioning; copy; media; and the mix of reach, frequency, and continuity.

Product Positioning Strategy. No product or brand can be all things to all people. Neither is there time in a brief commercial to explain all of the attributes of a product. Before deciding on the copy strategy, therefore, the product should be *positioned*; that is, we decide how we want it to be perceived in the marketplace relative to competition. A common approach to positioning is to identify the principal advantage, benefit, or strength of the product and then emphasize it in advertising and other forms of product promotion.* Some examples of brand and company positioning are:

- Coke—"The real thing" (implying that other colas are attempts to copy Coca Cola)
- Charmin toilet paper—softness
- Roundup—increases farm yields by controlling weeds
- Condé Nast—an important market is working women who read Condé Nast magazines
- ITT—ITT research improves the quality of life

An advertising executive has made the point that a positioning statement in an advertising plan should define the opportunity rather than dictate the creative (copy) strategy. He says it should answer these questions:

> To which market segment is the product to be sold? What are the product's unique benefits? Who are the competitors? Agreements on the opportunity will lead to a creative strategy that speaks clearly and forcefully to its intended audience.[14]

Copy Strategy. Copy is only one part of the creative process needed to develop advertising. The others are art, print production, and radio and television production.[15] Strictly speaking, copy is the written or spoken message, the encoding step of the market communications model. But since the message also is conveyed by illustrations in print advertising and by music, mood, and actors in television commercials, *copy* often is used as a term for the entire creative process. *Creative*, used like a noun, also refers to all aspects of advertising creation and development.

Copy strategy is concerned with how the advertising goals are to be achieved. It includes positioning, development of campaign themes, and deciding how the advertising will be presented. Media must be considered because, although the advertising goals may be the same, the copy will be different for television and print mediums. Or copy and media may be used to achieve different yet complementary goals.

> Sony, for example, in introducing the Walkman (portable cassette with headphones), followed two copy strategies (each linked to a different advertising medium) which Sony called the "soft" approach and the "hard" approach.[16] The soft approach used television for demonstrating the pleasures of listening to the Walkman. One commercial showed a small boy with his dog in a field listening to his Walkman. The hard approach used newspapers for ads that explained the technical superiority of the Walkman. Television ads enabled Sony to create awareness, interest, and desire, while newspaper copy was sufficiently detailed to overcome concerns that prospects might have about the product's technical qualities.

Ad campaigns are run for predetermined periods. While the central campaign

---

*See Chapter 16, page 439, for more on product and brand positioning (and repositioning) strategies.

theme may be portrayed differently in different ads, it can be used as long as it continues to "wear well."

> A successful long-term copy strategy can be illustrated by a campaign run by the General Foods Company's Sanka brand of decaffeinated coffee. Sanka was positioned as 100 percent real coffee for coffee lovers who find that regular coffee containing caffeine makes them nervous and irritable. The creative strategy or copy theme was carried out in a television commercial portraying before and after scenes of a regular coffee drinker overcoming irritableness by switching to Sanka brand after learning that Sanka is 100 percent real coffee with only the caffeine removed. The same theme replayed repeatedly in a campaign that ran for several years. The settings and actors changed while actor Robert Young provided continuity as the spokesperson who gave the reasons for trying Sanka.

Copy strategy should be approved *before* the advertising campaign is developed. In sophisticated companies, higher levels of management usually insist on approving copy strategy whether or not they later approve individual ads. Experienced managers know that successful advertising campaigns grow out of sound copy strategies that support the marketing strategy. The marketing vice president of a large consumer durable goods company said: "I constantly remind our people that every ad must help achieve a marketing objective and carry a strategy. No one shows me a storyboard ahead of showing me a strategy."[17] Examples of copy and media strategies are shown in **Marketing Note 21-3**.

Media Strategy. The task of media strategy is to match the characteristics of individual media with the market requirements of the product being advertised.[18] The goal is to select the most effective media for reaching the target audience while remaining within the media budget. Every media plan is a compromise between the ideal and what is practical and affordable. Media and copy strategies are closely related and should be considered together when developing advertising plans.

Each medium has its special strengths and weaknesses. Television is highly effective for products sold to mass markets because it reaches so many people at relatively low CPM. It is not as cost-effective for products sold to limited market segments. This drawback may be lessened, however, with the increase in cable systems programmed for special-interest segments. On the other hand, the increase of cable television may cause network coverage to be reduced, thereby reducing its effectiveness for mass market products.

Special-interest magazines provide a selective means of reaching market segments. Tennis magazines, for example, are ideal for advertising Spalding's tennis equipment; farm magazines are excellent for advertising Monsanto's herbicide Roundup. Print media such as magazines and newspapers also are good vehicles for products that require more explanation than can be carried in a brief radio or television commercial.

Radio, like magazines, is a selective medium. Furthermore, it has a relatively low CPM. Radio stations in large city markets design their programs to appeal to special segments based on age, ethnic background, or lifestyle. Newspapers are used primarily for local retail advertising. The newspaper is a mass medium that has

MARKETING NOTE 21-3

Planning Copy and Media Strategies

	Description	Examples of Possible Comments
II. COPY STRATEGIES		
1. Objectives	State who the target audience is and the basic message to be communicated to this audience.	· Convince mothers of young children that they will prefer our product because. . . . · Convince all teenagers that our product works twice as fast as Brand X.
2. Strategy		
· Basic Concept	If developed, describe the basic campaign idea that will be used to convey the above message to the target audience.	· For people who can't brush after every meal. · Leave the driving to us. · Put a tiger in your tank.
· Concept Support	Depending on the campaign approach, state the supporting reasons why the basic message should be believed.	· Contains GL 70. · Contains a combination of fast-acting ingredients. · 4 out of 5 doctors recommended. . . .
· Tone	If appropriate, describe the environmental setting in which the advertising is to be cast.	· Contemporary; sincere. · Masculine; humorous. · Soft, feminine; reassuring. · News announcement.
III. MEDIA STRATEGY		
1. Objective	State who the target audience is, the media weight to be applied to this audience, and any other comments that best define the media objectives to be achieved.	· Reach young mothers as often as practical. · Provide added emphasis in peak consumption periods. · Concentrate weight in high-growth markets.
2. Strategy	Indicate the media selected for this purpose; the reasons for their selection; and the reach and frequency they will deliver, if appropriate.	· TV will continue to be brand's primary medium because. . . . · Daytime network TV will be used to deliver year-round reach and frequency at maximum efficiency. · Nighttime spot will be used in major markets during the high-consumption season. · Major market newspaper ads will be used to support the summer promotions.

Source: F. Beaven Ennis, *Effective Marketing Management*, Association of National Advertisers, New York, 1973, pp. 160–161.

limited appeal to national advertisers except where the advertiser may wish to throw extra promotion into selected local markets.

There is more to media planning, of course, than merely selecting the medium. For television it means selecting the time of day, types of programs, and whether to buy *network* (national coverage) or *spot* (station-by-station coverage). The use of magazines requires decisions as to whether to select general-interest magazines or any of the hundreds of special-interest magazines; to use national coverage or regional editions; or to use Sunday newspaper magazine supplements such as *Parade* and *Family Weekly*. Furthermore, media planning must be done with an eye to coverage and costs.

Examples of company media strategies. Table 21-4 illustrates how media usage will vary by types of products and markets served.

Revlon, which sells packaged beauty aids to the women's market, spends over three quarters of its media budget in television and most of the balance in magazines, which reach the mass market and which also lend themselves to color and portrayal of beautiful models. Very little of the budget is spent for newspapers or radio, mediums which do not effectively portray glamour.

Du Pont, primarily a producer of industrial products, spends over half of its media budget in special interest magazines and farm publications read by industrial buyers. Most of the balance goes into network television in the form of corporate advertising or support of the company's consumer products.

American Airlines' advertising is directed to the business and personal travel markets. Two key things affect its selection of media. First, despite its large size, American does not serve all geographic markets. Therefore, it selects mediums whose coverage is primarily local (newspapers, spot TV, and spot radio). Second, air carriers' messages tend heavily toward influencing immediate and short-term customer travel plans, such as those caused by price and schedule changes or seasonal promotions. For

TABLE 21-4
Variations in Advertising Media Expenditures as a Function of Company Type

Medium	% of Advertising Budget		
	Revlon	Du Pont	American Airlines
Newspapers	1.1	1.5	41.5
Magazines	17.7	50.3	9.7
Farm publications		5.5	
Spot TV	36.0	5.5	26.0
Network TV	40.8	36.5	2.5
Total TV	76.8	42.0	28.5
Spot radio	1.7	0.1	19.0
Network radio	2.5	—	—
Total radio	4.2	0.1	19.0
Outdoor	—	—	1.3
Total	99.8	99.4	100.0

Source: Abstracted from "Marketing Profiles," *Advertising Age*, Sept. 10, 1981, pp. 4, 68, 129.

these, media with short deadlines are needed, such as newspapers, spot TV, and spot radio. Only 12 percent of American's media budget goes into magazines and network broadcasting, mediums characterized by national coverage and long deadlines.

Reach, Frequency, and Continuity Strategies. Closely related to copy and media planning is the question of how many in the target audience to try to reach and with what frequency. *Reach* is the number of people exposed to a single advertisement. *Frequency* is the number of times a person is exposed to an advertisement during a four week period. *Continuity* is the length of time a campaign is run in a medium.

Few advertisers can afford to reach as many people as they would like or with the desired frequency. It is thought that advertising effectiveness rises with increased exposure up to some point where it levels off and decline sets in. But there is conflicting evidence as to what the point is where the incremental costs of added exposure exceeds incremental effectiveness. Optimum frequency seems to vary by type of product, degree of current brand awareness, or the type and amount of competitive advertising. "In general the ideal frequency will be the number of advertising messages it takes to move a prospective customer to action."[19]

A study sponsored by Jos. E. Seagram & Sons and Time, Inc. found that the effectiveness of advertising continuity can continue for long periods. "The researchers were surprised to learn that awareness-level curves didn't flatten out over a period of time, but continued to rise even after 48 weeks."[20]

Because of the many variables that must be considered in media planning, computer models have been developed that help identify potential alternate plans. Most media experts seem to believe, however, that individual judgment plays the major role in media decisions. "Most media plans end up as a compromise between reach, frequency, and continuity, with the nature of the compromise being determined by the judgment of the media planner."[21] The media director of a leading advertising agency said:

> Computers, like the media research we program them with, provide only decision tools, not the decisions. Numbers have implications; they must be thought through. The same numbers can lead to opposite directions. Quantifying information makes it retrievable, retraceable, and open to clear discussion. Qualifying information with our involvement and understanding is what makes a great media plan.[22]

Budgeting

Despite years of talk about better methods of determining how much to spend for advertising, the decision remains largely judgmental. In a study of 260 U.S. companies, the Conference Board identified the following three broad methods used to develop advertising budgets:

> *The task approach*—Marketing objectives are established, for the company or division as a whole, or for individual products, services, or markets. The role advertising is to play in helping to achieve these objectives is spelled out, and the cost of producing this advertising, and disseminating it via media, becomes the tentative advertising budget.
> *Budgeting by fixed guidelines*—A formula is adopted which, when applied to some controlling figure, automatically established the advertising budget. The base figure is, most often, the volume of sales expected, and the formula is either a percentage or a specific amount per unit of sales.

Subjective budgeting—Management decides, largely by judgment and experience, how to divide an available sum between advertising and other activities, such as direct selling efforts, vying for shares of the corporate purse.[23]

The board notes that these methods are not necessarily exclusive; that is, a company may use more than one, but "judgment inevitably plays a part in the ultimate decision."

The Multi-Tier Budget. Robert Rechholtz, a brewery marketing vice president, suggests a multi-tier approach to budgeting. A model is shown in Figure 21-8. Tier I represents a maintenance budget to maintain current levels of advertising awareness. Tiers II and III are add-on budgets to achieve additional growth and market penetration. Rechholtz offers these reasons for his flexible approach:

> No matter how carefully prepared, most advertising budgets will conflict with brand and corporate goals. *The funds necessary to execute an agreed task invariably introduce a shortfall in operating profit objectives.* One of the major reasons is a "time lag response." Advertising funds are spent before the projected sales impact is realized. Management understands this relationship on new brands, but has difficulty with ongoing situations.
>
> An established brand with severe image problems will probably have a longer response rate than a fresh, new idea in town. The result is that management cuts the budget but still holds everybody to original objectives. Or, worse yet, the volume estimate is boosted to restore bottom line. Either way, the primary goals, *growth and profit*, are jeopardized.
>
> There is no sure way to cure the disease. It can be moderated by a multilevel budget system which allocates advertising coverage on several tiers and assigns risk/reward probabilities to each tier application.[24]

Research and Measurement

Most major advertisers make extensive use of research to assist with the planning and development of advertising and the measurement of its performance. Research is used to (1) identify the characteristics of the target market, (2) track brand

FIGURE 21-8. Multi-tier budget. *Source:* Robert A. Rechholtz, *Budgeting for Growth and Profit,* Association of National Advertisers, New York, 1978, p.11.

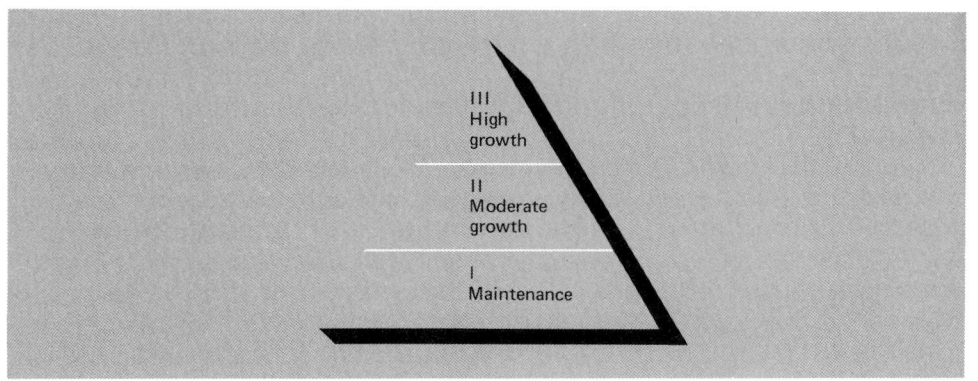

performance over time, and (3) measure the effectiveness of individual advertisements.

Market Characteristics. Facts about the target market for a product are essential if the copywriter is to avoid relying on guesses. The copywriter needs to know the market characteristics developed for the *situation analysis* of the marketing plan, such as size of market, market trends, who buys and why, purchase influencers, market share, attitudes toward brands (ours and competitors), frequency of purchase, and seasonal patterns. These are the kinds of information that are kept up to date by a competent market research department in a company with good planning procedures.

Tracking Performance. Tracking a brand's market standing over time is a good way of measuring the effects of the total market communications effort. Periodic interviews with consumers or industrial buyers can measure changes in brand awareness, brand perference, message retention, and buyer attitudes for both the company's and competitors' brands. This information can help determine whether to increase advertising, switch themes, or change media. For many years General Electric has measured on a quarterly basis ten elements which are combined into a single index of public attitudes toward GE. The index is said to be so sensitive that it will show the effect of a company-sponsored television series.

Testing Advertisements. Advertisements can be pretested and posttested to see how they perform against specified criteria such as gaining attention, creating interest, positioning, recall of brand and message, and attitude change. Called *copy testing*, this type of research is usually done by market or advertising research firms using a variety of research methods.

Pretesting can help in the creation of a new advertisement (testing, for example, the impact of concepts, themes, headlines, etc. with a real or simulated audience). It also helps to predict the performance of one or more proposed ads using some of the criteria listed in the paragraph above. Posttesting reveals how well audiences who were exposed to the ad remember the advertisement or campaign. Since the money has already been spent, posttesting principally helps to decide whether to continue with the basic copy strategy and helps to obtain ideas for developing better advertising in the future.

Copy-testing controversy. Copy testing is the subject of continuing controversy between researchers and creative people. The principal negative argument is that it does not measure effect on sales. The principal positive argument is that it does measure communication's effectiveness which (so the argument goes) should lead to sales. The most heated controversy surrounds "day-after recall measurement" (interviews conducted with television viewers the day after their exposure to a commercial).

An advertising agency creative director says "no research technique in existence can predict the effectiveness of advertising in the real world,"[25] and the Seagram/*Time* study concluded that "recall is a poor indicator of advertising effectiveness."[26] On the other side of the argument, the president of a research firm believes "the fundamental appeal of recall testing is its ability to help . . . sort out the winning television commercial from the losing ones in a real-world situation."[27] Many company and agency top managers with long advertising experience believe that copy research can aid decision making, but should not be used as a substitute for creative judgment.

SALES PROMOTION

The importance of sales promotion can be seen in the estimated $49 billion spent for this purpose in 1980. Sales promotion accounted for 60 percent of the combined expenditures for advertising and sales promotion in that year, having risen from 58.5 percent in 1974.[28] Figure 21-9 compares changes in the proportion of dollars spent by promotional categories between 1978 and 1980. It shows that the rise in total expenditures was caused by increases in consumer promotion, since a decline occurred in the percentages spent for trade promotion and media advertising.*

The reasons for the increased use of consumer promotion were the stagnant economy during this period, the high rates of inflation, and the need for greater incentives to encourage consumer spending. Whether the trend to more sales promotion continues depends in part on consumer purchasing power. Traditionally, advertising is the tool for the long-term brand image building needed to establish and maintain demand, whereas sales promotion is used to supplement advertising by triggering near-term buying action. Therefore, sales promotion increases when consumer spending requires stimulation.

Types of Sales Promotion

Sales promotion is a "catchall" category for all the types of market communications and persuasive devices not included in personal selling, advertising, or publicity. The number and diversity of these devices obscures the significance of the total activity, as does the common accounting practice of charging different items of sales promotion to the sales, advertising, discounts, or allowances accounts. Sales promotion can be classified under the broad headings of trade promotion, consumer and industrial user promotions, and sales force promotions.

*It should be noted that the $49 billion spent for sales promotion includes $7.6 billion in direct mail and $4.3 billion in media advertising for promotions. If these were included under advertising rather than sales promotion, as some compilers do (see Table 21-1), advertising dollars would exceed sales promotion dollars. In any event, there is little doubt that sales promotion has been growing faster than advertising.

FIGURE 21-9. Share of promotional dollars. *Source:* Donnelly Marketing Division of Dun & Bradstreet, shown in *Marketing Communications,* August 1981, p.44.

Calendar years	Media Advertising	Trade promotions	Consumer promotions
1978	43.6%	36.8%	19.6%
1979	40.6%	36.0%	23.4%
1980	40.4%	34.9%	24.7%

Trade Promotion. Trade promotions are particularly important in consumer goods marketing, and are designed to get retailers to stock, display, and otherwise feature the manufacturer's brand. Case allowances (a form of price discount) are used to encourage inventory stocking, point-of-purchase displays, and temporary price deals. Cooperative advertising payments are offered to obtain mentions of the manufacturer's brand in the retailer's local advertising. (Manufacturers' co-op ad budgets may be included in manufacturers' accounting records under either advertising or sales promotion.)

To some extent these allowances represent a cost of doing business in grocery, drug, and mass merchandising channels. The retailers may view allowances as price discounts and not perform the services for which they are offered. When a manufacturer has a missionary sales force, one of its key jobs is to convince the retailers to carry out their obligations with respect to stocking, display, advertising, and passing along special price offers to consumers. Other types of sales promotion to the trade are contests for wholesalers or store managers and "push money" or "PMs" payments to sales clerks, particularly those selling shopping goods, for pushing the manufacturer's brand.

Trade promotion is not as important to manufacturers of industrial goods as it is to consumer goods manufacturers, because retailers are not part of industrial distribution channels. However, manufacturers using industrial wholesale channels may offer stocking allowances to distributors. Also, they may offer PMs to distributor salespeople and run contests for both management and salespeople.

Consumer Promotion. Promotions directed at consumers are designed to get us to buy the manufacturer's brand while we are in the store or when we next go shopping. Promotions include cents-off coupons, price-off label offers, bonus packs, two-for-one offers, multiple packs, free samples, premiums, rebates, contests, and sweepstakes.

Industrial User Promotion. Sales promotions for industrial users may include temporary deals to encourage orders, but more commonly they are devices to create buyer interest, encourage requests for product information, and maintain awareness of the manufacturer's products. Gifts and entertainment are used to build goodwill with buyers and buying influences, although many companies have policies prohibiting their employees from accepting anything that could affect the buyer's objectivity. Gifts of small value—called "advertising specialities"—are given out frequently by industrial marketers; they include pens, letter openers, and calendars imprinted with company logos and slogans. Advertising specialty houses, located in many markets, offer a wide assortment of ideas for giveaways.

Sales Force Promotion. Sales force promotional methods include (1) incentives for the sales force such as contests and honor awards, and (2) selling aids such as catalogs, samples, price lists, and presentation devices (movie or slide projectors and flip charts). Instructional materials for sales meetings in the form of movies and slide films also are classed as sales promotion. Exhibits for trade shows and conventions represent a major sales force promotional expenditure for many companies. The costs involved in renting exhibit space; designing and building exhibits; professional models and demonstrators; and packing and shipping exhibits and products can run into many thousands of dollars for a single trade show.

Problems in Managing Promotion

Sales promotion is thought to be the most poorly managed element of the promotional mix by consumer packaged goods companies. The reasons apear to be lack of top management attention to the subject, diffusion of responsibility, uncoordinated planning, and poor record keeping and budgeting. Whereas advertising decisions are made at the division marketing manager level and above, sales promotion decisions often are delegated to the product manager.[29] The responsibilities for various sales promotion functions typically are divided among the advertising, sales promotion, and sales departments, and product managers.[30] A study of consumer goods companies concluded that sales promotion is poorly classified, accounted for, and planned, with inadequate attention given to budgeting.[31]

Hard Goods and Industrial Goods. Sales promotion appears better managed in those consumer hard goods and industrial goods companies where it is assigned to the advertising and sales promotion department for planning and execution. As described earlier, this department develops coordinated advertising and sales promotion plans for the approval of line management and sees that approved plans are executed.

Another reason that sales promotion fares better in these companies is the compatibility of print advertising and printed promotional materials. Most industrial advertising and much consumer hard goods advertising are carried in print media. Thus the same skills employed in print advertising are employed in print promotion; also, there is interchangeability of art and copy. By contrast, much packaged goods advertising is on television, and there is little duplication of skills and materials used for a television commercial and for print promotion. Furthermore, television remains the glamour medium and attracts more management interest at all levels than does print.

STRATEGIC SALES PROMOTION PLANNING

In most large advertiser companies, advertising planning is a well-developed management function; however, the same cannot be said for sales promotion. While it is generaly recognized that advertising and sales promotion should be complementary parts of broad strategy, in practice they are often planned for, budgeted, and carried out separately.[32]

We will now look at sales promotion planning in terms of goals, strategies, budgets, research, and evaluation. Our discussion will apply mainly to consumer goods (and particularly to packaged goods), since this is where the greatest amount of sales promotion (and advertising) occurs.

Sales Promotion Goals

Product or brand goals for consumer and trade promotions would include:

Consumer
 Increase trial
 Increase consumer inventory
 Encourage repurchase or reuse

Retail Trade
Obtain new distribution
Reduce out-of-stocks
Get prices reduced (i.e., get retailer to pass special case allowance prices on to consumers)
Build displays[33]

Since planning goals should be clearly stated and measurable, the above goals should be more specific. The first consumer goal, for example, might be restated as: "Within the two-month promotion period, increase trial rate for brand X by 20 percent." (*Trial* is defined as a purchase by someone who has not purchased brand X during the previous six months.) The retail display goal might be restated as: "To obtain floor displays of brand X in 75 percent of class A and B stores within the initial two weeks of the promotion period."

Sales Promotion Strategies

A sales promotion strategy might be designed to attain more than one goal. Continuing with the brand X example, the primary goal would be to increase trial by 20 percent while the secondary goal would be to obtain floor displays in 75 percent of class A and B stores. Consumer incentives in the form of coupons, price packs, or free mail-in premiums might be the strategy for achieving the primary goal, while a display allowance might be the strategy for achieving the secondary goal.

Coordination with Marketing Strategy. Sales promotion goals and strategies should always be tied in with the brand marketing strategy. Not only should they supplement the broader plan, but sales promotion itself usually needs help from other promotional functions such as advertising and personal selling.

Let's assume that the marketing goal is to increase unit sales of brand X by a certain percentage during a two-month period and that the sales promotion strategy is as described above. The consumer sales promotion strategy will be more effective if the regular advertising for brand X is increased during the period, if special ads are run announcing the consumer deal, and if inserts are prepared for use by retailers in their local co-op newspaper ads. The trade sales promotion strategy will have to be implemented by the sales force. Not only must the salesforce obtain retailers' permission to build floor displays in exchange for the display allowance, but company sales representatives are the ones who will actually build the displays.

Local Market Strategies. In Chapter 20 we discussed the sales strategy of targeting sales efforts to selected markets. Sales promotion usually plays an important role in implementing this strategy, because strategies and budgets can be tailored to the particular competitive situation in each market. Consumer incentives are needed to get users to switch from their regular brands, and trade incentives are required to obtain retailer support. You will recall how Keebler (described in the introduction to Part Five) used a mix of sales promotion, advertising, selling, and distribution to improve its market share in below-par markets. Keebler's sales promotion strategies included case allowances to get retailers to build their inventories and sampling, direct mail, and coupons to incease consumer trial.

Sales Promotion Budgets

Like advertising budgets, sales promotion budgets are based on a task approach, fixed guidelines (such as a percentage of sales), or subjective management decisions. A fixed guideline appears to be the most common approach. The Strang study concluded that "in most cases the major factor determining the allocation of funds to sales promotion or advertising for an established brand was the level of expenditures in the previous year."[34]

In a survey of ANA member companies, 76 percent report that the product manager is responsible for recommending the sales promotion budget. The remainder assign the responsibility to their promotion, advertising, or sales departments.[35]

The budgeting issue is partly a question of how much to budget and partly one of how to allocate promotional funds between advertising and sales promotion. Although the classic division is 60 percent advertising and 40 percent sales promotion, the ratio in each case can vary considerably, depending on the type of product, market conditions, and management philosophy. We noted earlier that expenditures for sales promotion have been rising faster than those for advertising. One of the reasons is pressure by top management on business managers for short-term results.

Marketing Note 21-4 lists a number of factors that packaged goods companies say influence whether a brand will receive a low or high level of sales promotion support relative to advertising. These offer at least a starting point for planning budget allocations.

MARKETING NOTE 21-4

Factors That Influence the Ratios of Advertising/Sales Promotion Expenditures

Lower levels of promotion relative to advertising are associated with brands that

1. Have profit contribution rate above the company average
2. Have a high level of brand loyalty
3. Have strong competitive differentiation
4. Have a high degree of perceived risk associated with purchase
5. Are in the growth and maturity stages of their life cycle
6. Have a large market share

Higher levels of promotion relative to advertising are associated with brands that

1. Have a profit contribution rate below the company average
2. Have little brand loyalty
3. Have little competitive differentiation
4. Are directed to children
5. Are purchased with little planning
6. Are at the introductory or decline stage of their life cycle
7. Have a marked seasonal sales pattern
8. Have a small market share
9. Face promotion-oriented competitors
10. Are in a market where private labels are important

Source: Roger A. Strang (with contributions by Robert M. Prentice and Alden G. Clayton), *The Relationship Between Advertising and Promotion In Brand Strategy*, Marketing Science Institute, Cambridge, Mass., 1975, p. 13.

More scientific approaches include market testing and modeling. The market testing of different advertising/sales promotion mixes appears to be little used for annual marketing planning purposes, however, even though the testing techniques are well known because of their extensive use in the test marketing of new products. Reluctance to use test marketing for planning purposes is due in part to the short-term goals of sales promotion and the fluid nature of consumer markets. Sales promotion plans may be changed quickly during the year because of competitors' actions. Under these conditions, time-consuming and expensive market tests may be impractical.

The use of models (particularly simulation models) appears to be increasing. The simulation model allows different advertising and sales promotion strategies to be pretested against different competitive responses. These models have gotten mixed reviews, however.[36] Most companies don't use them for planning their sales promotion budgets.

Research and Measurement

Loose management practices appear to carry over into research and measurement of sales promotion. Postevaluation of sales promotion programs "is often done on a rather superficial basis."[37] An indication of the low level of management interest in objective measurement of sales promotion performance is suggested by one survey which found that the market research department usually is not involved in the analysis and evaluation of promotion.[38]

An argument for avoiding the evaluation of sales promotion is that it is difficult (and very expensive) to isolate and measure the effect on sales and profits of one element of promotion. However, we have seen how this valid objection is bypassed in the case of advertising by setting goals that can be readily measured. The same can be done for sales promotion. Turning again to the brand X example, well-established consumer research procedures exist to measure trial. And the number of displays erected can be learned from a simple store count.

According to one consultant, trade promotion also can be measured for profitability:

> Some companies measure the profitability of trade promotions by making gross volume comparisons, some measure promotional effectiveness by changes in market share, and some by the level of retail ads. But in the final analysis, true short-term promotion profitability should only be measured one way—by calculating the difference between what was actually sold versus an estimate of what would have been sold had no promotion been run.
>
> Conceptually the approach to measuring incremental volume is straightforward:
>
> 1. An estimate of normal sales without promotions is calculated. This is called "base business."
> 2. Once the estimate is developed, subtract it from actual volume to get incremental sales.
> 3. Deduct losses in the *pre-* and *post-promoted* periods which must be subtracted to arrive at net incremental volume.
> 4. Once incremental volume is known, it is easy to apply the appropriate profit margins, deduct costs, and arrive at incremental profits.
>
> While this sounds straightforward, it is the calculation of an estimate of sales without promotions which has presented the greatest difficulty for most manufacturers.[39]

Sales promotion appears to offer major improvement opportunities through application of management principles, particularly in the areas of planning, organization, and control. Sales promotion, like advertising, is a creative art form, but this is no reason to forego management. Successful patterns already developed for advertising can be transferred to sales promotion. And in packaged goods companies, it is usually best to manage advertising and sales promotion jointly. At the very least, these two functions should be coordinated by a single executive.

PRODUCT PUBLICITY

Publicity is the fourth and last function of the promotional mix. Except for rare coups, it plays a more limited role than the other functions. "Public relations" is the broad term for all of the activities involved in promoting a favorable image for a company or institution. "Publicity" is a more narrow term. *Product publicity*, for example, relates to building favorable images for products and brands, primarily through coverage by the media in news and special-interest stories.

Advantages and Disadvantages

Product publicity has these advantages: (1) it is free; (2) it is more credible than a paid advertisement; and (3) media reports may be seen by potential buyers or buying influencers who do not see the product's advertising. The disadvantage is that the company has no control over what the editor decides to print or broadcast. Editors are resistant to pressure, and normally will report only what they think will interest their audiences.

A news release must be newsworthy and interesting to be used. Successful public relations practitioners know what the editors of different mediums are likely to consider newsworthy. They are also ingenious at coupling less interesting subjects (your company's new wrench) with pictures of or stories about movie and sports stars, babies, or puppies. **Marketing Note 21-5** offers advice from the editor of a trade magazine on how to prepare news releases that will get printed.

Types of Product Publicity

Here are some of the more common types of product publicity.

News Stories. One of the most effective ways to get publicity for a new or improved product is through stories in media that are likely to be read or seen by potential buyers. A news story normally is taken from a news release issued by the company's public relations office or its public relations consultants. Interested major media will usually seek more information from the source. Unless the subject is of general public interest (such as a breakthrough drug), it is unlikely to be picked up by the general news media. On the other hand, special-interest consumer and trade magazines consider it their responsibility to keep their readers informed of new product developments.

News Mentions and Pictures. To have a branded product mentioned, even incidentally, in a general news story or in a captioned photograph can produce good publicity. Showing astronauts eating certain food products on space flights can help a product's sales.

MARKETING NOTE 21-5

An Editor's Ten Public Relations Commandments

1. Thou shalt always identify individual photographs when submitted so that the recipient does not play "Editor's Bingo" in guessing who's who. Only send photos of people involved, not the person making the announcement. In group shots, indicate individual identifications as "left to right, standing."
2. Thou shalt not fold, staple, crease, or otherwise mutilate photos nor write on the front or back with a heavy hand, thereby damaging the photo.
3. Thou shalt know the publications to whom you send material so that you do not waste your company's money or the editor's time. Don't develop a reputation for sending out worthless material, or your important releases may one day be overlooked and consigned to file 13.
4. Thou shalt always provide needed information such as: the company's name and address (not just the PR or ad agency's name and address), the retail price or cost of the product so that the reader can evaluate its appeal and marketability, etc. Just the facts, no puffery.
5. Thou shalt not send too many releases at one time and then complain that the publication did not select "the most important." If one is most important from a product, marketing, design, or production standpoint, send that separately or identify it properly. It is really best to space out releases, as few publications maintain files to "space out" releases inasmuch as they receive hundreds each week.
6. Thou shalt be brief and provide a summary of the release so that it can be judged quickly (and properly) and written efficiently by someone not an expert in *your* field. Complete information *can* be briefly stated, you know—product description, etc., without reams of company history!
7. Thou shalt not confuse trade magazines with *Playboy*, etc. and use scantily dressed models. Frequently a picture will not be used if the models are too obviously selected to trap the viewer with blatant sex appeal.
8. Thou shalt be careful when placing on photos logotype, model number, etc., so that it can be cropped off without destroying the product image. Providing this information in a corner of the photo may solve your product or brand identification problem if intelligently used. Otherwise, your photo may not be used at all.
9. Thou shalt remember the timing of magazine publishing and not send out releases a week or so before a promotion takes place, expecting it to be used "in time" . . . nor should you ask a publication to run a new product or display item before you are in production and/or your sales organization has told the trade about it in regular personal calls. Thou makest thy customer mad when you spring such surprises.
10. Thou shalt not threaten editors with loss of advertising if they do not run your items . . . or bait them with promises of advertising if they do.

Source: The "Marketing Memo," issued by the editor and publication manager of *Hardware Retailing* magazine, Feb. 21, 1977.

Television Exposure. Getting exposure on television can range from professional sports figures using a branded product, such as a tennis racket, to products and services given away as prizes on a contest show. The exposure may be free, but the costs of endorsement by professional athletes and the cost of the prizes can be substantial.

Case Histories. Interesting stories about older products sometimes can be developed. Documented case histories of successful product applications can be used in press releases, advertising, or promotional literature. And direct mail is an excellent way to make publicity more effective by sending reprints of news stories to selected recipients.[40]

Movies. Even movies can provide excellent exposure for brands, particularly if a movie becomes popular. **Marketing Note 21-6** describes how Hershey Foods spent an estimated $1 million to capitalize on its Reese's Pieces candy used in the highly successful movie *E.T.*

> **MARKETING NOTE 21-6**
>
> **Hershey's Candy Baits an Extra-Terrestrial Being**
>
> If you saw the record-breaking 1982 movie *E.T.*, you may have thought the trail of small candies, laid down by little Elliott to entice E.T. to his home, was made with Mars, Inc.'s M&Ms. Actually they were Reese's Pieces, a product of Hershey Foods. Since the brand wasn't easily recognizable in the movie, Hershey used publicity and sales promotion to take advantage of *E.T.*s tremendous popularity. Actions and results included:
>
> Although not sold in movie theaters before *E.T.*, Reese's Pieces are now carried, and promoted with appropriate "E.T." point-of-sale material, in at least 800 theaters.
>
> Hershey offers "E.T." T-shirts, posters, and stickers, all available with Reese's Pieces proofs-of-purchase.
>
> Stories were carried by *People* magazine, the NBC "Today" show, and major newspapers.
>
> Sales of Reese's Pieces were up 70 percent in the month following the publicity and introduction of the promotions.
>
> Source: Joseph M. Winski, "Hershey Befriends Extra-Terrestrial," *Advertising Age*, July 19, 1982, p. 1.

Tactical Planning for Product Publicity

Product publicity should be included in the annual tactical marketing plan (see examples in Figures 10-3 and 10-4). The publicity plan should include objectives, action programs, budgets, schedules, and work assignments. A contingency budget should be included for unforseen stories or events that might turn up.

While not a substitute for personal selling, advertising, or sales promotion, product publicity can be an excellent supplement when initiated competently on a regular basis. Listing product publicity in the annual marketing plan outline helps ensure that it will not be ignored.

SUMMARY

In a free market it is rare when customers beat a path to the producer's door. Quite the contrary, producers first must inform potential buyers that their brands exist and then get them to try their brands. Even after people buy, producers must continue to remind customers of the benefits of their brands and discourage switching to competitive brands.

Securing and holding customers is the job of promotion. When the product is differentiated with desired attributes, is priced fairly, and is made available where people want to buy or consume it, then promotion can be highly effective at creating sales. But the best promotional program will be ineffective if the rest of the marketing mix is not right.

In Chapters 20 and 21 we have examined the role of promotion in the marketing mix. And we have looked at the roles played by personal selling, advertising, sales promotion, and product publicity in the promotional mix. We learned that personal selling (1) gets products into the channels in the case of products sold through wholesalers and/or retailers and (2) consummates the sale when the product is sold directly to the end consumer or industrial user. We saw how advertising helps to create sales by creating brand awareness, arousing interest, and suggesting action. We also saw how sales promotion covers a multitude of promotional activities and that one of its most important roles is to encourage buyers to purchase the company's brand now or at the time of next purchase. And finally, we noted how product publicity supplements the other three elements of promotion when it results in favorable mentions of a brand in media.

Marketing and Marketing Management

People who have not studied or practiced marketing usually think of it in terms of its promotional aspects, particularly selling and advertising. One of the purposes of this book has been to help you realize that marketing is far more than promotion. You should now be aware that marketing is the key to the entire process of securing and satisfying customers. Carried out well, this process results in profits for a business and the achievement of purpose by a nonprofit institution.

In a free market economy consumers have a variety of choices as to how they will satisfy their needs. Therefore, those institutions that survive are the ones that are most efficient at identifying and fulfilling the needs and wants of consumers and user organizations. In one way or another, every part of a producer's organization serves the organizational purpose of creating and retaining customers. Marketing management is the catalyst for these activities. It identifies market needs and wants, helps marshal the organization's resources to produce desired products or services, and persuades potential customers to buy because its offerings will satisfy them.

As the true role of marketing has become better understood, top managements of business and nonbusiness organizations alike have recognized the need for better marketing managers. It is my hope that some of the best of you who have read this book will be attracted to marketing. For those of you who have the qualifications and interest, marketing management can provide a rewarding career.

QUESTIONS

1. Define advertising, sales promotion, and publicity.
2. Name and explain the elements of the market communications model from source to response.
3. Name three common purposes of product advertising.
4. In the advertising development process, what are the principal roles of the client and the advertising agency?
5. Distinguish between organization patterns and decision-making patterns for advertising in (1) consumer packaged goods companies and (2) consumer hard and industrial goods companies.
6. Differentiate between the copy (or creative) strategy and the media strategy.
7. Give examples of the following types of sales promotion: trade, consumer, and sales force.
8. Why is it important that sales promotion strategy be coordinated with the brand marketing strategy?
9. Name some of the common types of product publicity.

REFERENCES

1. An American Association of Advertising Agencies Educational Foundation Study reported in *Marketing News*, June 27, 1980, p. 1.
2. "Advertiser Spending Picks Up," *Wall Street Journal*, Sept. 10, 1981, p. 1.
3. "100 Leading National Advertisers," *Advertising Age*, Sept. 9, 1982, p. 1.

4. "Advertising Supports Personal Selling at Only Pennies Per Contact," IAP Report No. 7020.4, McGraw-Hill Research, New York (undated).
5. Op. cit., "100 Leading Advertisers."
6. Edward G. Harness, "Some Basic Beliefs About Marketing," an address to the Conference Board, Inc. (undated).
7. Ibid.
8. U.S. Bureau of Census, *Statistical Abstract of the United States*, Washington, D.C., p. 595. Data supplied by *Advertising Age*, (copyright).
9. William M. Weilbacher, *Auditing Productivity, Advertiser-Agency Relationships Can Be Improved*, Association of National Advertisers, New York, 1981, pp. 22 and 24.
10. Victor P. Buell, *Organizing for Marketing/Advertising Success*, Association of National Advertisers, New York, 1982, p. 76.
11. Some of the information in this section is from ibid., Chaps. 3 and 4.
12. Russell H. Colley, *Defining Advertising Goals for Measured Advertising Results*, Association of National Advertisers, New York, 1961, p. 4.
13. Ibid., pp. 77 and 105.
14. R. Reed Saunders, "A Creative Sampler," *Advertising Age*, June 22, 1981, p. 50.
15. Maurice I. Mandell, *Advertising*, 3d ed., Prentice-Hall, Englewood Cliffs, N.J., 1980, p. 139.
16. Shu Ueyana, "The Selling of the Walkman," *Advertising Age*, Mar. 22, 1982, p. M-37.
17. Buell, op. cit., p. 23.
18. Kenneth E. Runyon, *Advertising*, Charles E. Merrill, Columbus, Ohio, 1979, p. 279.
19. Mandell, op. cit., p. 357.
20. "Major Study Details Ads' Effect on Sales," *Advertising Age*, June 21, 1982, p. 1.
21. Runyan, op. cit., p. 295.
22. Madeline Nagel, "Media Diversity Challenges Today's Ad Agencies," *Advertising Age*, Aug. 18, 1980, p. 38.
23. David L. Hurwood, *The Conference Board Record*, April 1968, The Conference Board, Inc., New York, 1968, p. 28.
24. Robert A. Rechholtz, "Budgeting for Growth and Profit," Association of National Advertisers, New York, 1978, p. 11. At the time, Mr. Rechholtz was vice president, marketing, for the Jos. Schiltz Brewing Co..
25. Kenneth Konecnik, "A Creative Sampler," *Advertising Age*, June 22, 1981, p. 50.
26. Op. cit., "Major Study Details Ads' Effect on Sales."
27. David Leach, "A Recall Debate," *Advertising Age*, July 13, 1981, p. 47.
28. Russell D. Bowman, "MC's 2nd Annual Report on Advertising and Promotion Expenditures," *Marketing Communications*, August 1981, p. 43.
29. Buell, op. cit., pp. 53 and 61.
30. William H. Lembeck, "Promotion Management Up-Date '78: Results of A.N.A. Survey," presented to an Association of National Advertisers Workshop, New York, Sept. 28, 1978.
31. Roger A. Strang, "Sales Promotion—Fast Growth, Faulty Management," *Harvard Business Review*, July-August 1976, pp. 115 and 119. Copyright © by the President and Fellows of Harvard College; all rights reserved.
32. Roger A. Strang, *The Relationship Between Advertising and Promotion in Brand Strategy*, Marketing Science Institute, Cambridge, Mass., 1975, p. 9.
33. William H. Lembeck, "Setting Strategies to Meet Objectives," a talk given to the Association of National Advertisers Sales Promotion Management Conference, Glen Cove, N.Y., Feb. 12–14, 1978.
34. Strang, op. cit., p. 23.
35. Lembeck, "Promotion Management Up-Date '78," p. 19.
36. Strang, op. cit., p. 26.
37. Ibid., p. 27.

38. Lembeck, "Promotion Management Up-Date '78," p. 17.
39. Robert G. Brown, "Measuring the True Effects of Promotion on Sales and Profits," presented to an Association of National Advertisers workshop, Miami, Fla., May 5, 1981.
40. John D. O'Connell and J. Robert Chernoff, "Public Relations Aspects of Marketing," in Victor P. Buell (ed.), *Handbook of Modern Marketing*, McGraw-Hill, New York, 1970, p. 13-78.

How consumer research and simulated test marketing can be used to help answer the question of whether to commercialize a new product.

Case 11

Paper Mate

The vice president of marketing for the Paper Mate Division of the Gillette Company, Derek Coward, was considering whether to recommend to top management the commercialization of a revolutionary new pen. He had just read the marketing plan presented by the product manager, David Melley, which proposed that the new pen—code named "Delta"—be introduced to the market. Delta represented a breakthrough in pen technology. It could be the first pen on the market containing truly erasable ink. Earlier pens, claiming erasability, had not sold successfully because the erasure resulted from abrading away the paper rather than removing the ink.

Paper Mate's technological breakthrough had been made several years earlier by Henry Peper of the Gillette R&D Department, who was credited as the author of the Paper Mate erasable ink patent. Mr. Peper described his invention as "a complicated process based on a simple idea." The idea was to combine ink with rubber cement. When erased, the ink adhered to the rubber cement rather than to the paper. Erasure could be made for several hours after writing, but after about 24 hours the ink became permanently absorbed in the paper. Although the combination of a special ink with rubber cement remained the basic technical concept, years of additional research and development had been necessary to bring the pen up to consumer use standards. To force the sticky fluid to flow around the ball point, for example, compressed nitrogen was sealed inside the ink container.

Paper Mate History

In 1955 the Gilette Company acquired the Frawley Pen Company, maker of the Paper Mate brand of ball-point pens; this company formed the nucleus of what was to become the Paper Mate Division of Gillette.

The first commercially produced ball-point pen, developed by Milton Reynolds, had gone on sale at Gimbels' department store in New York City, October 29, 1945. Ten thousand pens were sold that day at $20 each. While the pens did not work too well, the potential advantages of the ball point versus the conventional fountain pen obviously had captured consumer interest. The Frawley Co. had introduced the Paper Mate brand of ball-point pen in 1949. This pen overcame the principal disadvantages of earlier ball-point pens and led to Gillette's interest in acquiring Frawley. Paper Mate's success over the years had come about because of both internally developed innovations and improvements on the innovations of others. With the addition of its Flair porous pen, the Paper Mate Division became the leader of the pen industry in terms of dollar sales. Paper Mate's divisional and division marketing organization charts are presented as Exhibits 11-1 and 11-2.

Paper Mate's parent, the Gillette Company, had net sales of $1.7 billion in 1978 and net profit after tax of $94.6 million. Percent of sales and profit contribution by major lines of business were as follows:

Business	% of Sales	% of Profit Contribution
Blades and razors	33	72
Toiletries and grooming aids	25	13
Braun products (electrical)	24	13
Writing instruments	8	6
Other	10	(4)
	100	100

The Paper Mate Division accounted for sales of $141 million and profit contribution of $12.7 million. Sales growth had been at a faster rate than the industry.

The Writing Instrument Industry*

Total industry unit sales grew modestly from 2.2 to 2.7 billion units (23 percent) between 1972 and 1978. Dollar sales grew considerably faster, however, from $319 million to $582 million (82 percent), as can be seen in

---

*As defined by the Writing Instrument Manufacturers Association, the industry is composed of fountain, ball-point, and porous-tip pens; markers; mechanical pencils; and desk pen sets.

619

EXHIBIT 11-1
Organization of the Paper Mate Division

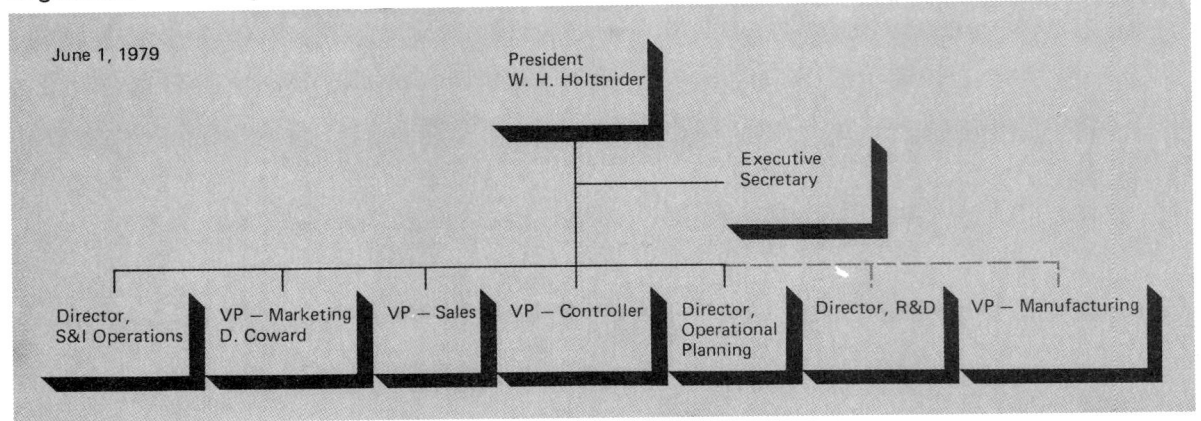

June 1, 1979

- President: W. H. Holtsnider
  - Executive Secretary
  - Director, S&I Operations
  - VP — Marketing: D. Coward
  - VP — Sales
  - VP — Controller
  - Director, Operational Planning
  - Director, R&D
  - VP — Manufacturing

Exhibit 11-3. Industry sales follow an uneven year-to-year pattern. Sales show a close correlation with gross national product. Inflation was partly responsible for the more rapid rise in dollar sales, but a more important reason was a shift in consumer demand toward higher-quality products. Exhibit 11-4 presents the percent change by product type in units and dollars between 1972 and 1978.

Exhibit 11-5 shows the breakdown of industry sales by type in 1978. The leading product is the ball-point pen followed by the porous-point pen. Ball-point and porous-point pens combined accounted for 88 percent of industry unit sales and 67 percent of dollar sales. Exhibit 11-6 shows an industry breakdown of writing instrument sales by channels and market segments.

Imports in 1974 were $23.6 million, but represented something less than 6 percent of the dollar value of domestic sales. Imports, however, were growing at a

EXHIBIT 11-2
Marketing Organization, Paper Mate Division

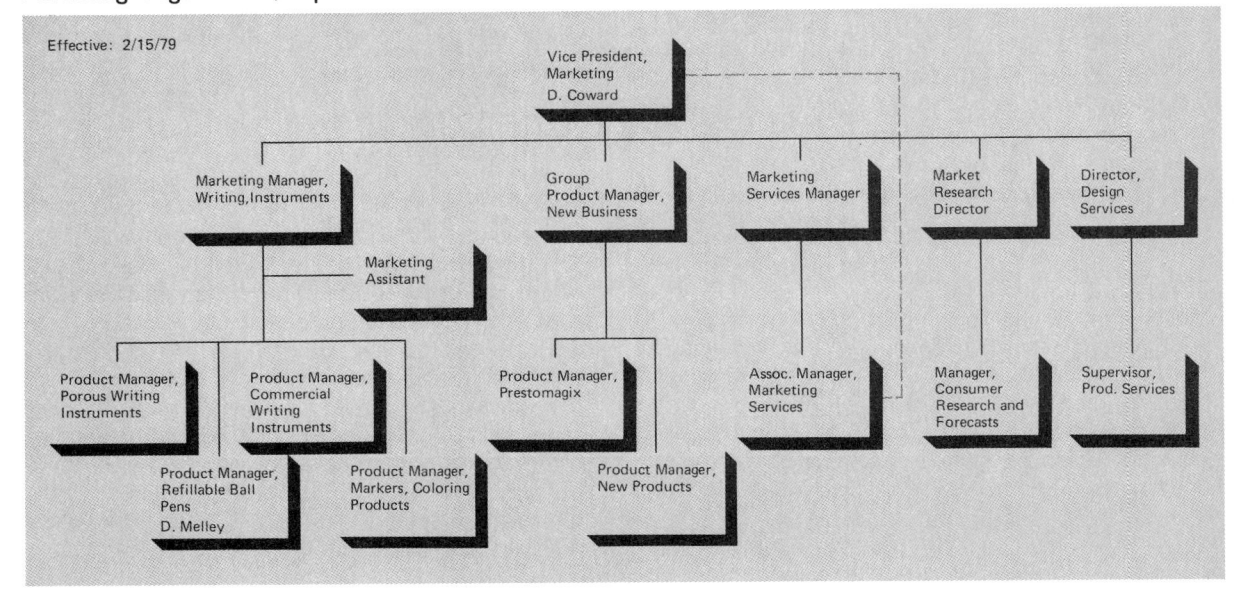

Effective: 2/15/79

- Vice President, Marketing: D. Coward
  - Marketing Manager, Writing Instruments
    - Marketing Assistant
    - Product Manager, Porous Writing Instruments
      - Product Manager, Refillable Ball Pens: D. Melley
    - Product Manager, Commercial Writing Instruments
      - Product Manager, Markers, Coloring Products
  - Group Product Manager, New Business
    - Product Manager, Prestomagix
    - Product Manager, New Products
  - Marketing Services Manager
    - Assoc. Manager, Marketing Services
  - Market Research Director
    - Manager, Consumer Research and Forecasts
  - Director, Design Services
    - Supervisor, Prod. Services

EXHIBIT 11-3
Estimated Writing Industry Instrument Sales, 1972–1978

Year	Millions of Units	% Change	Millions of Dollars	% Change
1972	2,159		319	
1973	2,341	8.4	353	10.7
1974	2,344		370	4.8
1975	2,120	(9.6)	365	(1.4)
1976	2,295	8.3	474	29.9
1977	2,438	6.2	538	13.5
1978	2,742	12.5	582	8.1

Source: Writing Instrument Manufacturers Association, Inc.

faster rate than the domestic industry between 1970 and 1974.*

Writing industry distribution channels are shown in Exhibit 11-7. Nearly half of industry shipments reach domestic consumers through a variety of retail outlets.

EXHIBIT 11-4
Percent Change by Type of Writing Instrument, 1972–1978

	% Change	
	Units	Dollars
Refillable ball point	(1.2)	67.1
Nonrefillable ball point	32.7	43.5
Total ball point pens	16.1	57.8
Total porous pens*	36.1	52.4
Markers	84.0	35.9
Mechanical pencils	17.3	21.9
Fountain pens	(34.7)	60.1
Desk sets	(19.5)	47.9
Total industry	22.7	82.3†

*Not broken out by type in 1972.

†Includes products not available in 1972. When these are excluded, industry sales for the categories shown increased by 59%.

Source: Writing Instrument Manufacturers Association, Inc.

Retailers purchase primarily from the four types of wholesalers shown; larger retailers may also buy direct from manufacturers. Over 30 percent of industry shipments are purchased by business organizations and institutions through channels such as commercial stationery dealers and specialty advertising houses. The latter imprint pens with company names and advertising messages. Approximately a fifth of total shipments go into export channels, and the remaining 5 percent are sold to government and military installations.

Market Shares. Exhibit 11-8 shows estimated market share rankings of leading pen companies in 1978 based on dollar sales at retail prices. The information is reported separately for ball-point and porous-point pens. It should be noted that share data cover retail sales only.

In 1978 five companies accounted for nearly 90 percent of the dollar value of ball-point pens sold at retail. Paper Mate and Bic were tied for first place. Paper Mate led in the medium- and higher-price refillable pen segments while Bic led in the lower-price non-refillable segments. Consequently, Bic was the industry leader in terms of units sold. Six companies accounted for approximately 75 percent of the dollar value of porous-point pens sold at retail. Paper Mate was the clear-cut leader in this pen segment, with Pentel in second place.

New Product Planning at Paper Mate

During the several years that the erasable ink pen, Delta, had been in technical research and development, the Market Research Department of Paper Mate had conducted several consumer research studies to try to measure the market potential for an erasable ink pen. The advantage of being able to make corrections when writing with an ink pen had seemed sufficiently obvious to justify continued investment in R&D in the early years. The question remained, however, whether the idea was powerful enough to create a new and profitable market.

The first consumer use studies confirmed that there was significant consumer interest in erasability, but that the writing quality of the pens tested was not acceptable. After R&D had made improvements in writing quality, Paper Mate continued with market research. Three projects which marketing management felt provided significant information are described briefly: (1) a consumer use test, (2) the B/EST test which provided information on trial and draw, and (3) the

*Source: U.S. General Imports, Schedule A, Commodity by Country. Bureau of the Census, U.S. Department of Commerce. Import data include categories of writing instruments not included in WIMA figures. For this reason imports probably were less than 6 percent if only the WIMA definition is used.

EXHIBIT 11-5
Percent of Industry Sales by Type of Writing Instrument, 1978

Instrument	% of All Units Sold	% of Total Dollar Sales
Refillable ball point	29.3	29.6
Nonrefillable ball point	34.7	16.1
Total ball point pens	64.0	45.7
Porous point writing	19.3	19.3
Porous point coloring	4.8	1.5
Total porous point pens	24.1	20.8
Markers	8.8	7.0
Mechanical pencils	2.6	8.4
Fountain pens	0.3	4.5
Desk pen sets	0.1	1.8
Other	—	11.7
Total	99.9	99.9
Total ball point and porous point pens	88.1	66.4

Source: Writing Instrument Manufacturers Association, Inc.

Yankelovich Laboratory Test which showed whether people would buy the new pen under simulated market conditions.

Consumer Use Test. This test was conducted by Market Facts—New York, Inc., who placed products with families in two national consumer mail samples for extended in-home testing. The samples were balanced with U.S. Census data with respect to geographic region, population density, sex, age (between 12 and 54), household income, number in household, and occupation and education of male head of household.

The Delta pen with eraser was placed in 400 households. A branded ball-point pen (the *control* pen) was placed in a separate but matched sample of 400 households. The control pen was a standard ball-point pen with no eraser. Some of the comparative results are shown in Exhibit 11-9. Respondents were questioned twice—April and June—to see whether there was a difference in response after longer use. For convenience in presentation the results of the two responses have been averaged. While attitudes toward the test pen were generally favorable, potential problem areas were revealed as well.

EXHIBIT 11-6
Percent of Manufacturer Dollar Shipments, 1977 (By channel of distribution*)

Retail	45.6
Export	19.3
Specialty advertising	15.9
Commercial-industrial	14.1
Government	2.9
Military	2.1
Miscellaneous	0.1
	100.0

*"Channel of distribution" is the heading used by the WIMA. Marketing students will recognize that some categories are user markets rather than channels.

Source: Special survey in 1977 for the Writing Instrument Manufacturers Association, Inc.

B/EST Test. This test is designed to give indications of the strength of a new product concept—i.e., will it change people's perception of the marketplace enough to cause them to buy. (A first purchase is called *trial* in marketing idiom.) The test was conducted with panels of 200 consumers in three different shopping malls. The participants were screened to ensure that the panels were balanced with the general population in terms of sex and age and that they were users of ball-point pens. Each panel was shown a display board of eight pens,

EXHIBIT 11-7
Distribution Channels for Writing Instruments

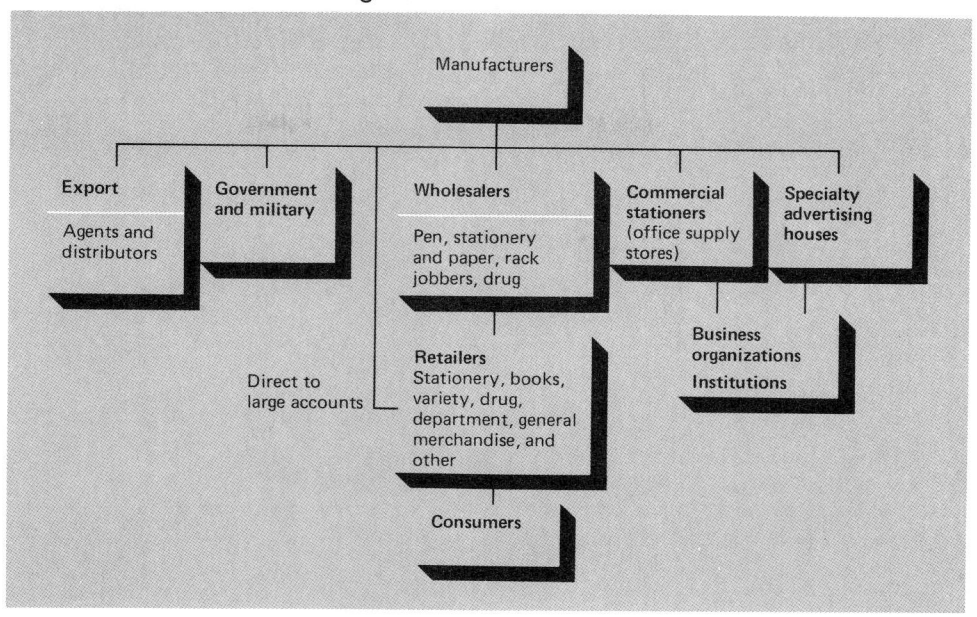

one of which was Delta. The balance consisted of a cross section of well-known brands of ball-point pens of varying prices. For purposes of the test, Delta was named "Ink Manager." It was presented differently to each panel as follows:

Panel A—$ .98 disposable

Panel B—$1.29 disposable

Panel C—$1.29 refillable

Respondents first read a description of each product and then were shown the display board containing the eight pens. Respondents were then given ten tokens

EXHIBIT 11-8
Market Share Rankings—Ball Point and Porous Point Pens at Retail Dollar Value, 1978

Ranking	Ball Point	Porous Point
1	Paper Mate and Bic (tied)	Paper Mate
2	Parker	Pentel
3	Cross	Sanford and Pilot (tied)
4	Sheaffer	Bic
5		Spree

Source: Market Research Department.

each, with instructions to choose the three products they would be most likely to purchase. Each product chosen was assigned a minimum of one token. The remaining seven tokens were to be distributed among the same three products to indicate intensity of purchase interest. The results for "Ink Manager" were as follows:

	Panel A, $.98 Disposable	Panel B, $1.29 Disposable	Panel C, $1.29 Refillable
% of respondents who assigned any tokens to "Ink Manager"	43%	38%	44%
% tokens assigned to "Ink Manager"	15	14	15

"Ink Manager" was the third choice of all panels. In addition to the third-choice ranking and the information on pricing, other findings were reported. Twenty-nine percent of respondents said they were willing to try "Ink Manager." Before exposure to the erasability feature, consumers rated this quality as unimportant, but raised it to important after learning that such a feature was available. The product drew from ball pen, porous pen, and pencil users. Purchasers were more likely to be female than male and more likely to be 40 or older.

EXHIBIT 11-9
Consumer Use Test—Delta versus Control Pen

(a) RATINGS RESULTS

Rating	% of Users	
	Delta	Control Pen
Very good	56	55
Good	39	37
Total	95	92
Fair	4	7
Poor		1
Don't know	1	
	100	100

(b) PREFERENCE COMPARED WITH PREVIOUS PEN USED MOST OFTEN

Preference	% of Users	
	Delta	Control Pen
Prefer test pen	78	62
Prefer previous pen	14	24
No preference	8	14
	100	100

(c) POSITIVE AND NEGATIVE COMMENTS

Qualities Judged—Positive	% of Users Commenting Favorably		Qualites Judged—Negative	% of Users Commenting Negatively	
	Delta	Control Pen		Delta	Control Pen
Erasability	85		Writing quality	50	24
Writing quality	34	76	Physical characteristics	13	20
Physical characterisitics	17	44	Erasability	6	
Writing immediacy and convenience	12	26	Writing immediacy and convenience	4	13

(d) USES OF PENS DURING TESTS

Used for	% of Users	
	Delta	Control Pen
Making lists	90	88
Addressing envelopes, signing cards	69	72
Personal letters	67	68
Short notes or memos at work	62	61
Signing checks, legal documents	59	75
Working with a lot of numbers	58	48
Taking notes at classes, work or meetings	60	45
Writing lengthy reports	33	24
Homework	34	20

Source: Consumer Use Tests conducted by Market Facts–New York, Inc.

Yankelovich Laboratory Test. YLT is a market testing service for new products which attempts to simulate real world market situations. It can be used by a company to determine whether to go to test market or as a partial substitute for test marketing where the company wishes to avoid market exposure of its new product to competition.

The YLT facility had interviewing rooms, a theater, an experimental store, and facilities for interviewing consumers by phone. Participants, drawn from various organizations such as PTAs and churches, visit the facility in groups. In all, 500 men and women aged 15 to 59 participated in the Delta test. Corrective factors were applied by YLT to compensate for demographic imbalances and biases introduced by the experimental technique. For purposes of this test Delta was named "Second Chance." It was presented in an attractive finished design as a refillable pen with an eraser on the top.

After obtaining demographic information on each participant—as well as the name, address, and phone number—the group saw a popular television show with its regular commercials, except that a commercial for the "Second Chance" erasable pen was also included. Following the show the participants were led into the convenience type store and permitted to make purchases using their own money. However, all items were discounted proportionally to encourage buying. The store contained a pen section stocked with a representative sample of brands and included "Second Chance." After having the opportunity to shop, the group was broken into small focus groups for discussions about why the participants purchased what they did and why they rejected other brands. Consumers who bought "Second Chance" were contacted at home later by telephone at 30-day intervals to check for product satisfaction and willingness to repurchase at varying prices. The key results of the YLT were as follows:

1. 38 percent bought "Second Chance."
2. Of the people buying some type of writing instrument, 60 percent bought "Second Chance."
3. On the 30-day call back to purchasers of "Second Chance":
   a. 66 percent were completely satisfied.
   b. The main source of satisfaction was erasability, which had exceeded the expectations of most users.
   c. "Ink smearing/smudging" and "too light a writing line" were the primary performance negatives.
4. The willingness-to-repurchase rate was: after 30 days, 57 percent; after 60 days, 64 percent; and after 90 days, 64 percent.
5. Purchasers confirmed a willingness to pay between $1.50 and $2.00 for the product.*

The Problem

As Derek Coward reviewed the marketing plan for the erasable pen, he was mindful of the high proportion of promising new products that never attain commercial success. He was aware that Delta faced many of the types of risks and tradeoffs characteristic of new product introductions generally. For example:

1. The new product had disadvantages as well as advantages.
2. The favorable results of the consumer sales tests had been obtained under simulated rather than real market conditions.
3. Consumers traditionally are skeptical before trial as to whether a new product will work as claimed.
4. Consumers' purchase habits are not easily broken.
5. Bankers' attitudes toward erasable ink might have an unfavorable effect on consumer purchases.
6. Erasability might prove to be a novelty that would wear off quickly.
7. Erasable pen sales could be expected to draw ("cannibalize") sales from existing Paper Mate products. If it drew from Paper Mate products, however, it should also draw from product sales of Paper Mate's competitors. The question was to what extent in each case.
8. The large commitment of promotional funds that would be required to support the new product introduction could have a disastrous effect on divisional profits if consumer purchases fell much below the sales forecast.

Mr. Coward decided to have one final meeting with his staff to weigh the pros and cons before making his final recommendations to the division president.

QUESTIONS

1. What are the key issues affecting the decision as to whether to commercialize?
2. List and evaluate the pros and cons of commercialization.
3. Should Mr. Coward recommend commercialization of the erasable pen? Support your answer.

*For comparative purposes, the most popular ball-point refillable pens marketed under the Paper Mate brand name at that time ranged in price from $.98 to $1.49.

A marketing plan is needed for a small company with a seemingly good product but poor sales. Marketing mix decisions are required for product, price, distribution, and promotion.

Case 12

The Gril-Kleen Corporation

"Well, where do I begin?" Marshall Hansen wondered as he surveyed the chaos before him. Boxes and bottles were piled all over the place, invoices and order forms cluttered the desk top and filled the drawers, and he couldn't seem to locate anything resembling an orderly set of books. Just a few days earlier Hansen had quit his job with a large management consulting firm to assume the presidency of the Gril-Kleen corporation and help get the young company off the ground.

The company's early efforts to market its innovative product, a liquid restaurant grill cleaner, had been extremely successful. Hansen felt that with a professional marketing approach, the product could capture a sizable share of a national market which he estimated at $60 million annually. The product, a chemical solution which could be applied directly to a working grill and would clean off burnt-on food and accumulated grease in a matter of minutes, represented a significant departure from the existing methods of cleaning restaurant grills. It appeared to have several major advantages over competing products, and initially it had generated such enthusiastic response from users that the product had practically sold itself.

Product Evolution

Gril-Kleen had been developed for their own use by two brothers who owned a small, busy restaurant in Hingham, Mass.. The restaurant's grill needed cleaning several times a day, especially during busy periods, and the brothers were disturbed by the amount of time and effort it took to clean the grill. They were also bothered by the orders they lost while the grill was being cleaned. Most grill-cleaning products then available could not be used on a hot grill, and the time required to cool, clean, and then reheat the grill varied from about 20 minutes to almost an hour, depending on the method being used and the condition of the grill.

Two of the most popular methods of cleaning grills used a carborundum "stone" or a wire mesh "screen" to scrub the grill clean. Though inexpensive, they required a great deal of physical labor, and both products tended to wear, with some danger of stone chips or metal particles ending up in food cooked on the grill. Spray foam oven-cleaner type products, similar to those sold for home use, were easier to use but considerably more expensive. Most had critical effective temperatures of around 160-200° Fahrenheit, compared to normal grill operating temperatures of around 350°, and often had objectionable odors which restricted their use in small or poorly ventilated restaurants.

Dissatisfied with the products then on the market, the two brothers decided to develop their own grill cleaner. They sought the advice of one of their customers in the chemical business, and from him learned of some chemicals which when combined might result in a solution which would give the desired results. They bought small quantities of these chemicals and began to experiment with different combinations in various proportions. The cleaner they were seeking would clean grills quickly, easily, and at normal operating temperature. It had to be economical, easy to mix, have no discernible odor or taste, and would have to pass safety requirements (i.e., be both nontoxic for use on food preparation surfaces and noncaustic to the user's skin). In addition, it had to leave the grill "seasoned" so that food wouldn't stick to the grill after it had been cleaned.

After experimenting and modifying the solution for a couple of years, the brothers finally arrived at a mixture having all the desired properties. It would work on both hot and cold grills, and the grill operator could clean a grill in less than 5 minutes by simply pouring the solution on, allowing it to dry, and then rinsing the grill with water. After a light seasoning with cooking oil, the grill was ready for use again. Soon, friends in the restaurant business heard about the product and began asking for samples, then coming back for more. As demand increased, the brothers started to sell the

---

This case was prepared by Professors Robert D. Hisrich and Michael P. Peters, Boston College.

product by the gallon, charging whatever price they felt the market would bear.

The Gril-Kleen Corporation

The product appeared to be so successful that the brothers began to think about marketing it on a larger scale. One of the restaurant's customers was impressd by the demand for the product, and urged the brothers to consider manufacturing and selling it on a regular basis. In early 1973, the three of them formed the Gril-Kleen Corporation of Hingham, Massachusetts.

Working out of the basement of the restaurant, the three new partners bottled and sold Gril-Kleen in their spare time and on their days off. The chemicals were mixed in a large plastic tub with a spigot, then transferred to gallon-size plastic bottles labeled "Gril-Kleen." On Tuesdays, when the restaurant was closed, the two brothers made sales calls to other restaurants, leaving behind samples of the product. Even with this minimal sales effort, orders began to increase to the point where larger facilities were needed to bottle and store the product. Less than a year after its incorporation, the Gril-Kleen Corporation moved to new and larger headquarters in the Hingham Industrial Park.

The new plant was a 1500-square foot cinderblock building, and the equipment consisted of a large stainless steel tub, formerly used for pasteurizing milk, capable of producing 450 gallons of Gril-Kleen per day. The company hired one part-time employee to mix the chemicals and fill the bottles. After one unfortunate experience with a traveling salesman, who offered to sell the product and instead sold several phony "exclusive distributorships" for Gril-Kleen throughout New England before he disappeared, the company had established relationships with half a dozen bona fide distributors of restaurant and cleaning supplies in New England.

As sales volume grew, the need for a full-time manager became increasingly apparent. Orders and invoices were piling up, billing was haphazard, records were disorganized and incomplete. With no regular system of record keeping, orders often went unfilled, or customers were never billed for orders that had been shipped. Recognizing that the company had grown too large to continue operating on a one-day-per-week basis, the owners hired a local individual to run the company and offered him a 25 percent interest in the business. As it turned out, he devoted little of his time and attention to running the business. After more than a year, with company sales declining, the other three partners bought him out and returned to running the business on their day off.

The Consultant

At this point, Marshall Hansen, a management consultant working on an assignment nearby, began patronizing the restaurant and became friendly with the owners. When he learned of the situation at Gril-Kleen, he suggested that the company hire his consulting firm to do a market study and map out an operating and marketing plan for the company. He also recommended that they utilize his firm's executive search service to find a new president for Gril-Kleen. Reluctant to deal with a large consulting firm or to hire anyone they didn't know to run the company, the brothers asked Hansen if he would take over the job himself.

Hansen, an MBA with extensive experience in marketing, advertising, and industrial management, was intrigued by the idea. He had grown up in a household with a small, family-owned business, and had long been interested in applying his management and marketing skills to running his own company. He agreed to consider the offer, and then began to research the product and its market. From library sources, he estimated the national restaurant cleaning market at about $60 million a year, and learned that no single company held a dominant share of the market.

From experience with the product and interviews with current users of Gril-Kleen, he became convinced of Gril-Kleen's performance superiority over competing products. Moreover, he was impressed by the apparent success of the company despite the lack of good planning, and concluded that the product could be developed successfully. After serious consideration and considerable research, he decided to accept the offer to become the new president of the Gril-Kleen Corporation.

The Situation

When Hansen took over, he found the product being manufactured in the small, one-story cinderblock plant in Hingham. The company's one part-time employee could mix and bottle up to 200 gallons a day to meet orders, and plant capacity could easily be increased by buying a larger mixing tank and hiring more labor. It was also possible to rent additional floor space if necessary.

The product was packaged in one-gallon size plastic containers in cases of four. It sold for $20 a case retail, $12 a case wholesale, F.O.B. the wholesaler's warehouse. Included with each case was a 16-ounce squeeze-type plastic applicator bottle. Sales volume at the time was approximately $20,000 a year. The average usage rate was approximately one case per month.

The company's primary customers were six wholesale distributors in Massachusetts: the Gantlin Company, a supplier of chemicals to restaurants and institutions; the

Downer Company, a paper products distributor; the Bay State Restaurant Equipment and Supply Company; Alden Sales Corporation, which supplies cleaning products to small restaurants; the Janitor Supply Company, selling to hotels and motels; and Theatres, Inc., a distributor of food products and supplies to theaters and drive-ins.

Hansen found few records, little financial data, and no regular flow of paperwork within the company. Prices were based on those charged by a competitive product with no regard for or knowledge of actual costs or profit margins. To apply for a working capital loan, Hansen had to develop a marketing plan and projected cash flow statements over the next 18 months, and then present his marketing plan and cash requirements to a bank.

Marketing Planning

Before he could develop a marketing plan, Hansen had to decide which markets to approach and determine realistic market-share goals for Gril-Kleen.

Additional Product Uses. There was considerable evidence that the product could do much more than just clean restaurant grills. Preliminary tests had indicated that the product was effective in cleaning stainless steel, ceramic tile, formica, vinyl, plastic, chrome, machine tools, clothing, and fiberglass. The last use suggested a possible application in cleaning boat hulls, a market which strongly appealed to the owners of Gril-Kleen. The product also appeared to be effective as a rust remover and preventative, suggesting a wide variety of possible industrial uses.

Hansen had to determine which markets to develop, which product lines to offer, and the degree of market penetration that could be achieved in each market segment before he could set profit targets and schedules. The restaurant, marine, and industrial markets required different selling methods and different channels of distribution and posed different pricing, packaging, promotion, and selling requirements. Before deciding which markets to pursue, Hansen needed additional information on the requirements of each market segment and the dollar and volume potential for each. Within each market, he had to decide whether to segment the market by uses, type of customer, or geographical territory. He wondered whether market testing would be useful in analyzing market need, product potential, and the habit patterns of users in the various markets, and if so, whether market testing should be accomplished by field product testing, field interviews, or mail or telephone surveys.

Hansen felt that Gril-Kleen could significantly increase its share in this market. Current sales of $20,000 a year represented about 0.5 percent of the potential market for restaurant cleaning products in the New England area alone. While the product appeared to fill a particular need in this market, there was considerable competition from similar products in the other markets under consideration (marine, industrial, consumer).

Pricing. To help determine standard costs, break-even volumes over a range of possible product prices, and profit margins, Hansen collected the cost data shown in Exhibit 12-1.

Hansen needed to determine a pricing strategy, set profit targets, determine the volume necessary to meet those targets, and establish a policy on trade discounts, allowances, and credit terms. He also needed further information on price elasticity (one dealer had tripled his sales from four to thirteen cases a month by lowering the retail price from $20 a case to $16). Checking the reorder rates, Hansen calculated the rate of usage of the product to be approximately one case every five weeks in a small, one-grill restaurant. Approximately 97 percent of the end users who had tried Gril-Kleen continued to order it.

Distribution. Among the distribution decisions to be made were whether to (1) hire a sales force, and if so, how large; (2) use manufacturer's representatives, and if so, how many and with what commissions; (3) sell exclusively to wholesalers; (4) sell directly to restaurants and large chain operations; or (5) grant exclusive privileges to any dealers, distributors, or representatives, and if so, what demands to make upon the holders of such exclusive rights in return.

Other decisions related to distribution included questions on consignment sales, volume discounts, and shipping costs. Hansen also had to decide whether to expand his distribution network geographically or to concentrate on getting a larger share of the New England market.

Promotion. To successfully promote the product, Hansen had to detemine which media to employ, how much to spend on advertising, and how to push or pull the product through to the ultimate user. In addition, he had to design some catalog sheets and fact sheets for Gril-Kleen similar to those of other companies shown in Exhibits 12-2 and 12-3. In designing these, he had to decide which product features to stress: price, convenience, effectiveness, safety, etc.

Patent and Trademark. Hansen also wondered whether he should try to patent the product. He didn't know if

EXHIBIT 12-1
Cost Data for Gril-Kleen

MATERIALS:

1 ounce = $.0028
1 batch = 32 cases = 1120 lbs. = $45.32
(83% water)

BOTTLES: (per thousand)

	quantity			
size	1000	5000	10,000	25,000
16 oz.	$ 90	$ 85	$ 78	$ 60.75
32 oz.	155	135	125	97.30
64 oz.	220	195	154.75	147.25
128 oz.*	245	202.75	184.75	178.95

(* = 1 gallon)

CAPS:

28 mm	$ 12			$ 10
33 mm	15			12
38 mm	20			15

PRINTING:

16 oz.	$ 17.50	$ 15	$ 12.50	$ 12.50
32 oz.	20	17.50	15	15
64 oz.	25	20	20	20
128 oz.	25	30	30	30

SPRAYER: (bought separately by customer)

for 28 mm cap	$ .48 ea.	$ .43 ea.	$ .39 each	$ .38 for 15,000 or more

SHIPPING COSTS: $2.00 per hundredweight

APPROXIMATE FIXED COSTS:		LABOR
Rent	$200/month	32 oz. $.046 per bottle
Travel	75/month	128 oz. .057
Telephone	40/month	
Gas	330/month	Sales costs estimated as
Insurance	100/month	400% of labor, G & A
Accounting	100/month	at 250% of labor.
Legal	100/month	
Depreciation	100/month	

it was patentable, if it infringed upon any existing patents, or if he could obtain a trademark on the name "Gril-Kleen" and/or on the product logo he planned to design. He wasn't sure that a patent would be valuable to the company, or even necessary, or whether it was worth all the trouble and expense required for a patent application. Legal costs alone, whether the patent were granted or not, would amount to about $2000 and would afford doubtful protection from imitators. The company would have the right to sue if it discovered anyone else using its formula, but patent litigation would be too time-consuming and expensive for a company of Gril-Kleen's size.

Competition. The most common grill-cleaning products then in use, especially in smaller restaurants, were

EXHIBIT 12-2
Sample Catalog Sheet

TECHNICAL DATA FOR OVEN CLEANER AND DEGREASER

GENERAL DESCRIPTION - DUBOIS OVEN CLEANER and DEGREASER is a light tan alkaline liquid which is highly effective for the removal of baked-on fats, greases and carbon deposits normally found in baking ovens. Also recommended for grills, deep fryers and undersides of range hoods or canopies, where grease and carbon accumulate. OVEN CLEANER is nonflammable and U.S.D.A. acceptable in meat and poultry plants.

PROPERTIES - Chemical Composition . . . . Caustic, soil suspending agents and foam boosting surfactants.
Biodegradable. . . . . Yes, all surfactants.
Caustic. . . . . Present
p II 1% Solution 11.7
Metal Safety . . . . Safe on iron, steel, stainless steel, nickel, porcelain and glass. May be used on enamel and paint (when diluted). It may etch aluminum, and will tarnish copper, brass, zinc, tin and galvanize on long contact.

USING PROCEDURE - Ovens & Equipment - For first time cleaning of heavy carbon and grease, use UNDILUTED. Thereafter, use 1:1 to 1:3 with water.

For best results, use on a warm oven (160° - 200°). Spray on with Trigger Spray Unit, direct from gallon bottle of solution. Foaming action allows product to cling to walls and top side of oven: thus, cleaner works harder. Allow cleaner to penetrate for five minutes. For heavy carbon, use oven brush, or Scotch Bright brand applicator on a handle. Rinse with wet sponge, to remove all grease and carbon residue. Can be applied with good results on cold oven when cleaner is allowed to set 15 to 20 minutes.

Heavily encrusted ovens may require a second application. One application will be adequate for periodically cleaned ovens.

Grills - use 1:1 to 1:3 with water
Hoods - use 1:4 with water
Fryers - use 1:15 with water
Steak Platter - use 1:1 with water

PACKAGING - 4- 1 gal. plastic bottles per case 35# net weight
6 gal. cans 53# net weight
30 gal. drums 264# net weight

CAUTION - ALKALINE. Do not take internally. Do not get in eyes or on skin. In case of contact, flush skin with plenty of water; for eyes, flush with plenty of water for at least 15 minutes and get medical attention. If swallowed drink a large quantity of water, followed by whites of eggs or mineral oil, and call physician.

DUBOIS CHEMICALS DIVISION   W.R. GRACE & COMPANY

DuBois Technical Representatives are located throughout the U.S., Canada, the United Kingdom, Latin America, Germany, France, Japan and Africa.

---

the "stone" and the "screen." The stone is a block of carborundum (hard soapstone) about the size of a brick, which was used to scrub the grill and remove grease and food residue. The screen was a wire mesh screen placed in a device similar to a sandpaper holder which was used to scour the grill much like home scouring pads. Both were inexpensive, but required a great deal of effort to use, took about an hour to clean a fairly dirty grill, and could not be used on a hot grill. Also, the stone tended to wear and chip, with some danger that stone chips might end up in food cooked on the grill.

There were also several chemical liquid and spray foam oven-cleaner-type products on the market that could be used to clean grills. Most of these were fairly expensive and had critical effective temperatures of around 160-200°F. These competitive products were generally marketed by fairly large companies with large advertising budgets and wide distribution networks. Among these were Swell, DuBois, Easy-Off, and Jifoam. Colgate-Palmolive and Lever Brothers also had plans to introduce new chemical oven cleaner products.

DuBois liquid oven cleaner (see Exhibit 12-2) was sold in 4-gallon cases for $21.80 a case retail, and the company employed its own sales force to sell directly to retailers. Swell was marketed via wholesale distributors for $5.00 a gallon or $18.75 a case retail, and the company used its own sales force to sell to wholesalers.

EXHIBIT 12-3
Sample Fact Sheet

FANTASTIK BOAT CLEANER
MARINE WHOLESALE FACT SHEET

Product: Fantastik Boat Cleaner
Manufacturer: Texize Chemicals, Inc. P.O. Box 368, Greenville, S.C. 29602

Packs:	32 oz. Spray Gun		64 oz. Refill
Code	#298		#299
Case Pack	12		6
Case Weight	31 lbs.		30 lbs.
Unit Retail:	2.59		3.29
Case Retail:	31.08		19.74
Wholesale Discount:		50%-10%	
Wholesale Cost:	13.99		8.88
Terms:		2% 10 Days	
		Net 30 Days	
		Prox.	

Wholesale Introductory Offer:
  Texize offers one case free with each five cases purchased on all orders
  Offer Dates: January 20, 1969 - May 30, 1969
  Billing: Free goods to be invoiced at no charge

Salesman Incentive Offer:
  Texize to pay $1.00 per case to salesman for each case sold to retail outlets.
  Offer Period: February 3, 1969 - June 27, 1969
  Payment: Payment to be made on a count and recount basis by Texize representative. Monies to be paid directly to individual salesman at the close of each month.

Wholesale Exclusive:
  Fantastik Boat Cleaner will be offered for sale only through bona fide wholesale distributors.

Sales Guarantee:
  Texize guarantees the sale of this product when adequately displayed at retail sales point.

Advertising:
  Fantastik Boat Cleaner will be advertised throughout 1969 with full and half-page spreads in the following publications: Boating, Motor Boating, Rudder, Yachting, Lakeland Boating, Boat Buyers Guide, Boating Industry, Marine Products, Marine Merchandising.
  (Plus: The bonus of a multi-million dollar Campaign that is making the Fantastik name a household by-word.)

Shipping Points: Texize plant or Warehouse
Product Liability Insurance: Yes

Developing a Marketing Plan. To develop a sound marketing plan, it was necessary to determine the size of the potential market in units and dollars, estimate the market share that Gril-Kleen could expect to attain, and then develop sales projections over an 18-month period.

Hansen needed to find out who and where the distributors of restaurant cleaning products in New England were, and determine the best means of selling to them. He had to calculate potential sales volumes at various prices, and price the product to maximize profits (or volume). He would need to construct volume discount schedules and determine the effects of any increase or decrease in price on demand and on profits. Hansen would have to consider whether any market or product testing was necessary, and if so, what type and how much.

These decisions would form the basis for Gril-Kleen's marketing plan, from which Warren Hansen could develop projected cash flow statements and estimate working capital needs over the next 18 months.

EXHIBIT 12-4

PROBLEM

Develop a marketing plan for Gril-Kleen including recommendations for product (e.g., packaging, patent, and trademark), pricing, distribution, and promotion. State your own assumptions with respect to such things as geographic area to be covered, market potential, distribution channels to be used, competition, and elasticity of demand.

New distribution channel strategies, proposed to meet shifts in consumer buying patterns, lead to changes in product, pricing, and sales strategies.

Case 13

Black & Decker Manufacturing Co., Consumer Power Tool Division

The management of Black & Decker's Consumer Power Tool Division was concerned about market developments that had begun to affect its financial results. During the previous decade sales had risen from $13 million to $113 million and each year's profits had exceeded those of the year before. Estimated market share measured by units sold at retail had grown to over 50 percent. The division's manufacturing plants, in spite of continuous expansion, could not keep up with demand.

But the situation changed abruptly in 1975. Division sales dropped 21 percent from the prior year. Profitability was significantly lower even after severe cost-cutting measures had been taken. Market share had fallen by four points. The effects of these developments on the total company financial performance are reflected in Exhibit 13-1.

Background

The Black & Decker Manufacturing Company was formed in Baltimore* in 1910 by Duncan Black and Alonzo G. Decker to make several types of machinery. The company introduced its first portable electric drill in 1916. This was a ½-inch drill with universal motor and a patented pistol grip and trigger switch—innovations which are standard on electric power tools today. In 1946 Black & Decker introduced the world's first line of popularly priced drills and accessories for the home and do-it-yourself market. Today the company is the world leader in the power tool industry. It produces and sells professional products for industrial, construction, and automotive markets as well as products designed for the consumer.

Black & Decker expanded into Canada in 1922 and England in 1928. Today it operates in most countries of the free world. Combined sales and earnings from international operations exceed those of the U.S. company. Organizationally the company is divided into three geographic areas as shown in Exhibit 13-2—U.S., Pacific, and European. The Consumer Power Tool Division with which this case is concerned is located in the Consumer Products Group which is a part of the U.S. company. An organization chart showing the Consumer Products Group and Consumer Power Tool Division is shown in Exhibit 13-3.

The U.S. Consumer Power Tool Division

The Power Tool Division's basic product line consisted of portable hand-held electric power tools: drills, jig saws, circular saws, and finishing sanders. These basic

EXHIBIT 13-1

Black & Decker Financial Performance, 1965–1975 (For total company)

Year	Sales, $millions	Net Earnings $millions	% ROI	Net Earnings per Share, ¢
1965	121.5	11.0	18.1	32.7
1966	146.8	13.0	19.2	38.4
1967	168.6	14.3	19.0	42.0
1968	189.7	15.4*	18.4*	42.4
1969	221.8	17.6	19.0	51.5
1970	255.4	19.5	18.4	55.8
1971	286.9	22.0	16.3	61.0
1972	345.7	26.6	15.7	71.5
1973	427.0	33.3	17.0†	86.7
1974	642.0	44.6	15.6	110.0
1975	654.0	35.4	10.7	85.0

*Before extraordinary charge of $850,000 from devaluation of foreign currencies—2.5¢ per share.

†Based on stockholders' equity before October 1, 1973, purchase of McCulloch Corporation.

*Company headquarters are now located in Towson, Md..

633

EXHIBIT 13-2
Black & Decker Organization Chart Showing the Breakout of the U.S. Company, June 1979

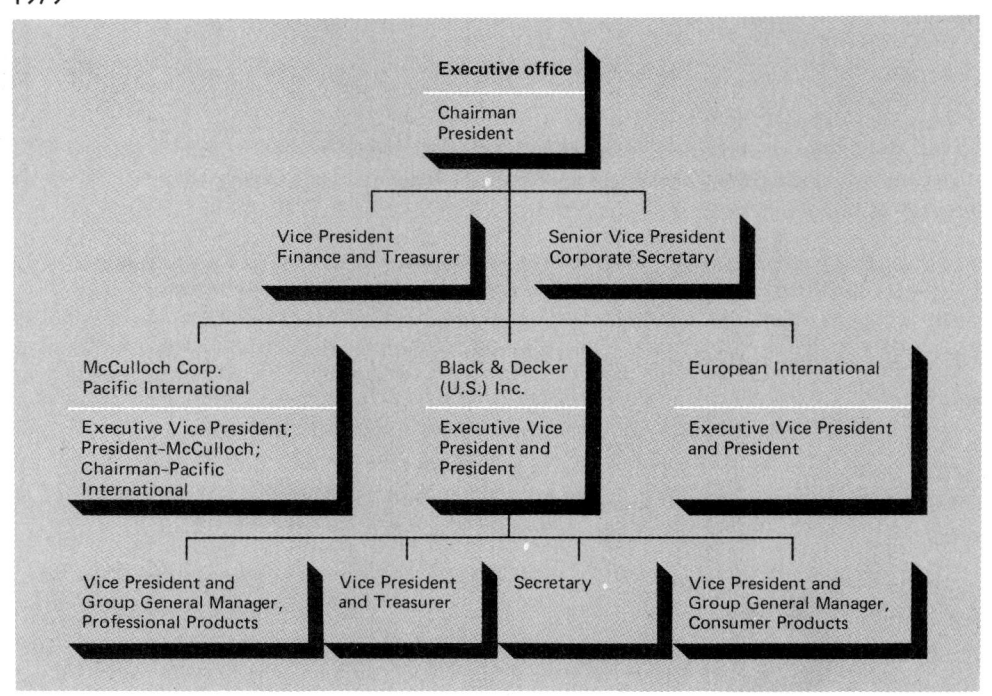

product lines varied by size, power, and other features, as well as by price.

While stressing quality, the division also is the industry price leader among advertised brands. The company is proud that its basic tools are better and sell for less than when they were first introduced. Black & Decker has made extensive use of the "learning (or experience) curve" concept in which unit costs of new products decline as unit production goes up and experience increases. Competitively low prices, along with heavy market promotion, produce the high unit sales which permit mass production. In addition to the cost benefits derived from volume production, cost reductions result also from continuing value analysis,* improved production processes, and plant modernization. Although employing a modest sales force of about 57 salespersons and supervisors—which concentrated almost exclusively on wholesale and major national accounts—Black & Decker products had achieved intensive distribution, particularly through hardware retail outlets. Hard-hitting price-oriented TV commercials were supplemented by local co-op advertising and retail promotions. Products were fair trade priced, where fair trade laws applied, which enabled company control over retail prices and margins and permitted the featuring of prices in national advertising that would be the same as prices presented in the local co-op ads.

Competitive Situation

Exhibit 13-4 shows the approximate unit shares at retail of Black & Decker and its principal competitors for the years 1973-1975.† Black & Decker's unit share had dropped in 1975, as had Sears'.

Rockwell International, a large, well-financed con-

---

*Value analysis at Black & Decker is an orgainzed team study of product and cost relationships. Groups consisting of representatives from engineering, manufacturing, and purchasing, with support from marketing, evaluate the company's products in great detail to identify cost reduction possibilities—or to hold cost and maintain quality while providing additional functions (consumer benefits). The company also encourages its suppliers to contribute their specialized knowledge to these efforts.

†Black & Decker held lower market shares when measured by dollar balue because its average factory and retail prices were significantly lower than the industry average.

EXHIBIT 13-3

U.S. Consumer Products Group, Showing Organization of the Consumer Power Tool Division, August 1979

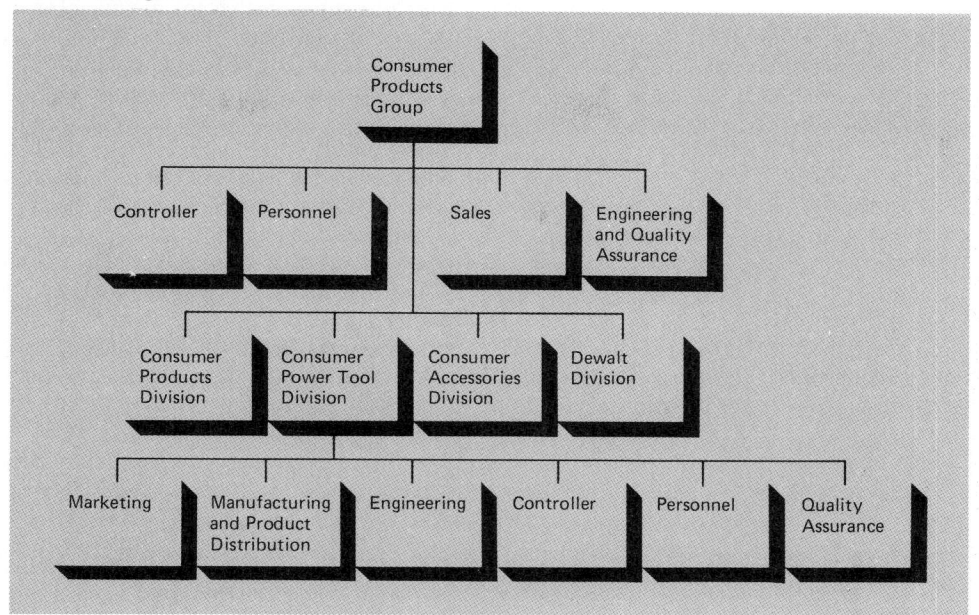

```
                        Consumer
                        Products
                         Group
        ┌───────────┬──────┴──────┬────────────┐
    Controller   Personnel      Sales      Engineering
                                           and Quality
                                            Assurance
        ┌───────────┬─────────────┬────────────┐
    Consumer     Consumer      Consumer     Dewalt
    Products    Power Tool    Accessories   Division
    Division     Division      Division
        ┌──────────┬──────────┬──────────┬──────────┬──────────┐
   Marketing  Manufacturing Engineering Controller Personnel  Quality
              and Product                                    Assurance
              Distribution
```

glomerate, had purchased Porter-Cable a few years before, a relatively small power tool manufacturer. Rockwell had just introduced a new line of low-priced power tools that competed head-on with the division's basic product line. It had also begun a major, well-financed marketing program aimed at Black & Decker's traditional hardware channels.

Black & Decker's sales force had little time for retail calls. Both Rockwell and Skil were expanding their sales forces and spending increasing amounts of time calling on retailers. These and other competitors were also outdistancing Black & Decker with new product innovations—relatively low priced tools such as bench grinders, belt sanders, and disc sander/polishers.

Sears Roebuck & Co., with a well-designed line of power tools manufactured by Singer & Co. on tooling owned by Sears, had become more aggressive with national TV and print advertising campaigns and major price reductions on key power tools, often as much as 50 percent off list price. There was also evidence that two major Japanese manufacturers—Makita and Hitachi—were planning to enter the U.S. power tool market.

The Changing Market

There was a feeling among Power Tool Division executives that the consumer power tool market was maturing and might already have peaked. Sixty-four percent of all U.S. households in 1975 owned a portable electric drill and 70 percent had at least one portable electric power tool of some type.

The Marketing Research Department had confirmed a significant change in the nature of the market. Most purchases were no longer the first purchase of a power tool, but were either a replacement purchase or the purchase of an additional power tool of the same type. The majority of these purchases were of the step-up variety—products offering extra features, higher power,

EXHIBIT 13-4

Estimated U.S. Consumer Power Tool Industry Market Shares (Core products—drills, saws, sanders)

	% of Units Sold at Retail		
Brand	1973	1974	1975
Black & Decker	50	54	50
Sears	20	22	20
Skil	10	8	10
Rockwell	2	4	5
All other	18	12	15
Total	100	100	100

and performance than offered by many products in the division's line. The market was moving rapidly away from basic products such as the single-speed ¼-inch drill upon which Black & Decker had built its consumer franchise toward step-up products such as the ⅜-inch variable-speed reversing drill.

Distribution and Pricing

Of all the problems facing the division, the most pressing were distribution and pricing. These two elements of the marketing mix were closely interrelated. Distribution channels had become fragmented and confusing. A simplified diagram of power tool industry channels is shown in Exhibit 13-5.

The Changing Hardware Wholesaler and Retailer. Since the end of World War II when the company entered the consumer portable power tool business, distribution had concentrated on traditional hardware channels, namely, the independent hardware wholesaler who distributed to the independent hardware retailer. Other competing channels had developed during the intervening years, which had caused independent hardware wholesalers and dealers to form alliances for combating the new competitors. These took the form of voluntary dealer chains (co-op) and alliances of wholesalers whose combined purchasing power placed leverage on suppliers for quantity price discounts and promotional funds. By 1975 more than half of all independent hardware and lumber/building material stores were affiliated with one of these groups.

Cotter & Company of Chicago was the largest of the *voluntary chains*, with about 5300 dealer members. Cotter operated as a national wholesaler and stocked both its own private True Value brand and selected manufacturers' brands. *Merchandising groups* were alliances of hardware wholesalers with voluntary dealer members. They included about 140 of the approximately 370 primary hardware wholesalers in the United States. The largest of these groups was Sentry Hardware Corp.

EXHIBIT 13-5
Distribution Channels, Consumer Power Tool Industry

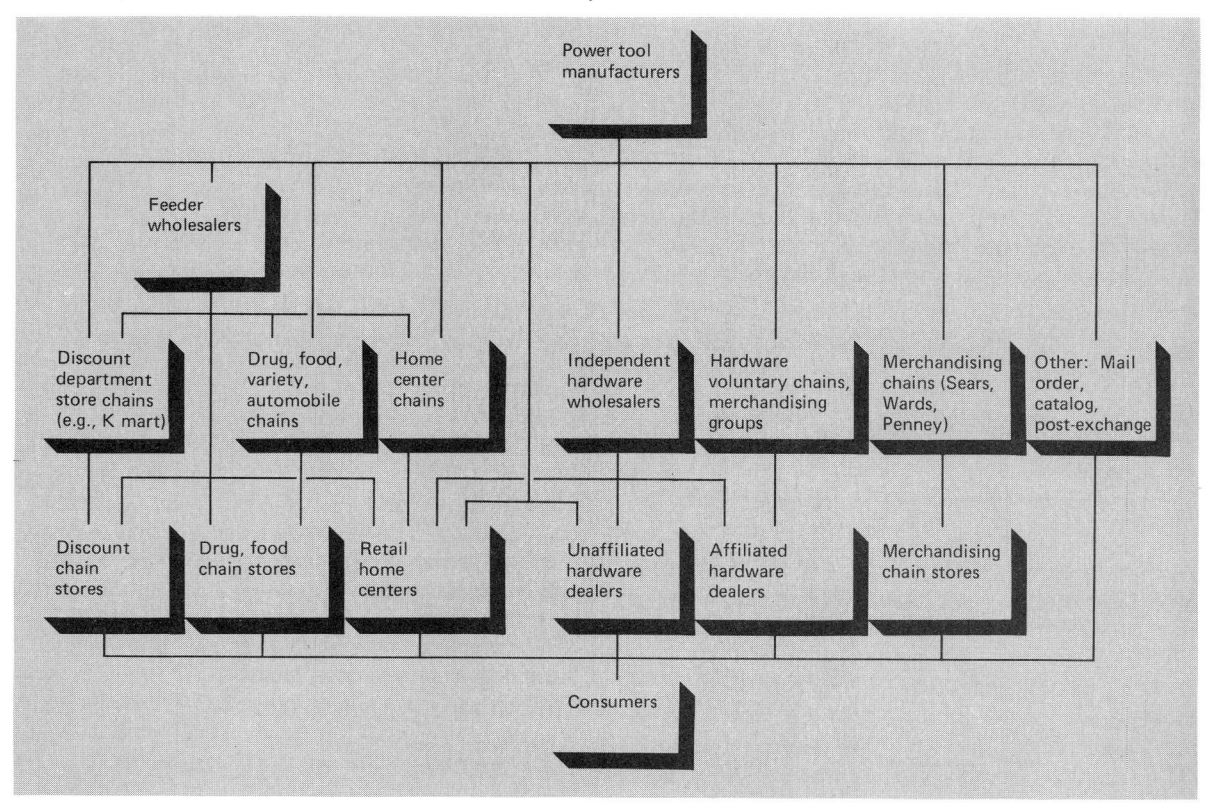

of Cleveland, with eleven affiliated wholesalers and approximately 4500 affiliated stores.

It was important to a national manufacturer to have its brands carried by the voluntary chains and merchandising groups because of their combined market power. At the same time, dealer members of these groups could and did buy from independent wholesalers not affiliated with a voluntary chain or merchandising group. Consequently, manufacturers could not ignore the need for distribution through unaffiliated wholesalers.

Another distribution channel development had been the *home center*. The home center was considerably larger than the typical hardware store. In addition to hardware it carried building supplies (lumber), home furnishings, and landscaping materials. The home center was set up primarily to serve the consumer rather than the building tradesperson. Regional home center chains had developed, and these chains were pressuring suppliers to sell to them at wholesale prices.

Major Chains. The Sears Roebuck, Montgomery Ward, and J. C. Penney chains accounted for a significant portion of national portable electric tool sales, although only Montgomery Ward and Penney carried any manufacturers' advertised brands in addition to their own private label brands. Black & Decker was not sold in the stores of these three chains.

Discount Department Store Chains.* These chains (the largest of which was K mart) had become important outlets for hardware items, including electric portable tools. In contrast to the typical hardware store, which carried complete product line inventories and sold at normal markups, the typical discount chain preferred to carry a manufacturer's best-selling items (called "cherry-picking" the line) and promote them at discounted prices. A national chain's feature promotion of a manufacturer's brand would often result in the sale of tremendous quantities of product.

Discount chains purchased some of their supplies direct from manufacturers and distributed them through the chains' warehouses. To supply the balance, *feeder wholesalers* had appeared on the scene. These wholesalers provided limited services and sold at a small markup, not only to discount chains, but to home center chains and large, merchandising hardware stores as well.

Other Channels. Catalog showrooms, military post exchanges, and even some drug, food, and variety chains distributed portable electric power tools.

Shift in Sales By Channel. For some time, mass merchandising chains had been taking a rising share of the consumer power tool market while hardware and other types of retailers were faced with falling shares. The trend is illustrated by comparing shares for the years 1972 and 1976:

Type of Retailers	% Share 1972	% Share 1976
Mass merchandising chains, e.g., Sears, Penney, K mart	56	62
Hardware, home center, and building supply	26	24
Other, e.g., catalog, mail order, P-X, miscellaneous retail chains	18	14
	100	100

Seventy-one percent of Black & Decker's consumer power tool sales in 1976 were being made through hardware wholesalers while only 29 percent went through the other channels. The primary accounts of these hardware distributors were the hardware, home center, and building supply dealers who accounted for 24 percent of all consumer power tool sales at retail. Consequently, the major share of the company's consumer power tool sales were going through a secondary and declining channel.

Divisional Distribution and Pricing Policies

The Power Tool Division's distribution and trade pricing policies had been established originally to serve the traditional (relatively small) independent hardware distributor and retailer. Quantity prices were offered only for "master packs," usually consisting of five units. By 1975, however, the division used two basic price sheets: the *wholesaler price list* and the *commercial-distributor price list*. The so-called commercial-distributor price list was primarily for major retail chains. It listed prices at 5 percent higher than the wholesaler price list because those on the commercial-distributor price list were classed as retailers. The wholesaler price (in master packs of five) for a no. 7004 ¼-inch drill, for example, was $9.45 each while the commercial distributor price was $9.95 each.

Terms of sale for both types of accounts were as follows:

---

*Often referred to as "mass merchandisers." The distinction is not always clear, since not all mass merchandisers (including Sears, Montgomery Ward, and Penney) consider themselves discounters.

1. Payment: 2% 10 prox., net 25th prox.*
2. Minimum order size: $50.00.
3. Orders for $1000 or more shipped freight paid.
4. Co-op advertising: 100 percent of approved advertising by retailers up to 3 percent of estimated purchases during the period.
5. Dating terms: Orders for $10,000 or more for shipment during the first two months of each program period (January-February and July-August) receive extended terms of 2 percent on June 10 and 2 percent on December 10, respectively.

The traditional distinction between retailers (particularly chain stores) and wholesalers was blurred, and it had become increasingly difficult to decide which of the price sheets to use for any given account. The dealer-owned co-ops and discount department store chains were replacing the traditional local and regional hardware wholesalers as the division's major customers. The co-ops and discount chains, although technically retailers, were performing many of the same functions as traditional hardware wholesalers, such as order processing, warehousing, distribution to retail stores, credit, and collection. Many of these types of accounts were pressuring to be sold at the wholesale list prices, but there were legal questions posed by these requests. The Robinson-Patman Act, for example, requires that the same classes of accounts be treated equally. The question was when are accounts essentially the same?

Compounding the trade pricing problem was the recent repeal of the federal fair trade laws. Without resale price maintenance, the traditional hardware wholesalers and retailers were finding it more difficult to compete with discounters selling the Black & Decker line. Consequently, Black & Decker was rapidly losing promotional support at the retail hardware store level.

A further problem for the division was that Black & Decker products were not well represented in regional shopping malls, which were accounting for a growing proportion of retail sales. The reasons were that (1) hardware stores usually were not located in shopping malls and (2) Black & Decker was not carried by many of the major department store and discount chains that normally were the primary retail outlets in these malls.

Physical Distribution. In the early 1960s the division had established six geographically decentralized distribution centers. Base warehouses at its four manufacturing plants fed finished product to the distribution centers which in turn distributed to wholesale accounts. This system provided rapid delivery service to hardware wholesalers at a time when rail transportation was the lowest-cost—though not the fastest—means of moving product around the country.

In the interim the trucking industry had become the major means of transport for finished goods. Truckloads could be delivered directly from the factories to major wholesaler and chain warehouses within acceptable time limits and at a lower cost than the decentralized distribution center system. While the distribution center served the smaller, local wholesaler well, it served the large buyer at a cost disadvantage to the division.

Management's Problem

In essence Black & Decker's power tool business had grown so successfully over the years that there had been little time for major strategy reviews. Although division executives were aware of the market changes going on, they had been dealt with largely by expedient modifications to existing policies rather than by new policies and strategies.

The falloff in sales and profits in 1975 had provided the incentive to take a hard look at the causes of the poor performance. One of the immediate reasons for the decline was the business recession brought on by the OPEC cartel's tripling of oil prices. Of deeper concern, however, was the decline in market share which appeared to be the result of external market factors—consumer interest in step-up products, changes in the places of consumer purchase, the effect on pricing of the demise of fair trade, and competitors moving to take advantage of Black & Decker's weaknesses.

Despite its problems, management did not feel the need to "press the panic button." Black & Decker remained the world's largest and most efficient manufacturer of portable electric tools, having made over the years extensive commitments to modern plants, automated equipment, cost-effective design and engineering, and favorable purchases of raw materials based on volume purchasing power. Its brand name was the best known and its products had the highest consumer preference ratings in the industry.

Product Line Changes. During 1975 the division already had taken an important step to help the traditional hardware channel battle the discount chains. A new *value line* of orange-colored, step-up power tools was introduced to hardware wholesalers and retailers. These

---

*"Prox."—an abbreviation for proximo. Terms are 2 percent discount if payment is made by the tenth day of the following month; net (not discounted) payment is required not later than the twenty-fifth day of the following month.

were different and better tools with higher prices and better margins for the trade. The value line would permit the hardware dealer to sell up and thereby avoid head-to-head price competition with discounters. The regular (green) power tool line, however, would continue to be available to any retailer that wished to feature price.

A longer-range product strategy under consideration was to offer several lines ranging from the lowest competitive price levels to the highest price and quality levels. The intent would be for the division to serve all major consumer power tool market segments using all principal channels. In this way, hardware channels and chain store channels would be able to offer tools of the quality and price preferred by their own particular clientele.

Distribution Problems and Possible Solutions

Going on the assumption that the product strategy decision would be made, division executives believed that the remaining problems were in the areas of distribution and sales policy. These included questions of which accounts could qualify for distributor prices, what the quantity discount structure and terms should be, whether the field distribution centers should be continued, and whether a special sales force should be formed to give support to retailers.

A team of executives appointed to study these problems recommended the following plan:

1. Establish a minimum order size of $1000.
2. Sell off of a single price list to any account (wholesale or retail) that can meet the minimum order test. The net effect of 1 and 2 would be that a retailer ordering in smaller than the minimum order size would order from a wholesaler or chain warehouse.
3. Provide incentives for accounts to order in larger quantities by offering quantity discounts. The plan suggested three price levels: (1) master pack, five units; (2) pallet load, 2 percent off the master pack prices; and (3) truckload, 5 percent off the master pack price. Under this plan the no. 7004 ¼-inch drill might be priced as follows:

Master Pack, 5 Units	Pallet Quantity	Truckload
$6.83	$6.69	$6.49

4. Revise payment terms to encourage larger orders and earlier payment. For example:
4% 10th prox.
2% 10th prox. + 60 days
Net 25th prox. + 60 days

Early shipment discount of 3 percent for shipments of orders in excess of $15,000 during the first two months of the semiannual special program periods.
5. Eliminate dating terms.
6. Eliminate any reference to "suggested retail prices" from all literature, price sheets, and advertising.
7. Vary the co-op advertising incentives according to the lines the division wishes to push, ranging from nothing on the lowest price lines to 75/25 (75 percent paid for by B&D, 25 percent paid for by the retailer) up to 4 percent of estimated purchases for a designated period.
8. Close the field distribution centers except for those serving the western states.
9. Establish a retail sales force to perform missionary sales functions with retailers.

Management Reactions

Division management had reviewed the study team's recommendations. While it could see advantages to the plan, it also had certain misgivings. The plan, for example, was thought to be legally sound and had the virtue of substituting one price list and a minimum size order for the present dual price lists with the resulting confusion over which accounts were to use which list. Yet this plan would seem to favor those larger accounts able to purchase the minimum $1000 order and qualify for quantity discounts.

The savings from closing the distribution centers could be used to offset the quantity discounts, to lower product prices, and/or for better promotional deals. However, it also would make for poorer delivery service to smaller wholesale accounts not able, or unwilling, to order in pallet size or truckload quantities.

The plans would seem to open the way for the division to deal successfully with dealer co-ops and discount chains. But it might downgrade Black & Decker's position with its traditional hardware retail accounts. The proposed new retail sales force could help offset dealer dissatisfaction by assisting with Black & Decker promotions that would be profitable for the dealer. And then there was the new orange value line designed to help hardware dealers differentiate their offerings from the discounters.

Although the recommended changes appeared logical and straightforward, the plan actually would fly in the face of long-established industry practices. Consequently, management recognized that the initial reaction to the plan by elements of the trade, and even by its own sales force, would probably be negative. There was a chance that such a plan might backfire and hurt rather than help sales.

Recognizing the high-risk nature of the decisions to be made, the division manager called a meeting of top divisional executives, including the division sales manager, to discuss the pros and cons of the proposed plan as well as other potential solutions to the division's problems.

QUESTIONS

1. What were the major problems facing the Consumer Power Tool Division in 1975, particularly with respect to distribution?
2. Analyze the proposals recommended to the division manager for solving the problems.
3. Should the division manager approve the proposals? If not, what alternatives should be considered? Explain the reasons for your answers.

New product introduction plan covering the marketing mix and budgets as recommended by the product manager.

Case 14

Eraser Mate

Derek Coward, vice president of marketing for the Paper Mate Division of the Gillette Company, had received approval to proceed with the market introduction of the company's new erasable ink pen (code named Delta).

Marketing Mix Decisions

In addition to the basic decision to go to market with Delta, several other important decisions had been made, including product design, name, logo, ink colors, packaging, distribution, and pricing.

Product Design. It was decided to offer the new pen in a refillable rather than a disposable model. A medium point was to be offered initially. The charcoal gray eraser was left exposed at the top of the pen for ease of use and to more readily differentiate the pen visually. The eraser was inserted in a metal ferrule which could be slipped in and out of the top of the barrel for easy replacement. There were to be four pen colors—black, blue, maroon, and yellow.

Name. Several hundred names for the new product had been generated internally as well as by the advertising agency and a name-generating consultant. Three names were selected for testing—Epic, Erasa Mate, and 2nd Chance. A number of attributes were tested; the key results are shown in Exhibit 14-1. The name chosen was Eraser Mate. The spelling was changed from the test name "Erasa Mate" on the advice of the division's trademark attorney.

Logo. To further avoid the possibility of confusion with any similar named products, the trademark attorney recommended that the logo incorporate the double hearts of the Paper Mate logo. The logo was to be carried on the pen's pocket clip. Trademark applications were submitted for the name and logo. The Eraser Mate logo is shown in Exhibit 14-2.

EXHIBIT 14-1
Consumers' Rating of Test Names

	% Making a Particular Evaluation		
Evaluation	Epic	Erasa Mate	2nd Chance
Excellent	5	18	17
Very good	18	29	17
Subtotal	23	47	34
Good	44	41	40
Fair	25	9	18
Poor	8	3	9
Total	100	100	101*
Name best describing product	18	59	23

*Does not add to 100% owing to rounding.
Source: Consumer research study.

EXHIBIT 14-2
Eraser Mate Logo

Eraser♥Mate™

Ink Colors. Based on purchase data from the Yankelovich Laboratory Test, and years of experience with permanent ink refills, the decision was made to offer three colors of refills—blue, black, and red. The pen itself was to contain a blue refill.

Packaging. All Eraser Mate pens and refills were to be packaged on blister cards. Front and back views of the card with pen are shown in Exhibit 14-3. Blister cards were chosen not only for purposes of retail display, but also because of the need to call attention to the uniqueness of the product. Also, the back of the card provides space for listing the features of the pen, the guarantee, and the recommendations of the American Bankers Association that Eraser Mate not be used to sign or endorse checks.*

Distribution and Sales. It was decided that Eraser Mate would utilize the Paper Mate Division's distribution channels and be sold by the division sales force.

Pricing. After reviewing estimated production costs and the results of the several consumer research studies, a recommended retail price of $1.69 was chosen for the pen and $1.19 for the refill and eraser. One research test had indicated that there would be little falloff in demand at $1.95. The $1.69 price was selected, nevertheless, to avoid the risk of pricing too high. Furthermore, this price would produce a normal profit contribution at the expected demand level. The refillable unit was priced using experience with other refillable pens in the Paper Mate line. In essence, the decision was made to price the pen somewhere between a *skimming* price and a *market penetration* price.

In pricing to the trade it was decided to follow the standard industry discount structure in which the manufacturer's selling price was 55 percent off the suggested retail selling price. The suggested trade discounts were 40 percent to the retailer and 25 percent to the wholesaler. Prices per dozen were as follows:

> *Paper Mate had faced up to the problem that erasable ink could cause with checks. While erasable pencil lead may be used legally for writing bank checks, people might not realize that ink could be erasable. Paper Mate's approach, after consulting with the bankers, was to warn consumers not to use the pen for negotiable instruments.

	Dollars per Dozen
Suggested retail list price	20.40
Suggested wholesale list price	12.24
Manufacturer selling price	9.18

Using a single unit as an example, the discount structure would work approximately (figures are rounded) as follows:

Retail list price	$1.69	
Less 40%	.68	(Retailer margin)
Wholesale list price	1.01	
Less 25%	.25	(Wholesaler margin)
Manufacturer list	$ .76	(55% off retail list)

Promotional Introduction Plans

The fundamental marketing mix decisions had now been made, with the exception of promotion. In summary, the decisions provided for:

Product—design, ink colors, name and logo, packaging

Pricing—recommended retail price and trade discounts

Distribution and sales—through regular channels using the division sales force

What remained was to determine (1) the promotional strategy; (2) the total promotional budget and how the funds were to be apportioned among the elements of the promotional mix—namely, among advertising, sales promotion, personal selling, and publicity; and (3) the tactical programs to support the strategy. The promotional section of the marketing plan submitted by the product manager, David Melley, made the following recommendations regarding promotional strategy and general objectives:

> To capitalize on the innovative nature of the *Eraser Mate* system in gaining quick distribution and display as well as early awareness and trial through maximum advertising, promotional, and public relations support

Sales Promotion

The sales promotion program would consist of promotion to the trade and sampling of the product among consumer opinion leaders.

Trade Promotion. The objective of the initial trade promotion would be to enable the sales force to obtain

EXHIBIT 14-3
Eraser Mate Package

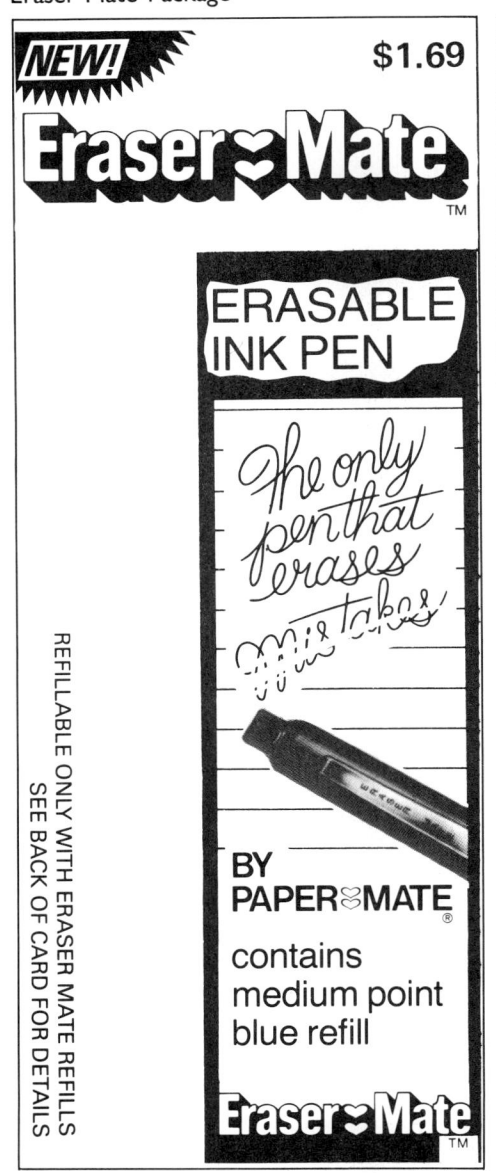

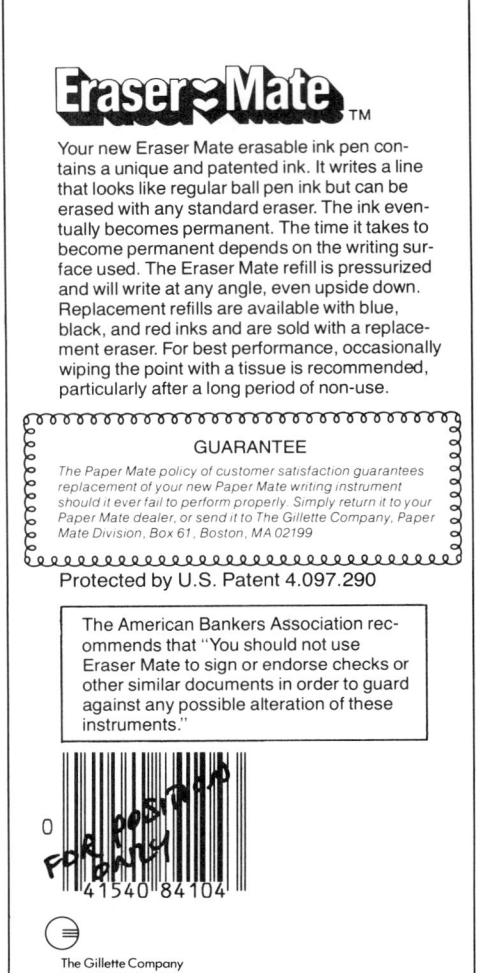

NEW! $1.69

Eraser Mate ™

ERASABLE INK PEN

The only pen that erases mistakes

REFILLABLE ONLY WITH ERASER MATE REFILLS
SEE BACK OF CARD FOR DETAILS

BY **PAPER MATE**®

contains medium point blue refill

Eraser Mate ™

Eraser Mate ™

Your new Eraser Mate erasable ink pen contains a unique and patented ink. It writes a line that looks like regular ball pen ink but can be erased with any standard eraser. The ink eventually becomes permanent. The time it takes to become permanent depends on the writing surface used. The Eraser Mate refill is pressurized and will write at any angle, even upside down. Replacement refills are available with blue, black, and red inks and are sold with a replacement eraser. For best performance, occasionally wiping the point with a tissue is recommended, particularly after a long period of non-use.

GUARANTEE
The Paper Mate policy of customer satisfaction guarantees replacement of your new Paper Mate writing instrument should it ever fail to perform properly. Simply return it to your Paper Mate dealer, or send it to The Gillette Company, Paper Mate Division, Box 61, Boston, MA 02199

Protected by U.S. Patent 4,097,290

The American Bankers Association recommends that "You should not use Eraser Mate to sign or endorse checks or other similar documents in order to guard against any possible alteration of these instruments."

0 41540 84104

The Gillette Company
Paper Mate Division
Box 61
Boston, Mass. 02199
Made in U.S.A.
© 1978

380-04-1-514

---

stocking of product and display units by 100 percent of key wholesale and retail accounts by the time the national advertising began.

Point-of-Sale Displays. Three different displays were to be offered the trade at no cost with initial orders of specified size:

1. A wire rack display for large retail outlets such as stationery, chain drug, and discount stores
   Minimum prepacked order to be shipped with each display rack:
   6 dozen pens
   2 dozen refills
   Order Incentives:

8⅓ percent off invoice and either a 5 percent ad/display allowance or 5 percent wholesaler PM (promotional money)
2. Counter display designed for smaller retail outlets such as independent drug stores and convenience stores
    Minimum order to be shipped with each display:
    3 dozen pens
    1 dozen refills
    Order Incentives:
    Same as for wire rack
3. Floor display—utility dump bin, holds six dozen pens and three dozen refills
    Order Incentives:
    Same as for other displays

Incentives were also to be offered for open stock orders as follows: 8⅓ percent off invoice for pens and refills; 5 percent ad/display or 5 percent PM allowance on pens only.

A counter card display rack is shown in Exhibit 14-4.

To ensure that incentives are used to increase consumer awareness and/or retail distribution, proof of account performance will be required as follows: the 5 percent ad/PM allowance will be paid on a performance billback basis; the wholesaler will be paid 5 percent PM only on the amount of merchandise moved through the warehouse in a 45-day period.

EXHIBIT 14-4
Eraser Mate Counter Display

The promotional incentives were to run from March 1 to April 15, 1979. The plan called for two similar programs to run later: a back-to-school promotion and a Christmas promotion.

Sampling. The objective of the sampling program was to obtain word-of-mouth advertising by influential people. Free samples, accompanied by a letter from division President William Holtsnider, were to be sent to some 175,000 VIPs including Gillette stockholders; congressmen; state officials; editors, TV executives, news commentators, and personalities; top executives of the *Fortune* "500," advertising agencies, banks, and associations; sports personalities; and well-known writers.

Advertising

The objective of the advertising program was to maximize consumer awareness and trial at as early a date as possible. The creative strategy was to generate significant consumer awareness through the use of dramatic and believable demonstration of the pen's ease of erasing and writing performance. The advertising (basically prime-time network TV) would break eight weeks after the start of shipments to allow sufficient time for the product to reach retail shelves. The launch flight was to last six weeks beginning April 19, followed by later flights in support of the back-to-school and Christmas promotions.

Advertising Services (a corporate department whose functions include making media buys for Gillette divisions) will be asked to "roadblock" the networks on a night early in the Eraser Mate advertising schedule—that is, buy time at the same time on all three networks, so that virtually anyone watching television will see the commercial. Additionally, an ad in *TV Guide* will be placed on that day referring to the TV ad and offering a 50¢ refund with proof of purchase of an Eraser Mate pen.

The media strategy for Eraser Mate had been developed based on experience will ball-point pens and results from the Yankelovich tests. The target audience was to be people 12 to 49, with a slight skew toward women 24 to 49. Since students comprised a key consumer group, targeting slightly toward mothers of school-age children was appropriate. A storyboard for a proposed Eraser Mate television ad is shown in Exhibit 14-5.

Public Relations

Paper Mate's public relations consultant, Robert Weiss Associates, had submitted a plan, the key objectives of which were to:

1. Assist the trade by providing maximum consumer visibility for Eraser Mate.

EXHIBIT 14-5
TV Storyboard, Eraser Mate "Father/Daughter"

ERASER MATE
"FATHER/DAUGHTER"

Client: THE GILLETTE CO.　　　　　　　　　　Length: 30 SECONDS

DAD: Argh! Not again!

DAUGHTER: Whatcha writing, Dad?
DAD: Mistakes

DAUGHTER: You need a pen that erases.
DAD: Pens don't erase, dear.

DAUGHTER: Eraser Mate erases.
DAD: I don't believe it.

ANNCR: (VO) Now there's a ball point pen that does the unbelievable. Erases.

The Eraser Mate Pen has a special patented ink.

that gives you time to erase mistakes this easily...

and eventually becomes permanent.

DAD: Eraser Mate... you're unbelievable!

ANNCR: (VO) Eraser Mate. The only pen that erases. New from Paper Mate.

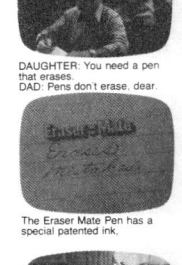

2. Maximize trade awareness of the significant technological breakthrough which Eraser Mate represented.
3. Increase consumer awareness of Eraser Mate through publicity mentions in the news media.

The program called for:

1. An announcement to the trade immediately following the announcement to the sales force.
2. At the same time, press releases, press kits, and product samples were to be sent to all major newspapers, TV stations, wire services, and trade and consumer magazines.
3. Press conferences would be held in New York, Chicago, and Los Angeles in conjunction with the sales department's trade briefings.

Sales Force

The primary product introduction objective of Paper Mate's sales force was to obtain stocking of displays with backup product in all major wholesale and retail accounts by the time the national advertising program began. The second objective was to get all major retail accounts to run local co-op advertising. The sales plan called for making special presentations to the top managements of all key accounts to enlist their enthusiasm and support. Preceding the sales calls, a telegram from William Holtsnider, division president, was to be

EXHIBIT 14-6
Sales Organization Chart, Paper Mate Division, Gillette Company

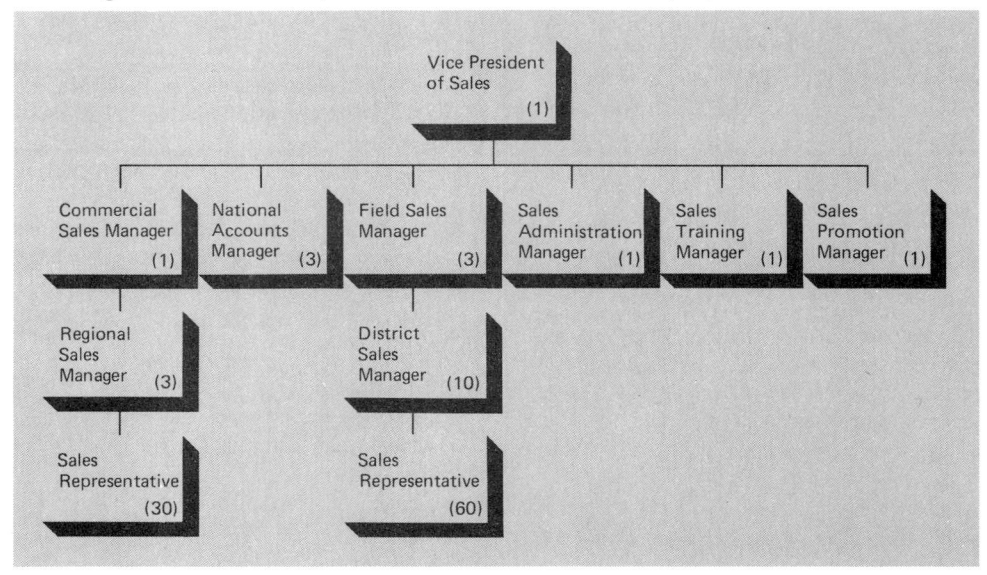

```
                        Vice President
                          of Sales
                            (1)
    ┌───────────┬───────────┬───────────┬───────────┬───────────┐
Commercial   National    Field Sales    Sales       Sales       Sales
Sales Mgr   Accounts     Manager     Administration Training    Promotion
            Manager                  Manager        Manager     Manager
   (1)        (3)          (3)          (1)           (1)         (1)
    │                       │
Regional                 District
Sales                    Sales
Manager                  Manager
   (3)                     (10)
    │                       │
Sales                    Sales
Representative           Representative
   (30)                    (60)
```

644

sent to the chief executives of major wholesale and retail accounts asking them to listen to the sales representatives' presentations of the new breakthrough in writing instruments.

The sales program would be launched at a national meeting of the sales force. Paper Mate's sales organization is shown in Exhibit 14-6. Sales representatives would be instructed to (1) gather together as many executives as possible on each account call to hear the Eraser Mate story, (2) create a "sense of urgency" about ordering and displaying, since advertising was scheduled to break April 19—only 8 weeks from the initial ship date and only 11 weeks from the first account call date, and (3) attempt to get the order on this initial call. The following instructions to sales representatives, from the sales training manual, were to be followed on each account call:

1. Use the suggested management presentation (shown in Exhibit 14-7 at the end of the case) and supporting samples and visual material.
2. Demonstrate Eraser Mate so that each person in attendance understands the nature of the breakthrough, the potential, and the profits to be made.
3. Suggest a major introductory distribution and display, drive, or promotion.
4. Close by asking for quantities of displays and open stock merchandise.
5. Write the order and immediately start to work with the sales and merchandising people to ensure that your final plan will be implemented.
6. Schedule an account sales meeting.
7. Check with the account principals for understanding and "next" action to be taken.
8. Thank everyone involved and tell them about your follow-up activities, including the next call, sales meeting, etc.

Reactions to the Promotional Plan

After studying the promotional section of the marketing plan, Derek Coward called David Melley into his office for discussion. Mr. Coward was generally complimentary about the product manager's plan. Although he was aware that many potentially successful products had failed because adequate resources were not put behind the market launch, he nevertheless wanted to double check the need for all of the proposed programs. He raised several questions, including:

PROPOSED SCHEDULE OF INTRODUCTORY ACTIVITES

Starting Dates, 1979	Activity
1/23	National sales meeting
1/23	Telegrams to account top managements
1/23	Press conferences
1/23	Release of press announcements to media
1/29	Sales calls on accounts
2/1	Sampling program
2/5	Shipments of orders and displays
4/19	National TV advertising program
5/20	TV Guide ad

PROMOTION BUDGET FOR 1979*

Item	Cost, $1000s
Media	3,250
Production	75
E&I (editing and integration)	21
Trade ads	50
Public relations (PR)	50
Couponing	50
Sampling	47
	3,543

*Does not include added costs for personal selling, which primarily would be for the national sales meeting.

1. What was the justification for the total budget?
2. Why were the advertising media limited to TV?
3. How important were the *TV Guide* couponing and the VIP sampling programs? Could these funds be better spent for a print media advertising campaign or for expanding the TV campaign?
4. What would David Melley recommend if it were necessary to reduce the total promotional budget by 20 percent?

Mr. Melley explained the general reasoning behind the plan, but asked for time to think out an alternative budget encompassing a 20 percent reduction in total expenditures.

QUESTION

If you were David Melley, how would you answer Derek Coward's questions? Explain your answers.

EXHIBIT 14-7   Management Presentation: The Great Breakthrough

WE WANT YOU TO TRY SOMETHING WHICH WILL DRAMATICALLY CHANGE PERSONAL HANDWRITING. IN TURN, THIS NEW WRITING INSTRUMENT WILL PROVIDE YOU AND YOUR COMPANY WITH A SUBSTANTIAL ADDITIONAL SOURCE OF SALES AND PROFITS.
(PRESENT A REFILL ALONG WITH A LEGAL PAD TO YOUR BUYER.)

TRY THIS! WRITE YOUR NAME.
(RETRIEVE THE REFILL)
(PRESENT A SHARPENED #2 PENCIL TO YOUR BUYER.)

WRITE YOUR NAME WITH THIS NUMBER 2 PENCIL.

ERASE BOTH INK AND PENCIL!

YOU'VE JUST TRIED THE GREAT PAPER MATE BREAKTHROUGH—IT WORKS! YOU'VE BEEN ONE OF THE FIRST PEOPLE EVER TO USE A PERMANENT YET ERASABLE INK PEN.
(RETRIEVE YOUR PENCIL AND PAD)

NOW LET ME TELL YOU SOMETHING ABOUT THE TECHNICAL ASPECTS AND THE BENEFITS TO BOTH CONSUMERS AND YOURSELF. YOU'VE ALREADY NOTICED THAT THE INK LOOKS AND WORKS LIKE ANY FINE INK.

SO THEN LET ME EXPLAIN ERASABILITY. WE ACHIEVE ERASABILITY THROUGH A PATENTED LATEX INK. JUST LIKE RUBBER CEMENT, THE INK ROLLS UP OR ROLLS OFF THE PAPER WHEN ERASED. THIS MEANS THAT USERS WHO HAVE MADE MISTAKES IN INK CAN NOW CORRECT THESE ERRORS YET PRODUCE QUALITY WRITING. JUST THINK OF THE VALUE THIS WILL BE TO THE STUDENT WHO HAS MADE AN ERROR ON A SPECIAL PAPER . . . OR TO THE PERSON WHO MADE A MISTAKE ON A SPECIAL OCCASION CARD.

NOW LET ME EXPLAIN THE WAY LATEX INK FLOWS FROM THE REFILL ON TO THE PAPER. THE BASIC MECHANISM IS IDENTICAL TO A REGULAR REFILL WITH BALL POINT; HOWEVER THE CARTRIDGE IS PRESSURIZED WITH GAS TO DELIVER A UNIFORM FLOW TO THE PAPER. THIS GUARANTEES THE CONSUMER A CONSISTENT HIGH QUALITY LINE.

NOW LET'S CONSIDER THE MATTER OF THE PERMANENT INK. USERS WILL BE ABLE TO CORRECT ERRORS OR MISTAKES FOR NEARLY 24 HOURS. AFTER THAT TIME THE INK PIGMENT HAS PERMANENTLY SET. TO PROPERLY POSITION OUR PRODUCTS ERASABILITY AND PERMANENCY WE HAVE COVERED POTENTIAL BANKING AND LEGAL PROBLEMS IN OUR PACKAGE GRAPHICS. AS YOU MIGHT UNDERSTAND, THIS ADVANCE IS JUST TOO IMPORTANT TO BE DEFERRED BECAUSE OF LEGAL SIGNATURES WHICH LIKELY MAKE UP LESS THAN 1/10 OF 1% OF OUR PERSONAL WRITING.
(HAVE ALL ERASER MATE COMPONENTS IN AN ENVELOPE)
(REMOVE THEM ONE AT A TIME AS NEEDED)

NOW LET ME BUILD FOR YOU A UNIQUE NEW PRODUCT. FIRST AND FOREMOST IS THIS REFILL - THE HEART OF THE SYSTEM. IT ONLY FITS THIS NEW INSTRUMENT. SECONDLY THE BARREL IS TRADITIONALLY SHAPED FOR COMFORTABLE WRITING. FINALLY WE ADD A QUALITY ERASER; NOTHING SPECIAL JUST QUALITY RUBBER. ANY ERASER WILL WORK SUCH AS THE ONE YOU USED ON THE NUMBER TWO PENCIL. HOWEVER LET ME BE CAREFUL TO POINT OUT THAT THE EXPOSED ERASER WILL CALL CONSUMER'S ATTENTION TO THIS UNIQUE NEW PRODUCT. THEY'LL KNOW IT'S DIFFERENT AND THAT THE INK IS ERASABLE.

THERE YOU HAVE IT! AN ERASER MATE ERASABLE INK PEN BY PAPER MATE!
(PRESENT THE ASSEMBLED PEN TO YOUR BUYER. THIS COULD BE THE SAMPLE YOU LEAVE BEHIND. BE CAREFUL HOWEVER TO REGAIN CONTROL OF THE CALL.)

NOW YOU CAN WRITE AND ERASE AGAIN. HOW ABOUT THAT?
(WAIT FOR REACTION AND COMMENTS.)

NOW HERE'S THE WAY THE ERASER WILL BE PACKAGED!
(SHOW AND EXPLAIN BLISTER CARD)
(SHOW DISPLAYS. EXPLAIN PRICING, PROMOTION, ETC. CLOSE AND WRITE ORDER.)

Developing the annual Marketing Plan for a government agency which is trying to get more people to participate in its health program.

Case 15

National High Blood Pressure Education Program

The National High Blood Pressure Education Program (NHBPEP) of the National Heart, Lung, and Blood Institute is a broad-scale public/private sector effort. The NHBPEP involves numerous other federal agencies, virtually all state health departments, more than 150 private sector organizations, certifying and accrediting bodies, pharmaceutical companies, labor and management groups, and insurance companies.

Hundreds of community high blood pressure efforts are allied with the NHBPEP and are involved in every facet of hypertension control.

The overall effort of the program is to reduce the morbidity and mortality attributable to high blood pressure through public, patient, and professional education. Currently, the program is concentrating much of its public and patient education efforts on communicating to those who know they are hypertensives the importance of *maintaining treatment regimens* prescribed by physicians to control the disease.

In 1972, when the NHBPEP was begun, large portions of the public were unaware of the prevalence and consequences of high blood pressure. In addition, detection and vigorous treatment efforts were lacking. It was estimated that half of all Americans with high blood pressure were undetected and did not know they had a problem. Among health providers there were considerable variations in treatment and patient management.

To meet these problems, activities were concentrated on public and professional awareness, improved and increased detection, and the development of a consensus among health care providers on treatment procedures.

Hypertension-control efforts to date appear to have contributed to the declines in death rates from cardiovascular diseases. Since 1972 the death rate from cardiovascular diseases (heart attack, stroke, heart failure) declined almost twice as fast as in the two previous decades. Moreover, hypertension-related cardiovascular disease deaths are primarily responsible for this decline; nonhypertension-related cardiovascular disease deaths are relatively unchanged (see Exhibit 15-1).

The decline in mortality rates from hypertension-related diseases (Exhibit 15-2) suggests progress in some important hypertension-control activities. Also, recent surveys suggest that general awareness and detection efforts have been effective in increasing the number of aware hypertensives seeking treatment. Nevertheless, getting aware hypertensives to maintain their treatment regimens remains a continuing problem. A summary statement of the problem, issued in January 1979, is presented in Exhibit 15-3.

Strategies for Public Audiences

In early years of the program, the communications strategy for public audiences was aimed at creating

EXHIBIT 15-1

Decline in Cardiovascular Deaths (thousands). *Source: National Center for Health Statistics.*

Hypertension related cardiovascular disease deaths: 897 (1970), 905 (1971), 919 (1972), 918 (1973), 891 (1974), 862 (1975), 843 (1976 Preliminary)

Nonhypertension related cardiovascular disease deaths: 135 (1970), 136 (1971), 141 (1972), 144 (1973), 144 (1974), 141 (1975), 143 (1976 Preliminary)

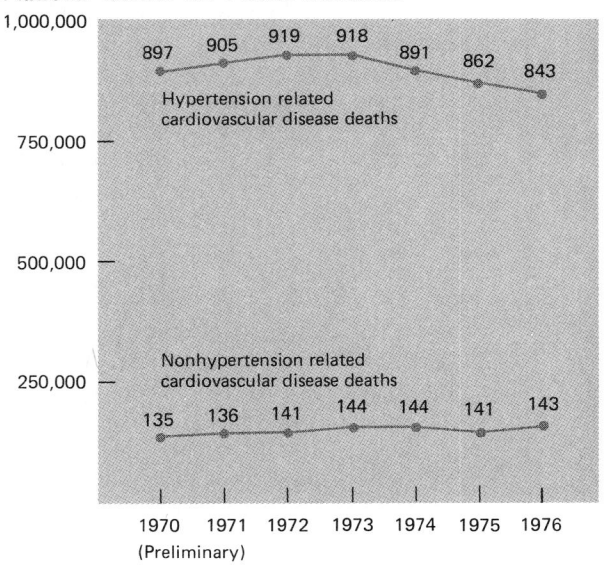

This case was prepared by Pamela W. Gelfand, associate, and William D. Novelli, president, of Porter, Novelli & Associates, Inc., Washington, D.C.

EXHIBIT 15-2

Percent Decline in U.S. Death Rates for Selected Cardiovascular Conditions by Age: 1970–1975

Condition	Age Range								
	All	15–24	25–34	35–44	45–54	55–64	65–74	75–84	>84
Hypertensive disease	35.4	0	55.6	55.6	43.4	32.7	31.1	32.4	29.3
Stroke	17.8	12.5	22.2	25.0	22.6	20.8	21.1	14.2	11.9
Coronary heart disease	14.0	33.3	28.6	19.3	13.8	14.3	16.4	12.0	8.4

Source: National Center for Health Statistics.

awareness of high blood pressure among the general population through messages which stressed screening and detection. To a large degree, this strategy was successful. As a result, data from studies like the Gallup survey (see Exhibit 15-4 at the end of the case) indicate that a high level of awareness about high blood pressure and its consequences has been achieved, but that compliance is lagging behind. Accordingly, the communications strategy has been revised to reach a primary target audience of aware hypertensives with messages designed to encourage them to get on and stay with proper therapy.

Current national initiatives are aimed at: (1) overcoming misconceptions about the disease among patients and the public which appear to inhibit therapy behavior; (2) assisting health professionals to develop effective approaches to patient management; and (3) developing new opportunities for high blood pressure control. A few of the newer areas of inquiry include: high blood pressure control in the work setting; high blood pressure

EXHIBIT 15-3

The National High Blood Pressure Education Program's Information and Education Strategies for Public and Patient Audiences

Problem

Approximately 35 million Americans, about one in six, have high blood pressure.* By properly treating their high blood pressure and thereby reducing it to recommended levels,† they can reduce their chances of stroke, heart disease, and kidney disease.

Because of improved detection efforts, many people now realize that they have high blood pressure. Studies indicate that public awareness of the serious nature of the condition has also increased. It is evident, however, that many who are aware of their problem fail to maintain the daily treatment necessary for control. The difficulty aware hypertensives have in adhering to prolonged treatment regimens is the major problem in high blood pressure control today.

Since there is no immediate benefit which motivates treatment, people who know they have high blood pressure need to be convinced to take daily medication or follow other physician-prescribed regimens. Long-term risk of catastrophic disease appears to have little emotional appeal. There are no symptoms that are relieved by treatment, nor does treatment make people feel better physically. Psychologically, it may even make them feel worse: the pills can become a reminder of sickness and evidence of disease.

*Estimated by the National Heart, Lung, and Blood Institute on extrapolations from national survey data.

†See "Report of the Joint National Committee on Detection, Evaluation, and Treatment of High Blood Pressure," DHEW Publication No. (NIH) 77-1088.

in rural populations; developing dietary and nutritional guidelines for high blood pressure control; and identifying means of improving patient compliance behavior with hypertension therapy.

Over the past five years the program has utilized mass media communication extensively to reach target audiences and has worked through health providers, community-based health agencies, and voluntary health organizations to stimulate interpersonal communication with public and patient audiences. In reviewing these areas, program managers concluded that while progress is evident, several problems must be addressed. See Exhibit 15-5 at the end of the case for a report on a meeting of program planners.

There is insufficient coordination between the information, messages, and materials aimed at public audiences and those directed through health providers* to patient audiences.

Research suggests that public and patient respondents recognize the widespread prevalence of hypertension, understand its severe impact, and perceive that it can be controlled with the help of a physician. Yet barriers appear to remain.

Beliefs persist that high blood pressure has symptoms. This myth seems to lead to other misconceptions which ultimately result in inadequate therapy behavior or even therapy discontinuance.

There appears to be lacking in many aware hypertensives a sense of personal susceptibility. It is as if they understand the general nature and consequences of the disease, but do not feel vulnerable themselves.

They imply that high blood pressure concerns are for "the other guy."

Although public service advertising is only a part of mass media public education, it is an important element because of the reach and frequency it can provide.

From 1974 through spring 1979, the program worked with the Advertising Council in the preparation and distribution of broadcast and print public service materials. (A storyboard of a TV public service announcement is shown in Exhibit 15-6, p. 654.) Currently, program staff hold the responsibility for message and materials development. Most recently, focus group interviews were conducted to test message concepts for the extension of the high blood pressure "Do It For Them" mass media campaign. (See Exhibit 15-7 at the end of the case for results of the focus group interviews.)

More must be done to support and stimulate community-based programs in their public education efforts. The current liaison consists of:

Meeting and exchanging views once each year at a national conference

Offering to tag the endings of national radio messages with local program names, addresses, and phone numbers if the local programs will place these announcements in their markets

A bimonthly newsletter about hypertension control which contains a modest amount of information on public education

Four field representatives who visit local programs with technical assistance and attend regional workshops on behalf of NHBPEP

PROBLEM

Jacquelyn Admire, the NHBPEP manager responsible for public education, is presently faced with the task of developing an annual plan for next year. She must set forth the objectives, strategies, and specific tactics for this area. These will later be integrated into the overall program plan. The history of the program must be taken into account, but close attention must be given to the progress and current issues.

A group from your class is working with Ms. Admire, and she has asked you to prepare the first draft of this plan. She stressed that it should be a comprehensive, actionable plan that contains sufficient detail for implementation. "Don't start with budget constraints," she advised. "That is too limiting. Do your plan and then we'll cost it out on a task by task basis."

Ms. Admire provided the attached materials as background. One of your group, a quantitatively oriented individual, asked for more. "Believe me," said Ms. Admire, "this is plenty."

In preparing the plan, keep in mind that solid justification for all recommendations is required for gaining the necessary approvals from the NHBPEP and NHLBI.

*Physicians, nurses, auxiliary health personnel.

EXHIBIT 15-4
High Blood Pressure Control: Data on Public Perceptions and Practices

Fewer Americans today than five years ago hold the mistaken impression that high blood pressure (hypertension) has readily identifiable symptoms, such as dizziness and headaches. A 1978 Gallup survey on high blood pressure also shows other significant changes in public knowledge and practices when compared to an earlier (Harris) study conducted in 1973.

"The decrease in the level of misunderstanding about nonrelated symptoms is good news," commented Graham W. Ward, Coordinator of the National High Blood Pressure Education Program (NHBPEP) at the National Heart, Lung, and Blood Institute. "Believing that high blood pressure has symptoms can work against an individual in two ways," Ward said. "First, the person may not experience the symptoms he thinks are part of high blood pressure, and therefore sees no reason to follow medical treatment. Or he may decide to follow treatment only when he feels tense or dizzy, or has a headache. None of these are reliable indications of high blood pressure."

Other survey findings are that:

1. The proportion of Americans who report having high blood pressure hasn't changed in the past five years. About one of every four adults considers himself in this category. Nine out of ten of these individuals report that they have been prescribed some form of medical treatment, and 60% claim to be continuing with their therapy.

2. Most people remain aware that high blood pressure is a serious disease that increases the risk of stroke and heart attack/heart failure. Also, most people understand that high blood pressure can be controlled.

3. While medication continues to be prescribed for seven out of every ten individuals who are given some form of therapy, most of these people report that they are also following other treatments prescribed by their physicians. These combination treatments are much more common today than five years ago, as reported by patients. Salt free diets, weight control, exercise, smoking cessation and stress avoidance have all gained significantly as treatments reported for high blood pressure.

4. Seven of ten hypertensives state that they take their medication every day, which is necessary to control the disease. Older Americans report better treatment compliance than younger people, and those at higher educational levels report following their treatment better than those at lower levels of education.

5. The reasons why people stop treatment are no clearer today than in 1973. The most frequent response given is that people simply don't know why they stopped. Physician-patient misunderstanding and the mistaken belief that their high blood pressure is cured or has returned to normal are other apparent reasons.

6. There is little, if any, difference in the amount of information people have about the disease and their resulting behavior. Aware hypertensives who are continuing therapy and those who have dropped out of treatment currently have about the same understanding of the consequences of the disease and that it can nearly always be controlled. "We operate from the basic assumption that knowledge alone is probably not enough to change behavior," Ward commented. "Information is probably necessary to set the stage for treatment maintenance, but it isn't sufficient to close the sale. A complete set of conditions is needed, with direct physician-patient communication, public and patient education, and family support all working together to motivate and reinforce long-term treatment compliance."

Analyzed and interpreted by the National High Blood Pressure Education Program, National Heart, Lung, and Blood Institute.

EXHIBIT 15-5

PORTER, NOVELLI & ASSOCIATES Inc.

MEMORANDUM

TO: Jacqelyn B. Admire   April 29, 1977

FROM: William D. Novelli

RE: <u>Meeting with State and Community HBP Program Planners and Resulting Recommendations</u>

I. <u>Background</u>

On April 13, the opening day of the National Conference on High Blood Pressure Control, a meeting was held on <u>high blood pressure public information and education</u>.

Participants were recommended by Bob and Gary, who also attended. The American Heart Association, the Kidney Foundation, state departments of health and community-based programs were represented (see attached list of participants and agenda).

II. <u>Summary of the Meeting</u>

The representatives described public education activities in which they are engaged. Examples of strategies and tactics include:

1. High Blood Pressure Month maintenance messages via the mass media.

2. Reaching compliance dropouts through mass media and community channels.

3. Promotion campaign to encourage viewing of "Silent Countdown" aired periodically on public television.

4. Demonstration of high blood pressure education in one school district for possible replication throughout the state.

5. Alternating strategies: six months of mass screening with media support followed by six months of referral/follow-up with media support.

3240 Prospect Street, N.W. □ Washington, D.C. 20007 □ (202) 342-7000

EXHIBIT 15-5 *(Continued)*

6. Multiple strategies (detection, follow-up, maintenance) all with heavy media and health promotion support.

7. Rural screening with no direct information/education component (this is left up to AHA).

8. Emphasis on professional education, based on assumption that health professionals will, in turn, educate patients. Only mass media effort centers on fear arousal.

9. Education of black audiences via churches and rural extension agents.

10. Regional coordination with many agencies and organizations, but independent media messages (AHA in Southeastern U.S.).

In reviewing how NHBPEP might better assist state and community-based programs:

1. There was general agreement on the need and utility of a compendium document which would provide an overview perspective of behavioral research, strategies, and approaches to public information and education.

There were numerous suggestions of areas to be covered in this document including:

   a. Statistics on hypertension incidence, deaths, state-of-control and other areas that can serve as a common basis throughout the country. Wherever possible, these data should be regionalized.

   b. Information and examples on what the national organizations (NHBPEP, AHA, NKF, etc.) are planning and doing in public education on high blood pressure.

   c. Information and examples on what the state and community programs are planning and doing in public education (the participants stated that the meeting itself was an example of the utility of sharing such information).

   d. Data on cost/benefits regarding hypertension control that can be used to motivate corporations to set up control programs in the worksetting.

   e. A variety of strategies, rather than just maintenance (many participants expressed the belief that multiple strategies are necessary in order to effectively promote high blood pressure control among mass, select, and patient audiences).

EXHIBIT 15-5 *(Continued)*

    f. Information on patient as well as public education. The differences between these two audiences are often blurred (sometimes the only difference is the medium used to reach the individual).

    g. Resources that can be tapped for materials, messages, case studies, examples, and further information.

2. Because of lack of time, the discussion of planning tools, such as a schema for pretesting print and broadcast messages, was not held. Participants were asked to review the poster paper on the Health Message Testing Service and told that they would receive further information on pretesting later.

3. The meeting participants appeared responsive to the concept of the NHBPEP developing prototype materials and messages which local programs can shape to meet specific community conditions. Again, messages stemming from multiple strategies were stressed. Several representatives used the Program's Ad Council TV and radio PSA's as an example of poor coordination. Their contention was:

    a. Competition for PSA time is more intense than ever before. Local programs with strategies keyed to local efforts must compete with the Ad Council spots.

    b. The Ad Council spots are sent directly to the media, bypassing local program staff. This causes:

        – confusion among the media.

        – difficulties in localizing the Ad Council spots (if this is desired).

        – embarrassment to local programs, supposedly the community's focal point for hypertension activities.

Examples of other prototype materials and messages were not discussed. However, several participants reiterated that the compendium (see 1. above) should identify what materials are available (from many sources) so that programs may inspect and use them if applicable.

4. Pilot testing and measuring public education efforts as part of an overall community hypertension control program was discussed. The concept was well received, with several qualifications:

    a. Such a test should be structured so that it can be <u>affordably</u> reproduced if it is successful.

    b. The test should be integrated into the local program in which it is conducted.

EXHIBIT 15-5 (Continued)

Following the meeting, several participants suggested that their areas may be appropriate for such a test.

5. In discussing ways to improve media coverage of high blood pressure, these points were made:

   a. This is not a high-interest subject, and most (if not all) media approaches have been exhausted. Fresh angles are needed and should be identified in the compendium.

   b. Concentrating media coverage on May-High Blood Pressure Month results in unnecessarily low media support during the rest of the year (several representatives agreed with this point; one disagreed; several did not comment).

   c. Better regional media coordination is needed. Regional and national interagency councils were suggested for the purpose of coordinating "who would approach the media with what."

   d. The need for media access and visibility among voluntary organizations was stressed. Since these groups rely on public awareness for fund raising, their media efforts must be continuous and intense.

   e. The need for coordinating the placement of Ad Council spots with local programs was reiterated.

EXHIBIT 15-6
TV Storyboard, National High Blood Pressure Education Campaign

NATIONAL HIGH BLOOD PRESSURE EDUCATION CAMPAIGN

"Take it for them" Public Service Announcements in :30, :10 Versions :30 SECONDS

ANNCR: (VO) It's foolhardy to fool yourself about High Blood Pressure.

It can only be controlled by daily medication.

SINGERS: Take it for him.

take it for her.

take it for your loving man.

If you don't take it for yourself,

take it for the loved ones in your life.

ANNCR: (VO): So take your daily medication daily. If not for yourself, for them.

SINGERS: Take it for the loved ones in your life.

A Public Service of This Station & The Advertising Council

NATIONAL HIGH BLOOD PRESSURE EDUCATION PROGRAM
CNBP-8130/CNBP-8110

Volunteer Advertising Agency: Norman, Craig & Kummel
Volunteer Campaign Coordinator: Sanford Buchsbaum, Revlon Inc.

EXHIBIT 15-7

PORTER, NOVELLI & ASSOCIATES Inc.

TO: Jacqelyn B. Admire

FROM: William D. Novelli

DATE: July 19, 1979

SUBJECT: Results of Focus Groups

This is to briefly summarize the results of the focus groups conducted in Atlanta and Pittsburgh on July 10 - 13. A full report will follow.

1. People with high blood pressure are perceived as being healthy. This perception was held by both aware hypertensive and social support respondents. Hypertensives are seen as "healthy" as long as:

    a. They are "functional," i.e., can get around, go to work, do what needs to be done (this applies to respondents' definitions of any healthy person, not just hypertensives).

    b. Their high blood pressure is under control. This control is seen as:

        - Following treatment, especially taking medication

        - Receiving a response from the physician that they are following his advice and are doing the right thing

    c. They are not doctor-dependent. That is, they don't spend a lot of their time at the doctor's office or in the health care system.

    Therefore, we seem to be on the right track in depicting aware hypertensives as healthy individuals, leading normal lives, even vigorous lives. This is not inconsistent with respondents' images of themselves and others as hypertensives. We don't want to overdo it, however. People should be shown as normally healthy in relation to others their own age (e.g., no 70 year old marathon runners).

2. Respondents, for the most part, seemed conscientious about taking their medication. This is seen as an essential part of therapy, and was clearly understood as a daily requirement despite other areas of confusion and misinformation.

3240 Prospect Street, N.W. ☐ Washington, D.C. 20007 ☐ (202) 342-7000

EXHIBIT 15-7 *(Continued)*

3. Many respondents believed that high blood pressure has symptoms--headaches, dizziness, and becoming ruddy-faced. However, the considerable confusion on this subject did not interfere with most people clearly and forcefully believing that daily medication is necessary, whether or not symptoms are present. Our communication to public and patient audiences that "high blood pressure (usually) has no symptoms" is neither totally understood nor accepted. Our message that you must take your medication daily, no matter how you feel, is well understood and accepted.

4. The majority of respondents strongly believe that tension is associated, and probably is a cause of, hypertension. Many claim to have been told by physicians of this direct association. To try to dispel this belief could be a serious mistake. The only reason to do so would be if there were evidence that non-tense individuals believed themselves free of hypertension and were not detected. Since there is evidence that most people are checked and detection levels are high, and since we are not on a <u>detection</u> strategy, it appears that we should not battle the tension issue as part of our <u>maintenance</u> strategy. To fight this battle:

    a. Would be very difficult

    b. Would put our messages in conflict with what people strongly believe

    c. Is not necessary to reinforce or stimulate compliance

5. There seems to be very little misunderstanding about substitute therapies. People understand that each element of a total program recommended by a physician is a necessary part of therapy. The several concepts that demonstrated substituting one part of a therapy for another met with high levels of disapproval. However, respondents are much more apt to take medication regularly than follow other, lifestyle forms of treatment. The majority of respondents reported being prescribed medication plus some other form of therapy.

    a. Salt restriction--this was the second-most frequently reported treatment among the Atlanta and Pittsburgh respondents, and was considered second-most important, after medication. However, it is a very inexact, non-quantified behavior. People tend to "watch their salt" or "cut down on it" but not in a measured way. A few were on salt-free diets. The rest tried to avoid table salt or at least reduce it as their effort in response to their doctor's advice. In our messages we should encourage salt restriction and reinforce those who practice this behavior.

    b. Weight control is next after salt as a reported form of therapy in addition to medication. Like salt restriction, weight control is an inexact behavior, and is even more difficult to achieve. Most of the

EXHIBIT 15-7 *(Continued)*

respondents were, to some degree, overweight, most wished they could reduce, and most reported little success. However, for most, the battle goes on. Few have completely given up. Also, most hypertensives reported that their doctors were not too adamant or admonishing about weight control, as long as drug therapy was adhered to. Related to weight control is exercise: few were prescribed exercise, but many saw it as one means of controlling weight. Far and away, the most frequent kind of exercise considered appropriate was walking.*

In our messages, we should consider showing some hypertensives who are a little overweight. They could be shown, among other things, as engaging in walking as a realistic form of exercise.

    c. Smoking reduction or cessation was not reported as a frequent therapy for high blood pressure. However, some respondents said that their physicians did recommend that they stop smoking, apparently for reasons of general health. The majority of respondents did not smoke, and most smokers were rueful about their habit. Although the trends in this area are favorable, we probably should not show smoking reduction/cessation as a recommended behavior in our messages:

      - We have too much else to get across

      - It is a very difficult behavior to change

6. Respondents were favorably disposed toward social support for hypertensives. It is frequent, and it is welcomed. For the most part, those who provide social support (spouses, small children, grown children, friends) are seen as loving and caring about the hypertensive. Even when it gets a bit heavy, it is as being done for "my (his/her) own good." However, it is possible to overstep the line and go from loving/concern into the area of nagging. This line or demarcation seems to differ among different couples/families/relationships. However, in one area the line is clear. It is almost universally drawn at weight control. People do not want to be encouraged, stimulated, pushed, nagged, or anything else about their weight. Both men and women are sensitive about this, but women appear to be the most sensitive. We must be very careful in social support situations in the area of weight control. Even a seemingly positive reinforcement ("You look better, you look thinner") is not well received.

---

*This was also seen in qualitative studies on exercise undertaken for the President's Council on Physical Fitness and Sports.

EXHIBIT 15-7 *(Continued)*

7. The word "program" is almost totally understood and accepted as a catch-all for a combination of therapies recommended by a physician. No other word or phrase is as good. "Regimen" is a distant second.

8. There is an ingrained sense of self-responsibility among hypertensives regarding therapy maintenance. Also, social supporters believe that they can provide support, but that the ultimate responsibility lies with the individual. Respondents were very positive and receptive to the "do it for them" family/loved ones protection appeal. But they stressed that you must do it for yourself as well as for them. Families can, do, and should help, but the burden should not be on their backs. This is not a divergent appeal--the two are linked. It represents an addition to an already strong approach. In essence, it is a call to "do it for yourself and all the loved ones in your life."

9. Showing a compliance "problem" did not appear to cause confusion or misunderstanding or weaken resolve. In some cases the respondents provided the solution ("That's wrong; she should take her pills all the time, not just when she's tense or headachey"). In other concepts, the solution was given and the respondents agreed with it ("He's telling him to stay on medication, and that's right").

10. Forward-looking concepts were well received. Examples are:

    a. Buying a house and having much to look forward to

    b. Teaching your son your business or trade

    c. An older couple with time together now that the children are grown

    The linkage between these scenes and the importance of blood pressure control was also understood and accepted.

11. For these respondents, their physicians were their primary sources of high blood pressure information. They were willing to wait as long as necessary, but they wanted as much time as they believed they needed to ask the doctor their questions. Some wrote their questions down, others thought them through in advance, others called back if something was unclear.

    Physicians were treated with respect, but there was no reported hesitation, among either race or sex, or any age group, to change doctors if performance was seen as unsatisfactory. Many respondents reported having changed doctors for that reason.

    The mass media were reported as the second most important source of high blood pressure information, including: PSA's, newspaper and magazine articles, and health segments on television.

EXHIBIT 15-7 *(Continued)*

Nurses had very low acceptance as sources of high blood pressure information. They were not seen as extensions of the physician's information and education role. Nor did respondents report that they were used as such. The most that nurses seemed to have done in relation to these respondents was to have taken blood pressures, in some cases.

Only a few respondents reported receiving any information or instruction regarding hypertension at their places of work.

Few respondents reported receiving information on high blood pressure from their pharmacists, but most seemed receptive to the pharmacist as a potential information source.

Few respondents reported receiving information on hypertension from their dentists, and most had trouble understanding what, if any, connection there might be between hypertension and dentistry. Several did report having their blood pressures checked before undergoing dental work.

We probably should minimize depiction of individuals in contact with the health care system. People do visit the doctor, but view themselves as healthy, leading normal lives, and not doctor dependent.

12. The response to the campaign song was extremely favorable. Recall of the campaign was very high, and respondents liked the music and the messages. Many could recall specific versions of the campaign and specific ideas (e.g., no symptoms). Black respondents especially favored the black version. Middle-aged and older respondents stated that the music was too youthful, too much rock and roll. The song is an important trigger for us in future campaigns. Some version of the music should be made more palatable for middle-aged and older audiences.

13. Numerous summary lines were presented. Both "High Blood Pressure . . . Treat It For Life" and "High Blood Pressure . . . Treat It and Live," were well received. Neither was especially preferred over the other.

    The line "Treat Your High Blood Pressure Every Day, For Yourself and the Ones You Love" seemed to best express the idea of self plus loved ones. We appear to have flexibility to develop and establish a good summary line in conjunction with the added dimension to "do it for them."

14. Those who dropped out of therapy or who were only occasionally in compliance were considered foolish, or worse, by most respondents.

    "My husband won't take his pills. I tried everything. I just hope when his warning comes it ain't too bad."

    "My brother-in-law wouldn't take his pills. They buried him."

EXHIBIT 15-7 *(Continued)*

Respondents who were not on therapy had a number of reasons, such as not having gotten around to getting under a doctor's care, being between physicians, being told by physicians that they could discontinue therapy, and others. None simply said they quit on their own and didn't intend to return. All respondents believed that high blood pressure is dangerous. Nearly everyone (ala Gallup) believed that hypertension could be controlled but not cured. Much of the reason for therapy discontinuance appears due to confusion and misunderstanding. Our best approach to "now and thens" and drop-outs may be along these lines: "If you've ever been told you have high blood pressure, but you aren't on regular treatment, for any reason, go to a physician and check it out. You probably should be on a regular program prescribed by a doctor."

A Sales Territory Layout requires a definition of the sales job and measurements of relative potential and account workload by geographic areas.

Case 16

The Quit-Smoke Company

You have just accepted a job as sales manager of the Quit-Smoke Company, a new company formed to manufacture a product that inhibits the desire of smokers to light up a cigarette. The chemical was developed by Walter Jones, a chemistry major. His father, a wealthy man, has put up the capital needed to build a plant and provide working capital until the company can begin producing income.

Although similar products have been on the market, tests with smokers indicate that this product is more effective. Tests showing that it has no harmful side effects have been submitted to the FDA, which has approved it for offering to the public. It does not require a doctor's prescription.

Walter has decided to offer the product as a mint-flavored lozenge that will be sold at retail at 99¢ a package, containing enough for a 3-day supply. The package can be sold to wholesalers at 45¢ and still provide a satisfactory profit margin. The markups available to wholesalers and retailers are quite attractive and should help to encourage them to stock the new product if they can be convinced the product will sell. Although the company expects to advertise, as of now, Quit-Smoke is an unknown brand.

Market Information

A marketing professor has been advising Walter on marketing matters while the new plant has been under construction. Through primary consumer research and secondary research into census and other data in the library, the following information has been learned:

1. The percentage of people who smoke is about the same in every part of the United States.
2. A sizable proportion of smokers would like to quit but lack the willpower to do so on their own.
3. A test with the Quit-Smoke product among a sample of smokers found that 72 percent who used the product regularly for 6 weeks were able to break the smoking habit.
4. A sample of smokers questioned indicated they would be most likely to buy such a product in a drug store and that they would be influenced by a doctor's or druggist's recommendation.
5. There are approximately 1,200 drug wholesalers (including drug chain buying offices) and approximately 13,000 drug and proprietary stores in the New England and Mid-Atlantic Census Divisions.
6. Casual discussions with drug retailers indicate they may be reluctant to stock the product because products making similar claims have not sold too well.

Before hiring you as a sales manager, Walter Jones has made the following decisions:

· The product will be introduced initially in only the nine states comprising the New England and Mid-Atlantic Census Divisions.

· The product will be sold initially through drug channels. An ad will be placed in *Druggist Digest*, read by many drug retailers and wholesalers.

· When the product is on retail shelves, an advertising program using newspapers and spot TV will begin in the twenty-two largest Metro Areas in the New England and Mid-Atlantic divisions. Examples: New York, Philadelphia, Boston, and Pittsburgh. *Sales and Marketing Management* magazine's Metro Areas are roughly equivalent to Standard Metropolitan Statistical Areas (SMSA).

· A direct mail piece with product samples will be sent to all doctors in the twenty-two Metro Areas three weeks before the consumer advertising program begins.

· Retail store point-of-sale materials will be made available through wholesalers for any drug store ordering one or more cases of Quit-Smoke. Each case contains forty-eight packages of lozenges.

· Jones had budgeted enough money to hire you as sales manager and to employ nine sales persons. No

This is a fictional case based partly on fact.

more salespeople can be hired until sales income is sufficient to pay for additional ones. He will not consider hiring manufacturer's agents.

He has decided tentatively that one salesperson should be assigned to each of the nine states that comprise the New England and Mid-Atlantic Census Divisions.

Jones has never defined a sales job, but he does realize that nine salespeople cannot call on all of the retail drug stores and probably not all of the drug wholesalers and drug chain headquarters in the nine states. He expects you to determine who the salesperson should call on, with what frequency, and what the salesperson needs to do on these calls to get orders and promote sales.

QUESTIONS

1. Would you be satisfied with Walter Jones's decision to use the nine states as boundary lines for the sales territories? Give reasons for your answer.
2. How would you go about laying out the nine territories? Illustrate with pertinent market data. Show your territories on a map. Indicate in your paper the reference source(s) used.
3. What instructions would you give to the salesperson with respect to the types and classes of accounts to be called on, frequency of call, selling tasks to be performed, and portions of the sales territory to concentrate on?

Note: Market data needed to help you answer these questions may be found in the reference section or government documents section of most university or city libraries, from such sources as the *Sales and Marketing Management* annual "Survey of Buying Power," the *Statistical Abstract of the United States*, the geographic atlas, the U.S. Census, and library reference works which abstract census data.

Market development problems of a new professional sports team which is faced with competition from better established sports, low public awareness, and high costs of operation relative to income.

Case 17

The Boston Bolts

The Boston Bolts, a new professional box lacrosse team, was hoping to capitalize on the tremendous growth occurring in spectator sports. Attendance at eighteen major sports had increased by 45 percent between 1966 and 1976, as shown in Exhibit 17-1.

During this period attendance at professional ice hockey games had grown by 365 percent and at professional basketball games by 270 percent. Because box lacrosse has elements of both hockey and basketball, John Kelly, the newly appointed manager of the Boston Bolts, was

EXHIBIT 17-1
Increase in Spectators at Sporting Events

	1966, millions	1976, millions	Percent Increase
1. Thoroughbred racing	40.9	51.2	25
2. Auto racing	39.0	50.0	28
3. Major-league baseball	25.2	32.6	29
4. College football	25.3	32.0	26
5. Harness racing	23.2	30.7	32
6. College basketball	17.0	25.5	50
7. Greyhound racing	11.1	19.0	71
8. Professional football	7.7	15.0	95
9. Major-league hockey	3.1	14.4	365
10. Minor-league baseball	10.1	11.3	12
11. Professional basketball	2.3	8.5	270
12. Professional wrestling	4.8	5.0	4
13. Minor-league hockey	2.9	4.9	69
14. College hockey	0.8	3.4	325
15. Professional boxing	1.7	3.2	88
16. Professional soccer	Negligible	2.8	
17. Professional golf	1.5	2.3	53
18. Professional tennis	Negligible	2.2	
Totals	216.3	314.0	45

Note: Attendance figures are for seasons ending 1966 and 1976 and include professional teams in Canada.

Source: A. C. Nielsen Company; National Research Center for the Arts; trade, sports, and other associations and publications; U.S. government agencies. Also, *U.S. News and World Report,* May 23, 1977, p. 63.

This case was prepared by Robert D. Hisrich and Michael P. Peters, Boston College.

convinced that the time was right to widen the Bolts' share of the greater Boston sports market.

The game of lacrosse originated among North American Indians. Its popularity as a school sport developed only since the 1960s. By 1980 there were over 400 high school teams and about 175 college varsity teams. Lacrosse is now played as an intramural club sport at many colleges. *Box lacrosse* is a variation of regular lacrosse and is played on a smaller field outdoors. Indoors it is played in a hockey rink on a wooden floor. The Canadians brought the game indoors a few years ago as an off-setting seasonal sport to better utilize indoor ice hockey facilities. The professional league of which the Boston Bolts are a part began in the mid-seventies. Play is indoors in the spring and summer.

A professional box lacrosse team consists of six players: a goalie, two defensemen, two forwards, and one center. The purpose of the game is to shoot a 2-inch hard rubber ball into a 4 foot by 4 foot goal. The stick, a raquet mounted with a loose net, is used to pass the ball from player to player, very much as in ice hockey. The offensive strategy, however, is similar to that used in basketball.

Since the box lacrosse playing season corresponds pretty much with the baseball season, the Bolts' principal competitor for sports fans is the Boston Red Sox baseball team. In addition to baseball being the third most popular sport in America (33 million paying customers), its prices are relatively low. Red Sox bleacher seats at $1.50 and reserved seats at $4.50 are priced lower than the Bolts can afford to charge.

The Red Sox have additional advantages compared to the Bolts. Fenway Park (the home of the Red Sox) is easily accessible via public transportation. Second, being outside usually makes for a more pleasant summer evening than being inside the Boston Garden (not air-conditioned) where the Bolts play. Finally, the Red Sox benefit from the promotional effects of regular television coverage, which the Bolts do not yet enjoy.

Baseball is the national sport. The public is familiar with the Red Sox, whereas the query, "Do you know what the Bolts are?" usually elicits the counter query, "A fleet of mechanics?" Because box lacrosse is not well known, much learning is necessary in order to fully appreciate the game.

John Kelly describes the Boston Bolts situation as follows: Athletic decisions are made by the general manager and coach. The presentation of the team pivots on their uniforms, the announcer, and their team program. Their image as part of the National Lacrosse League also contributes to their overall presentation.

The ticket prices of $6.50, $5.50, $4.50, and $3.50 are

EXHIBIT 17-2
Boston Newspaper Circulation and Costs

THE BOSTON GLOBE	
Circulation: (3/31/73)	
Morning (except Saturday)	278,126/day
Evening (except Saturday)	184,493/day
Saturday morning	374,055/day
Sunday morning	617,426/day
Retail advertising rates:	
Monday through Saturday	$1.70/line
Sunday	$2.00/line

THE BOSTON RECORD AMERICAN AND HERALD TRAVELER	
Circulation:	
Morning (except Saturday)	371,365/day
Saturday morning	301,717/day
Sunday	503,045/day
Retail advertising rates:	
Monday through Friday	$1.35/line
Sunday	$1.50/line
Holiday	$1.05/line

EXHIBIT 17-3
Selected Radio Audience and Rates

WBZ-Radio

Number of listeners
  Mornings 6:00 A.M. to 10:00 A.M. average of 147,600 during a ¼-hour period
  Total of 836,900 over a one-week period
Advertising rates
  6:00 A.M. to 10:00 A.M. $200.00/minute
  20-times plan   81.00/minute
    5 spots in morning
    5 spots in homemaker times
    5 spots in afternoon
    5 spots in evening
  8-times plan $660.00 total
    2 spots in morning
    2 spots in homemaker times
    2 spots in afternoon
    2 spots in evening
Coptor $1750.00/week
    5 spots in morning
    5 spots in evening

WRKO-Radio

Advertising rates
  Class AAA:
    6:00 A.M. to 10:00 A.M. Monday through Friday
    3:00 P.M. to 8:00 P.M. Monday through Friday
    8:00 P.M. to 9:00 P.M. Saturday
  Class AA:
    10:00 A.M. to 3:00 P.M. Monday through Friday
    8:00 P.M. to 11:00 P.M. Monday through Friday
  Class A:
    11:00 P.M. to 2:00 A.M. Monday through Sunday

	Class AAA*	Class AA*	Class A*
6 times	$87.00	$70.00	$35.00
12 times	83.00	66.00	33.00
18 times	79.00	61.00	30.00
24 times	69.00	56.00	28.00

*per spot cost

EXHIBIT 17-4
Selected Television Audience and Rates

WSBK-TV (Channel 38)	$ per 30 sec
Red Sox baseball games	650.00
Bruins ice hockey games	1,200.00
5:30 P.M. to 6:00 P.M.	130.00 to 220.00
6:00 P.M. to 6:30 P.M.	180.00 to 260.00

RKO General Broadcasting (Channel 7)	$ per 30 sec
9:00 A.M. to 12:00 A.M.	75.00
12:00 P.M. to 4:00 P.M.	150.00 to 175.00
4:00 P.M. to 6:30 P.M.	500.00
7:00 P.M. to 8:00 P.M.	600.00 to 1100.00
8:00 P.M. to 11:00 P.M.	1,500.00 (average)
11:00 P.M. to 11:30 P.M.	500.00
12:00 A.M. to sign-off	125.00 to 150.00
Weekend	125.00 to 400.00

the highest in the league. The main channel of distribution used so far is direct sales to walk-ins at games and people who go to the box office. The motivation of those people who buy their tickets direct is believed to be the product itself and the advertising which is concentrated on bumper stickers, the team's program, price schedules, and other printed matter. There is a publication, *Bolts Magazine*, which sells for a dollar and features advertising from enterprises which offer goods and services supplementary to sports. The main function of this publication is to introduce players, presenting them as individual personalities, and to explain the rules of the game.

Other types of sales include group sales to merchants. Group sales are done by Bolts salespersons. They receive 10 percent commission. Ticket agencies could also be used to sell Bolts tickets at a 50¢ markup. So far there has been no media advertising. (Space and time charges of typical local media are given in Exhibits 17-2, 17-3, and 17-4.)

The break-even point per game is $20,000. In their first season, the Bolts played a total of thirty-two games of which they won eleven. The average attendance for thirty-one games was 800.

The Boston Garden charges $4,000 per game or 15 percent or the gross, whichever is greater. The total expenses for the twenty-eight games normally played is $560,000 or an average of $20,000 per game. The players receive from $7,000 to $15,000 per season for an average of $10,000.

The primary target market is thought to be males 14 to 25 years of age; the secondary target market is thought to be hockey and basketball fans.

PROBLEM

Develop a marketing plan for the Bolts, bearing in mind that costs must be kept in line.

APPENDIX

Sources of Business and Marketing Information

Market and business analysts are frequent users of secondary data sources. You need to know where to find the same types of information that the professionals use. You may need it for your case analyses and course assignments having to do with the real world. In your job search, you will want to read up on certain industries and companies within those industries, and find the names of company executives, their job titles, and their addresses. There are vast amounts of mostly free information available to help you while you are in school and when you are out.

The purpose of this appendix is to describe briefly a selected list of data sources that my students and I have found most useful. It does not purport to be a complete list. If you are searching for some special information not covered by this list, check with your reference librarian. Sometimes you may be looking for information that doesn't exist or that is only in the private files of organizations. Executives of companies, associations, and research firms vary as to how willing they are to share private information. Many are surprisingly open. The only way to find out is to ask. But first check the available published sources.

This appendix is divided into four sections: (1) library sources (available in most major city and university libraries), (2) trade magazines, (3) trade associations, and (4) private sources. Sources are listed alphabetically within each section.

LIBRARY SOURCES

Business-Related Indexes and Bibliographies

Business Information Sources, Lorna M. Daniells, University of California Press.
   An annotated guide to sources of business information. Describes the basic kinds of business reference sources available, such as bibliographies, indexes and abstracts, directories, and statistical and financial sources, with particular emphasis on each specific management function.

Business Periodicals Index, H. W. Wilson Co.
   A subject index to approximately 150 business-related periodicals. Articles about specific companies are indexed by company name.

Encyclopedia of Business Information Sources, Gale Research Company.
   A detailed listing of information sources arranged according to alphabetical subject headings. A complete citation is provided for each source mentioned.

Funk & Scott Index of Corporations and Industries, Predicasts, Inc.

An index of company, product, and industry information that has appeared in over 750 business-related publications. Divided into an "Industries & Products" section arranged by Standard Industrial Classification (SIC) number and a "Companies" section arranged alphabetically by company name.

Monthly Catalog of United States Government Publications, Superintendent of Documents.
Contains an alphabetical listing of documents issued by each government agency. The list is compiled each month and indexed for access by author, title, subject, and series/report. The catalog also includes a stock number index and title key word index.

New York Times Index, The New York Times Company.
Indexes all issues of the *New York Times* from 1851 to date. Entries are made under subject headings and briefly describe article contents.

Public Affairs Information Service Bulletin, Public Affairs Information Service, Inc.
A guide to pamphlets, government publications, reports, and periodical articles which address contemporary public issues. Particularly helpful in locating those related to economics and political science. Arranged alphabetically by subject.

Wall Street Journal Index, Dow Jones & Company, Inc.
An index of all articles published in the *Wall Street Journal.* Entries are arranged alphabetically into two sections: "Corporate News" (by company name) and "General News" (by subject).

Sources of Statistical Information

American Statistics Index, Congressional Information Service, Inc.
An index to all of the statistical publications of the U.S. government. The index is divided into two sections: an "Index" section that contains subject and name, category, title, and agency report number indexes with references keyed to special ASI accession numbers; and an "Abstracts" section that contains descriptions of the content and format of each publication organized by the ASI accession number.

Census of Housing, U.S. Department of Commerce.
Includes detailed tabulations on the number and characteristics of U.S. houses.

Census of Population, U.S. Department of Commerce.
Provides information of the characteristics of the population for states, counties, cities, etc. in a series of reports. In addition, several series of short *Current Population Reports* are published. These provide summaries of population trends by age group, income, sex, etc. with extended forecasts of population growth.

County and City Data Book, U.S. Department of Commerce.
Offers a selection of recent statistical information for counties, SMSAs, cities, and other small geographic areas. Includes data on population, education, employment, aggregate and median income, housing, retail sales, and value of product sold. Source references are given for each item of data included.

Economic Censuses, U.S. Department of Commerce.
Includes censuses of manufacturers, retail trade, wholesale trade, selected service industries, mineral industries, construction industries, transportation, and others. Information is arranged according to the Standard Industrial Classification (SIC) for states, counties, SMSAs, major cities, etc.

Predicasts, Predicasts, Inc.
Includes short- and long-range forecasts for numerous industries and product categories, with each abstract giving the size of the individual forecasts and a reference as to their sources.

Predicasts Basebook, Predicasts, Inc.
  Contains approximately 25,000 time series of various products and industries. The series are arranged by SIC number under broad subject headings. Includes an alphabetical guide to SIC codes for products and services.

Statistical Abstract of the United States, U.S. Department of Commerce.
  Provides annual summary statistics on political, social, and economic aspects of the United States. Emphasis is given primarily to national data, although it does contain some information on states, SMSAs, and cities. Can be used as a reference as well as a guide to other statistical publications and sources.

Statistics Sources, Gale Research Company.
  An index to sources of statistical information on industrial, business, social, financial, and other topics for the United States and foreign countries. Arranged alphabetically according to subject or product.

Survey of Current Business, U.S. Department of Commerce.
  A monthly report on economic conditions and business activity in the United States. It is the prime source of national income and account statistics. A biennial supplement, *Business Statistics*, presents historical data for approximately 2500 series that appear in the S pages of the monthly issue. It includes explanatory notes and source references.

Company and Industry Sources

Annual Reports (of Publicly Held Companies).
  Provide financial and operating data and information related to policy considerations for a particular firm.

Form 10-K Securities and Exchange Commission.
  Reports filed annually by every publicly-held company. Provide information of financial and operating data, competitive conditions, R&D, employees, principal markets, and distribution methods. (May contain data not included in the annual reports.)

Million Dollar Directory, Dun and Bradstreet, Inc.
  A three-volume set of directories which list U.S. businesses with an indicated net worth of over $500,000. Each volume is divided into three sections: "Business Alphabetically," "Business Geographically," and "Business by Product Classification." Provides information on officers, products, sales volume, and number of employees.

Moody's Industrial Manual, Moody's Investors Service, Inc.
  Annually revised information of the history of companies, their operations, subsidiaries, products, and financial position. Company names are indexed in alphabetical order.

Reference Book of Corporate Management, Dun and Bradstreet, Inc.
  Provides an alphabetical listing of companies and their principal officers. Biographical data covering age, education, experience, and principal business affiliations are shown for each officer.

Standard & Poor's Industry Survey, Standard & Poor's Corp.
  Includes 33 industry segments which are divided into "Current Analysis" and "Basic Analysis" sections. Each "Basic Analysis" section includes an examination of the prospects for the industry, an analysis of trends and problems, and a comparative company analysis. The "Current Analysis" section provides latest industry developments; industry, market, and company statistics; and an appraisal of the investment outlook.

Standard & Poor's Corporation Records, Standard & Poor's Corp.
  Provides descriptions of various publicly-held corporations. Contains a cross-reference section which indicates the names of subsidiaries, affiliates, etc., of the described corporations as well as names of predecessor and merged companies and changes in company names.

Standard & Poor's Register of Corporations, Directors, and Executives, Standard & Poor's Corp.
    A three-volume set which includes addresses of companies; names, titles, and functions of executives and officers; SIC code; annual sales; and subsidiaries and divisions.

Thomas's Register of American Manufacturers, Thomas Publishing Company.
    A multivolume set which includes a listing of manufacturers by products and services, a list of trade and brand names, an alphabetical directory of manufacturers, and a company catalog file.

U.S. Industrial Outlook, U.S. Department of Commerce.
    Provides industry profiles and projections for over 200 industries. Offers data on production, sales, shipments, employment, productivity, imports, new products, developments, and regulations.

U.S. Regional, State, and Local Directories

There are numerous directories available which provide information on companies in specific regions, states, and localities. Most of the regional and state directories are arranged by geographic location and usually have both alphabetical and product indexes. Typical examples are:

Directory of New England Manufacturers, George D. Hall Company.
Directory of Massachusetts Manufacturers, George D. Hall Company.
Directory of Directors in the City of Boston and Vicinity, Bankers Service Company.

Others sources for local areas include chamber of commerce publications, city directories, and telephone directories.

Marketing and Marketing-Related Indexes and Bibligraphies

A.M.A. Bibliography Series, American Marketing Association.
    A series of annotated bibliographies which have been published on various marketing topics, such as market segmentation and industrial marketing.

Marketing Abstracts Section, Journal of Marketing.
    Each issue of the Journal contains an annotated bibliography describing selected articles and special studies. Arranged according to major subject areas.

Psychological Abstracts, The American Psychological Association, Inc.
    A guide to articles about psychology and related areas which have been published in journals, technical reports, scientific documents, dissertations, and books. Abstracts are arranged according to sixteen broad subject categories. Author and subject indexes are contained in each issue.

Sociological Abstracts, Sociological Abstracts, Inc.
    An index to the sociological journal literature and papers given at selected professional meetings. Each issue contains a subject, periodical, and author index.

Topicator, Thompson Bureau.
    A subject index to about twenty journals in the fields of advertising, communications, and marketing.

Marketing Information Sources

Commercial Atlas and Marketing Guide, Rand McNally & Co.
    Provides census data for SMSAs, states, counties, and principal cities. Includes marketing data and statistics on population, households, total retail sales, and total manufacturing.

Market Guide, Editor and Publisher Co., Inc.

Provides market information for 1500 American and Canadian cities. Includes data and projections on population, households, banks, autos, retail outlets, and newspapers. Arranged in alphabetical order by states and territories of the United States and Canada, with separate city entries listed thereunder.

Standard Directory of Advertisers, National Register Publishing Co., Inc.

Lists over 17,000 advertiser companies with annual appropriations for national or regional advertising campaigns. Includes two editions: classified (arranged in 51 product classifications) and geographical (companies arranged by state or city). Also includes a trademark index.

Standard Directory of Advertising Agencies, National Register Publishing Co., Inc.

Lists information (annual billing, breakdown by media, account executives) on approximately 4400 advertising agencies in the United States and overseas. Includes a geographical index as well as an alphabetical listing.

Standard Rate and Data Service.

This service offers a number of separate directories providing data on subscription rates, circulation, and advertising rates as well as specifications for publications, broadcast stations, etc. These directories include the following: *Business Publication Rates and Data, Consumer Magazine and Farm Publication Rates and Data, Network Rates and Data,* and *Newspaper Rates and Data.*

Survey of Buying Power Data Service, Sales & Marketing Management magazine.

Includes statistical information on population and household characteristics, total retail sales, effective buying income, and TV market data. Data are divided into 3 volumes.

Television Factbook, Television Digest, Inc.

Includes a directory of U.S. and Canadian television stations arranged geographically. Also provides statistics on TV production, sales to dealers, TV households, ranking of TV markets, and an index to advertisers.

Bibilographic and Statistical Data Bases

A data base is an organized collection of information which can be accessed through a computer-based retrieval system. Computer search services are available to students and businesses in many large public and university libraries.

A fee is generally charged for these services, and rates vary from one data base to another. The following are examples of special interest to business:

ABI/Inform, Data Courier, Inc.

Stresses general decision sciences information, but also includes specific product and industry information. Includes articles which have been abstracted from approximately 400 publications in business and related fields from August 1971 to date.

Management Contents, Management Contents, Inc.

Provides information from September 1974 to present on a variety of business and management related topics including accounting, finance, marketing, organizational behavior, and public administration. Articles from 200 U.S. and foreign journals are indexed and abstracted.

PTS F&S Indexes, Predicasts, Inc.

Covers both domestic and international company, product, and industry information from 1972 to present. Also provides on-line access to a comprehensive bibliography (known as "Source Directory") of more than 5000 publications cited in Predicasts' publications.

PTS Prompt, Predicasts, Inc.

Abstracts significant information since 1972 on the products and services of the following industries: chemical, communications, computers, electronics, energy, fibers, food, instruments and equipment, metals, paper, plastics, and rubber.

PTS U.S. Annual Time Series, Predicasts, Inc.

Includes two subfiles: Predicasts Composites and Predicasts Basebook. Predicasts Composites contains 500 times series on the United States providing historical data since 1957 and a projected concensus of published forecasts through 1990. Predicasts Basebook contains data from 1957 to date for about 30,000 series of U.S. business activity for a variety of industries, products, and services. Predicasts also offers a PTS U.S. Regional Time Series.

PTS U.S. Statistical Abstracts, Predicasts, Inc.

Includes abstracts of published forecasts for the United States from journals, business-related publications, newspapers, government reports, and special studies. Each abstract usually contains historical base period data, a short-term forecast, and a long-term forecast.

TRADE MAGAZINES

Current trends and developments in different products, companies, and industries may be covered in a wide range of trade and professional publications.

Many publish annual summaries of industry and product data, some of which may not be found elsewhere. It is a good idea to check the annual statistical issue first. Many libraries carry some trade magazines, but few, if any, would carry all because the list is extensive. You can write or call a magazine for help. Your library should have a list of the names and addresses of established publications.

Examples of magazines of particular interest to marketers are *Advertising Age* and *Sales and Marketing Management*. These magazines have excellent research departments and serve as data sources for many marketing analysts.

Advertising Age, Crain Communications, Inc.

A weekly publication which offers several annual surveys and special features. The following are examples: "Marketing Reports," which provides information on sales and earnings, leading product lines and brands, advertising expenditures, and ad agencies used by each of the top 100 national advertisers; "100 Leading National Advertisers"; "National Expenditures in Newspapers"; and "Profiles of the Top 100 Markets in the U.S."

Sales & Marketing Management, Sales & Marketing Management.

A widely-read magazine published monthly; in February, April, July, and October, it is published twice a month. Noted for its four annual statistical issues: (1) "Survey of Buying Power" (late July issue) which offers current estimates of U.S. and Canadian population, income, and retail business; (2) "Survey of Buying Power, Part II" (late October issue) which contains two marketing surveys—"Metropolitan Market Projections" and "Annual Surveys of TV, Newspaper, and Radio Markets"; (3) "Survey of Industrial Purchasing Power" (last April issue) which provides U.S. statistics by county; (4) "Survey of Selling Costs" (last February issue).

Examples of industry-specific trade magazines with annual issues summarizing industry data are *Drug and Cosmetic Industry, Progressive Grocer, Public Utilities Fortnightly, Iron Age, Chain Store Age Executive, The Discount Merchandiser, Men's Wear, Tennis* (player and tournament records), and *Merchandising* (electrical products). Some, such as *Hardware Retailing*, publish separate annual statistical reports.

TRADE ASSOCIATIONS

Trade associations can be a valuable source of information for specific industries and products. They often collect for their members such information as market trends, industry sales, and buyer characteristics. Some make this information public, and many will respond to student requests for information. The directories cited below can be found in most large libraries and can help you locate associations within particular industries.

Encyclopedia of Associations, Gale Research Company.
> A three-volume set. Volume 1 is a comprehensive list of all types of national associations arranged in broad categories such as trade, business and commercial, governmental, and educational. Volume 2 is a geographic and executive index to the associations listed in Volume 1. Volume 3 is a quarterly listing of new associations and projects.

National Trade & Professional Associations of the United States and Canada, Columbia Books, Inc.
> Lists more than 6000 organizations with national memberships. Information is arranged alphabetically by organization.

PRIVATE SOURCES

There are a number of commercial research services which undertake studies and surveys on a wide range of industries, markets, and brands. They are often done on a continuing basis. The findings are sold to organizations at relatively high subscription rates. These reports normally are not found in libraries, since making the data public would compromise the arrangements that research organizations have with their private clients. Some, however, such as the Simmons Study of Media and Markets, make year-old reports available to university libraries. For academic purposes the older data usually are quite acceptable.

A. C. Nielson Company.
> Noted for collection of data on products sold through food and drug stores. Retail data are obtained by auditing inventories and sales every 60 days in a sample of 2000 U.S. stores. Nielson provides national data as well as breakdownds by regions, cities, and by different types of outlets.

Market Research Corporation of American (MRCA).
> Provides data on products sold through food and drug stores. Data are collected through a national consumer panel of households and include information on sales by brands and type of outlet for the United States and major regions.

Study of Media and Markets, Simmons Market Research Bureau, Inc.
> This annual study provides information on media audiences and on consumption rates and brand usage of over 500 categories of packaged goods, durable goods, and services, tabulated by demographic characteristics of users and non-users.

Other commerical subscription services exist, often focusing on very specific areas of interest. The following directory can be used to help locate the market research reports which are available:

FINDex: The Directory of Market Research Reports, Studies, and Surveys, FIND/SVP.
> Lists and describes market research reports. Each entry includes a description of the subject matter, date of publication, price, and name and address of the publisher.

Name and Organization Index

A&P, 203, 520, 532
AT&T, 577, 590
Ackerman, Robert W., 91n.
Adams, J. S., 388n.
Adams, Walter, 209n.
Adler, Lee, 91n., 137n.
Admire, Jacquelyn B., 661
Advertising Council, 30n., 649
Alberto-Culver, 47
Alexander, Ralph S., 65n., 120n., 143n., 442n., 515n.
American Airlines, 83, 502, 603
American Association of Advertising Agencies Educational Foundation, 616n.
American Bankers Association, 641
American Broadcasting Co., 451
American Can, 19
American Express, 412, 517, 527, 590
American Motors, 23
American-Standard, 9, 83, 204, 242, 327, 333, 449, 516, 541
Amstutz, Arnold E., 143n.
Amway, 524, 525, 539
Anderson, M. J., Jr., 443n.
Anheuser-Busch, 429, 437, 502
Ansoff, H. Igor, 201n.
Anthony, Susan B., 374
Apple Computer, 69, 452
Aronson, E., 387n.
Armour and Company, 167
Armstrong World Industries, 437, 536
Arthur D. Little, 450
Assael, Henry, 98n., 112, 119n.
Associated Grocers, 519
Association of National Advertisers (ANA), 611
Avis, 83, 440
Avon, 524, 525, 531, 539n.

Bagozzi, Richard P., 582n.
Bali Company, 300, 311
Banks, Sharon K., 143n.
Bartos, Rena, 65n., 119n.
Bath Iron Works, 511
Battelle Memorial Institute, 450
Bauer, Judith, 209n.
Baum, Herbert M., 389
Beechnut, 45
Bell Telephone Companies, 358
Bellenger, Danny N., 143n.
Ben Franklin Stores, 519
Benny, Jack, 203
Bernacchi, Michael D., 442n.
Bernay, Elayn K., 119n.
Bernhardt, Kenneth L., 143n.
Bethlehem Steel, 484
Bic, 438, 449, 5-13
Bickmore, Lee, 549

Bird, Larry, 110
Birds Eye, 195
Birnbaum, Jeffrey H., 506n.
Black & Decker, 495, 500, 513, 549, 633
Black, Robert L., 515n., 547n.
Blair, Ed, 143n.
Blake, Robert R., 376n., 387n.
Blanchard, Kenneth H., 387n.
Blankenship, A. B., 143n.
Blood, M. R., 387n.
Boise Cascade, 189, 190
Booz-Allen & Hamilton (BA&H), 444, 445, 448n., 450, 453, 458, 460, 461n.
Borden, Neil H., 21
Borden Company, 416
Boston Bolts, 663
Boston Consulting Group (BCG), 425, 426, 428n., 429
Bower, Marvin, 4
Bowersox, Donald J., 546n., 547n.
Bowman, Richard D., 617n.
Boyd, Harper W., 403n.
Bradburn, Norman, 143n.
Branch, Ben, 426n.
Bristol-Myers, 68, 83, 457, 464, 590, 591
Brown, Robert G., 618n.
Bucklin, Louis C., 547n.
Buell, Victor P., 29n., 146n., 209n., 366n., 387n., 442n., 515n., 547n., 582n., 617n.
Buggie, Frederick D., 463n., 473n.
Bulova, 435, 541
Burck, Gilbert, 515n.
Burger Chef, 244
Burger King, 521
Burke, Warner, 366n.
Burlington Industries, 225, 306, 307, 310
Buskirk, Richard H., 582n.
Buzzell, Robert D., 254n., 442n., 515n.

CPC International, 454
Cacioppo, John, 119n.
Cadbury, N. D., 474n.
Caloric, 418
Campbell Soup, 362, 389, 412, 437, 502, 577
Canon U.S.A., 585
Carlson, Chester, 122
Carman, Hoy F., 168n.
Carroll, S. J., 388n.
Cary, Frank, 82
Caterpillar Tractor, 453, 464, 538
Chamberlin, Edward Hastings, 84n.
Chambers, John C., 167n.
Champion International, 243
Channing, Carol, 26
Chay, Richard F., 506

Chemers, M. M., 387n.
Chernoff, J. Robert, 618n.
Cheseborough-Pond, 438
Chevrolet Division, 86, 87
Chrysler, 23, 451
Citicorp, 191, 192, 534
Clark Paint Co., 123
Clarke, Darral, 168n.
Claycombe, W. Wayne, 168n.
Clayton, Alden G., 611n.
Cleland, David I., 473n.
Cluett-Peabody, 416
Coca-Cola, 19, 46, 590
Colley, Russell H., 598, 617n.
Collins, Thomas C., 442n.
Columbia Broadcasting System, 451
Combustion Engineering 156, 166
Condé Nast Publications, 597, 600
Conference Board, The, 187, 188, 200n., 256, 444, 445, 446n., 604
Conrail, 74
Consumer Product Safety Commission, 77, 148
Continental Group, 205, 243, 423
Control Data, 69
Cool, William R., 297n.
Cooper, M. Bixby, 546n., 547n.
Copeland, Ronald M., 498n.
Corley, Robert N., 515n., 547n.
Cotter & Co., 519, 532, 636
Count Digital, 452
Coward, Derek, 619, 625, 640, 645
Cowden Manufacturing, 505
Crain Communications, 588
Crawford, C. Merle, 443n., 473n.
Crissy, W. J. E., 443n.
Crown Cork & Seal, 429
Cross, James S., 120n., 515n.

Dartnell Corporation, 582
Data General, 451
Dataquest, Inc., 483
Davidson, William R., 547n.
Davis, H. L., 119n.
Davis, Kenneth R., 91n., 515n.
Davis, Robert T., 403
Davis, Stanley M., 367n.
Day, George S., 425, 443n.
Day, Ralph L., 143n.
Deere & Company, 502
Department of Commerce, 151
Department of Justice, 77, 496
Design and Manufacturing Corp., 418
Dhalla, Nariman K., 202n.
Diamond Tool and Horseshoe, 424
Diamond, Sidney A., 442n.
Digital Equipment, 69, 451
Disneyland, 454
Disney, Walt, 454

673

Disney, Walt, Productions, 454
Disney World, 454
Direct Selling Association, 523n.
Direct Selling Education Foundation, 523n.
Distribution by Design, 568
Donovan, Neil B., 254
Donnelly, James H., Jr., 547n.
Dow Chemical, 502, 513
Doyle, Stephen X., 582n.
Drucker, Peter F., 4, 388n.
Dun & Bradstreet, Donnelly Marketing Division, 607
Dunnette, Marvin D., 387n.
Du Pont, 22, 196, 204, 449, 452, 513, 590, 603

E. T. (movie), 614, 615
Eastman Kodak, 8, 122, 438, 453, 464, 502, 503, 534, 544, 577, 590
Electrolux, 73
Eldridge, Clarence, 202, 209n.
Ennis, F. Beaven, 602n.
Equitable Life of Iowa, 566
Equitable Life Insurance, 365
Erdos, Paul L., 133, 143n.
Estes, Bay E., Jr., 146n.
Exxon, 243

FDA (see Food and Drug Administration)
FTC (see Federal Trade Commission
Faris, Charles, 120n.
Federal Aviation Administration, 148
Federal Trade Commission, 77, 496, 499, 534
Ferber, Robert, 143
Ferrell, O. C., 515n.
Fiedler, F. E., 387n.
Fink, Daniel J., Dr., 30
Fischer, Paul M., 443n.
Food and Drug Administration, 77, 112, 661
Ford, Henry, 67
Ford Motor, 150, 451, 484
Foremost-McKesson, 532
Fox, John, 549
Frankel, Lester R., 143n.
Frankel, Martin L., 143n.
Friedman, William B., 582n.
Fuji, 503
Fuller Brush, 539
Futures Group, 147n.

Galbraith, Jay R., 366n.
Gale, Bradley T., 426n.
Gallop, George, 129
Gambles, 418
Gant, 416
Gelfand, Pamela W., 647
Gemmill, Gary R., 367n.
Genentech, 452
General Electric, 7, 8, 25, 69, 79, 86, 140, 188, 200, 201, 205, 206n., 423, 429, 430n., 437, 506, 577, 590, 606
General Foods, 8, 121, 197, 205, 244, 361, 362, 429, 437, 502, 538, 577, 585, 601
General Mills, 8, 49, 76, 549

General Motors, 7, 8, 22, 23, 67, 75, 205, 451, 484, 502, 585, 590
General Telephone and Electronics, 205
Gensch, Dennis, 474
Gerber, 45, 47, 148
Ghisselli, E. E., 387n.
Gillette, 9, 22, 83, 438, 462, 554, 557, 575, 576, 590
Glasrock, 449
Glidden, 537
Goldstucker, Jac L., 143n.
Goodrich, B. F., 423
Goodyear, 532
Gorn, Gerald T., 119n.
Granbois, Donald, 119n.
Greenberg, Herbert M., 582n.
Greenberg, Jeanne, 582n.
Gril-Kleen Corp., 626
Guiltinan, Joseph P., 547n.
Gulf Oil, 538
Gunn, William, 168n.

Haley, Russell I., 73n.
Hallmark Cards, 412, 502, 532, 542
Halloid Corporation, 122
Halpin, Andrew W., 387n.
Hamelman, Paul W., 443n.
Hamermesh, Richard G., 443n.
Hamilton, H. Ronald, 466n.
Hancock, Robert S., 84n., 209n.
Hanes, 75, 86, 210, 222, 227, 245, 267, 298, 307, 516, 531, 532, 574
Harness, Edward G., 11, 617
Harris, J. E., 443n.
Harris, John S., 474n.
Harris, Louis, 129
Hartman, William R., 242
Harvard University, 412
Hasbro Industries, 48
Haspeslagh, Phillippe, 443n.
Hayden, Spencer, 366n.
Heany, Donald F., 254n.
Heinz, H. J., 429
Hersey, Paul, 387n.
Hershey, Robert, 473n.
Hershey Foods, 484, 614, 615
Hertz, 83
Herwald, Seymour W., 442n.
Herzberg, Frederick, 387n.
Heublein, 122, 140, 171, 180, 457, 505
Hill, Richard M., 120n., 473n., 515n.
Hirschman, Elizabeth C., 546
Hisrich, Robert D., 626n., 663n.
Hitler, Adolf, 374
Hlavacek, James R., 473n.
Holiday Inns, 9
Holloway, Robert J., 84n., 209n.
Holtsnider, William, 643, 644
Hoover, 73, 449, 458, 464, 465, 480
Honeywell, 452
Hopkins, David S., 209n., 277n., 430n., 443n., 446n., 473n.
Hulin, C. R., 387n.
Hurwood, David L., 617n.

IBM, 8, 69, 78, 82, 122, 196, 219, 423, 451, 452, 453, 464, 467, 468, 511, 517, 526, 549, 566
IGA, 519, 532
IMS America Ltd., 147n.

ITT, 446, 598, 599, 600
Interco, Inc., 505
International Flavors and Fragrances, 505
International Harvester, 205
Interpace, 242
Isenberg, Martin I., 443n.

Johnson, Richard M., 443n.
Johnson, Robert W., 11
Johnson, Samuel, 473n.
Johnson & Johnson (J&J), 11, 74, 83, 438, 440, 452, 502
Johnson & Son, S. C., 458, 480, 506
Jones, Conrad, 473n.
Jones, Reginald H., 189n.

Kahn/Larsen/Walsh, 450
Kaldor, Andrew G., 17n.
Kassarjian, Harold H., 119n.
Katz, Gerald, 505
Kayser-Roth, 225, 306, 307
Keebler, 409, 410, 525, 532, 578, 610
Kellogg, 83
Keon, John, 506
Kendall, C. L., 442n.
Kentucky Fried Chicken, 180
Kimberly-Clark, 450, 452, 502, 541
King, Charles, 119n.
King, William R., 143n., 473n.
K mart, 53, 520, 532
Kodak (see Eastman Kodak)
Konecnik, Kenneth, 617n.
Kono, Ken, 442n.
Kotler, Philip, 119n., 143n.
Kress, Robert L., 389

Lambert, Douglas M., 546n., 547n.
Landon, E. Laird, 143n.
LaPlaca, Peter, 143n., 167n.
LaRue, Paul H., 498n.
Latham, Richard S., 442n.
Laurence, Paul, 387n.
Lavidge, Robert J., 95n., 119n.
Lawler, Edward E., 387n.
Lawrence, Paul R., 367n.
Lazer, William, 64n.
Leach, David, 617n.
Lego, 541, 542
Lembeck, William H., 617n.
Lesieur, F. G., 388n.
Lewin, Kurt, 372, 387n.
Lewis, Edwin H., 37n.
Levitt, Theodore, 10, 117, 120n., 442n.
Likert, Rensis, 373, 387n., 392
Lincoln, Abraham, 374
Lindsen, G., 387n.
Lippitt, Ronald, 387n.
Liptak, Thomas M., 468n.
Little, Robert W., 547n.
Lloyd, R. A., 168n.
Lockheed Aircraft, 167
Loews, 590
Loons, Alvin E., 387n.
Lorsch, S. W., 387n.
Louis Harris and Associates, 523n.
Lucier, Francis, 549
Luck, David J., 515n.
Luthans, Fred, 366

MRCA (see Market Research Corporation of America)
McAskill, James, 505
McCall, Suzanne H., 65n.
McCammon, Bert C., Jr., 547n.
McCann-Erikson, 588
McCarthy, Jerome E., 22n.
McDonald's, 94, 107, 502
McEnroe, John, 110
McFarland, James, 549
McKinsey & Co., 4, 11
McKinzie, J. R., 143n.
McLaughlin, Robert, 161n.
McNair, Malcolm P., 546n.
McNamee, Bernard J., 473n.
McNeil Laboratories, 464
McVey, Phillip, 547n.
Macy, R. H., 506
Maggard, John P., 443n.
Magic Chef, 418
Mahajan, Vijay, 443n.
Majers Corp., 409
Mallen, Bruce, 547n.
Management Decision Systems, 505
Mandell, Maurice I., 617n.
Mansfield, Edwin, 119n.
Market Facts, Inc., 622
Market Research Corporation of America, 308, 409
Mars (candy), 484
Marshall, Martin, 21
Martin, John E., 498n.
Martineau, Pierre, 91n.
Marx, Karl, 371
Mary Kay Cosmetics, 539
Maslow, Abraham, 96, 97n., 378n.
Mattel, 244
Mausner, Bernard, 387n.
May, Eleanor G., 547n.
Mayer, Charles, 137n.
Maytag, 537
Mazze, Edward M., 443n.
Melley, David, 619, 641, 645
Menzies, Hugh D., 582n.
Mercedes Benz, 483, 505
Michael, Stephen R., 366n.
Michelin, 98
Michigan Chemical Company, 148
Miles, Raymond A., 387n.
Miller Brewing, 439
Milton Bradley, 26
Minute Maid, 195
Mobil, 243, 450
Monroe, Kent B., 119n., 497, 498n., 515n.
Monsanto, 8, 358, 452, 459, 576, 601
Montgomery, David B., 139n., 443n.
Montgomery Ward, 52, 243
Morgan Guarantee Bank, 412
Mosler Safe, 9, 204
Mossman, Frank H., 443n.
Motorola, 454
Mouton, Jane S., 376n., 387n.
Mullick, Satinder K., 167n.
Munsterberg, Hugo, 372
Murphy, Patrick E., 111, 119n.
Murphy, Thomas A., 7

Nabisco, 83, 505, 525, 532, 549
Nagel, Madeline, 617n.
National Association of Hosiery Manufacturers, 231

National Broadcasting Co., 451
National Bureau of Standards, 115
National Cancer Institute, 412
National Center for Health Statistics, 648n.
National Heart, Lung, and Blood Institute, 647, 648n., 650n.
National Lead, 154
National Research Center for the Arts, 663n.
National Silver Industries, 506
Ness, Thomas E., 143n.
Newman, Derek, 366n.
New York Telephone Co., 93
New York Times, 597
Nielsen Co., A. C., 126, 308, 418–420, 421n., 663n.
Novelli, William D., 29, 647
Nystrom, Paul H., 209

Occupational Safety and Health Administration (OSHA), 115
O'Connell, John D., 618n.
O'Connor, Rochelle, 209n.
O'Dell, William F., 143n.
Odiorne, George, 366n., 387n.
Olshausky, Richard, 119n.
O'Meara, John J., Jr., 474n.
Opel, John, 549
O'Shaughnessy, J., 366n.
Outboard Marine, 244

P&G (see Procter & Gamble)
PIMS (see Profit Impact of Market Strategies)
Packard, Vance, 51n.
Pacific Gas and Electric, 166
Painter, John J., 119n.
Parker Hannifin, 162
Parsons, Leonard J., 143n.
Patton, George, 376
Paul, Gordon W., 547n.
Paul, Ronald N., 254n.
Pavlov, Ivan, 99
Penney, J. C., 52, 87, 224, 505, 517
Peper, Henry, 619
Dr Pepper, 204
Pepperidge Farm, 501
Pepsi-Co, 46, 243
Pessemier, Edgar A., 442n., 473n.
Peters, Michael P., 626n., 663n.
Petty, Richard, 119n.
Pfizer, 47
Pillsbury Co., 8, 76
Pine State Knitwear, 300, 311
Polaroid, 83, 196, 452, 453, 513
Powers, John, 505
Prentice, Robert M., 611n.
President's Council of Economic Advisors, 151
Pro Brush, 462
Procter & Gamble (P&G), 9, 11, 19, 25, 107, 121, 203, 356, 380, 417, 429, 437, 438, 445, 446, 452, 538, 541, 543, 549, 576, 577, 585, 586, 590
Proctor-Silex, 506
Profit Impact of Market Strategies, 411, 425, 431, 500
Provincetown-Boston Airline, 218

Questor, 169, 314

RCA, 69, 83, 205, 423, 453, 590
Radio Shack, 452
Raleigh (bicycles), 537
Ralston-Purina, 413, 440, 456
Ranard, Elliot D., 156n.
Rawnsley, Allan, 143n.
Ray, Michael, 119n.
Raytheon, 205
Rechholtz, Robert A., 605, 617n.
Reece, James S., 297n.
Reed, O. Lee, 515n., 547n.
Revlon, 502, 590, 603
Rewoldt, Stewart H., 442n., 547n.
Rexall, 462, 519
Rhor Industries, 244
Rich, Clyde L., 143n.
Richardson-Vicks, 449, 457, 554, 575, 576, 594
Richman, Barry M., 473n.
Rigaux, Benny P., 119n.
Ringling Bros., 244
Robinson, Patrick, 120n.
Rockwell International, 148
Rokeach, Milton J., 119n.
Rolls Royce, 483, 501
Roosevelt, Franklin, 374
Roper, 418
Rosak, Theodore, 119n.
Rosenberg, Larry J., 546
Rosenbloom, Bert, 547n.
Rosenblum, John W., 91n.
Runyon, Kenneth E., 119n., 617n.
Russ, Frederick A., 442n.

SAMI (see Selling Areas–Marketing, Inc.)
SCM, 506, 537
Saks Fifth Avenue, 98
Samsonite, 541–542
Saporito, D. A., 442n.
Saunders, R. Reed, 617n.
Sawyer, Alan, 119n.
Schewe, Charles D., 109n., 143n., 515n.
Schoeffler, Sidney, 254n.
Schwartz, George, 547n.
Scott, James D., 442n., 547n.
Scott Paper, 452, 462, 576
Seagram & Sons, Jos. E., 604, 606
Sears, Roebuck, 52, 224, 418, 476, 516, 517, 520, 585
Seiko, 503
Selling Areas–Marketing, Inc., 107
Sentry Hardware Corp., 636
Seven-Up Co., 102
Shanker, Marvin, 506
Shapiro, Benson P., 582n.
Shavel, Irwin, 506
Shell Oil, 365, 452
Sherwin-Williams, 532
Shocker, Allan D., 474n.
Silk, Steven B., 443n.
Simon, Leonard S., 474n.
Simmons Co., W. R., 126
Singer, 243, 244, 525
Skinner, B. F., 379
Smallwood, John E., 64n.
Smith, Adam, 371
Smith, Donald D., 167n.
Smith, George L., 547n.
Smith, Reuben M., 109n., 515n.
Smith, Wendell, 67, 91n.
Snow Crop, 195

675

Snydermann, Barbara Brock, 387n.
Sohio, 532
Sommer, Dale W., 163
Sony, 600
Southern New England Telephone, 508
Spalding, A. G., 169, 314, 544, 601
Sparks, David, 119n.
Standard Oil of Indiana, 484
Stanley Home Products (Stanhome), 524, 539
Stanton, William J., 582n.
Staples, William A., 111, 119n.
Steinbrink, John P., 582n.
Steiner, Gary A., 95n., 119n.
Steiner, George, 168n.
Sterling Drug, 68
Stewart, Wendell M., 547n.
Stocking, Carol, 143n.
Stogdill, Ralph M., 387n.
Stouffer, 438
Strang, Roger A., 611n., 617n.
Strategic Planning Institute, 411n., 426n.
Strauss, Levi, 45, 505, 517
Sudman, Seymour, 143n.
Sullivan, William G., 168n.
Summar, Polly, 119n.
Super Value stores, 519
Survey Research Center, Univ. of Mich., 154, 155n., 480
Swift, 450

TWA, 83
Talley, Walter J., Jr., 443n.
Tandy, 69, 452
Tappan, 418
Taylor, Donald A., 546n., 547n.
Taylor, Frederick W., 371
Taylor, James W., 254n.
Tellis, Gerald J., 443n.

Texaco, 8, 538
Texas Instruments, 196, 219, 462, 500
Thom McAn, 525, 532
Thompson, J. Walter, 418, 419n.
3-M, 446
Tigert, Douglas J., 119n.
Time, Inc., 83, 604, 606
Timex, 502
Tosi, H. L., 388n.
Toyota, 483, 502
Travelers Insurance, 437
Treasure Masters, 464
Tucker, W. T., 119n.
Tupperware, 539
Twedt, Dik Warren, 72n., 125n., 136n.
Tyson, Belzer and Associates, 523n.

Ueyana, Shu 617n.
U-Haul, 537
Union Camp, 429
Union Carbide, 590
United Airlines, 83
United Brands, 549
United Nations, 151
U.S. Patent Office, 417
U.S. Steel, 25, 83, 205, 484
Urban, Glenn, 139n.
Uyterhoeven, Hugo E. R., 91n.

Vroom, Victor, H., 387n.

Walter, Henry, Jr., 505
Warshaw, Martin R., 392n., 442n., 547n.
Wasson, Chester R., 209n., 442n.
Watson, Stuart D., 122, 143n.
Weber, Max, 371
Webster, Frederick E., 120n.

Weilbacher, William M., 617n.
Weinberg, Charles, 473n.
Weiss, Robert, Associates, 643
Wells, William D., 104n., 105n., 119n.
Wenz, Laurel, 107n.
Werner, Ray O., 515n., 547n.
Western Auto, 418
Western Electric, 196
Weyerhaeuser, 537
Wheelwright, Steven, 168n.
Whirlpool, 418
White, R. K., 387n.
Wiersema, Frederick D., 442n., 515n.
Wileman, David L., 367n.
Wilson, Aubrey, 137n.
Wind, Yoram, 116, 120n., 443n.
Winegardner, Roy E., 9
Winer, B. James, 387n.
Winski, Joseph M., 615n.
Woodward, Herbert W., 443n.
Worthing, Parker M., 443n.
Wren, Daniel A., 387n.
Wright Line, 463
Wrigley, William, Jr. Company, 79, 590
Writing Instrument Manufacturers Association, 619

Xerox, 82, 122, 449, 452, 464, 483, 484, 504, 526

Yamaha, 537
Yankelovich, Skelly & White, 471
Young, Robert, 601
Yuspeh, Sonia, 202n.

Zenith, 537
Ziff, R., 119n.

Cases and Readings Index

Numbers in parentheses indicate case/reading order in the text.

American-Standard: Changing Corporate Strategy (6), 327
American-Standard: The Stainless Steel Sink Problem (7), 333
Black & Decker Manufacturing Co., Consumer Power Tool Division (13), 633
Boston Bolts, The (17), 663
Eraser Mate (14), 640
Gril-Kleen Corporation, The (12), 626
Hanes Corporation, 222
Heublein, Inc.: Environmental Scanning for Strategic Planning (2), 171
Heublein, Inc.: Using Environmental Data at Kentucky Fried Chicken (3), 180
National High Blood Pressure Education Program (15), 647
National Relocation, Inc. (5), 321
New Patterns in Sales Management (9), 392
Organizing for Effective Advertising — Campbell Soup Company (8), 389
Paper Mate (11), 619
Quit-Smoke Company, The (16), 661
Sales Manager in Action, A (10), 403
Spalding Tennis Rackets (4), 314
Tennis Racket Market Segmentation (1), 169

Subject Index

Page numbers in *italic* indicate illustrations or tables.

Advertising:
  cigarette, 78
  classsifications of, 587–588
    cooperative (co-op), 588
    local, 587
    national, 587
  copy testing in, 606
  defined, 24, 583
  expenditures for: by company type, 603
    by medium, 588–589, *603*
    by product type, 589
    by total, 585
  by government, 30
  measurement of, 605–607
  nature of, 585–589
  organization of: by consumer hard goods, 594–597
    by consumer packaged goods, 592–594
    by corporate level, 597–598
    by industrial goods, 594–597
  as percent of sales, 22, *22*, 589, *590, 591*
  planning in: budgets, 604–605
    goals, 598
    multi-tier budget, *605*
    research and measurement, 605–607
    strategies (*see* Advertising strategies)
  ratio of, to selling expense, *25*
  research on: content, 126
    effectiveness, 126
    media, 126
Advertising agencies, 589–592
  client-agency problems, 592
  compensation of, 589
Advertising exposures, cost per thousand (CPM), 585, 601
Advertising strategies:
  continuity, 604
  copy, 600–601
  frequency, 604
  media, 601–604
  product positioning, 599–600
  reach, 604
Age changes by segments, 45
AIO (attitudes, interests, and opinions) (*see* Psychographic profile)
Attitudes, buyer's, 101–102, *101*
Average rate of return, 294

Balance sheet, 285–288, *287*
Birthrates, *45*, 47
Bottom-up sales forecasting, 154
Brainstorming, 463
Brand (*see* Product)

Brand strategies, 436–440
  brand extension, 438
  combination brand, 438
  family brand, 437–438
  individual brand, 437
  positioning, 439–440
    defined, 439
    preference/perception mapping with, 439–440, *439*
    repositioning, 440
Break-even analysis, 486–492, *486, 490*
Business cycle, 151
Business environment, 191
Business plan, 278*n*.
Business purpose:
  defined, 8, 194
  determining, 9–11, *9*
Business unit, 206*n*.
Buyer behavior, 92
  decision process: consumer, 94–95, *94*
    organization, 113–114, *113*
  external influences on consumer, 103
    cultural, 105–107
    economic, 103–104
    family life cycle, 110–111, *111*
    reference groups, 109–110
    social class, 108–109, *108*
    usage segment, 112
  influences on organizational buyers, 114–116, *114*
    environmental, 115–116
    interpersonal, 115
    marketer-initiated, 116
    organizational, 114
    personal, 114
  internal influences on consumer, 95–96, *96*
    attitudes, 101–102, *101*
    brand loyalty, 100–101
    learning, 98–100
    lifestyle, 103, *104, 105*
    motives, 96–97
    perceptions, 97–98
    personality, 102–103
  marketers' influences on, 112–113
  models of organizational buying, 116
    buyer-oriented, 117
    BUYGRID, 117
    price minimizer, 116
    vendor-oriented, 116–117
  random environmental factors and, 112
  types of buyers, 92
    consumers, 92
    organizations, 92
  types of consumer purchases, 93–94
    high-involvement, 94, *98*, 102
    low-involvement, 93–94, 102
Buyer-oriented model, 117

BUYGRID model, 117
Buying power index, defined, 56

Capital goods, 28
Cash flow, 285, 288–289, *288*, 295, 504
Caveat emptor (buyer beware), 416
Caveat venditor (seller beware), 416
Census:
  of business, 86
  of manufacturers, 80
  of population, 43
Census Divisions, 48, *48*
Census Regions, 48, *48*
Changes in business orientation, 5–8, *6*
Channel intermediaries (*see* Distribution, channel intermediaries for)
Channels of distribution (*see* Distribution, channels of)
Classical conditioning theory, 98–99
Clayton Act, 497, 533
Coefficient:
  of correlation, 164
  of determination, 164–165
Cognitive learning theory, 99–100
Communications model, *584*
Company divisions, types of, 12
  operating, 12
  staff, 12
Company market position, factors affecting, 90
Company organization, types of, 12
  divisional, 12, *13*
  functional, 12, *13*
Competition, 82–85
  degree of industry concentration on, 58–60
    by geographic location, 59, *60*
    by market share, 58, *59*
  as an external planning variable, 196
  monopolistic: defined, 83–84
    as factor in price change, 484
    features of, *84*
    industry examples of, *59*
    relevance of, to pricing, 88–89
  oligopolistic: defined, 83–84
    as factor in price change, 484
    features of, *84*
    industry examples of, *59*
    and price positioning, 502–503
    relevance of, to pricing, 88–89
  situation analysis, 219–220
  types and features of, *84*
Consignment inventory, 272*n*.
Consumer behavior (*see* Buyer behavior)
Consumer goods, 26
Consumer packaged goods, 28
Consumer trial, 610
Contribution pricing, 507–508

677

Control (see Managerial control)
Convenience goods:
  defined, 27
  and market coverage, 535–536, *536*
  and type of intermediary, 86
Cooperative (co-op) advertising, 588
Cost per thousand (CPM) advertising impressions, 585, 601
Costs:
  direct, 485–486
  fixed, 486
  full production, 292
  incremental, 292
  indirect, 485–486
  total, 292–293
  variable, 292–293, 485–486
  (*See also* Pricing)
CPM (*see* Cost per thousand advertising impressions)
Cross-impact analysis, 155
Cultural change, 75–76
  examples of, *76*
Cultural factors as buyer influences, 105–107
  foreign, 106
  subcultures, 106–107
Cultural values, 105–106
Cycle analysis, 160–161
Cycle forecasting, 161

Death rates, *45*
Decision making, 121, 122*n*.
  under risk, 121
  under uncertainty, 121
Delphi technique, 155
Demand, 477–491
  defined, 477
  derived, 195
  elasticity of, 477–478, *479*
  factors influencing, 213
  forecasting, 478–481
Demographic data on consumer markets, changes in, 43–50
  age segments, 45
  birthrates, *45*, 47
  death rates, *45*
  divorce rates, 46
  families, *47*
  households, *47*
  marriage rates, 46
  population, *44*, *46*, *49*, *50*
  senior citizens, 47
  working wives, 47
Demographic profile of heavy users of shotgun ammunition, *104*
Dependent variable, 164
Direct mail, 589
Direct response marketing, 589
Direction (management):
  communications and, 369
  coordination and, 369
  defined, 368
  managerial function of, 368–381
  organizational behavior and, 371–381
    group behavior, 372–374
    introduction to, 371–372
    leadership, 374–377, *376*, *377*
    motivation, 378–381
  personnel administration and, 370, 371

Discounted cash flow, 295
Discounts (*see* Price)
Distribution, 85–86
  changing channels, 516–517
  channel captain, 532–533
  channel conflict, 531
  channel intermediaries for, 24, 518–524
    agents, 519
    cash-and-carry wholesaler, 518
    chain buying offices, 520
    chain stores, 520
    dealer, 523
    direct to consumer, 522, 523
    distributors, 518
    electronic retailing, 522
    feeder wholesalers, 518
    franchised outlets, 521
    full service wholesaler, 518
    jobbers, 518
    limited service wholesaler, 518
    mail order, 522
    manufacturers' agents, 519–520
    manufacturers' branches, 519–520
    public warehouses, 519
    rack jobber, 519
    retailer-owned wholesaler, 519
    retailers, 520–521
    sales agents, 520
    service intermediaries, 524
    supply houses, 518
    vending machines, 522
    wholesaler voluntary chain, 519
    wholesalers, 518–519
  channel length, 528–529, *529*
  channels of, 24, 196, 524–533
    consumer goods, 524–525, *524*
    industrial goods, 525–526, *526*
    multiple channels, 528
    services, 527, *527*, *528*
    vertical channels, 532
    vertical systems, 532–533
  control of, by manufacturer, 196, *197*
  direct-to-consumer sales by industry, *523*
  drop-shipments, 518
  legal issues in, 533–534
    Clayton Act, 533
    exclusive dealing, 533
    exclusive territories, 533
    reciprocity, 534
    refusal to deal, 534
    Sherman Antitrust Act, 533
    tying sales, 533–534
  multiple suppliers in, 527
  relative costs of, by channel length, 529–531, *529*, *530*
  (*See also* Distribution strategies)
Distribution strategies:
  channel, 539–542
    direct, for consumer goods, 539
    direct, for industrial goods, 539
    indirect, for consumer goods, 539
    indirect, for industrial goods, 540
    multiple, 541–542, *542*
    single, 540–541
  for cost/performance tradeoffs, 542–545
    missionary sales, 543
    physical distribution, 543–545, *544*
    trade incentives, 543
  for market coverage, 535–538, *535*, *536*

Distribution strategies (*Cont.*):
  exclusive, 537–538
  geographic, 538
  intensive, 86, 536
  selective, 86, 536–537
Divorce rates, 46
Durable goods, 28

Economic data on consumer markets, changes in, 53–56
  family buying power, 55
  income: of black families, 55–56, *56*
    by geographic area, 54, *55*
    of white families, *56*
  key economic indicators, 53, *53*
Economic environment, 195
Economic factors as buying influence, 103–104
Economic forecasts, 213, *214*
Economic indicators, 53 *53*
Effective buying income, defined, 56
Elasticity of demand, 477–478, *479*
Evoked set of brands, 100
Evolution of marketing, 5–8, *6*

Fair trade laws, 270*n*., 498
Families:
  buying power of, 55
  changes in, *47*
Family life cycle as buying influence, 110–111, *111*
Fashion as an external planning variable, 198
Financial aspects of marketing, 284–296
  (*See also* Integrating marketing and business plans)
Forecast(s):
  business unit, 215–216, *216*, *217*
  capital investment, 290, 294–295
  of demand, 478–481
  economic, 213, *214*
  industry, 213–215, *214*
  of net profit, 290–293
  of return on investment, 290, 294–295
  of return on sales, 290–294, *294*
  (*See also* Sales forecasting)
Frequency distribution, 134
Functions:
  line, 12
  operating, 12
  staff, 12
  support, 12

Goods, types of, defined:
  capital, 28
  consumer, 26–27
  consumer packaged, 28
  convenience, 27
  durable, 28
  industrial, 26–27
  nondurable, 28
  shopping, 27
  specialty, 27
Government as external planning factor, 197–198
Gross national product (GNP):
  changes in, *54*
  defined, 53
  use of, in forecasting, 151

678

Hanes' case summary:
  addendum to, position in 1977, 309–313, *309–312*
  company performance, 299–302, *300–302*
  competitive reactions, 307
  evaluation of strategies and tactics, 307–309
  industry conditions, 298–299, *298, 299*
  management philosophy, 312–313
  tactics adopted, 302–306, *303–305*
Hawthorne studies, 372
Hierarchy:
  of effects, 95, 102
  of needs, 96–97
High-involvement purchases, 94, *98* 102
Households, changes in, *47*
Human relations, 372
Human resources administration, 370*n*.
Human resources and human relations, 372

Income:
  of black families, 55–56, *56*
  changes in personal, *55*
  by geographic area, 54, *55*
  national, 151
  of white families, *56*
Income statement, 285
Independent variable, 164
Index of consumer sentiment, 154, *155*
Industrial buyers:
  identification of, 58
  locating users and potential users, 58
Industrial goods, 26–27
Industrial market research:
  identifying buyers, 58
  locating users and potential users, 58
  potential by geographic location, 59
  primary market research, 58–59
Industry associations, 79
Industry shipments by company size, *59*
Industry structure, 79–82
Instrumental conditioning theory, 98–99
Integrating marketing and business plans:
  annual marketing department plan, 279–284
    applying planning format, 280–283
    budgets, 283, *284*
    consolidating plans, 283–284
    constructing planning format, 280, *280*
    content of plan, 281–283, *281*
    planning format, 279–280, *279*
  effect on financial statements, 284–289
    balance sheet, 286–288, *287*
    cash flow, 288–289, *288*
    income, 285–286, *285*
  financial impact of marketing plans, 289–296
    capital needs and return on investment, 294–296
    computing profit and return on sales, 291–293, *292–294*

Integrating marketing and business plans *(Cont.):*
  essential financial forecasts, 290–291, *290*
  understanding finance, 291
International marketing, 33–36
  approaches to, 35–36
    company-owned production, 35
    exporting, 35
    franchising, 35
    joint venture, 35, *36*
  compared to domestic marketing, 34–35
  job opportunities in, 33–34
Inventory, consigned, 272*n*.

Jobs:
  in international marketing, 33–34
  managerial, 3
  in nonbusiness marketing, 32
Jury of executive opinion, 153

Learning theories, 98–100
  classical conditioning, 98–99
  cognitive, 99–100
  instrumental conditioning, 98–99
Least squares method, 158
Legal environment as external planning factor, 197–198
  (*See also* Distribution, legal issues in; Pricing, legal factors in)
Lifestyles as buyer influences, 103, *104, 105*
Line responsibilities, 207
Linear extrapolation, 158
Low-involvement purchases, 93–94, 102

McGuire-Keough Act of 1952, 270*n*.
Magnuson-Moss Warranty Act, 416
Management, philosophy of, 199
Management by exception, 384
Management by objectives (MBO), 370–371
Management training, 3–4
Managerial control:
  control information, types of, 382–385, *384*
  control reports, types of, 381–382, *382, 383*
  corporate control system, 385
  defined, 381
  developing marketing controls, 385–386
  managerial function of direction (*see* Direction)
  marketing control system, 385
Managers, 3–4
Manufacturing, shift in geographic pattern of, *60*
Manufacturing states, leading, *60*
Market:
  broad characteristics of, 42, *42*
  communications, 583–585
  communications model, *584*
  defined, 18
  heterogeneous, 67
  homogeneous, 67
  indicators and data sources, 41–63, *41, 42*
  management of (*see* marketing management)

Market *(Cont.):*
  manager form of organization, 358–359
  research on (*see* Marketing research)
  for services (*see* Services markets)
  size and trends in, 195
  structure of, elements of, 75–90
    company position, 90
    competition, 82–85
    cultural change, 75–76
    distribution, 85–86
    governmental controls, 76–78
    industry, 79–82
    legal controls, 76–78
    price, 86–90
    technology, 78–79
  target, 19
  testing (*see* Test marketing)
Market segmentation, 66–75
  alternative approaches to, 68
  benefit segmentation, 73
  common sense approaches to, 74–75
  criteria for:
    identifiable, 69–70
    measurable, 70
    profitable size, 70
  defined, 66
  evolution of, 67
  reverse segmentation, 73–74
  strategic implications, 67
Market segments:
  consumer, 70–73, *71*
    demographic, 70
    economic, 70–71
    geographic, 70
    preference, 72–73
    price, 512
    psychological, 71–72
    social, 71–72
    use, 72–73
  defined, 19
  industrial, 74
    examples of, *74*
    types of, 74
Market share, 81, *81*
Marketing:
  concept of, 7
    acceptance of, 30
  consumer, defined, 15
  defined, 19–21, *20*
  elements of, as internal planning factors, 199–200
  of established products, 16
  evolution of, by periods, 5–8, *6*
    market, 6–7
    production, 6
    sales, 6
    societal, 7–8
  functions of, by organizational units, 4, *5*
  industrial, defined, 15, 57
  international (*see* International marketing)
  of new products, 16
  nonbusiness, 28–32, *31*
  organization (*see* Organization, forms of marketing)
  planning, 187
    (*See also* Planning; Strategic marketing planning)
  planning process, 210
    steps in, 210
  social (see nonbusiness, *above*)

679

Marketing *(Cont.)*:
  as system, 28–29
  defined, 28
  model of, *29*
  of utilities, *21*
    form, 20
    place, 20
    possession, 20
    time, 20
Marketing information system (MIS), 137–142
  building of, 140–142
  components of, 138
    hardware, 138
    information, 138
    people, 138
    procedures, 138
    software, 138
  defined, 137
  operating, 139–140
  structure, 139, *139*
  types of, 138
    data bank, 138, 141
    model bank, 138, 142
    statistical bank, 138, 141–142
Marketing management:
  coordinating functions of, 4
  decision-making model of, *10*
  defined, 11
Marketing mix:
  concept of, 21–22
  defined, 21–22
  pricing and the, 476
  situation analysis, 219–220
Marketing research:
  activities and applications of, *124–125*, 125, *137*
    advertising research, 126, 591
    frequency of occurrence, *124–125*
    market and economic analysis, 125
    pricing research, 126
    product research, 125–126
    sales research, 126–127
  defined, 123
  in new product planning, 445
  opinion surveys as, 129, *129*
  organization of, 136–137, *136*
  primary data, 130
  problem definition, *127*, 128
    symptoms vs. causes, 128
  with project strategy, 128–130
    analysis of data, 134, *135*
    collection of data, 129–130, *132*
    hypotheses, 128
    information needed, 128
    interpreting findings, 134–135
    report preparation, 135–136
    sources of data, 129–130
  questioning methods,
    direct, 130
    indirect, 130
  secondary data, 130
Marketing research survey, data collection methods for 132, *133*, 134
  focus group, 132, 134
  mailed questionnaires, 134
  personal interviews, 132
  telephone interviews, 134
Marketing services:
  centralized, 363
  functions of, 593–594
  managing, 593
Markup, 492–493, *494*

Marriage rates, 46
Metro Areas, defined, 56
Middlemen *(see* Distribution, channel intermediaries for)
Miller-Tydings Act of 1937, 270*n*.
MIS *(see* Marketing information system)
Monopoly *(see* Competition, monopolistic)
Motives, buying, 96–97
Moving average, 159–160, *160*
Multiple linear regression, 165

New product(s):
  criteria for, 464–465
  defined, 444–445
  failures of, 445–446
  internal development procedures for, 459–471, *460*
    brainstorming, 463, *463*
    business analysis, 465–466
    commercialization, 467–468
    cost by stage, *461*
    idea sources, 461–464, *461*
    ranking ideas, 466, *466*
    screening, 464–465, *460*
    strategy, 461
    technical development, 466–467
    testing, 467, 468–471
  organization for development of, 454–459
    guidelines, 455
    matrix organization, *455*
    new product committee, 458, *457*
    new product department, 457–458, *457*
    new product manager, 456–457, *456*
    new venture teams, 459
    problems of, 454–455
    product manager, 456
    task forces, 458–459
  pricing, 511–513
  research on, 125–126
  success rate of, *446*
  (*See also* New product strategies)
New product strategies, 446–454, *448*
  external development, 447–450
    acquisition, 448–449
    consultant, 449–450
    licenses, 449
    patents, 449
  internally driven, 453–454
    exploit technology in new way, 453–454
    innovate or follow, 453
  market-driven, 451–453
    defend market position, 451
    gain foothold, new market, 451–452
    preempt market position, 452–453
  [*See also* New product(s)]
Nondurable goods, 28

Objectives *(see* Planning, objectives in)
Oligopoly *(see* Competition, oligopolistic)
Opinion survey, *129*
Opportunity grid, 201
Organization:
  charting guidelines of, 350–353, *350*
  classic model of, 343–344, *343*
  defined, 344
  forms of marketing, 345–365, *363*

Organization *(Cont.)*:
  divisionalization, 360–363, *13*, *362*
  functional, 354–356, *13*, *354*
  geographic, 363–364
  market management, 358–360, *359*, *360*
  matrix, 364–365, *364*
  product management, 356–358
  fundamentals of design of, 345–350
    accountability, 345–346
    advisory authority, 347
    authority, 345–347
    decentralization of authority, 349–350
    functional authority, 347
    line authority, 345, *346*
    operating authority, 346*n*.
    staff authority, 346–347
  guidelines for design of, 347–350
  importance of, 344
  as internal planning variable, 199
  position descriptions in, 353–354, *352–353*
  reasons for change in, 344–345
  sample position description in, 352
Organizational behavior *(see* Direction)

Perceptions, buyer's, 97–98
Personal selling, defined, 24
Personality as buyer influence, 102–103
Planning:
  defined, 11, 187
  financial impact of marketing plans, 284–286
  integrating marketing and business plans, 278–284
  marketing department plan, 279–284
  objectives in, 239–241
    determining, 239
    management concurrence with, 240–241
    primary, 240
    quantitative vs. qualitative, 239
    secondary, 240
  situation analysis *(see* Situation analysis)
  tactical marketing plan, 256–267
    budget impact, 258–259
    checklist of ideas, 260–262
    Flavor, Inc. as example of, 259–264
    meshing tactics and strategies, 266–267, *267*
    objectives of, 256–258
    programs for, 258, 260–267
    schedules and assignments, 259
    situation analysis, 256
    worksheet, 257, *257*, *264–265*
  types of, described, 14
    individual, 14
    special projects, 14
    strategic, 14, 187–188
    tactical, 14, 188, 255–256
    (*See also* Integrating marketing and business plans; Situation analysis; Strategic marketing planning)
Planning gap, 213, 216, *217*
Planning strategies, 241–245
  checklist of alternatives, 242
  choosing best alternatives, 241, 244
  criteria for identifying, 194
  defined, 194
  developing alternatives, 241–244

Planning strategies *(Cont.):*
  management approval of, 244–245
  marketing strategies, 188
Plans, execution of, 11
  control, 11
  direction, 11
  organizing, 11
Policies, defined, 194
Population, shifts in, *44, 46, 49, 50*
Price, 86–90
  differences in, reasons for, 23–24
  elastic, 89
  inelastic, 89
  setting of, methods for: discount, 23
    markup, 23
    (*See also* Pricing)
Price minimizer model, 116
Pricing:
  administered prices, 507
  break-even analysis, 486–492, *486, 490*
  and channel structure, 492–496
  contribution, 507–508
  dating plans, 495
  defined, 475–476
  direct costs, 485–486
  effect of price on quantity sold, *478*
  elasticity of demand, 477–478, *479*
  factors in setting price, 89, 476–496
    cash discounts, 495
    competition, 481–485
    demand, 477–491
    functional discounts, 493
    markups, 492–493, *494*
    payment terms, 495–496
    promotional discounts, 496
    quantity discounts, 495
    trade discounts, 493–495, *494*
  indirect costs, 485–486
  leader, 484
  legal factors in, 496–500
    Clayton Act, 497, 533
    don'ts for the buyer, 499
    don'ts for the seller, 499
    fair trade laws, 270*n.*, 498
    Federal Trade Commission Act, 496
    FTC guidelines for retailers, 499–500
    price discrimination defenses, 497–498
    Robinson-Patman Act, 497–498, 508, 510
    Sherman Antitrust Act, 496
    state laws, 498–499
    Wheeler-Lea Act, 496
  and the marketing mix, 476
  profit analysis, 489–492
  profit maximization, *491*
  research on, 479–481
  responses to price cuts, *482*
  sensitivity, 482–483
  variable costs, 485–486
  (*See also* Pricing strategies)
Pricing strategies, 500–514
  administration, 509–511
    flexible, 509–511
    maintenance, 509–511
    negotiated, 511
  cost-based, 503–508
    cost-plus, 503–504
    marginal cost, 507–508
    target-return, 504–507
  new product, 511–513

Pricing strategies *(Cont.):*
  penetration, 513
  skimming, 512–513
  options within strategies, *501*
  positioning, 501–503
    by price segment, 501–502
    within price segments, 502–503
  trade positioning, 508–509
    normal discounts, 508
    variations in discounts, 508–509
    variations in terms, 509
Primary market research:
  in industrial markets, 58–59
  as source of information, 130
Product:
  attributes of, 414–416
  augmented, 413
  brand and generic shares, *421*
  brand image, 585
  brand loyalty, 100–101
  brand manager (*see* Product manager)
  brand name, 416, 585
  brand personality advertising, 585
  brands, types of: advertised, 417
    manufacturers, 417–418
    national, 417
    nonbrand (generic), 418–420
    private, 418, *420*
  defined, 23, 412
  described, 411–412
  generic, 418–420
  as an idea, 411
  manager (*see* Product manager)
  new (*see* New product)
  packaging of, 415
  parity, 413, *413*
  portfolio concepts for: Boston Consulting Group (BCG) model, 425–428, *428*
    cash cows, 426
    dogs, 426
    harvest/divest, 429
    impact of, on planning, 429–430
    invest/grow, 429
    limitations of, 426–429
    market share/ROI, *426*
    matrix, *427*
    multifactor assessment (GE) model, 429–430, *430*
    problem children, 426
    selectivity/earnings, 429
    stars, 425–426
  protecting trademarks, 417
  publicity for (*see* Product publicity)
  research on, 125–126
  as a service, 411
  trade name, 416
  trademark, 416–417
  warranties (guarantees) on, 415–416
  (*See also* Brand strategies; Product strategies)
Product differentiation, 412–413
Product life cycle (PLC), 420–425, *421*
  conditions by stage of, *422*
  decline period in, 424
  growth period in, 423
  introduction period in, 422–423
  maturity period in, 423–424
  renewal, 424
  use of, in strategy formulation, 424–425
Product line, 414

Product management (*see* Product manager)
Product manager:
  advantages of, 357–358
  in advertising, 593
  defined, 356
  in new product development, 456
Product mix, 414
Product publicity:
  advantages of, 613
  defined, 583
  disadvantages of, 613
  tactical planning for, 615
  types of, 613–615
    case histories, 614
    movies, 614
    news mentions, 613
    news pictures, 613
    news stories, 613
    television exposure, 614
  (*See also* Public relations; Publicity)
Product strategies, 430–436
  full- vs. limited-line, 432–433
  leader vs. follower, 432
  line filling, 435
  line pruning, 435–436
  line stretching, 433–435, *434*
  new product (*see* New product strategies)
  portfolio concepts (*see* Product, portfolio concepts for)
  product improvement, 431
  (*See also* Brand strategies)
Profit analysis, 489–492
Profit plan, 278
Promotion, 24
  (*See also* Sales promotion)
Promotional mix:
  defined, 24
  varying, 25
Psychographic profile:
  defined, 103
  of heavy users of shotgun shells, *105*
Public relations:
  defined, 613
  editor's ten commandments of, 614
  (*See also* Product publicity; Publicity)
Publicity:
  defined, 24, 26, 583
  (*See also* Product publicity)
Purchasing, organizational, 114
  centralized, 114
  decentralized, 114
Push-pull strategies, 25–26

Reference groups as buying influences, 109–110
Repositioning, 102
Research, pricing, 479–481
Residual analysis, 161
Retail trade:
  sales by kind of business, *87*
  (*See also* Distribution)
Return on investment (ROI), 290, 294–295, 504, 507
Return on sales (ROS), 290–294, *294*
Robinson-Patman Act, 497–498, 508, 510, 638
Rollout, defined, 268*n.*

Sales forecasting:
  defined, 144
  dimensions of, 144

681

Sales forecasting (Cont.):
  assumptions, 146–150, *147, 150*
  costs and benefits, 150
  scope, 145
  time period, 145, *146*
  techniques of, 153–157
    composite, 155–157, *156*
    judgmental, 153
    statistical, 154–155
    survey, 153–154, *155*
  tracking performance as step in, 157
  types of forecasts, 150–153
    macro, 150–151, *152*
    micro, 152–153
  (*See also* Statistical methods of sales forecasting)
Sales management:
  categories of sales jobs, *549*
  controlling the sales force, 569–572
    control methods, 570–572
    expense budgets, 572
    expense report, *572*
    sales call report, *571*
    setting quotas, 570
  cost per sales call, 585
  defining the sales job, 550–554
  directing the sales force, 558–569
    applicant evaluation form, *563*
    compensation of salespeople, 565–566
    designing territories, 566–569
    motivation of salespeople, 565–566
    qualifications for sales jobs, *561*
    recruiting salespeople, 558–561
    selection of salespeople, 558–561
    training salespeople, 562–565
    training schedule, *564*
  organizing the sales force, 554–558
  planning functions, 550
  responsibilities of field managers, 550–551
  sales manager's job, 549–551
  (*See also* Sales strategies)
Sales promotion:
  defined, 24, 26, 583
  expenditures for: compared to advertising, 611
    total, 607
    by type, *607*
  planning, 609–613
    budgets, 611–612
    goals, 609–610
    research and measurement, 612–613
    strategies, 610
  problems in managing, 609
  types of, 607–608
    consumer, 608
    industrial, 608
    sales force, 608
    trade, 608
Sales strategies:
  market coverage, 573–575
    exclusive, 574–575
    intensive, 573–574
    selective, 574–575
  organizational, 575–579
    full-line selling, 575–576
    specialized selling, 576–577
  targeting sales efforts, 578–580
    build on territory strengths, 580
    combination of strategies, 580

Sales strategies (Cont):
  strengthen weak territories, 578–580
  territory situation analysis, 578
Scatter diagram, 158, *159*
Seasonal analysis, 161
Secondary data sources, 130
Segments (*see* Market segments)
Senior citizens, changes in markets for, 47
Service, product as a, 411
Services, marketing (*see* Marketing services)
Services markets, 62–63
  defined, 62
  geographic patterns, 63, *63*
  selected industries, *62*
Sherman Antitrust Act, 496, 533
Shopping goods, 27, 86, 535–537, *536*
  (*See also* Goods, types of, defined)
Simple linear regression, 165
Situation analysis:
  defined, 210
  importance of, 210–211
  scope of, 211
  time period covered by, 211
  topical outline for, 211–222, *212*
    business unit forecasts, 215–216, *215, 216*
    buyer behavior characteristics, 217–218
    changes in market structure, 220
    competition, 219–220
    constraints, 220
    economic forecasts, 213, *214*
    forecasts, 213–216
    industry forecasts, 213–215, *214*
    marketing mix, 219–220
    markets not served, 216–217
    markets served, 216–217
    opportunities, 211
    planning gap, 213, 216, *217*
    strengths and weaknesses, 221
    summary of problems and opportunities, 222
Social class as buying influence, 108–109, *108*
Social variables in strategic marketing planning, 198
Specialty goods, 27, 535, *536*, 537
  (*See also*, Goods, types of, defined)
Staff:
  authority of, 346–347
  responsibilities of, 206
Standard Industrial Classification (SIC) system:
  description of, 60–61
  example of, *61*
Standard metropolitan statistical areas (SMSAs):
  defined, 49n.
  examples of use of, 59, 259, 567, 568, 573, 662
  map of, *52*
Statistical Abstract of the United States, description of, 43
Statistical methods of sales forecasting:
  computer simulation models, 166–167
  correlation, 162–164
    coefficient of correlation, 164
    coefficient of determination, 164
  regression analysis, 164–166
    multiple, 165

Statistical forecasting (Cont.):
  shortcomings of, 166
  simple linear, 165
  trend extrapolation, 158–162, *159*
    least squares, 158
    moving average, 159–160, *160*
    scatter diagram, 158
    time series, 160–162, *161–163*
    weighting methods, 159, *159*
Strategic business unit (SBU), 206n.
Strategic marketing planning, 187–209
  criteria for identifying strategies, 188–189, *190*
  distinction between strategy and tactics, 188
  divisional plan, example of, 208–209
  guides and formats for, 207
  model of, *193*
  organization for, 206–207
  planning environments, 194–200
    external, 194–195
    internal, 198–201
  reasons for adopting, 191–192
  role of, 188–193
  short- vs. long-range planning, 191
  situation analysis (*see* Situation analysis)
  strategic growth options, 201–205, *201*
    new products, new markets, 204–205
    new products, present markets, 203
    present products, new markets, 203–204
    present products, present markets, 201–203, *202*
  (*See also* Planning strategies)
Strategies (*see* Planning strategies; Situation analysis; Strategic marketing planning)
Survey of buying power, 56, 567
"Survey of Industrial Purchasing Power," 80, 567

Tactical plans, 14, 188, 255–256
  (*See also* Planning, tactical marketing plan)
Tactics, defined, 188
Target market, defined, 19
Technology:
  changing, 78–79, 112
  and the external environment, 196
Test marketing, 468–471
Time series analysis, 160–162, *161*
Top-down forecasting, 153
Trade, defined, 219n.
Trend analysis, 160
Trend impact analysis, 155
Trial, consumer, 610

U.S. Census Divisions, 48, *48*
U.S. Census Regions, 48, *48*
United States Trademark Act of 1946, 416

Value added by manufacturer, defined, 58n.
Value analysis, 431–432, 634n.
Vendor-oriented model, 116–117

Weighted data, 159, *159*
Wholesale trade:
  sales by kind of business, *88*
  (*See also* Distribution)
Wives, working, 47, *77*
  percentage of, 76n.